Rockin' Out

Canadian Edition

Reebee Garofalo
University of Massachusetts, Boston

with

Rob Bowman
York University

PEARSON

Prentice
Hall

Toronto

Library and Archives Canada Cataloguing in Publication

Garofalo, Reebee

    Rockin' out / Reebee Garofalo with Rob Bowman. — Canadian ed.

Includes bibliographical references and index.

ISBN 978-0-13-207210-6

1. Popular music—History and criticism. I. Bowman, Robert M. J. (Robert Maxwell James)
II. Title. III. Title: Rocking out.

ML3476.G237 2009   781.6409   C2008-906287-6

ISBN-13: 978-0-13-207210-6
ISBN-10: 0-13-207210-6

Vice President, Editorial Director: Gary Bennett
Editor-in-Chief: Ky Pruesse
Executive Acquisitions Editor: Christine Cozens
Executive Marketing Manager: Judith Allen
Senior Developmental Editor: Patti Altridge
Production Editor: Richard di Santo
Copy Editor: Martin Townsend
Proofreader: Allegra Robinson
Production Coordinator: Peggy Brown
Composition: Christine Velakis
Photo and Permissions Research: Sandy Cooke
Art Director: Julia Hall
Cover Design: Miguel Acevedo
Cover Image: Tim Mosenfelder / Getty Images Entertainment

1 2 3 4 5   12 11 10 09 08

Printed and bound in the United States of America.

Contents

Preface by Reebee Garofalo   **viii**
Preface by Rob Bowman   **xii**

Introduction: Definitions, Themes, and Issues   1

Into the Twentieth Century: Popular Music and Mass Culture   2
Rock 'n' Roll: The Birth of a New Era   4
Marketing and the Politics of Race, Language, and Gender   8
     The Language Barrier   11
     The Long, Hard Climb: Gender Discrimination   12
Regulating Popular Music   13

1   Mass Technology and Popular Taste: The Tin Pan Alley Era   15

Sound Recording: From Cylinder to Disc   16
Tin Pan Alley Constructs the Mainstream Tradition   22
     Tin Pan Alley Incorporates African American Music   23
     Tin Pan Alley Consolidates Its Power   26
Commercial Broadcasting: A Very Private Enterprise   29
     The Growth of Network Radio   30
     The Advertisers Versus the Programmers   32
Hollywood Bolsters Tin Pan Alley   34

2   Blues and Country Music: Mass Media and the Construction of Race   37

Blues and Country: More Equal Than Separate   38
"Race" Music: The Popular Sounds of Black America   40
"Hillbilly": The Music of the White Working Class   44
The Dissemination of Blues and Country: More Separate Than Equal   48
The Long Road Back for Records   53

3   "Good Rockin' Tonight": The Rise of Rhythm and Blues   56

The Publishers and the Broadcasters: ASCAP Versus BMI   57
Enter the Deejay: The Broadcasters Versus the AFM   59

From Big Bands to Solo Singers   61
The Major Labels Reclaim Country Music   63
The Independents Promote Rhythm and Blues   66
High Fidelity/Low Overhead   71
Television and the Suppression of FM Broadcasting   75
Independent Radio: Deejays in Your Face   77

4 Crossing Cultures: The Eruption of Rock 'n' Roll   82

Cultural Diversity: The Roots of Rock 'n' Roll   83
Structural Changes in the Music Industry   86
Sounds of the Cities   89
   New Orleans: The Fertile Crescent of Rock 'n' Roll   89
   Los Angeles: From Jump Blues to Chicano Rock   95
   Chicago: The Blues Electrified   99
   Cincinnati: The Crossroads of Blues and Country   105
   R&B Sanctified: The Gospel Connection   106
Doo Wop: The Intersection of Gospel, Jazz, and Pop   110
Rockabilly: The Country Strain   119

5 The Empire Strikes Back: The Reaction to Rock 'n' Roll   135

The Established Powers Fight Back   137
   Covering the Bases   139
   Pop Diversions: From Kingston Town to the Kingston Trio   143
Schlock Rock: Enter the White Middle Class   145
   Television's Greatest Hits   149
   The Brill Building: The New Tin Pan Alley   151
The Official Attack on Rock 'n' Roll   153
Surf's Up!   158

6 Popular Music and Political Culture: The Sixties   165

The Civil Rights Movement and Popular Music   166
   The "Girl Groups" and the Men Behind Them   167
   Motown: The Integration of Pop   172
   The Black Music Scene in Canada   177
   Folk Music: The Voice of Civil Rights   179
The British Invasion Occupies the Pop Charts   187
Breaking the Sounds of Silence   196
   Folk Rock: Adding Substance to Form   197
   Black (Music) Is Beautiful   200

Against the Grain: The Counterculture   203

    Blues on Acid: Psychedelic Rock   206

    Commercializing the Counterculture: The Monterey Pop Festival   211

    Riding the Storm   215

    Woodstock and Altamont: Reaching the Heights, Taking the Fall   219

7 Music Versus Markets: The Fragmentation of Pop   227

The Music Industry: A Sound Investment   228

    Merger Mania   229

    Expanding the Infrastructure: Counterculture as Commodity   230

Creativity and Commerce: Rock as Art   235

    Government Intervention and the Airwaves   245

Sweeter Soul Music   248

Singer/Songwriters, Soft Rock Solutions, and More   255

Women's Music: The Feminist Alternative   264

From Country Rock to Southern Boogie   269

Mad with Power: Heavy Metal   276

All That Glitters Does Not Sell Gold   286

8 Punk and Disco: The Poles of Pop   289

Punk Versus Disco   291

Punk: Rock as (White) Noise   293

    Born in the U.S.A.   295

    Canadian Punk   303

    Anarchy in the U.K.   304

    Flirtation with Fascism: The Underbelly of Punk   310

    Rock Against Racism: The Progressive Rejoinder   313

    Riding the New Wave   316

Disco: The Rhythm Without the Blues   321

    Proto-Disco: The Funk Connection   322

    Up from the Disco Underground   326

    Mainstream Disco: The Bee Gees Boogie Down   330

    The Hard Rock Reaction   332

9 Music Videos, Superstars, and Mega-Events: The Eighties   335

Early Music Television: They Want Their MTV   337

    MuchMusic: What Does It Mean to Make Canadian Music?   346

Superstars: The Road to Economic Recovery   351

Charity Rock and Mega-Events: Who Is the World?   359

Christmas in Ethiopia: The Advent of Charity Rock   361

Mega-Events: The Politics of Mass Culture   365

Technology and the New International Music Industry   373

10 Rap and Metal: Youth Culture and Censorship   375

The Continuing History of Heavy Metal   377

Heavy Metal: The New Wave   377

Metal Fragments   381

Hip Hop, Don't Stop   389

Old School Rap   390

Hip Hop: The Next Generation   392

Popular Music and the Politics of Censorship   406

The Parents Music Resource Center   408

The Issues: Sex, Drugs, and Rock 'n' Roll Revisited   410

11 Mainstreaming Alternatives: Packaging Pop in the Nineties and Beyond   422

Alternative as Mainstream   424

Seattle: From Sub Pop to Superstars   425

Alternative, Canadian-Style   432

Lollapalooza: Mainstreaming the Counterculture   437

Country: The Other Alternative   441

Packaging Pop Trends: The Search for The Next Big Thing   444

Electronic Dance Music   448

The Year(s) of the Woman and the Rage Rock Backlash   456

Teen Pop: Boy Bands and Teen Queens   461

The Year of Latin(o) Music(ians)   464

Black Music at the Base   468

Hip Hop with Soul: The New R&B   469

Rap: Still the Elephant in the Room   471

12 Welcome to the Terrordome: Music and Copyright in (a Time of) Crisis   485

They Want Their MP3   486

Legislation and Litigation   488

Piracy and Theft   491

The Music Industry in a Post-Napster World   493

Popular Music after 9/11   501

Corporate Radio and the New Patriotism   504

Country Music Goes to War   507

Dissent Unplugged   512

13 **Getting Back to Business: Popular Music in the New Millenium** **519**

And Now for Something Completely Familiar 521

The Return of Rock 521

Singer/Songwriters Emote 525

Idol Worship 532

Hip Hop: The New Rock 535
Reggaeton: The New Hip Hop? 543

Notes **548**
Bibliography **565**
Subject Index **574**
Music Index **598**

Listening Guides

LG 1 • **R&B** Ruth Brown, "(Mama) He Treats Your Daughter Mean" 72
LG 2 • **Rock 'n' Roll** Little Richard, "Tutti Frutti" 96
LG 3 • **Rock 'n' Roll** Chuck Berry, "Rock and Roll Music" 102
LG 4 • **Doo Wop** The Chords, "Sh'Boom" 112
LG 5 • **Rockabilly** Elvis Presley, "Hound Dog" 125
LG 6 • **Covers** Pat Boone, "Tutti Frutti" 142
LG 7 • **Surf** The Beach Boys, "Surfin' U.S.A." 161
LG 8 • **Motown** The Supremes, "Stop! In the Name of Love" 175
LG 9 • **Folk Revival** Bob Dylan, "The Times They Are A-Changin'" 182
LG 10 • **Soul** James Brown, "(I Got You) I Feel Good" 204
LG 11 • **Latin Rock** Santana, "Oye Como Va" 222
LG 12 • **Art Rock** Yes, "Roundabout" 242
LG 13 • **Soft Soul** Stylistics, "You Make Me feel Brand New" 251
LG 14 • **Singer/Songwriter** Carole King, "You've Got a Friend" 259
LG 15 • **Heavy Metal** Deep Purple, "Smoke on the Water" 280
LG 16 • **Punk** The Sex Pistols, "Anarchy in the U.K." 305
LG 17 • **Dance Pop** Michael Jackson, "Beat It" 344
LG 18 • **Heavy Metal** Metallica, ". . . And Justice for All" 386
LG 19 • **Rap** Run DMC, "Rock Box" 396
LG 20 • **Rap** Queen Latifah, "Ladies First" 402
LG 21 • **Alternative** Nirvana, "Smells Like Teen Spirit" 428
LG 22 • **Pop Country** The Dixie Chicks, "Not Ready to Make Nice" 511
LG 23 • **Singer/Songwriter** Norah Jones, "Don't Know Why" 527
LG 24 • **Rap** 50 Cent, "In Da Club" 538

Preface
by Reebee Garofalo

This preface marks the publication of the first Canadian Edition of *Rockin' Out*. When I was first approached by Kathleen McGill of Pearson Education Canada, I found the project immediately compelling culturally and politically. Kathleen's enthusiastic pitch only reinforced those feelings. I was especially pleased that Pearson recruited Rob Bowman to write the Canadian content. There is no one I would consider better suited to this assignment. While Canadian artists are certainly represented in earlier editions of *Rockin' Out*, Rob was charged with the difficult task of incorporating a deeper Canadian story—history, personalities, context—into a text that was not originally intended for that purpose. Given that challenge, I think Rob has done an excellent job of integrating Canadian content both substantively and stylistically.

In the process of revising *Rockin' Out* for a Canadian audience, I have tried, for my own part, to balance a sense of what I consider important with allowing for a large measure of Canadian self-determination. This exercise, in turn, has faced the additional challenge of length requirements; it was not just about what should be added, but also about what should be deleted. Although there have been moments where everyone involved in this process has deferred to the judgment of others, we have also achieved a remarkable degree of consensus regarding the final product. For this, I credit not only Rob's extensive knowledge, talent, and writing skill, but also Senior Development Editor Patti Altridge's editorial acumen and efficient management of the process. Before all was said and done, Kathleen McGill had passed the baton to Acquisitions Editor Christine Cozens, who saw the process through to a seemingly effortless completion. From the beginning there has been a shared sense of cooperation and flexibility. I feel proud to be a part of this venture and hope that *Rockin' Out*—the Canadian edition—sails as smoothly as the process through which we created it.

As I have said in previous editions of *Rockin' Out*, popular music—playing it, listening to it, learning from it, teaching others what I know—has been one of the organizing principles of my life ever since I can remember. It energizes me, provides the sound track for significant moments in my life, and helps me to navigate the world around me. In the society at large, discussions of its significance can be found everywhere from family dinners and Saturday night parties to corporate boardrooms and congressional chambers. There has also been an increasing interest in popular music courses on college and university campuses. The fact that popular music has been a source of pleasure for millions of people all over the world is reason enough for listening to it. But popular music is also a social and political indicator that mirrors and influences the society in which we live. This is the reason for studying it. *Rockin' Out* offers one way to do that.

In my view, popular music cannot be fully understood simply as a stand-alone musical text and then measured against some abstract aesthetic notion of quality. Although it is always important to explore the specificities of the music itself, it is equally important to recognize that the musical text is as much a product of its social and political context as any individual's creativity or talent. Because the enslavement and subsequent oppression of African Americans and resulting cultural interactions have had such a profound effect on the development of U.S. popular music, my inclination is to view popular music first through the lens of race. For this edition, we have also added notable Canadian themes and issues. Other crucial demographic variables include age, gender, and ethnicity. Technological advances and the political economy of the music industry have also been important in shaping the development of popular music. Finally, popular music invariably develops in relation to the prevailing political climate in a given era. These, then, are the themes that run throughout this book.

Because the notion of "popularity" has an obvious quantitative dimension, I attach a certain amount of importance to sales data. Accordingly, *Rockin' Out* is peppered with popularity chart listings and references to "gold" and "platinum" records. At the same time it is important to note that commercially successful artists and records may or may not be the most influential or artistically important. Historical accounts, musical analyses, critical reviews, and audience reactions are important qualitative indicators that must also be factored into any discussion of popular music.

Successive editions of *Rockin' Out* have not only updated popular music history with new research into current trends, but they have also added features designed to make the text more user friendly. The second edition of the book, for example, saw the addition of a song index, which made *Rockin' Out* more useful as a source book, as well as the conversion of a number of artist and song lists from the text into easy-to-understand tables that gave the reader a graphic sense of historical patterns and preserved the narrative for more important analytic points. The third edition included an accompanying compilation CD of songs selected to enhance the historical narrative.

In the fourth edition of *Rockin' Out*, we added a number of features to take advantage of recent technological advances that provide for a more engaging learning experience and make the music even more accessible. *Rockin' Out* now takes popular music history from the invention of the phonograph and the consolidation of Tin Pan Alley into the twenty-first century with commentary on everything from peer-to-peer file sharing networks and their implications for copyright to the crucial changes that have shaped popular music culture since 9/11. The compilation CD, which accompanied the third edition, has been replaced by two iTunes playlists that make nearly 200 songs from the book readily available for convenient download. In addition, we have added a number of carefully selected Listening Guides to deepen the analysis of musical elements and further enhance the narrative. And we are in the process of creating a Web site that will include additional Listening Guides with direct links to the musical selections, chapter outlines, and discussion questions, as well as pointers to regularly updated supplementary resources and other interactive features.

Naturally, a book of the scope of *Rockin' Out* does not fall from the sky. Although my name graces the cover, *Rockin' Out* is a work that involves countless others. In addition to drawing on original research and a wealth of primary and secondary source material, *Rockin' Out* has been shaped by discussions over the years with Bill Adler, William Barlow, Marcus Breen, Iain Chambers, Jannette Dates, Kai Fikentscher, Murray Forman, Simon Frith, Donna Gaines, Andrew Goodwin, Herman Gray, Larry Grossberg, Charles Hamm, Dave Harker, Simon Jones,

Steve Jones, Anahid Kassabian, Charlie Keil, George Lipsitz, Dick Lourie, Portia Maultsby, Susan McClary, Keith Negus, Deborah Pacini Hernandez, Richard Peterson, Tricia Rose, Danny Schechter, Larry Shore, Philip Tagg, Robert Walser, Peter Wicke, and many others too numerous to mention.

Dave Sanjek has demonstrated over and over that he is one of the most knowledgeable and forthcoming researchers in the field, and he also deserves special mention in his capacity as BMI archivist for helping to grace these pages with a treasure trove of photographs. The late Rick Dutka still occupies a special place in my heart and mind as someone whose knowledge of and love for popular music were as boundless as his political energy and activist spirit.

Brad Martin worked as my research assistant for the first edition, contributing everything from footnote corrections to substantive commentary. In preparation for the second edition, Craig Morrison offered challenging comments and a detailed review of the entire first edition. Students from my History of Rock 'n' Roll class at Tufts University contributed to the research for the second edition, including Ana Garnecho and Christina Lembo (teen pop), Lisa Wichter (women), Elise Podell (MP3), Matthew Baron (r&b), Mark Scholnick (rap), Laura Horstmann and Zach Berge (turntablism), Allie Schwartz and Alison Clarke (swing), and Suzanne Szwarc (Latin pop). More recent conversations with Kai Fikentscher, Murray Forman, and Deborah Pacini Hernandez have helped me to better understand electronic dance music, contemporary hip hop, and Latin(o) popular music, respectively. Marcus Breen gave the final chapter for the third edition a useful critical read. I am indebted to Andrew Ryan, my research assistant from UMass Boston, for his research contributions to the fourth edition, particularly in the area of hip hop. The guidance of Raquel Rivera, Wayne Marshall, and Deborah Pacini Hernandez was invaluable in shaping my understanding of reggaeton.

As to my own previous work, echoes of *Rock 'n' Roll Is Here to Pay,* the book with which I was first identified, can certainly be detected in *Rockin' Out.* In this instance, I owe a major debt of gratitude to senior author Steve Chapple whose pioneering contributions to popular music studies helped define the field and pushed me to formulate my own views. My chapter on the history of black popular music that appeared in *Split Image,* edited by Jannette Dates and William Barlow, informed the discussions of r&b, soul, and rap that appear in these pages. An earlier version of the discussion of popular music and the civil rights movement was published in *Radical America* and reprinted in my own *Rockin' the Boat.* More detailed versions of my research on mega-events have appeared in *Re-Imaging America,* edited by Mark O'Brien and Craig Little, *Technoculture,* edited by Constance Penley and Andrew Ross, and *Rockin' the Boat.* My research on censorship has been published in greater detail in the *Journal of Popular Music Studies.* It was originally funded by a grant from the Massachusetts Foundation for the Humanities and the Massachusetts Cultural Council, neither of which bear any responsibility for my opinions on the subject. My research for the chapter on Internet music in *Policing Pop,* edited by Martin Cloonan and me, provided the basis for earlier discussions of peer-to-peer file sharing networks in *Rockin' Out.* This work has been revised and updated for the current edition.

Taking *Rockin' Out* to a fourth edition has been a very interesting journey. I continue to be indebted to Susannah Brabant for bringing the original book proposal to the attention of Bill Bark at Allyn and Bacon, who published the first edition. Subsequent editions have been published by Prentice Hall; those corporate mergers I write about are not limited to the music industry. For the fourth edition of *Rockin' Out*, copyright was transferred to me and the editorial baton passed to my new editor Richard Carlin, with whom I became involved in a flurry of activity updating the text, adding new features, and integrating the whole endeavor with new cutting-edge technologies. Richard came to this new gig as a seasoned editor with a wealth of valuable experience, a congenial style, and a willingness to think outside of the box, all of which are most appreciated.

Richard and his colleagues at Prentice Hall assembled a new crack team of professionals to oversee every aspect of publishing the fourth edition. Angela Mariani-Smith deserves major credit for contributing the Listening Guides. Her insightful creations provide the reader with new dimensions of learning as she strengthens the existing narrative. Richard Kassel provided the iTunes links, which make the music immediately accessible. Watch for more Listening Guides and links as we move to develop supplementary Web-based materials. Angie also joined Dr. Robert Bonora, Guy M. Capuzzo, Joseph Kotarba, and Frank Retzel in submitting reviews that helped me shape the fourth edition. Debbie Prato provided invaluable services as copy editor, and Rich Genova's thoughtful overhaul and update of the Subject and Song Indexes promise even greater usability. For the third time, production designer Denise Hoffman created page layouts and graphic devices that compliment the tone and voice of the book perfectly. Working with Denise continues to be an absolute joy. And for the U.S. edition, the coordination of this whole package was in the able hands of production editor Jean Lapidus, whose scheduling genius was what enables the book to see the light of day.

As for me, I have finished my thirtieth year at the College of Public and Community Service at UMass Boston, and I continue to enjoy my affiliation with the American Studies Program. The college and U.S. public higher education generally are currently in rough shape. Still, I have been blessed with good friends, interesting colleagues, and a loving family. As always, Deborah Pacini Hernandez is not just my partner but also a colleague whose knowledge of popular music has added measurably to my own. Since the beginning of this project, she has offered perspective, insight, and criticism that have been incredibly valuable and emotional support I could not have done without. The family that I inherited from her, which includes daughter Radha and son Tai, continues to be a source of great joy and incredibly eclectic musical tastes. Although the loss of my dad in 1999 and my mom in 2004 was painful, I feel fortunate that I still have my brother Gary and his family in my life. And my granddaughter, Radha's daughter Soleil, now six years old, has filled me with a new sense of wonderment. I remain concerned about the world situation and the plight of those who struggle without reward. Fortunately, one look at Soleil is enough to melt hearts, inspire hope, and keep a vision of social justice alive as we move into an uncertain future.

Reebee Garofalo
September 2008

Preface
by Rob Bowman

Rock and roll and other forms of Western popular music were first taught at the university level in a few places in the United States in the mid-1970s. In 1979, I had the privilege of offering the first course at a Canadian university devoted to the academic study of rock music. I followed that in 1988 with the first course at a Canadian university that took rhythm and blues in the broadest sense (e.g., jump blues to rap) as its subject matter and in 1993 I introduced the first course at the graduate level in a music department in Canada that looked at approaches to the study of popular music.

For the first eighteen years of my teaching career there was no adequate text for an undergraduate course on popular music. While no textbook can be perfect, when Reebee Garofalo's *Rockin' Out* was first published in 1997, it went a long way toward providing a textbook that gave my students a good historical and social context for American popular music post-World War II. As good as Reebee's book was, though, it was written for American university students. While Canadians such as Neil Young and Alanis Morissette figured into the narrative, Leonard Cohen was mentioned in passing in a single sentence and the names of such seminal Canadian musicians as Lighthouse, Daniel Lanois, and the Tragically Hip didn't appear anywhere in the text. Perhaps even more important, the rich traditions of Canadian punk, hip hop, and alternative rock were notable by their absence.

It has been with this in mind that the Canadian edition of *Rockin' Out* was produced. We debated about how to include the new Canadian material. Should there be one or two separate chapters devoted to activity in Canada? Should we use sidebars to highlight discussions of Canadian content so that Canadian students could easily access this material? Both of these ideas were ultimately ruled out in favour of integrating the new Canadian content within the existing text. Sometimes that simply meant adding a sentence or even a few words on a given page. At other times, it meant adding one or two paragraphs, and in a few instances it meant writing passages that were two or three thousand words in length.

Much of this work involved reclaiming a space in popular music history for Canadian expressive culture, detailing the work of musicians who had substantial success in Canada but were not known internationally. Occasionally, I found myself moved to write about great Canadian music and fascinating Canadian scenes that did not even achieve substantial success in Canada but were nonetheless intrinsically interesting. In addition to doing my best to include at least a brief discussion of the contributions of the vast majority of important Canadian popular musicians, at various points in the text I discuss the impact of Canada's immigration laws on Canadian popular music, the creation of the Canadian Content regulations in 1971, and the differences between MuchMusic and MTV. Also, from 1970 onwards, I provide statistics on the Canadian recording industry to compliment the American statistics provided by Reebee.

The reader will note that while there is a small amount of Canadian material that has been added to Chapters 1–5, the majority of the Canadian content begins in Chapter 6, when the narrative reaches the 1960s. Unfortunately, due to the relatively small population of Canada, the absence of a developed recording industry in the country and the fact that popular music is by and large a commodified form, what popular music activity did exist prior to the late 1950s tended to be regional and attracted virtually no media attention. Consequently, with the exception of the country and classical recordings made by RCA Victor in Montreal beginning in the 1930s, there have been virtually no reissues of popular music recorded by Canadians in Canada before the 1950s. The paucity of available recordings has meant that there has also been virtually no research into Canadian popular music during the first five decades of the twentieth century. Even in the late 1950s, the main recording artists—Paul Anka, the Diamonds, the Crew-Cuts, and Jack Scott—were all signed to American record labels and made all of their significant recordings in the United States. While there is a significant increase in Canadian recording activity in the early and mid-sixties, the Canadian music industry was still in its infancy. It would not be until the early 1970s, largely due to the advent of the CanCon regulations, that a fully-fledged music industry developed in Canada.

While I knew the vast majority of this material prior to sitting down to write about it, I did find myself imbued with a sense of pride and occasionally a bit of wonder at just how much incredible popular music had been made by Canadians in the past 50 years. That in turn meant that I was often frustrated because there was not enough room to cover all of the material I would have liked to in as much depth as I would have preferred.

Adapting an already existing text has its own particular set of conundrums. As much as possible, I tried to follow the structure, spirit and literary aesthetic of Reebee's work. Some readers may feel that there are times when the Canadian material feels like it could have been more integrated. Perhaps they are correct. That said, I think it would be absurdly nationalistic not to acknowledge that the history of Western popular music in the twentieth century has been dominated by social, cultural, and musical developments in the United States. Unless one is teaching a course that is exclusively devoted to Canadian popular music (and I am not aware of such a course currently being offered), one has to look at a number of issues of history and race relationships in the United States, and one certainly has to discuss the political economy of the music industry in the U.S., the development of musical forms in the U.S., and a host of American artists. Reebee obviously already takes care of all of this. Along the way, he also writes about a number of general issues such as the dominance within the music industry of the English language and gender discrimination (both discussed in the introductory chapter) that are just as pertinent to the production and consumption of popular music in Canada as they are in the United States. As Reebee had already dealt with these issues and the amount of new material I could add was already limited, I felt no compulsion to rewrite such sections substituting Canadian examples for American ones. My new material was designed to compliment the material and the (largely American) story that already existed. With the above in mind, I should make note of two additional issues in adapting this book: (1) *Popular music* in Reebee's book does not include jazz. Consequently, such icons of Canadian jazz as Oscar Peterson, Sonny Greenwich and Lenny Breau are not included in this adaptation. (2) In the original book, in any number of discussions equally pertinent to both Canada and the United States, Reebee only refers to the United States. I initially substituted the word North America for all references to the U.S. that were equally applicable to both countries. Two reviewers quite correctly pointed out that North America would also include Mexico. Consequently, we opted in all of these instances to write "Canada and the United States."

I would like to thank a few people for their help in creating this edition. Len McCarthy provided valuable research assistance and Patti Altridge proved to be a very diligent yet light-handed editor. I greatly appreciate her work in shepherding this project to completion. Christine Cozens pulled the necessary strings to get this book out in time. For that I am grateful. I also appreciate Reebee Garofalo's openness to the idea of having a Canadian edition of his text and his responsiveness to the changes we proposed. I also would like to extend my thanks to my colleague, Matt vander Woude, who as is the case with much of my work provided a sounding board for some of my ideas and freely offered a few of his own. Finally, I would like to thank Kathleen McGill for selling me on this idea and for persistently working out details between the publisher and Reebee, and between the publisher and myself so that this project could actually get underway.

If you have any comments, suggestions, or factual corrections, I can be reached at *rbowman@yorku.ca*.

Rob Bowman
September 2008

Student Supplement

A Companion Website is available for students at *www.pearsoned.ca/garofalo*. This site provides students with an online study guide and chapter overviews to help organize key concepts. Seventeen additional Listening Guides are included. **The unique feature of the site is a link to the custom iTunes playlist for the text** (available for purchase through iTunes Canada).

Introduction: Definitions, Themes, and Issues

Broadly speaking, there have been two great eras of mainstream popular music in the United States and Canada in this century: the era dominated by the writers and publishers of Tin Pan Alley, which began at the turn of the twentieth century and continued through the end of World War II, and the era that began with the emergence of rock 'n' roll in the early 1950s and continues to the present day.[1] The term *rock 'n' roll* is thus used to describe both the particular music that became popular among youth in the 1950s and the paradigm that dominated popular music thereafter. *Rockin' Out* begins with the rise of Tin Pan Alley because all the technological advances (sound recording, radio broadcasting, and to a lesser extent, film and television) and all the musical styles (blues, jazz, country, rhythm and blues, and Tin Pan Alley pop itself) that contributed to the development of rock 'n' roll came to fruition during its reign.

While this book covers more than one hundred years of recorded music, its primary focus is on the second half of the twentieth century. The pivotal moment in this history was the emergence of rock 'n' roll in the 1950s, as the transition from Tin Pan Alley to rock 'n' roll revealed important social and cultural shifts in U.S. and Canadian society. If the music of Tin Pan Alley was lighthearted and urbane, the rock 'n' roll of the 1950s was heavy-handed and urban. While Tin Pan Alley appealed to middle-class

> *The rock 'n' roll that emerged in the fifties combined all the elements that would define the broad parameters of popular music in the United States and Canada for at least the next forty years.*

sensibilities, rock 'n' roll was decidedly working class in its orientation. Whereas Tin Pan Alley made no particular age distinctions among its listeners, rock 'n' roll was targeted at youth. Tin Pan Alley was identified with sheet music in the same way that rock 'n' roll was associated with records, and it was this difference that signified the beginning of an inextricable connection between popular music and advanced recording technology. Finally, the music of Tin Pan Alley evolved according to a Euro-American paradigm of music making, even when it incorporated

1

other cultural influences. In contrast, rock 'n' roll turned dramatically toward African American conventions. In short, the rock 'n' roll that emerged in the fifties combined all the elements that would define the broad parameters of popular music in the United States and Canada for at least the next forty years.

Into the Twentieth Century: Popular Music and Mass Culture

In its association with sheet music, Tin Pan Alley can be seen as a descendant of a popular culture that dates back to the invention of the printing press in fifteenth-century Europe.[2] When the music of Tin Pan Alley emerged, popular music was distinguished from both folk music and folk culture on the one hand and classical or art music and high culture on the other. These distinctions are a part of our inheritance that came with European colonization.

Prior to the advent of popular culture in Europe, European societies were characterized by a two-tiered system of culture composed of *folk culture* and *high culture.* While there is ample evidence to suggest that there was considerable interaction between the two, at the time, these different levels of culture were officially considered separate and distinct. Historically, folk culture has been associated with the poor and those lacking formal education—in European feudal societies, the peasantry; after the Industrial Revolution, agricultural workers and the urban proletariat. It was a collective and participatory culture, shared by a particular community of people. The music arising from it was comparatively simple in form and structure, performed by nonprofessionals, and passed along, usually anonymously, in oral tradition. Its production and consumption were noncommercial. At the other end of the European cultural spectrum was high culture, which was associated with the ruling classes—the feudal aristocracy, the capitalist bourgeoisie. Its music was more complicated in form and structure and composed by paid professionals who were commissioned through a system of patronage. Because this music was notated (written down), it required a certain literacy and training for its performance. High culture thus imposed a separation between artists and consumers that was unknown in folk culture. What was a community in folk culture became an audience in high culture. As the official culture of court and church, high culture was considered to be superior to folk culture.

Popular culture insinuated itself between folk culture and high culture as a third cultural category, a hybrid that was distinguishable from both but borrowed freely from each as needed. Tin Pan Alley provides an excellent example of these contradictory tendencies. In attempting to cater exclusively to popular (albeit narrow mainstream) tastes, Tin Pan Alley writers consciously sought to construct an alternative to the cultural dominance of European art music. In the process, these writers incorporated influences, however superficially, from a wide range of sources, including a number of African American genres. At the same time, however, these writers often took their cues from classical music and high culture. For example, the 1941 melody of "Tonight We Love," a popular song by Ray Austin and Bobby Worth, was lifted virtually note for note from the first movement of Tchaikovsky's *Piano Concerto No. 1.* Furthermore, in leaning heavily on upper-middle-class themes and images—dining at the Ritz, performing in black tie and tails—Tin Pan Alley writers further (and perhaps unwittingly) allied themselves with the high culture they sought to displace.

The invention of new mass communication technologies—records, radio, film, and eventually, television—inserted yet another distinction into the cultural lexicon, namely the concept of *mass culture.* The new term indicated cultural dissemination on a scale that increased by orders of magnitude. The question of scale had important implications for qualitative judgments about mass culture. Prior to its advent, it was possible to consider popular culture as historically continuous with folk culture, either slowly replacing folk cultures as the next stage of development following the Industrial Revolution or as coexisting with rural or industrial folk cultures in the modern era. When viewed in this way, popular culture, like folk culture, was a culture of the people. With the introduction of the mass media, however, the idea of a continuing historical progression came to an abrupt halt. In the eyes of most observers, the emergence of mass culture was accompanied by a subtle but important shift in orientation from a culture *of* the people to a culture *for* the masses. In this deceptively simple change there was a profound transformation of meaning. Mass culture was not seen as the lived culture of an identifiable group of people, which reflected their values and aspirations. It was instead a commodified culture produced by a centralized, corporate culture industry for privatized, passive consumption by an alienated, undifferentiated mass.[3] Thus, although the terms *mass culture* and *popular culture* are often used interchangeably today, most observers tended to distinguish between the two in language that was pejorative and/or politically charged until well into the 1960s. In 1959, for example, Oscar Handlin, among others, argued forcefully against "the misconception that the 'mass culture' of the present is but an extension of the popular culture of the past."[4] Indeed, as late as 1965, Stuart Hall and Paddy Whannel maintained that "the typical 'art' of the mass media today is not a continuity from, but a *corruption of,* popular art."[5]

Rock 'n' roll, of course, could be numbered among the victims of this largely false distinction. As an unabashedly commercial product clearly intended for mass consumption, the music was dismissed by most critics as inferior and unworthy of serious consideration. To avoid the mass culture stigma, critics and historians in the 1960s who became invested in the cultural importance of rock as the mature form of rock 'n' roll tended to characterize the music as something other than what it was. Historian Carl Belz, for example, argued that "rock is a part of the long tradition of folk art in the United States and throughout the world."[6] As the music took a turn toward greater sophistication, this characterization underwent further change. Discussions of Bob Dylan's lyrics as poetry and the Beatles' *Sgt. Pepper* as art reflected an attempt by some to "elevate" rock from folk music to art, thereby allying it with high culture. At the time, these efforts to categorize rock represented genuine attempts to understand the place of popular music in the hierarchy of cultural practices. Ultimately, however, there was no getting around the fact that rock was both a popular music and a mass cultural form. In 1981, music sociologist Simon Frith, among others, dismissed both earlier positions of rock as folk and rock as art.

In the eyes of most observers, the emergence of mass culture was accompanied by a subtle but important shift in orientation from a culture of the people to a culture for the masses.

"Rock is a commercially made mass music," he asserted, "and this must be the starting point for its celebration as well as its dismissal."[7] Since then, musical practices have been discussed more in terms of the death throes of the modern era and its uneasy segue into postmodernism, a period characterized by, among other things, the collapse of all cultural categories.

Rock 'n' Roll: The Birth of a New Era

The straightforward commercialism and mass appeal of rock 'n' roll did not set it apart from other popular music. What made rock 'n' roll different was its urban orientation, focus on youth culture, appeal to working-class sensibilities, and relationship to technology and African American musical influences and performance styles. As Charlie Gillett argues in his classic study *The Sound of the City,* rock 'n' roll was the first popular genre to incorporate the relentless pulse and sheer volume of urban life into the music itself. In his words, "Rock and Roll was perhaps the first form of popular culture to celebrate without reservation characteristics of city life that had been among the most criticized."[8] Here Gillett was referring to urban sounds that were perceived as "brutal and oppressive." It was in this world of droning machines that post–World War II adolescents "staked out their freedom . . . inspired and reassured by the rock and roll beat."[9]

Gillett's conflation of adolescence and rock 'n' roll highlights the fact that the emergence of the music as a genre coincided with the beginnings of youth culture as a phenomenon. Due to the convergence of a number of social forces in the 1950s, including postwar affluence and a demographic shift in the population toward youth, teenagers became an identifiable consumer group and one that possessed an ample amount of disposable income. The music industry learned, albeit not without considerable resistance, that targeting the musical tastes of this generation could be quite lucrative. As Simon Frith noted:

> The young had always had idols—film stars, sportsmen, singers like Frank Sinatra and Johnny Ray; the novelty of rock 'n' roll was that its performers were the same age as their audience, came from similar backgrounds, had similar interests; and the rise of rock 'n' roll meant a generation gap . . . . Rock 'n' roll records and radio shows were aimed exclusively at the young . . . and by the end of the 1950s most pop records were being bought by the young.[10]

Following the eruption of rock 'n' roll, the music industry identified young people as the primary audience for popular music. This new marketing strategy was later complicated by the fact that the baby boomers who comprised the initial rock 'n' roll audience kept on buying records well into their thirties and forties. Indeed, different generational preferences can be seen as a partial explanation for the fragmentation of popular genres in the 1970s. In the 1980s and 1990s, clear generational differences resurfaced as rap, metal, and alternative became the cutting-edge statements of youth culture. In response, many baby boomers have adopted the same critical tone toward this new music that their parents directed at early rock 'n' roll.

If rock 'n' roll was different from other forms of popular music in its unique relationship to youth, its connection to technology was also different. Different media have their own internal logic for such elements as composition, chronology, pacing, gesture, tone, inflection, and so forth. The power of filmmaking, for example, does not lie in the simple reproduction and transmission of an existing written work; rather, it is in exploiting the particular characteristics of the medium—camera angles, lighting, editing—that filmmaking becomes an art form in its own right. The same logic extends to the relationship between music and recording. However, while the artistic possibilities of filmmaking were recognized fairly early in the development of the medium, the incorporation of recording technology into the creation of music—as opposed to its simple reproduction—was slower to take hold. Initially, recording was thought of as a documentary process that sought only to preserve the quality of a live performance. Thus, while the success of popular music—even the music of Tin Pan Alley—depended to a large extent on mass communication technologies, these technologies were used in the dissemination of the music rather than its creation.

Unlike earlier forms of popular music, rock 'n' roll incorporated the capabilities of advanced technology into the creative process itself.

Unlike earlier forms of popular music, rock 'n' roll incorporated the capabilities of advanced technology into the creative process itself. Far from valuing the purity of the live performance, rock 'n' roll records consciously used the technical features of echo, editing, overdubbing, and multitracking to distort the reality of the performance. "Technical processes," as musicologist Peter Wicke has said, "became musical opportunities."[11] The emergence of rock 'n' roll, then, was characterized by a progressively more intimate relationship with the technologies used in its production and dissemination. This relationship continued as rock ventured toward art in the 1960s. Following the release of *Sgt. Pepper,* an album so dependent on studio technology that it couldn't be performed live, rock groups spent untold hours in the studio experimenting with technological gimmickry, overdubbing and adding special effects, and mixing each cut to perfection. Disco was further immersed in technological wizardry, becoming almost completely a product of the studio. In live performance, the use of feedback and distortion pioneered by Jimi Hendrix has become institutionalized in heavy metal through the use of voltage regulators, special effects boxes, and vocal distortion devices. Rap has pushed the envelope still further, first by using dual turntables as musical instruments, and then by using samplers, sequencers, and programmable drum machines as essential tools of the trade. To the extent that these creative uses of technology have been accepted as artistically valid, they have pushed the very definition of popular music beyond a traditional European conception of music as a pattern of *notes* toward a conception of music as organized *sound.*

Beginning with early rock 'n' roll, advanced technologies were married to musical elements that in themselves separated the music from earlier forms of mainstream popular music along lines of class and race. The prominence of rhythm, immoderate volume, slurred notes, grainy vocals, aggressive attack, and vernacular speech that characterized rock 'n' roll tended to place the music outside the reach of middle-class culture and beyond the purview of musicological investigation. Because the field of musicology derives its main categories of investigation from the "notated" tradition of European art music, there has been a tendency to dismiss most working-class forms of popular music (and certainly rock 'n' roll) as "formulaic" and therefore insignificant. Within the parameters valued by official tastemakers—melody, harmony, structure—rock 'n' roll was found wanting. However, as Richard Middleton has pointed out:

> *The formulaic processes operate within parameters relatively highly valued by traditional musicology: harmony, melodic shape, basic rhythm pattern. Variant processes, on the other hand, often take place in parameters little valued by traditional musicology (and much harder to notate): slight pitch inflection or rhythmic variation, timbre and timbre changes, accent, and attack.*[12]

The subtlety and sophistication of rock 'n' roll, then, were to be found in features of the music that were outside the frame of reference of the cultural elite.

Analyses of structure, melody, and chord progressions, of course, are not without value. They can offer important insights into the differences existing between popular music and other forms of music, as well as differences among popular genres themselves. Rock 'n' roll and Tin Pan Alley pop, for example, can be distinguished in these terms. However, a surface analysis of these elements alone cannot adequately capture the disjuncture that characterized the transition between the two. To get to this level of analysis, it is necessary to examine the full range of cultural practices and performance styles that constituted these respective musical eras. The ascendancy of Tin Pan Alley coincided with the emergence of a number of African American genres and subgenres, including ragtime, blues, boogie woogie, and jazz. Certain aspects of these African American sounds were appropriated by Tin Pan Alley songwriters who were somewhat open to outside influences. From ragtime to swing, one can find a hint of syncopation here, a blue note there. But while grassroots blues and jazz lured listeners toward Africa, mainstream pop interpretations of these genres quickly pulled them back to Europe. Tin Pan Alley appropriations were by and large superficial adaptations—what musicologist Charles Hamm has called "a touch of exotic seasoning"[13]—that were incorporated into an aesthetic framework defined by the European tradition. This, of course, was reassuring to some. It preserved the centrality of Western civilization and kept upstart African American artists in check. Conservative culture critic H. F. Mooney, for example, considered it fortunate that the influence of African American music was "limited by compromises with middle class conventions" and delighted in the fact that it was "'polished' . . . so as to conform to the standards of European rendition."[14] Revealing his bias further, Mooney noted, "The highest compliment most of the public could pay to big-band jazz between 1928 and 1950 was 'symphonic' or 'advanced.'"[15] He went on to describe the pressures on African American artists to toe the line:

By all accounts, the eruption of rock 'n' roll entailed a profound shift in cultural values on the part of mainstream youth, a shift away from Euro-American sensibilities toward African American ones.

> *Middle-class Negroes who desired to "come up," as they put it, during the 1930s and the 1940s responded to the smoothly harmonized arrangements of a white Jimmy Dorsey's watered-down jazz. Duke Ellington himself was influenced by Guy Lombardo's "sweetest music this side of heaven," and brought something of the sound of the Roosevelt Hotel ballroom to Harlem. Commercial orchestras of the period around 1920–50 followed more or less the "safe bet"—the aesthetic aspirations of the middle-class market—as did, indeed, most of the big Negro bands.*[16]

Rock 'n' roll, however, turned this situation on its head. By all accounts, the eruption of rock 'n' roll entailed a profound shift in cultural values on the part of mainstream youth, a shift away from Euro-American sensibilities and toward African American ones. The most important feature of this shift was an increased emphasis on rhythm. In the words of Christopher Small, "Rhythm is to the African musician what harmony is to the European—the central organizing principle of the art."[17] Although in the slave cultures of the Americas, this African tradition was complicated by considerable pressure to adopt European ways of music making (indeed, the history of African American music is fraught with this tension), rock 'n' roll is clearly descended from the tradition of organizing musical elements around a recurring rhythmic structure. In its early years, rock 'n' roll was often referred to as the Big Beat. With the ascent of rock 'n' roll, then, this "central organizing principle" came to define mainstream popular music in a way that it never had before.

The orientation toward an African American aesthetic also affected such musical elements as structure, chord patterns, and scales, as well as the more subtle features mentioned earlier. As music historian Iain Chambers has written:

> While the thirty-two bar format is the musical cornerstone of Tin Pan Alley, in the Afro-American tradition it is the twelve bar blues: three chords alternating in a fixed pattern. From the perspective of European classical harmony, this offers an even more rigid and correspondingly "poorer" musical frame than that used by the white popular music industry. The "blues scale" is also sparse: consisting of five rather than the seven notes of the official European scale. This produces a telling disorientation for our ears as the blues singer stretches and slides over those intervals ("blue notes") we are accustomed to expect. Such a sensation of "foreignness" is the most recognisable aural trait of the blues and Afro-American music in pop—the slides, slurs, bent, "dirty" and uncertain notes in the voice, guitar, saxophone and bass. It remains the irreducible testimony of the clash between a legitimised white European-derived tradition and a barely recognised Afro-American one.[18]

While there had been an awareness of African American influences among white jazz musicians and Tin Pan Alley composers, rock 'n' roll pushed performers toward the wholesale adoption of an African American orientation. As Peter Wicke has stated:

> Elvis Presley or Bill Haley were no longer merely taking set pieces from blues and rhythm & blues and imposing them as superficial effects on quite different musical categories. Their popularity was founded precisely on the fact that they were copying Afro-American music with all its characteristic features, including the performance style of black musicians, as closely as possible. What was happening was a complete reversal of the earlier situation. Whereas before white musicians had adapted elements of the Afro-American musical tradition to their own aesthetic ideas, now they were trying to suit their performances to the aesthetics of Afro-American music.[19]

If rock 'n' roll tipped the cultural balance toward an African American aesthetic, it was also a music defined by its hybridity. While Elvis Presley clearly drew on African American performance styles, he adopted the instrumentation of country music and was also driven by pop tendencies that were entirely consistent with Tin Pan Alley values. Chuck Berry and Sam Cooke, as well as many doo wop groups, enunciated clearly enough to pass muster with the harshest diction teacher. Indeed, doo wop harmonies and vocal styles defy any attempt to analyze rock 'n' roll solely in terms of race. In short, European cultural standards were never abandoned altogether; rock 'n' roll simply imposed a new cultural formula that favoured African American values.

Since the advent of rock 'n' roll, there has been a continuing debate regarding the relative proportions of African American and Euro-American influences in popular music. It was considered a mark of distinction by some critics that many of the San Francisco groups of the late 1960s did not sound like they were emulating African American performance styles. Art rock made its musical statement by looking to classical European influences. The concept of instrumental virtuosity in heavy metal derived from the same source. Punk, which ironically was formed in reaction to the excesses of art rock, stripped the music of whatever African American influences remained. Even disco, in the United States and Canada, was marked by the tension between funk and soft soul influences on the one hand and the influence of Eurodisco on the other. Popular music has been re-Africanized in rap, which has concentrated primarily on heavy beats and spoken word rhymes, eschewing melody almost completely. In fact, rap is the only form of U.S. popular music that became more Afrocentric as it gained in mainstream acceptance.

Marketing and the Politics of Race, Language, and Gender

If rock 'n' roll represented the triumph of African American culture, it did not automatically follow that African Americans would be the main beneficiaries of the victory. The way in which music actually unfolds as a social practice does not necessarily determine the way in which it reaches the ears of its audience. By the time a creative urge has been fed through the star-making machinery of the culture industry, all the biases of class, race, and gender have been brought to bear on it. Although rock 'n' roll proceeded from an aesthetic impulse that viewed cultural borrowing as both natural

If rock 'n' roll represented the triumph of African American culture, it did not automatically follow that African Americans would be the main beneficiaries of the victory.

and desirable, it developed in a commercial context that was subject to all the foibles and inequities of the larger society. In such a context, the natural process of cultural borrowing can become theft, and artists can be categorized incorrectly or excluded from the marketplace altogether for reasons that have little to do with talent or musical style.

The marketing categories of the music industry have often classified performers as much by race as by musical style. The beginnings of this practice date back to the 1920s, when the music industry organized popular music into three categories: "race" (African American popular music); "hillbilly" (white working-class rural styles); and "popular" (mainstream pop of the type produced by Tin Pan Alley).[20] Initially, *Billboard,* the leading music industry trade magazine, published popularity charts for only that music classified as "popular" by the industry. However, when *Your Hit Parade,* a radio program based on (and shaped by) listener preferences, became one of the most popular programs in the country in 1935, it became apparent that the commercial interests of the industry were not being served by only one chart. Thus, by the end of the decade, *Billboard* had inaugurated a popularity chart for "hillbilly" music and in 1942 added a chart titled "The Harlem Hit Parade." Three years later, the magazine changed this title to "Race Music."

Each marketing category was presumed to be a distinct musical style with its own audience. "The assumed mainstream pop audience," according to David Brackett, "was northern, urban, middle or upper class, and also white. The charts for the marginal musics also assumed an audience—African American for race and r&b [rhythm and blues], rural southern white for hillbilly, folk, and country and western (as these charts were variously designated during the 1940s)."[21] Initially, there was little overlap among the categories, which lent credence to the industry's assumption that these were separate, distinct styles. Indeed, these styles did develop regionally in a country that was segregated and racked by class divisions. It was, in fact, the social and cultural changes associated with World War II that began to render the barriers between marketing categories a bit more porous. As the categories "race" and "hillbilly" began to come to the attention of the mainstream audience, these styles were said to cross over.

The term *crossover* refers to that process whereby an artist or a recording from a secondary or specialty marketing category, such as country and western (c&w) or rhythm and blues (r&b), achieves hit status in the mainstream market. Although recently the term has been used simply to indicate multiple chart listings in any direction, historically it connoted movement from a marginal category to the mainstream. In writing of the golden years of r&b, music historian Arnold Shaw has noted:

> *The crossover concept was inherent in R&B from the start. In fact, acceptance by the pop market of an R&B disk (Cecil Gant's "I Wonder") generated the first mushrooming of R&B record companies. While these labels produced disks basically for ghetto consumption, they always hoped that the larger white market might be receptive.*[22]

The greater acceptance of African Americans in the mainstream market after World War II not only prompted some changes in music charting practices but also put the industry on the horns of a racial dilemma that has been the subject of heated debate ever since.

As late as 1949, most of the music by African American artists could be found under the heading *race music* in record company catalogues. As this music began to cross over to the white market, however, it was decided that a more palatable term was needed. Record companies toyed with labels like *ebony* and *sepia* for a while, but these too were obviously distinctions of colour, not musical style. Eventually *rhythm and blues* (reportedly coined by Jerry Wexler at *Billboard*) became the accepted term, and from 1949 until 1963 *Billboard* charted the music as such. *Billboard* discontinued its r&b charts from the end of 1963 until the beginning of 1965, presumably because the pop charts were becoming increasingly integrated. During this time, however, the number of African American artists on the pop charts actually declined. Accordingly, the r&b charts were reinstated by the magazine, and in 1969, r&b was replaced with the term *soul*. The industry came full circle in 1982 when the soul charts were renamed *black* music. *Billboard* later offered the explanation that "'soul' was too limited a term to define the diversity of musical styles appearing on the chart, and that 'black' was a better tribute to the music's cultural origins."[23] Ultimately, however, this term was as vulnerable to criticism as the term *race music* had been four decades earlier. Thus in 1990, *Billboard* reinstated the r&b category, explaining that it was "becoming less acceptable to identify music in racial terms."[24] And the beat goes on. . . .

Were it not for this artificial separation of the races, popular music history might read quite differently. When Syd Nathan, the founder of King Records, encouraged his r&b and c&w artists to record different versions of the same songs, he understood intuitively that pieces of music do not automatically have a genre, that they can be interpreted in many idioms. Still, in keeping with prevailing industry practices, he marketed his r&b releases only to black audiences and his country records only to white audiences. While Nathan was not limited in his choice of artists or material, he, like many others, accepted the notion that a separation of the races was "the way things were."

These same prevailing industry practices may have led Leonard Chess, head of Chess Records, to add "the rock beat of the Chicago blues" to Chuck Berry's more country-oriented audition performance of "Ida Red" ("Maybellene").[25] Chess was quite aware of the difficulties of marketing a black man as a country singer. Were it not for that reality, Chuck Berry might well have had a very different career trajectory. R&b artist Jimmy Witherspoon once argued, "Chuck Berry is a country singer. People put everybody in categories, black, white, this. Now if Chuck Berry was white, with the lyrics he writes, he would be the top country star in the world."[26] There have been any number of country-oriented versions of Chuck Berry songs, from Hoyt Axton's "Maybellene," Freddy Weller's "Too Much Monkey Business" and "Promised Land," Waylon Jennings' "Brown-Eyed Handsome Man," and Buck Owens' "Johnny B. Goode" to Linda Rondstadt's "Back in the U.S.A.," Emmylou Harris' "You Never Can Tell," and Johnny Rivers' "Memphis," but every one has been performed by whites.

Such music marketing practices were briefly challenged when Ray Charles recorded *Modern Sounds in Country and Western Music* (Volume I) and *Modern Sounds in Country and Western Music* (Volume II) for ABC-Paramount in 1962. Through these recordings, Charles proved that an artist does not have to be limited to a single performance style and a song can have more than one genre. He had long felt connections between the blues and country that rendered the rigid separation of markets suspect from a musical point of view. "I really thought that it was somethin' about country music, even as a youngster," Charles once remarked. "Although I was bred in and around the blues, I always . . . felt the closest music, really, to the blues [was country and western]. They'd make them steel guitars cry and whine, and it really attracted me."[27] These LPs turned out to be the two best-selling albums of his career. Volume I made the pop charts for fifty-nine weeks and was firmly ensconced in the number one slot for fourteen of them. The album also contained a recording of his best-selling single—Don Gibson's "I Can't Stop Loving You"—which went to number one on all three charts, perhaps the only record by an African American artist ever to do so. Even so, it was not until the end of the decade that another African American artist—Charlie Pride—made the country charts.

The identification of music with race, which has tended to exclude African American artists and others from certain marketing structures in the music industry, makes the task of unearthing an accurate history of U.S. and Canadian popular music quite difficult and encourages serious underestimates of the degree of cross-cultural collaboration that has taken place. For example, rockabilly, the country strain of rock 'n' roll in the 1950s, was a legitimate musical movement that integrated blues with country and western styles. It had its own identity, and in singers such as Elvis Presley, Carl Perkins, and Jerry Lee Lewis, performers of real originality and talent. But because rockabilly was one strand of a musical transformation that was most heavily indebted to African American culture, it is impossible to separate its popularity from a racist pattern in which styles pioneered by black artists are popularized, dominated, and even defined by whites as if they were the originators. This pattern is apparent in the history of popular music in the United States, from ragtime to jazz to swing. Rock 'n' roll was neither an exception—Presley was not merely crowned the King of Rockabilly—nor the end of the line. As a result, styles are often described (and defended) in terms that are clearly racial rather than musical. In 1984, Nick Tosches insisted that "rockabilly is hillbilly rock-and-roll. It was not a usurpation of black music by whites because its soul, its pneuma, was white, full of the redneck ethos."[28] Arnold Shaw had acknowledged a decade earlier that "it was that to a degree," but he went on to say that "it would probably be more accurate to describe [rockabilly] as the sound of young, white Southerners imitating black bluesmen."[29] The late 1960s were marked by endless debates over whether or not whites could sing the blues. The relative absence of African Americans in heavy metal and whites in rap suggests that racial divisions are still powerful determinants in social and cultural relations.

The Language Barrier

Because of the history of slavery in the New World, there is a tendency to think of racism, whether in the music industry or society as a whole, as a black/white issue. It should be recognized, however, that discriminatory practices have not been limited to African Americans alone. In many ways, the language barrier has proven to be even more intractable than the race barrier. Latin music, for instance, has always been an important influence in U.S. and Canadian popular music. In the 1950s, there was a series of popular mambos, rumbas, and cha-chas. Indeed, from Ritchie Valens to Santana to Los Lobos, there has always been a strong Latino presence in rock, and a recognizable Latin influence in dance styles from disco to hip hop. Even so, the number of Top Forty pop hits sung in Spanish in the United States or Canada could probably be counted on one hand. "La Bamba" (by Ritchie Valens and Los Lobos) and Santana's "Oye Como Va" readily come to mind, but precious few others. In fact, one could probably tally all of the non-English Top Forty pop hits on two hands. Four versions of "Volare" appeared on the charts, as did "Dominique" by the Singing Nun. Kyu Sakamoto's "Sukiyaki" was covered by Taste of Honey during the disco era. While one might quibble about whether to include Ray Barretto's "El Watusi" or Manu Dibango's "Soul Makossa" (both of which are primarily instrumental), the point is clear. Non-English hits in the United States and Canada are rare. As a result, artists who might sing in other languages feel compelled to record in English when they approach the U.S. or Canadian market. In the late 1970s and early 1980s, Spanish balladeer Julio Iglesias, a resident of the United States, was among the best-selling recording artists in the world, but he had never had a hit in the United States or Canada. The only way he could break into either market was with two English duets—one with Willie Nelson ("To All the Girls I've Loved Before") and one with Diana Ross ("All of You"), both in 1984. Linda Ronstadt, who achieved

In many ways, the language barrier has proven to be even more intractable than the race barrier.

U.S. and Canadian superstardom singing in English, provides an example of this logic in reverse. In 1988, Ronstadt, who is part Mexican, returned to her roots to record *Canciones de mi Padre.* The album never reached the U.S. pop Top Forty, even though it received the 1988 Grammy for Best Mexican/American Performance. Cuban-born Gloria Estefan's Top Ten pop album *Cuts Both Ways* (1989) included Spanish and English versions of "Don't Wanna Lose You" and "Here We Are," but only the English versions became Top Ten pop hits. The Swedish group ABBA charted fourteen Top Forty hits in the United States and Canada in the 1970s and 1980s, but all were sung in English. Norway's A-Ha broke into the U.S. and Canadian markets with "Take On Me," a cut with spectacular video animation and sung in English. When French Canadian Celine Dion, a veteran of the Quebec music scene, made a bid for international stardom in 1990, she did so on the basis of her first all-English LP, *Unison.* In 1993, she scored her first number one pop hit in the United States with "The Power of Love," which was, of course, sung in English. Similarly, with the exception of the progressive rock band Harmonium, French-language recordings by francophone artists have been unable to garner mainstream radio play or generate substantial sales. For the moment, language barriers in popular music remain strong. But, with the increasing diversity of both the U.S. and Canadian populations, this situation is bound to change. Ricky Martin did manage to include a dominant Spanish phrase in his blockbuster hit "Livin' La Vida Loca" (1999).

The Long, Hard Climb: Gender Discrimination

The barriers that women face in the music industry are equally formidable. Historically, the images of women in popular songs—from angel and baby to earth mother and sex goddess to bitch and "ho"—have been limiting or belittling, if not flat-out offensive and degrading.

Historically, the images of women in popular songs—from angel and baby to earth mother and sex goddess to bitch and "ho"—have been limiting or belittling, if not flat-out offensive and degrading.

Women performers have often been pressured by the industry to assume personas based on these stereotypes. Furthermore, the existence of a double standard regarding intimacy and sexual practices has made the social dynamics of life on the road more complicated and alienating for women than men. As if these difficulties were not enough, women have had to overcome the obstacles that stand between them and control over the creative processes. Technical processes such as record producing, engineering, mixing, and mastering are still overwhelmingly male-dominated.

While some women were able to achieve a certain status as vocalists in the decades preceding the emergence of rock 'n' roll, no woman ever achieved the status of Al Jolson, Bing Crosby, or Frank Sinatra, and it was almost never the case that a woman became successful as an instrumentalist. Whatever status could be achieved disappeared rapidly with the advent of rock 'n' roll. Indeed, rock 'n' roll actually reduced the presence of women in popular music. In the early 1960s, the women who were marketed as folk madonnas were channeled toward softer vocal styles, which were usually linked only to acoustic instruments. This trend continued among the female singer/songwriters of the 1970s, Bonnie Raitt being a notable exception. Even harder-rocking women in the 1960s—from the Crystals and the Ronettes to Grace Slick,

Janis Joplin, and Aretha Franklin—were promoted as vocalists who never touched electric instruments. While there were certain breakthroughs for women when the punk movement rewrote the rules of access, these gains were offset to some degree in the next decade by the misogyny displayed in rap and heavy metal.

By the late 1980s, women were fairly well represented in most styles (with the exception of heavy metal), and in the early 1990s, they had finally begun to compete on a roughly equal footing with men for lucrative recording contracts. However, as they have achieved greater acceptance in the popular market, they have had to confront an industry infrastructure that is fully owned and operated by men whose ideas about career development frequently push them to conform to male stereotypes of how female performers should act and sound. In other words, like African Americans and other people of colour, women performers must confront norms and social practices that limit their development and chances for success.

Regulating Popular Music

Because popular music always interacts with its social environment, it often serves as a lightning rod for the political controversies that invariably accompany change. The Tin Pan Alley pop that dominated the first half of the twentieth century, for example, was marked by a purposeful blandness and a studied inoffensiveness that, in retrospect, makes it difficult to imagine that anything about it, except its saccharine sweetness, could upset anyone. Still, the moral guardians of the early twentieth century felt that even Tin Pan Alley pop was too depraved for mainstream consumption, let alone the jazz that developed concurrently. As early as 1913, the well-known violinist Maud Powell told the National Federation of Music Clubs that the music of the United States had been

A compelling case can be made that popular culture—particularly popular music—has become the ideological battlefield upon which struggles for power, values, and identity take place.

> *thrown into disrepute through the unspeakably depraved modern popular song . . . which consists of brazenly suggestive words to a catchy rag-time accompaniment.*
>
> *Its effect on young folk is shocking. The vicious song is allowed in the home by parents, who, no doubt, have not troubled themselves to look at the words. As a result the suggestive meanings are allowed to play upon immature minds at the dangerous age. It is from the popular song that the popular suggestive dance sprang. Together and apart they are a menace to the social fabric.*[30]

The good Miss Powell went on to state that she was "heartily in favor of a board of censorship for the popular song."[31] Imagine the horror she would have felt had she been exposed to the rumblings of blues or country music, which surveyed more personal themes in a far more vernacular tone.

Throughout the second half of the twentieth century, popular music was connected quite explicitly with social change and political controversy. As millions of adults left the intensity of urban life in the 1950s for the new and expansive sprawl called suburbia, rock 'n' roll pulled their offspring back to the sounds of the city. While postwar youth may have found the new sound exciting and engaging, adults found it threatening and loosed criticisms far more damning than Powell's condemnations of Tin Pan Alley pop. Indeed, in the late 1950s, a conservative reaction against rock 'n' roll sought to turn back the musical clock by imposing rigid guidelines on radio.

A variation of this same social drama was played out in the 1980s and 1990s, as the custodians of culture became convinced that rap and heavy metal had gone too far and tried to regulate popular music through tactics ranging from a demand for warning labels on sound recordings to outright censorship. In fact, given the pronouncements of a whole range of public figures and elected officials during this period, a compelling case can be made that popular culture—particularly popular music—has become the ideological battlefield upon which struggles for power, values, and identity take place. Clearly then, popular music is potent cultural capital—aesthetically, economically, and politically. Unraveling and analyzing the complexities of its often contradictory social functions is the subject matter of *Rockin' Out*.

Mass Technology and Popular Taste: The Tin Pan Alley Era

In the late 1800s, a previously scattered conglomeration of songwriters and publishers began to converge on the Broadway and 28th Street section of New York City, an area that would come to be called Tin Pan Alley after the tinny output of the upright pianos there. The popular songsters who worked in the Alley and who would dominate mainstream popular music until World War II were not particularly interested in the tinfoil cylinder phonograph Thomas Edison, scion of a Canadian family, demonstrated for the staff of *Scientific American* in 1877. While they might have been aware of its possible use in the reproduction of music, this was not yet a practical consideration for them. Edison himself had placed this use third or fourth on his list of priorities. In his mind, the greatest potential for his machine lay in the reproduction of human speech. Consequently, he hailed his invention as a "talking machine." Along Tin Pan Alley, songwriters and publishers were far more preoccupied with the then leading form of musical reproduction—sheet music—than with Edison's invention. After all, sheet music was their primary source of revenue.

Middle-class home entertainment at that time centred on a symbol of decorum and upward mobility—the piano. In 1880 alone, two years after Edison had formed the Edison Speaking Phonograph

In its formative stages, the "music industry" could in no way be considered synonymous with the "recording industry" as it often is today.

Company, some 45,000 pianos were manufactured in the United States.[1] Over the next thirty years, annual production would increase eightfold, but there would still be those who imported their pianos from Europe. Accordingly, sheet music was the vehicle for the mass dissemination of music, and music publishers were at the centre of the music business. It was the publishers who turned the creations of songwriters and lyricists into commercial properties. It was the publishers who hired "song pluggers" and engaged the services of vaudeville stars—often for a hefty sum—to popularize their wares. All of the music publishers' practices (many of which existed in the grey margins of "ethical") were aimed at one goal—the sale of sheet music.

15

Sheet music retailed for thirty to forty cents a copy, and for the major publishers, sales in the hundreds of thousands of copies were not unheard of. Indeed, Charles K. Harris's "After the Ball," written and published in 1892, "quickly reached sales of $25,000 a week" and "sold more than 2,000,000 copies in only several years, eventually achieving a sale of some five million."[2] With potential sales such as these, it is not surprising that music publishers initially regarded the revolution in technology that eventually transformed the way in which popular music was produced and consumed as little more than a way to supplement their earnings.

In its formative stages, then, the "music industry" could in no way be considered synonymous with the "recording industry" as it often is today. At the time, it was, if anything, and industry of songwriting and music publishing. Of course, the writers of Tin Pan Alley, from Charles K. Harris, Paul Dresser, and Harry Von Tilzer to George Gershwin, Jerome Kern, and Irving Berlin, took notice of records and eventually pushed record companies to record their songs. But for a variety of reasons—practical, technical, legal, aesthetic, and economic—Tin Pan Alley never embraced records. Thus, while Tin Pan Alley and the recording industry intersected at many points and with increasing frequency over the years, in many ways they developed as separate industries. This is an important piece of historical data that begins to account for the disjuncture that marked the emergence of rock 'n' roll, a music that was issued primarily on records.

Following the decline of vaudeville in the 1920s, Tin Pan Alley tunesmiths turned to Broadway and Hollywood as natural successors to the promotional power of vaudeville. Even as records promised to become the dominant medium for the mass reproduction of music, Tin Pan Alley continued to identify itself primarily with the "literate" Broadway–Hollywood axis of popular music. In contrast, rock 'n' roll, which was derived from innovations in the oral tradition of African American music and country music, was a product of record companies; it owed its popularity to the existence of records. Just as record companies would come to replace publishing houses as the centre of the music industry, rock 'n' roll would push aside Tin Pan Alley pop as the dominant style of popular music. Thus, any social history of these changes in popular music must begin with a discussion of the development of sound recording and the uneven relationship that existed between music publishers and record companies.

Sound Recording: From Cylinder to Disc

When Edison first came up with his tinfoil cylinder phonograph, he envisioned marketing it as an office machine. In order to introduce it to the public, however, he decided to exploit its novelty value. In countless demonstrations in lecture halls, theatres, and vaudeville houses, members of the audience were invited to make live recordings. Scores of local vocalists, whistlers, and instrumentalists tried their hand at Edison's amazing "talking machine." But it was soon found that, although brass instruments reproduced reasonably well, the poor sound quality of the tinfoil cylinder severely hampered its commercial value. Once awed by its potential, Edison momentarily dismissed his phonograph as "a mere toy, which has no commercial value," and turned his attention to the invention of the electric light before once again returning to recording.[3]

The next steps in development were taken in the laboratories of Edison's fellow inventor, Canadian Alexander Graham Bell. Five years of research under the directorship of Charles

Sumner Tainter and Chichester Bell yielded a machine the inventors called a graphophone to distinguish it from Edison's phonograph. The graphophone used a floating stylus to cut "hill and dale" grooves into a wax-coated cardboard cylinder. The sound quality of the graphophone was significantly better than that of Edison's machine. Because at this time recording was a mechanical process rather than an electromechanical one, it was called *acoustic recording.*

In the late 1880s, corporate magnate Jesse Lippincott used nearly $1 million of his inheritance to consolidate the Edison patents and the national sales rights to the graphophone into a company called the North American Phonograph Company. It was to be a national office machine combined with local franchises, but it was clear within months that the phonograph did not have a future as a dictating machine. Mechanical problems and resistance from stenographers (who were mostly men at the time) constantly plagued the business. When Lippincott fell victim to infantile paralysis in the early 1890s, the struggling company was thrown into further disarray. Edward D. Easton's District of Columbia franchise—the Columbia Phonograph Company—would have to await a new direction for the talking machine before going on to become the oldest trademark in the record business.

It was Louis Glass, manager of the Pacific Phonograph Company, North American's West Coast licensee, who pointed the way to the future of the phonograph. In 1889, Glass had equipped some of his dictating machines with a patented, coin-activated mechanism and four sets of stethoscopic listening tubes and placed them in the Palais Royal Saloon in San Francisco. For a nickel per listener per play, patrons could avail themselves of the sounds of a prerecorded "entertainment" cylinder. These "nickel-in-the-slot" machines were so successful that within a year Glass had placed machines in eighteen other locations, some of which began bringing in as much as $1,200 annually. The enterprise not only pointed the way for the North American Phonograph Company but also won for Glass the title of "Father of the Juke Box."

Pay phonographs proved to be very popular in amusement parks, penny arcades, ice cream parlours, and drugstores, as well as saloons, train stations, and ferry-boat waiting rooms. However, because phonographs retailed for almost $150 and cylinders could not be economically mass-produced, a home entertainment market

In the genteel home entertainment market, the elegance of the piano and the simplicity of sheet music stood in sharp contrast to the ungainly phonograph with its awkward listening tentacles.

for prerecorded music did not seem feasible. There might also have been aesthetic considerations militating against the creation of a home-based market. "It was ludicrous in the extreme," recalled one phonograph company executive, "to see ten people grouped about a phonograph, each with a listening tube leading from his ears, grinning and laughing at what he heard."[4] In the genteel home entertainment market, the elegance of the piano and the simplicity of sheet music stood in sharp contrast to the ungainly phonograph with its awkward listening tentacles.

Among the early cylinders that caught on with the mainstream listening audience were those featuring brass bands; instrumental solos on cornet, piccolo, piano, and, especially, banjo; comic Irish tales; and so-called coon songs, novelty songs exploiting negative stereotypes of African Americans in caricatured black dialect. As the number of locations for coin-operated phonographs increased, so did the demand for prerecorded cylinders, but even so, a number of factors stood in the way of a natural alliance between Tin Pan Alley and the cylinder-recording companies that had come into being. Because of their limited sound quality, cylinders tended to favour spoken-word and instrumental selections; publishers did not receive royalties from the

John Philip Sousa, famous for his military marches, led the U.S. Marine Band to popular success during an era when the limitations of recording technology favoured the reproduction of brass bands. In the 1890s, Columbia catalogues listed scores of recordings by the Marine Band.

sale or use of recorded music; and the demand for prerecorded cylinders could not compete with the demand for sheet music. Thus, the companies manufacturing prerecorded cylinders grew independent of Tin Pan Alley.

Within this business, the Columbia Phonograph Company quickly distinguished itself as the leading producer of quality entertainment cylinders. Among the company's earliest popular cylinders were recordings by the U.S. Marine Band, which included Sousa marches, Strauss waltzes, and such popular Irish favourites as "Little Annie Rooney" and "Down Went McGinty." By 1892, Columbia had issued about one hundred recordings of the Marine Band, which sold for two dollars a cylinder. Second only to the Marine Band in popularity were the recordings of whistling virtuoso John Yorke Atlee, a government clerk who kept the nickels flowing with his renditions of tunes like "The Mockingbird" and "Home Sweet Home." New developments in recording technology had rekindled Edison's interest in the field. By the early 1890s, he was Columbia's main competition. During this period, improvements in sound reproduction came quickly, and within a few years, both Columbia and Edison had introduced affordable phonographs, which led to the creation of a home entertainment market for prerecorded cylinders.

By 1896, Columbia's catalogue of prerecorded cylinders listed thousands of titles, including, in addition to selections by the Marine Band and John Atlee, popular songs by Dan Quinn (who specialized in musical comedy), interpretations of sentimental love ballads by tenor George J. Gasken, and monologues by Russell Hunting, whose tales of Michael O'Casey became international favourites. Among Columbia's biggest artists was Henry Burr. Born January 15, 1882, as Harry McClaskey in New Brunswick, Burr was the number one star of recorded music between 1890 and 1930. As a soloist, in duets with Arthur Campbell and a number of other partners, and as a member of the Columbia Male Quartet, the Peerless Quartet, and the Sterling Trio, Burr made over 12,000 recordings, "far more than any other vocalist in history."[5] At the time of his death in 1941, Burr was a regular member of NBC's *National Barn Dance*.

Edison was not to be outdone and boasted George Washington Johnson—if not the first, then certainly the most successful black recording artist at the time—who achieved fame and fortune with two hits, "The Whistling Coon" and "The Laughing Song." Edison also hired Ontario-born May Irwin, the preeminent vaudeville star of the 1890s, who debuted such songs on stage as "Ta-ra-ra Boom Der-e," "The Bully," and "Mr. Johnson, Turn Me Loose." In 1907, she had a hit recording on Victor of "The Bully." In 1895, she shocked audiences with an early film titled "The Kiss," which was produced by Edison's Kinetoscope and at the time was considered risqué. Although both Columbia and Edison had great artists, the competition between the two companies was fierce; in fact, they spent so much time fighting each other that they paid little attention to the development of disc recording, an innovation that would eventually consign cylinders to the dust-filled corners of attics.

Emile Berliner, a German immigrant to the United States (who would move to Montreal in 1897), developed the flat recording disc that became the industry standard but was not the first to experiment with it. Edison himself had already considered and rejected the idea. Berliner had first perfected a method of engraving sound vibrations on wax-coated zinc discs which could produce a much louder playback volume than the cylinder machines, in 1887, but did not patent his work until 1896. When he had demonstrated his "gramophone" in 1888 at the Franklin Institute in Philadelphia, the machine had generated little interest, but it was at that meeting that Berliner prophesied the ability to make an unlimited number of copies from a single master, the use of discs for home entertainment on a mass scale, and a system of royalty payments to artists derived from the sale of discs. Thus, it was Berliner who first envisaged the contours of the modern music industry. Undaunted by the lack of interest in his gramophone, he set about the task of pursuing his vision.

Berliner delivered on his first prophecy when he made from the zinc masters negative discs, called "stampers," which were then pressed into ebonite rubber biscuits to produce an exact duplicate, or "record," of the master. A later improvement replaced the rubber discs with shellac-based, 78 rpm pressings, which then became the industry standard until the late 1940s. Berliner knew that to realize his second prophecy he would need someone with more musical ability than himself to coordinate talent and recording. He turned to Fred Gaisberg, who had been doing that at Columbia. Indeed, Gaisberg was, in effect, the first artist and repertoire (a&r) man in the infant industry. All it took to convince Gaisberg to jump ship was a single demonstration of the "beautiful round tones" of Berliner's disc.

Berliner then contracted with an enterprising machinist named Eldridge R. Johnson to manufacture the gramophones. Adding improvements of his own, Johnson soon began turning out machines by the hundreds. In 1901, the Berliner and Johnson interests were consolidated into the Victor Talking Machine Company with Johnson at the helm. Berliner was now based in Montreal, and it was in Canada that he registered as a trademark his company's logo: the famous "Little Nipper" (the comely pup listening attentively to his master's voice in front of a record horn), which was originally a painting by Francis Barraud that was given to Berliner and Johnson by William Barry Owen, head of The Gramophone Co., Ltd., Victor's European partner. Shortly after the formation of the Victor Talking Machine Company, whose recordings were pressed and distributed in Canada by the Berliner Corporation in Montreal, the major recording companies—Edison, Columbia, and Victor—decided to pool their patents and set about the business of making better records

Because of an elitist bias toward high culture, European art music was considered far superior to U.S. popular music.

and machines.[6] The first Canadian group to record was the Belleville Kilties Band, who cut their first record in 1902. Two years later, the Columbia Graphaphone Co. set up a Canadian branch in Toronto under the moniker Canadian Phonograph. From this point until the advent of commercial radio following World War I, acoustic recording enjoyed its golden era.

Because exclusive recording contracts were not yet the industry standard, artists were not tied to a single company. Consequently, Gaisberg had little trouble persuading Columbia's celebrities (Atlee, Gasken, and Hunting) to record for Victor. Indeed, he was not even limited to performers in the United States. Through the efforts of Owen, Gaisberg was soon recording in every music capital in Europe. Because of an elitist bias toward high culture, European art music was considered far superior to U.S. popular music. Accordingly, the British Gramophone catalogue contained songs and arias in every European language (Gaisberg even made recordings at the Imperial Opera in Russia) and many Asian languages as well. Victor imported these high-priced Red Seal recordings for sale in the United States and then began a domestic Red Label series of its own that featured the stars of the Metropolitan Opera in New York.[7] Producer C. G. Childs placed the jewel in the crown of the new series when he managed to sign Italian tenor Enrico Caruso to an exclusive Victor contract by offering him the unprecedented provision of a royalty on records sold, thereby fulfilling the last of Berliner's 1888 prophecies.

Priced higher than other records, Victor's Red Label series was clearly intended for the wealthy "carriage trade." Columbia, which by this time had entered the disc business, also featured a grand opera series of its own. However, by 1910, as Ian Whitcomb points out in his inimitable style, "It was quite clear to the record companies that the classics only brought in prestige and that the steady income was to be made from sales to the 'Cracker-Barrel Trade,' to the 'Good Old Coon Song—Sousa—Monologue—Sentimental Ballad—Bunch.'"[8]

The Clef Club, organized by James Reese Europe, was an African American musicians' union that could supply orchestras of varying sizes on request. In 1914, Europe's own Syncopated Society Orchestra was signed to Victor, becoming the first African American ensemble to secure a recording contract.

If the choice of recorded material was an indicator of class differences, the choice of format revealed a rural-urban split. "By the middle of the first decade of the twentieth century," writes C. A. Schicke, "the disc had distinctly succeeded in capturing the buying power of the upper and middle classes and the urban population. The cylinder's stronghold—and mostly Edison cylinders at that—was the poorer, rural market."[9] In both instances, however, the selection of recording artists was made with only the white population in mind. Even so-called "coon" songs, a staple of the recording companies from the beginning, were almost invariably sung by whites. With the exception of George W. Johnson and the great black vaudevillian Bert Williams, nearly all of "the other leading coon-song and black-dialect vocalists before World War I were white, the best known being Charles Asbury, David C. Bangs, Arthur Collins, Billy Golden, Silas Leachman, Bob Roberts, Len Spencer, Billy Williams, and the 'First Lady of Phonograph Records,' Ada Jones."[10] Indeed, prior to World War I, there was only one African American ensemble that had landed a recording contract: the Syncopated Society Orchestra led by James Reese Europe. Europe organized the Clef Club in New York as a black musicians' union of sorts that, according to musicologist Eileen Southern, "could furnish a dance orchestra from three to thirty men upon request at any time, day or night."[11] For special occasions, like their 1912 Carnegie Hall concert, a Clef Club orchestra could number as many as 145 players, including fifty-eight banjos, mandolins, and bandores, ten pianos, and five drum kits. Clef Club ensembles benefited from the dance fads that came into being in the early teens. Because of Europe's association with the cosmopolitan dance team of Vernon and Irene Castle, his Syncopated Society Orchestra was added to the Victor talent roster in 1914 and produced dance records that remained profitable for years.

While it is true that the golden age of acoustic recording drew on and preserved a broad range of musical styles, it also established one of the most troubling aspects of the contemporary music industry, namely, the fragmentation of the audience not only along lines of class but also along the lines of geography and, of course, race. It was also claimed that the existing technology favoured lower male voices, which clearly left women with few recording stars of their own. (One can only wonder how those piccolo solos got recorded.) Ada Jones was not simply the "First Lady of Phonograph Records"; she was one of the few ladies of phonograph records.

The technological advances of the late nineteenth and early twentieth centuries introduced what later critics of mass culture would see as the historical schism that marked the transition from active music-making to passive music consumption. In the popular image of a family gathered around the living-room piano, music is "consumed" through the active participation of all concerned. With the invention of recording, it was no longer necessary to have any musical ability whatsoever to re-create the sound of music. In playing to the earlier image of "family entertainment," the publishing houses of Tin Pan Alley were naturally at odds with the record companies. Like these companies, however, they had the same social and cultural biases that plagued the rest of society.

The technological advances of the late nineteenth and early twentieth centuries introduced what later critics of mass culture would see as the historical schism that marked the transition from active music-making to passive music consumption.

Irving Berlin lived to be 101 years old and became one of the most prolific songwriters of the twentieth century. Because he could play piano in only one key, he compensated by using a piano with a movable keyboard that could transpose into other keys.

Tin Pan Alley Constructs the Mainstream Tradition

Tin Pan Alley centralized the power of the American and Canadian popular music business at a time when European opera was the hallmark of taste. Although songwriters in the United States and Canada often took their cues from European high culture, they soon came to realize that the key to future profitability lay in catering to popular tastes. Unlike older, more traditional music publishing houses that issued a broad range of material, the song factories of Tin Pan Alley produced only popular songs, and in so doing, "Tin Pan Alley songwriters soon reached a stylistic plateau, a much more homogeneous style than had ever before been the case in the history of song in America."[12] Indeed, Tin Pan Alley actually availed itself of a much narrower range of material than the record companies and parlayed the undertaking into an overwhelming—and distinctly American—success. "Tin Pan Alley did not draw on traditional music," musicologist Charles Hamm has said; "it created traditional music."[13]

Typical of early Tin Pan Alley fare were graceful waltzes and spirited marches. Familiar tunes from the first category included Harry Von Tilzer's "Bird in a Gilded Cage" (1900), "In the Good Old Summer Time" by George Evans (1902), and Egbert Van Alstyne's "In the Shade of the Old Apple Tree" (1905). All sold millions. The marches of John Philip Sousa and the Marine Band were perhaps best echoed in popular song by the multitalented George M. Cohan. From "Give My Regards to Broadway" in 1904 to his World War I rally tune "Over There" in 1917, Cohan's up-tempo, lightly syncopated numbers won him enduring popularity.

One of the earliest Canadians writing in the Tin Pan Alley tradition was Toronto schoolteacher George Johnson, who penned the hit song "You and I Were Young, Maggie" in 1864 about his girlfriend, Stony Creek native Maggie Clark. Other important early Tin Pan Alley songwriters of Canada include Shelton Brooks, whose compositions included "Some of These Days" (1910) and "Darktown Strutters' Ball" (1916), the latter among the first jazz recordings ever when cut in 1917 by the Original Dixieland Jazz Band; Brantford lyricist Alfred Bryan, who co-wrote "Peg o' My Heart" (1913), "Come Josephine in My Flying Machine" (1910), "Oh You Beautiful Doll" (1949), and the controversial World War I song "I Didn't Raise My Boy to Be a Soldier" (1915); and Windsor native lyricist Raymond Egan, who co-wrote the World War I hit "Till We Meet Again" (1918), "The Japanese Sandman" (1920), "Ain't We Got Fun?" (1921), and "Sleepy Time Gal" (1925).

In 1919, the hit song "The World is Waiting for the Sunrise" was co-authored by London, Ontario, native Eugene Lockhart and a member of the faculty of the Toronto Conservatory of Music, Ernest Seitz. The song would be recorded more than a hundred times over the next several decades, with Les Paul and Mary Ford's 1949 recording for Capitol Records selling over 1 million copies. Another London-born composer, Claud L. Graves, penned the comedic topical song "Oh, What a Difference Since the Hydro Came" in 1913. Kingston native Geoffrey O'Hara wrote "K-K-K-Katy (The Stammering Song)" in 1918, selling over 1 million sheet music copies; Captain Gitz Rice from Montreal wrote another World War I hit, "Mademoiselle from Armentieres" (1917); and William Eckstein penned "Delirious Rag" and "Perpetual Rag" (both 1906) and co-wrote "You Are My All in All" (1917) and "Goodbye Sunshine, Hello Moon" (1919).

Tin Pan Alley was a songwriting enterprise dominated by Jews at a time when Jewish immigrants were considered racially different by many. If one had to choose a single artist who epitomized the Tin Pan Alley ethos, it would have to be Irving Berlin, about whom the *Literary Digest,* after praising his work, remarked with surprise: "And Berlin belongs to the Jewish race."[14] Born Israel Baline in 1888 in Russia, Berlin was just four years old when he and his family came to the United States after escaping the Russian pogroms. Like many Jewish immigrants of the time, the family settled in New York's Lower East Side, where they lived in abject poverty. By the age of eight, Berlin was already earning his own keep selling newspapers. "At fourteen, he was a singing waiter in the honky tonks of Chinatown and the Bowery, absorbing the rich sounds and rhythms of the musical melting pot."[15] Two years later Berlin landed his first Tin Pan Alley job, plugging songs for Harry Von Tilzer's publishing firm. There, he wrote his first published song, "Marie from Sunny Italy" (1907). This was soon followed by such classics as "Alexander's Ragtime Band" (1911), "A Pretty Girl Is Like a Melody" (1919), "Say It with Music" (1921), "Puttin' on the Ritz" (1929), "Easter Parade" (1933), "Cheek to Cheek" (1935), "Let's Face the Music and Dance" (1936), "I've Got My Love to Keep Me Warm" (1937), and "God Bless America" (1939), which captured the hearts and minds of generations and made Berlin a household name. Until he was unseated by Paul McCartney, Berlin was easily the most successful songwriter in history. "The range of his songs, in content and mood, if not in form," Charles Hamm has said, "is enormous. . . . Some take on a bit of the flavor of ragtime, of the blues, of country-western, Latin-American, or jazz."[16] His appropriations of multicultural sounds and rhythms—particularly those of ragtime and jazz—speak volumes about his uncanny ability to interpret diverse influences for the mainstream audience and the systematic cultural distortions that accompanied mainstream popularization.

Tin Pan Alley Incorporates African American Music

The rise of Tin Pan Alley paralleled the emergence of ragtime, and the connections between the two reveal the inequitable pattern of cultural borrowing and economic reward among black and white artists that has characterized much of the history of popular music in the United States and Canada. It is this pattern that is central to understanding the emergence of rock 'n' roll. Ragtime—as opposed to ragtime songs, which were creations of Tin Pan Alley—was a syncopated, African American piano music with structural ties to European marches. It employed, in the words of Gunther Schuller, "the polymetric . . . approach of the African native forced into the simple 2/4 pattern of European marches."[17] It evolved from a dance called the cakewalk, which was in itself a cultural form with a complicated history that involved blacks imitating whites imitating blacks. In the hands of its most famous practitioner, the African American pianist and composer Scott Joplin, ragtime was a self-conscious art form, a composed music. Joplin himself, Ian Whitcomb has noted, "presented the New Negro."[18] His "Maple Leaf Rag" (1899) remains one of the best-known ragtime compositions.[19]

For Tin Pan Alley, ragtime was a craze to be incorporated into popular song. As such, it is often difficult to separate ragtime songs from other Tin Pan Alley pop. In their affinity for slow march tempos, for example, ragtime songs tended to resemble George M. Cohan's most successful musical theatre numbers. It can also be argued that there is a historical and stylistic continuity from the so-called coon songs of minstrelsy to the ragtime songs of Tin Pan Alley, although the latter were clearly less offensive. Irving Berlin turned out dozens of ragtime songs, including "Play Some Ragtime" in 1909, "Stop That Rag," "Dat Draggy Rag," and "Oh, That Beautiful Rag" in 1910, and "Ragtime Violin" and his best-known "Alexander's Ragtime Band" in 1911. Although in "Alexander's Ragtime Band" Berlin did not marry syncopation and the march tradition the way Joplin might have, the catchy, well-crafted tune, which balanced "dash and energy," as Gilbert Seldes noted in 1924, with a "bow to negro music,"[20] proved to be so popular that Berlin was subsequently billed as the "Father of Ragtime." As Hamm has noted:

> *A pattern was established with the ragtime song that was to recur time and again in the twentieth century: white popular music skimmed off superficial stylistic elements of a type of music originating among black musicians, and used these to give a somewhat different, exotic flavor to white music. Though Scott Joplin and a handful of other black ragtime musicians realized a modest profit from their music, the important money went to the white publishers, performers, and composers of ragtime songs.*[21]

A similar, but far more complicated, pattern characterized Tin Pan Alley's use of blues and jazz. The blues appeared at about the same time as ragtime. "But, unlike ragtime," Gunther Schuller has noted, "the blues were improvised and as such were more successful in preserving the original and melodic patterns of African music."[22] Using, as writer Amiri Baraka (LeRoi Jones) has pointed out, a "three-line verse form [that] springs from no readily apparent Western source,"[23] and other African retentions, such as the call-and-response style and the flatted thirds and sevenths ("blue notes") that typify the singing of many West African tribes, the blues are clearly part of the African American musical tradition. Even so, this is not the impression one would have gotten once Tin Pan Alley grabbed hold of the so-called blues craze in the second decade of the twentieth century.

The so-called blues craze amounted to little more than a rash of blues-flavoured popular songs interpreted for a white audience by white vocalists. Early appropriations of jazz created the impression that jazz was actually the product of polite society's white dance bands.

In 1912, three blues compositions were published: Hart Wand's "Dallas Blues," Arthur Seals' "Baby Seals' Blues," and "Memphis Blues," by W. C. Handy. There has been considerable debate as to whether such compositions fit the strict definition of the blues. Handy, for example, who called himself the "Father of the Blues," was a trained composer. Still, he was as conversant with African American folkloric idioms as he was with musical notation. As Baraka (Jones) has argued: "W. C. Handy, with the publication of his various 'blues compositions,' invented [the blues] for a great many Americans and also showed that there was money to be made from it."[24] Handy had the most success with popular blues-influenced material and published his most memorable compositions, including "St. Louis Blues" (1914), "Joe Turner Blues" (1916), and "Beale Street Blues" (1917) during this period. According to William Barlow, "Handy's sudden success demonstrated [the] commercial potential [of the blues], which in turn made the genre attractive to the Tin Pan Alley song hacks, who wasted little time in turning out a deluge of imitations."[25] These Tin Pan Alley knock-offs were almost invariably performed by white singers. The so-called blues craze, then, amounted to little more than a rash of blues-flavoured popular songs interpreted for a white audience by white vocalists.

Early appropriations of jazz created the impression among the mainstream audience that jazz was actually the product of the white dance bands of polite society. While trying to pinpoint the precise influences and exact beginnings of jazz is an exercise in speculation that goes well beyond the scope of this book, it is safe to say that virtually all music historians acknowledge its African American origins. By the time the term came into popular usage, the style had been fed by a number of musical tributaries (minstrelsy, spirituals, ragtime, and blues, among others) that in themselves contained African as well as European elements. Indeed, many African American jazz musicians were well versed in the European classics. Still, there was an important distinction to be made between the oral tradition of improvisational, "hot" jazz and the written tradition of "sweet" dance music played by white society orchestras like Paul Whiteman's. The discussion is further complicated by the fact that performance styles varied not only regionally but also according to audience composition. Because high-society whites and middle-class blacks tended to shun the rough, hard-driving styles played in honky-tonks and brothels, jazz, as showcased in upscale venues, aspired to a cosmopolitanism not considered important in other places. Even pioneering black ensembles like King Oliver's band, a formative influence in New Orleans jazz, developed a more polished style as they gained mainstream popularity. As a result, there was an association in the minds of most mainstream listeners between jazz and sweet dance music, a connection that resulted in Paul Whiteman's designation as the "King of Jazz." Patterns of racial exclusion in the recording industry and, later, in broadcast radio, skewed

public perceptions of jazz even more. In 1917, for example, when Victor decided to take a chance on the new sound, the band it ended up recording was the all-white Original Dixieland Jazz Band. Although the ODJB was heavily influenced by King Oliver, the Oliver ensemble did not record until 1923.[26] Similarly, with few exceptions, radio broadcasts excluded black performers as a matter of

W. C. Handy was one of the first songwriters to bring a feel for the blues into the world of popular composition. Also a successful businessman, Handy established his own publishing house and record label with his partner, Harry Pace.

policy. To most mainstream listeners, then, jazz, which was what just about all dance music was called at this time, was the music played by white dance bands. Indeed, in the context of the times, even Irving Berlin was regarded as a jazz pioneer, a notion that would be rejected out of hand today.

The Tin Pan Alley songwriter who had the closest association with jazz in reality was George Gershwin. Thoroughly conversant with the European classics as well as with popular styles, Gershwin sought to bridge the gap between art music and popular music. He had a genuine affinity for and personal interest in the music of African Americans. One of the earliest and most familiar fruits of this interest was his "Rhapsody in Blue," written for "jazz band and piano" and originally performed at Aeolian Hall in New York in 1924 by Paul Whiteman's orchestra with Gershwin at the piano. While "Rhapsody" is clearly an extraordinary piece of music for its time, it is obvious in retrospect that it is much more a symphonic piece than a jazz composition. If, as culture critic Gilbert Seldes jested at the time, Gershwin was "a traitor to his class (the Tin Pan Alleyists),"[27] it was not because the siren call of African American culture had lured him too far from his European moorings but because he was a popular artist who attempted a work of "serious" music. Still, Gershwin was clearly more sensitive to and respectful of the subtle nuances of African American music than most of his contemporaries. Almost alone among Tin Pan Alley songwriters, his music found wide acceptance among black as well as white audiences. His "Summertime," originally written for the musical *Porgy and Bess* in 1935, quickly attained the status of a jazz classic. Indeed, it was the rare black jazz band that did not include a Gershwin tune in its repertoire.

Gershwin's identification with jazz is all the more dubious given the isolationist stance of Tin Pan Alley as a whole. Like his colleagues, Gershwin had little contact with musical developments outside of New York City. Certainly, he had little connection to the pioneering steps taken in New Orleans or the innovations of the territory bands in the Midwest and Southwest. The fact that he was able to assimilate African American influences in a way that resonated across racial lines says more about his musical instincts and talent than it does about the openness of the industry or society as a whole. In general, the image of "skimming off superficial stylistic elements" was a more accurate description of Tin Pan Alley's use of multicultural sounds.

Tin Pan Alley Consolidates Its Power

The institutionalization of Tin Pan Alley was coincident with the ascendancy of vaudeville. From its modest beginnings at Tony Pastor's Opera House in New York's Bowery, vaudeville had evolved by the turn of the century into a national network of hundreds of venues that were dominated in the East by the Keith-Albee chain and in the West by Martin Beck's Orpheum circuit, which ran from Chicago to the Pacific. Not surprisingly, vaudeville was a very popular form of entertainment in Canada as well. American chains such as Keith-Albee, Pantages, and Loew's built a number of theatres in Canada, while independent Canadian entrepreneurs such as Ambrose Small in Toronto, the Whitney family in southwestern Ontario, and C. P. Walker in Winnipeg (who owned the Red River Theatre Circuit) were also active, generally forming partnerships with one of the American chains. "Cleanliness, Courtesy, and Comfort," the slogan of the Keith-Albee theatres, described not only the principles of vaudeville houses but also the character of vaudeville performances. In 1900, the bookings for the majority of these theatres were centralized in the United Booking Office (UBO), a satellite organization of the Vaudeville Managers Association (VMA), which was controlled by Keith and Albee. Artists who were chosen to play the Keith-Albee chain or the Orpheum circuit enjoyed an unprecedented access to a national, mostly white middle-class audience. Clearly, then, those who influenced these artists' choices of material wielded tremendous power in determining what the mainstream public heard, and it was in its ability to influence these choices that Tin Pan Alley excelled.

The success of Tin Pan Alley's writers and publishers was due in equal measure to their distinctive songwriting style and their aggressive marketing strategies. Because popular songs were a staple of vaudeville, the gala shows produced in New York by the likes of F. F. Proctor, Oscar Hammerstein, Flo Ziegfeld, and of course, the Keith-Albee houses were regular stop-off points for the new Tin Pan Alley publishers. "They made fifty or sixty visits a week," Russell Sanjek has noted, "to pass around copies of their newest songs, buy champagne or beer, give out cigars, recommend tailors—in short, do everything they could to boost their newest publications."[28] "Everything," according to Charles Hamm, included "persuasion tactics" that ranged "from furnishing singers with free copies of new songs, to performing small or large kindnesses for them, to out-and-out payment by the publisher—a flat fee, or in some cases a promise of a percentage of profits from sales of sheet music."[29] It was not unheard of for performers like Al Jolson to be credited as writers of the songs they agreed to push. The practice of "paying for play"—legal at the time and considered a form of intelli-

The success of Tin Pan Alley's writers and publishers was due in equal measure to their distinctive songwriting style and their aggressive marketing strategies.

gent marketing rather than a shady business practice—eventually came to be known as "payola." For the publishers, investments in vaudeville's stars were often returned manyfold in sales. It is ironic that the Alleymen conveniently forgot the venerable history of payola a generation later, when they decried the ethics of the practice to discredit a cohort of deejays who had pushed rock 'n' roll and records past mainstream pop and sheet music.

As early as 1909, it should have been clear that records were a force to be reckoned with. According to Russell Sanjek, "In 1909, more than 27 million phonograph records and cylinders were manufactured, having a wholesale value of nearly $12 million."[30] While the larger proportion of their revenues would come from the sale of sheet music for years to come, publishers and a growing number of popular artists felt that there was no reason why this revenue should not be supplemented with revenues from record sales. Thus, in 1909, Victor Herbert, a successful composer of semiserious works, and John Philip Sousa led the charge for a revision of the copyright laws that mandated a royalty of two cents for each cylinder, record, or piano roll manufactured, in addition to the royalties already derived from live performances. Because the U.S. Copyright Act of 1909 used the term *mechanical reproduction,* these new fees came to be known as "mechanicals." When the printers' union went on a nationwide strike in 1919, mechanical royalties actually sustained the publishing industry for a time. In 1921, the Canadian Copyright Act legislated that the performing rights of musical works were a constituent part of Canadian copyright law.

Shortly after the passage of the U.S. Copyright Act, the recording industry and Tin Pan Alley began to cross paths regularly. This began with the dance fever that swept the country from 1910 to World War I and continued with the growth of musical theatre. Such Tin Pan Alley hits as Irving Berlin's "Everybody's Doin' It" and "Alexander's Ragtime Band" and Gilbert and Muir's "Waiting for the Robert E. Lee" were well suited to new dances like the turkey trot, the hesitation waltz, the tango, and the one-step. The dance-crazed public, eager to follow in the footsteps of Vernon and Irene Castle, gobbled up recordings of these songs to practise at home. Signed by Victor to supervise a series of dance records, the unconventional Castles hired as their music director James Reese Europe.

The value of the musical theatre market, which further linked Tin Pan Alley and the record companies, became apparent when British Victor made a recording of the songs from *Business As Usual,* a popular musical revue, for American soldiers and native Londoners during World War I. This was followed by recordings of two of Irving Berlin's shows, *Watch Your Step* and *Cheep,* which also sold well. U.S. Victor emulated the success of its British partner by recording the best-known stage entertainers in the United States. The success of these recordings led Columbia and Edison to follow suit. The singer who created the strongest bridge between Tin Pan Alley and the world of records was Al Jolson. Jolson's 1919 Columbia recording of Gershwin's "Swanee," which he usually performed live in blackface and white gloves, sold over 2 million records. This figure was equalled by a 1920 Victor recording of "Whispering" and "The Japanese Sandman," two Tin Pan Alley favourites performed by the Paul Whiteman Orchestra. With these successes, popular stage entertainers like George M. Cohan, Al Jolson, Nora Bays, and Sophie Tucker soon found themselves pushing Tin Pan Alley songs on records.

To recover all their codified sources of revenue, the Tin Pan Alley songsters organized the American Society of Composers, Authors, and Publishers (ASCAP) in 1914, five years after the passage of the 1909 Copyright Act. ASCAP is a "performing rights" organization that recovers royalty payments for the performance of copyrighted music. ASCAP did this by issuing a blanket licence for the use of any selection in the catalogue to live performance venues such as hotels and nightclubs (and, later, radio and television) and then distributing these royalties to writers and publishers according to a complex formula that favoured older and more successful members. Membership in the society was skewed toward writers of show tunes and semiserious works and included Richard Rodgers and Lorenz Hart, Cole Porter, George Gershwin, Irving Berlin, and George M. Cohan. Of the society's 170 charter members, only six were black: Harry Burleigh, Will Marion Cook, J. Rosamond, James Weldon Johnson, Cecil Mack, and Will Tyers.[31] While other black writers and composers who were schooled in musical notation (W. C. Handy, Duke Ellington) would be able to gain entrance to ASCAP, the vast majority of black artists were routinely excluded from the society and thereby systematically denied the full benefit of copyright protection. Until 1939, when a rival organization was formed, ASCAP was a closed society with a virtual monopoly on all copyrighted music. As proprietor of the compositions of its members, ASCAP could and did regulate the use of any selection in its catalogue. Thus, the organization, and therefore Tin Pan Alley, exercised considerable power in shaping public taste.

In Canada, the Canadian Performing Rights Society (CPRS) was formed in 1925 as a subsidiary of Britain's Performing Rights Society. For Canadian composers, lyricists, and publishers, CPRS served the same function that ASCAP did in the United States: collecting and

Membership in ASCAP was skewed toward writers of show tunes and semiserious works; the vast majority of black artists were routinely excluded from the society.

distributing royalties based on performances of their works. The CPRS would change its name in 1945 to the Composers, Authors and Publishers Associated of Canada Limited (CAPAC), which, in turn, would be succeeded by the Society of Composers, Authors and Music Publishers of Canada (SOCAN) in 1990.

Commercial Broadcasting: A Very Private Enterprise

At the beginning of the 1920s, the outlook for records was rosy. But while gross revenues in the United States hit an all-time high of $106 million in 1921, shrewd observers might have noticed a cloud on the horizon—radio. Two years after the advent of commercial radio broadcasting in 1920, annual record revenues showed a decline. By 1933, the height of the Great Depression, they had plummeted to an all-time low of $6 million.

The scientific properties of radio waves had been known since the latter half of the nineteenth century. In the early 1890s, Heinrich Hertz, the German scientist for whom the measure of the frequencies on the electromagnetic spectrum is named, had demonstrated how to set radio waves in motion, how to detect them, and how they passed through solid objects. It was Guglielmo Marconi who developed and implemented the first practical application of "Hertzian waves" to problems of communication. Initially rebuffed by the Italian government when he sought a patent, Marconi, with the help of his Irish mother, secured a British patent on "wireless" communication in 1896 and, a year later, established the Wireless Telegraph and Signal Company, Ltd. In 1899, he established American Marconi in the United States and set his sights on nothing short of a worldwide monopoly on wireless communication.

In its formative stages, wireless communication was used primarily for telegraphy, and its obvious application for ships in distress was demonstrated dramatically through continuous coverage of the *Titanic* disaster in 1912. The man who is usually credited with transforming the wireless into a technology for *telephony*—the basis of radio broadcasting—is Lee de Forest, the inventor of the audion, an early version of the vacuum tube that was capable of generating, modulating, amplifying, and detecting radio energy. In 1900, Canadian Reginald Fessenden (born in East Bolton, Quebec) formed the Wireless Telegraph Co. of Canada and transmitted "the sound of a voice over a distance of 50 miles using the principle of 'continuous-wave' transmission."[32] Six years later, Fessenden made a "continuous-wave" transmission from Boston to Scotland originating from a 420-foot mast at Brant Rock, Massachusetts, that was owned by the National Electric Signaling Company. While from a technical point of view this can be considered the birth of broadcasting, Fessenden's transmissions were far less dramatic than de Forest's experimental broadcasts of phonograph music from the Eiffel Tower in 1908 or his broadcast of Caruso from the Metropolitan Opera in New York in 1910. For all his brilliance, however, de Forest was a less than astute businessman, and in 1913, his United Wireless Company was bankrupted in a patent suit brought by Marconi.[33]

The commercial development of radio was halted during World War I in order to devote all further research and application to the war effort. A pooling of resources and a moratorium on patent suits during the war years encouraged technical advances that might not otherwise have been possible. Once the war was over, however, it was clear that there was a future for commercial radio and Marconi tried to pick up where he had left off. But when he began to negotiate for exclusive rights to General Electric's 200,000 watt Alexanderson alternator, the U.S. government intervened.

The Growth of Network Radio

Seeing international communication as a key element in the balance of world power, U.S. president Woodrow Wilson noted that a British-dominated monopoly on radio would not be satisfactory. In 1919, the president of American Marconi was forced to tell his stockholders: "We have found that there exists on the part of the officials of the [U.S.] Government a very strong and irremovable objection to [American Marconi] because of the stock interest held therein by the British Company."[34] Harnessing patriotism to the profit motive, Owen D. Young, a General Electric vice president, engineered a "solution," with the active support of the U.S. government. When all was said and done, the operations and assets of American Marconi were transferred to a new entity—the Radio Corporation of America—with Young as the first chairman of its board of directors. RCA was set up as a holding company for the major radio patent holders in the United States. In its first few years of operation, its stock was divided in varying proportions among General Electric (GE) and Westinghouse, which would manufacture radio equipment, American Telephone and Telegraph (AT&T), which would manufacture transmitters and control telephonic communication, and the former stockholders of American Marconi.

Harnessing patriotism to the profit motive, the operations and assets of American Marconi were transferred to a new entity— the Radio Corporation of America.

Despite these developments south of the border, on 20 May 1920, the Canadian Marconi Co. station XWA in Montreal transmitted the very first scheduled radio broadcast in the world (XWA would over time morph into CFCF and eventually CIQC). In November 1920, Westinghouse's KDKA went "on the air" from the roof of the company's Pittsburgh factory to broadcast the results of the Harding/Cox presidential election. Within two to three years, and with few precedents to guide their development, nearly 600 stations were licensed to operate across the country. Existing legislation, designed primarily to govern maritime telegraphy, did not anticipate the impact of commercialized telephonic broadcasting. Issues such as programming, financing, organization, ownership, networking, interference, and advertising were worked out in practice and over time.

By the mid-1920s, the structures and practices that would dominate radio for the next two decades, including network broadcasting and commercial advertising, were already in place. In 1926, AT&T bowed out of broadcasting and sold its flagship station, WEAF, and other assets to RCA for $1 million. That same year, RCA formed a new subsidiary, the National Broadcasting Company (NBC), the first company founded solely to operate a radio network. In November, a twenty-five station network, fed by WEAF in New York and extending as far west as Kansas City, went on the air with a most ambitious program. Broadcasting from the Grand Ballroom of the Waldorf-Astoria, the program featured the New York Symphony Orchestra, conducted by Walter Damrosh, and a number of "remote" features, including, among other things, the dance bands of Vincent Lopez, Ben Bernie, George Olsen, and B. A. Rolfe, the

Metropolitan Opera star Titta Ruffo, the comedy team of Webber and Fields, and a Will Rogers monologue. The formation of NBC marked the transition from radio as an ancillary corporate enterprise to radio as a profit-generating venture in itself.

By 1926, NBC was operating two semiautonomous networks, the Red Network and the Blue Network. The more powerful Red Network, originating at WEAF (later to become WNBC) in New York, offered broadcasts of news, semiserious works, and light opera. The Blue Network, fed by WJZ (later to become WABC), also in New York, presented what *Variety* magazine referred to as "the new school of entertainment, running more to the popular tune."[35] Both networks were headed by the American Marconi telegraph operator who had been in constant contact with the sinking *Titanic*—David Sarnoff, "wonder boy of the radio." Now a fast-rising executive at RCA, Sarnoff had envisioned consumer broadcasting as quality entertainment as early as the midteens. "I have in mind a plan of development which would make radio a 'household utility,' in the same sense as the piano or phonograph," he wrote in a memo to his superiors in 1916. "The idea is to bring music into the home by wireless."[36] Sarnoff became president of RCA in 1930, the year the company was severed from GE in a government-led antitrust suit, and went on to serve as chairman of RCA's board of directors from 1947 until his retirement in 1969.

A rival network had been formed in 1927, after Sarnoff had rejected a proposal by Arthur Judson, a violinist turned artist manager, to supply classical musicians to network radio. Enraged, Judson formed United Independent Broadcasters to book talent and, with financial backing from the Columbia Phonograph Company, began the Columbia Phonograph Broadcasting System. When the competition for advertising and programming got rough, however, Columbia pulled out. The fledgling network was put on a firm financial footing when it received an influx of cash from one of its main advertisers, the owner of La Palina cigars, whose son, William S. Paley, was installed as the network's new president in 1928. At this time, the name of the network was shortened to the Columbia Broadcasting System. Within months, CBS was NBC's major competition, and coast-to-coast broadcasting was a reality. Paley and Sarnoff were dominant figures in broadcasting for years, each controlling vast media empires.

Although radio in the United States developed in a generally laissez-faire fashion with little interference on the part of the government, its progress was closely monitored through a series of conferences on its development held by the National Alliance of Broadcasters (NAB), which actually recommended an extension of government regulatory powers. These recommendations were embodied in the Radio Act of 1927 and then extended in the Communications Act of 1934, which brought into being the Federal Communications Commission. Still, the law lagged behind the technological advances that had occurred and the patterns of ownership that were embodied in the predominance of network broadcasting. It was, according to Erik Barnouw, "based on a premise that had been obsolete in 1927 and by 1934 was totally invalid: that American broadcasting was a local responsibility exercised by independent station licensees."[37] By 1938, the networks were using 98 percent of the available nighttime wattage. A fourth network, the Mutual Broadcasting System, had been formed by the *Chicago Tribune* in 1934, but its chances for expansion were limited. CBS and the Red and Blue networks of NBC had already locked up fifty of the fifty-two clear channels—special frequencies allocated to stations with large transmitters positioned to broadcast over great distances with minimal interference—as well as 75 percent of the most powerful regional stations. In terms of owner-ship patterns, U.S. radio had developed as a very private enterprise indeed. Programming, how-ever, was another matter entirely.

The development of radio in Canada followed a somewhat different pattern. In 1924, Sir Henry Thornton, the president of Canadian National Railways, had radio receivers installed on all CNR transcontinental trains. He subsequently built a radio transmission studio in Ottawa using the call letters CNRO. Canadian Ted Rogers invented the 110 volt AC vacuum tube, thereby creating batteryless radio. In 1927, Rogers founded Toronto radio station CFRB, Canada's first batteryless station. That same year, festivities on Parliament Hill in Ottawa held to commemorate the sixtieth anniversary of Canadian Confederation, which included the inau-guration of the Peace Tower carillon, musical performances, and a speech from Prime Minister William Lyon Mackenzie King, were broadcast across the country. Two years later, the Royal Commission on Broadcasting, sometimes referred to as the Aird Commission, set in motion the founding of the Canadian Radio Broadcasting Company (the CRBC, later the Canadian Broadcasting Company or CBC) by recommending the establishment of a publicly owned broadcast system. The CRBC began broadcasting in 1932.

The Advertisers Versus the Programmers

In the market-driven U.S. system, those involved in radio, which was introduced at a time when Prohibition had forced the pursuit of alcohol-related pleasures underground, thought the new medium should nourish the spirit and raise the nation's general level of culture through programs of news, literature, drama, and concert music. While this belief did little for the fortunes of the popular songsters of Tin Pan Alley, or the cultural preferences of huge segments of the U.S. public, for that matter, it did affect the programming decisions of commercial stations. Commercial station owners were preoccupied with maintaining a sense of propriety and "good taste" in everything from program content to advertising. Direct advertising of a product was permitted only during business hours; at night, only a discreet mention of a program sponsor's name was allowed. When it appeared that such principles might somehow be compromised, "cultured" industry stalwarts like Lee de Forest

Fortunately for popular music, advertisers like Paley, who catered to "vulgar" popular tastes as a matter of necessity, ended up playing the major role in determining the course of radio programming.

> *lost no opportunity to cry out in earnest protest against the crass commercialism, the etheric vandal-ism of the vulger hucksters, agencies, advertisers, station owners—who lacking awareness of their grand opportunities and moral responsibilities to make of radio an uplifting experience, continue to enslave and sell for quick cash the grandest medium which has yet been given to man to help upward his struggling spirit.*[38]

As the twenties roared past most nineteenth-century conventions, however, the old guard of broadcasting often found itself locking horns with a new breed of unabashedly commercial advertisers. In many ways, Sarnoff and Paley personified the two camps. As a visionary corpo-rate executive, Sarnoff was immersed in the public service aspects of the medium. He viewed radio as an "electronic library" that brought useful information, uplifting literature, and tasteful music into the home "by wireless." Of course, as an equally good businessman, he was not oblivious to the fact that such services would sell millions of the radio receivers his company manufactured. Paley, on the other hand, came to radio as the advertising manager of his father's cigar factory. His product needed a harder sell, the kind that was considered crass by the old guard. Fortunately for popular music, advertisers like Paley, who catered to "vulgar" popular tastes as a matter of necessity, ended up playing the major role in determining the course of radio programming.

Since the birth of broadcasting, news had been a staple of radio programming, consistent with its instructional mission. Drama added another element to radio's aura of respectability. The bulk of radio programming, however, was music. While the old guard leaned toward concert music, advertisers paid more attention to mainstream popular tastes.

Of course, ever-vigilant concerning its economic self-interest, ASCAP recognized from the beginning that the preponderance of radio programming was musical and, early on, notified radio of its intention to include musical broadcasts among its sources of copyright royalties. Commercial advertising—even indirect advertising—had placed musical broadcasts within the public performance for profit provision of the 1909 Copyright Act. Station owners, however, rejected ASCAP's initial request for five dollars a day for a blanket licence. In fact, the NAB was organized in 1923 specifically to deal with ASCAP's "prohibitive" terms. By the end of 1924, Sanjek notes, "ASCAP income from 199 radio licences was $130,000, up from the previous year's $35,000 but far from the million predicted when the drive to collect from broadcasters began in the summer of 1922."[39] Dissatisfied with its share of the take, ASCAP complained that radio had not simply killed records and vaudeville; it had killed popular music itself. Publishers and broadcasters thus began an adversarial relationship that continued well into the 1960s.

In 1934, ASCAP's total radio royalties were $850,000, still not the threatened $1 million. By 1937, however, total radio royalties had jumped to $5.9 million. It was the advertisers, with their close attention to mainstream popular taste, who played a leading role in ASCAP's change of fortune. To draw listeners, and thus increase sales, the advertisers supported "dialect" comedy and popular song programs rather than dramatic series or concerts of classical or semi-classical music.[40] Pepsodent toothpaste (and popular demand), for example, turned Freeman Gosden and Charles Correll, the white creators of the "blackface" comedy series *Amos 'n' Andy*, into the highest-paid entertainers in all of broadcasting. (As usual, racial parody could be counted on to turn a profit.) Advertisers also provided the listening audience with "live" musical entertainment and skirted the stringent advertising code at the same time by promoting artists who included an identification of the sponsoring corporation in their group name, such as the Browning King Orchestra, the Cliquot Club Eskimos, the A&P Gypsies, the Ipana Troubadours, and the Gold Dust Twins, Goldy and Dusty.

One of the most interesting national prime-time experiments in popular music was sponsored on NBC by the American Tobacco Company, maker of Lucky Strike cigarettes. Company president, George Washington Hill, directed the show's featured attraction, B. A. Rolfe and his thirty-five piece orchestra, to play only popular dance music with "no extravagant, bizarre, involved arrangements," and invited listeners to send in their song preferences. With Hill's advertising budget of $20 million, even staid NBC executives "suffered his brash, boorish behavior and joined him at Sunday-morning rehearsals to test the 'foxtrotability' of every selection programmed."[41] The show evolved into the famous *Your Hit Parade*, one of the most popular programs ever to hit network radio. In focusing solely on musical selections that were popular among the listening audience, *Your Hit Parade* conferred on the consumer a measure of power in determining public taste. The show's admittedly flawed and probably rigged rankings foreshadowed the more "scientific" methods of rating that determine programming formats today.

The tension between "culture" and straight commercial entertainment in radio programming continued until the economic imperatives of the Great Depression put the advertisers more than the programmers in a position to determine the tone of radio. During the Depression, as Erik Barnouw has written, "Destitute families that had to give up an icebox or furniture or bedding still clung to the radio as to a last link with humanity."[42] Such loyalty tipped the balance of power in programming to the side of the advertisers. As a result, radio has tended to follow the popular tastes of consumers. This tendency had quite surprising consequences when rock 'n' roll dawned in the early 1950s.

Hollywood Bolsters Tin Pan Alley

If radio never quite measured up to ASCAP's musical or financial expectations (or so ASCAP claimed publicly), the creation of another new medium—"talking" films—held out the promise of even greener pastures for Tin Pan Alley composers.

The runaway success of MGM's Broadway Melody, released in 1929, made it clear that mainstream popular music (i.e., Tin Pan Alley compositions) would play a major role in talking films.

In 1924, AT&T's Western Electric developed the "vitaphone" process of synchronizing disc recordings with sound, which was purchased by Warner Brothers. Warner's classic 1927 film starring Al Jolson, *The Jazz Singer,* which is often remembered as the first "talkie," was in fact a silent film with songs. (The ill-fated Lee de Forest had experimented with sound on film as early as 1906 and had formed the Phonofilm Company in 1925. Unfortunately, this company too went into bankruptcy, this time because of inadequate financing.) GE developed a process for actually photographing sound onto film in 1922, and as usual, David Sarnoff was on the scene to manoeuvre RCA into the middle of the action.

In 1928, Sarnoff organized a new unit, RCA Photophone, to exploit the process. He also acquired stock in Film Booking Offices of America (FBO), a small film production company, and the Keith-Albee-Orpheum theatre chain. After ousting Albee, Sarnoff consolidated FBO and the Keith-Albee-Orpheum theatre chain into a single company, Radio-Keith-Orpheum (RKO), which controlled about 12 percent of all first-run outlets in the United States. By 1930, sound had been installed in 83 percent of the country's theatres.

The runaway success of MGM's *Broadway Melody,* released in 1929, made it clear that mainstream popular music (i.e., Tin Pan Alley compositions) would play a major role in talking films. Record companies rushed to record dance and vocal versions of the film's hit songs, "Give My Regards to Broadway," "You Were Meant for Me," "The Wedding Song of the Painted Doll," and, of course, the title song. The major motion picture companies—Warner, United Artists, Fox, Paramount, Universal, and MGM—all planned movie musicals. To secure entertainers with guaranteed appeal, they raided the most popular entertainment medium available to them—network radio. One of the first successful movie musicals, *The Big Broadcast*, even borrowed its theme from radio. Among the artists who journeyed westward in 1932 to film the movie were Kate Smith, the Boswell Sisters, and the Mills Brothers, making this film one of the few early Hollywood musicals to utilize African American talent. Another artist featured in the film was the singer who would set the standard for pop vocals until World War II—Bing Crosby. Originally steeped in minstrelsy (he actually appeared on film in blackface), Crosby began his singing career in 1926 as one of the Rhythm Boys in the Paul Whiteman band. Shortly thereafter, the Rhythm Boys were performing and recording independently as a vocal trio featuring Crosby. In 1931, Crosby launched his solo recording career and landed his first radio show. He proved to be so popular that Roy Turk and Fred Ahlert offered him a cut of the royalties on "When the Blue of the Night Meets the Gold of the Day" if he would make it his radio theme song. He recorded with everyone from Al Jolson and Louis Armstrong to Paul Whiteman and Duke Ellington. Hits like "Sweet Leilani" (1937), a pseudo-Hawaiian number written by Harry Owens for the Oscar-winning film *Waikiki Wedding*, and "San Antonio Rose" (1940), a western swing song penned by Bob Wills, fed the mainstream attraction for exotic cultural influences and furthered Tin Pan Alley's superficial treatment of them. Following *The Big Broadcast*, Crosby went on to star in over sixty musical films, including *College Humor* and *Going Hollywood* (1933), *Pennies from Heaven* (1936), and *Holiday Inn* (1942). His recording of Irving Berlin's "White Christmas" from the 1942 film sold more than 30 million copies and entered the pop charts eighteen years in a row.[43]

Among the major Hollywood studios, Fox was the first to ally itself with a Tin Pan Alley publishing house—De Sylva, Brown, and Henderson. The firm more than pleased its new Hollywood partner when it turned out a string of hit musical comedies: *Good News, Three Cheers, Hold Everything, George White's Scandals,* and *Sunny Side Up,* among others. In turn, Warner

Brothers acquired a dozen New York publishing houses. The studio utilized the songwriting team of Harry Warren and Al Dubin to score most of Busby Berkeley's extravaganzas, including *42nd Street, Gold Diggers,* and *Footlight Parade* in 1933, and *Dames* in 1934. Family-oriented Broadway musicals, such as Jerome Kern's *Babes in Toyland* and Rodgers and Hart's *The Merry Widow,* were reproduced for the silver screen in 1934. The indefatigable Irving Berlin, whose fee for a musical film score was $75,000 plus a percentage of gross receipts, contributed hit songs to films like *Mammy* and *Puttin' on the Ritz* (1930), *Top Hat* (1935), *Follow the Fleet* (1936), *On the Avenue* (1937), *Carefree* (1938), and *Second Fiddle* (1939). By 1937, the music publishing houses associated with Hollywood shared 65 percent of ASCAP's publisher dividends, and continued to do so for the next decade.[44]

Established Tin Pan Alley publishing houses thus consolidated their interests in every medium used to disseminate popular music—sheet music, radio, Broadway plays, Hollywood films, and, to a lesser extent, records. At times, Tin Pan Alley's relationship with the recording industry conflicted with its other interests. Radio and movies, for example, netted Tin Pan Alley a hefty sum but hurt the recording industry. After all, the consumer did not have to buy a record to hear the latest hit; he or she needed only to turn on the radio. Furthermore, movie music remained in demand for only as long as the film was in circulation. "When Hollywood created a glut of as many as six or eight songs in a single production, it led to a superabundance of recorded movie music, which sold pictures but not recordings. A Hollywood-connected publisher could no longer assure record makers that a specific song in a forthcoming film would be the plugged hit."[45] Therefore, what were profitable ventures for the Alley's songwriters and publishers may not have been equally lucrative for recording companies. During the 1920s and 1930s, then, record companies had to look elsewhere to realize the financial potential of their product. It may not be purely coincidental that they exploited the markets for blues and country music at precisely the moment when record sales began to decline.

Blues and Country Music: Mass Media and the Construction of Race

In the creation of their distinctive brand of popular music, the most creative of Tin Pan Alley's songwriters absorbed outside influences like aural sponges. For all their incredible breadth of influences, however, they were in many ways narrowly provincial, products of the urban Northeast and Hollywood. While their music was immensely popular, it reflected white upper-middle-class sensibilities and was actually known and accepted by a rather limited segment of the population. In the final analysis, as Charles Hamm has noted:

> *Tin Pan Alley songs were for white, urban, literate, middle- and upper-class Americans. They remained practically unknown to large segments of American society, including most blacks . . . and the millions of poor, white, rural Americans of English, Irish, and Scottish stock clustered in the South and scattered across the lower Midwest. These two groups had their own distinctive types of music, oral-tradition music. . . .*[1]

This oral-tradition music—primarily blues and country, which at the time the recording companies categorized as "race" and "hillbilly"—developed largely outside the orbit of Tin Pan Alley. It was recording companies, aided in some instances by radio and film, that brought this music to the public. That this music remained isolated for so long speaks more to the distribution of cultural power than to the music's artistic value.

A*s marketing categories, designations like race and hillbilly intentionally separated artists along racial lines and conveyed the impression that their music came from mutually exclusive sources. Nothing could have been further from the truth.*

37

Blues and Country: More Equal Than Separate

It is difficult to trace the myriad of cultural inputs that went into the creation of music from the grassroots in the first decades of the twentieth century. At street level, of course, there was considerable cross-cultural contact; it was a part of everyday life. To offer but one example: Polk Brockman owned a furniture store in Atlanta, Georgia. His customers cut across racial lines. In the early 1920s, Brockman, like other furniture store owners, expanded his business to include phonographs. To maximize his sales, it was in his interest to be somewhat attuned to the musical tastes of his diverse clientele. As a result, Brockman and others like him—Sam Price in Dallas and Henry C. Spier in Jackson—often served as local talent scouts for record companies.[2] In fact, Brockman had a very lucrative sideline supplying both black and white talent to the OKeh Record Company, an independent label founded by Otto Heinemann. At OKeh, however, black artists were assigned to the label's 14000 Race Series and white artists to its 15000 Hillbilly Series. As marketing categories, designations like *race* and *hillbilly* intentionally separated artists along racial lines and conveyed the impression that their music came from mutually exclusive sources. Nothing could have been further from the truth. Across the social divide of segregation, these artists were aware of and influenced by each other's work. In cultural terms, blues and country were more equal than they were separate.

The United States can be justifiably proud of the melding of African and European conventions that produced the blues, if not the circumstances of the music's creation. In its initial usage, the term *blues* was not a racially coded reference. As the description of a mood or feeling, the term dates back to sixteenth-century England. "In the nineteenth century, it was a common expression in the United States," Samuel Charters has reported. "The word was used occasionally in song titles, but as a slang expression, without reference to any Negro musical style."[3]

The evolution of the blues as a fundamentally African American musical genre can be traced back to the shouts, field hollers, and work songs of slavery, which followed the call-and-response style of, say, a work crew foreman, who set the pace of work by uttering a phrase that was answered in rhythm by the labourers in the field. These pre-blues forms, then, were a functional expression, rendered without accompaniment or harmony and unbounded by the formality of any particular musical structure.[4] Gradually, instrumental and harmonic accompaniment were added, reflecting increasing cross-cultural contact. The "Ethiopian airs" of early minstrelsy "with strange modal harmonies and sharply rhythmic dissonance"[5] and the "Negro spirituals" popularized later in the nineteenth century by the Fisk Jubilee Singers, who presented "spirituals in choral versions that were greatly influenced by white singing societies,"[6] were early codifications of this evolution.

Multicultural influences also shaped country music. In the words of country music historian Bill C. Malone:

> *The folk music of the South was a blending of cultural strains, British at its core, but overlain and intermingled with the musical contributions of other ethnic and racial groups . . . the Germans of the Great Valley of Virginia; the Indians of the backcountry; Spanish, French, and mixed-breed elements in the Mississippi Valley; the Mexicans of South Texas; and, of course, blacks everywhere.*[7]

As country music evolved into a commercial enterprise, its list of sources broadened to include the influence of German and Swiss yodelers, Italian mandolin players, and Hawaiian string bands.

Even a cursory look at the instrumentation used in blues and country music reveals multiculturalism at work. Of the two most common instruments used in early country music—the fiddle and the banjo—the fiddle was from Europe and the banjo was most probably of African origin. While the fiddle undoubtedly arrived with the earliest colonists, the instrument was soon mastered by others. Black fiddlers, for example, were quite well represented in the antebellum South. From the 1920s on, country fiddlers borrowed heavily from blues and jazz. Syncopated rhythms, improvisational styles, and call-and-response patterns were common in commercial country fiddling. An early form of what we know as the banjo—a four-stringed instrument with a long neck and a skin stretched over a hollow body, referred to as a *banza,* a *banshaw,* a *banjil,*[8] a *banjor,*[9] or a *banjar*[10]—was brought over from West Africa in the late seventeenth century. A fifth, or "drone," string and a fretted neck were added in the 1800s to produce the instrument that became a staple of country music, both hillbilly and blues varieties.

The guitar, another staple of both blues and country music, had been present in this country since the colonial period, when it was considered a classical instrument. It became a fixture in country blues accompaniment as well as a dominant instrument in country music. In fact, it found its way into country string bands through white musicians' fascination with the elaborate fingerpicking styles of black artists, which were characteristic of West African techniques but unknown in European folk music. Like the guitar, the mandolin, which was brought to the United States by Italian immigrants and concert musicians, was initially regarded as a polite, upper-class instrument. According to Bill Malone, it found its way into rural areas through the catalogues of Sears Roebuck and Montgomery Ward. The ukulele and steel guitar were introduced by the Hawaiian string bands that toured the country after Hawaii became a U.S. territory in 1900. The wail of the steel guitar in country music at this time echoed the sounds produced by black guitarists using knife blades, bottlenecks, and other devices.

Neither vocal style nor choice of material was limited by race. Yodelling, most readily identified with country music, has a more complicated history than one might suspect. Although German in origin, certain pre-blues shouts and hollers were described in John W. Work's *American Negro Songs* as a "fragmentary bit of a yodel, half sung, half yelled."[11] Yodelling became part of minstrelsy early on. Although the vocal technique was popularized on record by Jimmie Rodgers, black musicians had also learned it. Blues artists who were contemporaries of Rodgers, such as Stovepipe Johnson ("Devilish Blues," 1928) and Tampa Red ("Worried Devil Blues," 1934), can be heard yodelling on record.[12]

Familiar characters and folklore heroes also cut across racial lines. In the book *Country,* Nick Tosches' irreverent portrait of country music, he argues that the ballad of "Frankie and Johnny," a common tragic theme in blues and country, was written by a black singer named Mammy Lou. The tale of Casey Jones, recorded by both blues and country artists in the 1920s (and later by the Grateful Dead), was also written by an African American, Wallace Saunders. At the same time, black musicians were drawn to old folk tales of British origin. Tosches refers to a black version of "Barbara Allen" in which the Scottish lady is a black boy named Boberick Allen. There are also black versions of "The Maid Freed from the Gallows," "Lord Lovel," and

"Lady Isabel and Elf-Knight," three more British ballads that crossed the Atlantic Ocean in the eighteenth century.[13]

By the time the blues and country music were recorded in the 1920s and 1930s, these sorts of cross-pollinations were so common that artists were sometimes listed in the wrong racial category in record company catalogues. Nevertheless, because a separation of the races has been so prominent in U.S. social relations, the official histories of blues and country have treated these styles as separate and distinct and used designations such as *race* and *hillbilly* to emphasize differences.

"Race" Music: The Popular Sounds of Black America

Although all of what is now called *blues* was categorized as race music in the 1920s and 1930s, it is necessary for the purposes of this discussion to distinguish between *country blues* (also referred to as *down home* or *rural blues* or, in a more specific context, *Delta blues*) and *city*, or *classic, blues* (also known as *urban blues* or *vaudeville blues*). "Classic blues was entertainment," Amiri Baraka (LeRoi Jones) has said, "and country blues, folklore."[14] Country blues were intensely personal, highly improvised, and quite irregular in form. The music was usually performed by a single male vocalist with only banjo or guitar accompaniment, if there was any accompaniment at all. As Samuel Charters has noted, country blues styles were "related to the city-blues styles in the arrangement of the lyrics and the harmonic patterns, but the singing styles and the rhythms were from the music of the fields and work gangs."[15] In the cities, the myriad of blues styles were codified into an eight-bar and a sixteen-bar pattern, as well as the twelve-bar form that became the standard for classic blues. Classic blues followed a I, IV, V (tonic, subdominant, dominant) chord progression and was so constructed that each verse of the A/A/B rhyme scheme left enough space for either a vocal or an instrumental response. In this call-and-response pattern, there was considerable room for improvisation, but within a standardized musical framework. There also developed a "pianistic adjunct" to the city blues, which was known as boogie-woogie. It utilized repeated eighth-note figures in the left hand, which left the right hand free for blues improvisation.

One of the most unexpected developments of the post–World War I period was the discovery by recording companies of a significant and untapped African American market for classic blues recordings by black artists.

Boogie-woogie was a city blues piano style that had been pioneered before World War I in Chicago by Jimmy Yancey, a groundskeeper at Comiskey Park, home of the Chicago White Sox. Chicago also boasted Clarence "Pine Top" Smith, whose "Pine Top's Boogie Woogie" is often credited with naming the style, and Earl "Fatha" Hines, a classically trained pianist and veteran of a number of Louis Armstrong ensembles. Hines linked the propulsive left-hand rhythms of the ragtime pianists with melodic figures similar to those of Armstrong's trumpet in the right hand in developing a style that came to be known, naturally, as the "trumpet piano" style. In his sophistication, Hines could be considered the Chicago counterpart of the Harlem "stride" pianists such as James P. Johnson, Willie-the-Lion Smith, Luckey Roberts, and Fats

Waller, whose rhythmic figures jumped from bass notes to chords. Eventually, the solo piano styles were overshadowed by orchestral developments in jazz. But boogie-woogie in particular exerted a significant influence on the piano styles of early rock 'n' roll artists including Fats Domino, Little Richard, Huey "Piano" Smith, and Jerry Lee Lewis.[16]

One of the most unexpected developments of the post–World War I period was the discovery by recording companies of a significant and untapped African American market for classic blues recordings by black artists. The fact that this market was unrecognized says a great deal about U.S. race relations at the time. According to Robert Palmer, "The idea of making recordings by and for blacks hadn't occurred to anyone in a position to do anything about it when the so-called blues craze hit around 1914–15, so [W. C.] Handy's 'blues' and the blues of other popular tunesmiths, black and white, were recorded by whites, many of them specialists in Negro dialect material."[17] It wasn't until 1920, and then quite by accident, that this pattern changed. When a recording session that was to feature Sophie Tucker had to be canceled due to illness, the enterprising black producer/songwriter Perry Bradford, "the shrewdest and most determined of the colored blues writers," convinced executives at OKeh to let him do the session with a black contralto named Mamie Smith. Smith's recording of Bradford's "Crazy Blues" shocked and delighted company executives when it began to sell 7,500 copies a week, mostly to black buyers. OKeh thus became the first beneficiary of an incredible, previously untapped market among African Americans. Ralph Peer, the OKeh recording director who assisted at the sessions, dubbed these records "race records."[18] The label stuck and remained the designation for black music by black artists for a black audience until 1949.

Smith's singing style, while oriented toward the classic blues, "was more in the tradition of the vaudeville stage than it was 'bluesy.'"[19] Still, her overwhelming success ushered in an era of classic blues recordings that were sung almost invariably by African American women: Ida Cox, Chippie Hill, Sarah Martin, Clara Smith, Trixie Smith, Victoria Spivey, and Sippie Wallace, among others. Taking their cue from the style of Gertrude (Ma) Rainey, "Mother of the Blues," these women formed "the link between the earlier, less polished blues styles and the smoother theatrical style of the later urban blues singers."[20] All were veterans of traveling tent shows, circuses, carnivals, medicine shows, and later, the black-oriented TOBA (Theatre Owners Booking Association) theatre circuit, which booked tours in the larger cities throughout the American South and Midwest.[21] In contrast to the sparsely accompanied country blues singers, who were mostly men, these classic blues women were usually accompanied by "a red hot jazz band" or a "scintillating master of the keyboard."[22] As a group, they projected a polish and professionalism hitherto unknown in the blues. The bulk of their material—"upwards of seventy-five percent," according to one estimate—was sung from the point of view of women.[23]

Easily the most famous classic blues singer of her time was Bessie Smith, the "Empress of the Blues." A protégé of Ma Rainey, she spent years on the road perfecting her craft. Her singing style "combined the emotional fervor of country blues with the vigorous appeal of jazz."[24] After working with Ma Rainey as a chorus girl and then touring with the Rabbit's Foot Minstrels, she developed her own *Liberty Belles* revue and eventually became a vaudeville headliner with her own show, *Harlem Frolics.* Smith performed with some of the best jazz bands of the era, including those of Louis Armstrong and Fletcher Henderson. Signed to a failing Columbia in 1923, she recorded scores of sides (160 of which still survive) over the next decade. Her records sold so

The flamboyant and talented Bessie Smith rose to the pinnacle of classic blues success during the 1920s. Her career crashed along with the stock market at the end of the decade.

well—her "Downhearted Blues" (1923), for example, reportedly sold 780,000 copies in six months—that she was said to have saved the company from bankruptcy. One of the high points of Smith's career was the title role in the 1929 two-reel film *St. Louis Blues,* which was based on the W. C. Handy composition of the same name. That same year she recorded "Nobody Knows You When You're Down and Out"; it was her last big hit before the Great Depression wrecked her career.

The initial success of the various blues recordings encouraged the formation of a handful of black-owned, independent labels such as Black Swan, Sunshine, Meritt, and Black Patti. W. C. Handy and his publishing partner, Harry Pace, started Black Swan in 1921. Mayo (Ink) Williams, who was head of the race series for Paramount, a company owned by the Wisconsin Chair Company, which entered the record business in order to sell phonographs, struck out on his own and formed Black Patti in 1927. However, because these companies lacked sufficient resources for national promotion or for distribution outside their home territories, they were either bought up by the major labels or forced out of the industry. Not a single black-owned label survived the 1920s intact.

During the initial surge of classic blues recordings, country blues were all but forgotten. When the record companies began to test the limits of the new market, however, they discovered a considerable demand for country blues, particularly among southern blacks. Northern industrialization and World War I had caused many blacks to leave the South, which was still largely rural. Black rural musical tastes soon mingled with the urban sounds of the classic blues, creating new opportunities for the record companies. At first, these companies brought country blues performers to northern studios to record in the more sophisticated styles associated with the city blues. Later, they ventured south with mobile units to record local singers. While reaping considerable economic reward from this enterprise, the record companies became the unwitting folklorists of U.S. culture.

While reaping considerable economic reward, the record companies became the unwitting folklorists of U.S. culture.

First into the country blues breach was Paramount. In 1924, the company began its previously mentioned race series under the direction of "Ink" Williams and issued as its first release Papa Charlie Jackson's "Lawdy Lawdy Blues." This record was followed with releases by Arthur "Blind" Blake and Blind Lemon Jefferson, perhaps the most popular country blues singer of the decade. A native of Wortham, Texas, Jefferson was born blind but with a gift for music. While he led a chaotic and dissolute life as an itinerant bluesman, his style influenced just about every country blues artist of the 1920s. Over the course of four years, Jefferson made seventy-nine recordings for Paramount, including "Black Snake Blues" and a hymn titled "See That My Grave Is Kept Clean." His "Match Box Blues" was covered by rockers from Carl Perkins to the Beatles. As Charters has noted, many of his recordings "were direct reworkings of old field cries and work songs. He shouted the melody in a long, free rhythmic pattern, and the guitar sang behind the voice in a subtle counterpoint."[25]

Throughout the 1920s and 1930s, OKeh, Columbia, Victor, and Vocalion, a small independent label that tried to capitalize on the race boom, engaged in extensive field recording, thus documenting a crucial period in the development of African American music, a period that might otherwise have been lost forever. The person most associated with commercial field recordings was Ralph Peer, the man who had coined the term "race records" at OKeh. In the 1930s, the Library of Congress entered the field recording business through the efforts and documentary ambitions of John Lomax and his son Alan. As a result of all these field forays, both commercial and noncommercial, dozens of country blues artists—among them, Mississippi John Hurt, Sleepy John Estes, Blind Willie McTell, Son House, Charlie Patton, Leadbelly, and Robert Johnson—were brought to wider public attention. Their diverse, idiosyncratic styles ultimately evolved into a more classic mould with standardized structures, tunes, and even guitar breaks. Just as the pioneering guitar work of Blind Lemon Jefferson is echoed in the playing of Lightnin' Hopkins, Aaron "T-Bone" Walker, and ultimately B. B. King, there is a similar stylistic connection that can be traced from blues artists from the Mississippi Delta, especially Robert Johnson, to John Lee Hooker, Muddy Waters, and Howlin' Wolf.

Blind Lemon Jefferson was one of the first musicians to codify the country blues and was the most successful artist to record in the style. Although he was credited as the writer of many of his songs, he was probably paid a flat fee for most of his recording sessions, leaving his producer and record company to reap most of the profits.

As a group, these classic and country blues artists had a formative influence on rock 'n' roll that is undeniable. It is, therefore, fitting that Ma Rainey, Bessie Smith, Leadbelly, Robert Johnson, and Howlin' Wolf have been inducted into the Rock 'n' Roll Hall of Fame as "early influences." B. B. King, John Lee Hooker, and Muddy Waters have been admitted as rock 'n' roll artists in their own right.

"Hillbilly": The Music of the White Working Class

The first recordings of country musicians were as accidental as Mamie Smith's recording of "Crazy Blues." In fact, they were a by-product of the quest for black talent that dominated commercial field recordings, and once again it was Ralph Peer who opened the market for the music. In 1923, when Peer visited Atlanta in search of new black artists, Polk Brockman persuaded him to record a man who had been a mainstay of the North Georgia folk scene for some forty years, Fiddlin' John Carson. Although Carson was a veteran fiddle player and had won the Atlanta Old Time Fiddler's Convention numerous times, Peer was unimpressed with Carson's "The Little Old Log Cabin in the Lane" and "The Old Hen Cackled and the Rooster's Going to Crow." It was the sales figures of these recordings that convinced Peer of the commercial value of the music.

At the time, the music was never referred to as country music. Record catalogues used such labels as "old time music" (OKeh), "old familiar tunes" (Columbia), and "songs from Dixie" (Brunswick).[26] The word *hillbilly* had been used since the turn of the century as a catchall (and pejorative) term for southern backwoods culture. In 1925, however, a string band headed by Al Hopkins ventured to the OKeh studios in New York to record six songs for Ralph Peer. When Peer asked the name of the group, Hopkins responded: "Call the band anything you want. We are nothing but a bunch of hillbillies from North Carolina and Virginia anyway."[27] Peer thus listed the name of the band as the "Hill Billies," and the name soon became the generic term for commercial country music. The term, however, just like *race music,* was laden with contradictory meanings. According to Bill C. Malone,

The first recordings of country musicians were as accidental as Mamie Smith's recording of "Crazy Blues."

> Hillbilly music was not simply rural; it also came before the American populace as a southern art form. Like the South itself, hillbilly music suffered and profited from a conflicting set of images held by Americans that ranged from stability and enchantment to decadence and cultural degeneracy. The music took shape as a commercial entity during a decade when the South's reputation seemed at a particularly low ebb. To many people hillbilly music was just one more example, along with Ku Kluxism, Prohibition, sharecropping, racial violence, and religious bigotry, of the South's retarded and degenerate culture. On the other hand, many people no doubt responded positively to the South as a bastion of traditional values and orthodox religion in a nation given over to rapid and bewildering change.[28]

In the early period of commercial country music, string bands like the Hill Billies predominated, and among the finest bands of this period were Charlie Poole and his North Carolina Ramblers, and the Skillet Lickers. At first, the repertoires of these bands consisted of traditional, anonymous folk tunes, surprisingly few of which were of British origin.[29] Gradually, original composers began to appear, and as the music proved commercially viable, professional songwriters joined their ranks. By the time the Skillet Lickers began to record for Columbia in 1926, "in a wild, raucous, but highly infectious style," their repertoire included "everything from traditional ballads, breakdowns, and rural 'dramas' (humorous skits) to the latest popular hits from Tin Pan Alley."[30] Charlie Poole and the North Carolina Ramblers included such songs from the popular arena as "Goodbye Sweet Liza Jane," "Leaving Home," and "Milwaukee Blues." In fact, Poole's favourite singer was Al Jolson. Even so, it is important to note that the various sources, instruments, and sounds these artists drew on were incorporated into regional styles that were intensely familiar to their listening audiences.

Most of the early commercial performers were working people with day jobs who played country music in their off-hours. A few, like Charlie Poole, toured regularly on the vaudeville circuit, but it was rare for a "hillbilly" performer to have a career in show business that paid the rent. One such performer, Vernon Dalhart (who took his name from the towns of Vernon and Dalhart, Texas, where he had worked as a cowboy), actually entered the business through vaudeville and light opera. A graduate of the Dallas Conservatory of Music, Dalhart began recording for Edison in 1916, specializing in so-called coon songs. In 1924, he convinced Victor to record his "The Wreck of the Old 97" and "The Prisoner's Song." These became the first country music recordings to sell in the millions, and they established Dalhart as a country artist of note as well as one of the top-selling recording artists of his time in any category. By 1933, when his recording career ended, he had sold an estimated 75 million records.

In 1927, two of country music's most influential acts—Jimmie Rodgers and the Carter Family (A. P., his wife, Sara, and his sister-in-law, Maybelle)—were first recorded within days of each other by the tireless Ralph Peer, who had moved to Victor when OKeh was absorbed by Columbia in 1926. If Rodgers represented the archetypal "ramblin' man," the Carter Family

The Carter Family (from left, Maybelle, Sara, and A. P.) represented "family values" in country music even after Sara and A. P. divorced. Their traditional image corresponded with the treasure trove of traditional songs they helped to preserve.

projected family stability. (These two polar—and equally marketable—images of country music would be well represented for years to come.) Accordingly, while Rodgers roamed through vaudeville and the blues, the Carter Family explored the traditional folkloric component of country music. The Carter Family recorded for several labels, but principally for Victor, from 1927 until 1941. Sara's clear soprano defined the Carters' vocal sound. Maybelle's unique fingerpicking (which came to be known as "Carter picking") provided a distinctive instrumental base that incorporated blues licks and her signature "thumb-brush" style of picking the melody with her thumb on the bass strings while providing rhythm with a downward stroke of her fingers on the treble strings. A. P., who also sang bass and played some fiddle, collected, wrote, arranged, and copyrighted the Carter repertoire, which was published by Peer's Southern Music Company. Any number of their songs, including "The Wabash Cannonball," "Wildwood Flower," "Keep on the Sunny Side," "Worried Man Blues," and "Will the Circle Be Unbroken," have become country music classics. Although their records did not sell in the millions, the Carter Family kept alive a valuable repertoire of traditional music.

The first real star of country music was Jimmie Rodgers, the "Singing Brakeman." Rodgers learned to play the banjo and guitar at a very early age and dreamed of becoming a popular entertainer. Because his mother died when he was young, he often accompanied his father, a rail crew foreman, on extended journeys to different cities in the U.S. South. After a stint with a medicine show at the age of thirteen, Rodgers went to work for his father's crews and quickly learned the language and culture of the railroad men he later immortalized in song. In 1925, he joined a minstrel troupe and toured the South and Midwest as a blackface entertainer. He then moved to Asheville, North Carolina, and performed locally until 1927, when he first recorded for Ralph Peer. For his recording debut, Rodgers chose "The Soldiers' Sweetheart" and "Sleep, Baby, Sleep," two sentimental, traditional songs. Soon realizing that they had a potential star on their hands, Victor executives invited Rodgers to their Camden, New Jersey, studios. There he recorded the first of his twelve blue yodels, so called because they incorporated yodelling into the blues. Popularly known as "T for Texas," this recording became the country music hit of the year and Rodgers' only million seller. While his personal appearances were usually solo, Rodgers used a broad range of players and instrumentation in his recordings, including fiddles, banjos, ukuleles, pianos, and guitars, as well as brass and the one instrument that would become a defining characteristic of certain strains of country music, the steel guitar. His steel guitarists included Joe Kaipo, a real Hawaiian. He also recorded with the (black) Louisville Jug Band. On "Blue Yodel No. 9" (some blue yodels were simply numbered), Rodgers was joined by Louis Armstrong on trumpet and Lillian Armstrong on piano. Rodgers' blue yodels showcased the cultural diversity that informed his music, and his incorporation of yodelling and Hawaiian guitar into the blues influenced generations of musicians. Nothing corresponding to this particular combination of elements had ever before

Jimmie Rodgers played the "ramblin' man" to the Carters' stable family image. If the Carters stayed close to home musically, Rodgers' travels encouraged him to incorporate a greater diversity of influences into his music than any other country artist at the time.

appeared in country music or the blues. Like some of his blues contemporaries, Rodgers was inducted as an early influence into the Rock 'n' Roll Hall of Fame.

Rodgers had a seminal influence on Canada's first two country music stars, Wilf Carter and Hank Snow. Carter was born in 1904 in Port Hilford, Nova Scotia. After working for a brief period as a lumberjack, Carter headed out west to Alberta, became a cowboy, and began playing weekend dances. As was the case with most early country music stars, Carter developed an audience initially as a radio performer, debuting on CFCN in Calgary in 1930. He would later perform on Calgary station CFAC and nationally for the CRBC. By 1932, Carter had acquired enough of a name that he signed a contract with RCA Victor in Montreal. The top side of his first 78 rpm record, "My Swiss Moonlight Lullaby," clearly showed the extent of Rodgers' influence, with Carter demonstrating his yodelling skills. The flip side, "The Capture of Albert Johnson," was one of innumerable narrative ballads Carter wrote and recorded that drew on traditional Anglo-Saxon folk models as opposed to contemporary country music. The record proved to be Canada's first hit country recording.

Among the several hundred songs that Carter wrote over the course of his career, an inordinate number included cowboy, hobo, and prairie imagery. Between 1933 and 1949, many of Carter's songs were published in sheet music books with titles such as *Cowboy Songs*, *More Cowboy Songs* and *New Cowboy Songs*. While Carter spent most of his career in Canada, from 1935 to 1937 he lived in New York, where, under the moniker Montana Slim, he hosted a country music show on CBS. He would later host shows on both NBC and the CBC.

While Carter might have been the first Canadian country music star, Hank Snow was surely the biggest Canadian country music singer prior to the rise of Shania Twain in the 1990s. Born in Brooklyn, Nova Scotia, by the age of twelve Snow was on his own working on fishing boats and in the fish-processing plants in Nova Scotia. Heavily influenced by Jimmie Rodgers, Snow spent a short stint playing minstrel shows and first appeared on radio on CHNS in Halifax in the early 1930s. Following in Carter's footsteps, in 1936 he signed a recording contract with RCA Victor in Montreal, his first recording demonstrating Rodgers' influence on "Lonesome Blue Yodel" and the influence of cowboy culture on the flip side, "The Prisoner Cowboy." Both songs were written by Snow. In 1937, Snow embarked on his first cross-Canada tour. For the next decade, he plied his trade primarily in Canada, appearing regularly on the CBC and local Maritime radio shows and on recordings cut in Montreal for RCA Victor. In 1946, he relocated to Nashville, becoming a regular on the *Grand Ole Opry Show* for over forty years, beginning in 1950. That same year, he wrote and recorded the number one smash "I'm Moving On," one of the biggest country hits up to that time and later covered by the Rolling Stones. Between 1949 and 1979, Snow placed a staggering eighty-five singles on Billboard's country charts, six of which went to number one. Several of his earlier Canadian songs were published in sheet music folios such as *Cowboy Songs by Hank the Yodelling Ranger*.

As Richard Green has noted, "Carter, Snow, and later Earl Heywood introduced a unique style of country music that uses a lower, less nasal-sounding voice with clearer enunciation and fewer of the blues-like slurs and high whining sounds that dominate much American country music. Canadian singers have continued to rely more on the traditional ballad and story songs than on the 'cheatin'' and barroom songs often preferred in the U.S."[31]

In addition to Carter and Snow, there were any number of American country singers who were heavily influenced by Jimmie Rodgers.

Following Rodgers' success, groups like Roy Hall's Blue Ridge Entertainers and Roy Acuff's Smoky Mountain Boys established the steel guitar as a staple in country music. With the rise of such Texas "hillbillies" as Ernest Tubb, Lefty Frizzell, and Bob Wills, all of whom considered Rodgers to be their inspiration, country music took a turn to the West. The Texan who benefited the most from this "westernization" of country music was Gene Autry, the "Singing Cowboy," who began his career as a Jimmie Rodgers imitator. It was, however, Bob Wills and His Texas Playboys who popularized a brand of music called western swing, which became one of the formative influences on early rock 'n' roll.

Wills, who performed daily from 1934 to 1942 on KVOO in Tulsa, Oklahoma, was an outstanding fiddle player with eclectic tastes in music. In its various incarnations, the group included brass, reeds, drums, and electric guitars, all quite frowned upon in country music at the time. He always demanded a strong rhythmic base and hot improvisational solos from his players. By the end of the 1930s, Wills and his group could play anything from fiddle music to big band jazz with spirit. In 1939, his "San Antonio Rose" became a certified million seller for the group and a national sensation when it was recorded by Bing Crosby the following year.

Neither Rodgers nor the Carter Family toured extensively—the Carters by choice, Rodgers due to a running battle with tuberculosis, the disease that eventually took his life. The careers of both were propelled in large measure by their recordings and radio appearances. Although radio had devastating effects on the recording industry as a whole, early country musicians seem to have benefited from a complementary relationship between radio appearances and record sales.

The Dissemination of Blues and Country: More Separate Than Equal

While there were significant markets for jazz and blues on records, African American performers were almost never the beneficiaries of early developments in radio or film. Bessie Smith's starring role in *St. Louis Blues* in 1929 was successful enough to suggest more of the same, and the film's director, Dudley Murphy, followed his initial triumph one year later with *Black and Tan Fantasy,* a film built around a Duke Ellington composition. Shortly thereafter, Ellington himself filmed his entire *Symphony in Black.* In 1933, Murphy shot an operatic film version of Eugene O'Neill's *The Emperor Jones* with the incomparable Paul Robeson in the title role. As Thomas Cripps has noted, "Thus, in less than four years Murphy demonstrated the richness which sound film could bring to African American themes."[31] Unlike *St. Louis Blues,* however, these later efforts tended toward an art music mode, which was well within the bounds of mainstream acceptability, but far removed from the tastes of most African Americans. Because sound film raised the stakes for moviemaking, the Great Depression shut most independent black filmmakers out of the business, leaving Hollywood firmly in control, and Hollywood seldom cast African Americans in anything but subservient and/or degrading roles.

The situation was even worse on radio. The blues—particularly country blues—were seldom heard on the airwaves. "Radio broadcasts," as Nelson George has noted, "were rarely used to promote the grittier forms of music."[33] In 1932, however, Fats Waller's career received a significant boost when he played a long series of broadcasts, titled *Fats Waller's Rhythm Club,* over WLW in Cincinnati, Ohio. Two other blues performers, Sonny Boy Williamson (Rice Miller), a singer/harmonica player, and Robert Lockwood, a guitarist, were featured on the King Biscuit Flour Company's *King Biscuit Time,* which was broadcast from Helena, Arkansas, in the early 1940s. Given the population of the Mississippi Delta area, King Biscuit's choice of talent probably added measurably to its sale of flour.

When broadcast at all, African American jazz and dance music were usually relegated to late-night remote broadcasts from popular nightspots. Both jazz and dance music were popular with mainstream audiences. To white listeners, the race of the performers was probably unknown and, therefore, of little consequence.

Although radio had devastating effects on the recording industry as a whole, early country musicians seem to have benefited from a complementary relationship between radio appearances and record sales. African American performers were almost never the beneficiaries of early developments in radio or film.

> *If you liked swing in the 1920s and 1930s you could pick up live broadcasts of Duke Ellington at the Cotton Club and Chick Webb at the Savoy in Harlem, Earl (Fatha) Hines from Chicago's Grand Terrace, or maybe a late set from some California band from the West Coast Cotton Club. Significantly, these broadcasts weren't aimed at blacks. Broadcasters and advertisers were simply meeting America's demand for big-band music. These bands just happened to be black and popular.*[34]

Occasionally, an extremely talented African American musician could find work in radio as a composer or arranger. One such person was William Grant Still. With a music industry résumé that included positions at W. C. Handy's publishing house and the Black Swan record company, Still was an accomplished composer who had studied at the New England Conservatory as well as with the avant-garde French-born, but U.S.-based, composer Edgar Varèse. During the Depression, Still worked as an arranger and staff composer at both WCBS and WNBC in New York. His work at WCBS led to commissions from such popular entertainers as Artie Shaw, Sophie Tucker, and Paul Whiteman. Still supplied the arrangements for Whiteman's appearance on "The Old Gold Show" in California. On his return to New York, Still was hired by the "Deep River Hour" on WNBC and became the first African American conductor of a white radio orchestra. As in films, however, the employment of African Americans in radio was contingent on their ability to relate to European conventions and mainstream tastes.

There were a few attempts to air shows that featured well-known African American talent, but these attempts were short-lived. The *Ethel Waters Show,* sponsored by Amoco on NBC, was quickly canceled when the network's southern affiliates threatened to boycott the program. Fleischman Yeast sponsored the *Louis Armstrong Show* on CBS in 1937, but by this time Armstrong was doing comedy routines and singing Tin Pan Alley pop. Scheduled opposite the popular *Jack Benny Show* on NBC, the program lasted only thirteen weeks.

In contrast, country music was given a considerable boost by broadcasters and film producers. Since the dawn of commercial radio in the early twenties, stations throughout the

South and Midwest had broadcast country music. It was Fiddlin' John Carson's popularity on WSB, a station owned by the *Atlanta Journal,* that first convinced Polk Brockman there was a record market for country music. After WBAP in Fort Worth, Texas, broadcast a one-and-a-half-hour program of square dance music in 1923, the "barn dance" format quickly became the most popular showcase for country talent. The first such program of note was *National Barn Dance,* which was introduced in 1924 by the Sears Roebuck station, WLS (World's Largest Store), in Chicago. Combining country and folk material with older pop standards, the program had a broader appeal than most country-oriented shows.

Of course, the country music show that eventually overshadowed all country broadcasts was the *Grand Ole Opry,* which was the brainchild of George D. Hay, a popular columnist for the *Memphis Commercial-Appeal* and a veteran announcer on WLS. In 1925, Hay became the station manager for WSM in Nashville, a station owned by the National Life and Accident Insurance Company. Bypassing the cultural biases of the station owners and the Nashville elite, Hay launched the WSM *Barn Dance,* later renamed the *Grand Ole Opry,* and proved that country music could be an effective tool for selling life insurance to working-class people. Within weeks, the show's appeal was reflected in life insurance sales.

The Grand Ole Opry eventually went on to become the longest-running show on U.S. radio, a clear indicator of the commercial potential of country music.

As was common in the early days of commercial country music, the program emphasized instrumental music. Its first major singing star was David Harrison, "Uncle Dave" Macon, a gifted and unpretentious banjo player who had a vast storehouse of folkloric material. The program also introduced one of the first black stars of country music (and radio) to its audience, Deford Bailey, a country harmonica player who proved to be one of the show's most popular artists. In 1928, Bailey made twice as many *Opry* appearances as any other performer.

The entertainer who became the *Opry*'s biggest star was Roy Acuff. Acuff, a singer/fiddler who was raised on a tenant farm in the Smoky Mountains, achieved worldwide fame playing traditional mountain music. The Acuffs were a musical family; Roy's mother played piano and guitar, his father played fiddle, and all had fine singing voices. When near-fatal sunstroke dashed Acuff's hopes for a baseball career with the New York Yankees, his interests turned toward music. In 1932, he toured with Doc Hauer's Medicine Show, hawking Moc-A-Tan Compound in blackface. Later, he appeared with a variety of groups on stations WROL and WNOX in Knoxville, Tennessee. His first recording session in 1936, produced by Art Satherley, who would also produce Gene Autry's recordings, yielded two of his biggest hits: "Great Speckled Bird" and "Wabash Cannonball," which became a million seller. Joining the *Grand Ole Opry* in 1938, Acuff soon established the singer, rather than the string band, as the show's main attraction. When the show became a featured segment, sponsored by Prince Albert Tobacco, on the NBC radio network in 1939 (WSM had become a 50,000-watt clear channel in 1932), it was hosted by Acuff. The *Grand Ole Opry* eventually became the longest-running show on U.S. radio, a clear indicator of the commercial potential of country music.

Radio was also very important for country music in Canada. As noted earlier, both Wilf Carter and Hank Snow used first local and then national radio as springboards for their careers. Perhaps the Canadian country artist best-known for his radio work was Maritime fiddler Don Messer. Born in 1909 in Tweedside, Nova Scotia, Messer was somewhat of a child prodigy, playing publicly at local weddings and dances by the time he was seven. In 1929, when Messer

Gene Autry was not only the most famous singing cowboy on film, but he also made a successful transition to television with his own weekly series in the early 1950s.

was twenty, a local merchant sponsored a radio program for the young fiddler on CFBO, Saint John. Five years later, Messer's band, the New Brunswick Lumberjacks, numbering at times nineteen members, were broadcasting nationally on the CRBC. At the same time, Messer regularly performed in the northeastern U.S. and throughout the Maritimes with a smaller ensemble he called the Backwoods Breakdown.

Messer's most famous group was known as the Islanders, and was formed in 1939, when he became music director of radio station CFCY, Charlottetown. Over the next ten years, Don Messer and His Islanders developed into one of the most popular radio shows in Canada. In 1956, Messer, with a group fronted by vocalist Marg Osburne (who joined the group in 1947), took his show to television on CHBY-TV, Halifax. In 1959, *The Don Messer Show* was slotted in as a summer series on CBTV, where it continued in the fall under the name *Don Messer's Jubilee*. When the CBC cancelled the show ten years later, CHCH-TV in Hamilton produced a syndicated version that ran until Messer's death in 1973. In addition to Messer and His Islanders, the show included performances from every important Canadian country artist of the time, including Stompin' Tom Connors and Graham Townsend.

While the music Messer played aligns more closely with country music than any other popular genre, he always insisted that his music "was not Western or cowboy music. Our tunes have been around for two or three hundred years. They're folk tunes passed from generation to generation."[35] Messer's repertoire included traditional hornpipes, jigs, and reels as well as original tunes composed by himself and others. Between 1942 and 1952, Messer recorded thirty-five 78s for the Canadian record company Apex, and by the time of his death he had recorded over thirty LPs for Apex, MCA, and Rodeo.

For a generation of Canadians, *Don Messer's Jubilee* provided weekly entertainment that was distinctly Canadian. Its focus on Maritime culture helped serve both to promote this region of the country and to bind together its disparate regions.

As country music began to incorporate a western theme into its image, it was radio that helped to popularize the "singing cowboys." Woodward Maurice (Tex) Ritter, a native of Murvaul, Texas, who attended the University of Texas and Northeastern Law School, began singing western and mountain songs on KPRC in Houston in 1929. From there, he moved to a featured slot in 1932 on WOR's *The Lone Star Rangers* in 1932, one of the first western radio shows to originate in New York. Another well-known western group, the Sons of the Pioneers, which included Roy Rogers, the "King of the Cowboys," and New Brunswick native Bob Nolan, had an early-morning radio program on KFWB in Hollywood. (Rogers went on to host his own radio show with his wife, Dale Evans, in the mid-1940s.) Gene Autry got his start as the Oklahoma Yodeling Cowboy on KVOO in Tulsa, Oklahoma. After recording for Art Satherley, who released the singer on the Sears Conqueror label, Autry made a series of appearances on the *National Barn Dance* in Chicago and then landed his own radio show, *Conqueror Record Time,* on WLS, where he became one of the most popular entertainers in the station's history.

The cowboy image became so prevalent in country music that even performers who did not perform western-related material began to dress in garish western-style garb.

The cowboy image became so prevalent in country music that even singers who did not perform western-related material began to dress in garish western-style garb. For a time, the term *western* even became an alternative to the *hillbilly* designation used for country music. As Bill C. Malone has pointed out, however,

> In reality, except for the fabric of usable symbols which surrounded him, the cowboy contributed nothing to American music. The "western" music which became fashionable in the mid-thirties came from other sources. . . . in the Southeast: southern traditional and gospel music, popular music, commercial recordings of all kinds (including blues and jazz), and, crucially, black music. Southwesterners could draw additionally on Mexican, Cajun, German, and what generally was described as "Bohemian" music (that is, the polka-derived styles of people who emigrated to South-Central Texas from what is now Czechoslovakia).[35]

Hollywood also helped to popularize the image of the singing cowboy. In 1936, Tex Ritter made *Song of the Gringo*, one of dozens of cowboy movies. The Sons of the Pioneers and Bob Wills and His Texas Playboys also appeared in several westerns. Other western-style singers, such as Ernest Tubb, made occasional appearances in Hollywood films. By far the most successful of singing cowboys of films was Gene Autry. After a small part in *In Old Santa Fe* in 1934, Autry landed a starring role in an odd thirteen-episode cowboy/science-fiction thriller called *The Phantom Empire.* Following a featured role in *Tumbling Tumbleweeds* in 1935, he went on to star in more than 100 western films, most produced by Republic, which was considered the home of "class" Westerns. The song "Tumbling Tumbleweeds" had been written by Canadian Bob Nolan for his group the Sons of the Pioneers in 1934. After the Pioneers recording had become a hit, the film studio decided to build the film of the same name around the song. "Tumbling Tumbleweeds" was also sung by Roy Rogers in *Silver Spurs* (1943), by the Sons of the Pioneers in *Hollywood Canteen* (1944), and by Gene Autry again in *Don't Fence Me In* (1945). Both the Sons of the Pioneers and Gene Autry made hit recordings of the song, as did Glen Gray and his Casa Loma Orchestra, and in 1940 Bing Crosby's version helped establish the song as a pop standard.

The Long Road Back for Records

The Great Depression decimated the ranks of the independent specialty labels, as blues, jazz, and country music imprints were sometimes called. Independent, black-owned record companies had almost disappeared even prior to the Depression. Paramount had acquired the Black Swan catalogue in 1924, and Columbia had absorbed OKeh in 1926. Although country music continued to benefit from national radio exposure, the sale of 10,000 records was considered a hit. Things were no rosier for the major record companies. Already hurt by radio and confused by Hollywood, they were almost pulled under by the Depression. Edison ceased production altogether in 1930. Columbia, which was already in receivership, was picked up by the American Record Company for a mere $70,000 during the Depression. Convinced prematurely that records would be a good promotional vehicle for its film stars, Warner Brothers acquired Brunswick, Al Jolson's label. Sarnoff, as usual, planned for the future and slowly built his empire. In 1929, as vice-president of RCA, he engineered a merger between RCA and Victor records and emerged as president of the new company. At the time of the merger, Victor was one of the few record companies that was still holding its own.

For the record industry, the long road back to prosperity began with a machine that had been laid to rest more than two decades earlier—the jukebox. The nickel-in-the-slot phonograph manufacturers had developed a machine that used discs in 1908, but the machines quickly fell into disuse as phonographs and records moved into homes. A new incarnation of the coin-operated record player appeared in 1927 when the Automatic Musical Instrument Company (AMI) introduced its Selective Phonograph. Once Prohibition was repealed in 1933, bars and cocktail lounges opened by the thousands. Looking for low-cost entertainment and an additional source of revenue, owners were only too happy to consider the jukebox. A number of companies, Wurlitzer, Rockola (founded by Virdon, Manitoba, native David Rockola), and Seburg, among others, soon entered the business. By 1935, there were 150,000 jukeboxes in operation in the United States, and in that year, they accounted for 40 percent of the record trade.

Prior to the dramatic growth of the jukebox, record companies had taken their production cues from hits created in other entertainment media: vaudeville, Broadway, Hollywood, and radio. During the hard times of the 1930s, however, the jukebox emerged as a major source of public entertainment. It provided a guaranteed market for record companies and a valuable promotional vehicle for recording artists. To be sure they had something for everyone, jukeboxes included a much broader range of musical styles than most radio stations. Thus, the mass audience took on a new role in the determination of public taste. *Billboard* and *Variety*, the major entertainment industry trade magazines, soon began the practice of charting jukebox hits. Once this happened, radio producers began to use the charts as a basis for live music programming, and song-pluggers began to pay more attention to records.

Other technological advances also increased the desirability of records. Broadcast technology had ushered in the era of electronic recording in the mid-1920s. Microphones, vacuum tube amplifiers, and an electromagnetic cutting stylus replaced the acoustic recording horn. The better frequency response of the new technology created a more lifelike sound. No longer did musicians have to crowd around a single recording horn; recording studios became expansive, able to accommodate whole orchestras. Sound reinforcement meant that vocalists no longer had to project; they could croon, a practice soon elevated to a virtual art form by Bing Crosby, who used the microphone as if he were singing to a single listener. By 1925, both Victor and Columbia were issuing electrically recorded discs, but although the technology revolutionized the recording industry, with record sales falling it did not seem practical to market expensive new electric record players. In 1932, Ted Wallerstein, a veteran record executive who left Brunswick to join Sarnoff at RCA Victor, solved the cost problem when he offered the Duo, Jr.—an electric turntable with no tubes or speakers that could be "jacked" into a radio, for a list price of $16.50.

If the Duo, Jr., made hardware affordable, a price cut by Decca, a new label, made records once again available to masses of people. American Decca was formed in 1934 when E. R. Lewis, head of British Decca, bought the rights to Brunswick from Warner Brothers and used what remained of Brunswick's catalogue as a base to found the new company. Jack Kapp, who was creative director at Brunswick, was brought over to head the new label. Within months, he had assembled an impressive roster of talent, including Bing Crosby, the Dorsey Brothers, the Mills Brothers, Canadian Guy Lombardo, and Fletcher Henderson. While the talent roster certainly helped Decca, the key innovation that contributed to its success and to the revival of the record market as a whole was the slashing of the price of a record from seventy-five cents to thirty-five cents.

After supplying RCA Victor with the Duo, Jr., Ted Wallerstein began negotiations with William Paley and CBS. Wallerstein judged correctly that CBS, which had been operating without a record division until this time, would benefit from the acquisition of an established trademark, a pressing plant, and the rights to British-made Columbia recordings in the United States. Thus, he convinced Paley and CBS to purchase the faltering Columbia Records, Victor's main rival, as part of the acquisition of the American Record Company in 1938 for the seemingly outrageous price of $700,000, ten times its purchase price of a few years earlier. Abandoning RCA to become head of the new CBS record division, Wallerstein lured such talent as Benny Goodman, Duke Ellington, and Count Basie to the label. With the big band era in full swing, this was definitely a timely move.

One of the key players in the talent raids that brought Goodman and Basie to Columbia was John Hammond, a wealthy Vanderbilt on his mother's side, a staunch civil rights activist, an aficionado of African American music, and soon to become Benny Goodman's brother-in-law. Hammond, who accepted the job of producer at Columbia from Wallerstein in 1939 (the first full-time job he had ever held), was already a known quantity in the music industry, having produced Bessie Smith's final recording session and Billie Holiday's first session within months of each other in 1933. His years as a producer at Columbia spanned generations, and he influenced the careers of artists as diverse as Aretha Franklin, Bob Dylan, and Bruce Springsteen.

Hammond was widely respected among African American musicians (and widely considered to be a wealthy eccentric, if not an outright communist, in the music industry) for his attempts to break down racial barriers. And he put his expertise where his beliefs were. In 1938, Hammond had produced a landmark concert at Carnegie Hall, designed to showcase the entire history of African American music. Titled *From Spirituals to Swing,* the concert included music recorded in West Africa; boogie-woogie pianists Albert Ammons, Meade Lux Lewis, and Pete

Johnson; blues shouter Big Joe Turner; gospel singers Sister Rosetta Tharpe and Mitchell's Christian Singers; harmonica player Sonny Terry; Big Bill Broonzy; the Kansas City Six; and the Count Basie Orchestra, among others. The sophisticates of the New York jazz scene were finally treated to an evening with the real innovators of the music they professed to love. Hammond then repeated this successful event one year later. He was one of the few major label executives who truly believed that African American music should be accorded a place of prominence within U.S. popular culture. In his autobiography, he argued for a "lessening of differences between country and popular music, between folk, rock, jazz, gospel, and other categories."[36] He was clearly more attuned than most to the sounds that would eventually transform the character of popular music.

John Hammond was one of the few major label executives who truly believed that African American music should be accorded a place of prominence within U.S. popular culture. He was clearly more attuned than most to the sounds that would eventually transform the character of popular music.

With the advent of commercial radio and "talkies" after World War I, record companies found their sales slipping and looked about for new markets, discovering in the process a sizable African American market for blues recordings by black artists as well as an untapped market for so-called hillbilly music. While new labels such as OKeh, Black Swan, and Black Patti came into existence, most of these were forced out of business or absorbed by larger companies as record sales continued to fall. It was not until the rebirth of the jukebox, which gave the mass audience more of a voice in public taste, that the record companies made a real financial comeback. By the end of the Depression, Columbia, Victor, and Decca had emerged as the big three in recording. Although they faced virtually no competition, they saw no harm in protecting themselves from the possibility that small new companies would find new grassroots music. Thus, each company established a less expensive subsidiary to cover the grassroots. Victor created Bluebird for its so-called race and hillbilly artists. In 1940, Columbia revitalized OKeh as its specialty label. The more recently formed Decca acquired Gennett, an "old-time" label, in the late 1930s. This, then, was the situation as Canada and the United States prepared for their entrance into World War II.

"Good Rockin' Tonight": The Rise of Rhythm and Blues

The military buildup that preceded World War II greatly enhanced the prospects of both the United States and Canada for a complete economic recovery from the Great Depression. The nations' involvement in the war led in turn to profound social changes. Policies and practices concerning race and gender relations were successfully challenged, and as the two countries approached full employment, the improved financial status of the average citizen contrasted sharply with the hardship of the Depression. In the cultural arena, these social changes and other seemingly unrelated variables, such as population migrations, material shortages, and technological advances, all of which were associated with the war effort, played a major role in determining the course of popular music.

As the military buildup began, thousands of blacks and poor whites in the U.S. South abandoned the oppressive conditions of sharecropping and tenant farming and moved north and west to find better-paying jobs in defence plants. Naturally, they took their music with them. At the same time, countless eastern and midwestern G.I.s were put through basic training in southern military bases, where they heard musical styles that had not yet achieved mainstream popularity in the North. In this way, blues and country music received unprecedented exposure. While country music had done well on radio earlier, by the early 1940s there were hundreds of stations across the country that broadcast country music. The new audiences must have liked what they heard because Detroit jukebox operators reported that country music records were the most played of their selections, and in Europe the Armed Forces Radio Network voted Roy Acuff more popular than Frank Sinatra. It seemed even the enemy recognized Acuff's importance. A widely reported war story held that Japanese troops went into battle shouting: "To hell with Roosevelt, Babe Ruth, and Roy Acuff."[1]

The sweeping commodification of music that accompanied the development of recording and broadcasting had created possibilities for financial gain that could not have been imagined prior to the advent of mass culture.

56

Unlike country music, the blues, as a rule, had been excluded from radio in earlier years, but the exodus of more than 1 million African Americans from the South during World War II helped to loosen these restrictive programming policies. Wartime prosperity made these newly emigrated African Americans an identifiable consumer group. In areas with a high concentration of African American immigrants, it was in the interests of radio stations to introduce some programming that would cater to this audience. Gradually, some black-oriented programs, usually slotted late at night, began to appear on a few stations. It was this kind of programming that began to tear down the walls of the so-called race market toward the end of the decade.

In the music industry, economic recovery became the occasion for bitter and prolonged power struggles that revolved around a single question: Who should benefit, and in what proportion, from the profits derived from the use and sale of intellectual property? The key to understanding this question lay in the recognition that the music business in the 1940s had expanded far beyond the legal and organizational machinery that determined how to allocate the fruits of the market economy. The sweeping commodification of music that accompanied the development of recording and broadcasting had created possibilities for financial gain that could not have been imagined prior to the advent of mass culture. Neither the Copyright Act of 1909 nor the Communications Act of 1934 anticipated the complex interrelationships that would develop among the major interests in the music business—writers, publishers, performers, broadcasters, and record companies—let alone the relationships that would develop between these groups and consumers. As a result, these groups often found themselves in the midst of shifting alliances, competing interests, and dramatic cultural changes.

The Publishers and the Broadcasters: ASCAP Versus BMI

Broadcasters and publishers had been at odds ever since ASCAP had made its first demand for a $5-a-day royalty fee in 1922 and the NAB had been formed in reaction to the demand. Throughout the first decade of radio broadcasting, the major publishers had complained about declining profits. In point of fact, they had complained all the way to the bank. In the 1930s, according to Russell Sanjek, "ASCAP income from radio, of which the networks paid about 20 percent, had risen from $757,450 in 1932 to $5.9 million in 1937, and then dropped to $3.8 million the following year. It increased by 12 percent, to $4.3 million, in 1939."[2] That 1939 figure represented about two-thirds of ASCAP's total income for the year. Radio revenues were clearly substantial and their potential at the start of the 1940s was even greater.

As it had before, the prospect of windfall profits brought out the greed in ASCAP's 1,250 or so members, who controlled the performing rights to almost all of the best-known songs in the country. ASCAP's fee for a "blanket" licence (permission to broadcast any selection in the ASCAP catalogue) was 5 percent of the total receipts from all sponsored programs, including talk shows and sports broadcasts, which did not use music. Such terms naturally exacerbated the tension between ASCAP and the broadcasters. Their already strained relationship began to go up in flames in the summer of 1940 when ASCAP mailed out new contracts that were intended to take effect when the existing agreement expired on 31 December, 1940. The new contracts would have, in effect, doubled ASCAP's revenues. Designed to divide the broadcasters against themselves, the contracts included a sliding-scale fee that ranged from 3 percent for smaller stations to 7.5 percent for the networks. But ASCAP's divide-and-conquer strategy did not work; instead, the broadcasters closed ranks.

In 1939, anticipating the worst from ASCAP and dissatisfied with its own weak position at the bargaining table, the NAB, which then represented some 600 radio stations, had decided to challenge the ASCAP monopoly by forming a performing rights organization of its own. Some 256 stations raised close to $1.5 million to capitalize Broadcast Music Incorporated (BMI), which was launched in the United States on 13 October 1939 and in Canada a year later. "Taking advantage of ASCAP's stringent membership requirements, as well as its relative indifference to the popular and folk music being produced outside of New York and Hollywood," Nat Shapiro has written, "BMI sought out and acquired its support from the 'have not' publishers and writers in the grassroots areas."[3] Blues and country music songwriters and publishers found in BMI an inviting home for their work. By the time ASCAP's existing contract had expired, BMI had become a sizable operation, "turning out about 30 new songs a month under its own print" and acquiring "a number of existing catalogues—those of Hinds, Hayden & Eldridge, M. M. Cole, E. C. Schirmer, Ricordi, and [Ralph Peer's] Southern Music Publishing Co."[4]

For about ten months in 1941, no ASCAP music was heard on radio. As the broadcasters had predicted, there was no public protest.

With a catalogue of its own in place, the NAB responded to ASCAP's 1940 demands by announcing its intention to boycott the entire ASCAP catalogue. At first, ASCAP was not terribly rattled by the prospect of the boycott. The organization assumed that public demand for the likes of Irving Berlin, Cole Porter, and George Gershwin would soon bring the NAB back into the fold. The NAB held to the belief that there would be no public outcry when ASCAP music went off the air. "The music the people like is the music people hear," opined Neville Miller, president of the NAB, somewhat cynically. "It is likely that no one will notice the difference in character and quality of programs on and after January 1, 1941."[5]

For about ten months in 1941, no ASCAP music was heard on radio. In its stead, authentic regional styles, supplemented by melodies in the public domain, were broadcast to a national audience via mainstream outlets. As the broadcasters had predicted, there was no public protest. There were, however, a few key acquisitions by BMI that contributed measurably to the success of the boycott. Ralph Peer, who had moved into the international market, offered a catalogue of Latin popular music; Roy Acuff and Fred Rose (who had been members of ASCAP since 1928) offered Acuff-Rose Music, the first all-country publishing company; and E. B. Marks, an established Tin Pan Alley firm, offered the familiar pop fare that was required for network broadcasts. Although the broadcasters and the publishers came to terms in 1941, they did so only after a federally initiated criminal antitrust action forced ASCAP into a consent decree that regulated its dealings with its clients.

In the beginning, BMI came up with few songs of lasting significance. Still, by the end of 1941, its catalogue contained 36,000 copyrights from fifty-two publishers.[6] What was originally envisioned as a throwaway bargaining tool emerged as a valuable source of music and ASCAP's future primary competition. Moreover, for the first time, the Tin Pan Alley/Broadway/ Hollywood monopoly on public taste had been challenged. As writers from grassroots areas received encouragement from BMI, songwriting itself became more decentralized. By the end of the decade, BMI writers like Huddie Ledbetter (Leadbelly), Hank Snow, Arthur "Big Boy" Crudup, Roy Brown, Ivory Joe Hunter, Hank Williams, Ernest Tubb, Johnny Otis, Fats Domino, and Wynonie Harris had begun to play a major role in redefining popular music.

Enter the Deejay:
The Broadcasters Versus the AFM

Less than a year after the settlement of its dispute with ASCAP, the NAB found itself embroiled in another controversy, this time with the American Federation of Musicians (AFM). As a rule, the music heard on radio was performed live and often in formal concert settings with audiences in attendance. Searching desperately for less expensive programming during the Great Depression, however, some radio stations had begun to use records as an alternative to live talent. Although perhaps unrecognized by many at the time, records were a direct challenge to the primacy of live music and one that would change the face of popular music.

The records were played by a new figure in broadcasting, the disc jockey, a term that came to be defined as an individual who was "jockeying or riding a record toward success."[7] Until the advent of the disc jockey, radio had simply been a vehicle for transmitting the substance of other media—newspapers, religious pulpits, concert halls, and vaudeville and the legitimate theatre. The disc jockey's, or deejay's, show was unique in its combination of live announcing and "canned" (prerecorded) music. The earliest deejays appeared even before the stock market crash in 1929. There were, for example, three stations in Los Angeles, KGFJ, KMIC, and KPLA, that programmed records almost exclusively. The powerful X stations (those with X in their call letters), which broadcast from across the Mexican border and were exempt from U.S. wattage regulations, also relied heavily on records. "Doc" Brinkley, the first country deejay, beamed country music into millions of U.S. homes from the 100,000 watt XER in Mexico. The first black deejay, Jack L. Cooper, sold an incredible amount of Tip Top Bread in the 1930s, while spinning "jump, jam, and jive" records on his pioneering show *The Negro Hour,* broadcast from WSBC on the south side of Chicago. The first woman deejay on a commercially licensed station was Miss Halloween Martin (named after her birth date). Featured on Marshall Field and Company's *Musical Clock,* a wake-up show on KYW in Chicago, Martin played musical comedy, light classical, pop, and some jazz in between her time and weather announcements.

As deejays became more and more commonplace, the policy of prohibiting the use of records on radio became harder to enforce.

The archetypal deejay appeared in 1935 when the smooth-talking Martin Block began his show *Make Believe Ballroom* on WNEW in New York. Block, "whose facile tongue soon successfully defeated all record hiss or needle noise and made the time between records exciting with spellbinding monologues and irresistible advertising pitches," copied the concept for his program, which was sponsored by the makers of Retardo, a weight-reducing pill, from a Los

Angeles deejay named Al Jarvis.[8] Within months, the audience for Block's two-and-a-half-hour daily broadcasts had expanded to 4 million listeners. Block and Jarvis were more than mere technicians who filled "dead air" with recorded music. Focusing systematically on the most recent releases, they introduced the beginnings of "formula" radio.

As deejays became more and more commonplace, the policy of prohibiting the use of records on radio became harder to enforce. Indeed, after the formation of Capitol Records by record-store owner Glenn Wallichs, songwriter Johnny Mercer, and Paramount Pictures executive Buddy De Sylva in 1942, many programs and record companies openly ignored the policy. In a 1969 interview, Wallichs recalled the special consideration Capitol Records offered to deejays: "We typed special labels with their names on both sides, pressed them on expensive lightweights, unbreakable vinylite compound, and then had our limited employee force drive around and distribute each personally. It was a service that created a sensation. We made the jock a Big Man, an Important Guy, VIP in the industry."[9] Capitol also helped establish Los Angeles as an important music industry centre.

The same year that Capitol went into operation and became the first record company to send records to deejays free of charge, James C. Petrillo, president of the AFM, stepped up his war on "canned music." Petrillo had risen through the ranks of the Chicago local of the AFM during Prohibition. Reasoning correctly that recorded music would eventually put live musicians on radio out of work, Petrillo had tried a variety of tactics to deal with radio's use of records prior to 1942. He had begun by lobbying the Roosevelt administration to prohibit the use of records on radio. When that failed, he had forced Chicago radio stations to employ union musicians to operate turntables. As neither the musicians nor the record companies received royalties from record broadcasts, Petrillo had also convinced record manufacturers to join forces with the AFM to print on record labels a warning against airing commercial discs.[10]

Two things helped Petrillo in the early days of his struggle. First, a tacit assumption had built up over the years, fed by the FCC, that "live" programming was somehow more in the public interest than "canned" shows. Second (and possibly aided by this assumption), there had been a number of court decisions in the late 1930s that had prohibited radio from airing records. In 1940, however, a lower court decision restraining WNEW from broadcasting Paul Whiteman's records was reversed on appeal. Judge Learned Hand opined that "the common-law property of orchestra leader and corporation manufacturing phonograph records ended with sale of record, so that radio broadcasting company could not be restrained from using records in broadcasts."[11]

It is not surprising that the musicians held out for as long as they did in their struggle to preserve radio as a live performance medium. Radio provided steady work at a time when the vast bulk of most musicians' income came from live performances.

In 1942, Petrillo, not one to get overly bogged down in constraining legalities or past alliances, turned his wrath on the record companies, the ultimate source of the problem, rather than radio, the immediate offender. If no records were produced, Petrillo reasoned, recorded music could not be broadcast. He then warned the record companies that unless they could prevent radio stations and jukebox operators from playing records, his organization would strike the recording studios, a strategy intended to hurt record production and, at the same time, keep musicians working on radio. When the record companies were unable to comply, Petrillo ordered a ban on recording. No musicians were to enter recording studios in Canada or the United States until the AFM's demands were met.

Having anticipated the strike, the record companies had stockpiled unreleased masters.[12] As a result, they finished the year in reasonably good shape, but the musicians lost millions of dollars. As the demand for new releases far outstripped the supply, however, the musicians prevailed. Decca, which had been severed from its British parent, capitulated after thirteen months, but Victor and Columbia, expecting the government to intervene as it had in the ASCAP–BMI controversy, held out for about two years. The strike ended only when the record companies agreed to pay a royalty on record sales, which was used to finance a performance trust fund for out-of-work musicians. If Petrillo couldn't get radio to stop playing records, at least he could make somebody pay for the privilege. By 1950, when WINS in New York announced, over the objections of the AFM, that from now on it would program records exclusively, the era of live music network radio and the formality of its tuxedoed orchestras had clearly come to an end.

It is not surprising that the musicians held out for as long as they did in their struggle to preserve radio as a live performance medium. Radio provided steady work at a time when the vast bulk of most musicians' income came from live performances. Of course, at the time, live music on radio meant live music performed by white musicians for the most part, which the AFM did not seem to find unusual. Indeed, the AFM itself failed to extend its protection to all musicians equally. In 1944, as Arnold Shaw has pointed out, the "NAACP [National Association for the Advancement of Colored People] noted that, of 673 locals, 32 were 'colored.' Of the remaining 641 'white' locals, 8 had segregated subsidiary branches while many simply excluded Negro members . . . only 2 locals, those in Detroit and New York, admitted Negroes to full membership."[13]

Another group of musicians that remained outside the purview of the strike were the vocalists. The vocalists were covered by a different union—currently called the American Federation of Television and Radio Artists (AFTRA)—and AFTRA didn't join the strike. Throughout the strike, vocalists continued to record, but a cappella. By the time the musicians returned to the studios, the vocalists were in charge. Although the AFM strike probably was not a causal factor, it did mark something of a turning point in the rise of the solo vocalist and the decline of the big bands.

From Big Bands to Solo Singers

As swing music (a danceable amalgam of blues, jazz, and Tin Pan Alley pop) grew in popularity in the mid-1930s, nearly all the big bands had performed, sometimes grudgingly, with vocalists. Dance music was considered to be primarily an instrumental music. Vocalists were paid less than other members of the band and were often limited to one chorus of a tune. In fact, they were sometimes used simply to give instrumental soloists a rest. Audiences, however, enjoyed the vocal numbers, and the singers eventually became popular enough to begin solo careers. Bing Crosby ("Der Bingle," as the German soldiers in World War II called him), of course, had already established himself as the most successful vocalist of the era, totaling more than 300 hits between 1931 and 1954.

Others used their big band experience to launch careers that followed similar—if less spectacular—trajectories. Many singers were women. Mildred Bailey predated Crosby as a vocalist with the Whiteman band. Ella Fitzgerald started her career with Chick Webb; "A-Tisket A-Tasket" (1938) made her a pop star. Peggy Lee sang with Benny Goodman and Duke Ellington and then moved into songwriting and acting. Beginning as a country singer, Kay Starr launched a solo pop career after a stint with Charlie Barnet. Jo Stafford began with Tommy Dorsey and went on to record numerous pop hits that included folk and country material. Anita O'Day graduated from the Max Miller combo to the Gene Krupa and Stan Kenton bands and then to solo stardom.

The first pop vocalist to engender hysteria among his fans (rather than simple admiration or adoration) was an Italian American who refused to anglicize his name—Frank Sinatra, the "Sultan of Swoon." A song stylist with an unmistakable baritone, Sinatra won the *Major Bowes Amateur Hour* with the Hoboken Four in 1935 and then toured with Bowes for two years. He was even filmed performing in blackface. In 1939, an appearance on WNEW's *Dance Parade* led to engagements with the Harry James and the Tommy Dorsey bands. In 1940, Toronto songwriter Ruth Lowe wrote "I'll Never Smile Again." Recorded by the Tommy Dorsey Orchestra with Sinatra on vocals, the song was number one on the first-ever *Billboard* singles chart. Glenn Miller had a hit with the song in the same year, and thirteen years later the Canadian vocal group the Four Aces recorded a charting version. Sinatra also commissioned Lowe to write his closing theme, "Put Your Dreams Away for Another Day." According to pop legend, Sinatra's 1942 appearance at the Paramount Theatre with Benny Goodman uncorked a veritable teen frenzy. At his return engagement two years later, 25,000 screaming bobby-soxers blocked the street in what was referred to as the "Columbus Day Riot." From 1943 to 1945, Sinatra was the top vocalist on NBC's *Your Hit Parade*.

Sinatra was also unique among the pop vocalists of the day in that he was socially engaged. He supported Roosevelt for president and spoke out against racial and religious intolerance. He even excised the word *darky* from his recording of Jerome Kern and Oscar Hammerstein's "Ol' Man River." In the late 1940s, when he was accused of having both communist and Mafia ties, his career faltered, but it was revitalized by his Oscar-winning performance as Maggio in the 1954 film *From Here to Eternity*, a role he allegedly landed through Mafia influence. In the 1950s, Sinatra became a vicious opponent of rock 'n' roll. After that, his political leanings tended to take on the character of whoever occupied the White House.

*F*rank Sinatra's early success marked the transition from big bands fronted by singers to vocalists backed up by big bands.

Sinatra's early success is perhaps the strongest indicator of the ascendancy of the solo vocalist. His buy-out of his contract with Tommy Dorsey in 1942, the same year as the AFM strike, marked the transition from big bands fronted by singers to vocalists backed up by big bands. As rock 'n' roll historian Charlie Gillett has noted, "Records by the big bands dominated the best selling lists in 1937 to 1941. During this period band recordings accounted for twenty-nine of the forty-three records that sold over a million copies each."[14] With the rise of the vocalists, however, the pop market was taken over by such figures as Bing Crosby ("Swingin' on a Star"), Dinah Shore ("I'll Walk Alone," "Anniversary Song," "Buttons and Bows"), and Vaughn Monroe ("Rum and Coca Cola," "Let It Snow, Let It Snow, Let It Snow").

Although there were a number of pop-sounding black vocal acts that scored major hits in the pop market in the postwar 1940s—Nat "King" Cole ("For Sentimental Reasons"), Ella Fitzgerald ("My Happiness"), the Mills Brothers ("Across the Valley from the Alamo"), and the Ink Spots ("The Gypsy")—the period was dominated by Italian American men. In addition to Sinatra, there was Perry Como ("Long Ago and Far Away"), Frankie Laine ("That's My Desire," "That Lucky Old Sun," "Mule Train"), Vic Damone ("I Have but One Heart," "Again," "You're Breaking My Heart"), and later Tony Bennett ("Because of You," "Cold, Cold Heart," "Rags to Riches," "Stranger in Paradise"), Dean Martin ("That's Amore"), and Al Martino ("Here in My Heart").[15] The rich tradition of heart-wrenching emotionality that had long been part of Italian popular song seemed to be quite well suited to American popular styles in the 1940s and 1950s.

If the rise of the solo vocalist pushed the big bands into the background, postwar culture dealt them their death blow. At the end of World War II, initiatives in the mainstream culture encouraged women to leave the jobs they had taken and return to their homes. Visions of domestic bliss and fear of nuclear war encouraged a middle-class retreat from the frantic energy of swing. It was no longer feasible to support the elaborate production of twenty-piece orchestras as a regular attraction. Ballrooms disappeared, and unable to find steady work, the big bands gradually broke up. By 1947, they were almost gone. As Ian Whitcomb has written:

> [Glenn] Miller died in a wartime plane crash, but Herman, James, and Dorsey had folded their original bands in late 1946, together with Benny Goodman and many others. The straighter, less jazzy bands like Lawrence Welk's and Guy Lombardo's survived (for a specialist and aging public) but the Big Band Era, just over a decade, was finished.[16]

The African American jazz innovators, who had provided much of the impetus for the big band sound, were often conspicuous by their absence. While the better-known black bands, Count Basie's and Duke Ellington's, for example, could count on an occasional hit record, such as Basie's recording for Victor of "Open the Door, Richard," which was a best-seller in 1947, it was clear the big band era had ended. Between 1947 and 1949, sales dropped more than $50 million, which represented more than 20 percent of the dollar volume of the industry. The passing of the big bands created something of a void in popular music that contributed to the rise of rhythm and blues and, to a lesser extent, country and western.

The Major Labels Reclaim Country Music

The population migrations that had begun in the military buildup that had preceded World War II had opened the possibility of nationwide markets for specialty music. These markets had not existed prior to the war, and during the war the major record companies were unable to exploit them because shellac and vinylite shortages significantly affected the number of records that could be manufactured. Shellac, which was imported from India and was the principal ingredient used in making 78 rpm records, became almost impossible to obtain during the Pacific blockade. Vinylite, a superior material that the record companies had begun using more recently, was rationed because it was used for waterproofing raincoats and other war materials.

At the height of the shortage, to buy a new record it was often necessary to return an old one so that it could be recycled. Since the mainstream audience alone was capable of absorbing almost all the records that could be manufactured, the major companies concentrated their efforts in the mainstream market. The specialty fields—country to some extent but especially blues, jazz, and gospel—bore the brunt of the cutbacks.

Although the shellac and vinylite shortages had seriously limited the supply of specialty music, cross-cultural contact had, if anything, increased the demand for it. After the war and with the death of the big band era, the major labels tried to rebuild their control over the specialty fields. Naturally, the prospect of national markets for regional music titillated company executives who were concerned about their declining bottom lines. In the context of postwar affluence, however, the categories *race* and *hillbilly* seemed inappropriate, if not downright offensive. Many performers had come to resent being categorized in such demeaning terms. In 1949, *rhythm and blues* became the official designation for what was once called *race music.* A few years earlier, the industry had begun to use the designation *country and western* or *country* for what was once called *hillbilly.*

In the context of postwar affluence, the categories race and hillbilly seemed inappropriate, if not downright offensive.

In the country and western category, the strategies of the major companies for reclaiming the market proved to be remarkably effective, albeit somewhat dispiriting when viewed today. According to Gillett,

> the companies responded by heavily promoting various songs performed in versions of country and western styles. One tactic was to promote the strong southern accent of most country and western singers as a "novelty," as Capitol did successfully with Tex Williams' "Smoke That Cigarette" in 1947, and as Columbia did for several years with various Gene Autry songs, including "Rudolph, the Red-Nosed Reindeer" (1950). Alternatively, the country and western songs that were closest to the melodramatic or sentimental modes of conventional popular songs were promoted as popular songs—or, more frequently, recorded by popular singers in a style that was halfway between country and pop.[17]

Frankie Laine's "Mule Train" and "High Noon" are good examples of this latter strategy. Because of the effectiveness of their marketing, country and western music was soon firmly back in the hands of the major companies. The one exception to this rule was King Records in Cincinnati, Ohio, which boasted a strong roster of country and western artists like Cowboy Copas, Hawkshaw Hawkins, and Moon Mullican, who, as we shall see, came into regular contact with rhythm and blues and were heavily influenced by the western end of the country music spectrum.

The entry of two new big companies into the music industry during this period contributed to the major labels' firm hold on country and western music. The first entry was MGM Records, which was formed in Hollywood in 1946 as an outlet for the film company's movie soundtracks but soon expanded into other kinds of music. The second entry was Mercury, which began in Chicago in 1947. Founded as a specialty label that focused primarily on polka and rhythm and blues, Mercury operated with the flair of an independent. Only its ownership of a pressing plant and its own distribution system defined it as a major label. In 1947, the company signed Frankie Laine, who scored two hits that were million sellers for the company,

A veteran of life on the road, Hank Williams continued along the path pioneered by Jimmie Rodgers. His honky tonk swagger brought country music one step closer to rockabilly.

"Mule Train" (1949) and "Cry of the Wild Goose" (1950). Both recordings were in the ersatz country mould. It was, however, MGM that picked up Hank Williams, the biggest country and western star since Jimmie Rodgers.

Williams had begun his singing career at the age of thirteen on KSFA in Montgomery, Alabama. Working in roadhouses and honky tonks for years, he registered his original compositions with Acuff-Rose in Nashville. He first recorded for the independent Sterling label in 1946 but switched to MGM in 1947. Between 1949 and 1953, the year he died, eleven of the songs Williams recorded for MGM sold more than 1 million copies each. Fred Rose also "plugged" Williams' songs to pop producers, and numerous popular artists recorded the tunes as pop country hits, including Frankie Laine, who recorded "Your Cheatin' Heart" and "Tonight We're Settin' the Woods on Fire" as solo vocals and "Hey Good Lookin'" as a duet with Jo Stafford. Stafford did a solo version of "Jambalaya," and Tony Bennett recorded "There'll Be No Teardrops Tonight" and hit pop number one with "Cold, Cold Heart." Guy Mitchell did "I Can't Help It," and Rosemary Clooney scored with "Half as Much."

Altogether, Williams, who credited as his inspiration a black street singer nicknamed Tee Tot (Rufe Payne), penned about 125 songs. His honest, straightforward lyrics and catchy, well-crafted tunes lent his music to a variety of interpretations and established him as something of a folk poet. Although his producers tended to tone him down on record, his honky-tonk swagger, working-class sympathies, use of "backbeat" (accents on the second and fourth beats of a measure), and hot live performances make him one link in the musical chain that joins Jimmie Rodgers, Texas hillbillies like Bob Wills and Ernest Tubb, and Elvis Presley. Like Rodgers before him, Williams was inducted into the Rock 'n' Roll Hall of Fame as an "early influence" in 1987.

The biggest Canadian country singer in the late 1940s was Earl Heywood. Billed as "Canada's Number One Cowboy Singer," Heywood recorded a number of hits for RCA Victor in Montreal, including "Alberta Waltz" and "Tears of St. Anne."

The Independents Promote Rhythm and Blues

While the major labels were able to bring country and western music firmly under their sway, the African American music market proved much more difficult for them to capture. During the big band era, the majors had contented themselves with connections to the most prominent black innovators of the big band sound and had lost touch with other developments in the rich and constantly evolving African American culture. A number of African American musicians were now developing styles that were closer to the blues. As the swing era declined, the music that came to the fore in working-class black communities was rhythm and blues (r&b), described by Amiri Baraka (LeRoi Jones) as "huge rhythm units smashing away behind screaming blues singers."[18] Unlike country and western, which the major record companies easily domesticated for popular consumption, r&b was viewed as unsuitable for the mainstream because of its insistent rhythms and suggestive content. It was, however, a sound that would soon transform the very concept of popular music.

Unlike country and western, which the major record companies found could be rather easily domesticated for popular consumption, r&b was viewed as unsuitable for the mainstream because of its insistent rhythms and suggestive content. It was, however, a sound that would soon transform the very concept of popular music.

If there is one artist who signifies the transition from the controlled energy and smooth delivery of the big bands to the unbridled emotion that characterizes rhythm and blues, it is Louis Jordan. Signed to Decca in 1939, Jordan and his group, the Tympany Five (which actually fluctuated between five and seven members), anticipated the decline of the big bands and helped to define the instrumentation for the r&b combos that followed. With a much smaller horn section, rhythm became more pronounced. While Jordan's material was composed and arranged, selections like "Saturday Night Fishfry," "Honey Chile," and "Ain't Nobody Here but Us Chickens" evoked blues images that were not found in most black pop. "Chickens," for example, told the story of a farmer duped by a fox in his henhouse. "Those lyrics," according to George Lipsitz, "had their origins in the culture of . . . slavery. African legends about 'trickster-hero buffoons' provided the basis for slave stories in which animals or lesser gods outwitted stronger opponents."[19] At the same time, Jordan's performances were incredibly engaging, a factor that measurably increased his mainstream acceptance.

Between 1944 and 1949, Jordan furnished Decca with nineteen pop hits. His "G. I. Jive," backed with "Is You Is or Is You Ain't My Baby?" (1944), sold 1 million copies, as did "Choo Choo Ch'Boogie" (1946). The shuffle boogie beat that he used is one of the elements that followed r&b into rock 'n' roll. While, at the time, Jordan's music was described as "jumpin' the blues," he was not alone. Most of the r&b artists of the late 1940s screeched, honked, and shouted with themes that were often too raw for the mainstream market and thus for the major record companies. Still, the raucous sounds of such

Louis Jordan was a pivotal musician in the development of rhythm and blues. He and his group, the Tympany Five, brought African American working-class sensibilities into the mainstream with polish and humour. Film clips of their engaging performances were shown in movie theatres between features.

artists as Wynonie Harris ("Good Rockin' Tonight"), John Lee Hooker ("Boogie Chillen"), Eddie "Cleanhead" Vinson ("I'm Weak but I'm Willing"), Bullmoose Jackson ("I Want a Bow-Legged Woman"), Joe Liggins and the Honeydrippers ("Honeydripper"), saxophonist Big Jay McNeely ("Deacon's Hop"), drummer Roy Milton ("The Hucklebuck"), and pianist Amos Milburn ("Bad, Bad Whiskey") were a harbinger of sounds to come.

The success of these artists speaks to what Nelson George has referred to as "an aesthetic schism between high-brow, more assimilated black styles and working-class, grassroots sounds" that had existed in the black community for a long time.[20] A number of writers, notably Baraka [Jones], have written at length about class differences between jazz and blues. While jazz was an immensely popular and influential crossover music that introduced elements of the African American tradition into the mainstream, in some ways, it was also a product of the black middle class. Many of its most notable practitioners—Duke Ellington, Coleman Hawkins, and Fletcher Henderson, among others—were college educated. By the 1930s, jazz was a music that had "moved away from the older *lowdown* forms of blues, . . . [It was] a music that still relied on older Afro-American musical tradition, but one that had begun to utilize still greater amounts of popular American music as well as certain formal European traditions."[21]

The pioneer r&b artists of the 1940s were still close to their blues roots. While they often retained some semblance of the big band sound, their initial popularity in the black community in many ways represented a resuscitation of the blues, or race, market of the 1920s and 1930s. "While the term 'jazz' gave Whiteman equal weight with Ellington, and Bix Beiderbecke comparable standing with Louis Armstrong," George has written, "the term 'race' was applied to forms of black music—primarily blues—that whites and . . . the black elite disdained."[22] In the glow of postwar affluence, the African American working class imposed its tastes on black popular music, and the results were electrifying (and electrified).

> *Suddenly it was as if a great deal of the Euro-American humanist facade Afro-American music had taken on had been washed away by the war. Rhythm & blues singers literally had to shout to be heard above the clanging and strumming of the various electrified instruments and the churning rhythm sections. And somehow the louder the instrumental accompaniment and the more harshly screamed the singing, the more expressive the music was.*[23]

Since r&b did not readily lend itself to the bland pop vocal or ersatz country and western production styles of the major labels, company executives decided to ignore the burgeoning African American market. This made it possible for a large number of independent labels to enter the business. For the most part, these labels were hampered by a shortage of materials, a lack of funds, and inadequate distribution systems. Yet they persevered, and new independents came into the business because profits were substantial when a hit was produced. Modern, a Los Angeles-based company founded in 1945, was able to sell its blues singles for $1.05 in the late 1940s, while the major companies were getting only 78 cents for their pop singles. The most successful of the independent labels that survived the 1940s, particularly those with r&b experience, gained a foothold in the industry that would not be dislodged.

*I*ndependent companies produced r&b first for the black community and, with the aid of jukeboxes and independent deejays, brought the music to the attention of a national audience.

By the early 1950s, more than 100 independent labels were still in operation. The most important of these companies were Aladdin, Modern, Specialty, and Imperial, which were based in Los Angeles; Atlantic, based in New York; Savoy, based in Newark, New Jersey; King, based in Cincinnati, Ohio; Chess, based in Chicago; and black-owned Duke/Peacock, which was based in Houston. While some of these companies, most notably King, produced country and western music, all of them produced r&b. It was these independent companies, along with other important independents founded later (Herald/Ember and a dozen or so other labels in New York, black-owned Vee Jay in Chicago, and Sun in Memphis), that produced r&b first for the black community and, with the aid of jukeboxes and independent deejays, brought the music to the attention of a national audience. Indeed, these few companies produced the bulk of the repertoire that constituted the foundation of rock 'n' roll. Perhaps the best indication of their success in popularizing r&b can be seen in *Billboard*'s 1949 decision to drop the term *race music* in favour of the more descriptive term *rhythm and blues.*

King Records in Cincinnati could be distinguished from the other independent labels in its ability to produce rhythm and blues and country and western with equal success. No doubt, the particular character of the city, which offered significant outlets for blues, jazz, and country music, contributed measurably to King's good fortune. By 1937, Cincinnati's radio station WLW had offered a series of country barn dance programs, which evolved into the *Midwestern Hayride* in the mid-1940s. The city was also home to WCKY, a 50,000-watt clear channel that devoted a significant amount of airtime to country music. While African Americans had less access to the airwaves in Cincinnati than others—Fats Waller's WLW broadcasts in 1932 stand out as a notable exception—the entertainment needs of the city's sizable black population were addressed in live music venues, especially the Cotton Club, which featured the territory bands and jump blues combos that became popular in the late 1940s. The bands of Lucky Millinder, Todd Rhodes, and Tiny Bradshaw were among those that toured the region regularly.

The man who brought the city's divergent musical tendencies together under one recording roof was Syd Nathan. In 1945, Nathan left the department store business to start King Records. From the beginning, he was eclectic in his musical acquisitions and astute, if ruthless, in his business decisions. From WLW's *Midwestern Hayride*, Nathan signed the Delmore Brothers, Grandpa Jones, and Hank Penny, as well as the next generation of country singers, including Cowboy Copas, Moon Mullican, Hawkshaw Hawkins, and Wayne Raney. Mullican was a pioneer of country boogie who was known as the "King of the Hillbilly Piano Players." His influence on early rock 'n' roll can be heard in the piano playing of Jerry Lee Lewis and others. At the Cotton Club, Nathan met Lucky Millinder and, knowing that Millinder was under contract to Decca, signed his lead vocalist, Bullmoose Jackson, as a solo artist. At the same time, Nathan hired Millinder's arranger, Henry Glover, as a writer/producer. He also signed the Rhodes and Bradshaw ensembles, as well as vocalist Wynonie Harris, another alumnus of the Millinder band.

Initially, most of King Records' r&b artists were issued on the Queen label, a subsidiary Nathan had established to separate r&b releases from country releases. There was, however, an innovative wrinkle to this separation that added measurably to the company's profit margin. Nathan, largely for reasons of economic self-interest, encouraged his black and white artists to record each other's material. King was perhaps the only independent record company that had equally strong rosters of r&b and c&w artists. As Henry Glover once told Arnold Shaw:

King Records was covering R&B with country singers almost from the beginning of my work with Syd Nathan. . . . We were more successful in doing the reverse—covering C&W hits with R&B singers. In '49 . . . Bullmoose Jackson's hit "Why Don't You Haul Off and Love Me" was a cover of a Wayne Raney country hit. And Wynonie Harris' "Bloodshot Eyes"—on R&B charts in '51—was originally a Hank Penny country record . . . when a song happened in one field, Syd Nathan wanted it moved into the other.

You see it was a matter of Cincinnati's population. You couldn't sell Wynonie Harris to country folk, and black folk weren't buying Hank Penny. But black folk might buy Wynonie Harris doing a country tune. And since Syd published most of the tunes we recorded, he was also augmenting his publishing income and building important copyrights. He was a smart businessman and he didn't miss a trick.[24]

Nathan's primary motivation may have been more monetary than artistic, but his action produced a far greater cultural mix than might otherwise have been the case. As Bill Malone has noted, his "encouragement was no doubt instrumental in the decision made by such King artists as the Delmore Brothers and Moon Mullican to record their classic boogie tunes in the early fifties."[25] Of course, the key to the company's success in these crossover ventures was the free hand that Nathan gave Henry Glover in recording both r&b and c&w acts. No producer spanned the two fields more successfully than Glover. It was Glover, for example, who produced the r&b and c&w versions of "Why Don't You Haul Off and Love Me." The fact that Glover wrote and/or produced many of King's r&b hits marked him as successful. The fact that he consciously sought out country artists with whom to accomplish the same success moves him closer to the status of legendary. Under Glover's musical direction, the King empire not only maintained a foothold in country music but became one of the premiere r&b labels as well.

The fact that Henry Glover wrote and/or produced many of King's r&b hits marked him as successful. The fact that he consciously sought out country artists with whom to accomplish the same success moves him closer to the status of legendary.

Chess Records in Chicago was another instance where the collaboration between Jewish businessmen and black producers was a winning combination. Chess was launched in 1949 by Leonard and Phil Chess, two Jewish immigrants from Poland who had settled in Chicago in 1928. In the 1940s, the Chess brothers owned and operated the Macomba, a nightclub that presented at one time or another such talent as Louis Armstrong, Lionel Hampton, Billy Eckstine, and Ella Fitzgerald. Struck by the lack of adequate recording facilities in Chicago, the brothers bought into Aristocrat Records in 1947. In 1949, they took over the label and changed its name to Chess, eventually establishing three subsidiaries, Checker, Cadet, and Argo. With a small studio in the back room of its storefront record company, Chess was the quintessential shoestring operation, even distributing records from the trunks of the owners' cars. The lack of financing was reflected in the company's recording technique. "To add echo," Arnold Shaw has written, "inventive Leonard Chess hung an open microphone in their tiny toilet. . . . For tape echo effects and distortion, they suspended a ten-foot section of sewer pipe from the ceiling of their so-called studio."[26] Even with such modest equipment, Chess Records managed to turn out some of the most significant urban blues recordings and to later become one of the most important rock 'n' roll labels in the country.

One key to Chess' success was the presence of Willie Dixon, a Mississippi native who had been associated with the label as a singer, composer, bassist, talent scout, and producer since its days as Aristocrat. Leonard Chess thought of Dixon as "his right arm." Among the 200 or so songs written by Dixon were "Hoochie Coochie Man," "I Just Want to Make Love to You," "Little Red Rooster," and "Seventh Son." He also contributed in other capacities to any number of hits by Chess artists, including Muddy Waters and Howlin' Wolf.

Delta-born Muddy Waters (nee McKinley Morganfield) was one of Chess' earliest discoveries. A master of the slide guitar, Waters had been recorded for the Library of Congress by Alan Lomax and John Work before he left Mississippi for good in 1943. After settling in Chicago, he switched to electric guitar to compete with the sounds of the city. In the mid-1940s, he was presented by Big Bill Broonzy at Sylvio's. This appearance led to recordings produced by Mayo Williams at OKeh, but these were never released. Waters then switched to Aristocrat and recorded, among other songs, "I Can't Be Satisfied" and "I Feel Like Goin' Home." When the Chess brothers formed Chess Records, Waters followed them, recording one of his first hits, the immortal "Rolling Stone." Subsequent recordings included "Mannish Boy" (1955), "Got My Mojo Working" (1957), and "Baby Please Don't Go" (1958). Most of the next generation of Chicago blues musicians, including Buddy Guy, Junior Wells, and James Cotton, passed through Waters' band at one time or another. He was also a major inspiration for the white blues revival of the 1960s, which featured such artists as Paul Butterfield, Nick Gravenites, and Mike Bloomfield, who had heard him play at Smitty's Corner in the 1950s. When the Rolling Stones took their name from Waters' early Chess hit, he remarked: "They stole my music, but they gave me my name."[27]

Perhaps the most important of all the new independents was Atlantic Records, which was founded in 1947 by Ahmet Ertegun, the son of a prominent Turkish diplomat, and Herb Abramson, the former recording director for National Records, in Ertegun's one-bedroom Manhattan apartment. Abramson was drafted into the army in 1953 and some time later sold his interest in the company. Jerry Wexler, an r&b reviewer for *Billboard,* picked up where Abramson had left off and went on to become head of artist and repertoire for the company. In 1956, Ertegun's brother, Nesuhi, set up what would become a distinguished jazz division. Both brothers were avid jazz and blues collectors who had some 30,000 records in their private collection. Perhaps their own privileged position and their love of the music gave them an advantage over some of the other entrepreneurs who entered the business solely as a commercial gambit, for the Erteguns attracted outstanding talent and Ahmet, in particular, enjoyed a reputation for honesty and integrity, particularly in his treatment of black artists, that was unmatched in the business.

Ruth Brown began singing in church. The lure of rhythm and blues, however, led her to Atlantic Records, where she became the fledgling label's first big star. Although Atlantic was among the most reputable companies and Brown had a decent contract, years later she sued the label for back royalties and won.

After a few inconsequential releases, the fledgling company hit r&b pay dirt in 1949 with Stick McGhee's "Drinkin' Wine Spo-dee-o-dee." The company's first star was Ruth Brown. After her debut release "So Long" in 1949, which was a Top Ten hit, Brown turned out ten more Top Ten r&b hits over the next five years, including "Teardrops from My Eyes" (1950), "5-10-15 Hours" (1952), "(Mama), He Treats Your Daughter Mean" (1953), and "Oh, What a

Joe Turner's repertoire was clearly the stuff that rock 'n' roll was made of. By the time the phenomenon took hold, however, he had little inclination to break out of the comfortable r&b niche he already occupied.

Dream" (1954). She was rewarded for these efforts with a contract that guaranteed her $100,000 over five years. For a time, Atlantic was even nicknamed "the house that Ruth built." Big Joe Turner, perhaps the most celebrated of the blues shouters, was offered a contract in 1950. He also turned out a series of blockbuster r&b hits—"Chains of Love" (1951), "Sweet Sixteen" (1952), and "Honey Hush" (1953). By the early 1950s, Atlantic was the most important r&b label in the United States and had a talent roster that included LaVern Baker, Ray Charles, the Clovers, and the Drifters, among others. By 1954, Atlantic's releases began to cross over to the pop charts. Such hits as "Sh-Boom" by the Chords, LaVern Baker's "Tra La La," "Tweedlee Dee," and "Jim Dandy," Joe Turner's "Shake, Rattle, and Roll," and Ruth Brown's "Lucky Lips" made an imprint on rock 'n' roll that was unmistakable.

High Fidelity/Low Overhead

If the abandonment of the specialty fields by the major labels allowed independent labels to enter the business, a number of technological advances helped them to survive. The first of these was magnetic tape, an innovation that was "liberated" from the Nazis during World War II. Although the principle of magnetic recording had been known in the late 1800s, it was the Germans who had perfected it. The German magnetophone used plastic tape that was coated with iron oxide, which could be magnetized by amplified electrical impulses to encode a signal on the material. Playback simply reversed the process. Aside from the obvious technical advantages of editing, splicing, and better sound reproduction, magnetic tape recording was more durable, more portable, and less expensive than the existing technologies. In the United States, the Minnesota Mining and Manufacturing

With the advent of portable radios, teenagers, who would soon become an identifiable consumer group, could explore their developing musical tastes in complete privacy.

"(Mama) He Treats Your Daughter Mean"

Artist: Ruth Brown
Music / Lyrics by Herb Lance, John Wallace, Charlie Singleton
Label: Atlantic (1953)

"(Mama) He Treats Your Daughter Mean" was a big hit in 1953 for Ruth Brown and Atlantic. In terms of its driving dance rhythms, instrumentation and sixteen-bar blues structure, and its slightly suggestive lyrics, it's a classic example of 1950s rhythm and blues style.

Musical Style Notes

"(Mama) He Treats Your Daughter Mean" has a typical r&b text and rhythmic pattern. It begins with a "pickup" (if you were counting "And-a one, and-a two," the "and-a" is a pickup). The overall rhythmic pattern is subdivided into four-beat units, or measures:

(and-a)	1	2	3	4

In r&b, the primary accents fall on the second and fourth beats. The r&b "swing" feeling comes partly from the fact that each one of those four beats is subdivided into three equal parts, called "triplets."

Major beats in the measure	and-a	1	2	3	4
Subdivision of beat into triplets	1 2 3	1 2 3	1 2 3	1 2 3	1 2 3

The drumbeats can be shown with a slash representing an accented strike and a dash representing an unaccented strike:

Major beats in the measure	and-a	1	2	3	4
Subdivision of beat into triplets	1 2 3	1 2 3	1 2 3	1 2 3	1 2 3
Drum strikes here	/ –	/	/ –	/	/ –

The song's r&b rhythmic feel is heightened by the drummer's playing the "one" of each triplet "behind the beat"—in other words, the drummer actually hits the drum a fraction of a second after the ear expects the next downbeat, yielding a more loose, "relaxed" feeling to the rhythm. Meanwhile, the other instruments and the singer may put rhythmic accents in different places. For example, when Ruth Brown begins singing, the text accents fall on beats 1 and 3:

(and-a)	1	2	3	4	1	2	3	4
1 2 3	1 2 3	1 2 3	1 2 3	1 2 3	1 2 3	1 2 3	1 2 3	1 2 3
/ –	/	/ –	/	/ –	/	/ –	/	/ –
	Mama	- - -	- - -	- - he	treats	your	daugh-	ter mean

This use of layers of different rhythms, or *polyrhythms,* is one of the most prominent characteristics of African American music styles.

The song begins with the refrain, which then repeats after each verse. The melody of the verse is different from the melody of the refrain, although both are characterized by short melodic units that repeat several times and then are varied at the end. For instrumentation, the track uses drums, electric guitar, acoustic piano, and a "horn section"—in this case, saxophone and trumpet.

Musical "Road Map"

TIMINGS	COMMENTS	LYRICS
0:00–0:05	Drum introduction, two measures	
0:05–0:12	Introduction continues; saxophones and guitar join. Notice that they don't play exactly the same rhythmic accents as the drum. The saxes, for example, put the accent on the 3 in the triplet, which creates a *syncopation* with the drums. The guitar is emphasizing the triplet division of the beat.	
0:12–0:43	Refrain	
	Notice the vocal technique of "sliding" the pitch up in the second syllable of "Mama."	*Mama, he treats your daughter mean . . .*
0:17	Piano enters, also emphasizing the triplet division of the beat.	
0:36–0:37	Note how Brown "bends the pitch" on the word "meanest," wringing a great deal of expression from this one word.	
0:43–1:16	Verse 1 The actual sixteen-bar pattern begins on the word "treats."	*Mama, he treats me badly . . . makes me love him madly . . .*
1:07	The melody changes on the last line, *"All of my friends say they don't understand—what's the matter with this man?"*	
	Note that the horn section plays more sparsely on the verse. This helps to highlight the singer's part and differentiates the verse from the refrain.	
1:17–1:46	Refrain	
1:20	Full horn section enters here, providing sonic contrast with first refrain.	*Mama, he treats your daughter mean . . .*
1:47–2:21	Verse 2 The actual sixteen-bar pattern begins on the word "man."	*Mama, this man is lazy . . . almost drives me crazy . . .*
2:12	As in Verse 1, the melody changes on the last line, *"I've stood for all that I can stand—what's the matter with this man?*	
2:21–2:55	Refrain	*Mama, he treats your daughter mean . . .*
2:47–2:55	Ruth Brown varies the melody just slightly at the end, elongating the words "I've ever seen," to signal the end of the song. The band responds with an ending phrase that is almost a cliché in R&B: the ascending scale followed by a strongly accented keynote (tonic). Over that last sustained note, you can hear the keyboard add one last rhythmic "lick"—another characteristic of blues/rhythm and blues.	

Company (3M) came up with a tape, which the company marketed under its Scotch tape trademark, that surpassed the sound quality of the German product. At the same time, tape recorder manufacturers reduced recording speeds from thirty inches per second (ips) to fifteen ips and then to 7.5 ips without seriously compromising sound quality, thus quadrupling the amount of material that could be recorded on a standard tape. The advantages of tape were immediately apparent to recording companies and radio stations, and they invested in the technology as soon as it became available.

The transistor, introduced by Bell Laboratories in 1948, was a welcome companion to the new recording technology. The transistor was capable of performing all the functions of the vacuum tube but could do so in a solid environment. For this reason, it could be made smaller, required less power, and was more durable than the vacuum tube, which it soon replaced. With the birth of the transistor came the possibility of miniaturizing the cumbersome tube amplifiers that were essential to electronic recording. Smaller, more affordable, longer-lasting recording equipment encouraged decentralization in the recording field, which again aided independent production. Indeed, the transistor made truly portable radio receivers possible for the first time. With the advent of portable radios, teenagers, who would soon become an identifiable consumer group, could explore their developing musical tastes in complete privacy.

In the same year that the transistor was unveiled, a team of scientists who were working at CBS's laboratories under the leadership of Dr. Peter Goldmark and William Bachman invented high fidelity. This breakthrough, which developed out of their interest in classical music, yielded the microgroove, or long-playing, 33 rpm record (the LP), which increased the number of grooves per inch on a standard record from 85 to 300. Years later, Goldmark described the challenge the creation of the LP had presented to the group:

> First of all, to provide more playing time, it was necessary to change the number of grooves—which then necessitated changing the speed—which, in turn, required offsetting the resulting distortion—which then required offsetting the limitation of frequency response which would have occurred. . . . So we had to change the radius of the stylus. We went from sapphire to diamond. But, in order for the tiny radii not to chew up the record, we had to reduce the pressure. . . . Then you had wonderful sound quality, but you didn't have a microphone capable of creating wonderful sounds. . . . We . . . had to . . . develop a new kind of microphone, which turned out to be the condenser microphone . . . [that] the Germans already had invented.[28]

"In other words," Goldmark concluded, "we had to develop a whole new science."[29]

Shortly after the development of the LP, Columbia's Ted Wallerstein demonstrated its superiority to David Sarnoff and a few other RCA executives in the hope of making it the new industry standard. When the demonstration record played for twenty-three minutes without stopping, the RCA executives realized that Columbia had pulled off a coup of major proportions. Sarnoff, as was his wont, responded with polite approval and promptly directed his technical staff to come up with a similar record that played at a different speed. In what was to become known as the "battle of the speeds"—a battle that pitted Columbia's LP against RCA's newly developed 45—the two firms produced vinylite discs with excellent sound quality and maximum durability. The size of the 45 caught the fancy of jukebox manufacturers and soon became the preferred configuration for singles while the LP became the industry standard for albums. Both 45s and LPs were lighter and less breakable than the shellac-based 78s. Thus, they could be shipped faster and more cheaply than the 78s, which made them well suited to the rapidly changing pop market.

As a result of these technological advances, records emerged as a relatively inexpensive medium when compared with radio, film, and television, which were capital-intensive industries that required huge sums of money for the production of a product, elaborate systems for transmission, and/or complex bureaucratic interactions for such things as frequency assignments on the electromagnetic spectrum. It was in part for this reason that small independent labels were able to challenge the few giant corporations that had monopolized the music business. Records soon became the staple of all radio programming and the dominant product of the music industry as a whole. Indeed, in 1952, records finally surpassed sheet music as a source of revenue in the music industry. At about the same time, radio established its primacy over the jukebox as the number one hit maker.

In 1952, records finally surpassed sheet music as a source of revenue in the music industry. At about the same time, radio established its primacy over the jukebox as the number one hit maker.

Television and the Suppression of FM Broadcasting

It was, ironically, the development of television that opened the door to independent radio (and thus r&b) in the late 1940s by deliberately, if temporarily, sidelining a technological innovation that would have increased the quality of radio transmission measurably—FM broadcasting. Messages can be sent over the airwaves either by modulating, or varying, their amplitude, or size, or by modulating their frequency, or rate of propagation. Because early technical limitations favoured the development of amplitude modulation (AM), it was AM radio that was designated standard broadcasting in the United States. Although it was clear that frequency modulation (FM) broadcasting had certain advantages over AM broadcasting, its entry into the marketplace was intentionally suppressed because it conflicted with the development of television.[30]

Interference from either natural or man-made static or from stations on the same or adjacent frequencies had always been a major problem in broadcasting. Indeed, it had driven David Sarnoff to wish out loud that someone would come up with "a little black box to eliminate [radio] static."[31] Intrigued by the wish, inventor Edwin H. Armstrong, already the recipient of $1 million from RCA for the sale of his superheterodyne radio receiver, retired to his laboratory at Columbia University in 1923 to work on the project. He emerged ten years later with a whole new patented transmission system that utilized an FM signal in the very-high-frequency (VHF) range of the electromagnetic spectrum. Sarnoff was so impressed with the system that he moved Armstrong's operation to the RCA facilities atop the Empire State Building.

In 1935, however, Sarnoff reneged on his commitment to Armstrong's invention. Both television and FM transmission operated best in the VHF range, and Sarnoff, understanding even then that television would one day replace radio as the primary entertainment fixture in the home, made the decision to back the visual medium. Within days of evicting Armstrong,

Sarnoff and RCA announced a $1 million research initiative aimed at developing television. Realizing that the development of FM would conflict with the development of television, Sarnoff saw it as necessary to sever his ties to his friend Armstrong. The decision was not personal, just business. Although a series of patent wars, regulatory struggles over frequency assignments, and the imperatives of wartime production would slow the advent of television, the ubiquitous Sarnoff and RCA would be there when it arrived after World War II.

Meanwhile, Armstrong continued with the development of FM and, in 1936, approached the FCC in the United States with a plan for allocating spectrum space in the VHF range to his FM radio system. At the same hearing, Sarnoff presented plans for reserving the entire VHF band for television. C. B. Jolliffe, who only weeks earlier had been a ranking FCC executive, acted as counsel to the RCA executive. Not surprisingly, the FCC did not accept Armstrong's plan, but he was given permission to build a 50,000-watt FM transmitter in Alpine, New Jersey, which went on the air in 1939. That same year, Armstrong and the newly formed FM Broadcasters Association scored a small victory when the FCC assigned the frequency band that had been reserved for television Channel 1 to FM radio. (This is the reason why television receivers were initially built with no Channel 1.) The outbreak of World War II stalled the further development of television and FM, as RCA diverted its resources into the development of radar and Armstrong contributed his personal services and the use of his FM patents to the war effort.

In 1945, the FCC reassigned FM to a higher frequency band, between television channels 6 and 7 (88 to 108 megacycles), where it now thrives. At the time, however, the ruling was devastating; it placed FM into a band for which neither transmitters nor receivers existed. Investors in FM promptly withdrew from its further development and looked to television for potentially greater profits. The 430 applications for FM licences that were pending fell victim to bureaucratic shuffling. Furthermore, the end of the war allowed the pent-up wartime demand for new AM receivers to be assuaged, which at least temporarily satisfied the public need for radio. In the first three quarters of 1946, 6.5 million AM receivers but only 80,000 FM radios were manufactured. In suppressing FM radio to promote the development of television, Sarnoff may have insured the future of RCA's bottom line, but he stalled a medium that had significantly better sound quality, which could only have had positive implications for the transmission of music.

Television became a viable consumer item in the late 1940s. By 1951, there were nearly 16 million television sets in operation in the United States, and RCA was already showing a profit on its initial investment. The development of television was the death knell for network radio because the visual medium quickly attracted most of the national advertising that had been done on network radio. Independent radio, on the other hand, emerged as an effective medium for local advertisers, and it did so at a time when the number of radio stations in the United States had doubled from about 1,000 in 1946 to about 2,000 in 1948. Eventually, the most successful independent radio outlets pushed aside the more staid network stations and cemented a reciprocal arrangement with record companies that has defined the music industry ever since: inexpensive programming in return for free promotion.

Independent Radio: Deejays in Your Face

In the United States prior to 1948, radio had been dominated by four national networks that viewed the country as one monolithic listening audience. The prevailing marketing strategy was to create programming that could pull in as broad a slice of this total listenership as possible—hence the term *broadcasting*. Such programming naturally tended to favour middle-class, family-oriented fare that was largely the same from network to network. Although a considerable amount of popular music was broadcast, it was usually performed by studio orchestras that adhered strictly to swing era conventions, which made them virtually indistinguishable from one another. In Canada, the situation was somewhat different. The CBC was the only national broadcasting station. Being government funded, it tended to try to be all things to all Canadians, broadcasting a variety of news, drama, and comedy programs as well as classical and jazz music performances. The CBC's local affiliates routinely programmed local artists often performing more vernacular types of music. In addition to the CBC, every major market and many minor ones had a handful of independent stations, perhaps the most famous being CHUM AM in Toronto, which went on the air 1 October 1945.

In the United States, with the devastation of network radio (and motion pictures) effected by the growth of television, local radio became the primary vehicle for popularizing the music that was produced by independent record companies and then licensed to BMI, which technically the broadcasters owned. This link between BMI and the broadcasters outraged ASCAP almost as much as the "vulgarity," as ASCAP viewed it, of the music in question. Those publishers associated with ASCAP tried in vain to prove that the popularity of BMI music was due to its privileged status on radio and ardently advocated a return to so-called good music. It never occurred to them that perhaps the audience liked what it was hearing.

As national programming gave way to hundreds of locally programmed stations, each appealing to its own audience, the flawless, even-toned, accent-free "radio voice" of the typical announcer soon went the way of studio orchestras. Fast-talking deejays—"personality jocks," as they were called—whose stock-in-trade was their own eccentricity, took over. Far from being detached, generic voices, these deejays enjoyed a personal involvement with their listeners. "We were the stars in our hometown," said deejay Diggie Doo. "We went to the churches, we went to the clubs, to the schools, the little kids knew us."[32] These deejays not only talked to their fans, they talked like their fans. From his late night slot on WOV in New York, Jocko Henderson held forth in classic jive: "Eeeee tiddilee yok. Ho, this is the Jock. I'm back on the scene with the record machine. Saying goo bop-a doo, how do you do."[33] While hardly the King's English of an earlier generation of announcers, Jocko's rhymes are often cited as one of the formative influences in rap.

As they replaced the live entertainment personalities who had dominated national radio, these independent deejays became, for a time, pivotal figures in the music industry. Record companies routinely supplied free copies of new releases to them in the hope that they could

As national programming gave way to hundreds of locally programmed stations, each appealing to its own audience, the flawless, even-toned, accent-free "radio voice" of the typical announcer soon went the way of studio orchestras.

turn them into hits. Relying on their own inventiveness for popularity, independent deejays often experimented with specialty music as an antidote to the standard pop fare of network radio, and in most cases, the key to their success turned out to be r&b.

R&b radio represented a considerable departure from standard radio practices. As noted earlier, up to this point little black music had been broadcast at all, and there had been few African American announcers. As late as 1947, *Ebony* magazine had reported that out of an estimated 3,000 deejays around the country, only 16 were black.[34] Those who were deejays usually followed the example of Jack L. Cooper, an immensely successful, veteran black announcer from the 1930s who had eschewed all traces of black dialect in the pursuit of his conception of racial pride. According to Nelson George, Cooper's successors "tended to be conservative in their programming choices, leaning as heavily on Count Basie and Sarah Vaughan as on their vowels."[35] In r&b radio, however, there were black and white deejays from the start. While pay scales usually favoured white announcers, the tone of r&b radio was set by a new breed of black deejays who viewed themselves as entertainers, not just announcers.

> *[B]lack disk jockeys were a much more colorful group of platter-spinners than their white brethren, whose main concern seemed to be with dignity, decorum, and the King's English. Black jockeys tended to take over the manners and mannerisms of black preachers. They were showmen rather than announcers. Their job was to entertain, not just to introduce records. By the early '50s, there were quite a number who had made names for themselves on ghetto stations.[36]*

At first, the South was the major centre for r&b radio. Among the popular black deejays in this region were "Jockey Jack" Gibson in Atlanta, Georgia, "Professor Bop" in Shreveport, Louisiana, Larry McKinley and Vernon Winslow in New Orleans, Louisiana, "Sugar Daddy" in Birmingham, Alabama, "Spider" Burks in St. Louis, Missouri, Bruce Miller in Winston-Salem, North Carolina, and Nat D. Williams, "Bugs" Scruggs, Larry Dean, and George White in Memphis, Tennessee. Indeed, a number of southern r&b recording artists—Rufus Thomas and B. B. King, among others—had careers as deejays before they became performers. B. B. King acquired his initials from his radio moniker, "the Beale Street Blues Boy." There were also white r&b deejays who modeled themselves after the "preacher-emcees," as these popular black deejays were sometimes known. There was Zenas "Daddy" Sears in Atlanta, Bob "Wolfman Jack" Smith in Shreveport, Ken Elliott and Clarence "Poppa Stoppa" Hammon in New Orleans, Bill Gordon and Dewey Phillips in Memphis, and Gene Nobles and John Richbourgh in Nashville.

By the early 1950s, a number of so-called Negro stations in the South had proven to be quite successful. In St. Louis, Spider Burks addressed himself to the city's 328,000 African Americans over station KXLW. WOKJ went out to 107,000 blacks in Jackson, Mississippi. WDIA in Memphis, "America's only 50,000-watt Negro radio station," could broadcast to nearly 10 percent of the country's 12 million African Americans. WSOK in Nashville claimed to have several black stockholders. And in 1951, WERD in Atlanta became the first totally black-owned radio outlet in the country.

Of course, r&b radio was not limited to the South. It also flourished in those major cities of the North and West that had large concentrations of African Americans. In Los Angeles, a white deejay named Hunter Hancock had been playing jazz on station KFVD since 1943. In 1948, Hancock later recalled, a promo man from Modern records "told me that if I wanted to reach average Negroes, jazz wouldn't do it. Thank God that I had the good sense to listen to him and switched my shows to an exclusive diet of r&b disks."[37] Hancock remained among the top-rated r&b deejays in Los Angeles for twenty years. In the San Francisco Bay area, there was a black r&b deejay named Willie Mays on KSAN, and there were two white r&b jocks— "Jumpin'" George Oxford in Oakland and Phil McKernan (who sired the late Pigpen of Grateful Dead fame)—in Berkeley. In Chicago, Delta bluesman Muddy Waters held forth on WOPA before going on to record for Chess records. There was also a white r&b deejay on WOPA, Big Bill Hill, who sang the blues and sold Cadillacs in his version of highly stylized black speech: "Ah doan ca' if you got gahnashees on yo' gahnashees, ah cain p'choo in a big bread box by fo' o'clock dis aftanoon!"[38] However, Chicago's premier r&b deejay in the late 1940s was Al Benson, "Yo' Ol' Swingmaster," an African American. At the peak of his popularity, Benson hosted five shows on a number of stations and earned as much as $100,000 a year. According to Arnold Shaw, Benson delivered his radio jive in a Jamaican accent. "Benson killed the King's English," recalled one of Benson's young Milwaukee colleagues, "and I don't know if he did it on purpose or not. Everybody had to see Al if they wanted to sell to the black market in Chicago, whether it was beer or rugs or Nu Nile hair cream. . . . He wasn't pretending to be white. He sounded black . . . and most of us were proud of the fact."[39] He made something of a nationwide, if nonmusical, splash in 1956 when, as Passman has noted, "He hired two white men (because he feared violence to himself) to shower five thousand copies of the Constitution on Jackson, Mississippi, to emphasize the Supreme Court's antisegregation ruling."[40]

The Northeast also had its share of r&b deejays. There was George "Hound Dog" Lorenz in Buffalo, New York, who had an inordinate influence on Canadian teenagers in the Golden Horsehoe area of Ontario, and Danny "Cat Man" Stiles in Newark, New Jersey. "Symphony Sid" Torin moved from Boston to WMCA in New York, which was also home for Hal Jackson. New York was, of course, the centre for r&b radio in the Northeast. In addition to the white deejays just mentioned, the city also had a raucous contingent of black announcer/entertainers. Willie Bryant, "the Mayor of Harlem," and Ray Carroll broadcast their program *After Hours Swing Session* on WHOM, a foreign-language station by day. Jack Walker, "the Pear-Shaped Talker," appeared on foreign-language outlet WOV. Joe Bostic, who started at WBNX, held down a late-night slot for his program, *Harlem Music Shop,* on WINS. Tommy Smalls broadcast from WWRL, and Phil "Dr. Jive" Gordon from WLIB.

As this list of deejays indicates, r&b proved to be popular with white as well as black audiences. Unlike dance halls, record stores, and jukeboxes, the airwaves could not be easily segregated. If white teenagers wanted to turn their radio dials to the local r&b outlet, they were free to do so, and, apparently, that is exactly what they did. The new cross-racial appetite for r&b was soon reflected in record sales. As early as 1952, Dolphin's Hollywood Record Shop, a black retail outlet in Los Angeles, reported that its business was suddenly 40 percent white. The outlet's owners attributed this to independent deejays spinning r&b records. A similar pattern was developing

Unlike dance halls, record stores, and jukeboxes, the airwaves could not be easily segregated. If white teenagers wanted to turn their radio dials to the local r&b outlet, they were free to do so, and, apparently, that is exactly what they did.

Alan Freed was a reluctant convert to rhythm and blues, but once convinced, he embraced the music with a fervour that became part of his own undoing. Because of his crucial role in popularizing rock 'n' roll, Freed became the sacrificial lamb in the government investigations that robbed him of his livelihood and eventually ended his life.

at Mallory's Music in New Orleans and elsewhere. It signaled an impending change in popular music tastes, a change that made Fats Domino's "The Fat Man" (1950), Jackie Brenston's "Rocket 88" (1951), Lloyd Price's "Lawdy Miss Clawdy" (1952), and Joe Turner's "Chains of Love" (1951), "Sweet Sixteen" (1952), and "Honey Hush" (1953)—all recorded for independent labels—popular among both black and white audiences.

The most famous of all the r&b deejays was a classically trained trombonist named Alan Freed, who had grown up in Ohio and in high school had fronted a jazz band called the Sultans of Swing. After short stints on a couple of local stations, Freed began his radio career in earnest in 1946 as the host of *Request Review* on WAKR in Akron, Ohio. When his plans to convert the program to a television show in Cleveland failed, he became depressed, drank heavily, and vented his anger on current trends in popular music, saying that jazz had become too abstract and intellectualized to be "the people's music" and that "the run-of-the-mill, country-affected, pop-hit sound didn't do anything for him."[41] In 1951, his fortunes took a turn for the better. Leo Mintz, owner of the Record Rendezvous Shop in Cleveland and sponsor of a radio program of the same name on WJW, invited Freed to witness firsthand the strange new pattern of white customers buying records by black artists. Mintz convinced the initially reluctant Freed to take over the *Record Rendezvous* time slot and devote the entire show to r&b. Mintz had, of course, seen the future accurately. Freed bayed like a hound over Todd Rhodes' "Blues for Moon Dog" to introduce the show that became *The Moon Dog House Rock 'n' Roll Party.* His gravelly voice (due to damaged vocal chords from having some polyps cauterized) and colorful announcing style were well suited to his new material. "He was always drunk," said WJW morning man Soupy Sales. "It was late at night, but it was alright, he could handle it."[42] In fact, Freed handled it so well that he was soon hired by WINS in New York, which he turned into the number one popular music station in the city.

Freed is often remembered as the "Father of Rock 'n' Roll." He even claimed *rock 'n' roll* was a term he had invented. While there is ample evidence to suggest that he was the first to use the expression on radio, the phrase had been around the African American community for years. What is beyond dispute, however, is that the trajectory of Freed's career parallelled the rise and fall of this exciting new trend in popular music almost perfectly. "Anyone who says rock 'n' roll is a passing fad or flash-in-the-pan trend along the music road," Freed once said, "has rocks in his head, Dad!"[43] How right he was. Early in 1956, *Billboard* ran a retrospective piece on popular music trends for the previous year under the headline, **1955—THE YEAR R&B TOOK OVER POP FIELD.**

_____

In the 1940s, then, all the forces that would unleash rock 'n' roll were set in motion. The smoldering tension between ASCAP and radio burst into flames and set the stage for the structural realignments that affected the very character of popular music. There were subsequent struggles between radio and the musician's union and within the radio establishment itself (between network and independent stations). The death throes of swing created a void that signaled a culture in flux. Technological advances favouring decentralization allowed small independent record companies and flamboyant local deejays to become major players in the music business. Rivalries between giant record companies and competition between major and independent labels provided the corporate backdrop for the cultural developments that led to the rise of rhythm and blues in the late 1940s and the eruption of rock 'n' roll in the early 1950s.

Crossing Cultures:
The Eruption of
Rock 'n' Roll

Trying to pinpoint the beginning of rock 'n' roll is like trying to isolate the first drop of rain in a hurricane. The uninitiated may claim it began in 1955 when "Rock Around the Clock" by Bill Haley and His Comets became the best-selling record of the year. Others may want to date the phenomenon from the first rock 'n' roll record to make the pop charts, but there is no agreement about just which record that was. Charlie Gillett has said it was Bill Haley's "Crazy Man Crazy" in 1953.[1] Nick Tosches has argued for "Sixty Minute Man," which was recorded by the Dominoes in 1951.[2] Writer Jim Dawson and deejay Steve Propes decided "to go down the long list of great recordings that led up to the rock 'n' roll explosion of 1956 and pick out the milestones which have elements of rock 'n' roll in them— and which influenced the music that followed." They ended up devoting 200 pages to debating the merits of fifty contenders.[3]

Of course, part of the problem in determining the beginning of rock 'n' roll is the fact that rock 'n' roll evolved over time; it was not a one-time event. There is also a problem of definition. Which definition of rock 'n' roll should be used when trying to determine its beginning? There is

*P*art of the problem in determining the beginning of rock 'n' roll is the fact that rock 'n' roll evolved over time; it was not a one-time event.

rock 'n' roll, the musical genre unto itself; there is rock 'n' roll, the seemingly more acceptable term for rhythm and blues; and there is rock 'n' roll, the sexual metaphor. While Haley's "Crazy Man Crazy" fits the first definition well enough, the Dominoes' "Sixty Minute Man" highlights all three definitions. "Sixty Minute Man" was a popular r&b release that crossed over to the mainstream audience. R&b releases that did this were often called rock 'n' roll to obscure their origins. The protagonist in the song is a legendary lover who "rocks" and "rolls" his partners "all night long," leaving little doubt as to the sexual connotation of the term.

It is ironic that the term used by any number of white r&b deejays to give rhythm and blues a more wholesome veneer in the mainstream market was a slang term for the sexual act

82

common in African American music for years. With this in mind, one might date the start of rock 'n' roll from earlier releases that used the phrase in this way—Li'l Son Jackson's "Rockin' and Rollin'" in 1950, for example, or John Lee Hooker's "Rock 'n' Roll" in the same year. There is also Wynonie Harris' hit recording of Roy Brown's "Good Rockin' Tonight" in 1948 and Sister Rosetta Tharpe's "Rock Me," recorded with the Lucky Millinder Orchestra in 1942. For that matter, one could go all the way back to Trixie Smith's 1922 recording of "My Daddy Rocks Me (With One Steady Roll)." Tosches, taking the exercise to the extreme, has traced the sexual origins of the phrase back to medieval times.

> *Rock and Roll. Both verbs came to the English tongue during the Middle Ages, and were soon used as skin-thrill metaphors. "My throbbing heart shall rock thee day and night," wrote Shakespeare in* Venus and Adonis. *An early nineteenth-century sea chanty included the line, "Oh do, me Johnny Bowker, come rock 'n' roll me over." A lyric found in the ceremonial Fire Dance of Florida's obeah worshippers was, "Bimini gal is a rocker and a roller."*[4]

Suffice it to say, lest we get lost in history, that the music that came to be called rock 'n' roll began in the 1950s as diverse and seldom-heard segments of the population achieved a dominant voice in mainstream culture and transformed the very concept of what was popular music.

Cultural Diversity: The Roots of Rock 'n' Roll

In an age during which the virtues of multiculturalism constantly push against the limitations of a narrowly Eurocentric worldview, it is quite fashionable to focus self-righteously on the culturally diverse influences that gave birth to rock 'n' roll. Still, while there is no question that rock 'n' roll was profoundly multicultural, an analysis of its characteristics must also account for the proportionate influence of various cultures. Applying too simplistic a formula can easily distort the contributions of participating groups.

> *Unfortunately, when rock 'n' roll is discussed in terms of cross-cultural influences, it is often described in a way that could be represented by an algebraic formula: r&b + c&w = r&r.*

Unfortunately, when rock 'n' roll is discussed in terms of cross-cultural influences, it is often described in a way that could be represented by an algebraic formula: r&b + c&w = r&r. The formula is elegant in its simplicity and not without an element of truth—rhythm and blues and country and western were the primary styles that gave birth to rock 'n' roll—but it suffers from a number of shortcomings that render it less than useful for critical analysis, as Robert Palmer has noted:

> *The cliché is that rock & roll was a melding of country music and blues, and if you are talking about, say, Chuck Berry or Elvis Presley, the description, though simplistic, does fit. But the black inner-city vocal-group sound . . . had little to do with either blues or country music in their purer forms.*
>
> *The Bo Diddley beat . . . was Afro-Caribbean in derivation. The most durable . . . bass riff in Fifties rock & roll . . . had been pinched . . . from a Cuban* son *record. The screaming, athletic saxophone playing . . . was straight out of Forties big-band swing. . . . Traditional Mexican rhythms entered the rock & roll arena through Chicano artists. . . . Rock & roll proved an All-American, multi-ethnic hybrid, its sources and developing substyles too various to be explained away by "blues plus country" or any other reductionist formula.*[5]

Clearly then, the r&b + c&w formula overlooks too much, including the myriad of influences that comprise rhythm and blues and country and western, not to mention the other stylistic elements that contributed to rock 'n' roll. Also, in looking only at the dimensions of race, ethnicity, and musical culture, issues of class and gender are conveniently ignored. While rock 'n' roll certainly drew on a wide range of cultural inputs, all of its immediate musical sources were firmly rooted in the tradition of popular working-class styles. In fact, it resulted from a complex interplay of social and cultural forces that cannot be reduced to a simple algebraic formula. In attempting to capture this complexity, George Lipsitz has located rock 'n' roll at the intersection of urbanization, multiculturalism, and class:

> *Workers drawn to cities by the manpower needs of American industry retained elements from their traditional cultures, but also combined with others to form a polyglot, urban, working-class culture. The social meanings previously conveyed in isolation by blues, country, polka, zydeco, and Latin musics found new expression as they blended in an urban setting. . . . Rock and Roll music accelerated and intensified the interactions among ethnic groups, becoming the most visible expression of the increasing commonality of working-class experience.*[6]

A final limitation of the algebraic formula has to do with the relative values of r&b and c&w. Without specifying these relative values, one can infer that each style contributed equally to the new genre. Such an inference invariably undervalues the African American contribution. After rock 'n' roll erupted full-blown into the national pop market in 1956, it presented itself as a refreshingly integrated phenomenon, with performers such as Bill Haley and Elvis Presley sharing the stage equally with artists like Fats Domino, Little Richard, and Chuck Berry. Accordingly, Steve Perry may paint the early history of rock 'n' roll in racially glowing terms: "From 1955–1958, the roster of popular rock 'n' rollers was more racially equal than at any time before or since. Chuck Berry, Little Richard, the Coasters, the Platters, Fats Domino, Lloyd Price—major stars all, and on a rough par with the likes of Bill Haley, Jerry Lee Lewis, and Buddy Holly."[7] But this only happened after it had begun to expand to disruptive proportions among mainstream fans. As Greil Marcus correctly points out: "Most of the first rock 'n' roll styles were variations on black forms that had taken shape before the white audience moved in."[8]

The athletic honking saxophone, reminiscent of Illinois Jacquet ("Flying Home") and Big Jay McNeely, found its way into rock 'n' roll through Jackie Brenston's spirited solo on "Rocket 88" in 1951. That classic sound was soon echoed on countless rock 'n' roll records by such towering figures as Lee Allen and Herb Hardesty in New Orleans and King Curtis and Sam Taylor in New York. T-Bone Walker ("Call It Stormy Monday") practically invented electric blues guitar playing in the 1940s.[9] His picking style, which Robert Palmer has described as "clean, with a terse, dry tone, and minimal vibrato and sustain," had an obvious effect on Memphis-based B. B. King ("Three O'Clock Blues," "The Thrill Is Gone"), whose bent notes and single-string runs influenced generations of rock guitarists.[10] By merging T-Bone Walker's playing with jazz and pop influences, Chuck Berry created the definitive rock 'n' roll guitar style and, mixed with it, universal odes to teenage life: "School Day," "Rock & Roll Music," "Sweet Little Sixteen," and "Johnny B. Goode." This list of influences does not even include Muddy Waters ("Got My Mojo Working"), who had "electrified" the country blues in Chicago just to be heard above the din in the noisy honky-tonks and juke joints where he performed. Shortly thereafter, Bo Diddley ("Bo Diddley," "Say Man"), another Delta-born Chicago transplant, crossed over into the pop market as a rock 'n' roll star with a distinctive Afro-Caribbean variant of the style. New Orleans boogie pianist Professor Longhair, who described his own playing as a "combination of offbeat Spanish beats and calypso downbeats" and "a mixture of rumba, mambo and calypso," was a major influence on Fats Domino, whose successful r&b career was transformed into rock 'n' roll legend with such hits as "Ain't That a Shame," "I'm in Love Again," and "Blueberry Hill."[11]

On the vocal front, the assertiveness of such r&b performers as Joe Turner, Ruth Brown, and LaVern Baker helped to create the rock 'n' roll style. The emotional intensity of Roy Brown ("Good Rockin' Tonight"), for example, was carried to an extreme in the outrageous on-and-off-stage antics of archetypal rock 'n' roll screamer Little Richard ("Tutti-Frutti," "Long Tall Sally," "Rip It Up"). The jazz/gospel fusions of Ray Charles ("Hallelujah, I Love Her So," "I Got a Woman") and the more pop-oriented gospel stylings of such vocalists as Clyde McPhatter ("Treasure of Love," "A Lover's Question") and Sam Cooke ("You Send Me," "For Sentimental Reasons") brought the traditions of the black church into the secular world of rock 'n' roll. The elegant harmonies of urban vocal harmony groups like the Orioles ("Crying in the Chapel"), the Crows ("Gee"), the Chords ("Sh-Boom"), and the Penguins ("Earth Angel") ushered in a whole sub-genre of rock 'n' roll that was known as *doo wop*. Thus, in the well-intentioned and largely accurate celebration of rock 'n' roll's mongrel character, it is important not to lose sight of the fact that most of its formative influences, as well as virtually all of its early innovators, were African American. Among the artists who could have been considered rock 'n' roll musicians prior to 1955, there was only one white act that made a national impact—Bill Haley and His Comets.

If the tendency to systematically underestimate the African American contribution to rock 'n' roll is enough to give you pause, a consideration of what rock 'n' roll did to women can stop you in your tracks. The revolution that was rock 'n' roll just about eliminated

If the tendency to systematically underestimate the African American contribution to rock 'n' roll is enough to give you pause, a consideration of what rock 'n' roll did to women can stop you in your tracks.

women from the ranks of the best-selling recording artists. In the years immediately preceding the rock 'n' roll assault on the pop market, female vocalists had accounted for as many as one-third of the best-selling singles in a given year. Of course, these were women in the pop Tin Pan Alley mould who performed suitably inoffensive material, Patti Page ("Doggie in the Window," 1953), Kitty Kallen ("Little Things Mean a Lot," 1954), Rosemary Clooney ("Hey There," 1954), Doris Day ("Secret Love," 1954), and so forth. By 1957, however, only two women appeared on *Cashbox*'s list of the twenty-five best-selling records of the year, Debbie Reynolds ("Tammy") and Jane Morgan ("Fascination"). Not a single one of the eighteen or so rock 'n' roll records in the year-end top twenty-five list was by a woman. The breakdown for the following year was exactly the same, unless Connie Francis's recording of "Who's Sorry Now" is counted as rock 'n' roll. Occasionally, female performers did penetrate the weekly best-seller lists with rock 'n' roll material—LaVern Baker's "Tweedlee Dee" in 1955 and "Jim Dandy" in 1957 and Ruth Brown's "Lucky Lips" in 1957—but, overall, a pattern of overwhelming male domination prevailed.

Clearly, the sexuality that characterized rock 'n' roll's initial burst of energy was a male one. Women did not sing; they were sung about. Most often, they were referred to as babies—"Since I met you baby," "Honeycomb, won't you be my baby," "Be Bop a Lula, she's my baby," "Since my baby left me," "There goes my baby," and so forth. Without any models to make them question the double standard of the day, young male rock 'n' rollers were caught between the macho posturing of the "Sixty Minute Man" with his "Great Balls of Fire" and the passionate, even vulnerable, declarations of unconditional romantic love, delivered in teenage idiom. Accordingly, in some instances a woman could be portrayed as a wild "Party Doll," a promiscuous "Butterfly," or a "Devil in Disguise." Alternatively, she could be a heavenly goddess, "Venus" or "Diana," a "Dream Lover" with "Angel Eyes" sent to earth by a "Little Star," or a "Blue Moon." Either way, she was almost never a mature, down-to-earth being with a real personality. At best, women were treated as totally dependent creatures or ideal, unreal apparitions, perched high atop celestial pedestals.

Structural Changes in the Music Industry

Whatever else may be said about rock 'n' roll, in the early 1950s, the appearance in the mainstream market of African American artists recording rhythm and blues for independent labels turned all the rules of the music industry—especially those concerning artist and repertoire, recording techniques, marketing strategies, national distribution, and consumer preference—upside down. In 1953, for example, the Orioles, a black group originally from Baltimore, recorded "Crying in the Chapel," a sentimental country song, for Jubilee, an independent record label. Although there were already three versions of the song on the best-selling lists at the time, the Orioles' release, with its sparse accompaniment, a slight gospel tinge, and wordless falsetto swoops in the background, went to number one on the r&b charts and then crossed over to the pop market.

> *Lead singer Sonny Til's wavering tenor and the sighs and cries of the group were familiar to the black audience, but sounded appealingly strange to the popular music audience. Perhaps aided by the fact that Til didn't sound very "black," the record broke into the white popular music market, thereby establishing a precedent for independently produced records featuring black singers.*[12]

Prior to this, the mainstream market had been dominated by the major labels. It has been estimated that in 1948 and 1949, RCA, CBS, Decca, and Capitol released more than 80 percent of all the weekly Top Ten hits.[13] Company executives were firmly convinced that audiences responded favourably to gentle changes in popular styles, which made the market somewhat predictable. Accordingly, marketing categories were as simple and straightforward as they were narrow and limiting: there was popular music for the national market, country and western for the regional market, and rhythm and blues for the African American market. The advent of rock 'n' roll swept away this conventional wisdom in one fell swoop.

Of course, the major labels had been able to keep their hold on the market in part because they controlled the entire production process. Everything from songwriting, artist and repertoire management, arranging, production, and engineering to mastering, pressing, promotion, marketing, distribution, and, in some cases, retail sales was an in-house function and was performed according to a strict division of labour. The independent labels that came to life in the 1940s and 1950s had a far less highly organized system of production. Rock lore is rife with stories of enterprising label owners like Leonard Chess and Sam Phillips, who performed all the technical functions of producing and recording and then distributed their records from the trunks of their cars. There were, however, two events that permitted the independent labels to compete successfully for a significant share of the market. First was the creation of a series of poorly capitalized independent radio stations that were desperate for inexpensive programming. These stations had come into existence as the FCC had begun to clear away the backlog of applications for radio licences that had been put on hold during World War II. Second was the development of the lightweight, "unbreakable" 45 rpm record. Although Jack Gutshall, a Los Angeles distributor, had set up the first national independent distribution system in 1945, it was, for the independents, prohibitively expensive to ship shellac-based 78 rpm records because of their weight and fragility. With the introduction of the 45 rpm record, national distribution became a viable and cost-effective option for independent companies, which promptly began to supply independent radio stations with their music, thus introducing specialty music to the mainstream market.

Following the decline of network radio in the early 1950s, patterns of ownership in independent broadcasting began to change from individual stations to "chains," individually programmed stations that were brought together under one corporate roof. Chain owners were first and foremost businessmen for whom radio was just another investment. Said George Storer, the president of Storer Broadcasting,

> If the legend still persists that a radio station is some kind of art center, a technical museum, or a little piece of Hollywood transplanted strangely to your home town, then the first official act of the second quarter century [of commercial broadcasting] should be to list it along with the local dairies, laundries, banks, restaurants, and filling stations.[14]

Of course, these businessmen expected their investments to be profitable, thus programming not only had to be inexpensive but also had to appeal to a wide range of listeners. Although there was a lot of talk about a new youth market, astute businessmen could not help noticing that teenagers constituted only about 12 percent of the population and that they were unavailable as listeners (potential consumers) during school hours. While it was true that teenagers constituted a disproportionately large share of the record-buying public, it was not entirely clear that they paid their way in advertising dollars for other products. It was Todd Storz and Gordon McLendon, both of whom owned radio chains, who found the solution to this dilemma in a new format—Top Forty radio—which placed the forty best-selling records in constant rotation all day long.

There are, of course, numerous stories about how the Top Forty format came into being. One story has the format beginning as a cost-cutting measure at Storz's WTIX in New Orleans in 1953. According to this story, McLendon's KLIF in Dallas followed soon after.[15] A more dramatic story has the format originating in Omaha, Nebraska, when Storz and Bill Stewart, his program director at KOWH, were in a bar drinking and noticed that the patrons kept playing the same song in the jukebox over and over again. When at closing time one of the cocktail waitresses who had been subjected to the song all day walked over to the jukebox and selected it yet again, a new format was born. In the spirit of giving the public what it wants, Storz and Stewart reasoned, why not treat radio like a jukebox and play only the best-selling records? The Top Forty format was essentially *Your Hit Parade* on records; the weekly live broadcast simply became a daily programming concept. As a total "sound," the format integrated jingles, special effects, promotional gimmicks, and hourly news broadcasts into the music that was played. The format proved so successful that it soon dominated pop radio.

In the spirit of giving the public what it wants, Todd Storz reasoned, why not treat radio like a jukebox and play only the best-selling records? The Top Forty format was essentially Your Hit Parade *on records.*

With the success of Top Forty radio, the deejay became a replaceable element in a total sound formula. Naturally the personality jocks railed against the increasing rationalization. George "Hound Dog" Lorenz, the most popular deejay in Buffalo, left WKBW because, he said, "[t]his concept of radio programming is helping to kill the single-record business, is lowering radio listenership, and is decreasing a new artist's chances of making it."[16] To many, the inescapable conclusion was that the new format would restrict audience access to new music. While this would be the case over time, there is, paradoxically, ample evidence to suggest that in its initial stages, the format had precisely the opposite effect. As Richard Peterson has explained, "Because the charts were based not only on radio airplay but also on jukebox play and record sales, many r&b records as well as some country music records charted. Thus, for the first time, these sorts of records began to receive wide exposure via the radio."[17]

Because the aesthetic that had guided network radio programming had not kept pace with changes in popular taste, the format based on public appeal that had been created by independent chains had the effect, at least in the short run, of broadening the range of musical offerings that could be heard on a given station. Imagine hearing Little Richard's "Long Tall Sally," Patti Page's "Allegheny Moon," Carl Perkins' "Blue Suede Shoes," and Morris Stoloff's "Moonglow and Theme from Picnic" all on the same radio station—indeed, on the same show. It was possible in June 1956, when all four recordings were in the Top Forty simultaneously.

In the heyday of rock 'n' roll, there was a greater diversity of music on the radio than ever before.

In contrast to the United States, in Canada there are no national networks. Instead, Canadian broadcasting has always consisted of a combination of privately owned commercial stations and publicly owned not-for-profit broadcasters such as the CBC and, in more recent years, college and community radio stations. Eighty percent of Canadians live close enough to the United States that well into the 1960s many of them were regularly tuning into radio stations located across the border. Canada, in fact, did not have a station that played rock 'n' roll until CHUM-AM in Toronto adopted the Storz format on 27 May 1957. CHUM had existed since 1945, when Jack Q'Part purchased the frequency from the CBC. The station initially had only 1,000 watts of power and operated only from sunrise to sunset because of evening interference from a radio station in upstate New York that used the same frequency. For its first thirteen years, CHUM aired a programming hodgepodge of country, foreign language, and hits of the day. At the time, there were only three other stations in the Toronto market: CKEY, CFRB, and CBL, the last of these being a CBC station.

In 1954, CHUM was sold to Alan Waters. While on vacation in Florida in 1956, Waters became intrigued by the Top Forty format on the Todd Storz-owned 560 WQAM. With CHUM in a precarious financial state, Waters decided to go for broke. He boosted the station's power to 2,500 watts and, against the wishes of most of his staff, converted CHUM into Canada's first Top Forty rock 'n' roll–oriented station. After witnessing CHUM's phenomenal success, CKEY, as well as a number of other stations across the country, followed suit. Prior to this there were no radio stations or disc jockeys in Canada that regularly programmed rock 'n' roll or rhythm and blues.

Sounds of the Cities

The music that became rock 'n' roll issued from city centres in just about every region in the country. It was as disruptive in its degree of decentralization as it was exciting in its unpredictability. While there is always the temptation to trace the roots of rock 'n' roll to the South, perhaps because of the r&b + c&w formula, in the end, this tendency does not do justice to the geographical dispersion of the music or the variety of cultural inputs. In fact, there is no wholly satisfactory way to chart the course of the music. The one thing that can be said with certainty is that rock 'n' roll was an urban sound. Beyond that, the music often owed its characteristic sound to the magical ingredients of some bewitching musical brew—the distinctiveness of a particular region or city, the exceptional quality of a specific recording studio or record company, a unique vocal or instrumental style, even the creative genius of a particular writer, performer, producer, and/or engineer. One city where all these elements came together was New Orleans.

New Orleans: The Fertile Crescent of Rock 'n' Roll

New Orleans is one of those places where diverse cultural elements periodically come together to produce a distinct sound. The city had been home to people from incredibly varied backgrounds (French, Spanish, African, English, Native American, Cajun, and Creole) for many years before it was purchased by the United States in 1803. The resulting cultural blend, born of conflict, struggle, and accommodation, gave the city a distinctive cuisine, language, architecture, and musical culture. Known in legend as the birthplace of jazz, New Orleans was the site of a thriving r&b scene in the late 1940s and early 1950s. Thus, as Langdon Winner has noted:

> *Rock and roll performers nurtured in this fertile environment had a wealth of musical sources upon which to draw. The fabulous ensemble playing of the black funeral bands, the syncopated "second line" rhythms of Mardi Gras parades, the rugged country blues from the surrounding Mississippi delta, the raucous chords of barrelhouse piano players, the elegant styles of jazz improvisation—all became underlying elements of New Orleans rock.[18]*

One of the key figures in the construction of the New Orleans sound was an Italian American jukebox operator named Cosimo Matassa. Matassa was co-owner and chief engineer of J&M Studio, and from the 1940s until the late 1960s, almost every r&b record cut in New Orleans was recorded in one of his studios. Matassa began with a Duo-Presto disc recorder but soon moved up to tape, an Ampex 300 one-track machine, which afforded the possibility of some editing. There was, however, no overdubbing, no multitracking, and no electronic embellishment of any kind in Matassa's productions. His style was simple: he set the knobs at the desired level and let the band play. With this elementary philosophy, as well as brilliant sidemen, unique room acoustics, and some well-placed microphones, Matassa created classic New Orleans rock 'n' roll—heavy on bass and drums, light on horns and piano, with a strong vocal lead—that had independent labels from Aladdin, Imperial, and Specialty in Los Angeles to Chess in Chicago, Savoy in Newark, and Atlantic in New York flocking to New Orleans to record.

Cosimo Matassa's production style was simple: He set the knobs at the desired level and let the band play.

The first label to use Matassa's studio was De Luxe from New Jersey in 1947. It was, in fact, Roy Brown's recording of "Good Rockin' Tonight" (now a rock 'n' roll classic) for De Luxe that first focused national attention on New Orleans. Brown's version of "Good Rockin' Tonight" was outsold by Wynonie Harris' that same year, but Brown's record turned the industry spotlight on New Orleans. Brown himself became a significant influence on the vocal styles of artists from B. B. King and Bobby Bland to Jackie Wilson, the young James Brown, and even Little Richard. Charlie Gillett has said:

> *The most impressive quality of Brown's style was his intense involvement in his singing. Whereas the blues shouters were always evidently in control of the sounds they made, Brown's voice was shaped by the passions of despair or exhilaration. Rocking frantically to a boogie beat, or wracked by desolate doubt, he committed all he was to the song's message.[19]*

Another essential ingredient in the creation of the New Orleans sound was the city's fine array of session musicians. At the centre of this pool of talented sidemen was writer, producer, manager, arranger, trumpet player, and bandleader Dave Bartholomew. The son of a respected Dixieland tuba player and one-time trumpet player with Duke Ellington, Bartholomew started his own band (really an organization) in New Orleans in the late 1940s. From that point on, Bartholomew maintained a stable of first-rate musicians that included, among others, drummers Charles Williams and Earl Palmer, whose syncopated bass-drum style helped define rock 'n' roll drumming, and saxophonists Herb Hardesty, Red Tyler, and Lee Allen, "the Lester Young of rock." Allen was also a mainstay in the band of Paul Gayten, another noteworthy New Orleans bandleader and session musician.

Bartholomew and his organization found steady work at such clubs as the Dew Drop Inn and Club Tijuana and even had a minor r&b hit with "Country Boy" (1949) on De Luxe, but their most influential performances were as the house band at Matassa's studio. In various permutations, they could be heard as the backup band on Lloyd Price's "Lawdy Miss Clawdy" (1952), Shirley and Lee's "I'm Gone" (1952), the Spiders' "I Didn't Want to Do It" (1954), and Smiley Lewis's recording of "I Hear You Knocking" (1955), with Huey "Piano" Smith providing the piano introduction. Bartholomew's biggest successes, however, were with Fats Domino, for whom he acted as mentor, manager, co-writer, arranger, and producer.

Antoine "Fats" Domino was born in New Orleans in 1928. His first language was French. Taught to play piano by his brother-in-law, Domino quit school at the age of fourteen to work in a bedspring factory (he almost lost a few fingers in an industrial accident) and to play in local clubs at night, which is how he met Dave Bartholomew. Even today, Domino's music can be identified by his warm, inviting French Creole accent, Bartholomew's clear, well-constructed arrangements, and that steady boogie-woogie piano, which dates back to Albert Ammons, Meade Lux Lewis, and Pete Johnson but was influenced most immediately by Professor Longhair. "Domino, he was creative," Matassa noted. "No matter what he does comes through. He could be singing the National Anthem . . . you'd still know by the time he said two words it was him, obviously, unmistakably, and pleasurably him. . . . in fact he just hits an opening chord on his piano and you know it."[20]

Never a sex symbol or a musical iconoclast, Fats Domino managed to transcend to a great degree the racism that cheated so many African American artists and the ageism that plagued Bill Haley's career.

Domino began recording at Matassa's studio in 1949. Of the eight sides cut at his first session, "The Fat Man"—a cleaned-up version of Champion Jack Dupree's 1940 drug song "Junker Blues"—was released first. It hit the r&b charts in 1950. The next three releases flopped. On the fifth record, "Every Night About This Time," Domino introduced the piano triplets that became his signature. His rock 'n' roll breakthrough came in 1955 when Pat Boone's version of "Ain't That a Shame" went to number one on the pop charts and Domino's original followed it to number ten, establishing him as a full-fledged rock 'n' roll star with no change in his r&b style. From then on, Domino outdistanced almost all the competition. From 1955 to 1963, when he was well into his thirties, Domino charted thirty-six Top Forty pop hits, more than any other rock 'n' roll artist except Elvis Presley (unless Boone, who had thirty-eight, is counted as a rock 'n' roll artist). In addition to "Ain't That a Shame," eight other of Domino's records entered the Top Ten—"I'm in Love Again" and "Blueberry Hill" in 1956, "Blue Monday" and "Valley of Tears" in 1957, "Whole Lotta Lovin'" in 1958, "I Want to Walk You Home" and "Be My Guest" in 1959, and "Walking to New Orleans" in 1960. Never a sex symbol or a musical iconoclast, Domino managed to transcend, to a great degree, the racism that cheated so many African American artists and the ageism that plagued Bill Haley's career.

Somehow he was rock 'n' roll's safety valve, and all he was putting down was good time New Orleans music. . . . Fats' music had not changed in any way to meet his increased popularity. He was still a rhythm and blues singer whose music just happened to be the roots of rock 'n' roll. What he had in

Fats Domino's laid-back New Orleans r&b style brought him a devoted rock 'n' roll following even after he was well into his thirties. With the exception of Elvis Presley (and Pat Boone), he charted more Top Forty pop hits than any other rock 'n' roller.

abundance was a natural, mellow infectiousness which was instantly recognizable whether the songs were happy frolics or merely plaintive ballads. Relaxed good humor permeated his records, everything was so simple and danceable.[21]

All of Domino's hits, with the possible exception of "I'm Walkin'," were recorded in Matassa's studio, all were produced and arranged by Dave Bartholomew (indeed, most were co-written by Bartholomew), and all used some combination of the same session men. While the New Orleans scene certainly seemed to be a prescription for success, nobody successfully consolidated the package into a New Orleans record label. Matassa made a feeble attempt in 1958 when he founded Rex Records, but the company barely made a ripple outside of New Orleans. "I never did really get into the thing of being a producer as such," said Matassa, who went bankrupt in 1966. "I regret it now of course!"[22] The prodigious output of Matassa's modest studio was licensed to existing out-of-state independent labels. It wasn't until Bartholomew passed the creative baton to a second generation of producers, best exemplified by Allen Toussaint, at the turn of the decade that New Orleans developed any notable labels of its own.

The closest thing New Orleans had to a local label in the initial surge of rock 'n' roll was Ace Records, which was headquartered in Jackson, Mississippi, but centred in New Orleans. Founded in 1955 by Johnny Vincent (Vincent Imbragulio), who had been an artist and repertoire man for Specialty, the company had an immediate success with Earl King's "Those Lonely, Lonely Nights." King's second release, "Well-O, Well-O, Well-O, Baby," had that rocking New Orleans piano groove that had been made famous by Huey "Piano" Smith. Smith and his band, the Clowns, provided Ace with its first pop hit, "(I Got the) Rockin' Pneumonia and the Boogie-Woogie Flu" (1957). The recording featured Bobby Marchan as lead vocalist, Charles Williams on drums, and Lee Allen and Red Tyler on saxes. In 1958, the Clowns hit the Top Ten with "Don't You Just Know It." Following that, their biggest success was as the session band for Frankie Ford's "Sea Cruise." As Langdon Winner has pointed out, with this 1959 hit, "all of the elements of a sound which had been evolving for a decade are carried to their logical extremes. The New Orleans horns finally cook like their lives depend on it. The piano prances along, reaching the very essence of boogie-woogie. The lead vocal finally achieves the perfect mix of pure joke and pure hysteria."[23]

Ace's original recording of this song had featured Huey Smith's vocal, but the company had used Frankie Ford for the vocal in the final release in an attempt to find a teen idol who could compete with such white rock 'n' rollers as Elvis Presley and Ricky Nelson. This practice would become all too common in rock 'n' roll as the years went on. To Ford's credit, he had a genuine feel for r&b, and he delivered the song in a style heavily indebted to Bobby Marchan. This may explain why he was never able to repeat his success. Ace had more luck with a less influential white New Orleans rocker named Jimmy Clanton, who was managed by none other than Cosimo Matassa. Between 1958 and 1962, Clanton produced a string of pop hits, including three that made the Top Ten: "Just a Dream," "Go, Jimmy, Go," and "Venus in Blue Jeans." These three, especially the last one, removed him from his New Orleans roots and placed him in the company of such ersatz rockers as Fabian, Frankie Avalon, and Bobby Rydell.

The rest of the music recorded at Matassa's studio by New Orleans musicians was issued by more distant labels. Although Clarence "The Frogman" Henry's "Ain't Got No Home," "But I Do," and "You Always Hurt the One You Love" were issued by Argo, a subsidiary of Chess in Chicago, the bulk of the material went to Los Angeles–based labels, primarily Aladdin, Specialty, and Imperial, and at one time or another, Dave Bartholomew worked for all of them. Aladdin signed Shirley and Lee (Shirley Goodman and Leonard Lee), whose "Let the Good Times Roll" reached number twenty on the pop charts in 1956, even though some deejays thought it was too suggestive to play on the air. Imperial had Smiley Lewis ("I Hear You Knockin'") and the Spiders ("I Didn't Want to Do It"), both of whom were backed by Bartholomew's band. Imperial's founder, Lew Chudd, also signed Fats Domino, who turned Imperial into one of the most successful independent labels in the country. Art Rupe, the owner of Specialty, was so impressed with Domino that in 1952 he went to New Orleans to find some-one who could sing like him and found Lloyd Price. The seventeen-year-old Price was the last performer to show up for Rupe's public audition at Matassa's studio. Taken by Price's rendition of "Lawdy Miss Clawdy," a song he had written for a radio advertisement, Rupe spent the next four or five days putting together a band to record it professionally. Bartholomew rounded up the usual sidemen for the session, including Fats Domino on piano. "Lawdy Miss Clawdy" went to number one on the r&b charts and was followed up by two more Top Ten r&b hits— "Restless Heart" and "Ain't That a Shame" in 1952 and 1953. Before Price could hit his stride, however, he was drafted into the army. After finishing his tour of duty, he switched to ABC-Paramount and delivered nine Top Forty pop hits, including "Stagger Lee," "Personality," and "I'm Gonna Get Married," which were numbers one, two, and three, respectively, in 1959.

Rupe barely had time to mourn Price's departure from the label when he found two new artists to replace him, Little Richard and Larry Williams, both of whom are examples of the New Orleans–Los Angeles connection. Williams was a Little Richard soundalike from New Orleans who came to Rupe's attention when he was still employed as Lloyd Price's valet. Recording in Los Angeles with New Orleans session men, Williams turned out three pop hits, "Short Fat Fanny" and "Bony Maronie" in 1957 and "Dizzy Miss Lizzy" in 1958, and then faded from the scene. By this time, however, Little Richard had become the most colourful figure in rock 'n' roll.

Little Richard (born Richard Penniman) hailed from Macon, Georgia, where he sang and learned to play piano in the Pentecostal church. Forced to leave home when he was fourteen because of alleged homosexual activity, he toured with medicine shows for a while. In 1951, in a radio competition sponsored by Zenas Sears, a white r&b deejay in Atlanta, he won a record-ing contract with RCA Victor, which failed to ignite his career. At the suggestion of Lloyd Price, Richard sent a demo tape to Art Rupe in Los Angeles but heard nothing for almost a year. By the time Specialty's new producer, Bumps Blackwell, had decided to give Richard a try, he was already under contract to Peacock but still going nowhere. Rupe bought out the Peacock con-tract for $600 and sent Richard and Blackwell to New Orleans to record. Naturally, they went to Matassa's studio and used Bartholomew's sidemen. At the tail end of the session, which included nary a rocker, Richard began fooling around with a reportedly obscene song called "Wop Bop Aloo Bop." The song caught Blackwell's ear. He quickly brought in Dorothy La Bostrie, a local songwriter, to clean up the lyrics, and with fifteen minutes of studio time left, "Tutti Frutti" was recorded. It hit number twenty-one on the pop charts in 1956 and instantly established Little Richard as the most outrageous rock 'n' roller of them all.

Following the success of "Tutti Frutti," Little Richard turned out eight other Top Forty pop hits for Specialty, including "Long Tall Sally," "Slippin' and Slidin'," and "Rip It Up" in 1956, "Lucille," "Jenny, Jenny," and "Keep a Knockin'" in 1957, and "Good Golly, Miss Molly" and "Ooh! My Soul" in 1958. Each was as unrestrained as the one before it. Richard's outrageous personal appearance was the perfect complement to his uninhibited stage act. The eye-popping costumes, exaggerated pompadour, and heavy mascara defined a rock 'n' roll image with which few could compete. His stage antics would later be rivaled only by Jerry Lee Lewis; his fashion statement (minus the eye makeup) only by Elvis Presley. If Fats Domino was rock 'n' roll's safety valve, Little Richard was the steam that made it blow. In describing the difference between the two, Arnold Shaw has also noted the versatility of the New Orleans sound itself.

> *Fats had a friendly baritone and Little Richard's sound was strident and slam-bam. Fats' Cajun-inflected speech had an appealing musicality; Little Richard was a shouter. For Fats, the band played New Orleans jazz with an after beat while he boogied and barrelhoused at the piano. With Little Richard's crashing piano triplets, the band picked up drive and went "a-womp-bomp-a-loo-bomp a-lomp bomp boom" and "bama lama bama loo."*[24]

Little Richard's career came to an abrupt halt in 1958 when he unexpectedly quit the business to join the ministry. A number of not very convincing explanations have been offered for his sudden change in profession. Rupe blamed the first Russian satellite for Richard's departure. "He thought that the Sputnik was a sign from heaven," said Rupe. "That was it."[25]

According to another tale, the engine of an airplane Richard was on caught fire and he promised God he would leave the devil's music behind if he could be saved. Some have suggested more cynically that the artist was attracted to the idea that ministers did not pay income taxes. In any case, on board a ship while on tour in

If Fats Domino was rock 'n' roll's safety valve, Little Richard was the steam that made it blow.

Perhaps more than any other artist, Little Richard unleashed the energy of early rock 'n' roll. On a number of occasions, Richard left the world of music to pursue a higher calling. Fortunately for rock 'n' roll, however, his uncontrollable style and irrepressible spirit always won out in the end.

Australia, Richard plucked $8,000 worth of rings from his fingers and tossed them into the sea. "If you want to live with the Lord," he told an Australian reporter, "you can't rock 'n' roll it, too. God doesn't like it."[26] When he returned to the United States, he enrolled at Oakwood College, a Seventh Day Adventist school in Huntsville, Alabama, paying his entire four-year tuition in advance. Whatever the reason for Little Richard's conversion, it was one of a number of fateful occurrences in the late 1950s that signaled the decline of rock 'n' roll.

Los Angeles: From Jump Blues to Chicano Rock

The independent labels that were formed in Los Angeles in the late 1940s sought to satisfy a market that had been created by the cultural needs of waves of poor white, black, and Chicano migrants who had arrived to work in the shipyards and airplane manufacturing plants that had sprung up to meet wartime needs. Many of the artists who first recorded for these labels were pioneers in the transition from big band jazz to various styles of r&b. The first wave artists—Roy Milton, Amos Milburn, T-Bone Walker, and Charles Brown, among others—came from Texas. In Los Angeles, they encountered local jazz-cum-r&b musicians like Joe Liggins and Johnny Otis, who helped to shape their sound. As time went on, and a new wave of immigrants arrived from southern Louisiana, Los Angeles' independent labels began to explore the music of New Orleans. Perhaps they did so because New Orleans' early jazz sound, steeped in the blues, resonated well with the transition from jazz to rhythm and blues that was then occurring. As Johnny Otis once noted,

> In the early 40's a hybrid form of music developed on the West Coast. What was happening in Chicago was another kind of thing altogether. It was all rhythm and blues later, but the Chicago bands, the people that came up from the Delta, came up with harmonicas and guitars—the Muddy Waters and the rest of them. They had a certain thing, and we loved it, and we were influenced by it to a certain degree. But on the Coast, the people who were there, like myself and Roy Milton, T-Bone Walker, and Joe Liggins and the Honeydrippers, we all had big band experience. We all thought in terms of big bands, but when it became impossible to maintain a big band, . . . we didn't break down to just a guitar and a rhythm section. We still tried to maintain some of that sound of the jazz bands. We kept maybe a trumpet, a trombone, and saxes—this was a semblance of brass and reeds, and they continued to play the bop and swing riffs. And this superimposed on the country blues and boogie structure began to become rhythm and blues. And out of rhythm and blues grew rock 'n' roll.[27]

Even before Fats Domino and Little Richard recorded with some "semblance," as Otis called it, of the big band sound, Roy Milton (Specialty), T-Bone Walker (Imperial), Amos Milburn (Aladdin), and Joe Liggins and the Honeydrippers (Exclusive) had developed distinctive regional variants of Louis Jordan's jump blues. Charles Brown, the lead singer for Johnny Moore's Three Blazers, developed a smooth r&b style that was heavily influenced by Nat "King" Cole and Leroy Carr in "Driftin' Blues" (Aladdin, 1948) and "Merry Christmas, Baby" (Modern, 1949). Still, only Johnny Otis was able to make the successful transition to rock 'n' roll. Otis had been part of the West Coast r&b scene since its beginnings. He was, in fact, one of its formative influences. As a teenager in Berkeley, he was the

*J*ohnny Otis was clearly a catalyst for African American culture and talent. In his whole life, he has never been anything else, which is why it is sometimes surprising for people to learn that Otis happens to be white.

"Tutti Frutti"

Artist: Little Richard
Music / Lyrics by Little Richard
(and Dorothy La Bostrie)
Label: Specialty (1956)

Little Richard's first hits were recorded in Cosimo Matassa's famous studio in New Orleans with Dave Bartholomew's band, the same musicians who can be heard on recordings of Fats Domino and other New Orleans luminaries. "Tutti Frutti" hadn't been on the docket for that particular recording session, but Richard started singing it during a break:

> A wop-bop-a-loo-mop, a good goddamn,
>
> Tutti frutti . . . good booty . . .

Producer Bumps Blackwell decided that it would make a great single, once the lyrics were cleaned up (in addition to the obvious, "tutti frutti" was a contemporary slang term for a gay man). The task of rewriting the lyrics was given to Dorothy La Bostrie, an aspiring young New Orleans songwriter. The result was the now-famous "*A wop-bop-a-loo-mop, a lop bam boom, Tutti Frutti—oh Rootie. . . .* " "Tutti Frutti" was the first big hit for Richard and reached the Top Ten on both the r&b charts and the pop charts.

Musical Style Notes

"Tutti Frutti" is a classic twelve-bar blues structure. The last four bars of each verse are generally played as a *stop time chorus*: The band hits only the downbeat of each bar, highlighting the singer's lines. The last two bars of each verse feature the "*wop-bop-a-loo-mop, a lop bam boom*" line.

Vocal *cues* are an important part of Little Richard's style. If you listen to several of Richard's songs in a row, you'll notice that there's a particular "scream" that always cues in an instrumental solo verse.

In some ways, Little Richard is Fats Domino's alter ego: both played piano; both artists' records featured the same New Orleans–style instrumental combination, with its emphasis on sax and boogie-influenced piano rather than guitar; and both artists wrote accessible, catchy pop tunes. However, Fats' elegant New Orleans gentleman persona and smooth vocals were the polar opposite of Richard's outrageous stage presence and his manic yips and howls.

Musical "Road Map"

TIMINGS	COMMENTS	LYRICS
0:00–0:03	Begins with Little Richard's famous nonsense-syllable refrain, unaccompanied. The band stops each time this refrain is sung throughout the song, except for the lead into the sax solo (see below).	*"A wop-bop-a-loo-mop, a lop bam boom"*
0:03–0:19	"Tutti frutti" verse twelve-bar blues form, the last two bars of which are the *"wop-bop-a-loo-mop"* Note drum "pickup" to next verse—in other words, the drummer anticipates the next verse by starting a beat before the verse begins.	*Tutti frutti . . .*
0:19–0:34	Verse 1 twelve-bar blues form; last four measures are a "stop-time" chorus.	*I got a gal named Sue . . .*
0:35–0:50 0:37–0:39	"Tutti frutti" verse, as before Richard's trademark squeal and high-pitched "wooo"	*Tutti frutti . . .*
0:50–1:05	Verse 2, same form as Verse 1	*I got a gal named Daisy . . .*
1:05–1:20 1:18	"Tutti frutti" verse, as before, with one exception: Listen to the way the drummer plays "A wop-bop-a-loo-mop" with Richard, then does a drum roll to lead into the sax solo. Richard also leads into the sax solo with a scream, one of his favourite "cue-ing" techniques.	*Tutti frutti . . .*
1:20–1:36	Sax solo over the twelve-bar blues form of a verse. Listen to the drummer "ride" the high-hat cymbal; you won't hear this in Pat Boone's version.	
1:36–1:51	"Tutti frutti" verse	*Tutti frutti . . .*
1:51–2:07	Verse 2, same form as Verse 1	*I got a gal named Daisy . . .*
2:07–2:23 2:11	"Tutti frutti" verse Richard's trademark high-pitched "wooo" (copied later by Paul McCartney) Song ends with Richard's unaccompanied *A wop-bop-a-loo-mop, a lop bam boom."*	*Tutti frutti . . .*

drummer for Count Matthews' West Oakland House Rockers. He then moved to Los Angeles with Harlan Leonard and the Kansas City Rockets. In time, he started his own big band, "seven brass, five reeds, four rhythm," and two vocalists, sometimes three. The band's first recording session yielded its first hit, "Harlem Nocturne" (1945), on Excelsior, a subsidiary of Exclusive, one of the few black-owned labels in Los Angeles at the time. Otis was as much an entrepreneur as he was a musician. In the late 1940s and early 1950s, he was part owner of the Barrel House, an r&b club in Los Angeles; he also had a daily radio show and a weekly television show. His travelling road show, the Johnny Otis Show, a "rhythm and blues caravan," as he called it, featured vocalists Little Esther and Mel Walker, with whom he produced eleven hits for Savoy between 1950 and 1952. He is credited with discovering Hank Ballard, Little Willie John, Jackie Wilson, and Etta James. He also produced the ill-fated Johnny Ace[28] ("Pledging My Love," 1955) for Duke/Peacock, as well as Willie Mae "Big Mama" Thornton, for whom he claimed to have co-written the original version of "Hound Dog" with Jerry Leiber and Mike Stoller. (Otis claims that Leiber and Stoller cut him out when the song became a hit for Elvis Presley.) Otis finally hit rock 'n' roll pay dirt with "Willie and the Hand Jive" (Capitol, 1958), a novelty song played to the "Bo Diddley" beat, an Afro-Caribbean clave rhythm that Otis said he had learned from Count Matthews twenty years earlier.

In his heyday, Otis was clearly a catalyst for African American culture and talent. In his whole life, he has never been anything else, which is why it is sometimes surprising for people to learn that Otis happens to be white, the son of Greek immigrants, Alexander and Irene Veliotes. Otis identifies himself as "black by persuasion." When he speaks of African Americans, he uses the pronoun "we," and does so with credibility. "My friend, Johnny Otis, is genetically white, but in all other respects completely black," wrote black musician Preston Love in the preface to *Listen to the Lambs,* a book Otis wrote after the Watts rebellion in 1965. "His life has been that of a black man joined with other black men to combat the outside—the hostile and unjust white establishment."[29]

One of the musicians who worked at the Barrel House was Robert Byrd, who recorded as Bobby Day, Bobby Garrett (lead singer for the Hollywood Flames [aka the Satellites]), and Bob of Bob and Earl (Earl was Earl Nelson of the Flames). In 1957, the Hollywood Flames enjoyed pop success with "Buzz, Buzz, Buzz." That same year, Byrd wrote and recorded "Little Bitty Pretty One" under the name Bobby Day for the Class label. Class was another small subsidiary of Exclusive/Excelsior, which was owned by Otis and Leon René. It was Leon René who wrote "When the Swallows Come Back to Capistrano," which was, in fact, the flip side of "Little Bitty Pretty One." Although "Swallows" was expected to be the hit, deejays preferred "Little Bitty Pretty One." A nearly identical rival version of the song by Thurston Harris was put out by Aladdin and selected by Dick Clark for play on *American Bandstand.* It was Harris' only Top Ten pop hit and outsold Day's original four-to-one. The following year, René wrote another "bird" song for Day. This time nothing stood in his way. "Rockin' Robin" (1958) went to number two on the pop charts and became one of the all-time classic rock 'n' roll records.

Until the year "Rockin' Robin" came out, Los Angeles had produced a number of distinctive performers but never a specific "sound" that was identified with the city. In that year, how-

Los Angeles had produced a number of distinctive performers but never a specific "sound" that was identified with the city. In 1958, however, Los Angeles' rock 'n' rollers began to move toward styles that drew on Mexican rhythms.

ever, Los Angeles' rock 'n' rollers began to move toward styles that drew on Mexican rhythms. "Tequila" (which featured Glen Campbell on guitar) by the Champs, a white instrumental group that included Jim Seals and Dash Crofts (later Seals and Crofts), remained number one on the pop charts for five weeks in 1958. It was followed by "El Rancho Rock," a rocked-up version of the 1934 Mexican ballad "Alla en El Rancho Grande." There was one artist who might have developed this sound further—Ritchie Valens (Ritchie Valenzuela), the first

Ritchie Valens drew on his Chicano heritage to add another cultural source to the musical brew that was rock 'n' roll. Who knows how much further he might have taken that sound had he not been killed in a plane crash three months before his eighteenth birthday?

Chicano rock 'n' roll star. Recorded for Del-Fi, one of a number of labels owned at various times by Bob Keene, Valens' "C'mon, Let's Go" and "La Bamba," a rock 'n' roll version of the traditional folk song, hit the pop charts in 1958 and 1959. His biggest hit, however, was "Donna," a more mainstream ballad that he wrote for his girlfriend. Valens turned out two more hits for Del-Fi—"That's My Little Susie" and "Little Girl"—before he was killed in the same plane crash that took the lives of Buddy Holly and the Big Bopper. The date of that flight, 3 February, 1959, is sometimes eulogized as the day the music died. Valens' death slowed the development of Chicano rock, which made only sporadic inroads into the mainstream from then on.

Chicago: The Blues Electrified

Chicago was one of the main watering holes for urbanized blues musicians from the Mississippi Delta. The city had been receiving a steady influx of African American migrants from the South for decades, and included among its inhabitants were Big Bill Broonzy, Sonny Boy Williamson, Willie Mabon, Jimmy Reed, John Lee Hooker, Muddy Waters, and Howlin' Wolf. With the exception of Broonzy, all of these artists recorded for one or the other of Chicago's two main independent record labels, Chess and Vee Jay. Williamson, Mabon, Waters, and Wolf recorded for Chess, Reed and Hooker for Vee Jay.

According to legend, many of the Chicago blues greats simply walked into Chess Records off the street. Leonard Chess, however, was not one to sit and wait for talent to come to him. He made regular field trips to the South to find bluesmen in their natural habitat. It was on one such trip that he recorded Howlin' Wolf, with Ike Turner on piano and James Cotton on harp. Wolf subsequently joined the Chess stable in Chicago and began a professional rivalry with Muddy Waters that lasted until the day Wolf died. On another southern excursion in 1951, Chess acquired Jackie Brenston's recording of "Rocket 88" with Ike Turner's band, with Brenston playing sax and singing lead, from Sam Phillips, who later founded Sun Records. The song rocketed to the top of the r&b charts and provided a developing Bill Haley with the inspiration he needed to move in an r&b direction. Indeed, "Rocket 88" is sometimes cited as one of the first rock 'n' roll records.

If there is any question about Chess' pioneering role in advancing the new sound, it becomes moot when the label's next two major performers—Bo Diddley and Chuck Berry—are

Chuck Berry had it all: sex appeal, talent, wit, stage presence, and an incredible ability to relate to teen culture. Had the United States been more tolerant of racial differences, this "brown-eyed handsome man" would probably have been crowned the "King of Rock 'n' Roll."

considered. Like the early bluesmen who recorded for Chess, Bo Diddley (born Ellas Bates but reared as Ellas McDaniel after the family that raised him) came from Mississippi. He is distinguishable from his blues contemporaries in a number of ways, not the least of which is the fact that his first instrument was the violin—not the fiddle, the violin. Although Diddley moved to Chicago as a youngster in 1934, he did not record for Chess until 1955. Between 1955 and 1959, he turned out eight r&b hits, including the classic "Bo Diddley," backed with "I'm a Man," in 1955. In 1956, he set an attendance record at the Apollo Theatre. In 1959, his "Say Man" crossed over to the pop market, and in that same year his "Crackin' Up" made the pop charts but not the r&b charts, reflecting the beginning of the separation of rock 'n' roll from rhythm and blues.

Diddley was more influential than his chart entries indicate. A tall, heavyset man, he was an imposing figure on stage and usually performed in black with a black Stetson hat and oddly shaped square and triangular guitars. As if to emphasize the Afro-Latin quality of his clave-influenced rhythm, which is often incorrectly identified as the "shave-and-a-haircut" beat, he once appeared on the *Ed Sullivan Show* accompanied by a rhythm section that included maracas. His rhythmic signature, which is now known as the "Bo Diddley beat," was copied by Johnny Otis on "Willie and the Hand Jive," as well as by numerous other rock 'n' rollers. However, his importance at Chess, and in rock 'n' roll generally, was overshadowed by the label's biggest star and possibly the greatest rock 'n' roller of them all—Chuck Berry.

Were it not for the dynamics of racism in U.S. society, Chuck Berry probably would have been crowned king of rock 'n' roll. When Berry, the son of a carpenter from St. Louis, Missouri, walked into the offices of Chess Records on the recommendation of Muddy Waters, his demo of "Ida Red" (backed with "Wee Wee Hours," a blues number) had already been turned down by both Capitol and Mercury because it sounded "too country" for a black man. On the advice of Leonard Chess, Berry gave the tune a bigger beat and changed the title to "Maybellene," a name he took from a hair cream. Said Chess a few weeks before he died:

> *I liked it, thought it was something new. I was going to New York anyway, and I took a dub to Alan [Freed] and said "Play this." The dub didn't have Chuck's name on it or nothing. By the time I got back to Chicago, Freed had called a dozen times, saying it was his biggest record ever. History, the rest, y' know? Sure, "Wee Wee Hours," that was on the back side of the release, was a good tune too, but the kids wanted the big beat, cars, and young love.*[30]

For his part in popularizing the song, Freed and another deejay named Russ Fratto were credited as co-writers of the song, a practice that eventually contributed to the undoing of rock 'n' roll.

The country-tinged "Maybellene" went to number five on the pop charts in 1955. Still, success did not come quickly, as Berry's songs were far too socially relevant for many. As Charlie Gillett has written:

> *[Berry's] next four singles, performed in a blues style and presenting in their themes some strong criticisms of aspects of American life, showed his interests much more obviously. Judges and courts in "Thirty Days," credit and car salesmen in "No Money Down," high culture in "Roll Over Beethoven," and all these and more in "Too Much Monkey Business" were cause for complaint. Since these records were performed in a strong "blues" voice, the songs . . . received relatively little attention from disc jockeys.*[31]

"Too Much Monkey Business" was actually a two-sided r&b hit. On the back was "Brown-Eyed Handsome Man." The self-descriptive, thinly veiled racial commentary of this song no doubt added to the deejays' reluctance to push the record to a mainstream audience. Berry is best remembered for the simpler, teen-directed but socially relevant recordings that came later—"School Day" and "Rock & Roll Music" in 1957, and "Sweet Little Sixteen" and "Johnny B. Goode" in 1958. All of these reached the Top Ten on the pop charts. In his writing, Berry had the uncanny ability to relate r&b to white teen culture without disowning his blackness. His "duck walk" and other guitar gymnastics, indeed his comedic yet cool stage demeanor in general, added tremendous visual appeal to his performances without demeaning the substance of his music. "As rock & roll's first guitar hero," Nelson George has written, "Berry, along with various rockabilly musicians, made that instrument the genre's dominant musical element, supplanting the sax of previous black stars."[32]

Berry's career was interrupted in 1959 when he was arrested for a violation of the Mann Act and sent to prison. After returning from a tour in Mexico with an underage young woman in tow (ostensibly to check hats in his night club), he was arrested for transporting a minor across state lines for immoral purposes. The impulse to discredit rock 'n' roll was shown in a headline of the time, which read **ROCK 'N' ROLL SINGER LURED ME TO ST. LOUIS, SAYS 14 YEAR OLD**.[33] It took two trials to convict him. The first trial was vacated because of the blatant racism of the judge, who referred to Berry as "this Negro." The second trial, which ended in 1962, landed him in jail for nearly two years. Berry's songs continued to sell well in 1964 and 1965, but his career slipped in the late 1960s. He staged a comeback in 1972 with a song as commercially successful as it was puerile—"My Ding-a-Ling," his only number one pop hit. Although other heroes of rock 'n' roll may have had more and bigger hits than Chuck Berry, none matched his influence in defining the music's style.

"Rock and Roll Music"

Artist: Chuck Berry
Music / Lyrics by Chuck Berry
Label: Chess (1958)

Chuck Berry's 1950s singles represent what are in some ways the clearest combination of cross-cultural influences of early rock 'n' roll: the forms, harmonies, and pounding backbeats of rhythm and blues, and the twangy, clear-toned guitar solos of "hot country." Chuck Berry's music very much represents the musical *and* cultural boundary-crossing that went on in the music underworlds of Memphis and St. Louis.

Though he played the blues in East St. Louis clubs, Berry had clearly listened extensively to country artists as well—as can be heard on some of the sides he recorded in Chicago. While the rhythm section holds down a solid, behind-the-beat, triplet-laden blues shuffle ("tri-pl-et tri-pl-et tri-pl-et tri-pl-et"), Chuck's twangy guitar solos are in rock-hard straight-eighths ("dunka-DUNKA-dunka-DUNKA"). He never varied from this formula, and there was no reason to: he was the first rock guitar hero, and his twangy solos are the foundation of every young wannabe guitarist's first education.

Musical Style Notes

The strong drum backbeat, Berry's repeating guitar riff, and the boogie-woogie piano sound are all typical of 1950s rock 'n' roll style, as is the prominent echo effect. "Rock & Roll Music" begins as a typical twelve-bar blues form, but only the chorus maintains that structure; the verse is actually eight bars long. The lyric verses of "Rock & Roll Music" also form an interesting structural overlap with the music. The first line of the verse is actually sung over the last bar (measure) of the chorus's twelve-bar blues form. Likewise, the last line of the verse ("That's why I go for that—") could actually be considered the first line of the chorus rather than the actual words "rock and roll music," which occur on the downbeat of the first bar of the chorus's twelve-bar blues form.

Chorus, bar 11				Chorus, bar 12				Verse, bar 1			
1	2	3	4	1	2	3	4	1	2	3	4
if you	wanna	dance	with me	—I	got no	kick a-	gainst	mo-	dern jazz . . .		

The overall effect is a very seamless progression through the song; notice that there is no instrumental solo verse to interrupt the flow of the words.

Musical "Road Map"

TIMINGS	COMMENTS	LYRICS
0:00–0:25	Four quick guitar strums, directly into twelve-bar chorus. The lyric over the last measure is actually the first line of the verse.	*Just let me hear some of that rock and roll music . . .* *I have no kick against*
0:25–0:37	Verse 1 The last line of each verse, which occurs on the last measure, is actually a lead-in to the first line of the chorus.	*modern jazz . . .* *That's why I go for that*
0:37–0:57	Chorus	*rock and roll music . . .* *I took my loved one over*
0:57–1:09	Verse 2	*cross the tracks . . .* *That's why I go for that*
1:09–1:28	Chorus	*rock and roll music . . .* *Way down south they gave a*
1:28–1:41	Verse 3	*jubilee . . .* *And started playing that*
1:41–2:00	Chorus	*rock and roll music . . .*
2:00–2:13	Verse 4 Listen to the way that the drums and percussion change style here, from the rock backbeat to a Latin percussion beat; they're "commenting" on the reference to "tango" and "mambo" in the lyrics.	*Don't care to hear 'em play a tango . . .* *So I can hear some of that*
2:13–2:33	Chorus Rhythmic "tag" at the end—"cha-cha CHA" beat	*rock and roll music . . .* *If you want to dance with me,* *If you want to dance with me.*

Chicago's other main independent label was formed in the early 1950s by an African American couple, Vivian Carter and James Bracken; hence its name, Vee Jay. Carter was one of the few women deejays at the time, had won a 1948 talent contest and that had been sponsored by Al Benson. Bracken owned and operated a record store that was named after his wife. The label was a natural outgrowth of its founders' experience in the music business. One key to the company's success was the early installation of Calvin Carter, Vivian's brother, as producer. While not a musician himself, Calvin Carter's social and technical skills and fine ear for harmonies produced "a track record that Phil Spector would be envious of."[34] In 1955, Ewart Abner, who later went on to become the president of Motown, joined Vee Jay. Abner was the deal maker; his fast-and-loose style contributed to the rise and fall of the company.

Vee Jay began as a gospel recording label and included among its artists the Swan Silvertones, the Harmonizing Four, the Highway QCs, and the Staple Singers, who later moved to Stax. Like Chess, the company experienced some early success in doo wop, offering both the Spaniels and the El Dorados. However, the company's biggest-selling artist in the 1950s was Delta bluesman Jimmy Reed. Signed to the label in 1955, Reed produced thirteen r&b hits over the next six years, including "Honest I Do" (1957) and "Baby What You Want Me to Do" (1960), which crossed over to the pop Top Forty. After eight years of recording for other labels, most notably Modern in Los Angeles, John Lee Hooker joined Vee Jay in 1955. Although a more versatile performer, Hooker was less successful than Reed as an r&b artist. He did become better known in retrospect because of his Newport Folk Festival appearances and recordings, which were influential in the blues revival of the 1960s.

Vee Jay seemed destined for major success when the company signed the Impressions. The original Impressions group included Jerry Butler and Curtis Mayfield, who had met when Butler had joined the gospel choir in the church where Mayfield's grandmother was pastor. In 1957, Butler and Mayfield joined forces with the core of a group called the Roosters to form the Impressions. The group's audition at Vee Jay in 1958 yielded "For Your Precious Love," which was issued on the label's Abner/Falcon subsidiary (named after Ewart Abner). The song became a Top Twenty pop hit but contributed to the destruction of the group because the record was inadvertently credited to Jerry Butler *and* the Impressions. Butler stayed with Vee Jay as a solo artist, with Mayfield collaborating as a writer and arranger, but as recording artists, Mayfield and the rest of the Impressions switched to ABC-Paramount, where Mayfield penned a series of gospel-influenced "sermon songs" that rightfully belong to the era of the Civil Rights movement, discussed later in this book. Vee Jay made its mark on rock 'n' roll with hits by Dee Clark ("Hey Little Girl," 1959, and "Raindrops," 1961), Gene Chandler ("Duke of Earl," 1962), and Betty Everett ("The Shoop Shoop Song [It's in His Kiss]," 1964).

In terms of offering career direction to African American artists and displaying a knack for crossing black music over to a white audience, Vee Jay could have been what Motown became.

In terms of offering career direction to African American artists and displaying a knack for crossing black music over to a white audience, Vee Jay could have been what Motown became. Unfortunately, the company seemed to have a knack for losing many of its best acts. Gene Chandler, for example, signed with Constellation shortly after "Duke of Earl" ran its course. While Vee Jay introduced a number of name artists, including the Four Seasons, Gladys Knight and the Pips, and the Dells, many of these performers had their biggest successes after switching to other labels. Even the Beatles were first issued on Vee Jay in the United States, when Capitol initially passed on them. In 1966, the company unexpectedly folded amidst rumours of fiscal mismanagement.

Cincinnati: The Crossroads of Blues and Country

As a major rail stop situated along the Ohio River, Cincinnati had served for years as a gateway to northern iron and steel mills for blacks and poor whites from the South. As such, it was a crossroads for blues and country music. As noted, it was Syd Nathan's King Records that consolidated these influences into a diverse musical enterprise. Under the able direction of producer Henry Glover, Nathan's policy of encouraging his country and western artists and his rhythm and blues artists to record each other's songs provided early examples of the cultural cross-pollination that would yield rock 'n' roll.

Among King's country artists, the Delmore Brothers had first recorded blues-based country hits like "I've Got the Big River Blues" when they were with RCA. Still, it was Glover who continued the development of this music with a wealth of blues-influenced material that culminated in the country hit "Blues Stay Away from Me" in 1949. Glover's biggest country breakthroughs were with Moon Mullican. Mullican demonstrated his affinity for multicultural sounds early on, scoring country hits with "What Have I Done to Make You Go Away," which was "borrowed" from a Louis Jordan tune, and "New Jole Blon," a takeoff on the French Cajun "Jole Blon." "[U]nder Glover's influence," according to historian John W. Rumble, "Mullican expressed his fascination with black music on levels that few country artists had ever attained."[35] With Glover, Mullican found a blues-boogie groove on "Southern Hospitality" and also recorded hit country versions of Nat "King" Cole's "Mona Lisa" and Leadbelly's "Good Night Irene."

Ivory Joe Hunter was an African American artist who moved in the other direction. Hunter had recorded a number of early r&b hits, such as "Landlord Blues" and "I Quit My Pretty Mama," for King in the late 1940s. By the time he left the company in 1950, his smooth style had begun to appeal to country music fans as well. He achieved pop crossover success with his biggest hit, "Since I Met You Baby" (1956), on Atlantic, and ended his career more than a decade later as one of the few African American artists ever to become a regular on the *Grand Ole Opry*.

King Records eventually made a direct impact on the rock 'n' roll market with the Charms ("Hearts of Stone," 1954), Bill Doggett's combo ("Honky Tonk," 1956), and solo vocalist Little Willie John, who became a consistent hitmaker in the latter half of the 1950s with such Top Forty pop hits as "Fever" (1956), "Talk to Me, Talk to Me" (1958), and "Heartbreak (It's Hurtin' Me)" and the old Tin Pan Alley classic "Sleep" (1960). Needless to say, Henry Glover served as producer for all three acts. However, King's greatest influence on rock 'n' roll was exerted through its subsidiary, Federal, which was set up by Nathan in the early 1950s as part of a production deal with producer Ralph Bass. Bass quickly established a personality for the new label when he signed a number of gospel-influenced vocal harmony groups, including Billy Ward and the Dominoes, the "5" Royales, Hank Ballard and the Midnighters, and the Famous Flames, the group that sang backup for James Brown. These groups joined other African American performers in challenging the perceived morality gap between gospel music and rhythm and blues, and together, they contributed one of the major strands to that style of rock 'n' roll known as doo wop.

R&B Sanctified: The Gospel Connection

In the late 1940s, as r&b grew in popularity, a fair amount of gospel music was also recorded in major city centres throughout the country. In the Northeast, New York's Apollo label had Mahalia Jackson; Savoy in Newark had James Cleveland; and Gotham in Philadelphia had the Famous Ward Singers. Three other well-known groups—the Dixie Hummingbirds, the Silver Echoes, and the Skylight Singers—recorded for a succession of labels in New York City. In the West, the best-known gospel talent, including the Pilgrim Travelers and the Soul Stirrers, appeared on Specialty. Black-owned Peacock Records, founded by Don Robey in Houston, recorded the Five Blind Boys of Mississippi and the Bells of Joy, among others.[36] There was at the time a sharp distinction between gospel and rhythm and blues, if not in the music industry, then certainly in the African American community. "[R]hythm and blues was felt to be degrading, low," said Robey, "and not to be heard by respectable people."[37] Rhythm and blues artists did not perform in church and gospel singers were expected to steer clear of "the devil's music." In the early 1950s, however, some gospel-trained singers began to move into the secular world of rhythm and blues, retaining a gospel tinge that is best seen in their use of organs, soaring vocals, background choruses, and the call-and-response style. The first group to develop this style was the Dominoes, founded in 1950 by the multitalented Billy Ward. In 1951, the group had three r&b successes on the Federal label—"Do Something for Me," "I Am with You," and "Sixty Minute Man" (featuring Bill Brown's bass), which became a crossover classic whose sexual lyrics caused no small stir in the gospel community. "Sixty Minute Man" boldly confronted all the controversy associated with the secularization of church music. Subsequent gospel-flavoured releases, however, such as the Orioles' "Crying in the Chapel" (covered by June Valli for RCA) and "Shake a Hand" by Faye Adams, may have had a more profound effect than "Sixty Minute Man" because of their ambiguity. Both "Crying in the Chapel" and "Shake a Hand" were released in r&b and country versions, and both lent themselves to various interpretations along the sacred-secular continuum. "Here for the first time you were not sure exactly what ground you were on," r&b historian Peter Guralnick has written. "Were these love songs or devotionals? Was the second person singular you or You? It was an intentional ambivalence that was to persist."[38]

The Dominoes' early successes were due in large measure to the incredible leads of Clyde McPhatter, who had been gospel trained. In 1952, McPhatter capped his stay with the group with "Have Mercy Baby," a number one r&b hit. The following year, he left the Dominoes to form his own group, the Drifters. He was replaced by the equally talented Jackie Wilson, who delivered a Top Twenty pop hit in 1956 with "St. Theresa of the Roses" on Decca. In 1957, Wilson went solo, and Billy Ward took over as lead vocalist, scoring two more Top Twenty pop hits for the Dominoes that year with "Star Dust" and "Deep Purple" on Liberty.

McPhatter and the Drifters were signed by Atlantic. Every member of the group had a gospel background, and between 1953 and 1955, the group delivered six Top Ten r&b hits for

There was at the time a sharp distinction between gospel and rhythm and blues in the African American community. Rhythm and blues artists did not perform in church and gospel singers were expected to steer clear of "the devil's music."

the company, including "Money Honey" and the double-sided hit "Such a Night"/"Lucille." They also did a stirring version of "White Christmas" with lead vocals by both McPhatter and Bill Pinckney singing bass. After McPhatter was drafted in 1955, the group went through a number of personnel changes and then disbanded. It was later reformed with new personnel and a totally new sound. McPhatter continued with Atlantic as a solo act after serving in the army and became an immediate r&b and pop sensation with such hits as "Treasure of Love" (1956), "Without Love (There Is Nothing)" (1957), and "A Lover's Question" (1958), which was number six on the pop charts. He continued producing hits well into the 1960s.

It was also Atlantic that produced the most influential gospel-tinged vocalist—Ray Charles Robinson, a.k.a. Ray Charles, a.k.a. "the Genius." Blinded by glaucoma as a youth, Charles attended the St. Augustine School for the Deaf and the Blind in Florida, where he learned to compose and arrange in Braille, and then moved to Seattle. In Seattle, he dropped the Robinson to avoid confusion with Sugar Ray Robinson, who was then the middleweight boxing champion, and became Ray Charles. His musical influences were absolutely catholic, ranging from the Five Blind Boys of Mississippi to Chopin to legendary jazz pianist Art Tatum to jazz pianist cum pop vocal stylist Nat "King" Cole. Before leaving Florida, Charles had even joined a hillbilly band in Tampa and learned to yodel. After cutting some forty sides for Swingtime Records in the late 1940s and early 1950s, including a few r&b hits, he was signed by Atlantic in 1952.

Charles was one artist at that time who did not see a contradiction between gospel and r&b. "Now I'd been singing spirituals since I was three," he has said in his autobiography, "and I'd been hearing the blues for just as long. So what could be more natural than to combine them?"[39] After a couple of years of groping for his musical persona, the Genius began to hit his stride with a string of original r&b hits in 1954—"Don't You Know," "Come Back Baby," and the gospel-inflected "Hallelujah, I Love Her So." Often he mined the gospel repertory directly for new material: "Talkin' 'bout Jesus" became "Talkin' 'bout You"; "This Little Light of Mine" became "This Little Girl of Mine"; "How Jesus Died" became "Lonely Avenue." All the elements of his revolutionary jazz-gospel-r&b fusion were present by the time he released "I Got a Woman" (1954), one of his most influential, if not most successful, records. The impact of "I Got a Woman" has been remembered by popular music historians as nothing short of apocalyptic. "The very strategem of adapting a traditional gospel song, putting secular lyrics to it, and then delivering it with all the attendant fanfare of a Pentecostal service was, simply, staggering," Peter Guralnick has said. "It was like a blinding flash of light in which the millennium, all of a sudden and unannounced, had arrived."[40] The style reached its logical conclusion with the release of Charles' Top Ten classic "What'd I Say" (1959), "a culmination of the gospel blues style that Ray Charles had virtually created, an altogether secular evocation of an actual church service, complete with moaning, groaning, and speaking in tongues, a joyous celebration of an utterly profane love."[41]

By this time, Jackie Wilson had left the Dominoes to pursue a solo career at Brunswick. His first six solo hits, which included "Reet Petite" (1957), "Lonely Teardrops" (1958), and "That's Why (I Love You So)" (1959), were co-written by Berry Gordy, the founder of Motown. Wilson demonstrated his incredible versatility and vocal range in 1960 when Brunswick presented him with two new songs—"Night," based on "My Heart at Thy Sweet

With musical tastes ranging from Chopin to Nat "King" Cole, Ray Charles was a pioneer of the r&b/gospel fusion that has come to be known as rhythm and gospel. For many, his spirited live performances were, indeed, a religious experience.

Voice" from the opera *Samson and Delilah,* and "Alone at Last," taken from Tchaikovsky's "Piano Concerto No. 1." Both hit the Top Ten, and as Wilson has said, "Now they knew I wasn't just a screamer."[42] Wilson was still straddling the narrow line that separated gospel from rhythm and blues in 1967. His last Top Ten pop hit "(Your Love Keeps Lifting Me) Higher and Higher," projected the same sexual/spiritual ambiguity that made the fusion so exciting in the first place.[43]

Perhaps the most profound gospel "desertion" was Sam Cooke's. Until 1957, Cooke was still at the top of the gospel heap as the lead singer for the Soul Stirrers, a group that could date its origins to 1934. The son of a Chicago Baptist minister, Cooke was singing in the church choir before he was ten. He joined the Soul Stirrers in 1950 and quickly became, according to gospel historian Tony Heilbut, "the greatest sex symbol in gospel history."[44] Still, the lure of the material world was present. In 1956, Bumps Blackwell, Little Richard's producer at Specialty, which was also the Soul Stirrers' label, offered to "cut" Sam Cooke "pop." His first session yielded eight sides, one of which was "Lovable," which was then released, in a fairly transparent attempt to avoid the wrath of the gospel community, under the name of Dale Cook. Cooke agonized over what musical direction to take, but in the end the decision was made for him, as his outraged followers forced him to leave the Soul Stirrers.

Sam Cooke agonized over what musical direction to take, but in the end the decision was made for him, as his outraged followers forced him to leave the Soul Stirrers.

Fearing reprisals from his gospel constituency, Art Rupe, owner of Specialty, released both Cooke and Blackwell from the label and gave them Cooke's masters in return for back royalties. The masters were offered to Bob Keene, who had just launched the Keen label. Blackwell became Cooke's manager as well as the head of artist and repertoire for the new company. Cooke's first Keen release, "You Send Me" (1957), climbed straight to number one on the pop charts; his pop appeal seemed as effortless as the gospel-influenced melismas he used to embellish his vocals. Seven more of his Keen releases entered the Top Forty over the next three years. By the end of the decade, Cooke was one of the hottest musical properties in the popular market. In 1960, RCA, a label with virtually no African American artists that was looking for an answer to the black velvet tones of Columbia's Johnny Mathis, signed Cooke. His talent overpowered the generally pop material supplied by producers Hugo Peretti and Luigi Creatore, and he scored nineteen more Top Forty hits. "Chain Gang" (1960), "Twistin' the Night Away" (1962), "Another Saturday Night" (1963), and "Shake" (1964) all entered the Top Ten.

Cooke went on to become a business institution. In 1959, he took what was a rare step for an African American artist and formed his own publishing company, Kags Music, with his friend and mentor J. W. Alexander, tenor vocalist for the Pilgrim Travelers. A Kags audit of Keen's royalty statements bankrupted the label and ended Cooke's relationship with Bumps Blackwell. Cooke and Alexander used their earnings from Kags to finance a production company, an artists' management company, and SAR (Sam and Alex) Records, arguably the first soul label. SAR served as a vehicle for another side of Sam Cooke—the writer/producer. SAR issued not only straight gospel recordings by the Soul Stirrers but also more soul-oriented material by Johnny Taylor (later of disco fame), the Sims Twins, who prefigured Sam and Dave, and the Valentinos, featuring Bobby Womack, all of whom were gospel artists who had been turned out.

Meanwhile, a number of full-fledged gospel groups moved into the material world of rhythm and blues. These groups found an outlet for their music in the King subsidiary Federal, which was second only to Atlantic in the successful production of "rhythm and gospel." The Gospel Starlighters gave up spiritual trappings to become the Famous Flames, James Brown's backup group. The echoes of the group's gospel past could be heard on "Please, Please, Please" (Federal, 1956), the group's first recording with Brown and an eventual million seller. The Royal Sons emerged as the "5" Royales, and after recording two Top Ten r&b hits ("Baby Don't Do It" and "Help Me Somebody") for Apollo in 1953, moved to King, where the group recorded "Think" in 1957 and the original version of "Dedicated to the One I Love" in 1958. The latter song became a Top Ten pop hit for the Shirelles in 1961 and The Mamas and The Papas in 1967. After he had signed the "5" Royales, Syd Nathan changed the name of another group on his talent roster to avoid confusion; thus, the Royals became the Midnighters. The group's first recording under its new name, "Work with Me Annie" (1954) launched the erotic Annie series that rocked the gospel world to its foundations and shocked the rest of the nation in the process.

The Midnighters' lead singer, Hank Ballard, who had been heavily influenced by gospel as a boy, imbued the song with all the suggestiveness its title implied. If there was any doubt about the sexual connotation of the verb *work,* it was more than laid to rest in the two follow-up songs, "Sexy Ways" and "Annie Had a Baby," also released in 1954. All three were heavily censored, and all three were million sellers. "Work with Me Annie" was cited by at least one observer as "the Negro national anthem for 1954" because of its immense popularity.[45] The success of the trilogy spurred a number of decreasingly successful answer songs. The Midnighters themselves followed up with "Annie's Aunt Fanny," which fell flat. The El Dorados cut "Annie's Answer" for Vee Jay, which also fell flat. Even Buddy Holly recorded an Annie song called "Midnight Shift," which never went anywhere. A final bomb was offered by the Midnights (not to be confused with the Midnighters), who made "Annie Pulled a Humbug." There was, however, one answer song that was incredibly popular, Etta James' "Wallflower" (1955), popularly known as "Roll with Me Henry" (a reference to Hank Ballard). The song was so similar to the original "Work with Me Annie" that Ballard was credited as a co-writer along with Johnny Otis and Etta James. When pop singer Georgia Gibbs tried to eliminate all traces of James' eroticism for the mainstream audience by redoing the song as "Dance with Me Henry," Ballard and the Midnighters responded with "Henry's Got Flat Feet (Can't Dance No More)," which effectively ended the two-year affair.

Doo Wop: The Intersection of Gospel, Jazz, and Pop

To the average listener, the gospel-oriented vocal groups were virtually indistinguishable from those groups that employed a style of rock 'n' roll that came to be known as *doo wop.* Doo wop was the product of urban vocal harmony groups, mostly black and almost invariably male. The style owed as much of a debt to gospel, jazz, and pop as it did to the blues. Typical of the genre was a melodramatic, often gospel-inflected lead tenor who was bracketed by a distinctive bass and a soaring falsetto. Background vocals typically consisted of nonsense syllables, such as "Sha-na-na-na sha-na-na-na-na," "Buzz-buzz-a-doodle-lee," "Shoo-doo-shoo-bee-doo," or "Oodly-pop-a-cow pop-a-cow pop-a-cow cow" (or however you choose to spell these syllables). "Doo" and "wop" were the syllables used to name the style, but not until well after the fact. In terms of output, doo wop was the largest single subgenre of rock 'n' roll to come into existence, and according to Greil Marcus, "it was the first form of rock & roll to take shape, to define itself as something people recognized as new, different, strange, *theirs.*"[46] Doo wop came from just about every region in the country. While there were a few dozen groups that dominated the genre, hundreds more were destined only for obscurity. Among these were countless "bird groups" (the Ravens, the Orioles, the Larks, the Robins, the Swallows, the Flamingos, the Crows, the Cardinals, the Falcons, the Penguins, the Pelicans, the Jayhawks, and stretching the concept, the Feathers) and a slightly lesser number of "car groups" (the Cadillacs, the El Dorados, the Fleetwoods, the Continentals, the Impalas, the Imperials, even the Edsels).

Doo wop was the product of urban vocal harmony groups, mostly black and almost invariably male. The style owed as much of a debt to gospel, jazz, and pop as it did to the blues.

In addition to its gospel roots, doo wop had roots in two black pop/jazz vocal harmony groups that had achieved mainstream success in the 1930s and 1940s—the Mills Brothers and, to an even greater degree, the Ink Spots, who turned out nearly fifty hits for Decca between 1939 and 1951. Both groups utilized close barbershop harmonies and light rhythms. The Ink Spots' "If I Didn't Care" and "My Prayer" (1939), featuring lead singer Bill Kenny's high tenor and "Hoppy" Jones' talking bass, are, by almost any measure, proto doo wop.

In the late 1940s, a number of young black groups—among them, the Ravens, the Four Tunes, the Four Knights, and the Orioles—tried to emulate, with some innovations and varying degrees of success, the style of these artists. The Ravens pioneered the use of the bass lead, reportedly by accident (the nervous bass vocalist, Jimmy Ricks, came in too strong on "My Sugar Is So Refined" during an appearance at the Apollo). The Ravens then repeated the "mistake" on a recording of "Old Man River" (1946), which sold 2 million copies. Over the next several years, the group turned out a string of r&b hits, including "I Don't Have to Ride No More" (1950) for National and "Rock Me All Night Long" (1952) for Mercury, both of which achieved Top Ten r&b status.

Shortly after the Ravens' recording of "Old Man River," the Vibranaires came to the attention of Deborah Chessler, an astute manager-songwriter in Baltimore, Maryland. The group and its manager were truly unique in a number of ways. As Greil Marcus has said, "They made their piece of history—a young Jewish woman and five black men in an utterly segregated American city. . . . Together they found the new sound."[47] After a booking on Arthur Godfrey's talent show in 1948, Chessler took a demo of the group to Jerry Blaine, a former bandleader who had recently founded Jubilee Records. Blaine was clearly moved; he renamed the group the Orioles and fashioned a special subsidary label for them called It's a Natural. The group's very first recording—"It's Too Soon to Know," a Chessler tune that went Top Ten r&b in 1948— was Marcus' "new sound." Indeed, Marcus has suggested that this recording is a contender for "first rock 'n' roll record."

One pattern that is noticeable immediately in doo wop is the dazzling array of "one hit wonders," groups that disappeared after only one pop hit. There were also a significant number of doo wop groups that had just two pop hits before they were relegated to the revival circuit. This pattern is undoubtedly more a function of the treatment of these artists by their record companies than a statement about the talent of the musicians. Other groups, for example, the Harptones ("Sunday Kind of Love" [1953, Bruce], "Life Is but a Dream" [1954, Paradise], and "What Will I Tell My Heart?" [1961, Companion]) simply bounced from label to label before fading from the scene. The most interesting thing about these one- and two-hit groups is that, in many instances, they made the recordings that define the style. More than in any other genre, it was individual and unrelated records, rather than the special imprint of a particular artist or producer, that gave doo wop its overall character.

One pattern that is noticeable immediately in doo wop is the dazzling array of "one hit wonders," groups that disappear after only one pop hit.

If there was a centre for doo wop, it was definitely New York City. It has been said that Alan Freed had a particular affinity for vocal harmony groups, and perhaps this is why a greater number of groups and labels were based in and around New York than any other region. Herald/Ember, founded by Al Silver in 1952, generally recorded out-of-state talent, the Nutmegs and the Five Satins from Connecticut, and the Turbans and the Silhouettes from

"Sh'Boom"

Artist: The Chords

Music / Lyrics by James Keyes, Carl Feaster, Claude Feaster, Floyd McRae, and James Edwards

Label: Cat (1954)

"Sh'Boom" was an early doo-wop hit by a South Bronx group called The Chords: Jimmy Keyes, Carl Feaster, Claude Feaster, Floyd "Buddy" McRae, and Ricky Edwards, who supposedly wrote the song together while sitting in a Cadillac convertible.

In his book *A History of Rock Music: The Rock and Roll Era*, Glenn Gass (1994, 58) notes that many record company executives in the 1950s believed that the *song* is what sold and not the singer(s) or the particular performance. This belief fueled the unfortunate practice of re-recording an African American group's r&b hit with a new version by a white vocal group that would have been, in the 1950s, more attractive to white teenage listeners, the major market for this music.

The Chords' "Sh'Boom" is a famous and oft-cited example of this phenomenon. After reaching number five on the pop charts, it was trounced by a cover version that a white Toronto group called the Crew Cuts recorded for Mercury. But the story of "Sh'Boom" is actually a bit more complex. Ironically, the Chords' version had originally been the "B" side of a single, the "A" side of which was a cover of Patti Page's tune "Cross over the Bridge." Disc jockeys preferred "Sh'Boom," which became a huge hit. Patti Page's label, Mercury, then released the Crew Cuts' watered-down but highly successful version of "Sh'Boom," whereupon Atlantic, the parent label of Cat, re-released the Chords' "Sh'Boom" with a different flip side, dumping the Patti Page cover. The bottom line? The Chords still lost out; "Sh'Boom" was their only big hit. It has, however, become a beloved classic of the early doo-wop era.

Musical Style Notes

Like many doo-wop songs, the structure of "Sh'Boom" is loosely based on the tried-and-true template of verse-verse-bridge-verse: two initial verses both sung to the same melody, followed by a "bridge" section with a new melody, which then leads back into another verse with the original melody. This AABA form, as it's sometimes called, is one of the most common popular song forms, from Tin Pan Alley to doo wop to Beatles songs. However, the Chords vary it somewhat, adding short verses in which singer Carl Feaster "scats" (sings on nonsense syllables—a term taken from jazz), leading into a repetition of the "Life could be a dream" lyric. There is also an instrumental break over the chords of the verse, with a sax solo by Sam Taylor in the great, gritty r&b style sometimes called "dirty sax."

Musical "Road Map"

TIMINGS	COMMENTS	LYRICS
0:00–0:04	A cappella voices begin in harmony.	*Life could be a dream . . .*
0:04–0:08	Instruments enter.	*doo doot doot doot sh'boom . . .*
0:08–0:23	Verse 1 Background vocals add nonsense syllables, "Sh'boom."	*Life could be a dream . . .* *if I could take you . . .*
0:23–0:29	Singer Carl Feaster "scats" (sings on nonsense syllables).	
0:29–0:44	Verse 2	*Life could be a dream . . .* *if only all my precious plans . . .*
0:44–0:58	"Bridge" section; different melody, sung by bass Rocky Edwards; guitar plays fills; background vocals on "ahh."	*Every time I look at you . . .*
0:58–1:12	Verse 3 All voices sing lyrics in harmony.	*Life could be a dream . . .* *sh'boom if I could . . .*
1:12–1:22 1:18	Singer Carl Feaster "scats"; background harmonies. All sing.	*Life could be a dream; life could be a dream, sweetheart*
1:22–1:53	Sam Taylor plays sax solo over the chords of the verse, twice through.	
1:53–2:08	Verse 3 repeats, beginning with unison "wooooo. . . . " All voices sing lyrics in harmony.	*Life could be a dream . . .* *sh'boom if I could . . .*
2:08–2:26	Singer Carl Feaster "scats"; background harmonies. Vocals reenter.	*Life could be a dream; life could be a dream—doo, doot doot doot sh'boom.*

Pennsylvania. On the other hand, beginning in 1952, Rama's founder, George Goldner, tended to recruit directly from New York's streets. After his initial success with the Crows, he launched a subsidiary, Gee (named after the Crows' only hit), which had hits with the Mello-Tones, the Cleftones, and Frankie Lymon and the Teenagers ("Why Do Fools Fall in Love" and "I Want You to Be My Girl" in 1956 and "Goody Goody" in 1957). In 1957, Goldner formed two other labels, Gone and End, that listed Alan Freed as producer. It was Freed who changed the name of the Chesters to Little Anthony and the Imperials. The group's "Tears on My Pillow" (1958) became a Top Ten pop hit on the End label. The group reformed in the mid-1960s and scored two more Top Ten hits on the DCP label—"Goin' Out of My Head" (1964) and "Hurts So Bad" (1965).

The label that had the most luck with vocal harmony groups was Atlantic. The company's first successful group was the Clovers from Washington, D.C. From 1951 to 1954, the group had thirteen consecutive Top Ten r&b hits, including "Don't You Know I Love You" and "Fool, Fool, Fool" (written by Ahmet Ertegun), "One Mint Julep," "Ting-a-Ling," and the original rock 'n' roll versions of "Blue Velvet" and "Devil or Angel," which were later pop hits for Bobby Vinton and Bobby Vee, respectively. The group's first pop hit was "Love, Love, Love" (1956). Its last was "Love Potion No. 9" (1959), a rock 'n' roll classic that was written and produced by Jerry Leiber and Mike Stoller for United Artists after the group had left Atlantic.

The writer/producer team of Leiber and Stoller achieved greatness with two other of Atlantic's vocal groups—the Coasters and the Drifters. The Coasters had begun in Los Angeles as the Robins and had recorded as such with Johnny Otis on Savoy in New Jersey. The group's

The Chords were among the many "one hit wonders" who defined doo wop. Their "Sh'Boom" combines the jazz, pop, and r&b influences of the style and remains one of the most memorable songs of the rock 'n' roll era.

"Double Crossing Blues" (1950) was a number one r&b hit. Although Leiber and Stoller, who were also originally from Los Angeles, had had their first songwriting successes with Charles Brown ("Hard Times") and Big Mama Thornton ("Hound Dog"), when they met the Robins, they chose the group as the vehicle for their novelty r&b songs ("playlets" as Leiber used to call them) on their new Spark label. Atlantic was sufficiently impressed with such songs as "Smokey Joe's Cafe" and "Riot in Cell Block No. 9" that the company bought the Robins' catalogue from Spark, signed the group to its Atco subsidiary, and hired Leiber and Stoller as independent producers (among the first in the business). Once signed to the New York label, the group changed its name to the Coasters to reflect its West Coast origins. The first six releases—"Searchin'" and "Young Blood" (1957), "Yakety Yak" (1958), and "Charlie Brown," "Along Came Jones," and "Poison Ivy" (1959), all playlets written and produced by Leiber and Stoller and punctuated instrumentally by the "yakety sax" of King Curtis—made the pop Top Ten. The Coasters remained major hitmakers until 1961. Another Los Angeles group, the Olympics, came close to duplicating the Coasters' sound with such hits as "Western Movies" (1958, Demon) and "Big Boy Pete" (1960, Arvee).

After the original Drifters broke up, the group's manager, George Treadwell, who owned the name and had years remaining on contracts with the Apollo Theatre and Atlantic Records, persuaded another group that was known as the Five Crowns and featured Ben E. King on lead to take on the name. Produced by Leiber and Stoller, the new Drifters had immediate success with such hits as "There Goes My Baby" and "Dance with Me" in 1959 and "This Magic Moment" and "Save the Last Dance for Me" in 1960. When King left the group in 1960, he was replaced by the gospel-trained Rudy Lewis, who sang lead on "Up on the Roof" (1962) and "On Broadway" (1963). Lewis would have sung lead on "Under the Boardwalk" (1964), had he not died on the morning of the recording session. The emotionality of the group's performance at that session may well have had something to do with the intensity of the moment. The productions of Leiber and Stoller were so elaborate—often involving dozens of takes and significant editing to achieve the desired effect—that they must be seen as the start of the transition from the innocence and spontaneity (and amateurishness) of classic doo wop to the calculated products of the producer as an artist in his own right. It is this difference that separates the doo wop groups from the vocal harmony groups (chiefly, the "girl groups") of the 1960s.

New York, of course, was not the only place that produced doo wop, even during its formative stages. Both the Spaniels ("Baby It's You," 1953) and the Flamingos ("Golden Teardrops," 1953) started their recording careers with Chance Records in Chicago. The Spaniels then moved to Vee Jay, where they recorded their biggest hit, "Goodnight, It's Time to Go," in 1954. Vee Jay also had the El Dorados, a group that scored with "At My Front Door" one year later. The Flamingos also broke through to the pop market on the End label with "Lovers Never Say Goodbye" in 1957. The group's biggest hits came at the end of the decade with "I Only Have Eyes for You" (1959) and "Nobody Loves Me Like You" (1960). Chicago's Chess label had the Moonglows, a group founded in Cleveland by Harvey Fuqua in 1951. The group scored three Top Thirty hits—"Sincerely" (1955), "See Saw" (1956), and "Ten Commandments of Love" (1958)—for Chess in the classic doo wop mould before Fuqua became immersed in Berry Gordy's Motown empire as a writer/producer.

Under the tutelage of producers Leiber and Stoller, the Drifters took the vocal harmonies of doo wop to new heights and provided a gateway to the more produced r&b sounds of the early 1960s.

In Cincinnati, King Records also tried to exploit the doo wop sound. In addition to the rhythm and gospel groups on its Federal subsidiary, King had the Charms ("Gum Drop" and "Hearts of Stone," 1954, "Ling Ting Tong," 1955, and "Ivory Tower," 1956) on the company's De Luxe label, which Syd Nathan had purchased from a New Jersey firm in 1953. Unfortunately for King, the company lost the group that went on to become the most success-ful of all the vocal harmony singers—the Platters. Originally signed to Federal, the group was often used as backup for some of the other acts. When Buck Ram, the group's coach and man-ager, insisted on $100 a session for background vocals, however, Nathan released them. Ram, who also managed the Penguins, negotiated a near impossible contract that signed both groups to Mercury, a major label, in 1955. The Penguins died without a follow-up to "Earth Angel," but the Platters scored twenty Top Forty pop hits over the next seven years.

The Platters' first two releases for Mercury were Ram tunes: "Only You" went to number five in 1955 and "The Great Pretender" hit number one in 1956. It was the Platters, more than any other group, who carried the torch that had been lit by the Ink Spots two decades earlier. "My Prayer," a number one pop hit in 1956, was a virtual remake of the Ink Spots' 1939 origi-nal. Tony Williams' lead vocal paid homage to that of Bill Kenny before him. The Platters mined the past for other material as well. "Twilight Time," a number one hit in 1958, had been co-written by Ram in 1938 for a group called the Three Suns. In 1958, the Platters also went to number one with Jerome Kern's "Smoke Gets in Your Eyes." "Harbor Lights" (1960), the group's last Top Ten hit, had been first popularized by Rudy Vallee in 1937. The Platters actually sounded more pop than doo wop. Still, their music was accepted as rock 'n' roll.

Most of the doo wop groups were black. They were joined by a lesser number of white or integrated groups. Among the white doo wop groups, Italian Americans predominated.[48] The most popular Italian American doo wop group came from Belmont Avenue in the Bronx. Thus, they called themselves Dion (DiMucci) and the Belmonts. Performed in classic doo wop style, nonsense syllables and all, "I Wonder Why," the group's first of many releases on Laurie, became a Top Twenty pop hit in 1958. "A Teenager in Love" and "Where or When," the Rodgers and Hart classic, made the Top Ten in 1959 and 1960, respectively. In 1960, Dion left the group to pursue a solo career. By 1963, the handsome tenor had acquired thirteen Top Forty pop hits, a new wife (the inspiration for "Runaround Sue," recorded with the uncredited Del-Satins), and a drug problem that forced him out of the business for the next five years. The Belmonts had two more hits—"Tell Me Why" (1961) and "Come On Little Angel" (1962)—then faded from view.

Most of the doo wop groups were black. Among the white doo wop groups, Italian Americans predominated.

The Dell-Vikings, who met in the service, were the first racially integrated doo wop group (three black singers and two white in the group's original incarnation) to hit the pop charts. "Come Go with Me" and "Whispering Bells" both entered the Top Ten in 1957. The group then switched from Dot to Mercury and turned out a number of lesser-known hits. Frankie Lymon and the Teenagers were identified as a black group, but with Puerto Rican backup singer Herman Santiago, they represented a different kind of integration. Johnny Maestro and the Crests included an Italian American lead (John Mastrangelo), two African Americans (Tommy Gough and Jay Carter), and a Latino (Harold Torres). Honing their craft on the Lexington Avenue subway in New York, the Crests came to the attention of Coed Records, for which the group recorded five Top Thirty hits. The best was the first—"Sixteen Candles" in 1958. When the Crests faded, Johnny Maestro disappeared onto the supper club circuit with the Del-Satins, a group that merged with a show band called the Rhythm Method in the 1960s to produce a new group, the Brooklyn Bridge ("The Worst Thing That Could Happen," 1967), with Maestro singing lead.

Second in rarity to racial integration was gender balance.[49] Certainly, in 1956, Trudy Williams' lead on the Six Teens' "A Casual Look" was a rare occurrence. Female leads were repeated by Margo Sylvia of the Tune Weavers on "Happy, Happy Birthday Baby" in 1957, Barbara Lee on the Aquatones' "You" in 1958, and in 1960 by Kathy Young with the Innocents on "A Thousand Stars."

All-female groups, in the heyday of doo wop, were even fewer. Among the best were the Teen Queens ("Eddie My Love," 1956), the Bobbettes ("Mr. Lee," 1957), the Shepherd Sisters ("Alone," 1957), the Poni-Tails ("Born Too Late," 1958), the Quintones ("Down the Aisle of Love," 1958), and the Chantels ("Maybe," 1958). In some ways, especially in the way their songs defined male-female relationships, these groups prefigured the arrival of the early 1960s "girl groups." Interestingly, the producer most associated with the "girl group" phenomenon, Phil Spector, who was also an assistant to Leiber and Stoller, got his first big break as part of a vocal trio with a female lead, the Teddy Bears. "To Know Him Is to Love Him," a song Spector fashioned from the inscription on his father's tombstone, featured Annette Kleinbard's lead and went to number one in 1958. Spector duplicated the soothing vocal sound with the Paris Sisters ("I Love How You Love Me") in 1961 before his production style became completely devoted to his legendary "wall of sound." The Fleetwoods, a trio composed of one man and two women, moved vocal harmony groups further away from doo wop style. Still, their soft, elegant harmonies on "Come Softly to Me" and "Mr. Blue" in 1959, and "Tragedy" in 1961, were built around an almost seamless male-female blend.

Doo wop singing was also popular in Canadian cities such as Toronto and Ottawa. The Four Lads, consisting of Bernie Toorish (lead tenor), Jimmie Arnold (second tenor), Frankie Busseri (baritone), and Connie Coldarini (bass), started out singing in the choir at St. Michael's Cathedral in Toronto. After working local hotels and clubs, the group was signed in 1950 by Columbia Records in New York, where they were employed singing backup on numerous sessions, including Johnnie Ray's impassioned 1951 chart topper, "Cry" (cited by many as a candidate for the first rock 'n' roll record). Beginning in 1952, the Four Lads began recording as artists in their own right, placing twenty-eight records on the *Billboard* pop charts between 1952 and 1959. Seven of those, "Skokiaan," "Moments to Remember," "No, Not Much," "Standing on the Corner" (from the Broadway musical *The Most Happy Fella*), "Who Needs You," "Put a Light in the Window," and "There's Only One of You," reached the Top Ten.

The Crew-Cuts also hailed from Toronto. Formed in 1952 by brothers John (lead tenor) and Ray Perkins (bass), Pat Barrett (second tenor), and Rudy Maugeri (baritone), the group was signed to Mercury in Chicago. They initially found success with their 1954 cover of the Chords' "Sh'Boom." By removing the bass vocal lead in the bridge, replacing the gritty tenor sax solo of the original with a sixteen-bar section consisting of the group repeating a two-bar vocable riff, and omitting the bluesy guitar fills of the original, the Crew-Cuts largely succeeded

Dion and the Belmonts were one of the first white groups to pick up the torch of doo wop and carry it beyond the 1950s. Italian Americans all, they were true to the style and a testament to the hybridity of the music.

in removing the most overt rhythm and blues elements of the song. In the process, they also eliminated the sonic elements that at the time would have signified a heightened level of sexuality, thereby making the song "safer" and more readily accessible to mainstream white audiences in Canada and the United States. Backed by the Dave Carroll Orchestra, the resulting record enjoyed massive success, staying at the top of the pop charts for a total of nine weeks in the summer of 1954. The Crew-Cuts' recording was also a hit in the United Kingdom and was far and away the biggest pop song of the year. Over the next few years, the Crew-Cuts continued apace, charting with covers of "Earth Angel," by the Penguins, "Ko Ko Mo (I Love You So)," by Gene and Eunice, "Chop Chop Boom," by the Danderliers, "A Story Untold," by the Nutmegs, and "Gum Drop," by Otis Williams. By mid-1957, the cover era was long past and the Crew-Cuts' career as hitmakers had come to an end.

The other successful Canadian doo wop group, the Diamonds, was formed in Toronto in 1953. Original members Dave Somerville (lead tenor), Ted Kowalski (second tenor), Phil Leavitt (baritone), and Bill Reed (bass) signed first with Coral in 1955 before joining the Crew-Cuts on Mercury in 1956. Between 1956 and 1961, the group placed sixteen records on the *Billboard* pop charts. As was the case with the Crew-Cuts, a majority of the Diamonds' most successful recordings were covers of American rhythm and blues recordings. In 1957, they reached number two with their cover of the Gladiolas' "Little Darlin'." Other chart hits included their covers of Frankie Lymon and the Teenagers' "Why Do Fools Fall in Love," the Willows' "Church Bells May Ring," and the Rays' "Silhouettes." In early 1958, the Diamonds reached number four with one of the biggest dance records of the era, "The Stroll."

Doo wop was a phenomenon of the 1950s that spilled over somewhat into the next decade.[50] The Four Seasons, for example, could trace their musical roots to doo wop. Beginning as the Four Lovers in Newark in 1956, the group scored a minor hit with "You're the Apple of My Eye" that same year. As the Four Seasons, the group's first single was "Sherry" (1962). A number one pop hit for Vee Jay, "Sherry" received significant airplay on black radio before a live appearance on *American Bandstand* revealed a white Italian American vocal harmony group. Even so, the group, which featured the three-octave range of lead singer Frankie Valli (born Francis Castelluccio), turned out twenty-nine chart singles over the next fifteen years in addition to Valli's nine solo hits. Still, as a phenomenon, doo wop was over in 1961. As if to signal the end of the era, Little Caesar and the Romans released "Those Oldies but Goodies" that same year. The song went to number nine on the pop charts, and the designation "oldies but goodies" was immediately applied to songs that had been released in the previous decade, including some that had been hits a year earlier.

Rockabilly: The Country Strain

It was, of course, only a matter of time until some young entrepreneur figured out, after the initial surge of rock 'n' roll, that white artists who could merge r&b and c&w with credibility would have enormous sales potential. The person who is usually credited with this discovery is Sam Phillips, who founded Sun Records in Memphis, Tennessee, in 1953. According to Marion Keisker, Phillips' secretary, Phillips once said, "If I could find a white man who had the Negro

It was only a matter of time until some young entrepreneur figured out that white artists who could merge r&b and c&w with credibility would have enormous sales potential.

sound and the Negro feel, I could make a billion dollars."[51] The answer to his prayers was, needless to say, Elvis Presley, the man who was crowned the "King of Rock 'n' Roll." The rest, as rock 'n' roll lore would have it, is history—or at least a serviceable version of it.

In fact, Presley was not the first major white rock 'n' roll artist to reach the mainstream market with a fusion of r&b and c&w. That distinction belongs to Bill Haley and His Comets. Haley is often separated from Presley in the history of rock 'n' roll because of differences in musical style and public image. The music that Presley and the Sun artists who followed him played was called rockabilly after its amalgam of rocking African American and so-called hill-billy styles. According to Charlie Gillett, rockabilly differs from Haley's fusion in that it has "much looser rhythms, no saxophones, nor any chorus singing."[52] Haley's music, in contrast, sounds more arranged, more calculated. Haley related to his country roots through the instrumentation of a western swing combo; Presley's early Sun sides did not even include drums. If such musical differences are significant, the differences between Haley's public persona and that of the rockabilly artists are even more so.

In the mythology of rockabilly, there is always something appealing about white southern performers, roughly the same age as their fans, who record with pronounced regional accents for independent labels. Presley was the archetype even after he no longer fit the image. Bill Haley's celebrity was quite different. Already balding and looking somewhat middle-aged by the time his career took off, he was, in fact, a most unlikely candidate to become a rock 'n' roll sensation. Born in Highland Park, Michigan, and singing with no distinguishable regional accent, Haley's celebrity as a rock 'n' roller seems all the more unlikely in that he was signed by a major label, Decca, and his best-selling record, "Rock Around the Clock," was written by two Tin Pan Alley veterans (Max Freedman and Jimmy DeKnight) who registered the song with ASCAP.

Haley and his group, however, were clearly open to a variety of influences. Indeed, they experimented with various styles for ten years before coming to the attention of the mainstream public, and Haley once described his early sound as "a combination of country and western, Dixieland, and the old style rhythm and blues."[53] His heroes were Bob Wills and His Texas Playboys, who played western swing, and Haley's band approximated the pivotal sound of Louis Jordan. Haley's producer, Milt Gabler (who had been Jordan's producer in the 1940s), told Arnold Shaw that he had consciously modeled Haley's sound after Jordan's jump beat. "We'd begin with Jordan's shuffle rhythm," said Gabler. "You know, dotted eighth notes and sixteenths, and we'd build on it. I'd sing Jordan riffs to the group that would be picked up by the electric guitars and tenor sax. . . . They got a sound that had the drive of The Tympany Five and the color of country and western."[54]

In the early 1950s, Haley decided that r&b-flavoured dance music was the key to his future. He did well with his own versions of Jackie Brenston's "Rocket 88" and "Rock the Joint" by Jimmy Preston. It was just after his "Crazy Man Crazy" hit number fifteen on the pop charts in 1953 that he signed with Decca. There, with Gabler as his producer, he enjoyed his biggest hits, including "Dim, Dim the Lights" (1954), "Burn That Candle" (1955), and "See You Later, Alligator" (1956). With its lyrics cleaned up, his 1954 version of Big Joe Turner's "Shake,

Rattle, and Roll" became a classic rock 'n' roll recording and his first million seller. "Mambo Rock," a Top Twenty hit in 1955, was Haley's nod to the Latin dance craze that was then sweeping the nation.

Although it may now seem strange, when Haley's "Rock Around the Clock" was first released in 1954, it fizzled. Because of its Tin Pan Alley parentage, however, the song was selected as the theme for the Hollywood film *Blackboard Jungle*.[55] Within weeks of the film's release in 1955, the song went to number one on the pop charts. It remained there for the next eight weeks, eventually becoming one of the biggest-selling rock 'n' roll records in history, with sales of nearly 17 million copies. By the time Elvis Presley hit the pop charts, more than a year after "Rock Around the Clock" was first released, Haley was in his thirties and over the hill by teenage standards. His star was soon supplanted by the younger rockabilly artists from Memphis—Carl Perkins, Johnny Cash, Jerry Lee Lewis, and, of course, Presley himself.

Sam Phillips, the man who brought all these artists to the attention of the record-buying public, had a definite strategy in mind when he launched their careers. While Syd Nathan at King Records encouraged blues and country artists to record each other's songs, Nathan expected his country artists to record country versions of r&b hits and vice versa. He was not trying to break down racial barriers; he did not care if his white artists had "the Negro sound and the Negro feel" any more than he expected his African American artists to sound "country" (although some of this did happen). He was simply trying to maximize his income. Phillips, on the other hand, may have been just as economically motivated, but he

Sam Phillips deliberately sought to filter the black experience through white performers, thus making it more accessible to the mainstream audience.

Bill Haley and His Comets drew their inspiration from sources as disparate as Bob Wills and the Texas Playboys and Louis Jordan and The Tympany Five in constructing their country/r&b fusion. Adding outrageous stage antics to the mix, they earned a memorable niche in rock 'n' roll history.

deliberately sought to filter the black experience through white performers, thus making it more accessible to the mainstream audience. As Peter Guralnick has noted, "With Elvis, Phillips apparently found the key because following Elvis' success he had a succession of rockabillies who did just that. All of his major artists were poor whites who had not only lived in constant contact with black people all their lives but had obviously absorbed a great deal of their culture."[56] Phillips' strategy earned Sun Records a place of mythic proportions in the history of rock 'n' roll, but it also raises all sorts of questions about rip-offs and racism.

Phillips was a former radio engineer who got into the recording business when he started the Memphis Recording Service in 1950. For $2 a side, anyone could walk in and make a record. It did not take Phillips long to realize that he had the only convenient studio around for the Delta bluesmen who played the nearby Beale Street clubs. In the days when Leonard and Phil Chess from Chicago and Saul and Jules Bihari, the founders of Modern/RPM in Los Angeles, were scouring the South with portable machines in search of new talent, Phillips was already recording Howlin' Wolf, B. B. King, Bobby Bland, James Cotton, Little Walter, Little Junior Parker, Elmore James, Walter Horton, and Rufus Thomas, among others. At first, he leased all his masters to Modern and Chess. But after producing such notable r&b hits as Jackie Brenston's "Rocket 88" for Chess, he decided to launch a full-fledged record label of his own—Sun Records. In its beginnings in 1952, Sun was heavily invested in rhythm and blues releases. The label's first r&b hit was Rufus Thomas' "Bear Cat" (1953), the answer song to Big Mama Thornton's "Hound Dog," which went to number three on the r&b charts and occasioned a lawsuit for an infringement of the "Hound Dog" copyright. That same year, a young truck driver whose family had moved to Memphis from Tupelo, Mississippi, stopped in at the Memphis Recording Service and paid $4 to cut two songs. The truck driver was Elvis Presley, and a little more than a year later he would profoundly alter the operations of Sun Records and change the face of popular music forever. "When Elvis and Carl Perkins and Johnny Cash come along," Rufus Thomas once said, "just like he catered to black, Phillips cut it off and went to white. No more blacks did he pick up at all."[57]

Most of the white artists who gravitated toward Sun had grown up dirt poor and in close proximity to African Americans and their culture. Jerry Lee Lewis once explained how he

> used to hang around Haney's Big House, that was a colored establishment where they had dances and such. . . . we was just kids, we wasn't allowed in. So we'd slip around to the back and sneak in whenever we could. I saw a lot of 'em there, all those blues players. No, it wasn't anything about us being white, we was just too young. . . . it wasn't no big thing just because it was a colored place. Of course we was about the only ones down there.[58]

Carl Perkins explained his background by noting that he had been

> raised on a plantation in the flatlands of Lake Country, Tennessee, and we were about the only white people on it. I played with coloured kids, played football with socks stuffed with sand. Working in the cotton fields in the sun, music was the only escape. The coloured people would sing, and I'd join in, just a little kid, and that was coloured rhythm and blues, got named rock 'n' roll, got named that in 1956, but the same music was there years before, and it was my music.[59]

Elvis Aron Presley was born on January 8, 1935, the only child (a twin brother was born dead) of poor, white Mississippi parents Vernon and Gladys Presley. When he was ten years old, he placed fifth in a talent contest, singing "Old Shep," a sentimental country tune. He learned to play the guitar a year later when he received one as a birthday present. As a teenager in Memphis, Presley attended Pentecostal church services and, in a more secular vein, got turned on to the Delta bluesmen.

> *I'd play along with the radio or phonograph, and taught myself the chord positions. We were a religious family, going round together to sing at camp meetings and revivals, and I'd take my guitar with us when I could. I also dug the real low-down Mississippi singers, mostly Big Bill Broonzy and Big Boy Crudup, although they would scold me at home for listening to them.*
> *"Sinful music," the townsfolk in Memphis said it was. Which never bothered me, I guess.*[60]

It took Phillips more than a year to record Presley commercially, and there are at least two stories about the singer's first recording session for Sun. According to one, Phillips originally intended to work on a couple of sentimental ballads like the ones Presley had cut for his mother's birthday. When nothing gelled, Presley and session men Scotty Moore (guitar) and Bill Black (bass) started fooling around with Big Boy Crudup's "That's All Right." According to Presley, however, "That's All Right" was one of the songs Phillips had suggested. Either way, backed with Bill Monroe's classic bluegrass tune this song, "Blue Moon of Kentucky," set in motion a chain reaction that ultimately transformed the pop landscape. Within a day or so, a dub of the recording was sent to Dewey Phillips (no relation to Sam), a Memphis deejay, who liked it so much that he played it thirty times in one night. By the time Sam Phillips had the record pressed, he had orders for 5,000 copies.

From the beginning, Presley presented a marketing dilemma. No one knew exactly what to make of this "hillbilly cat," as he was described by one early billing that managed to capture the tension of his down-home yet wildly cool persona. "I recall one jockey telling me that Elvis was so country he shouldn't be played after 5 A.M.," said Sam Phillips. "And others said he was too black for them."[61] When Dewey Phillips interviewed Presley on the air, he made it a point to establish that the singer had attended the all-white Humes High School "because a lot of people listening had thought he was colored."[62] Though Presley's first release combined r&b and c&w (as did all his subsequent Sun releases), he was marketed as country. The record, which was a local hit, appeared only on the Memphis c&w charts.

The professional reaction to Presley's unorthodox style was mixed. After his debut at the *Grand Ole Opry,* he was told to go back to truck driving. He had better luck at the *Louisiana Hayride,* where he became a regular. Invariably, his live performances were electrifying, as country singer Bob Luman recalled.

> *This cat came out in red pants and a green coat and a pink shirt and socks, and had this sneer on his face and he stood behind the mike for five minutes, I'll bet, before he made a move. Then he hit his guitar a lick, and he broke two strings. I'd been playing ten years, and I hadn't broken a total of two strings. So there he was, these two strings dangling, and he hadn't done anything yet, and these high school girls were screaming and fainting and running up to the stage, and then he started to move his hips real slow like he had a thing for his guitar. That was Elvis Presley when he was about 19, playing Kilgore, Texas.*[63]

Presley recorded a total of ten sides for Sun. Each of the five records had an r&b song backed with a c&w song:

"That's All Right"/"Blue Moon of Kentucky" (1954)

"Good Rockin' Tonight"/"I Don't Care If the Sun Don't Shine" (1954)

"Milkcow Blues Boogie"/"You're a Heartbreaker" (1955)

"Baby Let's Play House"/"I'm Left, You're Right, She's Gone" (1955)

"Mystery Train"/"I Forgot to Remember to Forget" (1955)

In their innocence and seeming spontaneity, these recordings contributed measurably to the construction of the Presley legend, and in their unique blend of cultural influences, they contributed to the definition of the rockabilly style. Still, although each record sold better than the one before it, Presley never reached a mass popular music audience through them. It was not until the heavy-handed Colonel Tom Parker replaced deejay Bob Neal as Presley's manager in 1955 that a developing career was transformed into the stuff that myths are made of.

Parker engineered the sale of Presley's contract to RCA-Victor for the then–unheard of sum of $35,000 plus $5,000 in back royalties, which Presley used to purchase his fabled pink Cadillac. His first release for RCA, "Heartbreak Hotel" (1956), featuring Chet Atkins on guitar and Floyd Cramer on piano, went to number one on the pop charts and remained there for the next eight weeks. Later that same year, "Hound Dog"/"Don't Be Cruel," a double-sided hit, reached number one on the pop charts, the r&b charts, and the c&w charts simultaneously, perhaps the first record ever to do so.

It was not until the heavy-handed Colonel Tom Parker replaced deejay Bob Neal as Presley's manager in 1955 that a developing career was transformed into the stuff that myths are made of.

From that moment on, Elvis Presley enjoyed multiple Top Forty pop hits every year until he died. Parker's practice of allowing his star to record only songs with publishing rights assigned to Presley Music (BMI) or Gladys Music (ASCAP) restricted Presley's choice of material in later years but added significantly to his income. "When I first knew Elvis," Parker once said with pride, "he had a million dollars' worth of talent. Now he has a million dollars."[64] Under Parker's guidance, Presley's career options mushroomed to include records, TV appearances, movies, and finally a steady diet of Las Vegas club dates.

Following television appearances on the shows of Milton Berle, the Dorsey Brothers, and Steve Allen, and just weeks after Ed Sullivan had said he would never book Presley, Parker landed him a coveted $50,000 series of slots on Sullivan's show. Unlike other TV hosts, Sullivan tried to anticipate the objections of his family audience by ensuring that Presley would be filmed only from the waist up. However, mere cinematic censorship could not contain the popular appeal of "Elvis the Pelvis," as his detractors called him. Presley used one of his Sullivan appearances to debut the title song from his first film, *Love Me Tender*. The song became a number one pop hit and the film catapulted Presley to stardom in yet another medium.

While Presley's star would continue to rise as he became a pop idol, his influence as a seminal figure in the development of rock 'n' roll waned during his 1958 to 1960 stint in the army. Until that time, he had recorded some quality material and turned in more than a few memorable performances at RCA. After "Hound Dog," Leiber and Stoller were brought in to write "Don't" and "Jailhouse Rock," the title song for his third and probably best movie. Writer

"Hound Dog"

Artist: Elvis Presley

Music / Lyrics by Jerry Lieber & Mike Stoller
(possibly Big Mama Thornton)

Label: RCA (1956)

In 1953, Willie Mae "Big Mama" Thornton had a hit on the r&b charts with the song "Hound Dog," delivered with fearsome, gritty conviction by Thornton's huge voice, Johnny Otis' band, and Pete Lewis' smoking guitar work. The song was written by the well-known r&b songwriters Jerry Lieber and Mike Stoller (although both Otis and Thornton have claimed the actual songwriting credit). Sometime after that, Elvis Presley heard the song performed by a Las Vegas lounge musician named Freddie Bell. It was Bell's version, with its adapted lyrics, that Presley recorded for RCA in 1956 (as the "B" side of the single "Don't Be Cruel").

It was a common practice for white musicians to "cover" an African American musician's r&b hit, often replacing "suggestive" lyrics with more conservative fare that the major labels deemed more palatable for the white listening audience. (On Elvis's recording, the original lyrics, which were much more interesting and made more sense, are replaced with two verses that he alternates repeatedly throughout the song.) The financial success of white performers' versions of popular r&b tunes also frequently overshadowed the success of the original—an oft-repeated story in the history of American popular music, especially in the 1950s and 1960s. While it's said that Elvis consciously avoided covering r&b tunes that were still "on the charts," he recorded dozens of cover versions. After all, Elvis was not a songwriter, and his fame came from lending his own personal performance style to other people's music. "Hound Dog" was a huge hit for Elvis, staying at number one on the pop charts for eleven weeks in the summer of 1956.

Musical Style Notes

"Hound Dog" is a twelve-bar blues with the stepped-up tempo, slapping bass, and percussive, "twangy" guitar sound characteristic of the rockabilly style associated with Sun Records. However, Elvis had left Sun by the time he recorded "Hound Dog" and was now with RCA. With this change, we hear an important departure from Sun Records' rockabilly sound: the use of the drum set. Sam Phillips' early Sun recordings didn't emphasize drum-set percussion, but now, drummer D. J. Fontana is right up front in the mix, especially in the drum "roll" that you hear in the transition between verses. (You can also hear hand claps in the background during the sung verses.) Along with bass player Bill Black, the rhythm section provides a great foundation for the famous high-energy guitar solos Scotty Moore created for this track.

Musical "Road Map"

TIMINGS	COMMENTS	LYRICS
0:00–0:17	Verse 1 (twelve-bar blues form) As in Big Mama Thornton's original, Elvis starts singing a cappella (no instruments); the instruments come in on the downbeat at the words "hound dog." Note hand claps. Strong, foregrounded drum sound	*You ain't nothing but a hound dog, Cryin' all the time . . .* *You ain't never caught a rabbit—And you ain't no friend of mine.*
0:18–0:33	Verse 2	*When they said you was high classed, well, that was just a lie . . .*
0:34–0:50	Verse 1 repeats.	*You ain't nothing but a hound dog . . .*
0:50–1:06	Scotty Moore's guitar solo, over the verse form (Note background vocals singing "ah.")	
1:06–1:22	Verse 2 repeats. Hand claps return.	*When they said you was high classed . . .*
1:22–1:38	Another Scotty Moore guitar solo over verse form (Return of background vocals singing "ah")	
1:38–1:54	Verse 2 repeats. Hand claps return.	*When they said you was high classed . . .*
1:54–2:09	Verse 1 repeats.	*You ain't nothing but a hound dog . . .*
2:09–2:13	"Tag" (short phrase and final chord)	

By any measure, Elvis Presley—the rock 'n' roller who was crowned king—was a monster talent, albeit one who sometimes applied his considerable gifts to material that was of questionable value. He is pictured in a scene from Jailhouse Rock, *one of his better movies.*

Otis Blackwell followed up "Don't Be Cruel" with "All Shook Up" in 1957. In 1958, "One Night" (a cleaned-up version of "One Night of Sin," co-written by Dave Bartholomew for Smiley Lewis) came close to recapturing the excitement of his Sun recordings. At RCA, however, Presley's clear tenor, the stripped-down energy of early rockabilly, and the simplicity and straightforwardness of the Sun sound were overshadowed by vocal swoops from the higher to the lower register, bloated productions (supervised by Chet Atkins), and syrupy background choruses provided by the Jordanaires. This situation encouraged Presley to indulge the pop tendencies that had always been part of his musical aesthetic. After all, the blues and country aura of the Presley myth never adequately captured the range of styles that shaped the singer. The two songs he cut at the Memphis Recording Service in 1953 were "My Happiness" and "That's When Your Heartaches Begin," both stylized ballads that had been popular hits for the Ink Spots. At the time he made his first commercial recordings, his singing idol was Dean Martin. Following military service, Presley reentered popular music through a TV special with Frank Sinatra. His inclination toward pop conventions was already evident in his ardent gushing on "Love Me Tender," which was adapted from the folksong "Aura Lee." It emerged full-blown in a number of the releases he made after his military service, such as "Are You Lonesome Tonight," written in 1926, "Surrender," adapted from "Come Back to Sorrento," and his own reputed favourite, "It's Now or Never," a pop-oriented, Latin-flavoured number, based loosely on "O Sole Mio" by Mario Lanza, Presley's favourite opera star.

There has never been a career quite like that of Elvis Presley. All told, he charted 149 Top Forty hits on *Billboard*'s Hot 100 and 92 LPs on the album charts—all this with some of the most insipid material ever recorded. If he was able to infuse even his most middle-of-the-road recordings with some measure of exuberance, it did not come through in his films, which became increasingly more vacuous as the 1960s wore on. Indeed, Presley turned out some of the worst, although profitable, films imaginable. Still, the soundtrack albums, as shallow as they were, almost invariably entered the Top Forty. "The fact is, I think, that Elvis was too well suited to success," Peter Guralnick has said. "He was intelligent, adaptable, ambitious, and sure of his goals. . . . He soon settled in fact on a fairly comfortable and formulaic approach that took advantage of his wide-ranging musical background, facility in a number of styles, real talent as a quick study, and almost total lack of taste."[65] He briefly redeemed himself as the quintessential rock 'n' roller in a TV special taped in 1968. "If you're looking for trouble," sneered Elvis into the camera, completely outfitted in black leather and looking his greased-back best, "you've come to the right place." In addition to the obligatory big production numbers, he was joined on stage by such old musical friends as Scotty Moore and drummer D. J. Fontana. In those moments, he recaptured the "young Elvis" pictured on his 1992 memorial postage stamp.[66]

When Sam Phillips sold Presley's contract to RCA, he staunchly defended what, in retrospect, appears to have been a miscalculation of monumental proportions. At the time, Phillips needed the money to capitalize Sun properly, and he thought he had another artist waiting in the wings who would be bigger than Elvis. At first, it seemed that Carl Perkins, the son of a sharecropper, would not disappoint; his "Blue Suede Shoes" entered the *Billboard* pop charts on 10 March 1956, and climbed to number two, making it Sun's best-selling record to date. (It was followed immediately by "Heartbreak Hotel," Presley's debut release on RCA, the record that kept it from hitting pop number one.) "Blue Suede Shoes" is listed in Dawson and Propes' *What Was the First Rock 'n' Roll Record?* as a contender "because it kicked up dust in all markets. Occasionally an R&B or country record strayed onto the pop charts, and big pop songs often sloshed over into one of the specialized charts, but Perkins' little paean to fancy footwear was the first to capture them all."[67] It is this kind of cross-genre appeal that lands Perkins in the company of Jimmie Rodgers and Hank Williams.

Like Presley, Perkins was a poor white southerner whose musical influences crossed racial lines. At the top of Perkins' list of sources were the *Grand Ole Opry* and a black sharecropper named Uncle John Westbrook, who lived across the field from him. One of his early rockabilly recordings, "Gone, Gone, Gone," hinted at a fusion of blues and country. "That's what rockabilly music is," he once said, "a country man's song with a black man's rhythm."[68] With the success of "Blue Suede Shoes," it appeared as if Perkins might ride that formula to even greater heights than Presley, but just as he was about to take off commercially, he was nearly killed in a car crash on his way to New York for an appearance on Perry Como's show. Perkins never entered the Top Forty again, and his career never regained its momentum. Still, his influence on rock 'n' roll is undeniable. In 1964, the Beatles invited him to a recording session, where they recorded three of his songs—"Honey Don't," "Everybody's Trying to Be My Baby," and his adaptation of an old Blind Lemon Jefferson song, "Matchbox."

The rock 'n' roller who did the most to keep Sun operating in the black after Presley's departure and Perkins' misfortune was the uncontrollable Jerry Lee Lewis, who seemed to have a knack for revealing the underside of the fusion that made rockabilly. Typical of rockabillies, Lewis grew up poor amidst that convoluted southern mixture of music and religion, sin and depravity. Nicknamed "the Killer" in his adolescence, Lewis' personal life has been peppered with more than its share of debauchery and violence (two of his six wives died under mysterious circumstances). He quit high school after logging a record twenty-nine Fs and was then expelled from Bible school as well. By the time he was signed by Sun in 1956, he made Elvis look like a Boy Scout. There was, it could be said, a certain consistency between his personal life and his musical life; he rode his piano just as hard as he rode everyone around him. Once forced to take second billing to Chuck Berry at an Alan Freed show, Lewis reportedly closed his set with a frenzied rendition of "Whole Lotta Shakin' Goin' On" as he set fire to the piano. With the crowd boosted to fever pitch, he walked off stage and calmly said to Berry: "Follow *that,* Nigger."[69]

In terms of his music, Lewis came from a long line of hard-rocking piano men, including the boogie woogie greats on the r&b side and artists like Moon Mullican on the country side. With his boogie-powered "pumping piano," as his instrument was billed, Lewis turned out three Top Ten pop hits in a row for Sun, "Whole Lotta Shakin' Goin' On," "Great Balls of Fire" (1957), and "Breathless" (1958). "Whole Lotta Shakin'" not only went to number three on the pop charts, it topped the c&w and the r&b charts as well. Shortly after "Breathless," however, Lewis left his second wife and, without divorcing her, married his thirteen-year-old cousin, Myra, whose father played bass in Lewis' band. The press, of course, had a field day with Lewis, who was on tour in Great Britain with Myra in attendance. The remaining concerts in Britain were canceled and Lewis returned home to a career in shambles. He hit the pop charts three more times, but like Perkins, he was never a pop headliner again.

While Presley, Perkins, and Lewis were Sun's most notable artists, other white southern singers also passed through the company on their way to stardom or obscurity elsewhere. Warren Smith recorded the memorable (and racist) "Ubangi Stomp" and "So Long, I'm Gone," a minor pop hit, for Sun before settling for a short-lived country career on Liberty. Charlie Rich began as a session musician at Sun and had a pop hit with "Lonely Weekends" in 1960. He became a major country star a decade later. Conway Twitty recorded for the label under his real name, Harold Jenkins, but none of his recordings was released. Roy Orbison cut a version of "Ooby Dooby" at Sun before switching to Monument. Johnny Cash started at Sun in 1955. After a few country hits (including "Folsom Prison Blues"), "I Walk the Line" became a Top Twenty pop hit in 1956. A photograph of Cash, Presley, Perkins, and Lewis that year had as its caption "the million dollar quartet." Cash switched to Columbia in 1958 and embarked on a career that included gold and platinum albums, films, and even his own television show. Perkins did the same, though less successfully.

The sound Sam Phillips had created—soulful white singers from the grassroots, embellished by tape delay echo and backed by instrumentation (slap bass, electric guitar, pumping piano) that straddled c&w and r&b perfectly—defines one of the major strands of rock 'n' roll.

As the 1950s drew to a close, Sam Phillips began to treat Sun as something of a sideline. Still, the sound he had created—soulful white singers from the grassroots, embellished by tape delay echo and backed by instrumentation (slap bass, electric guitar, pumping piano) that straddled c&w and r&b perfectly—defines one of the major strands of rock 'n' roll. It was Phillips' introduction of the rockabilly style that set the stage for other white rock 'n' rollers who fell at various points along the r&b–c&w continuum and, thus, made possible the search for the "new Elvis" elsewhere.

Impressed by RCA's success with Presley, Capitol decided to take a chance on Vincent Eugene Craddock, better known as Gene Vincent, a former U.S. Navy enlistee from Norfolk, Virginia, who had injured a leg in a motorcycle accident. On Vincent's first release,

"Be-Bop-A-Lula" (1956), a song reportedly inspired by the *Little Lulu* comic strip, Capitol engineers pumped up Vincent's naturally gentle voice with "flutter echo" to achieve "a perverse, gothic performance."[70] Vincent intended the song to be the B side of the record, but "Woman Love" on the flip side was an "overtly sexual record, full of glottal twitches and orgasmic pantings" that was judged hardly suitable for mainstream airplay.[71] Capitol issued nineteen Gene Vincent records before he left the label in 1961. Only two more made the Top Forty in the United States—"Lotta Lovin'" (1957) and "Dance to the Bop" (1958). Although Vincent never hit his stride in the United States, he was revered in Great Britain and, hounded by the IRS, emigrated there in 1959. Eddie Cochran ("Summertime Blues," 1958), another would-be Elvis whose career followed a similar trajectory, joined Vincent for a British tour in 1960. The previous year, Cochran had recorded "Three Stars," a song commemorating the deaths of Ritchie Valens, the Big Bopper, and Buddy Holly. At the end of his British tour, Cochran was killed instantly as the limousine transporting him, his girlfriend Sharon Sheeley, and Vincent careened off the road while en route to the airport. Sheeley was hospitalized. Vincent suffered another injury to his bad leg and never recovered from the incident. The British, however, gobbled up Cochran and Vincent recordings just as they had earlier gobbled up those of Bill Haley and Little Richard.

Buddy Holly was another artist who enjoyed greater success in Great Britain than in the United States. Indeed, some of Holly's songs that were hits in Great Britain—"It's So Easy," for example—did not even chart on this side of the Atlantic. Still, at the time of his death, Holly was probably positioned better than anyone else to follow in Presley's footsteps. Holly was one of a number of Texas-born rockabillies to reach the pop audience. He started performing as part of a country duo, but it was his flair for rock 'n' roll that brought him to the attention of Decca Records in 1955. If Bill Haley, a balding man with a spit curl, could make hits, reasoned Decca, why not a younger man with "coke-bottle" glasses? Unfortunately, Holly was handled poorly by producer Owen Bradley and released from Decca at the end of 1956. Undaunted, Holly returned to his native Lubbock, Texas, where he formed the Crickets and then went to Clovis, New Mexico, to record with Norman Petty. Petty already had a notable rock 'n' roll success brewing with another Texas group, the Rhythm Orchids, for whom he produced "Party Doll" and "I'm Stickin' with You." Bandleaders Buddy Knox and Jimmy Bowen sold the masters to Morris Levy at Roulette Records in New York. Levy released the cuts separately as "Party Doll," by Buddy Knox, and "I'm Stickin' with You," by Jimmy Bowen with the Rhythm Orchids. "Stickin'" went to number fourteen, and "Party Doll" hit number one, establishing Roulette as a significant rock 'n' roll label and Petty as a producer to watch. The Petty/Holly/Crickets collaboration proved to be worthwhile for all concerned. The first release, "That'll Be the Day" (1957)— actually a revved-up, heavily electrified version of a number Holly had cut for Decca earlier—turned out to be the best and most successful recording any of them ever made. At the time, however, that outcome probably seemed highly unlikely to all of

The fact that Buddy Holly did not fit the description of a teen idol did not prevent him from becoming a rock 'n' roll legend. He and his group, the Crickets, were regular hit makers on the pop and r&b charts. Interestingly, they never had a country hit.

them. The song was turned down not only by Roulette but also by Atlantic, Columbia, and RCA. Ironically, Bob Thiele, a Decca producer, had engineered a contract for the Crickets on Brunswick and a solo deal for Holly on Coral, both Decca subsidiaries, after Holly's relationship with Decca was terminated. "That'll Be the Day" was finally released on Brunswick and promptly shot straight to number one, remaining in the Top Forty for sixteen weeks. Holly and the Crickets celebrated by recording fifteen more songs in Petty's studio. Their next release, "Peggy Sue," issued on Coral in 1957 and backed with "Everyday," was credited only to Buddy Holly. It was followed one month later by "Oh Boy!" backed with "Not Fade Away," which was credited to the Crickets, on Brunswick. Coral was a more conservative label that featured acts like the McGuire Sisters and Lawrence Welk. It is not surprising, therefore, that Holly's "softer" material was first released on Coral. Subsequent Coral releases such as "Early in the Morning" (recorded without the Crickets) and "Rave On," both in 1958, must have tested the label's limits.

Coral was a more conservative label that featured acts like the McGuire Sisters and Lawrence Welk. Releases such as "Early in the Morning" and "Rave On," both in 1958, must have tested the label's limits.

In retrospect, it seems difficult to imagine that anyone could mistake Buddy Holly and the Crickets for a black r&b act. In the 1950s, however, rock 'n' roll was an expression of cultural upheaval that was rife with racial ambiguities. As "country" as "That'll Be the Day" may sound today, it was an r&b hit in 1957. In fact, Holly was the only major rockabilly act who never had a country hit. As incredible as it may seem, Buddy Holly and the Crickets were booked, sight unseen, into the Apollo Theatre. Even if owner Frank Schiffman knew who they were, most of the audience did not. "I knew his records," recalled singer Leslie Uggams, who saw Holly's Apollo performance. "You thought, 'Hey, another brother out there doing his number.' Then this white guy comes out and everybody says, 'Oh, that's Buddy Holly!' . . . You know, here comes this guy with these glasses and funny-looking suit and stuff. I said, 'He's white, isn't he?' But he was terrific."[72]

Crossing racial barriers touched Holly's personal life as well. On one of his first trips to New York, he proposed to, and eventually married, Maria Elena Santiago, a Puerto Rican receptionist at Peer-Southern Music. A new wife and the lure of New York precipitated a split between Holly, the Crickets, and Petty. Holly's last Top Forty hit with the group was "It Doesn't Matter Anymore" (1959), a pop-oriented Paul Anka tune that hit the pop charts one month after Holly's untimely death.

Another Texas rocker with equally bad vision followed Holly. Roy Orbison's image complemented the pathos he evoked in his lead vocals. Like Holly, Orbison, who usually dressed in black, first recorded in Petty's studio. However, he quickly moved to Sun, RCA, and finally to Monument, where he made his biggest hits. "Only the Lonely" (1960), his first Top Ten pop hit, featured a heart-wrenching vocal in a call-and-response style with a hint of Latin flavour. It embodied the diverse cultural influences of rock 'n' roll in classic style. Orbison's incredible vocal range and crystal-clear upper register lent a distinctive sound to the releases that followed—"Blue Angel" (1960), "Running Scared" and "Crying" (1961), and "Dream Baby" (1962). Perhaps because of his unique vocal talents, Orbison was among the few rockabilly artists to ride out the British Invasion. His biggest hit, "Oh, Pretty Woman" (1964), became number one at a time when the U.S. pop charts were dominated by the Beatles and a host of other British groups.

While rockabilly and other early forms of rock 'n'roll were inarguably products of the black–white dialectic in American culture, the sounds of these musics were freely transmitted on a daily basis across the American–Canadian border via nearby U.S. radio stations and/or high-powered "clear channel" stations, such as the 50,000 watt WLAC in Nashville, Tennessee. The result was that a considerable number of young Canadian musicians were heavily influenced by the raucous sounds of rockabilly from the southern United States. Canadian labels such as Quality, Reo, Barry, Sparton, Apex, Regency, Delta, Zirkon, and others licensed various American releases for sale in Canada and by the late 1950s had begun to record dozens of made-in-Canada rockabilly records. Groups such as North Bay's Kenny and the Be-Bops ("Lindy Lou," released on Chateau in 1961), Edmonton's Barry Boyd and the Frantics ("Goin' Home to Memphis," released on Barry in 1961), Vancouver's The Hi-Fives ("Mean Old Woman," released on London in 1961), and Winnipeg's Gary Cooper ("Come on Pretty Baby," released on Quality in 1961 and featuring a young Randy Bachman) recorded rock 'n'roll records that were every bit as good as most of their American counterparts. Unfortunately, because of the size of Canada, its relatively small population, the undercapitalization of the companies that issued these records, and the state of transportation and communication technologies at the time, most of these singles were limited to regional success. Equally unfortunately, American chauvinism meant that, while Canadian companies were routinely licensing American recordings for release in Canada, in the late 1950s and early 1960s the reverse simply did not happen. The net effect today is that most of the records, the artists, and the companies that released rockabilly records in Canada in the 1950s and early 1960s have faded from Canadian popular music history.

There were two more significant practitioners of rock 'n'roll in Canada in the 1950s. Jack Scott was born in Windsor as Jack Scafone Jr. in 1936. Enamoured by the rocking sounds he heard on Detroit radio in the 1950s, Scott secured a contract with ABC-Paramount in 1957. Between 1958 and 1961, he placed nineteen singles on *Billboard's* pop charts, three of which, "My True Love," "What in the World's Come Over You," and "Burning Bridges," went Top Five. While Scott's biggest hits tended toward pop balladry, he also cut menacingly rocking rock 'n'roll records such as "The Way I Walk," which in the late 1970s would be immortalized by the psychobilly group the Cramps.

The Arkansas-born and bred Ronnie Hawkins would have fewer hits but arguably a much greater influence on Canadian popular music. Hawkins was a dyed-in-the-wool rockabilly singer who first came to southwestern Ontario under the auspices of a promoter and rather enterprising character from Hamilton, Ontario, named Harold Kudlets. Nicknamed the Colonel by Ronnie Hawkins, Kudlets had an operation going whereby he booked bands from the southern United States to play in southern Ontario, Quebec, and points along the Ontario–U.S. border such as Detroit, Cleveland, and Buffalo. Conversely, he also sent groups from Ontario down to Arkansas, Missouri, Oklahoma and Texas.

Ronnie Hawkins and The Hawks worked their way up to Canada a few times before Hawkins realized that in the South they were merely one of several good bands playing a rockabilly style that was rapidly becoming dated, whereas up in Toronto they were unique exotica. Hipper Torontonians felt that The Hawks played the fastest, most violent rock'n'roll ever heard. Logic and money being what they are, the group made Toronto their adopted home in 1958. The next year, Hawkins had two bona fide hits with cover versions of Chuck Berry's "Forty Days" and Young Jesse's "Mary Lou." His real historical importance, though, would be as the mentor for a series of Canadian musicians that would include future members of the Band, Crowbar, and Janis Joplin's Full Tilt Boogie Band.

In the United States, the Everly Brothers were among the most successful of country-influenced rock 'n' rollers. Their close harmonies were characteristic of country music, but their syncopated guitar riffs, positioned as instrumental responses to their vocal leads, suggested possible African American influences. Their father, Ike, was himself a blues-influenced guitar player. In the early 1950s, brothers Don and Phil went to Nashville to sing and write songs for Acuff-Rose. When "Bye Bye Love" (Cadence, 1957) went to number two on the pop charts, they gave Nashville a new profile in rock 'n' roll and launched a career that included twenty-six Top Forty pop hits, including four that went to number one: "Wake Up Little Susie" (1957), "All I Have to Do Is Dream" and "Bird Dog" (1958), and "Cathy's Clown" (1960).

The appeal of country-influenced rock 'n' roll enabled a number of major label country acts to experience success in the pop market. Columbia weighed in with Guy Mitchell and Marty Robbins. Mitchell's "Singing the Blues" (1956) and "Heartaches by the Number" (1959) both went to number one. In 1957, Mitchell recorded a song called "Rock-A-Billy" that hit the Top Ten. Robbins broke the Top Three three times with "A White Sport Coat (and a Pink Carnation)" (1957), "El Paso" (1959), and "Don't Worry" (1961). Capitol had Sonny James ("Young Love"), Tommy Sands ("Teen-Age Crush"), and Ferlin Husky ("Gone"), all of whom had their biggest hits in 1957. Everly soundalikes the Kalin Twins (Herbie and Hal) had a number five hit with "When" (1958) on Decca. Patsy Cline ("Walking After Midnight," "I Fall to Pieces," "Crazy"), also signed by Decca, was a straight country artist who crossed over to the pop market on the heels of country rock. Conway Twitty on MGM made the Top Ten three times with "It's Only Make Believe" (1958), "Danny Boy" (1959), and "Lonely Blue Boy" (1960). Don Gibson hit the Top Ten with "Oh, Lonesome Me" for RCA in 1958.

Although rockabilly broadened the appeal of certain country artists, it was no kinder to women than the rest of rock 'n' roll. It was not that women could not sing rockabilly. Charlene Arthur and Janis Martin ("the Female Elvis") on RCA, Rose Maddox on Capitol, and Barbara Pittman and Jean Chapel (a.k.a. Mattie O'Neill) on Sun had the force of personality to deliver the goods, but a lack of public interest in these women, a dearth of good material, weak promotion, and/or outright male hostility kept them from the attention of the mainstream.[73] Patsy Cline, like Kitty Wells ("It Wasn't God Who Made Honky Tonk Angels") before her, could get in touch with rockabilly sentiments, but she and the other female vocalists were restrained by the double standard of the culture that nurtured them. When Arthur, Martin, and Pittman went against those constraints, they paid the price of obscurity for their trouble. Maddox achieved regional fame, and Chapel appeared on the *Grand Ole Opry* as Mattie O'Neill. But except for Capitol's hard-rocking Wanda Jackson, who edged into the Top Forty three times, beginning with "Let's Have a Party" in 1960, there was only one nationally successful woman who could be included in a discussion of rockabilly—the diminutive Brenda Mae Tarpley, known professionally as "Brenda Lee." Signed by Decca at the age of eleven, she turned out twenty-nine Top Forty hits between 1960 and 1967, including the suggestive "Sweet Nothin's" and two number one ballads, "I'm Sorry" and "I Want to Be Wanted." Like Orbison, she rode out the British onslaught with dignity (and hits); then she returned to more traditional country roots for the remainder of her career.

Although rockabilly broadened the appeal of certain country artists, it was no kinder to women than the rest of rock 'n' roll.

Sam Phillips may have been the first rock 'n' roll producer to look for "a white man with the Negro sound," but he was not the only one. Ace Records tried for this with Frankie Ford, and in 1957, after years of promoting black artists exclusively, Atlantic signed Bobby Darin to the company's Atco subsidiary. Two of Darin's earliest releases on Atco, "Splish Splash" and "Queen of the Hop," hit the Top Ten on both the pop and the r&b charts in 1958. To their credit and the credit of the labels that signed them, these artists had at least some musical connection to the styles they interpreted. Unfortunately, the same cannot be said of the next generation of white rockers. Performers like Frankie Avalon, Fabian, and Bobby Rydell mustered little more in the way of talent than boy-next-door good looks and a feeble Elvis sneer. They had few if any identifiable links to previous rock 'n' roll styles, but youthful attractiveness and some semblance of rhythm enabled them to be successfully marketed as rock 'n' roll singers.

Such a musical development may have been inevitable, but it still served the purposes of those who were terrified by the cultural implications of rock 'n' roll. The energy of early rock 'n' roll had crossed lines of age, class, race, and culture in the United States, a country that seldom takes kindly to social upheaval and certainly did not do so during the conservative 1950s. As soon as rock 'n' roll captured the hearts, minds, and bodies of teenagers across all demographic categories, it was linked by some people to every perceived social ill from juvenile delinquency and miscegenation to atheism and communism. Asa Carter, executive secretary of the Alabama White Citizens Council, put the threat that some perceived in rock 'n' roll into stark words when he said in 1956, "the obscenity and vulgarity of the rock 'n' roll music is obviously a means by which the white man and his children can be driven to the level with a 'nigra'. . . . If we choose to call it the Communist ideology, I think we hit it fairly on the head."[74] While Carter's position was extreme, rhetoric like this pushed all the emotional buttons of most worried white middle-class parents. If some variant of rock 'n' roll was "here to stay," as Danny and the Juniors had prophesied in 1958, nowhere was it written that social pressures could not alter its character. The rock 'n' roll facelift of the late 1950s was but the most visible manifestation of a much broader reaction to the music.

The Empire Strikes Back: The Reaction to Rock 'n' Roll

By the late 1950s, rock 'n' roll had changed the popular music landscape irrevocably and, in so doing, had signaled the coming of still broader social change. It was the prospect of this change that precipitated unbridled enthusiasm and vicious backlash in equal proportions. Economically, the music had enhanced the fortunes of what seemed to some to be untutored writers and artists, upstart independent record companies, and wildly eccentric deejays. In essence, rock 'n' roll had turned the structure of the music business on its head. Aesthetically, the music had encouraged a tilt toward African American sensibilities and working-class styles. Thus, to some, it challenged the existing canons of cultural value and public taste. Socially, the music had threatened to upset the neat separation of the races that had guided not just the operations of the music industry but the dynamics of all social interaction to date. Depending on how one felt about these things, rock 'n' roll was either celebrated as a true democratization of culture or decried as the destruction of Western civilization.

Given rock 'n' roll's impact and the conservative political climate in which it developed, it is not terribly surprising that it became a target for repression. As surely as the 1950s are remembered musically as the decade of rock 'n' roll, they are remembered politically as the Eisenhower era. Two more diametrically opposed images would be hard to find. General, and then President, Dwight D. Eisenhower was as old-fashioned, conventional, bland, polite, and conservative as rock 'n' roll was youthful, innovative, wild, intrusive, and rebellious. By the mid-1950s, the general had developed a weak heart. Rock 'n' roll, in contrast, had nothing if not heart. If Eisenhower could be identified with golf (his favourite sport), rock 'n' roll could only be described as a demolition derby. The general, who had led the Allies during World War II, had become president in 1953 while U.S. troops were fighting communists in Korea and Senator Joe McCarthy was feverishly manufacturing them at home. The

Eisenhower was as old-fashioned, conventional, bland, polite, and conservative as rock 'n' roll was youthful, innovative, wild, intrusive, and rebellious.

135

communists, who had been allies during World War II, had now become the enemy, a necessary condition for the consolidation and expansion of U.S. capitalism. Eisenhower presided over the containment of communism, the operative strategy of the United States' postwar foreign policy. His secretary of state promised "massive retaliation" against anyone who violated U.S. turf. After the defeat of French colonialism in Vietnam, Eisenhower's vice president, Richard M. Nixon, pushed to implement the containment policy in that country, a course of action that precipitated cataclysmic political reverberations in the next decade.

In the same way that the U.S. government tried to contain communism, the powers that be also attempted to contain culture within a certain narrow framework of acceptability. Complementing the lackluster Eisenhower persona, the following bland releases were listed in *Billboard* as the ten best-selling records for the year he took office:

1. Song from Moulin Rouge—Percy Faith
2. Vaya Con Dios—Les Paul and Mary Ford
3. Doggie in the Window—Patti Page
4. I'm Walking Behind You—Eddie Fisher
5. You, You, You—Ames Brothers
6. Till I Waltz Again with You—Teresa Brewer
7. April in Portugal—Les Baxter
8. No Other Love—Perry Como
9. Don't Let the Stars Get in Your Eyes—Perry Como
10. I Believe—Frankie Laine

Uninspiring political leaders and insipid popular music ran in tandem with another aspect of American life in the 1950s—mind-numbing conformity. Battle-weary veterans, seeking to forget the ravages of war, aspired to little more than peace, quiet, prosperity, and what they remembered as "family life." In their quest for these things, they sought refuge from the harshness of city life, if not the horrors of nuclear war, in a new, and ultimately desperate, place—suburbia. Entrance to this tranquil environment did not come without a price. Each workday, according to the stereotype of the 1950s, men commuted to city centres as members of David Reisman's "lonely crowd." In the workplace, they became "organization men," mere cogs in the machine of the expanding U.S. economy; their wives stayed at home, usually even lonelier and more isolated than they were.

For the teenage children, the claustrophobic atmosphere of the workplace was replaced with the regimentation of school. In its essential features—the compartmentalization of knowledge, the passive reception of information, the pressure to achieve, the competition for grades, and the regulation of behaviour by bells—school was preparation for work. It was, in the eyes of many, the job of the school to inculcate the values of rigidity and conformity in future workers and their future mates.

Unfortunately, rigidity and conformity, so desirable in the workplace and the military, conflicted sharply with the demands of the new consumer economy. The Great Depression had ended with the United States' entrance into World War II, but the successful conversion to a peacetime economy depended in part on creating an increased demand for consumer items. The single most important strategy in this effort was (and remains) the pleasure principle:

people will buy that which they perceive as increasing their pleasure. The most obvious application of this principle could be seen in the growing use of sexuality to sell products. Thus, there was a contradiction between the social conditioning needed to produce a functioning workforce and the social conditioning needed to produce a model consumer who would be eager to absorb the surplus of manufactured goods. The values encouraged by the Protestant work ethic—discipline, frugality, asceticism, and abstinence—are best represented in a rather rigid, authoritarian, and sexually repressed personality. The ideal consumer, on the other hand, is an impulsive hedonist, given to boundless extravagance and insistent on instant gratification—that is to say, sexually more liberated. For teenagers in the 1950s, the conflict between this type of conditioning was experienced as a conflict between the official values of school/family/church and the reality of their leisure-time activities.[1]

Postwar prosperity enabled enough income to trickle down to teenagers to make them an identifiable consumer group, much to the surprise and joy of manufacturers, who began to produce products aimed specifically at a youth market. These products served to emphasize the growing chasm between teenagers and the adult generation. At the same time, dependence on parents became more and more extended as high school and university and, for some, graduate school, postponed entrance into adulthood and financial independence. Just as memories of wartime tragedies and the conditions of alienating work created the need for relaxation and escape in adults, teenagers sought relief from school and parental authority and found it in their leisure choices. Leisure became their alternative world, and rock 'n' roll its major port of entry. While adults tried to avoid facing the harsh realities of changing social mores and the threat of global thermonuclear war through backyard barbecues and family fallout shelters, teenagers sought to become engaged in their world through the sensuous ritual of dancing, the celebration of the sounds of urban life, and in multicultural explorations. Thus, in contrast to the vapid, unobtrusive popular music of the adult generation, rock 'n' roll represented everything that white, middle-class parents feared: it was urban, it was sexual, and most of it was black.

Rock 'n' roll represented everything that white middle-class parents feared: it was urban, it was sexual, and most of it was black.

As a cultural commodity, rock 'n' roll, like other products, prepared teenagers to be good consumers. (Indeed, the music has since been used to sell other products.) To adults, however, its message seemed to undermine the values of work, a necessary condition for consumption. "Rocking around the clock," not to mention rocking and rolling "all night long" in "sixty minute" intervals, hardly described the lifestyle of the upright citizen or the responsible employee. As a result, rock 'n' roll was frequently denounced by adults as the "devil's music," an NAACP strategy for recruiting young whites, or a communist plot to undermine the moral fibre of the younger generation.

The Established Powers Fight Back

To put the reaction against rock 'n' roll into proper perspective, it is necessary first to assess the degree to which the music actually encroached on the coveted pop terrain. The vintage rock 'n' roll years coincided with a period in which the fortunes of the music industry as a whole nearly tripled; revenues from record sales climbed from $213 million in 1954 to $603 million in 1959.

The question is, how much of this expansion can be attributed to rock 'n' roll? While market-share data broken out by musical style is difficult to come by, Charlie Gillett has offered a measure that gives at least some indication of relative proportions. Of the fifty-one records to make the pop Top Ten in 1955, only eight were rock 'n' roll. In contrast, in 1959, thirty-eight of the eighty-nine Top Ten records were rock 'n' roll. This means that rock 'n' roll jumped from 15.7 percent of the pop market in 1955 to 42.7 percent in 1959. In this same period, the total number of Top Ten pop hits produced by major record companies decreased from forty in 1955 to thirty in 1959, while those produced by independent record companies increased from eleven to fifty-nine. In other words, independent record companies went from a 21.6 percent share of the pop market in 1955 to a 66.3 percent share of a pop market that was roughly three times larger in 1959.[2]

Rock 'n' roll was one of those rare instances in which ideological blinders prevented the music industry from operating in its own economic self-interest.

The major labels had no one to blame for this situation but themselves. In the late 1940s and early 1950s, when countless independent labels came into existence to cash in on the growing demand for r&b, it should have been clear that these new developments in black popular music could be ignored only at one's own peril. Rock 'n' roll was one of those rare instances in which ideological blinders prevented the music industry from operating in its own economic self-interest. After it was clear that rock 'n' roll was here to stay, the industry giants responded with strategies that ranged from stances usually associated with ostriches to limited amounts of talent buying and the widespread practice of so-called cover records (alternative versions of original recordings). When these tactics did not improve things economically, some of the majors, principally RCA and Columbia, tried to divert audiences from the new sound by promoting alternative forms of music. When all these efforts failed, the established powers of the industry (artists, labels, and most prominently, ASCAP publishers) joined forces with the U.S. government in an attempt to suppress the music in what Russell Sanjek has labeled the "War on Rock."[3]

Given Columbia's historical connection to African American music (the company's vaults contained some of the best recordings of Bessie Smith, Robert Johnson, Louis Armstrong, Fletcher Henderson, Duke Ellington, and Count Basie), the label's comparatively lukewarm response to rock 'n' roll is somewhat surprising. After a reportedly feeble attempt at bidding for Elvis Presley's contract, Mitch Miller, Columbia's artist and repertoire chief, tried his best to ignore the music totally, although Columbia did sign Johnny Cash and Carl Perkins in 1958. It has been said that Miller despised rock 'n' roll, but to his credit, he never joined the chorus of industry malcontents who publicly denounced it. Instead, he devoted his time and energy to perfecting the pop production techniques that were used with artists like Frankie Laine, Jo Stafford, Rosemary Clooney, and Doris Day. These techniques had made Columbia the most successful label in the United States.[4]

Early in the 1950s, the emotionally unhinged Johnny Ray could have provided Columbia with a way into rock 'n' roll. His uninhibited stage performances, during which he routinely ripped off his shirt, were at least in part the result of tutelage by LaVern Baker and her manager. Following the phenomenal success of his heart-wrenching, tear-jerking recording of "Cry," which was number one on the pop charts for eleven weeks, Ray was switched from the OKeh subsidiary to the parent Columbia label. However, when ASCAP succeeded in having Ray's successful cover record of the Drifters' "Such a Night" banned from the airwaves in 1954 because of its sexual suggestiveness, Columbia may have thought that a deeper commitment to the performer and his current direction would be more trouble than it was worth. Except for a brief and inexplicable flirtation with the outrageous Screamin' Jay Hawkins ("I Put a Spell on You," 1956) on OKeh, the closest Columbia came to rock 'n' roll was the silken balladry of Johnny Mathis ("It's Not for Me to Say," "Chances Are," "The Twelfth of Never"). Produced in the same style as Columbia's other pop artists, the African American baritone (who was also a world-class athlete) was young enough and hip enough to appeal to the rock 'n' roll audience.

At RCA, Hugo Winterhalter was no better than Miller at producing rock 'n' roll, and artists like Vaughn Monroe, Dinah Shore, and Eddie Fisher were certainly no better at performing it than Columbia's artists.[5] However, in the Sarnoff tradition of covering all bases, RCA came up with a far more enlightened (and lucrative) strategy for dealing with the new sound. Recognizing that rock 'n' roll was not only a force to be reckoned with but also an idiom that required its own talents, RCA simply bought the most promising rock 'n' roll star it could get its hands on—Elvis Presley. It was the smartest move the company ever made. Presley carried the faltering record division for years.

Impressed by RCA's success, a number of other major labels tried to imitate the strategy. Capitol's search for the "new Elvis" yielded Gene Vincent. MGM had no connection to rock 'n' roll until they signed Conway Twitty in 1958. Like Presley before him, Twitty had served a classic, if undistinguished, apprenticeship at Sun Records in Memphis and had then moved on to an equally undistinguished career as a country singer at Mercury. However, at MGM, according to Charlie Gillett, "Twitty assumed a sonorous baritone, apparently satirizing the heavy breathing of Elvis Presley's 'Don't,' a hit earlier in the year."[6] Twitty's country background enabled him to create that delicate balance of country and pop that found acceptance as rock 'n' roll because of the success of rockabilly. His biggest hit, "It's Only Make Believe," "was one of the many records of 1958 that succeeded in absorbing elements of rock 'n' roll into the tradition of melodramatic ballads that popular music arrangers enjoyed working with."[7]

It is, perhaps, not surprising that MGM turned to Twitty. When the major labels decided to make a foray into rock 'n' roll territory, they naturally gravitated toward pop-oriented, country-influenced singers and material. This was a music to which they still had some connection, and given the racial fears that rock 'n' roll conjured up in some people, it was probably considered a safer move. Decca had first set the example by signing Bill Haley in 1953, a move that predated the other major labels by eighteen months. The company, however, couldn't quite bring itself to replicate the pattern. In 1957, Buddy Holly and the Crickets were turned down by Decca, although, as noted in Chapter 4, they were signed by Bob Thiele to two of Decca's subsidiaries, Coral and Brunswick. Coral had been founded in 1949 as an r&b label, but in the early 1950s it became one of the labels that engaged in a systematic attempt to blunt the crossover appeal of early rock 'n' roll through the practice of issuing cover records.

Covering the Bases

In the 1950s, major companies and some independents tried to capitalize on the growing popularity of r&b among white listeners by producing alternate versions of r&b hits using white artists and styles the companies thought would be more appropriate for and sell well in the mainstream market. In the vast majority of cases, black artists recording for independent labels were the victims of this practice.[8] Cover records not only altered stylistic elements but also often doctored lyrics as well. Bill Haley's 1954 cover of Joe Turner's "Shake, Rattle, and Roll," for example, sanitized the original version by replacing sexual phrases with fashion statements and moving the action from the bedroom to the kitchen. Cover records were often released during the expected chart life of the original, and owing to the superior distribution channels and promotional powers of the majors, frequently outsold the original.

The practice of making cover records began in earnest in 1953 when June Valli recorded "Crying in the Chapel" for RCA. At the time it was released, there were three other versions of the song out, two country and one r&b. The r&b release by Sonny Til and the Orioles had crossed over to the pop market and was enjoying considerable success until it was eclipsed by the Valli cover, which became one of the best-selling records of the year. RCA scored another coup with Perry Como's cover of "Ko Ko Mo," a lively novelty song originally recorded by Gene and Eunice for Combo in 1954, then rerecorded by the same group for Aladdin. This rerecording became an r&b hit and was covered by two independent labels—Checker, using the Flamingos, and Modern, using Marvin and Johnny—that hoped to use the song's novelty value to break into the pop market. Their efforts were thwarted when three major labels also covered the rerecordings. Mercury released a version by the Canadian group the Crew Cuts and Columbia used Tony Bennett, but the RCA recording by Perry Como became the most popular, giving the electronics giant another ersatz rock 'n' roll hit even before Presley was signed.

Bill Haley's "Shake, Rattle, and Roll" sanitized the original version by replacing sexual phrases with fashion statements and moving the action from the bedroom to the kitchen.

Of all the major companies, Decca and Mercury had the best luck with covers. Bill Haley's "Shake, Rattle, and Roll" cover for Decca went to number seven on the pop charts and became the artist's first gold record. Theresa Brewer and the McGuire Sisters on Decca's Coral subsidiary also made successful cover records. The McGuire Sisters' cover of "Sincerely" by the Moonglows hit number one on the pop charts and became the seventh best-selling pop single of 1955. Brewer's 1956 cover of Fats Domino's "Bo Weevil" went to number seventeen while Domino's reached only thirty-five.

Mercury, which had begun as an independent and had then made the transition to a major, knew the market well. The company used Georgia Gibbs to cover Etta James' "Wallflower" (popularly known as "Roll with Me, Henry") with a cleaned-up version called "Dance with Me, Henry." James' version sold 400,000 copies for Modern, but the Gibbs cover hit the 1 million mark. This was only the beginning for Mercury. The Chicago label really cashed in on cover records with two Canadian groups, the Diamonds and the Crew Cuts. The Crew Cuts systematically pillaged the r&b charts after their cover version of the Chords' "Sh'Boom" (originally on Atlantic's Cat label) became the fifth best-selling song of 1954. In addition to the previously mentioned "Ko Ko Mo," the group covered the Penguins' "Earth Angel" (Dootone), Nappy Brown's "Don't Be Angry" (Savoy), and the Charms' "Gum Drop" (Deluxe). Between 1956 and 1961, the Diamonds had hits with Frankie Lymon and the Teenagers' "Why Do Fools Fall in Love," the Gladiolas' "Little Darlin'," the Rays' "Silhouettes," and the Danleers' "One Summer Night."

The label that really worked the cover market was Dot Records, an independent with the pretensions of a major.[9] Launched by Randy Wood in Gallatin, Tennessee, in 1951, Dot's posture toward rock 'n' roll has been described as "predatory." Two of Dot's female acts were quite successful covering a wide variety of rock 'n' roll. The Fontane Sisters recorded "Hearts of Stone" by the Charms, "Seventeen" by Boyd Bennett and the Rockets, "Eddie My Love" by the Teen Queens, and "I'm in Love Again" by Fats Domino. Gale Storm had Top Ten hits with Frankie Lymon and the Teenagers' "Why Do Fools Fall in Love," Smiley Lewis' "I Hear You Knocking," and the Charms' "Ivory Tower," among others. The company also had on its roster the singer who represents the epitome of cultural theft, Pat Boone.

It is not simply the fact that Pat Boone has more covers to his credit than anyone else that makes him the lightning rod for all the criticism of the practice; it is the fact that he built his career by sanitizing the classics. His cover of Fats Domino's "Ain't That a Shame" (1955) was Boone's first number one single; "I Almost Lost My Mind" (1956), originally recorded by Ivory Joe Hunter, was his second. He also cleaned up the El Dorados' "At My Front Door" and the Flamingos' "I'll Be Home." His antiseptic versions of Little Richard's "Tutti Frutti" and "Long Tall Sally" alone would be enough to earn him the unyielding wrath of anyone who professes a love of rock 'n' roll. The "white buck" shoes that became his signature only reinforced the racist implications of his "white bread" delivery. Once he was firmly established in the rock 'n' roll market, Boone retreated into mainstream pop balladry ("Love Letters in the Sand," "April Love," "Moody River") and scored thirty-eight Top Forty hits. He was rewarded in 1957 with his own television show. That Pat Boone built his career on early rock 'n' roll is indisputable; that he did so more successfully than anyone but Elvis continues to rankle his detractors.

In the mythology of rock 'n' roll, the major labels are often portrayed as narrow, rigid companies that tried to insulate the mainstream from the complexities of difference, while the independent labels are portrayed as heroically pushed against the limits of public taste out of a love for the music from the grassroots. The truth, of course, is more complex than this. Record companies, whether majors or independents, frequently act in self-contradictory ways that are as likely to involve idiosyncratic choices and dumb luck as carefully crafted business plans or scientific market analyses. The appearance of Haley on Decca and Presley on RCA, let alone Lloyd Price on ABC-Paramount, certainly complicates the mythology. Given Columbia's aversion to rock 'n' roll, why did the company even bother to take a chance on a performer like Screamin' Jay Hawkins, whose stage act included rising from a burning coffin in full voodoo regalia? Capitol also nurtured an equally outrageous performer named Esquerita for a while. Toward the end of the 1950s, MGM signed two black rock 'n' roll acts—the Impalas ("Sorry [I Ran All the Way Home]," 1959) and Jimmy Jones ("Handy Man" and "Good Timin'," 1960)—to their Cub subsidiary. These are not the acts of companies that are trying to insulate the mainstream. By the same token, few independents entered the business solely for artistic reasons. If the independents had a progressive effect, it is because they were smart enough and flexible enough to respond to an unsated consumer demand that would have required a considerable shift in orientation for the

Pat Boone has served as the lightning rod for all the race-related criticism associated with the practice of cover records. This dimension of his questionable contribution to rock 'n' roll has prevented him from being inducted into the Rock 'n' Roll Hall of Fame.

"Tutti Frutti"

Artist: Pat Boone
Music / Lyrics by Little Richard
(and Dorothy La Bostrie)
Label: Dot (1956)

Musical Style Notes

Boone's smooth, mellifluous vocal style was part of his great appeal and owes more to pop crooners Bing Crosby or Perry Como than to Little Richard or Fats Domino. In terms of musical structure, tempo, and length, Boone's cover of "Tutti Frutti" is almost an exact copy of Little Richard's, but the vocal style and the clearly enunciated lyrics are utterly different from Richard's growling, high-tenor, powerhouse style.

Some of the lyrics have been changed here (even though Little Richard's had already been "cleaned up" for his recording). Richard's "She rocks to the east, she rocks to the west" was changed to "I've been to the east, I've been to the west."

One curious departure from the original comes at the end. Whereas Little Richard's version ends with Richard singing the "wop-bop-a-loo-mop" line by himself, the sax has the last word on Boone's version, punctuating the last line with one final note at the end.

Musical "Road Map"

TIMINGS	COMMENTS	LYRICS
0:00–0:02	Begins directly with a stop-time chord hit by the band and Boone singing the famous nonsense-syllable refrain.	A-wop-bop-a-loo-mop . . .
0:02–0:18	Refrain (twelve-bar blues—last two measures wop bop)	Tutti frutti . . . oh, Rootie . . .
0:18–0:33	Verse 2 (twelve-bar blues form—last four measures stop-time)	I got a gal her name's Sue . . .
0:33–0:49	Refrain (twelve-bar blues—last two measures wop bop)	Tutti frutti . . .
0:49–1:04	Verse 1 (twelve-bar blues form—last four measures stop-time)	I got a gal named Daisy . . .
1:04–1:19	Refrain (twelve-bar blues—last two measures wop bop)	Tutti frutti . . .
1:19–1:34	Sax solo over the twelve-bar blues form of a verse	
1:35–1:50	Refrain (twelve-bar blues—last two measures wop bop)	Tutti frutti . . .
1:50–2:06	Verse 2 (again, twelve-bar blues form—last four measures stop-time)	
2:06–2:22	Refrain (twelve-bar blues—last two measures wop bop) Note the one solitary sax note right at the end!	

majors. Dot's view of music simply as a product (a view that came to serve as a model for many of the independents that followed) was extreme, but even Dot was sufficiently attuned to the music to sign the Dell-Vikings, whose "Come Go with Me" and "Whispering Bells" (1957) are regarded as vocal harmony classics.

In this more complicated picture, there are also contradictory aspects of the practice of cover records that must be considered. Usually cover records are discussed only in terms of their destructive effects in the cultural arena. Under certain conditions, however, cover records in the 1950s could be beneficial to an artist, or more often, his label. A cover record often exposed a song to a larger audience through record sales and radio play. Such exposure could more than make up for a loss in record sales through an increase in writer's royalties for artists who wrote their own material. When royalty increases did not occur, it was often because independent label owners induced naive artists to sell their publishing rights for a few dollars or to sign them away for the "privilege" of recording. In any case, as teenagers became more familiar with rock 'n' roll and its roots, they became more adept at distinguishing originals from covers and covers became less valuable to the majors as a strategy for dealing with rock 'n' roll.

Record companies frequently act in self-contradictory ways that are as likely to involve idiosyncratic choices and dumb luck as carefully crafted business plans or scientific market analyses.

Pop Diversions: From Kingston Town to the Kingston Trio

One of the things that separated the majors from the independents was the fact that the majors—particularly Columbia and RCA—could rely on their catalogues or subsidies from other corporate divisions when they were not producing hit records. Thus, they could, in many instances, avoid dealing with such messy cultural practices as rock 'n' roll and cover records. In fact, Columbia and RCA were so reluctant to have anything to do with rock 'n' roll that they were less aggressive than others with cover versions. For a brief time, it appeared as though they might have other, more dignified strategies for dealing with the new music market. Chief among these was an attempt to divert popular tastes toward two other types of music, calypso and popularized folk music.

Beginning in late 1956, RCA and Columbia began promoting American interpretations of calypso, hoping that the new sound would supplant rock 'n' roll, which they viewed as a passing fad. There was, as Gillett has pointed out, a certain logic to the strategy.

> Given the way major record companies seemed to think and operate, calypso no doubt seemed to them a logical and clever answer to the dilemma of needing to divert their audience's attention from a product that the independent companies were best able to supply. Calypso was a black people's music, as jazz and rhythm and blues before it had been. Further, it had a Latin beat, which had always seemed to fit nicely into North American popular music. . . . Best of all, there were enough novelty songs in calypso with no sensual implications for the companies to escape having to deal with the disturbing content of rhythm and blues.[10]

Had it not been for the self-serving intervention of the AFM, the majors that decided to promote calypso might well have found they had a "tiger by the tail." In its original Trinidadian form, calypso had long been a highly politicized music that was based on topical social commentary and depictions of male–female relations that routinely brushed with lewdness. However, pressure from the AFM prevented such outspoken calypsonians as Lord Kitchener and the Mighty Sparrow from performing in the United States and left the task of representing West Indian culture to Harry Belafonte. The multitalented Belafonte, who was born in New York, started his singing career as a straight pop vocalist for Jubilee in 1949. In 1955, he was signed by RCA as a folk singer, recording material like "Scarlet Ribbons" and "Shenandoah." In 1956, he made the transition to what passed for calypso in the United States with the release of the LP *Calypso*, which stayed on the charts for eighty-four weeks and was firmly ensconced in the number one slot for thirty-one of them. This was an unprecedented chart run. The two hit singles from the album, "Jamaica Farewell" and "Banana Boat" (a.k.a ."Day-O"), established the tone and content of U.S. calypso. The sexual innuendo and pointed social commentary of Caribbean calypso was discarded and the novelty value of the sound was emphasized. The result was a series of well-crafted pop arrangements with a Latin rhythmic flavour. In retrospect, such apolitical pop calypso appears to be an ironic career choice for the man who would soon become a leading civil rights activist and an outspoken critic of injustice.

Columbia followed RCA's lead with Terry Gilkyson and the Easy Riders ("Marianne," 1957). Other notable pseudo-calypso hits included the Tarriers' "The Banana Boat Song" and Belafonte's "Mama Look-a Boo Boo." In the final analysis, however, U.S. calypso, not rock 'n' roll, was only a fad. Within two years, the sound had segued into popular folk music, a second diversionary strategy by the majors that yielded a new set of players. As noted earlier, before Belafonte took the plunge into calypso, he had recorded pop versions of traditional songs, and, in many ways, his calypso recordings were the Caribbean version of the same tendency. The Tarriers, before boarding the banana boat, had backed Vince Martin on "Cindy, Oh Cindy," another folk-sounding ditty with a vaguely Latin feel. However, it was not until a San Francisco group called the Kingston Trio unleashed their repertoire of popular folk sounds that the music industry realized the potential power of popular folk material. The Kingston Trio came up through the San Francisco folk scene but managed to avoid the left-wing taint that had haunted most folk artists since the McCarthy era. Perhaps their clean-cut image, brightly coloured matching shirts, and upscale college humour made it difficult to

Though Harry Belafonte began his career as a straight pop vocalist, he became the one to interpret a depoliticized version of Trinidadian calypso for the U.S. audience. Never one to be a pawn of the music industry, Belafonte soon took his considerable talent and progressive political views to the world stage, where he continues to champion humanitarian causes.

With coordinated preppy attire and college-oriented humour, the Kingston Trio swept the country with a pop folk repertoire that only hinted at the power of the folk revival yet to come.

think of them as politically subversive. Following the practice in folk circles, the Kingston Trio issued their material as LPs, not singles, but no other folk artists had ever before matched their success. Signed by Capitol in 1957, they released eighteen albums that made the Top Twenty, and a number of these remained on the charts for a year or more; five hit the number one spot. Rarer still, some of their LPs generated hit pop singles. "Tom Dooley," for example, from their first album, went to number one, which was almost unheard of for folk material.

Soon other, largely forgettable folk-oriented groups, including the Limeliters, the Highwaymen, and the Journeymen, tried their hand at the pop market. Columbia had moderate success with the Brothers Four ("Greenfields," 1960). During this period, college campuses became fertile grounds for talent scouts. By the time the folk revival got into full swing, however, with yet another roster of performers, it was allied with the burgeoning Civil Rights movement, and the music industry really did have a tiger by the tail.

Schlock Rock: Enter the White Middle Class

By the late 1950s, the initial rush of rock 'n' roll excitement was over. From a musical point of view, rock 'n' roll was a rather limited science that by then had been sufficiently absorbed into the collective unconscious that singers, songwriters, and producers with no particular feel for the music's roots or subtleties could still turn out commercially viable approximations. This new reality brought forth a new generation of white, middle-class teen idols—Fabian, Frankie Avalon, Bobby Rydell, Canadians Paul Anka and Bobby Curtola, and more—whose roots barely scratched the surface of pop. Along with many others, they ushered in a style of music I have referred to elsewhere as "schlock rock."[11]

In the rise of schlock rock, little separated the majors from the independents, save for market superiority. For every Tommy Sands ("Teen-Age Crush"), Connie Francis ("Who's Sorry Now"), and Sonny James ("Young Love") who recorded for a major label, there was a Charlie Gracie ("Butterfly"), Annette ("Tall Paul"), and Tab Hunter ("Young Love") who recorded for an independent. Warner and Colpix, new Hollywood-related labels, contributed Connie Stevens ("Sixteen Reasons") and James Darren ("Goodbye Cruel World"), respectively. Whatever higher morality or artistic integrity might have been attributed to the independents in the early days of rock 'n' roll had given way to a singular commercial pop orientation.

Whatever higher morality or artistic integrity might have been attributed to the independents in the early days of rock 'n' roll had given way to a singular commercial pop orientation.

The major hub for this commercial activity was Philadelphia, the home of three independent labels, Chancellor, Cameo/Parkway, and Swan, that had come into existence following Dot's success with cover records. These three labels transformed local teenagers into archetypal teen idols. Chancellor offered Fabian and Frankie Avalon; Cameo had Bobby Rydell; and Swan signed Freddy Cannon, who actually came from Lynn, Massachusetts, but contractually and aesthetically belonged to Philadelphia. "The focus in Philadelphia in particular was on image," Gillett has noted. "The unsophisticated white southern singers, and the unfashionable black ones, were supplanted by kids who could be the boy-next-door, whose visual appeal was more important than their musical ability."[12]

In this regard, Chancellor led the pack. According to critic Ed Ward, co-owner Bob Marcucci told *Billboard* in the late 1950s:

> *We now run a school where we indoctrinate artists into show business. We may sign them and spend three months schooling them before they cut their first record. We teach them how to walk, how to talk, and how to act onstage when they're performing. We worked with Frankie Avalon for three months before making "Dede Dinah."*
>
> *It was Frankie who introduced me to Fabian, a sixteen-year-old high school kid who likes to play football. Somehow I sensed that here was a kid who could go. He looks a little bit like both Presley and Ricky Nelson. I figured he was a natural. It's true that he couldn't sing. He knew it and I knew it.*[13]

By the time the rest of the world found out, however, Fabian had racked up eight Top Forty hits. In a few short years, rock 'n' roll had degenerated from Sam Phillips' dream of a white man who could sing black to a white high-school kid who couldn't sing at all.

"Showing a perverse wish to return to the standards of pre–rock 'n' roll days," Gillett has written, "the operators of the new independents scoured the same streets that had spawned the crooners who had been the core of major company rosters."[14] In so doing, they, like the majors, assembled a roster of vocalists who were, for the most part, pale imitations of the pop mainstays of the late 1940s and early 1950s. Once again, they were predominantly Italian American. Fabian (Fabiano Forte), Frankie Avalon (Francis Avalone), Bobby Rydell (Robert Ridarelli), Freddy Cannon (Frederick Picariello), Bobby Darin (Walden Robert Cassotto), Annette (Funicello), Connie Francis (Concetta Franconero), James Darren (James Ercolani), and Connie Stevens (Concetta Ingolia) were all of Italian descent. This is, perhaps, not surprising. At a time when ethnic succession still played a major role in white ethnic intergroup relations, entertainment and sports (as black artists and athletes knew only too well) offered the most promising avenues for upward mobility. It is interesting to note that all of these performers felt compelled to anglicize their names; still, they were not unaware of their heritage. Connie Francis toted up thirty-five Top Forty singles for MGM, but her two albums of *Italian Favourites* (the first of which charted for more than a year and a half) far outdistanced her two *Greatest Hits* LPs. One of Bobby Rydell's best-selling singles was "Volare" (1960). The problem was that this was not rock 'n' roll.

Frankie Avalon was one of a number of teen idols who turned boy-next-door good looks and a modicum of talent into a full-fledged rock 'n' roll career.

As in the 1940s, Italian American cultural tendencies seemed to work better with styles that were closer to mainstream pop, and among the new white rockers, connections to pop abounded. When Bobby Darin changed his singing style to record Kurt Weill's "Mack the Knife" (1959), Darin's first

In a few short years, rock 'n' roll had degenerated from Sam Phillips' dream of a white man who could sing black to a white high-school kid who couldn't sing at all.

number one single, it was because he aspired to be the next Frank Sinatra, not the next Elvis Presley. Bobby Rydell was actually discovered at the age of nine by bandleader Paul Whiteman. In addition to his stylistically questionable, but commercially successful, rock 'n' roll hits, Rydell hit pay dirt with "That Old Black Magic" (1961), a Johnny Mercer/Harold Arlen tune from the 1940s. Although there was an obvious, if narrow, connection between Italian Americans and pop/rock crooners, the new pop orientation in rock 'n' roll cannot be reduced to the function of a particular ethnic affiliation. In fact, the production of schlock knew no ethnic boundaries.

By the 1960s, the momentum of schlock rock had produced a second generation of white teen heartthrobs across ethnic lines who had varying degrees of talent. At the higher end of the scale, Del Shannon ("Runaway," "Hats Off to Larry") evidenced musical roots in the country sound of Hank Williams. Gene Pitney delivered some powerful, if pop-oriented, vocals on such hits as "(The Man Who Shot) Liberty Valence," "Only Love Can Break a Heart," "It Hurts to Be in Love," and "I'm Gonna Be Strong." He also distinguished himself as a writer of considerable note, penning such classics as "Hello Mary Lou" for Ricky Nelson and "He's a Rebel" for the Crystals. Paul Anka and Neil Sedaka also achieved success as songwriters for other artists in the 1960s. Among the female entries, Leslie Gore would also have to be positioned here, even though she performed one of the first feminist songs, "You Don't Own Me" (1963). In the end, an oversupply of artists, both male and female, contributed to what might be called *Schlock Rock's Greatest Hits, Volumes I and II.* Individual differences aside, the overwhelming social function of these artists as a group was to put a bland, white middle-class face on rock 'n' roll. Gradually, but decisively, strong regional accents gave way to neutral unlocalized voices. Raucous improvised riffs and solos on sax, guitar, or piano were overtaken by lavish

Schlock Rock's Greatest Hits, Volume I

Paul Anka   "Diana," "You Are My Destiny," "Lonely Boy," "Put Your Head on My Shoulder," "Puppy Love"

Frankie Avalon   "Dede Dinah," "Ginger Bread," "Venus," "Bobby Sox to Stockings"

Annette   "Tall Paul," "O Dio Mio"

Fabian   "Turn Me Loose," "Tiger," "Hound Dog Man"

Bobby Rydell   "We Got Love," "Wild One," "Swinging School"

Connie Francis   "Who's Sorry Now," "My Happiness," "Lipstick on Your Collar," "Everybody's Somebody's Fool"

Freddy Cannon   "Tallahassee Lassie," "Way Down Yonder in New Orleans," "Palisades Park"

Neil Sedaka   "Oh! Carol," "Stairway to Heaven," "Calendar Girl," "Happy Birthday Sweet Sixteen," "Breaking Up Is Hard to Do"

The biggest African American star to emerge from the Philadelphia scene of the late 1950s, Chubby Checker generated contradictory impulses in mainstream culture. His version of "The Twist" kicked off a national dance craze that the whole family could enjoy even as it anticipated more openly sexual dances.

strings and orchestral arrangements. The sexual double entendre was replaced by a highly romanticized vision of teenage love and/or angst. Bobby Vinton's "Blue Velvet" (1963) and Bobby Cartola's "Three Rows Over" (1963), among many others, are representative of the era.

Gradually, but decisively, strong regional accents gave way to neutral unlocalized voices. Raucous improvised solos were overtaken by lavish strings and orchestral arrangements. The sexual double entendre was replaced by a highly romanticized vision of teenage love and/or angst.

While the second generation of schlock was overwhelmingly white, there was one black superstar, Chubby Checker, whose "The Twist" was the first of a series of dance crazes that swept the country in the early 1960s. A funkier, original version of "The Twist" had been released two years earlier by Hank Ballard and the Midnighters and had sold extremely well in the r&b market. There was, however, little crossover into pop, and nothing hinting at the national fad that Checker triggered with his version. Unlike Ballard, Checker was a pop phenomenon. He was created as an image act in the corporate offices of Cameo/Parkway Records, which was, of course, located in Philadelphia. At the suggestion of Dick Clark's wife, the former Ernest Evans was given a name that sounded vaguely like Fats Domino (Fats = Chubby, Domino = Checker). "The Twist" reached number one on the pop charts twice, once in 1960 and then again in 1962. In fact, it was listed as the best-selling single of all time well into the 1970s.

Attempting to cash in on the craze the twist had set in motion, Cameo/Parkway concocted a seemingly endless series of new dance records, made by both black and white artists. Checker followed up with "The Hucklebuck," "Pony Time," "The Fly," and "Limbo Rock." Bobby Rydell contributed "The Fish." The Orlons offered "The Wah Watusi." The Dovells chimed in with the "Bristol Stomp" and the

Schlock Rock's Greatest Hits, Volume II

Bobby Vee   "Devil or Angel," "Rubber Ball," "Take Good Care of My Baby," "Run to Him," "The Night Has a Thousand Eyes"

Brian Hyland   "Itsy Bitsy Teenie Weenie Yellow Polkadot Bikini," "Sealed with a Kiss"

Johnny Tillotson   "Poetry in Motion," "Without You," "It Keeps Right on A-Hurtin'," "Talk Back Trembling Lips"

Bobby Vinton   "Roses Are Red," "Blue on Blue," "Blue Velvet," "There I've Said It Again," "My Heart Belongs to Only You," "Mr. Lonely"

Jay and the Americans   "She Cried," "Only in America," "Come a Little Bit Closer," "Cara Mia"

Sue Thompson   "Norman"

Little Peggy March   "I Will Follow Him"

Leslie Gore   "It's My Party," "Judy's Turn to Cry," "She's a Fool"

Paul and Paula   "Hey Paula"

"Hully Gully." Dee Dee Sharp announced that it was "Mashed Potato Time" and then told people to "Do the Bird." She was offered "The Loco-Motion" by Gerry Goffin and Carole King, but when Cameo passed on the song, the writers released a version by their babysitter on the Dimension label. Eva Narcissus Boyd became Little Eva and "The Loco-Motion" became a number one hit.

In its historical context, the twist craze was socially ambiguous. The dance was welcomed enthusiastically into conservative, white suburban America, even though its leading exponent was African American. Certainly, it anticipated more openly sexual dances like the monkey, the jerk, and the Philly dog. For a brief period, it served as an alternative port of entry to the pop market for African American artists, even as mainstream forces sought to turn back rock 'n' roll. In 1962 alone, Sam Cooke's "Twistin' the Night Away" and Gary "U.S." Bonds' "Dear Lady Twist" and "Twist, Twist Senora" broke into the Top Ten; the Isley Brothers followed their classic "Shout" with "Twist and Shout"; and Atlantic Records reissued an album of old Ray Charles material as *Do the Twist with Ray Charles*, which hit number eleven on the album charts. In the long run, however, Cameo/Parkway's faddish dance crazes tended to reduce rock 'n' roll to a novelty. As a Philadelphia independent, the company also had a close association with *American Bandstand,* the televised dance party that was primarily responsible for promoting the new teen idols.

Television's Greatest Hits

The program initially called *Bandstand* had begun in 1952 as a local Philadelphia broadcast on WFIL-TV, an ABC network affiliate. The program's first host, Bob Horn, was fired after he was arrested for drunk driving just as the *Philadelphia Ledger,* the owner of WFIL, was waging a vigorous campaign against the practice. Income-tax evasion and an unsubstantiated teenage vice charge added to Horn's career troubles. Looking for a replacement, the station asked Dick Clark, a Syracuse University graduate who had begun working there in 1952 as a news announcer, to take over in 1956. Although Clark, "the perpetual teenager," was twenty-seven years old, he looked as young as most of the teenagers who danced on the show, but he carried himself more like a big brother. This distancing served him well in the turbulent years that followed. Under his leadership, *Bandstand* quickly became one of the most important promotional vehicles in the music industry. By 1957, the show had been picked up by ABC-TV for national broadcast and had been renamed *American Bandstand.* As Russell Sanjek has noted, "Within two years, it was being broadcast by 101 affiliates to an audience of 20 million. . . . Because of program policy, [the performers who appeared on *Bandstand*] were invariably white in the early years."[15] As a result, "Dick Clark, the youthful, debonair host with the Dentyne smile," was remembered by Arnold Shaw "as the ballast to Alan Freed, representing cool white rock as Freed was the avatar of hot black rock."[16] Clark has maintained that associating him with only white rock is a cheap shot. "To write that the music we presented was all white bread is a fallacious premise. It's an easy angle," he has said. "It happens to be wrong."[17]

While it may be true, as Clark has pointed out, "that over two-thirds of the people who've been initiated into the Rock & Roll Hall of Fame had their television debuts on *American Bandstand,*"[18] there is no question that the show's Philadelphia location placed the local independents in a particularly good position to display their wares, which they did. Fabian, Frankie

Avalon, Bobby Rydell, and Freddy Cannon made regular appearances, and it seems unlikely that they would have become as popular as they were without such exposure. It is equally clear that Clark positioned himself to benefit from such successes. By the end of the decade, he was financially involved in thirty-three music-related corporations, including three record companies, a management firm, and a pressing plant. His publishing company held the copyright on 162 songs, many of which his show had helped to popularize. While a consummate businessman, Clark's financial entanglements often led him to the borders of ethical practice, as his handling of Duane Eddy illustrates.

Born in Corning, New York, Eddy relocated to Phoenix at the age of seventeen to work with producer Lee Hazelwood. Experimenting with echo in the studio, the two created the "twangy" guitar sound that became Eddy's signature. From 1958 to 1963, Eddy and his group, the Rebels, charted fifteen Top Forty hits, the best-known of which are "Rebel-'Rouser" (1958), "Forty Miles of Bad Road" (1959), and "Because They're Young" (1960). Between 1958 and 1961, Clark played eleven of Eddy's hits some 240 times on *Bandstand.* While Clark has claimed that he simply followed national trends on the show, there is no doubt that his promotion helped to propel the songs to hit status. Throughout this period, Eddy recorded for Clark's Jaime label, he toured under the auspices of Clark's management company, and all of his copyrights were owned by Clark's publishing company. Given this, it is not difficult to imagine how Clark's private holdings could have come into conflict with the promotional aspects of *American Bandstand.* Of course, television had long been used as a promotional vehicle for all kinds of music, including, on occasion, rock 'n' roll. Elvis Presley, Chuck Berry, Carl Perkins, Jerry Lee Lewis, Buddy Holly, and Bo Diddley, for example, had all appeared, albeit infrequently, on the many TV variety shows that then existed. However, these artists did not appear on national television until their musical abilities were proven. In the case of schlock rock, visual appeal itself became the basis for launching a musical career.

While *American Bandstand* may have been the primary culprit in this area, it was not the only one. Annette Funicello had been the *Mickey Mouse Club*'s most popular Mouseketeer since 1955. Still, the Disney show was an odd platform for launching a career in rock 'n' roll. Connie Stevens, who played Cricket Blake on the detective series *Hawaiian Eye,* teamed up with Ed "Kookie" Byrnes, the ultra-cool parking attendant on *77 Sunset Strip* who wowed millions of viewers each week with his hair-combing technique, for a duet titled, naturally, "Kookie, Kookie (Lend Me Your Comb)." The Top Ten single launched short-lived singing careers for both actors. Tommy Sands had the starring role in *The Singing Idol,* a TV play based very loosely on the life of Elvis Presley. Sands' first hit, "Teen-Age Crush," came from the telecast.

Although most of the teen idols of schlock were cast in something of an Elvis Presley mould, they seldom measured up. There was, however, one television artist who managed to project at least a tenuous continuity with his rockabilly forebears, the

In rock 'n' roll lore, Dick Clark is usually positioned as counterpoint to Alan Freed, promoting white middle-class schlock in opposition to Freed's penchant for black rhythm and blues. While too simplistic to hold up under scrutiny, such dichotomies helped Clark survive the official attacks on rock 'n' roll that destroyed Freed.

soft-spoken, soft-rocking Ricky Nelson. As rock 'n' roll became more mainstream, a less rebellious, more middle-class new "Elvis" was required, and for a time, Nelson filled the bill. Nelson grew up playing himself with his real-life family on a TV sitcom titled *The Adventures of Ozzie and Harriet,* a show about a so-called normal middle-class suburban family in the 1950s. In 1957, Verve Records hit on the idea of recording Nelson singing on the show. His mediocre cover of Fats Domino's "I'm Walking" broke into the Top Twenty, while the flip side, "A Teenager's Romance,"

> *Although most of the teen idols of schlock were cast in something of an Elvis Presley mold, they seldom measured up.*

unexpectedly went to number two. Imperial, which was Domino's label, was so impressed with Nelson's success that the company bought his contract from Verve and set about promoting him as a respectable alternative to Presley. Over the next seven years, Nelson released twenty-five Top Forty hits on Imperial, including "Be-Bop Baby" and "Stood Up" (1957), "Believe What You Say" and "Poor Little Fool" (1958), "It's Late (1959), and "Travelin' Man" backed with "Hello Mary Lou" (1961), as well as a few more on Decca before he was swamped by the British onslaught.

While there is no question that Nelson's clean-cut image and popular TV series figured heavily in his success as a singer, he was not simply a creation of the media. Unlike most of the teen idols of schlock, he was well rooted in music. His father was a multitalented big band leader in the 1930s with nearly forty hit records to his credit. His mother was the band's vocalist. His backup band included guitarist James Burton, who went on to join Presley, and most of his own early hits were written by Dorsey and/or Johnny Burnette, two over-the-top rockabilly artists whose backgrounds were similar to Presley's. Furthermore, Nelson had the capacity to grow as a singer. After his untimely death in 1985, he was eulogized as a country rock singer of some stature. Looking at the early days of his career, however, it is impossible to separate his success from the move to make rock 'n' roll both white and middle class.

The Brill Building: The New Tin Pan Alley

As rock 'n' roll became too popular for the established music industry to ignore, it also attracted a new breed of professional to its ranks—songwriters with a respect for the Tin Pan Alley tradition who could write (and sometimes sing) in teenage idiom. They put another nail in the coffin of early rock 'n' roll even as they tried to professionalize the genre. Paul Anka, a Canadian of Middle Eastern descent, aspired to a career as a professional songwriter and, as a brash teenager, was convinced he could sing as well. After an initial release on a local label in 1956, he took advantage of some indirect professional connections and, while in Los Angeles, pitched his next batch of tunes to Don Costa, a record executive at ABC-Paramount. Costa signed him immediately and produced Anka's first record, the Latin-inflected "Diana" (1957), written for an older babysitter from his childhood years. The song became a number one hit single. With Costa arranging and conducting, Anka continued to do well in the pop market until the British Invasion in 1964 swept away all the reigning popular styles. Undaunted, he segued into the role of adult songwriter, penning "Johnny's Theme" for the *Tonight Show* and the lyrics to "My Way" for Sinatra. "That was the turning point—in '68—for me, as *From Here to Eternity* was for him in '55," Anka once told an interviewer. "Suddenly, after years of sending out songs and demos, I was accepted and recognized as a writer—I mean, for others."[19] Such validation was

Paul Anka was one teen idol who got more gratification from being a songwriter. He was part of a stable of young writers who found a home near the Brill Building, the Tin Pan Alley of rock 'n' roll.

more important to Anka than his rock 'n' roll career.

Neil Sedaka was a concert pianist who studied at Julliard. Like Anka, he began his career as a professional songwriter, working in constant collaboration with Howard Greenfield, his high-school friend. Sedaka and Greenfield displayed a versatility and a breadth—ranging from "Stupid Cupid" and "Frankie" for Connie Francis to "Since You've Been Gone" for Clyde McPhatter and "I Waited Too Long" for LaVern Baker—that defy easy categorization. Sedaka's own singing career, however, was defined by a series of trivial teen-oriented songs, with his light tenor double-tracked over a moderate beat. Sedaka and Greenfield, like Anka, turned more toward adult pop following the British Invasion, writing for Peggy Lee, Johnny Mathis, and the Fifth Dimension, among others.

It is easy to associate writers like Anka and Sedaka and Greenfield with the death of rock 'n' roll—they wrote plenty of anemic material and effortlessly made the transition to adult songwriting. At the same time, they were part of a larger and more complicated effort to professionalize rock 'n' roll by restoring a Tin Pan Alley approach to popular music. This effort harked back to a division of labour in which writers wrote songs, singers sang them, and artists and repertoire men brought the two together. In this model, corporate executives could feel reasonably assured that the appropriate artist would be matched with a professionally written song. The physical and spiritual centre of this new enterprise was the Brill Building at 1619 Broadway, the new uptown location for a new Tin Pan Alley. In cramped quarters, songwriting teams like Gerry Goffin and Carole King, Barry Mann and Cynthia Weil, Howard Greenfield and Neil Sedaka, Jeff Barry and Ellie Greenwich, and Doc Pomus and Mort Shuman pounded out new melodies in much the same way that their Tin Pan Alley forebears had decades earlier. This new generation of composers were to rock 'n' roll what Richard Rodgers and Lorenz Hart and George and Ira Gershwin were to the popular music of an earlier time. The results were mixed.

Following the successful pairing of the song "Stupid Cupid" with Connie Francis, Sedaka and Greenfield went to work for Al Nevins and Don Kirschner at Aldon Music, the flagship company of Brill Building pop, which was actually located across the street. Like Sedaka and Greenfield, Aldon's other young writers (which included Goffin/King, Mann/Weil, and even Bobby Darin for a time) displayed consummate skill, real innovation, and genuine sensitivity one minute and a truly incredible flair for the insipid the next. It is difficult to imagine that the same Gerry Goffin and Carole King who wrote "Up on the Roof" for the Drifters and "Natural Woman" for Aretha Franklin also wrote "Her Royal Majesty" for James Darren and "Pleasant Valley Sunday" for the Monkees. How could Barry Mann and Cynthia Weil have turned out both "You've Lost That Lovin' Feeling" for the Righteous Brothers and "Blame It on the Bossa Nova" for Eydie Gorme? As contradictory as it seems, the Brill Building writers produced some of best rock 'n' roll of the era as well as some of the worst schlock imaginable.

Aldon's young writers displayed consummate skill, real innovation, and genuine sensitivity one minute and a truly incredible flair for the insipid the next.

The Official Attack on Rock 'n' Roll

As the ascendancy of schlock rock perhaps proves, by the mid-1950s, rock 'n' roll had become the focal point for all of society's fears of miscegenation, sexuality, violence, juvenile delinquency, and general moral decline. In the eyes of many, the danger was not simply that the music was urban, sexual, and black; such music had been around for a long time. The danger was that it was no longer contained on "the other side of the tracks." Rock 'n' roll's biggest sin was to bring styles of music that were considered class- and race-specific into the mainstream and in so doing to redefine our conception of popular music.

Indications of the racism that was explicitly part of the backlash against rock 'n' roll can be found in media coverage of the time. In reviewing a concert at Maple Leaf Gardens that featured Bill Haley and the Comets, Joe Turner, and Bo Diddley in April 1956, a reporter for *The Toronto Star* referred to the audience as behaving "like natives at a voodoo ritual." In the same review, the reporter described the concert as "a rock'n'roll orgy that resembled a wild west show, a jungle extravaganza, and a revival meeting all in one." Similarly, in reviewing another show at Maple Leaf Gardens in February 1957, the *Star* referred to the "jungle tempo" of the songs and described the event as follows: "Teen-agers swarmed around the stage, dancing in the aisles, cheering, screeching, flinging their arms, shaking their heads and looking like South American head-hunters getting warmed up for a party."

The opening salvo of organized opposition began in late 1954, even before the term *rock 'n' roll* had come into widespread usage. Opining that the rash of sexual double entendres entering the mainstream primarily through r&b crossovers was in poor taste, the entertainment trade papers called on the industry to police itself lest other forces do it for them. An editorial in *Variety,* one of the leading trade papers, coined the term *leer-ics* to call attention to the objectionable phrases. The editorial was widely reprinted and generated a considerable public response, allowing *Variety* to congratulate itself for having its finger on the moral pulse of the nation. Fearing reprisals, record companies, ranging from majors like RCA and Decca to independents like King, and radio stations, including prominent black-oriented outlets like WDIA in Memphis, announced campaigns to weed out suggestive lyrics. To keep them honest, Catholic youth organizations in Boston, Chicago, and Minneapolis, and fundamentalist religious groups all over the South supplied lists of objectionable records. As one might expect, such songs as "Sixty Minute Man" and "Work with Me Annie" made all the lists, but even the

Everly Brothers' "Wake Up Little Susie" managed to get banned in Boston. Municipalities set up review boards to screen new releases. When all else failed, police confiscated offensive records and jukeboxes.

Finding their concentration on "smutty" lyrics did not stop the music, opponents then changed their tactics. After 1955, according to Linda Martin and Kerry Segrave,

> *the anti-rock advocates moved into broader attacks on the music. Attacking with just a sexual brush could only "tar" a few songs. By moving into wider areas of attack the opposition hoped to tar the full spectrum of rock 'n' roll. Henceforth attacks would centre more on the poor and abysmal quality of rock music, its supposed effect in creating juvenile delinquency, and the lewdness of performers themselves.*[20]

To its credit, the industry was not uniformly in agreement on these matters. "American pop music today, despite the attacks upon it, is in its most vital period," editorialized the outspoken Paul Ackerman in *Billboard*. "It most broadly reflects the diverse elements making up musical America. It is rich and fresh in sound and content."[21] Still, the attacks on rock 'n' roll both within and outside the music industry created a climate that encouraged more official interventions. These interventions came about through a loosely coordinated series of government investigations and legislative actions that culminated in the infamous "payola hearings" of 1959 and 1960. As noted in Chapter 1, payola—the practice of "paying for play," that is, offering financial, sexual, or other personal inducements in return for promotion—was hardly a new-comer to the music business. Song plugging, as the practice was called earlier in the century, had been the linchpin of industry marketing since the heyday of Tin Pan Alley. As early as World War I, it was estimated that about $400,000 per year was paid to singers for the express purpose of pushing certain songs. Indeed, similar practices have characterized the development of most industries in their formative stages. In the 1950s, however, the focus on payola in the music industry became the operative strategy for neutralizing rock 'n' roll.

Beneath all the high-toned rhetoric lay a massive accumulation of ignorance and racism and a fair amount of unabashed economic and political self-interest.

Acting in concert, if not conspiracy, ASCAP and some of its most notable publishers, the major record companies and some of their biggest stars, and the U.S. government and some of its most tiresome elected officials waged a protracted public battle for a return to "good music." As most rock 'n' roll material was written by BMI writers, ASCAP, which had been at war with BMI since 1939, was more than happy to join in the fray. For them, the attack on rock 'n' roll was simply an escalation of their continuing efforts to put BMI out of business. For the major labels, the fight was an attempt to halt the expansion of the independents. Forty of the seventy records to make the Top Ten in 1957, for example, were produced by independent labels.[22] To conservative elected officials, jumping on the bandwagon with the likes of Frank Sinatra, Bing Crosby, Steve Allen, Ira Gershwin, and Oscar Hammerstein may have seemed like a sure way of grabbing some quick and memorable headlines. Beneath all the high-toned rhetoric, then, lay a massive accumulation of ignorance and racism and a fair amount of unabashed economic and political self-interest.

What was perhaps most frustrating to society's custodians of good taste and the established powers of the music industry was the fact that they could not understand how rock 'n' roll had gathered such momentum in the first place. For this, they had no one to blame but themselves. By initially ignoring the music in the hope that it was a passing fad, they had allowed it to gain a following that could not be turned around. As it had gained ascendancy, rock 'n' roll had brought with it a number of changes in the way popular music was produced and disseminated, changes that made it much more difficult to contain. Unlike the mainstream pop that had been produced by the major record companies according to a fairly precise division of labour and with fairly clear lines of power and authority, rock 'n' roll was the product of a highly decentralized and disorganized network of independent and very idiosyncratic writers, publishers, performers, producers, and distributors. In the world of rock 'n' roll, a single person often played multiple roles. As the beneficiaries of technological advances that encouraged low-cost, independent production and distribution, the entrepreneurs of rock 'n' roll precipitated major shifts in the economic infrastructure of the music industry. These shifts tended to democratize and decentralize the production of popular music, as a *Billboard* study comparing production in 1939 and 1959 illustrated. As Arnold Shaw notes:

> *Whereas the publishers of Top Ten songs in '39 were all located in New York, in '59 they were distributed in eight states. The songwriters now came from eighteen states instead of three. In '39 Top Ten disks were made by only three companies; in '59 by thirty-nine companies. And these companies, instead of all being located in New York, were distributed in ten states.*
>
> *The conclusion was inescapable: music business had broken out of Broadway, and Tin Pan Alley was gone as a shaper of trends and styles.*[23]

Although the established powers of the industry were certain that they wanted to eliminate rock 'n' roll, they were never sure, given the anarchy of its production, where or how to intervene. In the complex network of flamboyant personalities that produced rock 'n' roll, it was not easy to point to a particular place at which the flow of product could be stopped. Thus, as historian Trent Hill has argued, "One way to read the payola hearings is as an attempt—an attempt that was ultimately successful—to force a greater degree of organization and hierarchical responsibility onto the record industry so that the flow of music/product could be more easily regulated."[24]

ASCAP, which was in effect the organizational agent of Tin Pan Alley, led the charge. In 1953, thirty-three ASCAP members filed a $150 million antitrust suit against BMI, charging it with a conspiracy to dominate the market by keeping ASCAP music off the radio. Sydney M. Kaye, chairman of BMI, promptly pointed out that none of the radio stations that owned stock in BMI had ever received a dividend and that "all broadcasters have so-called blanket licenses from both ASCAP and BMI. . . . They cannot save one penny if they play more BMI and less ASCAP music. Broadcasters have, therefore, no incentive to discriminate against ASCAP music."[25] In sworn testimony, Stanley Adams, the president of ASCAP, could not identify a single station or network that had discriminated against ASCAP. Still, ASCAP continued to attack.

In 1956, under pressure from the Songwriters of America, a group of some 700 ASCAP writers, the Antitrust Subcommittee of the House Judiciary Committee, which was chaired by Congressman Emmanuel Celler, halted their investigation of rigged television quiz shows to ini-

Although the established powers of the industry were certain that they wanted to eliminate rock 'n' roll, they were never sure, given the anarchy of its production, where or how to intervene. In the complex network of flamboyant personalities that produced rock 'n' roll, it was not easy to point to a particular place at which the flow of product could be stopped.

tiate a probe into BMI. Officially, the committee was to investigate whether or not the structural relationship between BMI and radio had any influence on the music that was aired. However, Congressman Celler made clear the racial aspects of the investigation when he said: "Well, rock and roll has its place. There is no question about it. It's given great impetus to talent, particularly among the colored people. It's a natural expression of their emotions and feelings."[26] Although the committee heard testimony from a parade of influential ASCAP writers, it could find no evidence of wrongdoing on the part of BMI and referred the matter to the Justice Department.

The next battle occurred in 1958 when ASCAP succeeded in having introduced in the Senate a bill that would have prevented broadcasters from owning any BMI stock. To gather support for the bill, no less a figure than Frank Sinatra wrote:

> *My only sorrow is the unrelenting insistence of recording and motion picture companies upon purveying the most brutal, ugly, degenerate, vicious form of expression it has been my misfortune to hear—naturally, I refer to the bulk of rock 'n' roll.*
>
> *It fosters almost totally negative and destructive reactions in young people. It smells phony and false. It is sung, played and written for the most part by cretinous goons and by means of its almost imbecilic reiterations and sly—lewd—in plain fact, dirty—lyrics, and as I said before, it manages to be the martial music of every sideburned delinquent on the face of the earth. This rancid aphrodisiac I deplore.*[27]

Once again, a chorus of ASCAP sympathizers held forth. The Songwriters Protective Association, which was made up of ASCAP members, testified before the Communications Subcommittee of the Senate Committee on Interstate and Foreign Commerce, charged with gathering information relevant to the bill. If there were any doubts about the racial implications of Sinatra's statement, those doubts were certainly erased by Vance Packard, who, appearing at the hearing as a paid witness, declared that rock 'n' roll "was inspired by what had been called race music modified to stir the animal instinct in modern teenagers."[28] Even with 1,200 pages of such testimony, however, the bill died in committee.

In 1959, rock 'n' roll's opponents came closer to hitting its nerve centre when ASCAP convinced the Legislative Oversight Subcommittee of the House Committee on Interstate and Foreign Commerce to launch a new probe into payola just as the committee's investigation of rigged television quiz shows was coming to an end. Rock 'n' roll's opponents reasoned correctly that radio had been the primary vehicle for popularizing rock 'n' roll and that deejays had become powerful, largely unregulated figures in the process. Curtailing their freedom, opponents argued, could go a long way toward stopping the flow of music. While the committee, which was chaired by Arkansas Democrat Oren Harris, was convened to investigate abuses at all levels of the recording industry, deejays became the main targets of its hearings.

Ignoring all previous evidence, the payola hearings proceeded according to the assumption that no deejay would play a music as inferior and tasteless as rock 'n' roll unless he was handsomely rewarded for it. It never occurred to the committee that the deejays and their fans

The payola hearings proceeded according to the assumption that no deejay would play a music as inferior and tasteless as rock 'n' roll unless he was handsomely rewarded for it.

liked the music. The most damning indictment in the payola hearings was that of Alan Freed. While other deejays also fell victim to the probe, Freed was the most visible symbol of everything that many found threatening about the music and thus the most obvious target. He had played a major role in popularizing r&b among white teenagers to begin with, and he had continued to push original black recordings during the cover-record period. He had also refused to sign a statement saying that he had never received money or gifts to promote records. In fact, Freed had been a controversial figure in the music business since he had turned to r&b in 1951. He had first run afoul of the law when a concert he staged in 1952 at the Cleveland Arena was oversold and had to be canceled. Although he was charged with fraud (the charge was eventually dropped), the real issue had been that the crowd was half black and half white at a time when Cleveland was a segregated city. Freed ran into a similar problem in Boston in 1958 when a concert staged at the Boston Arena degenerated into violence outside the facility. This time Freed was indicted on two charges of inciting a riot. One week after the concert, he was no longer a WINS deejay. He moved to a slot at WABC radio and shortly thereafter also began hosting a dance party on WNEW-TV. In November 1959, after one of his Boston indictments had been dropped and he had pleaded no contest to the other, he was fired from WABC. Two days later, he lost his job at WNEW as well. By the time the payola hearings really took off, Freed's career was already on the ropes. In 1960, he was arrested for accepting $30,000 in payola and two years later was fined and given a suspended sentence. Unemployed and penniless, he was indicted again in 1964 for income tax evasion. He died of uremia the following year, a broken man.

Dick Clark, in contrast, came through the payola hearings without a smudge on his reputation. Clark was no cleaner than Freed, but he represented an acceptability that Freed did not. Clark was also toting up some $12 million in annual billings for ABC, compared with Freed's $250,000. As a result, ABC-TV issued a statement in support of Clark even after the radio division had fired Freed. Having voluntarily divested himself of the companies that would be most likely to show conflicts of interest, Clark was pronounced "a fine young man" by chairman Oren Harris. If anything, Clark's position within the music industry was strengthened by the hearings.

When all was said and done, the committee had unearthed little. A mail survey by the committee had revealed $263,245 in payola to deejays, but there was no hard evidence to back this figure. This was not even comparable to World War I levels of abuse, and so one cannot help but wonder what all the fuss was about. Still, the number of deejays who felt compelled to come forward and confess their sins was reminiscent of the worst aspects of the McCarthy era. Furthermore, as they had during the McCarthy era, reams of public testimony and extensive media coverage helped to create a climate so unfavourable to "down and dirty" rock 'n' roll that the music described here as schlock rock was encouraged further. Of course, by the time the committee had finished its deliberations, much of the work to contain rock 'n' roll had ceased to be necessary, as a number of the most prominent rock 'n' roll pioneers had already been neutralized in one way or another. Presley had been drafted in early 1958, and by the time he came home from Germany in 1960, his influence in shaping the genre had ended.

> The number of deejays who felt compelled to come forward and confess their sins was reminiscent of the worst aspects of the McCarthy era.

Indeed, through television appearances with Frank Sinatra and films like *Blue Hawaii* and *Viva Las Vegas,* he had become family entertainment, if not worse. Little Richard had quit rock 'n' roll in the late fifties to join the ministry. Jerry Lee Lewis' career had self-destructed in 1958 when he married his cousin. Buddy Holly had died in a tragic plane crash along with Ritchie Valens and the Big Bopper in 1959, the same year the committee began its hearings. Later that year, Chuck Berry's arrest for a violation of the Mann Act had effectively removed him from the rock 'n' roll scene.

In the end, the hearings were instrumental in passing a bill that outlawed payola. The most immediate effect of the bill was to impose on radio a tighter, more hierarchical structure that rendered the flow of popular music easier to control. Thus, in effect, mainstream radio was caught between a rock and a hard place. Severely chastised by the committee, which had delivered its racial message in no uncertain terms, and fearful of FCC reprisals that could affect licensing, rock radio became skittish about programming too many black artists. However, there was still a demand for the music, so rock stations could not afford to ignore it completely. In general, they responded by playing as few black artists as they could without losing their listenership.

Surf's Up!

In the early 1960s, as the second generation of schlock rockers pitted their dubious talents against the more complicated phenomenon of the "girl groups" and the emergence of Motown (two developments that will be dealt with in the next chapter), surf music emerged with vocal and instrumental variants. Its trajectory was remarkably short, essentially rising and falling from 1962 to 1964. While, on the one hand, surf music must take its historical place as part of the continuing trend to make rock 'n' roll both white and middle class, it has proven to be a more complex phenomenon than this. Certainly, nowhere is the imagery of white middle-class America more apparent than in surf music, and certainly in the early 1960s surfing became the central metaphor for an easygoing lifestyle based on the unabashed celebration of consumption. As Lillian Roxon has noted, the emergence of this sound "marked the first time in music history that a sport actually had its own music."[29] Its themes dealt primarily with images of affluence—expensive fast cars, attractive women and men at leisure on the beach, and, of course, surfing itself. Still, unlike schlock, which offered rock 'n' roll little more than a backward look to pop song stylists of an earlier era, surf music provided something of a gateway to the 1960s. It offered a vibrant, driving sound worthy of the name *rock 'n' roll.* As Steve Chapple and this book's American author have argued elsewhere:

> *The surfing music that appeared in the early sixties should not be seen as just another fad that softened rock 'n' roll. Rather it was a precursor to the psychedelic and underground progressive rock of the sixties. Several of the important people involved in surfing music—especially the Beach Boys . . . and Lou Adler, one of the first producers of Jan and Dean, became central figures in sixties rock. Surfing music represented an authentic West Coast rock 'n' roll culture that differed in one important way from earlier rock 'n' roll produced by urban blacks and Southern rockabillies: it was made by middle-class whites.*[30]

Of course, surf music should not be confused with the drivel that had issued from Hollywood "beach party" movies (*Bikini Beach, Beach Blanket Bingo*) a few years earlier. These movies, which began in 1959 with *Gidget,* starring Sandra Dee and James Darren, and reached their zenith in 1963 with *Beach Party,* starring Annette Funicello and Frankie Avalon, transformed the southern California surf cult into a national fad but trivialized the vitality and discipline of the sport with their focus on bikinis and middle-class teen dilemmas. They do represent, however, one instance in which Hollywood beat the record companies to the punch by nearly four years.

The prototypical surf music group was Dick Dale and the Del-tones from southern California. Working closely with Leo Fender, creator of the first solid-body electric guitars, Dale helped to develop the amplification and reverberation equipment that gave much of surf music its distinctive sound. He and his group were a powerhouse live combo with a dedicated following that had a local hit with "Let's Go Trippin'" in 1961. On the strength of the group's live shows, Capitol offered Dale and the Del-tones a contract with a hefty promotional budget in 1963, but the group failed to deliver any hits. By this time, the group's strong bass lines, sax-based instrumentals, and Dale's harsh vocal style—indeed, the very name of the band—seemed almost anachronistic in the national market. It would be left to other groups, primarily from southern California, to establish the style nationally. A number of these groups were instrumental ensembles. First out of the gate were the Marketts, who released "Surfer's Stomp" in 1962. That same year, a British group, the Tornadoes, effected a surf sound on "Telstar," a number one hit. Instrumental surf peaked in 1963 with the release of "Pipeline," by the Chantays, "Wipe Out," by the Surfaris, and "The Lonely Surfer," by session man Jack Nitzsche. The Pyramids scored with "Penetration" in 1964, and by this time, other groups from across the country, such as the Astronauts from Denver, had found their way into the pop market through the surf tag. But 1964 was really the swan song for surf as the British Invasion effectively washed away the entire genre.

In its short life, instrumental surf music was part of a venerable tradition of instrumental rock 'n' roll that began with talented musicians like organist Bill Doggett ("Honky Tonk," 1956), alto sax player Bill Justis ("Raunchy," 1957), who worked as a staff producer at Sun Records, and Bill Black, Elvis Presley's original bass player, who went on to record eight Top Thirty instrumental hits with his own combo. Initially, instrumental rock 'n' roll drew on a wide range of sources. The Champs' "Tequila" echoed the Chicano rhythms of the Southwest. Jazz drummer Cozy Cole broke into the rock 'n' roll market in 1958 with "Topsy (part II)," a revived Basie tune from the late 1930s. It was followed with "Topsy (part I)" and "Turvy (part II)" in 1958. In 1959, Santo and Johnny Farina from Brooklyn had a number one hit with "Sleep Walk," which featured a lilting Hawaiian steel guitar. In 1960, the Viscounts resurrected a version of the jazz classic "Harlem Nocturne" with enough tremolo and echo to qualify it as pure rock 'n' roll.

But it was as novelty music that instrumental rock 'n' roll had its greatest successes. In 1959, Johnny and the Hurricanes hit number five with "Red River Rock," a rock 'n' roll version of the traditional "Red River Valley." This was quickly followed by "Reveille Rock" (1959), an adaptation of the Army bugle call, and "Beatnik Fly" (1960), a remake of Burl Ives' "Blue Tail Fly." Kokomo pillaged a Grieg piano concerto to turn "Asia Minor" into a Top Ten rock 'n' roll hit in 1961. That same year, B. Bumble and the Stingers turned "The Flight of the Bumble Bee" into a boogie-woogie piano hit called "Bumble Boogie." The group followed up in 1962 with "Nut Rocker," a rock 'n' roll version of Tchaikovsky's "The Nutcracker." The subtlety and polish of Cozy Cole gave way to the novelty drumming of Sandy Nelson, whose adolescent pounding on "Teen Beat" (1959) and "Let There Be Drums" (1961) anticipates the classic surf drum solo that appeared on "Wipe Out."

There were two groups that dominated the guitar-based sound that eventually came to define instrumental rock 'n' roll—Duane Eddy and the Rebels, and the Ventures. Eddy and the Rebels were the most successful, but the Ventures were the most influential. Both, however, contributed to the effort to make rock 'n' roll, instrumental or not, white and middle class. In the hands of Dick Clark, Eddy became another teen idol. The Ventures, the pride of Seattle, established the instrumentation of the classic rock 'n' roll quartet—electric lead, rhythm, and bass guitars and drums, no horns, no keyboards, just electricity and rhythm. On their debut single, "Walk—Don't Run" (1960), the group evidenced polish and technical precision, without sacrificing excitement and drive. The group also had versatility, as its rock 'n' roll version of the Latin standard "Perfidia" in 1960 indicates. Overall, the Ventures enjoyed a longevity that was rare for an instrumental group, and they recorded more than fifty albums, sixteen of which made the Top Forty. In fact, neither the twist craze nor the turn toward surf music in the early sixties fazed the group. Surf even provided the Ventures with a new marketing hook in 1964, as they entered the Top Ten with a surf remake of their rock standard titled "Walk—Don't Run '64." As rock writer Greg Shaw has noted, however, "Surf music was the last hurrah for instrumental rock as a popular genre; after the British Invasion of 1964, vocals again assumed primacy in white rock."[31] By this time, surf music itself had become a vocally dominant music with hits such as the Hondells' "Little Honda," Ronny & the Daytonas' "G.T.O.," and the Rip Chords' "Hey Little Cobra."

As if to anticipate this development, the Beach Boys became the definitive surf group. The group was a family affair. In the early 1960s, brothers Brian Wilson (keyboards, bass), Carl Wilson (guitar), and Dennis Wilson (drums) teamed up with their cousin Mike Love (lead vocals) and their Hawthorne, California, neighbor Al Jardine (guitar, bass) to form the most popular self-contained vocal/instrumental combo in town. The only surfer in the group was Dennis, but he convinced Brian and Mike Love to write songs that elevated the sport and its cultural trappings to a metaphor for the American Dream. Their images, like surf music in general, were bound to a kind of affluence that was available to only a narrow segment of the population. In the early 1960s, such images contrasted sharply with those of the burgeoning Civil Rights movement. Seemingly oblivious to their own privilege or the social currents around them, the Beach Boys were hardly apologetic for their music. "We're white and we sing white," the group said.[32] Despite this comment, the group copped the tune (at least with attribution) for "Surfin' U.S.A.," their first Top Ten single, from Chuck Berry's "Sweet Little Sixteen." In many ways, however, it was fitting that the group should "collaborate" with Berry. After all, barring the suburban focus and a West Coast orientation, the Beach Boys constructed teen anthems in much the same way that Berry did. The group's sophisticated close harmonies and elegant counterpoint created a sound that was unique among white rock groups.

The Beach Boys constructed teen anthems in much the same way that Chuck Berry did. The group's sophisticated close harmonies and elegant counterpoint created a sound that was unique among white rock groups.

The Beach Boys first came to national attention in 1962 when their first release, "Surfin'," which had been a local hit the previous year, reached number seventy-five on the national pop charts. Signed by Capitol that same year, the group hit number fourteen with "Surfin' Safari." The group's biggest year was 1963, which was also the peak of the surfing fad. "Surfin' U.S.A.," backed with "Shut Down"; "Surfer Girl," backed with "Little Deuce Coup"; and "Be True to Your School," backed with "In My Room" all hit the charts between April and

"Surfin' U.S.A."

Artist: The Beach Boys
Music / Lyrics by Brian Wilson
and Chuck Berry
Label: Capitol (1963)

The Beach Boys' music is distinguished from the many "surf and sun" bands of the 1960s by the innovative production skills of leader/songwriter Brian Wilson. His methods of complex, multi-sectioned musical structures ("Good Vibrations"), multiple layers of overdubbed vocal harmonies, and sophisticated production techniques were emulated by many of their contemporaries. (The Beatles have often cited the influence of the Beach Boys' *Pet Sounds* LP on *Sgt. Pepper's Lonely Hearts Club Band*.)

"Surfin' U.S.A." is notable for having been included in the Rock and Roll Hall of Fame's list of *50 Songs That Shaped Rock and Roll*.

Musical Style Notes

The musical style of "Surfin' U.S.A." has three major elements: the influence of Chuck Berry, the musical conventions of "surf" music, and the Beach Boys' signature multiple vocal harmonies.

- The opening guitar riff, the chord progressions, and the refrain all borrow heavily from Chuck Berry's song "Sweet Little Sixteen"—so heavily, in fact, that Brian Wilson had to give Berry a songwriting credit on the LP to avoid a lawsuit.

- The "surf music" influence, which is obvious in the lyrics, can be heard in the instrumentation through the high, treble-dominated, and reverb-heavy guitar tone reminiscent of surf music "king" Dick Dale and the relentless, pounding, quarter-note pulse of the bass drum (meaning one drum hit per beat).

- On the refrain "Everybody's gone surfin'," we hear the Beach Boys' impeccable multiple vocal harmonies, with their wide range (from bass to falsetto). This refrain is a good example of a skill shared by both Brian Wilson and Chuck Berry: the ability to write a musical "hook," one of those phrases that gets stuck in your brain for the rest of the day.

Musical "Road Map"

TIMINGS	COMMENTS	LYRICS
0:00–0:02	Introduction—electric guitar riff, borrowed directly from Chuck Berry	
0:02–0:25	Verse 1 Note the vocal background harmony parts, singing on "oo" syllable.	*If everybody had an ocean,* *Across the USA. . .*
0:25–0:49 0:44	Verse 2 Vocal harmony parts acquire their own lyrics: "Inside, outside, USA" Harmony parts join refrain: "Everybody's gone surfin' . . ."	*You'd catch 'em surfin' at Del Mar* *Ventura county line . . .*
0:50–1:13 1:13	Verse 3 Vocal background harmony parts, singing again on "oo" syllable Typical surf-style drum "kick" into fourth verse	*We'll all be planning that route* *We're gonna take real soon . . .*
1:14–1:37 1:32	Verse 4 Vocal harmony parts repeat lyrics from verse 2: "Inside, outside, USA" Harmony parts join refrain: "Everybody's gone surfin' . . ."	*Haggerties and swamis,* *Pacific Palisades . . .*
1:38–1:51	Keyboard (organ) solo and guitar solo over form of the verse Guitar comes in	
1:57–2:26	Harmony parts join refrain: "Everybody's gone surfin' . . ." Refrain repeats five times (fades during fifth repeat)	

The Beach Boys made no bones about infusing rock 'n' roll with white middle-class themes and images. They managed to merge the squeaky cleanliness of Philadelphia schlock with the unbridled energy of a high-school garage band.

November. By 1964, the group's boldly conceived ideology of "Fun, Fun, Fun" was well established, if not quite believable. In pursuit of this ideology, the lyrics of the group's songs "shut down" all challengers on the dragstrip, defended the honour of their high school, and wished aloud that all (attractive) women could be "California Girls." Clearly, the group is vulnerable to the criticism that their songs offered primarily male-oriented, sexist imagery. At their worst, they were no better than the Hollywood beach blanket movies. At the same time, however, they were capable of expressing doubt ("When I Grow Up [To Be a Man]"), even insecurity ("Don't Worry Baby"). Even the most tired clichés became invested with a certain freshness and vitality. Although the group's songs were never quite cynical, they managed to convey the sense that propping up false myths was a task that could not be taken too seriously. In this spirit, they delivered all the raunchiness of a high-school garage band but still managed to sound as squeaky clean as the Philadelphia crowd. The job of managing these contradictions— transforming them into hits—fell mostly to Brian Wilson, a largely self-taught musical genius and an increasingly tortured soul.

Brian had emerged as the group's main writer, arranger, and producer (a rarity in the heyday of artist and repertoire men at major labels) following the extraordinary success of the group's second album, *Surfin' U.S.A.* Never fitting comfortably into the group's sun and fun image, he preferred the safety of the studio, where his demons could be more easily concealed.

He listened to the creations of his idol, Phil Spector, and became determined to perfect the oceanic version of Spector's "wall of sound" (see Chapter 6) based in the group's harmonic virtuosity. Starting with the complicated arrangement and unorthodox harmonies on "I Get Around" (1964), Brian began to push the limits of pop convention. By the time the style was fully developed on "California Girls" (1965), he had also begun testing the limits of his own consciousness with mind-altering drugs. The Beach Boys' *Pet Sounds* LP, released in 1966, experimented with advanced studio techniques well before the Beatles' *Sgt. Pepper* album. After the success of the fully "psychedelic" million-seller, "Good Vibrations," in 1966, Brian embarked on what was supposed to be his crowning achievement—a concept LP tentatively titled *Smile.* A short time into the project, however, his behaviour became erratic. After he had allegedly destroyed many of the album's vocal tracks in a fit of paranoia, the project became irrevocably stalled. The release of *Sgt. Pepper* was the final blow. Brian suffered a complete breakdown and withdrew from the group. The remaining members released a hastily assembled substitute LP called *Smiley Smile,* which included some fine cuts but failed to reach the Top Forty at all. Although the group continued to produce hits, it never regained the magic of Brian's peak years.

The only other act that came within striking distance of the surf crown was Jan and Dean. Jan (Berry), Dean (Torrence), and Arnie Ginsberg, a high-school buddy not to be confused with the deejay of the same name, had been active since 1959 when their performance of "Jennie Lee" became a Top Ten hit. It was released as "Jan and Arnie," since Dean was in the army at the time. A year later, however, Jan and Dean scored another Top Ten hit with a novelty rocker called "Baby Talk." The two did not really hit their stride, however, until 1963, when "Surf City," written by Jan and Brian Wilson, went to the number one slot. "Surf City" clearly established Jan and Dean as a surf act, a marketing label that the two rode to further chart success with "Drag City" in 1963, and "Dead Man's Curve" and "The Little Old Lady (From Pasadena)" in 1964, among others. Unfortunately, in 1966, Jan played out a variation of the story line from "Dead Man's Curve" in real life when he hit a parked vehicle at 65 mph, killing three passengers and sustaining brain damage himself. The tragedy effectively ended the career of Jan and Dean, but only after the genre itself had already self-destructed.

―――――――――――

Because it opened a new chapter in the social relations of class, age, and race (but not gender), rock 'n' roll became a target of attack by those who feared the changes the music signaled. Behind every attack—from cover records to government investigations—was an attempt to reclaim mainstream cultural space for white middle-class values, themes, and images. It can be said that this attempt was at least in part successful as the characteristics that had defined rock 'n' roll in the first place—strong regional accents, hot instrumental solos, and suggestive lyrics—gradually fell by the wayside. In all these changes, the connections between rock 'n' roll and its r&b heritage became more strained, which had the effect of imposing a separation on two genres that had been virtually indistinguishable.

Prior to 1959, rock 'n' roll had effected an extraordinary degree of overlap between the pop and the r&b charts. Not only had black artists gained unprecedented access to the popular market through rock 'n' roll, but white artists had sold to the black public in record numbers. In 1958, for example, more than half the records to make the r&b Top Ten were by white artists.[33] From 1959 on, however, bland white vocalists like Fabian, Frankie Avalon, and Bobby Rydell were marketed as rock 'n' rollers. Although they achieved considerable success as such, their styles were inappropriate for r&b radio, and as a result, white artists' penetration of the r&b market declined sharply. Black radio returned to a policy of programming more black artists than white. Somewhat paradoxically, the separation of rock 'n' roll and r&b contributed to a resurgence of rhythm and blues as a separate style with crossover potential. After 1959, artists like Wilbert Harrison ("Kansas City"), Barrett Strong ("Money"), Jimmy Jones ("Handy Man," "Good Timin'"), the Shirelles ("Will You Love Me Tomorrow," "Dedicated to the One I Love"), Gary "U.S." Bonds ("New Orleans," "Quarter to Three," "School Is Out"), the Crystals ("He's a Rebel"), Gene Chandler ("Duke of Earl"), and the Marvelettes ("Please Mr. Postman") provided a welcome change of pace (and race) in the popular market.

The percentage of black artists crossing over into the popular market remained uncommonly high until the onslaught of British performers in 1964. When the situation is seen in this light, not even the Beatles—the very musicians who breathed new life into the music—can be considered apart from the racist patterns that shaped rock 'n' roll. It is, in fact, impossible to understand the magnitude and immediacy of the Beatles' acceptance in the United States without some reference to this theme. At the same time, it would be a gross distortion of history to underplay their unique contribution to the music and the culture of the 1960s. The Beatles were refreshing, talented, and the harbingers of broad cultural and political change.

Popular Music and Political Culture: The Sixties

The conservative hegemony and control that rock 'n' roll challenged implicitly in the 1950s gave way to open social and political upheaval in the 1960s. Just as the Beatles marked the decade musically, a myriad of grassroots social and political movements—civil rights, antiwar, black power, student power, the counterculture, and later, women's liberation—signified a dramatic shift in the political centre of gravity toward the left. These changes were firmly grounded in contradictions that had been bubbling just beneath the surface of North American life for quite some time.

Throughout the 1950s, the growth of suburbia had been rivaled only by the frenzy of activity euphemistically called "urban renewal." Charges that suburbia could be culturally bankrupt and emotionally deadening and that urban renewal was often little more than neighbourhood removal were dismissed as the price of progress. It was expected that each generation of North Americans would be heir to a higher standard of living than the generation that preceded it. There were, however, a number of paradoxes in this ever-improving picture. In the United States, first and perhaps foremost was the "race problem," which was brought into bold relief by the historic Supreme Court school desegregation decision of 1954 (*Brown* v. *Board of Education*). The Court's decision was the most important government intervention in race relations since the previous century. Second, while Madison Avenue encouraged disciplined workers to become hedonistic consumers, there still existed throughout the country an almost Victorian attitude toward sexuality. In some ways, rock 'n' roll represented an initial (and partial) response to this paradox. Finally, although the country had entered a period of unprecedented affluence, there still existed a widespread, but largely invisible, poverty.

Given that rock 'n' roll crossed the lines of class, race, and age, it is ironic, in retrospect, that civil rights activists tended to avoid the music initially because its commercial bent seemed antithetical to the goals of the struggle.

165

Those who placed their faith in the security of the American Dream found it shaken to the core when the Soviet Union launched *Sputnik*, the first orbiting space satellite, in 1957. The event had implications for everything from military superiority to the computer revolution, still in its infancy. The country entered the era of high technology playing second fiddle to the Soviet Union. Education was seized upon as the key to the future, and there ensued a tremendous expansion of the college and university system nationwide. Because it was envisioned that the society of the future would require an educated labour force, higher education, once the province of the economic and intellectual elite, became available on a mass scale.

Thus, as the 1960s dawned, the United States was in the process of reinventing itself. The search for a new image led to the election of one of the youngest presidents in the history of the country, John F. Kennedy. He would assemble "the best and the brightest," as his advisers were called, to address all the problems of the country, and he would ask his supporters to give unselfishly of themselves in the restructuring of American values. The momentum of his vision and the political acumen of Lyndon Johnson, his vice president and then successor, yielded a spate of landmark legislation and social programming. It was in this context that young men and women of all classes, races, and ethnic backgrounds entered (and often dropped out of) college in record numbers. The participation of these young people—indeed, their leadership—in rethinking America produced the movements and the tumultuousness that defined the 1960s.

The Civil Rights Movement and Popular Music

The link between the civil rights movement, the movement from which all other movements took their cue, and music was first forged through early union songs and spirituals such as "Which Side Are You On," "This Little Light of Mine," "Keep Your Eyes on the Prize," "This Land Is Your Land," "Down by the Riverside," and, of course, "We Shall Overcome." Songs like these were, in the words of Bernice Johnson Reagon, the "songs that moved the movement."[1] Given that rock 'n' roll crossed the lines of class, race, and age, it is ironic, in retrospect, that civil rights activists tended to avoid the music initially because its commercial bent seemed antithetical to the goals of the struggle.[2] Still, while civil rights activists may have avoided rock 'n' roll, the civil rights movement had an impact on the larger musical culture, including rock 'n' roll, that went far beyond its own internal practices. In fact, it is possible to analyze the impact of the movement on the national consciousness by charting the trajectory of popular music during this period. Consider, for example, the mid-1950s. During this time, a new activist southern black clergy, led by Reverend Martin Luther King, Jr., began to form political alliances with such secular organizations as the National Association for the Advancement of Colored People (NAACP), the Congress on Racial Equality (CORE) and later, the Student Non-Violent Coordinating Committee (SNCC). At the same time, as Nelson George has noted, "The music world was witnessing the breaking of a longstanding taboo, as gospel began to fuse with rhythm and blues."[3] Thus, in popular music, as in the struggle for civil rights, the black church became a force to be reckoned with. Prior to the eruption of civil rights as a national issue, there were a number of regional struggles for equal rights. As these struggles, which were based primarily in the South, came to national attention, early rock 'n' roll, based on southern r&b styles, found a national audience. In Montgomery, Alabama, in 1955, Rosa Parks moved up to the front of a segregated bus and refused to relinquish her seat. Her defiance struck a blow for racial equality at the same time that Fats Domino, Little Richard, and Chuck Berry began to conquer the mainstream market as rock 'n' roll heroes. The rebellious tone of early rock 'n' roll mirrored the growing demand for political change in the black community.

> *W*hen Chuck Berry released *"School Day"* in *1957*, he had no problem conjuring up images of teachers teaching *"the golden rule"* even as President Eisenhower sent federal troops to Little Rock to enforce the Supreme Court's school desegregation edict.

With the advent of rock 'n' roll, the form and style of popular music changed dramatically and irrevocably. But these changes were not yet accompanied by analogous changes in lyric content. When Chuck Berry's "School Day" was released in 1957, he sang about teachers teaching "the golden rule" even as President Eisenhower sent federal troops to Little Rock to enforce the Supreme Court's school desegregation edict. Berry may have been a true storyteller in the folkloric sense of the term, but he was also a man of his time. As he would later tell his fans, "I said: 'Why can't I do as Pat Boone does and play good music for the white people and sell as well there as I could in the neighbourhood? And that's what I shot for writing 'School Day.'"[4]

The strategy of the early civil rights movement, like Chuck Berry's crossover dream, was integrationist; even at its most militant—the lunch-counter sit-ins of 1960 and the freedom rides of 1961—the demand was for social equality. Once that was attained, it was argued, full citizenship and assimilation into the mainstream of American life would follow naturally. Issues like institutionalized racism, white skin privilege, and black self-determination were not yet prominent on the political agenda. Society, it was widely believed, did not need a major overhaul but only some intelligent fine tuning. During this period, then, the influence of the civil rights movement on rock 'n' roll is not apparent in the content of its lyrics but in the ascendancy of black producers and black-owned record labels and in the appearance of black female vocal groups. There can be no question that the growing civil rights movement provided a climate that encouraged these developments.

The "Girl Groups" and the Men Behind Them

In the early 1960s, as civil rights activity heated up, r&b moved *uptown,* to use the term Charlie Gillett coined to describe the more polished, distinctly urban production style that came into being. Uptown r&b had been prefigured in Leiber and Stoller's pioneering work with the Drifters ("There Goes My Baby," "Dance with Me," "This Magic Moment," "Save the Last Dance for Me") in 1959 and 1960, and its crossover potential was immediately apparent. Using varying combinations of elaborate instrumentation, lavish studio production, and advanced recording techniques, the next generation of independent r&b producers, which included Luther Dixon, Phil Spector, and Berry Gordy, were able to deliver the forcefulness and emotional impact of rhythm and blues. In the process, they rekindled the spirit of early rock 'n' roll and brought to the forefront for the first time a score of black female vocal groups, known collectively as the "girl groups," that became overwhelmingly popular. In 1962, thanks primarily to the girl groups, there were more black artists on the year-end singles charts (but not the

Phil Spector is often regarded as the genius behind some of the most important "girl groups." The "wall of sound" he created for them produced the perfect marriage of technology and rhythm and blues. It remains one of the defining sounds of the early 1960s.

album charts) than at any time in history. Between 1962 and 1963 alone, for example, the best-seller lists included the Crystals ("He's a Rebel," "Da Doo Ron Ron," "Then He Kissed Me"), the Sensations ("Let Me In"), the Chiffons ("He's So Fine," "One Fine Day"), the Essex ("Easier Said Than Done"), the Ronettes ("Be My Baby"), Ruby and the Romantics ("Our Day Will Come"), and the Motown groups Martha and the Vandellas ("Come and Get These Memories," "Heat Wave," "Quicksand") and the Marvelettes ("Please Mr. Postman," "Playboy"). By 1964, Motown's Supremes had come into their own, and they turned out fifteen hit singles in a row over the next few years. The Orlons ("The Wah Watusi," "Don't Hang Up," "South Street") are often included in these lists, even though they had one male vocalist. The only significant girl groups that were white were the Angels ("My Boyfriend's Back") and the Shangri-Las ("Leader of the Pack"). Still, as talented as these groups were, it is virtually impossible to separate their artistic appeal from the genius of the producers who moulded their sound.

The Shirelles, from Passaic, New Jersey, were the prototypical girl group. They first recorded for the independent Tiara label, which had been formed by Florence Greenberg, one of the very few women to own her own record company. The Shirelles' first hit, "I Met Him on a Sunday," was written by the group; it sold so well locally that it was picked up by Decca for national distribution in 1958. Decca had no faith in the group, however, and their next records were put out on Greenberg's Scepter label. At Scepter, the group was placed under the tutelage of producer Luther Dixon. Combining a plaintive gospel call-and-response style with the urban sensibilities of uptown r&b, Dixon shepherded the Shirelles through a string of hits from 1960 to 1962. Among these recordings, which are now considered rock 'n' roll classics, were "Will You Love Me Tomorrow," "Dedicated to the One I Love," "Mama Said," "Baby It's You," and "Soldier Boy." By 1962, the commercial appeal of female vocal groups had been proven, and Dixon's production techniques, which had been developed simultaneously by Phil Spector and Berry Gordy, had become a virtual science.

Phil Spector, who produced two of the most important groups, the Crystals and the Ronettes, is the producer whose name is most readily associated with the so-called girl group phenomenon. Like Jerry Leiber and Mike Stoller, with whom he apprenticed, Spector was a white man whose vision was to harness the wizardry of studio production and the precision of a professionally written song to the energy and vitality of rhythm and blues. Certainly, there was no better cultural milieu than the unassuming integrationist stance of the early civil rights movement to nurture such a vision. Indeed, "Spanish Harlem" (one of Spector's first hits) and "Black Pearl" (his last) seem to underscore this connection. "Spanish Harlem," a song about a Latina named Rose with "eyes as black as coal," was written by Spector and Leiber within months of Spector's arrival in New York in July 1960. Spector then coproduced the song with Leiber and Stoller for Ben E. King, providing the singer with his first solo hit after leaving the Drifters. In 1969, Spector produced his last Top Twenty hit single for an integrated group called the Checkmates. The song "Black Pearl," which he had written with Toni Wine, was about a black woman who'd "been in the background too long." "Black Pearl and Rose are fascinatingly similar," David Hinckley has written in the liner notes to the Spector boxed set, *Back to Mono:* "shaded flowers to whom the singer offers sun. That Spector helped bring to life a rose that was Spanish and a pearl that was Black reflects a human rainbow pop music did not always acknowledge so sympathetically."[5]

Phil Spector's singular devotion to his recordings contributed greatly to the public perception of him as a Svengali-like producer who treated his artists as one more sonic element in the creation of a total sound. This perception encouraged the notion of the girl groups as replaceable entities on the assembly line of pop.

Spector's artistic vision and his genius for production were matched in equal proportion by his egotism and paranoia. He controlled every aspect of the production process. His resounding financial success (he was a millionaire before his twenty-first birthday) prompted conservative satirist Tom Wolfe to dub him "The First Tycoon of Teen" in an essay of the same name. Describing Spector's recording enterprise, Wolfe noted:

> *Spector does the whole thing. He writes the words and the music, scouts and signs up the talent. He takes them out to a recording studio in Los Angeles and runs the recording session himself. He puts them through hours and days of recording to get the two or three minutes he wants. Two or three minutes out of the whole struggle. He handles the control dials like an electronic maestro, tuning various instruments or sound up, down, out, every which way, using things like two pianos, a harpsichord and three guitars on one record; then re-recording the whole thing with esoteric dubbing and over-dubbing effects—reinforcing instruments or voices—coming out with what is known throughout the industry as "the Spector sound."[6]*

Spector clearly paid attention to detail, indeed, to every detail. While other companies issued multiple releases simultaneously, Spector laboured over and thoroughly promoted only a few records per year. This kind of singular devotion to his recordings contributed greatly to the perception of Spector as a Svengali-like producer who treated his artists as one more sonic element in the creation of a total sound. It was this perception that encouraged the notion of the girl groups as replaceable entities on the assembly line of pop. This notion was further reinforced by the interchangeability of the personnel within the groups that Spector produced. Darlene Love, for example, was and remains a formidable talent. She recorded only two Top Forty hits (both with Spector in 1963) under her own name: "(Today I Met) The Boy I'm Gonna Marry" and "Wait 'Til My Bobby Gets Home." However, she was part of the Blossoms, a group Spector used for background vocals, and a member of Bob B. Soxx & the Blue Jeans, another Spector group that had two Top Forty hits with "Zip-A-Dee Doo-Dah" (1962) and "Why Do Lovers Break Each Other's Hearts" (1963). She also sang lead on two of the Crystals' biggest hits in 1962—"He's a Rebel" and "He's Sure the Boy I Love"—even though she was never listed as a member of the group. In short, there exists something of a Darlene Love legacy that has been overshadowed by the producer's signature and the shoddy practice of crediting recordings incorrectly. Love's case is one of the more dramatic examples of this tendency to undervalue the individual talent of the women singers themselves, focusing instead on a consideration of the girl groups as a social phenomenon or their producers' overall sound.[7]

If the discussion of Phil Spector and the groups he produced seems to embody some of the dreams of the early civil rights movement, then this discussion cannot be complete without also considering the Brill Building songwriters discussed in Chapter 5. While at their worst these writers turned out more than their share of schlock, at their best they accomplished culturally what the early civil rights movement only dreamed of politically: white songwriters and black vocalists incorporating the excitement and urgency of rhythm and blues into the mainstream tradition of professional pop. Nowhere was this marriage better executed than in the classic hits of the girl groups listed on the next page. Gerry Goffin and Carole King wrote "One Fine Day" for the Chiffons, and "Chains" and "Don't Say Nothin' Bad About My Baby" for the Cookies, a trio that was often used for background vocals at Aldon Music. One of the best compositions of the era was their "Will You Love Me Tomorrow," the Shirelles' first number one hit in 1961. If Goffin's lyrics had seemed, up to that point, unusually progressive, he more than compensated for this a year or so later when he wrote "He Hit Me (It Felt Like a Kiss)," which was written for the Crystals but had to be withdrawn for obvious reasons.

By this time, Phil Spector, in partnership with Lester Sill, had formed his own company, Philles Records, and he soon became the Brill Building's best customer, working with top notch songwriting teams like Gerry Goffin and Carole King, Barry Mann and Cynthia Weil, and Ellie Greenwich and Jeff Barry for his top groups, especially the Crystals and the Ronettes. Spector, of course, had a special interest in the Ronettes, eventually marrying the group's lead singer, Veronica Bennett.

The production formula for the girl groups remained largely the same, whether the groups were black or white. When George "Shadow" Morton discovered the Shangri-Las, he called on his high-school friends Ellie Greenwich and Jeff Barry to help him write "Leader of the Pack," the group's best-selling single. The song, which tells the story of an impossible relationship that ends in tragedy as the outlaw biker protagonist speeds to self-destruction, was then recorded with the sound of a real motorcycle and a horrifying crash to emphasize the power of rock 'n' roll. Because gender roles had not yet been challenged, the Shangri-Las, like the other girl groups, were confined to singing about their relationships with men who were "rebels" and "leaders of the pack" and marketed as much for sexual appeal as for musical abilities. As late as 1968, *Rolling Stone*'s Richard Farrar remembered the Ronettes as

> *tough whorish females of the lower class, female Hell's Angels who had about them the aura of brazen sex. The Ronettes were Negro Puerto Rican hooker types with long black hair and skin tight dresses revealing their well-shaped but not quite Tina Turner behinds. . . . Ronettes records should have been sold under the counter along with girly magazines and condoms.*[8]

The British Invasion marked the beginning of the end for the girl groups. For Spector, however, the dream of a pop/r&b fusion continued. Turning his attention to the Righteous Brothers, a white male duo that was better able to stand up to the onslaught of British groups, Spector once again mined gold at the Brill Building, writing the duo's first and biggest hit, "You've Lost That Lovin' Feelin'" (1964) with Barry Mann and Cynthia Weil, and their second release, "Just Once in My Life" (1965), with Gerry Goffin and Carole King. The sound that Spector created for the Righteous Brothers was so successful that it commanded a new marketing category of its own—"blue-eyed soul." Other groups like the Young Rascals ("Good Lovin'," "Groovin'") on Atlantic and Mitch Ryder and the Detroit Wheels ("Sock It to Me, Baby") on

Selected Brill Building Girl Group Classics

SONGWRITERS	SONG	ARTIST
Gerry Goffin and Carole King	"One Fine Day"	Chiffons
	"Chains"	Cookies
	"Don't Say Nothin' Bad About My Baby"	Cookies
	"Will You Love Me Tomorrow"	Shirelles
	"He Hit Me (It Felt Like a Kiss)"	Crystals
(with Phil Spector)	"Is This What I Get for Loving You?"	Ronettes
Barry Mann and Cynthia Weil	"Uptown"	Crystals
	"He's Sure the Boy I Love"	Crystals
(with Phil Spector)	"Walking in the Rain"	Ronettes
Gene Pitney	"He's a Rebel"	Crystals
Ellie Greenwich and Jeff Barry		
(with Phil Spector)	"Da Doo Ron Ron"	Crystals
(with Phil Spector)	"Then He Kissed Me"	Crystals
(with Phil Spector)	"Chapel of Love"	Dixie Cups
(with Phil Spector)	"Be My Baby"	Ronettes
(with Phil Spector)	"Baby I Love You"	Ronettes
(with Phil Spector)	"Wait 'til My Bobby Gets Home"	Darlene Love
(with Phil Spector)	"Not Too Young to Get Married"	Bob B. Soxx & the Blue Jeans
(with Tony Powers)	"(Today I Met) The Boy I'm Gonna Marry"	Darlene Love
(with Tony Powers)	"Why Do Lovers Break Each Others' Hearts"	Bob B. Soxx & the Blue Jeans
(with Shadow Morton)	"Leader of the Pack"	Shangri-Las

New Voice also fit this bill. In these instances, the colour-blindness of the early civil rights movement was reinforced, for here was black-sounding music that was written by whites, produced by whites, performed by whites, and accepted by blacks. Thus, it was a crushing blow to Spector when he was unable to repeat these results with an African American act. "River Deep—Mountain High" (1966) had all the elements of success: it was written by Spector, Greenwich, and Barry; Spector, as producer, was at the height of his wall of sound powers; and the song was performed by Ike and Tina Turner, one of the hottest r&b acts in the business. At the time, it seemed like "River Deep—Mountain High" couldn't miss; Spector thought of it as his finest song, his crowning achievement. When it flopped, the millionaire boy genius of the music industry quickly became the Howard Hughes of rock.

The sound that Phil Spector created for the Righteous Brothers was so successful that it commanded a new marketing category of its own—"blue-eyed soul." The colour-blindness of the early civil rights movement was reinforced, for here was black-sounding music that was written by whites, produced by whites, performed by whites, and accepted by blacks.

The Ronettes belted out some of the most memorable songs of the early 1960s. Often, however, consideration of their talent seemed to be overshadowed by a focus on their sexuality. Too bad the two could not have been appreciated equally.

The girl groups were a short-lived phenomenon for several reasons. Despite their talent and the sophisticated production that accompanied their releases, these artists simply faced too many obstacles: they were, in many ways, a throwback to a 1950s style, they were women, and they were black. After the British Invasion, there were only two girl group releases that ever reached the Top Ten, the Shangri-Las' "I Can Never Go Home Anymore" (1965) and the Chiffons' "Sweet Talkin' Guy" (1966). The Motown blockbuster acts that survived and thrived did so because they transcended the "girl group" label, and they were able to do this because Berry Gordy did not just produce great records, he built long-term careers.

Motown: The Integration of Pop

In the early stages of the civil rights movement, it seemed to many that the primary task facing African Americans was assimilation into the mainstream of American life. It was in this context that Motown developed and defined itself. The company soon integrated the pop market with a success unmatched in the history of the music industry. Until its 1988 purchase by MCA and subsequent conglomerate merger with Matsushita (which eventually sold its interest to Seagram), Motown was the largest black-owned corporation in the United States. Its founder, Berry Gordy, was a tough, black, middle-class jazz buff from Detroit who preferred the world of music to life in the Ford Motor Company. Gordy, who was a regular at local jazz clubs, ran a small jazz record store in the mid-1950s. He was also a prizefighter with a number of wins to his credit. It was his association with Jackie Wilson, a Golden Gloves champion and r&b star, that brought these two strands of his life together. For about three years in the late 1950s, Gordy wrote Wilson's biggest hits, including "Reet Petite," "Lonely Teardrops," "That's Why

(I Love You So)," and "I'll Be Satisfied." During this period, Gordy also met Smokey Robinson of the Miracles. After Gordy wrote and produced a Top Thirty hit for Barrett Strong ("Money," 1960) that was issued on a small family-owned label named after his sister Anna and leased to Chess, Robinson convinced him to start his own company. This was the beginning of the Motown empire.

Motown, which was as private and secretive a company as there ever was, embodied the promise of the early civil rights movement in that it opened a new chapter in the treatment of African American artists in the music industry. With a few notable exceptions, such as session guitarist Joe Messina, virtually all of its creative personnel—artists, writers, producers, and session musicians—were African American, and all were groomed for long careers. At the same time, from its very beginnings, the company envisioned itself as a crossover label. For years, the company had one white employee, Barney Ales, the vice president for distribution, whose relationships with mainstream distributors were crucial to the label's financial health. It was Gordy's job to produce the records that would satisfy their pop needs.

*B*erry Gordy came up with a musical formula that was the perfect metaphor for the early civil rights era: upbeat black pop that was irresistibly danceable and threatening to no one in tone or content. This was the "Motown Sound."

To do this, Gordy, like Spector, evolved a production technique aimed at maximum crossover. Working closely with Smokey Robinson on the label's early releases, he multitracked compelling leads and rich gospel harmonies over strong rhythm and horn tracks and the signature bass lines of the legendary James Jamerson. In doing this, Gordy came up with a musical formula that was the perfect metaphor for the early civil rights era: upbeat black pop that was irresistibly danceable and threatening to no one in tone or content. This was the "Motown Sound," or, as the Motown label logo boasted, "The Sound of Young America." Gordy would later comment that any successful Motown hit sold at least 70 percent to white audiences.

The company was organized as a completely in-house operation totally under the control of Gordy. It included not only the Motown and Tamla labels but also the Hitsville USA studio, Jobete Publishing, and International Talent Management (ITM). ITM provided personal management, including choreographic training by industry veteran Cholly Atkins and lessons on etiquette from local beauty-school owner Maxine Powell, and tour bookings. Remembering Powell, Martha Reeves once recalled: "She taught us how to walk, how to sit proper, and how to get up. She'd have a line of us—the Marvelettes, the Supremes, and the Vandellas all learned together."[9]

To his credit, Gordy built all of his acts from the ground up; he did not simply bleed them for one or two hits, which had been an all too common experience for black artists in the past. As a result, first-generation artists at Motown enjoyed a longevity that was almost unheard of for black artists in the pop market. While other labels may have treated particularly successful groups with such care, Motown approached its whole

Selected Early Motown Top Ten Hits, 1960–1966

Miracles   "Shop Around," "You've Really Got a Hold on Me," "Mickey's Monkey"

Marvelettes   "Please Mr. Postman," "Playboy," "Don't Mess with Bill"

Mary Wells   "The One Who Really Loves You," "You Beat Me to the Punch," "Two Lovers," "My Guy"

Martha and the Vandellas   "Heat Wave," "Quicksand," "Dancing in the Streets," "Nowhere to Run," "I'm Ready for Love"

Temptations   "My Girl," "Beauty Is Only Skin Deep," "(I Know) I'm Losing You"

Four Tops   "I Can't Help Myself," "It's the Same Old Song," "Reach Out I'll Be There," "Standing in the Shadows of Love"

Junior Walker and the All Stars   "Shotgun"

Marvin Gaye   "Pride and Joy," "How Sweet It Is to Be Loved by You," "I'll Be Doggone," "Ain't That Peculiar"

Stevie Wonder   "Fingertips—Part 2," "Uptight (Everything's Alright)," "Blowin' in the Wind," "A Place in the Sun"

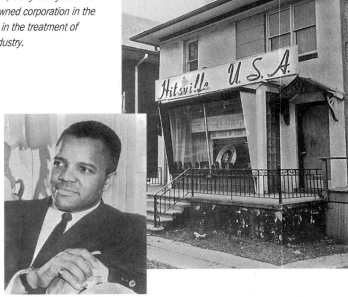

Beginning with a modest studio in Detroit, Berry Gordy built his Motown empire into the largest black-owned corporation in the United States. It opened a new chapter in the treatment of African American artists in the music industry.

roster in these terms, as just a sample of Top Ten Motown hits from 1960 to 1966 (see page 173) proves. From 1961 to 1971, the company placed well over one hundred singles in the pop Top Ten, not to mention hundreds more lesser hits.

Motown really hit its stride in 1964, when the Supremes were assigned to the writer/producer team of Holland-Dozier-Holland. The trio of Florence Ballard, Mary Wilson, and Diana Ross quickly became the jewel in the crown of the Motown empire. Beginning with the release of "Where Did Our Love Go," the Supremes turned out five number one singles in a row, including "Baby Love," "Come See About Me," "Stop! In the Name of Love," and "Back in My Arms Again," no mean achievement for an African American act during the first wave of the British Invasion. By the time Cindy Birdsong (formerly of Patti LaBelle and the Blue Belles) replaced Ballard in 1967, the group had turned out five more number one hits.

It was the company's understanding of the Top Forty radio format, as well as its outstanding artists, that permitted Motown to produce so many hits. On Top Forty radio, records are squeezed in between commercials and fast-talking deejays who sound like used-car salesmen. Understanding the constraints of this AM radio format, Smokey Robinson sought to exercise maximum creativity in a two- to three-minute time frame. In his own words:

My theory of writing is to write a song that has a complete idea and tells a story in the time allotted for a record. . . . I've just geared myself to radio time. The shorter a record is nowadays, the more it's gonna be played. This is a key thing in radio time, you dig? If you have a record that's 2:15 long it's definitely gonna get more play than one that is 3:15 at first, which is very important.[10]

Still, while there may have been a formula mentality for the structure of a song, the formula did not substitute for creativity. With songwriters like Eddie Holland, Lamont Dozier, Brian

"Stop! In the Name of Love"

Artist: The Supremes
Music / Lyrics by Holland-Dozier-Holland
Label: Motown (1965)

The Supremes (Diana Ross, Florence Ballard, Mary Wilson) were Motown's most successful "girl group," part of a roster that also included the Marvelettes and Martha and the Vandellas. Motown employed a whole team of music coaches, choreographers, fashion consultants, and modeling coaches for his artists to create the sleek, elegant image exemplified by the Supremes. Their sound, which took America by storm, was the combined result of their beautifully blended voices, Motown's roster of great recording session players and arrangers, and songwriters such as Smokey Robinson and the team of Eddie Holland, Lamont Dozier, and Brian Holland, who wrote "Stop! In the Name of Love."

"Stop! In the Name of Love" garnered a Grammy nomination in 1966. Gordy's formula for crossover appeal was bearing fruit in many ways: "Stop!" was nominated in the "Best Contemporary Rock and Roll Group Vocal Performance" category and *not* the "Rhythm and Blues" category, as the Supremes' "Baby Love" had been a year before.

Musical Style Notes

Motown's songwriters were masters of the Top Forty "pop song": a simple, familiar musical structure consisting of short verses and catchy, uptempo refrains, usually with one brief solo improvisation over an instrumental verse. Brevity was another consideration; few "pop" singles were over three minutes long. "Stop! In the Name of Love" is a classic example of this kind of structure and also features a signature Motown combination: a strong lead singer plus doo-wop-influenced background vocals, combined with slick, tightly arranged instrumental parts provided by a roster of virtuoso studio musicians known as the "Funk Brothers." The Funk Brothers' roster included a long list of distinguished players, including the unmistakable Motown "rhythm section" of drummer Benny Benjamin and bass player James Jamerson.

Musical "Road Map"

TIMINGS	COMMENTS	LYRICS
0:00–0:10	Electronic organ glissando (rapid slide up through several notes) leads into refrain.	*Stop, in the name of love* *Before you break my heart . . .*
0:10–0:19	Instrumental interlude between refrain and verse	
0:19–0:51	Verse 1	*Baby baby, I'm aware of where you go . . .*
0:28	Background vocals begin.	
0:43	Background vocals: "Think it over" (using same melody as refrain's last phrase)	
0:51–1:17	Refrain (repeated twice) (no instrumental interlude here)	*Stop, in the name of love* *Before you break my heart . . .*
1:17–1:51	Verse 2	*I've known of your . . . your secluded nights . . .*
1:26	Background vocals begin.	
1:42	Background vocals: "Think it over" (using same melody as refrain's last phrase)	
1:51–2:16	Refrain (repeated twice)	*Stop, in the name of love* *Before you break my heart . . .*
2:16–2:33	Verse 3	*I've tried so hard . . . hard to be patient . . .*
2:24	Background vocals begin. ("Think it over" phrase omitted in this verse—instead, they proceed directly into the refrain.)	
2:33–2:54	Refrain (repeated twice)	*Stop, in the name of love* *Before you break my heart . . .*

Holland, Norman Whitfield, and Nick Ashford and Valerie Simpson, Motown boasted an in-house staff that could rival the best of the Brill Building writers. A partial listing of their credits on the chart below more than makes the point.

In his quest for a mainstream audience, Gordy made sure his writers paid heed to the conventional, if unfounded, industry wisdom that controversial issues had no place in the lyric content of popular music. In this self-imposed constraint, Gordy was not alone. Motown took off at a time when the best rock 'n' roll was being composed by Brill Building songwriters, who wrote with intelligence, even wit, but, with few exceptions, an utter lack of substance. When these songs were hits, it was usually because of the distinctive performance of the artist. The pop/soul alliance between writer/producers Burt Bachrach and Hal David and song stylist Dionne Warwick, who recorded for Scepter Records, is a good example of this. Warwick soulful delivery of Bachrach and David's well-crafted tunes transformed lyric fluff into a thing of such beauty that even the British Invasion couldn't slow them down. From 1963 to 1970, Warwick recorded twenty-two Top Forty hits (including "Anyone Who Had a Heart," "Walk on By," and "I Say a Little Prayer") that never broached a topical issue.

Motown's songs were also well constructed and performances were invariably compelling, "but when it came to lyrics," as Gerri Hershey has said, Berry Gordy "had a larger constituency

> *In his quest for a mainstream audience, Berry Gordy made sure his writers paid heed to the conventional, if unfounded, industry wisdom that controversial issues had no place in the lyric content of popular music.*

Selected Hits, Motown Staff Writers

SONGWRITER	SONG	ARTIST
Holland-Dozier-Holland	"Heat Wave"	Martha and the Vandellas
	"Where Did Our Love Go"	Supremes
	"Baby Love"	Supremes
	"Stop! In the Name of Love"	Supremes
	"Baby, I Need Your Loving"	Four Tops
	"I Can't Help Myself"	Four Tops
	"Reach Out, I'll Be There"	Four Tops
Norman Whitfield	"Pride and Joy"	Marvin Gaye
	"I Heard It Through the Grapevine"	Marvin Gaye
	"Girl (Why You Wanna Make Me Blue)"	Temptations
	"(I Know) I'm Losing You"	Temptations
	"You're My Everything"	Temptations
Nick Ashford and Valerie Simpson	"Ain't Nothing Like the Real Thing"	Marvin Gaye and Tammy Terrell
	"Ain't No Mountain High Enough"	Diana Ross

to consider. . . . Gordy's demographics could countenance no overt militancy."[11] It should not be surprising, then, that socially relevant themes and images were no more prevalent in early Motown lyrics than in any other genre of pop, rock, or rhythm and blues. Stevie Wonder's 1966 cover of "Blowin' in the Wind"—six years after the founding of the label and well past the initial surge of the civil rights movement—was easily Motown's most prominent "topical" release. Thus, while the climate of the early civil rights movement encouraged the success of Motown, the company never became a voice for the cause. At the time, social commentary could be found in the folk arena and, to a lesser extent, in jazz. It is perhaps for this reason that the early 1960s saw the popular folk revival that the major labels had tried unsuccessfully to engineer from the top down just a few years earlier.

The Black Music Scene in Canada

The black music scene was very different in Canada. After both the American Revolution and the War of 1812, a few thousand newly emancipated black slaves from the United States moved to Atlantic Canada. The largest settlement was established on the outskirts of Halifax. Initially called Campbell River, the community's name was later changed to Africville. From this community, Brent Williams and Harry Cromwell were members of one of Canada's first bluegrass bands, recording in the early 1950s. Tellingly, after they forwarded a photograph of themselves they were turned down by the CBC for an appearance on *Don Messer's Jubilee*. Unfortunately, at least partially because there was a near total absence of local recording companies, until the 1980s there were no other recordings made by African Canadians from this area. In the 1980s, singer-songwriter Faith Nolan released an album called *Africville*, and vocal quartet Four the Moment (three-quarters of whom are black Nova Scotians) recorded a series of albums that included a handful of songs chronicling the black Maritime experience.

There was also a small black population from the eighteenth century onward in southern Ontario, as up until 1793 slavery had been legal in the area. After the passing of anti-slavery legislation, newly freed slaves in the area were joined by a number of escaped slaves who journeyed to southwest Ontario from the United States via the Underground Railroad. There appear to have been absolutely no popular music recordings made by members of this community.

Until 1967, Canadian immigration laws discriminated against people of colour. Consequently, the black populace in Canada was relatively small, and there were no recording companies of any size that focused on black music. Despite that, in 1963, two southern Ontario black artists, Shirley Matthews and Jackie Shane, released singles that enjoyed substantial chart success. Matthews was born near Windsor in Harrow, Ontario, and started out in the church choir. Moving to Toronto while in high school, upon graduation she began singing rhythm and blues in local clubs. It was while performing at the Toronto r&b mecca Club Blue Note that she was spotted by the producer of the Four Seasons, Bob Crewe, and Toronto record producer Stan Klees. The latter signed her to his Red Leaf Records and Crewe took the big-voiced singer into the studio to record her debut single, "Big Town Boy." A brassy, up-tempo girl group record that could just as easily have been cut in New York or Philadelphia, "Big Town Boy" took the alluringly nasal-voiced Matthews into the CHUM Top Five. A follow-up single, "Private Property," stalled at number eighteen. Although Matthews won a 1964 RPM Gold Leaf Award (the forerunner to the Junos) for "Female Vocalist of the Year," within a couple of years she had married and stopped performing.

Jackie Shane did even better with his 1963 cover of Stax artist William Bell's "Any Other Way." An expatriate American who was openly gay at a time when such behaviour was shocking to mainstream society, Shane was a Toronto favourite, his androgynous performances drawing packed houses of self-styled hipsters every week at the Sapphire Club. Accompanying Shane were Frank Motley and the Hitchhikers. Motley was also an expatriate African American and was famous for playing two trumpets at once. Although "Any Other Way" was a number two hit in Canada, when it was released in the United States on Sue Records, it failed to chart.

Shane was part of the vanguard of a sizable rhythm and blues scene in downtown Toronto in the 1960s and early 1970s. Audiences and musicians alike tuned into George "Hound Dog" Lorenz on Buffalo's WBLK to hear the latest in American rhythm and blues records, and they bought the singles at a local record emporium on Avenue Road that routinely imported black records from the States. Clubs such as Le Coq d'Or, the Bohemian Embassy, Friar's Tavern, and Club Blue Note routinely booked artists such as Shane, as well as local white r&b bands such as Jon Lee and the Checkmates, the Five Rogues, and Ronnie Lane and the Disciples, who hit the CHUM chart in September 1964 with their cover of African American artist Buster Brown's "Fannie Mae." The Five Rogues, featuring vocalists George Oliver and Roy Kenner and guitarist Dominic Troiano (later of the James Gang and the Guess Who), would morph into Mandala, who would enjoy three regional hits in 1967 and 1968, including a superb cover of "Love-Itis" by African American Harvey Scales.

Toronto's fascination with r&b would lead George Clinton and Parliament Funkadelic to relocate to the city between 1969 and 1971. Managed by Ron Scribner, who booked Le Coq d'Or, they recorded their seminal album *America Eats Its Young* in Toronto at Manta Sound, with the help of a bevy of musicians loosely associated with the Canadian band Dr. Music, including saxophonist Steve Kennedy, Prakash John, and vocalist Diane Brooks.

In 1967, under Prime Minister Lester B. Pearson, restrictions on non-white immigration were removed from Canada's Immigration Act. Toronto quickly became a destination for substantial Jamaican immigration. Among these immigrants were a handful of prominent Jamaican musicians, including original Skatalite Jackie Mittoo, producer Stranger Cole, vocalist Alton Ellis, and the singing duo Bob and Wisdom (often referred to as the Canadian Sam and Dave). Many of these artists hung out, rehearsed, and initially gigged at the West Indian Federation Club. Within a few years, private clubs such as Club Tropics, Club Trinidad, and Club Jamaica emerged to cater to the Jamaican expatriate community, and between 1967 and 1972, groups such as Jo-Jo and the Fugitives, the Cougars, and Bob and Wisdom recorded a handful of singles for small labels such as Summus Records, Tuesday Records, Records Tropical, Birchmount Records, Heart Records, Vintage Records, and so on. The majority of these recordings were much closer to American r&b than Jamaican reggae but, without local media oriented to the still relatively small immigrant populace, these records were rarely heard outside the Jamaican community and today are all but unknown. That is unfortunate, as many of these recordings were superb. The best of them, including Jo-Jo and the Fugitives' "Chips-Chicken-Banana Split," released in 1968 on Cobra Records, are among the great unknown Canadian recordings of all time. Other superb Jamaican-Canadian records from this period are Wayne McGhie's 1970s LP *Sounds of Joy*, Jackie Mittoo's 1971 LP *Wishbone*, and Bob and Wisdom's great 1972 cover of Mac Davis' "I Believe in Music." In the 1970s, Jamaican Canadian artists such as Ishan People and Leroy Sibbles were prominent in Toronto, while integrated ensembles playing Jamaican-inflected music such as V and the Satellites, and dub poets such as Lillian Allen and Curtis Joseph, were integral parts of Toronto's Queen Street scene in the 1980s.

For a short while, future funk superstar Rick James lived in Canada. Attempting to avoid the draft, James moved from Buffalo to Toronto, where for a brief period he and Neil Young played together in a group called the Mynah Byrds. While the group was popular locally after recording their solitary single for Motown, it was not long before James moved back to the United States. A short while later, Young would head to California with Bruce Palmer, where he formed Buffalo Springfield with Stephen Stills.

Folk Music: The Voice of Civil Rights

It is impossible to analyze the folk revival of this time without mentioning Woodie Guthrie and Pete Seeger. Avowed left-wing activists since the 1930s, Guthrie and Seeger were no strangers to insurgent political movements. Guthrie, an "Okie" who had been radicalized by the events of the Great Depression, wrote some of this country's most enduring folk songs, including "This Land Is Your Land" and "This Train Is Bound for Glory." His influence on folk music is incalculable. It was, in fact, Guthrie's radio show on KFVD in Los Angeles in the late 1930s that helped to create the association between folk music and leftist politics, an association perhaps bolstered by the statement on his guitar: "This machine kills fascists." Seeger was a college-educated New York radical who saw music as a means for helping to mobilize a mass movement. Together, Guthrie and Seeger formed the Almanac Singers in 1941 and pushed their progressive political message across the country. In the early 1950s, Seeger experienced the rush of million-selling records as a member of the Weavers. His disaffection with pop success and the specter of McCarthyism, however, forced his career into the background. By this time, Guthrie was seriously debilitated by Huntington's chorea. From the 1950s until his death in 1967, he was bedridden. Among his visitors was the young Bob Dylan, who described himself as something of a Woody Guthrie jukebox.

The civil rights movement was a natural outlet for Seeger's creative and political energies. It was Seeger more than anyone who tirelessly popularized the movement's anthem, "We Shall Overcome," to a global audience. While he was a folk purist who railed against commercialism in music and seldom basked in the pop limelight himself, his guiding hand was never far from view. "If I Had a Hammer," a song he had written in 1949 with Lee Hays, became a Top Ten hit in 1962 for Peter, Paul & Mary and then again in 1963 for Trini Lopez. The Kingston Trio also scored in 1962 with Seeger's "Where Have All the Flowers Gone."

In folk circles at the time, there was a fiercely argued, if not terribly relevant, distinction between performers who were "authentic" and those who were "commercial." For most, Pete Seeger defined authenticity while the Kingston Trio and most of the groups that garnered the Top Forty hits from popularized folk material—the Rooftop Singers ("Walk Right In," 1963), the New Christy Minstrels ("Green, Green," 1963), and the Serendipity Singers ("Don't Let the Rain Come Down," 1964)—were clearly commercial. The distinction, of course, was riddled with inconsistency. Eric Darling, the leader of the Rooftop Singers, had been a member of the Weavers with Seeger. Joan Baez was considered authentic even though she charted twelve Top Forty LPs, six of which were certified million sellers. As activist liberals with commercial success, Peter, Paul & Mary sort of straddled the fence. The one artist who openly challenged the distinction, and ultimately rendered it useless, was the newcomer who had sat at the feet of the ailing Woody Guthrie, the enigmatic Bob Dylan. Born Robert Zimmerman, the son of a middle-class Jewish family, Dylan grew up in Hibbing, Minnesota, listening to a 1950s mixture of rhythm and blues, country and western, rock 'n' roll, and pop. One of his boyhood dreams was to play in Little Richard's band. After knocking around the University of Minnesota for a while and reading Guthrie's autobiography, *Bound for Glory,* the young Zimmerman moved to New York. There, he visited the hospitalized folk legend and began building his own myth as a Guthrie-style folksinger. He also legalized his newly acquired surname and shrouded his earlier life in mystery. He was signed by John Hammond to Columbia in 1962, and over the next two years, issued three albums of highly unorthodox, mostly self-accompanied acoustic folk to critical raves.

With selections like "Oxford Town" (racism in a Mississippi town) from his second album, *The Freewheelin' Bob Dylan,* and "The Lonesome Death of Hattie Carroll" (the killing of a black domestic) from his third, *The Times They Are A-Changin',* Dylan was early on proclaimed a leader in the civil rights movement. In 1963, he performed "Only a Pawn in Their Game," his song about the murder of civil rights leader Medgar Evers, at the March on Washington, where

In folk circles at the time, there was a fiercely argued, if not terribly relevant, distinction between performers who were "authentic" and those who were "commercial."

After sitting at the feet of an ailing Woody Guthrie, the freewheeling Bob Dylan shrouded his past in mystery and set about building his own myth as a Guthrie-style folksinger. The early civil rights movement gave him the perfect springboard for success.

he stood next to Martin Luther King, Jr., and shared the stage with such folk luminaries as Pete Seeger, Joan Baez, and Peter, Paul & Mary. That same year, Peter, Paul & Mary had Top Ten pop hits with Dylan's "Blowin' in the Wind" and "Don't Think Twice, It's Alright." In two short years, then, Dylan was well along the road to transforming, almost singlehandedly, the lyric content of popular music. It was at this point that he made a musical decision that cost him his authenticity but brought him a mass audience. In 1965, he appeared at the Newport Folk Festival playing an electric guitar (a classic rock Fender Stratocaster, no less) and backed by an electric band (the Paul Butterfield Blues Band). Seeger was livid, and Dylan was booed off the stage.

But, as the song says, the times were "a-changin'," and Dylan knew that better than his critics. In a world of increasing student activism (Dylan released his first album just as Tom Hayden and a group of radical students were putting the finishing touches on "The Port Huron Statement," which announced the formation of Students for a Democratic Society [SDS]), folk offered an alternative to rock 'n' roll's lyric vacuity, but could never supplant the more primal urges that rhythm and blues and rock 'n' roll had turned loose. For this reason, folk could never capture the mass audience. Bridging that gap was Dylan's particular genius. *Bringing It All Back Home,* Dylan's next album, contained one whole side of electric music with uncommonly substantive lyrics that were held up by a hard-driving, straight-ahead rock 'n' roll beat. "Subterranean Homesick Blues,"

> *Folk offered an alternative to rock 'n' roll's lyric vacuity, but folk could never supplant the more primal urges that rhythm and blues and rock 'n' roll had turned loose. Bridging that gap was Bob Dylan's particular genius.*

the first cut on the electric side of the album, became his first Top Forty pop hit, and a roar of outrage arose from the folk community. Was Dylan the true seer the folkies had once thought he was or the consummate opportunist they now criticized? It depended on who was asked. Amidst charges that he had sold out not just the civil rights movement but the entire American left, Dylan took his own advice about following leaders and turned his back on politics. In this change of direction, he was often contrasted with Phil Ochs, whose songs, such as "Here's to the State of Mississippi" and "I Ain't Marching Anymore" from his second album, which

"The Times They Are A-Changin'"

Artist: Bob Dylan
Music / Lyrics by Bob Dylan
Label: Columbia (1964)

"The Times They Are A-Changin'" (1964), like the LP that shares its name, represents the Bob Dylan that became, perhaps somewhat reluctantly, a political and social spokesperson for his generation. Dylan captured in his lyrics a time when the youth movement was growing in strength, when the civil rights movement was making sea changes in the cultural landscape of America, and when we still thought that music might change the world.

Musical Style Notes

"The Times They Are A-Changin'" features a relatively short, repeated-verse structure with a simple acoustic guitar accompaniment. The occasional harmonica "comment" adds some colour to the arrangement and strengthens the listener's association with the American folk music tradition of Woody Guthrie and Pete Seeger. The time-honoured combination of solo voice with one accompanying instrument played in a relatively simple manner serves to foreground the lyrics, an effective combination for any genre that prioritizes lyric content over musical complexity.

Musical "Road Map"

TIMINGS	COMMENTS	LYRICS
0:0–0:03	Introduction; acoustic guitar	
0:03–0:32	Verse 1	*Come gather 'round people wherever you roam* *And admit that the waters around you have grown . . .* *For the times they are a-changin'.*
0:33–0:40	Harmonica bridge to second verse	
0:40–1:07	Verse 2	*Come writers and critics who prophesize with your pen . . .* *For the times they are a-changin'.*
1:08–1:18	Harmonica bridge to third verse	
1:19–1:45	Verse 3	*Come senators, congressmen, please heed the call . . .* *For the times they are a-changin'.*
1:46–1:52	Harmonica bridge to fourth verse	
1:53–2:19	Verse 4	*Come mothers and fathers throughout the land . . .* *For the times they are a-changin'.*
2:20–2:37	Harmonica bridge to fifth verse	
2:37–3:04	Verse 5	*The line it is drawn, the curse it is cast . . .* *For the times they are a-changin'.*
3:04–3:11	Harmonica fades to end of song	

spanned the civil rights and antiwar movements, remained true to the folk protest ideal. Ostracized by the true believers, Dylan soon left his detractors in the dust as he ushered in the era of folk rock. Ochs, in contrast, was tortured by his inability to become "the first left-wing star," a torment that eventually pushed him to take his own life in 1976.

The debate over commercial versus authentic performers tended to obscure a far more important issue at the time. From old-timers such as Pete Seeger to newcomers such as Joan Baez, Bob Dylan, and Peter, Paul & Mary, the best-known artists in folk music were white. Seeger, to his credit, included such African Americans as Odetta, Sonny Terry, and Brownie McGhee in his concerts and on his albums, and gradually, these artists became prominent as voices of the civil rights movement. However, they did not come to the attention of a mass public on their own. Indeed, during the initial surge of the folk revival, artists of colour who performed folkloric material, from Leadbelly to Josh White, seldom became well-known outside folk circles. Harry Belafonte, an outspoken activist and a director of Martin Luther King's Southern Christian Leadership Conference (SCLC), was, of course, an obvious exception. In 1960, he recorded a second million-selling live album at Carnegie Hall, this one including Odetta, Miriam Makeba, and the Chad Mitchell Trio. But Belafonte was already a pop star; his music and his acting/television career seemed curiously separate from his political choices. It was inevitable, given the times, that his commercial success would seem to taint his authenticity. Trini Lopez was also something of an exception. Like Ritchie Valens before him, the "Tex-Mex" pop singer included Mexican and American popular and folk material in his repertoire. His best-selling follow-up to Seeger's "If I Had a Hammer" was "Limon Tree" (1965), a song that he had adapted from the traditional Latin song "Hojita de Limon." Buffy Sainte-Marie, a Cree from Canada, might have received greater recognition early on if she had not been forced to take time off in 1963 because of ill health. Although identified as a folksinger, she was really more of a singer/songwriter. At the time, such original compositions as "Now That the Buffalo's Gone," "My Country 'Tis of Thy People You're Dying," and "Codeine" offered her limited audience a profoundly different view of Native Americans than that expressed by such pop fare as Johnny Preston's "Running Bear" or Larry Verne's "Mr. Custer."

In addition to Sainte-Marie, Canada had a long-standing tradition of amateur and professional folk musicians. The country's first folk group of note was the Travellers. The group first came together in the early 1950s at Camp Naivelt, which was located just north of Toronto and served as a summer retreat primarily for families from Toronto's left-leaning Jewish immigrant community. Naivelt hosted performances by labour-friendly American artists such as Paul Robeson and Pete Seeger, and it was Seeger's group, the Weavers, who served as the initial inspiration for banjo player and singer Jerry Gray and mandocello player Sid Dolgay to found the group. First recording in 1958 for Hallmark Records, in 1960 the Travellers became the first Canadian artists to be signed by the Canadian branch of Columbia Records. Primarily known for Canadianizing the words to Woody Guthrie's "This Land Is Your Land," the Travellers were ubiquitous performers on CBC television in the 1950s. The group tirelessly promoted all things Canadian, and to that end assiduously researched and learned a diverse repertoire of traditional Canadian folk songs from every region in the country in both official languages. Their repertoire also included many labour songs, several of which were recorded in 1967 for the LP *A Century of Song*. Although the Travellers never attained substantial commercial success and underwent numerous personnel changes over the years, they continued to perform into the twenty-first century.

The Mariposa Folk Festival, first held in the tiny Ontario town of Orillia in 1961, was an important conduit for the development of and propagation of Canadian folk music. Started in emulation of the Newport Folk Festival in the United States, Mariposa combined evening concerts featuring big-name headliners with afternoon workshops that pitted together performers of various statures from a variety of genres. Between 1964, when the festival moved to Toronto, through the late 1970s, Mariposa was regarded as one of the preeminent folk festivals in North America. Since the late 1980s, Mariposa's importance has been superseded by the Winnipeg, Edmonton, and Vancouver folk festivals.

The Travellers were among the headliners at the very first Mariposa Folk Festival, held in 1961, as were Ian and Sylvia. Ian Tyson, hailing from Victoria, British Columbia, and Chatham, Ontario, native Sylvia Fricker (later Tyson) first met in Toronto in the late 1950s. By 1963, they had secured a recording contract with Vanguard Records and were being managed by New York svengali Albert Grossman (who also managed Bob Dylan and later the Band and Janis Joplin). The title track of their second album, "Four Strong Winds," became a Top Ten hit single in Canada in the fall of 1963. With the lines "Think I'll go out to Alberta, weather's good there in the fall," "Four Strong Winds" has fallen into the realm of true folk music, being sung around campfires and in school classes throughout Canada by several generations of Canadians. Neil Young chose to perform the song at the legendary "Last Waltz" concert in 1976.

Ian and Sylvia also had Canadian chart success with Sylvia's "You Were on My Mind," which became a Top Ten American hit in the summer of 1965 when covered by the California group We Five. In addition to their original songs, Ian and Sylvia recorded traditional material, including "Un Canadien Errant," "V'la Le Bon Vent," and "Brave Wolfe," and were among the first artists to cover songs by Gordon Lightfoot and Joni Mitchell. Other notable Tyson originals included "Lovin' Sound" and "Someday Soon." By 1968, they had formed a group called The Great Speckled Bird and helped to pioneer the sound of country rock. Both Ian and Sylvia enjoyed successful solo careers after their split in the mid-seventies, Ian moving back west and recording a series of critically and commercially successful cowboy records for Canadian roots music label Stony Plain, and Sylvia attaining notable success with the all-female Toronto-based group Quartette.

Gordon Lightfoot appeared at the second Mariposa Folk Festival in 1962. Born in Orillia in 1939, Lightfoot came under the influence of the main practitioners of the urban folk revival in the early 1960s, most notably Bob Dylan. Although he recorded a live album as part of a duo with Terry Whalen in 1962, Lightfoot's recording career got underway in earnest with the recording of the *Lightfoot!* album in 1964. Amongst the album's fifteen songs were "For Lovin' Me" and "Early Morning Rain." Both songs charted in versions by American folk stars Peter Paul & Mary. In 1967, Lightfoot penned "Canadian Railroad Trilogy," a song that in five minutes cinematically chronicled the building of the cross-Canada railway. A year later, he wrote "Black Day in July," about the 1967 race rebellion in Detroit. By 1970, Lightfoot had signed with Reprise Records and released a series of acclaimed albums that included such international pop and country hits as "If You Could Read My Mind," "Sundown," "Carefree Highway," and "The Wreck of the Edmund Fitzgerald," the last of these about the sinking of a Great Lakes freighter. In the process, Lightfoot became one of the most successful singer/songwriters of the era.

Between October 1964 and June 1978, the Riverboat Coffeehouse in Toronto's Yorkville district was, alongside Club 47 in Cambridge and Gerde's Folk City in New York, one of the most important folk venues in North America. Owned and operated by Bernie Fiedler, the Riverboat was a showcase in the 1960s and early 1970s for a who's who of Canadian singer/songwriters including Gordon Lightfoot, Neil Young, Joni Mitchell, Bruce Cockburn, and Murray McLauchlan.

The folk music scene in Quebec, not surprisingly, was substantially different. For decades, the province had been the home to a rich fiddle tradition and a folk song tradition referred to as chanson. In the 1960s, the chanson tradition became highly politicized and tied to what became known as the Quiet Revolution. Its practitioners became known as chansonniers. For many in Quebec, the chansonnier tradition represents the only authentic Québécois music.

The Quiet Revolution gathered steam as the province became increasingly urbanized, Quebec society became increasingly secular, and the government expanded the number of universities and extended free education to postsecondary institutions. As more French-speaking Québécois moved to the cities and attained a university education, they began to realize the degree to which the English-speaking minority controlled the local government and business (80 percent of the province's population traced their roots to France, while only 10 percent traced their roots to the United Kingdom). The result was the beginning of a nationalist movement in Quebec, kick-started in 1961, when Premier Jean Lesage established L'Office de la Langue Française (The Office of the French Language). French became the official language of the government and increasingly became the language of business and popular culture in the province as well, and the term *French Canadian* was replaced by *Québécois*.

Chansonniers such as Félix Leclerc, Claude Gauthier, Gilles Vigneault, and La Bolduc wrote their own music and in performance combined songs and monologues that discussed Québécois history, culture, geography, people, and political aspirations. Popular songs included Vigneault's "Mon pays" ("My Country") and La Bolduc's "Nos braves habitants" ("Our Brave People"). Leclerc's career started in radio as far back as the 1930s. In the 1950s, he began performing as a professional musician and became so popular that he is referred to as "The Father of Chanson." His songs are still performed regularly in the province, and the Quebec music awards, the Félix Awards, were named after him.

At the end of the 1960s, the chansonnier tradition became more group and rock oriented. Electric chansonniers popular at the time were Claude Dubois, Jean-Pierre Ferland, Jacques Michel, and the province's superstar, Robert Charlebois. A French rock tradition would grow out of this shift, including groups such as Offenbach, Beau Dommage, and Harmonium. As part of the overt revitalization of Québécois identity, both the chansonnier and the French rock groups incorporated Québécois slang, known as joual, into their songs.

Chansonniers were integrally involved in the separatist movement. During both the 1980 and 1995 referendums on whether Quebec should become a sovereign entity separate from Canada, chansonniers participated alongside politicians at rallies organized to get the "yes" vote out. For example, in advance of the October 1995 referendum, Gilles Vigneault appeared on television performing at Premier Jacques Parizeau's home with Vigneault, Parizeau, and others in attendance singing "Tu peux raveler ta romance" ("You Can Take Back Your Romance"), described by Val Morrison as "a song that tells the history of Quebec-Canada relations in a mocking and provocative fashion, using the metaphor of an unhappy marriage in which the man (Canada) has done all in his power to alienate and take for a fool the woman (Quebec), who has finally wised up, telling him that she believes they are no longer 'from the same country.'" During the same referendum campaign, Paul Piche joined Lucien Bouchard (then leader of the federal opposition party, later the premier of Quebec) at a number of rallies in the Montreal area also designed to convince Québécois to vote yes.[12]

Although a number of African American artists had championed a merger of gospel and r&b styles in the 1950s, it was not until the mid-1960s that the social consciousness of folk music was linked to the popular appeal of the gospel/r&b fusion. The centre for this innovation was Chicago, and the often underappreciated Curtis Mayfield. Like fellow Chicagoan Sam Cooke, Mayfield had left the gospel choir for the secular world of popular music in the 1950s. After a series of hits with the Impressions—"For Your Precious Love" (1958), "Gypsy Woman" (1961), and "It's All Right" (1963)—Mayfield "got religion" once again. Beginning in 1964, he penned a series of successful folk-sounding but pop-produced "sermon songs" for the group, including "Keep on Pushing" and "Amen" in 1964, and "People Get Ready" in 1965. Through these, he became, in the words of Nelson George, "black music's most unflagging civil rights champion."[13]

Mayfield's fusion had actually been anticipated by the Staple Singers, a family gospel group that started in a Chicago Baptist church in 1950. In the late 1950s, they recorded gospel for Vee Jay with Pop Staples' understated guitar and daughter Mavis' compelling lead

Curtis Mayfield started as a talented writer and singer who effected a successful pop/gospel fusion in the 1950s with his group the Impressions. The civil rights movement provided the inspiration for some of his best music. He went on to become a producer, label chief, and solo artist, scoring Superfly, *one of the most successful so-called blaxploitation films of the early 1970s.*

vocals. In the early 1960s, the group demonstrated Mayfield's pop feel for the material, recording such spiritual classics as "Will the Circle Be Unbroken?" "Amazing Grace," and "We Shall Overcome" with electric guitar and drums. The Staple Singers did not make the pop charts until they signed with Stax in the 1970s, but even then, gospel-tinged songs like "I'll Take You There," "If You're Ready (Come Go with Me)," and "Touch a Hand, Make a Friend" were prominent among their hits.

Another look at Sam Cooke's career completes Chicago's musical connection to civil rights. Cooke had made a mild but successful foray into social commentary as early as 1960 when "Chain Gang" went to number two on the pop charts. Still, it was not until he heard Bob Dylan's "Blowin' in the Wind" that he felt compelled to relate to the civil rights movement more directly. In late 1964, he attempted a pop/folk fusion with "A Change Is Gonna Come." By the time the record was released as a single, however, Cooke had been shot to death under unsavoury circumstances. When his friend Malcolm X was assassinated only two months later, on 21 February 1965, "A Change Is Gonna Come" was moving up the charts to Top Forty status; it stands as Cooke's monument to civil rights.

The British Invasion Occupies the Pop Charts

The promise of President John F. Kennedy's "New Frontier," as his blueprint for America was called, was dealt a crushing blow when he was assassinated on 22 November 1963. In the aftermath of his death, the national mood was one of defeat and depression. It is noteworthy that in the six months between Kennedy's assassination and the passage of the Civil Rights Act of 1964, the Beatles' upbeat sound captured the cultural life of the nation. "In retrospect," as "gonzo" critic Lester Bangs has written, "it seems obvious that this elevation of our mood had to come from outside the parameters of America's own musical culture, if only because the folk music which then dominated American pop was so tied to the crushed dreams of the New Frontier."[14]

So dramatic was the Beatles' impact that, from a cultural point of view, there is a tendency to think that the sixties—that is, the cultural era rather than the chronological decade—began in 1964, the year the group first hit the U.S. pop charts.

The Beatles transformed popular music just as the issue of civil rights became permanently imprinted on the national consciousness. For both the Beatles and civil rights, the time was right; for both, the results were profound. So dramatic was the Beatles' impact that, from a cultural point of view, there is a tendency to think that the sixties (that is, the cultural era rather than the chronological decade) began in 1964, the year the group first hit the U.S. pop charts. It was as if the country had simply been marking time for four years, waiting for their arrival. There were many reasons for this perception.

First, the Beatles made their American debut at a time when the U.S. music industry was stagnating. While the industry had more than doubled in size between 1955 and 1959, record sales had decreased by 5 percent (to $600 million) in 1960. In 1963, sales were up by only 1.6 percent from the previous year. After 1964, however, the industry enjoyed double-digit growth every year until the end of the decade and, including tape sales, more than doubled its revenues (to about $1.6 billion). The Beatles, of course, did not rejuvenate the music business single-handedly, but other artists paled in the face of their impressive statistics and fresh sound. In 1964

The Beatles were not what they appeared to be. After they paid their dues in the rough-and-tumble nightclubs of Hamburg, manager Brian Epstein dressed them up in suits and ties and went to great pains to present them as clean-cut entertainers.

alone, they charted thirty songs and released six best-selling albums. From 1963 to 1968, the group sold an estimated $154 million worth of records worldwide.[15] Not even Elvis in his heyday could compete with numbers like these.

Second, the Beatles eclipsed all other talent so quickly and so completely that many people lost sight of the fact that, prior to the group's arrival, the most exciting developments in popular music had been in the African American realm. Indeed, the Beatles' first album in the United States, *Introducing . . . The Beatles,* which included five Top Ten singles, was released on the black-owned Vee Jay label. The early sound of the Beatles, as well as the Animals and the Rolling Stones, among others, was hard-driving rock 'n' roll, and much of their inspiration came directly from African American artists. Many of the Beatles' early recordings were nearly note-for-note reproductions of such African American rock 'n' roll classics as "Roll Over Beethoven," by Chuck Berry, "Long Tall Sally," by Little Richard, "Twist and Shout," by the Isley Brothers, "Money," by Barrett Strong, "Boys" and "Baby It's You," by the Shirelles, "You've Really Got a Hold on Me," by Smokey Robinson and the Miracles, and "Chains," by the Cookies. This is not to suggest that the Beatles could in any way be considered mere cover artists. The group brought a freshness and originality to popular music that was truly innovative. Their motivation in covering so many African American hits was less to cash in on black culture than to pay tribute to their musical heroes. The Beatles openly credited Chuck Berry, the Miracles, Chuck Jackson, and Ben E. King as formative influences. In fact, the Beatles (and even more the Stones and the Animals) introduced a whole generation of white, middle-class Americans to the rich tradition of African American music that had always existed within earshot. Still, it was a fact of American life that, while openly and repeatedly acknowledging their debt to African American music and touring with early rock 'n' roll greats like Little Richard, the Beatles and the other English groups that followed them were more marketable than the African American artists they admired. It was this particular contradiction in America that had created the need for the civil rights movement in the first place.

Prior to the arrival of the Beatles, British artists made the U.S. pop charts only one or two at a time: Lonnie Donegan ("Does Your Chewing Gum Lose Its Flavour [on the Bedpost Overnight]") in 1961, and Kenny Ball ("Midnight in Moscow") and Mr. Acker Bilk ("Stranger on the Shore") in 1962. When the Beatles first hit the U.S. pop charts in January 1964, their records were issued on six different labels. As of the beginning of February that year, they had become the country's hottest act, although they had yet to set foot on U.S. soil. By mid-April, they had twelve singles in the *Billboard* Hot 100, including the top five positions. *Billboard* reported that the group had accounted for nearly 60 percent of all singles sold for a period of about three weeks.

It is telling that the Beatles actually broke through as artists in Canada before they did in the United States. In the early 1960s, Capitol Canada executive Paul White inaugurated the 6000 series and effectively started Capitol Records' Canadian A&R department. White recognized that the majority of Canadians had roots in the United Kingdom and began to issue a series of Canadian-only record albums of pre-rock British artists such as Freddy Gardner, George Formby, and Vera Lynn. By the end of 1962, White began putting out current pop records from Britain that Capitol Records in Hollywood, who found it unthinkable that American teenagers would want to buy anything by a non-American artist, consistently passed on. The first successes were with Frank Ifield and Helen Shapiro in the fall of 1962, followed by Cliff Richard in the spring of 1963. The British Invasion, due to the foresight and aggressiveness of Capitol Canada, started a full year earlier in Canada than it did in the United States.

Over the next few years, Capitol Canada was to achieve a staggering 45 percent market share. This success, of course, was largely owing to the popularity of the Beatles. Capitol Records in the United States released its first Beatles single in early 1964. Capitol Canada, on the other hand, released "Love Me Do" nearly a full year earlier, thus playing a role in the history of the band that would change the world of music forever. While "Love Me Do" sold very poorly, Capitol Canada kept issuing Beatles records, gradually seeing chart action in London, Vancouver, Winnipeg, Kingston, Hamilton, and eventually Toronto, months before the group's American breakthrough.

Capitol Canada was so effective in its marketing that two Canadian-only Beatles singles, "All My Loving" and "Roll Over Beethoven," were exported into the United States in such vast numbers that they actually reached the American *Billboard* Hot 100 chart in March 1964, the only time in history records have charted on Billboard that wasn't actually issued in the U.S. In the meantime, Capitol Canada was charting north of the border with a slew of British hits by the likes of the Dave Clark Five, the Yardbirds, Gerry and the Pacemakers, Freddie and the Dreamers, the Swinging Blue Jeans, Billy J. Kramer and the Dakotas, the Hollies, and Manfred Mann (all of whom Capitol U.S. had passed on). Even the initial releases by the Animals and Herman's Hermits were issued first in North America by Capitol Canada.

Over the next two years, no fewer than two dozen British groups would appear on the U.S. pop charts. At its best, the British Invasion recalled the enthusiasm of early rock 'n' roll and pointed the way to numerous future developments in popular music. At its worst, the taste for anything British became so indiscriminate that acts like Chad and Jeremy ("Yesterday's Gone") and Ian Whitcomb ("You Turn Me On") had Top Ten pop hits in the United States while remaining completely unknown at home. The assault also overshadowed all other developments in popular music. There was, for example, a Mexican American influence in popular music during this period. "Pop"ularized as "Ameriachi" by Herb Alpert and the Tijuana Brass, one of the best-selling bands of the era, this trend also showed a clear connection to rock and soul. In 1962, Chris Montez, a protégé of Ritchie Valens, scored a Top Ten hit with "Let's Dance" and was signed by Alpert's A&M label. In 1966, he scored four more Top Forty hits.

At its worst, the taste for anything British became so indiscriminate that acts like Chad and Jeremy and Ian Whitcomb had Top Ten pop hits in the United States while remaining completely unknown at home.

Another Chicano act from Los Angeles, Cannibal and the Headhunters, released the defining arrangement of "Land of 1000 Dances" in 1965, well over a year before Wilson Pickett had a Top Ten hit with the song. A Chicano group from Detroit, ? (Question Mark) & the Mysterians, hit number one with "96 Tears" in 1966. Indeed, from 1965 to 1967, Sam the Sham & the Pharaohs, from Memphis, Tennessee, turned out six Top Forty hits, including "Wooly Bully" (1965) and "Lil' Red Riding Hood" (1966). There was something of a "sound" to this music (including the prominent use of Farfisa organ on many cuts), but it was totally overpowered by the craving for all things British. So great was this hunger that another Tex-Mex–influenced rock band, the Sir Douglas Quintet ("She's About a Mover," 1965), led by a white local, Doug Sahm, from San Antonio, Texas, was actually promoted as a new British group.

The groups identified with the first wave of the British Invasion came from far and wide. There were the Zombies ("She's Not There") from Hertfordshire and the Moody Blues ("Go Now!") from Birmingham. Peter and Gordon ("A World Without Love") came from Scotland. The group Them ("Here Comes the Night," "Gloria") was Irish. The Seekers ("I'll Never Find Another You") were Australian. If it seems odd that the Sir Douglas Quintet came from San Antonio, it is equally ironic that the Nashville Teens ("Tobacco Road") hailed from Weybridge, Surrey. In the minds of many fans, even the Beau Brummels ("Just a Little") from San Francisco were associated with the British onslaught. Mostly, however, the British Invasion came from three cities: Liverpool, Manchester, and London.

The Beatles, of course, came from Liverpool, as did the Searchers ("Needles and Pins"), Gerry and the Pacemakers ("Don't Let the Sun Catch You Crying," "Ferry Cross the Mersey"), Billy J. Kramer and the Dakotas ("Little Children"), Cilla Black ("You're My World"), and the Swinging Blue Jeans ("Hippy Hippy Shake"). Although Liverpool is a dreary, grey, industrial seaport town located along the Mersey River, there was at the time a flourishing rock 'n' roll culture among its working-class residents nourished by the steady stream of American merchant seamen who brought records over. Once absorbed, rock 'n' roll mingled with British folk styles and achieved pop status in a type of music known as *skiffle*. (Skiffle was fleetingly exposed to American audiences in Lonnie Donegan's "Rock Island Line" in 1956.) It was skiffle that John Lennon, Paul McCartney, George Harrison, and Stuart Sutcliffe, who later died of a brain hemorrhage, played as the Quarrymen. This was the musical amalgam that shaped the Beatles and their Merseybeat comrades, but they paid their dues playing rock 'n' roll in the rough-and-tumble nightclubs of the German port city of Hamburg. Hamburg was the crucible that forged their professionalism. By the time they journeyed to Hamburg, the Quarrymen had metamorphosed into Johnny and the Moondogs, then to the Silver Beatles, and at last to simply the Beatles, with Pete Best on drums. When they returned home, they were showcased with the best-known Liverpudlian groups at a dingy basement club called the Cavern, which is where they first came to the attention of record-store owner cum manager Brian Epstein. Like all beat groups, the Beatles had mastered a standard rock 'n' roll repertoire of Chuck Berry, Little Richard, Elvis Presley, and Buddy Holly and the Crickets, as well as such r&b classics as Barrett Strong's "Money" and the Isley Brothers' "Twist and Shout," and material from the girl groups. Unlike many of the beat groups, however, Lennon and McCartney wrote original songs right from the beginning.

Once under the brilliant tutelage of Epstein, the Beatles, who had been turned down at other labels, were signed by producer George Martin to EMI. Their first single, "Love Me Do" (with Ringo Starr replacing Best on drums), went Top Twenty in Great Britain in 1962. "Please, Please Me" hit number two there in 1963. "From Me to You" went all the way to number one that same year. All three of these hits were Lennon-McCartney tunes. When another Lennon-McCartney original, "She Loves You," became the best-selling single in British history in late 1963 and enjoyed similar success in Canada, Epstein decided the group was ready to take on the United States. The "fab four" arrived in New York on February 7, 1964 when "I Want to Hold Your Hand" was the number one single in the country. For the next six months, they occupied the number one slot on the U.S. pop charts. Once again, eight of their nine Top Ten hits during this period were Lennon-McCartney tunes. Their first movie, *A Hard Day's Night,* a black-and-white film by director Richard Lester about a day in the life of the group, opened in August to rave reviews. The soundtrack album of the same name yielded two Top Ten singles—the title song and "Can't Buy Me Love." Beatlemania, as the frenzied reaction to the group was called, was no less dramatic in Canada and the United States than it had been in England, and the group quickly established a beachhead for the rest of the British Invasion.

Unlike Liverpool, the city of Manchester turned out some of the most mindless drivel ever associated with the British Invasion, with the exception of Wayne Fontana and the Mind-benders, who spent one glorious week in 1965 at number one with "The Game of Love." Herman's Hermits ("Mrs. Brown, You've Got a Lovely Daughter," "I'm Henry VIII, I Am") presented an alternative to the rock 'n' roll/skiffle fusion of the beat groups that showed just how low a pop interpretation of the British music hall tradition could sink. Even so, between 1964 and 1970, the group charted eighteen Top Forty singles and

Herman's Hermits presented an alternative to the rock 'n' roll/skiffle fusion of the beat groups that showed just how low a pop interpretation of the British music hall tradition could sink.

ten albums in the United States. Freddie and the Dreamers ("I'm Telling You Now," 1965) elevated vacuity to an art form, as Freddie Garrity's stage act of flapping both arms while lifting each leg outwardly—a set of moves requiring no skill and less grace—became a dance craze that guaranteed another hit, "Do the Freddie." With close harmonies that set them apart from other Manchester groups, the Hollies were a first-rate group, but their biggest hit by the end of the first wave of the British assault was the insipid, if clever, hit single "Bus Stop" (1966). When Graham Nash left the group in 1968 to "make records that say something" with David Crosby and Stephen Stills, it was evident that music in the United States was heading in a new direction.

London, which was far more eclectic than either Liverpool or Manchester, offered artists ranging from the jazz-influenced Manfred Mann ("Doo Wah Diddy Diddy," 1964), who was born in South Africa, to Dusty Springfield ("I Only Want to Be with You," "You Don't Have to

Say You Love Me"), one of the two women who held her own from the beginning of the British Invasion to the end of the decade. (The other was thirtysomething Petula Clark from Epsom, Surrey, who charted fifteen Top Forty singles, winning Grammys for her first two, "Downtown" and "I Know a Place," both in 1965.) A London woman who did not fare as well was Honey Lantree, drummer for and namesake of the Honeycombs, a group whose only big hit, "Have I the Right?" (1964), sounded vaguely like the Dave Clark Five, a group from the London suburb of Tottenham. Clark became the drummer for his group mostly because they didn't have anyone else. His rudimentary pounding, the defining characteristic of the group's sound, was likened by *Time* magazine to an "air hammer." Beginning with "Glad All Over" and "Bits and Pieces," both Top Ten hits in 1964, the Dave Clark Five brought new meaning to the term "beat" music. The quintet relied on a series of r&b classics for success, as did many other British groups. In 1965, they scored with covers of Chuck Berry's "Reelin' and Rockin'" and Chris Kenner's "I Like It Like That." The group's last Top Ten hit was a remake of Marv Johnson's "You Got What It Takes."

One London group that had the talent and creativity to be truly influential was the Kinks. Under the leadership of writer/vocalist/guitarist Ray Davies, the group took the United States by storm in late 1964 with three original Top Ten hard rockers ("You Really Got Me," "All Day and All of the Night," and "Tired of Waiting for You"). After these, the group seemed to stall. This may have happened because they encountered such problems with the American Federation of Television and Radio Artists (AFTRA) on their first U.S. tour that they could not return for four years, or because the group never really had an effective promotional apparatus, or because the group's follow-up hits ("A Well Respected Man" and "Dedicated Follower of Fashion"), while brilliant contributions to popular music, were so distinctly British that they were lost on U.S. audiences. Whatever the reason, the Kinks never attained the stature that should have been their due.

The London groups that had the most influence on U.S. music were the white blues revivalists. Blues aficionado Alexis Korner, owner of the London Blues and Barrelhouse Club, had been jamming with visiting African American bluesmen since the mid-1950s. In the early 1960s, Korner went electric and formed Blues Incorporated. At about the same time and at Korner's request, John Mayall moved to London to form the Bluesbreakers. These two ensembles served as catalysts for some of the best blues-based rock Britain has ever had to offer. Among the musicians who passed through the Korner/Mayall brotherhood were Mick Fleetwood, John McVie, and Peter Green of Fleetwood Mac; Eric Clapton, Jack Bruce, and Ginger Baker, who went on to become Cream; Ray Davies of Kinks fame; future members of Pentangle, Free, and Led Zeppelin; and two founders of the British rock band that has outlasted all of them, drummer Charlie Watts and lead singer Mick Jagger of the Rolling Stones.

The Animals, from Newcastle, a town every bit as tough as Liverpool, was another influential blues-based group. They had begun as a combo bearing the name of its organizer, organist Alan Price, but the early addition of Eric Burdon as lead singer and the group's wild stage act led to the name change. After the release of their first album, *The Animals* (1964), which included the hit single "House of the Rising Sun," Burdon's hard, bluesy delivery prompted *Ebony* magazine to devote five pages to the group's funky sound, rare coverage for white singers. In hindsight, it is possible to say that what appeared to be authenticity at the time was in fact Burdon's obsession with blackness.

Like most British rockers at the time, the Animals and the Rolling Stones included a good deal of African American music in their repertoires. The Rolling Stones did "Walking the Dog" by Rufus Thomas, "Under the Boardwalk" by the Drifters, "Hitchhike" and "Can I Get a Witness" by Marvin Gaye, and a number of Chuck Berry tunes, including "Carol," "Talking About You," and "Around and Around." They also ventured into the country blues with Slim Harpo's "I'm a King Bee." The Animals brought back Ma Rainey's "See See Rider" and John Lee Hooker's "Boom Boom"; Nina Simone's "Don't Let Me Be Misunderstood"; Shirley and Lee's "Let the Good Times Roll"; Fats Domino's "I'm in Love Again"; Chuck Berry's "I'm Talking About You" and "Around and Around"; a number of Ray Charles hits, including "Hallelujah, I Love Her So," "Mess Around," and "Hit the Road, Jack"; and Sam Cooke's "Bring It on Home to Me" and "Shake." There were, however, important differences in the ways in which Jagger and Burdon approached the material. In Britain, where social divisions are more clearly expressed in class terms than in the United States, Jagger could pull off his self-mocking delivery of African American styles without the slightest embarrassment at being white. While the Stones displayed the typical British fascination with African American culture, they had a sufficient distance from it that their involvement with the music was primarily aesthetic. It was not so for Burdon, whose relationship to blackness seemed to be a never-ending source of frustration.[16]

> *While the Stones displayed the typical British fascination with African American culture, they had a sufficient distance from it that their involvement with the music was primarily aesthetic. Not so for Burdon, for whom blackness loomed as an unattainable personal goal and a never-ending source of frustration.*

In the United States, where race tends to dominate the discourse of social division, the revival of African American styles that the British onslaught set in motion had immediate race-based implications for commercial viability and touched off endless debate about white people singing the blues.[17] It was during this period that the r&b charts were briefly discontinued, at least in part as a result of the integrationist impulse of the early civil rights movement. For African American artists, the results were disastrous. In 1962, 42 percent of the songs on the year-end singles charts were by African Americans. In 1966, African Americans declined to 22 percent, the lowest point since the initial surge of rock 'n' roll in the mid-1950s. Only three of the top fifty albums for the years 1964 and 1965 were by black artists. In contrast, nearly one-third of the Top Ten releases for 1964 belonged to British artists; one year earlier there had been none. Among African American artists, only the Motown acts survived the first wave of the British Invasion. They did so not only because of the freshness of the Motown sound, but also because the businessman in Berry Gordy intuitively understood that his interests would be best served by an alliance with popular British acts. It was no coincidence that the Supremes' third album, *A Bit of Liverpool* (1964), showcased cover tunes from British groups, especially the Beatles. In two important telecasts, *T.A.M.I.* (1964) and *TNT* (1965), the Supremes, Smokey Robinson and the Miracles, and Marvin Gaye appeared with British groups Gerry and the Pacemakers and the Rolling Stones.[18] *Ready Steady Go!*, a television pop music variety show in Great Britain, devoted an entire episode to the Motown sound in 1965. When Motown launched a tour of Britain featuring a number of the company's best-selling artists that same year, everybody gushed. The Beatles lauded the music at every opportunity. Even the *Sunday Times* was enthusiastic. If there had been any misconceptions about where Berry Gordy sought to position Motown on the pop music continuum, his remarks laid them to rest: "We are very honored the Beatles should have said what they did. . . . They're creating the same type of music as we are and we're part of the same stream."[19]

The politics of class and culture played itself out further in the tension between Liverpool and London, or more specifically, between the Beatles and the Rolling Stones. As revolutionary as the Beatles' music may have sounded, Brian Epstein took great pains to present the group as middle-class family entertainment. Their first U.S. appearance was on the *Ed Sullivan Show.* The press marveled at their wit. Even parents liked them—they were "cute." They wanted only "to hold your hand." The Stones were anything but cute. If Epstein extracted an image of innocence from the Beatles, Andrew Loog Oldham, the Stones' manager and earlier an Epstein employee, cultivated precisely the opposite image for his group. The Rolling Stones took longer to arrive in the United States than the Beatles (the country's thirst for Beatles clones had to be quenched first), but when they did, they were embraced as the menacing, street-toughened alternative to the playful mop-tops. The Stones scowled at the camera; they were surly. Their music was full of disdain, mostly for women. After they played the *Ed Sullivan Show,* Sullivan vowed that they would never return. Of course, neither the Beatles nor the Rolling Stones were quite what they appeared to be. The Beatles came from solid working-class backgrounds. Prior to their Epstein manicure, they had played Hamburg in slicked-back hair and black leather jackets. In contrast, only two of the Stones—Bill Wyman and Charlie Watts—had working-class backgrounds. Brian Jones, the Stones' first rhythm guitarist, who drowned in 1969, was an upper-middle-class dropout. Keith Richards attended art school, and Mick Jagger remained a student at the London School of Economics until the group became a going concern. These were no more "street-fighting men" than the Beatles were wholesome, carefree mop-tops. The respective image of each group was based on strategic career choices.

If anything, the Stones were bohemians; the terrain that the group staked out—the tradition they wished to explore and the musical statement they wanted to make—was based in the

As revolutionary as the Beatles' music may have sounded, Brian Epstein took great pains to present the group as middle-class family entertainment.

The Rolling Stones arrive in New York for the first time in 1964 with Brian Jones (second from left) as rhythm guitarist. In retrospect, the bad boys of sixties rock look more youthful than tough. They have gone on to become one of the longest-running self-contained rock acts in the business.

blues. It was down and dirty, replete with exaggerated aggressiveness and overt sexuality. It almost demanded a tough, streetwise, working-class image. Almost a year after the Beatles were presented with MBE (Members of the British Empire) awards by the Queen herself at Buckingham Palace (over the loud protests of outraged upper-class conservatives), the Rolling Stones were still cultivating their working-class identities at New York's Academy of Music, a venue that recalled Alan Freed's week-long, walk-in rock 'n' roll shows at the Brooklyn Paramount. For the Beatles, who were steeped in working-class culture and destined to remain within its confines until Epstein's arrival, the wholesome, mop-top image offered a way out of their class-determined fate. Epstein's strategy of scrubbing them clean and dressing them up in suits and ties was, as always, on the mark.

As was the case throughout the Western world, in Canada the British Invasion inspired legions of young teenagers to learn to play guitar, bass, and drums and form bands. In Winnipeg, Chad Allen and the Expressions got together in 1962. In 1965, they recorded a stunning cover of British group Johnny Kidd and the Pirates' "Shakin' All Over." Recognizing that Canadian radio stations were suffering from what is called in Third World countries the "colonial mentality" and were not liable to give a fair shake to a domestic recording by a Canadian artist, Quality Records sent out promotional copies in blank sleeves with the words "Guess Who?" printed on the cover. When the record when to number four on the CHUM chart in April 1965 and a month later peaked at number eleven in the United States, the group's name was officially changed to the Guess Who.

In January 1966, Burton Cummings replaced the original keyboard player and also assumed duties as co-lead singer. When Chad Allen left a few months later, Cummings became the group's sole lead singer. Together with guitarist Randy Bachman, he co-wrote a substantial

In 1970, the Guess Who single "American Woman" was the first record by a Canadian band to become a number one hit in the United States.

number of Canadian hits through the spring of 1970. Beginning with "These Eyes," "Laughing," and "Undun" in 1969, the group, now produced by Jack Richardson for Nimbus Nine Productions, became successful internationally. Their biggest record, "American Woman" backed with "No Sugar Tonight," was the first record by a Canadian band to become a number one hit in the United States.

Bachman left the group in May 1969 and was replaced by two guitarists, Kurt Winter and Greg Liskiw. Winter and Cummings went on to co-write a number of subsequent hits, including "Hand Me Down World," "Share the Land," "Hang On to Your Life," and "Albert Flasher" in 1970 and 1971. After a number of personnel changes, the Guess Who finally called in quits in 1975.

Less successful were innumerable and now legendary Canadian artists such as Toronto groups Robbie Lane and the Disciples and the Ugly Ducklings, both influenced by the Rolling Stones and the Animals, Montreal's the Haunted and the Rabble, Edmonton's King Beezz, and the West Coast-based Five Canadians. More generically British Invasion–influenced bands included Halifax's The Stitch in Tyme, who actually charted with a cover of the Beatles' "Got to Get You into My Life" on Yorkville Records in 1967, and Toronto's The Paupers and Kensington Market.

Breaking the Sounds of Silence

Given the folk revival's stringent requirements for authenticity, it would have been difficult for Bob Dylan to trumpet his admiration for the Beatles in 1964, even though he had experienced electric ensemble recording as early as 1962 on "Rocks and Gravel." It was, however, precisely his attraction for the group that started him thinking more seriously about recording with other musicians and moving in a rock 'n' roll direction. As he later confessed to Anthony Scaduto, his first serious biographer:

> *I had heard the Beatles in New York when they first hit. Then, when we were driving through Colorado we had the radio on and eight of the ten top songs were Beatles songs. In Colorado! I Wanna Hold Your Hand, all those early ones.*
>
> *They were doing these things nobody was doing. Their chords were outrageous, just outrageous, and their harmonies made it all valid. You could only do that with other musicians. Even if you're playing your own chords you had to have other people playing with you. That was obvious. And it started me thinking about other people.*
>
> *But I just kept it to myself that I really dug them. Everybody else thought they were for the teenyboppers, that they were gonna pass right away. But it was obvious to me that they had staying power. I knew they were pointing the direction where music had to go.* [20]

On the other hand, it was not difficult for the Beatles to acknowledge their high regard for Dylan. When the folksinger toured England in May 1964, the Beatles, as well as the Rolling Stones and Eric Burdon, went to see him. According to popular music lore, two important things happened. First, Dylan allegedly turned the Beatles on to marijuana.[21] Hallucinogenic drugs had an obvious influence on their future development, and, therefore, the rest of popular music. Second, Dylan heard the Animals' "House of the Rising Sun" before it was released in the United States. It knocked him out. "My God, ya oughtta hear what's going down over there," he told a friend when he returned to New York. "Eric Burdon, the Animals, ya know? Well, he's doing *House of the Rising Sun* in rock. *Rock!* It's fuckin' *wild!* Blew my mind."[22] The Animals had, in fact, mined Dylan's first album for their first two recordings, redoing "Baby Let Me Follow You Down" as "Baby, Let Me Take You Home" and then transforming "House" into electric, transatlantic magic. Dylan appreciated its significance immediately. "You see, there was a lot of hypocrisy all around," he told Scaduto, "people saying it had to be folk or rock. But I knew it didn't have to be like that."[23]

Folk Rock: Adding Substance to Form

Dylan credited the Animals with concocting the alloy that would yield folk rock, even though he might have looked to the earlier model of Ritchie Valens and "La Bamba." Still, it was the Byrds who turned folk rock into a full-fledged genre (marketing category). The Animals had come at folk mat-erial from a rock and blues direction. The Byrds were folkies who, like Dylan, embraced rock. Leader Jim (later, Roger) McGuinn had arrived in Los Angeles through the Chicago folk circuit. Guitarist and vocalist David Crosby was a California-bred folksinger from the start. Chris Hillman picked up the electric bass after laying down his bluegrass mandolin. Together, they evolved a self-conscious sound (defined by McGuinn's electric twelve string Rickenbacker) that was clearly based in a rock aesthetic. Like Dylan's Newport 1965 debacle, the Byrds' sonic conception challenged a number of orthodoxies, as Lillian Roxon has pointed out:

The Byrds showed how rock could transform folk. They are pictured in an airport about to begin the journey that would take them eight miles high.

Until the Byrds, the very notion of a group of folk singers strengthening their sound with rock devices was unthinkable. Folk was highminded, pure and untouched by sordid commercial values. Rock was something you played for a quick buck. The most important thing the Byrds ever did was to recognize that rock could revitalize folk—with a finished product that was considerably more than the sum of its parts.[24]

At the beginning of their career, the Byrds drank heavily from the well of Dylan's creativity, recording rock versions of four of his songs on their first album. When the group's version of "Mr. Tambourine Man," the title song from their debut album, became a number one pop hit in

It was well understood by almost everyone that in the mainstream market, the social consciousness that folk brought to the table would be folded into a commercialized rock aesthetic, not the other way around.

1965, folk rock became a "thing." The Lovin' Spoonful ("Do You Believe in Magic"), Barry McGuire ("Eve of Destruction"), Sonny and Cher ("I Got You Babe"), and Simon and Garfunkel ("Sounds of Silence") all debuted in 1965. Donovan also came into his own with "Sunshine Superman" that year, although he had been dogged by comparisons with Dylan earlier. In Los Angeles, it paid to be Dylan-influenced, as the Turtles discovered when "It Ain't Me Babe" quickly followed the Byrds' "Tambourine Man" up the charts. Cher even offered Dylan to the teenyboppers in 1965 with her version of "All I Really Want to Do," which was also a hit for the Byrds that year.

To say that 1965 was *the* year for folk rock does not mean that folk rock died after 1965; it simply means the electrification of folk in the rock market was more or less taken for granted from that point on. It was well understood by almost everyone that in the mainstream market, the social consciousness that folk brought to the table would be folded into a commercialized rock aesthetic, not the other way around. Lillian Roxon correctly chastised *Newsweek* for referring to the Byrds as "Dylanized Beatles when the whole point was that they were Beatlized Dylans."[24] In the marriage of folk and rock, rock was in control, with all the contradictions that such a statement implies. For those artists who could not reconcile themselves to these contradictions, the results could be disastrous, as the untimely death of Phil Ochs proves. Others unwittingly expressed their uneasiness in their music. Peter, Paul & Mary's tentative ode to rock, "I Dig Rock and Roll Music" (1967), reveals both their musical discomfort with the genre and their political distrust of its unabashedly commercial bent.

At the time, folk rockers were usually considered to be "thinking musicians," which in the rock market, until the Beatles, was a virtual contradiction in terms. It was not that there had never been topical songs in rock 'n' roll. From Chuck Berry's "Brown-Eyed Handsome Man" to the Crystals' "Uptown," rock 'n' roll had occasionally flirted with the notion of something more, but folk rock offered a steady diet of such material, be it about personal relationships ("All I Really Want to Do") or social commentary ("Sounds of Silence"). In this way, folk rock pointed the way for the singer/songwriters who would go on to capture one strand of the fragmented audience of the 1970s. Perhaps nothing illustrates the transition from one era to the other better than the career of Simon and Garfunkel.

Paul Simon and Art Garfunkel first performed in the late 1950s as Tom and Jerry. Eight years later, when their producer Tom Wilson added drums and electric backing to an acoustic recording of "Sounds of Silence" without their permission, their careers took off. The song shot to number one and established Simon and Garfunkel (now performing under their real names) as a folk rock act. After racking up five gold or platinum albums and ten Top Thirty singles (including their number one hit from *The Graduate,* "Mrs. Robinson"), the duo turned the decade with the moving, if sentimental, social commentary of "Bridge over Troubled Water," from the six-Grammy-Award-winning album of the same name. When they broke up over artistic differences around 1972, both men segued easily into solo soft rock careers, with Simon eventually leaving his former songmate far behind.

In addition to the social consciousness embedded in its songs, folk rock held out the elusive possibility of rock protest. The energy of rock 'n' roll had always been identified with rebellion but never with a cause. Folk rock was different. Here for the first time was a mainstream music that could be used explicitly in the service of thoughtful protest and creative opposition. Folk rock thus brought not only the poetic leanings but also the predominantly left-wing political inclinations of folk music to a mainstream audience. In its earliest and most didactic form, there was Barry McGuire's raspy "Eve of Destruction," which rose to the top

The energy of rock 'n' roll had always been identified with rebellion but never with a cause.

of the pop charts. Such doomsday fears, however, were met with rejoinders. Within six months, "Ballad of the Green Berets," by Sgt. Barry Sadler, who was himself a Green Beret, had also risen to the top of the charts.[26] The battle lines that would soon separate the hippies from the hard hats were already being drawn.

Oddly enough, given the tenor of the times and the propensities folk rock's roots, a good deal of this music had an uncommonly sunny disposition, even while President Johnson was committing U.S. forces to Vietnam irrevocably. Two groups in particular—the Lovin' Spoonful and the Mamas and the Papas—seemed to offer as large a dose of good old Tin Pan Alley escapism as they did folk protest. Interestingly, both groups came from a common source. John Sebastian, Cass Elliot, and Canadians Zal Yanovsky and Dennis Doherty had been a group called the Mugwumps (the name was borrowed from a group of nineteenth-century liberal reformers who had, for the most part, left the Republican Party). When the group split up after one forgettable LP, Sebastian and Yanovsky formed the Lovin' Spoonful, and Elliot and Doherty joined John and Michelle Phillips to become the Mamas and the Papas. Just as the Mamas and the Papas launched their career with the cheerful "California Dreamin'" in 1966, the Lovin' Spoonful began with two unbelievably lighthearted singles, "Do You Believe in Magic?" and "You Didn't Have to Be So Nice." The group's carefree "Daydream" (1966) continued the trend. Even the distrustfulness of "Monday, Monday" by the Mamas and the Papas and the cynicism of the group's "Words of Love" were delivered congenially. About the closest either group came to rock grittiness was the Spoonful's "Summer in the City" (1966), which was recorded with street sounds and a real jackhammer to give it a convincingly urban sound.

Even groups that were more given to social commentary than these two sounded fairly lighthearted. Compare, for example, the Byrds' "Chimes of Freedom" with Dylan's original. Dylan's half-spoken, half-sung delivery with sparse acoustic accompaniment sounds almost ominous when it is contrasted with the brightness of McGuinn's electric twelve-string and the Byrds' upbeat falsetto harmonies. Indeed, the music may have been more effective than so-called pure folk precisely because of its lightness and wit. Perhaps for all its folkiness, folk rock never lost sight of the sheer delight of rock entertainment, or perhaps its spirit emanated from those innocent "years of hope" before they turned, as Todd Gitlin has said, to "days of rage."[27]

Black (Music) Is Beautiful

If 1965 was a pivotal year for folk rock, it was even more so for the civil rights movement. Sam Cooke's posthumous tribute to the early phase of the movement, "A Change Is Gonna Come," ironically coincided with the assassination of Malcolm X. The passage of the Voting Rights Act was significant, but it did little to paper over racial injustice. This was the year that activists marched in Alabama from Selma to Montgomery to protest racial discrimination, and it was the year that rebellion broke out in the Watts neighbourhood of Los Angeles, signaling an era of urban unrest. The phrase *black power*—coined by Stokely Carmichael that year and invested with new meaning by the Black Panther Party, which was formed one year later—would soon occupy a prominent place in the American political lexicon. Nina Simone captured the tenor of the times with her 1964 recording of "Mississippi Goddam," which foreshadowed the militancy that was about to erupt just as her "Backlash Blues" anticipated the reaction to it. This transformation in the tenor of the times was reflected in changes in the form, the tone, the production style, and eventually the lyrics of black popular music.

When southern soul crossed over to the pop market, it was not because the music had changed; it was because black pride had created a cultural space in which unrefined r&b could find mainstream acceptance on its own terms.

As the themes of black pride and black self-determination gradually supplanted the call for integration, Motown's hegemony over black pop was successfully challenged by a resurgence of closer-to-the-roots, hard-driving rhythm and blues recorded in the Memphis–Muscle Shoals region of the South. Chiefly responsible for the popularization of southern soul, as this grittier r&b was called, was a temporary but highly successful collaboration between Atlantic Records and a number of southern studios, most notably Stax-Volt in Memphis, Tennessee, and Fame in Muscle Shoals, Alabama. The fruits of this collaboration captured the spirit of the emerging black militancy in tone rather than content. From 1965 on, artists like Otis Redding ("I've Been Loving You Too Long"), Wilson Pickett ("In the Midnight Hour"), Sam and Dave ("Soul Man"), Arthur Conley ("Sweet Soul Music"), and Percy Sledge ("When a Man Loves a Woman") were the new chart toppers. Their recordings were raw, basic, almost angry, and much less "produced" than the cleaner, brighter Motown sound.

Stax-Volt, Motown's chief competitor, was founded around 1960, about the same time as Motown. It was, however, as open and disorganized as Motown was opaque and tightly controlled. Originally, Stax was a white-owned company, named after its founders, Jim Stewart and Estelle Axton. With integrated units like Booker T. and the MGs and the Memphis Horns as session musicians, creative functions were as likely to be handled by whites as by blacks. The "Memphis sound" that these musicians spawned was almost invariably the product of cross-racial teamwork. Initially, the credits on all Stax recordings read simply "produced by the Stax staff." Motown, on the other hand, was clearly a haven for black talent. Even so, Motown is remembered by Nelson George as being "totally committed to reaching white audiences," while Stax aimed its recordings "at r&b fans first, the pop market second."[28]

In many ways, it was the simplicity and straightforwardness of southern soul production that gave the music its claim to authenticity. In the quest for black pride, Motown's lavish use of multitrack studio production to achieve a more "pop" sound seemed out of sync with the search for African roots. Commenting on the difference in style between Stax-Volt and Motown, Otis Redding said:

Motown does a lot of overdubbing. It's mechanically done. At Stax the rule is: whatever you feel, play it. We cut together, horns, rhythms, and vocal. We'll do it three or four times and listen to the results and pick the best one. If somebody doesn't like a line in the song we'll go back and cut the whole song over. Until last year [1967], we didn't even have a four track tape recorder. You can't overdub on a one track machine.[29]

It is somewhat ironic that it was this largely integrated effort that came to signify black power at its most militant. When southern soul crossed over to the pop market, it was not because the music had changed; it was because black pride had created a cultural space in which unrefined r&b could find mainstream acceptance on its own terms.

Between 1965 and 1967, the Stax roster grew from a dozen or so acts to about a hundred, with a concomitant expansion in sales. A good deal of the credit for the increase in sales has to go to Al Bell, a former deejay and Stax's first black executive. Bell, who was hired as head of sales in 1965, opened promotional doors Stax did not know existed. In his outgoing, flamboyant style, Bell was the perfect foil to Jim Stewart's inherent conservatism. "To most of the blacks in the company," music historian Peter Guralnick has said, "Al Bell was a kind of secret hero, the 'Jesse Jackson' of in-house politics."[30] The internal tensions that would eventually prove to be Stax's undoing were not apparent in 1966, when Al Bell toted up sales of 8 million records. At that moment, all was right with the world, and Al Bell was on everybody's A-list at Stax.

Of the many artists who passed through Stax on their way to fame, Wilson Pickett is perhaps most illustrative of the magic of the marriage with Atlantic Records. Signed to Atlantic in the early 1960s, Pickett was sent by producer Jerry Wexler to Memphis to record with Booker T. and the MGs. The results were immediate. "In the Midnight Hour" (co-written in typical cross-racial Stax fashion by Pickett and guitarist Steve Cropper) went to number one on the r&b charts in 1965 and also achieved significant crossover to the pop market. Pickett's next song, "634-5789," replicated the same success one year later. When relations between Atlantic and Stax became strained in 1966, Wexler simply sent Pickett over to Fame studios in Muscle Shoals, Alabama, and repeated the same success. Over the next few years, Pickett tallied a couple of dozen more pop hits, hitting the Top Ten with "Land of 1000 Dances" in 1966 and "Funky Broadway" in 1967. Pickett's hits were straight-ahead dance tunes. While the coarse grain of his voice and the rhythmic insistence of southern soul clearly signified the forcefulness of the new black militancy, it would be left to others to combine the passion of southern soul with explicit social consciousness.

Aretha Franklin was one artist who would do just that. After floundering at Columbia for years, she was signed to Atlantic in January 1967 by Jerry Wexler and taken immediately to Muscle Shoals where, after one legendary session, she found her sound. The resulting single, "I Never Loved a Man (The Way I Love You)," became her first of many Top Ten releases for Atlantic. Later that spring, she cut a version of the song that had been Otis Redding's signature tune. "Respect" went straight to number one and was instantly "transformed from a demand for conjugal rights into a soaring cry of freedom."[31] Shortly thereafter, she was crowned "Lady Soul." Aretha herself projected a presence that confirmed the slogan "Black Is Beautiful." The

Aretha Franklin earned the title "Lady Soul," as she took the fusion of gospel and r&b to new heights. Her music was as powerful and uplifting as the civil rights movement at its best.

vocal and emotional range of her early Atlantic releases ("Baby, I Love You," "Natural Woman," "Chain of Fools," and "Think," to name a few) express the fervour of the era dramatically. As Hettie Jones once remarked,

> Aretha did not pray like Mahalia for the endurance to make it on through, nor make you believe her pain as Billie Holiday had. The statement black artists wished to make had changed, the blues had been transfigured by anger and pride. Aretha's music was a celebration, she was "earthmother" exhorting, preacher woman denouncing, militant demanding, forgotten woman wailing. She was black, she was beautiful, and she was the best. Someone called that time in 1967 the summer of "Retha, Rap, and revolt."[32]

An even more dramatic parallel to the trajectory of black politics can be found in the career of James Brown. In the 1950s, Brown was an ambitious and headstrong r&b artist whose music was intended for, and in many ways confined to, the black audience. At the time of his first Top Ten crossover single, "Papa's Got a Brand New Bag" (1965), he billed himself with some justification as "the hardest working man in show business." By 1968, he was "Soul Brother No. 1." When he came to the attention of the white audience, he did so without compromise. His string of Top Ten pop hits ("I Got You," "It's a Man's Man's Man's World," "Cold Sweat," "I Got the Feelin'") made fewer concessions to mainstream sensibilities than any music in the pop market. Critic Robert Palmer has described it as follows:

> With no chord changes and precious little melodic variety to sustain listener interest, rhythm became everything. Brown and his musicians and arrangers began to treat every instrument and voice in the group as if each were a drum. The horns played single-note bursts that were often sprung against the

James Brown's performances were unparalleled and got him billing as "the hardest working man in show business." By the late 1960s, his stripped down, rhythmically charged proto-funk echoed the forcefulness of the black power movement.

downbeats. The bass lines were broken up into choppy two- or three-note patterns, a procedure common in Latin music but rare in r&b. Brown's rhythm guitarist choked his guitar strings against the instrument's neck so hard that his playing began to sound like a jagged tin can being scraped with a pocketknife. Only occasionally were the horns, organ or backing vocalists allowed to provide a harmonic continuum by holding a chord.[33]

This was prototypical "funk." In taking every instrument to the limit of its rhythmic capabilities, Brown carried the Africanization of popular music to its logical extreme. It was a musical statement that strongly echoed the cultural nationalism that was developing as part of the new militancy in the African American community. If, by chance, a listener missed the significance of Brown's music for black pride, it became explicit in the lyrics of his 1968 hit single, "Say It Loud—I'm Black and I'm Proud," which became an anthem in the struggle for black liberation.

Against the Grain: The Counterculture

The ascendancy of the black power movement reflected the growing separation between blacks and whites in their struggles for power, identity, and meaning. As the movement for black liberation became more traditionally militant, record numbers of white youths began to experiment with alternatives to middle-class life. The making of the counterculture, as it has been labeled, was based on a rejection of the competitive, achievement-oriented culture surrounding them in favour of free-living, free-loving lifestyles and shared communities of choice. It is noteworthy that the citizens of the counterculture were called "hippies," an inversion of "hipster," a black term from the 1940s and 1950s for urban

The making of the counterculture was based on a rejection of the competitive, achievement-oriented culture in favour of free-living, free-loving lifestyles and shared communities of choice.

"(I Got You) I Feel Good"

Artist: James Brown
Music / Lyrics by James Brown
Label: King (1965)

James Brown was the most influential African American bandleader between Duke Ellington and Prince, and like them, he understood what makes great dance music: focus, discipline, and precision. James developed a complex, polyrhythmic ensemble approach in which all instruments—basses and drums, guitars, horns, and vocals—functioned as parts of a percussive whole. Rooted in the tap-dancing and gospel singing of Brown's childhood, his musical approach evolved swiftly and radically, putting ever more attention on the rhythmic "groove," his show-stopping stage theatrics, and the complex improvised interactions between himself and the band.

Brown's genius was particularly minimalist: He stripped the rhythmic grooves of R&B, blues, and gospel down to their barest bones. With a succession of great rhythm sections, including most notably the great bass player Bootsy Collins and horn soloist Maceo Parker, Brown developed the layered, double-timed rhythmic interaction that was the basic foundation of funk.

Musical Style Notes

"I Got You" has all the elements of soul: the strong backbeat (accent on the second and fourth beats of the bar), emotional intensity, the "wailing" call-and-response vocals of gospel, impeccable horn arrangements, and rhythmic drive that just won't quit. In its percussive bass line, and the way the horns "punctuate" the musical line with short, precise phrases, it also foreshadows funk. Brown was a master of vocal "cues"—in other words, vocalizations that would cue the stopping and starting of phrases by the instrumentalists. Brown's cues help the musicians execute these "breaks" with razor-sharp precision:

"So good" — (bomp bomp)

"So good" — (bomp)

"I got you" — (bomp-bomp-*bomp-bomp*-BOMP)

In Brown's live performances, you can see that many of his wails and screams are accompanied by certain physical gestures that serve as further cues for the band. This ensemble precision was a signature part of James Brown's style.

Musical "Road Map"

TIMINGS	COMMENTS	LYRICS
0:00–0:20	Song starts with one of Brown's signature vocal screams: "Wow! I feel good—" Verse 1 Note call and response between voice and horn section at the end of the verse.	*I feel good* *Like I knew that I would . . .* *So good — —* *So good — —* *I got you — — — — —*
0:20–0:40	Verse 2 Again, note call and response.	*I feel . . . nice* *Like sugar and spice . . .* *So nice — —* *So nice — —* *I got you — — — — —*

TIMINGS	COMMENTS	LYRICS
0:40–0:47	Saxophone break (transitional musical phrase leading into bridge)	
0:47–0:59	Bridge Note how the instruments stop completely when Brown sings, "My love won't do me no harm—" This cues the next verse.	*When I hold you in my arms . . .* *. . . my love won't do me no harm—*
0:59–1:20	Verse 2 repeats. (Call and response between voice and horn section at the end of the verse)	*I feel . . . nice* *Like sugar and spice . . .* *So nice — —* *So nice — —* *I got you — — — —*
1:20–1:26	Reprise of saxophone break leading into bridge	
1:26–1:39	Bridge Instruments stop again at 1:36—"my love can't do me no harm."	*When I hold you in my arms . . .* *. . . my love won't do me no harm—*
1:39–1:59	Verse 2 repeats.	*I feel . . . nice* *Like sugar and spice . . .* *So nice — —* *So nice — —* *I got you — — — —*
1:59–2:19	Verse 1 repeats.	*I feel good* *Like I knew that I would . . .* *So good — —* *So good — —* *I got you — — — —*
2:19–2:30	Reprise last line twice. Horns play extended line, then stop.	*So good — —* *So good — —* *I got you — — — —* *So good — —* *So good — —* *I got you — — — —*
2:30	Brown screams, "Hey!" (This vocalization is Brown cueing the band for the last chord.) Band hits last chord.	*Hey!*

outsiders. A number of philosophical tendencies and social and political developments framed the counterculture, including a Christian belief in "loving thy neighbour" and a fascination with Eastern religions and music, the mass availability of reliable birth control (the Pill), and the escalation of the war in Vietnam. The one unifying element that held this myriad of forces together was the widespread use of mind-expanding drugs.

By the mid-1960s, statements about drugs had become so clear that uninformed conservatives no longer had to go so far as to identify the Beatles' "Yellow Submarine" as a submarine-shaped barbiturate known as a "yellow jacket," or to transform Peter, Paul & Mary's "Puff the Magic Dragon" into a drug song by changing "puff" into a verb. The Association's "Along Comes Mary" (1966) as a code for marijuana or the Stones' "Jumpin' Jack Flash" (1968) as methedrine were much easier connections. When the Byrds flew "Eight Miles High" in 1966, none of the radio stations that banned the song thought the group was referring to an airplane ride. A year later, there was no question about the function of the pills in the Jefferson Airplane's "White Rabbit" or in the "Purple Haze" that swirled around Jimi Hendrix. By now all of this was a part of the "Journey to the Centre of the Mind" (Amboy Dukes, 1968). Of course, sensational media coverage notwithstanding, not all the drug songs were in favour of drugs. It seemed fitting to many that the first Top Ten antidrug song, "Kicks" (1966), came from Paul Revere and the Raiders; at the time they were the house band for Dick Clark's television program *Where the Action Is.* It was simply bewildering when Donovan, the "Sunshine Superman" himself, whose "Mellow Yellow" (1966) had unintentionally initiated a short-lived and highly unproductive banana-smoking craze, suddenly denounced drug use. In that same year, the Rolling Stones spoke to the problem of middle-class prescription drug abuse in "Mother's Little Helper," a song that pointed out the hypocrisy of those who criticized the use of marijuana. Merle Haggard's "Okie from Muskogee" (1969), which chided marijuana-smoking hippies for their anti-American values while extolling the virtues of "white lightning," was as hypocritical as it was humorous. Later, the Stones' "Sister Morphine" and James Brown's "King Heroin" would capture the downside of inner-city addictions, a theme that would become much more prevalent in the 1980s and 1990s. For the counterculture, the focus on mind-expanding drugs seemed to offer the possibility of greater self-awareness and consciousness, which would in turn lead to a world without war, competition, or regimentation.

Blues on Acid: Psychedelic Rock

By the late 1960s, a number of musical strands (folk rock, a home-grown blues revival, and the second wave of the British Invasion) seemed to become emblematic of a larger cultural change going on in North America. Although there were inputs from major city centres such as New York, Chicago, and Los Angeles, the spiritual mecca for the counterculture was San Francisco, the site of a burgeoning rock scene that could boast of such groups as the Charlatans, the Jefferson Airplane, the Grateful Dead, Country Joe and the Fish, Quicksilver Messenger Service, Moby Grape, Sopwith Camel, Big Brother and the Holding Company, The Electric Flag, and Sly and the Family Stone.

The Jefferson Airplane was the only San Francisco group ever to have Top Ten singles in the 1960s. In 1967, primarily because of the powerful vocals of Grace Slick, "Somebody to

The sense of community that the Grateful Dead created was easily as important as the music they played. From the beginning, they were first among equals in giving of themselves to the counterculture.

Love" and "White Rabbit" moved into the upper reaches of the pop charts. Even before Slick replaced Signe Andersen as lead singer of the group, the Airplane was the first San Francisco band to get a major label contract and the first to get national exposure. Still, more than any other group, it was the Grateful Dead, who never registered a Top Ten album or single until 1987, who embodied all the elements of the San Francisco scene and came, therefore, to represent the counterculture to the rest of the country. The story of the Grateful Dead is one that combines the anticommercial tendencies of disaffected white middle-class youth with the mind-altering properties of lysergic acid diethylamide (LSD, acid), a chemical first synthesized by a Swiss chemist during World War II. After Timothy Leary, a Harvard psychology professor, was dismissed from the school in 1962 for his controversial experimentation with the drug, he turned his back on academia and set about convincing the world (or, at least, young people) to "turn on, tune in, and drop out." The attractiveness of this philosophy was immediately apparent to California novelist (and former state wrestling champion) Ken Kesey and his extended family, the Pranksters. Before LSD was declared illegal, Kesey, the Pranksters, and the Grateful Dead (then called the Warlocks) organized the first Trips Festival, one of a number of public LSD gatherings, which has been chronicled by Tom Wolfe in *The Electric Kool-Aid Acid Test.*

The Dead came from a smorgasbord of musical influences. Leader Jerry Garcia had played folk and bluegrass. Ron "Pigpen" McKernan, the son of a white r&b deejay, brought his blues background to bear in his keyboard and harmonica playing. Bassist Phil Lesh had studied classical music. The group's sound was rounded out by Bill Kreutzmann on drums, Bob Weir on guitar, and the later addition of eclectic percussionist Mickey Hart. The band's first LP, *The*

Grateful Dead (1967), was a straightforward rock album with a distinct r&b flavour. Ever open to the beckoning of psychedelia, the Dead went on to become one of the most experimental and improvisatory bands in rock.

One of the most endearing qualities of the band was their undying commitment to a sense of community. Never ones to impose a distance between themselves and their fans, the Dead lived in the Haight-Ashbury district, the heart of the hippie scene. The Haight was dedicated to the provision of free goods and services for all who needed them, including free lodging, free food, free medical care, and free music. The Dead were first among equals in giving unselfishly of themselves to hippie culture, performing "more free concerts than any band in the history of music."[34]

It was this sense of community, of contributing to the collective good, that made the counterculture, and San Francisco in particular, unique. It was reflected in the way bands now named themselves. Prior to the counterculture, groups invariably used plural nouns to describe themselves (the Temptations, the Rolling Stones). All the San Francisco groups (the Dead, the Airplane, Quicksilver, Big Brother, Moby Grape) and, after 1967, the most important groups from elsewhere (the Who, the Jimi Hendrix Experience, Led Zeppelin, Blood, Sweat, and Tears, Cream, Chicago, War) chose either the singular form of a noun or a collective noun for their names. While the plural form of a noun indicates an aggregate of individuals, the singular form or a collective noun describes a single entity, a unified whole, which was far more in keeping with the communal philosophy of the counterculture.

The music that emerged from the psychedelic experience came to be known, logically enough, as acid rock. Efforts to reproduce the effects of the psychedelic experience naturally resulted in a new kind of swirling concert poster art and light shows, attempts to incorporate colourful moving images as an integral part of the music a band was playing. Sometimes, simply the presence of these extra musical elements was enough to categorize music as acid rock. In fact, as Lillian Roxon has noted, "Much of the San Francisco music of that period came out of the blues, but because of the whole psychedelic coloring of that culture, it moved out of blues into the wider realms of acid rock."[35] In fact, blues-based rock enjoyed a surge among white rockers throughout the United States and Canada during this period. The blues revival had its beginnings in Chicago, where white teenager Paul Butterfield served as the American counterpart to Britain's Alexis Korner. Butterfield jammed with blues greats like Muddy Waters, Howlin' Wolf, and others, and eventually formed his own integrated blues band in 1963 with Mike Bloomfield on guitar. By 1965, New York folk-blues artists Danny Kalb, Tommy Flanders, Steve Katz, and Al Kooper had followed suit and formed The Blues Project. Both groups recorded reasonably successful LPs that included classic blues numbers. In Los Angeles, Canned Heat began in 1965, but the group did not get off the ground until "On the Road Again" hit the Top Twenty in 1968. By then, Butterfield had added horns to his group, thus anticipating Katz and Kooper's formation of Blood, Sweat, and Tears.

The first blues bands of note in Canada were the Downchild Blues Band, McKenna Mendelson Mainline, and the Dutch Mason Trio, the first two from Toronto, the third from Nova Scotia. While all three bands formed around the same time in the late 1960s, McKenna Mendelson Mainline, fronted by idiosyncratic vocalist Joe Mendelson and guitarist extraordinaire Mike McKenna, were the first to record, issuing the *Stink* album on Capitol Records in 1970. Both Downchild and Dutch Mason would issue their first albums a year later. While

Mainline enjoyed substantial radio play for the next few years, by 1972 McKenna and Mendelson had gone their separate ways.

Downchild would have a surprise hit single in 1974 with a cover of Big Joe Turner's 1950s r&b classic "Flip Flop and Fly." The single was taken from the group's second album, *Straight Up*, which also included two originals by Donnie "Mr. Downchild" Walsh: "(I Got Everything I Need) Almost" and "Shot Gun Blues." Both of these songs were covered in 1978 by the Blues Brothers on their million-selling *Briefcase of Blues* album. Both Downchild and Dutch Mason continued to record and perform across the country well into the twenty-first century.

In addition to the three bands noted above, Hamilton harmonica wizard Richard "King Biscuit Boy" Newell was an important participant in the late 1960s/early 1970s blues revival in Canada. Influenced by Little Walter, Newell found his first important gig in 1967 when he joined Ronnie Hawkins' backup band, the Hawks. It was Hawkins who nicknamed him "King Biscuit Boy" after the Helena, Arkansas, radio show which for many years had featured harmonica player Sonny Boy Williamson. In 1970, the then-current edition of the Hawks quit and became Crowbar. King Biscuit Boy played with Crowbar for a while and can be heard on their first album, 1971's *Bad Manors*, but in 1970 he embarked on a solo career, recording the classic *Official Music,* backed by Crowbar for Daffodil Records. Until his death in 2003, Biscuit remained one of the most gifted blues harmonica players alive. Unfortunately, he was plagued by personal demons and wasted much of his professional life wrestling with substance abuse.

In the late 1970s, the Powder Blues Band emerged from Vancouver to hit pay dirt with "Doin' It Right." British blues pioneer Long John Baldry emigrated to Canada at the turn of the decade, settling in Vancouver in 1985, and recorded the seminal *It Still Ain't Easy* album in 1991 for Stony Plain Records. Over the course of the 1970s, '80s, and '90s, Canada would continue to produce a number of blues-based popular musicians, including Moncton-born Matt Minglewood, Toronto's Jeff Healey and Paul Reddick, and Vancouver's Colin James. The late Jeff Healey, blind from the age of one, was a guitar virtuoso who played the instrument across his lap, fretting the strings "overhand." In 1988, with a style heavily influenced by Jimi Hendrix and Eric Clapton, he exploded internationally with the album *See the Light* and the Top Ten U.S. hit "Angel Eyes." Healey's 1990 album, *Hell to Pay*, was equally successful. Combined, the two albums sold over four million units. Healey died of cancer at the age of forty-one in March 2008.

Also in 1988, Regina-born Colin James released his eponymously titled debut platter, which included Canadian hits "Voodoo Thing," "Five Long Years," and "Why'd You Lie?" Sharing Healey's interest in blues-based music, James was picked to open U.S. shows for Keith Richards, Steve Winwood, and ZZ Top. In 1993, James released the first of three *Little Big Band* CDs, drawing on 1940s jump blues and pre-dating the swing revival craze by a few years.

At first, the music these blues rockers played was largely derivative. If it was connected to the psychedelic experience, it was primarily by virtue of its association with the counterculture ethos. It was the British group Cream that married the authenticity of the blues to the commercial appeal of the new rock aesthetic. Cream was the first of the supergroups (groups that were composed of top musicians from previously existing groups) in that it brought together drummer Ginger Baker, bassist Jack Bruce, and virtuoso blues guitarist Eric Clapton. Bruce and Baker had played together in the early 1960s as part of the Graham Bond Organisation, an organ-based group with jazz and blues influences. Clapton had embraced the blues so thoroughly as a member of the Yardbirds that he left the group (and was replaced by Jeff Beck) just as the blatantly commercial "For Your Love" (1965) rocketed to number six. Clapton then joined the more "authentic" Bluesbreakers. The group united Bruce and Clapton until Bruce left to join the more commercial Manfred Mann. Cream became a reality in 1966 when Clapton met Baker at a summer jam and the two decided to recruit Bruce and start a new band.

As the first of the power trios (a configuration that later proved very attractive to heavy metal groups), Cream provided its three members with more room to move than they had ever enjoyed before. In live performance, all three soloed extensively at deafening volumes, and through all the calculated distortion that drove listeners to new musical places, their musicianship was impeccable. The group combined psychedelics and the blues at the production level, defying listeners to figure out how many times Clapton had overdubbed himself. The layers of sound on the group's first LP, *Fresh Cream,* added a new dimension to the music, and yet somehow Delta bluesman Skip James' "I'm So Glad" could still be related to its originator. The group's second album, *Disraeli Gears,* yielded a Top Ten single, "Sunshine of Your Love," in 1967. *Wheels of Fire* went to number one on the album charts before the group disbanded in 1968. Although other British blues groups followed—most notably the Jeff Beck Group, which included Rod Stewart and Ron Wood, and Traffic, which featured Steve Winwood—Cream set the standard to which all others had to measure up.

Of course, San Francisco attracted its share of white blues enthusiasts as well. Steve Miller was a veteran of the Chicago blues scene who was lured to San Francisco by the prospect of lucrative recording contracts. His band included fellow Chicagoan Boz Scaggs. Eventually, Mike Bloomfield also left Chicago for the West Coast, where he teamed up with drummer Buddy Miles to form the Electric Flag. Janis Joplin, conspicuous as one of the few white female blues singers, came to the city from Port Arthur, Texas. Paired with Big Brother and the Holding Company, Joplin covered Big Mama Thornton's "Ball and Chain" and Irma Franklin's "Piece of My Heart" in 1968. Never one to save herself for the future, Joplin poured everything she had into every performance, but the intensity of her lifestyle took its toll. Having become a symbol of rebellion for millions of white middle-class youths, she died of a heroin overdose in 1970. She would have been proud to see her last album, *Pearl* (released posthumously), and its hit single, "Me and Bobby McGee," rise to the top of the pop charts in 1971.

The San Francisco scene peaked, so to speak, during the 1967 Summer of Love. When Los Angeles singer Scott McKenzie advised the young people heading to San Francisco that year to "wear some flowers in your hair," thousands upon thousands did just that. In the minds of the majority of the population, "flower power" became the hippie analog to "black power." Just as

the Black Panthers in neighbouring Oakland were identified with confrontational male posturing in the extreme and often depicted brandishing twelve-gauge shotguns over the slogan "Power comes from the barrel of a gun," the hippies were shown exploring the gentler, perhaps more female, side of resistance. One of the most memorable images of the counterculture pictured hippies planting daisies in the rifle barrels of the National Guard troops who were deployed to police mass demonstrations.

Janis Joplin gave her life to rock 'n' roll—literally. The intensity of her bluesy performances mirrored the tumultuousness of her life. In the end hers was a flame that burned out all too soon.

Commercializing the Counterculture: The Monterey Pop Festival

The commercial possibilities of the counterculture became apparent when the first Human Be-In Festival drew some 20,000 fans to San Francisco's Golden Gate Park in January 1967. Almost immediately, some hip capitalist rock entrepreneurs from Los Angeles, hoping to produce a profit-making festival along the same lines, booked the Monterey fairgrounds for the weekend of June 16 through 18. It was John Phillips of the Mamas and the Papas who convinced them to turn it into an artist-run, nonprofit, but still very commercial, event. Gradually, Phillips' manager, Lou Adler, took over, and the Monterey International Pop Festival was born. It was the perfect opening event for the Summer of Love.

In the hands of Adler and Phillips, the Monterey Pop Festival took shape as a decidedly West Coast event. About half of the two dozen or so artists who performed at the festival came from Los Angeles (the Byrds, Buffalo Springfield, the Mamas and the Papas, Canned Heat, Scott McKenzie) or San Francisco (the Jefferson Airplane, Country Joe and the Fish, the Grateful Dead, Big Brother and the Holding Company, [which featured Janis Joplin], Quicksilver Messenger Service, Steve Miller). New York singer/songwriters were represented by Laura Nyro and Simon and Garfunkel, although Nyro's overly laid-back performance earned her a place on the cutting room floor when a film of the festival was made. Although Eric Burdon and the Animals appeared, it was the Who that advanced the British Invasion as well as the ideology of the counterculture with a blistering performance of "My Generation." Canada was represented by Toronto group the Paupers and two members of Buffalo Springfield, Neil Young and Bruce Palmer. Not surprisingly, there was a dearth of black artists, but those who performed—Otis Redding, Jimi

Throughout the weekend, a range of countercultural impulses was on display, everything from the violent spectacle of the Who smashing their equipment to the curious sexuality of Jimi Hendrix making love to his guitar as he set it ablaze.

Hendrix, Lou Rawls, and Hugh Masekela—represented a broad range of styles. Even though Smokey Robinson sat on the festival board, not a single Motown act materialized, but then Berry Gordy seldom allowed his artists to participate in anything that he didn't control.

Whatever its shortcomings, the Monterey Pop Festival was a landmark event. As the first huge rock festival (30,000 fans in attendance), it pointed the way for all others. The event was patronized by the "hip-oisie" of the counterculture and by the elite of the recording industry, both of whom took it extremely seriously. It launched the U.S. careers of the Who and Jimi Hendrix, and it provided Otis Redding with the ideal springboard for crossover success, which unfortunately ended when he died in a plane crash later in the year, just three days after recording "(Sittin' on) The Dock of the Bay," his only number one single. Janis Joplin emerged from the festival as nothing short of a white blues goddess and was promptly signed to a lucrative contract by Clive Davis, president of CBS Records. The flowering San Francisco scene had already earned the Grateful Dead and the Jefferson Airplane contracts with Warner and RCA, respectively, and Vanguard had picked up Country Joe and the Fish. Later, Capitol signed both Quicksilver Messenger Service and the Steve Miller Band, reportedly for the then-unheard-of sum of $40,000 in advances.

If the Monterey Pop Festival confirmed the creeping commercialization of the counterculture, it also provided a platform for the politics of its adherents. David Crosby introduced the Byrds' "He Was a Friend of Mine," a song about the Kennedy assassination, with a direct challenge to the Warren Commission's official version of the story. "When President Kennedy was killed, he was not killed by one man," Crosby said. "He was shot from a number of different directions by different guns. The story has been suppressed, witnesses have been killed and this is your country."[36] Crosby also waxed eloquent about the joys of acid. His words infuriated McGuinn and marked the beginning of the end of Crosby's association with the Byrds. Undaunted, Crosby sat in with Buffalo Springfield, which included Stephen Stills and Neil Young, who were equally outspoken, and laid the groundwork for the supergroup configurations of Crosby, Stills & Nash and Crosby, Stills, Nash & Young.

Monterey Pop was, in fact, peppered with artists who had taken an antiestablishment stance in their music for some time. Earlier in the year, Buffalo Springfield had scored a Top Ten hit with "For What It's Worth (Stop, Hey What's That Sound)," a Stephen Stills song protesting the brutal treatment of peaceful demonstrators by police. Country Joe (McDonald) had been performing his anti-Vietnam "I-Feel-Like-I'm-Fixin'-to-Die Rag" in various folk and jug band versions since 1965. Together with the Fish, he performed it as rock at rallies and demonstrations long before it was released on record. The Animals' "We Gotta Get Out of This Place" had already become an early anthem protesting the constraints of urban life. The Who's "My Generation" solidified the generation gap.

Lyric content was not the only source of antiestablishment statements. One look at a stoned Mama Cass drinking in Janis Joplin with her eyes made it abundantly clear that applying the label *acid rock* to music required little more than music and acid. Indeed, throughout the weekend, a range of countercultural impulses was on display, everything from the violent spectacle of the Who smashing their equipment to the curious sexuality of Jimi Hendrix making love to his guitar as he set it ablaze. More bluesy than Clapton, louder than Cream, and more bizarre sexually, on stage at least, than Jim Morrison of the Doors could ever hope to be,

Hendrix was a left-handed, African American expatriate virtuoso guitarist from Seattle who started in his teens as a sideman for acts like Little Richard and the Isley Brothers. After he was lured to London by ex-Animal Chas Chandler, dressed up in "mod" gear, and paired with Noel Redding on bass and Mitch Mitchell on drums, he proceeded to dazzle British audiences with both his technical ability and his image, which Lillian Roxon has described as "the Wild Man of Borneo . . . crossed with all the languid, silken, jewelled elegance of a Carnaby Street fop."[37] In 1968, Eric Clapton described Hendrix's rise to popularity with a racist hipness that was all too common at the time:

> *He had the whole combination in England. It was just what the market needed, a psychedelic pop star who looked freaky, and they're also hung up about spades and the blues thing was there. So Jimi walked in, put on all the gear, and made it straight away. It was a perfect formula.*[37]

After his first single, "Hey Joe," hit the British Top Ten early in 1967, Hendrix brought his trio, known as the Jimi Hendrix Experience, back to the United States. His debut album, *Are You Experienced,* promptly climbed to number five on the charts. After performing at the Monterey Pop Festival, Hendrix and his band toured as the opening act for the Monkees ("Last Train to Clarksville," "I'm a Believer," "Daydream Believer"), a group of white, squeaky clean, mostly nonmusicians who were created by NBC-TV to fill the teen void left by the Beatles' maturity. It seems more than likely that audiences for the Monkees were ill-prepared to see Hendrix on stage "doing things to his guitar so passionate, so concentrated and so intense that anyone with halfway decent manners had to look away," as Roxon has said. "By the time it was over he had lapped and nuzzled his guitar with his lips and tongue, caressed it with his inner thighs, jabbed at it with a series of powerful pelvic thrusts. Even the little girls who'd come to see the Monkees understood what this was about."[39]

While Hendrix, who died unexpectedly in 1970, never attracted a substantial black U.S. audience to his music during his lifetime, he was considerably more important to music than his commercial, psychedelic, oversexed black man image indicates. He was a fine writer. He pioneered the incorporation of distortion and feedback into the language of popular music. His interpretation of Dylan's "All Along the Watchtower,"

Jimi Hendrix hovered above most other musicians. With his group, the Jimi Hendrix Experience, he elevated rock to new highs.

his only single to break the U.S. Top Twenty, added measurably to the music. "I liked Jimi Hendrix's record of this and ever since he died I've been doing it that way," said Dylan in the liner notes to *Biograph*. "Strange though how when I sing it I always feel like it's a tribute to him in some kind of way." During Hendrix's lifetime, however, the commercial interests surrounding him kept him tied to the formula that had made him a star, even when he wanted to expand his musical horizons. The pressures of the situation drove him not only to chemical excesses but also to his Electric Ladyland studios, where he logged some 800 hours of tape exploring fusions of jazz, rhythm and blues, and contemporary rock styles with Miles Davis, John McLaughlin, and other avant-garde jazz notables. None of these tapes was released during Hendrix's lifetime, and it is only recently that black artists and audiences have begun to recover the music with which he was identified.

At Monterey (as in the counterculture generally), psychedelia was the common thread that bound a Scott McKenzie, a Janis Joplin, an Otis Redding, a Jimi Hendrix, and a Ravi Shankar together. Nowhere was the power of this bond more apparent than in the recorded music that was played between performances. That music was the Beatles' recently released *Sgt. Pepper's Lonely Hearts Club Band*. *Sgt. Pepper* was a masterpiece. Eight months in the making, the album epitomized all the creativity (and the excesses) of the counterculture. As the first concept LP (an album designed as a coherent whole, with each song segueing seamlessly into the next), *Sgt. Pepper* established a new plateau in record production. It was an album conceived as a single, it required hundreds of hours of studio time, and it utilized special effects so sophisticated that the music could not be performed live. Of course, the Beatles had flirted with such developments in earlier albums. The release of *Rubber Soul* in 1965 had allowed Lennon and McCartney to show the new level of maturity they had reached in their songwriting. "Nowhere Man" hinted at Lennon's frustration with the group's lack of political engagement. At the same time, Harrison pioneered the use of the sitar in rock on "Norwegian Wood," introducing a sound that would become more familiar in the psychedelic era. (It was later marketed, somewhat sacrilegiously, as raga rock, referring to the Indian sitar music from which it took its name.) It was also at this point that George Martin went from being an excellent producer to being an indispensable creative force for the group; he was now called the "fifth Beatle," a title once used promotionally by deejay Murray the K. *Revolver* (1966), an even more experimental album, continued these trends. Harrison developed his sitar playing further under the tutelage of Ravi Shankar. "Taxman," the first Beatles song to contain an explicit political reference, chastised British government officials by name. George Martin polished every layer of sound to perfection. Released as a single early in 1967, "Penny Lane," backed with "Strawberry Fields," once again confirmed the Beatles' artistry and clearly prefigured the sound of things to come. But all of these merely hinted at the impact that *Sgt. Pepper* would have as its connection between music and psychedelics came to full fruition. It was not just transparent references like "Lucy in the Sky with Diamonds," or "With a Little Help from My Friends," or the cannabis plants hidden among the flora on the album cover collage; it was the whole sonic presentation of the album, from the hurdy-gurdy effects on "Mr. Kite," which were created by cutting a tape of steam organ music into foot-long sections and splicing them back together at random, to the seemingly interminable decay of the final mesmerizing chord on "A Day in the Life." Rounded out with military marching band regalia, *Sgt. Pepper* presented an artful and engaging foray into new musical terrain and represented the spirit of a way of life.

Riding the Storm

If the Beatles usually brought out the optimistic, upbeat aspects of the counterculture, the Doors were the avatars of its darker side. John Lennon might have tended toward a hostile surrealism at times, but Doors leader Jim Morrison actually embraced madness and terror in both his art and his life. The Doors had begun as an underground Los Angeles rock band. Morrison had met keyboardist Ray Manzarek in some of his classes when he was a student at UCLA. Manzarek had then recruited guitarist Robby Krieger and drummer John Densmore from the Third Street headquarters of Maharishi Mahesh Yogi, where they practised transcendental meditation. The group took its name from Aldous Huxley's *The Doors of Perception,* a book about the liberating aspects of drug use. After knocking around the Los Angeles club scene for a while, the group came to the attention of Jac Holzman, who signed them to his Elektra label in 1967. Their self-titled debut LP was an immediate smash. "Break on Through (To the Other Side)," the album's hard-rocking first single, defined the group's music and captured their image perfectly. The final cut, "The End," was an Oedipal fantasy that ran eleven minutes, forty-one seconds and got the group banned from the Whiskey-A-Go-Go before the record was released. What seems incredible is not that such material proved attractive to the Los Angeles underground but that the group became the number one teenybopper band in the country when "Light My Fire" (written by Krieger) rocketed to the top of the charts in 1967. Spreads in teenage magazines that cast Morrison as a teen idol were juxtaposed against a real-life, dramatic, on-stage sex-related bust in New Haven, Connecticut, and warrants for "lewd

> *If the Beatles usually brought out the optimistic, upbeat aspects of the counterculture, the Doors were the avatars of its darker side. John Lennon might have tended toward a hostile surrealism at times, but Doors leader Jim Morrison actually embraced madness and terror in both his art and his life.*

Led by poet/vocalist Jim Morrison, the Doors explored the darker side of rock, made headlines for their sex- and drug-related escapades, and much to the dismay of parents, became teen idols in the process.

and lascivious behavior" in Miami. The Doors' teen success spoke volumes about 1950s sexual repression coming undone in strange ways.

Throughout the late 1960s, as the group's next five albums made the Top Ten, the Doors remained one of the most in-demand acts in rock. Even Ed Sullivan felt compelled to book them, a move he regretted when they defied his censors and included a reference to getting "higher" in their performance of "Light My Fire." Although Morrison's constant brushes with the law served to bolster the group's outlaw image, the intensity of his lifestyle took its toll on all concerned. In 1971, he left the band for a temporary sabbatical in Paris. It became permanent when he died on July 3, most probably from a drug-induced heart attack. Three weeks later, the Doors' final hit single, "Riders on the Storm," began its ascent into the Top Twenty.

For observers of the American scene, the storm had begun several years earlier. In 1968, the Tet Offensive in Vietnam had shattered all hopes of a short stay, let alone the oft-promised "imminent victory" for U.S. forces. At home, Martin Luther King, Jr., was assassinated just after the Kerner Commission on Civil Disorders, which had been created to address the issue of increasing urban violence, warned that the country was "moving toward two societies, one black, one white—separate and unequal." Shortly thereafter, Robert Kennedy was murdered just as he was about to make a bid for the presidency. (That night David Crosby wrote "Long Time Coming," lamenting his death.) To some it seemed that revolution was just around the corner. King's assassination on 4 April 1968 provoked violent reactions in over one hundred American cities. As the most politically credible black artist at the time, James Brown was courted by the political establishment as ambassador to the streets. On the day King was assassinated, Brown was scheduled to perform at the Boston Garden. Faced with a potentially uncontrollable outburst of sorrow and rage, the city made it possible for the show to be broadcast on public television, which kept Boston cool, at least for one evening. Brown was later flown to Washington, D.C., to appeal to rioting youth there.

Other artists of all styles and personal backgrounds responded to race-related tensions in their own ways. Releases such as "Abraham, Martin, and John" (1968), by Dion, and "Everyday People," by Sly and the Family Stone (1969), picked up the "black and white together" theme of the early Civil Rights movement. The difficulties of interracial relationships had already been explored in sixteen-year-old Janis Ian's "Society's Child," released in 1967. The Rascals had taken an increasingly antiracist stance even before the group released "People Got to Be Free" in 1968. Reportedly, they refused a slot on the *Ed Sullivan Show* when the host refused to book a black opening act. Curtis Mayfield and the Impressions continued a series of socially conscious "sermon songs" with "We're a Winner" and "This Is My Country" in 1968 and "Choice of Colors" in 1969. Even Elvis Presley's rather unlikely entry, "In the Ghetto" (1969), went to number three on the pop charts. The Temptations' "Ball of Confusion (That's What the World Is Today)" (1969) captured the restlessness of the era and the state of the civil rights movement after King's death. "The civil-rights struggle was not dead," Nelson George has written, "but its energy was increasingly scattered. The Black Panthers embraced communism. Ron Karenga's U.S. organization advocated an Afrocentric cultural nationalism. . . . Black Power came to mean whatever its user needed it to . . . the assimilationists pressed on."[40] In 1971, the entropy of the movement was clearly

Aretha Franklin's stirring recording of Nina Simone's "Young, Gifted, and Black" captured the spirit of a community that had weathered a torrent of urban violence and provided the musical capstone for a decade of civil rights struggle.

reflected in popular music. While John Lennon's exhortation, "Power to the People," and The Chi-Lites' "(For God's Sake) Give More Power to the People" represented attempts to recall the heyday of the Black Panthers, Bob Dylan's tribute to the memory of slain black leader George Jackson made clear that the more radical elements in the struggle for black liberation had already been neutralized. Dylan's "George Jackson" was released in the aftermath of the massacre (thirty-three prisoners and ten hostages killed by police bullets) that followed the Attica State Prison uprising, which had begun as a silent vigil protesting Jackson's death. The disillusionment of the period was best expressed in Marvin Gaye's "What's Goin' On" and "Inner City Blues." Still, Aretha Franklin's stirring recording of Nina Simone's "Young, Gifted, and Black" captured the spirit of a community that had weathered a torrent of urban violence and provided the musical capstone for a decade of civil rights struggle.

Meanwhile, the social and political consciousness that the civil rights movement had awoken found its way into an increasingly broad range of concerns. For countercultural whites, the issues fell roughly into three categories: the open celebration of sex with or without love; spiritual transcendence; and a call for social change, which was expressed in terms of a revolution in consciousness, a call to arms, a commemoration of particular individuals or incidents, or opposition to the war in Vietnam.

The Beatles' 1964 willingness to just "hold your hand" had by 1967 escalated to the Rolling Stones' open call to "spend the night together" (even though they complied with the censors' directive to change the lyric to "spend some *time* together" for their appearance on the *Ed Sullivan Show*). In that year, the social complexity of Janis Ian's conception of interracial intimacy in "Society's Child" was washed away by the Beatles' simpler maxim "All You Need Is Love." Even teenyboppers were included in the new sexual freedom, as they "tumbled to the ground," embracing each other in Tommy James and the Shondells' "I Think We're Alone Now" (1967). There was little doubt as to what was going on in "Itchycoo Park" in 1968. One year later, even the Beatles wondered aloud: "Why Don't We Do It in the Road." While the sexual revolution was real enough, it did not liberate men and women equally. There was something about the energy of the Rolling Stones' music that could move both male and female bodies, but many of the group's songs—"Stupid Girl," "Under My Thumb," and later "Honky-Tonk Women" and "Brown Sugar"—were downright nasty toward women. Although the National Organization for Women (NOW) was founded in 1966, the best women could do on their own behalf that year musically was Sandy Posey's defeatist "Born a Woman" or Nancy Sinatra's more aggressive "These Boots Are Made for Walkin'." Even when Helen Reddy roared "I Am Woman" in 1972, it was less than ferocious, although it was explicitly feminist. In music, women had limited roles; they could be groupies or they could be go-go dancers, which indicates a good deal about their positions in society as a whole. Janis Joplin and Grace Slick held out to their listeners the possibility of a stronger voice for women, but only Aretha Franklin demanded respect. As a group, women declined on the year-end singles charts from an all-time high of 32 percent in 1963 to 6 percent in 1969.

In some ways, the call for social change split the counterculture into two groups: those who favoured militant political action (the so-called politicos) and those who favoured a strategy of individual consciousness-raising. The popular slogan "The revolution is in your head" reflected the counterculture's preoccupation with self-awareness and consciousness expansion, which sometimes intermingled the call for social change with spiritual transcendence. For some, revolution was an act of self-development, not the overthrow of one political system by another. Nowhere is this definition of revolution better illustrated than in the Beatles' "Revolution" (1968), which rose to number twelve as the flip side of "Hey Jude," the group's best-selling single. In their anti-Maoist rhetoric, Lennon's lyrics represented a rejection of militant political action in favour of individual consciousness-raising, which would then make everything "all right." Criticized by New Left activists, Lennon made a barely perceptible but highly significant change in the song when a slower version was included on the so-called *White Album* (1968). Where the single had spoken of "destruction," Lennon had said "count me out." On the album cut, he added "in" to the line, which was then sung as "count me out/in." Confronted with a real dilemma about the value of political action, Lennon could only leave the choice up to the listener. After the Beatles went their separate ways, Lennon tried to connect to grassroots political movements and to assume, in his own way, a more activist stance. There were, for example, the "bed-ins" he staged with Yoko Ono to protest the war in Vietnam, and anthems like "Give Peace a Chance" and "Power to the People," which were clearly intended for mass participation. While beautifully expressed in "Imagine" (1971) with the Plastic Ono Band, Lennon's vision was ultimately utopian. For the real "politicos," who were more grounded in the here-and-now of radical transformation, the Doors' "Five to One" (1968), referring to the notion that *our* "numbers" were more powerful than *their* "guns," or the Jefferson Airplane's "We Can Be Together" (1969), which called together those who were "out-laws" in the eyes of their country, had more appeal.

In the summer of 1968, radical activists turned their eyes toward Chicago, which was to be the site of the Democratic National Convention. For radicals, Chicago was to be the occasion to embarrass the government for its repressive policies at home and abroad. With front-runner Hubert Humphrey cloaking himself in outgoing President Lyndon Johnson's mantle, there was only mild-mannered Senator Gene McCarthy to carry the antiwar banner to the convention. Anticipating little support from within the Democratic Party, a most unlikely group of "co-conspirators" (who were later tried, and acquitted, for inciting a riot) vowed that their constituents would descend on the windy city in great numbers. The "Chicago Eight," as they were called, represented everyone from conscientious objectors and student radicals to yippies and Black Panthers. Todd Gitlin recalls thinking of Chicago as a "grand fusion between radical politics and counterculture—drugs, sex, rock 'n' roll, smash the State."[41] Protesters who came for the music were sorely disappointed. Political stalwart Phil Ochs did his part, but of all the prominent rock bands that were invited, only the MC5 was there to "Kick Out the Jams." Their appearance may have had something to do with the fact that their manager was White Panther leader John Sinclair. Those who came for the mayhem got more than they bargained for. The Chicago police spared no quarter in suppressing all dissent outside the convention hall. The theme music for these confrontations could have been the Rolling Stones' just released "Street Fighting Man" (despite its own disclaimers), if most of the Chicago rock stations had not refused to play it. If there had been any innocence among the demonstrators before the convention, it was lost forever, especially because a good part of the American population seemed to approve of the brutality they saw on their television screens. In the end, McCarthy's bid for the nomination failed, Humphrey ran, and Richard Nixon was elected. In the eyes of those who demonstrated in Chicago, this was simply adding the ultimate political insult to considerable physical injury.

Chicago '68 was a watershed event. For many activists, it confirmed the bankruptcy of the American political system; some withdrew from politics altogether, others became radicalized. Once beyond the pale of electoral politics, radicals explored various paths toward revolutionary change. The resulting sectarianism fragmented the New Left beyond hope, as the 1969 SDS National Convention (the organization's last convention) proved. The meeting was torn by bitter factionalism between Progressive Labor Party (PL) delegates and the Revolutionary Youth Movement (RYM)–Weathermen faction, and their third world allies, the Young Lords, Brown Berets, and Black Panthers. When a Panther took to the stage to announce that the only position for a woman in the revolution was prone, the new voice of feminism rose to a deafening roar. In the end, the largest and most visionary organization of the New Left was irrevocably shattered. But just as the Weathermen were gearing up to "bring the war home" by "fighting in the streets," Woodstock offered a fleeting pastoral approximation of the countercultural utopia.

Woodstock and Altamont: Reaching the Heights, Taking the Fall

The Woodstock Music and Art Fair took place in August 1969 on Max Yasgur's 600-acre farm in Bethel, New York. Despite a solid financial base and considerable advanced planning, the festival was a prime example of Murphy's Law—everything that could possibly go wrong did so. The crowd was expected to number 50,000 or so. There were instead seven or eight times that number. Roads were obstructed for miles; food and water were insufficient; medical and sanitary facilities were dreadfully inadequate; and there was the potential for a security nightmare. And then it began to rain. For all of this, Woodstock was the counterculture's finest hour. It was not just that there was no violence; it was that a spirit of cooperation infused the entire event. The three accidental deaths that did occur were balanced, at least symbolically, by three births. Bad acid to be avoided was announced from the stage. Wavy Gravy and the Hog Farm Commune offered practical guidance and makeshift medical attention and even managed to stretch the food supply to provide "breakfast in bed for 400,000," as Gravy described it. On the last day of the festival, Yasgur was moved to tell "the largest group of people ever assembled in one place" that "you have proven something to the world . . . that half a million kids can get together and have three days of fun and music and have nothing *but* fun and music."[42] With some exceptions, police and local residents described the crowd in terms as glowing as Yasgur's. Here, then, was the counterculture made real, the spontaneous temporary community that was later lionized by Chicago Eight defendant Abbie Hoffman as the "Woodstock Nation."

The symbolism of Woodstock was overpowering, and its music was compelling. Creedence Clearwater Revival and The Band (parodoxically, a Canadian group) represented good old American rock 'n' roll. Together, they summed up an era of rock styles in much the same way the festival summed up the counterculture. Arriving from England, where the group's groundbreaking rock opera, *Tommy,* had just been released, the Who began with "Touch me,

Roads were obstructed for miles; there was insufficient food and water, dreadfully inadequate medical and sanitary facilities, and the potential for a security nightmare. And then it began to rain. For all of this, Woodstock was the counterculture's finest hour.

feel me . . ." from *Tommy* and then burst into a memorable performance of "Summertime Blues." Roger Daltrey's bare-chested costume with the long white fringes provided one of the most lasting visuals of the event. Ten Years After did a more than credible job of representing the second wave of British blues bands. Also riding the second wave of the British Invasion was Joe Cocker, who had just embarked on his first U.S. tour after the release of his first LP, *With a Little Help from My Friends* (which included Jimmy Page and Steve Winwood). His soulful, spastic performance of the title song at the festival has been imprinted on the national consciousness ever since. The following year, he played to sellout crowds on a tour organized by Leon Russell and billed as Mad Dogs and Englishmen.

San Francisco offered the Jefferson Airplane, Country Joe and the Fish, and Santana. The Jefferson Airplane delivered some of the more political material from their *Volunteers* album. Country Joe and the Fish introduced "I-Feel-Like-I'm-Fixin'-to-Die-Rag" with a rousing version of the "Fish Cheer." Like most of the San Francisco groups, Santana had begun in 1967 as a blues band but because of their Latin roots they quickly outgrew the genre. Their performance of "Soul Sacrifice" at Woodstock introduced them to a new mass audience and earned them a recording contract with Columbia. Their self-titled debut album, which was released a month later, rose to number four and included the hit single "Evil Ways." The group's second album, *Abraxas* (1970), went all the way to number one, acquainting a national audience with a Latin rock version of Peter Green's "Black Magic Woman" and a stunning interpretation of Tito Puente's "Oye Como Va."

The festival also had the expected deficiencies. Aside from Melanie, Grace Slick, and Janis Joplin (none of whom were included in the original film), there was only one other female headliner—Joan Baez. (Nine months later, Joplin would front the four-fifths Canadian Full Tilt Boogie Band.) Performing "Joe Hill," a song about the martyred labour organizer, Baez introduced a new generation of rock fans to the music of the labour movement. There were also only three African American acts for three days of morning-to-evening performances—Richie

Hendrix delivered a political message of sorts. His searing performance of "The Star-Spangled Banner," which replicated the sounds of "bombs bursting in air" on the guitar as only Hendrix could, turned the national anthem into an antiwar song.

Havens, Jimi Hendrix, and Sly and the Family Stone. As much an anomaly as Hendrix, Havens, a black folkie, opened the festival as the organizers were still putting the finishing touches on logistics. Asked to stall until the next act was ready, the artist ran out of material. He closed his set with "Freedom," a song that he improvised on the spot and felt captured the ethos of the day. Hendrix also delivered a political message of sorts. His searing performance of "The Star-Spangled Banner," which replicated the sounds of "bombs bursting in air" on the guitar as only Hendrix could, turned the national anthem into an antiwar song.

The only act that could be considered a black act with a substantial following in the African American community was Sly and the Family Stone. Combining black and white women and men, they managed to marry the funk and rock cultures in a way that other artists had been unable to. Between 1968 and 1971, Sly and the Family Stone recorded a series of Top Ten pop hits—"Dance to the Music" (1968), "Everyday People" and "Hot Fun in the Summertime" (1969), "Thank You (Falletinme Be Mice Elf Agin)" (1970), and "Family Affair" (1971)—that transcended the confines of musical style, much as the band crossed the boundaries of race and gender. Based in San Francisco, the group was a model of racial and sexual

Sly (second from left) and the Family Stone created socially relevant music that crossed the boundaries of r&b, jazz, and psychedelic rock as boldly as the group transcended the divisions of race and gender. It was an ambitious project for the late 1960s, and for a while, the group pulled it off better than anyone.

harmony. The group's 1969 LP, *Stand!,* illustrated both the band's growing maturity and Sly's growing militancy. The album contained not only the all-inclusive number one single "Everyday People" but also the bolder title song and the more provocative "Don't Call Me Nigger, Whitey." The group's 1971 LP, *There's a Riot Goin' On,* was considered even more controversial, but by this time Sly's militancy was more than offset by his drug-induced unreliability. Following a number of personnel changes, the group slowly disintegrated. "Family Affair" was the group's last Top Ten pop single.

It was Crosby, Stills & Nash who got the most out of their Woodstock appearance. The supergroup had begun to form in the summer of 1968, when an informal jam at singer/songwriter Joni Mitchell's house in Laurel Canyon turned into serious talk about starting a group. After David Geffen was brought in to help with contractual arrangements (most of the principals were already signed to various labels), the new group, which consisted of David Crosby (from the Byrds), Stephen Stills (from Buffalo Springfield), and Graham Nash (from the Hollies), was signed to Atlantic. The self-titled debut album showcased all the talents of the group's members: their obvious writing ability, elegant harmonies, penchant for social commentary, and seasoned professionalism. Heralded by critics as the best LP of the year, the album included the seven-minute single they performed at Woodstock, "Suite: Judy Blue Eyes," as well as "Marrakesh Express," Crosby's "Long Time Coming," and "Wooden Ships," written by Crosby, Stills, and Paul Kantner of the Jefferson Airplane about the horrors of nuclear war. "Long Time Coming" and "Wooden Ships" were both used on the opening audio track for the *Woodstock* film. At the suggestion of Ahmet Ertegun, Canadian Neil Young (also from Buffalo Springfield) was recruited for the group's second effort. *Déjà Vu* (1970) was, if

"Oye Como Va"

Artist: Santana
Music / Lyrics by Tito Puente
Label: Columbia (1970),
from the LP *Abraxas*

Composed by New York–based salsa percussionist Tito Puente, "Oye Como Va" is quite literally a song about rhythm. Its text celebrates the great dances of Afro-Cuban music, and its music is based on a distinctive Afro-Cuban "cha-cha" rhythm. "Oye Como Va" was made famous among Anglo audiences in this particular 1970 version by Santana, which married a traditional Afro-Cuban percussion section (timbales, congas, guiro) to the slightly "distorted" sound of the Hammond organ and the singing, bent-note guitar solos of late 1960s rock. In this performance, guitarist and bandleader Carlos Santana, the offspring of Mexican-born parents, illustrated that he did not need to "invent" Latin roots for rock music; they had been there all along in jazz, r&b, and (eventually) disco and hip hop.

The players on the *Abraxas* LP were Carlos Santana, guitar and vocals; Rico Reyes, percussion; Mike Carabello, percussion and conga; José Chepitó Areas, percussion, conga, and timbales; Michael Shrieve, drums; Alberto Gianquinto, piano; David Brown, bass and guitar; and Gregg Rolie, keyboards and vocals.

Musical Style Notes

"Oye Como Va" is a good example of a piece that is constructed of several repetitive melodic and rhythmic formulae over which improvisation can happen. Harmonically, it is simple: two chords are played over and over again. The complexity lies in the layering of musical elements: over those two chords, we hear the percussion section playing Latin polyrhythms (multiple rhythms layered over each other and played simultaneously), to which are added improvisations by the guitar and organ.

The Afro-Cuban rhythm is a very important part of the stylistic footprint of "Oye Como Va." The beginning consists of a "vamp" (a short musical phrase, usually with a distinct rhythm, that repeats a number of times, sometimes through an entire song). The vamp begins right at the introduction. Here's the rhythm the organ plays:

1 + 2 + 3 + 4 +	1 + 2 + 3 + 4 +
/ / / /	/ /

Overlaid with this, you can then hear the distinctive "cha-cha" rhythm in the *sheee-yuk-shuk-shuk shee-yuk-shuk-shuk* sound of the guiro, a grooved percussion instrument played with a stick:

1 + 2 + 3 + 4 +	1 + 2 + 3 + 4 +
/ /// //	/ /// //

Transitions between musical sections are marked by a short, percussive phrase played in rhythmic unison. This has been indicated in the Road Map as "rhythmic transition."

Musical "Road Map"

TIMINGS	COMMENTS	LYRICS	
0:00–0:06	Hammond organ "vamp"		
0:06–0:15	Percussion enters. Guiro enters at 0:08.		
0:15–0:30	Guitar enters, layered over organ, bass, percussion; guitar plays the same phrase four times.		
0:30–0:37	Rhythmic transition (short, percussive phrase played in rhythmic unison)		
0:38–0:53	Verse	*Oye como va . . .*	
0:53–0:57	Rhythmic transition		
0:57–1:45	Guitar solo (based on opening phrase)		
1:45–1:53	Rhythmic introduction "vamp" returns as transitional passage.		
1:53–2:08	Volume drops; organ plays repetitive riff; section ends with another unison passage played with percussive rhythm, forming transition to organ solo.		
2:08–2:48	Hammond organ solo		
2:48–3:00	Rhythmic "vamp" (as in introduction)		
3:00–3:14	Verse	*Oye como va . . .*	
3:14–3:22	Rhythmic transition		
3:22–4:06	Guitar solo		
4:06–4:14	Rhythmic transition, ending with vocal "huh!" and final chord		

anything, received even more warmly by the critics as it climbed to the number one position on the charts. Side two began with "Woodstock," a song that Joni Mitchell had written about the festival for the quartet. The group also released a single that year that was not included on the album. When the National Guard opened fire on a demonstration at Kent State University in Ohio, killing four students and wounding nine others, the group responded immediately with "Ohio," a protest song written by Young that named Nixon as the guilty party. The single was released within weeks of the shooting and quickly became a Top Twenty hit.

One of the things that made Crosby, Stills, Nash & Young attractive to its members was the freedom to work on solo projects throughout the life of the group. As individuals, each member turned out quality music, often using topical material, as in Neil Young's "Southern Man," a warning to Alabama's racist Governor George Wallace, Crosby and Nash's "Immigration Man," Stephen Stills' "Love the One You're With," and Graham Nash's "Chicago," written about the 1968 Democratic National Convention for a benefit for the Chicago Eight. Individually and as a group, Crosby, Stills, Nash & Young represented the creativity and positive political impulses of the 1960s as well as the commercial potential of topical material.

Between Woodstock and Altamont, it seemed like the apocalypse might be approaching. Having promised "days of rage," the Weathermen tore up Chicago's upscale Gold Coast just as Charles Manson and his tribe were emerging from the California desert to kill actress Sharon Tate, reportedly inspired by the Beatles' "Helter Skelter." In Washington, D.C., at the Vietnam Moratorium on November 15, Pete Seeger led three-quarters of a million antiwar activists in a chorus of John Lennon's "Give Peace a Chance." On December 4, Chicago police shot Black Panther Fred Hampton dead in his bed. Two days later, there was California's Altamont.

Altamont might well have turned into a Woodstock-like miracle save for two key differences. First, the concert was held in an area that was a fraction of the size of Max Yasgur's farm. Second, the San Francisco chapter of the Hell's Angels was hired to do security for $500 worth of beer.

Altamont was a free concert that the Rolling Stones had planned as the climax to their 1969 U.S. tour promoting their *Let It Bleed* album. Held at the Altamont Speedway just outside San Francisco, the concert was captured in all its gory detail in a documentary titled *Gimme Shelter*. There are, in fact, a lot more similarities between Woodstock and Altamont than it is comfortable to remember—an audience numbering in the hundreds of thousands, inadequate food, water, and toilets, shifting sites at the last minute, traffic jams, equal numbers of deaths and births. Altamont might well have turned into a Woodstock-like miracle save for two key differences. First, the concert was held in an area that was a fraction of the size of Max Yasgur's farm. Second, the San Francisco chapter of the Hell's Angels was hired to do security for $500 worth of beer.

Initially lukewarm to the idea of a free concert, the Stones had become more comfortable with it as the tour wore on. It was the group's first tour in the United States since 1966 and Mick Taylor's introduction to the American audience. The concert was originally slated for Golden Gate Park in San Francisco, but the site was then shifted to the Sears Point Raceway, where all the logistical planning and on-site construction were completed. Unfortunately, final negotiations with the owners of the raceway broke down at the eleventh hour. Upscale San Francisco attorney Melvin Belli was brought in to set things straight. He promptly negotiated an alternative deal with the Altamont Speedway, which meant that all the logistics had to be redone and all the staging had to be torn down and reassembled at the new site. The idea of hiring Hell's Angels to do security was not rejected by the Stones for a number of reasons. First, the British Hell's Angels had done security without incident for the free concert the group had staged in London's Hyde Park the previous summer. That concert had attracted some 300,000 fans. Second, the Grateful Dead—however naively, optimistically, or stupidly—had advised the Stones that it would be "cool" to use the group. The romantic outlaw biker image in mid-1960s films like *Easy Rider* fascinated Americans, and the Stones probably felt that using the Angels for security would complement their own outlaw image. However, the British Hell's Angels the Stones knew were pale imitations of their U.S. counterparts, who came armed with knives and lead-filled pool cues, which they used at the slightest provocation.

From the beginning, the concert was marred by bad drug trips and violence. Instructed to keep people off the stage, Hell's Angels treated the area as if it were a military stronghold. Marty Balin, the Jefferson Airplane's lead singer, was punched unconscious by one of the Angels during the group's performance of "Somebody to Love," when Balin found himself caught between the security force and a group of fans who had climbed onto the stage. The violence continued unabated throughout the day, reaching its apex when a black student named Meredith Hunter was murdered. Hunter, who was brandishing a pistol, was stabbed several times by one of the Angels and then clubbed to death during the Stones' plodding performance of "Under My Thumb." Sporting an orange-and-black cape and a T-shirt emblazoned with an appropriately prophetic Greek letter *omega* ("the end"), Mick Jagger made feeble attempts to calm the crowd. Nothing could have made it clearer who were the real street-fighting men and who were the rock 'n' roll pretenders, and it was all captured on film.[42]

The violence at Altamont reflected the deterioration of political movements and served notice of the counterculture's impending demise. Within months, New York City construction workers would attack antiwar activists and hippies in the street with the tacit approval of the Nixon administration. With hundreds of Panthers already dead or in jail, Bobby Seale, having just weathered the Chicago Eight debacle, would find himself on trial for murder. The U.S. military would bomb Cambodia illegally, and a state of outright repression would become a public spectacle with the killing of student demonstrators at Kent State and, shortly thereafter, at Jackson State. These students' deaths would have the same chilling effect on direct political action that the deaths of Hendrix, Joplin, and then Morrison would have on popular music.

In 1970, Motown made a rare sortie into social commentary when it released Edwin Starr's "War." "War," proclaimed the artist, bellowing the song's title, was worth "absolutely nothing." As the song became a number one pop hit, its message obviously struck a chord among listeners, but it fell on deaf ears among Washington policymakers. Starr's follow-up hit, "Stop the War" (1971), also failed to translate into social policy, even though it echoed the sentiments of millions of Americans. It was clear that the era was coming to an unsatisfactory end and that the "return to normalcy" would be marked by an enforced decline in urban violence with no alleviation of its root causes, and a separation of popular music from political ferment.

Music Versus Markets: The Fragmentation of Pop

The 1960s rolled into the 1970s, leaving behind a series of unresolved issues. As a result, the 1970s are often viewed as a decade of retreat. While it is true that the two great movements of the previous decade—the civil rights movement and the antiwar movement—were in decline, lasting social and cultural (if not structural) changes did occur. Society was not radically transformed in the manner the New Left wanted, but neither did conservatives reestablish the cultural and political hegemony that they had enjoyed in the early 1950s. There were advances in environmental politics (ecology and the antinuclear movement) and, particularly, the women's movement. The oppression of poor people, people of colour, and women would not disappear, but these constituencies would never again be silent or invisible. Finally, the 1970s called into question all traditional notions of masculinity and femininity.

The music industry, like the population at large, had been swept up in the political currents of the 1960s, as popular music was used to fuel every impulse from explorations of awakened sexuality and flights of psychedelic fantasy to furious discharges of political spleen. But the industry never lost its footing as an enduring capitalist enterprise. Any internal tensions the industry felt were expressed, predictably, in terms of culture versus commerce, music versus markets, the electric version of the authentic-commercial debate of the folk revival. The more astute observers of the scene understood that this contradiction had always been inherent in rock 'n' roll. "From the start," Michael Lydon said in 1970, "rock has been commercial in its very essence. . . . It was never an art form that just happened to make money, nor a commercial undertaking that sometimes became art. Its art was synonymous with its business."[1] Just as the radical movements of the 1960s depended, in part, on the affluence provided by the war effort,

> *The music industry, like the population at large, had been swept up in the political currents of the 1960s, as popular music was used to fuel every impulse from explorations of awakened sexuality and flights of psychedelic fantasy to furious discharges of political spleen. But the industry never lost its footing as an enduring capitalist enterprise.*

popular music was bound to the capitalist interests that produced it. Thus, to understand the trajectory of popular music in the 1970s, it is necessary to explore commercial and technological developments that began in the music industry in the late 1960s.

As popular music in the late 1960s began to incorporate blues, jazz, classical, East Indian, and electronic sounds, the boundaries separating audiences became somewhat murky. Because of the technical development of FM rock radio, which led to short-lived experiments in free-form programming, there was a brief moment in the late 1960s when it was not out of the ordinary to hear the Beatles, Stevie Wonder, Janis Joplin, Aretha Franklin, Jimi Hendrix, Pink Floyd, Simon and Garfunkel, and the Grateful Dead on the same radio program or to find them in the same record collection. At the time, all these artists were included in the umbrella category of progressive rock, which presumably distinguished them from less interesting formulaic pop. A few years later, however, as the industry tried to rationalize production, such a range of artists would be spread over a number of more discrete, less overlapping audiences. It is for this reason that *Rolling Stone*'s Steve Pond remembers the 1970s as a time when rock

> *became diffuse, scattered and unfocused, fragmenting into little genres whose fans paid less and less attention to other little genres. In the Seventies, rock had a hundred different focal points: Elton John for popsters; Led Zeppelin for hard rockers; Emerson, Lake and Palmer for the art rockers; Joni Mitchell for the singer/songwriter contingent; David Bowie in the glam rock corner; Stevie Wonder for soul aficionados. Instead of a center, rock had a batch of radio formats.*[2]

Keeping its capitalistic roots in mind, the music industry moved to a strategy of trying to target fans with the most disposable income. Thus, the art of marketing became more and more tied to the science of demographics.

The Music Industry: A Sound Investment

By 1973, the music business had become a $2-billion-a-year industry, about as large as the sports and film industries combined. The Canadian record industry was also rapidly expanding, growing 50 percent between 1970 and 1973. The total value of tapes (in all formats) and LPs shipped in Canada in 1973 was $105.1 million. Having learned from their rock 'n' roll mistakes, major record companies in both countries no longer resisted the creative impulses of offbeat artists or upstart independent labels. Instead, they happily signed acts directly, made label deals, entered into joint ventures, or contracted for distribution. When the Jefferson Airplane left RCA to set up Grunt records, the group did not hesitate to look to its old label for distribution. Capitol contracted with the Beach Boys to distribute Brother Records. Frank Zappa's Bizarre label, which was distributed by Warner, developed new talent. When Zappa directed Alice Cooper to Warner in the early 1970s, the company was smart enough to listen, and the outrageous metal ensemble became one of the label's best-selling acts. Warner also entered into a lucrative distribution deal with Chrysalis, which had Jethro Tull and Procol Harum. At the same time, distribution deals with Stax and Philadelphia International profitably provided CBS Records with entrée to the soul market.

By 1973, the music business had become a $2-billion-a-year industry, about as large as the sports and film industries combined.

What had begun in the late 1960s as a period of political awakening with a cultural flourish for the rock 'n' roll audience was, for the music industry, a period of commercial expansion and corporate consolidation. While the industry learned to "go with the flow" to a great extent, the impulse to engineer trends from the top down was never completely extinguished. Sometimes the magic worked, as in the creation of the Monkees and their cartoon cousins the Archies. Sometimes it did not, as in the ill-fated effort to create the "Bosstown Sound," an attempt to replicate the San Francisco experience in Boston that cost MGM an estimated $4 million.

Merger Mania

Even with the occasional failure, Wall Street finally came to view the music industry as a sound investment. Thus, there ensued a period of unprecedented merger activity, not just large record companies gobbling up smaller ones but huge conglomerates, unrelated to music, acquiring properties in the music industry. RCA, CBS, Capitol-EMI, and their related labels, which had long been divisions of multinational electronics firms, simply expanded their holdings. Phillips, the Dutch electronics conglomerate, acquired Mercury and MGM. Gulf and Western bought Paramount. GRT, the tape company, purchased Chess. Omega Equities bought Roulette.[3] By far the most interesting merger, however, was the one that created the Warner Communications empire.

Warner Brothers Records had been a rather lacklustre label that was created in 1958 as a division of the film company. In 1963, the purchase of Frank Sinatra's Reprise label, which was run by Mo Ostin, put the corporation on a firmer footing financially, but its place in the burgeoning youth culture was not secured until promo man Joe Smith, soon to become the company's president, signed the Grateful Dead in 1967. In that year, through a series of merger techniques, the combined labels were bought by the smaller Seven Arts film company, which also acquired Atlantic Records. (At the time it was bought, Atlantic was consolidating its hold over southern soul with Aretha Franklin and the Stax-Volt roster and moving into new terrain with second-wave British acts like Cream.) Warner-Seven Arts, as the newly formed company was called, then ran headfirst into Steve Ross. Ross had just parlayed his wife's family funeral business into a modest empire that included rental cars and the Kinney parking lot system. It was the subsequent purchase of a talent agency that whet Ross' appetite for the music business. Within months, his Kinney Corporation, as the conglomerate was called, had bought Warner-Seven Arts and its associated labels. Shortly thereafter, Jac Holzman's Elektra label was added. Elektra had been launched as a folk label in the 1950s, but it became a more attractive property financially after Holzman signed the Doors in 1967. In 1973, David Geffen's Asylum Records was acquired by Ross and amalgamated with Elektra in the following year. Geffen then replaced Holzman at the helm. Asylum had started as a refuge for softer acts such as Joni Mitchell, the Eagles, and Jackson Browne, many of whom Geffen had managed with his partner, Eliot Roberts.

By this time, Ross had reorganized the company as Warner Communications. In addition to a couple of dozen associated labels, the corporation had extensive holdings in film and television, *Mad* magazine, sixty-three comic books, and a piece of *Ms.* magazine. Its national record distribution was set up as Warner-Elektra-Atlantic (WEA). In addition to the talent mentioned earlier, the company had Led Zeppelin, Deep Purple, Black Sabbath, the Faces, Crosby, Stills &

Nash, Arlo Guthrie, Van Morrison, James Taylor, Randy Newman, the Mothers of Invention, and Canadians Gordon Lightfoot, Neil Young, an Joni Mitchell. While the committee of record executives that coordinated the music operation—Joe Smith and Mo Ostin from Warner-Reprise, David Geffen from Elektra-Asylum, and Ahmet and Nesui Ertegun from Atlantic—had little contact with Steve Ross, their combined efforts turned him into one of the most powerful men in the recording industry as well as American business as a whole.

By the time gasoline shortages miraculously led to record profits for the oil companies between 1973 and 1974, structural realignments had produced a level of concentration in the music industry that had not been witnessed since the postwar 1940s. The top four record corporations accounted for over 50 percent of all records and tapes sold. CBS and Warner Communications alone took in about 40 percent of the total. The industry had also consolidated vertically. For example, CBS, Inc., in addition to its own labels, recording studios, pressing plants, national distribution, and publishing division, owned the Columbia Record and Tape Club, Pacific Stereo and the Discount Records chain, Fender Guitars, Leslie Speakers, Rhodes Pianos, and Rogers Drums. EMI in Great Britain had an analogous set of holdings. Because of the predominance of electronics corporations in the field, there was a wrinkle to this corporate structure that seemed particularly antithetical to the ideology of popular music at the time: the unexpected connection between music and the military. Ever since the invention of the wireless, electronic communication had developed according to its military applications. "Audio is a fairly obscure backwater of electronics," producer Peter Williams has explained. "When people do go out to design a new chip they're not thinking how many recording studios can we sell it to. They're thinking how many missiles can we stick this in. Most electronic development is highly military."[4] The connection between music and the military was driven home dramatically to Keith Richards when he discovered that Decca, the Stones' label, had diverted the profits it made from the sale of Rolling Stones records to precisely this kind of research and development.

> *We found out, and it wasn't years till we did, that all the bread we made for Decca was going into making little black boxes that go into American Air Force bombers to bomb fucking North Vietnam. They took the bread we made for them and put it into the radar section of their business. When we found that out, it blew our minds. That was it. Goddamn, you find you've helped to kill God knows how many thousands of people without even knowing it. I'd rather the Mafia than Decca.[5]*

In the headiness of the late 1960s and early 1970s, such connections were not always apparent. This was the time when rock became art, when it became progressive—indeed, revolutionary. The industry rose willingly to the challenge of accommodating the new aesthetic.

Expanding the Infrastructure: Counterculture as Commodity

Developments in recording technology had a dramatic impact on the production of music. By the late 1960s and early 1970s, high-fidelity stereo records had become the industry standard (with various tape configurations vying for acceptance) and had increased the public desire for high-quality sound. In the search for better sound, the two four-track tape machines that had been used to record *Sgt. Pepper* in 1967 were rendered obsolete by the appearance of eight- and sixteen-track studios. Multitrack recording had immediate consequences for the social relations of musical production. No longer was it necessary for musicians to perform together to make a record. Indeed, a single musician could now play all the instruments. Overdubbing, layering, mixing, and the addition of special effects such as reverb, equalization, and compression removed increasingly important aspects of the creative process from the studio performance and located them in the control room, elevating the producer to an artistic status equal to that of the musicians he produced. As a result, the term *production* in the music industry, as Peter Wicke has astutely pointed out, came to have two related but distinct definitions: "the production of music and the manufacture of records."[6] By the early 1970s, the major record labels had narrowed their focus essentially to the manufacture and sale of records. Virtually all of the creative aspects of music-making were contracted out. "The mechanics of a record company are just that—the mechanics," said Joe Smith in 1974.[7] On the creative end, record companies were involved primarily in talent acquisition, marketing, and promotion. And promote they did. The record companies were quick to pick up on the antiestablishment fervour of the late 1960s and early 1970s in promoting some of the more creative strands of rock that were being labeled *progressive rock,* a term that resonated nicely with the radical rhetoric of the era. In 1968, CBS introduced an ad campaign that promoted some of its rock acts as "The Revolutionaries." Advertisements were headlined with slogans like **THE MAN CAN'T BUST OUR MUSIC.** Warner released a compilation LP called *The People's Album* that was largely a repository for their singer/songwriters and soft rock acts. The album cover art, however, had lettering intended to look like Chinese characters and depicted heroic, banner-waving protesters in Mao jackets, thus suggesting an association with the cultural revolution that was occurring halfway around the world.

By the early 1970s, the major record labels had narrowed their focus essentially to the manufacture and sale of records. Virtually all of the creative aspects of music-making were contracted out.

The appearance of a whole new industry infrastructure greatly enhanced the promotional power of the record companies. Once experimentation with psychedelic drugs introduced a new visual dimension to live rock performances, a touring circuit of ballrooms and small clubs opened up to showcase the new progressive rock acts. Taking their cue from promoter Bill Graham's Fillmore Auditorium in San Francisco, clubs like the Electric Circus in New York, the Electric Circus in Toronto, the Boston Tea Party, the Electric Factory in Philadelphia, the Grande Ballroom in Detroit, and the Kinetic Playground in Chicago embellished rock performances with strobe effects and undulating, amoeba-like light patterns that pulsated to the beat of the music. When the psychedelic clubs and ballrooms folded after only a few years, it was largely because the progressive rock market had outgrown such small venues. Established promoters simply moved into arenas or stadium-size venues and huge outdoor festivals. They could do so because advances in sound reinforcement technology had opened up the possibility of mass audience events on the scale of Woodstock. Many of those sound advances were the result of the pioneering efforts of Canadian Pete Traynor. Yorkville Sound, incorporated in 1963 by Jack Long (of Long and McQuade) and Traynor, pioneered the development of the portable P.A. system (including column speakers, mixers, and amplifiers), portable stage lighting, the guitar amp master volume control, reliable high-powered bass amplification, bass cabinets with eight ten-inch speakers, contract concert sound, the "wedge" floor monitor, and the multi-patch cord snake. Although there were a handful of Canadian competitors, including

Garnett Amplifiers in Winnipeg and GBX (a division of Arc Sound) and Tagus in Toronto, from the 1960s until the present, Yorkville Sound has been the dominant company in the Canadian market. While the Traynor name is not as well-known as that of Fender or Marshall, vintage amp collectors around the world rank Traynor gear among the finest sounding, most durable amps and speaker cabinets ever built.

A burgeoning rock press, including the U.S.-based *Rolling Stone* and the Canadian-based *Beetle Magazine*, and the advent of FM rock radio completes the picture of the music industry's growing infrastructure. Prior to the mid-1960s, popular music was geared to the Top Forty AM radio format. The format was perfected when programmer Bill Drake, who learned his trade at KYA in San Francisco and KYNO in Fresno, California, developed tight, distinct *sound* for his stations by encouraging his stereotypically fast-talking deejays to eliminate what he termed "dead air." The format reduced the power of deejays by forcing them to adhere rigidly to a limited list of forty or fewer songs that were rotated all day long and liberally interspersed with commercials.

As Smokey Robinson at Motown recognized early on, the unit of pop production for AM Top Forty was the three-minute single. However, the new lyric substance that the folk revival of the early 1960s had brought to popular music and concept LPs like *Sgt. Pepper* did not readily lend themselves to the fast-paced AM radio format. It was at this point that FM rock radio opened up to accommodate this new musical style.

After the postwar decision to reassign FM to the 88–108 MHz band, which rendered a half million FM receivers instantly obsolete (see Chapter 3), FM radio continued to develop but as a service that was clearly ancillary to AM broadcasting. In the 1960s, however, in the United States, two FCC rulings transformed the importance of FM for rock. In 1961, the FCC authorized FM "multiplexing," a process of broadcasting two signals simultaneously on a single channel. It is this process that makes possible a stereo broadcast. Although the fifty-seven multiplex stations that existed in 1961 were broadcasting primarily middle-of-the-road and classical music, the multiplexing process itself soon became attractive to a larger audience for whom rock was art. It was the second FCC decision in 1965 that married FM and rock. At this time, the FCC ruled that FM programming in cities with a population greater than 100,000 had to differ from AM programming at least 50 percent of the time. In effect, the ruling forced station owners to divide their AM and FM properties or release their FM stations altogether. Station owners promptly decided to use FM to explore new styles of music. Progressive FM rock began more or less simultaneously on the East and West coasts around 1967, although a number of college stations had used the format even earlier. One of its commercial pioneers was "Big Daddy" Tom Donahue, who initiated a laidback, "free form" music show in the 8:00 p.m. to midnight slot on station KMPX in San Francisco. Within months, Donahue was programming the whole station. He described the format as one that "embraces the best of today's rock and roll, folk, traditional and city blues, raga, electronic music, and some jazz and classical selections."[8] By 1970, there were over 670 FM outlets in the United States and Canada, and a goodly number of them—WBCN in Boston, WABC and WNEW in New York, WBBM in Chicago, WKNR in Detroit, KSAN in San Francisco, KMET in Los Angeles, CKLG in Vancouver, CHUM in Toronto, and CHOM in

The existing trade magazines—Billboard, Cash Box, Record World—shared AM radio's inability to incorporate new developments in music. They could no more fashion a music journalism that could relate to progressive rock contextually than the counterculture could confront the downside of its own antiprofessionalism.

Montreal, among others—were playing rock.

Born of the counterculture, progressive FM rock radio exhibited a unique blend of culture and politics in its formative stages. Within a few years, the better FM stations even rivaled some AM outlets in commercial success, but as soon as they did, they fell victim to the same corporate pressures toward homogenization that affected AM radio. *Rolling Stone*'s Ben Fong-Torres, who did some moonlighting as a deejay, detailed the process in 1973:

> *The typical FM station goes on with waves of good vibes, building an audience of loyal listeners by playing album cuts unheard on AM, by talking with, instead of to, listeners, and by opening up the station to the community. As the audience builds, however, the ratings, "the numbers," climb, and the station owners suddenly have a marketable commodity. Suddenly the air is filled with increasingly uptight advertisers, administration takes over, and everything is sterilized. Suddenly there are playlists; certain records have to be banned. No more interviews—can't stop the flow of music. No politicizing—remember the Fairness Doctrine. Got to have that license in order to do your thing, you know. Suddenly there's no community out there, but a "share" of the "quarter hour audience." And in the end, FM rock stands naked. It is, after all, just another commercial radio station.*[9]

The rock press followed much the same trajectory. The existing trade magazines—*Billboard, Hit Parader, Cash Box, Record World*—shared AM radio's inability to incorporate new developments in music. They could no more fashion a music journalism that could relate to progressive rock contextually than the counterculture could confront the downside of its own antiprofessionalism. It is hardly surprising, then, that dozens of alternative magazines (for example, *Crawdaddy!* in Boston [proving ground for Jon Landau, Peter Guralnick, and Ed Ward] began appearing around 1966 to fill the void. Robert Christgau, Ellen Willis, and Richard Goldstein cut their journalistic teeth at *Cheetah* in New York. Most of the alternative rags, such as San Francisco's *Mojo-Navigator R&R News,* were completely disorganized and folded within months. Some, such as *Creem,* watering hole for Dave Marsh and Lester Bangs, published sporadically but with considerable impact. On 18 October 1967, Jann Wenner launched the magazine that would outlast them all—*Rolling Stone.* From its very beginnings, it ran counter to the antibusiness culture of rock.

Wenner, whom Robert Draper has described as a dedicated and driven journalist, an unabashed and insecure social climber, a fawning stargazer, and a ruthless businessman "who cut a multitude of ethical corners," was a Berkeley dropout and rock 'n' roll fanatic who found himself immersed in the eruptions of mid-1960s San Francisco.[10] Through the efforts of his friend and mentor, Ralph Gleason, the *San Francisco Chronicle's* music critic, Wenner landed a job as entertainment editor for the radical *Sunday Ramparts* at a time when the magazine's political leadership had not grasped, to Wenner's satisfaction, the full cultural importance of rock. At the invitation of Chet Helms, manager of the Avalon Ballroom, a psychedelic club in San Francisco, Wenner then joined a group that, by his standards, was taking an interminably long time to start a counterculture magazine called *Straight Arrow.* After attending a few meetings, Wenner stole the group's mailing list and started his own magazine. Cofounder Ralph Gleason christened the magazine *Rolling Stone,* and it was published by Wenner's own company, which he named Straight Arrow. Helms was flabbergasted.

It was Gleason who gave the magazine legitimacy in progressive rock circles. He had been a tireless advocate of the alternative rock scene at a time when few established critics ventured out onto that limb. With Gleason's name on *Rolling Stone's* masthead, musicians were willing to grant interviews to the magazine and record companies were willing to buy ads. Forget that 34,000 of the 40,000 copies of *Rolling Stone's* premiere issue were returned unsold. Within months, the magazine was carrying ads from almost every major record company. Taking both rock and journalism seriously, Wenner managed to attract the best stable of writers of any rock magazine; his first generation of writers included Michael Lydon, Jon Landau, Greil Marcus, Langdon Winner, and Jim Miller, among many others.

In the first issue of *Rolling Stone,* which pictured John Lennon in an army uniform on the cover, as the film *How I Won the War,* in which he appeared, was premiering at the San Francisco Film Festival, Wenner told his readers, "*Rolling Stone* is not just about music, but also about the things and attitudes that the music embraces."[11] This hint of a connection to politics seemed to be borne out in Ralph Gleason's piece on racism in television and Michael Lydon's exposé of the Monterey Pop Festival, which he criticized as being "done for a cost plus songs, not for a song plus costs."[12]

Rolling Stone, which soon became required reading in the music industry, was considered authoritative from the start, and Wenner never missed an opportunity to distance his publication from all others. The trade magazines, he had opined in his first editorial, were "inaccurate and irrelevant" and fanzines "an anachronism, fashioned in the mold of myth and nonsense."[13] *Cheetah,* he observed elsewhere, was "dull, poorly-conceived, and pointless."[14] While his magazine could be influential, as was proved by an article on Texas rock that plugged the then-unknown albino blues guitarist Johnny Winter and netted him a $600,000 advance from Columbia Records, Wenner could also be spiteful. He reportedly refused to grant Simon and Garfunkel favourable coverage because a former girlfriend had taken up with Paul Simon.

Wenner's editorial condemning the Yippie protest at the 1968 Democratic National Convention in Chicago for "using methods and means as corrupt as the political machine it hopes to disrupt" clearly separated him from the more radical political tendencies of his generation. To the outrage of the New Left, Wenner said, "Rock and roll is the *only* way in which the vast but formless power of youth is structured, the only way in which it can be defined or inspected."[15] For the New Left, this kind of mystification of rock was precisely what was wrong with the counterculture. Following the Chicago '68 editorial, the magazine was regularly bombarded with angry letters that denounced it as a capitalist shuck, the ultimate 1960s insult. Wenner tried to redeem himself with a fake to the left in *Rolling Stone's* 1969 issue on "The American Revolution," in which he grudgingly editorialized, "These new politics are about to become part of our daily lives, and willingly or not, we are in it," but it was too late.[16] The magazine had long since staked out its relationship to politics. As Robert Draper has said:

> *While the nation buried Martin Luther King, Jr.,* Rolling Stone *published an obituary of . . . Frankie Lymon; while America cried for Robert F. Kennedy, Jann Wenner fired bullets at the new Cream album.* Rolling Stone *responded to the rapid escalation of the Vietnam War with an article showing how soldiers were smoking good weed overseas. Nixon's election—a brutal blow to the counterculture—did not warrant a mention, as the magazine was preoccupied with John Lennon's foreskin.*[17]

By the time of the magazine's fourth anniversary in 1971, Wenner no longer cared about taunts from the left but instead embraced the term *capitalist,* trying to invest it with a positive spin. "As long as there are bills to pay, writers who want to earn a living by their craft, people who pay for their groceries, want to raise children and have their own homes," he editorialized, "*Rolling Stone* will be a capitalistic operation."[18] By this time the magazine was firmly ensconced in its new $7,000-a-month Third Street offices; had already lost some of its best writers, including Marcus and Winner, largely over political differences; and had entered a new phase of corporate expansion with the addition of millionaire computer magnate Max Palevsky to its board of directors. Politics at *Rolling Stone* now meant electoral politics, as in Hunter Thompson's "gonzo" coverage of the Nixon-McGovern race in 1972, the magazine's endorsement of Jimmy Carter in 1976, and some good investigative pieces on particular issues throughout the decade. After all, music had always been *Rolling Stone*'s primary mission, and Wenner had reasoned early on that, to realize his vision, the magazine would have to be built on a solid economic foundation, even if that meant distancing it from the political upheaval that provided its context. This was not too high a price for him to pay. He never trusted movement politics any more than he tolerated countercultural inefficiency. What was important to Jann Wenner was the surety that the music he loved was taken seriously and that there was a place for him in the scene.

Creativity and Commerce: Rock as Art

In the new music industry, rock enjoyed a privileged position. Technological advances and journalistic seriousness invested it with the status of art. The signal event for this development had been, of course, the 1967 release of the Beatles' *Sgt. Pepper* album. With 900 hours of studio time required for completion at a then unheard-of price of $100,000, *Sgt. Pepper* became the Sistine ceiling of rock and George Martin its Michelangelo. Meticulous attention had been paid to every detail of composition, balance, and technical execution. It was, in the modest opinion of guitarist Lenny Kaye, "an artistic statement in a music that was never regarded as art before."[19] Even established academics stood up and took notice. Noted musicologist Wilfred Mellers called it "the most distinctive event in pop's brief history."[20] Clearly the days when the Beatles, or any other rock group, could release six best-selling albums in one year were gone forever. Rock artists now laboured over every cut, experimenting with new sounds, adding special effects, and overdubbing to perfection. Joe Smith told a

In the new music industry, rock enjoyed a privileged position. Technological advances and journalistic seriousness invested it with the status of art.

story of how the Grateful Dead said they wanted to "record thirty minutes of air in the summertime, when it's hot and smoggy. Thirty minutes of heavy air. Then we could go to the desert and record thirty minutes of clean air. Then mix the two together, get a good sound, and record over it."[21] The Dead found themselves in trouble with (and in debt to) Warner after they ran up a $120,000 tab in various studios around the country before a single album resulted.

As the counterculture and the social movements that accompanied it deteriorated in the early 1970s, rock increasingly found refuge in its newly acquired status as art. If rock-as-counterculture had existed outside market relations, then rock-as-art hovered above them. This was, of course, a hopelessly contradictory belief, but it echoed the anticommercialism of the period and made musicians central to the creative process. Critics friendly to the music began to construct their own versions of *auteur* theory in popular music. "The criterion of art in rock," said Jon Landau, "is the capacity of the musician to create a personal, almost private, universe and to express it fully."[22] This focus tended to carry rock in the direction of European art music, drawing on classical influences, delving into opera, exploring the possibilities of orchestration, and stressing the technical aspects of musicianship. George Martin's training as a classical oboist had doubtless played more than a small role in the appearance of cellos, piccolo trumpets, and classical string quartets on Beatles' records. *Sgt. Pepper* "marked the turning point," Wilfred Mellers has said, "when the Beatles stopped being ritual dance music and became music to be listened to."[23] It was in this sense, then, that rock was said to be the mature form of rock 'n' roll. However, the adjective was laden with extra-musical baggage.

In the context of U.S. race relations, rock's artistic explorations were not simply neutral forays into a broader musical terrain; they mirrored the separation of the races that had begun in the late 1960s. "No one who can hear today," proclaimed *Rolling Stone* editor Ralph Gleason in January 1968, "can possibly find any way in which the Beatles imitate Black musicians."[24] In May of that year, Gleason extolled the virtues of the San Francisco groups for much the same reason:

> *One of the most encouraging things about the whole hippie scene and rock music in San Francisco which grew out of it is that no one is really trying to be anything other than what he is. The white sons of middle class America who are in this thing are not ashamed of being white. They are the first American musicians, aside from the country and western players, who are not trying to sound black.*[25]

These sentiments were later echoed by Eric Clapton, who built his career covering B. B. King guitar licks. "My whole attitude has changed," said Clapton. "I listen to the same sounds and records but with a different ear. I'm no longer trying to play anything but like a white man."[26] Such comments devalued the contributions that black artists made, placing them outside the definition of progressive music and, therefore, beneath the critical attention of the rock press. Progressive rockers headed off in new artistic directions, relating to black music as a touchstone of historical significance rather than a continuing source of artistic inspiration.

Progressive rockers headed off in new artistic directions, relating to black music as a touchstone of historical significance rather than a continuing source of artistic inspiration. Black music had provided the foundation; now progressive rock would construct the edifice.

Black music had provided the foundation; now progressive rock would construct the edifice. By 1971, Motown chronicler Dave Morse was able to observe, rather bitterly, "Black musicians are now implicitly regarded as precursors who, having taught the white men all they know, must gradually recede into the distance as white progressive music, the simple lessons mastered, advances irresistibly into the future."[27] Jon Landau argued that black music "provides rock with the continuity which allows developments like the rise of San Francisco to take place."[28]

San Francisco's psychedelic clubs, of course, were some of the places where rock began its advance toward art. When George Hunter formed the Charlatans, one of the progenitors of the San Francisco scene, he was studying electronic music and staging "happenings" at San Francisco State College. The Charlatans' good-time electric folk had less of an impact than the group's vintage gold-rush cowboy fashions and innovative poster art, which had been inspired by turn-of-the-century illustrator Maxfield Parrish. These images found a ready home in the city's psychedelic clubs, where designers, sculptors, visual artists, and electronics experts were as important to the "total environment" as the music itself. A more systematic impetus for combining these elements came from British art schools, which had long been a haven for bohemian students who went on to become rock stars. Said Keith Richards, who did a stint at the Sidcup Art School, "I mean, in England, if you're lucky you get into art school. It's somewhere they put you if they can't put you anywhere else."[29] As Peter Wicke has pointed out, a remarkable number of British rock musicians took this path to stardom:

> *John Lennon was registered at the Liverpool College of Art from 1957 to 1959; Pete Townshend studied at London's Ealing Art College at the same time as Ron Wood, later a member of the Rolling Stones, and Freddie Mercury of Queen; Ray Davies of the Kinks was from London's Hornsey Art College; Jeff Beck, guitarist with the Yardbirds, and Eric Clapton were both educated at London's Wimbleton College of Art; and even David Bowie and Adam Ant were art school graduates, from St. Martin's School of Art and Hornsey Art College, respectively.*[30]

In their engaging study *Art into Pop,* Simon Frith and Howard Horne have noted that British art schools promoted a nineteenth-century Romantic notion of (high) art as an autonomous, personal statement operating within (and sometimes resisting) the shifting demands of capitalist culture. The schools thus encouraged an atmosphere of experimentation and self-indulgence that enabled would-be musicians to bring "into music-making attitudes that could never have been fostered under the pressures of professional entertainment."[31]

Alongside the fine arts courses, somewhat more practical courses in industrial and fashion design and photography allowed students to investigate the aesthetic dimensions of image and style within modern mass media. For those who were interested and talented, rock offered the potential for bringing all of these elements together in a single, total experience (and held out the possibility of earning a living from it). Pete Townshend, for example, applied what he had learned from avant-garde lecturers in theatre, poetry, and film to the Who's stage act, treating it as performance art. In this spirit, the Who experimented with noise and destroyed instruments and

The Who were the first pop art band. From Pete Townshend's Union Jack jacket to the use of real radio ads and jingles on record, they pioneered the use of popular signs and symbols as an artistic statement in music.

sound systems. Pop artist Peter Blake (who designed the *Sgt. Pepper* cover) played a key role in determining the image of the Who (badges, medals, targets, the Union Jack on Townshend's jacket), which established the group as the first pop art band. When the Who released the first rock opera, *Tommy,* in 1969, it placed them in an artistic realm that would have been considered a contradiction in terms a few years earlier.

The use of national symbols (the Union Jack on Townshend's jacket, the Stars and Stripes on hippies) for graphic embellishment paralleled the appearance of Campbell Soup cans and comic book images in fine art galleries. While pop art was blurring the distinctions between high art and mass culture, Andy Warhol, mass culture's most famous practitioner, was working to neutralize the contradiction between all art and commercial necessity. He saw "commercial art as real art and real art as commercial art."[32] While his position displayed both disturbing cynicism and considerable insight, it also addressed the needs of the music industry.

> *By the end of the 1960s, LP sleeve designers were roaming across the history of modern art, film and fashion as knowingly (and for much the same reason) as advertising agencies—the sleeves, like the rock posters and group images, at first glimpse the most obvious sign of a high art presence in rock, were, in fact, designed to sell the product.*[33]

Warhol became directly involved in rock through his tutelage of the Velvet Underground, a group with a discomforting sound that would become influential in the void that yielded punk. There was a perversely interesting connection between his famous banana cover for the debut Velvet Underground album, which allowed the consumer to peel off the skin revealing the fruit beneath, and his cover design for the Rolling Stones' *Sticky Fingers* (1971), which pictured Joe Dallesandro's jean-clad midsection with a real zipper for a fly.

For a time, the move to elevate rock to art was balanced by a sense of humour. When the Beatles acknowledged the Mothers of Invention's *Freak Out* as one of the inspirations for *Sgt. Pepper,* Frank Zappa returned the favour with a complete send-up of *Sgt. Pepper'*s cover art on an album titled *We're Only in It for the Money.* The Who followed with the tongue-in-cheek *The Who Sell Out,* which simulated a commercial radio broadcast and included ads and jingles, some made up and some real. Pete Townshend's pop art strategy, Frith and Horne have said, was to use "the vitality of commerce itself, the bombardment of sales patter, to both heighten the 'realism' of the Who's music and draw attention to its spuriousness."[34] As the 1960s turned into the 1970s, however, a new generation of British art rockers brought "high seriousness" to full fruition, and the music abandoned its sense of humour. "It was the abstract chimera of 'art' surrounding the music of such groups as Yes, Jethro Tull, Genesis, Emerson, Lake & Palmer, and the Moody Blues," contends Iain Chambers, "that continued to exert a disproportional influence on the direction and sense of much pop music, distributing judgment and dividing the musical field into frequently quite rigid divisions."[35] At this point, art rock emerged as a new marketing category that distinguished these groups from other progressive rock acts. There was perhaps a greater tendency to "dignify" the music with classical references in Britain, where class distinctions are more sharply felt than in the United States. The Moody Blues kicked off this trend when the group's *Days of Future Past,* which was recorded

Certainly, art rock was vulnerable to the criticism that it pandered to middle-brow cultural sensibilities in a vain effort to gain acceptance among people who would have regarded the two words as mutually exclusive. At the same time, however, it has to be acknowledged that this music worked.

with the London Festival Orchestra, reached number three on the charts in 1968. They followed up with six gold LPs in a row. With keyboardist Jon Lord's *Concerto for Group and Orchestra* in 1970, which was recorded at the Royal Albert Hall, Deep Purple was headed in the same direction until guitarist Ritchie Blackmore intervened and changed the group's direction. At their worst, musicologist Rob Walser has said, these classical appropriations reeked of upper-class pretension. In this regard he has been particularly critical of Emerson, Lake & Palmer:

> *[N]eoclassical extravaganzas, such as their rendering of Mussorgsky's* Pictures at an Exhibition *(1972), were intended as elevations of public taste and expressions of advanced musicianship. Keith Emerson's attraction to classical resources was unabashedly elitist; he considered ordinary popular music degraded and took on the mission of raising the artistic level of rock.*[36]

Certainly, art rock was vulnerable to the criticism that it pandered to middle-brow cultural sensibilities in a vain effort to gain acceptance among people who would have regarded the the words *art* and *rock* as mutually exclusive. At the same time, however, it has to be acknowledged that this music worked. If the reaction of the critics was any indicator, it worked artistically; if the response of the fans counted, it worked commercially. Indeed, it worked beyond the wildest fantasies of the record companies. "Emerson, Lake & Palmer have no faults," said the *Cash Box* review of the group's first New York City appearance in 1971.[37] Apparently fans concurred; all the albums the group released in the 1970s were certified gold.

Emerson, Lake & Palmer was a supergroup that had drawn its members from existing rock bands: keyboardist Keith Emerson from the Nice, an earlier rock/classical fusion group, guitarist Greg Lake from King Crimson, and drummer Carl Palmer from the Crazy World of Arthur Brown. Lake and Palmer's blues orientation provided the group with a hard rock base, but it was Emerson who was the group's guiding force. As a boy he had taken classical piano lessons, which had introduced him to the percussive piano sound of Béla Bartók. Indeed, Bartók's influence coloured their self-titled debut album. As the group matured, Emerson took the concept to new heights, typically rushing around amidst a bank of keyboards (at one point a piano, a Moog synthesizer, two electric organs, and other unnamed sound-producing devices), stabbing at them with staccato 32nd-note runs. Four of the group's next five albums reached the Top Ten. In the mid-1970s, group members took time out for a number of solo projects, including Emerson's failed attempt to record a piano concerto with the London Philharmonic. In 1977, they staged a comeback with the release of two volumes of mostly solo material. *Works, Volume I* and *Works, Volume II* sold well enough, but the seventy-piece orchestra assembled for the group's comeback tour had to be laid off because of poor ticket sales. By this time, disco was making far more efficient use of the synthesizer and punk had stripped rock down to its bare essentials. Art rock extravagance seemed bloated by comparison. Emerson, Lake & Palmer disbanded in 1979, to regroup only at the end of the next decade.

Yes, another art rock group, had actually begun before Emerson, Lake & Palmer. The group, which had several members who were well versed in the classics, had first started recording for Atlantic in 1968, but had then undergone a number of personnel changes. By the time their third LP, *The Yes Album,* was released in 1971, they had edged into the U.S. Top Forty, but the group didn't hit its stride until keyboardist Tony Kaye was replaced by Rick Wakeman, a classically trained pianist from the Royal Academy. The next album, *Fragile* (1972), hit the Top

Ten and yielded one of the group's few successful singles of the decade, "Roundabout." Critical response to the album was one of unbridled enthusiasm, and there was no denying the commercial appeal of the music. From *Fragile* on, every Yes album reached the Top Twenty. Wakeman ventured out as a solo artist in the mid-1970s and confirmed the pretentiousness of art rock with such weighty titles as *The Six Wives of Henry the VIII, Journey to the Center of the Earth* (recorded with the London Symphony Orchestra), and *The Myths and Legends of King Arthur and the Knights of the Round Table* (recorded with the English Chamber Choir).

Perhaps because the life of the group was divided into two distinct phases with different cultural referents, Pink Floyd was more eclectic in its influences than either Emerson, Lake & Palmer or Yes. From 1965 to 1968, the group was dominated by writer/guitarist Syd Barrett, a Camberwell Art School student with an unusual flair for combining kinky imagery ("Arnold Layne," the group's debut single about a transvestite, was banned by the BBC) with all the psychedelic trappings of San Francisco. Indeed, Pink Floyd was the first British group to perform with an accompanying light show. By 1968, however, Barrett had succumbed to the psychic perils of LSD experimentation and had been replaced by David Gilmour. *A Saucerful of Secrets,* released that year, was the band's first real introduction to the U.S. audience and marked the ascendancy of bassist Roger Waters as the spiritual centre of the group. Under Waters' leadership, the group eschewed Barrett's three-minute forays into psychedelia in favour of long-winded, spacy sonic voyages that were often based on a single chord. This tendency earned

Ultimately, the canon of art rock that emerged, like the canon of the classical music from which much of it drew inspiration, was a social construct. Inclusion in the art rock category was linked to art school training, to the appropriation of classical and other esoteric resources, even to being British.

Pink Floyd equal measures of critical praise as the quintessence of art in rock and out-of-hand dismissal as the purveyors of psychedelic muzak. The group reached its zenith in 1973 with the release of *Dark Side of the Moon,* one of the darkest and best-selling rock albums ever. Some 566 weeks and 10 million copies after its release, the album still registered on the pop charts. It was during this period that the group introduced its 360° sound system. The system drew on Waters' background as an architecture student at Regent Street Polytechnic and the expertise of the Light/Sound Workshop from Hornsey Art College. Shortly after its introduction, the group was playing "concert halls to audiences as hushed as if they were at a classical event."[38] The group continued in this vein throughout the punk era, crowning the decade with *The Wall* (1979), a number one album that yielded their only number one single, the anthemic critique of formal education, "Another Brick in the Wall."

Ultimately, the canon of art rock that emerged, like the canon of the classical music from which much of art rock drew inspiration, was a social construct. Inclusion in the art rock category was linked to art school training, to the appropriation of classical and other esoteric resources, even to being British. Using these criteria, Procol Harum, with its nod toward Bach on "A Whiter Shade of Pale" in 1967, was an easy entry. The Bach influence was also enough to place Deep Purple in the art rock category for a while, even though the group was heading toward the border of the emerging and much less prestigious category of heavy metal. Because hip critics could not find a constructive way of positioning themselves in relation to Led Zeppelin's ultra-macho presentation this group was excluded from the art rock category despite their broad range of influences. Concept LPs and theatrical stage shows that were more intelligent than most allowed Genesis to be categorized as art rock. Ian Anderson's spirited flute playing and religious musings propelled Jethro Tull into the category. The release of the Who's second rock opera, *Quadrophenia,* was enough to continue the group's association with art. On the other hand, few American groups seemed to meet the criteria.

Quebec had long been a hotbed of support for progressive rock bands such as Emerson, Lake & Palmer and Yes. In fact, the Strawbs, Supertramp, and to a lesser degree, Genesis, all received substantial radio play and record sales in Quebec well in advance of achieving similar success in the rest of North America. Therefore, it is not surprising that in the early 1970s a handful of bands with similar progressive tendencies began to emerge within the province. Foremost among these was Harmonium. Formed in 1973 by guitarist, flautist, and composer Serge Fiori, Harmonium recorded their first LP in 1974. By 1976, they had expanded to a seven-piece ensemble and recorded *L'Heptade*, which featured seven original songs connected by orchestral segments composed by the fifty-six-year-old Saskatoon composer and conductor Neil Chotem and recorded by members of the Montreal Symphony Orchestra. The album was extremely successful, and Harmonium toured extensively in parts of English-speaking Canada as well as Europe. Other groups that were popular in Quebec at the time but did not necessarily play progressive rock were Beau Dommage, Offenbach, Mashmakan, and Michel Pagliaro. All four of these owed a large debt to Robert Charlebois, who, with *L'Osstidcho* in 1968, fused the French chanson tradition with 1960s rock.

Groups such as Blood, Sweat and Tears, Chicago, and Lighthouse, while not classified as art rock or prog rock per se, attempted to fuse elements of jazz and to a lesser degree classical music

Extremely ambitious, Lighthouse attempted to create a fusion of rock, jazz, and classical music.

"Roundabout"

Artist: Yes

Music / Lyrics by Jon Anderson
and Steve Howe

Label: Atlantic (1971),
from the LP *Fragile*

"Art" or "progressive" rock was identified with large musical structures, layers of overdubbed sound, experimentation with instrumentation and electronic effects, and compositional techniques borrowed from classical music. These musical elements were often paired with poetic, philosophical, weighty, or somewhat surreal lyrics. The English group Yes, with its team of virtuoso players and production wizard Eddie Offord, was a classic English "prog" rock band, and "Roundabout" is a classic example of the style.

Musical Style Notes

One of the hallmarks of Yes's style lay in their collaborative compositional method. The members all contributed to compositions and arrangements, which partly accounts for the "sectional" sound of a lot of their music. Yes guitarist Steve Howe once noted that another one of the "secret ingredients of Yes" was the "intensity of the color," referring to the use of tone and timbre (the quality of the sound) to create vivid sonic effects. This is illustrated beautifully in "Roundabout," as the different sections of the piece are marked by changes in tone and timbre as well as rhythm.

Another important aspect of Yes's style is the focus on multiple layers of beautifully executed harmony vocals, as precise in live performance as they were on record. The lyrics to "Roundabout" were written during a drive from Aberdeen to Glasgow in Scotland ("Roundabout" is the British name for a traffic circle), and much of the imagery is literally taken from the countryside ("mountains come out of the sky"; "in and around the lake," which happened to be Loch Ness).

Yes lineup on the *Fragile* LP was Jon Anderson, vocals; Steve Howe, guitar and vocals; Chris Squire, bass and vocals; Rick Wakeman, keyboards; and Bill Bruford, drums.

Musical "Road Map"

TIMINGS	COMMENTS	LYRICS	
0:00–0:07	Introduction: sound effect created by reversing a recording of a grand piano		
0:07–	Free-rhythm introduction on guitar, beginning with "harmonics," created by lightly touching the sixth, third, second, and first strings of the acoustic guitar at the twelfth fret		
0:40	Descending acoustic guitar line, providing a transition into the first verse		
0:44 0:58	Verse 1—melody "A"; instruments begin. Vocal enters.	*I'll be the roundabout . . .*	

TIMINGS	COMMENTS	LYRICS
1:18–1:44 1:25	Verse 2—melody "A" Vocal enters (lyrics begin at 1:25). Note how additional vocals are layered in.	*The music dance and sing . . .*
1:44–2:15	Transitional or "bridge" verse—melody "B"	*In and around the lake . . .*
2:15–3:21 2:34	Verse 3—melody "A" Instrumental beginning is extended in length. Vocal enters.	*I will remember you . . .*
3:21–4:57 3:40 4:36	Instrumental section, featuring a repeating bass and guitar riff over a complex, "polyrhythmic" drum part (several different rhythms being played simultaneously) Vocals in multiple harmonies are layered over the bass/guitar/drum riff. Melody "A" returns, also sung over the bass/guitar/drum riff.	 *Along the drifting cloud* *The eagle searching down on the land . . .* *I'll be the roundabout . . .*
4:57– 5:33	Return of acoustic guitar introduction, played over a repeated, very fast synthesizer riff; sonic texture is much more sparse. Keyboard riff continues, while vocal enters with truncated version bridge "B" melody—last vocal line cues following instrumental section.	 *In and around the lake . . .* *. . . twenty-four before my love* *and I'll be there . . .*
5:50–6:16	Instrumental section: blues-style organ solo, while bass/guitar/drums play the instrumental lines from the transitional "bridge"	
6:16–7:05	Another instrumental section; solos traded between organ and guitar Instruments "cue" the return to the verse with a passage that ascends up the scale.	
7:05–7:25	Verse 1—melody "A" returns.	*I'll be the roundabout . . .*
7:25–7:53	Transitional or "bridge" verse—melody "B"	*In and around the lake . . .*
7:53–8:21	Multiple harmony vocals enter over an acoustic rhythm guitar part, singing "da-da-da" syllables. The harmonies are layered in two groups. The first sings a simple, repetitive melody; the second enters with a short countermelody (the first three notes of "Three Blind Mice").	
8:21–8:29	Return of the descending acoustic guitar line from the end of the song's introduction, ending on a single chord	

with late sixties rock. All three bands featured horn sections staffed by college-trained jazz players, and all three groups consequently tended to include in some of their original material extended and altered chords, jazz-inflected arrangements, and a swing or shuffle feel in terms of their approach to time. While Chicago had the most hit records, Blood, Sweat and Tears, fronted by Toronto's David Clayton-Thomas, was the first jazz-rock group to hit the charts in late winter 1969 with "You've Made Me So Very Happy," followed a few months later by a Clayton-Thomas original called "Spinning Wheel." Clayton-Thomas had been experimenting with the idea of jazz rock in Toronto as early as 1966 with the Bossmen, best-known for their AM hit, "Brainwashed."

Lighthouse took a slightly different approach. In addition to grafting jazz horns onto a rock rhythm section, the group also had a small amplified string section. The resulting sound veered from pop to jazz to ersatz classical. Formed in 1969 by Skip Prokop, former drummer of the Paupers, and keyboard and vibes player Paul Hoffert, the group signed with RCA Records and soon received enough FM airplay to turn them into rising stars in Canada. In 1970, they collaborated with the Royal Winnipeg Ballet on *A Ballet High* and that summer made a legendary appearance at the Isle of Wight Festival in England alongside groups such as Jimi Hendrix, the Doors, and the Who. By 1971, with Bob McBride singing lead, Lighthouse, now signed to GRT, managed to fuse their progressive tendencies with a pop sensibility, producing radio-friendly AM hits such as "Hats Off (To the Stranger)," "One Fine Morning," "Sunny Days," and "Pretty Lady." In September 1973, at Lighthouse's annual free concert at Nathan Phillips Square in Toronto, 50,000 fans watched as Mayor David Crombie presented the group with a platinum record for *Lighthouse Live!* Lighthouse was the first Canadian group to sell over 100,000 copies of an album in Canada. Saxophone player Howard Shore went on to become the original music director for Saturday Night Live and to write the scores for such Hollywood blockbusters as *Lord of the Rings*.

There was, in fact, a jazz rock, or fusion, category that emerged in the early 1970s after Miles Davis' *Bitches Brew* (1970) reached number thirty-five on the pop charts. At the time, a gold jazz album was virtually unthinkable. A full-page ad in *Rolling Stone* boasted: "Critics agree Miles Davis has found a new audience. Or is it that Rock has just found Miles Davis?"[39] Jazz rock differed from art rock in that entrants into the category were jazz musicians who were enjoying a brief flirtation with the mainstream audience rather than rock musicians who were drawn to jazz influences. There was virtually no overlap between the two categories. John McLaughlin, who played guitar on *Bitches Brew*, reached the mainstream audience with his Mahavishnu Orchestra on *Inner Mounting Flame* (1971) and *Birds of Fire* (1973). He also teamed up with fellow Sri Chimnoy devotee Carlos Santana for *Love Devotion Surrender* in 1973. Another Davis alumnus, Herbie Hancock, scored with the platinum *Headhunters* in 1974 and finished the decade with three more Top Forty albums. While jazz artists like George Benson and Chuck Mangione achieved mainstream success in the late 1970s, their sound is better described as pop jazz than jazz rock. Jazz rock was almost invariably a repository for black or racially integrated groups, while art rock remained the exclusive province of white men.

Art rock was also separate from other forms of black music in significant ways. At a time when most black music was still built around the hit single, art rock focused on extended compositions and LP suites. Typically, art rockers sold far more albums than singles. (Among the most successful groups, Emerson, Lake & Palmer registered eight Top Forty albums between 1971 and 1978; Yes, eleven between 1972 and 1983; Jethro Tull, sixteen between 1969 and 1982; Pink Floyd, seven between 1973 and 1983; and the Moody Blues, thirteen between 1968 and 1986.) Art rock groups routinely tallied Top Ten album entries and gold record certifications, but throughout the 1970s only one of them ever had a Top Ten single—the Moody Blues' "Nights in White Satin" hit number two in 1972. Jethro Tull never even hit the Top Forty with a single, and Pink Floyd and Yes made it to the Top Ten singles charts once, but not until the 1980s. By the late 1960s, however, LPs had surpassed singles as a source of revenue in the music industry. By the early 1970s it was estimated that about 80 percent of the sales dollars (and therefore the lion's share of promotional budgets) was in albums. Thus, black music was marginalized financially.

There was also an aesthetic/social dimension to this financial separation. Art rock was often a music of ponderous introspection; it underscored the connection between rock and hallucinogenic drugs. At its most ethereal, it was called "head" music. Clearly, this was a music of the mind, not a music of the body. Nourishment for the body—the "ritual dance music" that drew on increasingly distant African resources—was devalued accordingly. Aside from the racist implications of homologies that suggest the superiority of European/art/mind over African/entertainment/body, the marginalization of black music carried with it the virtual disappearance of stylized partner dancing, which remained on the periphery until it resurfaced with a vengeance during the disco craze. In the interim, it was replaced by the broadly interpretative and highly individualized free-form swirling that sometimes accompanied "journeys to the centre of the mind."

Government Intervention and the Airwaves

Throughout the 1960s, it was virtually impossible for a Canadian musician to make a decent living playing music without moving to the United States. Part of the problem was that the sheer size of the country coupled with its relatively small population made it very difficult to tour nationally and make a profit. Consequently, most bands gigged on a regional basis in Ontario, Quebec, the Maritimes, the Prairies, or British Columbia. Perhaps even more problematic was the "colonial mentality" that existed with radio programmers in Canada. The majority of Canadian radio stations either hired U.S. programming consultants or watched closely what records American stations were playing. Either way, they tended to see Canadian recordings and Canadian artists as inherently inferior to their U.S. and British counterparts. Together, these problems militated against the development of a music industry infrastructure consisting of highly skilled recording engineers, producers, recording studios, record companies, management, booking agents, and a music press. Lacking such an infrastructure in their homeland, in the 1960s Canadian artists such as Neil Young, Joni Mitchell, Steppenwolf, and the Band moved to the United States. While Leonard Cohen and Gordon Lightfoot remained in Canada, both artists were signed to American record companies, which meant that every time one of their albums sold in Canada, profits flowed to the United States rather than remaining in their own country. The one major exception to this was the Guess Who, who remained in Canada and were signed to Jack Richardson's Nimbus Nine label.

This situation forced talented Canadians to move south of the border and had significant financial consequences for the country. Moreover, it meant that Canadians were largely consuming popular culture that in no way, shape, or form reflected anything about their country, their culture, or their identity. This had long been a concern of the Canadian government, leading as early as 1932 to the establishment of the Canadian Radio Broadcasting Company (CRBC). At the time, Prime Minister R. B. Bennett stated, "This country must be assured of complete Canadian control of broadcasting from Canadian sources, free from foreign interference or influence."[40] In 1957, the government established the Royal Commission on Broadcasting (a.k.a. the Fowler Commission). This body concluded that broadcasting policy should be used to develop a sense of Canadian identity. A year later, an administrative body known as the Broadcast Board of Governors (BBG) was formed to oversee the broadcasting industry and create regulations to promote Canadian talent. The BBG concluded that implementing such regulations was impractical.

In 1968, the Canadian Radio and Television Commission (CRTC), headed by Pierre Juneau, replaced the BBG. Four years earlier, Stan Klees and Walt Grealis had started the trade journal *RPM Weekly* in Toronto. *RPM* was designed to service the needs of the Canadian recording and broadcast industries, such as they existed. Both Klees and Grealis were staunch supporters of Canadian popular music and virtually from the beginning of their magazine had been lobbying Canadian radio stations to play more Canadian content. When the CRTC was established, Klees embarked on a ten-part series entitled "An In-Depth Study of Legislated Radio," in which he pointed out:

> *Too many stations have been vocal in their disregard for any attempt to encourage Canadian content in radio . . . We can offer a smidget [sic] of art to the world, a little bit of literature, very little theatre, very little dance, and next to no music. We have failed as a cultural power in the world and we have failed to provide ourselves with a cultural background distinct to our people.*[41]

In the course of researching his series, Klees surveyed nine top Canadian radio stations, noting that only 6.5 percent of the programming on these stations featured Canadian artists. When Klees looked beyond the artists to the composers and producers of the recordings being played on these stations, he concluded that only one-half of one percent of their programming was wholly Canadian. These figures were shocking. Grealis sent copies of the series to every one of the Commission's members, feeling that they were not necessarily knowledgeable enough about the Canadian recording and broadcasting industries.

Worried that the CRTC would legislate the amount of Canadian content to be broadcast, thirteen Canadian stations banded together to form the "Maple Leaf System." In 1971, Stan Klees designed the MAPL logo and method of categorization (music, artists, production, lyrics), so that recordings could be classified as to the degree of Canadian participation involved in their creation. The Maple Leaf System involved conference calls once a week during which the thirteen stations would debate the merits of new Canadian releases, the idea being to add a handful of Canadian releases to each station's playlist at the end of the call. In reality, this effort didn't lead to much more Canadian content being played on the respective stations, since the programmers regularly concluded that the Canadian recordings they were listening to simply weren't good enough.

By 1971, Prime Minister Pierre Trudeau made multiculturalism the official policy of Canada. In January 1971, the CRTC mandated that Canadian pop stations must make

Canadian recordings 30 percent of their station playlists (classical and jazz stations had to play 10 percent Canadian content, ethnic stations 7 percent). This figure was increased to 35 percent in 1991, and the regulations were tightened so that stations could not make up most of their Canadian content in off-peak hours such as midnight to 6:00 a.m.

To be considered Canadian content, a record typically had to fulfill at least two of the following conditions based on the MAPL system: (1) M (music)—the music had to be composed entirely by a Canadian; (2) A (artist)—either the music or the lyrics had to be performed principally by a Canadian; (3) P (production)—the performance had to be recorded wholly in Canada or be a live broadcast from a Canadian location; and (4) L (lyrics)—the lyrics had to be written entirely by a Canadian. There were four "special cases" where a recording could qualify as Canadian without meeting two of the above cited criteria: (1) if the performance was recorded before January 1972 and met one of the four criteria cited above; (2) if the recording was an instrumental performance of a musical composition written or composed by a Canadian; (3) if the recording was a musical composition that a Canadian composed for instruments only; or (4) if the selection was recorded after 1 September 1991 and, in addition to meeting the criterion for either artist or production, a Canadian who collaborated with a non-Canadian received at least half of the credit for both the music and lyrics.

While Canadian broadcasters argued vehemently that such regulations were unconstitutional and tantamount to censorship, and that they were going to be forced to play inferior recordings, the regulations ultimately achieved their goals. The first single released under the new CanCon regulations was Hamilton-based boogie band Crowbar's "Oh What a Feeling." Issued on a new Canadian independent label, Daffodil Records, "Oh What a Feeling" reached *RPM*'s Top Ten and gave Crowbar the biggest hit of their career. Within a few years, established Canadian artists such as Montreal's April Wine,[42] Vancouver's Chilliwack, and Toronto's A Foot in Cold Water received significantly increased radio play due to the CanCon regulations, resulting in several charting records. Over the next few years, newer artists such as Calgary's The Stampeders and Toronto's Max Webster were able to enjoy multi-year careers as stars in their native land without ever making a dent in the United States.

Over the course of the next two decades, the possibility of radio play and the consequent possibility of Canadian artists being able to tour nationally served as a catalyst for the creation of the previously non-existent music industry infrastructure leading to the establishment of state-of-the-art recording studios, engineers and producers, independent record labels, professional management and booking agents, and a music press. Of course, the CanCon regulations also motivated major record companies such as Columbia, Capitol, and Warners to create Canadian A&R positions and cultivate and sign Canadian artists.

It is safe to say that without the CanCon regulations, groups such as Blue Rodeo and the Tragically Hip would not have been able to become superstars in Canada while selling at only moderate levels in the United States. These days, many superstar Canadian artists, such as Celine Dion and Rush, are signed to Canadian recording companies (although Dion is signed to Sony, her contract is with Sony Canada rather than Sony in the United States). This means that every time one of these artists sells a CD in the United States or any other foreign country, substantial profits come back to Canada, where, of course, they trickle down via the salaries of record company employees into the Canadian economy at large.

Today in Canada, at least 35 percent of popular music selections broadcast by commercial AM and FM radio stations must be Canadian, while 10 percent of what the CRTC calls "traditional and special interest music selections" (e.g., classical, jazz, world music, and so on) broadcast by commercial radio stations must be Canadian. In Quebec, 65 percent of the selections broadcast on French-language AM and FM radio stations must be in the French language. Further, 55 percent of the popular music vocal selections broadcast between 6:00 a.m. and 6:00 p.m. on French-language stations must be in French. To combat the early habit some broadcasters had of fading out Canadian recordings partway through, the CRTC regulations state, "Popular Canadian selections and French-language selections must be played in their entirety for the purpose of meeting Canadian content and French-language vocal music requirements."[43]

In 1982, the Canadian government established the Foundation to Assist Canadian Talent on Record (FACTOR). FACTOR's mandate was to use their funds to "assist Canadian recording artists and songwriters in having their material produced, their videos created and support for domestic and international touring and showcasing opportunities as well as providing support for Canadian record labels, distributors, recording studios, video production companies, producers, engineers, directors—all those facets of the infrastructure which must be in place in order for artists and Canadian labels to progress into the international arena."[44] FACTOR grants have supported numerous Canadian artists, including Alanis Morissette, Great Big Sea, Nickelback, Sara McLachlan, the Tragically Hip, and Blue Rodeo.

In addition to lobbying for CanCon, *RPM Magazine* sought to promote a Canadian star system by establishing national music awards in 1964. Initially voted on by *RPM* readers and called the "RPM Gold Leaf Awards," the awards were in 1971 renamed the Junos, recognizing the efforts of the head of the CRTC, Pierre Juneau, in creating the CanCon regulations. In 1973, the Canadian Academy of Recording Arts and Sciences (CARAS) took over the administration of the Junos. Two years later, *RPM* established the Big Country Awards, which eventually became the Canadian Country Music Association (CCMA) Awards. Six years later, the Félix Awards were established to separately recognize achievements by largely French-speaking Quebec artists. Beginning in 1989, the East Coast Music Awards (originally known as the Maritime Music Awards) began to similarly recognize achievements by artists in Nova Scotia, New Brunswick, Prince Edward Island, and Newfoundland. In 1978, CARAS began inducting musicians into the Canadian Music Hall of Fame. The first two inductees were Guy Lombardo and Oscar Peterson. Recent inductees have included producer Bob Rock, Bryan Adams, and the Tragically Hip.

Sweeter Soul Music

African American artists seldom shrank from their role as entertainers since that role allowed their creativity to shine. In the black community, commercial success was regarded less as a compromise than as a necessity. As differences in material reality and political strategy occasioned a separation of black and white communities in the late 1960s, however, the music press often decried the commercialism of black popular music while praising the artistry of rock, even r&b-based rock. "The soul and R & B strains of Janis Joplin, Rod Stewart, Joe Cocker, and Van

Morrison were praised," Iain Chambers has said, "while Ray Charles and Aretha Franklin, not to mention the unredeemable Tamla Motown stable (with the precise exception of the 'progressive' Stevie Wonder), were accused of decaying in the swamps of a commercial jungle."[45] If the music press tended to deprecate black music, radio tended to ignore it entirely. Jerry Wexler, Atlantic's primary rhythm and blues producer, has said that by 1971, radio stations did not want to "burden" their listeners "with the sound of breaking glass in Watts or the sirens coming from Detroit, which is what r&b music meant at the time . . . so they took most of it off the radio."[46] Hardly above criticism itself, Atlantic responded to this situation by changing direction to focus primarily on its British rock acts, just as its former soul partner, Stax, was about to begin its long and tortuous descent into bankruptcy, a saga that paralleled the trajectory of the civil rights movement itself.

As differences in material reality and political strategy occasioned a separation of black and white communities in the late 1960s, the music press often decried the commercialism of black popular music while praising the artistry of rock, even r&b-based rock.

Wexler's comment suggests there was a connection between the decline of r&b on the radio and the political shift that marked the end of the tumultuousness associated with the 1960s. Certainly by the early 1970s, the Civil Rights movement appeared to have run its course, and civil rights themes declined in popular music. While War scored with "The World Is a Ghetto" in 1972, by 1973, only the Spinners' "Ghetto Child" and Stevie Wonder's "Living for the City" were noticeable in the pop singles market. There was a corresponding decline in the popularity of southern soul, the militant-sounding strain of r&b from the deep South. Arthur Conley, Percy Sledge, and Sam and Dave disappeared from the Top Forty after 1968, and by then Otis Redding had died. Wilson Pickett lasted until 1972 and then faded from pop view. That same year, Ike and Tina Turner had their last Top Ten hit of the decade. Soul music had not disappeared completely; instead, outside social forces had altered its character.

As radicalism in the black community was repressed, either by the co-optation of key leaders or by the more sinister effectiveness of the FBI's COINTELPRO (Counter-Intelligence Program) operation, there was a fleeting attempt to use the music industry as a proving ground for black capitalism, which was then pushed as an alternative to urban violence. The music industry was quite aware of discrimination within its own ranks. At the 1969 convention of the National Association of Television and Radio Announcers (NATRA), Stan Gortikov, then president of Capitol, had accused the industry of being "too damn white."[47] Earlier that year, at a conference held by the Recording Industry Association of America (RIAA), New York Senator Jacob Javits had expressed the "hope that the industry . . . will move forward . . . by striking a resounding note for black capitalism."[48]

The flurry of rhetoric and action that ensued over the next few years produced some interesting, if paradoxical, results. Having declined on the singles charts from 34 percent in 1968 to 24 percent in 1971, artists of colour then accounted for an all-time high of 44 percent of the best-selling singles in 1972. From a dramatic decrease on the album charts to just 12 percent in 1971, they rebounded to 24 percent one year later. During this time, there had been a short-lived and highly controversial breakthrough of sorts for African Americans in Hollywood in the form of black-oriented movies like *Shaft*, *Superfly*, and *Troubleman* (the so-called blaxploitation films). The soundtracks for these movies were scored by Isaac Hayes, Curtis Mayfield, and Marvin Gaye, respectively. Still, soundtrack albums alone do not account for the substantial presence of African Americans on the pop charts in 1972. There are two other developments that come closer to explaining the dramatic increases: the emergence of a number of African American artists as album-oriented acts and the popularization of softer soul sounds that would provide one of the building blocks for disco.

If there was a dominant black sound that reflected the seemingly quieter mood of the early 1970s, it was Philadelphia soft soul, which was pioneered by the writer-producer team of Kenny Gamble and Leon Huff and producer-arranger Thom Bell, who joined forces with Sigma Sound Studios. The three men collaborated in the tripartite administration of Mighty Three Music, the publishing company they formed for their music. Having come of age in Philadelphia in the early 1960s, Gamble, Huff, and Bell were no strangers to a predominantly white music scene. Gamble had sessioned for Leiber and Stoller in New York and had helped to produce Danny and the Juniors' "At the Hop." When he returned to Philadelphia, he formed the Romeos with Thom Bell on keyboards. After Bell was replaced by Huff, Gamble teamed up with Huff to do freelance production projects for Atlantic and other labels. The two scored their first Top Ten hit with the blue-eyed Soul Survivors' "Expressway to Your Heart" on Crimson. Bell worked at Cameo and, when the label folded in 1968, moved to Philly Groove with the Delfonics. There he produced the group's blockbuster hit, "La La Means I Love You." Gamble and Huff quickly followed suit with a series of novelty songs for the Intruders, "Cowboys to Girls" and "(Love Is Like a) Baseball Game." After these, they resuscitated the

In the long run Gamble and Huff infused the market with romantic ballads and stylish dance music more than they rejuvenated the civil rights movement with a message of black liberation.

flagging career of Jerry Butler with a new persona—The Iceman— and smoothed out the rough edges of soul on his "Only the Strong Survive," "Moody Woman," and "What's the Use of Breaking Up." In doing so, they perfected the production style that would be described in *Rolling Stone* as "not as bluesy as the Memphis/Muscle Shoals stuff, not as pop as Detroit."[49]

In a five-year period, Gamble and Huff produced 30 million-selling singles, with twenty-two records on the charts in 1968 alone. In 1970, the duo grossed over $1 million. Even so, the two did not hit their stride until 1971. In that year, Gamble and Huff formed Philadelphia International Records (PIR) and made a distribution deal with CBS Records. The deal was important to the team financially because it offered economic self-sufficiency, but it was also important to Gamble personally. Gamble was a nationalist with inclinations toward Islam. He saw PIR as a platform for pushing a message; thus, in the words of Nelson George, "Gamble and Huff contemplated slavery (the O'Jays' mini-epic "Ship A'Hoy"), ecology ("The Air I Breathe"), spiritual enlightenment ("Wake Up Everybody"), corruption ("Bad Luck"), and the male-dominated nuclear family ("Family Reunion")."[50] In the context of the increasingly conservative Nixon–Ford era, however, certain aspects of nationalism (economic self-sufficiency, for example) resonated as well with Nixon's call for black capitalism as with the development of a strong opposition movement. In the long run, Gamble and Huff infused the market with romantic ballads and stylish dance music more than they rejuvenated the Civil Rights movement with a message of black liberation.

Gamble and Huff's two biggest groups—Harold Melvin and the Blue Notes ("If You Don't Know Me By Now,") and the O'Jays ("Back Stabbers," "Love Train," "I Love Music,"

"You Make Me Feel Brand New"

Artist: Stylistics

Music / Lyrics by Thom Bell and Linda Creed

Label: Avco (1973), from the LP *Rockin' Roll, Baby*

"You Make Me Feel Brand New," with its lush vocal harmonies, string arrangements, smooth production, and relaxed rhythmic feel is a perfect example of Philadelphia soft soul. It was a huge hit for the Stylistics, reaching number two on the pop charts in 1974. An important part of the Stylistics' sound was the work of producer Thom Bell, who had also enjoyed great career success producing the Delfonics. The song was written by Linda Creed, a well-known songwriter who worked extensively with Bell and wrote hits for a number of pop and soul artists before her untimely death from breast cancer in 1986.

While an important development in the history of African American soul music, Philly soft soul was a style that crossed over into a number of markets. A song like "You Make Me Feel Brand New," a hit on the pop and soul charts, was as likely to be heard on Adult Contemporary radio or found in the Easy Listening section of a record store. The widespread popularity of this particular single can also be illustrated by its frequent use in the early 1970s as a wedding song by couples of all creeds and colors.

Musical Style Notes

The beautifully crafted musical and lyrical structure of "You Make Me Feel Brand New" was a variation on popular songs' typical verse-chorus pattern, and it became a model for subsequent ballads. The verse itself is divided into two sections marked on the Road Map below as "A" and "B," each of which has a different melody and features a different vocalist (Airrion Love on the "A" section and the Stylistics' lead singer, Russell Thompkins Jr., on the "B" section and chorus; the other members of the group are James Dunn, Herbie Murrell, and James Smith). The instrumental texture is dominated by keyboards (electric and acoustic piano and synthesizers), with the typical Philly soft soul string orchestra layered in at various points.

Musical "Road Map"

TIMINGS	COMMENTS	LYRICS
0:00–0:13	Introduction: synthesizers and keyboards, with "sitar-like" synth sound	
0:13–0:26	At the "whoosh" of the cymbal, tremolo strings enter.	
0:26–0:37	Entrance of full string orchestra	
0:37–1:29	Verse 1, section "A," with vocal by Airrion Love Instrumental texture reduced to just keyboards, bass, synth, basic percussion	*My love . . .* *I'll never find the words, my love . . .* *. . . taught me how to live again . . .*
1:29–1:55	Verse 1, section "B" Lead vocal switches to Russell Thompkins Jr.	*Only you . . .* *Cared when I needed a friend . . .*
1:55–2:34	Chorus (multiple voices in wide harmony; Thompkins' vocal most prominent) Synth orchestra enters right at the "God Bless You."	*God Bless You . . .* *You make me feel brand new . . .*
2:34–2:44	Transitional instrumental passage Note "glockenspiel" sound at transition.	
2:44–3:54	Verse 2, section "A" Airrion Love vocal Note that this verse is instrumentally much thicker than verse 1—strings, synth, additional keyboards.	*My love . . .* *Whenever I was insecure . . .*
3:54–4:04	Verse 2, section "B" Russell Thompkins' vocal	*Without you,* *Life has no meaning or rhyme . . .*
4:04–4:37	Chorus (multiple voices in wide harmony; Thompkins' vocal most prominent) Synth orchestra continues through chorus.	*God Bless You . . .* *You make me feel brand new . . .*
4:37–4:47	Track fades.	

"Use Ta Be My Girl")—were produced throughout the 1970s with what critic Jim Miller called an "urbane glossiness."[51] During the same time, Thom Bell drew on the classical training he had received as a youngster to provide lush orchestral arrangements over a polite rhythmic pulse for the Stylistics ("Betcha by Golly, Wow," "Break Up to Make Up," "You Make Me Feel Brand New") on the Avco label, and the Spinners ("I'll Be Around," "Could It Be I'm Falling in Love," "The Rubberband Man," "Working My Way Back to You/Forgive Me, Girl") on Atlantic. By the mid-1970s, MFSB (Mother Father Sister Brother), the massive integrated house band at Sigma Studios, and its backup vocal trio, The Three Degrees, had become hitmakers in their own right. In 1974, their recordings of "TSOP (The Sound of Philadelphia)" and "When Will I See You Again," were numbers one and two, respectively, on the charts. Together, these groups set the standard in black popular music for the first half of the decade and anticipated one strand of the disco craze that was about to erupt.

If Philadelphia soul had supplanted its rougher southern variant, it was also clear that the heyday of vintage Motown had ended. The Supremes were performing without Diana Ross, and the Miracles without Smokey Robinson. David Ruffin and Eddie Kendricks had left the Temptations (in 1968 and 1971, respectively) because of disputes with the record company. The Marvelettes and Martha and the Vandellas were already groups of the past. After a $22 million lawsuit, Holland-Dozier-Holland, Motown's top producer team, left the label to form their own Invictus imprint. The Four Tops followed them to the new label in 1971. Two years later, Gladys Knight and the Pips moved to Buddah, where white singer/songwriter Jim Weatherly supplied them with some of their biggest hits, including their only number one single, "Midnight Train to Georgia."

Still, while Motown may have been down, it was not out, thanks to the Jackson 5. Their first four releases on the label—"I Want You Back," "ABC," "The Love You Save," and "I'll Be There"—all rose to number one on the pop charts in 1970. The next two—"Mamma's Pearl" and "Never Can Say Goodbye"—went to number two in 1971. This kind of success with debut releases was almost unheard of. From Berry Gordy's perspective, the success of the Jackson 5 proved that his upbeat pop orientation still worked. To some critics, however, such releases appeared to be a throwback to Motown formula production. "One has the feeling, whether it's true or not," said Jon Landau, "that Berry Gordy passes personal judgment on every single that comes out on his label."[52] For many of the label's veterans, however, Gordy's centralized control, once necessary to the survival of the organization, was artistic constraint. Gordy would have to be dragged, kicking and screaming, toward a new point of view. It was Stevie Wonder and Marvin Gaye, two important exceptions to the initial talent drain at Motown, who accomplished this.

When he turned twenty-one in 1972, Stevie Wonder demanded the royalty payments that had been held in trust for him by Gordy since he was a child. Wonder spent about $250,000 of this money on the production of *Music of My Mind* (1972), which reintroduced him to the white audience as a progressive act. At about the same time, Wonder gained control of his own publishing; he was the first Motown artist to do so. Subsequent progressive albums—*Talking Book* (1972), *Innervisions* (1973), *Fulfillingness' First Finale* (1974), and *Songs in the Key of Life* (1976)—were all top five albums and confirmed Wonder's position as a crossover star. Gaye spent years trying to convince Gordy to back him as an album artist. He finally succeeded in 1971 when *What's Goin' On* was released. It was followed by *Let's Get It On* (1973). Both of Gaye's albums went Top Ten. Although Motown released smash hit singles by the Jackson 5, the new Temptations, and the solo Diana Ross throughout the 1970s, it was Stevie Wonder and Marvin Gaye who introduced the company to the financial joys of independent production and album-oriented releases.

It was not just the album-oriented releases of Stevie Wonder and Marvin Gaye that did well. War, which had been Eric Burdon's backup band on MGM until the group went out on their own on United Artists (UA) in 1971, released eight albums between 1972 and 1977, four of which made the Top Ten, all of which were certified gold or platinum. UA tried to take credit for the group's success, pointing to the label's nondiscriminatory policy of promoting black acts no differently from white ones. Jerry Wexler, however, had a different explanation: "The old myth used to be that an r&b record could sell maybe 200,000 copies and, in order to get any real muscle in sales, [it] had to sell pop (to whites). But now I think millions of sales are possible on 'secret service' hits—records that whites may not really be familiar with."[53] Whatever the truth, War's mellow grooves seemed consonant with the tenor of the new times. The group's music ("Slippin' into Darkness" and "The Cisco Kid") tended toward a laid-back rhythmic base with a funky r&b feel.

James Brown adapted to the new political era by singing a new political tune. The political establishment had been wooing Brown since the late 1960s, but the streetwise artist had always seemed to project a clear sense of where his sympathies lay. In 1970, *Rolling Stone* quoted him as saying, "Me and Nixon don't get along. He asked me to go along to Memphis in the campaign. I don't want to be his bullet-proof vest. I didn't want to protect him from my people, deceive them. Make them think he's with me and I'm with him."[54] In 1972, however, his loyalties changed. Whether it was Nixon's support for black capitalism or his alleged six-figure contribution to Brown, in that year Brown endorsed Nixon for the presidency, a move that compromised Brown's credibility in the traditionally Democratic black community. "Soul Brother No. 1" became, in the eyes of his detractors, "Sold Brother No. 1." He had his last pop hits of the decade in 1974, the year Nixon resigned, and did not return to the Top Forty until the film *Rocky IV*

propelled "Living in America" to number four in 1986.

Aretha Franklin also faded from the Top Ten charts. She hit the Top Ten for the last time in the seventies in 1974 with "Until You Come Back to Me (That's What I'm

Stevie Wonder began his career as a multitalented, twelve-year-old musical genius with the prefix "Little" attached to his name. By the early 1970s, he had secured his own publishing rights, successfully challenged Motown's formula mentality, and was well on his way to becoming an international superstar.

Gonna Do)" in 1974 and did not achieve that position again until 1985 with "Freeway of Love." It was not that her career dissolved; there were a few lesser hits and some successful albums. Still, between 1976 and 1981, she did not place a single entry in the Top Forty albums or singles. To be sure, there were personal problems that affected her recording career, but perhaps more important, in the less militant 1970s, her sound no longer appeared to be the compelling force it once was. Indeed, by the early 1970s, a good deal of rhythm and blues seemed to have lost its edge. Almost everywhere, black popular music seemed less feisty than it had been. It wasn't that there was no great black popular music being produced; there was, but it no longer had the insistence of southern soul. The operatic Roberta Flack hit the number one slot three times in three years for Atlantic with singles as soothing as they were beautiful—"The First Time Ever I Saw Your Face" (1972), "Killing Me Softly with His Song" (1973), and "Feel Like Makin' Love" (1974). Her duets with Donny Hathaway were equally delicious. Taking romantic sincerity all the way to self-parody, Barry White, backed by his Love Unlimited female trio and the forty-piece, string-laden Love Unlimited Orchestra, produced hits such as "I'm Gonna Love You Just a Little More Baby" and "Never, Never Gonna Give Ya Up" (1973) and "Can't Get Enough of Your Love, Babe" and "You're the First, the Last, My Everything" (1974). Both Flack and White joined the ranks of successful album artists. Flack had eight gold records to her credit; White had five gold and two platinum.

By the early 1970s, a good deal of rhythm and blues seemed to have lost its edge. Almost everywhere, black popular music seemed less feisty than it had been. It wasn't that there was no great black popular music being produced; there was, but it no longer had the insistence of southern soul.

White's saccharine grunting and groaning had actually been anticipated by Isaac Hayes on *Hot Buttered Soul,* which had been released on Stax's Enterprise label in 1969. Hayes' eighteen-minute version of "By the Time I Get to Phoenix," with its extended spoken word intro of murmured declarations of love, made the album the best-selling LP in Stax's history and might have provided the company with an entrée to the softer sounds of the 1970s if it had not been about to be buried under the pressures of high finance. By the start of the decade, Stax had become a multimillion-dollar corporation, built on practices that were no more disreputable than those of the rest of the industry, but no less either. Under the leadership of Al Bell, the company had entered a new period of political engagement, with ties to Richard Pryor and the Reverend Jesse Jackson. Sales were fine, and a new distribution deal with CBS provided the company with $6 million in capital advances.

In 1972, the label undertook its most ambitious project, Wattstax, a spectacular benefit concert in Los Angeles to commemorate the 1965 Watts uprising. The concert featured all the Stax stars, and in many ways it was a success. A feature-length film and a six-sided album resulted from it, and almost $100,000 in charitable contributions were divided among such organizations as the Sickle Cell Anemia Foundation, the Martin Luther King, Jr., General Hospital in Los Angeles, and Jesse Jackson's Operation PUSH (People United to Save Humanity) in Chicago. Without question, the concert underscored the connection between southern soul and black power. At the same time, however, it revealed identity problems and political tensions within the company. Why was Stax promoting a benefit in Los Angeles? What had they done for hometown Memphis? As these questions were being raised within the company, the IRS launched an investigation into Stax's business operations and turned up a number of highly unorthodox business expenditures. Over the next few years, Stax—Al Bell in particular—was dogged by a series of grand jury investigations into a variety of money-laundering and kickback schemes. The unceremonious firing of Clive Davis as president of CBS Records in 1973 because of alleged high-level drug improprieties did not help; CBS was distributing Stax at the time. By the time Bell was cleared of all charges against him in 1976, Stax had already closed its doors. Jim Stewart, Stax's conservative white founder, defended his partner's honesty, adding that Bell "got too involved in politics and not enough in the record business."[55] Given what Stax's music signified politically, it may well have been impossible for any black man to avoid doing this. Still, it was clear that the times demanded a new cultural orientation. Philadelphia provided soft soul sounds; white singer/songwriters provided soft rock.

Singer/Songwriters, Soft Rock Solutions, and More

The singer/songwriters of the 1970s were intensely personal—at times intimate, at times introspective, at times confessional. In the aspirations of rock toward art, they represented an attempt to apply lyric poetry to semiautobiographical themes. As a trend in popular music, these artists were born of the 1960s and edged toward a break with that same era. In them, the introspection of the drug culture manifested itself in a level of self-disclosure that, a decade before, only a psychiatrist would have heard. At the same time, this turning inward signaled a retreat from—or was it a reevaluation of?—the politics of the 1960s.

In the radical movements of the 1960s, personal concerns were often treated as psychological inadequacies that got in the way of revolutionary transformation. It was, of course, women who figured out that this usually meant that men did not have to deal with their own oppressive tendencies at the level of interpersonal relations, which meant in turn that the complete liberation of women would be deferred until after the revolution. The articulation of the powerfully simple feminist maxim "the personal is political" rendered all such thinking invalid. Now power relations had to be considered at all levels. Vulnerability was no longer a sign of political weakness; it was an essential ingredient in any trusting relationship. For radicals, of course, this was a tricky proposition. Openness and honesty could undermine revolutionary discipline; the lack of it could destroy the bonds of trust. At its best, a successful resolution of this tension tended toward equalizing power, at least among individuals, although frequently positions on all sides were exaggerated beyond parody along the way. At its worst, such thinking was considered soft. And soft was not the stuff that revolutions were made of.

Soft was also not the stuff that rock was about at the turn of the decade. Indeed, until the appearance of the singer/songwriters, the words *soft* and *rock* would not have appeared in the same sentence. Surprisingly, at a time when most rock was rough, this new music was gentle; when most rock was deafening, its amplification was modest; while rock sought to let it all hang out, its tone was reserved. At the time hard rock was perceived as male in its loud, aggressive tone and phallic connection to instruments; soft rock represented the female side of the equation. The results were mixed. On

Soft was not the stuff that rock was about at the turn of the decade. Indeed, until the appearance of the singer/songwriters, the words soft and rock would not have appeared in the same sentence. Hard rock was perceived as male in its loud, aggressive tone and phallic connection to instruments; soft rock represented the female side of the equation.

the plus side, soft rock was the first style since the advent of rock 'n' roll that allowed women to sing in their own voice and encouraged men to try on new personas. On the minus side, its gentleness could sound mousy and its self-revelations could approach masochism or the cliché.

If an appearance of vulnerability is used to define soft rock, then Canadian singer/songwriter Joni Mitchell heads the list. Her romantic involvements (with David Crosby, producer of her first album, *Songs to a Seagull* [1967], Graham Nash, the inspiration for "Willy" on *Clouds* [1969], and James Taylor, "My Old Man" on *Blue* [1971]) were more widely noted than her music and frequently submerged consideration of her artistry beneath the tabloid tales of her life. Mitchell bore some responsibility for the situation herself, since she devoted much of her considerable talent—a near three-octave range, intricate melodies, original harmonic voicings, and elegant lyrics—to exploring the exquisite pain of her amorous ups and downs. Still, critic Robert Christgau saw the influence of feminism at work, even if Mitchell herself would not have worn the label. Said Christgau, commenting on *Blue:*

> *Like her voice, Joni Mitchell's lyrics have always suggested emotional life with startling highs and lows and an attenuated middle. Just because she knows herself, she reveals how dangerous and attractive such a life can be, especially for women. . . . In a male performer such intense self-concern would be an egotistic cop-out. In a woman it is an act of defiance.*
> *Not that Mitchell herself has always perceived it that way.*[56]

Born in 1943 in Fort Macleod, Alberta, Mitchell grew up in Saskatoon. Moving to Toronto in the mid-1960s, she first played the Mariposa Folk Festival in 1965. Signed to Reprise in 1967, Mitchell had her first big break in 1968, when Judy Collins scored a Top Ten hit with Mitchell's "Both Sides Now." As her career progressed, Mitchell moved from acoustic accompaniment to a soft rock band and switched to Asylum, where she was more protected from prying reporters. While she generated a handful of Top Forty hits—"Big Yellow Taxi," "You Turn Me On, I'm a Radio," "Help Me"—she was first and foremost an album artist (she even painted a number of her own album covers). After turning out eight gold or platinum LPs in the 1970s, Mitchell turned toward jazz. She had hoped her crowning achievement of the decade would be a collaboration with jazz bassist Charles Mingus, but he died before recording could commence. *Mingus,* her tribute album, broke her run of gold certifications. She returned to more accessible material in the 1980s, recording for Geffen, and in 2007 for Hear Music.

Over the course of her career, Joni Mitchell has continued to courageously forge new paths as an artist. She remains one of the most gifted singer/songwriters in popular music.

Second only to Mitchell in self-absorption was James Taylor, another singer/songwriter and Mitchell's one-time lover. As a performer, he was unquestionably talented. On stage he was always polite if somewhat wooden, the antithesis of in-your-face 1960s rockers. To the trained observer, his overly laid-back demeanour may have suggested the frequent bouts of depression or the heroin addiction that characterized his late teens. To his critics, however, his demeanour exuded the kind of mellowness that Woody Allen was talking about when he said something to the effect that he did not like getting too mellow because he was afraid he would ripen and rot. Robert Christgau once recounted a story of how the late Lester Bangs had wanted to run Taylor through "with a broken-off Ripple bottle," and went on to say, "Me, I only took the poster from his third album and ripped it into four or five pieces. Then I hung the face on my wall and scrawled upon it slogans from imaginary Maoist comic books, e.g.: 'Eat felt-tipped death, capitalist pig!'"[57]

Of course, the response to Taylor would not have been so virulent had he not become so famous. Originally signed to the Beatles' Apple label by Peter Asher, Taylor's self-titled debut album caused little stir even with the appearance of Paul McCartney and George Harrison. It was not until Taylor returned to the United States with Asher in tow as his new manager and switched to Warner that his star began to rise. His first album for the company, *Sweet Baby James* (1970), became one of the defining sounds of the soft rock genre and went platinum to boot. For the next eleven years, Taylor enjoyed nothing less than gold album sales. His 1972 marriage to Carly Simon simply heightened his visibility. Despite Taylor's skill as a songwriter (*Sweet Baby James* contained some of his best material, including the title song, "Fire and Rain," and "Country Road"), most of his hit singles were covers of other artists' material—Carole King's "You've Got a Friend" (1971), Marvin Gaye's "How Sweet It Is (To Be Loved By You)" (1975), and Jimmy Jones' "Handy Man" (1977). Taylor also joined Simon and Garfunkel on Sam Cooke's "What a Wonderful World" and hit number five with Carly Simon on Charlie and Inez Foxx's "Mockingbird" in 1974.

Carole King was neither consumed by politics nor driven to share the intimate details of her private life with the record-buying public. She never tried to become "one of the boys," but she also never felt compelled to ooze sex. She seemed at home with herself, a calm during the storm. She appeared forthright and genuine. She projected contentment at a time when most listeners were suspicious of it in their own lives. She wrote with a personal touch, sang in a conversational tone, and in 1971 outsold everyone in the music business. But then, she had been in the business much longer than most of her contemporaries. While most of soft rock's singer/songwriters could trace their roots to the folk revival of the early 1960s, King was a seasoned Brill Building professional before that movement even started. By 1961, before she was out of her teens, she and Gerry Goffin, her lyricist husband, were already collecting royalties on their first major hit, the Shirelles' "Will You Love Me Tomorrow." In 1962, she had her own pop hit as a solo vocalist, "It Might as Well Rain until September." After she and Goffin were divorced, King and their two daughters moved to the West Coast, where she continued to write songs. By the end of the decade, she was both composer and lyricist. A contract with Lou Adler's Ode Records launched her career as a full-fledged singer/songwriter. Her first outing, *Carole King: Writer* (1970), failed to crack the Top Forty, but her second, *Tapestry* (1971), broke all existing records.

Tapestry contained its share of sentimentality, but it was never disingenuous. On an artistic level, all of its elements worked in synergy—King's genius as a songwriter, the understated sensuality of her lightly r&b-inflected piano playing, the warm and friendly voice you could believe in. Another key ingredient was Adler's uncluttered production. *Tapestry* "was a very naked sounding album," he said. "I wanted it to sound like she was in the room playing piano for you."[58] In its first year, *Tapestry* ended up in 5 million rooms. It remained in the Top Forty for sixty-eight weeks and was located at number one for fifteen of them. Within five years, the album had sold 13 million copies, becoming the best-selling record of all time. It also garnered an impressive four Grammies: Album of the Year, Song of the Year ("You've Got a Friend"), Record of the Year ("It's Too Late"), and Best Female Pop Vocalist.

Tapestry was such an outstanding achievement—"a triumph of mass culture," said Christgau—that it would be difficult to fault King for not repeating its success. The album provided her with the means to withdraw from touring almost completely, and she did. She adopted a strict no-interview policy, becoming, in the words of Katherine Orloff, "a housewife who writes songs."[59] While she turned out seven more Top Forty albums before the decade was out, by the late 1970s she had moved to Idaho and had limited her live performances to occasional appearances at benefits. Despite the substantial presence of women among the singer/songwriters, life on the road was still largely the province of men.

Australian-born Helen Reddy is seldom classified as a singer/songwriter because she was essentially a nightclub singer who introduced material by singer/songwriters into her act. But she also wrote, and it was her composition "I Am Woman" (co-written with Ray Burton) that announced feminism to the mainstream audience in 1972. As a feminist, Reddy took heat from all sides. The obvious connection of "I Am Woman" to feminism angered conservatives and prompted radio to demur from playing it; the easy-listening, pop feel of the song made it odious

"You've Got a Friend"

Artist: Carole King

Music / Lyrics by Carole King

Label: Ode (1971), from the LP *Tapestry*

The early 1970s saw a trend away from lyrics that focused on social and political commentary toward those that expressed the highly individual emotions of the singer-songwriter. Carole King is a master of the songwriting craft; in the 1960s she and her then-husband, Gerry Goffin, were churning out number one hits for other artists as members of the songwriting staff at Aldon Music (known collectively as the "Brill Building" songwriters after the New York building that housed Aldon).

King's ability to write songs that were simultaneously universal and deeply personal made her one of the era's most beloved singer/songwriters, and *Tapestry* was one of the most popular recordings of the early 1970s (it was virtually required listening in women's dorms at colleges across the United States). The musical cast featured the cream of the crop of L.A. session musicians (including drummer Russ Kunkel and guitarist Danny "Kootch" Kortchmar) and a team of backup singers that included James Taylor and Joni Mitchell. It swept the Grammy Awards for 1971. These accolades were a fitting tribute to a songwriter who had provided classic hits for so many artists (her own versions of two of her former hits, Aretha Franklin's "You Make Me Feel Like a Natural Woman" and the Shirelles' "Will You Love Me Tomorrow," are also included on *Tapestry*).

Musical Style Notes

The style of "You've Got a Friend" is dominated by Carole King's clear and beautifully understated vocals and her tasteful and soulful piano style. Producer Lou Adler's addition of a touch of string orchestra heightens the sentimentality without overpowering the sound texture. The song has several classic elements of a popular hit: the honest, forthright emotions of the lyrics; a simple verse-and-chorus structure; and a chorus that has one of those "hooks" ("Winter, spring, summer, or fall . . . ") that remain on "replay" in your mind for the rest of the day.

Musical "Road Map"

TIMINGS	COMMENTS	LYRICS
0:00–0:10	Piano introduction	
0:10–0:58	Verse 1	*When you're down and troubled . . .*
0:58–1:38	Chorus	*You just call out my name . . .*
1:20		*Winter, spring, summer, or fall . . .*
1:38–1:48	Piano interlude (same as introduction)	
1:48–2:34	Verse 2 (Note entrance of string orchestra to sound texture.)	*If the sky above you . . .*
2:34–3:13 2:56	Chorus	*You just call out my name . . .* *Winter, spring, summer, or fall . . .*
3:13–3:42	Bridge (new melody)	*Now ain't it good to know that you've got a friend?*
3:42–4:25 4:05	Chorus	*You just call out my name . . .* *Winter, spring, summer, or fall . . .*
4:25–5:04	Last line of chorus, "You've got a friend," followed by King's vocal improvisations over this line, which continue until the end of the song	

to radicals. In her own way Reddy was committed to the women's movement (at one point she even started her own Hollywood Hills consciousness-raising group), but she never strayed far from its more centrist tendencies. She also set her priorities carefully. "I am first and foremost a singer," she told historian Gillian Gaar. "That's how I earn my living. I don't earn my living as a feminist."[60] All the same, Reddy would be the first to admit that the women's movement had an obvious effect on her career, as it did on the careers of other female performers of the era.

In the early 1970s, all the women in rock (and a good many men) were affected by the women's movement to some degree, and whether they were singer/songwriters or not, the women rockers who came into their own during this era—among them, Maria Muldaur, Melissa Manchester, Bonnie Raitt, and Linda Ronstadt—all took a soft rock approach in their music. Maria Muldaur knocked around the acoustic folk scene for years with her husband, Jeff, as members of Jim Kweskin's Jug Band before she achieved solo success with the balmy "Midnight at the Oasis" in 1974. Melissa Manchester studied under Paul Simon at the High School of Performing Arts in New York before moving on to middle-level soft rock success on her own. Bonnie Raitt always seemed destined for superstardom, but at the beginning of the 1970s it was still some twenty years away. Her love of blues and proficiency on electric slide guitar—as well as her Quaker upbringing and political activism—set her apart from most of her contemporaries. Still, she did not overwhelm her audiences (in the beginning she performed sitting down), she communicated with them . . . respectfully. Linda Ronstadt found a pop niche much earlier. She had already experienced major success as the lead singer for the Stone Poneys ("Different Drummer," 1967). She went solo at the end of the 1960s, steadily built her career, and achieved number one status with her album *Heart Like a Wheel* and its hit single "You're No Good," released in 1974. Ronstadt went on to become one of the most successful solo female vocalists of the decade with nothing but gold and platinum albums to her credit, including two more that were number one—*Simple Dreams* (1977) and *Living in the USA* (1978). Ronstadt combined Carly Simon's penchant for "cheesecake" photographs on her album covers with Joni Mitchell's inability to separate her personal life from her professional life. "I have no self-control," she told an interviewer in 1974. "When I meet somebody I really admire and I trust, which has to be somebody I'm involved with businesswise, I always end up having a sexual relationship with him. Then it blows it."[61] Ronstadt's sexpot image—one reviewer referred to her as "an impossibly cuddly chicklet"—may have advanced her career on one level, but it tended to overshadow a determined personality and a considerable talent.

Linda Ronstadt's sexpot image—one reviewer referred to her as "an impossibly cuddly chicklet"—may have advanced her career on one level, but it tended to overshadow a determined personality and a considerable talent.

All of these women had an awareness of themselves as female performers, all of them wrestled with the contradictions of life on the road, and all of them grappled publicly with the difficulties of expressing their sexuality comfortably. The fact that they all were channeled toward soft rock solutions presented a different kind of dilemma. To the extent that soft rock offered a vehicle for more personal communication, it was progressive for women. But to the extent that it looked to acoustic folk as its model, it was regressive in form, and not just for women but for rock as a whole. Many of the men who were categorized as soft rockers or singer/songwriters—from major stars like James Taylor and Paul Simon to lesser-known artists like Jonathan Edwards, Jim Croce, Harry Chapin, Mac Davis, and Canadians Valdy and Dan Hill—were identified with a retreat from rock. "[James] Taylor is leading a retreat," said

Christgau in 1972, "and the reason why us rock and rollers are so mad at him is simply because the retreat has been so successful."[62] Artists like British-born Cat Stevens and Canadian Gordon Lightfoot, both of whom began recording in the mid-1960s, added to the perception of regression. Influenced by the hippie mysticism of Donovan, Stevens, who was described by one reviewer as "the English James Taylor," came to the attention of the U.S. market in 1971 with the release of *Tea for the Tillerman,* which included the hit single "Wild World." As critic Stephen Holden has noted, "Although his records were pretty, they were quite vacuous."[63] Nine Top Forty albums later, Stevens began to tire of the music business. After his 1979 conversion to Islam, he withdrew from it completely. Lightfoot was a folkie who had written songs for Peter, Paul & Mary, Marty Robbins, and others in the mid-1960s. His seven Top Forty albums between 1971 and 1978, including the number one *Sundown* (1974), set him up for a comfortable recording career in the 1980s, even though his music seemed to be a throwback to an earlier time. Similarly, (Jim) Seals and (Dash) Crofts ("Summer Breeze," 1972) sounded far more reserved than they had when they first started playing with the Champs in 1958. Nevertheless, six gold albums established them as a solid soft rock act. Even more successful were folk-rockers America ("A Horse with No Name," 1972), who had eight Top Forty albums to their credit.

The singer/songwriter category also included some variation, particularly among the critics' choices for the "next Dylan"—David Bromberg, Loudon Wainwright III, John Prine, Steve Goodman, even the early Bruce Springsteen, and a range of cult-figure types, including Leonard Cohen (the poet), Tom Waits (the beatnik barfly who claimed to have slept through the 1960s), and Randy Newman, whose wry humour more than balanced the earnestness of most others in the field. Many of Newman's compositions were clever dramatic narratives that dealt with such issues as racism and other forms of discrimination ("Sail Away," "Rednecks," "Short People,") but often from the point of view of the perpetrators, which left the listener to grapple with an uncomfortable ambiguity. The narrator on "Rednecks," for example, boasted about "keeping our 'nigras' down" and poked fun at the "smart-ass New York Jew." Newman was too talented to be dismissed out of hand, but one often had to wonder whether his Swiftian irony crossed the line.

Montreal's Leonard Cohen was an acclaimed poet and novelist for a decade before he recorded his first album, *Songs of Leonard Cohen*, for Columbia Records in late 1967. On the strength of era-defining songs such as "Suzanne" and "Hey, That's No Way To Say Goodbye," Cohen played the Mariposa and Newport Folk Festivals. His second album, 1969's *Songs From a Room*, contained another classic in "Bird on a Wire." A reluctant performer with a rabid if small fan base, Cohen continued to release albums sporadically, attaining much greater popularity in the late 1980s when his former background singer, Jennifer Warnes, recorded a whole album of Cohen covers named after his 1971 song "Famous Blue Raincoat." Cohen capitalized on his newfound notoriety with strong albums such as *I'm Your Man* (1988) and *The Future* (1992) that saw the former folk-based singer-songwriter exploring electronic keyboards and European folk and popular music traditions. The results were rich and uncategorizable. Along with Bob Dylan, Cohen brought a literary quality to popular song that was unprecedented.

In 1969, Bernie Finkelstein, former manager of the Toronto groups the Toronto groups the Paupers and Kensington Market, established True North Records largely as a vehicle for singer-songwriter Bruce Cockburn, whom he also managed. Cockburn had been a member of the Ottawa-based 1960s rock group The Children before he went solo in 1969. An extraordinary guitarist who tended to sing about nature and spirituality, Cockburn wrote songs from an unquestionably Canadian perspective. As the decade progressed, Cockburn began playing more and more electric guitar, and in the 1980s, after a series of visits to Third World countries, his lyrics became increasingly political. His 1984 album, *Stealing Fire,* included songs such as "Lovers in a Dangerous Time," "Nicaragua," and "If I Had a Rocket Launcher," all of which expressed no-holds-barred outrage at the U.S. government's activities in Central America. "Call It Democracy," from 1985's *World of Wonders,* was probably the first song to criticize the International Monetary Fund. In 1989, with "If a Tree Falls," from *Big Circumstance,* Cockburn addressed the subject of rainforest depletion.

Over the years, Cockburn became an icon of Canadian folk and popular music, and beginning in 1979, achieved substantial international acclaim. Other important Canadian singer-songwriters who have recorded for True North include Murray McLauchlan, Luke Gibson, Stephen Fearing, and Colin Linden. In 1979, True North ventured into the world of post-punk alternative rock, releasing hit albums by Carol Pope and Rough Trade. Subsequent rock artists signed to the label have included the Rheostatics, 54-40, the Cowboy Junkies, and the Golden Dogs. More recently, the company has enjoyed substantial national and international success with CDs by Zubot and Dawson, Lynn Miles, and Blackie and the Rodeo Kings.

Bruce Springsteen can be classified as a singer/songwriter in the same sense that Van Morrison or the solo John Lennon can be. They all composed personal, poetic verse. They also belted it out with incredible intensity; they were hardly soft. Following the breakup of Them, Morrison tasted success on his first solo album, *Blowin' Your Mind* (1967), which had the hit single "Brown Eyed Girl." After a dry spell that included the failure of the critically acclaimed *Astral Weeks,* he regained his footing in 1970 with *Moondance* and *His Band and the Street Choir.* The latter of these yielded the single "Domino," which made the Top Ten. At his most confessional, Lennon transformed months of primal scream therapy into singles like "Cold Turkey" and album cuts like "Mother" from his first solo LP, *John Lennon/Plastic Ono Band* (1970), the album that included "Working Class Hero." Springsteen was that working-class hero.

Bruce Springsteen demonstrated that singer/songwriters did not have to be hamstrung by the parameters of soft rock.

There were a number of reasons for promoting Bruce Springsteen as the new Dylan. Springsteen was signed to Columbia by the same John Hammond who had brought Dylan himself (not to mention Billie Holiday and Benny Goodman) to the label. Furthermore, on his first two albums—*Greetings from Asbury Park, N.J.* (1973) and *The Wild, the Innocent, and the E Street Shuffle* (1974)—he exhibited Dylan's tendency to fill a song with more words than a line could hold. At the same time, Springsteen, who grew up in the resort towns of the Jersey shore, could evoke images of everyday working-class lives that were as powerful as they were sympathetic.

His live shows were raw, brash, and full of energy, often extending to the three-hour range. Songs like "Rosalita" from his second album were absolute showstoppers. More than any other performer, Springsteen demonstrated that singer/songwriters did not have to be hamstrung by the parameters of soft rock. To his followers, he was a legend even before Jon Landau wrote in 1974, "I saw rock and roll's future and its name is Bruce Springsteen."

It was *Born to Run* (1975) that provided Springsteen with the creative and commercial breakthrough he needed to crack the Top Ten, but the breakthrough did not come without a price. Always a disciplined artist and an exacting craftsman, Springsteen hit a creative block in the midst of *Born to Run,* and Landau was brought in to guide the album to completion. For his work, he shared a coproducer's credit with Springsteen and Mike Appel, Springsteen's manager. On its release, the album was hailed as a rock masterpiece. "Thunder Road" and "Jungleland" became instant rock classics. The LP hit number three and propelled Springsteen to national fame. In the last week of October that year, both *Time* and *Newsweek* pictured him on their covers (perhaps one of the ancillary benefits of having a critic as a producer). At about this time, however, Springsteen began to part ways with Appel over career direction. When the artist insisted on using Landau as the producer for his next album, his manager refused. The ensuing lawsuits kept Springsteen tied up in court for the next year. By the time *Darkness on the Edge of Town* was released in 1978, a number of its cuts—including the title track, "Badlands," and "The Promised Land"—were already live performance favourites.

Throughout the remainder of the 1970s, Springsteen matured both musically and politically. He pared down his music, unleashed the fury of his guitar, and created ever more vivid images. In 1979, he took a step that moved him closer to the activism that would characterize his career in the 1980s. As a favour to his friend Jackson Browne, he agreed to headline two shows for No Nukes, a weeklong series of concerts protesting the construction of nuclear power plants in the wake of the Harrisburg, Pennsylvania, Three Mile Island disaster. The concerts were held at Madison Square Garden and sponsored by Musicians United for Safe Energy (MUSE). MUSE represented a coalition of antinuclear groups. Bonnie Raitt was among its active artists. John Hall, formerly of Orleans ("Dance with Me," "Still the One"), was also a central figure and provided the group with its anthem, "Power." Jackson Browne sat on the MUSE Board. Browne had come into his own as a solo vocalist with "Doctor My Eyes" in 1972. In the latter half of the decade, *The Pretender* (produced by Landau) and *Running on Empty* moved him into the Top Ten as an album-oriented artist. As a singer/songwriter he was as self-confessional as any of them, but he had an activist spirit. He joined the antinuclear movement in the mid-1970s and

Bruce Springsteen combined working-class roots and social consciousness with riveting live performances. Even as a superstar in the age of video, he remained essentially a live artist who could project working-class solidarity with credibility.

performed for the Clamshell Alliance in New Hampshire and the Alliance for Survival in California. Eventually, he was arrested with demonstrators at California's Diablo Canyon nuclear power plant.

At first glance, No Nukes appeared to be soft rock heaven. Along with Raitt, Hall, and Browne, James Taylor, Carly Simon, and Crosby, Stills & Nash were on the bill, but it also included Springsteen, the Doobie Brothers, and newcomer Tom Petty, not to mention African American artists such as Chaka Khan, Sweet Honey in the Rock, and Gil Scott-Heron. In fact, it was Scott-Heron who had first raised the issue of nuclear power in song. A political singer/songwriter if there ever was one, Scott-Heron had started as a poet and novelist and then began to collaborate with musician Brian Jackson to deliver his message in a new medium. He is perhaps best known for his antiapartheid "Johannesburg," from the album *From South Africa to South Carolina* (1975). The South Carolina half of the title referred to the song "South Carolina (Barnwell)," which protested plans to build a reprocessing plant for nuclear waste in Barnwell. Two years later, Scott-Heron raised the issue even more forcefully in "We Almost Lost Detroit."

The only sellout nights in the No Nukes series were the nights that Springsteen played. On one of those nights, a frustrated Chaka Khan walked off the stage, thinking that the cries for "Broooce" were boos. No Nukes yielded a documentary film and a triple LP that sold moderately well. The California Alliance was even more ambitious. It staged over fifty shows that included Joan Baez, Peter, Paul & Mary, Bob Dylan, Gil Scott-Heron, Bruce Springsteen, Jackson Browne, Minnie Ripperton, Bette Midler, and Stevie Wonder. These artists can claim some small share of the credit for the success of the movement. Robin Denselow has noted that by 1982, "Every single [nuclear power] station ordered in the USA since 1974 had either been canceled completely or indefinitely postponed."[64] The connection between songwriting and activist politics was applied most forcefully in a concert that was staged in Harvard Stadium on July 21, 1979. *Amandla: Festival of Unity* was a benefit concert for the liberation organizations in all the front line states in South Africa. It was headlined by Bob Marley and the Wailers and featured Patti Labelle, Eddie Palmieri, and Olatunji, among others, with Dick Gregory as MC. Bob Marley had already distinguished himself in his native Jamaica as a songwriter and performing artist of genuine talent, moral authority, and political principle by the time Chris Blackwell signed him to Island Records in 1971. Marley and the Wailers broke into the U.S. Top Thirty with two albums—*Rastaman Vibration* (1976) and *Exodus* (1977). By 1979, Marley had become the first black international superstar. For Amandla, he demonstrated the power of his political convictions, performing songs such as "Slave Driver," "Get Up, Stand Up," "No Woman, No Cry, " and a stirring rendition of "War/We Don't Need No Trouble."

Women's Music: The Feminist Alternative

Throughout the 1970s, the sexist nature of rock was openly debated in the feminist press. Those who felt that rock was irrevocably sexist gravitated toward softer styles. There were some, however, who felt that rock could be a valuable cultural asset for them. Feminist critic Ellen Willis wrote:

Music that boldly and aggressively laid out what the singer wanted, loved, hated—as good rock-and-roll did—challenged me to do the same, and so, even when the content was antiwoman, antisexual, in a sense antihuman, the form encouraged my struggle for liberation. Similarly, timid music made me feel timid, whatever its ostensible politics.[65]

In 1972, in a concrete attempt to harness the energy of rock in the service of feminism, the Chicago Women's Liberation Rock Band and its East Coast counterpart, the New Haven Women's Liberation Rock Band, recorded *Mountain Moving Day* for Rounder Records, an independent label. While the creation of the record was an overtly political act, even in circles that were less political, women began to venture into territory that had been exclusively male. A number of regionally known all-female rock bands came and went. Eyes and the Enchanted Forest were too short-lived to make any impact. Ace of Cups never landed a contract. Although Goldie and the Gingerbreads had been popular in Great Britain since the early 1960s, the group was never able to make a dent in the U.S. market. Isis ventured into jazz rock with a full horn section. The Deadly Nightshade recorded *The Deadly Nightshade* (1975) and *Funky and Western* (1976) for RCA and then folded. There was also a group from Berkeley—Joy of Cooking—that showed promise. It was a mixed-gender group, but it was led by two women, electric guitarist Terry Garthwaite and electric keyboardist Toni Brown. Garthwaite and Brown's music was not political in the narrow sense, but it was compelling in that it reflected the experiences of two literate, adult women. With two well-received albums to their credit by 1971 (*Joy of Cooking* and *Closer to the Ground*), Garthwaite and Brown looked like they might be the beginning of a non-sexist tradition in commercial rock. Christgau opined: "Many vaguely feminist women have no special connection to rock not out of ideology but simply because it has never really spoken to them. Joy of Cooking can end that."[66] However, after a disappointing third album (*Castles* [1972]), the group dissolved. Brown and Garthwaite headed to Nashville to record *Cross Country* as Toni and Terry before embarking on solo careers.

For the members of Fanny, becoming a rock band and developing a feminist consciousness were mutually exclusive choices. The group chose to become a rock band and, in so doing, helped eliminate one of the biggest obstacles facing women in music—access to electric instruments.

Fanny was the first self-contained, all-female rock band to be signed to a major label and the only one of its generation to hit the Top Forty. The group was started by two sisters from the Philippines, June and Jean Millington, who had formed bands with their female classmates throughout their high-school years. Signed to Reprise in 1969 by Richard Perry, the band faced an almost impossible situation. Within the women's movement, their impolitic name and such double entendre album titles as *Charity Ball* (1971) and *Fanny Hill* (1972) made them something of an embarrassment. A promotional campaign that included **GET BEHIND FANNY** bumper stickers did not help. In the music business, the band was seen as a novelty group; when their concerts were well received, the sentiment was "not bad . . . for chicks." The fact that the title cut from *Charity Ball* reached the Top Forty was remarkable.

June Millington eventually came to resent the fact that the quality of Fanny's music was measured by the group's ability to play like men. At the time, however, it never occurred to the members of Fanny that the women's movement might be a natural point of reference for them. Feminism "was such a dirty word!" said Millington.[67] Fanny was thus caught between rock and a hard place. The sector of the music business the band had chosen to enter was so male-dominated there were no female referents, let alone a support network. "You had to prove that you could play like a guy, or play as good as a guy," Millington later recalled. "That's really all there was. The whole attitude, what you wore, the way that you projected, every note that you played, was male territory."[68] In such a milieu, the women's movement could never have presented itself as a refuge. For the members of Fanny, becoming a rock band and developing a feminist consciousness were mutually exclusive choices. The group chose to become a rock band and, in so doing, helped eliminate one of the biggest obstacles facing women in music—access to electric instruments.

Fanny was the model for the Runaways, an all-female rock band made up of four southern California teenagers. Like their predecessors, they were never able to transcend their novelty status (with releases like "Cherry Bomb," written by Kim Fowley, the group's manager, it is hardly surprising) and eventually broke up. Still, the band was the proving ground for Joan Jett and Lita Ford, who would go on to achieve some measure of solo hard rock success in the 1980s. The group's one-time vocalist, Micki Steele, later surfaced as one of the Bangles. Suzi Quatro, the group's fourth member, also ventured into hard rock with some success during this period. Again, however, the progress she represented was trivialized by her role as Leather Tuscadero on the television series *Happy Days.*

The failure of all-female rock bands and the hostility of the music industry toward women in rock bands in general led to the development of explicitly feminist, mostly folk-oriented alternative music. For the most part, it was music Ellen Willis would have found timid. Women's music, as this new sound came to be called, was institutionalized in 1973 when a group of politically active women from Washington, D.C., started Olivia Records at the suggestion of singer Cris Williamson. Olivia's first release was a single that featured Williamson's "If It Weren't for the Music," backed by Meg Christian's rendition of "Lady," by Carole

King/Gerry Goffin. The single sold 5,000 copies through mail order. The revenue it generated was used to relocate the operation to San Francisco and to finance the label's first album, Meg Christian's *I Know You Know* (1975), which sold 70,000 copies. Olivia's second album, Cris Williamson's *The Changer and the Changed*, sold over 250,000 copies. While the album was in preparation, Williamson

The male-dominated music industry was sufficiently exclusionary that there were no career paths to positions of power for women; there were no female record company presidents or record producers to serve as role models.

had invited June Millington, who had left Fanny in 1973, to play. Millington's appearance served as her introduction to a career in women's music; she began touring with Williamson and became a regular session player at Olivia. "I decided to just get into working with other women," she said.[69]

Sales of *The Changer and the Changed* revealed the existence of an untapped feminist market. Other women's labels soon filled the void: Margie Adam launched Pleiades, and Kay Garner founded Wide Woman/Urana. Seeking to avoid the mainstream music industry completely, women's music formed its own subindustry. Olivia established a network of volunteers to distribute its records at concerts, in feminist bookstores, and door-to-door. As other women's music labels came into existence, Olivia's volunteers formed a network called WILD (Women's Independent Labels Distributors) that distributed these labels as well as Olivia's. Festivals like the Michigan Womyn's Music Festival began to attract thousands of feminists annually. In 1978, Roadwork, Inc., a national booking agency, was created to coordinate tour bookings.

Women's music was originally conceived as music by women, for women, and about women. It was, for all intents and purposes, lesbian music. However, lesbians had experienced discrimination not only in society at large but also within the women's movement. Thus, the term "women's music" was used because it was less threatening to the public as a whole. "Women were less likely to be harassed for listening to or performing 'women's music' than 'lesbian music,'" said feminist music historian Cynthia Lont.[70] Because of the women's movement, there was a tendency to think of women's music in separatist terms. Tactically, a separatist orientation was probably necessary, at least in the short run. The male-dominated music industry was sufficiently exclusionary that there were no career paths to positions of power for women; there were no female record company presidents or record producers to serve as role models. As a way of life, however, separatism limited the audience for the music and led to damaging internal tensions within the movement. The experience of Holly Near and Redwood Records is a case in point. In political circles, Near was originally known as an antiwar activist. She started Redwood Records as an outlet for political material after visiting North Vietnam in 1973. Because of her involvement with the women's movement, however, she and the men who recorded for Redwood were stocked in the women's music section in record stores. When Near "came out" as a lesbian in 1978 on *Imagine My Surprise* (1978), she was criticized for using Jeff Langley, her long-time piano player, on the album. Political differences of this sort sapped an inordinate amount of time and energy from women's music.

As often happens in situations like these, the marketplace serves as the final arbiter. By the 1980s, the market for women's music had become saturated, leaving the alternative industry with no alternative but to expand its audience or die. "Ironically," Gillian Gaar has written, "Olivia now found itself trying to break out of the 'women's music' genre they worked so hard to create."[71] Abandoning its earlier position of using only female musicians, the label responded by launching Second Wave to diversify its roster. The move was less a compromise of principles than a part of the natural evolution of a business. Olivia could be justifiably proud of having helped create a cultural space for postpunk feminists from Tracy Chapman to Two Nice Girls.

While a handful of Canadian artists such as Ferron and Heather Bishop have participated in the women's music movement in the United States, in Canada feminist-oriented musicians have tended to be integrated into either the folk music or post-punk alternative scenes. Perhaps the first explicitly feminist songs by Canadian artists were Jacqueline Lemay's "La Moitié du monde est une femme" and Rita MacNeil's LP *Born a Woman*, both issued in 1975.

For some, it might be a stretch to describe Carol Pope, the lead singer and lyricist of the Toronto band Rough Trade, as a feminist artist. Fascinated with all things sexual (in fact the band's name resulted from Pope's interest in gay male iconography), Pope—with partner Kevan Staples, in first O, then the Bullwhip Brothers, and from 1974 with Rough Trade—sang what at the time were shocking songs that expressed in no uncertain terms explicit sexuality and desire. Presenting herself at all times as firmly in control, Pope represented a level of female sexual liberation that was simply unprecedented in popular music.

Rough Trade's debut album, aptly titled *Rough Trade Live!*, was cut in 1976 for producer Jack Richardson's Umbrella Records label. The album has the distinction of being the first direct-to-disc recording by a rock band. A few years later, the group signed with True North Records, and in the early 1980s, surprisingly garnered substantial airplay in Canada with singles such as "High School Confidential," "All Touch," and "Crimes of Passion." With lyrics

Parachute Club's 1983 hit "Rise Up" served as a welcome anthem of empowerment.

such as "She's a cool, blond, steaming bitch / She makes my body twitch" expressing lesbian desire, "High School Confidential" was many years ahead of its time. It's hard to believe that the single reached number twelve on the Canadian singles charts in late spring 1981. Although the group played spot gigs in Australia, Europe, and New York, outside Canada they were never able to achieve substantial success.

In 1977, Mama Quilla II, named after an Inca moon goddess who was the protective deity for married women, was formed by Lorraine Segato (guitar, vocals), Laurie Conger (keyboard), Linda Robitaille (sax), Susan Sturman (guitar), Jacqui Snedker (bass), and Billy Bryans (drums). Fixtures on Toronto's Queen Street scene, in 1981 Mama Quilla II recorded a three-song EP produced at Grant Avenue Studios in Hamilton by a very young Daniel Lanois. Featuring three originals by Susan Sturman, including the lesbian-positive "Angry Young Woman," the EP was released on the group's own Tupperaros Records. When Segato and Bryans were asked to put together a group for the 1982 Festival of Festivals and several members of Mama Quilla II were unavailable, in tandem with Conger and several other local Toronto musicians, they formed the Parachute Club. Signed to Martha and the Muffins' Current Records in 1983, Parachute Club combined politically conscious lyrics with world beat rhythms. In the summer of 1983, "Rise Up," produced by Daniel Lanois, became a Top Ten Canadian hit and an anthem for all kinds of empowerment. Two years later, "At the Feet of the Moon" peaked at number eleven.

The Toronto "no boy" collective Fifth Column was formed in 1981. Taking their name from a 1938 play by Ernest Hemingway, the group's members were publicly known solely by their first names and last initials, not wanting to be tied to their father's surnames. Fifth Column's first three albums, beginning with *To Sir with Hate* in 1986, were issued through their own feminist magazine, *Hide*. With songs such as "All Women Are Bitches: Repeat" and a sound that typified the Riot Grrrl movement of the 1990s, Fifth Column was several years ahead of its time.

In poems/songs such as "Sister Hold On," "Nellie Belly Swelly," "Birth Poem," and "Mrs.," Lillian Allen consistently articulated the concerns and experiences of African Canadians in general and African Canadian women in particular. Born in Jamaica, Allen moved to Toronto in her twenties. One of the originators of dub poetry, she released her first album, *Dub Poet: The Poetry of Lillian Allen,* in 1983. By 1986's *Revolutionary Tea Party*, released on Allen's own Verse to Vinyl label, she was being accompanied by members of the Parachute Club while being produced by Billy Bryans. That year, she won the Juno Award for Best Reggae/Calypso album. She won a Juno again in 1988 for *Conditions Critical.*

From Country Rock to Southern Boogie

In the late 1960s, *country rock* became yet another term in the growing lexicon of hybrid rock styles. Country music had long been one of a number of significant influences in popular music. Rockabilly had been a major strand of rock 'n' roll in the fifties and was carried into the 1960s by artists like Roy Orbison and Brenda Lee. Ray Charles' two volumes of pop country and western tunes were his best-selling albums. The late 1960s brought down-home, traditional Nashville sounds into the rock idiom. The artist who kicked off this trend in 1968 utilized clean, unfettered production, accompaniment that was laid back and spare, and sang in a voice sounding uncharacteristically throaty. On first hearing, it would have been difficult to tell it was Bob Dylan.

Dylan had been on hiatus since *Blonde on Blonde* had been released following his 1966 motorcycle accident. In the interim, Columbia had issued a greatest hits album. By 1968, then, Dylan's new album had been long awaited. When it came, it was totally unlike anything anyone had been expecting. At a time when rock was immersed in technological overindulgence, Dylan's *John Wesley Harding* was as spartan as his earlier acoustic efforts. At a time when the counterculture was as free-spirited and antiestablishment as it could be, *John Wesley Harding* was recorded in Nashville, a bastion of traditional values. Dylan had, once again, thrown his fans a curve, one of his most successful. *John Wesley Harding* rose to number two on the album charts, Dylan's highest position to date. If there were any doubts about the seriousness of his new artistic direction, he laid them to rest with the release of *Nashville Skyline* in 1969, which included the Top Ten hit single "Lay Lady Lay" and a duet with country legend Johnny Cash on "Girl from the North Country." As Bill Malone has written, "Dylan lent respectability to a musical form, and to a body of musicians, that had been perceived as 'corny' or old-fashioned."[72]

Nashville soon became the hot "new" recording centre, and country rock became a new trend. The top session players in the country music capital, those "Nashville Cats" the Lovin' Spoonful sang about, began getting so much work that they started their own performing ensemble called Area Code 615. Over the next few years, folk and rock musicians, from Canadians Buffy Sainte-Marie and Ian and Sylvia to the Nitty Gritty Dirt Band to the Byrds, followed Dylan into country, thus putting an end to its association with socially regressive values. Buffy Sainte-Marie and Ivan and Sylvia journeyed to Nashville to record *I'm Gonna Be a Country Girl Again,* the title song of which became a hit single in 1972. That same year, the Nitty Gritty Dirt Band recruited country greats Roy Acuff, Doc Watson, Merle Travis, Maybelle Carter, and Earl Scruggs, among others, for a three-record album titled *Will the Circle Be Unbroken.* Because the artists who traveled to Nashville treated country and western music without condescension, they began to soften the negative view that Acuff and other country performers had of hippies.

Nashville soon became the hot "new" recording centre, and country rock became a new trend. Because the artists who traveled to Nashville treated country and western music without condescension, they began to soften the negative view that Acuff and other country performers had of hippies.

Most prominent among Dylan's fellow travelers on the road to country rock at the end of the 1960s were four Canadians and one "good ole boy" from Arkansas who were known collectively as the Band. Guitarist Robbie Robertson, organist Garth Hudson, bassist Rick Danko, and pianist Richard Manuel had been fans of country music from childhood, even though they had been born and raised in Canada. Drummer Levon Helm from Marvell, Arkansas, could not have avoided country music even if he had wanted to. One by one, beginning in the late 1950s, these players joined the Hawks, the backup band for rockabilly artist Ronnie Hawkins, with whom they toured for years, honing their craft. "There were only three kinds of rock then: rhythm and blues, corny white rock, and rockabilly," said Robertson. "We played rockabilly."[73] The Hawks were hired by Dylan on the suggestion of Mary Martin, a Torontonian who was working for Dylan's manager, Albert Grossman. At the time, Dylan was moving toward electric

The Band started as a rockabilly outfit and became Bob Dylan's backup band for his first electric tour. Their breakup on Thanksgiving Day, 1976, was immortalized in The Last Waltz, *one of the best concert films ever made, directed by Martin Scorsese*

music. Hired as the backup band for his 1965–66 tour, the musicians withdrew with him to Woodstock, New York, after his accident. There they collaborated—jammed, really—on music that became rock's first significant bootleg, later released by Columbia as *The Basement Tapes.* The Band's official debut album, *Music from Big Pink* (1968), a reference to their Woodstock home, and their second release, *The Band* (1969), introduced a number of country rock classics, including Lefty Frizzell's "Long Black Veil," Dylan's "I Shall Be Released," and Robertson's "Up on Cripple Creek," "Rag, Mama, Rag," "Across the Great Divide," and "The Night They Drove Old Dixie Down." This last song became a Top Ten hit for Joan Baez in 1971. Their third and again critically acclaimed album, *Stage Fright,* continued in the country rock mold.

In 1973, Dylan and the Band recorded their first official album together. *Planet Waves* was recorded in three days and rose to number one on the album charts almost as fast. In January 1974, Dylan and the Band embarked on Dylan's first full tour in eight years. The tour was captured on the two-disc LP *Before the Flood.* Since Dylan's contract with Columbia was in limbo at this time, both albums came out on Asylum, a major coup in the eyes of the industry for David Geffen. However, Dylan returned to Columbia for *Blood on the Tracks* (1975) and *Desire* (1976). Both of these albums, which went to number one on the charts, would have been introspective enough to land Dylan back in the singer/songwriter category had it not been for the hit single "Hurricane," a political protest song dedicated to boxer Rubin "Hurricane" Carter, whom Dylan believed had been wrongly convicted of murder.

There were a series of groups, mostly from southern California, that picked up on Dylan's turn toward country. The Byrds, having been keenly aware of Dylan's importance when they transformed his acoustic material into folk rock earlier in the decade, again followed his lead.

By this time, the group had recruited Gram Parsons. Parsons, a Harvard Divinity School dropout, became a pioneer of country rock. His influence on the Byrds' *Sweethearts of the Rodeo,* which was recorded in Nashville, helped the group to become the first rock band to play the Grand Ole Opry. Although the album did not reach the Top Forty, it was a milestone for country rock.

Parsons left the Byrds when the group planned a tour of South Africa and formed the Flying Burrito Brothers with Chris Hillman and Gene Clarke, two alumni of the Byrds. Although they had only one album that charted (*Last of the Red Hot Burritos*), they played to packed houses and rave reviews, merging rock and country as no other group had done. The group further emphasized the fusion of cultures by performing in striking sequined Nudie suits that were embroidered with marijuana leaves instead of the cactus plants and wagon wheels selected by most country artists. By the time he died from heart failure in the mid-1970s, Parsons had been credited with influencing everyone from Emmylou Harris (his protégé) to the Rolling Stones.

Fronting the Stone Canyon Band, Rick (Ricky) Nelson made a country rock comeback with "Garden Party" in 1973. At various points, his new ensemble included members of Poco, Little Feat, and the Eagles, the group that would come to dominate country rock in the 1970s. The Eagles were accomplished writers and vocalists, as well as multi-instrumentalists. Sixteen Top Forty singles and four number one albums in a row attest to that. Indeed, the group's credentials were impeccable; bassist Randy Meisner had been a founding member of Poco, and guitarist Bernie Leadon had played with the Burritos. Along with drummer Don Henley and guitarist Glenn Frey, who became the group's main writers when Meisner and Leadon departed, all had backed up Linda Ronstadt at one time or another. There was, however, something about the group that was unsettling. When rockers like Creedence Clearwater Revival or Neil Young performed country-flavoured material, there was a certain southern ethos, a down-home earthiness, in the way they sang. The Eagles were slicker, more polished. The group was certainly talented enough to replicate the sound of country music, but they brought it out of the backwoods and into the big city. The word that most readily comes to mind in describing them is *corporate.* Somehow, the Eagles placed country rock in a new social context. With *John Wesley Harding,* Dylan had responded to the election of Richard Nixon by reclaiming the music of the heartland for rock 'n' roll. The Eagles were different. From their signature song "Take It Easy" (co-written by Jackson Browne in 1972), about the joys of an unencumbered life on the road, to the music on *Hotel California* (1976), their seminal statement about the California good life, they used country rock as a vehicle for embracing the hedonism of the 1970s. "The Eagles are the ultimate in California dreaming," said Christgau, "a fantasy of fulfillment that has been made real only in the hip upper-middle-class suburbs of Marin County and the Los Angeles canyons."[74]

It was not that the group was unaware of politics; there were direct political influences in their lives. Once Linda Ronstadt started dating Jerry Brown, who was then governor of California, she pulled the group into the electoral arena, and Jackson Browne exerted an environmental influence in the latter part of the decade. The very fact that group took its name from Native American folklore suggested an awareness of some kind of transcendence. In the

The Eagles were certainly talented enough to replicate the sound of country music, but they brought it out of the backwoods and into the big city. The word that most readily comes to mind in describing them is corporate.

context of the early 1970s, however, the name did not reflect that truth, nor did it ring with irony as it might have a few years earlier. During the culmination of the war in Vietnam and Nixon's final years, the eagle was as likely to represent a bird of prey as a symbol of liberation. Still, the group was politically astute enough to know that with a name like the Eagles, they should have a major album out in 1976, the bicentennial year. *Hotel California,* musically their best effort, commercially their biggest hit (15 million copies sold), was the pinnacle of their success. Eventually, the years of "Life in the Fast Lane," as the Eagles termed it, took their toll on the group. "I think the underbelly of success is the burden of having to follow things up," Frey told an interviewer. "We started to run out of gas. Don [Henley] sort of blew his literary nut on *Hotel California.*"[75] The result was the nightmarish three-year effort it took to produce the group's final studio LP, ironically titled *The Long Run.*

If Bob Dylan had recovered country for the mainstream rock scene, southern boogie returned rock 'n' roll to the soil.

The success of country rock paralleled that of its pop/country variants. Glen Campbell and John Denver were the biggest beneficiaries of this trend. Campbell parlayed such songs as "Wichita Lineman" and "Galveston" into major pop stardom in the late 1960s. Between 1968 and 1978, he tallied eleven gold albums, which brought him his own television program. Denver scored fifteen Top Forty albums and placed thirty-two singles in the Hot 100 between 1971 and 1982. A number of his biggest singles—"Take Me Home, Country Roads," "Rocky Mountain High," "Thank God I'm a Country Boy," and "Sunshine on My Shoulders"—suggested country themes, which his jeans-and-flannel image reinforced. Other artists cashed in as well. Canadian Anne Murray placed "Snowbird" in the pop and country Top Ten in 1970, kicking off an eleven-year run as a hitmaker.

As rock artists made a move toward country, a number of country artists were drawn to rock. At the centre of this movement were a number of country artists who sought to challenge the conservative hegemony of Nashville. For their insolence, they came to be known collectively as "the outlaws." They wore the label proudly and marketed it to their advantage and RCA's. In 1976, the company released *Wanted: The Outlaws,* a compilation LP with songs by Willie Nelson, Waylon Jennings, Tompall Glaser, and Jessi Colter. The album became the first certified platinum country album.

Nelson and Jennings were the most famous of the so-called outlaws. By the time he began to tire of Nashville's slickness in the mid-1960s, Nelson had toed the country mark for over a decade. He had achieved great success as both a writer—he wrote "Crazy," Patsy Cline's biggest hit—and a performer. Before the 1960s ended, he had more than a dozen albums to his credit. It was when he moved back to Texas in the early 1970s that he began to change his image, growing his hair long and discarding his western suits and ties in favour of jeans and T-shirts. His new look suited both his laid-back, conversational singing style and his refusal to be pigeonholed for commercial reasons. He first came to the attention of the rock press with *Shotgun Willie* and *Phases and Stages,* which he recorded in the early 1970s. He crossed over to the pop market with *Red Headed Stranger* in 1975, his first of more than thirty albums to make the pop charts. In 1978, he recorded his best-selling album of the decade, *Waylon and Willie.*

Waylon Jennings' country roots had first led him toward rock in 1958 when he joined Buddy Holly on bass. In fact, it was Jennings who gave up his seat to the Big Bopper on the flight that killed him, Holly, and Ritchie Valens. Although RCA's Chet Atkins had tried to fashion Jennings in the mould of a respectable country singer, it was his tough rockabilly past that defined the character he portrayed in the film *Nashville Rebel* in 1966. Throughout the sixties, Jennings fought hard for artistic freedom; his influences ran as far afield as Dylan and the Beatles. He even had a minor hit with "MacArthur Park" with the Kimberleys in 1969. Jennings, like Nelson and the rest of the outlaws, resisted easy categorization and musical limitations, but he was always respectful of his roots. "The ultimate irony of the Outlaws," Bill Malone has said, "may be that, while drawing upon a diverse array of musical sources and reaching out to new audiences, they did more to preserve a distinct identity for country music than most of their contemporaries who wore the 'country' label."[76]

Malone's comment was directed at artists like Kenny Rogers and Dolly Parton, who achieved incredible mainstream success with material that hugged the middle of the pop/country road. Emmylou Harris took a different route. Harris was a truly eclectic performer who managed to stay grounded in tradition even as she explored rock-based material with her versatile (and aptly named) Hot Band. While the group was adept at playing traditional acoustic country, their electric numbers were bold enough to be linked with a more extreme development in country-identified rock, which came to be known as redneck rock or, more politely, southern boogie.

Little distinguishes southern boogie bands—the Allman Brothers, the Marshall Tucker Band, Lynyrd Skynyrd, the Charlie Daniels Band, Molly Hatchett, and ZZ Top—from hard rock bands other than a truculent identification with the South. Like other hard rock bands, these groups were based in blues and country, their music was loud and sometimes crude, and they exhibited the same macho posturing, albeit with a bit of "good ole boy" flair. However, at a time when much of rock had become a pale imitation of its former self, these bands, even with their reactionary tendencies, sounded refreshing. If Dylan had recovered country for the mainstream rock scene, southern boogie returned rock 'n' roll to the soil.

The prototypical southern boogie band was the Allman Brothers, which featured brothers Duane and Greg Allman on guitar and keyboards, Dickie Betts on guitar, Berry Oakley on bass, and Jai Johanny "Jaimo" Johanson and Butch Trucks on drums. Duane had been a session player at Fame Studios in Muscle Shoals, backing artists such as Aretha Franklin and Wilson Pickett. He was also the second lilting lead guitar on Eric Clapton's *Layla.* At their best, the Allmans were a tight, disciplined unit with intricate instrumental harmonies over a strong percussive base. The group first came to the attention of the national audience with *Idlewild South* (1970). *Eat a Peach* (1972) was the band's first Top Ten album and contains Duane's last recordings. (Duane was killed in a motorcycle accident before the album was completed; a year later, Berry Oakley died in a similar accident.) The band continued after Duane's death, recording their best-selling album *Brothers and Sisters,* which hit number one on the album charts and yielded the number two hit single "Ramblin' Man" in 1973. That same year, along with two other acts—the Band and the Grateful Dead—the group headlined a single show at Watkins Glen, New York, that attracted some 600,000 fans, dwarfing even Woodstock in audience size. Although commercial success continued unabated throughout the decade, greatness, that very elusive quality, remained out of reach for the group after the loss of Duane.

The Marshall Tucker Band, which took its name from the owner of the band's rehearsal space, was softer and more laid-back than the other southern boogie bands but still in the

Heavy metal represented an absolute rejection of the peace and love ethos. It was the critics' worst nightmare: hard rock taken to the extreme, with no socially redeeming features—or so it seemed.

The Allman Brothers were the prototypical southern boogie band. Except for its identification with the South, there was little that separated southern boogie from hard rock in general. The Allmans' signature sound included rhythm and blues influences and intricate instrumental harmonies.

mould of country rock. Like the Allmans, the group was signed to Phil Walden's Capricorn label. Guitarist Toy Caldwell's playing was often compared to that of the Allmans' Dickie Betts. The group toured with the Allmans, and along with other Capricorn acts, did benefits for Jimmy Carter. The Tucker Band was respectable enough to be rewarded with gigs at the White House after Carter's victory, but other southern rockers lived life closer to the edge.

Lynyrd Skynyrd, a phonetical spelling of the name of the high-school gym teacher who suspended the group for wearing long hair, were fiercely proud to be southern. The band's first two albums—arguably their best—were produced by Al Kooper. The first contained "Freebird," a ten-minute tribute to Duane Allman, that became something of a signature song for the group. The second had the group's best-selling single, "Sweet Home Alabama," an explicit defence of the southern way of life in response to Neil Young's "Southern Man." If southern rock had an ideological component, this was it. (It would pop up again in Charlie Daniels' "The South's Gonna Do It Again.") With four gold and four platinum albums by 1980, Lynyrd Skynyrd found a ready audience, if not critical praise, for their music, which was as wild and rowdy as their personal lives. The beginning of the end for the group came in 1977 when a plane crash claimed the lives of lead singer Ronnie Van Zant and band members Steve and Cassie Gaines. The band's natural successor was Molly Hatchett, a group that first entered the Top Twenty in 1979 with the platinum-selling *Flirtin' with Disaster.*

ZZ Top was a Texas-based trio that took southern rock into the 1980s. Their influences ranged from acid rock to the down-home blues of John Lee Hooker and Elmore James. Album titles like *Tres Hombres, Fandango!, Tejas, Deguello,* and *El Loco* suggested a Tex-Mex cultural location. They had flirted with heavy metal as early as 1975, when they included the metal classic "Tush" on *Fandango!* In the 1980s, when the trio adopted their anonymous bearded look, they attempted a more conscious blues-based metal/pop fusion. When all was said and done, the southern rockers could be distinguished from their hard rock contemporaries only by geography and, in some cases, personal appearance.

Mad with Power: Heavy Metal

Depending on one's perspective, the softer rock and soul styles of the 1970s represented either a withdrawal from the political engagement of the 1960s, a reevaluation of its efficacy, a foregrounding of music as entertainment, or a new strategy for making the world a better place. In contrast, heavy metal represented an absolute rejection of the peace and love ethos. The music was too intense to be regarded as entertainment, and it was too self-absorbed to worry about making the world a better place. It was the critics' worst nightmare: hard rock taken to the extreme, with no socially redeeming features. Or so it seemed.

The origins of the genre's name can be traced to a number of sources. It is used in chemistry to describe the heavier elements in the periodic table. In literature, the term has been ascribed incorrectly to the William Burroughs novel *Naked Lunch* and correctly to the later novel *Nova Express.* Most agree that its first appearance in popular music occurred in the line "heavy metal thunder" from Toronto group Steppenwolf's "Born to Be Wild" (1968), a Top Ten single that became a biker anthem after it was featured in the film *Easy Rider.* In rock journalism, the term is usually credited to the incomparable Lester Bangs, one of the few critics who would touch the music with a less than ten-foot pole.

By the time heavy metal coalesced into a genre in the early 1970s, it had developed several distinctive elements. Chief among these was sound quality: "The essential sonic element in heavy metal is power, expressed as sheer volume," Deena Weinstein has claimed.[77] "If there is one feature that underpins the coherence of heavy metal as a genre," Robert Walser has noted, "it is the power chord" (a chord that is strummed at deafening volume and held to maximum sustain).[78] The power of heavy metal was intended to overwhelm its listeners, to flood them in a kind of sonic tidal wave. Heavy metal was not a violent break from hard rock; rather, it was a logical extension of hard rock with sufficient variation to defy its detractors' simplistic characterization of it as a wall of noise.

According to Weinstein, the origins of heavy metal lie in blues-based rock and psychedelic music.[79] Walser concurs with Weinstein's analysis but adds classical music to the list of sources.[80] Thus, heavy metal bears the influences of Muddy Waters, Howlin' Wolf, B. B. King, and Chuck Berry at one extreme, and Bach, Beethoven, Mozart, and Vivaldi at the other. As always, genre boundaries are a matter of subjective judgment at the fringes. Black Oak Arkansas occupied the territory between metal and southern boogie. The J. Geils Band played hard blues-based rock, but their Boston contemporaries, Aerosmith, moved into heavy metal. The Canadian band Bachman-Turner Overdrive, which was formed after guitarist Randy Bachman left the Guess Who ("These Eyes," "American Woman"), pushed boogie to the limit on "Takin'

Care of Business" and unleashed Who-like power chords on "You Ain't Seen Nothin' Yet," but with jazz-based guitar on songs such as "Lookin' Out for #1," fell just short of metal in the eyes of most observers. According to Walser, "The sound that would become known as heavy metal was definitively codified in 1970 with the release of *Led Zeppelin II,* Black Sabbath's *Paranoid,* and *Deep Purple in Rock.*"[81] The ascension of these three pivotal bands illustrates the diversity of sources that produced the genre.

Metal's immediate acid and blues rock antecedents are what one might expect. From Eric Clapton and Jeff Beck to Jimmy Page, the lead guitarists who fronted the Yardbirds marked the path. Clapton and Beck had always been blues aficionados. Beck enhanced blues licks with a daring use of distortion. As a founding member of Cream, Clapton overlaid his taste in blues with the psychedelic experience. Cuts like "Sunshine of Your Love" began to pull together the elements that define heavy metal: pounding bass and drums, blaring guitar, and screeching vocals. Hendrix was a parallel acid/blues influence who added incredible virtuosity to deafening sonic distortion. A number of groups in North America, including Blue Cheer ("Summertime Blues," 1968) and Steppenwolf ("Magic Carpet Ride," "Rock Me Baby," "The Pusher," "Born to Be Wild") also pushed the boundaries of volume and distortion. In metal, these elements were fueled by power chords, which were already evident in the music of the Kinks and the Who. These were the influences that guided Jimmy Page when he sought to extend the work of the Yardbirds in a new configuration.

For American audiences in particular, Led Zeppelin—Jimmy Page (guitar), Robert Plant (vocals), John Paul Jones (bass), and John Bonham (drums)—became the archetypal heavy metal group. Initially billed as the New Yardbirds, Led Zeppelin (reportedly, the Who's immodest drummer Keith Moon quipped that the group's music would go over like a "lead zeppelin," thus the name) filled the void for fans looking for a new intensity in rock. From the release of the group's first self-titled album in 1969, the band was a hit. Each of the eight subsequent albums released before the end of the 1970s rose to number one or two on the pop charts. Aided by the business acumen of manager Peter Grant, the group set concert attendance records all over the United States. They were, however, ignored by the rock press. "[A]cclaim," Plant once said, "always came from the street, never from the written critique."[82]

Black Sabbath followed a similar heavy metal road and enjoyed an equally poor relationship with the press. The group started as Earth, a working-class, hippie blues rock band from Birmingham, England. They changed their name to Black Sabbath after writing a song with that title, which was taken from an old Boris Karloff horror movie. The name change coincided with a move to a louder, more aggressive style and something of a break with the group's hippie past. In their new incarnation, the group paralleled Zeppelin's success and had five platinum albums in a row in less than four years, peaking with *Master of Reality* in 1971. For this feat, they were charged with a "complete lack of subtlety, intelligence, and originality."[83] Continued *Los Angeles Times* critic John Mendelsohn, "Black Sabbath's . . . new songs are as indistinguishable from its old songs as its old songs are from one another."[84]

As in the 1950s, complaints that the music was too loud, that you couldn't hear the words, that it all sounded the same, overlooked the considerable variation in the music itself.

While Black Sabbath may have been as good a target as any for such condemnation, this type of blanket dismissal was reminiscent of the things parents and critics had said about rock 'n' roll when it first emerged. Complaints that the music was too loud, that you couldn't hear the words, that it all sounded the same, sounded like the 1950s and overlooked considerable variation in the music itself. Led Zeppelin, for instance, was influenced by everything from U.S. soul music to Celtic mysticism. Zeppelin's first album ran the gamut from sluggish blues to ethereal ballads. Page even played pedal steel on "Your Time Is Gonna Come." *Led Zeppelin III* (1970) balanced the hard rock riffing on cuts like "Immigrant Song" with a whole side of largely acoustic music. On "Gallows Pole," for example, Page played banjo. A folkish influence continued on the group's fourth album, which featured "The Battle of Evermore," a vocal duet between Plant and folk rocker Sandy Denny, for which Page used a mandolin. *Led Zeppelin IV* (1971) also included the group's seminal "Stairway to Heaven," which builds from an acoustic intro to a blistering climax with Plant's piercing tenor soaring over Page's deafening salvo of raw guitar licks.

Deep Purple had an even broader range of influences as well as a strong psychedelic bent and the beginnings of that conscious incorporation of classical virtuosity that would become increasingly important to the genre. The group first hit the Top Ten with "Hush" in 1968. The use of an organ gave the group a fuller sound than most of their contemporaries and landed them at first in the company of groups like Vanilla Fudge, who described their music as "psychedelic symphonic rock," and Iron Butterfly. Vanilla Fudge interpreted songs like the Supremes' "You Keep Me Hanging On" and the Beatles' "Eleanor Rigby" as if they were being played at a speed slower than most turntables could go, thereby creating in listeners the feeling of a drug-induced effect. Working in a similar way, Iron Butterfly parlayed the droning seventeen-minute "In-A-Gadda-Da-Vida" from their debut album of the same name into Atlantic's best-selling record. Deep Purple evidenced a similar psychedelic connection on *The Book of Taliesyn*. Music from this album was used in the science-fiction drama *2001: A Space Odyssey,* the ultimate filmic acid trip. Classical influences also became evident in Deep Purple's music early on.

For many Americans, Led Zeppelin defined heavy metal. Despite a broad range of influences, however, they were not accepted in art rock circles. Instead, they were trashed from the left for their sexism and condemned by the right for their fascination with the occult.

Both guitarist Ritchie Blackmore and organist Jon Lord had studied classical music in their youth. The critical and financial success of Lord's *Concerto for Group and Orchestra* (1970) suggested that the group would follow the trajectory of an art rock ensemble, but Blackmore balked, feeling "that the whole orchestra thing was a bit tame. I mean, you're playing in the Royal Albert Hall, and the audience sits there with folded arms, and you're standing there playing next to a violinist who holds his ears every time you take a solo. It doesn't make you feel particularly inspired."[85] Blackmore clearly felt put off by the ambiance of the concert hall; he wanted to make use of classical resources but in the context of heavy metal.

Blackmore's guitar playing became a hallmark of the precision and virtuosity that defined the next generation of metal guitarists. It shows up clearly on *Machine Head* (1972), Deep Purple's best-selling album, which includes the group's best-known single, "Smoke on the Water." In a direct reference to the classical sources the group drew on in the album, Blackmore described the chord pattern for his solo on "Highway Star" as "a Bach progression." After he left Deep Purple to form Rainbow, the liner notes for Rainbow's first LP included the credit: "Inspiration: J. S. Bach." These classical influences would continue. As Robert Walser has pointed out, "A few years later Blackmore even took up study of the cello, and Rainbow's 1981 release featured a very direct use of classical music in its title cut, 'Difficult to Cure,' an instrumental built around the 'Ode to Joy' from the last movement of Beethoven's *Ninth Symphony*."[86]

By the mid-1970s, there was a whole generation of heavy metal acts that wore the label proudly; they had found their way into the genre through the paths that their predecessors had followed. Some came from psychedelia. When Judas Priest released *Rocka Rolla* in 1974, they were a hard acid rock band. By the time they released *Sad Wings of Destiny* one year later, however, they were squarely in the heavy metal camp. Uriah Heep took a similar road. Ted Nugent made a more gradual break from his psychedelic past as the leader of the Amboy Dukes to a solo career that reached a heavy metal peak with the release of *Cat Scratch Fever* in 1977. Some acts came from blues-based rock. When Aerosmith was first signed by Columbia in 1972, the group was considered Boston's answer to the Rolling Stones. Lead singer Steven Tyler even looked (and pranced) a bit like Mick Jagger. By the time *Toys in the Attic* made the Top Forty in 1975, the group had begun edging toward the lighter side of heavy metal, a niche that they then occupied successfully throughout the 1980s. Humble Pie, a blues-based rock ensemble aimed at younger fans, was beginning to move toward metal when guitarist Peter Frampton left to become a solo superstar. The James Gang from Cleveland had been aiming at metal with more eclectic influences when guitarist Joe Walsh left for a stint with the Eagles and his own solo career. Bad Company, a group under the tutelage of Zeppelin's manager, Peter Grant, played predictable heavy blues-based rock. Although they could emulate Zeppelin's stance on cuts like "Can't Get Enough" and "Ready for Love," they could not match their talent or success.

Categorizing the Toronto power trio Rush is even more problematic. While the group's roots clearly are in the heavy rock, proto-metal camp, by the mid-1970s guitarist Alex Lifeson, bassist/vocalist Geddy Lee, and drummer Neal Peart had developed a style of writing and playing that was as complex and virtuosic as any self-styled progressive band. Not only was the group's music exceedingly progressive, but Peart wrote intellectually oriented lyrics that drew upon the writings of libertarian Ayn Rand.

"Smoke on the Water"

Artist: Deep Purple

Music / Lyrics by Ritchie Blackmore, Ian Gillan, Roger Glover, Jon Lord, and Ian Paice

Label: Warner Bros (1972), from the LP *Machine Head*

If you were between the ages of 13 and 20 in 1972, and you had an electric guitar, you learned the opening riff of "Smoke on the Water." This compelling, repetitive, distortion-soaked guitar riff is one of the hallmarks of hard rock and heavy metal, and aspiring young electric guitar players in the 1970s honed their craft by learning it. Thanks to the success of this song, Deep Purple is included in most discussions of "proto-metal," but this classification doesn't really give the big picture of their complex stylistic background.

At the end of the 1960s and the beginning of the 1970s, the lines between "heavy metal" and "hard rock" were not clearly defined. To add confusion to the issue, many proto–heavy metal bands shared certain elements with "art" or "progressive" rock bands: complicated musical structures, orchestral electronic effects, and an obsession with technical virtuosity. Deep Purple navigated several of these channels. After experimenting with blues and art-rock, the band regrouped in the early 1970s with a new bassist and vocalist, and the new band (Ritchie Blackmore, guitar; Jon Lord, keyboards; Ian Paice, drums; Roger Glover, bass; and Ian Gillan, vocals) had a somewhat "harder" rock sound, even though they never completely let go of their classical leanings.

Musical Style Notes

The famous opening guitar riff of "Smoke on the Water" has all the hallmarks of a blues "lick": the movement from the keynote to the lowered third note of the scale, the flatted fifth note of the scale sliding back down to the fourth, and the use of rhythmic syncopation (see for example the second bar, where the first note appears on the "and" between the first and second beats).

Beat:	1 + 2 + 3 + 4 +	1 + 2 + 3 + 4 +	1 + 2 + 3 + 4 +	1 + 2 + 3 + 4 +
Scale Degree	1 ♭3 4 1	♭3 ♭5 4	1 ♭3 4 ♭3	1 1
Actual Note	G B♭ C G	B♭ D♭ C	G B♭ C B♭	G G

Note: "♭3" indicates the flattened third step of the scale.

When the rhythm section enters, however, we know it's rock and roll just from the driving rhythmic pattern. Listen for the bass player's relentless repeated tonic note (tonic being "do," the first note in a major or minor scale).

Ian Gillan's vocal sound is strongly associated with hard rock and heavy metal—a high tenor sound with a certain amount of raspiness—and is a perfect complement to the distorted guitar tone, accomplished by raising the volume to a level in excess of what the amplifier can handle ("overdriving" the amp), resulting in a gritty sound.

"Smoke on the Water" is also a good example of instrumentation built up in layers, a technique used by a number of art rock and heavy metal bands. (Led Zeppelin's "Stairway to Heaven" is another very famous example.)

Musical "Road Map"

TIMINGS	COMMENTS	LYRICS
0:00–0:18	Begins with the famous distorted guitar riff, henceforth referred to as the "SOTW riff."	
0:18–0:27	Another guitar track is layered in, with high-hat cymbal.	
0:27–0:35	Drum adds backbeat to texture (drum strike on second and fourth beats of each bar).	
0:35–0:52	Bass layered in, playing steady "eighth notes" (one-and-two-and-three-and-four-and)	
0:52–1:26	Verse 1	*Well, we all came out to Montreux . . .*
1:26–1:55	Refrain, "Smooooke on the waaaa-ter," followed by SOTW riff, twice	*Smoke on the water . . .*
1:55–2:29	Verse 2	*They burned down the gambling house . . .*
2:29–2:58	Refrain, "Smooooke on the waaaa-ter," followed by SOTW riff, twice	*Smoke on the water . . .*
2:58–3:39 3:39–3:56	Ritchie Blackmore guitar solo over the structural form of the verse Solo ends over the SOTW riff.	
3:56–4:29	Verse 3	*We ended up at the Grand Hotel . . .*
4:29–5:39	Refrain, "Smooooke on the waaaa-ter," followed by SOTW riff, four times; music fades as guitar begins to solo.	*Smoke on the water . . .*

One of the most successful bands in rock 'n' roll history, Canadian power trio Rush have carved a singular path at various points in their career embracing prog rock, heavy metal, reggae, and power pop.

Formed in 1968 as a four-piece group playing covers of songs by British hard rock groups such as Cream and Led Zeppelin, Rush recorded its debut album as a three-piece in early 1974 for their own Moon Records. Shortly after the album was issued, original drummer John Rutsey left because of health issues and was replaced by St. Catharines, Ontario, native Neal Peart. In 1977, their management team of Ray Daniels and Vic Wilson formed Anthem Records. In addition to Rush, Anthem's roster included Max Webster, Beatles tribute group Liverpool, and A Foot in Cold Water. Over the years, Rush has won many Juno Awards, including the 1975 Juno for Best New Band and the inaugural Juno for Best Hard Rock/Metal album for *Presto* in 1991. In the course of their forty-year career, Rush has continued to evolve. With their *Permanent Waves* album in 1980 the group began to explore aspects of reggae and new wave. The result was a Top Five album on the *Billboard* charts. In the early 1990s, beginning with *Roll the Bones,* hip hop and funk influences began to work their way into the band. On 1996's *Test for Echo,* Peart began exploring jazz grooves. One of the biggest groups in rock 'n' roll history, Rush has sold well over 40 million albums worldwide.

In the classical realm, there was one guitarist in particular who followed in Ritchie Blackmore's footsteps and rewrote the book on virtuosity and sophistication, thus helping to usher in the new wave of heavy metal guitarists that dominated the 1980s: Eddie Van Halen.

Just as it is important to recognize the range of influences that heavy metal drew on, it is important to recognize that these influences were utilized in the service of the blustering, sexist, hard-rock scene that provided its context.

Van Halen and his drummer brother, Alex, were born in the Netherlands but raised in California, where they were trained to become classical musicians until the lure of rock won out. With Michael Anthony on bass and David Lee Roth on vocals, Van Halen was a high-energy act right from the beginning. After the group was signed by Warner in the late 1970s, their debut LP, *Van Halen* (1978), made the Top Twenty. Every subsequent album charted higher than the one before until the group hit number one in 1985. While Van Halen owed its early success partially to Roth's athletic, overtly sexual (some would say sexist) performances, the group's defining and sustaining force was Eddie Van Halen's pathbreaking guitar style.

Like many of his contemporaries, Van Halen was drawn to hard rock through the blues. It was the combination of the emotionality of the blues feel, the aggressiveness of hard rock, the discipline of his classical training, and his sophisticated knowledge of music theory that enabled him to propel metal guitar playing to new heights. According to Walser, Van Halen's solo on the appropriately titled "Eruption," from the group's debut album, heralded the arrival of the new virtuosity in heavy metal. Walser describes the solo as "one minute and twenty-seven seconds of exuberant and playful virtuosity, a violinist's precise and showy technique inflected by the vocal rhetoric of the blues and rock and roll irreverence. Here and elsewhere, Van Halen's guitar playing displays an unprecedented fluidity."[87] As a result, *Guitar Player* magazine chose Van Halen as the best rock guitarist for five years in a row.

Just as it is important to recognize the range of influences that heavy metal drew on, it is important to recognize that these influences were utilized in the service of the blustering, sexist, hard rock scene that provided its context. Perhaps the best example is Zeppelin's rip-off of Willie Dixon's "You Need Love," "Whole Lotta Love," which appeared on *Led Zeppelin II.* While the thundering rhythm underpinning Plant's insistent, shrieking vocals and Page's chugging guitar and buzzsaw fills laid out the parameters of classic metal, the song itself illustrates why most critics were so antagonistic to the music. "I have felt over the past year and a half a steadily increasing disaffection with rock's male chauvinism," wrote Robert Christgau shortly after the song's release. "I am acutely uncomfortable with songs of cock-pride (Led Zeppelin's "Whole Lotta Love," for instance)."[88] For a number of groups (and critics), Plant's macho posturing and Page's phallic guitar thrusts defined heavy metal.

There was only one North American band that could rival Led Zeppelin in its unique combination of macho swagger, commercial success, and critical disdain: Grand Funk Railroad, a group that began in Flint, Michigan. Grand Funk played raw, basic rock that was not terribly distinctive and, as often as not, out of tune. There were dozens of antecedents for their brand of rock, and they added little to the corpus of this music other than a few tunes by guitarist Mark Farner. The fact that the group achieved any success at all is surprising; the fact that they became one of the top five rock bands in the world in their heyday is astounding. Grand Funk tallied eleven gold albums in a row—eight of them Top Ten—peaking with *We're an American Band* and a number one single of the same name in 1973. It is all the more incredible that the band achieved this status with virtually no radio play and an almost total lack of press coverage. The only possible explanation is that near-unanimous condemnation conferred on the group the ultimate in outsider status. This status was hyped to the fullest by the group's manager Terry Knight.

The lack of critical recognition for the heavy metal genre meant that most acts had to support their albums with grueling tours. These live shows tended to be ear-splitting spectacles of testosterone-drenched rock that aroused aggression more than sexuality. As a result, the audiences for metal concerts were predominantly young, white, working-class men, engaging in rites of male bonding with abandon. It was in the milieu of live performance that metal earned its nickname—cock rock. In the context of a burgeoning women's movement, it was a damning indictment, although in certain metal circles it probably would have been taken as a compliment. Heavy metal was a bastion of male dominance and privilege. There were no women in heavy metal. The only women who even came close to the genre were the Wilson sisters, Ann and Nancy, who rose to prominence as key members of Heart. Even though Heart's debut release, *Dreamboat Annie* (1976), pictured Ann and Nancy bare-shouldered on either side of a red heart, their combination of ballads and near–heavy metal rock propelled them past novelty status all the way to number seven on the pop charts. Subsequent hits like "Barracuda" confirmed the group's ability to rock with the best of them. In time, the group achieved a superstar status that carried them through the 1980s. In the 1970s, however, Heart was an anomaly.

If heavy metal was condemned, or more likely avoided in progressive circles for its sexism, it was assaulted from the right for its fascination with the occult. The title of *Led Zeppelin IV* appeared nowhere on the album's jacket, but one group of runes printed on the liner looked like it spelled Zoso, the name of the three-headed dog that guards the gates of hell. Armed with such evidence, fundamentalist groups accused Zeppelin of including satanic messages on "Stairway to Heaven" through backmasking, the process of recording passages backwards. Groups like Black Sabbath and Judas Priest (formed in 1974) attracted attention simply by virtue of their names. Album titles like *Sabbath Bloody Sabbath* and *Sin After Sin* only added fuel to the hellfire. Police agencies argued that Australia's AC/DC (also founded in 1974) stood for Anti-Christ/Devil's Children. Given metal's preoccupation with power, the more obvious reference to electric current might have been considered as equally likely to have inspired the acronym. In 1990, Zeppelin's Robert Plant chastised Americans for their inability to understand the British sense of irony and sarcasm. "There was . . . a lot of humor in the music," he explained in a retrospective interview. "Not all this glowering satanic crap. . . . It's very American. Nowhere else in the world has anybody ever considered it or been concerned or bothered at all about that."[89] Still, Black Sabbath's Ozzy Osbourne marketed the connection with satanism most effectively, particularly in his solo career in the 1980s, when the issue became even more volatile.

Faced with a widespread lack of industry support, if not outright hostility, metal came to wear its outsider status like a badge of honour; part of its mission was to fly in the face of respectability. Blue Öyster Cult, a New York metal group in the Black Sabbath mould, used occult-style lyrics written by critic Richard Meltzer, who was also a vocalist for the group. They also sought to capitalize on the disreputable character of the music by adding Nazi paraphernalia to their metal regalia. Even with such trappings, their biggest hit, "(Don't Fear) The Reaper," tended toward a pop sound, with sweet harmonies and just a hint of metal in the instrumental break. In the eyes of the critics, Rush made a more considered nod toward fascism with its recording of *2112,* which was based on right-wing novelist Ayn Rand's *Anthem,* even though a closer listen reveals a more complex theme. Subsequent recordings led the group into the realm of platinum-selling bands. Some groups, such as Blue Öyster Cult and Motörhead, added gratuitous umlauts to their names to conjure up a more generic gothic horror, a practice that continued into the 1980s with Mötley Crüe and others.

It was not just that the shows got harder and heavier or that strange animal rituals and awesome pyrotechnics were added; it was that heavy metal began to challenge the traditional concept of masculinity from within its exclusionary male environment. It was the last place one would have expected to find cracks in the facade of male sexuality.

Other heavy metal artists pushed the limits of decorum through performance and personal appearance. It was not just that the shows got harder and heavier or that strange animal rituals and awesome pyrotechnics were added; it was that heavy metal began to challenge the traditional concept of masculinity from within its exclusionary male environment. It was the last place one would have expected to find cracks in the facade of male sexuality. By the early 1970s, women and gays had become sufficiently vocal that gender roles and sexual preferences were no longer beyond question. While Mick Jagger had long played with androgyny, it was most unexpected to find the beginnings of gender-bending in that area of heavy metal that blossomed into glitter or glam rock. Among the weirdest acts was a group of white middle-class suburban athletes from Phoenix, Arizona, who named themselves after their leader, a minister's son who called himself Alice Cooper. Alice Cooper represented a clear break with the counter-culture. "Even hippies hated us," Alice has said, "and it's hard to get a hippie to hate anything."[90] They made no pretense to authenticity or blues roots. Television was their main influence. Musically the group was as subtle as a train wreck; they simply plastered their fans against the wall with noise. The group's big break came the night they cleared the posh club Cheetah after only three songs. Frank Zappa was sufficiently impressed that he signed them to his label, which then brought them to the attention of its parent, Warner.

By 1976, the group had brought out eight gold or platinum albums, including the number one *Billion Dollar Babies* (1973), and a few memorable hit singles like "Eighteen" (1971) and "School's Out" (1972). Still, Alice Cooper's importance to rock history has much more to do with their outrageous stage antics than their music. These antics, which included cutting the heads off baby dolls, were invariably embellished by the press. The boa constrictor that Alice performed with became the biggest snake in the world. When a chicken was trampled by the audience, it became, in the eyes of the press, Alice biting the heads off live chickens and drinking their blood. (There was a similar story about Ozzy Osbourne biting the head off a bat. The story simply fed the quest for evidence of Satanism.) Stranger yet, the group's members performed in spandex, high-heeled boots, and makeup. Forget that they looked about as feminine as Frank Sinatra; these guys wore makeup at a time when "real men"—especially a bunch of heterosexual ex-athletes from Phoenix—did not wear makeup. It was a perverse challenge to the security of fixed gender roles.

Kiss, a group that played metal as heavy as anyone with a posture that was just as macho, made makeup their trademark. As with Alice Cooper, the fact that Kiss racked up eight gold or platinum albums in the 1970s and were still going strong at the end of the following decade is less important to rock history than the image the group presented. Members of Kiss did not just apply cosmetics, they donned whole personas. Bassist Gene Simmons (the "tongue") became a

Kiss played metal as heavy as anyone and were eminently successful at it. Their equally heavy use of makeup suggested a connection to the ascending glam rock movement that challenged traditional gender roles as never before.

ghoulish monster; drummer Peter Criss, a cat; guitarists Paul Stanley and Ace Frehley, a clown and a spaceman. The group's gimmick of never being photographed without their makeup—to which they held fast until 1983—added measurably to their mystique.

All That Glitters Does Not Sell Gold

The success of Alice Cooper and Kiss proved that the limits of decorum and personal appearance could be pushed, and during the early 1970s, there was a short-lived movement in rock that pushed these limits over the edge. Glam, or glitter rock, challenged traditional notions of masculinity and femininity as no other music had. As Iain Chambers has written, "'Glam' or 'glitter' rock's inroads into the public figure of male sexuality, in which the chameleon figure of David Bowie was seminal, seemed to crack an image brittle with repression."[91] In the United States, the focal point for the developing glitter scene was New York's Mercer Art Center, where groups like the Forty-Second Street Harlots, the Miamis, Teenage Lust, and the transvestite Wayne County held forth. It was here that the New York Dolls became local favourites. The New York Dolls played a brand of rock that would have placed the group somewhere near the Rolling Stones on the popular music continuum, but the music was tinged with the kind of informed cynicism that could be bred only in New York. Mostly burned-out, working-class dropouts, the singers performed in full drag—high heels, tights, miniskirts, and bright red lipstick. Why they were surprised when people related to them as a "bunch of transsexual junkies or something" is baffling. Even with albums produced by Todd Rundgren (*New York Dolls*, 1973) and girl group veteran Shadow Morton (*Too Much Too Soon*, 1974), the Dolls never really got beyond cult status. Lead singer David Johansen did achieve some measure of pop success in the 1980s as Buster Poindexter.

The glitter scene in England was more developed, extending the music's reach to the rarefied atmosphere of art rock in one direction and teenybopper pop in another. When the tantalizing Marc Bolan shortened the name of his group from Tyrannosaurus Rex to T. Rex, he signaled a move to an electric hard rock style ("Bang a Gong [Get It On])," 1972) and brought the world of sequins and platform boots to teen fans. By the time of Bolan's death in 1977, many of his fans had switched their allegiance to The Sweet ("Little Willy," "Ballroom Blitz," "Fox on the Run," "Love Is Like Oxygen"). The portly Gary Glitter was another British star who excited teenagers with Elvis-style sequined costumes and lacklustre pounding rock. Alvin Stardust was similarly camp. Neither performer made a dent in the North American market.

The glam rocker who invested the music with its most lasting artistry and memorable theatrics was David Bowie. As Iain Chambers stated:

> His "feminine" pose and extravagant attire speak an indeterminate language, an androgynous code. But the narcissistic atmosphere this image invokes is in turn richly ambiguous. . . . Such a public display in self-fascination gestures towards the possibility of loosening the sexed male subject from previous, more predictable, moorings.[92]

Born David Jones, Bowie took his surname from the Bowie knife to avoid being confused with the Monkees' lead singer Davy Jones. When Bowie's early hard rock style failed to capture a substantial following, he turned his attention to creating new personas for himself, mindful that such brazen artificiality represented a break with the rock authenticity he had once embraced. Drawing on influences as diverse as mime, the Beat poets, Dylan, the bohemianism of Oscar Wilde, and Warhol's pop avant-gardism, Bowie pointed the way to the future.

No artist marketed sexual ambiguity more successfully than Bowie did. Originally included in his 1969 album *Man of Words, Man of Music,* "Space Oddity," which became his first Top Forty hit when reissued in 1973, established Bowie as an extraterrestrial, an outsider looking in. The original cover of his follow-up album, *The Man Who Sold the World* (1970), pictured the artist in drag, but it was withdrawn (at that point, it was ahead of its time) and a different cover was used. In addition to tributes to Dylan and Warhol, *Hunky Dory* (1972) contained "Changes" and "Oh! You Pretty Things," both of which celebrated the sexual subterfuge of glitter as a defining characteristic of the new counterculture and provided great copy for questions about Bowie's own preferences. His chiseled good looks, offset by orange hair and platform boots, presented a most androgynous package. By 1972, Bowie was more than ready to inhabit his alien alter ego, Ziggy Stardust. The tour supporting the release of *The Rise and Fall of Ziggy Stardust and the Spiders from Mars* was a lavish glam rock extravaganza. It was during this period that Bowie announced his bisexuality to the press. Never one to milk a persona for too long, he continued projecting sexual ambiguity through other protagonists on *Aladdin Sane* (1973) and *Diamond Dogs* (1974).

Credit for Bowie's marketing triumph was due, at least in part, to his manager, Tony De Fries, who was also the manager for Lou Reed, Iggy Pop and the Stooges, and Mott the Hoople. This network not only placed Bowie in a line that led directly to punk, but it also drew the other artists into the orbit of glam. *Aladdin Sane* included "Jean Genie," a tribute that linked Iggy Pop with Jean Genet. In 1972, Bowie produced Iggy Pop's *Raw Power,* as well as Lou Reed's *Transformer,* which included his only hit single, "Walk on the Wild Side," a darkly focused paean to sexual adventurism. That same year, Bowie produced Mott the Hoople's *All the Young Dudes,* the album that gave the group a new lease on life. The association with Bowie and the juxtaposition of the album's title cut with songs like "One of the Boys" and Lou Reed's "Sweet Jane" (about

> *When David Bowie's early hard rock style failed to capture a substantial following, he turned his attention to creating new personas for himself, mindful that such brazen artificiality represented a break with the rock authenticity he had once embraced.*

With his androgynous good looks and flair for ambiguity, David Bowie elevated sexual subterfuge to an art form and provided critics with a seemingly endless list of questions regarding his own sexuality.

a New York transvestite) located the straight (in all senses) rock group in the middle of the "trendy gayness" of glam. The group was appreciative of Bowie's input, even if somewhat confused by its effects.

If, in the construction of himself as an ever-changing media icon, Bowie took a lesson from Warhol's pop art manipulations, Bryan Ferry of Roxy Music was even more deliberate in his application of pop art principles. Ferry's early lyrics used "throwaway clichés and amusing phrases that you found in magazines or used in everyday speech—stylistic juxtapositions."[93] "Virginia Plain" (1972), the group's first hit single from their self-titled debut album, was a rambling pop narrative that took its title from a brand of cigarettes. As per the Warhol maxim that real art is commercial art, Ferry was also concerned with packaging, both of himself in the finest glam tradition and of his album covers. The cover for *For Your Pleasure* (1973) had seductive black satinlike surfaces. The cover for *Country Life,* the group's 1975 introduction to the American mainstream, originally pictured two scantily clad models.

Roxy Music's early sound resulted from the tension (musical and otherwise) between Ferry and Brian Eno. Armed with a Revox tape recorder, a VCS 3 synthesizer, and no musical training, Eno joined the group in 1971 as a "technical expert" rather than a musician. Eno's input moved the music in a direction that held sound and style to a higher value than musicianship per se. After leaving Roxy Music, Eno joined Bowie on a retreat to Berlin, where the two collaborated on three albums of avant-garde synthpop. By this time, Roxy Music had had its only Top Forty single in the United States, "Love Is the Drug" (1976), and glam was about to be stripped naked by punk, a development Eno had anticipated on his solo single "Seven Deadly Finns" in 1974.

Between his Ziggy Stardust period and his Berlin reclusiveness, Bowie went through a number of changes. In embracing the artificial, Bowie had led the way from hippie idealism toward the eruption of punk. In 1975, he took another unexpected turn, swapping "the sci-fi future" of his glam period "for the uniform of white soul boy."[94] After *Diamond Dogs* he decided to venture to Sigma Sound Studios in Philadelphia, the spiritual centre of soft soul. There he recorded *Young Americans,* an album that Peter York would later describe as "avant-garde disco."[95] The title cut became a hit, and "Fame" provided Bowie with his first number one American single. Lou Reed had anticipated the move in *Sally Can't Dance* in 1974, but Reed's outing was sandwiched between other experiments in heavy metal and white noise and no one noticed. It was Bowie who became the first white performer of note to straddle both punk and disco.

By the early 1970s, the established music industry had consolidated its hold over the rock and soul styles that grew out of the 1960s. In the fragmentation of popular music that ensued, audiences that might have overlapped in an earlier time were treated as discrete entities. This trend reached its zenith in the late 1970s in the emergence of punk and disco, genres whose audiences were viewed as mutually exclusive. Punk and disco were thus positioned as the two poles of pop that would define the extremes of a decade in which rock began to lose its status as outsider art.

Punk and Disco: The Poles of Pop

8

When the U.S. music business passed the $2 billion mark and the Canadian music industry passed the $100 million mark in the early 1970s, many assumed that sales would continue to climb indefinitely. When the U.S. industry doubled in size between 1973 and 1978 and surpassed $4 billion in annual sales in 1978 and the Canadian industry expanded by 150 percent in the same period, surpassing $250 million in 1978, years ahead of official growth projections, the assumption appeared correct. An era of mergers, it seemed, had consolidated the industry into a rationalized music machine. Industry marketing suggested that, with a generous expenditure of promotional dollars, sufficient exposure on radio, and a tour supporting his or her release, any proven artist could almost guarantee millions of dollars in return. It seemed to many that the rock 'n' roll rebellion that had begun in the 1950s was on the verge of being tamed. Popular music was becoming centrist, corporate, safe.

If popular music could be drawn as a bell curve, the centre of the curve would house a number of middle-of-the-road artists who borrowed soft rock styles for pop-sounding lounge acts. Beginning with "(They Long to Be) Close to You" in 1970, the Carpenters, for example, parlayed a clever combination of rock covers and originals into twenty Top Forty hits in just over a decade. Barry Manilow, who began as the piano accompanist in the gay bathhouse where Bette Midler got her start, produced twenty-five Top Forty singles and became one of the industry's biggest stars. At the height of his career, he had three albums in a row—*This One's for You* (1976), *Barry Manilow Live* (1977), and *Even Now* (1978)—that sold more than 3 million copies each. Neil Diamond topped both of them. Between 1970 and 1986, he scored thirty-six Top Forty singles and twenty gold and platinum albums. It is a telling commentary on the state of popular music in the 1970s that the most popular singles of the year between 1974 and 1976 were "The Way We Were" by Barbra Streisand, "Love Will Keep Us Together" by the Captain and Tennille, and "Silly Love Songs" by Paul McCartney and Wings.

The pop rockers of the time were only slightly more adventurous. The album that dominated the charts in 1976 was Peter Frampton's *Frampton Comes Alive!* As a member of Humble

> *It seemed to many that the rock 'n' roll rebellion that had begun in the 1950s was on the verge of being tamed. Popular music was becoming centrist, corporate, safe.*

Pie, Frampton had flirted with heavy metal; as a solo artist, he became a teen idol, more interested in melodic sweetness than volume. His first Top Thirty album, *Frampton* (1975), showcased the songs that would become his major hits ("Show Me the Way," "Baby, I Love Your Way," and "Do You Feel Like We Do") as melodic rockers with an acoustic feel. *Frampton Comes Alive!,* recorded live at the Winterland in San Francisco, made a nod toward his origins by including the same songs at hard rock volume. The LP charted for nearly two years, selling more than 10 million copies.

Fleetwood Mac was a more mature version of these same rock tendencies. With their roots in John Mayall's Bluesbreakers, Fleetwood Mac really gelled when Britons Mick Fleetwood and John and Christine McVie added the acoustic/electric guitar stylings and sweet harmonies of Americans Lindsay Buckingham and Stevie Nicks to the group. The self-titled debut album of the reconstituted Fleetwood Mac hit number one in 1975, but it was *Rumours* (1977) that earned the band a mythic place in rock lore. *Rumours* was a straight-ahead, upbeat pop rock album that hit number one and generated four hit singles, including the number one "Dreams." The album sold 10 million copies in the United States and 25 million worldwide. When the group's follow-up album, *Tusk,* sold 4 million copies, there was a tendency to preface the accomplishment with the word "only." But then, in the mid-1970s, the music industry was basking in sales figures like these. Between Frampton's and Fleetwood Mac's hits, the Eagles released *Hotel California,* selling 11 million copies. Also released in 1976, Stevie Wonder's *Songs in the Key of Life*, Linda Ronstadt's *Hasten Down the Wind*, Boz Scaggs' *Silk Degrees*, and Boston's *Boston* all sold more than 3 million copies. The platinum releases that same year by Bob Dylan, Chicago, the Doobie Brothers, the Rolling Stones, Kansas, Ted Nugent, Rush, Foghat, Rod Stewart, and Elton John seemed almost routine by comparison.

As a gay man, Elton John added a bit of spice to the mainstream. With his Presleyesque glitter tendencies and wild array of custom-made eyeglasses, he was something of the Liberace of rock. Well before *Blue Moves,* his first platinum album, he was a bona fide rock star with seven number one albums to his credit, five of them in a row. With his long-time collaborator, Bernie Taupin, he was also a prolific writer whose compositions captured the spirit of vintage rock 'n' roll with a sense of humour. Early standout hits like "Rocket Man," "Crocodile Rock," "Goodbye Yellow Brick Road," and "Bennie and the Jets" celebrated the entertainment value of a well-crafted song without succumbing to the self-importance of art rock. Throughout the late 1970s, John produced hit singles and platinum albums, always remaining a cut above the formula mentality of the time. He brought something of the flair and showmanship of glam into the mainstream during one of rock's most colourless periods.

There were a few other artists who also had something to offer in the way of rock artistry during this period. Billy Joel, a piano man like Elton John, was an intensely personal songwriter who was able to muster a bit of John's flamboyance in concert. Like Bruce Springsteen, Joel added a rock edge to the craft of the singer/songwriter, but he projected more of a mainstream image. On *The Stranger* (1977) and *52nd Street* (1978), which rose to numbers two and one, respectively, he explored cultural themes and created portraits of everyday life with drive and sophistication, laying the groundwork for a career that would carry him past the next decade.

Borrowing from jazz, r&b, and rock, Steely Dan introduced a level of instrumental sophistication that was rare in the mainstream market. Named after the dildo in William

Burroughs' *Naked Lunch,* Steely Dan was essentially a studio band founded by quirky writer/instrumentalists Walter Becker and Donald Fagan, who assembled different sidemen for various album projects. Although the group almost never toured, their fluid rhythms, cryptic lyrics, and exacting production generated sales. *Pretzel Logic* (1974), *Aja* (1977), and *Gaucho* (1980) all went Top Ten.

Montreal-born Gino Vanelli was also writing and producing sophisticated jazz-inflected pop. Wrapped in elaborate arrangements dominated by multiple synthesizers, hits such as "People Gotta Move" and "I Just Wanna Stop" were totally bereft of guitars. Vanelli's music challenged notions of pop and rock authenticity and hipness, and consequently Vanelli was never a favourite with the *Rolling Stone* wing of rock critics. Nonetheless, he managed to rack up ten *Billboard* pop hits, seven of which also charted Adult Contemporary and three of which crossed over to the r&b charts.

Aside from the occasional burst of creative energy offered by these artists, however, the centre of rock had begun to take itself and its audience for granted. Beginning in the mid-1970s and continuing well into the 1980s, American groups like Bob Seger and the Silver Bullet Band, Foghat, Styx, Foreigner, Journey, Air Supply, and REO Speedwagon and Canadian groups such as Prism, Triumph, Trooper, Saga, Loverboy, Honeymoon Suite, and Glass Tiger relied on tried-and-true music and business practices to produce guaranteed sales. It wasn't that their music was incompetent, it's that it was uninspired. It appeared that the mainstream music industry had become such a well-oiled music machine that, with precious little in the way of innovation and next to nothing approaching passion, any second-rate rock group could be assured of radio play, full stadiums, and platinum record sales. There were, however, other styles of music still in their formative stages that were positioned at the periphery of the cultural continuum. There were initially few suitable venues for them and they were well beyond the pale of radio play. At one extreme there was punk, at the other, disco. In different ways and for different reasons, they would shake rock out of its complacency, at least for a time.

It appeared that the mainstream music industry had become such a well-oiled music machine that, with precious little in the way of innovation and next to nothing approaching passion, any second-rate rock group could be assured of radio play, full stadiums, and platinum record sales.

Punk Versus Disco

There are, of course, a number of obvious distinctions between punk and disco. While disco was smooth, sleek, and sensual, punk was dense, discordant, and defiant. While disco depended on technological sophistication and studio production, punk's three chords could be hammered out by any garage band that could get its hands on an electric guitar. While disco dancers aspired to the controlled energy of the gymnast or the precision of group choreography, punks in the "pit" approximated the antics of a tag-team wrestling match. "[P]ogo dancing—jumping up and down and flailing one's arms," observed Charles M. Young, "is as far as one can get from the Hustle."[1] Disco proudly took its place among other black dance music styles. *Rolling Stone*'s Mikal Gilmore suggested that those "rock purists" who dismissed it as "a frivolous form of expression might do well to remember that rock & roll and rhythm & blues were dance styles, too, before they became art forms."[2] Punk, however, had a different agenda.

Punk's aim was to deconstruct rock 'n' roll, bleeding it of its black rhythmic influences until only the elements of noise and texture remained. Robert Christgau noted that punk "differentiates itself from its (fundamentally black and rural) sources by taking on the crude, ugly, perhaps brutal facts of the (white and urban) prevailing culture, rather than hiding behind its bland facade."[3] Needless to say, these differences were mirrored in fashion statements that pitted the sheen of polyester leisure suits against the chill of black leather bondage gear and ripped T-shirts held together by safety pins. Fans of each culture viewed each other with surprise. "It was funny," Legs McNeil, cofounder of *Punk* magazine, has said. "You'd see guys going out to a Punk club, passing black people going into a disco, and they'd be looking at each other, not with disgust, but 'Isn't it weird that they want to go there.' "[4]

Differences as obvious as these tend to obscure the fact that there were certain similarities between the punk and disco cultures. Both were initially shunned by radio (albeit for different reasons) and forced to develop their own countercultural networks. Both were seen as contributing significantly to the destruction of Western civilization—punk with its nihilism, disco with its decadence. Both encouraged active—indeed, fanatical—participation among their audiences. Finally, both arose in reaction to the complacency of the music that preceded them. Compare, for example, Andrew Kopkind on disco with Simon Frith on punk. "Disco in the '70s is in revolt against rock in the '60s," Kopkind explained. "Disco is 'unreal,' artificial, and exaggerated. It affirms the fantasies, gossip, frivolity, and fun of an evasive era."[5] Frith, describing the impetus for punk, told his readers that "the reason why teenage music must be *remade* is because all the original rock'n'rollers have become boring old farts, imprisoned by the routines of show biz. . . . I'd rather listen to a good punk rock'n'roll band like the Jam or the Boomtown Rats than to either the old or new work of their original models, the Who and the Stones. But I'm still listening for the old reason—to feel good."[6] The motivation and effect of both genres were quite the same—to intensify the feeling of the moment in an otherwise uncertain world.

Still, most critics at the time decried disco as escapist and embraced punk as a political statement. According to Frith, "The return to rock'n'roll roots is, in itself, a radical rejection of record company habits and punk's musical simplicity is a political statement. The ideology of the garage band is an attack on the star system."[7] Although disco spawned its own multibillion-dollar subindustry and punk barely registered a blip in sales, disco made no overt political statement. Herein lies the source of the distortion in the way in which the histories of punk and disco have been recounted. It was punk's political possibilities, real or imagined, that captured the attention of rock critics who had cut their teeth on the political movements of the 1960s. Never has so much been written by so many about so little. As Andrew Kopkind complained in 1979, "John Rockwell was still writing Hegelian analyses of the Sex Pistols in the Sunday *Times* when two-thirds of the city was listening to Donna Summer and couldn't tell Mr. Rotten from Mr. Respighi."[8]

Although disco was seldom intentionally political, in the long run it may have scored a larger political victory than punk. While a good deal of punk, particularly its British variant, was conceived politically, the conflict between its progressive urges and its flirtation with Nazi imagery often led to mixed results in its ability to pull people together. Disco, especially in the United States, brought people together across racial lines, not to mention lines of class and sexual preference. It was disco that, as critic Abe Peck has noted, enabled "black artists [to] conquer the pop charts in a way they never did even during the height of rhythm and blues."[9] In such a context, antidisco slogans like "Death to Disco" and "Disco Sucks" have to be regarded more as racial (and sexual) epithets than as statements of musical preference, and the systematic avoidance of disco by the rock critical establishment can be construed only as racist, as Mikal Gilmore suggested in 1977:

Anti-disco slogans like "Death to Disco" and "Disco Sucks" have to be regarded more as racial (and sexual) epithets than as statements of musical preference, and the systematic avoidance of disco by the rock critical establishment can be construed only as racist.

> *[W]henever a phenomenon is given blanket dismissal, you can be sure something deeper is at work. And what's going on here is that rock fans, like the proverbial cake, have been left out in the rain. Disco's principal constituents have been gays, blacks, Hispanics. . . . Then coincident with* Saturday Night Fever, *disco achieved anthem-like status with urban, working-class youth. So, in effect, disco had done what punk was supposed to accomplish. . . . rock pride was wounded. Somehow, an entire grassroots movement had passed us by: No wonder Clash fans cry, "Disco sucks!"*[10]

By the time the decade had ended, disco had swamped the music business, and punk had imploded. While disco would collapse shortly thereafter, punk would be born again as new wave, incorporating such a wide range of influences that it included disco itself.

Punk: Rock as (White) Noise

If the history of punk has been distorted in favour of its political impact, there has been a corresponding tendency to emphasize its British origins because its arrival in Britain coincided with right-wing advances and decaying social conditions that gave the music a more critical political edge. In the United States, where the Carter presidency offered a brief and ultimately fruitless respite from the preceding eight years (and subsequent twelve) of conservative government, punk was less disruptive and more easily incorporated into the star-making machinery of the music industry once it got off the ground. Thus, in putting punk's best political foot forward, critics usually look first to the Sex Pistols, a British group that caused a political furor in their home country even before releasing their first single in 1976. While political impact is certainly one valid measure of the importance of a cultural form, it may not be the best way to trace its origins. "It's the Before and After Sex Pistols debate," Caroline Coon wrote in *Melody Maker* in 1976. "'We saw Johnny Rotten and he CHANGED our attitude to music' (the Clash, Buzzcocks), or 'We played like this AGES before the Sex Pistols' (Slaughter and the Dogs), or 'We are miles better than the Sex Pistols' (the Damned)."[11] Comments like Coon's, which fail to mention a single U.S. or Canadian group, limit discussion to the development of British punk and consign even British groups like the modish Jam (formed in 1974) to the category of "1960s revivalists." While there was something of a rivalry between London and New York in the competition for the punk throne, the emergence of U.S. punk does, in fact, predate its British eruption by nearly two years. While the Sex Pistols may have set the standard

The Sex Pistols never registered on the Top Forty album or singles charts in the United States and broke up before completing their only U.S. tour. The fact of the group's celebrity reveals one of the most important features of punk: its myth was always more powerful than its reality.

in England, their debut album, *Never Mind the Bullocks,* never registered on the Top Forty album or singles charts in the United States, and the group broke up before completing their only U.S. tour. (Indeed, it was rare in the United States for a punk group to transcend cult status, much less to have a hit record.) The fact of the group's celebrity reveals one of the most important features of punk: its myth was always more powerful than its reality.

Central to the myth of the Sex Pistols is Malcolm McLaren, the group's manager. McLaren, who claimed he had managed the New York Dolls before returning to England to create the Sex Pistols, enjoyed picturing himself as a Machiavellian manipulator with a master plan to use the power of the music industry against itself, in the service of radical social change. In fact, he was never a committed activist. He was, however, fascinated by the 1968 student revolts in Paris (he even claimed to have been there) and intrigued by the tactics of the French situationists who created media-savvy situations as a way of transforming everyday life.

McLaren began as a sophisticated rag merchant with a keen eye for youth fashion. He and his partner, Vivienne Westwood, had a shop at 430 Kings Road. In its first incarnation, it was called Let It Rock, and it appealed to impeccably attired teddy boys. When that fad began to fade, McLaren and Westwood changed the name of the shop to Too Fast to Live, Too Young to Die and oriented its fashions toward leather-clad rockers. While in McLaren's myth he fashioned the Sex Pistols from nothing, in reality guitarist Steve Jones and drummer Paul Cook had already started the prototype group, the Strand (named after the Roxy Music song), before they began to frequent number 430. Bassist Glen Matlock joined later. It was Jones and Cook who went looking for McLaren to be their manager, not McLaren who went looking for them. Further complicating the picture was the addition of John Lydon (Johnny Rotten) as lead singer. Everyone knew that Lydon couldn't sing and had no sense of rhythm, but according to *Rolling Stone*'s Charles M. Young, he had three qualities to recommend him: "1) his face had the pallor of death; 2) he went around spitting on poseurs he passed on the street; and 3) he was the first to understand the democratic implications of punk."[12] While Lydon and McLaren would vie for control of the group until the end, at the time Lydon joined the group, McLaren and Westwood had reopened Too Fast to Live, Too Young to Die as a shop called Sex, hence the group's name, the Sex Pistols. At this point in their development, McLaren saw the group more as a vehicle for selling T-shirts and trousers than as point men in an anarchist revolt.

McLaren's claim that he managed the New York Dolls was equally distorted. He had met the Dolls' guitarist Sylvain Sylvain, who had been a clothing manufacturer, in 1973 when he visited New York to exhibit clothing from Let It Rock. Through Sylvain he met the rest of the group, which was then the toast of the underground. Having garnered the approval of the Dolls, McLaren was given the keys to the subterranean city: a room at the Chelsea Hotel, an invitation to meet Andy Warhol, and an interview in *Interview.* McLaren became completely obsessed with the Dolls, joining them on a tour of Europe later that year. It wasn't until the fall of 1974 that he revisited New York. By this time the group was in trouble. The Mercer Art Center had physically collapsed a year earlier, leaving the Dolls without their major venue; the group's second album had stalled at number 167 on the charts; drummer Billy Murcia had died of a drug overdose; guitarist Johnny Thunders and drummer Jerry Nolan had serious heroin habits; and bassist Arthur Kane was well along the way to becoming a complete alcoholic. Finally, Marty Thau, the group's manager, dropped them. It was at this point that McLaren entered the picture. As a friend, he did right by the group, finding hospitals and drug treatment programs for those who needed them. As a manager, a relationship that was never formalized, he simply orchestrated the Doll's last gasp. Drawing on his interest in radical politics, he dressed the group in red patent leather with hammer and sickle flags for a backdrop and sent the press a manifesto rather than an invitation to their upcoming shows. "Out went Glam, in came Communism," said historian Jon Savage.[13] By most accounts the band was tight, but with no substance to their posture their newest attempt at outrage had no beneficial effect. "You get beat up for being a fag," observed photographer Bob Gruen, "but you get killed for being a Commie."[14] Metaphorically speaking, this is exactly what happened to the Dolls, as their three-year run at celebrity abruptly came to a halt.

Born in the U.S.A.

During the descent of the Dolls, New York trash rock had gotten considerably more stripped down. As 1973 was crossing over into 1974, club owner Hilly Kristal was in the process of reopening his hangout for bikers and winos on the Bowery as a bar called Country Blue Grass and Blues (CBGB). Although Kristal expected country music to be the next big thing, Tom Verlaine and Richard Lloyd from the band Television convinced him to book underground rock acts. Within months, CBGB, the dingy Bowery bar, became the heart of the New York rock underground. Its only competition was Max's Kansas City. By the time McLaren returned to New York to preside over the Dolls' demise, Hilly Kristal was already playing host to Television and the scene that would yield Patti Smith, Blondie, the Ramones, and the Talking Heads.

One thing that the first wave of punk rockers on both sides of the ocean had in common was a sense of rock 'n' roll history that recognized the importance of the Velvet Underground and Iggy Pop and the Stooges. At the poles of the Velvet Underground's creative axis were Lou Reed and John Cale. The Brooklyn-born Reed appeared to be your average college student. His tastes in music ran from doo wop and rhythm and blues to jazz. After graduating from college, he even became an assembly-line songwriter at Pickwick Records for a while. In 1965, however, songs like "Heroin"

> *One thing that the first wave of punk rockers on both sides of the ocean had in common was a sense of rock 'n' roll history that recognized the importance of the Velvet Underground and Iggy Pop and the Stooges.*

needed a more unorthodox vehicle than Pickwick could provide. Cale had a degree in classical music; his tastes ran more to the avant-garde sounds of Stockhausen, John Cage, and La Monte Young. The buzzsaw sound of Cale's modified electric viola became part of the early Velvet trademark sound and an inspiration to a generation of punks. The group's sound was rounded out by Sterling Morrison, a classically trained guitarist, and female drummer Maureen Tucker.

The Velvets' repertoire, instrumentation, and avant-garde excursions into feedback and white noise were in place before their fabled association with Andy Warhol began, providing an early model for McLaren's Sex Pistols myth. Warhol provided the group with a slot at the Factory (his umbrella for diverse multimedia projects), which was undoubtedly the best offer a band with material like "Heroin," "Venus in Furs," and "Black Angel's Death Song" could get in 1966. His only direct intervention was to install the striking Hungarian-born blonde singer Nico in the band as a more visually appealing focal point than the deadpan Reed. The new lineup was captured on the group's debut album, *The Velvet Underground and Nico,* in 1967.

During this period, the group was incorporated into Warhol's touring multimedia show, the Exploding Plastic Inevitable.

Iggy Pop (born James Osterberg) was an uncultivated working-class kid from Ypsilanti, Michigan, who spent his high-school years playing in bands. It was at a performance of the Exploding Plastic Inevitable at the Ann Arbor Film Festival in 1966 that he was first exposed to the New York underground. His introduction to Warhol, affair with Nico, and subsequent induction into the art rock scene must have been interesting for all concerned. In 1968, Pop founded the Psychedelic Stooges (later shortened to just the Stooges) with the "unremittingly inept" Asheton brothers (Ron on guitar, Scott on drums). By this time he had already developed a style that, according to MC5 manager John Sinclair, "had gone beyond performance—to the point where it was really some kind of psychodrama."[15] The group's material seldom included songs in the conventional sense; instead they were unstructured ramblings with titles such as "The Dance of Romance," "Asthma Attack," "Goodbye Bozos," and "Search and Destroy," a selection with a somewhat discernible structure. Six months after the band was formed, the Stooges were signed to Elektra by a&r man Danny Fields. Fields had ventured to Detroit to sign the MC5, and at the group's urging, had caught the Stooges' stage act. He was blown away by the group's "saber-toothed fury." Two weeks later he returned with Elektra's president, Jac Holtzman, and signed both groups. From Elektra's point of view, Iggy Pop must have seemed like a logical next step in the progression from the Doors to the MC5. Iggy's choice of John Cale as producer of his group's first album created a direct link between the Stooges and the Velvet Underground. Shortly thereafter, Iggy was engaging in the acts of self-mutilation on stage (he once closed a New York date by making cuts in his chest with two drumsticks) that would earn him the title "Godfather of Punk."

By the end of the 1960s, the Velvet Underground had two more albums to their credit—*White Light/White Heat,* which included their classic seventeen-minute tale of horror "Sister Ray," and *The Velvet Underground*—and Elektra had issued the Stooges' self-titled debut album. There were, however, so few venues that would book either act that it was almost impossible to promote their releases. Thus, they were frequently ignored. Only *White Light/White Heat* managed to scrape into the Top 200. By the early 1970s, the Stooges had disbanded and, of the original Velvet Underground, only Sterling Morrison remained. Two years later, David Bowie convinced the Stooges to reunite, but they could never keep it together for very long. By the time CBGB took off, the Stooges and the Velvets had more value as historical referents than as current practitioners. Still, the new generation of underground rockers who came to dominate the scene recognized their influence.

Punk usually followed the maxim, Whatever is popular, do the opposite. If hippies wore bell-bottoms, punks would wear straight legs. If hippies ate brown rice and health food, punks would embrace fast-food, junk-food diets. If 1960s rock was inspired by psychedelic drugs (marijuana, LSD), punk's attitude and performance style would be defined by amphetamines (speed) on the way up and heroin coming down. If there was a politics to punk, it was the politics of refusal—the refusal to conform, the refusal to act with decorum, and in some cases, the refusal to learn how to play music. Aside from this fragile unity,

The most distinctive thing about the early New York punk groups was just how different they were from each other. Consider Patti Smith's spoken-word rock poetry and mannish attire against Blondie's breathy pop and lead-singer Deborah Harry's peroxide persona; the Ramones' bikers-on-speed sound and image against the preppiness of the Talking Heads.

the most distinctive thing about the early New York punk groups was just how different they were from each other. Consider, for example, Patti Smith's spoken-word rock poetry and mannish attire against Blondie's breathy pop and lead-singer Deborah Harry's peroxide persona; the Ramones' bikers-on-speed sound and image against the preppiness of the Talking Heads. The group that paved the way for all these opposites was Television.

Television, the first CBGB group to make a splash, was a ramshackle outfit that followed the Stooges' lead and pioneered the punk practice of learning on the gig. Although the group's guitarist, Tom Verlaine, cited John Coltrane and the free jazz of Albert Ayler among his influences and claimed that the Stones' "19th Nervous Breakdown" was his favourite rock 'n' roll song, an early review proclaimed that the group had "no musical or socially redeeming characteristics, and they know it."[16] At the time, this might have been taken as something of a backhanded compliment. Key to this endearing set of attributes was the presence of bass player Richard Meyers, a former poet, who took the name Richard Hell and lived up to it. Anticipating punk fashion, Hell supplied the look of Television—ripped T-shirts and close-cropped hair. The look was true to punk's maxim; it was as antiglam as it was antihippie. Hell also contributed the punk classic "Blank Generation"—an answer song of sorts to the Who's "My Generation"—to Television's early repertoire. While the song was taken as an early indicator of punk nihilism, Hell insisted that its message was misunderstood. "People misread what I meant by 'Blank Generation,'" he once told Clinton Heylin. "To me, 'blank' is a line where you can fill in anything. It's positive."[17] By the time Television had released its first independent single, "Little Johnny Jewel," tension between Verlaine and Hell had forced Hell out of the group. (Hell was also thrown out of his next group, the Heartbreakers.) It was not until 1977 that a reconstituted Television was able to follow "Johnny Jewel" with the album *Marquee Moon,* one of the more interesting artifacts of the era. That same year, Hell committed "Blank Generation" to vinyl on an album of the same name with his new group, The Voidoids. By this time, punk was being called *new wave.*

Patti Smith was the first artist associated with CBGB to become famous. Smith attended Pratt Institute, an art school in Brooklyn, in the late 1960s. There she met her first mentor, photographer Robert Mapplethorpe, and became acquainted with the New York scene when she and Mapplethorpe took up residence at the Chelsea Hotel, which was then frequented by Andy Warhol and William Burroughs, among others. While immersed in the Chelsea scene, she fell in love with playwright Sam Shepherd, with whom she wrote *Cowboy Mouth* early in 1971. By this time, Smith was becoming known as a poet and had a burgeoning career as a rock journalist, writing primarily for *Creem* and *Rolling Stone.* Smith had already begun performing her work, accompanied by Lenny Kaye, a well-known rock journalist, on electric guitar when *Creem* took the unorthodox step (for a rock paper) of publishing a portfolio of her poetry late in 1971. One more boyfriend (Allen Lanier, keyboardist for Blue Öyster Cult) and an extended sabbatical in Paris, where she visited Jim Morrison's grave, took her several steps further in her journey toward the fusion of poetry and rock 'n' roll. Upon her return from Paris, she opened for the New York Dolls during the final days of the Mercer Art Center. After its collapse, she and Kaye began appearing regularly as a duo. However, it was not until they added pianist Richard Sohl that they began to approximate the amalgam of free verse and improvisatory rock with which Smith would become identified. After attending a performance of Television at CBGB in the spring of 1974, the trio recorded their first single, "Piss Factory," which, with an assist from Tom Verlaine on lead guitar, was backed with "Hey Joe." "Piss Factory" was an autobiographical account of the horrors of working in a New Jersey plant. The meaning of "Hey Joe" was transformed by an introductory poem about Patty Hearst's exploits with the Symbionese Liberation Army, which had created an instant myth in 1974. By using an independent single to attract major label attention, Smith pioneered what would become the strategy of choice for punk groups from Television to the Sex Pistols. The release of the single coincided with Smith and Television sharing a memorable residency at Max's Kansas City. In the spring of 1975, this same double bill established CBGB as New York's premier rock club. It was around the time of the CBGB residency that the Patti Smith Group was signed to Arista. By the time *Horses* was released in 1976, the group had added Ivan Kral on bass and Jay Dee Daughterty on drums. The ubiquitous John Cale served as producer. *Horses* was not only the first punk album of note; it was one of the few ever to enter the Top Fifty. Smith, whose trademark of a man's white shirt and tie also suggested possible new roles for women, was well on the way to stardom when she fell off a ten-foot stage while promoting the group's second album, *Radio Ethiopia,* and broke her neck. *Easter* (1978), the album that marked her return, included the decidedly unpunk hit single "Because the Night," which was supplied by Bruce Springsteen.

While Television and Patti Smith were in residence at Max's in 1974, Blondie and the Ramones were making their debuts at CBGB. The Ramones were formed by a group of middle-class kids from Forest Hills, New Jersey. Jeff Hyman (Joey), John Cummings (Johnny), Doug Colvin (Dee Dee), and Tom Erdelyi (Tommy) each adopted Ramone (Paul McCartney's first pseudonym) as his *surnom de punk*. Unlike other punk groups, the Ramones played only original material. "We couldn't figure out how to play anybody else's songs," explained Johnny.[18] Stylistically, the group stripped rock 'n' roll naked with unadorned, rapid-fire guitar bursts, pneumatic drumming, and abrupt, minimalist lyrics. Lyrically, the group filled in the blank of Richard Hell's generation with a repertoire of refusal, including "I Don't Care," "I Don't Wanna Be Learned, I Don't Wanna Be Tamed," and "I Don't Wanna Go Down to the Basement." "We didn't write a positive song until 'Now I Wanna Sniff Some Glue,' " Dee Dee later quipped.[19] The group usually ran through a set with dizzying speed. Songs rarely lasted for more than two minutes and lyrics were seldom longer than eight lines.

Critical praise in the *SoHo Weekly, Rock Scene, Hit Parader,* and the *Village Voice* was not long in coming for the group. When London's *New Musical Express* did its first spread on the New York punk scene in 1975, the Ramones were the featured artists. It was the CBGB Festival of Unsigned Bands in the summer of 1975 that had prompted the spread. The festival also led

The Ramones played faster songs with shorter lyrics than anyone connected to the New York punk scene. Their rapid-fire delivery pointed the way for British punk.

Sire Records to sign the group, which became the second punk act after Patti Smith to secure a record contract. Seymour Stein of Sire played a pivotal role in developing punk, eventually signing not only the Ramones but also the Talking Heads, the Dead Boys, Richard Hell and the Voidoids, and the Pretenders.

The Ramones' eponymous debut album, released in 1976, delivered all the manic energy of the group's live performances. The album bombed in the United States, but in London it was the talk of the town, at least in part because there was no similar domestic product. When the Ramones went to London to promote the album, they played the Roundhouse, an auditorium-sized venue. Reportedly, Malcom McLaren was thrown bodily down a flight of stairs by the concert's promoter for asking if the Sex Pistols could be the opening act. In the race to lay claim to punk, New York was well ahead of London at this juncture.

Although the Ramones pointed the way for British bands, it was not until Rocket to Russia *(1978) that the group finally broke into the U.S. Top 100 LPs. By this time, British punk/new wave was in full swing, and London had overtaken New York as the cutting edge of the new trend.*

The Ramones' second album, *Leave Home* (1977), did even more poorly in the United States than their first, but it cracked the Top Fifty in Great Britain and yielded a hit single there, "Sheena Is a Punk Rocker." Although the Ramones, more than any other U.S. group, pointed the way for British bands, it was not until *Rocket to Russia* (1978) that the group finally

Higher, faster, louder, briefer—it's the Ramones!

The Ramones were at the same time the simplest and, one might say, the most abstract of punk bands. Recognizing their own musical limitations, they set out to recover the brevity, simplicity, and hammer-headed directness of earlier "punks" like Jerry Lee and Elvis. Though some thought they came across as complete knuckleheads, their musical style and ethos made great sense as a sly-yet-ferocious assault on bloated late 1970s art rock. Where art rock was deemed pretentious, the Ramones were defiantly modest. Where art rock sought symphonic breadth and staged extravaganzas, the Ramones kept everything short (their sets at New York's famed CBGB's club rarely exceeded a half-hour). Where art rock was ruled by banks of pedals and stacks of electronic keyboards, the Ramones kept it to the guitars, the chords, and the (bellowingly loud) amps. The Ramones' uncomplicated yet defiant lyrics are vaguely political yet not nearly as direct an affront as those sung by groups like the Sex Pistols or as consciously intellectual as punk poets like Patti Smith. Not by accident, the Ramones also borrowed the straightforward forms, repetitive melodies, and pounding four-on-the-floor rhythms of surf music.

"I Don't Wanna Be Learned, I Don't Wanna Be Tamed" was originally recorded as a demo and was included as a bonus track on Rhino's rerelease of the 1976 LP *The Ramones.*

Musical Style Notes

The structure of "I Don't Wanna Be Learned" couldn't be more straightforward: three twelve-bar sections, the second and third of which contain lyrics sung over the first eight bars, followed by the first four bars played instrumentally. The abrupt ending sounds sudden because the harmonic resolution to this point has been coming at the end of the twelve-bar form, and they never get there (but then, that's the whole point). The entire song lasts only one minute.

The sound characteristics—driving drum hits on every beat, loud and extremely distorted guitars, and unpolished vocals—are all typical of early punk rock, New York-style. The ersatz British accents on the other hand were a Ramones' specialty.

Musical "Road Map"

TIMINGS	COMMENTS	LYRICS
0:00–0:01	Countdown	*"One, two, three, four—"*
0:01–0:18	Introduction, instrumental, twelve bars	
0:18–0:34	Verse Same form as introduction Lyrics last eight bars, four-bar instrumental transition into next "verse"	*"And I don't wanna be learned* *And I don't wanna be tamed—"*
0:34–0:51	Verse Exactly the same as 0:18–0:34	*"And I don't wanna be learned* *And I don't wanna be tamed—"*
0:51–1:00	Instrumental, consisting of the eight-bar verse, but with no lyrics sung—song ends abruptly where the sung verse would have ended.	

broke into the U.S. Top 100 LPs. By this time British punk/new wave was in full swing, and London had overtaken New York as the cutting edge of the new trend.

Blondie also found London to be the best launching pad for success in North America. The group was formed by singer Deborah Harry and guitarist Chris Stein from the remains of their former group, the Stilettos. After recording with a forgettable folk rock group called Wind in the Willows in the late 1960s, Harry had done stints as a bartender and a Playboy bunny. As lead vocalist for Blondie (the name was taken from the comic strip character), she projected a Marilyn Monroe image. Stein had joined the Stilettos primarily because of his interest in Harry. As part of Blondie, he became more career directed, but the group's success was slowed by a number of early personnel changes. Between their debut at CBGB and the release of their first LP, bassist Fred Smith left to join Television, Ivan Kral was stolen by Patti Smith, and drummer Billy O'Connor quit to go to law school. The five-piece Blondie lineup that recorded the group's self-titled debut album included only Harry and Stein from the original group. The album was issued on the small Private Stock label. The addition of Jimmy Destri on Farfisa organ gave the group a distinctive camp feel that harked back to the pop sounds of the 1960s. Blondie had pop ideals from the beginning, but the group was still a good bit ahead of the mainstream. Although the album did not generate a ripple in U.S. sales, it brought the group to the attention of Chrysalis, which then purchased their contract for $500,000. The group's second album, *Plastic Letters,* also flopped, although it included a remake of Randy and the Rainbow's "Denise," changed to "Denis," which went to number two on British charts. For their third outing, Blondie switched producers to Mike Chapman, formerly of the sure-bet British bubblegum producer/songwriter team of Chinn and Chapman. *Parallel Lines* (1978) marked the group's breakthrough in North America. It peaked at number six and yielded four hit singles in Britain.

Combining breathy pop vocals with a Marilyn Monroe persona, Blondie's Deborah Harry added disco and rap influences to punk.

Although the Talking Heads were formed in 1974 like other first-generation groups and achieved mass market success in North America before either Blondie or the Ramones, they are considered part of a second wave of CBGB groups. Unlike most of the first wave of punk groups, Talking Heads already knew how to play by the time they took to the CBGB stage in the spring of 1975. From the group's live debut on, there was a structure, even a rigidity, to a Talking Heads set that made them unlike all other CBGB groups. The group also embraced rhythm and blues as one strong element in what they envisioned as an otherwise pop rock sound. Still, their presentation was sufficiently minimalist and self-conscious to earn them a place on the art rock side of punk.

The group had begun to take shape at the Rhode Island School of Design when guitarist and vocalist David Byrne and drummer Chris Frantz came together to form the Artistics in 1973. The following year, Byrne, Frantz, and Tina Weymouth, Frantz's girlfriend, headed for New York to seek their artistic fortunes. It was the CBGB scene that reignited Byrne's desire to use music as his vehicle. Frantz also liked the idea, and the two rounded their rhythm section with the addition of Weymouth on bass. They were an instant hit. Hilly Kristal loved them; the press loved them; other groups were jealous of them. Within two months of their debut, they were headlining with the Ramones. The following year, they were signed to the Ramones' label, Sire. Before they recorded their debut single, "Love Goes to Building on Fire," in 1976 they added to the group Jerry Harrison, a keyboardist from the proto-punk band the Modern Lovers. *Talking Heads '77,* the group's first album, made it into the Top 100. Although primarily a pop-sounding LP, singles like "Psycho Killer" showed an ironic punk edge. The group's next three albums were produced by Brian Eno, who would see the band through the punk era into the next decade. *More Songs About Buildings and Food* (1978) included a Top Thirty cover of Al Green's "Take Me to the River" that showcased the Talking Heads' affinity for African American music, which would become a cornerstone of their sound in the 1980s.

By the time the Talking Heads played their first CBGB gig, it was apparent that New York was not the only punk mecca in North America. There had been hints of activity elsewhere when the New York well ran dry for the Velvet Underground in the late 1960s and a Boston club called the Boston Tea Party became their second home. In fact, it was Boston that had given birth to the first proto-punk band to embrace the Velvets fully—the Modern Lovers, led by Jonathan Richman. In 1972, however, the country was no more ready for the Lovers than it had been for the Velvets. After one album, the group sank without a trace, leaving keyboardist Jerry Harrison to resurface as a Talking Head. Cleveland, another city that provided an occasional respite for the exiled Velvet Underground, was also a burgeoning scene in the early 1970s. The Mirrors, the Electric Eels, and Rocket from the Tombs all began there. Peter Laughner of Rocket from the Tombs had done a stint with Television after arranging for the group to play Cleveland. While the Mirrors and the Eels went the way of the Modern Lovers, the Rockets split into two groups that earned a place in punk history: Pere Ubu and the Dead Boys. The Dead Boys' "Sonic Reducer" and Ubu's "Thirty Seconds over Tokyo," "Life Stinks," and "Final Solution" had been part of the Rockets' repertoire before the fracture.

In Akron, Ohio, Devo (the name was a contraction of deevolution) was formed at Kent State University in 1972, two years after the National Guard had opened fire on student antiwar protestors. With inverted flowerpot hats and jerky robotic movements defining their

Even though the Talking Heads fashioned a minimalist arty sound, they never lost their affinity for African American music. This combination of influences served them well in the 1980s.

image, the group found early acceptance in Britain. Devo was signed to Virgin in 1978, and Brian Eno was recruited to produce the group's first album, *Are We Not Men? We Are Devo!* The album's title was taken from the anthemic line from "Jocko Homo," one of the group's first singles. "Jocko Homo" and Devo's punk send-up of the Rolling Stones' "Satisfaction" were hits in Britain, but the group remained a cult item in the United States until the next decade.

Canadian Punk

Toronto was also a hotbed of punk activity, with the Diodes and the Viletones issuing records in 1977, followed by Hamilton's Teenage Head in 1978, the Forgotten Rebels in 1979, and London, Ontario's the Demics in 1979. The Diodes formed in 1976 and a year later opened Canada's first punk club, the Crash'n'Burn, in downtown Toronto. Although the club was forced to close at the end of the summer of 1977 because of noise complaints by the principal tenants of the building, the Liberal Party of Ontario, it served as the initial focal point for a scene that included the Demics, the Viletones, Teenage Head, the Poles (whose 1977 single "CN Tower" on Nimbus 9 was one of the great moments of Canadian punk), and the all-girl punk band the Curse. In July 1977, the Diodes, the Viletones, Teenage Head, and the Curse played four nights in New York City at CBGB's, ads for the show billing them as "outrageous punk bands from Toronto, Canada."

The Viletones truly were outrageous. Their lead singer, Steven Leckie, a.k.a. Nazi Dog, would hang from the rafters, hurl himself into the audience and regularly engage in self-mutilation, cutting himself onstage *à la Iggy* Pop. The group's first two singles, containing songs such as "Screamin [sic] Fist" and "Swastika Girl," further fueled their notoriety, helping to garner them coverage in music magazines around the world.

Hamilton's Teenage Head was perhaps the most popular Canadian punk band. In contrast to the Toronto bands, the group was heavily influenced by rockabilly, and their original songs tended to have humorously goofy lyrics. Their second album, 1980's *Frantic City*, featuring the singles "Let's Shake" and "Somethin' on My Mind," received substantial national radio play. Their appearance at Toronto's Ontario Place that summer ended in a riot, prompting nationwide headlines and leading Ontario Place to ban rock concerts for a number of years.

Anarchy in the U.K.

CBGB showcased over thirty new groups at its 1975 Festival of Unsigned Bands, months before the Sex Pistols played their first gig. But while punk developed earlier in the United States, the conditions to which it responded were more profoundly disturbing on the other side of the Atlantic. In Britain, a growing sense of foreboding accompanied the development of British punk bands. Unemployment had already reached record highs, and the country was plunged into its deepest recession since World War II. Although there was considerable labour unrest, the fascist National Front was growing stronger and the conservative Margaret Thatcher had become prime minister. The optimism of the postwar years was giving way to a knowing cynicism, and the consensus of values and behaviour that had regulated social and political life was coming unraveled.

It was at their second Manchester date that the Sex Pistols unleashed "Anarchy in the U.K."— the call to arms that would establish them as the vanguard group in a nationwide movement.

In such a climate, even the name Sex Pistols, with its obvious connections to youth, violence, and sex, caused a stir. Thus, finding suitable venues for the group was a problem from the moment they started performing in 1975. The pub rock scene was already dominated by Dr. Feelgood, the Stranglers, and Eddie and the Hot Rods, groups that played loud, fast, aggressive rock, but who would never quite make it into the inner circle of punk. The Pistols' initial tour of Britain was staged mostly in college venues, and attendance seldom reached triple figures. Still, by the summer of 1976 they had built a small following and were ready for slightly larger events. The most notable of these concerts occurred in Manchester, where the group shared the stage with such local Manchester favourites as Slaughter and the Dogs and the Buzzcocks. It was at their second Manchester date that the Sex Pistols unleashed "Anarchy in the U.K."—the call to arms that would establish them as the vanguard group in a nationwide movement. Manchester also led to an appearance on Granada TV's *So It Goes,* where the Sex Pistols again performed "Anarchy," this time on national television.

Joe Strummer, a guitarist for a group called the 101ers, was positively inspired by this event. The 101ers, who had been playing the pub rock circuit, had taken their name from the number of the torture room in George Orwell's *1984.* With the guidance of manager Bernie Rhodes, a colleague of Malcom McLaren, Strummer teamed up with Mick Jones and Paul Simonon, from a group called London SS, to form the Clash. The group took its name from the word most often used in tabloid headlines concerning class and race relations in Britain. If, as chronicler Jon Savage has suggested, "Punk's breakthrough was to unite people who saw pop in terms of social realism and those who viewed it as artistic expression," it was the Clash, more than any other group, who took social(ist) realism to its artistic and political limits.[20] At the

"Anarchy in the U.K."

Artist: The Sex Pistols
Music / Lyrics by Paul Cook,
Steve Jones, Glen Matlock,
and Johnny Rotten
Label: EMI (1976)

John Lydon/Rotten understood, better than anyone in rock 'n' roll since John Lennon, the way that one generation's scandal could be the next generation's opportunity. Just as Lennon had told a Command Performance audience to "rattle your jewelry" in lieu of applause, John had put a safety pin through a photocopy of Queen Elizabeth's portrait. Both were purely symbolic acts—working-class anger masquerading as mere impudence—but both carried a powerful symbolic message. Neither of these "angry young men" was prepared to accept the previous generation's sense of propriety, and each built a career out of calculated (and brilliantly musical) outrage. Both Lennon and Lydon saw rock 'n' roll as a way out—and a chance for a few swipes at the ruling class along the way.

The players in this 1976 incarnation of the Sex Pistols were Johnny Rotten (aka John Lydon), vocals; Steve Jones, guitar; Glen Matlock, bass; and Paul Cook, drums. "Anarchy in the U.K." was released as a single in 1976 and was also included on the LP *Never Mind the Bollocks, Here's the Sex Pistols.*

Musical Style Notes

The driving, drum-hit-on-every-beat and the high-volume guitar distortion of the Sex Pistols place them squarely in the sonic category of punk rock, but claims that the Sex Pistols were unable to play their instruments are highly exaggerated. The musical structure of "Anarchy" is not simple but contains a typical verse-chorus pop-song construction with two contrasting guitar solo sections. Further, while it may rely on the three primary chords in a major key—what musicians call I, IV, and V—it's no less harmonically sophisticated than many blues songs or British invasion–style songs from the previous decade. The most frequent chord progression here (the one you hear while Johnny's singing "I am an antichrist") is a frantic, sped-up version of the same chord progression that repeats endlessly in Muddy Waters' "I'm a Man," although the distortion and the different rhythm may render it unrecognizable. The first guitar solo is played over a completely different set of chords (for musicians, the II and III chord in the key). The second guitar solo modulates (changes key) a whole step and is, whether intentionally or not, an almost complete replica of the guitar part from the Searchers' 1964 hit "Needles and Pins" (which, interestingly enough, was also covered by the Ramones in 1978). Rotten's lyric style may be confrontational and coarse, but his delivery is impeccable and "in sync" with the rhythm and the harmonic changes of the music, right down to the last snarl.

Musical "Road Map"

TIMINGS	COMMENTS	LYRICS
0:00–0:06	Instrumental introduction	
0:06–0:14	Instrumental introduction	[spoken] Right . . . now! . . . ha ha ha ha ha . . .
0:14–0:28	Verse 1	*I am an antichrist . . .*
0:28–0:43	Chorus	*I . . . wanna be . . . Anarchy . . .* [spoken] No dog's body!
0:43–1:00	Verse 2	*Anarchy for the U.K. . . .*
1:00–1:12	Chorus	*I . . . wanna be . . . Anarchy . . .* [spoken] In the city!
1:12–1:31	Guitar solo #1	
1:31–1:45	Verse 3	*How many ways to get what you want? . . .*
1:45–2:00	Chorus	*I . . . wanna be . . . Anarchy . . .* [spoken] It's the only way to be!
2:00–2:14	Guitar solo #2 ("Needles and Pins" quote)	
2:14–2:29	Verse 4	*Is this the M.P.L.A. . . .*
2:29–2:43	(Chorus, with new words)	*just . . . another country . . .* [spoken] Another council tenancy . . .
2:43–3:11	Chorus (four times)	*I . . . wanna be . . . Anarchy . . .* *I . . . wanna be . . . Anarchy . . .* *I . . . wanna be . . . Anarchy . . .* *I . . . wanna be . . . an anarchist—* [spoken] Oh, what a name . . . *Get pissed . . . DESTROY!*

Johnny Rotten's painful engagement with his music captures the aesthetic of the Sex Pistols. The "destroy" T-shirt with the swastika juxtaposed against the Union Jack speaks to their contradictory politics.

time, Simon Frith wrote that punk's message "comes most powerfully and most ambiguously from the Sex Pistols, but it comes most clearly from the Clash."[21] The group was the Sex Pistols' major competition and, in fact, outlasted the Sex Pistols by years.

Under the tutelage of Bernie Rhodes, the Clash seemed somehow more grounded in the real world than other punk outfits. While the Sex Pistols staked out the territory of nihilism with songs like "Pretty Vacant," "Seventeen," "Problems," and "Submission," the Clash appeared more socially engaged with material like the self-explanatory "London's Burning," "I'm So Bored with the U.S.A.," a searing commentary on popular culture, and "White Riot," which was inspired by the clashes between young blacks and police at the Notting Hill Carnival. In the spirit of punk, the Clash's "1977" proclaimed an end to Elvis, the Beatles, and the Rolling Stones. The group took on the issues of racism ("Police and Thieves") and unemployment ("Career Opportunities") and cast the theme of youth identity in distinctly class terms ("What's My Name").

Another punk group of note that formed at this time was the Damned. The group as a whole was apolitical. Its members just liked speed and noise. Still, they were the first unmistakably punk group to land a record contract in Britain (Stiff Records) and the first to hit the Top Thirty ("New Rose," an amphetamine rush, ostensibly about the excitement of a new romance). The Vibrators were equally lacking in moral authority, but they also beat the Sex Pistols to the recording punch with the slightly off-colour "We Vibrate," also on Stiff. Stiff had been founded in 1976 by two pub rock entrepreneurs, Dave Robinson and Andrew Jakeman, better known as Jake Riviera. Robinson had distinguished himself in rock lore earlier in the decade when he had flown 150 British journalists to New York's Fillmore East to catch Brinsley Schwarz, a pub rock group he was then managing. The grandiose scheme yielded nothing but bad press. Robinson had gone on to manage Graham Parker, whose intense r&b sound (*Howlin' Wind,* 1976) straddled the fence between pub rock and punk. Parker's backup group, the Rumour, was led by Brinsley Schwarz on guitar. Brinsley vocalist Nick Lowe became the house producer at Stiff and an artist in his own right. His "So It Goes" was Stiff's first release. Lowe produced the Damned's first album and eventually supervised all of Elvis Costello's early work. Jake Riviera, Stiff's other principal, doubled as Costello's manager.

While McLaren knew that the Sex Pistols needed a record contract, he was grooming the group for the big leagues as part of his plan for worldwide subversion, and Stiff was a mere independent in his eyes. Hoping to capture the attention of the major labels, McLaren turned to the idea of a punk festival. It was an idea that had always appealed to him. CBGB and Max's had benefited from their punk showcases and, even though a recent punk festival in the south of France had failed, McLaren felt he could pull it off in England. The Punk Rock Festival was staged at the 100 Club in September 1976. It featured, among others, the Sex Pistols, the Clash, the Buzzcocks, the Damned, the Vibrators, and Siouxsie and the Banshees, a group that was assembled at the last minute from the Bromley contingent of Sex Pistols hangers-on.

> *The Punk Rock Festival as a whole was plagued by technical difficulties, professional rivalries, political differences, violence, and several arrests. In short, it was a roaring success.*

Siouxsie and the Banshees originally included Sid Vicious, who later joined the Pistols, and Marco Pirroni, who joined Adam Ant. Billy Idol (later of Generation X) also agreed to be part of the group but disappeared before the festival. Vocalist Siouxsie Sioux was the group's focal point. At such a late date, the group saw no point in trying to learn any songs, so they debuted without a repertoire. Their set was a mess, but a memorable one.

The festival as a whole was plagued by technical difficulties, professional rivalries, political differences, violence, and several arrests. In short, it was a roaring success, especially for the Sex Pistols. In October, the group was signed to EMI; in November, "Anarchy in the U.K." was released as a single. A tour with the Clash, the Damned, and Johnny Thunders' Heartbreakers was planned to promote the record. In December, however, the Sex Pistols were interviewed on Thames TV's *Today* show by Bill Grundy, who goaded Steve Jones into calling him a "dirty fucker" and a "fucking rotter" on the air. In the ensuing scandal, deejays all across Great Britain (with the notable exception of John Peel) refused to play "Anarchy." Of the twenty-one dates booked for the Anarchy tour, the Sex Pistols were banned from all but three. Even so, with sales of more than 50,000, "Anarchy" entered the Top Twenty before Christmas, confirming that a good scandal can generate a great deal of free publicity.

In the punk tradition, Siouxsie Sioux performed with the Banshees before the band had a repertoire. A testament to their staying power, Siouxsie and the Banshees went on to play the first Lollapalooza Festival in 1991.

In January 1977, amidst the fallout from the Grundy appearance, EMI dropped the Sex Pistols, which cost the company its £50,000 advance. A&M picked the group up in March for another £50,000 and dropped them a week later for an additional £25,000 buyout. Not bad for a group with only one single. The Grundy interview had finally put punk over the top, and the music industry was finally beginning to take notice of it. A new club called the Roxy became the CBGB of London. Manchester began to mirror Cleveland as punk's second home when the Buzzcocks issued an EP called "Spiral Scratch" on their own New Hormones label and sold 15,000 copies of it. Stiff signed a distribution deal with Island Records just in time to push the Damned's first album, *Damned Damned Damned,* into the U.K. Top Forty. United Artists had already signed the Stranglers, and Polydor had picked up the Jam. The biggest news, however, was that the Clash had been signed to CBS for an advance of £100,000.

The Clash's self-titled debut album was released in April 1977, a month after they had signed with CBS. It was a surprisingly accessible creation that clearly stamped punk with the imprint of social realism. It was, in the words of Jon Savage, "the first major Punk statement."[22] Unfortunately, it was not released in the United States. It wasn't until the beginning of the 1980s that the Clash did well in the U.S. market. *London Calling* (1980) and *Sandinista!* (1981) charted Top Thirty, and *Combat Rock* (1982) went Top Ten, yielding the group's only U.S. Top Ten single, "Rock the Casbah."

While CBS was promoting the Clash, Malcom McLaren was scrambling for a new contract for the Sex Pistols, eventually going with Virgin. By this time, Sid Vicious had replaced Glen Matlock on bass. In 1977, Queen Elizabeth II's silver jubilee provided the perfect opportunity for the Sex Pistols to reassert their primacy. The record they planned to release was "God Save the Queen," which baldly accused the monarchy of being a "fascist regime." It was

The Clash had their sights set on nothing short of a socialist revolution through music. Not surprisingly, they were accompanied by heavy security whenever they arrived in the United States.

recorded immediately after the Virgin signing but proved difficult to get out. The CBS pressing plant held up production, the platemakers refused to make the plates for the liner notes, radio and television stations rejected advertisements, retail outlets refused to place orders, and the single itself was banned from the airwaves. Needless to say, all of this provided incredible publicity. "God Save the Queen" was finally released in late May (still a few weeks in advance of the planned celebrations) and was selected as the "Single of the Week" by all four British music weeklies. By the end of Jubilee Week, it had sold 200,000 copies. It would easily have gone to the top of the British charts except for some official tampering that resulted in listing a blacked-out song title and group name in the number one slot for the week of 18 June 1977. "God Save the Queen" was the only serious critique of the Jubilee. It uncovered cracks in the social facade that had been remarkably well papered over by official pomp and ceremony. The effectiveness of the song, however, thrust the Sex Pistols' rhetoric up against the politics of the real world. Verbal attacks became physical, and the group, which had not even recorded an album yet, could tour only in secret. The Sex Pistols had definitely made rock 'n' roll "dangerous" again, and the movement they helped to set in motion had barely hit its stride.

If the Sex Pistols tended toward anarchism, the Clash headed straight for the far left. At different times, Strummer endorsed both Germany's extremist Baader-Meinhoff group and Italy's Red Brigades. Far more than any other punk group, the Clash took up the cry of the British working class. By the fall of 1977, they were announcing the apocalypse, with slogans like "Hate and War," "White Riot," and "Sten Guns in Knightsbridge" stenciled on their new black jumpsuits. When CBS released a weak single called "Remote Control" without the group's permission, the Clash retaliated with "Complete Control," an attack on CBS Records that was also a pronouncement of punk power. When Strummer screamed at the end of the song that taking control means "you," he was talking to his fans, his comrades-in-arms.

Flirtation with Fascism: The Underbelly of Punk

In their rush to shock, punks on both sides of the Atlantic often seized on any image that could be counted on to produce a strong reaction. No image fit that bill as well as the swastika. If 1960s rock had been marked by its associations with the leftist leanings of the counterculture, punk gravitated toward symbols at the other end of the political spectrum. For most punks, although certainly not all, flaunting the twisted cross was an exercise in confrontational art rather than a political endorsement of fascism per se. However, that fine distinction, which is rife in punk's recapitulations of itself, overlooked the importance of historical meaning.

For most punks, flaunting the twisted cross was an exercise in confrontational art rather than a political endorsement of fascism per se. However, that fine distinction, which is rife in punk's recapitulations of itself, overlooked the importance of historical meaning.

It was Ron Asheton of the Stooges who pioneered the utilization of swastikas, iron crosses, and jackboots on stage. Asheton's fascination with the trinkets and jargon of Nazism was mirrored in other groups. One of the high points of the fledgling Cleveland scene in 1974 was an event titled Special Extermination Night, which featured Rocket from the Tombs, the Mirrors, and the Eels. Swastikas adorned the poster advertising the event. Of the three groups, the Eels, whose members often appeared in ripped T-shirts with white power logos and swastikas, were easily the most offensive. The lyrics to "Spin Age Blasters," one of the group's songs, were taken from a slogan displayed at Cleveland's American Nazi Party Headquarters that read "Pull the Triggers on the Niggers." Even when these groups disbanded, the use of Nazi symbols did not disappear. After Pere Ubu rose from the ashes of the Rockets, the group released a song called "Final Solution" (the title taken, of course, from Hitler's plan to exterminate the Jews) as a single in 1976. The Dead Boys showed up at CBGB's 1976 Festival of Unsigned Bands wearing Nazi uniforms. (It was at this event that Hilly Kristal agreed to manage the group, which led to a contract with Sire.)

After he left the Stooges, Ron Asheton went on to form his own band, The New Order. The Dictators, a group from upstate New York that formed at about the same time as the early Cleveland groups, played a brand of rapid-fire rock that occupied a cultural space somewhere between the New York Dolls and the Ramones. In 1977, The Dictators released their first (of two) albums on Asylum. It was titled *Manifest Destiny.* The Ramones were packaged by Arturo Vega, a Mexican artist who made dayglo swastikas. Early song titles, "Blitzkrieg Bop" and "Today Your Love, Tomorrow the World," for example, contained explicit references to Nazism.

Per their situationist leanings, Malcolm McLaren and Vivienne Westwood had already noted that the swastika could be used quite effectively to disrupt the flow of everyday life. At one point, they had landed a commission to fashion the costumes for the film *Mahler,* which included an Aryan anima decked out in a leather miniskirt with a swastika emblazoned on her backside in brass studs. When the New York Dolls had toured Europe in 1973 with McLaren in tow, the group had added the occasional swastika to their trash drag queen attire. In Germany (of all places), a blathering Johnny Thunders had told the press that the Dolls wanted to play a benefit at Bergen-Belsen "for all the Nazis who gotta hang out in trees in fuckin' South America."[23] McLaren had observed the reaction and filed it away for future reference. In fact, McLaren and Westwood had a stock of Nazi memorabilia at their shop. The groups that arose from the Bromley contingent of Sex Pistols fans were heavily influenced by the fashion fare at Sex. Adam Ant was criticized early on for Nazi references in his lyrics. Sid Vicious wore T-shirts with swastikas. Siouxsie Sioux had a particular affinity for her swastika armband. The Clash, in fact, had objected strenuously to the Banshees' use of the swastika at the 100 Club festival. Nevertheless, these tendencies continued. In 1977, the Sex Pistols themselves started performing a song called "Belsen Was a Gas," which had been written earlier by Sid Vicious. The next generation of British groups included Joy Division, whose name was taken from concentration camp brothels; they evolved into New Order, a reference to Hitler's plan for the future.

The swastika, it should be noted, was only one of a number of disruptive symbols used by punks. For McLaren and Westwood in particular, fashion served as a part of their larger political strategy. When the Sex Pistols first performed the song that would become "Anarchy in the U.K.," McLaren and Westwood had designed a shirt to complement it. The "Anarchy" shirt combined small portraits of Karl Marx and flying swastikas with slogans like "Only Anarchists Are Pretty." The ensemble was completed with an armband that read "Chaos." "The intention was the group should not be politically explicit, but instead should be an explosion of contradictory, highly charged signs."[24] It was in this politics of confusion that punk irony became complicated.

Like the Sex Pistols, the Ramones did not limit themselves to fascist symbols in their attempts to outrage. Anyone with an intimate knowledge of the group's repertoire, which conjured up images across the landscape of the grotesque, could only interpret their antics as rock 'n' roll parody. As Robert Christgau has pointed out:

> *Unless you think the Ramones identify with Charlie Manson, the Texas chain-saw killer, CIA men, SLAers, geeks, glue-sniffers, and electroshock patients—an absurd misreading as far as I'm concerned—then you must conclude that their intention is satiric, and the same applies when they turn to fascist characters.*[25]

"The problem," Christgau noted, "is that irony is wasted on pinheads."[26] It was Lester Bangs who made one of the more cogent arguments against the use of the outrageous: "Another reason for getting rid of all those little barbs is that no matter how you intend them, you can't say them without risking misinterpretation by some other bigoted asshole; your irony just might be his cup of hate."[27] Bangs drove the point home by recounting the story of Miriam Linna of the Cramps, who was quoted in a punk fanzine called *New Order* as saying: "I love the Ramones [because] this is the celebration of everything American—everything teenaged and wonderful and white."[28] She was pictured in leather and shades, brandishing a pistol in front of the Florida headquarters of the United White People's Party. In such a context, the intended irony of Patti Smith's "Rock & Roll Nigger" might well have been lost on many of her fans. Nico was being unmistakably clear when she told an interviewer that she "didn't like negroes" after performing "Deutschland Uber Alles" at CBGB.

The political climate of the 1970s further confused any punk attempts at irony. In the United States at this time, the curious concept of "reverse discrimination" began to come into popular usage. The logic of the Civil Rights Act of 1964 was turned on its head when the Supreme Court ruled in 1978 that Alan Bakke's civil rights as a white person had been violated by the University of California's affirmative action policy. The landmark decision signaled the beginnings of a concerted attack on affirmative action and a tremendous resurgence of white supremacist organizations that would extend well past the next decade. In such a climate any punk attempts to deconstruct racially loaded terms and symbols could have only unintended consequences. In Britain, the fascist National Front had already begun to make disturbing inroads into parliamentary elections. In response, a confused Paul Weller of the Jam, the group that had opened for the Clash on their White Riot Tour, told his fans that he would be voting Tory in the next election.

With the rise of the National Front in Britain, it did not take much to fan the flames of racial hatred. However, the most inflammatory statements by musicians came not from the punks but from within the ranks of the British rock aristocracy.

Not even the Clash were above misinterpretation. "White Riot" had been intended as a statement that the white working class should stand up for its rights in the same way that blacks at Notting Hill Gate had. In the atmosphere of racially charged conservatism, however, it was sometimes taken as a racist rallying call to oppose such insurrection. The Sex Pistols, of course, traded on misinterpretation. Taken literally, the lyrics to "God Save the Queen" could be (mis)heard as a call to save the "fascist regime." This is exactly what happened at an early

Clash/Sex Pistols concert when the Student Union at Lanchester Polytechnic in Coventry refused to pay the groups, calling them "these fascists."

With the rise of the National Front in Britain, it did not take much to fan the flames of racial hatred. However, the most inflammatory statements by musicians came not from the punks but from within the ranks of the British rock aristocracy. In the spring of 1976, David Bowie was quoted as saying, "I think I might have been a bloody good Hitler."[29] He then staged his return from Berlin to London with what appeared to be a Nazi salute at Victoria station as he and his entourage piled into a Mercedes limousine. While Bowie later apologized for his flirtation with fascism, Eric Clapton did not. Clapton interrupted a concert in Birmingham in August 1976 to make a drunken speech urging support for Enoch Powell, the most rabid antiblack member of Parliament there was at the time. In response, a letter of protest signed "Rock Against Racism" was fired off to all the popular music weeklies, precipitating well over 100 enthusiastic replies in the first week alone.

Rock Against Racism: The Progressive Rejoinder

Rock Against Racism was organized as a broadly based mass movement that had as its sole purpose opposition to the National Front. According to RAR historian David Widgery, the organization had a multilevel strategy.

> On one level Rock Against Racism was an orthodox anti-racist campaign simply using pop music to kick political slogans into the vernacular. But on another level, it was a jail break. We aimed to rescue the energy of Russian revolutionary art, surrealism and rock and roll from the galleries, the advertising agencies and the record companies and use them again to change reality, as had always been intended. And have a party in the process.[30]

The energy and creativity for RAR came from graphic and fashion designers, photographers, actors, and punk and reggae musicians. Political direction was supplied primarily by the Socialist Workers Party, which later formed the Anti-Nazi League, which then merged with RAR.

At about the same time the Sex Pistols released "Anarchy in the U.K." in late 1976, RAR began staging concerts. By the following year, the organization was producing major events that attracted hundreds of thousands of fans. RAR's antiracist strategy of showcasing the new multicultural Britain in a positive light necessitated packaging black and white acts together. In doing so, a tilt toward reggae predominated. As Jon Savage has explained, "Any fascist ambiguity in Punk was fueled by the way that the style had bled Rock dry of all black influences; one way to overcome any taint of white supremacy was to affirm visible links with Reggae."[31] Thus, major RAR events paired reggae groups with punk bands: Aswad with the Adverts, the Cimarrons with Generation X, Steel Pulse with the Clash. Reggae was, of course, prevalent in Britain's West Indian enclaves, but it was also popular since the late 1960s with disaffected British white youth who were attracted to its hypnotic rhythms and unflinching "rude boy" stance. Its trajectory among white youth, however, was not always progressive. In the late

1960s, skinheads who were prone to racist attacks adopted reggae as the marshall music to accompany their violent rages. By the time skinheads resurfaced in the media in the 1970s, they were adherents of punk. Some were racist Nazi sympathizers; others liked the music and opposed its fascist leanings. Thus, part of RAR's mission was to claim punk for the Left, thereby driving a wedge between racist skinheads who were drawn to the National Front and those with more progressive tendencies.

The skinhead affinity for punk and violence often put RAR in a delicate situation. Sham 69 was a sizzling punk band that performed a number of RAR benefits. But Sham also had a sizable skinhead following who wreaked havoc at their concerts by chanting "Sieg Heil," destroying property, and plastering Nazi emblems everywhere. Lead singer Jimmy Pursey was genuinely concerned about skinhead racism but sufficiently desperate to be a star that he was hesitant to cut himself off from his diehard fans. Rock Against Racism was able to turn the tables to some degree by booking Sham with a Southall reggae outfit called Misty, thus forcing skinheads to attend an antiracist benefit to see their favourite group. "I believe that black and white must live together," said an emboldened Pursey, who appeared wearing a Jamaican tam.[32] Sham and Misty then joined forces in a performance of an old skinhead favourite, Desmond Dekker's "The Israelites."

The punk/reggae convergence projected a unique symbolic power that contributed significantly to the "black and white together" feeling of many RAR events. At one show in 1977, a member of Generation X and a member of the Cimarrons joined hands aloft while the entire audience chanted "Black and white. Black and white." Billy Idol remembered the experience as "one of the greatest nights of my life";[33] the Cimarrons responded by recording a single called "Rock Against Racism."

Key to the widespread appeal of reggae was the influence of Bob Marley. Following in his wake, successful Jamaican reggae artists—from the polemical Burning Spear and the anthemic Peter Tosh to the more pop-oriented Jimmy Cliff and Third World—contributed to a virtual subindustry of reggae influences that affected not only the music of black Britons but that of white punks as well. The Clash included a punk/reggae cover of Junior Murvin's "Police and Thieves" on their first album. For the reggae feel on "Complete Control," the group contracted Jamaican producer Lee "Scratch" Perry.

In the United States, where conditions favoured the influence of rhythm and blues, reggae never had a terribly profound impact in the pop market. Jimmy Cliff might have become a superstar before Marley because of his starring role in the cult classic film *The Harder They Come;* Cliff eschewed reggae in favor of undistinguished soul material after the film's 1973 U.S. release. Prior to this, the only Jamaican releases to crack the U.S. market had been Millie Small's "My Boy Lollipop" (1964), produced by Chris Blackwell, and Desmond Dekker's "The Israelites" (1969). In the late 1960s, Johnny Nash, a middle-of-the-road r&b singer from Austin, Texas, made a dramatic turn toward reggae and recorded Bob Marley's "Guava Jelly." Nash then hit number twelve on the U.S. charts with a version of Marley's "Stir It Up" in 1973. His own reggae-inflected "I Can See Clearly Now" (1972) went all the way to number one. For the most part, when U.S. white artists gravitated toward reggae, it was for a touch of

It was a discouraging testament to the prevailing distribution of cultural resources that Eric Clapton's number one cover of Bob Marley's "I Shot the Sheriff" (1974) outsold the Wailers' original not only in England and the United States but also in Jamaica.

exotica, as in Paul Simon's "Mother and Child Reunion" (1971). It was not until 1980 that Blondie embraced the style on "The Tide Is High," which became a number one hit. Throughout the 1970s, white British artists were more conversant with the style than their U.S. counterparts and often more successful at using it than its Jamaican originators. It was a discouraging testament to the prevailing distribution of cultural resources that Eric Clapton's number one cover of Bob Marley's "I Shot the Sheriff" (1974) outsold the Wailers' original not only in England and the United States but also in Jamaica. Clapton never repaid this debt by supporting RAR, preferring instead a safer charitable path that stretched from George Harrison's Concert for Bangladesh to his memorable appearance at Live Aid. Bob Marley, on the other hand, was sufficiently taken with RAR's reggae/punk alliance that he released "Punky Reggae Party" in solidarity.

As the RAR push to unite black and white met the reggae explosion, a number of integrated bands were formed. These bands delved into ska, the lighter, faster form of Jamaican dance music that had preceded reggae. From Coventry came Selecter and the Specials, from London, Madness, and from Birmingham, the English Beat. The groups recorded for a label called 2-Tone; its name was an obvious indicator of the interracial character of the bands and their music. UB 40, another ska-influenced band, came shortly thereafter, taking its name from the British unemployment form.

In attempting to build as broad a base as possible, RAR also reached across lines of gender and sexual orientation. It was a gay activist named Tom Robinson who unfurled the first "Rock Against Sexism" banner at an RAR concert. Robinson played it safe (and made the U.K. Top Ten) with his first single, "2-4-6-8 Motorway," but "Up Against the Wall," from his first album, captured the politics of punk as well as any song. At RAR concerts, he moved even straight audiences to tears with his heart-wrenching performances of "Glad to Be Gay." RAR's endorsement of progressive sexual politics dovetailed nicely with a potential that had been inherent in punk on both sides of the Atlantic from the beginning: the creation of new cultural spaces for women. When *Sideburns* magazine pictured an A chord, an E chord, and a G chord with the instructions, "This is a chord; this is another; this is a third; now form a band," in 1976, the message was almost as liberating for young women as it was for young men. Punk was aimed at destroying convention from its beginning; there was nothing that prohibited women from taking part. In New York, women began to appear in groups like DNA and Mars wearing black jeans, boots, T-shirts, and leather jackets, the same defiant image used by the men. They put out the same angry, dissonant sound as the men. It was christened "no wave" in opposition to new wave. "It was liberating," exclaimed Adele Bertei, organist for the Contortions, "we were just like the boys, finally, we could do what the fuck we wanted to, without any sexist bullshit."[34] X, a Los Angeles group, was led by a poet named Exene Cervenka and her husband, John Doe. Dissecting Los Angeles with a caustic wit and a rapid-fire beat, the group was able to make the jump to a major label, Elektra, and producer Ray Manzarek.

In London, there was Siouxsie Sioux and the Banshees, and the Slits, an all-female band that translated a maelstrom of noise into a message of female power. Members of the Slits joined early RAR benefits. Poly Styrene, a portly biracial woman with braces and an acid wit,

The Rock Against Racism movement provided a context that could nurture the more progressive impulses in punk. In return, punk and reggae musicians supplied the Left with the cultural politics needed to reach youths. It was one of the most successful marriages of music and politics ever to occur.

formed X-Ray Spex by placing an ad in *Melody Maker.* After only three performances, they released their first record, "Oh Bondage! Up Yours!" In 1978, as the group joined the Clash, Steel Pulse, the Tom Robinson Band, and others as headliners of RAR's biggest event at Victoria Park, "The Day the World Turned Dayglo" made the U.K. Top Thirty. By then, even Siouxsie and the Banshees had publicly distanced themselves from fascist icons. RAR had had its intended effect.

In the British general election of 1979, the National Front was soundly defeated. To be sure, Margaret Thatcher's exploitation of white Britain's worst racial fears ("this country might be rather swamped by people with a different culture") had a major impact on bringing the conservative vote back to the Tories, but the effect of RAR cannot be discounted. The Rock Against Racism movement provided a context that could nurture the more progressive impulses in punk. In return, punk and reggae musicians supplied the Left with the cultural politics needed to reach youth. It was one of the most successful marriages of music and politics ever to occur.

Riding the New Wave

For the most part, the RAR movement coincided with the heyday of punk's first generation of performers. By the time there was a second generation, punk had been born again as "new wave." While the wit, irony, flair for the outrageous, and politics of the absurd that were a part of punk were never completely abandoned, the new artists were somewhat less oriented toward shock for its own sake, a bit more adept musically, and infinitely more successful commercially. In the United States, Blondie and the Talking Heads easily assumed the new label. The Clash made the transition while touring North America so extensively they lost contact with their home base. In Britain, the new wave label was assumed by Elvis Costello, the Police, and the Pretenders, all of whom were connected in their own way to some form of political activism.

If there was any single performer who bridged the gap between punk and new wave and embodied all the contradictions contained therein, it was Declan Patrick McManus, also known as Elvis Costello. When Costello started recording for Stiff, he was married, had a son, and had not given up his day jobs, the most legendary of which was as a computer operator for Elizabeth Arden, a company he skewered as a "vanity factory" on "I'm Not Angry." Costello combined the words of a poet with the temper of a madman. He told the press "revenge and guilt" were his primary motivations for his songs.

In 1977, Costello joined Nick Lowe, Dave Edmunds, and Ian Dury on a U.S. tour that Stiff sponsored for its artists. Edmunds and Dury, who were well into their thirties at the time, were too old to be punks and they had retained a good bit of rhythm and blues influence in their sound. Edmunds had cracked the U.S. Top Ten in 1971 with a cover of Smiley Lewis' "I Hear You Knockin'." Dury had experienced British success with the anthemic "Sex and Drugs and Rock and Roll" and had given Stiff its first number one U.K. hit with "Hit Me with Your Rhythm Stick." Nick Lowe would eventually hit U.S. number twelve with "Cruel to Be Kind" in 1979. The tour may have been a turning point for Costello, who left Stiff in late 1977. His debut album, *My Aim Is True,* was issued on Columbia, as were all of his subsequent releases in the United States. Costello had genuinely catholic tastes in popular music. He released more than a dozen original homages to American r&b on *Get Happy!!* (1980) and packaged his favourite country songs on *Almost Blue* (1981). Only Joe Jackson, who was compared (unfavourably) to Costello on "Is She Really Going Out with Him" (1979), rivaled his eclecticism. Jackson explored reggae on *Beat Crazy* (1980), paid homage to Cab Calloway and Louis Jordan on *Jumpin' Jive* (1981), and delved into r&b, salsa, jazz, and funk on *Night & Day* (1982), which also yielded his biggest U.S. hit, "Steppin' Out." Costello generated hit after hit in Britain but managed only one Top Forty single, "Every Day I Write the Book" (1983), in the United States. His albums, however, usually garnered respectable chart positions, which placed him ahead of most of the British new wave pack.

There was no topic that was outside the reach of Costello's acerbic wit or immune to his incredible hostility. He bit the hand that fed his success on "Radio, Radio" and vented his misogyny on "Green Shirt." As he was no less contradictory than the punks who had preceded him, he was a staunch supporter of RAR. Inspired by RAR's punk/reggae fusion, his first big hit in Britain, "Watching the Detectives" (1977), was a lively reggae track backed by the Rumour. He contributed a number of songs about fascism to the RAR movement ("Less Than Zero," "Oliver's Army," and "Two Little Hitlers," among others) and shared the stage with Aswad at RAR's Brixton Carnival Two in 1978. None of this, however, kept him from getting into trouble in the United States the following year when Bonnie Bramlett belted him for muttering racial slurs about Ray Charles. Although Costello's anger often got the best of him, he remained a darling of the critics throughout his career. At the end of the 1980s, he was still charting respectably in the lower reaches of the U.S. Top Forty.

While the Police had little sympathy in the punk community, they achieved more commercial success than most groups in the punk/new wave category. After they peaked, they went their separate ways, with Sting remaining in the limelight as a solo artist.

Like Costello, the Police—Sting (bass and vocals), Andy Summers (guitar), and Stewart Copeland (drums)—rose from the punk scene, but unlike Costello, the group had little support in the punk community, which viewed them as too commercial. The Police were willing to appear in television advertisements. In fact, Sting's image was fashioned when he dyed his hair blond for a chewing-gum commercial. The group was managed by Stewart Copeland's brother Miles, who owned a record company called Illegal. (The Copelands' father had worked for the CIA, which may or may not have some bearing on the name of the group and the record company, not to mention the group's biggest hit, "Every Breath You Take" [1983], which has the listener being stalked by someone who was watching every move she or he makes.) Miles had been watching the New York and London punk scenes for some time and had signed a number of punk bands to one of his labels before the Police made their debut as the backup band for Cherry Vanilla, a second-rate transvestite act from New York. The Police were thrown into the new wave category primarily because of their nod toward reggae, which was then fashionable in Britain. A distant touch of reggae seasoning can be heard in such early hits as "Can't Stand Losing You" (a suicide threat) and "Roxanne" (about a prostitute). *Reggatta de Blanc,* the title of the group's second album, is patois for "white reggae."

Also like Costello, the Police broke into the U.S. market by touring small clubs on a shoe-string. But they were not parlaying an already solid British base into U.S. success. Instead, the Police entered both markets simultaneously, and when they hit, their success was immediately mainstream. Sting's rugged good looks were broadly appealing, and the group's white reggae style was sufficiently rock to be appreciated by the critics. Furthermore, the material the group wrote was good. "Message in a Bottle" and "Walking on the Moon," from *Reggatta de Blanc,* and "Every Little Thing She Does Is Magic" and "Spirits in the Material World," from *Ghost in the Machine,* rank among the more engaging songs of the era.

In the early 1980s, the members of the group took time off to embark on a number of solo projects—Sting as an actor, Summers as a photographer, Copeland as his musical alter ego Klerk Kant. They reunited for *Synchronicity* in 1983, which remained in the number one slot for seventeen weeks and turned them into one of the biggest rock acts in the world. Since then, members have gone their separate ways, and Sting has drawn most of the attention. In the late 1980s, having missed the RAR movement, he became active in Amnesty International.

If members of the Police used the new cultural possibilities offered by the punk/reggae fusion to become successful, Chrissie Hynde walked through the door that punk had opened for women. Born in Akron, Ohio, Hynde attended Kent State (like Devo) for three years without becoming aware of the punk scene that was developing in her own backyard. In 1973, she headed to London to live out her rock 'n' roll fantasies. After stints as a writer for *New Musical Express* and a clerk for McLaren and Westwood, she headed for Paris, thinking the new wave in music was going to break there first, as it had in film. She returned to London as soon as the Sex Pistols took off, and there she formed the Pretenders. The group started with a cover of the Kinks' "Stop Your Sobbing" and two moderate tempo singles, "Kid" and "Brass in Pocket." "Brass in Pocket" promptly went to number ten in Great Britain. The group was also an immediate success in the United States. "Brass in Pocket" made it into the Top Twenty, and the group's eponymous debut album entered the Top Ten with material ranging from aggressive, no-holds-barred rock ("Tattooed Love Boys," "Precious") to reggae ("Private Life") and ballads

("Lovers of Today"). *Pretenders II* also went Top Ten and was followed by the group's biggest single, "Back on the Chain Gang" (1983).

As the front woman for the Pretenders, Hynde projected a "tough-chick-in-leathers" image with uncommon grace and dignity. In 1983, she had her first child, who then regularly accompanied her on tour. While her lifestyle owed a lot to the women's movement, Hynde's views on marriage and the family were quite conventional. As she later told an interviewer, "It's not sexist to say that a woman's place is in the home looking after children."[35] In 1985, she married Jim Kerr of Simple Minds and took time off to have another baby. Though feminism was not among her strongest motivations, Hynde did pursue vegetarianism and animal rights vigorously toward the end of the decade.

As new wave journeyed toward mainstream success, there were other artists who sought to retain the edge and anticommercialism of early punk. Prominent among them were Black Flag, X, the Minutemen, Fear, the Germs, and the Circle Jerks. These groups saw their mission as one of increasing punk tempos to the limits of human endurance while they railed against the conditions of everyday life. This was hardcore; the dance that accompanied it was called slamming. To the uninitiated, slamming could easily be mistaken for fighting, and indeed, fueled by their fans, many of the hardcore bands seemed more interested in concert brawls than making records. Penelope Spheeris' 1981 documentary film, *The Decline of Western Civilization,* remains to date the best study of early hardcore bands. In addition to L.A., post-punk stalwarts also held forth from other locales, notably Minneapolis, where Hüsker Dü came from; San Francisco, home of the Dead Kennedys; and Washington, D.C., which spawned Fugazi.

Key to the development of hardcore was SST, an independent label that was started by Black Flag in 1981. The label was also the musical home to the Minutemen and Hüsker Dü. Black Flag had been through a number of personnel changes before arriving at the lineup that featured Henry Rollins as lead singer. A bodybuilder and poet, Rollins unleashed a fury in his vocals that was well suited to the hardcore beat. On Black Flag's debut LP, *Damaged,* Rollins

> *As new wave journeyed toward mainstream success, there were other artists who sought to retain the edge and anticommercialism of early punk. These groups saw their mission as one of increasing punk tempos to the limits of human endurance while they railed against the conditions of everyday life. This was hardcore.*

seemed to delight in celebrating depression and inflicting pain (mostly on himself). Before the group released its second album, *Slip It In,* Rollins left to form his own group.

Given the speed of their music, the Minutemen were aptly named. "On their first few recordings," Robert Palmer noted in the *New York Times,* "the Minutemen got through every song in under two minutes, many in under one, and still had time to sing each song through once, insert a manic guitar break and sing the song again."[36] Early Hüsker Dü were often compared to the Minutemen. On *Land Speed Record* (1982), one of their first releases, they more than lived up to the comparison.

The Washington, D.C., variant of hardcore was no less hyper than its L.A. counterpart, but it was called *straightedge* because its adherents were encouraged to avoid drugs, alcohol, and promiscuous sex. If hardcore reacted against the overproduction of 1960s rock, straightedge also eschewed its freewheeling lifestyle. The straightedge philosophy was perhaps best captured in "Out of Step," by Minor Threat. After Minor Threat's founder, Ian MacKaye, disbanded the original group, a new group, Fugazi, was formed. Fugazi took hardcore in a more political direction, railing against racism, sexism, and environmental destruction.

The most politically oriented band in the hardcore scene was the Dead Kennedys. The group was founded in 1978 by Jello Biafra, the group's lead singer and a dedicated left-wing activist. On their first album, *Fresh Fruit for Rotting Vegetables* (1980), Biafra's biting satire was applied to issues ranging from poverty ("Kill the Poor") to U.S. involvement in Southeast Asia ("Holiday in Cambodia"). "California Uber Alles" skewered Jerry Brown, who was then governor, and other "zen fascist" devotees of the California lifestyle. For the group's second outing, *In God We Trust, Inc.* (1981), they rewrote "Über Alles" as "We've Got a Bigger Problem Now" to apply the same caustic wit to Ronald Reagan. According to punk enthusiast Vic Bondi, that song "defined the lyrical agenda of much of hardcore music, and represented its break with punk."[37]

Vancouver had a very active scene during the second wave of punk with bands such as the Young Canadians, D.O.A., SNFU, and the Dayglo Abortions, all releasing seminal hardcore records between 1979 and the mid-1980s. Art Bergman's Young Canadians were first on the scene, regularly playing the legendary Vancouver club the Smilin' Buddha Cabaret and recording songs such as "Automan" and "Fuck Your Society" under the auspices of producer Bob Rock (who a few years later would gain fame producing Metallica's breakthrough album).

D.O.A., along with Black Flag, the Bad Brains, and Minor Threat, were among the first important hardcore bands. Their second album, *Hardcore '81*, may be the first time the term was used in print. As was the case with many hardcore bands, D.O.A.'s founder, Joey "Shithead" Keithley, has consistently maintained a political stance that is both anarchist and populist in nature, and the band has actively supported antiracism, antiglobalization, freedom of speech, and environmental efforts. D.O.A. are also remembered for their early single "Disco Sucks." Given their outsider stance, they must have been surprised in 2003 when Vancouver's Mayor Larry Campbell declared December 21 as "D.O.A. Day," marking the band's twenty-fifth anniversary.

SNFU (which originally stood for Society's No Fucking Use) formed in Edmonton in 1981, relocating to Vancouver a few years later and releasing their first EP in 1984. Lead singer Ken Chinn, a.k.a. Mr. Chi Pig, sang lyrics that were gross to the point of being humorous ("The Cannibal Cafe"), violent ("Bodies in the Wall"), or satirical of pop culture ("Bobbitt," "Quentin Tarantino Can't Act").

Victoria, B.C.,'s Dayglo Abortions, their name inspired by a raft of then-current headlines in the *Victoria Times* about attacks on abortion clinics, were the most extreme Canadian punk band. Financed by a friend's lottery winnings, in 1981 they recorded an independent twelve-inch release entitled *Out of the Womb* (Sharpe Records). Consisting of ten original songs sporting such titles as "Stupid Songs," "Argh Fuck Kill—Die Sinner Die," "Dogfarts," "Stupid World," and "Ronald McRaygun," the record was lyrically and musically hardcore in the extreme. Much of the recording, including "Wake Up America" and "Proud to Be a Canadian," was highly political in nature. All of it, including the cover art, was designed to shock. The latter was especially offensive, playing off both the group's name and the EP's title, portraying a topless, gut-slashed woman in a bondage shot.

Two later albums, *Feed U.S.A. Fetus* (1986) and *Here Today, Guano Tomorrow* (1987), released by Toronto's Fringe Records, landed the group and their record company in court, charged with violating Canada's obscenity laws. The former album came replete with a cover shot of Ronald and Nancy Reagan sitting down to a dinner consisting of a fetus covered in sauce and garnished with jelly beans. The cover of the latter sported a photo of a hamster with a gun pointed at his head hovering over a heart-shaped box of chocolates nestled innocently on a pink bedspread. The back cover contained a photo ostensibly taken several seconds later of the same scene, only now the gun has been fired and the hamster's blood, guts and fur are strewn all over the chocolates and pink bedspread.

On November 8 1990, a jury ruled that, in distributing these two albums, Fringe Records had not in fact violated Canada's obscenity laws. While Fringe owner Ben Hoffman was not convicted and, legally, neither he nor the band had done anything wrong, the costs of the trial crippled his record company in the short term, and ultimately Fringe never recovered its position as the country's dominant cutting-edge alternative label. Such was the way censorship went in the late 1980s and early 1990s.

While hardcore was pushing the boundaries of punk to the limit, new wave was incorporating other influences that pointed the music in an entirely different direction. Early punk had strayed as far from black music as one could get; new wave rebuilt the connection, primarily through reggae in Britain and rhythm and blues in the United States. The Talking Heads, for example, had always maintained a strong connection to rhythm and blues. It was, then, a logical extension of the group's sound to employ African drummers on *Fear of Music* (1979). Their unique synthesis of black and white reached its zenith on *Remain in Light* (1980), which featured Nona Hendryx (formerly of LaBelle) guesting on vocals and Bernard Worrell (formerly of Parliament) on keyboards. Some new wavers even began to make strange alliances with the dance craze that was threatening to swallow the music industry whole—disco. Blondie's breakthrough single in the United States, for example, was the disco-oriented "Heart of Glass" (1979). Blondie had always been based on a send-up of 1960s pop. "Heart of Glass" had, in fact, begun as a parody of disco, but in the hands of pop producer Mike Chapman, it became a genuine dance floor hit and a number one single. That same year, Third World released a full-fledged disco hit called "Now That We Found Love." One year later, Devo scored their only U.S. hit single with "Whip It," another dance floor favourite. Disco was what was happening, and at the beginning at least, the site of enormous creativity. "I'm cynical about rock music," said canny new waver David Byrne. "The innovations in popular music seem to be more often in disco and funk in the last ten years."[38]

Disco: The Rhythm Without the Blues

"After 1970, when psychedelia gave way to a vogue for downers," Stephen Holden has written, "public dancing hit a low point. About the only people who didn't stop dancing were blacks and gays."[39] If one adds Latinos to Holden's list, it becomes more complete. The clubs frequented by the dancers were called discos from the French word *discothèque.* Discos had been around in the United States since the early 1960s, and many—New York's Peppermint Lounge, among others—booked live acts like Joey Dee and the Starlighters, whose forty-five minute versions of songs like "Shout" and the "Peppermint Twist" propelled patrons into a sweat-drenched dance frenzy. This was the defining element of disco. By the early 1970s, the discos had borrowed light shows from the psychedelic era; most featured records rather than live performances, primarily for economic reasons; and the dancers had added their own pharmacological embellishments to heighten the experience. Unlike the hallucinogens favoured by 1960s rockers or the downers preferred by heavy-metal fans or the speed that fueled punk, the disco drugs of choice were cocaine and poppers (amyl and butyl nitrate). "It was about communal dance ecstasy," Tom Smucker has written of the disco craze. "A new brew of 1970s self-absorption and 1960s collectivity, mixing aerobics, the pick-up singles bar, drug highs and light shows . . . made the dance floor, rather than the concert hall, the locus of orgasmic revelation."[40]

Long before it became a genre unto itself, disco, the music, was whatever was played in dance clubs. "At the start, it was an amalgam of pirated songs," Barbara Graustark reported in *Newsweek* in 1979. "In black, Latino and gay all-night clubs on Fire Island, in New York City, and San Francisco, club deejays would create non-stop sequences of dance music by weaving together twenty minute medleys of tunes by Diana Ross, Barry White, The Temptations and Marvin Gaye."[41] Isaac Hayes and MFSB were also early favourites. At this point, disco was simply called "party music." As the sound began to evolve into its own musical genre, its sources of inspiration came from far and wide. "From Latin music, it takes its percolating percussion, its sensuous, throbbing rhythms; from the '60s 'funk' music of James Brown and Sly Stone, it borrows a kicky bass-guitar line; from Afro-Cuban music, it repeats simple lyric lines like voodoo chants; and like early rock 'n' roll, it exploits the honking saxophones of black rhythm and blues," Graustark noted.[42] Often, nuances of musical taste indicated sexual preference. In the words of club deejay Danae:

> *Straight disco is heavy-duty funk, the driving sound, that has all the power without much of the emotion. Gays like to hear black women singers; they identify with the pain, the irony, the self-consciousness. We pick up on the emotional content, not just the physical power. The MFSB sound was gay, Barry White was a gay sound, so is Donna Summer, Gloria Gaynor.*[43]

As has often been the case in the United States, where the language barrier can be as intractable as the race barrier, Latin music made itself felt primarily as an outside influence. Salsa was just coming into its own, and it developed as a separate subindustry with its own record labels (notably, Fania), distribution networks, and performance venues. Although Fania All Stars compilations like *Spanish Fever* and *Crossover* contained disco material, there was little direct crossover. KC and the Sunshine Band included a Latino conga player, but aside from Disco Tex and His Sex-O-Lettes ("Get Dancin'," 1974) and Foxy ("Get Off," 1978), both of whom hit the Top Ten, disco produced few Latino stars, probably because of the difficulties of interacting with the mainstream culture. These difficulties were well documented after the fact in Rubén Blades' poignant film *Crossover Dreams*.

Proto-Disco: The Funk Connection

The impact of funk was more direct but also limited. By the early 1970s, soul, not unlike the rest of popular music, had splintered. In the centre, Stevie Wonder had a firm hold on the pop soul audience, just as the Jackson 5 appealed to their younger brothers and sisters. At one end of the soul spectrum was the lavish, sweet sound of Philadelphia. At the other was funk, the more caustic, percussive sound descended from James Brown, whose choppy, jagged rhythms interrupted the smooth forward motion of its Philadelphia cousin. Early on, it seemed as if such self-contained funk bands as Kool and the Gang, the Ohio Players, and Earth, Wind & Fire would make a major contribution to disco. Even a white funk band from Scotland, Average White Band ("Pick Up the Pieces," "Cut the Cake"), and a mixed unit from Oakland, California, Tower of Power ("What Is Hip"), appeared to be cutting a good bit of funk mustard. However, as the dance floor mania developed into a more and more upscale trend, the cruder sensuality of post-Sly, James Brown–inspired funk was eclipsed by the more polished sound associated with Philadelphia and the controlled, high-tech energy and propulsive (some would say relentless) 4/4 beat of what came to be known as Eurodisco. In many ways, dance music was at its most creative when it combined elements of all these styles: the sweet soul tenor vocal over Earth, Wind & Fire's funky instrumental on "Shining Star" or Donna Summer's soulful delivery over producer Georgio Moroder's clean, clear, driving synthesizer tracks on "Hot Stuff," which won a rock Grammy at the height of disco.

As the dance floor mania developed into a more and more upscale trend, the cruder sensuality of post-Sly, James Brown–inspired funk was eclipsed by the more polished sound associated with Philadelphia and the controlled, high-tech energy and propulsive (some would say relentless) 4/4 beat of what came to be known as Eurodisco.

The funk sound had been a long time coming and was absorbed all too soon. Like a number of their Philadelphia soul mates, the Ohio Players had formed in the 1950s and laboured for years before hitting the Top Forty in 1973 with "Funky Worm." Although they recorded five gold albums and a handful of hit singles—"Skin Tight," a dance-floor favourite, and "Fire" and

Earth, Wind & Fire's sweet soul vocals over their funky instrumental base propelled the group through the disco era with nothing but gold and platinum albums to their credit.

"Love Rollercoaster," which hit number one—they disappeared from the Top Forty in 1976, even before disco peaked. Wild Cherry, another funk band from Ohio, picked up where the Ohio Players left off with "Play that Funky Music" in 1976. Following a similar, if more successful, trajectory, Kool and the Gang formed in the mid-1960s and first hit the Top Forty in 1973 with "Funky Stuff." Although the group seemed to be really taking off with two follow-up Top Ten singles ("Jungle Boogie" and "Hollywood Swinging"), they also disappeared from the Top Forty in 1975. The inclusion of "Open Sesame" on the *Saturday Night Fever* soundtrack gave the group a new lease on life in 1978. At this point, Kool and the Gang came back strong with three Top Ten singles in a row—"Ladies Night," "Too Hot," and the classic "Celebration"—that took them successfully into the 1980s.

Earth, Wind & Fire was formed later than either the Ohio Players or Kool and the Gang, but the group did better than its predecessors. Throughout the disco era, they turned out nothing but platinum-selling Top Ten albums. The group was founded in 1969 by Maurice White but did not have a stable lineup until 1973, when Philip Bailey was added as colead vocalist. White had started as a session drummer at Chess records. By the 1970s, he had absorbed a catalogue of styles that ranged from American jazz and soul to African folk drumming. In 1975, the group released *That's the Way of the World,* their first number one album and the soundtrack to a documentary film about the band. The album contained all the musical elements that would wrestle for prominence in disco—funk guitar and horn licks punctuating African American and Latin rhythms, all providing a bottom for lavish strings and sweet harmonies with a James Brown tightness that could be rivaled only by the studio precision of Eurodisco. *That's the Way of the World* included the group's only number one single, "Shining Star" (see accompanying CD).

Under White's leadership, Earth, Wind & Fire, who called themselves "the Creator's band," transformed their spiritual interests in Egyptology into a media-savvy image. (White had first become interested in Egyptology while touring with jazz pianist Ramsey Lewis in the late 1960s.) Pyramids and other Egyptian symbols became trademarks of the group. While they had a keen eye for commercial opportunities, they never lost sight of their funk roots. Their rendition of the Beatles' "Got to Get You into My Life," from Robert Stigwood's film version of *Sgt. Pepper,* was one of the few bright spots in an otherwise abysmal movie. The group was also one of the first African American acts to tour with theatre sets and special effects. The band's 1979 world tour had Maurice White dueling on stage with a kind of Darth Vader character. Even at their most outrageous, however, Earth, Wind & Fire seemed to be well within the bounds of soul orthodoxy when compared with George Clinton.

George Clinton was to funk what glam was to rock. His first group, the Parliaments (formed in 1955), had a straight soul hit called "(I Wanna) Testify" in 1967 on Berry Gordy's Revilot label. Following a contract dispute, Clinton found his way to white hippies, LSD, and the music of Jimi Hendrix and added these influences to his storehouse of sources. The new George Clinton (a.k.a. Dr. Funkenstein, Maggot Overlord, Uncle Jam) could be viewed as either a black Frank Zappa or a psychedelic James Brown. Attired in sequined jumpsuits and a blond wig, he could rival any of David Bowie's science-fiction fantasies. At the same time, his express purpose was to "rescue dance music from the blahs."[44] In many ways, Clinton was the missing link between the 1960s focus on consciousness expansion and the 1970s preoccupation with the body. An early album exhorted "Free Your Mind and Your Ass Will Follow."

George Clinton is either a black Frank Zappa or James Brown on acid, depending on how you look at it. The mission of his P-Funk empire was to "rescue dance music from the blahs."

With a core of sidemen (Eddie Hazel, Gary Shider, and Mike Hampton on guitars, Bernard Worrell and Junie Morrison on keyboards, James Brown alumni Bootsy Collins on bass, and Fred Wesley and Maceo Parker on horns), Clinton presided over an extensive and hopelessly complicated Parliament/Funkadelic empire. Funkadelic recorded Clinton's wild psychedelicized funk excursions for Warner. Parliament (essentially the same group) recorded shorter, if not simpler, material for Casablanca. Spin-off projects, which Clinton encouraged, were signed by any number of other labels. The Horny Horns, led by Wesley and Parker, were signed to Atlantic, as were the Brides of Funkenstein. Worrell also issued a solo LP on Arista before joining the Talking Heads. Hazel recorded as a solo artist for Warner, who also signed Bootsy's Rubber Band. The P-Funk vocal chorus constituted Parlet, a group who recorded three albums on Casablanca.

All things considered, Parliament/Funkadelic had a prodigious output with reasonably impressive sales figures. At the height of the disco craze, six of Parliament's albums placed in the Top Thirty, as did two of Funkadelic's. Still, the music was not all that accessible to those who lived only for the dance floor. Disco was primarily a singles medium. Parliament/Funkadelic had only three Top Thirty singles—"Tear the Roof off the Sucker (Give Up the Funk)" and "Flash Light" as Parliament, and "One Nation under a Groove" as Funkadelic. By the late 1970s, their brisk album sales in the pop market stood more as an alternative to disco than as one of its formative influences.

Up from the Disco Underground

When disco first began to emerge as a genre, most of the initial releases were by black artists. In this sense, early disco was part of the continuing development of black dance music. Among the records that made the rare crossover from clubs to radio was "Soul Makossa" (1973), an obscure French import by a Cameroonian artist named Manu Dibango. Dibango thus became the first African musician to have an international hit. "Rock the Boat" by the Hues Corporation and "Rock Your Baby" by George McRae followed a similar path. B. T. Express had a couple of early hits with "Do It ('Til You're Satisfied)" and "Express," as did Tavares with "It Only Takes a Minute." By 1975, when Van McCoy and the Soul City Orchestra established the "Hustle" as the most important new dance craze since the Twist, disco was already showing signs of respectability, but the music industry had not yet taken notice of it.

Perhaps the first hit to reach the charts as disco was Gloria Gaynor's "Never Can Say Good-Bye" (1975), reportedly one of the first records especially mixed for club play. Gaynor should have had a shot at the disco crown, but she was unable to follow up her first hit until 1979. In that year, her aptly titled "I Will Survive" went all the way to number one. "Six months ago," marveled her publicist, "we couldn't give Gloria Gaynor away."[45] Gaynor's mistake had been to record a dynamite disco hit before the music industry recognized disco as a trend. It was Donna Summer who became the first disco diva. Summer was a high-school dropout from Boston who fell into a fortuitous alliance with Europroducer Georgio Moroder when a part in the German production of *Hair* took her to Munich. Summer, who had done musical theatre for years, could really belt out a vocal, but for what would become her first hit single in the United States, Moroder created a symphonic mix of drum machine rhythms and synthesized sounds and then cleared the studio so that Summer could repeat the song's one-line lyric over and over in a breathy whisper while simulating the sound of orgasm twenty-two times. While the widespread popularity of "Love to Love You Baby," which rose to number two early in 1976, moved disco closer to the surface, the established recording industry continued to ignore it. According to Andrew Kopkind of the *Village Voice:*

> The record companies seemed bewildered by what they had, and promo people continued their quirky disregard of the disco category in their portfolios. Instead, they inflated passing fancies into seismic cultural events: Peter Frampton, reggae, and punk, for example. Not that some of those sounds or stars lacked merit; certainly Springsteen, Bob Marley, and the best of the New Wave deserve seats high in rock and roll heaven. But disco would soon swamp them all, and nobody was watching.[46]

With no promotional support forthcoming from the major record companies, disco was rarely heard on the airwaves. The one exception to this was New York's top black station, WBLS, where deejay Frankie Crocker (the Alan Freed of Disco) played many of the early disco hits from clubs. However, WBLS was clearly an exception. Forced to remain underground in this way, disco continued to receive its primary exposure in clubs, popularized only by the creative genius of the disco deejays who "prided themselves on psyching out a crowd and then programming them into an ecstatic frenzy, slip-cuing records into a continuous sequence and equalizing them for dancing by boosting the bass. The top DJs became taste-making alchemists-engineers with cults that followed them from club to club."[47]

Like the music they played, the disco deejays were initially shunned by record companies. To get records, they were expected to make the rounds to each label individually. Eventually, they organized themselves into "record pools" that served as central distribution points where new releases could be discussed and new tastes created. There were about fifty functioning pools in major markets scattered across the country as late as 1979. Much to the surprise of the mainstream music industry, which had not been taken by surprise since early rock 'n' roll, this network of record pools and nightclubs quickly became an alternative to the airplay marketing structure of the music business. Disco deejays were able to break out hits from the dance floor. Such hits were capable of selling upwards of 100,000 copies in New York City alone with virtually no radio play—no mean achievement in an industry that had committed billions of dollars to the airplay system of marketing. In the absence of sustained national exposure through radio play, many disco releases achieved hit status through regional sales. As late as 1979, one record company executive noted:

> *A year ago, we couldn't sell dance records outside the disco belt: New York, Boston, Philadelphia, Baltimore, Washington, and Miami. . . . With a group like the Trammps, who were one of the most successful disco groups, we would sell 100,000 to 150,000 LPs in New York, but only 5,000, say, in Detroit. Our total sales would be about 300,000.*[48]

Such middling sales figures, however, demonstrated record company unwillingness or inability to promote disco more than they demonstrated the music's lack of commercial potential.

Disco's following was not just a fleeting, if dedicated, underground party culture; it was a significant record-buying public. In 1976, the year-end pop charts were bursting with disco acts: Johnny Taylor ("Disco Lady"), Walter Murphy and the Big Apple Band ("A Fifth of Beethoven"), Silver Convention ("Fly, Robin, Fly," "Get Up and Boogie"), the Andrea True Connection ("More, More, More"), Sylvers ("Boogie Fever," "Hot Line"), Hot Chocolate ("You Sexy Thing"), K. C. and the Sunshine Band ("Shake Your Booty," "That's the Way I Like It"), Maxine Nightengale ("Right Back Where We Started From"), Rhythm Heritage ("Theme from S.W.A.T."), the Bee Gees ("You Should be Dancing"), and Vicki Sue Robinson ("Turn the Beat Around"). All of these artists' records were listed among *Billboard*'s forty most popular of the year. Over the next couple of years, disco continued to swell its ranks on the pop charts.[49]

Although as many of these acts were signed by major labels as by independents, the majors neither promoted the music nor supplied any of its key innovations. When disco hit, the majors simply contracted with the independents for distribution or rode the disco wave with their own artists. By and large, disco's creative energy came from independent producers and upstart independent labels. Consider, for example, Richard Finch and Harry Wayne Casey, who made TK Records one of the premier disco labels. Casey was a songwriter who worked for a record distributor in Miami, Florida, and he knew the club scene well. Finch was a bassist who worked as an engineer at TK Records in Hialeah. Together they wrote and produced George McRae's "Rock Your Baby" for TK, which gave the small independent its first entrée to disco. Finch and Casey then went on to form KC and the Sunshine Band, an integrated (black, white, and Latino) ten-piece unit that established TK's position in disco. In 1975, the band released

Donna Summer clutches one of her four Grammy awards. While Summer had the talent to rise above her disco queen image, the pressures of fame and fortune ultimately caused her to turn her back on disco altogether.

three singles that, like "Rock Your Baby," hit number one on both the pop charts and the r&b charts: "Get Down Tonight," "That's the Way (I Like It)," and "Shake Your Booty." By the end of the decade, Finch and Casey had turned out two more number ones—"I'm Your Boogie Man" and "Please Don't Go"—as well as a number of lesser hits. Their strong r&b feel, which came to be known as the "Miami Sound," contributed significantly to the funk side of disco.

When Georgio Moroder wanted to introduce Donna Summer to North America, he took a three-minute demo of "Love to Love You Baby" to Neil Bogart, who had distinguished himself in the previous decade as "the Bubblegum King," producing groups like Ohio Express and the 1910 Fruitgum Company for Buddah. Bogart had recently founded Casablanca Records with a roster that included two bands that had almost nothing in common: the heavy metal group Kiss and George Clinton's Parliament. The addition of Summer would point Casablanca in yet another direction. It was perhaps Bogart's inclination to take chances that attracted Moroder to his label. Summer, of course, became the Queen of Disco and a mainstay of Casablanca's financial health. At her peak, she delivered three number one albums and eight Top Ten singles in a row, including "MacArthur Park," "Hot Stuff," and "Bad Girls," which reached the number one position. "Last Dance," from the film *Thank God It's Friday*, earned her the first of four Grammys in 1978. Summer had trouble rising above her sultry disco seductress persona, but she had enough talent and persistence to seek more. In 1979, she dueted with Barbra Streisand on "No More Tears (Enough Is Enough)." Her ambition was also evident, if not fully realized, on her autobiographical disco mini-opera, *Once Upon a Time.* Under the pressures of fame and fortune (and a lawsuit against Casablanca), she became a born-again Christian in the early 1980s and turned her back on her disco queen image and the gay following who adored it.

Bogart continued to build his quirky roster with the addition of the Village People in 1978. The Village People were a gay-oriented novelty act whose members costumed themselves as a cowboy, an Indian, a hard hat, a soldier, a cop, and a leather freak. The group was assembled by Jacques Morali, a French producer who parodied European perceptions of gay fantasy characters as "a protest against Anita Bryant," the notorious Florida orange juice queen turned antigay activist. Morali's upbeat, anthemic melodies and the group's animated, karate chop delivery were presented as camp disco to the general public. For those in the know, however, the irony of such hits as "Macho Man," "Y. M. C. A.," and "In the Navy" was not particularly subtle. With worldwide sales of 10 million albums, the Village People added measurably to Casablanca's fortunes. In 1978 alone, the fledgling company grossed $100 million.

In 1979, *Billboard* referred to Montreal as being second only to New York City as an important centre for disco music in North America. The city sported over fifty dance clubs in the late 1970s and was the home to independent record companies specializing in disco such as Inter-Global and Les Disques Parapluies. Memphis soul musicians such as former Bar-Kays guitarist Michael Toles were flown up to Montreal for numerous disco sessions in this period. In Toronto, Direction and Rio Records also specialized in disco. Important Canadian disco recordings of the time include Gino Soccio's "Dancer," the THP Orchestra's "Too Hot for Love," Claudja Barry's "Boogie Woogie Dancin' Shoes" and "Can't You Feel My Heart Beat," the Black Light Orchestra's "Once Upon a Time," and Laurie Marshall's "Disco Spaceship." According to Will Straw, in 1979 "it was estimated that some 90 stations across Canada were playing disco music as part of their programming, including CHIC-AM in Toronto, which broadcast disco music 24 hours a day."[50]

If disco was largely a product of independent record companies, the independent producer was equally important to its creative drive, especially in Europe, where producers like Cerrone and Alec Costandinos made such quasi-symphonic disco concept LPs as *Love in C Minor* and *Love and Kisses,* respectively. Costandinos also turned to literary sources to create *Romeo and Juliet* and *The Hunchback of Notre Dame.* There were, in fact, significant differences between Eurodisco and its U.S. counterpart. U.S. disco was more song-oriented and more r&b-based than Eurodisco. Disco albums produced by Freddie Perren in the United States, for example, contained ballads and dance cuts that varied in tempo and mood, with no segues between songs. Perren had begun as a staff producer at Motown, a label dedicated to the concept of

In some ways, the album-length compositions of the European producers attempted to do the work of the club deejays for them. In North America, where the success of disco depended on the dance-club environment and deejay creativity, the music developed as a singles medium.

crossover. As an independent producer, his first successes included the Sylvers' Jackson Five-ish "Boogie Fever" and Tavares' pop-oriented "Heaven Must Be Missing An Angel" and "Who Dunit." In the late 1970s, he produced Gloria Gaynor's "I Will Survive" and Peaches and Herb's disco hit "Shake Your Groove Thing." Still, neither Gaynor's nor Peaches and Herb's albums were all disco. In contrast, Georgio Moroder thought of himself as a composer. On Donna Summer's *Live and More* LP, "MacArthur Park" was followed seamlessly by "Heaven Knows," a song Moroder wrote expressly to complement the rhythm and feeling of "MacArthur Park," thereby maintaining the same tempo and emotional edge for the entire album side.

In some ways, the album-length compositions of the European producers attempted to do the work of the club deejays for them. In North America, where the success of disco depended, at least at first, on the dance club environment and deejay creativity, the music developed as a singles medium. In fact, a whole new subindustry of twelve-inch, 45 rpm singles (the so-called disco mix) opened to accommodate the specific needs of club deejays for extended play and heavy bass. It was this particular innovation that would provide the foundation for rap records in the next decade.

Mainstream Disco: The Bee Gees Boogie Down

In keeping with the popular music tradition of black innovation and white popularization, it was not until a white supergroup—the Bee Gees—came to dominate the scene that disco finally took on the mantle of respectability. According to Andrew Kopkind, 1978 saw

> *several disco stars achieve the necessary "crossover" effect, bringing the music out of the subcultural ghettoes into mainstream life. The Bee Gees were crucial to that passage; they made disco safe for white, straight, male, young, and middle-class America. What Elvis Presley did for black rhythm and blues . . . the Brothers Gibb have done for disco.*[51]

By the time that Barry, Maurice, and Robin Gibb struck disco gold, they had already been through at least three musical incarnations. They began their hit-making career as a Beatles sound-alike act with "New York Mining Disaster 1941/Have You Seen My Wife Mr. Jones" in 1967. After a few more hits in the Beatles' style but lacking the Beatles' depth, the three brothers embarked on undistinguished solo careers. Their reunion in the early 1970s produced a few more hits ("How Can You Mend a Broken Heart" became number one) but still no distinctive voice of their own. It took Atlantic's producer Arif Mardin to help them create their disco-era Bee Gees persona. On *Main Course,* Mardin encouraged an r&b feel that is evident on cuts like "Jive Talkin'," a number one hit in 1975. On "Nights on Broadway" (later covered by Candi Staton), Barry unveiled the falsetto that would become the Bee Gees' disco trademark. The sound was perfected on "You Should Be Dancing," which rose to number one in 1976. Still, while they moved steadily up the ranks of the disco artists, the group did not capture the disco crown until Robert Stigwood commissioned them to write the soundtrack for *Saturday Night Fever,* a feature film starring John Travolta as Brooklyn disco king Tony Manero.

The Bee Gees had been associated with Stigwood from the start of their careers. In 1967, they were signed to a five-year management contract with Brian Epstein's NEMS company when Stigwood was its director. Reportedly, Stigwood paid $2,500 for a 51 percent interest in their publishing.[52] Beginning with *Main Course*, all Bee Gees recordings were released on Stigwood's RSO label. Stigwood was a master at what the industry was beginning to call "crossover media," a product in one medium that can sell a product in another. With the purchase of all the performance rights to the *Jesus Christ Superstar* album in 1970, he perfected a crossover media pattern that *Newsweek*'s David Ansen described as "album sells theater ticket, play sells movie rights, soundtrack album sells movie, movie sells soundtrack album."[53] Stigwood was involved in similar ways with the production of the film version of *Tommy,* the Who's rock opera, in 1975 and with *Grease, Evita,* and *Sgt. Pepper's Lonely Hearts Club Band* in 1978, months after he produced *Saturday Night Fever,* a film whose music he already owned.

As envisioned by Stigwood, the crossover media process was more than the popularity of a Broadway play or a Hollywood film generating sales for a subsequent soundtrack album. Stigwood consciously used each product as a marketing tool to sell the other. The plan was orchestrated to perfection with *Saturday Night Fever.* "How Deep Is Your Love," from the soundtrack album, rose to number one about two months before the film's scheduled Christmas release. By the time the film broke in 504 theatres just before Christmas, "Stayin' Alive," the song that opens the movie, was in the number one position. "Every time the deejay announced 'Stayin' Alive'," crowed RSO Records president Al Coury, "he said, 'That's from the movie *Saturday Night Fever* starring John Travolta.' It was millions and millions of dollars of free publicity."[54] Two months later, "Night Fever," the song from which the film took its name, occupied the number one slot. This, of course, had the effect of keeping the film in circulation that much longer. This kind of marketing would become the rule in the 1980s, a decade dominated by video clips and movie tie-ins.

The success of *Saturday Night Fever* was unprecedented. The film grossed $130 million in its first U.S. run and the soundtrack of the same name sold 15 million copies in the United States and 30 million worldwide, becoming the best-selling record of all time. In addition to the Bee Gees' three number one hits, the LP generated hits for Tavares ("More Than a Woman") and the Trammps ("Disco Inferno"), and a number one single for Yvonne Elliman ("If I Can't Have You"), all within the film's initial run. The film even showcased the Latin side of disco with David Shire's "Salsation," the selection that accompanied the Latino couple who danced circles around Travolta. Under Stigwood, even the Bee Gees' younger brother, Andy Gibb, also on RSO, tallied three number one singles in a row, peaking with "Shadow Dancing" in 1978. Midway through the year, RSO estimated that its 1978 revenues would be somewhere between $300 million and $500 million. The biggest winner of all, however, was Polygram, the Netherlands-based conglomerate that distributed both RSO and Casablanca.

After *Saturday Night Fever*, it became impossible to ignore disco. Artists of all persuasions jumped on the disco bandwagon. Cher's "Take Me Home" on Casablanca reached number eight on the charts. Dolly Parton contributed "Baby I'm Burnin'." Jazz flautist Herbie Mann had a disco hit with "Superman." Even the Rolling Stones and Rod Stewart became disco converts. The Rolling Stones' "Miss You" sold 2 million copies, and Rod Stewart scored the best-selling single of his career with "Da Ya Think I'm Sexy?" (Stewart had actually turned his attention toward the disco market the previous year with "Hot Legs.") With such guaranteed hit-making artists as these on board, radio and television soon followed suit.

The commercial potential of disco came to full bloom when WKTU, an obscure soft-rock station in New York, converted to an all-disco format. Within months, WKTU went from a dreary 0.9 share of the market to an unbelievable 11.3 share, making it the most popular station in the country.

The commercial potential of disco came to full bloom when WKTU, an obscure soft rock station in New York, converted to an all-disco format. According to David Rapaport, the station manager, the conversion was simple: "We sent the program director out to a record store with a credit card Monday morning and he came back with 400 and some odd dollars worth of disco records. That night we changed our format from soft rock to disco."[55] Within months, WKTU went from a dreary 0.9 share of the market to an unbelievable 11.3 share, making it the most popular station in the country. This was in December of 1978. By March 1979, there were some 200 disco stations broadcasting in almost every major market from Miami to Los Angeles, and syndicated television programs such as *Disco Magic* and *Dance Fever* brought the dancing craze to the heartland. Of the fourteen pop Grammy awards in 1979, disco records captured eight. Some 36 million adults thrilled to the musical mixes of 8,000 professional deejays who worked just a portion of the estimated 20,000 disco clubs. Depending on the estimates one believed, disco accounted for 20 to 40 percent of *Billboard*'s chart action. All in all, the disco phenomenon spawned an industry with annual revenues ranging between $4 and $8 billion.

Having seen the profits that disco could produce, the music business soon replicated the successful 120-beat-per-minute formula ad nauseam. The entire disco apparatus was harnessed in the service of industry profits. Record pools, first organized as a collective response to industry indifference, now served as indispensable marketing tools, supplying the record companies with crucial demographic data. Everything from Glenn Miller's "Chattanooga Choo-Choo" to the theme from "Star Wars" to Stravinsky's "Firebird Suite" fell prey to the relentless disco beat. Beethoven's "Fifth Symphony" was an early victim. Canadian middle of the road veteran Percy Faith even recorded a disco version of "Hava Nagila." In the hands of the industry, disco seemed to gobble up everything in its wake.

Of course, by this time, disco had come to symbolize all of the mindless overindulgence its critics had complained about in the first place. Even disco sympathizers had to acknowledge "its empty excesses, its superficiality, its desperate trendiness."[56] The disco underground, once a haven for the disenfranchised, had surfaced as affluent-chic. Disco "is the height of effete snobbery," snapped one observer, "the ultimate in mindless narcissism. Disco is Margaret Trudeau, Truman Capote, Cher, and all their vacuous Studio 54–*People* magazine cronies."[57] Many black artists began to complain that they had no alternative but to submit to the demand for disco. "We're in a period of the McDonald's of music, where it's mass-marketed like junk food," lamented Melba Moore, whose "You Stepped into My Life" was a disco hit. "I don't know what *good* is any more."[58] In a given week, as many as forty of *Billboard's* Hot 100 were disco releases. With the market saturated to this degree, there was bound to be a backlash, and given disco's particular history, it was bound to have racial overtones.

The Hard Rock Reaction

The most visceral antidisco reactions came from the hard rock/heavy metal axis of popular music. As John Travolta won the urban white youth market for disco, and scores of radio stations across the country converted to a disco format almost overnight, FM rock radio responded almost instinctively to its loss of audience share by initiating various antidisco campaigns. Dave Marsh, writing in *Rolling Stone*, explained their motivation in the following way:

> As competition becomes fiercer, each station must settle for a narrower demographic range. Right now the goal is males, ages eighteen to thirty-four. . . . White males, eighteen to thirty-four, are the most likely to see disco as the product of homosexuals, blacks, and Latins, and therefore they're the most likely to respond to appeals to wipe out such threats to their security. It goes almost without saying that such appeals are racist and sexist, but broadcasting has never been an especially civil-libertarian medium.[59]

Marsh was not the first to note the racial dimension of these campaigns. Georgia Christgau had pointed out these tendencies in New York six months earlier.

> Three progressive FM rock stations in New York run anti-disco campaigns. It's not hard to do—radio is already segregated black from white. At a sellout show of Twisted Sister, a local group with a white following, a banner displayed from the balcony read, "We hate disco because it sucks." This isn't opinion, it's willful ignorance, racism feeding on paranoia. . . .[60]

The height of antidisco mania occurred on July 12 1979 when Chicago deejay Steve Dahl staged a "Disco Demolition Night" for station WLUP (the "Loop") at a White Sox double-header. Drawn by the Loop's non-stop hype, 47,795 fans (more rock than baseball) paid their way into Comiskey Park, while about half as many more either crashed the gate or swarmed around the streets outside. As soon as Dahl blew up a cache of disco records between games, hordes of rock crazies stormed the field, tearing up turf and chanting "disco sucks" at the top of their lungs. When Comiskey Park security was unable to restore order, the Sox were forced to cancel and subsequently forfeit the second game.[61]

In the frenzy of the antidisco campaigns, hard rock fans generalized their antidisco feelings to include all black music. While rock radio could have demonstrated the connections between hard rock and black music for its listeners, it fanned the flames of racism instead. As Robert Hilburn has written:

> *Where young rock fans traditionally find identity or strength in the communal celebration of specific genres of rock (punk, heavy metal), much of the energy in the mid and late '70s was suddenly directed against something. "Death to Disco" became a rallying cry. In its enthusiasm, a large percentage of this white audience equated anything black with the dance-floor trend.*
>
> *Rock-oriented radio stations could have educated this young audience on the historical link between rock and black music by programming classic Motown-Stax-Hendrix tracks or the rock-oriented tracks by such contemporary black stars as Stevie Wonder, Prince, Donna Summer, and Rick James. Eager to be culturally in tune with their listenership, however, the stations carelessly picked up on the anti-disco sentiment and fell into racist programming policies: They simply stopped playing all black records.*[62]

Although FM rock radio, which was called album-oriented rock (AOR) at the time, viewed disco as a serious threat to its well-being, it was in no real financial danger. As originally developed by consultant Lee Abrams, AOR was programmed on the basis of sophisticated market research techniques that targeted the record-buying habits of the demographic population with the most disposable income. Needless to say, the use of these techniques meant that black music was usually excluded from programming. WKTU in New York may have been the most popular station in the country in 1979, but with an estimated "annual pretax income of about $6 million on revenues of $9 million," AOR station KMET in Los Angeles was by far the most lucrative.[63] The economic reality for radio was that "disco pulled in an audience that was older, younger, more female or less affluent than desired. And it was easy to see that stations that had stuck to hard rock—KMET in Los Angeles, for instance—were prospering in just the demographic areas radio needed. So rock rose."[64]

As originally developed by consultant Lee Abrams, AOR was programmed on the basis of sophisticated market research techniques that targeted the record-buying habits of the demographic population with the most disposable income. Needless to say, black music was usually excluded from programming.

As disco declined and rock radio reasserted its primacy, black-oriented radio stations were forced to adopt a new format—Urban Contemporary. Black radio had often had to attract a white listenership just to maintain respectable ratings. In the competitive environment of the 1970s, however, there was also pressure to appeal to a more affluent demographic. To do so, these stations retained those black artists in the soul, funk, and jazz idioms—Stevie Wonder, Donna Summer, Rick James, Third World, Funkadelic, Quincy Jones, and George Benson—

who were central to their playlists and added white acts—David Bowie or Hall and Oates—that fit the format. As the strategy began to show returns, bewildered black listeners called to ask why their stations were programming more and more white artists. While listeners were assured of the continuing commitment to the black audience, the stations continued to drift toward the mainstream market. According to Pablo Guzman: "To satisfy everyone in the spirit of the lowest common denominator and to appease big-budget advertisers who were still nervous about the 'black' tag, black references were dropped, music that was 'too funky' was abandoned in favor of white 'crossover' and UC was born."[65]

It must be admitted that the format Urban Contemporary was an interesting concept in that it was designed as a multiracial format. It was also quite successful, surpassing even AOR stations in many instances. Still, while Urban Contemporary programmers succeeded in providing greater access to white musicians on what had been black-oriented stations, black performers did not gain any greater access to rock radio. Thus, Urban Contemporary may well have been a net loss for black artists.

By the end of the 1970s, punk, which had been born again as new wave, had assimilated such diverse musical influences (everything from Jamaican ska to electronic music to disco itself) that it had expanded beyond categorization. Dance-oriented cuts like Blondie's "Rapture," the Clash's "Magnificent Seven," and Spandau Ballet's "Freeze" found their way into disco clubs, further blurring the lines between genres. Concurrently, disco, as a distinct musical style, became so bloated that it began to collapse under its own weight, and black artists began to move in different musical directions. Such traditional soul artists as Smokey Robinson and Stevie Wonder began to reappear on the year-end pop charts. At the same time, a whole new style of black music, known as rap, was born. Artists like the Sugar Hill Gang, Kurtis Blow, and Grand Master Flash and the Furious Five transformed the street poetry of Harlem and the South Bronx into black popular culture. Other black artists—most notably Prince—moved in a rock-oriented direction. Indeed, the artist who dominated in the 1980s was Michael Jackson, the best-selling pop star in history. Jackson's ascent to superstardom was initially hampered by technological advances that allowed the transfer of radio's restrictive programming policies to the new medium of music television. As economic imperatives propelled the music industry toward a strategy of globalization, however, the 1980s witnessed a significant reshuffling of the musical deck. Even as the industry moved toward greater concentration, African American artists achieved superstar status in unprecedented numbers, and popular music became more politically engaged than in any period since the 1960s.

Music Videos, Superstars, and Mega-Events: The Eighties

9

The murder of John Lennon on 8 December 1980 put the big chill to any vestiges of 1960s idealism that had survived the Me Decade, just as the election of Ronald Reagan in the United States one month earlier made it clear that the country was moving in a new political direction. Because of the faltering economy that had plagued the Carter administration, the Keynesian economic strategies of pump priming and deficit spending that had defined the fiscal policy of the Democratic Party since the 1930s no longer held sway among the electorate. Reagan's laissez-faire new federalism, which some labeled "voodoo economics," promised that deregulation of big business and supply-side manipulations would yield a balanced budget. Instead, this approach plunged the U.S. government into the worst deficit in its history.

At the time Reagan was elected, the music industry, like society as a whole, was already in a state of flux. Disco had fallen victim to the predictability of its own formula and the racist backlash of hard rock fans. At the same time, punk had evolved into new wave, an umbrella category so diverse that it was virtually meaningless as a genre. As a result, the marketing categories of the music industry were temporarily thrown into disarray—a disturbing state of affairs for an industry that depends on targeting particular audience demographics. For a time, "new music" was used to describe everybody from Blondie to Michael Jackson. Just to add to the confusion, in 1979, the U.S. music industry suffered its first major recession in thirty years. The phenomenal growth curve of the industry in the mid-1970s had led many to believe that it was virtually recession-proof.

The murder of John Lennon on 8 December 1980 put the big chill to any vestiges of 1960s idealism that had survived the Me Decade, just as the election of Ronald Reagan one month earlier made it clear that the United States was moving in a new political direction.

335

Between 1978 and 1979, however, revenues from the sale of recorded music in the United States declined by 11 percent from an all-time high of $4.1 billion to $3.7 billion one year later.[1] In Canada, revenues similarly declined. Between 1979 and 1980, they dropped by 10 percent from an all-time high of $303.5 million to $270.1 million. The French-language pop music industry in Quebec was especially hard hit by the change in fortune in the industry at large. In 1978, multi-national record companies released 180 LPs by French-language Québécois artists, accounting for 61 percent of the total production of French-language recordings in Quebec. By 1987, releases of French-language popular music albums by multinational record companies had dropped to thirty-eight CDs, accounting for a mere 5.5 percent of all French-language recordings in Quebec. With a number of independent labels that had started in the 1970s going bankrupt in the early 1980s, the total number of French language recordings by both major and independent labels dropped a shocking 54 percent between 1978 and 1983. Overall in the early 1980s, in the U.S. and Canada sales fluctuated, bottoming out in the U.S. at $3.6 billion and in Canada at $240.6 million in 1982. The international music industry followed a similar trajectory. International sales fell 18 percent in three years from $11.4 billion in 1980 to $9.4 billion in 1983.[2]

Although hardly the stock market crash of 1929, the decline in revenues was significant for an enterprise that had more than doubled in size in the preceding five years, and the industry was quick to respond. Within the first five months of decline, 700 record-company employees lost their jobs.[3] Between 1980 and 1986, CBS alone eliminated over 7,000 positions worldwide.[4] Production became more restrictive, making it harder for new acts to break into the business. One estimate suggests that record companies signed about 50 percent fewer artists during the recession than they had previously.[5] Accordingly, the number of new releases in the United States was cut nearly in half during this period from 4,170 in 1978 to 2,170 in 1984.[6]

Any number of reasons were proffered for the slump. The industry itself favoured home taping and piracy as the best explanations. Home taping (consumers illegally taping records instead of buying them) was, by far, the weaker of the two explanations, as market research showed that the people who were buying blank tapes were precisely the people who were buying records. The introduction of portable cassette players in Walkmans, boom boxes, and car stereos had opened up new opportunities for listening to music. Consumers showed their preference for the new configuration by taping their own record collections. By 1983, the year the U.S. music business recovered from the recession, prerecorded cassettes surpassed record albums in unit sales. (In Canada, cassette sales would not surpass those of record albums until 1985.) The figures on piracy were more convincing. In 1979, when the U.S. industry was plagued with returns because records were being shipped at 1978 levels, Al Coury, president of RSO, estimated that 20 to 40 percent of the returns to his company were illegal duplicates.[7] In 1982, the International Federation of the Phonographic Industry (IFPI) estimated piracy at 11 percent of the total market in the United States and Canada, 21 percent of the market in Latin America, 30 percent in Africa, and 66 percent in Asia.[8]

What the industry tended to leave out of its explanations, however, were the possibilities of a less than exciting period in music, a saturated market, and the failure of the industry's own promotional apparatus. It also failed to note the diversion of its own investment capital into other profit-making ventures, including the burgeoning home video market for films and games. The introduction of the video cassette recorder (VCR) in the late 1970s had opened up the possibility of a home market for films on video. By 1980, *Billboard* had started its Video Sales chart, which was followed in 1982 by a Video Rentals chart. Having recognized the potential of films to promote music and Robert Stigwood's success with cross media marketing, many record companies, ranging from such independents as RSO, Casablanca, and Island to such major conglomerates as Warner Communications and CBS, had developed film divisions and were betting that there would be stronger connections between film, video, and music in the near future. VCR penetration grew modestly at first but approached 75 percent by the end of the decade.

While the video-game market seemed to open a new path to profits for some in the industry, this market followed a boom and bust cycle that was even more dramatic than that of records. By 1982, the manufacture of arcade and home video games had become a $7 billion per year enterprise in which Warner Communications' Atari division (maker of Pac Man and other popular entries) led the way. In the first quarter of 1982, Atari's $400 million plus in sales accounted for two-thirds of Warner's total profits at the same time that its record and music publishing subsidiaries posted losses of over $100 million.[9] Noting this, the conglomerate staked its future on the development of video games but was completely unprepared for the intense competition and consumer backlash that occurred. A year later, Warner's Atari division faced losses in the hundreds of millions of dollars. During this same time, the pared-down record division rebounded significantly and was once again on its way to financial health.

By the early 1980s, advances in satellite transmission had opened the door to the possibility of instantaneous national exposure for recording artists, as well as the worldwide simultaneous broadcast of performances. At the same time, the global penetration of portable cassette technology provided for individualized reception anywhere in the world.

If nothing else, the new leisure diversions of the late 1970s and early 1980s pointed out the importance of technological advances that were about to transform the way in which music was produced and consumed. By the early 1980s, advances in satellite transmission had opened the door to the possibility of instantaneous national exposure for recording artists, as well as the worldwide simultaneous broadcast of performances. At the same time, the global penetration of portable cassette technology provided for individualized reception anywhere in the world. In the United States, new transmission capability became apparent in 1981 with the creation of the most powerful music outlet ever to be developed—MTV.

Early Music Television: They Want Their MTV

While it is theoretically possible for music to exist as a solely auditory phenomenon, its presentation within some kind of accompanying visual context, be it dancing in a disco or attending a live concert, has long been seen as an indispensable part of its promotion. There is a sense in which a pop performance is a visual experience. Fans ask, "Have you ever *seen* Springsteen live?" not "Have you ever *heard* Springsteen live?" It is the visual impact of a performance, whether on film, stage, or television, that enables music to deliver its full measure of pleasure. This is a fact that the music industry has long recognized. Music played a prominent role in many of the first sound films. Louis Jordan, among others, made promotional music film clips in the 1940s that contributed measurably to his popularity and sales. For a brief time in the 1960s, there were even video jukeboxes (the Scopitone in France and the ColorSonics machine in the United States) that showed groups performing the selected record. Given the technological advances of the late 1970s, however, it was only logical that the visual context for music should become television.

Of course, television had been used to promote popular music for quite some time. Rock 'n' roll stars had made regular appearances on family variety shows in the 1950s, and *American Bandstand* had provided national exposure for recording artists for years. In the 1960s, shows like *Shindig, Hullabaloo, The Monkees, The Archies,* and *The Partridge Family* were organized around rock. The Beatles' promotional film clips for "Penny Lane" and "Strawberry Fields" were, in fact, produced for television and anticipated some of the videographic techniques used in the 1980s. Indeed, the 1975 film clip for Queen's "Bohemian Rhapsody" is often remembered as the first music video. Still, music television in the 1980s ushered in a new era, an era in which the medium was used in new ways and video became the standard method for marketing popular music.

It was the deregulation of television at the start of the 1980s that encouraged an incredible expansion of cable services throughout the United States and Canada and a dramatic increase in the sheer number of available channels, all of which required new forms of programming. At the same time, technological developments enabled the hitherto unconnected media of television, film, and computer games to converge under the rubric of home video. It was only a matter of time before the home stereo would be added to the mix, a fact which Robert Pittman, MTV's founding father, recognized when he announced the creation of MTV in 1981: "We're now seeing the TV become a component of the stereo system. What we're doing is marrying those two forms so that they work together in unison. . . . MTV is the first attempt to make TV a new form, other than video games and data channels."[10]

The U.S. music industry was fairly slow to warm up to the idea of music videos. They were a high-budget item, and it was not clear that there would ever be a substantial market for them. Indeed, music videos have never become consumer commodities in quite the same way as records, tapes, and compact discs have. Even in 1989, sales of music videos were a paltry $115 million in the United States, while the sales of sound recordings were $6.5 billion. Still, Pittman and his colleagues recognized that music videos, like sound recordings on the radio, could promote an interest in the music itself and deliver potential consumers to advertisers.

Thus, with an initial investment of $20 million, MTV, the first twenty-four-hour music video cable channel, was launched on 1 August 1981 by Warner Communications and the American Express Company. The channel, described by Marshall Cohen, who was then vice president of marketing, as "the most researched channel in history," was devoted to the science of demographics or, to use Pittman's term, *psychographics.* With 85 percent of its mostly white suburban viewers falling between the ages of twelve and thirty-four, MTV promised to deliver the perfect consumers for a tight economy.[11] In its first year of operation, 125 sponsors gambled that the channel would do just that, and the gamble paid off handsomely. With only 40 percent of the United States wired for cable at the time, MTV expanded from an initial 2.5 million subscribers to 17 million in 1983, becoming the fastest growing cable channel in history. It was unquestionably the most effective way for a record to get national exposure.

In his book *Dancing in the Distraction Factory,* Andrew Goodwin identified three historical periods in the development of MTV.[12] The first, 1981 to 1983, was characterized by a twenty-four-hour continuous flow of music with little in the way of discrete programs. During this period, MTV was, in essence, a visual radio station with an AOR format, no news, and continuous music punctuated only by advertisements and the bland patter of the on-camera "vee-jays" (video jockeys). This was hardly surprising, since Pittman had come to the cable channel from a career in radio. The second period, 1983 to 1985, marked a "second launch," as the channel became available in the New York and Los Angeles markets for the first time. During this period, a number of new music video outlets were created to fill in the gaps left by MTV's rock-oriented programming. Black Entertainment Television (BET) devoted about six hours per week to its *Video Soul* program, which was the primary outlet for video exposure for black artists. USA Cable Network's *Night Flight* played longer clips than MTV and showcased the work of some black and Latino acts. The Nashville Network, which went on the air in 1983, offered about eighteen hours of country music per day. WTBS inaugurated *Night Tracks,* a program that used a kind of Top Forty format. The networks also moved into the music video game with NBC's *Friday Night Videos* and ABC's *Hot Tracks.* Similar services—for example, MuchMusic in Canada and Music Box and the Power Station in Europe—soon began to appear elsewhere in the developed world.

MTV bested its U.S. competition at this time by entering into exclusivity arrangements with a number of major record companies. Under these arrangements, MTV had exclusive broadcast rights to certain videos for one month in return for cash payments in the hundreds of thousands of dollars annually. This period marked the beginning of a major commitment to heavy metal and the ascendancy of the "performance clip," essentially a video of a live performance in which the interaction between the band and their fans served as an indicator of metal authenticity. The third period saw a broadening of musical scope and a deeper commitment to youth culture. Videos aimed at those between the ages of twenty-five and fifty-four were transferred to the adult-oriented VH-1, a second MTV Networks music video channel. This period also witnessed the departure of Robert Pittman as MTV's auteur and the abandonment of the continuous flow of music format in favour of discrete programming that would eventually rival the cluttered schedules of the networks.

Goodwin has astutely pointed out that most studies of MTV have a postmodernist bent in that they focus disproportionately on the channel's first period and Pittman's tenure. During the first period, according to Goodwin, the relatively small number of videos available to the channel contributed to a "high degree of repetition," and the continuous flow of music "blurred the categories of art-rock and pop, thus contributing toward a conflation of popular and high-cultural discourses."[13] The relatively small number of videos resulted from the reluctance of the U.S. music industry to enter the video market and forced MTV to rely on British music videos, which "tended toward the abandonment of narrative" as groups "eschewed the bland realism of performance videos."[14]

Music videos had developed earlier in Britain because the paucity of radio stations in Britain and throughout Europe had caused British record companies to seek exposure for their artists on

Britain was swept up in the new romantic movement, which, in its reaction to punk, combined black-influenced dance music, synthesizer pop, and a sense of disco glitz in a strikingly visual and unabashedly commercial package that was well suited to televisual presentation.

television programs such as Britain's *Top of the Pops.* With the coming of MTV, the videos (or promo clips, as they were called) offered a way of gaining entrance to the U.S. market that was more cost-effective than mounting cumbersome and chancy transatlantic national tours. Because the videos were conceived as a form of promotion, their producers and directors were drawn from the ranks of advertising. Thus, the videos were dominated by the aesthetic of advertising—fast cuts, ever-changing camera angles, eye-catching visuals, and a panoply of special effects. It was this aesthetic that was at the heart of the perception that postmodernism had arrived. The fact that Britain, at the time, was swept up in the new romantic movement (which, in its reaction to punk, combined black-influenced dance music, synthesizer pop, and a sense of disco glitz in a strikingly visual and unabashedly commercial package that was well suited to televisual presentation) only added to this perception. Drawing on the repetitive electronic sounds of Can and Kraftwerk from Germany, British acts like Gary Numan and Ultravox made dance-oriented synth-pop safe for Spandau Ballet, Depêche Mode, Soft Cell, and other new romantics. While the new romantic movement itself was short-lived, MTV exposure contributed heavily to the success of Spandau Ballet's "To Cut a Long Story Short" and Depêche Mode's "Just Can't Get Enough." Indeed, Soft Cell's "Tainted Love" became a Top Ten hit at least in part because of its MTV exposure.

Throughout Pittman's tenure, MTV devoted a significant portion of its airtime to introducing white rock acts from other English-speaking countries. The channel's first video, appropriately titled "Video Killed the Radio Star," was by Buggles, a British group, and Australia's Men at Work owed their American success completely to MTV. In fact, beginning in 1982, the channel showcased so many English groups (Adam Ant, Billy Idol, A Flock of Seagulls, New Order, After the Fire, Thomas Dolby, and ABC, among many others) that it contributed significantly to what can only be described as a second British Invasion. In doing so, the channel propelled Human League's "Don't You Want Me?" to number one on the charts and prolonged

The Eurythmics (Dave Stewart and Annie Lennox) look pleased with themselves after their performance of "Sweet Dreams Are Made of This" at the 1984 Grammy Awards. In challenging gender roles as she did, Lennox added an effective political statement to her considerable musical gifts.

the musical lives of the Kinks and the Hollies. It also rejuvenated the career of the supremely telegenic David Bowie when it placed his video of "Let's Dance" in heavy rotation (about half a dozen plays per day) in 1983, giving him his first Top Ten hit in seven years. Other British groups that were proponents of what was now called the new pop (the Eurythmics, Culture Club, and Duran Duran, among others) also made their U.S. debuts in 1983 on MTV and parlayed their exposure into international superstardom. Annie Lennox of the Eurythmics played with androgyny from a female point of view on the video of "Sweet Dreams," while Boy George of Culture Club performed gentle, soulful dance cuts like "Do You Really Want to Hurt Me?," "I'll Tumble 4 Ya," and "Karma Chameleon" decked out in heavy makeup and flowing female frocks. In both instances, the music was as satisfying as the visual images were striking. It was, however, Duran Duran that used the visual medium to greater advantage than any other act.

The physical attractiveness of the group, which was formed in 1978, was an early indicator of one of the prime requirements for video success. Shortly after the recruitment of the alluring, almost pretty Simon Le Bon as lead vocalist in 1980, the group had become the favourite of the teeny bopper set in Britain. The group's first video, "Girls on Film," directed by former musicians Kevin Godley and Lol Creme, was so steamy/erotic/sexist (depending on one's perspective) that it was limited in its ability to get public exposure, which naturally identified Duran Duran as a group to watch, so to speak. The videos for "Rio" and "Hungry Like the Wolf," released in the United States in 1983, established the group as international superstars. Though group members tried to defend their aesthetic choices as parody, in the eyes of the critics, Duran Duran was clearly eschewing the oppositional politics of punk in favour of jet-set images (yachts, sailboats) in exotic locations (Rio, Sri Lanka). The video of "Wild Boys," directed by ad-man Russel Mulcahy, was a surrealistic, science-fiction montage that epitomized the advertising technique of connecting disparate images formally, a common characteristic of early British music videos.

The second British Invasion was a fact of life in the music business by 1985, thanks in large measure to MTV. According to *Billboard,* the invasion "became a certifiable matter of public record on 16 July 1983, upon which date no fewer than eighteen singles of British origin charted in the American Top Forty, topping the previous high of fourteen, set on July 18, 1965."[15] While it was true that a good number of British videos were visually more interesting than their U.S. counterparts, it must be noted that MTV's selection process favoured British groups at the expense of American artists, especially African American artists. Indeed, Britain's Thompson Twins ("In the Name of Love") was one of the few integrated groups to appear on the channel. A tally of *Billboard*'s MTV listings for the week of 16 July 1983 showed that, of nearly 100 videos aired that week, there were no African American artists in heavy rotation and none in medium rotation, and that no new videos by African Americans had been added to the playlist. Needless to say, in the history of the channel, no concerts or specials by African American artists had been shown. Of the American videos shown, the only African American one was Donna Summer's "She Works Hard for the Money," which was in light rotation. Overall, there were only three black acts (all from other countries) in medium or heavy rotation.[16] The channel was roundly trashed in the popular

If MTV executives claimed that few black artists recorded the kind of rock 'n' roll the channel played, how could they explain programming Phil Collins' note-for-note cover version of the Supremes' "You Can't Hurry Love" when Motown acts were getting no airplay? On what basis was Hall and Oates' r&b crossover music considered rock 'n' roll if the r&b crossovers of African American artists were not?

press for its racism, which *People* magazine summed up in one line: "On MTV's current roster of some 800 acts, 16 are black."[17] MTV executives defended their practices by claiming that few black artists recorded the kind of rock 'n' roll that the channel's format required. The argument was, of course, circular. If the channel was formatted according to extensive market research that targeted the tastes of a largely white suburban audience in the first place, then the format could not be used to explain away the racial bias. The format was the *cause* of the racial bias. Furthermore, if MTV executives claimed that few black artists recorded the kind of rock 'n' roll the channel played, how could they explain programming Phil Collins' note-for-note cover version of the Supremes' "You Can't Hurry Love" when Motown acts were getting no airplay? On what basis was Hall and Oates' r&b crossover music considered rock 'n' roll if the r&b crossovers of African American artists were not? The channel's racism was exposed on the air when David Bowie caught veejay Mark Goodman off guard with a question about the lack of black artists on the channel. Replied Goodman: "Of course, also we have to try and do what we think not only New York and Los Angeles will appreciate, but also Poughkeepsie or the Midwest. Pick some town in the Midwest which would be scared to death by Prince, which we're playing, or a string of other black faces, or black music."[18]

Perhaps the most blatant act of racial exclusion was MTV's rejection of five Rick James videos at a time when his album *Street Songs* had sold almost 4 million copies. An MTV spokesperson gave the standard reply: "We play rock and roll. We don't play Rick James because he's funk."[19] The response was particularly unconvincing because MTV was (perhaps reluctantly) playing Prince heavily at the time. While the case could certainly be made that James had a "blacker" sound than Prince, trying to set a rigid outer limit on rock 'n' roll somewhere between Prince's "Little Red Corvette" and James' "Superfreak" could only be considered an exercise in hair splitting. Of course, one possible explanation for this seemingly irrational distinction was the fact that Prince was signed to Warner, one of MTV's parent companies, while Rick James recorded for Motown. In any case, MTV steadfastly continued its refusal of Rick James videos at the time. "The tragedy," said Chris Blackwell of Island Records, "is that here's an opportunity to break down the barriers and they don't do it."[20]

It was Michael Jackson and the incredible success of *Thriller* that finally blew MTV's format argument out of the water. Jackson had already demonstrated his crossover appeal as a member of the Jackson 5 on Motown and as a solo artist on Epic. His first Epic album, *Off the Wall* (1979), produced by Quincy Jones, sold multiplatinum and yielded four Top Ten singles.

He launched into a dance routine that married the fluidity of Fred Astaire to the acrobatics of break-dancing, unleashing his now fabled "moonwalk" on millions of awestruck viewers for the first time. With a single performance, Michael Jackson boosted the sales of Thriller *beyond all known records.*

Still, the album was only a warm-up for *Thriller,* which was number one for thirty-seven weeks in 1983 and generated an unprecedented seven Top Ten singles. It also accounted for a record twelve Grammy Awards in 1983, eight for Jackson himself and four more for Jones as producer. In fact, *Thriller* set so many records and was implicated in so many issues concerning the operations of MTV and the music industry that any consideration of its artistic merit can easily get buried under its impressive statistics. While there is no doubt that it was a marketing achievement of the highest order, the fact is that *Thriller* was a musical tour de force. Its songs and arrangements were well crafted, its production was crisp and uncluttered, its dance grooves were positively infectious, and Jackson's vocals were flawless. On *Thriller,* Michael

Because of criticism over reported physical alterations, charges of alleged child abuse, and unfavourable coverage of his failed marriage to Lisa Marie Presley, it is easy to lose sight of the fact that Michael Jackson once broke down racial barriers, set unimaginable sales records, and provided the inspiration and leadership for charity rock in the United States.

Jackson demonstrated the versatility that might have earned him the title "King of Pop," but given the racial politics of fame, that was a throne he could capture only by crowning himself a decade later.

The album had something for just about everyone. Its first hit was "The Girl Is Mine," an upbeat pop duet with Paul McCartney that was guaranteed to pull in a middle-of-the-road, adult rock audience. It was followed by "Billie Jean," an exquisitely pulsing rocker with obvious dance floor appeal that was number one for seven weeks. The song that displaced it was "Beat It," an overture to hard rockers that used Eddie Van Halen on guitar. As "Beat It" was beginning its descent from the number one slot, Jackson proved once and for all his televisual appeal in an appearance on *Motown 25,* a TV special celebrating Motown's twenty-fifth anniversary. The show, which was aired 16 May 1983, was intended to reunite such first- and second-generation Motown acts as Stevie Wonder, Marvin Gaye, the Supremes, the Temptations, the Four Tops, and the Jacksons, all of whom, with the notable exception of Stevie Wonder, had long since departed the label. For the most part, the celebration proceeded with spirit, although with twenty-five years of contract and royalty disputes, Flo Ballard of the Supremes dying on welfare, and bad blood between Jackson and his brothers, it would have been impossible for the show to be trouble free. Michael had agreed to appear on the condition that he be allowed to perform "Billie Jean," the only non-Motown song of the evening. The Jacksons' set went smoothly, and Michael even effected an on-screen reconciliation with Jermaine. Then Michael's brothers left the stage and he sheepishly introduced "Billie Jean." As the song's throbbing rhythms came up from the band and a black fedora appeared from nowhere, Jackson teased his audience to shrieks of delight. He then launched into a dance routine that married the fluidity of Fred Astaire to the acrobatics of break dancing, unleashing his now fabled "moonwalk" on millions of awestruck viewers for the first time. With a single performance, Michael Jackson boosted the sales of *Thriller* beyond all known records.

Even after Jackson won this kind of acceptance and showed such obvious televisual charisma, MTV at first refused to air the videos of "Billie Jean" or "Beat It." On "Billie Jean," adman Steve Barron portrayed Jackson as a shadowy figure who leads a private detective through a surreal street scene and vanishes into thin air just as he is about to be captured. Bob Giraldi, also from the world of advertising, shot "Beat It" as a straight ensemble dance number that reportedly used real Los Angeles gang members as well as professional dancers. Both videos made as good use of the medium as any of the British videos that were being aired, and their appeal should have been self-evident, but still MTV resisted. Whether it was the overwhelming

"Beat It"

Artist: Michael Jackson

Music / Lyrics by Michael Jackson
(with Quincy Jones)

Label: Epic (1983),
from the *LP Thriller*

Funk, disco, and metal meet with visceral force in "Beat It," one of the many huge hits from Michael Jackson's 1983 LP, *Thriller*. The precision disco beat and catchy "hook," laid down by L.A.'s finest studio musicians, was further enhanced by a pyrotechnic metal guitar solo by Eddie Van Halen (who, honoured and excited by being asked to participate on a Michael Jackson song, reportedly refused to take any money for the session).

Often considered the high point of Jackson's career, *Thriller* and its spin-off videos married the masterful production and arrangement skills of producer Quincy Jones with the James Brown–influenced dance and vocal virtuosity that was evident in Jackson even as a ten-year-old Motown star. Both the LP and the videos were lavish, expensive productions, and the associated musical mini-movies raised the bar for music videos in general. *Thriller* catapulted Jackson through the race barrier of white-dominated AOR radio and 1980s MTV and broke the field of music video wide open for the next wave of funk-influenced African American artists such as Prince.

Musical Style Notes

The backbone of the song "Beat It" is provided by a disco-style electronic drum track, synthesizers, and drum set (played by Steve and Jeff Porcaro of the band Toto), over which a repetitive and compelling melodic vamp is played by bassist Steve Lukather (also of Toto) and guitarist Paul Jackson. Adding to the texture are multiple keyboards, played by Bill Wolfer and Greg Phillinganes (of Stevie Wonder's Wonderlove Band). Layered over this are Michael Jackson's multi-tracked vocals and Eddie Van Halen's guitar solo.

The musical structure is straightforward and typical of song forms found in both rock and disco—verse-verse-chorus—with an improvisatory section (the guitar solo) followed by the repetition of several choruses (see below).

Fun fact: At 2:45 you can hear something that sounds like knocking on a door and then a door closing. Legend has it that this was an engineer who didn't realize that Van Halen was about to begin recording his solo.

Musical "Road Map"

TIMINGS	COMMENTS	LYRICS
0:00–0:11	Introduction—synthesized "gong" sound followed by sharp rhythmic synth "hits"	
0:11	Synthesized "disco" style Drum track enters.	
0:25–0:39	Repeating guitar/bass "vamp" begins.	
0:39–0:53	Verse 1	*They told him . . .*
0:53–1:06	Verse 2	*You better run . . .*
1:06–1:27	Chorus (All parts sung by Jackson)	*Beat it . . .*
1:27–1:41	Verse 3	*They're out to get you . . .*
1:41–1:55	Verse 4	*You have to show them . . .*
1:55–2:29	Chorus	*Beat it . . .*
2:29–2:49	Instrumental interlude providing a transition to the guitar solo (Listen for the knocking at 2:45.)	
2:49–3:18	Eddie Van Halen's guitar solo.	
3:18–4:17	"Beat it" chorus begins again and repeats until the end of the track.	*Beat it . . .*

popularity of the record or the widespread but officially denied rumour that CBS Records threatened to pull all of its videos from MTV unless they aired the Jackson videos, the fact is that MTV finally changed its mind and "Billie Jean" and "Beat It" proceeded to become two of the most popular videos the cable channel ever aired. "Billie Jean" is widely remembered as the video that broke the colour line on MTV.

Having spent $150,000 on the production of "Beat It"—at a time when the cost of most videos was in the $35,000 to $45,000 range—Jackson went on to push production costs to the limit by hiring film director John Landis to shoot a $300,000, fifteen-minute version of "Thriller." Although the move threatened to price other artists out of the video market, Jackson recovered his investment when a long-form documentary called *The Making of Michael Jackson's Thriller,* which included the video of the song, sold nearly one-half million copies, becoming the third best-selling video of 1984, behind *Jane Fonda's Workout* and *Raiders of the Lost Ark.*

While charges of racism provided MTV with its first controversy, it is the treatment of women and the portrayal of gender roles in music videos overall that have engendered the longest running debates. Particularly in MTV's early years, the vast majority of videos the channel aired were by white men trying to appeal to a similar audience demographic. Women appearing in these videos were used as visual hooks to encourage young male viewers to continue watching. Early examples of this practice include the J. Geils Band's "Centerfold," ZZ Top's "Legs," Van Halen's "Hot for Teacher," and Robert Palmer's "Addicted to Love." Given the promotional nature of the videos and the fact that many of their directors came from advertising, where it had long been considered axiomatic that sex sells, the sexism involved in these efforts cannot be attributed to the innocent experimentation with a new art form. As Kevin Godley, codirector of Duran Duran's "Girls on Film," has noted, "People are always accusing that video of sexism, and of course they're right. . . . We were very explicitly told by Duran Duran's management to make a very sensational, erotic piece that would be for clubs, where it could get shown uncensored, just to make people take notice and talk about it."[21]

It should be noted, however, that the objectification of women in music videos was not uniform, monolithic, or fixed. Madonna was routinely taken to task for objectifying herself in her early videos ("Like a Virgin," "Material Girl"). She defended the practice on the basis that she was in control of her image, and she has since been claimed by critics and her audience as a progressive rock star. "Material Girl," in particular, has been subjected to more scholarly (and mostly feminist) rereadings than any other video.[22] At the same time, male stars did not always exploit female images. Lionel Richie's "Hello" or Phil Collins' "One More Night," for example, displayed a respect for women. Furthermore, early music videos sometimes challenged the traditional images of men and women. Annie Lennox and Boy George played with androgyny. Girl-next-door Olivia Newton-John released one of the most popular, if overexposed, videos of the decade. "Physical" had middle-aged fleshpots in a gym metamorphosing into buff he-men as Newton-John fondled their muscles. At first glance, the video appeared to be little more than a shallow attempt on the part of the singer to spice up her image, but its ending had a touch of irony as the men left the gym arm-in-arm as gay couples. Diana Ross' "Muscles" included the muscles without the irony.

Cyndi Lauper, Donna Summer, and Pat Benatar tried different ways of giving a voice to women. The title of Lauper's debut album, *She's So Unusual* (1984), aptly described the singer with the extreme New York accent, rainbow-coloured hair, and thrift-shop fashions, but it was her three-octave range that gave her four Top Ten hits in a row and propelled her to instant, if short-lived, superstardom. On the video of her first hit, "Girls Just Wanna Have Fun," which was shot in her own home with her real mother, Lauper resisted the confines of traditional feminine roles and used imaginative computer graphics to make the point. Donna Summer's "She Works Hard for the Money" depicted a single working mother oppressed on the job and faced with the drudgery of housework and ungrateful kids at home. The bleakness of the mother's life is eased at the end of the video as women from all walks of life gather together to dance in the streets. Pat Benatar's "Love Is a Battlefield" took a similar line. In the video, Benatar portrays a young woman who is thrown out of her suburban home by unbending parents and forced to work in an urban brothel. She finds strength when she intervenes on behalf of a friend who is threatened by a surly patron. The video ends with the women dancing defiantly into the street, expressing both female solidarity and the pleasure of dancing together.

MTV was fraught with racist and sexist practices, but it went on line at exactly the right time for a music industry battling a recession. By late 1982, record companies could count on a 10 to 15 percent increase in sales for acts that made their debut on MTV. Stray Cats sold about 2 million copies of *Built for Speed* (1982) on the strength of the videos accompanying "Rock This Town" and "Stray Cat Strut." Except for "The Breakup Song" in 1981, the Greg Kihn Band had been virtually hitless for eight years when an engaging video of "Jeopardy" shot the single to number two in 1982. By the week of 10 October 1983, seventeen of *Billboard*'s Top Twenty albums had videos on MTV. Artists took the power of the new medium very seriously. Stevie Nicks scuttled an elaborate Civil War drama shot for "Stand Back" at a cost of $85,000 because she thought she looked overweight in the video.

Radio took notice of MTV's power and often added new artists on the basis of video success. The music industry could have taken this trend as an indicator that breaking new artists could point the way out of the recession, but the major record companies perceived their growth potential to be tied to a different and far less democratic strategy.

Given its impact, then, MTV could have had a major effect on the music industry's star system, particularly because it differed from radio in one significant way. "We play 80 percent new music, 20 percent old," boasted Robert Pittman. "Radio is just the opposite."[23] Radio took notice of MTV's power and often added new artists on the basis of video success. The music industry could have taken this trend as an indicator that breaking new artists could point the way out of the recession, but the major record companies perceived their growth potential to be tied to a different and far less democratic strategy.

MuchMusic: What Does It Mean to Make Canadian Music?

Inspired by the success of MTV, in early 1984 CHUM's John Martin and Moses Znaimer applied to the CRTC to start a Canadian cable television video channel devoted to popular music. A licence was granted to MuchMusic in April, making the station one of the first Canadian cable specialty channels. Much (as it is commonly referred to) went on air 31 August 1984, its debut video being Rush's "The Enemy Within." In those early days of cable TV, Much reached approximately 300,000 homes. Today, it delivers programming to millions of Canadian households.

Although the premise of MuchMusic was based on MTV's success, from the beginning there were significant differences between the two stations. Governed by the CRTC's Canadian Content regulations, Much aired a significant number of videos by Canadian artists. Paradoxically, because of economic imperatives and the fact that there had been few outlets for broadcast prior to MuchMusic, there were relatively few videos being made by Canadian artists at the time. Consequently, Much initially had to adopt a policy that if it was Canadian and it was a video, they would play it. As a result, the programming in its first several years was somewhat quirky, and compared with MTV, extremely varied in terms of musical style and the production quality of the videos being aired.

This state of affairs also meant that a number of artists who had virtually no chance of getting played on commercial radio in Canada had a national outlet for their videos on MuchMusic. A good example is the Montreal group Deja Voodoo. Intrigued by the possibilities offered by the new cable channel, they produced a couple of low-budget videos that were subsequently aired by Much. When the group did their first cross-country tour, they found that people who came to their shows were shouting out for the songs that were on video. Given that Deja Voodoo was receiving absolutely no radio play, it was clear that even a limited amount of exposure on Much had helped the band become a going concern.

The case of the Pursuit of Happiness hit "I'm an Adult Now" is even more compelling. Via MuchMusic's steady play of the video, the song became a national hit before it had even been released on vinyl or cassette. When a friend of the band, Lou Guira, offered to shoot a video for the group, lead singer and songwriter Moe Berg played Guira some demos that the band had recently recorded and asked the director which song he wanted to work with. Guira picked "I'm an Adult Now."

Berg picks up the story: "When it was done we took it over to MuchMusic, really clueless, and handed it to them thinking they might play it on [the late-night alternative show] *CityLimits*. We were really lucky, because this was a time when MuchMusic's programming policy was kind of loose." When Much put the video into regular rotation, the Pursuit of Happiness started packing shows right across the country. The problem was that fans kept asking to buy the record and it didn't exist. Borrowing money from their parents, the band rushed-released a twelve-inch single of the song. In the words of MuchMusic's James Booth, "It was shot for very little money, but it was a great song and the video itself is just a cool little storyline that really works for it. You can be cynical and think to do something like that you need to have a marketing team pushing it, but that was one that was just a total grassroots thing. People liked the video and it went into rotation, then got bumped up and played all the time, and probably still gets played every so often as sort of a golden oldie. It pretty much made their career in a sense; it helped them get signed and helped them become a big Canadian band at that point in time."

As Barclay, Jack, and Schneider write in *CanRock Renaissance*, "MuchMusic allowed Canadian youth to see reflections of themselves in their compatriot musicians, which did a lot to increase the importance of Canadian celebrity. Videos made Canadian musicians look much more interesting than they were previously perceived to be."[24]

In her dissertation, "An Analysis of the Construction of National, Racial, and Gendered Identities on MuchMusic (Canada) and MTV (US)," Karen Pegley asks whether MuchMusic has "a televisual aesthetic that reflects Canadian as opposed to American cultural articulations."[25] Examining in great detail a week of fall 1995 programming on both MuchMusic and MTV, she concludes that while the programming on both stations was dominated by white males (largely performing alternative rock on MTV but mainstream rock on MuchMusic), in many respects MuchMusic was more open and inclusive, and consequently the range of videos that the station aired was more diverse.

This diversity manifested itself on Much via a deeper repertoire and a broader sense of history and racial diasporas in the videos that the station chose to program. Much programmed more videos in languages other than English and also more videos made by people from a wider range of nationalities than did MTV. The more inclusive approach to nationalities was largely a result of MuchMusic's willingness to broadcast "world music" videos. Pegley also noted that women artists were featured in Much in a wider range of videos and music genres, performing on a wider range of instruments. Finally, she found that videos by Canadian artists (which of course were featured in much greater numbers on MuchMusic than on MTV) made much greater use of techniques such as film colouring, blurring effects, and film grain than their American counterparts. While Pegley felt that the use of such techniques was an extension of the Canadian documentary tradition, the more open, inclusive policy evident in MuchMusic's programming is most likely tied to norms evident in Canadian society, partially reflected in the government's official policy of two official languages and multiculturalism.

A further example of MuchMusic's openness is that the station had historically been more lenient than MTV when it came to censorship, even airing videos on *Too Much 4 Much* specials that it had "banned" from regular rotation. On *Too Much 4 Much,* each otherwise excluded video was followed by a discussion of why it should or should not be censored.

In September 1986, the French-language version of MuchMusic, MusiquePlus, began broadcasting eight hours a day. At the time, there were only twenty-six French-language videos to show. Consequently, in the earliest days of MusiquePlus, half of its programming was created by MuchMusic in Toronto. In September 1988, MusiquePlus was launched as a twenty-four-hour channel. By 1994, it could choose from over 600 French-language videos, and today at least 35 percent of the videos broadcast on MusiquePlus are in French. Quebec's low birth rate has created a situation where over 71 percent of MusiquePlus's audience are between 18 and 49. Consequently, the station has a very different broadcasting style than MuchMusic or MTV.[26] In 1998, MusicMax was created as an analogue to MTV's VH-1, with popular music programming aimed at an adult audience. In English-speaking Canada, a similar function was served by Much More Music, which began broadcasting in October 1998.

In the 1990s, Much launched affiliated stations in Argentina, Brazil, Finland, the United States, the Middle East, Malaysia, and Indonesia. As well, blocks of Much programming began to be regularly broadcast in Colombia, Mexico, and Singapore.

The differences in programming by MuchMusic and MTV raise the question of differences in the psychology, mythologies, and expressive culture of the two countries. These comparisons in turn bring up an age-old question: what is Canadian about Canadian music?

Not surprisingly, music seems most obviously Canadian when Canadian place names, Canadian people, or Canadian events are referenced. Country artist Stompin' Tom Connors spent most of his career in the late 1960s and early 1970s writing about Canadian places, events, and people in songs such as "Tillsonburg," "Sudbury Saturday Night," "The Black Donnellys," and "The Hockey Song." His "rediscovery" in 1986 had a profound effect on a number of Canadian independent rock musicians, leading many of them to write about Canadian places and people.

There are numerous other examples of songs by Canadian artists that reference Canadian places. Neil Young famously referred to the town of Omemee when he sang "There's a town in North Ontario," in Crosby, Stills, Nash & Young's "Helpless"; Ian Tyson wrote of Alberta in "Four Strong Winds"; singer-songwriter Murray McLauchlan referred to a famous sculpture in downtown Toronto in the song "Down by the Henry Moore"; and the Guess Who sang about "Running Back to Saskatoon." More recently, the Tragically Hip wrote about the town of "Bobcaygeon" and the Rheostatics referred to a hockey legend and his birthplace, Kelvington, Saskatchewan, in the song "The Ballad of Wendell Clark."

Canadian events are chronicled in any number of songs, including Gordon Lightfoot's "Canadian Railroad Trilogy" (about the opening up of the country through the building of coast-to-coast railroad lines) and Weeping Tile's "Westray" (about a tragic mining disaster in the Maritimes). Perhaps the most powerful example of a song chronicling an event in Canadian history is the Band's "Acadian Driftwood," Robbie Robertson's account of the Acadians' expulsion from the East Coast in 1755.

Canadian musicians have often commented on what they feel makes Canadian popular music Canadian. In 1989, Lorraine Segato of Mama Quilla II and the Parachute Club wrote that most of the great Canadian musicians "seem to have emerged from the folk and country tradition, and common ground is their use of narrative—the sense of place that comes through the broad expanses of the music, that makes me think of Canada."[27] This prominence of narrative in Canadian popular song may be a result of the fact that Canada developed without a significant number of people of colour, which meant that the influence of African-derived musics was minimal for much of the nation's history. Instead, the Anglo-Celtic ballad tradition, which is largely narrative, has historically been the dominant influence on Canadian folk and popular music. Narrative continues to inform the work of many current Canadian singer/songwriters, such as Ron Sexsmith and Feist.

A number of musicians feel that the relative sparseness of Canada's population and the vast expanses of forest and plains that dominate Canadian geography have had a marked influenced on the sound of Canadian music. Bruce Cockburn told *Saturday Night* writer Myrna Kostash that he felt that space was what distinguished his own songs and those of other Canadians from American songs. "Space may be a misleading word because it is so vague in relation to music, but maybe it has to do with Canadians being more involved with space around them," asserted Cockburn, "than trying to fill it up as the Americans do. I mean physical space and how it makes you feel about yourself."[28] Barclay, Jack, and Schneider echo Cockburn's thoughts in *CanRock Renaissance* when they write that what makes producer Daniel Lanois' production work so captivating "is that his sense of space in many ways reflects Canada's own vast distances."

Various regions and peoples in Canada have produced music that sounds like it could only have come from Canada. Inuit musicians such as Charley Panagoniuk and Susan Aglukark and the Innu group Kashtin have at various times made extremely popular records that tap into tropes and gestures from mainstream culture while at the same time retaining elements of their own cultures. A good example of this would be Aglukark's "Big Feeling," which contains traces of muted Inuit throat singing.

The Maritime region has also produced distinctive Anglo-Celtic-based popular music that is fundamentally different from anything being recorded in the United States and qualitatively different from anything being recorded in Britain or Ireland. Ashley MacIsaac's hybridized fiddle style is a good example of this, as are the Newfoundland chin rhythms heard in Great Big Sea's "Ordinary Day."

Canadian hip hop and r&b artists are also distinctive. For example, Michie Mee, the Dream Warriors, and Jully Black have all written and recorded music that, while clearly inspired by American hip hop, is infused with Caribbean influences, particularly from Jamaica, stemming from the massive immigrant Caribbean population that lives in Toronto.

Of course, there are many quintessential Canadian artists, such as Leonard Cohen, Rush, the Tragically Hip, and the Barenaked Ladies, who have nothing in common with Innu, Inuit, Jamaican, or Celtic music. Does that make them any less Canadian? Of course not, but it is also arguable that there is nothing about any of those artists that is in any way quintessentially Canadian. The problem comes down to the question of what is (or isn't) Canadian in an officially multicultural country?

The above discussion doesn't even touch on the fact that Canada has two official languages. The chansonniers of Quebec have influenced French Canadian rock and folk music for the past fifty years, leading to particular ways of phrasing both vocally and instrumentally, different approaches to the articulation of time, and different timbral aesthetics. Pagliaro, Harmonium, and even Roch Voisine could be from nowhere else but Canada, but they all make music that is clearly distinct from that made by 80 to 90 percent of Canadian artists.

Part of the problem with the concept that there must be something Canadian in the music made by Canadians is that part of the raison d'être of popular music is to write and perform music with at least the possibility of mass appeal, which, by and large, means adhering to normative musical practices dominant in the United States. This very goal mitigates against regional idiosyncrasies. A colleague recently recalled a conversation between two record executives about Maritime fiddler Ashley MacIsaac's second album. One of the executives was saying that MacIsaac was going to have to rerecord it because it sounded too "ethnic." The irony of course was that MacIsaac's first album sounded very "ethnic" (in this case Celtic), and that is precisely why it was popular. When no one at the record company had expectations of large-scale sales, they were happy to put out what MacIsaac chose to give them. Once he demonstrated with that first album that he had the potential for substantial sales, they felt a need to micromanage the product, in the process denuding it as much as possible of any regional Maritime or Canadian influences. They effectively killed the goose that laid the golden egg.

That said, it could be argued that the majority of Canadians starting out hoping for a career in popular music do not expect to receive any airplay on mainstream radio or to be signed by a major label (as of spring 2008, it has been four years since any Canadian artist was signed to a major label contract in Canada). Consequently, these artists are freed from the imperatives of making formula-based hit recordings and instead can experiment as they try to figure out just what their own music might sound like. This leads to a great deal of diversity in the sounds of popular music being made by Canadians. While there is no single Canadian "sound," there are a number of sounds that are distinctively Canadian. In many ways, it is not surprising that this simply parallels the multicultural reality of the country itself.

Superstars: The Road to Economic Recovery

By 1983, the combination of the recession, the U.S. music industry's slowness in embracing music videos, and MTV's reliance on white British product and their unwillingness to air African American artists had resulted in U.S. pop charts that listed little U.S. music. Writing somewhat jingoistically in the *Boston Globe,* Steve Morse noted, "The American pop charts these days have a shocking lack of true American music—especially country rock, blues, soul, rockabilly, folk and rhythm and blues. Or for that matter, black funk and rap music—two more recent styles that have been unable to transcend cult status."[29]

At the same time, as a result of the multiracial programming of Urban Contemporary stations and MTV's preponderance of new music, AOR radio, which was now the most conservative and segregated format in radio, experienced a significant decline. A resurgence of Top Forty radio in its new incarnation, Hot Hits, further hurt AOR. As Paul Grein explained in a five-part *Billboard* series on radio programming: "AOR used to be a broad-based no-holds-barred format where you could play a wide variety of music and make it all work. But AOR got a little too structured and researched in the '70s and Top 40 took the ball and started playing the wide variety of music AOR once did."[30] Responding to pressures on all fronts, Lee Abrams, the founder of AOR, unveiled a new format called Superstars 83. By the end of the year, even the new format had been radically revised—ironically, following MTV's reluctant and belated lead—to include black crossover acts like Lionel Richie, Donna Summer, Eddy Grant, Prince, and, of course, Michael Jackson. The appearance of black artists on AOR stations suggested some new developments in the music industry.

In 1978, five transnational music corporations—RCA, CBS, Warner, EMI, and Polygram—controlled through ownership, licensing, and/or distribution more than 70 percent of an international music market that was worth over $10 billion.[31] While both CBS and RCA had reported in 1977 that more than 50 percent of their sales were coming from their international divisions, at the time there was still a marked division between artists who were aimed at the domestic market and those who were marketed primarily outside the United States. The surprisingly high international sales figures of the late 1970s were the result of international artists outselling artists intended for the domestic market (Spanish balladeer Julio Iglesias, for example, barely made a dent in the U.S. market in the 1970s, even though he lived in the United States and was the best-selling artist in the world at the time). Disco tended to transcend national boundaries, but it was, in many ways, a transnational music right from the

While international sales provided a handsome source of additional revenue for U.S.-based record companies in the 1970s, the domestic market was still their main focus. The systematic exploitation of the world market as a condition of further growth did not become dominant until the 1980s.

beginning. Its global success was based more on the ubiquity of its international connections than the marketing strategies of U.S.-based record companies. While international sales provided a handsome source of additional revenue for U.S.-based record companies in the 1970s, the domestic market was still their main focus. The systematic exploitation of the world market as a condition of further growth did not become dominant until the 1980s.

At this time, these companies developed a conscious strategy for internationalization that was based on the systematic exportation of Anglo-American popular music that was originally produced for the domestic market. Key to this development was the recognition, as reported in *Billboard,* that the economic recovery of the music industry that began in 1983 "was due more to the runaway success of a handful of smash hits than to an across-the-board pickup in album sales."[32] Of course, nothing better embodied this reality than the success of Michael Jackson's *Thriller.* By 1984, when total domestic sales of $4.4 billion indicated that the U.S. music industry had at least returned to its 1978 level of prosperity, Jackson's *Thriller* was well on its way toward earning a place in the *Guinness Book of World Records* as the best-selling LP of all time, eventually reaching sales of some 40 million units worldwide. The success of *Thriller* signaled an era of blockbuster LPs featuring a limited number of superstar artists as the solution to the industry's economic woes. *Thriller* thus underscored the two most salient aspects of the industry's recovery: concentration of product and expansion into new markets.

Of course, the globalization of the music industry had implications for the treatment of artists at home. "Increasingly, the big record companies are concentrating their resources behind fewer acts," reported the *Wall Street Journal,* "believing that it is easier to succeed with a handful of blockbuster hits than with a slew of moderate sellers."[33] Accordingly, in 1984, Warner Records dropped over thirty artists from its roster, including Arlo Guthrie, Van Morrison, and Bonnie Raitt, who were not quite up to par in terms of sales. Some of these artists (for example, Raitt and Carly Simon, who left the label shortly after her) went on to achieve their greatest successes at other labels. The major labels could have taken the push toward globalization as the occasion for scouring the world for new, exciting, and diverse talent, but instead, that became a research and development task for independent labels. In the cost-cutting fever generated by the recession, major companies looked to reap greater rewards from fewer artists.

If 1983 belonged to Michael Jackson, then 1984 was the year of Prince. Just as Jackson would become the (self-proclaimed) "King of Pop," Prince was the heir-apparent to Little Richard, Jimi Hendrix, and Sly Stone. He synthesized funk and rock just as masterfully as Sly and the Family Stone had before him. As singer, guitarist, and producer, Prince was able to do all by himself what Michael Jackson needed Quincy Jones and Eddie Van Halen to do for him. Born of an interracial union in middle-class, middle-American Minneapolis, Prince Rogers Nelson, better known at the time simply as Prince, was signed to Warner in 1978 and was granted an unprecedented degree of artistic autonomy for a teenager who used music as a vehicle for some very strange notions about sexuality and religion. His first albums were entirely self-written, played, sung, and produced. "Soft and Wet" from *For You* (1978), an album that was dedicated to "God," gave an early taste of the themes that would be included on *Dirty Mind* (1980), which contained odes to incest ("Sister") and oral sex ("Head") as well as other ditties that radio would not touch with the proverbial ten-foot pole. Still, he seemed quite at home in concert, appearing in black lace underpants, backed by the provocative female trio Vanity. For the double LP *1999*

(1982), Prince moved closer to the rock main-stream, producing three major hits including "Little Red Corvette," which became one of the first videos by an African American artist to air on MTV. However, it was not until the release of *Purple Rain* (1984) that Prince was finally crowned. For *Purple Rain,* Prince assembled the Revolution, a new band that was integrated racially and sexually, like Sly and the Family Stone. Released as both an album and a film of the same name, *Purple Rain* was the kind of triumph of cross-media mar-

Despite the fact that Prince projected a mysterious and seductive R-rated persona in the early 1980s, his music still took the mainstream by storm.

keting that Robert Stigwood would have envied. Parallels to the marketing of *Saturday Night Fever* abounded. Before the movie opened, "When Doves Cry," the first single from the album, had already reached number one. It was followed by "Let's Go Crazy," which hit number one shortly thereafter. Once Prince's sound and image were firmly implanted in the public mind, the title song was released and rose to number two. All in all, the album yielded five hit singles for Prince, and the film produced two more for the Time, the group that appeared as his musical competition in the film. *Purple Rain,* the album, sold some 14 million copies, while the video of the movie sold half a million units within six months of its release. Clearly, Prince and *Purple Rain* were more profitable for Warner than most of their other artists combined; not surprisingly, the release of the album coincided with the 1984 purge of the label's talent roster. Still, the artistry of *Purple Rain* should not be overlooked. The stark rhythms of "When Doves Cry" and the frenzied pace of "Let's Go Crazy" seemed to play fast and loose with the rules of pop, yet both reached number one. On video, Prince unleashed some dance moves that approached Jackson's finesse, and guitar playing that rivaled the best of the heavy metal virtuosos. It was Prince's finest hour.

Purple Rain's occupation of the number one position for twenty-four weeks delayed Bruce Springsteen's entrance into the top slot. *Born in the U.S.A.,* which was released about the same time as *Purple Rain,* ascended to number one and accomplished for Springsteen in 1985 what *Purple Rain* had done for Prince in 1984 and *Thriller* had done for Michael Jackson in 1983. *Born in the U.S.A.* tied *Thriller*'s record of generating seven Top Ten singles and remained in the Top Forty for nearly two years, eventually selling some 11 million copies. In 1985, Springsteen was the hottest artist of the year.

Unlike many other superstars, Springsteen always felt more comfortable on stage than on video. An early clip for "Atlantic City," from his acoustic *Nebraska* album, was a black-and-white collage of mundane images of the Atlantic City boardwalk, parking lots, and casino scenes. Springsteen himself never appeared. "The music is left to speak for itself," observed *Newsweek*'s Jim Miller, "a strategy that makes most other videos seem like garish distractions."[34] In his music and in his live perfor-mances, Springsteen combined the image of a hard-driving, blue collar rock 'n' roller with that of a socially conscious 1960s romantic so effectively that he was able to project a "working-class hero" per-sona without pretense, even as he carried home tens of millions of dollars from the sale of *Born in the U.S.A.* On this album,

In his music and in his live performances, Bruce Springsteen combined the image of a hard-driving, blue collar rock 'n' roller with that of a socially conscious 1960s romantic so effectively that he was able to project a "working-class hero" persona without pretense, even as he carried home tens of millions of dollars from the sale of Born in the U.S.A.

Springsteen brought together the unbridled energy of *Born to Run* and the sober portraits of everyday life that constitued *Nebraska.* In "Glory Days," he sang with passion about the trials and tribulations of a former high-school baseball star and a divorced prom queen. "My Hometown" was a thoughtful, searching ballad about the deindustrialization of small-town America. "Born in the U.S.A." was a wail about the racism and senselessness of the war in Vietnam and the cruel fate that befell its veterans. The song's hook line was so powerful (and so ambiguous) that both the Republican and Democratic candidates for president in 1984 (Ronald Reagan and Walter Mondale) tried to appropriate the song as a patriotic anthem, conveniently sidestepping the deeper issues it raised. Springsteen wisely avoided endorsing either of them, concentrating instead on the more grassroots approach of playing benefit concerts to raise money for food banks, soup kitchens, striking miners, and unemployed steelworkers.

Whitney Houston outsold Springsteen and set more industry sales records than he did, but she never reached his heights as a political icon or culture hero. As the daughter of soul singer Cissy Houston and a cousin of Dionne Warwick, Houston came by her talent and gospel roots honestly. Because she had worked as an actress and a model before coming to the attention of Clive Davis at Arista Records, she was, in some ways, made for music television. Given the paucity of black acts, particularly black female acts, that were aired, however, her promotional clips were few and far between. Even so, the playful video for "How Will I Know" helped to maintain her 1985 self-titled debut album in the Top Forty for seventy-eight weeks after it entered the charts at number one. By the time she released "Where Do Broken Hearts Go," from her second album, *Whitney,* she had tallied seven number one hit singles in a row, a feat that had not been accomplished since the Beatles.

Needless to say, Jackson, Prince, Springsteen, and Houston were not the only superstars of the period. Lionel Richie had started as a founding member of the Commodores. He began by playing saxophone and then became lead vocalist and main songwriter. He was a versatile performer whose goal had always been maximum crossover. The Commodores' songs routinely registered in the upper reaches of the pop and r&b charts in the 1970s. "Three Times a Lady," a Grammy-nominated number one hit, even earned Richie a country songwriter award from ASCAP in 1978. He went solo in 1981 under the tutelage of Kenny Rogers' manager, Ken Kragen. In 1983, Richie released *Can't Slow Down,* which went all the way to number one in the middle of Michael Jackson mania and remained in the Top Forty for seventy-eight weeks. The album generated five Top Ten singles, including "All Night Long (All Night)" and "Hello," which, aided by videos on MTV, reached number one. Had it not been overshadowed by *Thriller, Can't Slow Down* (which sold more than 10 million copies) would have been the talk of the industry. Richie repeated his success with *Dancing on the Ceiling* (1986), which also went to number one. This time, he capitalized on the popularity of the title song's video by issuing a "making of" documentary, as Jackson had with "Thriller." After "All Night Long (All Night)," all of Richie's hits tended to be well within the bounds of pop convention, including those with movie tie-ins ("Say You, Say Me" from *White Nights,* 1985) and high-tech videos ("Dancing on the Ceiling," 1986). Richie wanted to cross over in a big way and he got his wish.

Madonna combined good promotion, danceable material, engaging choreography, and visual appeal into just the kind of superstar package that the industry wanted. Between 1984 and 1987, she had twelve Top Ten hits in a row. Nine of them came from two albums, *Like a*

Virgin (1984) and *True Blue* (1986). Both albums hit number one and remained in the Top Forty for a year. Madonna began her career as a disco diva with such dance floor hits as "Holiday," "Borderline," and "Lucky Star" and then used music videos to make the transition to rock star with "Like a Virgin" and "Material Girl." In her videos and live performances, she displayed an adult sexuality that inspired lust in teenage boys, emulation in young girls (dubbed Madonna-wannabees by the media), and outrage in their parents. Her penchant for Christian iconography sometimes recalls Prince's uneasy marriage of sex and religion. Over the years, she has continued to push sexual expression to the limit of public acceptability and sometimes beyond. Ambitious to the core and one of the most astute businesswomen in the industry, Madonna has always managed to use controversy to generate sales—all of her albums have been certified platinum.

In the 1980s, albums were carefully constructed repositories of quality material, designed not as single conceptual wholes like Sgt. Pepper but as time-release capsules, with individual cuts marketed to the public at precise moments. The aim was not to sell the single itself—singles had become largely promotional by this point—but to keep the album in circulation for months.

There were a handful of other artists whose extraordinary chart runs generated similar mega-sales and rounded out the profile of a small group of superstars who could carry the entire music industry. Their multiplatinum figures represented a dramatic statement of how concentrated the industry had become. During this period, the music industry realized a significant proportion of its revenues from about two dozen or so artists. Interestingly, for many of these artists—the Pointer Sisters certainly come to mind—this period represented some of their best work. In some respects, the industry came full circle and returned to the days before rock became art, when albums were aggregates of singles. In those days, however, LPs were crammed with filler because they were designed simply to sell the artist's current hit at a higher price. In the 1980s, albums were carefully constructed repositories of quality material, designed not as single conceptual wholes like *Sgt. Pepper* but as time-release capsules, with individual cuts marketed to the public at precise moment. The aim was not to sell the single itself—singles had become largely promotional by this point—but to keep the album in circulation and on the pop charts for months on end as illustrated on page 356. Of course, music television and cross-media marketing, particularly movie tie-ins, were crucial to this development.

Selected Albums with One-Year Top Forty Chart Runs, 1983–1986

ARTIST	ALBUM (YEAR)	TOP FORTY CHART RUN
Michael Jackson	*Thriller* (1983)	ninety-one weeks
Huey Lewis and the News	*Sports* (1983)	seventy-one weeks
Lionel Richie	*Can't Slow Down* (1983)	seventy-eight weeks
Madonna	*Like a Virgin* (1984)	fifty-two weeks
	True Blue (1986)	fifty-two weeks
Billy Ocean	*Suddenly* (1984)	fifty-seven weeks
Pointer Sisters	*Breakout* (1984)	sixty-five weeks
Bruce Springsteen	*Born in the U.S.A.* (1984)	ninety-six weeks
Tina Turner	*Private Dancer* (1984)	seventy-one weeks
Wham!	*Make It Big* (1984)	fifty-six weeks
Phil Collins	*No Jacket Required* (1985)	seventy weeks
Whitney Houston	*Whitney Houston* (1985)	seventy-eight weeks
Anita Baker	*Rapture* (1986)	seventy-two weeks
Janet Jackson	*Control* (1986)	seventy-seven weeks
Steve Winwood	*Back in the High Life* (1986)	sixty weeks

As Chris Blackwell explained in 1986, "If you're in the entertainment business on the music side, you really need to be in films as well because I think they're really joining into one business."[35] Again, the industry had come full circle in some respects. Just as Tin Pan Alley had solidified its dominance through its relationship with Hollywood films in the thirties and forties, record companies now accomplished the same goal in the 1980s, as illustrated on page 357. As Simon Frith pointed out, "Few hit films are released these days without an accompanying title song promotion."[36] Indeed, music had become so integral to films that it even affected how the films were made. In the 1970s, *Saturday Night Fever* had made it difficult to hear the Bee Gees' "Stayin' Alive" without imagining John Travolta strutting down the streets of Brooklyn. *Flashdance* and *Footloose* permitted similar associations in the 1980s, but it was the release of the 1987 sleeper hit *Dirty Dancing* that completed the fusion of music and film. In this film the music that constituted the soundtrack actually became the focal point of the film, Bob Buziak, the RCA president who authorized the film and the soundtrack, noted at the time:

I had a lot of experience with soundtracks and had seen what worked and what didn't. The movie Back to the Future *grossed $150 million and had a No. 1 single with Huey Lewis; the soundtrack album only sold 600,000. That's because the music was "wallpapered" into the movie, and the songs were not an essential part of the emotional experience. For a soundtrack to be really successful—like* Top Gun *or* The Big Chill—*you have to hear what you see.*[37]

By harnessing all the technology and marketing tools at its disposal, the music industry created a small but internationally popular roster of superstars who were capable of generating unheard-of profits. In the United States, revenues increased steadily from 1983 on, even though total unit sales declined from 680 million in 1984 to 618 million in 1986. In other words, the U.S. music business was making more money selling fewer sound recordings overall. The same was true in Canada, where the total number of units shipped declined from 83.3 million in 1984 to 59.1 million in 1986, yet revenues increased from $294.3 million in 1984 to $310.8 million in 1986. This development was aided by another technological advance—the compact disc (CD), which was introduced simultaneously by Sony and Phillips in the late 1970s. As a digital configuration, the CD promised greater fidelity and ease of use than either records or tapes. Although CDs cost no more to produce than records or tapes, demand allowed record companies to charge more for them. In 1986, in the United States, "The sale of 53 million CDs generated almost as much income ($930 million) as the 125 million LPs sold ($983 million)."[38]

Perhaps what was most striking about the star system that generated these profits was the fact that a significant number of the new international superstars—Michael Jackson, Prince,

Selected Top Ten Hits with Movie Tie-Ins, 1984–1986

ARTIST	SONG (YEAR)	MOVIE
Phil Collins	"Against All Odds (Take a Look at Me Now)" (1984)	*Against All Odds*
Kenny Loggins	"Footloose" (1984)	*Footloose*
Pointer Sisters	"Neutron Dance" (1984)	*Beverly Hills Cop*
Huey Lewis and the News	"The Power of Love" (1985)	*Back to the Future*
Billy Ocean	"When the Going Gets Tough, the Tough Get Going" (1985)	*Jewel of the Nile*
Lionel Richie	"Say You, Say Me" (1985)	*White Nights*
Tina Turner	"We Don't Need Another Hero (Thunderdome)" (1985)	*Mad Max: Beyond Thunderdome*
Berlin	"Take My Breath Away" (1986)	*Top Gun*
Kenny Loggins	"Danger Zone" (1986)	*Top Gun*
Madonna	"Live to Tell" (1986)	*At Close Range*

Lionel Richie, Tina Turner, Whitney Houston, Billy Ocean, the Pointer Sisters, Janet Jackson, Anita Baker, and to a certain extent, Stevie Wonder, Kool & the Gang, Luther Vandross, and Diana Ross—were African American. This may have been the first indication that the greater cosmopolitanism of a world market could produce some changes in the complexion of popular music at home. International acceptance, it appeared, gave access to the kind of promotional clout that could lead to superstardom at home. In 1985, nineteen of the Top Fifty albums of the year were by black artists. In 1986, in the United States eight of the twelve most popular hits of the year were by African American artists, four of whom were women. As *Billboard*'s Paul Grein noted in 1986:

> *Black music has been setting the pace in pop for the past four years, with Michael Jackson, Lionel Richie, and Prince & the Revolution leading the way. . . . In 1986 . . . female artists came to the forefront. . . . The popularity of black female singers was dramatized in June, when "Whitney Houston," Patti LaBelle's "Winner in You" and Janet Jackson's "Control" held down the top three spots on the Top Pop Albums chart. It was the first time that black artists—or female artists, for that matter—had ever achieved that monopoly.*[39]

During this time, the talents of such African American producers as Quincy Jones, Nile Rogers, Narada Michael Walden, Jimmy Jam, and Terry Lewis also came to the forefront and paved the way for LA Reid and Babyface Edmunds toward the end of the decade.

Most of the white artists who achieved superstardom during this period were heavily influenced by black music. Madonna started as a disco artist and kept abreast of developments in the urban dance music scene throughout her career. Phil Collins had enjoyed a fruitful relationship with the Earth, Wind & Fire horn section since his earliest solo hits. Wham! evidenced a Motown influence even before George Michael left to launch a solo career that regularly crossed him over to the black music market. In 1989, Michael actually won the American Music Award for Best Black Male Vocal. Bruce Springsteen's on-stage interplay with sax player Clarence Clemmons foregrounded the r&b roots of his music. Indeed, according to *Billboard,* the rest of the white rock scene was "in something of a sorry state. Urban/dance-oriented rock sounds seemed to garner the lion's share of chart success in 1986, with major names such as Robert Palmer, Peter Gabriel, and Steve Winwood all leaning more toward r&b than rock on their platinum releases."[40]

Record companies came to realize in the 1980s that the longevity of a particular product was the key to their financial well-being. If black artists could demonstrate that kind of staying power, then they would become superstars. Second in importance to longevity was to appeal to as broad a range of audience demographics as possible. Thus, the record companies adopted a deliberate strategy of appealing to different demographics simultaneously. This strategy became a virtual science with the release of a number of well-calculated cross-racial ethnic duets from 1984, as illustrated on page 359.

When Paul McCartney teamed up with Stevie Wonder in 1982 to record "Ebony and Ivory," with its transparent (and saccharine) appeal to racial harmony, the recording appeared to be something of a breakthrough and was discussed as such. McCartney then dueted with

Michael Jackson on "The Girl Is Mine" in 1982 and "Say, Say, Say" in 1983. This latter recording was supported by one of the few interracial videos on MTV, although one did have to wade through the trappings of minstrelsy in the video's staging, costuming, and blackface makeup to appreciate its significance. These projects can be viewed optimistically, as attempts to break down the segregation of the music industry, or cynically, as two commercial giants cashing in on each other's superstar audiences. Julio Iglesias, as another example, was introduced to the U.S. mainstream through two 1984 duets, one with Willie Nelson ("To All the Girls I've Loved Before"), to see if he might spark the country end of the market, and one with Diana Ross ("All of You"), to test his appeal among black listeners. Other cross-racial pairings ranged from pop-oriented commercial gambits to socially conscious anthems. The successes encouraged record companies to spread single acts around to multiple marketing categories. In 1985, Kool & the Gang released *Emergency,* which, on the strength of three Top Ten singles, remained in the Top Forty for nearly a year. The group finished the year in the number one position on the black music charts and among the top twenty acts on the pop, adult contemporary, and dance charts. Madonna registered on the same four charts in that year, topping both the pop and dance categories. Stevie Wonder also found acceptance in these marketing categories when his "Part-Time Lover" reached number one on all four charts at various times during the year. As a whole, in their attempts to consolidate cross-racial markets, these projects brought a new dimension to the very term *crossover.* There were a few crossover projects that seemed to have a higher purpose. "Sisters Are Doin' It for Themselves," (1985) by the Eurythmics and Aretha Franklin, included a video that portrayed women in a broader range of leadership roles than had ever been aired on music television. Proceeds from the sale of the number one single "That's What Friends Are For," by Dionne Warwick and Friends (Elton John, Gladys Knight, and Stevie Wonder), went to finance AIDS research. But these efforts had the benefit of hindsight, as they ventured down a trail that had been blazed some eight months earlier by the ultimate crossover recording—"We Are the World."

Selected Top Ten Cross-Market Pairings, 1984–1987

James Ingram/Michael McDonald "Yah Mo B There" (1984)

Julio Iglesias/Willie Nelson "To All the Girls I've Loved Before" (1984)

Julio Iglesias/Diana Ross "All of You" (1984)

Philip Bailey/Phil Collins "Easy Lover" (1984)

Kenny Rogers/Kim Carnes/James Ingram "What About Me" (1984)

The Eurythmics/Aretha Franklin "Sisters Are Doin' It for Themselves" (1985)

Dionne (Warwick) and Friends "That's What Friends Are For" (1985)

Patti LaBelle/Michael McDonald "On My Own" (1986)

Aretha Franklin/George Michael "I Knew You Were Waiting for Me" (1987)

Linda Ronstadt/James Ingram "Somewhere Out There" (1987)

Charity Rock and Mega-Events: Who Is the World?

International superstars and technological wonders like satellite transmission and the incredible portability of cassettes had, by the mid-1980s, made popular music truly global. Perhaps nothing illustrates this phenomenon better than the string of socially conscious mass concerts and all-star performances, known as mega-events, that began in 1985 with Band Aid, Live Aid, and "We Are The World." Because these projects, which were somewhat cynically dubbed "charity rock," also aided transnational record companies in their quest to find new markets, construct new audiences, and deliver new consumers, they have sometimes been written off as politically irrelevant. More often than not, however, this judgment is too facile.

In their relentless pursuit of higher profits, record companies have tended to relinquish artistic control and move further and further away from the creative process.

While it is true that a handful of major corporations have always been able to exercise tight economic control over the international music market, acquiring the lion's share of the market is not synonymous with determining the form, content, style, and impact of popular music. If anything, in their relentless pursuit of higher profits, record companies have tended to relinquish artistic control and move further and further away from the creative process. By the beginning of the 1980s, music, to the transnational corporate giants, was no longer limited to the manufacture and distribution of a fixed sound product. Instead, it had become a "bundle of rights" for things like television, movies, and advertising. Content to focus its energy on the development of these new sources of income for music, the industry evidenced little inclination to intervene in its content except when forced to do so (see Chapter 10). Thus, in the mid-1980s, popular music tended to develop according to two opposing principles that correspond roughly to the extremes of the commercialism/authenticity continuum. On the commercial front, record companies discovered that their back catalogues were gold to filmmakers and advertisers. Ben E. King's "Stand By Me" was featured in a film of the same name and Levi used it to sell jeans in Britain. As a result, the 1961 r&b classic reentered the British charts and generated brisk sales in the United States as well. Cream's "I Feel Free" was used to sell cars, the Doors' "Riders on the Storm" to sell tires. The Beatles' "Revolution" turned up as the soundtrack for a Nike commercial. When the 1990s finally rolled in, even Bob Dylan's "The Times They Are A-Changin'" was used to promote an accounting firm. "What's new about the rock/ad agency tie-in," said Simon Frith, "is not the exploitation of stars' selling power as such (Coca-Cola has been using rock and pop idols that way for at least thirty years) but the use of anticommercial icons to guarantee the 'authenticity' of the product they're being used to sell."[41] If the meaning of authenticity was confounded by this commercial bent, it was recovered somewhat by the more humanitarian impulse of charity rock, which was coloured, according to John Rockwell of the *New York Times,* by the left-leaning aura that had characterized popular music since the advent of rock 'n' roll.

> *Rock's leftist bias arose from its origins as a music by outsiders—by blacks in a white society, by rural whites in a rapidly urbanizing economy, by regional performers in a pop-music industry dominated by New York, by youth lashing out against the settled assumptions of pre-rock pop-music professionals.*
>
> *That bias was solidified by the 1960's, with its plethora of causes and concerns. . . . Rock music was the anthem of that change—racial with the civil-rights movement, and also social, sexual, and political.*[42]

Christmas in Ethiopia: The Advent of Charity Rock

The story of charity rock begins with the energy and imagination of Bob Geldof, leader of the Boomtown Rats, an Irish punk group. Inspired to action after seeing a BBC documentary on Ethiopian famine, Geldof, in collaboration with Midge Ure of Ultravox, wrote "Do They Know It's Christmas?" and then organized the biggest names in British popular music to record the song as Band Aid, with all proceeds donated to famine victims. "Do They Know It's Christmas?" became the biggest-selling U.K. single ever, totaling 7 million copies worldwide. Based on its success, Geldof tried to organize a similar project in the United States but was stonewalled by some of the artists he contacted. "Look, they viewed me as a minor pop singer from England," he told *Rolling Stone.* "From their point of view, its like Joe Blow calling up. . . . But if Ken Kragen calls up, they know it's kosher. They know that Lionel [Richie] and Quincy [Jones] will be there and that you're gonna have a good show."[43] This is, of course, exactly what happened.

In the United States, charity rock was initiated by African Americans, with Michael Jackson providing much of the leadership and musical direction. Although Jackson may have felt a growing ambivalence about his own "blackness," his career had opened doors for African American artists. The videos for "Beat It" and "Billie Jean" had played pivotal roles in breaking the colour line on MTV, and *Thriller* pointed the way out of the recession for the music business. Jackson then enabled the industry to put its best international foot forward by taking the first American giant step in charity rock. "We Are the World" was co-written by Jackson and Lionel Richie and produced by Quincy Jones, with Jackson playing the role of music director. It was released by an all-star ensemble recording as U.S.A. (United Support of Artists) for Africa, which was also the name of the umbrella organization set up to administer the profits from the record. Organizational input came from Harry Belafonte and Ken Kragen, who, as manager for both Lionel Richie and Kenny Rogers, covered a broad range of pop terrain with the credibility that Geldof lacked. He was the perfect choice for president of U.S.A. for Africa.

There was a distasteful element of self-indulgence in the "saving our own lives" line in that the performers were proclaiming their own salvation for singing about an issue they would never experience on behalf of a people most of them would never encounter.

"We Are the World" was an upbeat pop ditty structured around cameo appearances by the biggest names in U.S. popular music—Michael Jackson, Lionel Richie, Bruce Springsteen, Kenny Rogers, Billy Joel, Madonna, Cyndi Lauper, Diana Ross, Huey Lewis, Bob Dylan, Stevie Wonder, Ray Charles, and more. Because it fit promoter Bill Graham's description of 1980s rock as "the voice of corporate America," it proved to be an easy target for the critics. "With *We Are the World,* I know what they *meant,*" said Jackson Browne. "But on the other hand, that's the problem with North America. We think we *are* the world!"[44] When the song was released, Greil Marcus argued that it

> sounds like a Pepsi jingle—and the constant repetition of "There's a choice we're making" conflates with Pepsi's trademarked "The choice of a new generation" in a way that, on the part of Pepsi-contracted songwriters Michael Jackson and Lionel Richie, is certainly not intentional, and even more

certainly beyond the realm of serendipity. In the realm of contextualization, "We Are The World" says less about Ethiopia than it does about Pepsi—and the true result will likely be less that certain Ethiopian individuals will live, or anyway live a bit longer than they otherwise would have, than that Pepsi will get the catch phrase of its advertising campaign sung for free by Ray Charles, Stevie Wonder, Bruce Springsteen, and all the rest.[45]

There was also a distasteful element of self-indulgence in the "saving our own lives" line of the song in that the performers were proclaiming their own salvation for singing about an issue they would never experience on behalf of a people most of them would never encounter. Even so, "We Are the World" became for charity rock what "We Shall Overcome" was to the civil rights movement and helped to clear the way for Live Aid, the largest single event in human history.

Live Aid made Marshall McLuhan's global village something of a reality for at least sixteen hours. It was organized as an act of will by Geldof, who conned, cajoled, and even resorted to what he called "moral blackmail" to convince more than sixty artists (not to mention promoters, ticket sales agencies, merchandising concerns, sponsors, satellite operators, and radio and television stations) to donate their time and/or money to the cause. The event, which capitalized on the international appeal of superstars, just as "We Are the World" and "Do They Know It's Christmas" did, was organized as a Band Aid project. U.S.A. for Africa did not participate as an organization, and neither Michael Jackson nor Lionel Richie appeared at the event, even though the concert closed with an ensemble rendition of "We Are the World." The concert

"We Are the World" brought together a range of artists who might not otherwise have appeared on the same stage. In so doing, the project opened the door to bolder undertakings like "Sun City."

was staged simultaneously at Wembley Stadium in London and JFK Stadium in Philadelphia on 13 July 1985, and was broadcast either live via fourteen satellites or pretaped to more than 1.6 billion people in 160 countries.

Although the widely rumoured Beatle reunion with Julian Lennon sitting in for John never happened, Live Aid had its share of classic rock 'n' roll moments. Keith Richards and Ron Wood of the Rolling Stones joined Bob Dylan for an all-star performance of "Blowin' in the Wind." Mick Jagger teamed up with Tina Turner for what one newsweekly called a "delightfully lascivious" version of "State of Shock." The Who played together for the first time in three years, and there were welcome Led Zeppelin and Crosby, Stills, Nash & Young reunions, although time and other indulgences had taken their toll. Daryl Hall and John Oates joined former Temptations David Ruffin and Eddie Kendricks for some show-stopping choreography. Phil Collins managed to perform at both Wembley and JFK by zooming across the Atlantic on the Concorde, the supersonic jetliner that Geldof felt for some reason symbolized the potential triumph of technology over human suffering. Geldof's own magic moment occurred when he was hoisted onto the shoulders of Paul McCartney and Pete Townshend on stage for all the world to see.

In both the popular press and the trade press, the concert was celebrated and criticized at the same time—celebrated for "weld[ing] together popular art and humane politics, for using the power, energy and invention of rock & roll to accomplish something of practical social value,"[46] and criticized for its paucity of black and Latino artists and its trivialization of the issues. MTV, which carried the sixteen-hour telecast in its entirety, was the primary target for criticism in the United States because its vacuous veejays seemed more intent on displaying themselves than any knowledge of or interest in the issues at hand or the value of rock history. As the reunited Led Zeppelin launched into their seminal "Stairway to Heaven," the cameras cut to Martha Quinn looking enraptured. The performance of rap group Run-D.M.C., one of the few youth-oriented black groups booked for the event, was short-shrifted so that MTV could cover Sting's backstage arrival. If the veejays could not be blamed for directorial decisions, their commentary, which amounted to little more than the 1980s equivalent of "Wow!" and interview questions that never asked more than "What does Live Aid mean to you?," was no one's fault but their own. The event's hype, glitter, and industry gossip routinely took precedence over education, analysis, and a call to action.

> *Woodstock was the product of a bygone era; it was experienced as participatory, communitarian, and anticommercial. Live Aid was an unabashed celebration of technological possibilities in a period of yuppie conservatism.*

Because Live Aid was a benefit, comparisons with other humanitarian events abounded. While the issue of starvation recalled George Harrison's Concert for Bangladesh, the most obvious comparison was to Woodstock. Indeed, Joan Baez opened the Philadelphia show with the words: "Good morning, you children of the 1980s. This is your Woodstock and it's long overdue." In point of fact, however, Baez's comments reflected wishful political thinking. To the extent that Woodstock helped usher in the big business/mass music/techno-culture of the 1980s, there was certainly a historical connection between the two events, but they had little else in common. Woodstock was the product of a bygone era; it was experienced as participatory, communitarian, and anticommercial. Live Aid was an unabashed celebration of technological possibilities in a period of yuppie conservatism. Live Aid made use of corporate sponsors—AT&T, Eastman Kodak, Chevrolet, and Pepsi—which would have been anathema to the Woodstock

Shared by 1.6 billion people in 160 countries, Live Aid was the largest single event in human history. The live concert was staged simultaneously at Wembley Stadium in London and JFK Stadium in Philadelphia.

generation. "The politics of Woodstock were antiauthoritarian, antiestablishment, antiwar," said commentator Pete Hamill. "The American Live Aid audience was part of a new American generation that thinks Ronald Reagan is a wonderful president, Rambo a wonderful role model, and Grenada a wonderful war."[47]

Still, as Will Straw pointed out, "The most underrated contribution rock musicians can make to politics is their money, or ways in which that money might be raised," and although sometimes overlooked in the hype, the most important function of Live Aid had been that of fund-raising.[48] The actual take was $67 million. By anyone's fund-raising standards, that is a staggering amount of money to be generated from a single event. Even so, Geldof, who was nominated for the Nobel Peace Prize for his efforts, recognized its limitations: "I'm aware that a million dollars is a lot of money, but when 130 million people are affected by this problem, even $67 million is nothing."[49] Furthermore, there remained the question of the extent to which Live Aid served the issue at hand and the extent to which it served capital. At the 1986 ceremony of the British music industry's BPI awards, Norman Tebbitt of the Thatcher administration "extolled Live Aid as a triumph of international marketing."[50] On this side of the Atlantic, John Costello, vice president of Pepsi, said, "Live Aid demonstrates that you can quickly develop marketing events that are good for companies, artists, and the cause."[51]

Mega-Events: The Politics of Mass Culture

To many, charity rock was a contradictory phenomenon. While it provided activist musicians with a platform for political expression on a scale that was previously unthinkable, at the same time it enabled the music industry to exploit a gold mine of untapped markets. Embedded in this contradiction, which went well beyond popular music and mega-events, was a new view of mass culture. Far from being considered a cultural wasteland that promotes mindless consumption, mass culture came to be seen as "contested terrain," an ideological cauldron in which new values could be forged.

Band Aid, Live Aid, and U.S.A. for Africa created a climate in which musicians from countries all over the world felt compelled to follow suit with African famine relief projects of their own. The Canadian effort, entitled "Tears Are Not Enough," actually was written and recorded before "We Are the World." Issued under the name Northern Lights, as was the case with Bob Geldof's "Do They Know It's Christmas?," the recording brought together an unprecedented gathering of pop, rock, jazz, country, and classical musicians, in this case from Canada. The music for "Tears Are Not Enough" was written by David Foster (ironically, originally for an American film), while long-time songwriting partners Bryan Adams and Jim Vallance penned the English lyrics. French lyrics were provided courtesy of Rachel Paiment, and the whole project was organized by Adams' manager, Bruce Allen.

The backing track for the song was cut by Foster in Vancouver, and on 10 February 1985, the fifty-plus singers who participated in the recording gathered at Manta Sound in Toronto. Superstars such as Gordon Lightfoot, Burton Cummings, Anne Murray, Joni Mitchell, Dan Hill, Neil Young, Bryan Adams, Corey Hart, Bruce Cockburn, Geddy Lee, and Mike Reno (from Loverboy) all took solo lines, while r&b diva Liberty Silver, country singer Carroll Baker, Ronnie Hawkins, Murray McLauchlan, Veronique Beliveau, Robert Charlebois, Claude Dubois, jazz singer Salome Bey, Lorraine Segato, Paul Hyde (of the Payolas), and Carole Pope were featured as either duos or trios. Classical guitarist Liona Boyd, country musician Tommy Hunter, jazz pianist Oscar Peterson, Paul Shaffer (band director for David Letterman), Tom Cochrane, Kim Mitchell, Jane Siberry, and Sylvia Tyson all participated on the chorus.

"Tears Are Not Enough" was originally issued as a twelve-inch single by CBS in March 1985. By late April, it was number one in Canada. The song would go on to sell more than 300,000 copies and was included on U.S.A. for Africa's *We Are the World* album later that year. Both the video for the song and a ninety-minute documentary, originally broadcast on CBC and eventually issued on home video, were extremely popular. With lyrics such as "If we could pull together, we could change the world forever, don't you know that tears are not enough," the record was as full of banal "feel good" platitudes as "We Are the World." Nonetheless, "Tears Are Not Enough" raised over $3.2 million over the next five years, 10 percent being allocated to Canadian assistance programs, the remainder being directed to Ethiopian famine relief.

A partial list of such other projects includes West Germany's all-star Band fur Ethiopia, which released "Nackt im Wind," and Chanteurs Sans Frontières, a group of thirty-six French singers who offered "Ethiopie." Belgium contributed "Leven Zonder Honger," the Netherlands "Samen," Australia "E.A.T." (East African Tragedy), and fifty African artists, including Youssou

N'Dour, Hugh Masakela, Manu Dibangu, and King Sunny Ade, recorded "Tam Tam Pour L'Ethiopie."[52] As politically cautious as some of these humanitarian efforts were, they created the cultural space for progressively bolder projects, including some that brought the issue of economic devastation closer to home. An offhand comment by Bob Dylan about the plight of the U.S. family farm made from the stage at Live Aid prompted Willie Nelson, John Cougar Mellencamp, and Neil Young to organize Farm Aid two months later. Nelson secured the use of the football stadium at the University of Illinois from Governor James R. Thompson and cajoled country artists ranging from Kenny Rogers and Glen Campbell to Alabama and the Charlie Daniels Band to Merle Haggard and Loretta Lynn to perform. Young and Mellencamp pulled in rockers ranging from Billy Joel and Don Henley to Eddie Van Halen and Sammy Hager to X and the Blasters. The concert brought together a unique coalition of rock and country artists who were uncommonly respectful of one another, raised $10 million in the process, and eventually made Farm Aid an annualized event.

Other, more politicized ventures followed, including Sun City, the two Amnesty International tours, and two tributes to African National Congress leader Nelson Mandela. Using "We Are the World" as a model, guitarist Little Steven, fresh from Bruce Springsteen's E Street Band, assembled more than fifty rock, rap, r&b, jazz, and salsa artists to create the recording "Sun City," a politically charged anthem in support of the UN-sponsored cultural boycott of South Africa, which was then under white minority rule. "Sun City" urged musicians not to perform at the lavish Las Vegas–like entertainment complex that was located in one of the so-called South African homelands. Symbolically, it upped the political stakes of all-star recordings significantly.

In some ways, "We Are the World" was the logical extension of the crossover strategy developed in the mid-1980s. It was a pop-oriented tune that primarily utilized artists who, while drawn from the often mutually exclusive categories of rock, country, and r&b, had achieved mainstream acceptance. By including heavy metal acts like Judas Priest and Ozzy Osbourne, new wave groups like Simple Minds and the Boomtown Rats, r&b artists like Patti LaBelle and Ashford and Simpson, and rappers like Run-D.M.C., Live Aid had broadened the politicization of mass culture a bit more. "Sun City" pushed it even further. It was a forceful composition with an explicitly antiapartheid message. It included a broad range of artists (jazz great Miles Davis, salsa stars like Ray Baretto and Rubén Blades, rappers like Afrika Bambaataa and Run-D.M.C., and two South African groups, the Malopoets and Via Afrika, who risked personal reprisals as a result) as well as artists who were known to be politically outspoken, including Jackson Browne, Bonnie Raitt, Peter Garrett from Midnight Oil, and Bono from U2. Its video masterfully intercut scenes of the horrors of apartheid with cameo appearances of the performing artists. It climaxed with the ensemble cast singing the anthemic chorus at an actual divestment rally at CitiBank in New York and then segued seamlessly to a demonstration of black South Africans singing "Nkosi Sikelel' iAfrica," the (unofficial) black South African national anthem, as the video faded, thus linking the participating artists with the antiapartheid movements in the United States and South Africa.

Not content with just presenting an antiapartheid message, the creators of "Sun City" also sought to encourage an activist audience response. The album jacket, for example, was filled with facts and figures about apartheid, and a teacher's guide showing how to use the record and the video in the classroom was issued. As part of its educational effort, the guide reported on numerous antiapartheid student projects that had been inspired by the recording. In creating a teacher's guide, the Sun City project was attempting to build on the familiarity of a mass cultural product to create exercises that could be tailored to local use.

The "Sun City" project was not the only one to encourage political activism on the part of its audience. In 1986, U2, then an up-and-coming Irish rock band from Dublin, headlined a U.S. tour, titled The Conspiracy of Hope, for Amnesty International. As a group of politically progressive devout Christians from strife-torn Ireland, U2 was the perfect choice to represent the organization that acts as an advocate for prisoners of conscience around the world. Formed in 1977, U2 first cracked the U.S. Top Forty in 1983 with *War,* which included "Sunday Bloody Sunday," the group's most poignant political commentary. With the release of *The Unforgettable Fire* (1984), which included the hit single "Pride (In the Name of Love)," they began their ascent to superstardom. By 1987, they were the hottest rock act in the world, with millions of devoted followers, including Bruce Springsteen. *The Joshua Tree,* which was released in 1987, went to number one and then charted in the Top Forty for more than a year, winning the 1987 Grammy Award for album of the year.

The Unforgettable Fire was produced by Daniel Lanois. A Canadian guitarist who was born in Montreal and raised from the age of 12 in Hamilton, in the early 1970s Lanois was a member of Tranquillity Base. In 1974, in partnership with his brother Bob Lanois, he opened Hamilton's Grant Avenue studios producing seminal albums by Martha and the Muffins, the Parachute Club and Ian Tyson. In 1983, British experimental pop composer Brian Eno recorded *Apollo: Atmospheres & Soundtracks* at Grant Avenue. Impressed by Lanois' unique approach to timbre and soundscape, Eno invited Lanois to co-produce U2's *The Unforgettable Fire.* Lanois would go on to produce or co-produce several future albums with U2 including their breakthrough disc, 1987's *Joshua Tree.* He would also produce Bob Dylan's two finest albums in the 1980s and 1990s, *Oh Mercy* (1989) and *Time Out of Mind* (1997), as well as Robbie Robertson's first solo album and discs by Emmylou Harris, Willie Nelson, and the Neville Brothers. Beginning with 1989's *Acadie,* Lanois has also periodically recorded solo albums drawing on both English and French folk and popular traditions.

It was Jack Healy, then executive director of Amnesty International USA, who organized the Conspiracy of Hope Tour and engineered the connection between rock and the human rights movement. One of the tour's goals was to recruit new "freedom writers" who would participate in the letter-writing campaigns Amnesty uses to call attention to the plight of prisoners of conscience.

Thus, as a part of the event, the tour targeted six political prisoners, three of whom were freed within two years as a result. In addition, Amnesty USA added some 200,000 new volunteers to the organization. "Previous to 1986, we were an organization post forty," said Healy. "Music allowed us to change the very nature of our membership."[53] In 1988, Healy organized a world tour, called the Human Rights Now! tour, that featured Bruce Springsteen, Sting, Peter Gabriel, Tracy Chapman, and Youssou N'Dour as headliners who were supported by a variety of local and national acts from host countries. Healy's choice of artists was well calculated. Sting, who had left the Police in the mid-1980s, was riding high from the success of *The Dream of the Blue Turtles* (1985) and *. . . Nothing Like the Sun* (1987), both collaborations with jazz saxophonist Branford Marsalis. Gabriel's *So* (1986), the best-selling album of his solo career, had catapulted him to international superstardom, and he was already well respected in international circles as the prime mover of WOMAD, the international World of Music, Arts, and Dance Festival. Chapman's self-titled debut album hit number one in 1988, enabling Healy to add some diversity (musical and otherwise) to the bill. Youssou N'Dour was Senegal's most popular artist and a master of the African funk, rock, and jazz fusions that were becoming popular on the international stage. His presence conferred that much more credibility on the Human Rights Now! tour. Springsteen was Amnesty's best-selling artist, but the tour had as big an effect on him as he had on it. As Healy recalled:

> *I remember Bruce Springsteen saying that he'd played to his first black audiences on the Human Rights Now! Tour in Zimbabwe and the Ivory Coast. We played to Shintos in Japan, Hindus in India, uptight Orthodox Christians in Greece, a mix of religions in Zimbabwe and a lot of Muslims in the Ivory Coast. And Bruce was loved by all of them; he rocked the stadiums everywhere.*[54]

After the Human Rights Now! tour, Amnesty boasted 420,000 members worldwide, with an average age of twenty.

There were also two massive international concerts staged at Wembley Stadium on behalf of Nelson Mandela. The first was held on 11 June 1988 to celebrate Mandela's seventieth birthday. The second was held on 16 April 1990 to celebrate the end of his thirty years of imprisonment. The eleven-hour Nelson Mandela Seventieth Birthday Tribute, as the first concert was officially named, featured a remarkably diverse roster of first-rate talent.[55] It was broadcast whole or in part to an estimated 600 million people in more than sixty countries. In calling for the release of the imprisoned leader of the African National Congress (ANC), an organization considered illegal by most of the countries that broadcast the concert, the Mandela Tribute raised the political stakes for mega-events once again. The stage was adorned by a thirty-foot scrim of Mandela's image perched tastefully atop the slogans "Isolate apartheid" and "The struggle is my life." The massive speaker columns were flanked by exact replicas of the late Keith Haring's "Free South Africa" poster. Just as "Sun City" pushed against the limits of politicized pop, the Mandela shows eschewed charity in favour of structural change.

> *J*ust as "Sun City" pushed against the limits of politicized pop, the Mandela shows eschewed charity in favour of structural change.

Like all political events, the first Mandela tribute had found it difficult to balance the need to recruit stars who could ensure the financial success of the event with the need to present those artists who had demonstrated commitment to the issue at hand. In the push to book name acts, lesser-known but politically more active artists like Billy Bragg and South Africa's Johnny Clegg were passed over for Whitney Houston and others. Houston was the biggest star booked for the event and thus attracted the most criticism, particularly because industry rumours suggested that her management had urged concert organizers to downplay the political aspects of the event as a condition for her appearance. For her part, Houston delivered the most animated performance of the day. While she was vulnerable to the charge of playing it safe both musically and politically, she was one of the first artists to commit to the festival. Her overwhelming popularity contributed significantly to making the event attractive to broadcasters all over the world, and she was a favourite of the imprisoned ANC leaders. Ahmed Kathrada, an ANC rebel who was serving a life sentence along with Mandela, sent a message that was distributed by the local Anti-Apartheid Movement and quoted in *Rolling Stone:* "You lucky guys. What I wouldn't give just to listen to Whitney Houston! I must have told you that she has long been mine and Walter's [Sisulu] top favourite. . . . In our love and admiration for Whitney we are prepared to be second to none!"[56]

Organizers of the second concert, An International Tribute for a Free South Africa, were in a particularly good position to learn from the criticisms of the first tribute. With only fifty-four days to produce the concert, there were problems in booking artists. Still, with stars like Peter Gabriel, Tracy Chapman, Bonnie Raitt, Anita Baker, Neil Young, Natalie Cole, and Lou Reed among many others agreeing to appear, an impressive lineup of artists was assembled on short notice. The 72,000 tickets for the live event sold out faster than any other event in the history of Wembley Stadium. Of course, the real headliner of the event was Nelson Mandela, and it was widely assumed that his presence, which without question gave the event political credibility, would make the concert irresistible to broadcasters the world over. That assumption turned out to be largely accurate; broadcasters from some sixty-three countries signed on to broadcast the four-hour concert. Even South Africa proposed to carry the show, a proposal that was eventually rejected by the ANC in support of the cultural boycott. It was, therefore, all the more shocking that not a single U.S. broadcaster could be persuaded to air the event. The only North American broadcast of the show was by Canada's MuchMusic, which broadcast the concert in its entirety.

Using the international platform that the event offered, Mandela, with his dignified but forceful demeanour and steadfast refusal to compromise his principles, drove home his antiapartheid message to hundreds of millions of people all over the world. He indicated his understanding of the power of mega-events when he thanked the performing artists backstage for their efforts:

Over the years in prison I have tried to follow the developments in progressive music. . . . Your contri-bution has given us tremendous inspiration. . . . Your message can reach quarters not necessarily interested in politics, so that the message can go further than we politicians can push it. . . . We admire you. We respect you, and above all, we love you.[57]

The international political agenda of mega-events was not limited to issues affecting only the African continent. Global environmental concerns were also important. Early in 1989, Geffen Records and cable music channel VH-1 teamed up to promote a project for Greenpeace, the environmental group. As its part of the project, VH-1 produced more than two dozen sixty-second spots, called "World Alerts," that featured celebrities discussing a range of environmental issues. Artists ranging from U2 and Talking Heads to John Cougar Mellencamp and Belinda Carlisle donated twenty-seven hit songs to a compilation album titled *Rainbow Warriors,* which was released under the title *Breakthrough* in what was then the Soviet Union. It became the top-selling record there, with all proceeds split between Greenpeace and the Soviet Foundation for Survival and Development of Humanity. Our Common Future was another environmental extravaganza that was staged at Lincoln Center in the spring of 1989. Participants included Bob Geldof, Richard Gere, Sting, Midnight Oil, and Herbie Hancock, among others. In addition to entertainment, the show provided a platform for a number of scientists and world leaders to voice their concerns over global environmental decline. It was a little unnerving for some, however, to see Margaret Thatcher delivering a pretaped message about Britain's concern for the environment. It may be that the politics of the show were complicated by the sponsorship of multinational corporations, including Sony, Panasonic, and Honda, all of whom had their corporate logos prominently displayed during the syndicated telecast.

By the end of the 1980s, there was scarcely a social issue that was not associated in a highly visible way with popular music and musicians.

Critic Dave Marsh has been particularly critical of corporate involvement in mega-events, claiming that such involvement robs "charity-rock of one of its most important selling points: the selflessness of its motivation."[58] Given the scale of mega-events, however, most would be impossible without some kind of corporate sponsorship. Amnesty's Human Rights Now! tour would have gone bankrupt had not Reebok bailed it out at the last minute. Furthermore, the mega-events of the 1980s developed a kind of momentum that obliged corporations and world leaders to accommodate initiatives that were essentially humanitarian or progressive. Indeed, this momentum exerted an effect on the culture of popular music in general. As Simon Frith and John Street have noted: "The paradox of Live Aid was that while in the name of 'humanity' it seemed to depoliticise famine, in the same terms, in the name of 'humanity' it politicised mass music."[59] There was a clear connection between John Cougar Mellencamp's involvement in Farm Aid and his "Rain on the Scarecrow," a song about the despair of modern rural life. Jackson Browne's interest in Central America led to "Lives in the Balance," a moving criticism of U.S. intervention in Central America. Bruce Cockburn was similarly moved by his experiences in Central America to the point of writing songs such as "If I Had a Rocket Launcher." Likewise, there was a resonance between Sting's involvement with Amnesty International and his "They Dance Alone," a song about the widows of "disappeared" political activists in Chile, which became all the more poignant when he brought Chilean women onstage to dance with him as he toured that country. With "Luka" (1987), singer/songwriter Suzanne Vega brought the issue of child abuse to the attention of many. A number of rap groups, including Public Enemy, Boogie Down Productions, and Stetsasonic, participated in "Self-Destruction," the anthem of the Stop the Violence movement, which protests black-on-black crime. In recording "Fight the Power" for Spike Lee's *Do the Right Thing,* Public Enemy contributed the soundtrack for the most powerful statement about racism in the 1980s. By the end of the 1980s, there was scarcely a social issue that was not associated in a highly visible way with popular music and musicians.

The mega-events of the 1980s also had an unintended but no less progressive side effect on the music industry itself. In the United States, the formats for most music programs are designed to cater to the tastes of a fragmented audience. While these divisions ostensibly represent differences in musical taste, they correlate highly with divisions of class, race, age, and ethnicity. Because the artists who participated in the mega-events crossed a broad range of audience demographics and music programming formats, the media outlets that carried the performances contributed significantly to breaking down the apartheid of the music industry itself. "Whoever buys ['Sun City']," remarked coproducer Arthur Baker, "is going to be turned on to a new form of music, just as whoever sees the video is going to be turned on to an artist they've never seen before."[61] For a brief time in the 1980s, the internationalization of the music industry became a two-way process, albeit a limited one. While Anglo-American music may have been disproportionately broadcast to a worldwide audience, artists like Youssou N'Dour and Sly and Robbie did gain greater access to the world market. It was more than a coincidence that the emergence of world music (also known as world beat) in developed countries paralleled the development of charity rock. A greater awareness of world cultures, in turn, influenced the character of mainstream popular music at home. Peter Gabriel had long been credited with tasteful appropriations of African rhythms. Jackson Browne incorporated Central American sounds on *Lives in the Balance.* David Byrne of Talking Heads developed an interest in Brazilian music.

Perhaps the best-known—and most controversial—fusion of mainstream popular music and international music styles is Paul Simon's *Graceland,* which was in many ways a pivotal album of the 1980s. Released in 1986, the album was based primarily on South African musical styles and incorporated an incredible diversity of cultural influences, ranging, in the words of ethnomusicologist Steven Feld, from

> *quirky 1960's Long Island/Brill Building Simon lyrics, pedal steel guitar riffs from a Nigerian Jùjú band player via Nashville recordings, vocals from Senegalese Youssou N'Dour on break from recording projects with British pop star Peter Gabriel, and everything else from Synclavier samplers and drum machines to the Everly Brothers and Linda Ronstadt . . . with exemplars of zydeco . . . and East Los Angeles Chicano rock and roll. . . .*[61]

Historically, the album has taken its place as one of the defining contributions to that amorphous category of world music or world beat. As such, it has been at the heart of highly politicized discussions concerning musical appropriation and ownership on the one hand and cultural imperialism on the other.

On *Graceland,* Simon demonstrated his talent as a musician with a fine ear for exotic sounds. He was respectful of South African music and worked with such notable black South African artists as Ladysmith Black Mambazo and other first-rate studio musicians. He offered three times union scale for sessions and gave appropriate co-writer credits on collaborative songs. The album also featured performances by Los Lobos and zydeco legend Rockin' Dopsie. The result was a hauntingly beautiful compilation that effectively linked South African rhythms with a range of regional ethnic U.S. influences. Still, as critics noted, most of the album was recorded in South Africa, in violation of the UN cultural boycott. (This may explain why Simon agreed to appear as a soloist on "We Are the World" but refused to participate in the more radical Sun City project, which directly opposed violating the cultural boycott.) In using Linda Ronstadt, who had performed at Sun City without apologies, as a backup vocalist, Simon simply added to the insult of his own violation of the cultural ban. If his purpose was to showcase black South African music, one had to wonder why he had named the album after the estate of a white American who had captured the rock 'n' roll crown by employing (some would say imitating) African American musical styles. Simon was also taken to task for registering the producer's credit and all the copyrights in his own name, which ensured that he would receive any music awards that were given as well as the lion's share of subsequent royalty income. Contributing the lyrics for many of the songs, he was also vulnerable to the charge that he avoided political content. Under considerable international pressure, he added such explicitly antiapartheid performers as Miriam Makeba and Hugh Masakela to his 1987 Graceland Tour.

Because Simon considered himself to be antiapartheid (he did refuse to perform in South Africa), he and many others tended to dismiss the criticisms of *Graceland* out of hand, a position that receiving the 1986 Grammy Award for Album of the Year reinforced. The producer's Grammy Award for record of the year for the same album in 1987 seemed to be the final refutation of the criticisms. As a result, *Graceland* was variously celebrated, according to Feld, as "a melding of mainstream 'world' pop and African 'folk' musics; the major anti-apartheid consciousness-raising and publicity event of 1987; and a major international market breakthrough for the South African musicians."[62] Still, five years later, on the eve of Simon's 1992 South African tour—the first such tour by a major U.S. artist after cultural sanctions were lifted—the offices

On the eve of Simon's 1992 South African tour—the first such tour by a major U.S. artist after cultural sanctions were lifted—the offices of the promoter and sound company were bombed. Simon was considered an appropriate target because of the controversy that surrounded Graceland.

of the promoter and sound company were bombed by the Azanian National Liberation Army. While the tour was supported not only by the white minority government but also by two of South Africa's main black organizations (the ANC and the Inkatha Freedom Party), many in South Africa felt that the lifting of the sanctions was premature, and Simon was considered an appropriate target because of the controversy that surrounded *Graceland*. In the international community, *Graceland* produced passionate responses on both sides of the political divide, reinforcing the notion of mass culture as contested terrain.

Technology and the New International Music Industry

By the mid-1980s, the music industry had bounced back from the doldrums of worldwide recession and had resumed its pattern of more or less steady growth now tied to international sales. In 1990, according to *Billboard,* the United States alone boasted year-end sales of $7.5 billion in a world market worth well over $20 billion.[63] Given the reconfigurations of the global cultural economy, however, this recovery did not come without some profound structural changes in the ownership patterns of the transnational music industry that pointed to the beginnings of a decline in U.S. dominance. EMI Records, a division of the British electronics firm Thorn-EMI, also controlled Capitol, Chrysalis, IRS, and Rhino, among others. Japan's Sony Corporation had purchased CBS Records (renamed Sony Music) for $2 billion. The Netherlands-based Phillips Electronics Corporation owned Polygram, which included Polydor, Deutsche Grammophon, Mercury, and Decca, and acquired A&M and Island. The German publishing conglomerate Bertelsmann had purchased RCA Records and its affiliated labels from General Electric after GE had taken over RCA. In 1990, Matsushita purchased MCA, which included Geffen Records and Motown, for $6.6 billion. Thus, by the early 1990s only one of the major transnational record companies—WEA (Warner Bros./Elektra/Atlantic), a division of Time-Warner—remained in U.S. hands, and in 1991, Time-Warner entered into a $1 billion partnership agreement with Toshiba and C. Itoh. From the point of view of international capital, however, business was booming.

The internationalization of the music industry was also accompanied by some dramatic shifts in consumer preference for various playback configurations. By 1989, cassettes were outselling LPs in the United States nearly thirteen to one (446.2 million units against 34.6 million) as the vinyl configuration began its descent into virtual extinction. The reasons for the decline of vinyl were twofold. First, as a medium with recording, editing, and playback capabilities, cassettes were simply more versatile than LPs. Second, in the realm of sound quality, resistance to wear, and ease of use, CDs were far superior to LPs. Buyers quickly realized this. While in 1987, unit sales for LPs and CDs were about equal, two years later the CD, which was sold for a higher price, was outselling the LP by a factor of six (207.2 million to 34.6 million units).[64]

Technology, of course, has played an indispensable role in the economic recovery of the music industry. But while technological advances have served to further the industry goals of expansion and concentration, music-related interests have not been monolithic in these developments. In the late 1980s, the introduction of digital audio tape (DAT), a digital tape configuration that held out the possibility of making studio quality recordings in one's living room, was threatening to record companies, whose primary task was to protect the "integrity" (i.e., financial viability) of the "artistic property" that was their economic lifeblood. A number of summit meetings were held between hardware manufacturers and record companies to try to arrive at a solution to the potential impact of DAT on record sales. This tension sometimes played itself out among different departments of the same corporation—for example, Sony, which made DAT recorders and owned CBS Records. The flap over DAT was but one small part of a larger historical pattern—that the electronic items that have caught the public's fancy have usually been those that delivered improved sound quality and offered consumers maximum flexibility and portability of use. In this sense, technology is a double-edged sword; its development has been rife with unintended consequences. In the words of writer Simon Frith:

> *The major disruptive forces in music in this century have been new devices, technological breakthroughs developed by electronics manufacturers who have very little idea of their potential use. The only lesson to be learned from pop history (besides the fact that industry predictions are always wrong) is that the devices that succeed in the market are those that increase consumer control of their music.*[65]

A similar pattern exists on the creative end. The same electronic innovations that have accompanied increased revenues in the music industry as a whole have encouraged decentralization in the creative process. As producer Nile Rogers has explained:

> *We're working out systems where if somebody who lives in England, say, has a system similar to what I have, and he's got a track and he wants me to play on it, well, he can send it to me over the satellite to New York. My system can then pick it up. It will go down on tape. I can listen to it, put my guitar overdub on it, send it back to him, and it'll all be digital information. It will sound exactly the same as when I played it. . . . I can play on your record if you're anywhere.*[66]

Technology, then, has altered the social relations of music production with the result of greater and greater degrees of artistic freedom. However, it has left unanswered the question of whether or not a broad range of new cultural products will find acceptance in the marketplace.

If Michael Jackson's Thriller *represented the revitalization of the music industry as an international cultural force,* Graceland *embodied all the contradictions involved in trying to manage the unequal distribution of cultural power. Technological advances had brought the cultures of the world closer together, and, while these developments created possibilities for musical expression that were new and exciting, they also allowed the music industry to centralize its operations. In attempting to use the power of popular music to foster greater understanding and empathy among different cultures, mega-events politicized popular music and, at the same time, provided the music industry with access to new international markets. In both instances, mega-events generated considerable controversy. During this period in the United States, new developments in rap and heavy metal became the focus for controversy. By the late 1980s, rap and metal had become the defining elements of a new disaffected youth culture and in the process had precipitated the most concerted attempt to regulate popular music since rock 'n' roll's payola hearings.*

Rap and Metal: Youth Culture and Censorship

In the mid-1980s, there was an interesting convergence of forces in popular music. Aided significantly by technological advances, mega-events politicized popular music to a greater extent than at any time since the 1960s. At the same time, MTV—itself a product of new technology—launched a companion outlet, VH-1, aimed at an older audience, and thus renewed its focus on youth culture. As in the 1960s, there emerged a connection between youth, music, and politics that soon became most apparent in the phenomenal expansion of rap and heavy metal. It was at this cultural moment that the Parents Music Resource Center (PMRC), a Washington-based pressure group that boasted Tipper Gore, wife of then Senator Albert Gore, as one of its founding members, launched its campaign against explicit lyrics in popular music. No sooner had the music industry recovered from the recession of the early 1980s than it found itself embroiled in a pitched battle with conservative forces over the values and principles that would guide popular music into the next

> *As in the 1960s, there emerged a connection between youth, music, and politics that became most apparent in the phenomenal expansion of rap and heavy metal.*

decade and perhaps the next century. The PMRC initially targeted heavy metal as the prime offender of decency and decorum. As rap gained in prominence, however, it became the focal point of conservative wrath.

Technology, of course, has been a central factor in forging the connection between youth, their music, and its politics. As different as rap and metal may sound, both have enjoyed a particularly intimate relationship with the tools of their production. While it is safe to say that just about all successful popular recording artists make use of advanced technology, rap and metal artists, more than others, have incorporated advances in technology into the very essence of their music. In neither case have these advancements been appropriated straightforwardly. Rather, both styles have sought to turn the logic underlying technological advancement on its

375

head. While the history of sound recording—from the acoustic recording horn to the digitization of sound—can be read as a quest to eliminate noise, both rap and metal have used this "cleaner" technology precisely to achieve a "dirtier" sound. Metal has used it in the service of volume and distortion; rap in the very organization of its disparate sonic elements.

Given the heavy metal preoccupation with power, technology has long been an indispensable tool in the continuing development of the music. The heavily distorted guitar sound that has become the most obvious sign of heavy metal power occurs when an amplifier is overdriven—that is, driven beyond its capacity to deliver a clean sound. In the 1960s, Jimi Hendrix achieved this effect through the creative use of feedback, using the operating noise of the amplifier to overwhelm the signal of the guitar. In the 1980s, Eddie Van Halen used a voltage regulator to increase power to his amp. Heavy metal vocalists often use vocal distortion boxes to create a menacing growl.

Both rap and heavy metal have used the power of noise to assault traditional musical conventions and to trace the boundaries of youth culture.

In the case of rap, dual turntable rigs were transformed into full-fledged musical instruments and boom boxes became localized radio stations, often to the dismay of nearby listeners. In the mid-1980s, rap artists began to use samplers, digital devices capable of recording, storing, and reproducing any sound in nature perfectly, and drum machines to construct the basic building blocks of a rap composition—rumbling bass tones that can destroy car radio speakers, familiar beats looped into endless repetition, and found sounds and prerecorded tracks reshuffled into an original sound collage.

If there is an aspect of rap that is analogous to power in heavy metal, it is the concept of noise. As rap has strayed further and further from middle-class conventions, it has come to be defined less by such traditional concepts as melody and harmony and more by the notion of organized sound or noise. In titling her definitive analysis of rap *Black Noise,* Tricia Rose has used the noun to explicate not only rap's relationship to technology but also a new development in the history of black orality and a cultural device for political resistance.[1] Public Enemy's "Bring the Noise," for example, assaults the listener with a dense mix of samples and synthesized noise. Borrowing from the gospel call-and-response style, Chuck D's vocal exhortation "Turn it up!" is answered by DJ Terminator X with furious record scratching (back cueing a record with the sound system turned on). As a whole, then, "Bring the Noise" mounts a defiant challenge to mainstream listeners through its intentionally aggravating use of noise.

Both rap and heavy metal have used the power of noise to assault traditional musical conventions and to trace the boundaries of youth culture. In doing so, they have provided highly visible, if fast-moving, targets for the custodians of good taste. At the same time, however, both genres have their defenders. Once reflexive dismissals of metal's racism and misogyny—common during its first wave—have tended to give way to more complex rereadings of the music in an effort to understand the youth culture of the 1980s and 1990s. In a similar move, issues of violence and sexism in rap have become part of a heated dialogue concerning class, age, and gender differences within the black community and the relationship of black youth to the mainstream culture. As a result, both genres have become the arenas for what can be viewed as a battle for modern-day values.

The Continuing History of Heavy Metal

After an initial surge in the early 1970s, it appeared as if heavy metal might be a short-lived phenomenon. First-generation fans began to move on to new styles, and the succeeding generation of (white) youth gravitated toward punk. Still, metal never disappeared completely. Artists like Ted Nugent, Aerosmith, and Kiss had consistent runs of gold and platinum releases throughout the late 1970s. As the statement of a more or less coherent subculture, however, the music was in decline. Feminist dismissals of metal's misogyny had caused many thinking fans to reevaluate the music, and punk had supplanted metal's "empty virtuosity" with a more defiant political statement. But just when it appeared that metal might be destined for the dustbin of music history, a resurgence of the music beginning at the turn of the decade transformed it into the dominant expression of youth culture in the 1980s.

Heavy Metal: The New Wave

One key to this development was the cluster of groups that *Sounds* magazine dubbed and promoted as "the new wave of British heavy metal." These groups—Iron Maiden, Def Leppard, Motörhead, Saxon, Venom, Angelwitch, Diamond Head, and so on—filled the void that was left when first-wave British metal groups like Deep Purple and Led Zeppelin ceased touring or went into tax exile. Judas Priest, still in its ascent, had temporarily abandoned the British audience following the success of their U.S. tour as the opening act for Zeppelin in 1977. (They redeemed themselves partially with the release of *Stained Class* in 1978.) As a result, British fans were deprived of the opportunity to see their favourite artists in live performance, which was still the dominant mode of reception for heavy metal. It took a new generation of metal acts to fill this void. Two of the new groups—Iron Maiden and Def Leppard, which were formed in the midst of punk—went on to achieve worldwide success. AC/DC, which was formed in Australia in 1974 around a core of British expatriates, rode the new wave in the United States. The nucleus of AC/DC was brothers Angus and Malcolm Young on guitars and Bon Scott on lead vocals. Having achieved Australian and British chart success with such early releases as *Let There Be Rock* and outrageous stage shows, AC/DC broke into the U.S. Top Forty with the more occult-oriented *Highway to Hell* (1979), just before Scott died from alcoholism. With Brian Johnson as his replacement, AC/DC's momentum continued unabated with three Top Ten LPs in a row, climaxing with *For Those About to Rock, We Salute You* in 1981, which went to number one. Def Leppard shared AC/DC's management. Their debut album, *On Through the Night* (1980), established the group as part of the new wave in Britain. Aided by MTV's broadcast of its promotional videos, Def Leppard's *High 'n' Dry* (1981) broke into the U.S. Top Forty. While Iron Maiden got a significant boost when they opened for Judas Priest, which helped push their debut album to number four in Great Britain, the group did not hit the U.S. Top

Forty until 1982. At that point, Bruce Dickinson was installed as the lead singer on *The Number of the Beast,* another album that appealed to the North American fascination with the occult.

It should be noted that there was no particular brand of metal that dominated the British new wave. Motörhead was able to attract a punk following with pounding cuts—for example, "Overkill" and "Bomber"—played at breakneck speed. This style aligned the group with the speed metal style that grew out of L.A. hardcore. The group continued in this vein throughout the 1980s, peaking early in the decade with *Ace of Spades* and the live album *No Sleep Till Hammersmith.* Iron Maiden, which was pegged by *The Number of the Beast* as a Satanist group, was more eclectic in its references and musical moods. In using Satanism as one of a number of biblical, occult, and mystical sources to explore a range of dilemmas involving morality, power, and chaos, however, the group leaned toward more traditional heavy metal. "Run for the Hills" addressed the plight of Native Americans; "Stranger in a Strange Land" and "Sea of Madness" spoke to the alienation of youth. Def Leppard guitarist and composer Steve Clark brought his classical training to bear on the group's music. On *High 'n' Dry,* producer Mutt Lange played up the melodic elements of Leppard's music, propelling the group toward a more pop sound, which has been described somewhat disparagingly by Philip Bashe as "metal pop" and by Deena Weinstein as "lite metal."[2] Even with such variation, however, there were elements that united the new wave groups under the heavy metal banner. "What all the new bands did share," Weinstein has written, "was a general heavy metal sensibility, along with youthfulness and a strong emphasis on visual elements."[3] According to Robert Walser, "the new wave of metal featured shorter, catchier songs, more sophisticated production techniques, and higher technical standards."[4] In the United States, Van Halen was the embodiment of these characteristics. Throughout the 1980s, the group turned out nothing but Top Ten platinum albums. *1984* was on the charts for more than a year and yielded the number one single, "Jump." Until he was replaced in the mid-1980s, lead singer David Lee Roth provided a striking, if vacuous, visual focus with his macho aerobic performances, and lead guitarist Eddie Van Halen had been, of course, the standard bearer of technical proficiency for years.

Among the standout guitar virtuosos of heavy metal, there was also Randy Rhoads. Like Van Halen, Rhoads was a classically trained guitarist who could claim influences that ranged from Alice Cooper to Vivaldi. He first made a name for himself as a member of Quiet Riot, a hard-rocking metal act from Los Angeles. He then became Ozzy Osbourne's lead guitarist, a move that promised to link the new virtuosity with traditional British heavy metal. Rhoads' classical influence can be heard on two 1981 recordings, "Goodbye to Romance" and "Mr. Crowley," and a live recording of "Suicide Solution," which was released on *Tribute* in 1987, five years after Rhoads' death in a plane crash. Following Rhoads' death, the torch of technical proficiency was picked up by Sweden's Yngwie Malmsteen. Although his debut release in 1984 led *Guitar Player* to name him Best Rock Guitarist in 1985, Malmsteen did not break into the U.S. Top Forty until three years later with *Odyssey.* More of a musician's musician than a commercial success, Malmsteen "adapted classical music with more thoroughness and intensity than had any previous guitarist, and he expanded the melodic and harmonic language of metal while setting even higher standards of virtuosic precision."[5]

Of course, virtuosity in heavy metal, indeed in the context of Western music generally, as Walser has astutely pointed out, "has always been concerned with demonstrating and enacting a particular kind of power and freedom that might be called 'potency.' Both words carry gendered meanings, of course; heavy metal shares with most other Western music a patriarchal context wherein power itself is construed as essentially male."[6] Walser allowed that some women might also be able to identify with this power as signifying "a more general sort of social capability," but in such instances, women would be forced to adapt a phenomenon coded as male in our society to suit their own needs and experiences.

Throughout its first generation, heavy metal was the exclusive province of young, white males. There were no female heavy metal musicians to speak of unless the genre's boundaries are extended far enough to include the Wilson sisters from Heart. Indeed, there were precious few female fans who attended metal concerts. Those who did were accepted as subcultural equals only when they conformed to the masculinist codes of dress (jeans and black T-shirts) and evidenced the proper knowledge and love of the music. Women who appeared in "feminine" garb were usually regarded as groupies who were there to service the band sexually. It wasn't until 1980 that an all-female metal band released an album in the United States—*Demolition,* by Girlschool, which emerged in Britain as part of the British new wave and achieved some measure of respect and chart success there after touring with Motörhead. U.S. success, however, never came their way.

> *There were precious few female fans who attended metal concerts. Those who did were accepted as subcultural equals only when they conformed to the masculinist codes of dress (jeans and black T-shirts) and evidenced the proper knowledge and love of the music.*

Around 1983, the next wave of metal began to arrive from Los Angeles. Groups like Mötley Crüe and Ratt tended toward a glam rock appearance, harking back to the New York Dolls, and a lite metal sound. "What happened in the punk rock days was that the girls looked very much like the boys," punk/metal documentary filmmaker Penelope Spheeris has noted. "In the metal scene, the boys looked more like the girls, with the big poofy hair and the makeup and the plucked eyebrows."[7] Mötley Crüe ascended to national fame after opening for Kiss in 1983, which helped to push the group's *Shout at the Devil* album into the Top Twenty. Ratt first hit the Top Ten with *Out of the Cellar* in 1984. Other L.A. groups included Quiet Riot, Dokken, and W.A.S.P. Quiet Riot scored two hit singles from their *Metal Health* album, "Cum on Feel the Noize" (1983) and "Bang Your Head (Metal Health)" (1984), which was rare for a metal band at the time. Dokken's *Tooth and Nail* (1984) failed to crack the Top Forty but did earn the group a spot on *Hit Parade*'s Top 100 Metal Albums, as did their Top Twenty *Back for the Attack* (1987), which promoted a consistent image of male victimization at the hands of the femme fatale, an oft-used misogynist device in metal. Though they had a hardcore following, W.A.S.P. never had a major hit in the United States. The group's importance was blown out of all proportion when right-wing critics of heavy metal discovered "Animal (F**k like a Beast)," a song that was disturbing to many in its celebration of only the sheer physicality of sex.

The Los Angeles metal scene was given a boost by the U.S. '83 Festival, which was organized by Steve Wosniak, founder of Apple Computer. Originally envisioning a festival that would pay tribute to Woodstock, Wosniak took heed of the audience fragmentation that had occurred since the 1960s and organized the event around different genres on different days. The heavy metal day, which featured Ozzy Osbourne and Judas Priest from Britain, the Scorpions from Germany, Triumph from Canada, and Van Halen, Quiet Riot, and Mötley Crüe from Los Angeles, drew the largest audience. The festival and the fact that the major U.S. groups were from Los Angeles prompted other metal acts, including Poison and Guns 'N' Roses, to relocate.

Poison, in particular, was well suited to the glam look and the lighter sound that characterized much of the Los Angeles scene. The group's carefully tended, artfully moussed, blow-dried hair led it, along with Ratt and the lesser-known White Lion, to be dubbed "hair" bands. Still, the Los Angeles scene created space for the emergence of female artists like Lita Ford and Vixen, who achieved a measure of metal fame in the late 1980s.

What was crucial to the growth of metal, particularly the Los Angeles variety, was its exposure on MTV. The genre had been largely excluded from radio since its beginnings. While some AOR stations had begun to program metal in the late 1970s, it was significantly cut back in the early 1980s when these stations found themselves in ratings wars with other formats like Urban Contemporary (UC), Contemporary Hits Radio (CHR), and Adult Contemporary (AC). Even MTV was reluctant to air heavy metal during its first phase of operation, preferring instead the cutting edge antinarratives of British newpop (see Chapter 9). During its second period, however, MTV "programmed heavy metal with a vengeance."[8] Among the more prominent metal groups that MTV aired were Mötley Crüe, Quiet Riot, Dokken, Twisted Sister, and the Scorpions. MTV shifted its orientation, according to Andrew Goodwin.

> *The New Pop had gone out of fashion and . . . as MTV expanded from the main urban centers of the United States on the coasts into midwestern cities and towns, it needed to reach out with music that appealed to the rockist tastes of its new demographics. Furthermore, the network was no longer dependent on a relatively small number of clips originating in Europe. These factors colluded to generate MTV's embrace of heavy metal music.*[9]

The success of heavy metal on MTV led to increased programming on radio, particularly AOR and CHR stations. The real payoff, of course, was in sales. In a special section on heavy metal, *Billboard* reported that the music's market share jumped after a year of heavy play on MTV from about 8 percent in 1983 to 20 percent in 1984.[10]

Metal's advance was slowed temporarily in 1985 when a loose confederation of right-wing Christian fundamentalist groups and various conservative civic, professional, and watchdog organizations pressured MTV into cutting back on its programming of the genre. Although MTV tried to explain away its action by claiming that it had cut back on metal to focus on more "cutting edge" product, according to Linda Martin and Kerry Segrave, "as most of the industry saw it . . . MTV was bowing to the pressure of various conservative watchdog groups who had been complaining."[11] This campaign—a prelude to the PMRC hearings held in Washington, D.C., later that year—had immediate results. In the first quarter of 1985, metal's market share dropped to 15 percent.[12] By this time, however, metal had begun to develop a momentum that could not be turned around. Gradually, it began to drift back into MTV's programming, and by the end of 1986, the demand for it had become so great that MTV created a weekly late-night program, Headbangers' Ball, devoted solely to metal, that gave the music its due and placed some of its more objectionable videos in an after-hours slot. Headbangers' Ball generated a weekly audience of 1.3 million viewers, becoming MTV's most popular show.

For a music defined in part by transgression, increased acceptance into the mainstream of U.S. popular culture was a mixed blessing. The bonds of the heavy metal subculture had been forged in the cauldron of exclusion. Musicians and fans alike found strength in their outsider status.

For a music defined in part by transgression, increased acceptance into the mainstream of U.S. popular culture was a mixed blessing. In many ways, the bonds of the heavy metal subculture had been forged in the cauldron of exclusion. Musicians and fans alike found strength in their outsider status. Prior to the beginning of mass acceptance, metal was free from the constraints of pop convention. Songs could be longer, instrumentals (favouring extended guitar solos) could be privileged over vocals (typically less prominent in the mix than in pop), the raw energy of live performance could be accorded a higher cultural value than the precision of studio production, and there was no need to produce hit singles. Mainstream acceptance brought with it pressure for higher "production values," sophisticated recording techniques, higher technical standards, and a more polished (commercial) sound. Thus, the expansion of the music beyond its original subcultural following paralleled the fragmentation of the genre.

Metal Fragments

By the late 1980s, the metal press became rife with distinctions between categories. *Traditional* or *classic heavy metal* was used to describe the original sound of wildly distorted guitar, heavy bass and drums, and raw, unadorned vocals; *lite* or *pop metal* emphasized sweeter vocals, even harmony; *glam metal* was defined by a particular look; *thrash* and *speed metal* featured faster tempos that were derived from punk; *death metal*, a subcategory of speed/thrash, focused on the issue of death; *black metal* focused on Satanic themes; and *white metal* was its Christian counterpart. For all these distinctions, however, there were really only two camps, each claiming their rightful place in a lineage that led back to the grand old groups of the genre Led Zeppelin, Black Sabbath, and Deep Purple. At one end of the spectrum was lite metal and at the other were the groups lumped together as speed/thrash metal.

It was the lite metal of groups like Def Leppard, Quiet Riot, Van Halen, Mötley Crüe, and Bon Jovi that was favoured by MTV, gained greater access to radio, and expanded the music into arena and stadium-sized venues. It was lite metal that initially transformed the metal audience from subculture to mass and altered its gender balance as well. As late as 1984, the metal audience consisted primarily of male high-school teenagers. A year later, however, *Billboard* reported, "Metal music is no longer the exclusive domain of male teenagers. The metal audience has become older (college-aged), younger (pre-teen), and more female."[13] A number of lite metal album releases signaled the transition. Def Leppard's *Pyromania* (1983) reached number two and remained on the charts for more than a year. The album's three hit

The lure of androgyny as a transgressive social practice was strong in metal, particularly among glam metal groups. It complicated metal's masculinist codes, and in conferring prestige on traditionally female signs, may have accounted for some of metal's positive appeal among young women.

singles generated sales of 7 million units, a sure sign that metal was beginning to move beyond its subculture status. Quiet Riot's *Metal Health* and Van Halen's *1984* made similarly impressive showings, peaking at numbers one and two, respectively.

These albums also mark the period when the performance clip came into frequent use on MTV. This was, according to Goodwin, "a direct result of the need for heavy metal acts to establish an 'authentic' (i.e., documentary rather than fictional) set of images and to display musical competence."[14] According to E. Ann Kaplan, these performance clips were typical of what she has called the "nihilist heavy metal video," in which

> *the male body is deliberately set up as object of desire: zoom shots pick up male crotches and bare chests in an erotic manner and instruments are presented as unabashed phallic props. . . . these videos . . . adopt a challenging, aggressive stance toward the fans and spectators. . . . The camera often*

sways with the male bodies, and figures are filmed in slow motion, often jumping in the air, spread-eagled, as in Van Halen's "Jump."[15]

While Kaplan aptly describes metal's macho preoccupation with reinforcing an unstable and insecure masculinity, which was certainly a part of the heavy metal subculture, there was, as she acknowledges, "a more complicated set of discourses" involved in the way metal worked to shape identity. David Lee Roth, who was let go as Van Halen's lead singer shortly after "Jump" became the group's most popular single, argued that "a lot of what I do can be construed as feminine. My face, or the way I dance, or the way I dress myself for stage."[16] The lure of androgyny as a transgressive social practice was strong in metal, particularly among glam metal groups. It complicated metal's masculinist codes, and in conferring prestige on traditionally female signs, may have accounted for some of metal's positive appeal among young women.

Romance was another theme that was adopted in the mid-1980s that clearly extended metal's appeal to females. Prior to the mid-1980s, themes of romantic love had been conspicuously absent from metal. This was one of the features of the music that helped maintain metal as a bastion of male bonding. Offering a broader analysis, Walser notes: "Until the mid 1980s one of these three strategies—misogyny, exscription, androgyny—tended to dominate each heavy metal band's 'aesthetic.' A fourth approach, increasingly important in recent years, 'softens' metal with songs about romance; this kind of music has drawn legions of female fans to metal."[17] The pivotal album in this regard was Bon Jovi's *Slippery When Wet* (1986).

Bon Jovi (named after lead singer Jon Bon Jovi) was formed in New Jersey in the early 1980s. In its first incarnation, the group sported many of the characteristics of the standard heavy metal band—doom and gloom lyrics, macho performances, a leather/mascara look, and the powerhouse sound of distorted guitar. In keeping with metal's preoccupation with power and phallocentric imagery, the group's first Top Forty album was named *7800° Fahrenheit,* the temperature of an erupting volcano. For *Slippery When Wet,* however, Bon Jovi reconstructed their image and their sound. In trading in their leathers and makeup for a more casual bluejean look, they consciously sought the broader appeal of rock authenticity. From pop they drew on a long tradition of songs about love and romance, which they could do effectively because Jon Bon Jovi himself projected a vulnerability that was rare among heavy metal artists. Put together, these new elements, which

Jon Bon Jovi, leader of the group that bears his surname, started out as a leather-clad rocker who then drew legions of female fans to heavy metal with themes of romance and his vulnerable good looks.

had been anathema to metal until this time, had enormous appeal for female fans, and *Slippery When Wet* became one of the best-selling albums of the decade. It rose to number one on the charts and stayed in the Top Forty for well over a year, generating two number one hit singles. The album's biggest hit, "Livin' on a Prayer," was, as far as its content went, a classic love-conquers-all composition. How to position it musically was more complicated. In part because the group included keyboards, Bon Jovi's inclusion in the heavy metal genre is controversial in certain circles. However, Walser has convincingly argued that "Features of heavy metal are evident in the timbres and phrasing of both instruments and vocals. . . . The sustained and intense sounds of heavy metal are channeled behind the romantic sincerity of pop, while smooth, sometimes poignant synthesizer sounds mediate the raw crunch of distorted guitar."[18]

Against this backdrop of upbeat, forward-looking pop crossover, speed/thrash metal, which had come into being in reaction to the perceived compromises of lite metal, turned inward, consciously seeking to position itself outside the parameters of mainstream acceptance in an attempt to forestall the further dilution of the genre. If lite metal was the expansionist wing of metal, seeking to broaden its audience base beyond the young white male demographic, speed/thrash metal was the preservationist side, seeking to fortify and defend the boundaries of an exclusionary male subculture. In the words of Deena Weinstein:

> *Speed/thrash can be understood as an attempt to reclaim metal for youth and especially for males by creating a style that is completely unacceptable to the hegemonic culture. Speed metal represents a fundamentalist return to the standards of the heavy metal subculture. But like all forms of fundamentalism, speed metal is at least as much a new beginning as it is a continuation of what it seeks to revive.*[19]

Speed/thrash metal began as a West Coast phenomenon (primarily in Los Angeles and San Francisco) with groups like Metallica, Slayer, Testament, Megadeth, Exodus, and Possessed, bands that eschewed the glamour and popularity of lite metal in favour of an underground club scene, where the subculture could be maintained more easily for white male teenagers. They were later joined by other groups, including Anthrax, Nuclear Assault, Suicidal Tendencies, Annihilator, and Sepultura. The creators of speed/thrash metal were influenced as much by hardcore punk as by earlier forms of heavy metal. From punk came speed/thrash metal's faster tempos, more hostile posture, and menacing vocals; from heavy metal came sheer volume and ensemble virtuosic precision. Lyric content, according to Weinstein, "specializes in chaos. Sex is rarely mentioned, alcohol and drugs are judged to be bad rather than pleasurable. . . . Themes of lust and romance are ceded to lite metal."[20] The resultant fusion, according to the *Boston Globe,* was "ugly, nasty, angry."[21] Still, while it is true that speed/thrash metal tended to focus on the darker side of life, as evidenced in the growth of death metal, it was not, as many of its detractors have claimed, simply empty nihilism. Themes of justice and environmental concern ran through the music and tended to resemble the content of protest songs: "Environmental destruction has almost become as standard a theme for this subgenre as sex is for lite metal."[22] Nuclear Assault's "Inherited Hell," Testament's "Greenhouse Effect," and Metallica's "Blackened" all raised environmental issues. Metallica's *. . . And Justice for All* expressed a concern for justice.

Metallica became the best-known speed metal group. Formed in Los Angeles in the early 1980s, the group had been influenced by the speed of L.A. hardcore. They began by playing covers of British new wave metal bands at breakneck speed. Among the practitioners of speed metal, Metallica parlayed its outsider status into greater sales than any other group in the category. *Master of Puppets* (1986) became the first platinum-selling speed/thrash album, which suggests significant crossover success. Still, in the eyes of most fans and critics, Metallica remained loyal to the subculture. "Remaining true to a tough identity incompatible with MTV, AOR, or even college radio," wrote one critic, "Metallica are the first in years to build a big career in American rock disregarding the dictates of all three. They've called their own shots, kept their integrity, and rallied their support on the strength of their music and non-image."[23] True to form, . . . *And Justice for All* (1988) achieved Top Ten status and platinum sales with virtually no radio play.

By this time, metal's popularity had exceeded all expectations. In 1987, Bon Jovi's *Slippery When Wet* became the most popular record of the year, and after its success, as *Billboard* reported, "Five more metal bands cracked the top five: Cinderella, Poison, Whitesnake, Mötley Crüe, and Def Leppard. At one point in June, five of the top six albums were by metal-leaning acts."[24] These included the Ozzy Osbourne/Randy Rhoads *Tribute* LP, Mötley Crüe's *Girls, Girls, Girls,* Poison's *Look What the Cat Dragged In,* Bon Jovi's *Slippery When Wet,* and Whitesnake's *Whitesnake.* In 1988, metal accounted for eleven of the fifty best-selling albums of the year, and in 1989, ten of the top forty most popular albums were metal. At this level of success, the genre was impossible to ignore. Accordingly, in 1988, the National Academy of Recording Arts and Sciences (NARAS) established a new Grammy Award for Best Hard Rock/Metal Performance. Metallica delivered a sizzling performance of "One" at the awards telecast and was widely expected to be the recipient of the new Grammy. By including hard rock in the category, however, NARAS was able to appease its conservative elements and award the prize to the largely irrelevant Jethro Tull. Metal was not given its full due until the following year, when NARAS separated hard rock from heavy metal and Metallica finally walked off with a Grammy.

Among the ten most popular albums of 1989 were two LPs by Guns 'N' Roses, a new Los Angeles group. *Appetite for Destruction,* the group's Top Forty debut, rose to number one and remained on the charts for seventy-eight weeks, generating three Top Ten singles. The album was aptly titled, as Guns 'N' Roses showed a strong propensity for stirring up trouble wherever they went. In record time, they became the new bad boys of heavy metal. Rising as they did from the ranks of the L.A. street scene, their raw emotion resonated with the experiences of many alienated white young people. As *Rolling Stone* put it, "You didn't have to be a runaway to relate to the feelings of dislocation, terror and excitement that mingled in the likes of 'Paradise City' or 'Welcome to the Jungle.' "[25] At the same time, however, on "One in a Million," the group tapped into (or exploited) the racial/sexual fears, insecurities, and hostilities of some of their fans when lead singer Axl Rose spoke of African Americans and homosexuals as "niggers" and "faggots." While the group incurred the wrath of the more progressive elements of the rock critical establishment, its popularity continued unabated into the next decade. *Use Your Illusion I* and *Use Your Illusion II* both finished among the twenty most popular albums of 1992.

Although Canadian fans certainly bought British and American heavy metal albums in significant numbers, very few Canadian heavy metal bands have been able to achieve international reputations and sales. In the 1970s and 1980s, there were a number of Canadian bands who approached the hard rock end of the heavy metal continuum, including Rush, April Wine, Bachman-Turner Overdrive, Haywire, the Headpins, Loverboy, Max Webster, Toronto, Saga, and Triumph. At the heavier end of the spectrum were Thundermug, from London, Ontario, and the Hendrix-influenced Frank Marino and Mahogany Rush from Montreal. These were followed by Anvil, Goddo, Moxy, Helix, and Lee Aaron in Toronto, Sword from St. Bruno, Quebec, the Killer Dwarfs from Oshawa, Ontario, Voivod from Jonquière, Quebec, and Annihilator from Vancouver. Voivod parlayed an interesting amalgam of thrash metal and science fiction lyrics into a cult following on an international level, peaking with *Nothingface* in 1989. The speed metal kings of the West Coast, Annihilator, also managed to sell significant numbers of *Alice in Hell and Never Neverland* for Roadracer Records in 1989 and 1990. Helix's *Walking the Razor's Edge,* in 1984, and Lee Aaron's *Bodyrock,* in 1989, were the only Canadian heavy metal albums to achieve gold status in their native country. Finally, it should be mentioned that there have been a number of Canadian hard rock and heavy metal musicians and singers who have achieved prominence in American and British groups. Montreal native Corky Laing manned the drum kit for Mountain, Toronto's Pat Travers had a successful British-based career in the 1970s and early 1980s, and Peterborough's Sebastian Bach became the lead singer of Skid Row in 1987.

By the end of the 1980s, metal had become so expansive that there was even space for a handful of African American and female artists. Most prominent among African American groups was Living Colour, which was led musically and spiritually by guitar virtuoso Vernon Reid. Reid was a founder of New York's Black Rock Coalition, which had as its express purpose the reclamation of the black roots of rock 'n' roll. Living Colour was the perfect articulation of the organization's position. Reid and company drew on every major movement in black

"...And Justice for All"

Artist: Metallica

Music / Lyrics by James Hetfield, Lars Ulrich, and Kirk Hammett

Label: Elektra, from the LP *...And Justice for All* (1988)

Musical Style Notes

Music Terminology Demystifed: What Is a "Riff"?

A "riff" is a *repetitive* musical phrase characterized by a memorable melody and a compelling rhythmic pattern. It can be used as an introduction or as a steady pattern that repeats throughout a piece. Three classic but quite different examples can be found in the Beatles' song "Birthday" from the *White Album;* the two-bar riff that permeates Run-DMC's tune "Rock Box," and the memorable guitar riff Duane Allman wrote for Derek and the Dominoes' song "Layla." In the case of heavy metal, a song's signature riff often features a driving rhythm and considerable speed and energy, like the signature riff in Metallica's "...And Justice for All."

Writer Richard Gehr has described Metallica's music as "mini-epics of ear-shattering volume and mind-boggling speed." These "epics" are actually created by assembling sections of music based on instrumental riffs. James Hetfield has stated that the members of Metallica regularly create musical riffs, which they often write down or record for future use, partnering song lyrics with instrumental riffs that seem to fit the mood and adding additional riffs and patterns that correspond with the changing content or mood of the different lyric sections. This creative method works well to produce these musical "mini-epics," with their multiple contrasting sections, just as classical composers crafted melodic "themes" that would then be manipulated and reiterated in different sections of large-scale musical compositions.

Musical "Road Map"

TIMINGS	COMMENTS	LYRICS	
0:00–0:22	Introduction: electric guitar		
0:22–0:28	Second guitar added.		
0:28–0:34	Drums and bass enter.		
0:34–0:39	Drums out—guitars continue.		
0:39–0:45	Drums and bass reenter.		
0:45–0:56	Introduction form repeated with all instruments.		
0:56–1:01	Transition section, characterized by percussive texture and full "stops"		
1:07–1:21	Introduction ends—the actual song form begins here, with the steady "speed metal" percussion style, marked by occasional "syncopations" (accents placed between the beats).		
1:21–1:41	The song's signature riff begins here. (Note the use of syncopations and sophisticated and complex rhythms.)		
1:41–2:11	Another guitar is "layered" into the sound texture.		

TIMINGS	COMMENTS	LYRICS
2:11–2:31	Verse 1, "A" section of melody	*Halls of Justice . . .*
2:31–2:55	Verse 1, "B" section of melody	*The ultimate in vanity . . .* *. . . I can't believe the price you pay . . .*
2:55–3:16	Chorus	*Nothing can save you . . .* *Justice is lost . . .* *. . . seeking no truth . . .*
3:16–3:37	Signature riff returns.	
3:37–3:58	Verse 2, "A"	*Apathy their stepping stone . . .*
3:58–4:21	Verse 2, "B"	*The ultimate in vanity . . .* *. . . I can't believe the price you pay . . .*
4:21–4:53	Chorus	*Nothing can save you . . .* *Justice is lost . . .* *. . . seeking no truth . . .*
4:53–5:05	Return of percussive transition section heard at 0:56	
5:05–5:29	Guitar solo, part 1	
5:29–5:55	Guitar solo, part 2	
5:55–6:22	Tempo begins to slow down.	
6:22–7:27	Beginning of new instrumental section, with slower tempo, repeating melody, and descending chord pattern (the bass notes of the chords move progressively lower in pitch)	
7:27–7:47	Signature riff returns.	
7:47–8:09	Verse 3, "A"	*Lady Justice has been raped . . .*
8:09–8:33	Verse 3, "B" (same lyrics in each verse)	*The ultimate in vanity . . .* *. . . I can't believe the price you pay . . .*
8:33–8:54	Chorus	*Nothing can save us . . .* *. . . seeking no truth . . .*
8:54–9:07	Riff continues, with additional guitar sound layered in.	
9:07–9:41	Final section—repeat of the last section of the chorus, followed by the repetition of the signature riff leading to the end off the song	*Seeking no truth . . .*
9:41–9:43	Ending "tag"—guitar plays alone, followed by three percussive chords.	

music—from the blues and jazz to hip hop, from Jimi Hendrix and Sly Stone to James Brown and George Clinton—to fashion their brand of metal. At the same time, they paid tribute to the British contributions to the genre by choosing the British spelling of "color" for the group's name. Living Colour first hit the Top Ten with *Vivid* in 1989 and finished on the year-end pop charts for that year just a couple of notches below Guns 'N' Roses. That same year, the group received the Hard Rock Grammy for "Cult of Personality."

Living Colour's metal success made the absence of other African Americans that much more conspicuous, especially since most heavy metal musicians had found their way into the genre through the blues and nearly all of them cited Hendrix as an important influence. From Thin Lizzy in the 1970s to King's X in the 1980s, even the number of racially mixed groups could be counted on one hand. Historians of the genre have tried to explain the absence of black musicians in various ways. While Walser has pointed to the music's history as a British working-class style, Weinstein has argued that it is the result of black "cultural self-segregation."[26] Weinstein's argument, in particular, contradicts the founding principle of Living Colour, and it does not adequately account for why the group had so much difficulty in getting signed to a label or why their label had so much trouble marketing them afterwards. In the end, the group was assigned to a new marketing category called *funk metal,* as were other black metal artists who, according to Weinstein, "brought the contribution of their separate musical culture to metal, grafting themselves onto it."[27]

In assessing the significance of racism in heavy metal, it is important to note that, except for isolated examples such as Guns 'N' Roses' "One in a Million," explicitly racist themes, as Walser has observed, seldom show up in the content of the music.[28] Still, one must wonder how much the antidisco campaigns of hard rock radio stations in the late 1970s served to widen the already existing racial divide. Racial tensions flared between Living Colour and Guns 'N' Roses when the groups opened for the Rolling Stones in Los Angeles in 1989. Both groups traded harsh, racially charged barbs on and off stage, which, given the pattern of racial exclusion in metal, created the impression that metal was foreign territory for black artists.

For female artists of any nationality, the road to metal success was almost impassable, a reality that has been amply documented in most accounts of the genre. While the explosion of lite metal and the inclusion of romantic themes contributed significantly to creating more gender-balanced audiences, they opened few doors for female performers. Even at the height of metal mania, there were few women in the genre. In the second half of the 1980s, Heart had a run of LPs that reached numbers one, two, and three and scored with a number of singles, beginning with "What About Love" (1985), that approached the sound of a power ballad. Joan Jett and the Blackhearts also hit the Top Twenty in 1988 with *Up Your Alley,* but the inclusion of either group in heavy metal would be hotly contested by most fans.

There were only two female acts that were incontrovertibly metal and achieved national recognition—Lita Ford and Vixen. Ford had performed with Joan Jett as a member of the Runaways in the mid-1970s. After years as a solo artist, she released her first album, *Out for Blood,* on Polygram in 1983, but she did not garner national attention until she changed labels

Lita Ford is one of the few women artists who has achieved any measure of success or respect within heavy metal. To get to that point, she paid her dues for more than a decade.

and managers. She felt the switch to RCA and Sharon Osbourne, manager of husband Ozzy Osbourne, allowed her the freedom to be herself. *Lita* (1988) brought her into the Top Thirty, and its hit single, "Close My Eyes Forever," co-written by Ozzy Osbourne, entered the Top Ten. When Ford said in a *Metal* interview, "I wear my balls on my chest," she spoke volumes about the contradictory demands placed on a female performer in a masculinist subculture.[29] Vixen worked as an unsigned performing ensemble for years before landing a contract with EMI. The group's eponymous debut album, released in 1987, was among the most popular albums of 1989, eventually selling more than 1 million copies.

By 1990, there was a glut of metal bands in the marketplace, and metal sales experienced something of a slump. By this time, the pop charts were dominated by black pop, and rap had begun to push metal aside as the cutting edge statement of youth culture.

Hip Hop, Don't Stop

Rap music must be understood historically as one cultural element within a larger social movement known as hip hop, which also includes break dancing, and to some extent, graffiti art. The movement was nothing short of a new way of life. As Tim Carr has noted:

> *Hip hop is to funk what bebop was to jazz . . . a new strain of an old form, stripped down and revved up, rejuvenated. The Young Turks challenging the old masters. Just as bebop replaced stiff collared swing orchestras with Zoot-suited combos . . . so has hip hop emerged as a musical style with a brand new way of walking, talking, dancing, and seeing the world.*[30]

Hip hop, which has its roots in the gang cultures and ghetto communities of the South Bronx and Harlem, originated at the same time as disco but developed for more than five years in almost complete isolation. According to David Toop, "Since nobody in New York City, America, or the rest of the world wanted to know about the black so-called ghettos—the unmentionable areas of extreme urban deprivation—the style was allowed to flourish as a genuine street movement."[31]

Old School Rap

The early culture heroes of hip hop, like those of disco, were the disc jockeys—or, as the hip hop movement called them, DJs. Following the norms of gang culture, certain DJs dominated particular geographical territories. As early as 1973, pioneer Bronx-style DJs such as Kool Herc, who was soon followed by Afrika Bambaataa and Grandmaster Flash, had already begun to distinguish themselves from their disco counterparts. The new DJs played hardcore funk such as Jimmy Castor's "It's Just Begun," the Incredible Bongo Band's "Apache," and James Brown's "Get on the Good Foot." More important, they developed a new way of handling records. While disco deejays concentrated on segueing smoothly from one cut to the next, hip hop DJs experimented with different ways of playing records. Kool Herc, for example, played only a record's hottest, most percussive portion, known as the "break." These sustained peaks of dance beats created a musical collage that came to be called break-beat music, and the young "b-boys" and "b-girls" who danced to it came to be known as break dancers. While this was happening in New York, on the West Coast, the dance troupe the Original Lockers, introduced the robotic movements known as popping and locking that would help to rejuvenate hip hop dancing in the 1980s.

These sustained peaks of dance beats created a musical collage that came to be called break-beat music, and the young "b-boys" and "b-girls" who danced to it came to be known as break dancers.

Hip hop DJs tried to outdo each other by spinning outrageous combinations of records. One of Afrika Bambaataa's sets, for example, might include the theme from the *Pink Panther*, the Beatles, the Rolling Stones, Grand Funk Railroad, Kraftwerk, and the Monkees in addition to James Brown, Sly and the Family Stone, and the Jackson Five. "Hip hop," David Toop has noted, "was the new music by virtue of its finding a way to absorb all other music."[32] By 1976, the DJs had transformed records and turntables from mere sound carriers into full-fledged rhythm instruments through the introduction of such technical innovations as scratching.

As their popularity increased, the best Bronx-style DJs outgrew the small house parties they worked and moved into clubs, community centres, and finally into auditoriums, some of which could accommodate up to 3,000 people. In these larger venues, the DJs began to use members of their crews as "MCs" who could provide some sort of vocal entertainment as a means of crowd control. Like break dancing, "MCing," as it was first known, started as a solo art; there would be one DJ and one MC. Like DJs and break dancers, MCs soon developed their own unique styles, which eventually came to be known as rapping. Among the first solo MCs were Eddie Cheeba, DJ Hollywood, and later Kurtis Blow, all of whom used a disco-oriented style. The first Bronx-style MC was, again, Kool Herc. It was Grandmaster Flash who expanded the idea to include whole groups of MCs. Soon rap groups were popping up all over the Bronx and Harlem, using names like Double Trouble, the Treacherous Three, and the Funky Four Plus One. One of the best-known rap groups, the Furious Five, was started by Flash. Afrika Bambaataa worked with a number of rap groups,

Out of his love of music and his experiences as a South Bronx gang member and a follower of the Black Panthers, Afrika Bambaataa, a pioneer hip hop DJ and leader of the Soulsonic Force, fashioned the Zulu Nation as an inclusive hip hop posse.

including the Jazzy Five, the Cosmic Force, and finally, the Soulsonic Force. By around 1978, MCs had begun to surpass DJs in cultural importance.

Although the style of these early rap groups evolved spontaneously, it is important to note that the roots of rap can be traced through various traditions of the Caribbean islands back to the griots of West Africa. In the United States, the ancestors of rap include field hollers, work and prison songs, competitive urban word games like "signifying" and the "dozens," scat singing, the rhymes of Muhammed Ali, the politically potent verse of the Watts Prophets and the Last Poets, and, finally, the lyrics of such artists as James Brown and Gil Scott-Heron. While the development of rap clearly followed an African American progression, there was also a strong Latino presence in the hip hop movement. Early hip hop sources—for example, Jimmy Castor—routinely included Latin influences in their music. DJs like Kool Herc and Afrika Bambaataa incorporated Latin music into their mixes just as Puerto Rican DJs like Charlie Chase played funk at block parties that combined disco and hip hop. Graffiti artists spanned all racial/ethnic groups. Taki 138 was of Greek lineage; Julio 204 was Chicano; the internationally known Lee Quinones was Puerto Rican. The most famous of the break-dance crews, the Rock Steady Crew, was predominantly Puerto Rican.[33]

Although Bronx-style rapping had been around since 1976, it was not recorded commercially until 1979. Prior to that, rapping existed only in live performance or on the homemade cassettes that blared from boom boxes in the South Bronx. It is surprising, therefore, that the first two rap records did not come from that neighbourhood. "King Tim III (Personality Jock)" was recorded by the Fatback Band, which was from Brooklyn, and "Rapper's Delight" was made by the Sugar Hill Gang, which was based in New Jersey. Edging into the lower reaches of the pop Top Forty, "Rapper's Delight" utilized classic hip hop rhymes recorded over "Good Times" by Chic and eventually sold some 2 million copies.

Given its lineage, it was inevitable that rap would include topical themes. The first recorded rap to deliver a serious message was "How We Gonna Make the Black Nation Rise" (1980), by Brother D and Collective Effort. The style and political priorities of message rap had been antici-pated by two earlier albums, *Hustler's Convention* and *Rappin' Black in a White World. Hustler's Convention* was recorded in New York by Lightnin' Rod, a pseudonym for Jalal Nuridin, who had been the leader of the Last Poets. His powerful prison poetry over tracks by members of Kool and the Gang inspired many early MCs. *Rappin' Black in a White World* was recorded by the Watts Prophets, the Los Angeles analogue to the Last Poets. Though the Prophets and the Poets were unknown to each other until 1969, both had come to the attention of the FBI's infamous COINTELPRO operation, and neither received their artistic or commercial due at the time. Two decades later, samples of their work could be found on albums by such hip hop artists as Def Jeff, Too Short, Tim Dogg, and A Tribe Called Quest.

Flashdance made it appear as though break-dancing techniques were invented by Jennifer Beals or, to be more accurate, her uncredited body double. The only hints of historical accuracy in the film were the brief scenes in the park in which Beals looks on as the Rock Steady Crew performs to Jimmy Castor's "It's Just Begun."

It was the phenomenal success of "Rapper's Delight" that first alerted the mainstream media to the existence of hip hop. More than five years after the subculture had come into being, hip hop was discovered by the music business, the print media, and the film industry in turn. Camera crews and print journalists scoured the South Bronx in search of untold stories, and Bronx DJs entered the downtown New York club scene. Afrika Bambaataa was invited to spin at the Mudd Club, the Ritz, the Peppermint Lounge, Negril, Danceteria, and finally the Roxy, where, on a good Friday night, he would host crowds of up to 4,000 people. Films like the low-budget *Wild Style,* the blockbuster *Flashdance,* and *Breakin'* and *Beat Street* soon followed, bringing hip hop to the attention of a mass audience. Unfortunately, the mass media have a way of ripping any cultural phenomenon out of its historical context. *Flashdance* made it appear as though break-dancing techniques were invented by Jennifer Beals, or to be more accurate, by her uncredited body double. The only hints of historical accuracy in the film were the brief scenes in the park in which Beals looks on as the Rock Steady Crew performs to Jimmy Castor's "It's Just Begun." Similar disjunctures were evident on vinyl. The first so-called rap record to reach number one on the pop charts was "Rapture," by Blondie. Although lead singer (rapper?) Deborah Harry tried to be respectful of hip hop, there was simply no way her musical roots could be traced to the Last Poets, let alone the Yoruba. That same year, Chris Frantz and Tina Weymouth of Talking Heads formed Tom Tom Club and recorded "Wordy Rappinghood," which was followed by the hip hop–influenced "Genius of Love." During this same time, however, some of the most enduring Bronx-based rap records were also produced. "Planet Rock," by Afrika Bambaataa, and the Soulsonic Force and "The Message," by Grandmaster Flash and the Furious Five, were released in 1982 and showcased all the innovations of hip hop culture. Borrowing freely from Kraftwerk's "Trans Europe Express," "Planet Rock" utilized a Roland TR 808 drum machine and rhymes that were, according to Steven Hager, "a dreamy, utopian throwback to the 1960s" to create a formidable dance floor and retail hit.[34] "The Message" heralded greater lyric sophistication and a tilt toward topical themes. It was quickly followed by "Problems of the World," by the Fearless Four, and "White Lines (Don't Do It)," by Grand Master Melle Mel and the Furious Five.

Shortly after these releases, critics began to debate whether or not rap would continue. In the final analysis, these debates were irrelevant. Hip hop had already infected everything, from ballet and modern dance to fashion design and studio art, to pop, rock, funk, soul, and jazz. As critic Stephen Holden noted:

> *Last season's synthesizer-pop has been dressed up and rhythmically charged with elements of "hip hop," the New York–originated dance music style that embraces rapping, scratching, breakdancing, and harsh, electronic sound effects. In fashion industry terms, the mood of these records might be described as one of elaborate severity, in which high technology meets the streets.*[35]

David Toop's description of Herbie Hancock's "Rockit" illustrates the ubiquity of rap's sources: "In among the Fairlight, Chroma, Emulator and alphaSyntauri, the bata drums and the DMX, the Led Zeppelin guitar chord and the Vocoder, Grandmaster D.ST is featured cutting in rhythmic fills with turntable scratching of a record of the Ketjak Balinese Monkey Dance."[36] More straightforwardly, Chaka Khan used Grandmaster Melle Mel to deliver a rapid-fire rap introduction on "I Feel for You," which hit the Top Ten in 1984.

Hip Hop: The Next Generation

By this time, there was a second generation of New York rap artists, including Whodini, The Force MDs, The Fat Boys, and Run-D.M.C. There was also a fledgling hip hop scene developing in Los Angeles. A crew of mobile DJs called Uncle Jam's Army (after the Funkadelic album *Uncle Jam Wants You*) played music at street parties, while such clubs as Radio served the downtown crowd. Prominent among the local DJs were Dr. Dre and Yella from the World Class Wrecking Cru, the group that would eventually metamorphose into N.W.A. (Niggas With Attitude). Also on the scene were Ice-T and Kid Frost. Ice was a New York transplant who rapped harder than most of his contemporaries at Macola Records. He had been the star of the documentary *Breaking and Entering*, a West Coast version of *Wild Style*. Kid Frost was hip hop's first Chicano nationalist. Both Ice and Frost at first played to predominantly Chicano audiences. In 1984, station KDAY made a significant commitment to hip hop when through the efforts of Greg Mack, the station's program director, all the popular New York groups performed in Los Angeles.

The growth of New York hip hop moved rap from the twelve-inch single, the industry standard for dance music since disco, to the album. Key to this transition was the success of *Run-D.M.C.* (1984), which was the first gold rap album. The group that gave its name to the album represented a departure from first-generation rappers in a number of ways. Joseph Simmons (Run), Darryl McDaniels (DMC), and Jason Mizell (Jam Master Jay) came from the lower-middle-class neighbourhood of Hollis in Queens. They were college educated, and they had their sights set on nothing short of conquering both the rock and rap markets. On their second album, *King of Rock,* they proclaimed their conquest and backed it up with hard, boastful rapping complemented by the Hendrix-like live guitar of Eddie Martinez. While hip hop DJs had always used rock tracks in their mixes, Run-D.M.C.'s use of live guitar was novel. The presence of Martinez, who also appeared on "Rock Box," from the group's first album, served as a bridge to rock and a reminder of the Latino presence in hip hop. The Latino connection was further emphasized on *King of Rock* in the use of mixes by Tony Torrez and the Latin Rascals.

In 1986, Run-D.M.C. released *Raising Hell,* which went to number three on the charts and sold 3.5 million copies. The album contained, among other things, an interesting version of "Walk This Way." Like other hip hop DJs, Jam Master Jay had long used rock cuts in the mixes he created for the group. One of his favourite selections was Aerosmith's 1977 hit "Walk This Way." For the album, producer Rick Rubin suggested remaking the song as a duet between Run-D.M.C. and Aerosmith's Steven Tyler and Joe Perry, who were just returning to music from an extended bout with drugs and alcohol. The video of the song is a metaphor for all the contradictions inherent in crossing over. It opens with Run-D.M.C. and Aerosmith performing to audiences on opposite sides of a brick wall. As Run-D.M.C. become intrigued by the noise on the other side, they crash through the wall and end up performing with Aerosmith, leaving their own audience behind.

The only album to rival the sales of *Raising Hell* was *Licensed to Ill* by the Beastie Boys, a group of white bohemians from Manhattan who were branded as rap's first major affront to human decency because of their on- and off-stage antics and the content of their first hit single, "You've Got to Fight for Your Right to Party." Signed to black-owned Def Jam, the Beasties were the first significant white performers in rap. They did not, however, become its kings. Over the next few years, such East Coast rap releases as UTFO's *Lethal*, L. L. Cool J's *Bigger and Deffer*, Whodini's *Open Sesame*, Heavy D. & the Boyz' *Living Large*, Eric B. & Rakim's *Paid in Full*, Salt-N-Pepa's *Hot, Cool & Vicious*, and the Fat Boys' *Crushin'* continued to make significant inroads into the album and cassette markets. Eight of *Billboard*'s Top Thirty black albums for the week of 28 November 1987 were rap albums.

The Beastie Boys, a group of white bohemians from Manhattan who were branded as rap's first major affront to human decency, were the first significant white performers in rap. They did not, however, become its kings.

By this time, the Los Angeles rap scene, which featured harder rhymes set to the slower pace of L.A. cruising, was beginning to come into its own. In 1986, Ice-T recorded "Six in the Morning," which spoke of early morning police raids and threw in a bit of gratuitous misogyny for male posturing. The recording led to a six-year association with Warner that produced *Rhyme Pays* (1987), *Power* (1988), *Iceberg* (1989), and *OG* (1990). It was also in 1986 that a sixteen-year-old Ice Cube wrote "Boyz N the Hood." It was recorded with Eazy E providing the vocals over a grinding, bass-heavy rhythm track created by Dre and Yella. It was this association that led to the formation of N.W.A. and the music that has come to be called *gangsta rap*. Although Los Angeles is usually considered home to gangsta rap, the style can be traced to earlier artists, including Philadelphia's Schoolly-D and the single "PSK," which projected a chilling image of gang membership, and New York's KRS-One and Scott La Rock of Boogie Down Productions and the album *Criminal Minded*, which included cuts like "South Bronx" and "9mm" that employed the gangsta vocabulary.

As the Los Angeles rap scene began to bloom, Public Enemy, the group responsible

Public Enemy are among the most socially conscious and politically controversial groups in rap. Their early albums elevated production values and political commentary to a new level.

for the most politically advanced lyrics in rap, was formed in New York. The group, which hailed from Long Island, or Strong Island as they called it, was an extended posse that included leader Chuck D, MC Flavor Flav, DJ Terminator X, a production team (affectionately called the Bomb Squad) composed of Bill Stephney, Hank Shocklee, and Eric "Vietnam" Sadler, Professor Griff as minister of information, and a paramilitary troop of bodyguards known as Security of the First World. Public Enemy sought to advance the cause of black nationalism and Afrocentricity with tracks as compelling and technically advanced as they were controversial. After cutting their teeth on *Yo! Bum Rush the Show,* the group hit its stride with *It Takes a Nation of Millions to Hold Us Back* (1988) and *Fear of a Black Planet* (1990). Writing of *Nation of Millions,* David Toop has said, "The droning loops, screams and word-blitz of [this] album . . . elevated the art of rap onto a level that was simultaneously abrasive and seductive; the texture of its noise and the polysemic, labyrinthine maze of imagery were relentless."[37] On the album, PE positioned themselves among a host of black leaders, including Marcus Garvey, Rosa Parks, Steven Biko, Martin Luther King, Malcolm X, and Nelson and Winnie Mandela. "This literal act of insertion by Public Enemy into the tradition of black resistance," Brian Cross has written, "collapses the boundary between popular culture and politics."[38]

As 1988 continued, it became clear that message rap had embarked on a course that would raise the consciousness of its fans and the blood pressure of its enemies in equal measure. The cover for *Nation of Millions* had included a logo that pictured a bereted silhouette caught in the crosshairs of a rifle sight. That same year, KRS-One, who was recovering from the shooting death of his partner Scott La Rock, released *By Any Means Necessary.* Invoking the famous Malcolm X photograph, the cover of the album pictured KRS-One looking out the window with a gun. Thus, by the time N.W.A. released *Straight Outta Compton* in 1988, hip hop culture had already become highly politicized and controversial. N.W.A. added to the controversy by portraying the seamier side of Los Angeles gang life without any distance or moral judgment. Brian Turner, president of Priority, the label that distributed N.W.A., defended the group, saying,

> *What impressed me about N.W.A. and Eazy-E was that these guys lived the things they talk about. All I was hearing on the news was the perspective of the police and outsiders—you never get the perspective of the actual guy they're talking about. When I saw what these guys wrote, it really hit me that their side of the story is important to tell.*[39]

While Turner may have felt it was important to tell the other side of the story, it seemed that not everyone agreed with him. Even a cursory look at rap's audience made it clear that something of a generation gap had developed in black music. Nowhere was this gap more apparent than in the programming on black radio. At the time, *Billboard* maintained charts that distinguished between sales and airplay for the Top Forty black singles. Of the twenty-eight rap songs that reached *Billboard's* Top Forty sales chart in the first forty-six weeks of 1988, only sixteen registered on the magazine's airplay chart.[40] Clearly, rap was not receiving airplay commensurate with its sales. Tony Gray, the program director at WRKS in New York, tried to explain the reasons for this:

"Rock Box"

Artist: Run-D.M.C.
Music / Lyrics by Larry Smith, Joseph ("Run") Simmons, Darryl ("D.M.C.") McDaniels
Label: Def Jam (1984), from the *LP Run D.M.C.*

Founded in the early 1980s by Joseph "Run" Simmons, Darryl "D.M.C." McDaniels, and Jason "Jam Master Jay" Mizell, Run-D.M.C. is often credited with breaking down the barrier between hip hop and mainstream rock 'n' roll, introducing hip hop to a huge listening audience that had previously either been unaware of it or viewed it as an exclusively urban, African American "street" phenomenon. Run-D.M.C.'s cover of Aerosmith's "Walk This Way" was a huge crossover hit. This was the first "rap" video played on MTV. However, a strong rock element was present from the very beginning in their music, as we can hear on "Rock Box," which is from their first LP.

Musical Style Notes

"Rock Box" contains many stylistic elements of hip hop:

- A sampled drum rhythm track (although the actual beat is a hard-rock style)
- Rap-style vocals, with dialogue between Run and D.M.C., voice doublings and echo effects used to highlight certain words, and rhythmic lyric repetitions
- Turntable "cuts" from Jam Master Jay

In addition to this, however, a definitive "rock" element is present. The prevailing drum rhythm is a trap-set style, hard-rock backbeat (with the emphasis on beats 2 and 4, as opposed to the relentless "1-2-3-4" equal quarter notes heard in some sampled drum tracks). The opening "riff," doubled on guitar and bass (first occurring at 0:12), would sound completely at home on any heavy metal album. Layered over this is the guitar work of Eddie Martinez, whose wailing solos on "Rock Box" were played live in the studio and were reminiscent of a sound more likely to be associated with Hendrix or Stevie Ray Vaughan than with hip hop mixes.

Musical "Road Map"

TIMINGS	COMMENTS	LYRICS
0:00–0:08	Rap intro—Run Electric guitar and sampled drum rhythm track is established, then stops.	*Run: Run — Run — D — DM — MC — C* *Rock — rock — rock* *For you — for you — for you* *Fresh — fresh — fresh*
0:08–0:32 0:12	Rhythm track reestablished. Repeating bass-guitar heavy metal–style riff established. Electric guitar solo (Eddie Martinez)	
0:32–1:11	Part 1 Run begins. Echo effects and D.M.C.'s added. Voices are used to highlight and accentuate certain words. The word *fade* is both a verbal conclusion and a musical cue that leads into the instrumental break.	*Run: For all you sucker MC's perpetratin' a FRAUD . . .* *. . . Jam Master cut the record up and down and cross-FADE!*

TIMINGS	COMMENTS	LYRICS
1:11–1:29	Instrumental section: Overdubbed electric guitar solo Sampled rhythm track Synthesizer	
1:30–1:54 1:36	Part 2 Run begins. D.M.C. enters over Run's "Never, never."	*Run: Because the rhymes I say . . .* *D.M.C.: Took a test to become an MC . . .*
1:54–2:03	Run jumps in with "Bust into the party . . ."	*Run: Bust into the party, come in the place . . .*
2:03–2:32	DMC begins. Run joins occasionally to punctuate a word or phrase. Echo effects are used again to highlight certain words.	*D.M.C.: So listen to this . . .* *You might think that you have WAITED . . .* *. . . STATED . . .* *. . . GRADED . . .* *. . . DEBATED . . .*
2:32–3:15	Run–D.M.C. dialogue (Turntable cuts from Jam Master Jay.)	*Run–D.M.C.: So move your butt . . .* *D.M.C.: We want to see y'all all in motion* *Run–D.M.C.: Just SHAKE, WIGGLE, jump up and down . . .* Outcue: *Run–D.M.C.: Our DJ's better than all these bands* *HUH!!*
3:15–3:34	Dialogue between Run and D.M.C.	
3:34–3:58	Improvised rap, with lots of rhythmic repetition of words, syllables.	*Jay Jay Jay Jay Jay Jay . . .* *We don't . . . we don't . . . we don't stop! . . .*
3:58–4:27	Guitar solo can be heard under rap lyrics.	*My, my man Jam Master . . .*
4:27–5:27 5:11	Synth chord "pops" and cues next section of rap; guitar continues at intervals throughout. (Lyrics and music begin to fade.)	*Re, remember you don't stop . . .* *Kickin' it, and you don't stop . . .* *. . . Homeboys . . .* *Hollis Crew . . .*

Those records appeal to a specific demographic, primarily 12- to 18-year-olds, or perhaps 12- to 24-year-olds. The battle that [black] radio stations have is that they do need to play popular music, but for marketing reasons they have to be concerned with the 25-plus listeners as well. You don't want to alienate those listeners because that's where the bulk of your revenue comes from.[41]

Although black radio had often been caught between rock and a hard place in the struggle for a viable listenership, in the case of rap, black stations were exhibiting a reluctance to play cuts that were clearly outselling other selections on their lists. To some, it seemed that the split between rap and other forms of black popular music was more than a generation gap; it was an indicator of class divisions within the black community. Bill Adler, publicist for Run-D.M.C., L. L. Cool J, and Public Enemy, among others, put it rather starkly: "Black radio is run by 'buppies' [black urban professionals]. They've made a cultural commitment to a lifestyle that has nothing to do with music on the street. . . . This music very rudely pulls them back on the street corner, and they don't want to go."[42] Artists themselves often identified "bourgeois blacks" as the main source of resistance to rap.

Of course, rap's detractors had no lack of issues to point to. From different quarters, rap was roundly chastised for bigotry, sexism, and/or violence. The cries of anti-Semitism that were directed at Public Enemy's Professor Griff reached a peak when he claimed in an interview with the *Washington Times* that Jews were responsible for "the majority of wickedness that goes on in the world."[43] (Griff was subsequently fired and then rehired as liaison to the black community.) At the time, critic Jon Pareles berated Professor Griff for his misguided prejudices in the *New York Times*, but he also noted that Public Enemy's "overall message is one of self-determination for blacks."[44] As to rap's sexist tendencies, Harry Allen noted:

When Ice-T releases a record called "Girls, Let's Get Buck Naked and Fuck" ("Girls, L.G.B.N.A.F." on the album cover), when 2 Live Crew on a cut called "S & M" calls to women to bring their "d _ _ k-sucking friends," when Ultramagnetic M.C.'s Kool Keith on "Give the Drummer Some" talks about smacking up his bitch in the manner of a pimp, sisters understandably scream.[45]

"Hip-hop is sexist," Allen concluded, but he added, "it is also frank."[46] One wonders if rap would have been so upsetting if it had not been so frank. Still, while it should be noted that sexism has never been a stranger to any genre of popular music or any aspect of life in America, rap's sexism should not be excused.

Evidence of a change in the sexual politics of hip hop started to become apparent in 1985 when Roxanne

As one of the original gangsta rappers, Ice-T was controversial from the start. Still, he has been able to fashion a credible film career and make a bridge to heavy metal with Body Count. While some of his political decisions may be open to debate, his business sense has been unerring.

Shanté's "Roxanne's Revenge," the answer track to "Roxanne Roxanne," UTFO's insult song, beat the original at its own game. It was, however, the overwhelming commercial success of Salt-N-Pepa's double platinum debut LP, *Hot, Cool & Vicious* (1988), that finally convinced some rap labels to promote female rappers, many of whom had been part of the hip hop underground for years.

> *After six years of releasing records, Def Jam finally recorded Nikki D's "Daddy's Little Girl," their first track by a female rapper, and Public Enemy recruited Sister Souljah to the ranks. In Los Angeles, Ice Cube put his support behind Yo Yo, co-producing her scorching* Make Way for the Motherlode. . . . *Yo Yo, who had already show[n] her capacity for fightbacks on Ice Cube's "It's a Man's World," founded the Intelligent Black Woman's Coalition, hoping to reverse the low status and self-esteem that women were clearly suffering in the face of such a concerted shut-out by men.*[47]

By the end of the decade, women had added a new public voice to hip hop. With releases like "Paper Thin" (MC Lyte), "Independent Woman" (Roxanne Shanté), and "Ladies First" (Queen Latifah), critics tended to portray women rappers as a female corrective to adolescent male sexual ranting. However, the reality is more complex.[48] After all, not all male raps were sexist. Consider, for example, "Date Rape" by A Tribe Called Quest. Furthermore, trying to shoehorn groups like Hoes with Attitude or Bitches with Problems into a feminist mould is obviously problematic. In fact, even the most progressive female rappers resisted the feminist tag, perceiving it as a label for a white middle-class movement that existed in tension with their commitment to racial solidarity. It was perhaps this commitment, more than a tacit approval of male sexism, that made most female rappers reluctant to speak out publicly against their male counterparts.

*E*ven the most progressive female rappers resisted the feminist tag, perceiving it as a label for a white middle-class movement that existed in tension with the rappers' commitment to racial solidarity.

The woman who best managed this conflict between racial solidarity and feminism was Queen Latifah. Projecting a powerful and dignified image, Latifah developed "a forthright rapping approach that sidestepped the dissing clichés."[49] Through cuts like "Dance for Me" and "Come into My House," she was able to establish herself as a rapper whose talent was commensurate with that of her male counterparts. She released her first album, *All Hail the Queen,* on Tommy Boy in 1989. On the video for the album's most popular cut, "Ladies First," which was performed as a duet with her "European sister," Monie Love, Latifah positioned herself as a military strategist in the company of such historical black women activists as Sojourner Truth, Angela Davis, and Winnie Mandela and offered a pro-female version of the predominantly male lineage portrayed in other political rap videos. Still, these gains were offset by the continuing objectification and exploitation of women, expressed most straightforwardly by the Miami-based 2 Live Crew on *Move Something* (1988) and *As Nasty as They Wanna Be* (1989).

Violence was the third issue that rap's critics frequently decried. The confrontational stance and uncompromising lyrics of Public Enemy ("Fight the Power") and N.W.A. ("_ _ _ _ tha Police") and skirmishes at rap concerts fueled the notion in the minds of some that rap promoted violence. Violence had occurred at some rap concerts, but that, in and of itself, did not distinguish them from rock concerts or, for that matter, soccer matches in Britain. Furthermore, rappers themselves addressed this problem head-on. In 1989, following the leadership of critic Nelson George, a number of rap groups—Stetsasonic, Boogie Down Productions, and Public

Queen Latifah is one of the most intelligent and articulate women in rap. Her forceful rhymes added measurably to the chorus of female voices that began to emerge in the late 1980s. In the 1990s, she went on to star in the television sitcom Living Single.

Enemy, among others—initiated a campaign called Stop the Violence, which was aimed specifically at black-on-black crime. As one of their projects, these groups contributed their time and talent to "Self-Destruction," the all-star rap recording that became the anthem of the movement. The following year, West Coast rappers followed suit with "We're All in the Same Gang."

Ironically, the West Coast effort occurred amidst bitter splits among the N.W.A. posse. Following the success of *Straight Outta Compton,* Ice Cube left the group over disputes about creative control and money. Looking toward the Public Enemy orbit for support and inspiration, he "sought to bring the gangsta style of rhyming from the west to the apocalyptic beats of the Bomb Squad."[50] The result was *Amerikkka's Most Wanted*, one of the best-selling albums of 1990. The album launched Cube on one of the most successful solo careers in rap and led to his best-selling LPs, *Death Certificate* (1991), *Predator* (1992), and *Lethal Injection* (1993). N.W.A. responded with *Efil4zaggin* in 1991, after which Dr. Dre also left the group. He returned as a solo act the following year with *The Chronic* (the term for a particularly strong strain of marijuana). The N.W.A. split made it clear that gangsta conflicts in the music community were as likely to be resolved in lawyers' offices as on the streets.

While the press frequently decried gangsta violence and hip hop misogyny, the fact remains that a good deal of rap spoke positively to real issues.

While the press frequently decried gangsta violence and hip hop misogyny, the fact remains that a good deal of rap spoke positively to real issues. "Any examination of rap's lyrical content," wrote David Nathan in *Billboard*, "reveals a very high percentage of anti-violent, anti-drug messages, many aimed at improving self-esteem, encouraging the youth of the 80s to continue their education and approach adulthood with a positive approach."[51] Unfortunately, this side of rap, which stood in sharp contrast to the lyric vacuity of most other forms of black pop at the time, tended to get lost in the controversy. "Self-Destruction" sold nearly 500,000 units and never even registered in the black airplay Top Forty. Writing for a *Billboard* special on "The World of Black Music" in the summer of 1989, Dan Stuart pointed out, "Today it's virtually impossible to find a non-rap song in the black top 40 that contains lyrical content that deals with any topic besides dancing and romancing."[52]

The turmoil surrounding rap may have presented a problem for the population at large and black radio in particular, but major record companies were quick to recognize the financial potential of the sound. While few majors signed rap acts directly, buy-ins and distribution deals with successful rap indies soon became commonplace. The first to make a move was Columbia Records, which concluded a custom label deal with Def Jam (L. L. Cool J, Oran 'Juice' Jones, the Beastie Boys, Public Enemy) in 1985. Jive Records (Whodini, Kool Moe Dee, Steady B., D.J. Jazzy Jeff & the Fresh Prince, Boogie Down Productions) entered into distribution arrangements with both RCA and Arista. Cold Chillin' Records (Marly Marl, Roxanne Shanté, Biz Markie, M. C. Shan) signed a distribution deal with Warner in 1987. Warner also bought a piece of Tommy Boy (Stetsasonic, Force MDs, De La Soul, Queen Latifah, Black by Demand,

Digital Underground). Delicious Vinyl (Tone Loc, Def Jef, Young M.C.) concluded a national distribution deal with Island. National distribution for Priority (N.W.A., Eazy E, Ice Cube) went to Capitol. By and large, these majors left creative functions at street level and simply provided the rap independents with superior distribution, which increased rap's access to mainstream outlets. As a result, rap tended to get more support on pop radio than on black radio. Even MTV initiated a rap show. Although at first buried in a late-night weekend slot, *Yo! MTV Raps* soon moved to a daily afternoon slot and became one of the channel's most popular programs. By 1988, rap had entered the mainstream to such an extent that NARAS added a rap category to the Grammy Awards. However, the academy refused to include the first rap award in its live telecast, which led four of the five nominees, including the winners, D.J. Jazzy Jeff & the Fresh Prince, to boycott the show. Shortly thereafter, *Billboard,* unceremoniously and with no editorial comment, added a rap chart to its pages.

As usual, entrance into the mainstream led to exposure in other media, such as television and film. After being awarded the first rap Grammy, Will Smith (the Fresh Prince) received a starring role in the prime-time sitcom *The Fresh Prince of Bel Air.* Rappers also began to show up on other African American sitcoms, including *A Different World* and *Cosby.* The poignant comedy/variety show, *In Living Color,* which was clearly grounded in a hip hop aesthetic, featured regular appearances by such artists as Monie Love and Queen Latifah, who later landed a starring role in her own television sitcom, *Living Single.* Quincy Jones, producer of *Fresh Prince,* also attempted "to bridge generations and traverse musical boundaries" in the production of his award-winning 1989 LP, *Back on the Block,* which brought together such diverse musical talents as Sarah Vaughn, Ella Fitzgerald, Siedah Garrett, Al Jarreau, Bobby McFerrin, Take 6, Ray Charles, Chaka Khan, Al B. Sure, James Ingram, and Barry White with rappers like Ice-T, Melle Mel, Big Daddy Kane, and Kool Moe Dee.

There appeared a rash of black-directed films about life in the "'hood." These films were far more realistic in their portrayal of urban life and far more demanding in their political analysis than either the break-dance movies of the mid-1980s or the "blaxploitation" films of the early 1970s.

It was in film, however, that rap made some of its most powerful statements. When Kid N Play parlayed their LP *Funhouse* into the film comedy *House Party* (and a sequel as well as a Saturday-morning cartoon show), they only hinted at the connections between rap and topical film. It was Spike Lee's *Do the Right Thing,* powered by the hip hop force of Public Enemy's "Fight the Power," that tied rap and topical film tightly together. Following the success of Lee's devastating treatment of race relations, there appeared a rash of black-directed films about life in the "'hood," including *Straight Outta Brooklyn, Juice, New Jack City,* and *Boyz N the Hood.* The latter two of these starred Ice-T and Ice Cube, respectively, and featured their music. As a group, these films were far more realistic in their portrayal of urban life and far more demanding in their political analysis than either the break-dance movies of the mid-1980s or the "blaxploitation" films of the early 1970s.

In 1990, rapper/dancer Hammer (then M.C. Hammer) scored another first for rap with his album *Please Hammer Don't Hurt 'Em,* which logged twenty-one weeks at number one on the pop charts and became the best-selling rap album ever. With sales of more than 10 million copies, it outdistanced its nearest competitor by a factor of two. Ambitious to the core, Hammer set his sights on nothing short of toppling Michael Jackson. Roundly "dissed" by the hip hop nation for playing to mainstream sensibilities, Hammer enlisted the services of no less a

"Ladies First"

Artist: Queen Latifah

Music / Lyrics by Dr. Shane Faber, Mark James (DJ Mark the 45 King), Simone Johnson, Dana Owens (Queen Latifah), Anthony Peaks

Label: Tommy Boy, from the CD *All Hail the Queen* (1989)

Queen Latifah's music is an example of the immediacy and the community basis in which hip hoppers develop their rhymes. A talented, disciplined, and hardworking musician, she came under the influence of Kris Parker, otherwise known as KRS-One, who as a producer and rapper with Boogie Down Productions had developed an explicitly Afrocentric, antiviolent, and "conscious" hip hop approach. As part of this group, Latifah, whose stage name means "delicate and sensitive" in Arabic, fashioned a proud, empowered female response to the misogyny and "gangsta" violence of much hip hop. In "Ladies First," Queen Latifah and guest artist Monie Love use the medium of hip hop, a genre that in many cases objectifies women, to deliver a message about the strength and autonomy of women, creating a powerful, courageous new identity for women in hip hop and leaving no question as to whether female rappers can compete with the guys.

Musical Style Notes

The instrumental tracks of "Ladies First" feature the trademark hip hop techniques of synth programming and sampling, in which digital samples of extant sound files are used as building blocks for a new composition, often repeating or "looping" the samples. These samples can be anything from turntable scratching to preexisting recordings (see Puff Daddy's "I'll Be Watching You"), to the funky horns and the sampled alto sax squeal heard on "Ladies First."

Vocally, we hear another hallmark of hip hop, which is a dialogue between two rappers, each reinforcing the other's point of view and adding to the argument.

Musical "Road Map"

TIMINGS	COMMENTS	LYRICS
0:00–0:18	Introduction Synthesized, funk-style horn and drum samples	
0:18–0:29	Verse 1	Queen Latifah: *The ladies will kick it,* *the rhyme that is wicked . . . (etc.)*
0:29–0:53	Verse 1 (response)	Monie Love: *A-yo, let me take it from here, Queen . . .* *Excuse me but I think I'm about due . . . (etc.)* *. . . Let me state the position: Ladies first, yes? (Yes)* Male voice: *(Yeah, there's going to be some changes in here.)*
0:53–1:12	Verse 2	*Believe me when I say being a woman is great, you see . . . (etc.)*
1:12–1:30	Verse 2 (response)	Queen Latifah: *I break into a lyrical freestyle* *Grab the mic, look into the crowd and see smiles . . .* *(etc.)*
1:30–2:04	Instrumental interlude—same material as introduction	
2:04–2:14	Verse 3	*Who said the ladies couldn't make it, you must be blind . . . (etc.)*
2:14–2:24	Verse continues, with dialogue between Latifah and Monie Love.	*. . . A female rapper with the message to send the* *Queen Latifah is a perfect specimen . . .* Monie Love: *My sister, can I get some?* Queen Latifah: *Sure, Monie Love, grab the mic and get dumb.*
2:24–2:59	Verse 4 (response)	Monie Love: *Yo, praise me not for simply being what I am . . .* *(etc.)* *. . . And next up is me, the M-O-N-I-E L-O-V-E* *And I'm first cause I'm a L-A-D-I-E.*
2:59–3:13 3:13	Verse 4 (response)	Queen Latifah: *Contact and in fact, the style, it gets harder . . .* *(etc.)* *. . . And I'll recite the chapter in verse* *The title of this recital is "Ladies First."*
3:17	Horn samples continue. Break at 3:35; sound reduced to only drum and alto sax samples Music fades; ends 3:56.	

figure than James Brown to bolster his credibility. In the long-form prologue to the "2 Legit to Quit" video, Brown anoints Hammer as his "godson" and directs his heir apparent to "bring back the glove," an obvious reference to Michael Jackson and, therefore, to the pop crown.

Ironically, Hammer's pop tendencies may have created cultural space for his main competition, Vanilla Ice. After touring as Hammer's opening act, Ice's LP *To the Extreme* skyrocketed to number one on the pop charts and multiplatinum certification, temporarily displacing Hammer himself. At this point, however, Ice ran into credibility problems when it was discovered that part of his biography had been falsified to make him look more "street." This drive "to appear more 'authentic,'" according to Kristal Brent Zook, "demonstrates that an increasing sense of African-American solidarity seems to inspire an increasingly blatant demand for inclusion among (some) white people who now sense themselves uncomfortably shifting from center to margin."[53] Another group of white rappers, called Young Black Teenagers, actually included a song called "Proud to be Black" in their debut album, pushing the identification with black culture to the limit. Other white rap groups, such as Third Base, were taken at face value. Their acceptance by other rappers seemed to be based on a certain repudiation of white skin privilege in their own lifestyles.

Los Angeles gangsta rap tended to push toward harder rhymes, and its success led both Hammer and Vanilla Ice to follow up their earlier successes with harder images—Hammer looking like a gangsta, Ice wearing dreadlocks and publicly embracing marijuana. However, gangsta rap was also home to an incredible diversity of rappers. In 1989, Kid Frost, a Chicano veteran of Los Angeles hip hop, recorded the bilingual *Hispanic Causing Panic.* He was joined in short order by Cubanos Melloman Ace and Skatemaster Tate. Named after the discharge of a shotgun, the Boo Yaa Tribe, a group of Samoans who grew up among blacks and Chicanos in southeast Los Angeles, were a formidable looking group of ex–gang members. David Toop notes that their "raps are written in hardcore prison slang, with joy, pleasure, identity and emergence expressed in metaphors of death, violence, intimidation, fear and imprisonment."[54] Against this background, the members of the group have talked openly about respect for women in their culture. The most diverse posse in the Los Angeles hip hop scene were the groups associated with the Soul Assassins. At the centre of the Soul Assassins posse was Cypress Hill with Grandmixer Muggs, an Italian, B-Real, a Chicano, and Sen Dogg, a Cuban. Known for their "old school" hook lines and harmony approach to rap and B-Real's characteristic nasal whine, Cypress Hill's 1991 debut single "How I Could Just Kill a Man" propelled the group to national recognition. Songs dealing with such hot-button issues as drugs ("I Wanna Get High") and violence ("Cock the Hammer") brought further recognition. Their second album, *Black Sunday* (1993), debuted at number one on the pop charts. Following the group's initial success, Muggs set up the Soul Assassins as a production company that included FunkDoobiest and House of Pain. Among the members of FunkDoobiest were Puerto Rican and Sioux MCs and a Mexican DJ. House of Pain was Irish with a Latvian DJ. With the release of the 1992 single "Jump Around" and the LP *Fine Malt Lyrics,* House of Pain achieved national fame, bringing something of the Irish experience to hip hop.

By the early 1990s, then, hip hop had become, in the words of Brian Cross, "a voice for many different subjectivities—women, Chicano, Cubano, Asian, Irish, gay, and all the variants covered by black, Jamaican, Dominican, etc."[55] According to Cross, far from detracting from the African American cultural priorities that determined the trajectory of rap, the expansion of the music "brings the struggle of African-Americans to many new ears, thereby providing a new perspective on one's own problems."[56] From an isolated street culture, hip hop had expanded in less than twenty years into a global phenomenon.

Things were not so easy for Canadian rap artists. By the late 1980s, active hip hop scenes had developed in Toronto, Halifax, and Montreal. Given the preponderance of Caribbean immigrants to Canada in the late 1960s and early 1970s, the majority of participants in Canadian hip hop had a West Indian background. Unfortunately, their quest for national, let alone international, success was stymied by the total lack of an infrastructure for black Canadian music. Until 2000, there was not a single radio station in Canada oriented towards the country's black populace. Consequently, established Canadian record companies had zero interest in signing black artists. If there was no way to market these artists through radio, there was no way such signings could be profitable. With no contracts being signed and no commercial radio outlets, there was also little to speak of in terms of management, promotion people, or booking agents.

Stepping into the void in 1987 was Ivan Berry, who established Beat Factory Productions in Toronto. That same year, KRS-One and Scott La Rock of New York City's Boogie Down Productions produced the first Canadian hip hop compilation, optimistically entitled *Break'n Out*. A year later, Berry was able to place one of his early signings, Michie Mee (Michelle McCulloch) and LA Luv (Phillip Gayle), with American and European labels. Their reggae-inflected singles such as "On This Mike," "Elements of Style," and "Victory Is Calling" achieved a modicum of international success.

In 1989, Wesley Williams, using the stage name Maestro Fresh Wes, became the first really successful Canadian rapper, breaking into the Canadian Top 40 with "Let Your Backbone Slide" from the album *Symphony in Effect*, released on LMR Records through Attic. The single remains the only certified gold single in Canadian hip hop history, and the album remains the biggest-selling album in the history of Canadian rap. Two years later, the Dream Warriors emerged from Toronto's Jane-Finch community, featuring King Lou and Capital Q.

Influenced by the jazz–hip hop experiments of Gang Starr and Guru, in 1991 the Dream Warriors issued *And Now, The Legacy Begins*, containing the singles "My Definition of a Boombastic Jazz Style," "Wash Your Face in My Sink," and "Ludi." The engaging "My Definition of a Boombastic Jazz Style" was cleverly built on

Maestro Fresh Wes became the first Canadian rap star in 1989 with the single "Let Your Backbone Slide."

a sample from Quincy Jones' "Soul Bossa Nova," which was being used at the time as the theme music for a Canadian game show called *Definition*. The Dream Warriors achieved significant success in Europe while remaining virtually unknown in the U.S.

The rap scene in Montreal was different from that in Toronto in that the majority of black immigrants were French speakers from Haiti. In 1990, the bilingual and interracial Laymen Twaist achieved popularity with a rap version of Lou Reed's "Walk on the Wild Side." A year earlier, the first French Canadian rap song of note, the topical "Je m'en souviens," addressed Quebec's controversial French language law Bill 101. In 1990, the Mouvement rap francophone duo released "M.R.F. est arrivé," which they followed in 1991 with "Le Boyfriend" and "Rapper chic." In the early 1990s, Montreal was also home to a white Muslim rapper, Malik Shaheed, who recorded politically infused songs in Spanish, French, and English. In 1997, Dubmatique became the first rap group from Quebec to have a major hit on the francophone pop charts. A year later, Vancouver's Rascalz partnered with Kardinal Offishall, Thrust, and Choclair for the single "Northern Touch." A shout-out anthem to Canadian hip hop, "Northern Touch" became the first Canadian rap hit since 1991.

In 2000, the CRTC finally granted a licence to Milestone Communications for the first urban radio station in Canada. Prior to the debut of Milestone's Flow-97 in 2001, Toronto's urban community had been forced to tune in to Buffalo's WBLK for a steady dose of hip hop and r&b. Not surprisingly, WBLK felt no compunction to play recordings by Canadian artists. In the rest of Canada, with the exception of specialty shows on community stations, there was simply no radio access for hip hop. Following the success of Flow, a handful of urban stations were established in other major Canadian cities, providing for the first time outlets for airplay for Canadian hip hop and r&b artists. Among the many groups to benefit from this were Swollen Members, K-Os (whose "Crabbuckit" was featured in the trailer for *Shrek the Third*), Halifax's Buck 65, and Edmonton's Cadence Weapon. A number of francophone rap artists, such as Muzio and Prince Ayman, have followed in the wake of Dubmatique's success, releasing recordings that have become hits in Quebec and, at times, France.

Popular Music and the Politics of Censorship

Popular music has never been a stranger to controversy or opposition. Herman Gray has noted three periods of particularly strong opposition: the response to jazz in the early part of the twentieth century, the reaction against rock 'n' roll in the 1950s and 1960s, and the most recent wave of controversy associated with heavy metal and rap.[57] No matter what the genre, certain themes such as a fear of the connection between music and sexuality tend to run through all three periods. Such concerns may be expressed either as the fear that sensual rhythms can overcome rationality or that lyrics that push the boundaries of decorum can undermine moral values. Because of these fears, each genre has been linked at various times to drug abuse, lawless behaviour, and general moral decline. In turn, all of these problems have been projected to some degree onto race.

Lawrence Grossberg has ascribed the most recent round of attacks on popular music to the new conservatism espoused, in his view, by Christian fundamentalists, conservative elitists, and organizations like the PMRC.[58] His view is shared by Nan Levinson, a Tufts University professor and correspondent for the *Index on Censorship* journal. "Though usually played as revolts of the fed up," Levinson has said, "these skirmishes are likely to be nurtured or orchestrated by organizations of the extreme moralist right."[59] Both Grossberg and Levinson believe these conservative groups are not monolithic but rather linked by common themes, such as an adherence to a narrow interpretation of the "Christian way of life," and certain sound-bite concepts, such as "family values," that have become media codes for conservatism.

These conservative groups are not monolithic but rather linked by common themes, such as an adherence to a narrow interpretation of the "Christian way of life," and certain sound-bite concepts, such as "family values," that have become media codes for conservatism.

Picking up on the initiatives of the new conservatism, the popular press began to cast music as a social irritant and its detractors as defenders of a decent society. It should also be noted that the shift in the political centre of gravity toward the right during the Reagan-Bush years made essentially conservative arguments that much more persuasive to many would-be liberals. The assumption—often made tacitly—was that popular music communicated an intentional message, usually through its lyrics (although visual images, hypnotic rhythms, subliminal suggestions, and sheer volume were also mentioned), to an impressionable young audience with little will or inclination to resist, thus producing a direct and uniform effect on human behaviour. Of course, the way in which popular music communicates is far more complicated than this. As Susan McClary and Robert Walser have pointed out:

> *Music relies on events and inflections occurring on many interdependent levels (melody, rhythm, harmony, timbre, texture, etc.) simultaneously. Each of these has something of a syntactical dimension—a grammar of expectations, normal continuity, etc.—and also a wide-open semiotic dimension. . . . When all these levels are operating at the same time, whether reinforcing or contradicting one another or both, we are dealing with a tangle that pages and pages of words can only begin to unpack.*[60]

Add to this the visual dimension of music video, which frequently eschews narrative organization altogether, and the complexity of communication increases significantly. Popular music is polysemic; it communicates on many levels at once. Its meaning may be different for different people in different places, and that meaning may change over time. This is not to suggest that popular music has no effects. In its association with the social movements of the 1960s, popular music was certainly related in some way to the social transformations of the era. Today, however, that same music is used to sell beer, cars, and running shoes. During the mega-events of the 1980s, popular music clearly served as a vehicle for mobilizing masses of people toward particular political ends. At the same time, it opened new markets for and delivered new consumers to transnational corporations. The proposition that lyrics and images glorifying violence or the degradation of women contribute to those same proclivities in the society as a whole must be taken seriously. However, it must be considered in proportion to all of the forces that bear on the problem. In other words, the lyrics and images of popular music would have to be considered as one of a number of variables, including such things as class, age, race, gender, ethnicity, sexual orientation, employment status, housing, education, religion, drug laws, obscenity standards, health status, nutrition, the availability of social services, the state of the economy, and the prevailing political climate. In the 1980s and 1990s, however, as in the jazz era and the heyday of rock 'n' roll, the reaction to popular music seemed to lack such a sense of proportion. Indeed, there seemed to be a compelling drive to treat popular music as if it were solely responsible for (and actually more harmful than) the social problems it referenced. The signal event for this treatment was the high-profile government investigation in the United States that was initiated by the PMRC in 1985.

The Parents Music Resource Center

The PMRC was founded in early 1985 by a group of prominent women in Washington, D.C. Founding members included, in addition to Tipper Gore, Sally Nevius, whose husband had chaired the city council; Pam Howar; and Susan Baker, whose husband, James Baker, was then secretary of the Treasury. Indeed, of the twenty original members, seventeen were married to influential Washington politicians.[61] They were immediately dubbed "the Washington wives" by the press in recognition of their access to political clout. Concerned, as they said, "about the growing trend in music toward lyrics that are sexually explicit, excessively violent, or glorify the use of drugs and alcohol"—as evidenced in the lyrics to songs like Prince's "Nikki Darling" and Madonna's "Like a Virgin"—these women decided to exploit their personal connections to "educate and inform parents about this alarming trend as well as to ask the industry to exercise self-restraint."[62] The PMRC consistently maintained that it was in favour of voluntary measures, not censorship, and that it was not opposed to all forms of popular music.

With a cash contribution from Mike Love of the Beach Boys and office space donated by Coors Beer, a company already well-known for its anti-union tactics and conservative funding practices, which included contributions to the Contras and the Heritage Foundation, the group set up shop and formed an alliance with the national Parent/Teacher Association (PTA). Having gained through this alliance instant access to the PTA's base of 5.6 million members, the PMRC then set about trying to convince the music industry to publish the lyrics to all new releases and institute a rating system similar to the one used for movies ("X" for explicit lyrics, "V" for violence, "O" for occult, and so on). In August, 1985 Stan Gortikov, then president of the RIAA, offered a compromise generic warning, "PARENTAL ADVISORY/EXPLICIT LYRICS," in response to the PMRC's demand. Acknowledging the legitimacy of the PMRC's concerns, he cited only legal and logistical problems as the reason for the compromise.

Whatever one's position on labeling, there were, as Gortikov pointed out at the time, a number of legal and logistical problems with the PMRC's original proposal. "Unlike the motion picture industry, which rates about 325 films a year," Gortikov noted, "the recording industry releases 25,000 songs annually, which would require a process for rating 100 tunes a day."[63] He then went on to point out that publication of lyrics without the permission of the publisher would violate the copyright laws. Beyond such mechanical problems, however, there were the more pressing difficulties of interpretation. Popular music often resists a single, fixed meaning that can be read off its surface. As Simon Frith asserted long ago, "Different consumers *use* rock differently,"[64] which is to say that different consumers may attach a range of competing meanings to their experience of music. Such meanings might be based on a knowledge of subcultural codes, mediations in fanzines and the music press, and/or individual subjective judgments and emotional responses. The use of such recording practices as echo, distortion, and "backward masking" (the process of recording passages backward), which has led to charges of musicians intending subliminal messages, makes any discussion of meaning still more complex. The mind boggles at the thought of a committee trying to make definitive cultural sense out of all of this in a timely fashion, especially given some of the confusion over meaning that the music industry itself reported during the hearings. Frank Zappa recalled one record company executive who forced his group to excise the phrase "*And I still remember mama with her apron and her pad/ Feeding all the boys at Ed's Cafe*" because he thought that the word *pad* referred to a sanitary napkin.[65]

To the average onlooker, Gortikov's compromise suggested that the music industry had surrendered to minimal pressure. Gortikov's willingness to compromise, however, began to make some sense when the PMRC rejected his suggestion and decided to unleash its full powers, or, more accurately, the powers of its mates. In September, the Senate Committee on Commerce, Science, and Transportation held public hearings on the PMRC's charges. Among the members of the committee were John Danforth, who was its chairman, Fritz Hollings, and Albert Gore. Their wives were members of the PMRC. Gortikov immediately saw that the industry faced the dual threats of legislation and regulation if it did not cooperate. Adding further impetus to the industry's desire to cooperate was the home taping bill (H.R. 2911), which the record companies wanted passed. The bill would have levied a tax on blank tape, enabling record companies to recover millions of dollars in revenues presumably lost because of home taping. Representative Thomas Downey was an early sponsor of the bill and a past recipient of the RIAA's culture award. His wife was a member of the PMRC. When hearings on the bill were stalled, the industry looked to the Senate for help. Charles Mathias, Chairman of the Senate Subcommittee on Copyright Laws, had authored a bill (S. 1739) similar to the House version. The cosponsor of the Mathias bill was Albert Gore.

The character of the 1985 PMRC hearings was reminiscent of the payola hearings of 1959. Once again, morally high-toned critics advocated protecting innocent children from the evils of popular music. Testimony from the young people allegedly affected was notably absent.

The character of the 1985 PMRC hearings was reminiscent of the payola hearings of 1959. Once again, morally high-toned critics advocated protecting innocent children from the evils of popular music. Testimony from the young people allegedly affected was notably absent. Unlike the 1959 payola hearings, however, the players did not fall into neatly defined interest groups, such as major record labels and independent record labels or liberal and conservative artists and politicians. Important labels, including MCA, A&M, and Geffen, initially broke ranks with the RIAA and joined a group of smaller labels to form an anticensorship group called the Musical Majority. While Smokey Robinson and Mike Love spoke out against so-called porn rock, artists ranging from Frank Zappa and Dee Snider of Twisted Sister to John Denver and Donny Osmond denounced the rating system.

Denver testified about the dangers of being overly literal in the interpretation of lyrics, recounting how some radio stations had refused to broadcast his "Rocky Mountain High" because they thought it was about drugs. PMRC cofounder Susan Baker had attempted to anticipate any warnings about overly literal interpretations by pointing out earlier that Cole Porter's "The Birds Do It, The Bees Do It" could hardly be compared to the heavy metal group W.A.S.P. singing "F-U-C-K Like a Beast."[66] However, Baker neglected to mention that the W.A.S.P. song had never been released in the United States, or that the Porter classic could be compared to the

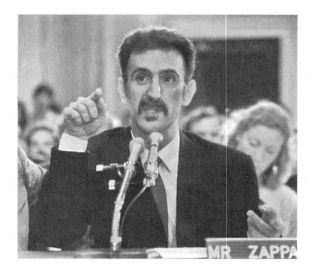

As the leader of the Mothers of Invention, Frank Zappa was as creative and idiosyncratic as he was uncompromising and disciplined. In 1985, he played a prominent role at the PMRC hearings as an outspoken defender of First Amendment rights.

Captain and Tennille's "Do That to Me One More Time," which, according to Zappa, had appeared on the PMRC's original hit list.[67] Omissions like these left many people openly suspicious of the proceedings. "Beneath the 'save the children' rhetoric," editorialized *Rolling Stone*, "is an attempt by a politically powerful minority to impose its morality on the rest of us."[68]

In November 1985, shortly after the hearings, a compromise was hammered out between the RIAA and the PMRC and announced publicly. Essentially, the PMRC ended up agreeing to Gortikov's original proposal. With a "voluntary" rating system now in place, the question remained as to what was considered offensive and how serious it was. It was in this area that the PMRC scored its greatest victories in terms of framing the issues and capturing public attention.

The Issues: Sex, Drugs, and Rock 'n' Roll Revisited

In 1988, the PMRC produced *Rising to the Challenge,* a video in which the group outlined "five major themes" in popular music that were of concern to it. The themes were:

1. Abuse of drugs and alcohol
2. Suicide
3. Graphic violence
4. Fascination with the occult
5. A sexuality that is graphic and explicit[69]

The PMRC claimed that the five themes listed above "occurred consistently in some rock music and especially in heavy metal."[70] While they would later add rap to their list of music to be watched, at the time, the organization maintained that heavy metal was "the most disturbing element in contemporary music," claiming that "much of it dwells on themes that glorify rape, sado-masochism, violence, and suicide."[71] According to Robert Walser, however, "Heavy metal lyrics dealing with these topics are uncommon. For example, examination of eighty-eight [heavy metal] song lyrics reprinted by *Hit Parader* reveals relatively little concern with violence, drug use, or suicide."[72]

To bolster its claims in its video, the PMRC drew attention to the unsavoury lifestyles of certain heavy metal groups like Mötley Crüe, using lead singer Vince Neil's conviction in a drunk driving accident that took the life of another musician as an example. While Neil certainly projected the image of a profoundly irresponsible person, such behaviour is hardly limited to heavy metal artists, and the vast majority of incidents surrounding heavy metal artists far less dramatic. While the PMRC argued that times had worsened since Elvis ground his pelvis into the consciousness of an adoring generation, the fact was that Elvis could match drug habits and violent outbursts with the best of the heavy metal artists. As to the music itself, *People* magazine reminded its readers that "Cole Porter's 'Love for Sale' was considered so 'blue' that it could be broadcast only in instrumental form. . . . Duke Ellington's 'The Mooche' was considered so provocative that some blamed it for a national rise in incidents of rape."[73]

While the PMRC themes have, to a large degree, defined the terms of debate over popular music since they were issued, the fact is that, from Shakespeare's *Romeo and Juliet* to Dante's *Inferno,* sex, drugs, violence, suicide, and the devil have always been compelling themes in Western art and common obsessions in the lives of its practitioners, whether they are painters, sculptors, writers, or musicians. "Berlioz made no bones about his use of opium," Walser has noted. "His program for the *Symphonie Fantastique*

In targeting heavy metal, and later, rap, to the extent that they did, the PMRC and their allies were drawing a line between themselves and youth.

explicitly connects opium use with the rhetorical splendor of his music. Abuse of alcohol is well documented for composers such as Schumann, Schubert, and Mussorgsky."[74] Mozart was also no saint; his depiction in the movie *Amadeus,* while somewhat caricatured, was well within the bounds of historical accuracy. Wagner's music has long been associated with imperialism and violence. It is no coincidence that director Francis Ford Coppola selected Wagner's "The Flight of the Valkyries" to accompany the destruction of the Vietnamese village in *Apocalypse Now*. The composition, which tells of warrior maidens who preside over battles and transport fallen heroes to Valhalla, effectively made the statement Coppola wished to make about U.S. involvement in Vietnam.

In targeting heavy metal, and later, rap, to the extent that they did, the PMRC and their allies were drawing a line between themselves and youth. In so doing, they made it clear that other forms of music—even other forms of popular music—would not be subjected to the same scrutiny. Country music, for example, remained largely untouched by the PMRC, even though it has often dealt with themes of sex, violence, and alcohol. Critic Dave Marsh noted this double standard when he wrote, "Imagine how the rapper Ice Cube would be denounced for a song about drunkenly disrupting an old girlfriend's wedding and threatening the groom, then setting out on a bender with his crew. That is exactly the story line of Garth Brooks' 'I've Got Friends in Low Places.'"[75]

In some ways, the country music industry relished the attacks on rap and heavy metal. "Every morning when they play that stuff," said Jimmy Bowen, head of Nashville's Liberty Records, "people come running to us."[76] Frank Zappa went so far as to suggest that the rating system would "have the effect of protectionist legislation for the country music industry."[77] Occasionally, there were explicit political connections between country music and the new conservatism, as with Randy Travis' 1990 hit, "Point of Light," written expressly for Bush, but the real payoff for country music was in expansion and sales. Albums by country artists like Randy Travis, George Strait, Clint Black, and Garth Brooks began to appear regularly among the best-selling pop albums of the year, historically a rare occurrence for country product. In 1992, Garth Brooks alone had five albums among the year's most popular, including *Ropin' the Wind* at number one, the first time a country album had ever been cited as top pop album of the year.

This is not to suggest that the increase in the appeal of country music was only the result of the reaction to other forms of popular music or that the PMRC had not identified some real issues. However, in the selective application of their research to rap and metal, the PMRC raised serious questions about their commitment to freedom of expression. The logic of the First Amendment suggests that it is the most unpopular ideas and expressions that are most in need of protection. In his testimony at the PMRC hearings, Stan Gortikov—easily the most cooperative industry spokesman—had expressed the "fear that the only acceptable translation of the wishes of the PMRC will somehow constitute a de facto first stage form of censorship."[78] Since the creation of the rating system in 1985, many retail record outlets had, in fact, refused to carry stickered product, fearing organized consumer protest. These outlets included department stores like Sears and J. C. Penney as well as music chains like Record World, Disc Jockey, and Camelot Music, the second largest in the country. The influential Wal-Mart chain took the practice one step further, refusing to carry a growing list of nonstickered records as well.[79] (Wal-Mart had distinguished itself prior to this by refusing to stock thirty rock magazines, including *Rolling Stone, Creem,* and *Tiger Beat,* on the basis that they were "pornographic."[80] This policy was implemented while the giant warehouse chain was still selling guns.) By 1990, as many as nineteen states had considered legislation requiring lyric labeling, and some of them—Louisiana, for example—used the appearance of a stickered product in a store as grounds for criminal liability.[81] (There was at the same time a spate of proposed legislation aimed at regulating live concerts and volume levels on boom boxes.) In 1992, the police chief of Guilderland, New York, sent a letter to local music stores, warning about the legality of selling stickered records, even though the practice was not illegal.[82] That same year, four record outlets in Omaha, Nebraska, were actually charged with violating the state's harmful to minors law when they sold stickered LPs to teenagers.[83] If the warning label was designed simply to alert parents to controversial material, as the PMRC contended, why was it being used as a basis for criminalization? The fact is that the 1985 PMRC hearings marked the beginning of an intensified effort to put popular music on trial.

Shortly after the 1985 hearings, singer Ozzy Osbourne was sued by the parents of a California teenager, when it was alleged that Osbourne's song "Suicide Solution" had caused their nineteen-year-old son, John McCullom, to shoot himself. The case became a cause célèbre for the PMRC, and the song and McCullom's death were highlighted in *Rising to the Challenge* a few years later. Because the lyrics, which referred to suicide as "the only way out," were admittedly ambiguous, Osbourne's claim that "Suicide Solution" was actually an antisuicide song whose lyrics were inspired by the alcohol-related death of a friend did not convince the public at large, although the lawsuit was thrown out of court. The arguments over the meaning of the lyrics of "Suicide Solution" simply underscore the fact that the way in which popular music communicates is complex. As Walser has pointed out, "Music does not simply inflict its

> *If the warning label was designed simply to alert parents to controversial material, as the PMRC contended, why was it being used as a basis for criminalization?*

meanings upon helpless fans . . . indeed, the evidence suggests that only a tiny minority of fans found 'Suicide Solution' depressing rather than sobering and thought-provoking."[84]

A late 1980s broadcast on the impact of heavy metal by ABC's *20/20* corroborated Walser's view. The show addressed a suicide case involving Metallica's "Fade to Black," another song that had caught the PMRC's attention when two Chicago teenagers, Nancy Grannan and Karen Logan, were found dead clutching a note that contained the lyrics to the song. The PMRC blamed the song for encouraging suicide. The *20/20* segment included interviews with students from a New Jersey high school and journalist Charles M. Young. Said Young, "Heavy metal speaks to the anger and despair of teenagers today the same way the blues used to speak to the despair and anger of black people in the South. Without heavy metal, there would probably be more suicides because metal and certain other forms of rock give teenagers something to believe in that they get no place else."[85] While Metallica acknowledged the tragedy of the case in an interview in *Parade* magazine, bassist Jason Newsted also said, "I wish you could hear all the kids that come up to us and say, 'If it weren't for "Fade to Black" . . . I'd be dead now.' Or, 'You guys helped me through those times, to want to continue my life.' And there's hundreds of those."[86]

The most celebrated suicide case was the 1992 lawsuit in which it was alleged that subliminal messages on Judas Priest's *Stained Class* caused Ray Belknap and Jay Vance of Reno, Nevada, to kill themselves with a shotgun. Because lyrics about suicide had already been ruled as protected speech in the Osbourne trial, the plaintiffs built their case around subliminal commands to "do it" and backward messages exhorting "try suicide," "suicide is in," and "sing my evil spirit," which they claimed were part of the LP. When it was revealed that Vance and Belknap came from severely troubled backgrounds that could have easily accounted for their self-destructive behaviour, Judas Priest was cleared of all charges. The judge found that whatever subliminal messages were on the album were neither intentional nor necessary to explain the suicide pact. He did, however, leave the door open to future lawsuits in ruling that "subliminal messages and 'backmasking' . . . are not protected speech under the First Amendment."[87]

Subliminal messages and backmasking also figured heavily in charges of Satanism, an issue that clearly reveals the affinity between the PMRC and the religious right. Prominent among the Christian fundamentalists who were attempting to link popular music and Satanism were James Dobson, leader of Focus on the Family, Dan and Steve Peters, two ministers in St. Paul, and the Reverend Donald Wildmon, head of the Mississippi-based American Family

Association, which claimed to have 380,000 members at the time. In the late 1980s and early 1990s, Focus on the Family campaigned vigorously to remove "objectionable" records from stores. At the time, the PMRC's Susan Baker was a member of their board of directors. The Peters brothers, who lectured widely on the evils of popular music, were endorsed by PMRC cofounder Sally Nevius, who said, "It was guys like them who got the rock & roll wrecking ball rolling in the right direction."[88] While there was no structural connection between Wildmon's group and the PMRC, a 1990 *Time* magazine article titled "No Sympathy for the Devil" suggested an ideological one, describing the campaigns of both groups in similar terms.[89]

There have been wildly divergent estimates as to how widespread and how dangerous Satanism is. In 1985, Darlyne Pettinicchio, a consultant on gangs for police agencies who worked at the Back in Control centre, a counseling program that advocated, among other things, "deprogramming" youth who had fallen under the spell of heavy metal, estimated that there were approximately 135,000 covens of nine to thirteen people each in the United States, bringing total occult membership to well over 1 million.[90] In contrast, David Alexander, writing in *The Humanist,* placed the number of actual Satanists in the United States at fewer than 1,000. Alexander also pointed out that Satanists were members of a religion protected by the First Amendment and that none of them had been charged in any ritual crimes.[91] Law enforcement agencies, in particular, have tended to view Satanism as dangerous. Writing in *The National Sheriff,* Robert J. Barry maintained that "Satanism is on the rise in America. Hardly a day passes without reports of violent acts conducted by Satanists. Across the country law enforcement organizations are receiving reports of homicide, mayhem, assault, suicide, child abuse and animal mutilations that are linked with the satanic occult."[92] Barry went on to claim, "One of the major contemporary movements exploiting Satanism is the music industry and its punk rock and 'heavy metal' productions."[93] However, there is little to validate Barry's claim other than the sensational arrest of Richard Ramirez, the alleged "Night Stalker," who was described by the press as "an AC/DC fan who had apparently been obsessed by Satanism."[94]

Even without corroborating evidence, the issue of Satanism in popular music continued and reached fever pitch in 1990 when New York's Cardinal John J. O'Connor warned his flock that "diabolically instigated violence is on the rise."[95] The cardinal's message came three weeks after J. Gordon Melton, head of the Institute for the Study of American Religion in Santa Barbara, California, reported that "press reports of satanic activities showed no increase and that upon investigation many of the most dramatic reports turned out to be without basis."[96] Nevertheless, in his sermon, the cardinal said that "some kinds of rock music" were a tool of the devil and singled out Ozzy Osbourne's "Suicide Solution" as an example.[97] "The Cardinal's observations on rock music," reported the *New York Times,* "followed closely those of Tipper Gore."[98]

If one were looking for any religious connections between popular music and violent crime, one would do well to look at white supremacist organizations that espouse some form of Christian fundamentalism rather than Satanism. The White Aryan Resistance (WAR), for example, consciously used a variant of punk rock called "oi" to recruit skinheads. In 1989, Tom Metzger, a former Ku Klux Klansman and leader of WAR, and his son John, organized an "Aryan Woodstock" for their skinhead followers. A year later, the Metzgers and two skinheads were found liable for the 1988 beating death of an Ethiopian student named Mulugeta Seraw, in Portland, Oregon. The crusaders who attacked heavy metal, how-ever, seemed to overlook problems of racism and bigotry. Where, for example, were the PMRC and the religious right when Jon Pareles, music critic for *The New York Times,* took Public Enemy to task for their anti-Semitism and challenged Guns 'N' Roses for their use of "nigger" and "faggot"?[99] Because neither the religious right nor the PMRC had included racism or bigotry in their list of con-cerns, these incidents were largely unmentioned in their campaigns. They did not begin to speak to such concerns until after Pareles' criticism forced a partial reframing of the issues.

The crusaders who attacked heavy metal, however, seemed to overlook problems of racism and bigotry. Where, for example, were the PMRC and the religious right when Jon Pareles, music critic for The New York Times, *took Public Enemy to task for their anti-Semitism and challenged Guns 'N' Roses for their use of "nigger" and "faggot"?*

Clearly, then, the way in which a problem is framed can determine the response. Nowhere is this more apparent than in the PMRC's concern over "a sexuality that is graphic and explicit." In phrasing its concern in this way, the PMRC made sexuality itself the concern. While this may have appealed to conservative fundamentalists, it permitted no distinctions between a sexuality that is violent and degrading to women and a sexuality that is gentle and sensuous. In this phrasing, it matters not whether a woman is a passive victim or actively in control of her sexual choices. The only thing that matters is that sex has taken place. Within this all-inclusive scattershot approach, the PMRC, of course, hit some worthy targets. But their inability to make distinctions led only to the conclusion that "sex is bad," a message that is dis-orienting and repressive to teenagers at a crucial stage in their own sexual development.

Madonna, of course, was the main target of the PMRC's concerns about sexuality. Susan Baker said that it was Madonna's "Like a Virgin" that moved her to become a founding mem-ber of the PMRC. Pam Howar expressed the concern that Madonna was teaching young girls "how to be porn queens in heat."[100] Madonna had expressed her sexuality consistently and boldly in her musical performances and videos. She had also been forthright in her promotion of safe sex, speaking out publicly on the issue, performing at AIDS benefits, including informa-tional materials in her albums, and distributing condoms at her concerts. In so doing, she had become a major source of irritation for the PMRC and the religious right. Transforming the role of undergarments in fashion and taking liberties with Christian iconography in her visual pre-sentations only added to the ire of her detractors.

It was her "Justify My Love" that was, for some, the final straw. The video presented the viewer with graphically implied, but not quite explicit, sex, which was made more complicated by insinuations of homosexuality and group sex. Its artful black-and-white cinematography recalled Fellini's *La Dolce Vita.* Madonna was aware that she was pushing the boundaries on the video. Still, its sexuality was soft and gentle, and it forced her fans to grapple concretely with the com-plexities of sex that her critics would sooner have avoided by preaching abstinence. There was certainly room for discussion concerning her choice of images, but in the PMRC's conception of the problem, the issue was closed before any questions could be raised. "Justify My Love" earned the singular distinction of being the first video ever to be officially banned by MTV, a status that quickly turned it into the best-selling music video in history. Rather than take on the more com-plex questions of sexuality, the battles over sex in popular music tended to pit First Amendment defences against fundamentalist dismissals of all provocative material as obscene.

In December 1985, shortly after the PMRC's hearings, a young girl from Los Angeles pur-chased the Dead Kennedys' *Frankenchrist* album, which also included the poster "Penis

Landscape," by the award-winning Swiss artist H. R. Giger. Her parents were so horrified at the graphic portrayal of ten male appendages that they called the California Attorney General's office to complain. In April 1986, Jello Biafra, the leader of the group, was arrested for distributing harmful material to a minor. Criminal charges were also leveled at his record company, his distributor, the Los Angeles wholesaler, and even the sixty-seven-year-old owner of the pressing plant that manufactured the record. The retail outlet that actually sold the record was not charged because, according to the police, "They were cooperative and took the record off the shelves."[101]

The Dead Kennedys bust had all the markings of a test case. The police may have thought that Biafra and his label, Alternative Tentacles, would be an easy target because the label was a small, self-managed and self-supported company that could ill afford a protracted legal battle. Biafra quoted a police official as saying: "We feel this is a cost-effective way of sending a message that . . . we are going to prosecute."[102] Biafra, however, decided to fight. Defending his artistic choices as political speech, he argued that the Giger poster resonated with themes that ran through the *Frankenchrist* album. Whatever the courts may have thought of the wacky, activist history of the Dead Kennedys, it had to be admitted that Jello Biafra was a serious political figure. In 1979, he had actually run for mayor of San Francisco and placed fourth in a field of ten candidates. The case ended with all defendants cleared, but the legal battle, which dragged on for a year and a half at a cost of tens of thousands of dollars, bankrupted Alternative Tentacles and ended the career of the Dead Kennedys.

The Biafra obscenity case was followed by several others that received nationwide coverage. In June 1988, Tommy Hammond, the owner of a small record store in Alabama, was arrested on obscenity charges for selling 2 Live Crew's *Move Something* to an adult undercover agent. At the time of his arrest, the album had not been declared obscene in any court of law. In fact, Hammond kept the album behind the counter and refused to sell it to minors because it carried a warning sticker, as did all of 2 Live Crew's albums. Nevertheless, four months after his arrest, Hammond was fined $500 by a municipal court judge who declared the album obscene on the spot. While Hammond appealed and, after several postponements, was acquitted, neither 2 Live Crew nor sellers of the group's albums were done with obscenity charges.

Henry Louis Gates, Jr., testified that 2 Live Crew's risqué rhymes were part of the venerable tradition of "signifying" and "playing the dozens," and that judging the legal status of 2 Live Crew's work, therefore, required a familiarity with "black codes," which had been absent in the original determination of obscenity.

In 1990, 2 Live Crew's LP *As Nasty As They Wanna Be* became the first recording to be declared legally obscene in a federal district court. After Judge José A. Gonsalez handed down the ruling, the group was arrested for performing some of the material from the album at an adults-only nightclub. Charles Freeman, an African American record-store owner from Fort Lauderdale, was also arrested for selling the LP. Like the Dead Kennedys, 2 Live Crew was thought to be an easy target. Cuts like "Me So Horny," from an album that detailed sex in every imaginable position, were bound to be considered offensive by many, and the record was produced by a small independent label (Luke Records, owned by group leader Luther Campbell), which did not have the financial resources for an extended legal battle.

The 2 Live Crew case is important not only because it tested the strength of the First Amendment, but also because it confronted all the racism associated with the application of the obscenity laws. There is at present a three-pronged test for the legal determination of obscenity.

To be judged obscene by a court of law, a work must (1) lack serious literary, artistic, political, or scientific value; (2) when taken as a whole, appeal to prurient interest; and (3) be patently offensive, as judged by community standards.[103] Given this third standard, what the Supreme Court has called the "dim and uncertain" line separating obscenity from constitutionally protected speech can change from one locale to another. A work that has been judged obscene in Florida may be perfectly legal in New York, which was, in fact, the case with the 2 Live Crew recording. It is, of course, the determination of community standards in a multicultural community that has made obscenity rulings questionable, and it was this ambiguity that served as the basis for 2 Live Crew's defence. Appearing as an expert witness for the defence, eminent African American scholar Henry Louis Gates, Jr., testified that 2 Live Crew's risqué rhymes were part of the venerable tradition of exaggeration found in such competitive African American word games as "signifying" and "playing the dozens," and that judging the legal status of 2 Live Crew's work, therefore, required a familiarity with "black codes," which had been absent in the original determination of obscenity.[104] The defence prevailed, and the obscenity ruling was overturned in May 1993. Although there was strong sentiment that Gates' eloquence had papered over some deficiencies in both the quality of 2 Live Crew's production and their treatment of women, the question of obscenity was finally laid to rest when the U.S. Supreme Court refused to challenge the appellate decision.[105] Unfortunately, in their ecstasy over 2 Live Crew's acquittal, civil libertarians hardly noticed that Charles Freeman, the record-store owner, was convicted and fined $1,000 for selling the group's album two months later. In London, Ontario, City Lights bookstore owner Marc Emery was also convicted for selling 2 Live Crew's album.

Charges of obscenity in rap have been second only to charges of violence. These charges of violence became particularly loud in the 1992 election year, primarily because of the political fallout surrounding the uprising in Los Angeles that followed the not guilty verdict given to the police who had beaten Rodney King. In that charged atmosphere, the righteous anger that had led to the uprising ran headfirst into political expedience that required candidates to respond to what was said and done. Cultural and political differences between speakers resulted in a considerable distortion of what was actually being said. When President Clinton characterized Sister Souljah's comments about the situation in Los Angeles as being "full of hatred," David Mills, the *Washington Post* reporter who had interviewed her, noted in an article for *Essence,* "Clinton really *did* take her comment out of context. Souljah was describing the attitude of the L.A. rioters, not prescribing future action."[106] Far from being an easy target, Souljah turned out to be a formidable opponent, trading blows with the likes of Bryant Gumbel, Larry King, and Phil Donahue, and eventually landing on the cover of *Newsweek.*

A few weeks later, the rap/metal song "Cop Killer" from Ice-T's *Body Count,* which he had been performing for more than a year, sparked further national debate over rap's seeming encouragement of violence. To some people, the song captured all the outrage and dissatisfaction associated with the Rodney King verdict. At the same time, its violent imagery prompted others, including dozens of police agencies all over the country, to call for a boycott of Time Warner, then the parent company of Ice-T's record label. In the ensuing controversy, public figures ranging from George Bush and Dan Quayle to Mario Cuomo jumped on the bandwagon to denounce the record. Sixty congressmen wrote to Time Warner about the song. Oliver North joined forces with Jack Thompson, the Florida attorney who had gone after 2 Live Crew, to try (unsuccessfully) to have the record declared illegal under federal sedition laws. Charlton Heston, a member of the Time Warner board, read the lyrics aloud at a board of directors meeting. Among the directors, Beverly Sills was publicly critical of the company while others proposed "screening" future releases. "Maybe I underestimate my juice," said a bewildered Ice-T, "but there's people out there with nuclear bombs, people with armies, and the president has time to sit up and get into it with me?"[107]

While in some ways the furor over "Cop Killer" was similar to the furor over N.W.A.'s "_ _ _ _ tha Police" a few years earlier, the environment was quite different. Most of the world had seen the video of Rodney King's beating by the police and knew the outcome of the subsequent trial. These events recontextualized the messages of both songs. Although the album had long since peaked in sales, the publicity surrounding the song in the aftermath of the riots boosted *Body Count* from number seventy-three back up to number twenty-six on the pop charts. While it is easy to understand why some police officers found the song unsettling, it is interesting that the National Black Police Association denounced the Warner boycott, noting that "Cop Killer" "did not happen in a vacuum. People have always expressed their feelings and opinions through songs, and they are talking about how African-American people have been victimized by police brutality. And that is very real. Where were those organizations when Rodney King was beat up and when that verdict came in?"[108] The association was disappointed when Ice-T agreed to pull the song from future pressings of the album. Like many other groups, it feared that the action would send "a negative message to other artists."[109]

No sooner had this controversy begun to subside than three more rappers made headlines for allegedly crossing the line into violence in real life. In August 1993, Snoop Doggy Dogg was charged in connection with the fatal shooting of Philip Woldemarian in Los Angeles. In October, Tupac Shakur was arrested for aggravated assault in the shooting of two off-duty Atlanta police officers. Three weeks later, he was arrested again with two friends on charges of sexual assault, for which he eventually did time. Public Enemy frontman Flavor Flav was arrested for attempted murder and criminal possession of a firearm.

Flavor Flav had confronted his girlfriend's alleged lover with a gun. In a jealous rage, he had fired one shot into the ground. Fortunately, he had enough presence of mind to check himself into the Betty Ford Clinic for crack abuse. Still, his irresponsible behaviour compromised the effectiveness of Public Enemy, which had consistently put forth a message of self-determination for African Americans. For Tupac Shakur, both incidents initially seemed out of character. Described by others as quiet and shy, Shakur was a formally trained actor who had received an NAACP Image Award nomination for his role in the film *Poetic Justice.* His hit single, "Keep Ya Head Up," according to Havelock Nelson, "speaks urgently and respectfully about the struggles of black women."[110] Thus, many observers of the hip hop scene found Shakur's behaviour troubling. The NAACP deflected criticism by giving the Image Award to Denzel Washington. Havelock Nelson took a harder line, arguing that "Shakur . . . is endangering more than just his own career. He and other rappers who can't get a grip are also helping set the stage for hip hop's last blast. With their buck-wild actions, these artists are unwittingly playing into the hands of forces fed up with heightened levels of black achievement."[111]

Rap had been roundly criticized when its art simply imitated life. The media blitz following these incidents seemed to suggest the more disturbing possibility that there was no difference between the two.

Although Snoop Doggy Dogg was only indirectly involved in violence, his case received more publicity than the others because he had just made music history. On 11 December 1993, his debut album, *DoggyStyle*, became the first debut album ever to enter the *Billboard* pop charts at number one. In its first week of release, the LP sold more than 800,000 units. Snoop Doggy himself entered the music business as a protégé of rapper/producer Dr. Dre, formerly of N.W.A. A veteran of the Los Angeles streets, Snoop was no stranger to gang violence. In the incident in question, it was Snoop Doggy Dogg's bodyguard who actually shot Woldemarian; Snoop was driving the car. The rapper pleaded not guilty, claiming the shooting was in self-defence.

One of the things that distinguished Snoop from other rappers was his style, which was described in *The New York Times* as "gentle"; "where many rappers scream," said *Times* reporter Touré, "he speaks softly." Touré then added, "While Snoop delivers rhymes delicately, the content is anything but."[112] Snoop's work on Dr. Dre's rap hit, "Deep Cover," from the film soundtrack of the same name, supports this assessment. On this cut, Snoop's laid-back vocal drawl smoothed the edges from what had been perceived as the song's chilling refrain, "cuz it's 1-8-7 on an undercover cop." The number referred to the California police code for homicide, which, of course, prompted a number of comparisons between "Deep Cover" and Ice-T's "Cop Killer." None of the comparisons appearing in the media, however, mentioned that the line in the movie was delivered in sympathy for a good cop who was tragically slain at the end of the film.

Rap had been roundly criticized when its art simply imitated life. The media blitz following these incidents seemed to suggest the more disturbing possibility that there was no difference between the two. According to this logic, rap could be held responsible for all social disintegration. As David Toop has pointed out, however, "Children carry automatic weapons like Uzis and sell crack in the streets. Babies are born with AIDS and teenagers are shot dead for their shoes. Music may be powerful and influential but no music is strong enough to create this kind of social decay."[113] When James Brown ran afoul of the law, he went to jail, but no one said funk was to blame. The fact that Tupac Shakur served jail time for some of his actions should be no different. Such instances cannot be used legitimately as the occasion for indicting a whole genre of music.

Following these incidents, media outlets began falling over themselves to outdo each other's antiviolence policies. Black radio station WBLS in New York banned violence and profanity from its broadcasts. The rap magazine *Rap Sheet* stopped carrying advertisements that pictured guns. Black Entertainment Television (BET) instituted a policy of no guns in the videos they aired. The Box, a pay-to-view channel, initiated a "guns suck" campaign that exhorted: "Wake up and smell the roses before they toss 'em on your grave."[114] These moves coincided with an escalation of protests against gangsta rap from within the black community. In late December 1993, the National Political Congress of Black Women (NPCBW), which boasted a membership of 2,500, staged demonstrations in Washington, D.C., against two record retail outlets, Nobody Beats the Wiz and Sam Goody. The organization was joined in civil disobedience by activist Dick Gregory and endorsed by the National Council of Negro Women, the NAACP, and Jesse Jackson's National Rainbow Coalition, among others. In addition to direct action, the NPCBW took the well-worn path of advocating government hearings. Beginning in February 1994, both the House and the Senate scheduled hearings to gather testi-

The question is not why some rappers are so offensive but rather, why so many fans find offensive rappers appealing.

mony on gangsta rap. In some ways, these proceedings re-called the 1985 PMRC hearings. Senator Carol Moseley Braun, who chaired the Senate committee, proposed a rat-ing system like the one used for movies—the same idea that was abandoned in 1985 as too unwieldy—"to prevent records from getting into the hands of children."[115] In the first round of hearings no rappers were invited to offer testi-mony. Instead, the hearings relied on comments from people like Dr. C. DeLores Tucker, national chairwoman of the NPCBW, and entertainer Dionne Warwick, thus rais-ing questions of class and age divisions within the black community. At the time, Darryl James, the founder of *Rap Sheet,* said: "Frustrated men and women like the Rev. Jesse Jackson and Dr. C. DeLores Tucker, who misrepresent themselves as representatives of the masses, only serve to fan the flame of controversy."[116] There was one aspect of the hearings that differed significantly from the PMRC hearings. While none of the participants who criticized rap—most of whom were African Americans—condoned violent or misogynist lyrics, nearly all recognized the legitimacy of black rage and placed their comments in the context of societal disintegration. "The issue is not whether to spurn, regulate, restrict, segre-gate, or otherwise curb the distribution of hip hop music," said David W. Harleston of Rush As-sociated Labels. "Rather, the issue is whether we, as a community and nation, are prepared to address the very issues that have given rise to the lyrics that some find so troubling."[117] In fram-ing the issue as he did, Harleston put a rather different spin on the problem than was the case in 1985. The question that follows logically is not why are some rappers so offensive but rather, why do so many fans find offensive rappers appealing? It is this question that suggests a consideration of popular music as one variable among the myriad of social forces that affect the quality of life.

After 1994, in the absence of an election year, government hearings on rap began to sub-side, only to pick up again two years later, when the violence associated with gangsta rap cli-maxed with the shooting deaths of Tupac Shakur and then Biggie Smalls. At the time of his death on 13 September 1996, Shakur's fourth album, *All Eyez on Me*, which debuted at number one, had sold three million copies, placing him squarely in the company of top-selling artists. With considerable high drama along the way, Shakur had built his career steadily to this point with the release of three previous albums—*2pacalypse Now* (1991), *Strictly 4 My N.I.G.G.A.Z.* (1993), and *Me Against the World* (1995)—and well-received appearances in a number of films—*Juice* (1992), *Poetic Justice* (1993), and *Above the Rim* (1994), with two more films in the can: *Gridlock* and *Gang Related.* The final escalation began in late 1994 when Shakur was shot five times during a robbery in New York. The rapper implied that Biggie Smalls and Sean "Puffy" Combs, the head of his label, Bad Boy Records, were somehow involved or at least knew the identity of the shooter, a charge which Smalls and Combs denied. The accusation nevertheless placed the shooting within the age-old East Coast/West Coast rap rivalry; Shakur recorded for LA-based Death Row Records, founded by Dr. Dre and run at that time by Marion "Suge" Knight, who was himself widely suspected of having ties to organized crime. Knight had publicly insulted Combs and Bad Boy at the 1995 *Source Awards* show in New York. For his part, Shakur had baited Smalls viciously on "Hit 'Em Up," on which he claimed to have had sex with Smalls' estranged wife, Faith Evans, with the line "You claim to be a player, but I fucked your wife." Shakur was shot on 7 September 1996 in Las Vegas while riding in the passenger seat of Knight's BMW 750, after the two left the Mike Tyson/Bruce Seldon fight. He died one week later.

Biggie Smalls, who recorded as the Notorious B.I.G., grew up big and tough on the streets of Brooklyn but had a gift for constructing rhymes, which Combs had noticed and nurtured. If Shakur displayed a siege mentality on *Me Against the World*, B.I.G. foretold his own death on his debut album, *Ready to Die* (1994). In the aftermath of Shakur's death, Puffy Combs tried to lay the enmity between Bad Boy and Death Row to rest, as he and Smalls prepared for the release of the Notorious B.I.G.'s second album, *Life After Death*. Both felt that the rapper was on the verge of a major breakthrough. Riding high and trying to put Shakur's death behind them, Smalls and Combs ventured to Los Angeles (with extra security) in March 1997 to present an award to Toni Braxton at the *Soul Train Awards*. The following night, after leaving a party, Biggie Smalls was shot dead in his car, with Combs not far behind. As 2001 dawned, there had been no arrests in either shooting. By then Combs was in court battling his own transgressions. For Combs, B.I.G.'s death was something of a wake-up call in which he manifested genuine remorse as well as irrational fits of his own violence. He paid tribute to his friend and protégé on a chart-topping duet with Faith Evans titled "I'll Be Missing You." It was a single from his own debut as rapper Puff Daddy. Still feeling somewhat trapped by recent events, he titled the album fittingly *No Way Out*.

Against the odds, metal had risen from the embers of a dying 1970s subculture. Rap emerged from one of the most dispossessed communities in the country. By the late 1980s, they had become the primary musical expressions of youth culture. Working from the bottom up, these styles seemed to thrive on the indifference, even hostility, of the music industry. They engendered fanatical devotion among their fans and a ferocious backlash among their detractors. In this sense, these styles were decidedly political, whether they intended to make an overt political statement or not. The intensity of feelings generated by rap and metal resonated with the profound rethinking of North American values that characterized the period. In the 1990s, a new sound that was labeled alternative *began competing for national attention among youths. For many,* alternative *was the fulfillment of the political promise of punk a decade later. Alternative emerged as an intensely personal music with a discordant sound, and its artists initially adopted a doggedly anticommercial posture. Paradoxically, the music became wildly successful.*

Mainstreaming Alternatives: Packaging Pop in the Nineties and Beyond

The success of rap and metal at the dawn of the 1990s reminded many of precisely that aspect of rock 'n' roll that had so distressed the moral guardians of the 1950s: that the music of the most disenfranchised elements of society—angry blacks and irreverent working-class whites—could be the most compelling culturally, politically, and economically. Accordingly, *Rolling Stone*'s Mikal Gilmore remembered 1990 as "the year in which rock & roll was reborn."[1] There was also something of a postmodern twist to this particular rebirth that became apparent as the major market breakthrough of what had been called *alternative music* brought about a further disintegration of the barriers between cult and mass, margin and mainstream, underground and commercial, and, ultimately, serious art and popular culture. As boundaries collapsed, the music business faced a crisis of categories and found itself packaging musical trends in the latter half of the decade according to tried-and-true—if divisive—marketing categories based on age, gender, ethnicity, and of course race.

The success of rap and metal at the dawn of the 1990s reminded many of precisely that aspect of rock 'n' roll that had so distressed the moral guardians of the 1950s: that the music of the most disenfranchised elements of society—angry blacks and irreverent working-class whites—could be the most compelling culturally, politically, and economically.

Prior to rock 'n' roll, there had been an attempt to separate rhythm and blues from pop and country (the other two major marketing categories of the music industry) along racial lines. At first, rap and metal developed according to this division, but as was the case with rhythm and blues, fissures in the race barrier began to occur when rap artists laying hard-edged urban rhymes over hot rock tracks began to cross over to the mainstream audience. Still, joint efforts like the now classic Run-D.M.C./Aerosmith collaboration on the remake of Aerosmith's "Walk This Way" were rare. Except for their respective commitments to technology and transgression, the genres developed in fairly distinct ways—rap based on technologically sophisticated electronic beats and def(t) linguistic juxtapositions; metal based on virtuosic precision on the guitar and sheer volume. Beneath these two main youth cultural trends, however, lay an underground of post-punk alternative sounds in which genre boundaries were not always so clear or well defended.

Cross-genre influences were starting to become more conspicuous as the 1990s dawned. According to Mikal Gilmore, Living Colour's second LP, *Time's Up,* "fused punk rhythms and speed metal leads with a complex harmonic architecture derived from the avant-garde sensibility of legendary jazz saxophonist Ornette Coleman."[2] Living Colour's mission was to reclaim rock 'n' roll as black music, less in the interest of cultural separatism than historical accuracy. Cuts like "History Lesson" (reminiscent of Keith LeBlanc's "No Sell Out"—the Malcolm X rap record) and "Pride" drove the point home. At the same time, Faith No More, an all-white post-punk band, released *The Real Thing,* which Gilmore noted "took a personalized, raplike delivery and intercut it with hard-edge metallic textures."[3] Faith No More had been knocking around the San Francisco underground for more than eight years with two previous albums to their credit—*We Care a Lot* (1985) and *Introduce Yourself* (1987). Bolstered by MTV support for the single "Epic," *The Real Thing* went gold. "Between these two bands," Gilmore said, "the face of modern rock was virtually overhauled this last year."[4]

Both Living Colour and Faith No More ended 1990 among the best-selling pop artists of the year and enjoyed substantial sales in the mainstream market. What is interesting is that the label *alternative* was applied to both groups, although for different reasons. That same year, Sinéad O'Connor, another mainstay of alternative music, released her second album, *I Do Not Want What I Haven't Got,* which, propelled by her heart-wrenching video of Prince's "Nothing Compares 2 U," entered the *Billboard* pop charts at number twenty-four and logged six weeks at number one, achieving double platinum certification within months of its release. Combining as it did Irish pathos with punk rage, O'Connor's 1987 debut album, *The Lion and the Cobra,* had won her a devoted following in the alternative category. With even more challenging material, *Do Not Want* sold millions of copies. This level of success raises the question: alternative to what?

There is a sense in which loud, grainy-voiced, rhythm-based rock 'n' roll could have been considered an alternative to melodic Tin Pan Alley pop smoothness even after rock 'n'

Sinéad O'Connor displays the Video of the Year, Best Female, and Post-Modern video awards she won for "Nothing Compares 2 U" in 1990. It was that kind of recognition that began to collapse alternative into the mainstream.

roll had succeeded in outselling the music it displaced. The best-selling music of the 1960s signified an alternative to mainstream values even as it dominated sales. In this sense, the term *alternative* could be used to connote opposition or resistance to established norms, or a countercultural lifestyle. While the mainstream music industry can control the marketplace economically, this is not synonymous with determining the meaning of the music. For all the saccharine teen pop that clogged the airwaves, it was still possible for the targeted polemics of Rage Against the Machine to sell platinum. As established (and aging) a rocker as Bruce Springsteen could still shake up the status quo with something like "American Skin (41 Shots)," about the murder of New York City resident Amadou Diallo. Content to focus on the revenue-generating aspects of popular music production, the major record companies had long since chosen to distance themselves from the creative process. As a result, popular musicians enjoyed a greater degree of artistic autonomy than most other popular artists. It was the failure to understand this fact that was at the heart of people's inability to grasp the contradictions inherent in the notion of alternative music. The idea that music can only retain its integrity before it reaches a mass public leads to the tendency to lionize artists when they are least successful and to dismiss them precisely at the moment of their greatest impact.

The idea that music can only retain its integrity before it reaches a mass public leads to the tendency to lionize artists when they are least successful and to dismiss them precisely at the moment of their greatest impact.

There has been a culture war of sorts going on since the appearance of rock 'n' roll, and most often the battles have been fought in the arena of popular music. The music industry has responded differently at different times. In the 1950s, the major record companies aligned themselves for the most part with the more conservative elements of society in resisting rock 'n' roll. The writers, performers, deejays, and independent record companies that produced and disseminated the music were essentially in competition with the established powers of the industry. Thus, the victory of rock 'n' roll was perceived as a victory for independent production, and there has been a continuing tendency to depict independent labels as heroic underdogs, even though the structural relationship between independents and majors has long since been transformed. The beginnings of this transformation lie in the mid-1960s, when the majors realized that rock and soul were key to the future success of the industry. Far from fighting the independents, major companies began to rely on them for research and development. Today, independent labels do the groundwork of ferreting out niches of unsated consumer demand and/or test-marketing new musical forms. If this activity becomes successful, the majors are there to buy the independents, distribute their product, or sign their most successful artists. This was the pattern with punk and disco in the 1970s, and it was the pattern with rap and metal in the 1980s. The only things that changed in the 1990s were the speed and efficiency with which the mainstream music industry was able to incorporate new trends.

Alternative as Mainstream

In the 1980s, the music that was usually labeled *alternative* had its roots in the punk movements of the 1970s and their 1980s post-punk (as opposed to new wave) variants. Still, it should be noted that the label was applied in one way for African American artists and in another for white artists. The fact that African American artists as diverse as the metallic Living Colour, the folk-oriented Tracy Chapman, bluesman Robert Cray, and soul singer Terrence Trent D'Arby were labeled alternative speaks more to race-based marketing strategies than to a shared aesthetic among the groups in question. Chapman outgrew the confines of the label quickly when her self-titled debut LP went to number one on the pop charts, but as a black female acoustic folksinger, she was still in a class by herself. Her search for a musical home led her to headliner status on the Amnesty International tours and eventually to Farm Aid V, where she shared the stage with Living Colour's Vernon Reid. It was fitting that she should collaborate with Reid (and Bobby Womack) on her third album, *Matters of the Heart,* in 1992. In 1991, Reid and his group, still falling through the cracks of conventional industry marketing categories, could be found among the headliners of the first Lollapalooza tour, adding breadth to the alternative festival. When Living Colour first previewed their 1992 lineup, which featured Doug Wimbish on bass, they chose the legendary New York punk club CBGB to do so, again challenging the limitations of forced racial confinement.

While white alternative groups also sounded different from one another, they derived from a more coherent lineage of forebears, including those groups associated with the hardcore SST label (Black Flag and the Minutemen from Los Angeles, Sonic Youth from New York, Dinosaur, Jr., from Massachusetts, and Hüsker Dü from Minnesota), the Dead Kennedys from San Francisco, Fugazi from Washington, D.C., and R.E.M. from Athens, Georgia. Athens and Minneapolis had established the viability of regional alternative scenes, but it was Seattle that put the music over the top.

Seattle: From Sub Pop to Superstars

If Seattle seemed like an unlikely place for a guitar-based post-punk explosion, one had only to remember that the city had earlier spawned those fathers of guitar-based instrumental rock 'n' roll, the Ventures, and the greatest psychedelic guitarist of them all, Jimi Hendrix. In fact, Seattle had a thriving, if isolated, alternative scene for years. At its centre was Sub Pop records, which was founded by Bruce Pavitt, a former deejay and local promoter, and Jon Poneman, who published a fanzine called *Sub Pop* in the early 1980s. Among the groups that got their start on (or at least passed through) Sub Pop were Soundgarden, Nirvana, Pearl Jam, Alice in Chains, the Smashing Pumpkins, Mud Honey, L7, the Afghan Whigs (actually from Cincinnati), Screaming Trees, and from Halifax, Eric's Trip, Jale, and Hardship Post. These groups were supported by Seattle's radio stations KCMU and KJET early on and by a developed alternative press that included the now-defunct *Backlash* and the *Seattle Rocket.* Prior to the 1990s, all the groups lived in and around Seattle and played to local audiences. In 1991, however, Nirvana released *Nevermind,* an album that announced alternative to the mainstream with a vengeance. Aided significantly by MTV's decision to push the video of the album's haunting single "Smells Like Teen Spirit" to anthem-of-a-generation status, *Nevermind* managed to displace Michael Jackson's *Dangerous* from the number one slot on the pop charts, if only for a week. Nirvana's album sold 3 million copies in four months and thereafter continued to sell at the rate of 100,000 copies a week. If the connection between the title of the Nirvana LP and the Sex Pistols' historic *Never Mind the Bollocks* seemed striking, it is important to

Like the Sex Pistols, Nirvana embodied all the contradictions of alternative music, but whereas the Pistols embraced the tension until they self-destructed, Nirvana fell victim to its pressures early on.

note that just as the Pistols recorded for the major label EMI, *Nevermind* marked Nirvana's major label debut on David Geffen's DGC imprint. Like the Sex Pistols, Nirvana embodied all the contradictions of alternative music, but whereas the Pistols embraced the tension until they self-destructed, Nirvana fell victim to its pressures early on. The beginning of the end began with the group's inexorable ascent to rock superstardom once Seattle was discovered.

Although Nirvana is the group that most readily comes to mind when considering the collapse of alternative into the mainstream, the Seattle gold rush actually began with the signing of Soundgarden to A&M in 1988. Soundgarden had contributed three tracks to a 1986 compilation album called *Deep Six*. It was this album that marked the rise of the Seattle scene. Before signing with A&M, Soundgarden had recorded two EPs for Sub Pop and a full-length, Grammy-nominated LP for SST entitled *Ultramega OK*. Kim Neely has described the album as "a pastiche of psychedelia, blistering hardcore and wrecking-ball blooze wrapped up with odd

It was the promise of Soundgarden in the late 1980s that prompted a slew of major label a&r men to descend on Seattle in search of The Next Big Thing.

tunings and time signatures [that] was a sonic fuck-you to the candy-ass poodlehead bands that were clogging the charts at the time."[5] Due to a number of personnel changes, a poorly timed European tour, and the death of a close friend of the band, Soundgarden's A&M debut, *Louder Than Love* (1989), failed to set the music world ablaze. The group did better with *Badmotorfinger* (1991) and *Superunknown* (1994). Still, it was the promise of Soundgarden in the late 1980s that prompted a slew of major label a&r men to descend on Seattle in search of The Next Big Thing. Columbia signed Alice in Chains, Pearl Jam went to Epic, and Nirvana eventually signed with DGC.

On the surface, the story of Nirvana, especially that of the late Kurt Cobain, the group's leader and spiritual centre, seems quite out of proportion with the impact the band made. As rock 'n' roll hard luck tales go, Nirvana's was not atypical. The group originally hailed from Aberdeen, Washington, a dying lumber town that passed on to its inhabitants depression, disillusionment, and dysfunction. Cobain was a product of all three. The group played around Olympia, Tacoma, and Seattle before coming to the attention of Sub Pop, which, as it usually did, issued a test single (now a collector's item), "Love Buzz" backed with "Big Cheese," in 1988. That same year, the group contributed one obscure cut, "Spank Thru," to a sampler called *Sub Pop 200,* an early anthology of the dark, brooding guitar-based sludge that came to be known as *grunge*. The following year, Sub Pop released Nirvana's first full-length LP, *Bleach*. The album was a shoestring production but had respectable regional sales and showcased the promise of Cobain's songwriting. On the strength of this run-of-the-mill track record, Nirvana was signed by DGC. By this time, Cobain and bassist Krist Novoselic had settled on Dave Grohl as the band's permanent drummer. It was this lineup that recorded *Nevermind* and its hit single, which, in the words of Anthony DeCurtis, captured "a defining moment in rock history." As DeCurtis argued in his eulogy for Cobain, "Nirvana announced the end of one rock & roll era and the start of another. In essence, Nirvana transformed the '80s into the '90s."[6] The impact of *Nevermind* was a huge burden to Cobain. How could he be the spokesperson for a generation when he could barely keep his own life together? Ultimately, what he called "medicating myself" (with heroin) and being photographed with the barrel of an M-16 in his mouth said more about his pain than wearing a T-shirt that read "Corporate Magazines Still Suck" for Nirvana's *Rolling Stone* cover said about his integrity.

With the release of Nevermind, *Nirvana introduced alternative to the mainstream with a vengeance. Kurt Cobain shrinks at the prospect of fame while Krist Novoselic sports a T-shirt advertising Sonic Youth, their labelmates at DGC.*

Following the runaway success of *Nevermind,* alternative bands, particularly those from Seattle, began to enter the mainstream as never before. Pearl Jam's debut album, *Ten,* went straight to number two, and with sales upward of 7 million copies, could still be found among the top 100 albums three years later. The group's follow-up album, *Vs.* (1993), entered the charts at number one. Alice in Chains enjoyed similar success. In October 1992, with their 1990 debut, *Facelift,* still on the charts, the group's second album, *Dirt,* entered the *Billboard* 200 at number six. That same week, Pearl Jam's *Ten* held the number seven slot, and the soundtrack to Cameron Crowe's *Singles,* the film that put Seattle on the big screen, was at number ten. If Seattle had any smell at this point, it was the sweet smell of success, and for a fleeting moment it looked as if Cobain might enjoy it. With the 1993 release of *In Utero,* Nirvana's long-awaited studio follow-up to *Nevermind,* Cobain tried his level best to portray his life as one worth living. "I've never been happier," he told *Rolling Stone,* this time appearing on the cover of the magazine in a suit and tie and embracing his mass following. Why? "Pulling this record off. My family. My child. Meeting William Burroughs and doing a record with him."[7] This, of course, was the other side of Cobain: the brilliant singer/songwriter who tried to exorcise his demons through his art; the genuine misfit who longed for the normalcy of love and family, which he tried to find in his marriage to Courtney Love, leader of the female-dominated punk band Hole, and the raising of their child Frances Bean. Ultimately, however, the picture he tried to paint for *Rolling Stone* was the forgery of a man in serious denial. His relationship with Love was a tumultuous and well-publicized foray into co-dependency, complete with guns, drugs, domestic violence, overdoses, detoxes, and police interventions. Neither were things much rosier on the artistic front. The release of *In Utero* had been fraught with last-minute title and track changes. Cobain had originally wanted to title the album *I Hate Myself and Want to Die* after a song he had written for the LP, but he pulled the song just prior to release because he

"Smells Like Teen Spirit"

Artist: Nirvana

Music / Lyrics by Kurt Cobain, Dave Grohl, Krist Noveselic

Label: DGC, from the CD *Nevermind* (1991)

The debut album of the power trio Nirvana, led by the intelligent, talented, and unhappy twenty-four-year-old Kurt Cobain, established "grunge" as a popular style. Nirvana's 1991 disc, *Nevermind*, chock-full of dark, angry, powerful, and hook-ridden rock anthems, garnered extensive critical acclaim and sold over 3 million copies in six months. The album's hit single "Smells Like Teen Spirit" reached the Top Ten, and in some cases the number one position, internationally.

In contrast to some of the *poseurs* who throughout rock's history had made a profession of portraying the anguished artist, Cobain was both truly brilliant and truly tormented, and the wave of angst, rage, and despair unleashed in his lyrics gained him a reputation as spokesperson for Generation X, a title he regarded with ambivalence. Chronically depressed and a heroin addict, Cobain ended his life in 1994.

Musical Style Notes

Nirvana's instrumentation falls into the category of "power trio"—guitar (Kurt Cobain), bass (Krist Noveselic), and drums (Dave Grohl)—a combination that has a long history in the world of rock 'n' roll, although it was used in different ways. For power trios like the Jimi Hendrix Experience, it was all about the virtuoso lead guitarist; for others, the guitar was primarily employed as a rhythm instrument, while the bass laid down structurally simple but prominent lines, and the drums were the "star" attraction that filled the extensive available sonic space. Like the Who's Keith Moon or Led Zeppelin's John Bonham, Dave Grohl's drums are the instrumental power engine driving Nirvana's guitar-riff-based songs.

"Smells Like Teen Spirit," though perceived at the time as a new "alternative" musical phenomenon, is in many ways a classic pop single, with a fantastic guitar hook, simple repeated chord progression, and cathartic shout-along chorus. The song's signature succession of chords is in a dark, "minor" key, and functions somewhat outside the normal harmonic expectations of rock 'n' roll (for those who have studied music theory, the chord progression is i–iv–III–VI).

Structurally, it has a verse-chorus form, but the verse has two parts: an "A" section that features new lyrics each time and a "B" section with the same hypnotic, repetitious "hello" lyric each time. The chorus continues the technique of repetition but moves from hypnotic to a litany of rage and despair. This combination of introspective, atmospheric, soft verse and hard, screaming chorus is a strong stylistic marker of "grunge" rock.

Musical "Road Map"

TIMINGS	COMMENTS	LYRICS
0:00–0:25	Introduction: electric guitar begins with the song's signature chord progression. Drums enter at 0:07. Other instruments join at 0:09, including guitar now playing with distortion.	
0:25–0:34	Introduction ends with reduced volume, transition to verse.	
0:34–0:50	Verse 1	*Load up on guns* *Bring your friends . . .*
0:50–1:06	"B" section, which provides transition from the verse to the chorus	*Hello, hello, hello, how low . . .*
1:06–1:31	Chorus Note the change in energy and sonic texture—harder rock sound, "screaming" vocals.	*With the lights out* *It's less dangerous* *Here we are now,* *Entertain us . . .*
1:31–1:47	Instrumental transition to Verse 2	
1:47–2:04	Verse 2	*I'm worst at what I do best . . .*
2:04–2:20	"B" section	*Hello, hello, hello, how low . . .*
2:20–2:45	Chorus	*With the lights out . . .*
2:45–2:53	Instrumental transition	
2:53–3:33 3:25–3:33	Guitar solo over musical content of verse Ends with instrumental transition to Verse 3	
3:33–3:50	Verse 3 (Note feedback in background.)	*And I forget just what it takes . . .*
3:50–4:05	"B" section	*Hello, hello, hello, how low . . .*
4:05–4:58	Chorus Last line repeats several times. Sound fades on last chord, with guitar feedback.	*With the lights out . . .* *. . . A denial – A denial . . .* *(9 times)*

feared no one would get the joke. (The prophetic single subsequently appeared as the lead track on the otherwise lacklustre *The Beavis and Butt-Head Experience.*) After the album's release, he authorized Geffen to make changes that appeared uncharacteristically compromising. First, the record company removed the collage of fetuses from the back cover of the album that had caused chains like Kmart and Wal-Mart to refuse to stock it. Then they changed the title of "Rape Me," the album's most controversial song, to "Waif Me." Because Cobain equated compromise with selling out, these changes must have eaten away at his artistic soul.

That Cobain was prone to suicide came as a surprise to no one. Even so, people were unprepared for what they discovered on 8 April 1994. Cobain had apparently barricaded himself in the greenhouse above his garage a couple of days earlier, pressed the barrel of a 20-gauge shotgun to his head, and pulled the trigger. He could be identified only by his fingerprints and the wallet he left open showing his driver's licence. Commentators spoke of Cobain's death with a profound sense of loss. At the same time, however, they did not pass over lightly or excuse the suicide. Aware that his actions might be seen as something to be emulated by troubled teens at a time when teen suicide had reached epidemic proportions, Courtney Love repeatedly called her late husband an "asshole" as she read his suicide note aloud. Donna Gaines, author of *Teenage Wasteland,* a superb book on teen suicide, took a more analytic perspective in an article for *Rolling Stone.* "Despite his compassion, he wasn't an altruist who died for anybody's sins," she wrote. "His suicide was a betrayal; it negated an unspoken contract among members of a generation who depended on one another to reverse the parental generation's legacy of neglect, confusion and frustration. Cobain broke that promise. He just walked."[8] Thus was cut short Nirvana's contribution to the chapter of popular music history that bore their imprint. What made the whole story sadder was that there were role models—Sonic Youth and R.E.M., among others— who could have pointed the way for Nirvana and, perhaps, Cobain.

In some ways, Sonic Youth was to 1990s alternative what the Velvet Underground had been to 1970s punk—a formative influence with a distinctly New York posture and avant-garde tendencies. The group was formed in the early 1980s, and two of its members, guitarists Thurston Moore and Lee Ranaldo, had previously played with avant-garde musician Glenn Branca's group. From this group they learned to use unconventional tunings to bend otherwise standard pop songs completely out of shape, a trademark of Sonic Youth that, in Seattle, resonated as well as the dark side of their musical vision. Sonic Youth recorded a number of albums for independent labels before being signed by DGC later in the decade. Nirvana's

Sonic Youth was to 1990s alternative what the Velvet Underground had been to 1970s punk—a formative influence with a distinctly New York posture and avant-garde tendencies.

respect for the group was, in fact, one of the factors that made DGC attractive to them. Sonic Youth's vocals were split between Moore and bassist Kim Gordon, who can best be described as something of a female Lou Reed. On cuts like "JC" and "Swimsuit Issue," from *Dirty* (1992), the group's second DGC album, Gordon combined an overt sexuality with uncompromisingly feminist lyrics about women's issues. In her seemingly contradictory mix of femininity and feminism, she served as a role model for many other post-punk female bands, including Babes in Toyland, L7, and Hole. Just as it had for 1970s punk, the rules-don't-apply attitude of the alternative scene created a cultural space for women to experiment with new roles and sounds. At the time of Cobain's death, Sonic Youth had just released *Experimental Jet Set, Trash and No Star,* the group's third DGC album. At the time,

Gordon and Moore were also expecting their first child, which prevented the band from touring in support of the LP. The decision to put family ahead of fame and fortune was one that Cobain should have been able to relate to, but he acted otherwise.

R.E.M. was another group Cobain could have looked to for help. Just prior to his death, he had been in regular contact with Michael Stipe, R.E.M.'s enigmatic leader. Indeed, the two had talked about collaborating. Stipe had enormous respect for Cobain, and Cobain was an unabashed R.E.M. fan. In fact, R.E.M.'s career was the model that Cobain would have liked for Nirvana. R.E.M. had mainstream success at a pace that could be handled without the abandonment of artistic or personal integrity. At the time of Cobain's death, R.E.M. were at work on their ninth and most abrasive album, *Monster,* which was dedicated to River Phoenix, the rising young actor who had recently died of an accidental drug overdose. The group's 1992 outing, *Automatic for the People,* had already logged seventy weeks on the pop charts, after peaking at number two. R.E.M. had been formed in Athens, Georgia, in 1980 as a jangly inaccessible folk rock unit, as beholden to 1960s-era Byrds as to any punk influences. It might have been possible to anticipate their future success when *Rolling Stone* selected their first full-length album, *Murmur* (1983), as album of the year over Michael Jackson's *Thriller.* The *Village Voice* lavished similar "best of" praise on the album. At the time, however, *Murmur* had sold only 150,000 copies. R.E.M. built their career slowly from the bottom up, broadening their fan base through live performances and support on college radio. From *Murmur* on, most of R.E.M.'s albums sold slightly better than the one before. In 1987, *Document* became the band's first million seller, prompting a move from independent IRS to major Warner. *Green,* the group's 1988 major label debut, occasioned their first arena-level tour. *Out of Time* (1991) became their first album to reach number one, making it, along with *Nevermind,* one of the releases that pushed major labels into taking alternative acts more seriously. *Out of Time* actually beat out *Nevermind* in 1991

Throughout their career, R.E.M. have kept their personal lives out of the limelight and have tried to be musically and politically progressive.

R.E.M. has enjoyed success at a pace they could handle without compromising their artistic or personal integrity. If Kurt Cobain could have done likewise, it might have changed the course of his life.

for the Grammy Award for Best Alternative Music. The band also received nominations for Album of the Year, Record of the Year, and Song of the Year, the recording industry's highest pop honours, which further erased the distinction between alternative and mainstream. In all, R.E.M., which had never been nominated for a Grammy before, tallied seven nominations in 1991, more than any other artist, and walked away with additional trophies for Best Pop Performance and Best Short-Form Video for "Losing My Religion," *Out of Time*'s hit single.

Throughout their career, R.E.M. have kept their personal lives out of the limelight and have tried to be musically and politically progressive. Michael Stipe, for example, has been involved with environmental causes, animal rights, and antinuclear campaigns. He also founded his own nonprofit film company, C-00, which has produced public service announcements about AIDS, homelessness, and racism. A number of the group's songs have had explicitly political themes. For example, "Fall on Me" (from *Life's Rich Pageant,* 1986) deals with acid rain, *Document*'s "Welcome to the Occupation" protests U.S. intervention in Central America, and "Ignoreland" is an anti-Republican anthem from *Automatic for the People.* Other songs, such as "The One I Love," which deals with opportunism in love, "Losing My Religion," which was banned in Ireland, and "I Took Your Name," which concerns relationships that can breed resentment, have leaned more toward the politics of the personal.

For a group with the longevity and achievement of R.E.M., their career has been remarkably trouble-free. Of course, there have been a few bumps on the road to success. While members proclaimed early on that they would never play arenas or lip sync, to the dismay of some diehard fans, they broke both vows with the *Green* tour and the video for "Losing My Religion." Still, on the cooptation scale, these were fairly minor infractions. Overall, it was a testament to the strength of the group's fan loyalty and artistic staying power that, some fifteen years later, R.E.M. was still being reviewed as a model of musical integrity.

Alternative, Canadian-Style

In the book *Have Not Been the Same: The CanRock Renaissance,* Michael Barclay, Ian Jack, and Jason Schneider suggest that the mid-1980s to mid-1990s was a golden period for independent and alternative music in Canada. They make a convincing case. Halifax, Montreal, Toronto, Vancouver, and to a lesser degree, Edmonton all had dynamic scenes that produced more than a few substantial hits. Perhaps more importantly, each of these cities provided a context and an infrastructure that allowed a number of musicians to create wondrously innovative music that in turn helped to define a particular scene and to provide a focal point for the lives of thousands of young Canadians. The big stars of the era were Sloan, Great Big Sea, Men Without Hats, the Cowboy Junkies, Blue Rodeo, The Tragically Hip, Skinny Puppy, and Sarah McLachlan. But groups like Eric's Trip, the Gruesomes, Deja Voodoo, the Bourbon Tabernacle Choir, A Neon Rome, Change of Heart, the Rheostatics, Jr. Gone Wild, and Moev made incredible music that helped pave the way for more recent alternative stars such as Godspeed! You Black Emperor, Arcade Fire, Broken Social Scene, and Feist.

One of the first groups to make a name for itself was Montreal's Men Without Hats. Led by Ivan Doroschuk, Men Without Hats achieved international notoriety with "Safety Dance"

With their classic rock sound and lyrics chronicling aspects of Canadian culture, history, and place names, the Tragically Hip have been embraced in their native land as the quintessential Canadian rock band.

in the winter of 1983. Drawing on various threads of new wave, post punk, and the electronic innovations of Kraftwerk, Men Without Hats made poppy, cheerful, electronic dance music using a drum machine and multiple synths. On top of the layered electronics, Doroschuk delivered a knowingly ironic, somewhat tongue-in-cheek vocal that owed more than a little to the B-52's and perfectly captured the zeitgeist of the time.

At the other end of the alternative spectrum in Montreal was the deliberately primitive-sounding, Cramps-influenced Deja Voodoo, formed in 1981. Drummer Tony Dewald and singer guitarist Gerard Van Herk pioneered what they lovingly referred to as *sludgeabilly*. Taking a page out of the Ramones' notebook, they kept most of their songs under two minutes in length. As great as the band was, Dewald and Van Herk were equally important for founding Og Records and releasing a series of incredibly influential discs they called *It Came from Canada*. These compilations included cuts by bands from coast to coast. In addition to helping many of the bands included on the compilations to tour nationally, the *It Came from Canada* series gave notice to musicians, booking agents, club owners, and music fans alike that there was exciting independent music being made in Canada that was the equal of anything coming out of the United States and the United Kingdom.

Other Montreal groups of note from this period were the electronic, politically-tinged Rational Youth; the platinum-selling the Box who, like Men Without Hats, sang in both French and English (leading some members of the press to refer to them as "Pierre Trudeau's dream come true"); rockabilly mad men Ray Condo and His Hardrock Goners; "psycho-country-gospel-punk" artist Jerry Jerry and the Sons of Rhythm Orchestra; punk rock groups the Doughboys and the Nils; and 1960s garage punks-extraordinaire the Gruesomes.

Jerry Jerry and the Sons of Rhythm were originally from Edmonton. While the city produced a number of fine bands, there was no local indie record company of note. Consequently, many of Edmonton's finest musicians moved elsewhere in search of fame and fortune—or at least the chance to make a record. Moe Berg, who led the Pursuit of Happiness, and torch and twang chanteuse kd lang both moved to Toronto, while the rootsy Jr. Gone Wild and the hardcore punks SNFU headed to Vancouver.

As discussed in Chapter 8, Vancouver had a very active hardcore scene, dominated by seminal groups such as the Young Canadians, D.O.A., SNFU, and the Dayglow Abortions. In the early 1980s, Tom Ferris and Cal Stephenson, influenced by the European electronic underground, formed Moev. After two releases on the short-lived Noetix and Go Records labels, in 1984, Moev's *Toulyev* EP became the first release on Terry McBride and Mark Jowett's fledgling Nettwerk Records. A short time later, McBride and Jowett signed industrial upstarts Skinny Puppy. Formed in 1982 by cEvin Key (Kevin Crompton), late of Images in Vogue, and Nivek Ogre (Kevin Ogilvie), between 1984 and 1992 Skinny Puppy sold over two million albums worldwide for Nettwerk. Over those eight years, the group developed a substantial following in Europe and the United States with their politically charged lyrics about animal rights and chemical warfare and their over-the-top theatrical performances. The folk-rock oriented Grapes of Wrath, hailing from Kelowna, B.C., rounded out Nettwerk's early lineup.

When Nettwerk signed Halifax's Sarah McLachlan in 1988, their future was set. McLachlan (discussed elsewhere in the context of Lilith Fair) released a series of increasingly successful singer/songwriter albums that were influenced by Kate Bush and Peter Gabriel, including 1991's *Solace*, 1993's *Fumbling Towards Ecstasy*, and 1997's *Surfacing*. By *Surfacing* she had blossomed into an international superstar.

While bands like the October Game, featuring a teenage Sarah McLachlan, had been active in Halifax in the mid-1980s, the city's scene took off during the 1990s, beginning with the founding of Sloan in 1991. The following year, the members of Sloan—Chris Murphy, Andrew Scott, Patrick Pentland, and Jay Ferguson—started their own record label, Murderrecords, and released their debut EP, *Peppermint*. Although they were courted by Nettwerk, the group opted to sign with Geffen Records, releasing the grunge-infused "Underwhelmed" as the lead single off their major-league debut, *Smeared*. With ample support from MuchMusic and Canadian radio stations coast to coast, "Underwhelmed" made Sloan instant darlings in the world of Canadian rock. When the band fell out with Geffen over the direction of their second album, 1994's *Twice Removed*, they opted to remain independent, releasing albums at regular intervals on Murderrecords up to and including 2008's *Parallel Play*.

Over the course of the late 1980s and the 1990s, Halifax was also home to Jellyfishbabies, Eric's Trip (originally from Moncton, New Brunswick), the all-female Jale, Hardship Post (from Newfoundland), and Thrush Hermit. Eric's Trip, Jale, and Hardship Post were all signed to Seattle's ultra-cool Sub Pop label, leading many to feel in the second half of the 1990s that Halifax would be the next Athens, Georgia, or Minneapolis. Unfortunately, while well received critically, none of these bands sold in significant numbers. The same fate befell Thrush Hermit, who had signed with Elektra Records. Thrush Hermit's leader, Joel Plaskett, would find much greater success in the first decade of the twenty-first century with the Joel Plaskett Emergency.

Not surprisingly, Toronto had the largest and arguably the most diverse independent music scene in Canada in the 1980s and 1990s. Handsome Ned, Blue Rodeo, and kd lang presented various forms of country as alternative music. Their music resided side by side with the collective funk and soul mania of the Bourbon Tabernacle Choir; the singer/songwriter eccentricities of Jane Siberry, Bob Snider, and Mary Margaret O'Hara; the grungy rock of Change of Heart; and A Neon Rome's revisioning of the Velvet Underground. It was an unbelievably exciting time to be making and listening to music on Queen Street West.

Handsome Ned, a.k.a. Robin Masyk, grew up in Stony Creek, Ontario. After spending time in Austin, Texas, in 1978, Ned became enamoured with country music, and upon his return to Toronto, in various guises—most notably as the Handsome Neds—he began performing country music on joint bills with punk groups such as the Viletones. Although Ned left only a handful of recordings behind, his embrace of American roots music filtered through an alt-rock sensibility influenced a host of other groups, including the Cowboy Junkies and Blue Rodeo.

Blue Rodeo, headed up by Jim Cuddy and Greg Keelor, evolved out of two earlier groups, the Hi-Fi's and Fly to France. In 1986, they were signed to Risque Disque (with distribution through WEA). Their debut album, *Outskirts*, included the earlier Fly to France song "Try," which became a major Canadian pop and country hit. With a roots-oriented sound grounded in country music, the Canadian singer/songwriter tradition, rich harmony singing, and modern rock, the band had subsequent hits with "Day After Day," "Diamond Mine," and "Till I Am Myself Again." Between 1986 and 2008, Blue Rodeo issued one live album, 1994's classic *Five Days in July*, and eleven other studio albums, received numerous industry awards, and, alongside the Tragically Hip, became superstars in their native country without achieving substantial success in the United States. As such, in many ways the group are a product of Pierre Juneau's dream (jump-started by the CanCon laws he helped to enact in 1971) of a self-sufficient Canadian popular music industry where Canadian artists could avail themselves of promotion on Canadian radio and could consequently carve out successful careers without having to leave the country.

The Cowboy Junkies were formed in 1985 by brothers Michael Timmins and Peter Timmins, sister Margo Timmins, and bassist Alan Anton. Infatuated with roots music, the Junkies developed a minimalist sound that featured Margo delivering enigmatic vocals at extremely low volume. Their first two albums, *Whites Off Earth Now* and *The Trinity Sessions*, were issued in 1986 and 1987, respectively, on their own Latent Records. Both albums were recorded and produced by Peter Moore using a single Calrec Ambisonic microphone. The *Trinity Sessions* was cut in one fourteen-hour session at Toronto's Holy Trinity Church and featured an amalgam of originals by Michael and Margo, and sultry, melancholic covers of songs such as Patsy Cline's "Walking After Midnight," Hank Williams' "I'm So Lonesome I Could Cry," and Lou Reed's "Sweet Jane." In each case, the Junkies' idiosyncratic take on what were iconic songs in the world of popular music invested the material with completely new meaning. RCA Records signed the band in 1988 and reissued *The Trinity Sessions* to substantial critical acclaim in both the United States and the United Kingdom. The influential *Los Angeles Times* critic Robert Hilburn listed the LP as one of the Top Ten albums of the year. The Cowboy Junkies would go on to have a number of Canadian hits and continue in the latter years of the first decade of the twenty-first century to sell hundreds of thousands of albums with each new release and to regularly headline venues such as Carnegie Hall in New York and Massey Hall in Toronto.

The artist known as k.d. (Kathryn Dawn) lang was born in Edmonton and grew up in Consort, Alberta. Back in Edmonton to attend university in the early 1980s, lang would tell anyone who would listen that she was the reincarnation of country singer Patsy Cline. To that end she called her backup band the Reclines. As James Hale has written, in the early days lang's shows were "equal parts performance art and rockabilly."[9] In 1984, she recorded a rockabilly album that betrayed hints of punk influence, entitled *A Truly Western Experience*, for the indie Bumstead Records. After breakthrough performances in Toronto and New York, lang was signed to Sire Records, releasing *Angel with a Lariat* in 1987. That same year, she recorded a duet with Roy Orbison on a remake of Orbison's "Crying," which became an Adult Contemporary hit. Her third album, 1988's *Shadowland*, broke into the Top Ten in both Canada and the United States. A year later, she won the Grammy for Best Female Country Vocal Performance. A staunch vegetarian, lang ran afoul of country fans in her native Alberta and in Nashville for a series of antimeat campaigns she participated in. In 1992, she came out as a lesbian, further challenging the country music establishment. That same year, she remade herself into a singer of Adult Contemporary pop with *Ingenue*, winning the Grammy for Best Female Pop Vocal Performance. In 2008, lang had her biggest hit in years with *Watershed*, which went to number eight in the United States and number three in Canada.

The Tragically Hip were formed in 1983 in Kingston, Ontario, by Gord Downie, Rob Baker, Paul Langlois, Gord Sinclair, and Johnny Fay. The group was signed to MCA Records after a gig at the Horseshoe Tavern, Toronto's legendary Queen Street West club, and their second album, 1989's *Up to Here*, went triple-platinum in Canada and produced the hits "Blow at High Dough" and "New Orleans Is Sinking." Referencing Canadian place names, historic events, and hockey, by 1991, with the release of their third album, *Road Apples*, the Hip (as their fans affectionately called them) had become "unquestionably the People's Band of Canada," according to Barclay, Jack and Schneider. The group's live shows were phenomenally intense, marked by lead singer Gord Downie's unpredictable lyric improvisations in the middle of songs. These improvisations would often evolve into fully fledged new songs.

In 1993, in support of *Fully Completely*, an album that contained songs detailing a recent Canadian murder trial and the story of legendary Toronto Maple Leafs hockey player Bill Barilko, the Hip began the first of a series of festival tours they dubbed Another Roadside Attraction. Each tour featured the Hip headlining a bill that included several of their favourite Canadian independent bands. The Canadian equivalent of Lollapalooza, the Another Roadside Attraction tours served to promote and potentially expand the fan base of each of the bands on the bill and were just one example of the Tragically Hip's staunch pro-Canadian stance. The band routinely sells out arenas across Canada, is able to play small theatres in border cities such as Detroit, and is relegated to clubs in the rest of the United States. In 2005, the Hip were inducted into the Canadian Music Hall of Fame, and they remain godlike heroes to rock youth in their native country.

The final major indie success to emerge out of Toronto in the early 1990s was the Barenaked Ladies. Formed as an acoustic duo in 1988 by Ed Robertson and Steven Page, by 1991 the group was a five-piece band notable for their unusual name, energetic live shows, and zany sense of humour. That year ,they recorded and released a five-song independent cassette. Titled, appropriately enough, *The Yellow Tape,* and featuring stark versions of such whimsical future Canadian hits as "Brian Wilson," "Be My Yoko Ono," and "If I Had $1 000 000," the cassette received regular airplay on Toronto's alternative rock station CFNY-FM, displaced Michael Jackson to take the number one spot at HMV records, and sold a whopping 83,000 copies. For an indie release in Canada, especially one on cassette, this was a phenomenal achievement that served to open up Canadian retail to stocking independent releases that bands would bring in and leave on consignment.

In 1992, the Barenaked Ladies signed with Sire in the United States and released their first full-length album, *Gordon*. In Canada *Gordon* shot straight to number one, where it remained for eight weeks. Altogether, the album generated four hit singles and sold 800,000 copies in Canada, while barely making a dent in the United States. It would take a few years, but by 1998, with the album *Stunt* and the single "One Week," the Barenaked Ladies became a Top Ten act south of the border. *Stunt* would go on to sell 4 million copies. As was the case with Blue Rodeo, the Tragically Hip, and Sarah McLachlan, audiences in Canada understood the Barenaked Ladies as being quintessentially Canadian and supported the band with unprecedented fervour.

In the late 1980s, Celtic musicians in the Maritime provinces produced a fusion variously titled Celtic-pop or Celtic-rock that has proven to be quite successful. Ironically, Vancouver's Spirit of the West were actually the first group to forge such a style at a national level, with hits such as "Political," from 1988's *Labour Day*, and "Save This House" and "Home for a Rest" from the group's major label debut, 1990's *Save This House*. In 1993, Cape Breton fiddler Natalie McMaster achieved gold status with her third independent release, *Fit as a Fiddle*. Three years later, she signed a major label deal with Warner Music Canada. A distant cousin of McMaster's, Ashley MacIsaac, combined "virtuoso fiddling with modern dance rhythms and punk rock excitement"[10] on his 1995 release *Hi, How Are You Today?* Fueled by MacIsaac's "energetic, kilt-swirling live performances" and the hit single "Sleepy Maggie," *Hi How Are You Today?* sold 300,000 copies in Canada alone.

The most successful Celtic-rock artists were unquestionably Newfoundland's Great Big Sea. Formed in 1993 by Alan Doyle, Bob Hallett, Sean McCann, and Darrell Power, collectively the group members play guitar, bass, bouzouki, mandola, mandolin, banjo, fiddle, whistles, pipes, accordion, concertina, tin whistle, bodhran, bones, and harmonica. Adapting traditional Newfoundland music to the structures of contemporary pop music, "in the tradition of the convivial Newfoundland 'kitchen party,'" Great Big Sea's "concerts are as much communal celebrations as they are musical events."[11] The net result has been that, beginning with their major label debut, *Up*, in 1995, every Great Big Sea album has gone either gold or platinum in Canada. This is a remarkable achievement for a group specializing in traditional music.

Lollapalooza: Mainstreaming the Counterculture

Alternative music thus took its place, along with rap and metal, as one of the predominant voices of youth culture. From a certain point of view, rap, metal, and alternative had developed separately at least in part because the industry that produced them, like society at large, was divided along lines of race and culture. It could easily be argued that the fans who listened to rap, metal, and alternative had a fair amount in common, including, certainly, their age and their alienation from the establishment. These styles were themselves united in their commitment to

From a certain point of view, rap, metal, and alternative had developed separately at least in part because the industry that produced them, like society at large, was divided along lines of race and culture.

transgression—transgression of musical conventions, societal values, and behavioural norms. If rap, metal, and alternative were already individually threatening and controversial, what could be more upsetting than putting them all together? No doubt these thoughts crossed the mind of Perry Farrell, the leader of Jane's Addiction, when he organized the first Lollapalooza festival in 1991.

The idea of Lollapalooza came to Farrell and booking agent Marc Geiger in 1990 while they were in Europe marveling at the routine success of annual multiact summer music festivals like the Reading Festival in England. While these types of festivals had never caught on in the United States in any big way, Farrell and Geiger felt certain they could pull one off and joined forces with Ted Gardner and Don Mullen to do so, picking the worst concert season in recent memory to launch the tour. Jane's Addiction, who had recently broken into the Top Twenty with their album *Ritual de lo Habitual,* headlined the event. It was, in fact, the group's farewell tour (or, perhaps, parting shot), as Farrell moved on to begin work with his new group, Porno for Pyros. Other acts included Living Colour, Nine Inch Nails, Ice-T and Body Count, the Henry Rollins Band, the Butthole Surfers, and Siouxsie and the Banshees. In a summer when mainstream acts flopped or lost money on multiple dates, the seven-act, twenty-one-city Lollapalooza tour—assault, really—played to a total of 430,000 people and grossed $10 million. "Lollapalooza became," as *Boston Globe* critic Jim Sullivan wrote, "the surprise smash summer tour of 1991, an artistic success and a substantial moneymaker in a recession-plagued season."[12]

To capture the unifying element that seemed to run through the tour, *The New York Times* titled Jon Pareles' review "Howls of Rage." Henry Rollins delivered the vein-popping punk fury that had characterized his stage demeanour since fronting Black Flag in the early 1980s. The Butthole Surfers bashed away at acid-induced, punk-influenced, three-chord garage rock. Over a mechanized industrial beat, Trent Reznor continued the nihilistic rants that had pushed Nine Inch Nails' *Pretty Hate Machine* to platinum sales. Siouxsie and the Banshees, the only female-fronted act, carried forward the punk spirit of an earlier generation. (The tour boosted the group's new LP, *Superstition,* into the weekly Top 100 albums.) Living Colour delivered messages about everything from racism to the environment, and their music was as scorching as ever. Jane's Addiction matched them in fury and multicultural influences, drifting, in Pareles' words,

Perhaps more than its music, what made Lollapalooza "alternative" was the continual projection of political messages concerning everything from censorship to the Gulf War, and the presence of many left-leaning activist organizations.

"from heavy metal stomps to scrabbling funk to finger-picking folk rock. . . . Mr. Perkins added a touch of Latin Timbales to rock rhythms, while Morgan Fichter on violin brought hints of country and Arabic music to some songs."[13] In many ways, however, it was Ice-T who put the show over the top, both musically and politically. After rapping for half his set, he brought out his new thrash metal band, Body Count, for the second half. It was at Lollapalooza that he first performed "Cop Killer," the song that got him in so much political hot water one year later. Like the Butthole Surfers, he openly brandished firearms on stage, vowing to avenge police brutality. In Atlanta, he tested the limits of racial tolerance when he teamed up with Farrell for a provocative version of Sly Stone's "Don't Call Me Nigger, Whitey." "That was really intense," remarked an awestruck Henry Rollins.

Perhaps more than its music, what made Lollapalooza alternative was the continual projection of political messages concerning everything from censorship to the Gulf War, and the presence of many left-leaning activist organizations. Among the organizations present at the festival, which occurred in the midst of the first Bush administration, were the National Abortion Rights Action League; Refuse and Resist; the Hyacinth Foundation, an AIDS group; and Handgun Control, Inc. (apparently Ice-T and the Surfers did not get the message of that organization). The tour may well have been an early harbinger of the slight shift to the left that accompanied Clinton's election the following year (a shift that was more than undone in the Republican landslide in the midterm elections of 1994). The potential for making an impact at the polls in an election year was not wasted on festival organizers the following year. "We got a lot of people registered [to vote] last year," Don Mullen said, "and this year signing people up is even more important."[14] The political booths for Lollapalooza '92 included Rock the Vote and College Democrats, as well as the more radical gay activist organization ACT-UP, the environmental organization Greenpeace, the controversial animal rights group PETA (People for the Ethical Treatment of Animals), the Cannabis Action Network, and the Coalition for the Homeless.

Because the first festival had been such a success, the production group for Lollapalooza '92 initially tried to land bigger (and more mainstream) headliners like Neil Young and R.E.M. and expanded the festival from a twenty-one-city tour to a thirty-six-city tour. In some ways, organizers felt like they had to settle for a lineup that included the Red Hot Chili Peppers, Pearl Jam, Soundgarden, Ice Cube, Ministry, The Jesus and Mary Chain, and Lush. In the five months it took to put the show together, however, the vagaries of pop stardom smiled on the event. By the time the tour hit the road, Pearl Jam's *Ten* and the Chili Peppers' *Blood Sugar Sex Magik* were both riding the Top Ten, peaking at numbers two and three, respectively. At that moment, either group could have sold out shows the size of Lollapalooza. Furthermore, Soundgarden's *Badmotorfinger* had already gone Top Forty, and Ice Cube's *Death Certificate*, which had peaked at number two, was still riding the charts. The festival nearly doubled its audience (to 800,000) and its take (to $19 million) and propelled Ministry's *Psalm 69* into the Top Thirty. The 1992 festival also featured a second stage for lesser-known acts like Cypress Hill, the Boo Yaa Tribe, and Sharkbait.

The Red Hot Chili Peppers provided some of the most interesting music on the tour, their sound recalling at times early hip hop sources like Jimmy Castor and Parliament-Funkadelic grafted onto heavy metal. Lead singer Anthony Kiedis hovered somewhere between rapping and singing. Formed in the early 1980s, the group had been a part of the Los Angeles underground for years. "Loved and scorned in equal measure as tattooed punk-funk loons obsessed with the horizontal rumba," David Fricke has said, "the Chili Peppers are skateboard-culture heroes, recognized even by their detractors as early pioneers of the mosh-pit marriage of funk, rap, and thrash that Living Colour and Faith No More took to the bank."[15] Following their self-titled debut LP in 1984, they recorded *Freaky Styley* and *The Uplift Mofo Party Plan*, before hitting pay dirt with *Mother's Milk* in 1989. During this period, the band struggled through the death of guitarist Hillel Slovak, caused by a heroin overdose, and Kiedis's own heroin addiction. *Blood Sugar Sex Magik* marked the group's Warner debut in 1991. "Under the Bridge," the unlikely hit single that kicked them into the Top Ten, detailed Kiedis's ordeal with drugs.

In terms of musical range, Lollapalooza '92 was similar to its predecessor. Although there were differences between them, Pearl Jam and Soundgarden carried the banner of Seattle grunge. Pearl Jam was a safer, more straightforward blend of heavy metal and psychedelic rock.

By the time Lollapalooza '92 hit the road, Pearl Jam was so well-known that the alternative festival was well on its way to becoming a mainstay of the summer concert circuit. Lead singer Eddie Vedder is held aloft by the crowd as he explores the darker side of life.

The group's lead singer, Eddie Vedder, was dark and brooding as he agonized over questions of sanity and personal existence. Soundgarden was more dissonant, with irregular tempos and time signatures. Lead singer Chris Cornell segued from angry growls to high, piercing tones. Concerned about Ice-T's removal of "Cop Killer" from *Body Count,* Soundgarden performed the song. Ice Cube, the reigning king of gangsta rap, supported the sentiment with a new rap line, "Rappers don't kill people. Cops do." Ministry dispensed industrial rock, with as many as four guitars pounding frenzied riffs. The Jesus and Mary Chain played nihilistic Ramones-derived punk. Lush supplied the only female voices of the day, offering ethereal introspective punkish folk rock.

As varied as the music was, however, there was already a kind of formula mentality setting in. Anthony Kiedis, in particular, was critical of the 1992 lineup, insisting it was "way too male" and, especially on the main stage, "way too guitar-oriented."[16] By 1993, the festival had become an institution. Headline positions on the main stage became slots to be filled. Alice in Chains replaced Soundgarden, just as Dinosaur Jr. occupied Pearl Jam's slot. (Nirvana spurned the event.) Arrested Development, with their multiplatinum 1992 debut album, *3 Years 5 months & 2 days in the Life of . . . ,* still on the charts, represented rap as Ice Cube and Ice-T had done in years past. Fishbone, from Los Angeles, was the West Coast ska to gospel to heavy metal answer to New York's Living Colour. Front 242 took over the industrial niche vacated by Ministry and Nine Inch Nails. Primus closed the show, although not as successfully as the Red Hot Chili Peppers, with snappy, quirky, quasi-funk. Again, there was only one female act, Babes in Toyland, a group from Minneapolis. With Perry Farrell playing a lesser creative role, Lollapalooza '93 became, in the words of critic Steve Pond, "the year Lollapalooza doesn't like to talk about."[17]

By 1993, Lollapalooza had become so successful that other artists began to develop alternatives to the alternative festival, the most notable being Alternative Nation. The tour featured the Spin Doctors, Soul Asylum, and Screaming Trees. By tour time, the Spin Doctors' 1991 debut, *A Pocket Full of Kryptonite,* had gotten a second wind, which propelled it to platinum status. Soul Asylum's *Grave Dancer's Union* had already gone platinum. The group's video for the single "Runaway Train" featured listings of missing children and led to a gig at the White House as President Clinton signed the youth service bill. Screaming Trees' *Sweet Oblivion* album and "Nearly Lost You" single, from the *Singles* soundtrack, announced the group's arrival after eight years and six albums. Like Lollapalooza, Alternative Nation was a summer-long tour that played to hundreds of thousands of fans in sold-out shows across the country. It was dubbed by *Rolling Stone* "the Little Lollapalooza That Could."

While it lasted, Lollapalooza presented a reasonably representative cross-section of what was going on musically in youth culture, and each tour did so with far more heart and spontaneity than the festival held on the twenty-fifth anniversary of Woodstock.

In 1994, Farrell again played an active planning role, and Lollapalooza regained its artistic footing. Nirvana had agreed to play, but the commitment was derailed by Cobain's suicide. Still, the festival featured the Smashing Pumpkins, the Beastie Boys, George Clinton and the P-Funk All Stars, the Breeders, A Tribe Called Quest, L7, Green Day, and others. Because the Smashing Pumpkins' *Siamese Dream* was already double platinum and the Beastie Boys' *Ill Communication* entered the charts at number one before the tour began, the festival was as vulnerable as its predecessors had been to the criticism of being too mainstream. However, the fact is that all the Lollapalooza tours crossed lines of class, race, and gender in ways that most tours would have avoided like the plague. Lollapalooza faded into oblivion in the late 1990s, survived by other ensemble tours, like H.O.R.D.E. and Lilith Fair, that were aimed at more specialized audiences. While it lasted, however, Lollapalooza presented a reasonably representative cross-section of what was going on musically in youth culture, and each tour did so with far more heart and spontaneity than the festival held on the twenty-fifth anniversary of Woodstock. Because Woodstock '94 performances were broadcast only on pay-per-view, MTV was temporarily reduced to the rock equivalent of the Home Shopping Network, with its incessant merchandising schemes to make up for the lack of performances. It was so not alternative.

Country: The Other Alternative

All the column inches devoted to alternative music tended to obscure the biggest commercial breakthrough of the 1990s—country music. If the early part of the 1990s belonged to any one artist, it was Garth Brooks, of country music fame. *Billboard* listed Brooks as Top Pop Album Artist and Top Country Album Artist for the years 1991, 1992, and 1993. In 1992, NBC aired a Garth Brooks special opposite a CBS Michael Jackson special. Jackson's show placed sixty-sixth in the ratings while Brooks's finished among the ten highest-rated shows. In 1993, all six of his albums—*Garth Brooks, No Fences, Ropin' the Wind, In Pieces, Beyond the Season,* and *The Chase*—could be found among the 100 most popular albums of the year. By the end of the year, *No Fences* and *Ropin' the Wind* had sold about 10 million copies each. It was Brooks' *Ropin' the Wind* that caused the pop side of the industry to stand up and take notice. Released in September 1991, the album went straight to number one (the first country album to do so in ten years) and remained there for eight weeks. After fending off challenges from Hammer, Guns 'N' Roses, U2, Michael Jackson,

Brooks' fame caused a shake-up in Nashville and highlighted a generation gap in country music. Not only was he a best-selling country artist under the age of forty, but his material challenged some of country music's most sacred cows.

Garth Brooks, more than any other artist, dominated the early 1990s and turned country music into the biggest commercial breakthrough of the decade. With his roots in the country tradition, he packs his live performances with all the glitz of an arena rock show.

and Nirvana, *Ropin' the Wind* regained the number one position in January 1992 for another ten weeks.

Brooks was neither your average superstar nor your average country singer. A paunchy, slightly balding singer from Yukon, Oklahoma, he made it big with no major tale of woe to hang his considerable hat on. While there was no question that he was exposed early on to country greats like Merle Haggard and George Jones, his tastes ran as far afield as Kiss, Kansas, ELO, and Styx. His music is to be distinguished from the music of such "new traditionalists" as Ricky Skaggs and Emmylou Harris, both of whom achieved a certain amount of crossover appeal in the early 1980s by updating honky-tonk heroes like Hank Williams and Lefty Frizzell, as well as from the embarrassment of country riches that followed the success of the film *Urban Cowboy*. Brooks came from a generation of country artists whose blend of folk, country, and rock 'n' roll ran the gamut from the songs of singer/songwriter James Taylor to the mellow country rock of the Eagles to the raucous southern boogie of Lynyrd Skynyrd. His performance style was steeped in the arena rock aesthetic, including theater smoke, pyrotechnics, and sophisticated lighting effects. Teenagers wearing Megadeth and Cinderella T-shirts have been known to attend his shows.

Needless to say, Brooks' fame caused a shake-up in Nashville and highlighted a generation gap in country music. Not only was he a best-selling country artist under the age of forty (indeed, the ten best-selling country artists of 1992 were all under forty), but his material challenged some of country music's most sacred cows. In 1991, the Nashville Network (TNN) refused to air the video of "The Thunder Rolls," which ends with a woman shooting her abusive husband. "We Shall Be Free" was written as a response to the Rodney King beating and includes lines supportive of gay rights. After completing the video for the single, Brooks played two benefits that raised $1 million for South Central Los Angeles and shrugged off any criticism of his actions as "Garthbashing." He also defended his music as real country. "No one could doubt that we did country music," he told one interviewer in 1993. "One thing was who I surrounded myself with: two guys from Kansas, three from Oklahoma. Out in front you've got steel guitar, fiddle, you got hats, we're all wearing Wranglers and Ropers." While he acknowledged the arena rock mentality of his shows ("I got guys smashing guitars, I got guys doing leads while running across the stage"), he came back to what, for him, was the bottom line—the fact that he and his band were "just a bunch of country bumpkins who got lucky. And *know* that they got lucky."[18]

Brooks' crossover triumph opened up unprecedented space on the pop charts for other country artists. Between 1991 and 1994, Clint Black, Reba McEntire, Travis Tritt, Vince Gil, Trisha Yearwood, Dwight Yoakam, George Strait, Billy Ray Cyrus, and Mary Chapin Carpenter could all be found among the best-selling pop artists of the year. The following year, Tim McGraw joined the list with *Not a Moment Too Soon,* and one year later his wife-to-be Faith Hill scored with *It Matters to Me.* By 1992, country radio had become the second most listened to music format in the country. It had an 11.6 percent share of the market, which was second only to Adult Contemporary's 18.1 share. TNN's 1.6 cable channel share of the market may not have set any records, but it was higher than MTV's 0.6 percent piece of the action. In some ways, Brooks' overwhelming popularity may have created a permanent space for country crossovers on the pop charts. With the exception of 1997, at least two Garth Brooks albums could be found among the best-selling albums of the year for every year of the decade. The year Brooks was absent, a teenaged LeAnn Rimes placed three albums among the fifty best-selling albums of the year, including *Blue,* at 5.7 million copies and counting. Rimes was bracketed on both sides by Shania Twain, whose *The Woman in Me* and *Come On Over* were among the ten best-selling albums of 1996 and 1998, respectively. *Come On Over* could still be found among the twenty best-selling albums of the year two years later.

Like Garth Brooks, Ellen "Shania" Twain—her nickname taken from the Ojibway Indian word for "I'm on my way"—was not your average country artist. In the first place she was not a product of Nashville. Born in Windsor, Ontario, both her parents were killed in a car crash when she was in her early twenties. She turned to music to help support the family. Her self-titled debut album earned her little in the way of critical praise, but her sexy video for "What Made You Say That" caught the attention of producer Mutt Lange, who went on to become her producer and her husband. With credits that included AC/DC, Def Leppard, and the Cars, Lange was not your average country producer. But it was his guiding hand that propelled Twain's next two albums to multiplatinum success. At twelve times platinum, *The Woman in Me* was a very good start. Interestingly, Twain achieved this level of sales without touring. She was a superstar before most of her fans had any opportunity to see her live. It wasn't until 1998 that she corrected this situation, finally mounting a two-year world tour in support of *Come On Over.* There were actually two versions of *Come On Over*: a country version for the U.S. audience and a pop-oriented "international" version that wasn't released in the United States until several of its remixes became pop hits. Clever marketing of this kind allowed Twain to make a pop record without risking a backlash from her country audience. By the end of the decade, *Come On Over* had sold 34 million copies worldwide, the most ever by a female artist. Twain and Lange then retreated to their new home in Switzerland to concentrate on raising a family.

Shania Twain distinguished herself not only as a country artist but also as a woman in pop and, more specifically, a Canadian woman in pop. But more on that later. Meanwhile, the female partner of another couple—Faith Hill and Tim McGraw, both top country performers and touring partners who were married in 1996—also scored in the late 1990s. Following a string of country crossover successes in the mid-1990s, Hill unveiled a new, sexier image and more pop-oriented material for *Breathe* (1999), whose title song became the best-selling single of 2000. Like alternative, country was now fully pop.

Packaging Pop Trends: The Search for the Next Big Thing

Interestingly, the unlikely success of such a diversity of groups and sounds in the early 1990s—Boyz II Men, Sinéad O'Connor, Living Colour, Nirvana, and Garth Brooks, to name a few—did not cause the music industry to alter its marketing strategies in the least. "Instead of investing in and nurturing a wide range of new talents," observed Anthony DeCurtis in 1992, "record companies are betting wildly like drunks at the roulette table, hoping that one big score—whether by an old favorite or a new lucky number—will cover all past debts."[19] In its current form the music industry needs stars—superstars, really—like fish need water. Superstars are what make everything else work for the industry—the formidable marketing apparatus, radio promotion, music videos, and live performance touring circuits. The major labels are prepared to risk millions of dollars in search of that one artist or group who will make it worth their while. When one of these acts pays off, they make up for dozens of others who, according to record company accounting, lose money. This strategy leads to the culturally unappealing logic that a single artist who can sell 40 million units—as Michael Jackson did with *Thriller*—is actually worth more to a label than forty acts that sell 1 million units apiece. This is because banking on a single artist saves the record company from having to duplicate the costs of marketing and promotion forty times. It is by design, then, that record companies have a vested interest in promoting as few artists as possible.

> *In its current form, the music industry needs stars—superstars, really—like fish need water. Superstars are what make everything else work for the industry—the formidable marketing apparatus, radio promotion, music videos, and live performance touring circuits.*

As a result, it may often appear as if a given year is dominated by a single artist, even though there are thousands of musicians recording and performing for their life's work. In the same way that 1983 was the year of Michael Jackson, and Nirvana put their imprint on 1991, it was Sweden's Ace of Base who reigned over 1994. Hootie and the Blowfish ruled in 1995. Britain's Spice Girls dominated 1997—after taking Europe the previous year. (And who could forget the "Macarena" in 1996, even if they wanted to?) Such overwhelming dominance can obscure the fact (at least for that moment) that these may not be the artists (or the songs) that are the most important artistically or that make the most lasting impact. But then, it has never been a requirement that popular music be great art. A cursory look at the entries for these groups in the *All Music Guide to Rock* is sufficient to illustrate the point. "Ace of Base's strong point is not versatility—all of their hit singles have exactly the same beat. But that doesn't matter."[17] "Hootie and the Blowfish aren't innovative . . . . None of the tracks [on *Cracked Rear View*] transcend their generic status. . . ."[20] "*Spice* doesn't need to be original to be entertaining. . . . None of the Girls have great voices . . . ."[21] None of this mattered. In 1994, Ace of Base's Eurodance album, *The Sign,* was everywhere, parlaying heavy radio play in a variety of formats—Top Forty, Adult Contemporary, Urban, and Modern Rock—into sales of 8 million units. Hootie and the Blowfish eventually achieved sales of 13 million units on *Cracked Rear View,* essentially by convincing audiences everywhere that they were their local bar band. *Spice* sold more than seven times platinum in the United States alone. All these groups logged more than respectable sales on follow-up albums. But what lasting effect have they had? Even Hootie's own guitarist, Mark

Bryan, once remarked: "There are so many other bands that I listen to and think, 'This band is great, and no one knows who it is. This guy can play guitar better than me, and these people can write better songs than us, so why do we get to sell 5 million records?'"[23]

In the 1990s, the artist for whom the power of the music industry was harnessed to the greatest economic advantage was one who combined incredible talent and potential for follow-through with the best business plan on the planet—Mariah Carey. With her multioctave range and no shortage of good pop/dance/r&b material, Carey was paired with top-notch professionals and approached by Columbia as a major investment and a long-term artist from day one. Columbia's Don Ienner made the label's position perfectly clear when he announced in Carey's debut year: "We don't look at Mariah Carey as a dance-pop artist. We look at her as a franchise."[24] (Accordingly, Ienner must have regarded Carety's subsequent marriage to label head Tommy Mottola as a corporate merger.) Carey's 1990 eponymous debut album did not disappoint when it rolled out four number one singles in a row. Two of them, "Vision of Love" and "Love Takes Time," hit number one in three different markets—pop, adult contemporary, and r&b. Since that time, every one of Carey's albums has been launched with a single that went to number one.

Choosing to debut "Vision of Love" on *The Arsenio Hall Show*—then the late night last word in black New York hipness—suggested that Carey (and Columbia) felt secure enough about her pop appeal to play to her black audience. During this period there was as much press devoted to Carey's biraciality—she is the product of a white New York opera singer mother and a black Venezuelan father—as to her music. The fact that her black father's Venezuelan's nationality also made her a Latina did not seem to make an impression on anyone at the time, perhaps because it was not germane to the marketing strategy of black/white crossover. Carey's second album, *Emotions,* also followed the same formula of r&b and ballads with cross-market appeal. Beginning very early in Carey's career, one got the impression of a monster talent following a calculated program of career development—from her appearance on *MTV Unplugged,* which yielded a number one cover of the Jackson 5's "I'll Be There," to her rendition of "All I Want for Christmas Is You," which hit the pop charts for the 1994, 1995, and 1996 holiday seasons. *Daydream* (1995) straddled the r&b and Adult Contemporary audiences perfectly with hit singles like "Fantasy," which sampled the Tom Tom Club's "Genius of Love," and "One Sweet Day," a duet with Boyz II Men.

As her marriage to Mottola began to fray at the edges and Carey expanded her social and leisure activities, she came out with *Butterfly* (1997), with the unreleased single of the same name hitting the Top Twenty. The album following her split with Mottola was *Rainbow* (1999), featuring the number one single "Heartbreaker." In between there was a greatest hits compilation, *#1's,* with a very provocative Mariah pictured on the cover. *Butterfly* added a bit more hip hop and r&b to Carey's usual mix, as in its first single, "Honey," in addition to a bit more cheesecake, as in her sultry pose for the "Butterfly" video, which was reminiscent of Caroll Baker's promo poster for the 1950s movie *Babydoll.* She continued her move toward hip hop and r&b on *Rainbow*—which featured guest shots by Jay-Z, Snoop Dogg, Da Brat, and Missy Elliott—without losing one iota of her pop appeal.

Mariah Carey has had more number one singles than any other female artist in any genre—including at least one in every year of her debut decade—and, as the new millennium began, she had racked up sales of an incredible 105 million units in less than ten years. Given

Mariah Carey was considered a hot property at Columbia from the moment she was signed. She lived up to expectations when her multiplatinum self-titled debut album brought her the Grammys for Best New Artist and Best Pop Vocal Performance, Female, in 1990.

this kind of success, it is perhaps not all that surprising that the major labels stuck like glue to their tried and true marketing strategies. Consequently, even with the acceptance of a rather broad range of genres pointing toward a decentralized grassroots strategy, record companies continued to hang on to the concept, ponying up millions for contracts in the 1990s that were surely unprecedented, and perhaps unrecoverable, hoping to find the next Michael Jackson, or was it now the next Mariah Carey?

Janet Jackson initiated the 1990s round of high-stakes contracts when she switched from A&M to Virgin in 1991. With only two albums (admittedly both number ones) and one tour to her credit, Jackson scored a reported $30 million deal. At the time, Richard Branson, chairman of Virgin Records, compared the signing to buying a Rembrandt. When Aerosmith left Columbia for Geffen in 1985, the band was broke. In 1991, they signed a new deal with Columbia worth upwards of $30 million. That same year, Mötley Crüe renewed their agreement with Elektra for a $25 million guarantee to be paid over four albums. ZZ Top scored $30 million at RCA. The Rolling Stones topped all of these with a $40 million three-album deal with Virgin. As large as these contracts may seem, they paled in comparison with the deals that were eventually offered to Madonna, Michael Jackson, and Prince, all of which were reportedly worth more than $60 million in guarantees. The frenzied bidding peaked in August 1996 when R.E.M., of all groups, scored an $80-million five-album deal with Warner—the largest contract in record company history.

These artists and their handlers were cashing in on the outlandish sums of money that had changed hands in the recent spate of record company mergers, such as Matsushita's 1990 purchase of MCA and its affiliated labels for $6.6 billion. "When you hear that your record company has been sold for 20 or 30 times its earnings," said Tim Collins, Aerosmith's manager, "you think, 'I want a piece of that.'"[25] The sale of so many record companies for such incredible sums of money led artists to begin to think of themselves as major factors in the overall profitability of a company, a thought that had not been factored into contract negotiations prior to this. A new realization of the value of catalogue sales simply added to the performers' awareness of their role in profitability.

The sale of so many record companies for such incredible sums of money led artists to begin to think of themselves as major factors in the overall profitability of a company, a thought that had not been factored into contract negotiations prior to this.

Back catalogue had always been a valuable commodity because when an artist has a hit record, it often boosts the sales of his or her previous recordings. Following Kurt Cobain's death, Sub Pop reaped an unexpected windfall when sales of *Bleach* jumped from 150,000 to 800,000 copies. With the advent of the compact disc, the industry had slowly shifted to a new standard, and back catalogue became even more important as consumers began buying recordings they already owned in the new configuration. In the early 1990s, catalogue sales were estimated to be as much as 40 percent of all album sales. Thus, for many artists, back catalogue was their most valuable asset. Aerosmith, for example, had recorded seven Top Forty albums on

Columbia before switching to Geffen. According to the group's original contract with Columbia, the rights to previous recordings reverted to the group after twenty years. Had Columbia not managed to pull these rights back from Geffen, it would have lost not only earnings from the band's current popularity but also any interest in previous recordings. Knowing this, Aerosmith managed to negotiate a very good deal.

For both artists and companies, a second and perhaps more attractive aspect of back catalogues came from the practice of linking particular groups and songs with particular films or products. The success of *Singles,* both the movie and the soundtrack, again demonstrated the value of cross-media marketing and the symbiotic relationship between film and popular song. Advertising proved to be even more lucrative, whether it was the Beatles selling sneakers, Elton John crooning for Sassoon, or Madonna shilling for Pepsi. By this time, record companies had begun to think of themselves more as exploiters of rights than producers of records. Their new mission was to develop as many "revenue streams" as possible. For a while, they were on a roll. Then the bottom fell out—well, sort of.

In his 1996 front-page, year-end wrap-up for the *New York Times*, Neil Strauss noted, "Growth in the $12 billion [U.S.] record industry, which for more than a decade has ranged from 12 to 20 percent annually, has slowed to a virtual standstill."[26] Strauss and others offered a number of explanations for the phenomenon: record companies chasing hit singles rather than building long-term careers; the industry focusing on new technologies instead of the music; a natural decline in catalogue sales as baby boomers completed the replacement of their black vinyl collections; the failure of the industry to recognize the potential of "urban music"; and the industry's typical reliance on a handful of superstars.

Interestingly, some of the biggest superstars no longer sold like superstars. In the early 1990s, new releases by Madonna and Prince (who, after his adoption of an unpronounceable name, was called "the artist formerly known as Prince" or simply "the Artist") rose and fell on the charts as never before. Prince sustained himself with three greatest hits packages; Madonna, with a $50 "art" book—*Sex*—of suggestive photographs of herself. Pearl Jam outsold Michael Jackson. By 1996, the industry's superstar strategy seemed like it might be in need of an overhaul, as many multiplatinum artists turned in products that fell far short of previous releases and record company expectations. Hootie and the Blowfish, who owned 1995 with *Cracked Rear View* (9.2 million units sold), followed up with 1996's *Fairweather Johnson* at only 2 million. Sheryl Crow's sales went from 3.8 million for her blockbuster *Tuesday Night Music Club* (1993) to a mere half million for *Sheryl Crow* (1996). Even Pearl Jam, whose *Vs.* and *Vitalogy* catapulted them to the top of the charts, sold less than 1 million units of *No Code* in 1996. Following the success of *Monster* at 2.7 million units sold, R.E.M. kicked off their new $80 million contract with *New Adventures in Hi-Fi* way below expectations at under 1 million. There is a particular note of irony in this brand of industry-think that is worth calling attention to: it is only in the context of sales of 5 to 10 million units that sales of "only" 1 million can be considered "disappointing." Most artists would be deliriously happy with such figures.

Nevertheless, with an overall pattern of flat sales, it was clear that the industry was in trouble, even if only temporarily. Within eighteen months of each other, the Wherehouse, Peaches, and Camelot outlets, three of the largest record retail chains in the country, filed for bankruptcy. Four of the six major labels responded to the crisis with significant staff cuts.

Those who remained had their musical antennae out for signs of The Next Big Thing. As 1996 drew to a close, all the indicators seemed to point toward urban dance music. These suspicions were seemingly confirmed when WKTU, New York's Top 40/Dance station, became the number one station in the market, with the largest listening audience in the country (which is exactly what happened when the same station converted to an all-disco format some twenty years earlier). For a good part of 1997 then, the music industry tried to engineer a top-down campaign to promote what it called *electronica,* a catch-all term that included everything from hip hop, dance pop remixes, and r&b-flavoured dance music to the sounds of acid house, techno, and their multiple variants, which had been seeping into the United States from England and the continent for a number of years. During this period, this music was the subject of countless news articles and, subsequently, of a number of academic books as well.[27]

Electronic Dance Music

The story of house and techno, the major styles that constituted *electronica,* is a complex and convoluted tale of transatlantic cross-fertilization and ever-evolving substyles and scenes, which were complicated further by multiple, and at times conflicting, interpretations of musical categories, cross-racial codes, sexual etiquette, the significance of drug use, and the meaning of subcultural style.[28] Although the British and continental styles of these musics have dominated both academic discourse and public understanding of these sounds, their formative influences date back to late 1970s/early 1980s Chicago, Detroit, and New York. Long before pivotal British figures such as Paul Oakenfeld, Danny and Jenni Rampling, and Nicky Holloway returned from a rented villa in Ibiza to revitalize the stagnant British club scene with fashionable dance-oriented nightspots such as Spectrum, the Trip, and Shoom (named after the sensation of an Ecstasy rush)—all precursors to Britain's rave culture—the music that had captured their bodies and spirits issued from seminal DJ/producers like Frankie Knuckles in Chicago, Larry Levan in New York, and Juan Atkins, Derrick May, and Kevin Saunderson (the Belleville Three) in Detroit.

Knuckles had moved to Chicago to spin at the dance club the Warehouse in 1977 (where he remained until 1983), after the position was turned down by his New York colleague, the legendary Larry Levan. The audience at the Warehouse, which was located in what was then a desolate industrial area, favoured up-tempo disco mixes drawn from a mixture of Philadelphia soft soul, New York dance music, and Eurodisco, played at

Frankie Knuckles is credited with developing the sound of house music at the Warehouse in Chicago.

around 124 beats per minute. The original music that developed from this sensibility was called *house music* after the Warehouse, its place of origin. Knuckles assembled his disco remixes on reel-to-reel tape, adding his own machine-made four-to-the-floor kick drum (a defining sound of house), beefed-up bass, and other special effects like his signature locomotive steam engine sound. Two labels—Trax and DJ International—handled most of the output of Chicago house. Jesse Saunders and Vince Lawrence's remix of First Choice's "On and On" (Trax, 1983) is generally acknowledged to be the first commercially available house recording, and "Love Can't Turn Around," by Farley "Jackmaster" Funk and Jesse Saunders (on DJ International), became house's first international hit, breaking into the U.K. Top Ten in 1986. The predominant dance style at the Warehouse was called *jacking*, referring to a type of frenzied, sexualized body movements. As house became popular in Britain, a number of "jack tracks" actually made the British charts. In 1987, "Jack the Groove," by Raze, hit U.K. number twenty and Steve Silk Hurley's "Jack Your Body" went all the way to U.K. number one. Chicago made it clear that disco hadn't died; it had simply returned underground. And underground meant it had returned to its roots in mostly black and Latino gay club culture. "House didn't just resurrect disco," asserts Simon Reynolds, "it intensified the very aspects that most offended the discophobes: the mechanistic repetition, the synthetic and electronic textures, the rootlessness, the 'depraved' hypersexuality and 'decadent' drugginess."[29]

Chicago made it clear that disco hadn't died; it had simply returned underground. And underground meant it had returned to its roots in mostly black and Latino gay club culture.

Meanwhile, in New York, Larry Levan was spinning for a more upscale gay crowd at the Paradise Garage, home to the slower, more soulful variant of the music, which came to be known as *garage.* There he transformed his remixes of Loose Joints' "Is It All over My Face" (1980), Taana Gardner's "Heartbeat" (1980), ESG's "Moody" (1981), and N.Y.C. Peech Boys' "Don't Make Me Wait" (1982) into dance floor magic. When Frankie Knuckles sent him a copy of Jamie Principle's "Baby Wants to Ride" (Trax, 1984), Levan "flipped over it and started playing it at the Garage," thereby exposing house to a broader audience.[30]

In the Detroit area, Atkins, May, and Saunderson, three middle-class blacks from the suburb of Belleville, had cut their musical teeth on the sounds of radio deejay Charles "the Electrifyin' Mojo" Johnson's heady, eclectic mixes of everything from Prince and Parliament/Funkadelic to Kraftwerk and electropop from Europe on his "Midnight Funk Association" show on WGPR. Each went on to start his own record label and recording ensemble. Atkins began transforming Mojo's eclectic tastes into a fresh original sound when he started the DJ collective/record label/publishing company Deep Space (with May and others). With partner Rik Davis, he began releasing his own records as Cybotron, whose "Alleys of Your Mind" (1981)[31] shares the spotlight with the lesser-known "Sharevari" by A Number of Names as the first techno recording. With appropriate props to Kraftwerk, Cybotron produced funkier, rhythmically more complicated tracks, featuring Atkins' deep, resonant vocals and a background of murky psychedelic sounds. In 1983, Cybotron released its first album, *Enter,* whose single "Clear" hit number fifty-two on the *Billboard* Top Black Singles chart. Derrick May established Transmat Records in 1986 and hit his stride performing as Rhythim Is Rhythim in 1987. Using the rich bank of bass guitar sounds in the Yamaha DX-100 keyboard to produce complex staccato bass lines, overlain with other purposefully electronic sounds, May's 1987 releases, "Nude Photo" and "Strings of Life," the latter of which sampled strings from the Detroit

Symphony Orchestra, became defining moments in the evolution of techno. While Atkins became the spiritual leader of techno and May its chief alchemist, it was Kevin Saunderson who achieved the greatest commercial success. Forming the group Inner City to record his pop/dance crossover single, "Big Fun," issued on his own KMS label, Saunderson released *Big Fun* in 1989. It spawned four hit singles ("Big Fun," "Good Life," "Ain't Nobody Better," and "Do You Love What You Feel"), all of which went to number one on the dance charts, with "Good Life" crossing over to pop as well.

These, then, were the sounds that took British club culture by storm in the late 1980s, aided significantly by the warm, feel-good rush provided by the drug Ecstasy, or E for short. By then, Americans had begun to import some homegrown British product, such as M/A/R/R/S' "Pump Up the Volume," which went to number eleven on the U.S. pop charts in 1988. In British club culture, that summer became known as the "Second Summer of Love." Given the physio-psychedelic qualities of Ecstasy and its central role in the scene, the music came to be known as *acid house.* The particular mix of cultural elements also produced some remarkable gender-bending effects. According to Simon Reynolds, "Gay behavioural codes and modes of expression were entering the body-consciousness of straight working-class boys, via Ecstasy."[32] This new sensibility was evident in "Acid Trax," by Chicago's Phuture, and was based on the gooey bass bleep produced by the Roland TB-303 synthesizer and reflected in popular British dance club singles such as Jolly Roger's "Acid Man" and D-Mob's "We Call It Acieed," which went to number three on the British charts.

If the influence of Ecstasy tended to bend gender roles, the white-dominated (but racially more integrated) club scene in Britain tended to obscure the origins and formative influences of the music. Techno originally entered Britain as a subset of house imports; it was codified as black dance music but was not specifically labeled *techno* until Virgin Records released the compilation *Techno: The Dance Sound of Detroit* in 1988. After imports from the U.S. melded with homegrown product and morphed into acid house, the scene outgrew the confines of downtown clubs and expanded to all-night events—raves—with crowds of up to 20,000 "turning on, tuning in, and freaking out" in aircraft hangers, abandoned warehouses, and open fields along London's M25 Orbital highway. There ensued a moral panic about the drug excesses of the burgeoning rave culture. In this context, the term *acid house*—given its explicit drug reference— became less serviceable as a category. After applying numerous alternative adjectives to the word *house,* the movers and shakers in the scene settled on the term *techno,* but as an umbrella term that included the various electronic dance styles coming out of Britain and the continent—a definition far removed from the music's Detroit origins. As Sarah Thornton puts it, "the shift from the first to the second kind of techno, from a 'black' to a 'white' sound, is accompanied by a shift in the discourses about their places of origin. Later techno was said to be a musical Esperanto. It was not considered to be the sound of any particular city or any definite group but rather as a celebration of rootlessness."[33] Thus, when this later techno was fed back into the United States following its immense overseas popularity, it was bundled with an aura of white Europeanness. "In Detroit," asserts Simon Reynolds, "everybody assumed Cybotron were white guys from Europe," a perception that was no doubt fed by the group's liberal appropriation of Kraftwerk and other sounds associated with the European avant garde.[34]

When techno was fed back into the United States following its immense overseas popularity, it was bundled with an aura of white Europeanness.

As British rave culture fragmented into progressively narrower scenes, the house/techno sound underwent further transformations into various substyles including deep house, hardcore, ambient, hip house, jungle (a.k.a. drum and base), and trip hop, among others. For active participants within the scene, these changes represented subtle but important nuances in the continual evolution of usage and meaning. As a second generation of young energetic ravers pushed the heart rate of house toward its more up-tempo and anthemic variant hardcore that rocked the body to new extremes with tracks such as Unique 3's "The Theme," Shut Up and Dance's "Raving I'm Raving," and the Prodigy's "Charly" and "Everybody in the Place," there was also a resurgence of interest in chill-out ambient music to replenish the spirit. Examples include the KLF's *Chill Out,* 808 State's "Pacific State," S'Express' "Mantra for a State of Mind," and the Orb's "Fluffy Little Clouds," "Backside of the Moon" (a thinly veiled reference to Pink Floyd), and "A Huge Evergrowing Pulsating Brain That Rules from the Centre of the Ultraworld." For the more sedentary, there was Warp's self-described "electronic listening music" compilation, *Artificial Intelligence* (1992).

From another point of view, these scenic changes also signaled social and aesthetic divisions along the fault lines of class, sexual orientation, and, in particular, race. One of the initial splits in class-sensitive British rave culture came when the first generation of the upper working-class trendy in-crowd expanded to include the less hip "acid teds"—a disparaging play on the teddy boys of the 1960s, used to describe clueless, and presumably lower-class, newcomers. In gender terms, Sarah Thornton points out that "in America, house and acid house were perceived first and foremost as gay and could be heard only in gay clubs until they were re-exported back to the United States as 'English acid house.'"[35] As for race, genre names such as *rock* and *rhythm and blues* have always been racially coded. Rave culture was no different. When adjectives like *progressive* or *intelligent* were used to prefix a style—as in progressive house or intelligent techno—they were often indicators that the music had been drained of its African American influences and also marked something of a retreat from dance culture itself. Warp's *Artificial Intelligence* compilation could be described in such terms.

As the hypersyncopated breakbeats of hardcore attracted more black Britons to the rave scene, more black influences started showing up in the music. Jungle was such a phenomenon. Lacking the metronomic four-to-the-floor kick drum that underpins much of house and disco, jungle combined samples from reggae imports with deep hip hop baselines and layers of percussion so dense that for many ravers it was too polyrhythmic for them to find the beat. Credit for the first use of the term probably goes to black promoter Paul Chambers, proprietor of the Ibiza label, who released a white label (uncredited) single called "Jungle Techno" around 1992, borrowing the title from James Brown's *In the Jungle Groove* album. Curiously, according to Matthew Collin, jungle was immediately understood as "black youth reasserting control over what was originally the black music of Chicago, New York and Detroit," even though it was widely known and accepted that half the DJs and producers contributing to the style were white.[36] Among junglists, the substances of choice went from Ecstasy and speed to marijuana and champagne. If the stereotype of the hardcore raver had been "a sweaty, shirtless white teenager," the stereotypical junglist was "a head-nodding, stylishly dressed black twenty-something with hooded eyes, a joint in one hand, and a bottle of champagne in the other."[37] If the term *jungle* was complicated, it was also controversial, conjuring up images of primitivism, urban violence, and miscegenation.

If the term jungle was complicated, it was also controversial, conjuring up images of primitivism, urban violence, and miscegenation. For many in the scene, the term drum and bass was a more acceptable alternative, since that was primarily what the music was about anyway.

There were plenty of pejorative examples of the term in popular culture to point to, from the fear of the "jungle rhythms" of 1920s jazz and early rock 'n' roll, mesmerizing young followers by inverting the Eurocentric primacy of melody over rhythm, to the depiction of mid-1950s school violence in films like *Blackboard Jungle,* or Spike Lee's take on the difficulties of miscegenation in *Jungle Fever.* Shut Up and Dance, a highly politicized rave duo ("White White World," "Autobiography of a Crackhead," "Raving I'm Raving"), who described themselves as "a fast hip hop group," denounced the term as racist. For many in the scene, the term *drum and bass* was a more acceptable alternative, since that was primarily what the music was about anyway.

The first artists to experiment with the jungle style of distilling breakbeats into complex percussive webs were DJs like Fabio and Grooverider, who drew on a panoply of influences including house, hardcore, reggae, hip hop, soul, jazz, ambient, and techno. But it was Goldie who put the sound over the top. A veteran of the hip hop break-dancing and graffiti art scene, Goldie joined 4 Hero's Reinforced label crew, where he participated in marathon sessions of "sampladelic research" and released tracks as part of Rufige Cru and under his own alias, Metalheadz. Goldie made his mark with a track called "Terminator," on which he perfected the junglist technique of time-stretching—using pitch control to create the illusion of changing tempos that actually remain constant. Goldie's masterpiece, "Timeless," the title track of the 1995 album of the same name, appeared shortly after two other concept jungle albums—4 Hero's *Parallel Universe* and A Guy Called Gerald's *Black Secret Technology. Timeless*, in the words of Simon Reynolds, stands as jungle's *Sgt. Pepper*—"half genre-bending brilliance, half ill-advised attempts to prove Goldie's versatility."[38] Because jungle tended to explore the underside of rave culture, it was labeled *dark* and invariably linked—as were black youth more generally—to violence and the use of harder drugs. At this point, the scene split, again along racial lines, with white ravers gravitating toward the more upbeat sounds of happy hardcore in a nostalgic attempt to regain the feel-good vibe of the Ecstasy culture.

Just as the term *jungle* proved difficult, the term *trip hop* was reviled both by its practitioners, who considered it a media invention, and by its detractors, who saw nothing new in the music. Trip hop, based primarily in Bristol, was an ethereal, down-tempo form of hip hop, designed mostly for listening. Contrary to the attitude and the "keepin' it real" imperatives of U.S. hip hop, trip hop's goal was to keep it as unreal as possible. Its best-known practitioners included Massive Attack, Tricky, Portishead, and LA-based DJ Shadow. The style was defined with the 1991 release of Massive Attack's *Blue Lines,* which included raps by Tricky and instrumental programming by Portishead's Geoff Barrow. While *Blue Lines* retains the essence of hip hop—breakbeat rhythms and looped samples—it also includes atmospheric guitar riffs and trance-like melodies and proceeds at a disarmingly tranquil 90 bpm or less. If the tempo of the music was any indicator of the pace of the group's life, it should not be surprising that it took Massive Attack three years to record a follow-up. *Protection* (1994) was less well received than *Blue Lines*, but its sequel, *No Protection* (1995), fared considerably better. Portishead's *Dummy* (1994) effectively employed Beth Gibbons' bluesy vocals and elements of house and film soundtrack music to create an album with broad appeal that went beyond the rave culture to include alternative rock and world beat fans as well. *Dummy* received the prestigious Mercury

Music Prize and sold 150,000 copies in the United States after "Sour Times" went into regular rotation on MTV. DJ Shadow, a white b-boy from southern California, gained attention abroad (but not in the United States) as a master sampler on the strength of singles like "Entropy," "In Flux," "Lost and Found," and "What Does Your Soul Look Like?" His debut album, *Endtroducing* (1996), issued on Mo'Wax, was greeted with critical acclaim, even though Shadow remained a virtual unknown in the U.S. hip hop scene.

Tricky was easily the most colourful figure in the trip hop scene. Appearing at times in a wedding dress and mascara, Tricky played with gender as much as he played with genre. Following the success of his first single, "Aftermath," on which he established a full-time collaboration with vocalist Martina, his debut album, *Maxinquaye* (1995), entered the British charts at number two. In this album, he tackled issues of the drug culture that were often sidestepped and combined a sense of social consciousness with ponderous rhythms, orchestral arrangements, and ominous background sounds. All in all, this was quite a package. In the words of Simon Reynolds: "Racially, stylistically, sexually, Tricky is one slippery fellow. *Maxinquaye* is an unclassifiable hybrid of club and bedroom music, black and white, rap and melody, song and atmospherics, sampladelic textures and real-time instrumentation. It sucks you into the polysexual, transgeneric, mongrelized mindspace inside Tricky's skull."[36] Following his second album, *Nearly God,* a collection of tracks featuring Björk, Neneh Cherry, Cath Coffey, Alison Moyet, and others, Tricky was signed by Polygram for *Pre-Millennium Tension* (1996).

> *Tricky was easily the most colourful figure in the trip hop scene. Appearing at times in a wedding dress and mascara, Tricky played with gender as much as he played with genre.*

These, then, were the rough contours of the house/techno scene abroad as the U.S. music industry began to take notice and tried to lump everything into the catch-all category *electronica*. As 1997 dawned, the groups to watch were the Prodigy, the Chemical Brothers, Underworld, and the most recognizable DJ/producer of them all—Moby. The prodigy behind the Prodigy, Liam Howlett—a classically trained pianist turned hip hop b-boy—burst onto the rave/hardcore scene with "Charly" (1991), which hit number one on the British dance charts and crossed over to pop number three. Harnessing rave energy to pop appeal, titles like "Hyperspeed," "Full Throttle," and "G-Force" captured the youthful exuberance of Prodigy's music. Their debut album, *The Prodigy Experience* (1992), which was picked up by Elektra in the United States, added polished pop hooks to the breakbeat foundation already evident in hardcore. While Prodigy may have been considered hopelessly commercial by the ultra-hip—they were playing at rock festivals by this time—Howlett continued to release underground singles that passed muster on the dance floor and the group's 1994 double album, *Music for the Gilted Generation,* launched an all-out assault against the British Criminal Justice and Public Order Act's crackdown on illegal raves. Following the success of their nonalbum single, "Firestarter" (U.K. number one, U.S. number five), there ensued a bidding war for their contract, with Madonna's Maverick label ultimately winning out. The Prodigy's aptly titled third album, *The Fat of the Land* (1997), went straight to number one in the United States—and just about everywhere else.

The Chemical Brothers rose to popularity on the wings of a rave-meets-rock 'n' roll hybrid called *big beat,* which also included artists like Fatboy Slim and Bently Rhythm Ace. Beginning musical life as the Dust Brothers (a name that had to be abandoned for legal reasons), Chemicals Ed Simmons and Tom Rowlands debuted with *Exit Planet Dust* (1995), a compilation of bombastic guitar-laden, siren-screeching, but still dance floor–friendly techno for headbangers. They extended their rock credentials on the follow-up single, "Setting Sun," a collaborative effort with Oasis' Noel Gallagher supplying the vocals. *Dig Your Own Hole* (1997)—which entered the British charts at number one, and U.S. charts at number fourteen—was an even more eclectic, hard-rocking album, under-pinned with layered rhythms and sophisticated electronics. In a similar vein, Underworld started as a funk rock group but evolved toward a more techno (but still rock-oriented) sound with the addition of DJ Darren Emerson. Following the success of *Dubnobasswithmyheadman* (1994), Underworld scored a U.S. deal with TVT. *Second Toughest in the Infants* (1996) was released to critical acclaim, with the nonalbum single, "Born Slippy"—featured in the soundtrack to *Trainspotting*—boosting sales of the album. While these groups were built on a firm foundation of electronic dance music, part of what enabled them to succeed in the U.S. pop market was their more rock-like presentation as bands. The lure of even their limited success was strong enough to convince veteran rockers like U2 to flirt with the techno style, as they did on the techno-influenced *Pop* (1997). And, of course, there was Madonna, who had always kept at least one foot in the dance market.

New York–based Moby took a somewhat different tack. Born Richard Melville Hall, Moby became a radical Christian and a vegan activist. While he was the first techno producer to become a full-fledged pop celebrity, he also aspired to be an everyman. He tried to blend into his surroundings the same way his music blended into its various cultural settings. Based on his successful remix of the theme from *Twin Peaks,* which he titled "Go," and his high-energy eponymous debut techno album in 1992, Moby came to the attention of Elektra Records, for whom he recorded *Everything Is Wrong* in 1994 to critical raves but no corresponding commercial success. In 1996, he abandoned the techno to pursue an agenda of political activism and progressive rock on *Animal Rights*. While he returned to techno for *I Like to Score* (1997), it wasn't until 1999, after parting company with Elektra, that Moby hit his stride with *Play*, released by the independent V2 label. *Play* was a master stroke of musical production—Robert Christgau called it "the Moby album we've been waiting for"—as well as a marketing triumph for Moby's handlers. With tracks that worked as well in restaurants and movies as in clubs, the ubiquitous *Play* eventually achieved multiplatinum certification. But if there was genius in the tracks, it was equaled by the genius of the marketing strategy. All eighteen of the tracks on *Play* were licensed for use in films, television programs, and advertisements before the album peaked on the charts. According to *Wired*: "The dozen and a half songs on *Play* . . . have been sold hundreds of times for commercials, movies, and TV shows—a licensing venture so staggeringly lucrative that the album was a financial success months before it reached its multi-platinum sales total."[40]

Richie Hawtin, from Windsor, Ontario, while never a superstar in mainstream circles, is an internationally renowned DJ who played an important role in the second wave of techno artists associated with Detroit in the early 1990s. In partnership with John Acquaviva from London, Ontario, Hawtin founded the influential Plus 8 record label. His early recordings under the moniker Plastikman and later albums under his own name, such as 1999's *Decks, EFX & 909,* are among the finest techno recordings ever made.

Montreal has also been an influential centre of electronica, with DJs such as Kid Koala and Marc Leclair, a.k.a. Akufen, achieving global prominence. It is significant that both the Force Inc. and Ninja Tune labels decided to locate their North American offices in Montreal. Force Inc.'s *Clicks and Cuts* compilations were seminal in the establishment of the concept of glitch. During the 1990s, Toronto had a major rave scene and was home to techno wizard DJ Algorithm (Jeff Milligan). Although operating on a smaller scale, Vancouver, Winnipeg, and Halifax also had active electronica scenes, each with their own labels and DJs.

Electronica as an enterprise never became The Next Big Thing the music industry had hoped for. Ultimately, it had to be admitted that electronic dance music, in its most effective form, was the product of master turntablists and remixers—propeller-heads working with samplers, drum machines, and computers (Moby was more likely to grace the cover of *Wired* than *Rolling Stone*), rather than the charismatic frontmen and -women who fit more easily into the industry's conception of superstars. As such, electronica remained the province of the underground, in the able hands of DJ crews like San Francisco's Invisibl Skratch Piklz and New York's X-ecutioners. Aside from 808 State's "Bombadin," Jam and Spoon's "Right in the Night," and a handful

Ultimately, it had to be admitted that electronic dance music in its most effective form was the product of master turntablists and remixers—propeller-heads working with samplers, drum machines, and computers, rather than the charismatic frontmen and -women who fit more | easily into the industry's conception of superstars. As such, it remained the province of the underground.

of other foreign imports, the cuts that dominated the American and Canadian dance charts in the late 1990s were club remixes of artists from other genres: Björk, who later married Goldie ("Big Time Sensuality"), Canadians k.d. lang ("Lifted by Love," "Sexuality"), and Celine Dion ("Misled"), Reba McEntire

As a DJ, Richie Hawtin was noted for constructing intelligent techno sets that creatively fused turntablism, drum machines, and various digital effects.

("You Keep Me Hanging On"), Gloria Estefan ("You'll Be Mine [Party Time]," "Tres Deseos [Three Wishes]," "Reach"), and Toni Braxton ("You're Making Me High," "Un-break My Heart," "I Don't Want To"). *Billboard*'s Marilyn Gillen had already summed up the fate of electronica as a commercial trend at the end of 1997: "The planned phenomenon of 'electronica' was still being assessed as the year closed out, though its impact on cash registers seemed less than electric."[41]

Veterans in the music business are not at all shy about admitting that nobody ever knows what The Next Big Thing will be before it happens. The trick from their point of view is to be able to spot a trend as soon as it happens and ride the wave for as long as they can. In this, the majors, with deeper pockets to see them through a drought and superior marketing and distribution to cash in on a trend, are particularly well positioned. When grunge looked like it might take off, major label talent scouts were all over Seattle. The industry tried to engineer a trend with electronica, but as a dance music based on studio-produced singles, there was little hope that it could be effectively adapted to the superstar strategy. In the second half of the decade, then, the music industry found itself following and trying to exploit trends based not so much on genre but rather on gender, age, and ethnicity—The Year of the Woman, The Year of Teen Pop, and The Year of Latin(o) Music—only to realize, once again, that rap was still the biggest thing.

The Year(s) of the Woman and the Rage Rock Backlash

Although women make up more than 50 percent of the population, they are usually underrepresented in the upper reaches of most fields of endeavour, including popular music. Consequently, when women break through, it is considered a trend. Writing in the *Boston Globe,* Steve Morse identified this trend when he opened his year-end roundup with the sentence: "Time to call 1996 what it was: pop music's Year of the Woman."[42] Morse noted not only the superstar entries of two Canadians—Alanis Morissette with *Jagged Little Pill,* the best-selling album of the year, and Celine Dion with the multiplatinum *Falling into You*—but also the impact of lesser-known artists like Joan Osborne, Natalie Merchant, Ani DiFranco, Tori Amos, Suzanne Vega, and Shawn Colvin, as well as women fronting mixed-gender groups such as Delores O'Riordan (the Cranberries), Gwen Stefani (No Doubt), and Lauryn Hill (Fugees). In fact, the six best-selling albums of the year were by women or woman-fronted groups. In addition to albums by Morissette and Dion, there were Mariah Carey's *Daydream,* the Fugees' *The Score,* Shania Twain's *The Woman in Me,* and the all-female soundtrack to *Waiting to Exhale.* The following year revealed a similar pattern, with women taking five of the six top spots. Newcomers included the Spice Girls (*Spice*), No Doubt (*Tragic Kingdom*), Jewel (*Pieces of You*), and LeAnn Rimes (*Blue*).

A number of things were striking about the Year of the Woman trend. One was the number of different genres that were represented, including pop/dance (Mariah Carey, Spice Girls), alternative/pop rock (Alanis Morissette), folk rock (Jewel), country (Shania Twain, LeAnn Rimes), and hip hop (Lauryn Hill). Equally interesting was the number of women at the top of pop stardom who hailed from Canada. Given that Canadians Alanis Morissette, Celine Dion, and Shania Twain were three of the six biggest sellers of the year, 1996 might well have been called the Year of the Canadian Woman. Celine Dion carried the Canadian torch into 1998, dominating the top two slots with a central presence on the soundtrack to *Titanic,* followed by

Sarah McLachlan rose to prominence in the Year(s) of the Woman and founded Lilith Fair, the most important women's tour of the decade.

her own *Let's Talk About Love*, with Shania Twain close on her heels at number five with *Come On Over,* the album that eventually set an all-time sales record for a female artist. They were joined by fellow Canadian singer/songwriter Sarah McLachlan, whose aptly titled *Surfacing,* (released on Vancouver's Nettwerk Records) which began its ascent in 1997, announced her entrance into the elite of pop superstars.

McLachlan had developed a solid career as a singer/songwriter beginning with her debut album, *Touch,* in 1989. After returning from a journey to Southeast Asia, where she worked on a Canadian documentary about poverty and child sexual abuse, she was inspired to return to the studio. She hit her stride on *Fumbling Towards Ecstasy* (1994). In 1996, she turned her energy to founding Lilith Fair, which she described as a "Celebration of Women in Music," featuring only female-led acts (although at times male backup musicians outnumbered the women on stage). Lilith Fair was the most successful concert tour of 1997. Between 1997 and 1999, the final year of the festival, it grew into a multicity, multidate event featuring dozens of artists on multiple stages. Lilith Fair was to women what Lollapalooza was to alternative: a spectacular showcase that demonstrated that women could succeed against all odds. And as with Lollapalooza,

> *Lilith Fair was to women what Lollapalooza was to alternative: a spectacular showcase for women that demonstrated that it could succeed against all odds. And as with Lollapalooza, there was an attempt to inject a social consciousness into the event, to give something back.*

there was an attempt to inject a social consciousness into the event, to give something back. With one dollar from every ticket sold being donated to a charitable organization, Lilith Fair was able to distribute some $700,000 in 1997 alone to a variety of progressive women's organizations such as Planned Parenthood, the Breast Cancer Fund, the Rape, Abuse and Incest National Network, and LIFEbeat, an AIDS awareness group. Throughout the fair's run, McLachlan maintained a hands-on relationship to the festival and was the only headliner to perform every date. While she is to be credited with selfless devotion to the cause, this success came bundled with a considerable financial payoff. *Surfacing* was released just prior to the 1997 blockbuster tour. Her strong presence at the festival helped propel the album to four times platinum sales, generating three hit singles in the process. By the time she called it quits in 1999, her *Mirrorball* album was in the Top Ten.

Lilith Fair was criticized for gravitating toward the softer end of the female performance spectrum, focusing primarily on singer/songwriters like Fiona Apple ("Criminal"), Paula Cole ("Where Have All the Cowboys Gone"), Shawn Colvin ("Summer Came Home"), Joan Osborne ("One of Us"), and Suzanne Vega ("Luka"). "The cartoon image of Lilith," wrote

James Sullivan retrospectively in the *San Francisco Chronicle,* "has been one of anguished young maidens with wispy songs to sing."[43] As the festival grew in popularity, however, it also grew in diversity. In 1998 and 1999, it included performances by Erykah Badu ("On and On"), Missy "Misdemeanor" Elliott ("Hot Boyz"), Lauryn Hill ("Doo Wop [That Thing]"), Queen Latifah ("Ladies First"), Me'Shell Ndegéocello ("Wild Night," with John Mellencamp), and the Dixie Chicks ("There's Your Trouble"), as well as Bonnie Raitt, Sinéad O'Connor, and the Pretenders. Even teen sensation Christina Aguilera came on board briefly in 1999. Asked where all this variation had been in 1997, McLachlan responded: "We asked them all last year and they said no."[44] By 1999, it looked like Lilith would be concluding with a more powerful sound. Comic Sandra Bernhard captured this spirit as she railed against the previously softer sound in a caustic comic routine at 1999's San Francisco show, actually naming Alanis Morissette and Fiona Apple as offenders. "Will somebody please give me an old fashioned, sweaty, bitch of rock 'n' roll?" she bellowed.[45]

During this period, female artists not only demonstrated that they could compete with men on an equal footing commercially but also proved to be a superior artistic force dominating the 1999 Grammy Awards. In a sweep that the *Globe*'s Morse dubbed, once again, the Year of the Woman, top honours went to Sheryl Crow, Alanis Morissette, Shania Twain, the Dixie Chicks, Madonna, Celine Dion, whose single "My Heart Will Go On," from the film *Titanic,* dominated the airwaves, and Lauryn Hill, who went home with five trophies, a new record for a female artist. Crow took Best Rock Album for *The Globe Sessions* and Morissette walked away with Best Rock Song (and Best Female Rock Vocal Performance) for "Uninvited." The Dixie Chicks upset Shania Twain for Best Country Album, but Shania shared the writing credits for Best Country Song and walked off with Best Female Country Vocal for "You're Still the One." Madonna picked up Best Pop Album and Best Dance Recording for *Ray of Light.* Additional awards to women included Brandy and Monica ("The Boy Is Mine") and Patti LaBelle ("Live! One Night Only") in the r&b category, and Deniece Williams and Cissy Houston in gospel. Patti Page won Best Traditional Pop Vocal Performance.

The youngest of fourteen children, Celine Dion had been a veteran of the francophone Quebec music scene since she began performing in her parents' club at age five. When she made her bid for international stardom, she did so on the strength of her first all-English album, *Unison,* referred to as a "bold declaration of independence" on her record company website. When the album crossed over national and linguistic boundaries as planned, Dion scrambled to appease her French-speaking base by very publicly refusing to accept the Canadian Félix Award for Anglophone Artist of the Year. Still, it was clear that, to some extent, her career choices were subject to the dictates of U.S. tastemakers. On her second all-English album, *Celine Dion* (1992), she was paired with such notable songwriters as Diane Warren and Prince, who supplied "With This Tear." The album also includes "Beauty and the Beast," the title song from the animated film of the same name. While Dion continues to record in both languages, she was confirmed as an international superstar with *Falling into You* (1996), which became the best-selling album of the year and won both the Album of the Year and Best Pop Album Grammys. The album to date has sold more than 25 million copies worldwide. *Let's Talk About Love* (1999) was released on the same day as the soundtrack of the motion picture *Titanic.* The ubiquitous "My Heart Will Go On," featured on both albums, pushed them to sales of 27 million units internationally.

Lauryn Hill had more options than most people. Before she was out of high school she had appeared at an amateur night at the Apollo Theater, landed a recurring role on the soap opera *As the World Turns,* and had a part as a high school diva in the Whoopi Goldberg film *Sister Act 2.* In addition, she wrote poetry, played on her high school basketball team, ran track, and was a cheerleader and homecoming queen. Clearly, she could have gone in many directions. She chose to go to Columbia and continue to work with childhood friends Wyclef Jean and Prakazrel ("Pras") Michel as a member of the Fugees, whose album *The Score* (1996)—at 17 million units—was the best-selling hip hop album ever. Propelled by Hill's infectious vocal on the commercially oriented cover of "Killing Me Softly," *The Score* was the socially conscious hip hop album of the year, its combination of deep beats and insightful commentary juxtaposed with an incredible musicality. Before launching her solo career, Hill took time off to give birth to her son, Zion, fathered by Bob Marley's son Rohan, a move she was advised against by career-conscious naysayers. Throughout all this, she never forgot the activism that defined the Fugees, as she continued to work with the Refugee Project, an organization she started in 1996 to assist underprivileged and at-risk youths.

The Miseducation of Lauryn Hill (1998) was Hill's solo debut—a big-band jazz-meets-hip-hop extravaganza incorporating soul, rap, reggae, and hip hop into its own hybrid. It earned her the Album of the Year, Best New Artist, R&B Song, R&B Album, and R&B Vocal Performance Grammys. The album's title was inspired by *The Miseducation of the Negro,* by Carter G. Woodson, and critical praise was nearly unequivocal. Hill's largely autobiographical work touched on issues ranging from racism and sexism to spirituality and self-confession, eliciting comparisons to such touchstone works as Marvin Gaye's *What's Goin' On* and Joni Mitchell's *Blue.* In addition to the warmth and sensitivity of her delicious vocals, Hill also brought considerable savvy to the studio as the album's producer and incredible grace to the Grammy Awards. Still, she had no illusions about the orientation of the music industry. "This is a very sexist industry," she exclaimed. "They'll never throw the genius title to a sister. They'll just call her 'diva' and think it's a compliment. It's like our flair and vanity are put before our musical and intellectual contributions."[46]

Perhaps it was the overwhelming success of Lilith Fair or the continued dominance of women in the pop arena, but 1999 definitely marked the beginning of a backlash to the preponderance of women in high places. While even some of the female singer/songwriters like Alanis Morissette had been described as "angry"—in her case because of her Catholic schoolgirl torments and the uncensored lyrics of "You Oughta Know"—they did not compare to the fury that issued from a collection of rock bands who were labeled *rage rockers* by the press. The acts most often mentioned included Korn, Limp Bizkit, and Kid Rock.

Alanis Morisette's 1995 hit single "You Oughta Know" represented the epitome of the angry female post-punk singer/songwriter.

All came from white working-class and mostly southern backgrounds, all combined elements of rock and rap in their music, and all had achieved platinum sales. They came together at an event that was reported in the press as the antithesis of Lilith Fair—Woodstock '99. "If Lilith catapulted women front and center in the popular culture," opined the *Boston Globe*'s Joan Anderman, "Woodstock '99 flung them not merely back into the wings but to a far darker place, where men rule with iron—and if it suits them, violent—fists."[47]

Woodstock '99 was staged at Griffis Air Force Base in Rome, New York, essentially a slab of concrete surrounded by barbed wire, with nary a shade tree in sight. The promoters could not have selected a more inhospitable site. While nudity abounded in 1967, the vibe in 1999 was different. Here the scene was more like an amphitheatric strip club, with shirtless goons demanding that women "show us your tits," forceably for those who did not do so willingly, or in exchange for cigarettes, beer, drugs, or water. In the sets by Korn and Limp Bizkit, the mosh pit seemed more violent than usual; women were routinely groped and dozens of fans were carried off to the emergency tent with physical injuries, including cracked ribs and broken wrists. "Don't let anybody get hurt," said Limp Bizkit's seemingly concerned Fred Durst, who then added, "but I don't think you should mellow out. That's what Alanis Morissette had you motherfuckers do," referring to her earlier, admittedly sluggish performance.[48] Limp Bizkit then broke into their hit single "Nookie" and the mosh pit exploded. In all, four rapes were reported at Woodstock '99, one of them allegedly occurring in the pit during Limp Bizkit's set.

Woodstock '99 was staged at Griffis Air Force Base in Rome, New York, essentially a slab of concrete surrounded by barbed wire, with nary a shade tree in sight. The promoters could not have selected a more inhospitable site.

The Red Hot Chili Peppers closed the Sunday night show. In another context, the group's bursting on stage buck naked could have been celebrated as an act of sexual freedom. Juxtaposed against scenes of female spectators being asked by concessionaires to bare their breasts for a bottle of water, their exuberance became part of a different reality. Closing their set with a rendition of Jimi Hendrix's "Fire" might also have taken on a different meaning were it not linked to a growing number of bonfires that prompted the health services to begin abandoning the site. The festival eventually degenerated into a finale of arson and rioting by fans, who were justifiably outraged at the poor sanitary conditions, the lack of appropriate shelter from the sun, and the $4.00 bottles of water and $12.00 one-person pizzas.

There was also another kind of rage expressed at Woodstock '99 and elsewhere during this period—that of rock-rap ensemble Rage Against the Machine. During their set at Woodstock '99, Rage tried to educate fans in the mosh pit about the plight of American Indian activist Leonard Peltier. At other shows; the band intervened when men harassed women. While the group's music is laced with rage, it is a directed rage. As

Limp Bizkit became one of the focal points for male rage in the late 1990s. With an aggressive stage show and titles like "Nookie," is anyone surprised?

self-defined socialists, Rage have also taken up the causes of the Zapatista rebels in Chiapas, Mexico, and imprisoned black journalist Mumia Abu-Jamal. Like the other rage rockers, Rage have incorporated rap into their music, but with a political edge, as in songs like "Vietnow," from *Evil Empire* (1996). Led by Mexican-American vocalist Zac de la Rocha and biracial guitarist Tom Morello, Rage has criticized the macho posturing of gangsta rappers like Tupac and Notorious B.I.G. as well as the misogynistic lyrics of a number of artists (including Wu-Tang Clan, with whom they toured very briefly in 1997). Following the success of *The Battle of Los Angeles* (1999), Rage released *Renegades,* an album of covers that includes versions of the Rolling Stones' "Street Fighting Man," Afrika Bambaataa's "Renegades of Funk," and Cypress Hill's classic "How I Could Just Kill a Man," all recorded with the group's signature political edge. The group had always been an explosive combination of strong personalities, and it was unfortunate but not surprising that de la Rocha felt it necessary to leave the band just prior to the release of *Renegades.*

Teen Pop: Boy Bands and Teen Queens

If the rage rockers stood in opposition to the imagined "lacy lilting ladies" of Lilith Fair, they were also described as the antithesis of another, larger phenomenon—teen pop, represented most visibly by such artists as the Backstreet Boys, 'N Sync, Britney Spears, and Christina Aguilera. But as usual, there is more to such stark dichotomies than meets the eye. With rage rock described by the press as everything that is aggressive, hateful, and misogynistic in life and teen pop as wholesome family entertainment—complete with autograph sessions and photo ops with the stars—one might assume that the audience for the former is limited to angry white men, while that of the latter is made up of young girls. The reality is far more complex. "Contrary to popular opinion," says Joan Anderman, "not every adolescent heart is aflutter for the Backstreet Boys and 'N Sync. Girls from the suburbs and girls from the city, girls who live in tiny hamlets overseas and in Midwestern trailer parks, are dedicated followers of the new crop of coarse, venomous rockers."[49] Indeed, many of the young women at Woodstock '99 were willing participants in their own sexual (mis)adventures. In this context, the results of the 1999 *Rolling Stone Readers Poll*—which bestowed top honours on the Backstreet Boys and Christina Aguilera as well as on Korn, Limp Bizkit, Kid Rock, and Eminem—cannot automatically be read as a simple gender division.[50] It is quite likely that young women as well as young men voted for all of these bands.

While there is a striking image of innocence and sexuality about the new teen sensations, it is in some ways a throwback to an early 1960s image of pent-up sexuality—a preoccupation with titillation, as in the Frankie and Annette beach party movies. The rage rockers manifested a rougher sexuality (some would call it sexism)—a combination of Marlon Brando and James Dean's alienated hoodlums and the Stones' "Street Fighting Man" taken to the extreme—but it clearly had its appeal. Teenage sexual fantasies have never been limited to boy- or girl-next-door types. For young women, the attraction of the

> *While there is a striking image of innocence and sexuality about the new teen sensations, it is in some ways a throwback to an early 1960s image of pent-up sexuality—a preoccupation with titillation, as in the Frankie and Annette beach party movies.*

dangerous, adventurous, outlaw bad boy has always been there, in popular culture and in everyday life. Christina Aguilera has talked openly about wanting to date a "roughneck." She has been linked in the press to Fred Durst (of Limp Bizkit) and Eminem and admits to thinking they are "cute," even though the latter absolutely skewered her sexual reputation on "The Real Slim Shady."[51]

There is a certain incestuousness to the formation of the new teen pop infrastructure and a shared ethic among the most successful artists about their role as teen idols. Most apparent is the Orlando/Disney connection. Britney Spears and Christina Aguilera, as well as 'N Sync's Justin Timberlake and JC Chasez, were members of the *Mickey Mouse Club* class of 1993. Backstreet Boys Howie Dorough and Nick Carter had auditioned. Both the Backstreet Boys and 'N Sync shared management with Lou Pearlman's Continental Management Company. BSB became disillusioned when Pearlman created 'N Sync without telling them and then sued for back royalties. 'N Sync also flew the coop over money. When they landed, they joined Johnny Wright's Wright Stuff management company, the firm that started with the New Kids on the Block and moved on to Britney Spears. 'N Sync then left RCA and inked a deal with Jive Records, the label that is home to both Britney Spears and the Backstreet Boys, and all three acts have worked with the crack writer-producer team headed by the late Denniz Pop and his protégé, Max Martin, at Sweden's Cheiron Studios. Auditions for *Star Search* and a Southern Baptist upbringing are themes that run through many of these artists' backgrounds. There is also an intense work ethic and rigorous sense of discipline that characterizes all the successful careers; it is a curious combination of youthful energy and seasoned professionalism, accompanied by an acute sense of their responsibilities as role models to a generation.

There is, of course, nothing particularly new about the teen pop phenomenon. Ever since Motown presented the Jackson 5 and producer Maurice Starr switched his focus from the New Edition to the New Kids on the Block, there has been a market for teen pop, from the mall tours of Tiffany andd the r&b–flavoured pop of Debbie Gibson to the "girl power" feminism of The Spice Girls and No Doubt. The difference at the end of the decade was just how systematic and all-pervasive it seemed to be. In addition to the above-mentioned boy bands and teen queens, there were also the funkier 98 Degrees, LFO, Mandy (Moore), Jessica Simpson, and the well-respected Hanson. Monica and Brandy, and more recently Destiny's Child, were among the few African American acts who could be considered part of the phenomenon. Teen pop peaked in 1999. That year, three of the four best-selling albums of the year were *Millennium* (Backstreet Boys) at number one, . . . *Baby One More Time* (Britney Spears) at number two, and *'N Sync* in the number four slot, with Christina Aguilera edging into the Top Forty with her self-titled debut. The year 2000 showed a slight shift, with 'N Sync taking over the top slot and Spears' *Oops! . . . I Did It Again*

Britney Spears has combined sexual innuendo, disciplined professionalism, and a strong business plan into one of the most successful careers in teen pop.

and Aguilera's debut making the Top Ten. By this time, the Backstreet Boys had slipped due to contractual problems.

Britney Spears burst onto the charts in late 1998 and took the music to new heights over the next two years. As 2000 came to a close, her first album, *. . . Baby One More Time,* had been certified thirteen times platinum and was still riding the charts, and her second, *Oops! . . . I Did It Again,* was at number five and climbing, eventually reaching sales of 9 million units. The title songs from both albums, like her stage act, were loaded with sexual innuendo. The fact that the hook line from ". . . Baby One More Time" was prefaced with the words "hit me" raised concern that it could be interpreted as a masochistic come-on, a charge that Spears shrugged off as nonsense. "It doesn't mean physically hit me," she told Steven Daly. "It means just give me a sign."[52] Deeply religious (she prays at night) and very athletic (she did her own backflip in the ". . . Baby One More Time" video), Spears made her stage debut at age five. From the moment that Jive signed her, every aspect of her career has been thoroughly mapped out—advertising campaigns, promotional tie-ins, 800 numbers, email addresses, websites. Jive even sent her out on a twenty-six-date mall tour (à la Tiffany) before the release of her first album. Throughout her career, Spears has been more than just a willing participant in her fate; she has been a full collaborator, actively calling many of the shots. As her co-manager Larry Rudolph explains, "She knows exactly what her audience wants. She is her audience."[53]

Like 'N Sync, Britney Spears sought to project a more grown-up image for her third album. And like 'N Sync, she brought in the Neptunes to produce one of the album's singles, "I'm a Slave 4 U." Released in late 2001, *Britney* became her third album in a row to debut at number one. By this time, she was dating Justin Timberlake, and the media attention lavished on their romance, however short-lived, added to the celebrity status of both singers and laid to rest any lingering doubts about how chaste their off-stage lives were. During this period, Spears also landed a lucrative Pepsi endorsement. But even this level of exposure was not enough to propel *Britney* past the sales figures of her first two albums. *Britney* ran out of steam at around 4 million copies, and none of the album's singles—"I'm a Slave 4 U," "I'm Not a Girl, Not Yet a Woman," or "Overprotected"—was able to break into the Top Ten, even with the steamy video for "I'm a Slave 4 U." Clearly feeling the pressure, Spears decided to take a much-needed sabbatical after a complete onstage meltdown on the final date of her summer 2002 world tour in Mexico City.

With obvious similarities to Britney Spears, Christina Aguilera had often been compared to her fellow former Mouseketeer. But given her vocal range and power—which earned her the right to record "Reflection" for the Disney soundtrack to *Mulan* before her first album was released—comparisons with artists like Whitney Houston and Mariah Carey are not out of line. It was her vocal abilities that enabled her to beat out both Britney Spears and Macy Gray for the Best New Artist Grammy in 2000. Her upset victory was all the more incredible in that RCA had reined her in for her freshman outing, keeping the album well within the bounds of teen pop conventions. Her 1999 eponymous debut entered the charts at number one and sold better than 8 million copies before it peaked. Its first single, "Genie in a Bottle," whose infectious hook line propelled it straight to number one, became the most popular single of the year. It was the perfect metaphor for the state of her career and the bottled-up teenage sexuality that typified so much of the music. Still riding the charts in 2000, *Christina Aguilera* generated two more number one singles—"What a Girl Wants" and "Come On Over Baby (All I Want Is You)." Aguilera capitalized further on the success of the album by recording a version of it in Spanish. With an Ecuadorian-born father, Aguilera is part Latina, a side of her identity she decided to explore in more depth. As 2000 came to an end, Aguilera had three albums in the Billboard 200: *Christina Aguilera* at number twenty-six with a bullet, *My Kind of Christmas,* her holiday entry, and *Mi Reflejo* (My Reflection), the Spanish version of her debut album. And she hadn't even recorded what the press was calling her sophomore album yet.

Aguilera took two years to complete her second studio album, *Stripped.* During this period, she came of age in a most extroverted fashion, going so far as to brag to one interviewer that her genital piercings had "gotten a lot of compliments," to which she quickly added, "From my gynecologist."[54] Aguilera was certainly entitled to celebrate her newfound adult sexuality, but on *Stripped*, as in real life, she seemed overwhelmed by it, compelled to flaunt it, unable to place it in any kind of perspective. Despite her protestations that the album title referred to her "stripped of all the hype, the gloss, the controversy, the rumors,"[55] rather than her body, her nude photos on the album cover as well as the cover of *Rolling Stone* suggested otherwise, as did "Dirrty" with two Rs, selected as the first single from the album. "Dirrty" stalled at number 48. Her Linda Perry collaboration, "Beautiful," fared much better, breaking into the Top Ten. Although *Stripped* quickly rose to number two on the album charts, it failed to generate sales even approaching the success of her first album. Tracks like "I'm OK," about her father's abuse of her mother, revealed the pain of a young woman in transition working through serious childhood issues. Gone was the pretty, perky Christina of nineteen; replacing her was the alter ego she called Xtina (tattooed on the back of her neck), who represented her "dark, mysterious, kind of edgier side."[56] One of her main difficulties was that she had to do her growing up in public. In the time it took to record her second album, the teen pop space in popular culture was already being taken over by a generation of somewhat more serious, less overtly sexual female artists, ranging from Norah Jones and Vanessa Carlton to Canadian Avril Lavigne and Pink. While Christina and Xtina struggled to come to an accommodation, Aguilera could still rely on one of the best vocal instruments in the business, and she still had all that Latin music to explore.

The Year of Latin(o) Music(ians)

It was no accident that Christina Aguilera became interested in her Latin roots shortly after her own debut in 1999. It was not just a good year for teen pop. In a season of "Years of . . . ," it was the long-awaited Year of Latin Music, or more correctly, Latino/a musicians doing all types of music. It was the year that Ricky Martin shook his bon bon into the hearts of millions. And it was the year that Carlos Santana recorded *Supernatural*, which earned him a record-tying eight Grammys. Among the Latino/a artists who had Top Ten pop hits that year were Christina Aguilera ("Genie in a Bottle," "What a Girl Wants"), Marc Anthony ("I Need to Know"), Gloria Estefan ("Music of My Heart," with 'N Sync), Enrique Iglesias ("Bailamous"), Jennifer Lopez ("If You Had My Love," "Waiting for Tonight"), and of course, Martin ("Livin' La Vida Loca," "She's All I Ever Had," "Shake Your Bon Bon"), and Santana ("Smooth," featuring Rob Thomas). The following year, the Latin Academy of Recording Arts and Sciences (LARAS, an offshoot of NARAS, the Grammy organization) staged its own separate prime-time telecast of its recently established Latin Grammys. Several developments that had been bubbling just beneath the surface for years had conjoined to bring this moment to fruition.

Beginning in 1997, NARAS gave its blessing to the formation of LARAS and also established a new Best Latin Rock/Alternative Grammy of its own, essentially to recognize the fact that the *rock en español* of groups like Mana, Los Fabulosos Cadillacs, Café Tacuba, and Molotov had gained a foothold in the United States. During this period, several other unrelated events also served to raise the profile of Latin music in the mainstream. First, the opening of *Selena,* a feature-length Hollywood biopic about the Queen of Tejano Music (following her untimely death in 1995), catapulted Jennifer Lopez (in the title role) to pop stardom. Then came the release of Ry Cooder's accidental blockbuster, *The Buena Vista Social Club,* whose stylistic assortment of *son, descarga, danzón, mambo, cha-cha-cha, guajiro,* and *bolero* elevated a forgotten group of aging traditional Cuban musicians like Ibrahim Ferrer and Compay Segundo to international star status. Finally, the opening of Paul Simon's well-promoted but ultimately flawed Broadway production of *The Capeman* provided a crossover platform for artists like Marc Anthony, Ednita Nazario, and Rubén Blades with its mixture of everything from doo wop and gospel to modern *salsa* and *merengue.* Throughout this period, Gloria Estefan continued to turn out her signature *salsa*-fied dance music, and even Puerto Rican rapper the late Big Pun(isher) hit the Top Thirty with "Still Not a Player." By 1999, the floodgates had opened, allowing a torrent of Latino/a artists to wash over the pop charts with a full range of material. The biggest winners, of course, were Ricky Martin and Carlos Santana.

Ricky Martin's career was the Puerto Rican version of the teen pop superstars. At age twelve, he was already a star as a (replaceable) member of the international teen sensation Menudo. Following some successful soap opera work (*General Hospital*), a stint on Broadway (*Les Misérables*), and a string of four successful solo albums (totaling sales of 15 million units), Martin jump-started the late-1990s Latin pop explosion with his electrifying performance of "Cup of Life" at the Grammys. In May 1999, Columbia released Martin's first English-language album, *Ricky Martin,* which shot to number one, and he began "Livin' La Vida Loca" in earnest; it was so loca, in fact, that 2001 found him sharing the stage with Wayne Newton and Destiny's Child at the Bush Inaugural, where he "persuaded Bush to come onstage and give his pelvis a twitch or two (albeit small, tastefully presidential ones)."[57]

At the time of Martin's ascent, Santana appeared to be a superstar of the sixties who was quite possibly past his prime. He had not recorded a new studio album since *Milagro* in 1992 (in part to get out of his contract with Columbia), and he had not had a Top Forty album or single since 1982. Some seventeen years later, an angel named Metatron, whom Santana says visits him frequently, told him, "You will be inside the radio frequency for the purpose of connecting the molecules with the light," which Santana immediately understood to mean a new album that would be on the radio, connecting people with their spiritual selves.[58] Santana delivered Metatron's message, verbatim, to Arista president Clive Davis, who, being a veteran of the sixties himself, also understood. If Santana was the spiritual force behind *Supernatural,* Davis was its architect, planning the album as half vintage Santana and half collaborations—with Rob Thomas from Matchbox Twenty, Dave Matthews, Everlast, Lauryn Hill, Cee-Lo, Mana, Eagle Eye Cherry, and Eric Clapton. Arista released the album in June 1999, with "Smooth" (featuring Rob Thomas) as its first single. Both the album and the single went to number one, taking *Supernatural's* sales past 10 million copies. If Martin was the brash young Latino crossover heartthrob of the moment (despite the rumours of his being gay), Santana comported himself more like an elder statesman of music, with a new, and much appreciated, lease on life. Interestingly, both men stressed the importance of family and spirituality in their lives.

The success of Martin and Santana created the space for other Latin artists on the pop charts—most notably Jennifer Lopez and later Shakira. Following her starring role opposite George Clooney in the film *Out of Sight* (1998), Lopez had established herself as one of the highest paid actresses in Hollywood, commanding up to $9 million per movie. She had also become a celebrity of the highest order whose every move was chronicled in the press. In 1999, she turned her attention to music to record *On the 6* (after the number of her childhood New York subway line), with major label backing from Epic and producers of the calibre of Emilio Estefan and Sean "Puffy" Combs, with whom she also had a high-profile, tortured affair. The album's first single, "If You Had My Love," hit number one and *On the 6* eventually reached sales of 6 million copies. For her second outing, *J.Lo*, she continued in the dance/pop vein with singles such as "Love Don't Cost a Thing," although expectations were higher than the album delivered. Still, its release landed her on the cover of *Rolling Stone,* albeit in strangely revealing Viking attire. A compilation of remixes followed, with J.Lo entering politically sensitive territory by using the word "nigger" on the Murder, Inc. remix of "I'm Real" (featuring Ja Rule). With "street cred" as something of an issue, the first single selected from her third full-length studio album, *This Is Me. . . Then,* was "Jenny from the Block," on which the unabashedly mainstream Lopez tried to convince her listeners that she was still just plain folks from the 'hood.

Shakira Isabel Mebarak Ripoll was born in Barranquilla, Colombia; her father, who was born in New York, is of Lebanese descent. She had already become a pop superstar throughout Latin America, performing her own rock-oriented compositions in Spanish before ever coming to the attention of U.S. music fans. In Barranquilla, at the age of thirteen, she auditioned for a Sony executive who was so impressed that he signed her to a three-record deal. For Shakira's third outing, Sony allowed her to record an entire rock album. Influenced by rockers such as Aerosmith, Nirvana, and Tom Petty, Shakira's *Pies Descalzos* ("Bare Feet"), which was released in 1995, went to number one in eight different countries and kept generating hit singles until it reached sales of nearly 4 million units. In 1998, she hired Miami Latin music mogul Emilio Estefan as her manager and producer to record *Dónde Están Los Ladrones?* ("Where Are the

The success of Martin and Santana created the space for other Latin artists on the pop charts—most notably Jennifer Lopez and later Shakira.

Thieves?"), which became a bigger worldwide hit than her previous album. It also spent eleven weeks at number one on the U.S. Latin album chart. Poised for crossover success in the United States, Shakira allied herself with impresario Freddy DeMann (who had helped nurture the careers of Madonna and Michael Jackson). Her *MTV Unplugged* special was the channel's first Spanish-language cablecast. Released as an album in 2000, *MTV Unplugged* became her third platinum album in a row and earned her a Grammy for Best Latin Pop Album.

Determined to overcome all remaining obstacles to achieving mainstream pop superstardom, Shakira dyed her brown hair blond and taught herself English well enough to sing and write in it. Then she recorded *Laundry Service,* her first (mostly) English album, for which she wrote or co-wrote every song. Within a year of its release in 2001, *Laundry Service* had achieved triple platinum sales, propelled by the infectious Latin dance rock groove of "Whenever, Wherever." Shakira had earned a reputation as a serious *rockera* and a writer of poetic lyrics, described by one critic as "emphatically self-expressive and somewhat surreal."[59] Clearly a woman to be reckoned with, Shakira remained quite in charge of managing a career in which she, like other Latin rockers, could engage her commitment to rock while maintaining a coherent Latina identity in the United States.

The disparate events and variations of style that created the late 1990s Latin boom not only showcased the diversity of artists and rhythms that constituted the Latin music category. They also raised the question: what is Latin music?

The disparate events and variations of style that created the late 1990s Latin boom not only showcased the diversity of artists and genres that constituted the Latin music category. They also raised the question: what is Latin music? Shakira is a case in point. Clearly a rocker, albeit one grounded in Latin rhythms, Shakira is listed in the *All Music Guide* only in the "Latin" genre, primarily because of her ethnicity. Rock is not mentioned as one of the styles she employs, even though it is the driving force of her current music. In what sense, then, is music like Shakira's Latin? LARAS addressed and neatly sidestepped the question, describing the inadequacy of the term in the opening line to one of the pages of their website: "'Latin Music' has never been more than a shorthand for a universe of rhythms and styles as diverse as the people who created them. For a while it was a useful convention. Not any more. As technology and communications continue to erode borders, we are all fast becoming next-door neighbors."[60] Operationally, Latin music has been defined as music made by Latinos for Latinos. Such a statement suggests another question: what is a Latin(o)? Even as Latin music was positioned to become yet another Next Big Thing, the variations in style and difficulties of categorization became as apparent as the complexity of the term *Latino* itself.

In the United States, *Latino* is used as an umbrella term referring to people of Latin American descent who live permanently in the United States. It is a social construct that purports to describe a number of very different cultures and ethnic groups, each of which has a different historical relationship to the United States and its various racial and ethnic formations, as well as to each other. According to ethnomusicologist Deborah Pacini Hernandez, the major social function of the term is to distinguish people of Latin American descent from others in the United States.[61] But, as Pacini Hernandez points out, Cubans, Puerto Ricans, Mexicans, Colombians, Salvadorans, Dominicans, and so forth cannot be reduced to a single ethnic category any more than Western Europeans can. The experiences of Chicanos who have been a major presence in the U.S. Southwest since the Spanish-American War have been quite different from those of newcomers from the Spanish Caribbean, whose major waves of immigration didn't start until after World War II, with the inauguration of "Operation Bootstrap." Clouding the waters further, the term *Latino* is often used synonymously with the more prevalent (and more controversial) term *Hispanic,* which extends the umbrella to include peninsular Spain. It is in this sense that Enrique Iglesias—son of Julio—can be described as Latino. There is also some debate as to whether *Latino* includes immigrants from Portuguese-speaking Brazil, whose musical styles are well represented in the Latin Grammy categories.

The relationship between language, culture, and identity is of particular importance in a country like the United States, where pop hits are English-only. The term *Latino* is clearly associated with the Spanish language. But many Latino/a musicians, such as Jennifer Lopez, were either born in or have been raised in the United States and grew up speaking little Spanish. Those who do speak it know that crossing over to the U.S. pop charts will probably require recording in English. To the extent that language is an integral part of one's identity, it surely affects an artist's relationship to his or her music. The eruption of salsa in the 1970s, in an era of emergent ethnicity, was not simply the start of a hot new dance music; as a Spanish-only music, it was also a referendum on political allegiances and cultural authenticity. The Rubén Blades film *Crossover Dreams* offers a powerful explication of these complexities. Thus, while one could argue that musical influences from the Spanish Caribbean—mostly Cuban, dating back to the mambo, rumba, and cha-cha-cha crazes of the 1950s—have had a greater effect on the course of U.S. popular music overall, it is also the case that Chicano musicians, who have been more willing to engage the English language and the rock idiom, have had more access to chart success as a result. Santana created a best-of-both-worlds hybrid when he first married Spanish Caribbean rhythms to the rock idiom in the late 1960s.

Black Music at the Base

In the focus on the sensationalized murders of Tupac Shakur and Biggie Smalls, the feeding frenzy for alternative, and the ascent of country, it was easy to lose sight of the fact that in most instances it was African American musical styles that powered the pop machine. The music industry was criticized by more than a few critics for ignoring "urban" sounds (code for black music) in the downturn that followed the incorporation of alternative. Although the major labels tried to impose electronica in 1997, it was largely a defensive move and one that didn't fit their marketing strategies especially well. However, the major labels must have noticed that hip hop aesthetics, performance styles, and production techniques had contributed significantly to the development of popular music ranging from rage rock and teen pop to dance and r&b. Throughout this period, rap itself continued to develop real muscle in sales. But rap had long been the elephant in the room—the music industry preferred not to notice rap, even as it benefited enormously from its CD sales. Rap had continued to be a Big Thing throughout the period that the industry was searching for one. By the opening years of the new millennium, hip hop–related artists—especially rappers—had become the predominant trend on the year-end pop charts. This phenomenon had its

In the focus on the sensationalized murders of Tupac Shakur and Biggie Smalls, the feeding frenzy for alternative, and the ascent of country, it was easy to lose sight of the fact that in most instances it was African American musical styles that powered the pop machine.

beginnings in the explosion of gangsta rap that occurred in the early 1990s and the marriage of rap and traditional r&b that the music industry even-tually dubbed r&b/hip hop. It was also accompanied by a sharp distinction between the hardcore rap of the gangstas and thugs and the smoother rap-influenced r&b sound.

Hip Hop with Soul: The New R&B

Rounding out the diverse array of musical tastes that surfaced in the early 1990s were r&b vocal styles that combined the smooth balladry of seasoned r&b veterans like Barry White and Luther Vandross with the hip hop inflected harmonies of artists like Boyz II Men, En Vogue, TLC, Color Me Badd, Jodeci, Mary J. Blige, and Silk. This smooth r&b sound—referred to at the time as *hip hop doo wop* or *hip hop soul*—often bore the signatures of African American writer/producers: Teddy Riley, who had been credited with inventing new jack swing with his group Guy ("Groove Me" and "Teddy's Jam," 1987); Sean "Puffy" Combs, who established the signature sound of Mary J. Blige (*What's the 411?,* 1991) before he ascended to the status of mogul; and Antonio "L.A." Reid and Kenneth "Babyface" Edmunds, who in 1989 founded LaFace Records, the label that became home to TLC and Toni Braxton. Braxton's self-titled 1993 debut eventually sold eight times platinum, generating five hits in the process. She hit her stride on her sophomore outing, *Secrets,* featuring the erotic "You're Makin' Me High," backed with the Diane Warren–penned blockbuster, "Un-break My Heart," both of which hit number one in 1996 and earned her Grammys as well. TLC were discovered by Reid's writer/producer wife, Pebbles, and signed to LaFace in 1991. They were launched as a sexy novelty act with *Ooooooohhh . . . On the TLC Tip,* whose pop/rap/hip hop singles "Ain't 2 Proud 2 Beg," "Baby, Baby, Baby," and "What About Your Friends" propelled the album to multiplatinum status. *CrazySexyCool* (1994) revealed a more seasoned group with a polished, smooth r&b sound. Generating four Top Ten

singles—"Creep" and "Waterfalls" at number one—the album eventually sold about 11 million copies. Following *CrazySexyCool,* personal dramas and financial troubles kept the group out of circula-tion until their spectacular comeback with *Fan Mail* in 1999.

Destiny's Child picked up where TLC left off, complete with high drama among its personnel. Destiny's Child had formed in Houston in 1990 and paid seven years of dues before getting signed to Columbia in 1997, while still in their teens. Their eponymous debut sold well, but it was their second

High drama and personnel changes did not keep Destiny's Child from becoming superstars.

The multitalented R. Kelly could have achieved upward mobility through sports, but he chose music instead.

outing, *The Writing's on the Wall* (1999), and one of its hit singles, "Say My Name," that established them as pop superstars. Unfortunately, it was also at this point that the original group self-destructed. Following a series of high-profile lawsuits and verbal exchanges in the press, the lineup that took the group into the new millennium included Beyoncé Knowles, who had long since become the group's focal point, her cousin Kelly Rowland, and newcomer Michelle Wallace. Their aptly named third album, *Survivor*, debuted at number one in 2001.

If there was one artist who left the biggest imprint on this new sound, it was writer, producer, performer, and pro basketball player R. Kelly. Raised in South Side Chicago, Kelly early on saw music and/or sports as avenues out of poverty. Through the efforts of his high-school music teacher, music gained the edge (although Kelly did sign a contract with the Atlantic City Seagulls). Over the course of his career, Kelly has written and/or produced music for artists such as Toni Braxton, Mary J. Blige, Whitney Houston, Boyz II Men, and Michael Jackson, and by 1991 had released his own platinum solo debut, *Born into the 90s.* It was overshadowed by the controversy that greeted his five times platinum second album, *12 Play* (1993), whose sexually explicit singles "Sex Me (Parts I and II)," "Bump N' Grind," and "Your Body's Callin'," coupled with his equally suggestive stage show, both delighted and enraged fans across the country. It didn't help that the following year he produced fifteen-year-old Aaliyah's debut, *Age Ain't Nothing But a Number,* amidst rumours that he had married the underage star, a charge which they both denied but which later proved to be true.

Raised in South Side Chicago, Kelly early saw music and/or sports as avenues out of poverty. Through the efforts of his high-school music teacher, music gained the edge.

While the explicit material from *12 Play* clearly established Kelly's image in the popular mind, there was also another side to the artist—one that recalls the sacred/secular binary that had caused a breach between gospel music and rhythm and blues in the 1940s. In 1994, Kelly formed a bond with gospel singer Kirk Franklin. His eponymous third album, while still sexually charged, reflected Franklin's influence. In 1997, he appeared at one of Franklin's concerts proclaiming: "Every day I seem to be falling in love with the Lord. . . . I used to be flying in sin—now I'm flying in Jesus."[62] By then he had written the G-rated "I Believe I Can Fly" for the *Space Jam* soundtrack (reportedly at the behest of Michael Jordan himself), which he performed at the Franklin concert to wild applause. The move certainly did no harm to his career. *R. Kelly* was his first album to hit pop number one. It sold four times platinum and generated three platinum singles—"You Remind Me of Something," "Down Low (Nobody Has to Know)," and "I Can't Sleep Baby (If I)." At the end of the decade, he was still riding high with the two-disc *R.* (1998), which sold seven times platinum, propelled by a duet with Celine Dion titled "I'm Your Angel," which had a six-week run at number one. *TP-2.com* (2000) also went to number one on the album charts, extending Kelly's popularity into the new millennium.

A collaboration with Jay-Z on a remix of "Fiesta," from *TP-2.com,* led to the idea of creating a whole album together. "The best of R&B. The best of rap. Let's put it together and see what happens," said Kelly.[63] *The Best of Both Worlds* was expected to be the crowning achievement of the music that *Billboard* had officially dubbed r&b/hip hop in 1999, renaming the r&b charts to reflect this evolution in the music. On the eve of its release, *Vibe* magazine called the album "the ultimate union of hip hop and r&b."[64] One might have thought that Kelly was at the top of his game as he belted out "The World's Greatest," his hit single from the *Ali* soundtrack, at the opening ceremony of the Winter Olympics in Salt Lake City, draped in an American flag. But that very morning, the *Chicago Sun-Times* had broken a story about a videotape of Kelly allegedly having sex with a fourteen-year-old girl. As the lurid details of the sex and urination video became public, along with other tapes and civil suits, plans for *The Best of Both Worlds* suddenly took a new turn. Those who thought the collaboration was a bad idea to begin with now felt vindicated. A tour would be out of the question. The song "Come to Daddy" was jettisoned, although other tracks like "Naked" and "P***y" made the cut. There were mushrooming legal problems, such as the twenty-one-count indictment relating to the original tape, and, in addition, many of the critics felt that the album simply didn't measure up artistically. For whatever reason—or for all of them—*The Best of Both Worlds* flopped. R&b/hip hop continued to develop in the able hands of artists like Mary J. Blige, whose *No More Drama* (2001) revealed a mature r&b diva with a hip hop edge. Closer to the teen market was Destiny's Child, whose *Survivor* marked the end of their own group's drama, selling four times platinum, with "Bootylicious" at number one. But Kelly's career was seriously destabilized; his 2002 single—"Heaven, I Need a Hug"—said it all.

Rap: Still the Elephant in the Room

By the 1990s, hip hop geography had expanded beyond the East Coast/West Coast poles that had figured into the deaths of Tupac Shakur and Biggie Smalls, creating new vocabularies of place and space. Rap was not simply a buck wild street culture; it was a major corporate enterprise, with the most successful artists often playing the multiple roles of performing artist, writer, producer, and label head, as they took on appellations like *mogul* and *impresario*. As Keith Negus astutely pointed out, "rappers who have often been identified solely with 'the street' are also executives."[65] Even though mainstream commentary about (and opposition to) rap remained largely a discourse of the street, dedicated hip hop magazines such as *The Source* and *Vibe,* as well as business journals such as *Forbes,* included countless discussions of career development and business plans.

> *Rap* was not simply a buck wild street culture; it was a major corporate enterprise, with the most successful artists often playing the multiple roles of performing artist, writer, producer, and label head, as they took on appelations like mogul and impresario.

If there was any artist who best exemplified the move from the street to the executive suite, it was Sean "Puffy" Combs, a.k.a. Puff Daddy (later to become P. Diddy, and then just Diddy). "I strive to be known as a mogul entrepreneur," he told *Rolling Stone* in 1997, but even then he was plagued by the notion that "I've gotten my fame through tragedies. My successes have been overlooked."[66] For Puffy, the tragedies began in earnest in 1991, when an oversold celebrity basketball event that he promoted in New York resulted in a stampede that left nine people dead. In 1999, he was accused of breaking the arm and jaw of Interscope executive Steven Stoute over a dispute about a video. Then there was his arrest (along with his then-girlfriend Jennifer Lopez and rapper Shyne) for a shootout that occurred at Club New York in January 2000, in which one woman was shot in the face and two other people were injured. None of these incidents was played out in the press as dramatically as Puffy's connection to the assassination of Biggie Smalls. For most of 1997, it was the only thing the press could focus on when it came to Puffy. But if trouble seemed to follow Puffy wherever he went, so did success.

By 1997, he presided over a Bad Boy Entertainment empire that grossed $200 million and employed 300 people. That year, having made the decision that he was "going on for B.I.G. and everyone else," Combs—who, as producer, had already launched the careers of Mary J. Blige, Mase, Lil' Kim, Foxy Brown, Jodeci, and of course, the Notorious B.I.G. (Biggie Smalls)—came out from behind his mixing board to record his first album, *No Way Out,* as rapper Puff Daddy. Credited to Puff Daddy and the Family (which included other Bad Boy artists such as Mase, Lil' Kim, the Lox, 112, Black Rob, Faith Evans, and Notorious B.I.G. himself), *No Way Out* was certified seven times platinum. Its first single, "I'll Be Missing You," a duet with Faith Evans (the late Biggie Smalls' estranged wife), was a eulogy to his friend and protégé that was based on a sample of the Police's "Every Breath You Take." On "Pain," Puffy recalled a number of the tragedies in his life, including the murder of Smalls. "Is This the End" marked his decision to carry on as B.I.G.'s heir. Another single from the album, "It's All About the Benjamins" (after the picture of Benjamin Franklin on the $100 bill), became an anthemic metaphor for the unabashed materialism at the center of the new hip hop culture. Puffy was roundly considered to be a lightweight rapper and a sample-heavy producer, having borrowed from David's Bowie's "Let's Dance" (for "Been Around the World") and Love Unlimited Orchestra's "I Did It for Love" (for "The Benjamins"); he even teamed up with Jimmy Page to use the melody from Led Zeppelin's "Kashmir" for "Come with Me." Defending the practice on *Forever* (1999)—on which he sampled Earth, Wind & Fire's "Fantasy" (for "Angels with Dirty Faces"), and Christopher Cross' "Sailing" (for "My Best Friend")—Puff Daddy often asked reporters rhetorically: If what I do is so easy, why haven't others followed suit?

After a couple of years of fending off his legal problems, Combs reinvented himself as P. Diddy in 2001 and released two albums: a gospel album titled *Thank You* and a rap album called *The Saga Continues.* The latter was a production extravaganza that featured more than a score of rappers and singers and yielded the rock-inflected "Bad Boy for Life," Diddy's biggest single in a long time. Intended to announce that Bad Boy was still in the house, the album also made clear that the label had lost some of its most talented rappers—most notably Biggie Smalls to murder and Shyne Barrow to prison—since its last major release. Diddy's empire suffered another setback in 2002 when Arista dropped Bad Boy. Although Diddy soon scored another distribution deal with Universal, he had already been dislodged from his position of dominance.

In 1998, Combs was edged aside for standout "mogul entrepreneur" of the year by one Percy Miller, a.k.a. Master P. That year, P, as he calls himself, recorded his fourth and what he claimed would be his last album, the multiplatinum *MP Da Last Don.* It wasn't because he was finished with hip hop—in fact, he kept recording—but because he wanted to build "the profile of a businessman, not a gangsta."[67] By 1998, P had built the No Limit record store into a label and a multimedia empire, earning $56 million that year, compared to Puffy's $53.3 million. The No Limit Army, as its stable of artists was called, included the production team Beats by the Pound, and P's younger brothers Silkk The Shocker and C-Murder, as well as Mo B. Dick and Mia X, who also recorded collectively as TRU (The Real Untouchables). Master P had grown up in what was then called the Calliope projects in New Orleans, a tough neighbourhood in one of the most violent cities in the country; tales of crime and violence were commonplace in his music. Master P had seen the future when No Limit's first release, *The Ghetto Is Trying to Kill Me*—a straight-ahead gangsta rap album with hard beats, deep bass, and NC-17 lyrics—became a substantial underground hit. Since that became No Limit's signature sound, it was only natural that Master P would expend part of his energy in 1998 to get Snoop Dogg out of his Death Row contract and on to No Limit. Snoop reinforced the point with "Still a G Thang" from *Da Game Is to Be Sold, Not to Be Told,* which debuted at number one.

As to his own career, *Only God Can Judge Me* (1999), P's follow-up to *MP Da Last Don,* peaked at number two on the album charts, but then his chart position began to slip with the release of *Ghetto Postage* (2000) and *Game Face* (2002). During this period, P had gone way beyond being a recording star and label head to become an actor-writer-producer-director (co-starring in his own Miramax film, *I Got the Hook-Up!*), an author (with a book called *Animal Rights* in the works), and a sports agent (representing Derek Anderson of the Cleveland Cavaliers and, later, Ron Mercer of the Boston Celtics). A serious athlete himself, P spent part of the summer of 1998 playing basketball in a UCLA summer league, and then in 1999 joined the Charlotte Hornets as a player but was dropped just four days before the season opened. In addition to No Limit Records, No Limit Films, and No Limit Sports Enterprises, a No Limit clothing line (Soldier Gear) and a multimillion dollar deal with Converse, Inc. completed the picture. While the ancillary commercial enterprises of rap impresarios like Master P and others like him often proved difficult to maintain, they seemed to confirm what Keith Negus emphasized as the "need to be wary of the increasingly routine rhetoric and romanticization of rap musicians as oppositional rebels 'outside' the corporate system, or as iconoclasts in revolt against 'the mainstream'—a discourse that has often been imposed upon rap and not necessarily come from participants within hip hop culture itself."[68]

No Limit's location in New Orleans highlighted another aspect of the new era of hip hop—that its production was no longer confined to New York and Los Angeles. In 1992, Nelson George had written that "rap's gone national and is in the process of going regional."[69] George was referring to the fact that a national audience had been getting rap from a number of regional sources: Miami (2 Live Crew), Houston (Geto Boys), Seattle (Sir Mix-A-Lot), and San Francisco (Too Short). By the mid-1990s, the geography of hip hop had

No Limit's location in New Orleans highlighted another aspect of the new era of hip hop—that its production was no longer confined to New York and Los Angeles.

shifted markedly to include the Mid-West and what Tony Green referred to as "The Dirty South."[70] New Orleans boasted not only Master P's No Limit Army, but also Mystikal on Jive Records, and the Cash Money label with Juvenile, B.G., Turk, Lil' Wayne (who recorded solo and collectively as the Hot Boys), and Big Tymers. The LaFace label (OutKast, Goodie Mob) and So So Def (Jermaine Dupri, Lil' Bow Wow, Da Brat) were headquartered in Atlanta. Then in 2000, Def Jam opened a subsidiary there with Scarface as its president and Ludacris as its flagship artist. Timbaland and Magoo represented Virginia Beach, as Bone Thugs-N-Harmony did in Cleveland, and later Eminem in Detroit. There was also a next generation of labels in rap's historical strongholds. Dr. Dre had launched Aftermath in Los Angeles. New York boasted two significant new rap labels as well— Roc-A-Fella (Jay-Z) and Ruff Ryders (DMX). These developments pushed Nelson George's analysis further toward the local. Observed Murray Forman:

> *Today the emphasis is on place, and groups explicitly advertise their home environments . . . or else they structure their home territory into titles and lyrics, constructing a new internally meaningful hip hop cartography. The explosion of localized production centres and regionally influential producers and artists has drastically altered the hip hop map and production crews have sprung up throughout North America. These producers have also demonstrated a growing tendency to incorporate themselves as localised businesses (often buying or starting companies unrelated to the music industry in their local neighborhoods, such as auto customising and repair shops) and to employ friends, family members and members of their wider neighborhoods. Extending Nelson George's observation, it now seems possible to say that rap, having gone regional, is in the process of going local.*[71]

Just as Puffy opened Justin's Restaurant and hired Sister Souljah to run his $2 million Daddy's House social programs, Master P started a basketball foundation for underprivileged youth and donated $500,000 to keep a number of schools and churches in his neighbourhood from closing.

To some extent, the decentralization of rap could be recognized in regional production styles. The New York sound of the 1980s, as exemplified by the frenetic layered sounds that the Bomb Squad produced for Public Enemy, represented the pace and density of New York life and could be distinguished from the more laid-back, bass-heavy productions of N.W.A. in Los Angeles, where car culture allowed for cruising and the installation of powerful sound systems that could take advantage of the deeper bass. By the release of Dr. Dre's *The Chronic* (1992), the sound had been codified into the G-funk production style that emphasized slow beats underpinning lengthy samples of traditional late 1970s funk. Florida, being something of a car culture centre as well, also favoured deep, sub-woofer bass sounds referred to there as "booty bass" or "booty boom." After the death of Biggie Smalls, the production style at Bad Boy became softer, even more sample heavy, and more pop oriented. The gangsta style reasserted its primacy after Dr. Dre's discovery, mentoring, and production of Eminem turned the white rapper from Detroit into the country's most successful hip hop artist at the end of the decade.

Into the new millennium, with the Dirty South still in its ascendancy, the style that most defined the region was called *bounce,* as in Mystikal's 2002 hit "Bouncin' Back (Bumpin' Me Against the Wall)." The style could be traced back to a number of sources, including Luther Campbell's booty bass in Miami. Campbell offered some additional insight when he noted that "Miami is not really a Southern city; it's a Caribbean city—Jamaicans, Cubans, Haitians, Puerto Ricans, Bahamians. So what I did was add all those elements together. I took the Jamaican driving bass . . . and the Latin flavor—that brought it to be uptempo and dance-oriented. . . ."[72] British critic and bounce producer Nik Cohn took bounce back to the 1980s and located the style in New Orleans, also in many ways a Caribbean city. Said Cohn: "Before Master P or Cash Money, there was bounce. It started in the late 1980s, a wild mix of rap and Mardi Gras Indian chants and second line brass-band bass patterns and polyrhythmic drumming and gospel call-and-response."[73] Most commentators could agree that bounce was about beats made for dancing, but beyond that it was difficult to encapsulate a region as large as the South within a single production style.

The major labels, of course, were only too happy to distribute these overwhelmingly successful new rap indies. Arista distributed Bad Boy and LaFace. Aftermath, Ruff Ryders, Roc-A-Fella, and Cash Money were linked to Interscope and Def Jam, both of which were part of Universal. Still, there were a number of social practices that prompted the majors to keep rap at arm's length. Aside from the constant political pressure from conservative watchdog organizations and elected officials concerned about lyrics, rap's propensity to sample other copyrighted records presented a real headache for the copyright-conscious major companies. Moreover, the tendency of hip hop artists to operate as extended social groups—posses, crews, collectives of all types—rather than readily identifiable musical entities was confusing to an industry that is structured around precisely worded contracts and easy identification and tracking of an artist or band for the purposes of determining such things as chart position, market share, and royalty rates. At Bad Boy, the collectivity of artists was called the Family, Master P referred to the No Limit Army, Snoop Dogg had Tha Dogg Pound, and Wu-Tang was a Clan. These loose alliances manifested themselves in the continual appearance of rap artists on each other's recordings, sometimes across label affiliations. The credits on Bad Boy records—particularly those of Puffy, who considered himself more of a "vibe giver" than an MC—routinely consisted of half a

Aside from the constant political pressure from conservative watchdog organizations and elected officials concerned about lyrics, rap's propensity to sample other copyrighted records presented a real headache for the copyright-conscious major companies.

Wu-Tang Clan has combined group efforts, solo projects, and incredible merchandizing into a loose-knit hip hop operation that almost defies description.

dozen names or more, as in the case of "It's All About the Benjamins," which listed as its artists not only Puff Daddy and the Family but also The Notorius B.I.G., Lil' Kim, The Lox, Dave Grohl, Perfect, FuzzBubble, and Rob Zombie.

Perhaps the most collective operation in rap was Wu-Tang Clan. Wu-Tang was consciously assembled as a loose confederation of MCs—RZA, Genius (GZA), Ol' Dirty Bastard, Method Man, Raekwan the Chef, Ghostfaced Killah, U-God, Inspectah Deck, and Masta Killa—who would act collectively as Wu-Tang Clan and also record as solo artists. Started by Genius (GZA) and Ol' Dirty Bastard, it was the musical genius of producer RZA (pronounced Rizza), whose signature sound of menacing beats, sparse samples, and surrealistic soundscapes, underpinning the group's violent martial arts humour, enabled Wu-Tang to realize its vision. Following the success of Wu-Tang's *Enter the Wu-Tang: 36 Chambers* (1993), released on their own Loud label, they landed the perfect label deal with RCA, which allowed each individual member to record solo with anyone and any label he wanted to. Any number of solo projects followed: Method Man's *Tical* in 1994, Ol' Dirty Bastard's *Return to the 36 Chambers (Dirty Version)*, Genius (GZA)'s *Liquid Swords*, and Raekwan's *Only Built 4 Cuban Links* in 1995, and finally, Ghostface Killah's *Ironman* in 1996.

After releasing their second group effort, *Wu-Tang Clan Forever* (1997), the group had achieved major crossover success coupled with ancillary merchandizing ventures that included a clothing line (Wu Wear), a video game for Playstation (*Wu-Tang: Shaolin Style*), and a comic book (*The Nine Rings of Wu-Tang*). Other solo projects followed: Method Man's *Tical 2000: Judgement Day* and RZA's *Bobby Digital in Stereo* in 1997; Genius (GZA)'s *Beneath the Surface*, U-God's *Golden Arms Redemption*, Inspectah Deck's *Uncontrolled Substance*, Ol' Dirty Bastard's *Nigga Please*, and Raekwan's *Immobilarity* in 1999; and Ghostface Killah's *Supreme Clientele* in 2000. The group's prodigious output, produced mostly by RZA, occurred amidst continual skirmishes with the law, usually related to weapons or assault charges and usually involving Ol' Dirty Bastard. By the end of 2000, the Clan was hard at work on a new group project, *The W*, with all the original members participating except Ol' Dirty Bastard, who was a fugitive from a court-ordered drug rehabilitation program at the time. ODB nevertheless still appeared on the album via previously recorded rhymes. The full Clan—minus ODB, who had struck a deal with prosecutors that included jail time—assembled once again in 2001 to record their fourth group album, *Iron Flag*, which was released in December.

In the collective ethos of hip hop, the later half of the 1990s witnessed the beginning of a number of successful ensemble tours. Bad Boy's No Way Out tour featured Puffy and the entire Bad Boy Family, plus other artists like Jay-Z, Foxy Brown, Busta Rhymes, and Usher, and played to sold-out houses everywhere. But it was the 1999 Hard Knock Life tour that set the standard. Headlined by Jay-Z, whose third album, *Vol. 2 . . . Hard Knock Life,* had gone quadruple platinum, the fifty-four-date tour also featured DMX as co-headliner, the duo of Method Man and Redman, and DJ Clue. By this time, DMX had distinguished himself as the only artist (hip hop or otherwise) to have his first two albums—*It's Dark and Hell Is Hot* and *Flesh of My Flesh*—debut at number one on the *Billboard 200* in the same year. The tour itself was distinguished among rap tours in that it earned an impressive $18 million, suffered no cancellations, no artist drop-offs, or any incidents of violence to speak of. It gained further respectability by donating money to the families of the victims of the Columbine shootings.

The Hard Knock Life tour served as the model for other tours to follow, like the Ruff Ryders/Cash Money tour of 2000, which featured Ruff Ryders' DMX and Cash Money's Juvenile as co-headliners, and both labels' other artists as support. By this time, Juvenile's *400 Degreez* had been certified triple platinum. While the tour had fewer scheduled dates than Hard Knock Life, they were booked into larger, mostly coliseum-level venues with greater ticket sales potential. But the tour was marred by a violent backstage brawl in Boston that left six people stabbed, two of them critically.

One of the most successful (and controversial) tours of the period was Up in Smoke, featuring as headliners Snoop Dogg, Dr. Dre, and Dre's protégé, who, had recently stepped out from under his mentor's shadow—Eminem. The tour also featured appearances by Ice Cube and MC Ren, who joined Dr. Dre occasionally as a reunited N.W.A. After keeping a low profile for a number of years, Dre had released *Dr. Dre—2001* in 1999 to show the world that he hadn't lost his touch. By the end of 2000, it had been certified six times platinum. Dre gained equal if not greater notoriety for bringing Eminem to the world. If Dre had found a new sensitivity for himself following his disillusionment with gangsta rap earlier in the decade, Eminem more than filled the void. Eminem (born Marshall Mathers III) grew up mostly around Detroit in what he describes as a dysfunctional family situation. He quit school in the ninth grade, fathered a child, and lived with Haile and her mother, Kim, in a crack-ridden Detroit neighbourhood. In short, Mathers had what is known in the business as "street cred." He came to Dre's attention when the latter heard a copy of the *Slim Shady* EP that Eminem had released independently in 1997. In 1999, the duo worked together on the full-length *The Slim Shady LP,* which entered the charts at number two and was certified three times platinum before the year was out. Slim Shady was the alter ego that allowed Eminem to take revenge on the world, and take revenge he did, killing his mother, killing the mother of his child, getting even with the high-school bully who beat him up, ripping Pamela Anderson's breasts off, and taking every drug imaginable at the same time. For his second outing, Eminem came out from behind his Slim Shady persona to assume his real identity on *The Marshall Mathers LP* (2000). With material as venomous as his first album, *Marshall Mathers* sold 7 million copies in its first year of release.

The fact that both *Slim Shady* and *Marshall Mathers* were overwhelming commercial successes outraged most observers of the cultural scene. The fact that both albums were also released to critical raves—to Dre for his skilled production and, Eminem for his verbal dexterity—was like pouring gasoline on a fire. "When Ice-T sang about murdering a cop, he got dropped from his record label," wrote Renée Graham. "When Eminem raps about butchering his wife and brutalizing homosexuals, he gets

The fact that Eminem achieved both commercial success and critical acclaim with violent, misogynistic rhymes outraged many.

a Grammy nod for album of the year."[74] The fact that Eminem was white was even more troubling for different people for different reasons. For some, it meant that a double standard was being applied to rap—one for black artists and another for white. From another point of view, it meant that the Up in Smoke tour would reach an unprecedented crossover audience. Everyone's fears were realized. Up in Smoke played to predominantly white audiences, and the more provocative the material, the louder the cheers. At the same time, the shows were well produced and the audiences well behaved. The white rapper from Detroit had succeeded in turning himself into a superstar, in the process bringing to hard-edged rap a new generation of middle-class teens. He then stepped in front of the camera to film *8 Mile,* not exactly a biopic, but a movie based loosely on his rap persona.

Up in Smoke played to predominantly white audiences, and the more provocative the material, the louder the cheers. At the same time, the shows were well produced and the audiences well behaved.

If the Up in Smoke tour rekindled a focus on Los Angeles—and more importantly, on Eminem—New York was still the centre for hardcore rap. But in a more dispersed rap world, New York itself had become significantly more decentralized. In its rundown of the fifty most influential hip hop players, *Rolling Stone* went so far as to identify the particular borough or 'hood that each New York artist "represented"—Beastie Boys (Manhattan), Busta Rhymes (Brooklyn), KRS-One (the Bronx), Mase (Harlem), Wu-Tang Clan (Staten Island), etc.[75] Puff Daddy and his Bad Boy empire may have been getting most of the notoriety, but Russell Simmons had parlayed Def Jam (LL Cool J, Method Man, Redman, Foxy Brown) into a multimedia empire that included film (*The Nutty Professor*), television (*Def Comedy Jam*), a clothing line (Phat Farm), and distribution deals with Roc-A-Fella and Ruff Ryders, home to Jay-Z (Brooklyn) and DMX (Yonkers), respectively. Nas (Queens) had scored a major label deal with Columbia/Sony.

With literate rhymes and tough beats, Nas evoked the harsh reality of street life in the Queensbridge projects on his major label debut, *Illmatic.* Jay-Z, from Brooklyn's Marcy projects, was a promising student who also found himself immersed in the seamier side of street life until rap showed him a way out. His debut album, *Reasonable Doubt* (1996), a classic of the genre, is often compared to Nas' *Illmatic.* The two singers sparred repeatedly for New York's rap throne in the aftermath of Biggie Small's death. Jay-Z also entered the East Coast/West Coast fray with "Brooklyn's Finest," a vicious response to Tupac's "Hit 'Em Up." At the same time, he ventured across turf lines to collaborate with the hottest rappers in the business: the Notorious B.I.G., Ja Rule, and DMX on the East Coast, Ludacris and Missy Elliott in the South, and Snoop Dogg and Too Short on the West Coast. Nas enjoyed a steady stream of hits by some of the best producers in the business—"If I Ruled the World" (the Trackmasters), "Hate Me Now" (Puff Daddy), "Nas Is Like" (DJ Premier), and "You Owe Me" (Timbaland)—before his career started to go into decline. Sensing weakness, Jay-Z called Nas out on "Takeover," to which Nas responded with a direct frontal assault on "Ether" (from *Stillmatic,* 2001), which then prompted Jay-Z's comeback, "Super Ugly." Though the release of *Stillmatic* represented something of a valiant comeback for Nas, he never quite regained an undisputed position of prominence in New York rap. Jay-Z became so successful that his Roc-A-Fella label (founded with Damon Dash) became a corporate empire that included its own talent roster (Beanie Sigel, Cam'ron, M.O.P.), a stable of in-house producers (Just Blaze, Kanye West), a clothing line (Roca Wear), and a film division (*Paid in Full, State Property*). Even with all this commercial success, he never lost his focus on the music.

Even as Jay-Z launched side projects, it was all about the music.

Jay-Z hit his stride on *Vol. 2 . . . Hard Knock Life,* part of a trilogy bracketed by *In My Life, Vol. 1* (1997) and *Vol. 3 . . . Life and Times of S. Carter* (1999). For *Vol. 2,* he featured numerous fellow rappers including DMX ("Money, Cash, Hoes") and Ja Rule ("Can I Get A . . .") and collaborated with some of the best-known producers in the business, such as Puffy and Teddy Riley, whose memorable, radio-friendly hooks generated a string of hit singles, such as "Hard Knock Life (Ghetto Anthem)," that doubled his audience. He scaled back somewhat for 2000's *The Dynasty: Roc la Familia,* which mostly featured Roc-A-Fella's in-house stable of rappers. Still, the album hit number one and went platinum. For *The Blueprint* (2001), Jay-Z gave his fans just what they had been looking for since *Reasonable Doubt,* an album of just Jay-Z. There is only one guest shot on *The Blueprint*—Eminem on "Renegade." Propelled by demand for "Izzo (H.O.V.A.)," one of the hottest singles of the year, *The Blueprint* went to number one and multiplatinum certification. When Jay-Z first laid claim to the New York rap throne on 1997's "The City Is Mine," many wondered if he was serious. By 2001, there was no longer any doubt that he was. His ill-fated collaboration with R. Kelly on *Best of Both Worlds* seemed like a mere bump on the road to an ever brighter future that included a committed relationship with Beyoncé Knowles of Destiny's Child and his eventual ascension to the presidency of Def Jam.

DMX, from Yonkers, spent part of his childhood in several group homes and by his early teens was no stranger to the criminal justice system. Touré described him as "tough at a glance . . . sonic testosterone . . . a direct descendent of Tupac." Continued Touré: "He raps in the roughest and grimiest voice in hip hop, the sound of gravel hitting the grave. His records speak of death constantly, crime casually, moral consequences occasionally."[76] After a few unrewarding years at Ruffhouse, DMX switched to Def Jam, where his first album, *It's Dark and Hell Is Hot* (1998), debuted at number one on the pop charts. His second album, *Flesh of My Flesh,* which also entered the charts at number one, pictured him covered with blood. DMX, however, was also a devoted husband and father who shunned publicity and avoided overly high drama in his personal life, despite a number of skirmishes with the law. His 2000 entry, *. . . And Then There Was X,* became his third album in a row to enter the charts at number one, eventually selling 5 million copies. By this time, the singer had also broken into acting, with major supporting roles in the Jet Li action film *Romeo Must Die* and Steven Segal's *Exit Wounds.* He repeated his chart success on *The Great Depression*, which debuted at number one in 2001, his fourth straight album to do so.

DMX's success marked the entry of a new producer on the block—Irv Gotti, a man who had once been Jay-Z's DJ. Gotti started out as Irv Lorenzo, a small-time drug dealer from Hollis, Queens, the same neighbourhood that spawned Def Jam founder Russell Simmons and

Run-D.M.C. Because he always acted like a boss, Jay-Z called him Gotti, after the New York crime boss, and the name stuck. It was Gotti who brought DMX and Ja Rule to Def Jam and helped restore the label's fading glory. It was also Gotti who convinced Jennifer Lopez to use the word "nigger" on "I'm Real." Additionally, he is credited with launching Ashanti's career. Gotti makes what he calls "chick records . . . records that niggas ain't mad at and women love."[77] Examples include "Always on Time" (Ja Rule and Ashanti), "What's Luv" (Fat Joe and Ashanti), "Foolish" (Ashanti), "Baby" (Ashanti), "Ain't It Funny" (Jennifer Lopez and Ja Rule), "I'm Real" (Jennifer Lopez), and "Down for You" (Ja Rule, Charli Baltimore, Vita, and Ashanti).

In 1997, Gotti formed a joint venture with Def Jam, which he called—what else?—Murder, Inc. and signed Ja Rule as its flagship artist. In Gotti's hands, Ja Rule scored an early success with *Venni Vetti Vecci* (1999), an album modeled after DMX's hardcore style. For his second outing, *Rule 3:36* (2000), Gotti took Ja in a more pop direction, adding a chorus of female background singers to the mix. This was a formula he perfected on Ja's third album, *Pain Is Love* (2001), which featured collaborations with Jennifer Lopez ("I'm Real") and Ashanti ("Always on Time"). While the move toward pop added measurably to Ja Rule's crossover appeal, it cost him at street level. DMX attacked him relentlessly in the press. Ja retaliated with "Fuck with Us" on his fourth album, *The Last Temptation* (2002). By this time, Ja Rule had become one of the most financially successful rap artists of the early 2000s. But if he was smarting all the way to the bank, he was also watching his back.

The ascension of the new generation of hardcore New York rappers returned the most publicized rap back to its gangsta roots. Unlike the rappers who had dominated New York, from Run-D.M.C. to Public Enemy, all of whom were college graduates from middle-class backgrounds—even Puff Daddy attended Howard University and donated $500,000 to his alma mater—the new rap stars came from the school of hard knocks. Their frustrations were often directed toward each other in the form of verbal jousts, like the ones between Jay-Z and Nas and DMX and Ja Rule. The attacks on Ja Rule escalated in the hands of Eminem and his New York protégé, 50 Cent, who punched Ja Rule in Atlanta, called him out on "Wanksta" (from the *8 Mile* soundtrack), and began one of his concert sets with a montage of snippets from Ja Rule music videos, between each of which he commented: "I know that's not hip hop, you know that's not hip hop."

Unlike the rappers who had dominated New York, from Run-D.M.C. to Public Enemy, all of whom were college graduates from middle-class backgrounds, the new rap stars came from the school of hard knocks.

50 Cent began life as Curtis Jackson, in Hollis, Queens. According to his bio, he became a second-generation crack dealer at age twelve, earning up to $5,000 a day. At twenty-four, he was shot nine times at point black range; one of the bullets pierced his jaw, producing his signature slur on record. With street cred like that, is it any wonder that the bidding for his contract reached a reported $1 million, as Eminem and Dr. Dre signed 50 Cent to the Shady/Aftermath label? That's when the war with Ja Rule and Murder, Inc. really heated up. 50 Cent's first album on his new label, *Get Rich or Die Tryin'*, went double platinum in three weeks, largely on the strength of the Dr. Dre–produced party anthem "In Da Club." The album also included "Back Down," part of the continuing salvo of insult songs directed at Ja Rule. Ja did not sit idly by. He responded on record with "Loose Change," on which he took on not just 50 Cent but Eminem and Dre as well. 50 Cent was also reportedly stabbed by Ja Rule's crew at the Hit Factory. A trio of Eminem, 50 Cent, and Busta Rhymes

then verbally ganged up on Ja Rule, setting new rhymes to the instrumental track of Tupac's "Hail Mary." Ja fired back with "Guess Who Shot Ya."

If all of this had been just verbal sparring, a time-honoured tradition in rap, it would not have been especially disturbing. But as 50 Cent himself said: "This ain't no rap war."[78] It began to get more intense when the press started connecting the dots to the 2002 real-life, execution-style murder of Jam Master Jay (of Run-D.M.C.) in his studio in—you guessed it—Hollis, Queens. 50 Cent had met Jay back in 1996 when he was making mix tapes that had earned him something of a reputation on the underground party circuit for tracks such as "How to Rob" (now an underground classic), which details ripping off hip hop and r&b stars from Mariah Carey to Jay-Z. Jam Master Jay was apparently instrumental in brokering a deal for 50 Cent with Columbia Records, for which Jay got the lion's share of the advance. Before Jay helped 50 Cent to reorient his life's work toward music, 50 Cent admitted to having a long-standing feud with drug distributor Kenneth "Supreme" McGriff, who was being investigated for bankrolling Murder, Inc. at the time of Jay's murder. The question being asked was whether 50 Cent's subsequent beef with Murder, Inc. and Ja Rule was somehow a link in the chain that led to Jay's murder. There were other theories as well. Whatever the truth, 50 Cent and his six-year-old son spent the early 2000s wearing bullet-proof vests wherever they went. Rap was capitalizing more than ever on its connections, both literal and metaphorical, to the street, even as it became more fully implicated into the social and corporate fabric of American life.

While the most publicized rap of the era was drenched in testosterone, it is important to note that there were other tendencies as well. In OutKast's *All Music Guide* entry, for example, John Bush credits the group with taking rap in a more upbeat direction without losing its edge. "OutKast's blend of gritty Southern soul, fluid raps, and the rolling G-funk of their Organized

Noize production crew epitomized the Atlanta wing of hip-hop's rising force, the Dirty South, during the late 1990s. Along with Goodie Mob, OutKast took Southern hip hop in bold, innovative new directions: less reliance on aggression, more positivity and melody, thicker arrangements, and intricate lyrics."[79] By 2000's *Stankonia,* OutKast had already enjoyed a run of hit singles and platinum sales. Also from Atlanta, Ludacris had emphasized the "dirty" in Dirty South with his first hit single "What's Your Fantasy" (2000) and more so with its remix.

The eccentric Outkast are credited with taking rap in a positive direction.

Other hit singles, such as the Neptunes-produced "Southern Hospitality," followed. For his third album, *Word of Mouf* (2001), Ludacris modulated his gangsta style (if not his sexism) with more subtlety and humour, as in "Area Codes." *Word of Mouf* aspired to pop rap mass appeal featuring a broad range of styles. Meanwhile, in New Orleans, Mystikal had been recording since 1995, including a stint at No Limit. By the time he was signed to Jive in the late 1990s, however, he had begun distancing himself from No Limit's thuggishness. For *Let's Get Ready* (2000), he incorporated Southern soul in the album's James Brown-influenced lead single, "Shake Ya Ass." He continued in this same vein on "Bouncin' Back (Bumpin' Me Against the Wall)," from *Tarantula* (2001). It is significant that both singles were produced by the Neptunes. If these artists retained their edge as they crossed over to the mass audience, the most popular rap artists of 2001 and 2002—Shaggy and Nelly, respectively—were unabashedly pop.

Shaggy's *Hot Shot* was the second most popular album of 2001, behind the Beatles' *1*. By the end of the year, *Hot Shot* had been certified six times platinum. Born in Jamaica but raised in Brooklyn, Shaggy was the antithesis of the New York gangsta: he was polite, well mannered, and completely non-threatening. His breakthrough single, "Oh Carolina" (1993)—a remake of Prince Buster's original, with Latin percussion over a sample of the theme from *Peter Gunn*—was recorded while he was in the U.S. military and was released after he had served a term in Kuwait during the first Gulf War. Shaggy continued recording in what he called his "dog-a-muffin" style (acknowledging his debt to dance hall) throughout the 1990s but did not achieve pop stardom until the success of *Hot Shot.*

Nelly picked up where Shaggy left off. In 2001, he was two notches down from Shaggy as the fourth most popular pop artist in *Billboard*'s tally. In 2002, he ascended to the number one artist on the year-end pop charts. Nelly was born in St. Louis, but moved to the suburbs before street life could take its toll. He burst onto the rap scene in 2000 with the blockbuster album *Country Grammar* and its lead single of the same name. With his laid-back Southern drawl, tongue-twister rhymes, and infectious pop hooks, Nelly was regarded by many onlookers as a passing fad who would soon fade from view. But *Country Grammar* caught fire. By the time Nelly was signed by Universal one year later, the album had already been certified eight times platinum. His first outing for Universal, *Nellyville* (2002), went straight to number one on the pop charts, propelled by the Neptunes-produced single, "Hot in Herre," and stayed there for seven weeks. Indeed, the week *Nellyville* was released, Nelly occupied the number one position on ten different *Billboard* charts. Even with some minimal gangsta posturing, Nelly did nothing that would risk losing any segment of his vast pop audience. If anything, including a duet with Justin Timberlake ("Work It") served only to consolidate his base among teens.

It is also the case that many women rappers rose to fame during this period, representing a geographical dispersion similar to the men. Foxy Brown, Lil' Kim, and Charli Baltimore, the latter two of whom were lovers and protégés of Biggie Smalls, hailed from New York. Missy "Misdemeanor" Elliot presided over her own record company empire in Virginia. Eve, a former stripper from Philadelphia, became the lone woman in the Ruff Ryders crew. Da Brat, from Chicago, hooked up with Jermaine Dupri's So So Def in Atlanta. Solé came from Kansas City, and Mia-X was discovered by Master P in New Orleans. Most of these new female rappers paid homage to their elder sisters like Queen Latifah but started out taking a much more over-the-top

Missy Elliott established herself as a rapper, producer, and woman to be reckoned with.

sexualized approach to their craft. Referred to early on as "hard-edged harlots" and "the reigning divas of raunch," these women have been celebrated and criticized not only for their street-tough raps and NC-17 lyrics but also for their stage outfits and demeanour that "leave little to the imagination." After a few false starts, Eve prevailed in a rap competition to be admitted to the Ruff Ryders crew. A relative newcomer to the Bronx, Eve could be as sexy as Lil' Kim or Foxy Brown or as competitive as her male counterparts. She scored double platinum on *Let There Be Eve . . . Ruff Ryders First Lady* (1999), her first full-length album for Ruff Ryders, which entered the pop charts at number one and was the first rap album by a woman to do so. But it was her duet with No Doubt's Gwen Stefani on "Let Me Blow Ya Mind" (from *Scorpion*, 2001) that really broke Eve to the mainstream audience and earned her a Grammy as well. From there, she continued her successful career as a rapper on *Eve-Olution* (2002), broke into film (*XXX, Barbershop*), and contracted with the UPN network to produce and star in a multiracial sitcom bearing her name, based on a Miami fashion designer.

Before breaking away from the pack as an artist, Missy Elliott had already established herself as a writer and producer of note, owning her own company, The Gold Mine, and working alongside producer and friend Timbaland, creating hits for other artists such as "One in a Million" for Aaliyah. As a rapper, she hit platinum on her first outing, *Supa Dupa' Fly* (1997) and more than held her own with *Da Real World* (1999), on which some critics say she reclaimed the word *bitch* as a term of strength for women. "Elliott doesn't sling the b-word around in the misogynistic way of her male hip hop cohorts," says Vanessa Jones. "Instead, Elliott reclaims it, making it the description of choice for strong women."[80] From there, the hits just kept coming: "She's a Bitch" and "Hot Boyz" from *Da Real World*; "Get Ur Freak On" and "One Minute Man" from *Miss E . . . So Addictive* (2001); and "Work It" from *Under Construction* (2002). Elliott's vocal talents—she is a consummate rapper and an able soul singer—over Timbaland's appealing digital dance grooves have made Elliott one of the few artists to span the worlds of rap, r&b/hip hop, and electronic dance music. Her artistic accomplishments stand as one vision of what a rap that remains hard, sexy, playful, and danceable could be, unencumbered by the encroachments of the thug life.

Despite the media's single-minded focus on the violent side of rap, there clearly existed a range of styles—some more uncompromising than others—that spoke to other tendencies as well.

Despite the media's single-minded focus on the violent side of rap, there clearly existed a range of styles—some more uncompromising than others—that spoke to other tendencies as well. There were also hip hop's forays into political territory, the most notable of which was the

Hip Hop Summit Action Network. Founded in 2001 with Def Jam founder Russell Simmons at the helm, the Action Network mobilized support among rappers and hip hop executives, and across the spectrum of black political leaders, from Ben Chavis, then of the NAACP, to Louis Farrakhan of the Nation of Islam. Even with its own internal tensions and divisions, the Action Network managed to take on issues such as freedom of speech and social injustice as well as concrete political campaigns, such as reforming the punitive Rockefeller drug laws in New York and voter registration on a national scale. Such efforts showcased the positive activities of the citizens of the hip hop nation—activities that were seldom reported with the same gusto as the sensationalized acts of violence.

———

The music industry began the 1990s with the pleasant surprise that a local music scene from Seattle could spawn a national market that would define a generation. The fact that the major players were unable to follow up this success with another such mass phenomenon coincided with a downturn in industry fortunes at mid-decade that was reflected in flat sales. To regain its lost footing, the industry tried packaging a number of trends based on age (teen pop), gender (women), ethnicity (Latino/a), etc., but to no lasting avail. Of course the staples in the industry marketing bag, from country to rap, continued to sell, but such music had long since established identities that would not permit promoting the singers as Next Big Things. Country still had a regional aura that smacked of Nashville commercialism, even as it dominated the national pop charts. Rap had always been kept at arm's length by the major labels for a variety of reasons, ranging from the uncomfortable gaze of conservative watchdog organizations to the impossible collectivity of its business and artistic practices, as rappers routinely collaborated with one another across contractual lines. The failure of the music industry to completely pigeonhole consumers spoke to a truth that the major labels have never fully grasped: that most consumers' tastes are far more diverse than music industry marketing strategies permit.

The year 2000 ended with the Beatles' greatest hits compilation, 1, at number one, prompting one record store owner to query: "How many times can people buy what they already have?" At the time, the answer to that question appeared to be, We don't know yet. One year later, the music industry was confronted with the nightmare that the answer might be none, as digital file swapping became a popular method for acquiring music and the music industry was unable to evolve toward a business model that would accommodate the practice.

Welcome to the Terrordome: Music and Copyright in (a Time of) Crisis

By 1999, according to the International Federation of the Phonographic Industry (IFPI), the international music business was worth $38.5 billion annually in worldwide sales. The industry's renewed good fortune became the occasion for another round of mergers that made the acquisitions of a decade earlier seem downright small-time. In 1998, Seagrams combined the holdings of MCA (acquired from Matsushita in 1995) and PolyGram (purchased for $10.4 billion) into a single corporate entity called, modestly enough, the Universal Music Group. Among the properties that UMG would control were MCA, Universal (formerly PolyGram), Geffen, A&M, Motown, Island, Mercury, London, and Interscope, not to mention forty wholly owned publishing houses. Operating in forty-eight countries, the new mega-firm boasted a 23 percent market share of worldwide sales. This was followed in short order by the $165 billion takeover of Time-Warner by America Online. Meanwhile, the unexpected demerger of Thorn-EMI had set the record division

The music industry initially regarded the Internet with caution and suspicion, which soon erupted into outright hostility.

afloat as a prime takeover target. What had been "The Big Six" in the early 1990s was rapidly moving toward becoming "The Big Four" as the new millennium began. These mergers were accompanied by a significant downsizing of staff (as these new gigantic companies moved to capitalize on economies of scale) and significant cutbacks in artist rosters (as they set about constructing a global marketing apparatus that demanded superstardom for success). In the merger that created Universal, for example, the artist roster at affiliated label A&M was cut from ninety artists to eight.

485

The AOL/Time-Warner merger marked the first music industry merger involving an Internet company. It was doubly significant that AOL was the senior partner, not the other way around. Indeed, the online companies that survived the bust of the late 1990s dot-com boom couldn't help but take notice of recording companies in their life-or-death search for "content." The music industry, for its part, initially regarded the Internet with caution and suspicion, which soon erupted into outright hostility. In the mid-1990s, while certain artists and record companies were still trying to figure out how to turn a profit from enhanced CDs (which never amounted to much more than a novelty), the music industry as a whole was largely unaware of the research on file compression that had been going on for years at Germany's Fraunhofer Institute. In 1992, the audio portion of this work was approved by the Motion Picture Experts Group (MPEG) as a standard that was designated MPEG 1—Audio Layer 3, or MP3 for short. But it wasn't until modem and computer clock speeds increased enough to permit efficient downloads of MP3 files toward the end of the decade that the incredible potential of MP3 was finally realized. By the late 1990s, music enthusiasts—indeed, artists themselves—were converting audio CD files to MP3s and posting them on websites for easy, and most often unauthorized, download. For a time, the term *MP3* became second only to the word *sex* as the most requested item on Internet search engines. More importantly, as the full impact of this new software became apparent, MP3 threatened to become the Trojan horse that could topple the music business.

It wasn't until modem and computer clock speeds increased enough to permit efficient downloads of MP3 files toward the end of the decade that MP3 threatened to become the Trojan horse that could topple the music business.

As if that weren't enough for the music business to contend with, the events of September 11, 2001, had a devastating effect on an economy that had already entered a bust cycle, and pushed the country into questionable and possibly protracted wars in Afghanistan, Iraq, and wherever else the government's assessment of a terrorist threat might lead. These events had the effect of introducing a new role for music of the rock and rap era, as patriotism became *de rigeur* and protest and dissent were muffled in the name of individual sensitivity and/or national security.

They Want Their MP3

For the uninitiated, MP3 is file compression software that can shrink an audio CD file to one-tenth its original size without appreciable loss of quality. MP3 files are small enough to send as email attachments. Before online etailer MP3.com was forced into bankruptcy by the major record labels, the self-described "premier music service provider" posted thousands of MP3 files on its website for easy download. This became a particularly popular activity in areas with convenient access to high-speed, high-capacity connections to the Internet—places like college campuses. In such an environment, the development of so-called peer-to-peer technologies like Napster, Gnutella, and Freenet utilized the potential of MP3 to the fullest. Napster, developed by Northeastern University drop-out Shawn Fanning, was a combination search engine, communication portal, and file-sharing software that facilitated sharing MP3 files by granting to any user who logged on to its central database access to all other Napster users and the MP3 files they chose to share. As early as 2000, estimates of the size of the worldwide Napster community were as high as 40 million users. Newer technologies, such as Gnutella and Freenet, took the

Shawn Fanning developed the software that could revolutionize the music industry. Apparently he does not hold a grudge against the band that sued him for his trouble.

process one step further. While Napster users first had to log on to a central server to access other users' MP3 files, Gnutella and Freenet allowed direct user-to-user contact (peer-to-peer), which made it much more difficult to track users or the files they were trading/sharing. Freenet was designed to enable such direct transactions not just with MP3s but also with any file type—audio, video, text, spreadsheets, databases, etc.—and added the capacity for file encryption and user anonymity to the mix.

It was not difficult to see why the music industry would be concerned. In its push toward globalization, the industry had become significantly more concentrated at a time when technological advances demanded a model of decentralization. The Internet and MP3, in contrast, held out the possibility of a business model that could link consumers directly with the artists and music of their choice, bypassing the record companies completely. Furthermore, as an unprotected format, MP3 left the industry with no way to regulate the software's use. With articulate industry critics like Chuck D and forward-looking artists like Sheryl Crow leading the way, MP3 quickly generated a momentum that the industry couldn't help but notice. According to a 1999 article in *Wired* magazine, "About 846 million new CDs were sold last year. But at least 17 million MP3 files are downloaded from the Net *each day*. That adds up to almost 3 billion in the first six months of 1999."[1] And that was before Napster was unleashed. A later study by Webnoise estimated that Napster users downloaded 1.3 billion songs in September 2000 alone and that at any given moment there were 640,000 Napster users online together.[2]

In its push toward globalization, the music industry had become significantly more concentrated at a time when technological advances demanded a model of decentralization. The Internet and MP3, in contrast, held out the possibility of a business model that could link consumers directly with the artists and music of their choice, bypassing the record companies completely.

Rather than embracing the potential of the Internet and taking the lead in developing convenient, affordable, user-friendly methods of downloading music, the music industry retreated instead into a protectionist mode, seeking to prop up its dated business model of manufacturing and selling a particular piece of physical property. Terrified that computer users sharing and downloading music tracks for free over the Internet would seriously cut into CD sales, the industry adopted a two-pronged strategy of legislation and litigation, advocating for laws that would extend the reach of copyright and filing lawsuits against alleged infringers. There followed a spate of restrictive legislation, designed to strengthen corporate copyright protection on the one hand and narrow the terrain of fair use on the other, as well as a flurry of legal actions primarily targeting MP3.com and Napster and demonizing the users of these services as pirates and thieves.

Legislation and Litigation

To grasp the severity of these actions, it is important to understand that copyright law has never simply mandated an exclusive contract to exploit the fruits of one's creativity. Instead, has been a balancing act, weighing the legal protection of intellectual property and providing an incentive for creative work against the public rights of access to information and freedom of expression. As framed in the U.S. Constitution: "The Congress shall have power . . . to promote the progress of science and useful arts, by securing for limited times to authors and inventors the exclusive right to their respective writings and discoveries."[3] According to Harvard legal scholar William Fisher, the most popular school of thought regarding the intent of the founding fathers holds that their primary concern was the promotion of learning; the protection of authors was simply a means to that end.[4] This perspective has been reaffirmed over the years in provisions regarding the public domain, personal use, fair use, and rights of access. It was reiterated in the late 1980s in the House report on the Berne Convention Implementation Act of 1988, which stated: "'The constitutional purpose of copyright is to facilitate the flow of ideas in the interest of learning' . . . [T]he primary objective of our copyright laws is not to reward the author, but rather to secure for the public the benefits from the creations of authors."[5]

Copyright law has never simply mandated an exclusive contract to exploit the fruits of one's creativity. Instead, it has been a balancing act, weighing the legal protection of intellectual property and providing an incentive for creative work against the public rights of access to information and freedom of expression.

The legislation of the late 1990s inverted these priorities by serving the interests of corporate capital over those of the general public. The No Electronic Theft Act of 1997 was enacted to prosecute and punish persons who accessed copyrighted materials electronically without authorization, whether or not they realized any "commercial advantage or private financial gain."[6] In eliminating commercial gain as a necessary condition for unlawful behaviour, the law criminalized a range of practices that had once been considered fair use. The Digital Millennium Copyright Act of 1998, narrowed the terrain of fair use still further by making it illegal to circumvent technological measures for protecting sound recordings and other copyrighted material. Seemingly in the interest of creative artists, the law created, in effect, a new owners' right to control access to a work. In 1998, Congress enacted the Sonny Bono Copyright Term Extension Act, a sweeping revision spearheaded by Disney because under the existing law, Mickey Mouse was about to enter the public domain. This law extends U.S. copyrights owned by corporations to ninety-five years and individually held copyrights to the life of the author plus seventy years, effectively eliminating the public domain for anything written in the twentieth century.

Armed with a daunting array of new as well as previous legislation, the music industry launched its first legal salvo against online music in October 1998, targeting Diamond Multimedia's Rio, a portable, Walkman-like digital MP3 player capable of downloading, storing, and playing back sixty minutes of music. The Rio caused the music industry to stand up and take notice because it was this product that first moved MP3 beyond the computer desktop. Fearing piracy on a grand scale, the Recording Industry Association of America (RIAA) was quick to seek an injunction against the Rio, claiming a violation of the Digital Audio Home Recording Act of 1992. The Audio Home Recording Act itself had been the result of a compromise between manufacturers of audio recording hardware and record companies; it imposed levies on blank digital audio recorders and media to compensate the music industry for lost revenues allegedly due to home taping. Significantly, the law permits copying for personal use, effectively taxing consumers for the privilege. In the Rio case, the courts came down on the side of users' rights, but in this instance it was because Diamond squeezed through a loophole by successfully arguing that the legislation targeted only recording devices and the Rio was a storage device. With the injunction quashed, other portable MP3 players were rushed to market, including Creative Labs' Nomad, Pontis' MPlayer3, and Empeg's Empeg Car, capable of storing up to 5,000 songs.

Undaunted by this setback, the RIAA trained its sights on MP3.com, at the time the best-known source of online MP3 files. In late 1999, MP3.com constructed an online database of some 60,000 commercially available CDs and gave free access to users who inserted a corresponding CD into the CD-ROM drive on a computer and "beamed" its contents to MP3.com. This action prompted MP3.com to place a copy of that CD's content into the user's password-protected "music locker" on the My.MP3.com website. The service allowed users to listen to the music of any given CD on any web-enabled computer, anywhere in the world. The RIAA brought suit against MP3.com, alleging that the service infringed the copyrights of all the major label recordings in the database. Since MP3.com had failed to negotiate permissions or licensing arrangements to construct the database in the first place, it was almost a foregone conclusion that they would lose the suit. Still, their use argument was interesting. In its defence, MP3.com argued that once a consumer buys a recording, the music industry should no longer have control over how it is used. If that person chooses to upload the contents of that CD to an online database, he or she should have the right to do so since the Audio Home Recording Act allows copying for personal use. This argument is still a point of debate.

> *MP3.com argued that once a consumer buys a recording, the music industry should no longer have control over how it is used.*

Artists themselves were divided on the question. While singers such as Paul McCartney sued MP3.com and others such as Puff Daddy/P. Diddy spoke out against services that facilitated MP3 file swapping, Prince praised Napster as "an exciting new development in the history of music."[7] And unsigned artists were turning overwhelmingly to the Internet as an alternative vehicle for self-promotion. Roger McGuinn, founder of the Byrds and a veteran of twenty-five albums on four different labels, testified at the July 2000 U.S. Senate hearings on digital music that: "In most cases a modest advance against royalties was all the money I received for my participation in these recording projects."[8] Regarding his experiences with MP3.com, in contrast, he stated:

> *They offered an unheard of, non-exclusive recording contract with a royalty rate of 50% of the gross sales. . . . MP3.com not only allowed me to place these songs on their server, but also offered to make CDs of these songs for sale. They absorbed all the packaging and distribution costs. So far I have made thousands of dollars from the sale of these folk recordings on MP3.com, and I feel privileged to be able to use MP3s and the Internet as a vehicle for my artistic expression. MP3.com has offered me more artistic freedom than any of my previous relationships with mainstream recording companies. I think this avenue of digital music delivery is of great value to young artists, because it's so difficult for bands to acquire a recording contract. When young bands ask me how to get their music heard, I always recommend MP3.com.[9]*

By the end of 2000, MP3.com had settled with all the major labels for an estimated cost of about $170 million and had revived its My.MP3.com venture, hoping to turn it into a lucrative subscription service. Competing etailers such as myplay and Musicbank were moving ahead with similar licensing arrangements. But at the end of the day, these services could not compete with the power and potential of peer-to-peer file-swapping networks like Napster. It was Napster that crystallized all the music industry fears about piracy and theft.

The RIAA filed suit against Napster on behalf of eighteen powerful record companies in December 1999, alleging "contributory and vicarious" copyright infringement. Another suit, brought by the heavy metal group Metallica (which was joined by Dr. Dre), further polarized a situation already fraught with tension. Upset by reports that unfinished songs from the sound-track to *Mission Impossible II* were already being traded over the Internet, Metallica hired NetPD to monitor three days of Napster activity. Drummer Lars Ulrich then hand-delivered the results to Napster headquarters—60,000 pages of screen names, documenting 330,000-plus Napster users, who downloaded 1.4 million Metallica songs during the three-day period.[10] The group then demanded that Napster remove the violators from their service in a lawsuit that also named Yale, Indiana University, and the University of Southern California. The Metallica suit was somewhat neutralized when Napster, as per its own antipiracy policy, complied and removed all 330,000-plus users. As required by law, however, Napster also issued a disclaimer stating that any users who felt that they had been falsely identified could petition the company and be reinstated. Within days, 30,000 users petitioned and were reinstated, placing Metallica in the awkward position of having to initiate 30,000 individual lawsuits against some of their most ardent fans to maintain their legal position.

Perhaps the most surprising aspect of the case was the posture of the music business and prosecuting bands toward their own consumers. In the campaign to shut down Napster, the major labels, and groups like Metallica in particular, squandered valuable cultural capital demonizing their core fan base as pirates and thieves. After the first 17,000 users dropped in the Metallica suit petitioned Napster to be reinstated, for example, Metallica's lawyer decried: "What Napster has done is create 17,000 liars."[11] Statements like that had the effect of alienating the most dedicated segment of the record-buying public. Wrote P. J. Huffstutter in the *LA Times*: "The industry's crusade to block techno-logical innovation has been taken as a declaration of war against young music fans, traditionally its most fervent customers. Fighting back, computer-savvy kids have united and are turning a business dispute into a holy war."[12]

In the campaign to shut down Napster, the major labels, and groups like Metallica in particular, squandered valuable cultural capital demonizing their core fan base as pirates and thieves.

As 2000 drew to a close, Napster was still in court facing major suits from Metallica, Dr. Dre, and all the major labels. Curiously, at the same time, Napster also announced an alliance with one of its plaintiffs, BMG, to develop a new, secure subscription service as a joint venture that the other labels could join. Under the terms of the deal, Bertelsmann, parent of one of the five major music companies suing Napster, agreed to withdraw its lawsuit once Napster success-fully introduced the membership-based commercial service. At the time, Napster estimated that a $4.95 monthly user fee could generate some $500 million for record companies and musi-cians.[13] As the months crept into 2001, however, the other majors had shown little interest in the concept, perhaps preferring to make an example of Napster. Accordingly, on 6 March 2001, Judge Marilyn Hall Patel successfully issued an injunction requiring Napster to take all "reason-able" steps to block any copyrighted songs from its network on receiving notice from the record companies. The RIAA quickly provided Napster with a list of some 675,000 protected works with 8 million file names that it said should be blocked. Try as it might, Napster was unable to comply with such demands. By summer 2001, the wildly popular file-swapping network had been effectively shut down, despite continued attempts on the part of Bertelsmann to help revive it as a commercial pay service.

Piracy and Theft

Loaded terms like *piracy* and *theft,* of course, cannot simply be taken at face value. The music industry tried to make the case that file swapping and digital downloading were tantamount to stealing. Had they been able to understand these practices in more value-neutral terms, however, they might have been able to see the value of Napster as a promotional vehicle. A study conducted by the Norman Lear Center at USC in June 2000 in the wake of the Napster hearings suggested that downloading did not reduce students' CD consumption patterns. Fully 73 percent of students who downloaded MP3s reported that they still bought either the same number of CDs or more.[14] This finding squared with a *Playboy* study of downloaders in which a surprising 87 percent of the respondents reported buying the same number of CDs or more.[15] Indeed, according to the industry's own mid-year 2000 figures—a period of heavy Napster activity—an RIAA press release stated: "The number of full-length CDs . . . is at an all-time high, growing 6.0% from this time last year . . . which suggests once again that consumer demand for music in the form of a CD remains the mainstay."[16] The importance of this pattern cannot be emphasized enough: during Napster's heyday, before the lawsuits began to take their toll, CD album sales were still on the rise. Who, then, were the pirates and thieves?

The degree to which the music industry projected terms such as *piracy* and *theft* onto consumers tended to deflect attention from its own less than ethical practices. While the music industry often cast its policing actions in terms of legal protection for creative musicians, the evidence suggested that corporate bottom lines were a much higher priority. The history of popular music has been rife with tales of one-sided contracts that have included low royalty rates, unfair publishing arrangements, multiyear renewals that kept an artist tied to a particular label, and advances against royalties that kept artists perpetually in debt. Indeed, the major sources of revenue for artists have most often been concert ticket sales and merchandizing. Income from royalties has usually accrued to record companies as repayment of advances. In 1999, the music industry added a significant item to this catalogue of abuse with the passage of the Work for Hire amendment. At the behest of the RIAA and unbeknownst to Congress, Mitch Glazier, then majority counsel to the House Judiciary Subcommittee on Intellectual Property, slipped a three-line amendment into an omnibus appropriations bill that made all recordings works for hire, reducing all artists, in effect, to hired hands of the record companies. Master recordings, which previously reverted to artists after thirty-five years, became the property of the record companies forever. President Clinton signed the bill into law without debate. Mitch Glazier then left his government post to become the RIAA's chief lobbyist. The law wasn't reversed until the following year, under intense pressure from artists like Don Henley and Sheryl Crow, who organized the Recording Artists Coalition to protect the rights of artists.

> *While the music industry often cast its policing actions in terms of legal protection for creative musicians, the evidence suggested that corporate bottom lines were a much higher priority.*

In May 2000, the Federal Trade Commission settled a suit against all the major labels involving a price-fixing scheme known as minimum advertising price programs (MAPS), whereby these companies routinely paid a store to advertise a particular CD in return for specifying a required minimum retail price in the ads. Referring to what the FTC called "coercive agreements," FTC Chairman Robert Pitofsky stated, "There was no plausible business justification for this other than to get prices up."[17] According to the suit, consumers were overcharged $500 million for CDs in a two-and-a-half-year period. While the majors admitted to no wrongdoing, the terms of the settlement obligated them to refrain from imposing MAPS-like requirements on retailers for seven years, resulting in potential savings for consumers of an estimated $17 million per month.

Such behaviour called into question the uncritical acceptance of music industry logic and reinforced the notion that terms like *piracy* and *theft* were relative terms to begin with. Using such terms also had the effect of putting a narrowly negative spin on issues that were considerably more complicated. If terms such as *piracy* and *theft* had been replaced by phrases such as *file sharing* and *community building,* for example, a very different picture would have emerged, one that emphasized the more positive aspects of the Napster community. It was clear from the beginning that there were any number of features of Napster that the music industry simply had to incorporate if it was to survive.

In the first place, the Napster interface made the process of locating and downloading a song so easy that even a neophyte could do it. Napster set the standard for user-friendliness that the industry then had to match. More importantly, Napster and other similar services offered users a music library that cut across artists, songs, and labels. As such, it was a library that individual labels—organized and divided by imprint, genre, race, language, etc.—couldn't duplicate. Music fans do not have any label loyalty. In most cases, they neither know nor care what label an artist records for. They know that they like a particular song and they want access to it as easily as possible. Napster enabled users to construct their own customized compilation CDs of exactly the music they wanted. Record companies, as structured, could not have easily duplicated such a service. Finally, Napster users did not simply trade music files; they communicated with each other. They shared ideas and feelings, argued passionately about music, and turned each other on to new sounds. In short, they self-selected into communities of taste, which, without spending a dime, constituted a better promotional vehicle than anything the music industry ever had at its disposal.

Throughout the Napster controversy, many industry observers felt that the major labels were using their legal victories to buy time until they could figure out how to enter the online record business on their own terms. Key to this prospect was the industry's search for a secure digital format to use for commercial music downloading. Interestingly, the Secure Digital Music Initiative (SDMI) was headed by Leonardo Chariglioni, founder of the Motion Picture Experts Group (MPEG), which certified the MP3 specification in the first place. SDMI was envisioned as a standard that would encode a sound file with a digital watermark, identifying its owner and origin, as a way of discouraging piracy on the Internet. After nearly two years of experimentation with four types of watermarks, SDMI had borne little fruit. A challenge issued by Chariglioni in September 2000 that offered up to $10,000 to anyone who could crack the SDMI code was flatly refused by the hacker community.[18] Then in October, Princeton computer scientist Edward Felten and a team of students defeated all four watermarks.[19] Two years after the SDMI began, then, there was still no music being secured by the watermarking technology.

The Music Industry in a Post-Napster World

Despite the disappointing results of SDMI and the prospect of declining sales, by 2001, the need for a meaningful online presence was becoming unmistakably clear to the music industry. Following a few false starts and the devastation of 9/11, but just in time for the year-end holiday season, the major labels inaugurated two new online music services. Pressplay, a joint venture of Sony and Vivendi Universal, included deals with Yahoo, Roxio, the Microsoft Network (MSN), and, interestingly, MP3.com. MusicNet, a competing project of AOL Time Warner, BMG, and EMI, partnered with RealNetworks and reportedly agreed to allow Napster itself to license its catalogue. At launch, both services were restricted to the catalogues of the participating labels and offered only limited access to digital music for a monthly fee. For $24.95 a month, pressplay, for example, allowed a user to stream 1,000 songs, download 100, and burn 20, but no more than 2 by any given artist. Industry analysts were quick to point out that both services were likely to enjoy little success as long as they offered limited catalogues and restricted how music could be used. Meanwhile, the U.S. Department of Justice launched an antitrust investigation of MusicNet and pressplay to determine if the major labels had been colluding illegally to set rates and terms for the use of their music.

> *By 2001, the need for a meaningful online presence was becoming unmistakably clear to the music industry.*

A more troublesome limitation arose from the fact that the two services aligned themselves with bitter Internet rivals Microsoft and RealNetworks, which could only hamper collaboration and cross-label licensing. Pressplay was based on Microsoft's Windows Media Player, while MusicNet used RealNetworks' RealOne Player. "It's a crying shame that the Microsoft-RealNetworks rift has spilled over to the major labels," said Aram Sinnreich of Jupiter Media Metrix. "The end result is that it will be a longer time before consumers will have access to a music-subscription service that offers them enough music."[20] Not surprisingly, a number of next-generation Napster clones, such as Grokster, Morpheus, and KaZaA, jumped in to fill the void left by the major labels. For the first week of 2002, for instance, the RealOne Player was downloaded 18,000 times from software library Download.com, compared with 1.5 million downloads for Morpheus and 1 million for KaZaA.[21] Despite upgrades to pressplay and MusicNet that liberalized the terms of both services, the limiting features of restricted CD burning, inadequate transfers to portable MP3 players, and "tethered downloads" that disappeared from the user's hard drive on termination of service made it impossible for these industry offerings to compete. As of the year ending September 2002, the free KaZaA software had been downloaded 120 million times.

Facing competition of this magnitude, the RIAA never wavered from its strategy of prosecuting alleged offenders, even as the major labels tried to strengthen their online presence. Beginning in October 2001, the RIAA had joined forces with Hollywood's Motion Picture Association of America (MPAA) to nip the threat of new file-swapping services in the bud, following essentially the same strategy that was used against Napster. But as its suits against Grokster, Morpheus, and KaZaA worked their way through the court system, the RIAA received a series of stunning setbacks. First, an appeals court in the Netherlands ruled that distributing the KaZaA software there did not violate copyright law, stipulating that "Insofar as there are acts that are relevant to copyright, such acts are performed by those who use the

computer program and not by KaZaA."[22] Then, in April 2003, a federal judge in Los Angeles
ruled that Grokster and Morpheus were not liable for infringing practices on the part of their
users. In what amounted to a complete reversal of the Napster decision, Judge Stephen Wilson
ruled that Grokster and Morpheus were "not significantly different from companies that sell
home video recorders or copy machines," an argument that file-swapping services had been
making for years. Basing his decision of the famous Sony Betamax case, which recognized that
these technologies are capable of "substantial non-infringing uses," the judge distinguished the
defendants from Napster in noting that Napster opened itself to liability
by playing an active role in connecting its users, whereas Grokster and
Morpheus had no control over the actions of their users once they downloaded the software.[23]

> *Denied the legal basis for eliminating the new peer-to-peer services, the music business felt it had no alternative but to pursue a strategy that was guaranteed to raise the ire of the entire record-buying public—suing thousands of individual consumers.*

Denied the legal basis for eliminating the new peer-to-peer
services, the music business felt it had no alternative but to pursue a
strategy that was guaranteed to raise the ire of the entire record-buying
public—suing thousands of individual consumers. As part of this new phase of their antipiracy
campaign, in April 2003, the RIAA surprised hundreds of thousands of file swappers with an
email message that read:

> *It appears that you are offering copyrighted music to others from your computer. . . . When you break
> the law, you risk legal penalties. There is a simple way to avoid that risk: DON'T STEAL MUSIC,
> either by offering it to others to copy or downloading it on a 'file-sharing' system like this. When you
> offer music on these systems, you are not anonymous and you can easily be identified.*[24]

As a warning, the message was somewhat disingenuous. That same month, the RIAA had already filed lawsuits against four college students from Princeton, Michigan Tech, and Rensselaer for allegedly uploading between 27,000 and 1 million songs each. The lawsuits asked for damages of $150,000 per song (the maximum allowable under the terms of the Digital Millennium Copyright Act), effectively suing the students for billions of dollars.

In fact, the RIAA had begun the process of suing individuals six months earlier, when it subpoenaed Verizon to get the name and address of a KaZaA file trader who used Verizon as his Internet service provider. The RIAA targeted the ISPs because peer-to-peer systems like KaZaA made it possible for a user to identify the Internet address of fellow swappers. By staking out such systems, the RIAA was able to intercept these Internet addresses. Then, by working back to the relevant Internet companies, they could subpoena the ISPs to get the names and addresses of the subscribers who were assigned those particular Internet addresses at a particular point in time.

Verizon fought the case vigorously, not because it wanted to encourage copyright infringement, but because of the controversial fast-track subpoena process the RIAA sought to employ. An obscure provision of the Digital Millennium Copyright Act allowed copyright holders to obtain subpoenas from court clerks without going before a judge and without first filing a lawsuit. Envisioning literally thousands of lawsuits, the music industry was counting on this streamlined process; without it, the cost of pursuing individual lawsuits would have been prohibitive. Civil liberties groups quickly signed on to the case, concerned about issues of privacy and due process. Verizon and other commercial ISPs were also concerned that, increasingly, the burden of copyright enforcement would fall to them. By the time the case came to a head, more than 100 commercial ISPs and universities had been subpoenaed, including Comcast, Time Warner Cable, RCN, Earthlink, Massachusetts Institute of Technology, Boston College, Loyola, DePaul, and Bentley College. Some colleges and universities readily turned over the contact information of the alleged student violators. Others, like MIT and Boston College, opposed the subpoenas on procedural grounds, arguing that they violated provisions of the Family Education Rights and Privacy Act.

The music industry also experimented with more draconian measures during this time period. Some of the major labels piloted copy-proof CDs, which were in effect corrupted audio CD files that not only couldn't be copied but wouldn't even play in certain computer CD-ROM drives. Some industry defenders took to posting corrupted files on the various P2P networks. Senator Orrin Hatch, chairman of the Senate Judiciary Committee, who earned $18,000 in songwriting royalties for the year, actually endorsed developing the technological means for destroying the computers of downloaders during a government hearing on copyright violation.[25]

In June 2003, Verizon lost the fight against the subpoenas on appeal, and though it had not yet exhausted its legal options, by July the company was preparing to turn over the contact information of 150 subscribers who had been fingered by the RIAA. The Verizon case was considered a decisive victory for the RIAA, opening the floodgates to over a thousand new subpoenas. These translated into 261 individual lawsuits, those fingered including a twelve-year-old honour student from a New York public housing project and a seventy-one-year-old grandfather from Texas. Preteen Brianna Lahara, whose mother settled the case out of court for

$2,000, quickly became the poster child for the heavy-handed tactics of the music industry. Grokster President Wayne Rosso offered to pay the bill, denouncing the RIAA as "the show-business version of the Taliban."[26]

By the end of the year, however, the legal landscape had changed. In December 2003, the appeals court ruled that the music industry's mass subpoenas would be permissible only in instances where the allegedly illegal files were stored on the ISP's own servers. By this time, the RIAA had already modified its tactics to sending a demand letter with an option to settle out of court before going to trial. During this period, the RIAA also promoted an amnesty program called Clean Slate, which reportedly protected users against prosecution if they agreed to sign a statement saying they had illegally downloaded files and would refrain from ever doing so again. The program was immediately denounced as a sham by the Electronic Frontier Foundation (among others), who correctly pointed out that the RIAA did not have the authority to prohibit lawsuits by its member labels or other rights holders and that signing the Clean Slate affidavit would be tantamount to providing them with a signed confession.

Although the appeals court decision put an end to the DMCA-related mass subpoenas, the RIAA continued the tactic of targeting one individual at a time, using the traditional subpoena process under the supervision of a judge. Undeterred by a constant stream of bad press, the RIAA pursued this practice relentlessly for the next few years. As of October 2005, most of the 3,300 alleged file traders who had settled out of court had forked over sums ranging from $3,000 to $11,000 apiece.[27] By May 2006, more than 18,000 people had been sued in the United States alone, with another 5,500 in eighteen other countries.[28] Perhaps the most interesting thing about all these cases is that, as of June 2006, none of them had been adjudicated in a court of law, which is to say that not a single person had yet been convicted of any wrongdoing. Indeed, the first case ever to go to trial was still pending. It targeted Patricia Santangelo, a single mother of five, whom the judge described as "an Internet-illiterate parent, who does not know Kazaa from kazoo, and who can barely retrieve her e-mail."[29] Until Santangelo surprised industry lawyers by insisting on going to trial even after her lawyer resigned, the music industry had simply been intimidating individuals into settling out of court, creating a handsome new revenue stream for itself in the process.

While the initial threat of lawsuits reportedly precipitated a dramatic—if not a sustained—drop in music downloading over the summer of 2003, file sharing had already grown to proportions that even the Napster community couldn't have imagined. The RIAA estimated that 2.6 billion copyrighted song files were being traded over P2P networks every month, with KaZaA leading the pack with more than 230 million users, up from 100 million one year earlier.[30] Moreover, statistics from Big Champagne, a market research firm specializing in P2P technology, showed a steady increase in the number of users who were online at any given time from 3.8 million in August 2003 to 6.7 million in October 2004.[31]

While there was no question that CD sales had declined during this period, there were many questions regarding just how much they had declined, what portion could be attributed to free downloading, and whether, in its relentless pursuit of file swappers, the music industry had lost sight of its primary mission. Industry figures of decline ranged from 26 percent to 31 percent over the three-year period marking the start of the new millennium, and file sharing was always cited as a major source of the problem. According to statistics from Forrester Research, however, the decline in sales since 2000 had been 15 percent, with only 35 percent of that amount due to unauthorized downloading.[32] A more definitive study, undertaken by economists at the Harvard Business School and the University of North Carolina at Chapel Hill, concluded somewhat dramatically, "Downloads have an effect on sales which is statistically indistinguishable from zero."[33] Indeed, for the most popular albums—"the top 25 percent that had more than 600,000 sales"—the study actually found a positive correlation between downloading and sales. "For every 150 songs downloaded, the study showed, sales jumped by one CD."[34] The thing that made this particular study so compelling was that it did not rely on subjective user testimony at all, but rather on a comparison of data from 1.75 million downloads during a seventeen-week period in fall 2002 with actual sales data from Nielsen SoundScan during the same period.

In addition to being perceived as a cultural schoolyard bully, the industry also gave the sense that it was exaggerating both its losses and the proportion of the losses that could be attributed to file swapping.

In addition to being perceived as a cultural schoolyard bully, the industry also gave the sense that it was exaggerating both its losses and the proportion of the losses that could be attributed to file swapping. Seldom did the music industry analysis attribute the decline to competition from DVDs and video games or to the fact that so many record labels were in play that industry executives were more concerned about cutting costs, trimming artist rosters, and managing bottom lines than about producing music. Nor did anyone mention that the music industry's losses were comparable to the decline in the economy as a whole following the devastating effects of 9/11. Moreover, implicit in the music industry's logic was an unproven assumption that a CD downloaded was a CD not bought. If anything, there were more studies showing that downloaders bought more music than nondownloaders, rather than the other way around. Whatever the actual figures, it finally had to be admitted that while punitive lawsuits might make file swappers fearful of downloading for a time—at best, a temporary reprieve awaiting better user anonymity—these lawsuits certainly were not designed to stimulate CD sales. The San Jose *Mercury News* put it best when it editorialized, "Suing your customers, as a long-term strategy, is dumb."[35]

It appeared as if the most popular file trading services might begin to suffer a reversal of fortune beginning in early 2004, when the Australian music industry decided to go after KaZaA on its home turf. The first question, however, was where KaZaA called home. While its domain name was registered to an Australian company called LEF Interactive—which took its name from the French slogan *liberté, égalité, fraternité*—its software was licensed to a company in Estonia, its servers were in Denmark, and its web interface was owned by Sharman Networks, officially located in the island nation of Vanuatu. The major labels used an obscure Australian law known as Anton Pillar to get court permission to raid Sharman's offices and the homes of its executives to search for evidence of copyright infringement. In September 2005, the court ruled that Sharman Networks had encouraged copyright infringement on KaZaA. The major labels were expected to petition for several billion dollars in damages, in addition to which the court ruled that Sharman would be liable for 90 percent of the music industry's legal fees, which had already run to millions of dollars. Seeing the writing on the wall, KaZaA took steps to prohibit Australians from downloading its software and began negotiations to settle with the music industry and make the transition to a legally sanctioned pay service, which eventually cost the company an estimated $115 million.

By this time, Grokster and its co-defendant, StreamCast Networks (owner of Morpheus), had experienced a similar defeat. In June 2005, the U.S. Supreme Court unanimously ruled that companies that actively encourage or induce users to engage in illegal file trading are liable for their users' illegal actions. Wrote Justice David Souter: "We hold that one who distributes a device with the object of promoting its use to infringe copyright, as shown by clear expression or other affirmative steps taken to foster infringement, is liable for the resulting acts of infringement by third parties."[36] While the Court did not rule that Grokster and Morpheus were guilty of anything, instead referring the case back to the lower court, Souter's decision made the Court's feelings on the matter unmistakably clear, stating that "Grokster and StreamCast are not . . . merely passive recipients of information about infringing use. The record is replete with evidence that from the moment Grokster and StreamCast began to distribute their free software, each one clearly voiced the objective that recipients use it to download copyrighted works, and each took active steps to encourage infringement."[37] StreamCast pledged to continue fighting the case. Grokster quickly settled for $50 million in damages and the agreement to stop distributing its software. And the Grokster website (www.grokster.com) went dark, except for the following statement:

> *The United States Supreme Court unanimously confirmed that using this service to trade copyrighted material is illegal. Copying copyrighted motion picture and music files using unauthorized peer-to-peer services is illegal and is prosecuted by copyright owners. There are legal services for downloading music and movies. This service is not one of them.*

Interestingly, that was not what the Supreme Court had said. The legal doctrine that underpinned the Grokster case was similar to the Napster suit for "contributory and vicarious copyright infringement." It is important to note that these are court-created legal theories; there is nothing in the copyright law itself that uses this language. Both theories have tests for liability that have been developed in the practice of case law over the years. Since 1984, the Sony Betamax standard of "substantial non-infringing uses" had been seen as the primary limitation on the degree to which a service provider could be sued for "contributory and vicarious infringement." At the district and appellate levels, Grokster and the other second-generation P2P services were judged to have met this standard. Congress tried to bypass this standard by proposing the so-called INDUCE Act, which would have legislated that companies could be held liable simply for encouraging their users to engage in illegal activity. Even though the legislation failed, the Supreme Court applied the principle in the Grokster case. Souter's opinion, which "premises liability on purposeful, culpable expression and conduct," clearly narrowed the broader interpretation of "substantial non-infringing uses" that had been applied to Grokster by a court of appeals one year earlier.[38] Said Souter, "We agree with MGM that the Court of Appeals misapplied Sony, which it read as limiting secondary liability quite beyond the circumstances to which the case applied."[39]

In the end, it was not entirely clear what effect the Grokster decision would have on P2P and technological innovation generally. Grokster and KaZaA agreed to stop distributing their software, but given the decentralized nature of these services, users were still able to continue trading files with the versions of the software they had already downloaded. Since StreamCast continued to maintain that it had not broken any laws, Morpheus continued to operate as before, only now with multinetwork support and better user anonymity. More important, by the time the Grokster decision was handed down, these second-generation file-swapping networks had already been superseded by a third generation of more sophisticated and further decentralized P2P services like Bit Torrent and eDonkey, both of which initiated talks with the entertainment industry to determine if they could make the transition to legitimate pay services. While the Grokster decision was undoubtedly a motivational factor in these discussions, it was also the case that the Apple iTunes Music Store had already provided a successful model for legal downloading.

Launching its iTunes Music Store in the spring of 2003 over the slogan "Downloads done right," Apple began with a catalogue of some 200,000 songs culled from the rosters of the five major companies and offered users simplicity, affordability, convenience, and flexibility. The iMS interface proved to be as user-friendly as any file-sharing service, the songs sold for $.99 per single ($9.99 for most albums), and the user was permitted easy transferability to Apple's iPod portable music player, as well as unlimited CD burning. With that simple formula, the iMS shocked and delighted record company executives when it sold 1 million songs in its first week of operation and then duplicated the same sales figures for the second week. A few weeks later, Apple invited 150 representatives from independent labels to participate in the iMS on an equal footing with the majors.

The thing that was most remarkable about the success of the iMS was that it began as a Macintosh-only enterprise; there was no PC version of the required iTunes software. Apple's share of the computer market was well under 5 percent at the time. Of that 5 percent, only about 20 percent had migrated to Mac OS X, Apple's new operating system, required for using iTunes—which is to say that Apple was able to sell 1 million songs per week to less than 1 percent of the record-buying public. The computer maker promised and delivered a PC version of iTunes by year's end.

Clearly, what Apple accomplished was most impressive; it also had some limitations. The sound files that Apple made available for download at the iMS were copy-protected AAC files, not MP3s. AAC is a version of the newer MP4 format. On the upside, unlike MP3, MP4 is public domain software; it boasts better compression and better sound quality than MP3. But this means the files will not play on traditional MP3 players. AAC also includes the capability of Digital Rights Management (DRM), which allowed Apple to "authorize" loading the files onto only three computers at a time. In order to authorize an additional computer to play the files, one of the first three had to be deauthorized. Under pressure from the record companies, Apple was also compelled to disable the "rendezvous" function from iTunes, which allowed users to make their iTunes songs available to other iTunes users for streaming (but not downloading) on the Internet. While limitations such as these were minimal and easily managed, it was not difficult to see how additional restrictions imposed by the music industry could propel users back toward unrestricted peer-to-peer networks. The international developer community lost no time in aiding this flow by creating new systems that offered more encryption and user anonymity.

Apple's success with such a small market share encouraged other companies to try to beat them to the more lucrative PC market.

Apple's success with such a small market share encouraged other companies to try to beat them to the more lucrative PC market. The most interesting venture in this regard was the one proposed by Roxio, best-known as a maker of CD-burning software. After Napster liquidated its assets in bankruptcy, Roxio was able to acquire the remaining rights to the brand at fire sale prices. Then in May 2003, Roxio bought pressplay and made plans to launch a competing online music store, using the pressplay technology and the Napster brand name. "With our acquisition of Napster we obtained the most powerful brand in the online music space," said Roxio's chairman and CEO, Chris Gorog. "Now, with our acquisition of pressplay, we have the most complete and scaleable legal technology infrastructure to use as a platform to relaunch Napster."[40] The online music industry had thus come full circle with the once venerable—or, depending on one's perspective, reviled—Napster brand reemerging as a commercial pay service. The supreme irony of a commercial online music store called Napster was hardly wasted on industry observers.

Apple vanquished all competitors over the next few years, maintaining a market share in the 80 percent range, with the new Napster in a distant number two position and other online services dividing the remains. Other services simply found it difficult to beat Apple's combination of style, ease of use, and seamless hardware/software integration. Since its debut in 2001, Apple's iPod had established itself as the icon of digital music (and then photo and video) players. In the last quarter of 2005 alone, Apple sold 14 million iPods, dwarfing even the revenues from the sale of the company's Macintosh computers. By this time, the Music Store was even outselling some bricks-and-mortar outlets like Tower Records and Sam Goody. In July 2006, Microsoft decided to go toe-to-toe with Apple in announcing the development of a new product called the Zune. Despite Microsoft's formidable resources, it faced an uphill battle in unseating Apple for a number of reasons. In the first place—the Xbox notwithstanding—Microsoft had never been much of a hardware company. It was going after the de facto industry standard. And it would also be competing with its own third-party partners that made digital music players based on Microsoft's Windows Media software. A more serious threat could come from Yahoo Music, which began experimenting with selling online music as unprotected MP3s, or from the major labels themselves, once they figured out that they didn't need Apple to create an online music store. But they had a lot of catching up to do. A few months earlier, the iTunes Music Store had just sold its billionth song.[41]

In capturing the imaginations of digital downloaders, the iPod became the gold standard for digital media players and a cultural icon for portable music (and video).

Popular Music after 9/11

If the death of Napster in the summer of 2001 sent reverberations throughout the virtual world, it paled in comparison with another catastrophe during the same season that rocked the material world to its core—the terrorist attacks that felled the twin towers of the World Trade Center and left a gaping hole in the side of the Pentagon. The events of 9/11 shook the United States out of its complacency regarding national security, prompted a moving, if short-lived, outpouring of sympathy from nations around the world, and sent the economy into a tailspin from which it has yet to fully recover. These events also ushered in something of a new role for contemporary popular music. Historically, the rock and rap axis of U.S. popular music has most often been associated with rebellion, defiance, an oppositional stance, and resistance to authority. Post-9/11, this same music was also conscripted into the service of mourning, healing, patriotism, and nation building. At least since Elvis, this was a new role for this music.

> *Historically, the rock and rap axis of U.S. popular music has most often been associated with rebellion, defiance, an oppositional stance, and resistance to authority. Post-9/11, this same music was also conscripted into the service of mourning, healing, patriotism, and nation building.*

Music outlets monitored listener call-ins closely as indicators of their audience's frame of mind—all within the market segmentation of their format-driven programming. While classic rock stations fielded requests for old chestnuts like John Lennon's "Imagine" and Simon and Garfunkel's "Bridge over Troubled Water," heavy metal outlets pushed the sonic envelope with Jimi Hendrix's "The Star Spangled Banner" and Metallica's "Don't Tread on Me." Songs in demand at country stations leaned toward patriotic anthems like Johnny Cash's "Ragged Old Flag," Brooks and Dunn's "Only in America," and Lee Greenwood's "God Bless the USA." MTV sought to establish a nonviolent tone with Lennon's "Imagine," Bob Marley's "One Love," Prince's "When Doves Cry," and Pearl Jam's "Alive."

Artists' involvement in this enterprise ranged from individual financial contributions to huge mega-events. Dr. Dre simply donated $1 million of his own money to a victim relief fund in Los Angeles. Other artists who were playing New York at the time, like the Black Crowes and Incubus, donated the proceeds from their New York dates. Prior to the attacks, Bono had already teamed up with hip hop producer Jermaine Dupri to produce an ensemble version of Marvin Gaye's 1971 classic, "What's Goin' On," with Christina Aguilera, Backstreet Boys, Mary J. Blige, Wyclef Jean, Michael Stipe, and others, for Artists Against AIDS Worldwide. In the aftermath of 9/11, the artists added the United Way's September 11 Fund as a beneficiary. Arista re-released Whitney Houston's stirring 1991 Super Bowl performance of the "The Star Spangled Banner," with proceeds earmarked for New York firefighters. The Houston single shot up the charts, peaking at number six, and sustained enough momentum to finish 2002 as the ninth most popular song of the year. Recalling his anthemic contribution to the issue of hunger and starvation in Africa, "We Are the World," Michael Jackson weighed in with an ensemble cast to record his new composition, "What More Can I Give." His chosen performers included Destiny's Child, Backstreet Boys, Tom Petty, and Seal, among many others, with proceeds slated to go to a number of unnamed 9/11 relief agencies. Sony ultimately refused to release the record when they discovered that Jackson hired a producer of gay pornography videos to oversee the project, but not until the song was performed at the October 22 United We Stand benefit in Washington, D.C., which raised $3 million. The day before, Paul McCartney, who had been sitting in a plane on a New York runway when the World Trade Center was hit, headlined the Concert for New York City in Madison Square Garden, which raised $30 million for the New York Fire Department. The Beastie Boys organized New Yorkers Against Violence as a two-night fundraiser at the Hammerstein Ballroom, with guests Moby, Michael Stipe, Bono, Mos Def, and the Strokes. Significantly, this was the only effort of the lot that was explicitly committed to nonviolent solutions.

The concerts staged to benefit the victims of 9/11 were organized with remarkable efficiency and cooperation among all sectors of the entertainment business.

The concerts staged to benefit the victims of 9/11 were organized with remarkable efficiency and cooperation among all sectors of the entertainment business. Perhaps the most impressive was America: A Tribute to Heroes. Plans for the tribute, which was staged on September 21, were set in motion three days after the attacks. The event featured twenty-two artists, with fifty actors staffing the telephones, and was transmitted over the big four commercial networks as well as thirty cable channels, without any credits and without commercial interruption. Artists participating in the *America: A Tribute to Heroes* telethon included Bruce Springsteen, Celine Dion, Mariah Carey, U2, Sting, Stevie Wonder, Neil Young, Paul Simon, Tom Petty, Billy Joel, Jon Bon Jovi, Richie Sambora, Sheryl Crow, Dave Matthews, Eddie Vedder, Limp Bizkit, Enrique Iglesias, Alicia Keys, Wyclef Jean, Faith Hill, the Dixie Chicks, and Willie Nelson. The show was coordinated by former MTV *Video Music Awards* producer Joe Gallen, with Interscope's Jimmy Iovine booking talent, and producer Don Was and bandleader Paul Shaffer assembling the backup bands. The telethon generated an estimated $160 million from its East Coast broadcast alone, making it the largest single fundraising event in history even before the compilation CD was released.

From the hushed tones of Tom Hanks' introductory call for "a simple show of unity" to Willie Nelson's closing ensemble rendition of "America the Beautiful," America: A Tribute to Heroes was an understated, reverential event whose very attempt at tastefulness encapsulated the new role for music. If overt political statements of patriotism were downplayed during the telecast, it was because they were unnecessary. The United States had just been attacked on its own soil, and patriotism and security were already the show's main agenda. Significantly, punk, rap, and metal, as performance styles, were excluded, despite their popularity among youth. There were no heavy rockers, aggressive rhymes, or sonic distortions that might have signified discord or disunity. In an effort to achieve the proper tone, the tribute's dominant aesthetic was that of *MTV Unplugged.* For security reasons, the program was broadcast from undisclosed locations in New York, Los Angeles, and London. There were no stage risers—and, as another security precaution, no audience—to elevate the performers above the crowd or to call attention to their star power. Indeed, with no artist introductions or credits, celebrity was consciously obscured to engender a sense of what Tom Hanks called "our larger American family." Stage sets for the tribute were unadorned, bathed in soft backlight in the red/orange and blue/green ranges of the spectrum and illuminated by the white light of candles, creating a hint of the colours of the American flag. These sets were then transformed into American flag banners for the closing ensemble performance of "America the Beautiful."

To be sure, there were some poignant moments, such as Will Smith's introduction of Muhammad Ali as a Muslim, or the footage of Muslim children in America expressing fears of retaliation. In the children's defence, Stevie Wonder chastised those who "hate in the name of God or Allah" in his intro to "Love's in Need of Love Today." If Tom Petty's muted, but still somewhat pugnacious, rendition of "I Won't Back Down" was a call to arms for the nationalist project that was about to get under way, it was offset by Neil Young's stirring performance of John Lennon's "Imagine," which conjured up visions of a world with neither religions nor countries and "nothing to fight or die for." A number of songs, such as Enrique Iglesias' "Hero" and Billy Joel's "New York State of Mind" (performed solo at a grand piano with a firefighter's helmet perched atop the soundboard) were irrevocably re-signified by the event. And if something like Celine Dion's bloated arrangement of "God Bless America" was considered obligatory for a moment like this, noticeably absent was the "The Star Spangled Banner"; it must have seemed clear to the producers that, on this occasion, the "purple mountains majesty" and "amber waves of grain" of "America the Beautiful" would play far better than the "rockets' red glare" and "bombs bursting in air" of the U.S. national anthem. It should also be noted that the all-cast version of "America the Beautiful" that closed the show included the second verse, which calls on America to "Confirm thy soul in self-control/Thy liberty in law."

If America: A Tribute to Heroes attempted to be a measured response to the tragedy of 9/11, the Concert for New York City was a loud, commercialized, public extravaganza staged at Madison Square Garden on behalf of the city's police, fire, and health workers. With minimal diversity provided by Jay-Z and Destiny's Child, the bill was dominated by British and American rockers, including Billy Joel, Bon Jovi, John Mellencamp, David Bowie, Eric Clapton, the Who, Mick Jagger and Keith Richard, Elton John, and Paul McCartney. Musically, the concert was a tribute to brash, white, male, mostly guitar-based rock in both its lineup and performance styles.

The finale of America: A Tribute to Heroes *both celebrated and challenged the country in a time of crisis.*

Karen Pegley has pointed out that the Canadian benefit concert for the 9/11 tragedy, Music Without Borders: Live, was equally dominated both in the actual concert itself and, more dramatically, in its television presentation by white male rock artists. Pegley goes on to note that media spectacles such as Music Without Borders: Live go a long way toward constructing a notion of national music, which in turn plays a significant role in socially defining the nation. In terms of its benefit concerts, Canada is routinely presented as masculine, white, and rock-oriented, raising serious questions about privilege and power relations.

The increased testosterone level of the Concert for New York City was a clear indicator of the change in mood, emotional tone, and political will that was taking place as the United States invaded Afghanistan. McCartney's presence as the headliner of the event was significant in that he was seen as the primary link between the first British Invasion and the present alliance between Britain and the United States. McCartney performed three Beatles songs and showcased "Freedom," a new song that included the cautionary line "Anyone who tries to take it away, they'll have to answer." The theme of revenge for the September 11 attacks had already been previewed in Bon Jovi's earlier performance of "Wanted Dead or Alive," echoing Bush's statements about Osama bin Laden. But it was the Who, the group that practically invented the on-stage release of violent emotion, who drove the message home. Opening their set with classic Pete Townshend power chords on "Who Are You?"—now a query to the terrorists—the group performed their high-energy single in front of a Union Jack background, as if to recall their use of the British flag as a pop cultural icon in the 1960s. As they segued into "Baba O'Reilly" the background changed to an American flag. They closed their set with "Won't Get Fooled Again"—perhaps now a message to al Qaeda—performing before a Union Jack flanked by two American flags, signifying the special relationship between the two countries.

As talk of helping and healing gave way to the rhetoric of revenge and retribution, those who chose to dissent found that a new reality had taken hold.

Given the imperative for emotional healing following the 9/11 tragedy, it was not surprising that the historical antiestablishment role of rock might have appeared inappropriate to the crisis at hand. Still, as artists rushed to show their support for a grieving nation, many seemed to retreat from previously held positions. U2, whose defining moments included images of Bono carrying a white flag as he ranted against war on "Sunday Bloody Sunday," adopted a very different stance at the Super Bowl XXXVI halftime show in 2002, where the world-famous lead singer visibly displayed the American flag lining of his jacket and the band unfurled a larger-than-life scrim that listed the names of all the 9/11 victims. At that same halftime show, Paul McCartney, who had seriously criticized the British occupation of Northern Ireland when he wrote and recorded "Give Ireland Back to the Irish" in 1972, related differently to the long-term implications of an impending invasion thirty years later on his new song, "Freedom." As talk of helping and healing gave way to the rhetoric of revenge and retribution, those who chose to dissent found that a new reality had taken hold.

Corporate Radio and the New Patriotism

If America: A Tribute to Heroes attempted to be a measured, balanced response to the tragedy of 9/11, it was soon eclipsed by a more fervent patriotism in the popular cultural offerings—and the government rhetoric and actions—that followed. In the music field, corporate radio, in particular, played a major role in narrowing the range of cultural expression that would bear on the policies of the Bush administration. In the days immediately following the attacks of 9/11, for example, Clear Channel, the largest radio chain in the United States, issued a list of nearly 200 songs to its member stations that executives felt might be inappropriate to play. Defended by Clear Channel as a simple act of sensitivity toward the victims' families, and denounced by its critics as an act of suppression, the list quickly took its place as part of a running battle pitting civil liberties and freedom of expression against the need for national unity and internal security. One thing was clear: given how centrally Clear Channel was organized and programmed, any list of songs to be avoided that was sent out from corporate headquarters was likely to be read as more than a suggestion.

The list included some obvious choices, like Metallica's "Seek and Destroy" and AC/DC's "Shot Down in Flames," that could be credibly defended as sensitivity, and some not so obvious selections, such as Carole King's "I Feel the Earth Move" and the Bangles' "Walk Like an Egyptian," which made people wonder. The fact that the list also included all Rage Against the Machine songs further raised the spectre of censorship, for here was a whole body of work by a single group being eliminated, rather than a particular grouping of their songs that might have been considered offensive. Most surprising to many observers, "Imagine" was also included on the list, which made it all the more interesting that it was the song Neil Young chose to perform at America: A Tribute to Heroes the following week.

> *One thing was clear: given how centrally Clear Channel was organized and programmed, any list of songs to be avoided that was sent out from corporate headquarters was likely to be read as more than a suggestion.*

"Imagine" was an interesting choice that shed some light on Clear Channel's thinking. In the days and weeks following 9/11, all media outlets were concerned about what they broadcast. Rather than focusing on the negative and singling out songs to be eliminated, many outlets concentrated on what would be appropriate to play, what should be added. An MTV spokesperson reported, "The music department started picking through the playlist in the library to figure out what we might add, what would be meaningful."[42] Most of the outlets that took this approach included "Imagine"—alongside other selections like Bob Marley's "One Love" and Prince's "When Doves Cry"—among the songs to emphasize. "Imagine" was clearly regarded as a song of peace by most programmers and listeners alike. Interestingly, John Lennon himself thought of the song as "virtually the Communist Manifesto. . . . But because it is sugar-coated, it is accepted."[43] Perhaps there was a method to Clear Channel's seeming madness.

What made the Clear Channel list so important—and the touchstone for the debate on civil liberties—was the power of its network, which derived from the terms of the 1996 Telecommunications Act in the United States. The 1996 law, twelve years in the making, was the first major overhaul of the telecom landscape since the Communications Act of 1934; it covered everything from radio, television, and telephone to cable TV and the Internet. Often cited as a model of bipartisan cooperation, the legislation altered the telecom sector in ways that were not always beneficial to the consumer. The controversial Communications Decency Act, which was inserted as part of the legislation (and declared unconstitutional by the Supreme Court one year later), drew considerable attention away from one of the central provisions of the Act—the relaxation of the rules of ownership for media corporations.

The media have become significantly more concentrated since the passage of this landmark bill. When Ben Bagdikian wrote *The Media Monopoly* in 1983, he expressed concern that fifty corporations controlled most of the major mass media outlets. By the 1990s, that number had shrunk to fewer than twenty. At stake, according to Bagdikian, was nothing short of the very concept of a free press. In 2003, the FCC, under the direction of Michael Powell, son of Secretary of State Colin Powell, sought to relax the rules of ownership still further. It wasn't until hundreds of thousands of irate voters—and a list of organizations that included such a diversity of groups as the National Rifle Association, the Catholic Conference of Bishops, and the National Organization for Women—complained to their elected representatives that Congress halted, if only temporarily, this headlong rush toward further media consolidation.

One provision of the 1996 Telecom Act repealed cross-ownership laws for radio. As a result, according to one major news outlet, by the early 2000s, consolidation in radio had reached the point where four companies controlled 90 percent of the ad revenue.[44] This level of concentration had serious implications for programming. Though there were about 30,000 CDs released in the United States in 2001, each of which contained on average more than a dozen songs, national radio hardly noticed. "In one recent week," reported *Rolling Stone* in August 2001, "the forty top modern-rock stations added a total of sixteen new songs, and the biggest forty-five Top Forty stations added a total of twenty."[45] Clear Channel was the poster corporation for these developments. In 1995, prior to the passage of the Telecom Act, Clear Channel owned forty-three radio stations. By the early 2000s, the corporation posted revenues in excess of $8 billion; it had acquired more than 1,200 U.S. stations which took in more than $3 billion, or 20 percent of the industry dollar volume, in 2001; it had a lock on outdoor advertising, owning over 700,000 billboards; and it controlled 65 percent of the U.S. concert business, with a $1.1 billion gross from concert tours alone in 2002.[46] By this time, the music industry was rife with stories of record companies decrying the difficulty of breaking new artists on the centrally programmed chain and artists complaining that if they chose not to perform at a Clear Channel concert venue, they would pay the price in radio play.

As the U.S. went to war against Iraq, Clear Channel adopted an activist posture that marked a new role for corporate radio. During this period, there were a number of grassroots demonstrations protesting the war as well as a number of counterdemonstrations expressing support for the Bush administration's policies. In cities like Atlanta, Cleveland, San Antonio, and Cincinnati, there were pro-administration demonstrations organized under the banner of "Rally for America," that attracted up to 20,000 participants. At first, these rallies appeared to be organized from the ground up as spontaneous local events and were reported as such. It was then revealed that the rallies were being organized and sponsored by Clear Channel. At least two of them were promoted on the company's website. In Chicago, where Clear Channel owned six radio stations, Tim Jones wrote in the *Chicago Tribune*, "While labor unions and special interest groups have organized and hosted rallies for decades, the involvement of a big publicly regulated broadcasting company breaks new ground in public demonstrations."[47] Added former FCC Commissioner Glen Robinson, a law professor at the University of Virginia, "I can't say that this violates any of a broadcaster's obligations, but it sounds like borderline manufacturing of the news."[48]

It was not difficult to imagine that Clear Channel's support for administration policy might have been motivated by the fact that the company had upcoming business before the

It was not difficult to imagine that Clear Channel's support for administration policy might have been motivated by the fact that the company had upcoming business before the FCC—business that would have allowed the radio giant to expand considerably, particularly into television.

FCC—business that would have allowed the radio giant to expand considerably, particularly into televsion. Interestingly, an even more troubling connection to the Bush family presented itself. While a number of investigative reporters were connecting the dots between the Bush administration and Middle Eastern oil—not just between Vice President Cheney and Haliburton but between the Bush and bin Laden families as well—Paul Krugman, writing in the *New York Times*, also traced a direct connection from President Bush to Clear Channel:

> *Experienced Bushologists let out a collective "Aha!" when Clear Channel was revealed to be behind the pro-war rallies, because the company's top management has a history with George W. Bush. The vice chairman of Clear Channel is Tom Hicks, whose name may be familiar to readers of this column. When Mr. Bush was governor of Texas, Mr. Hicks was chairman of the University of Texas Investment Management Company, called Utimco, and Clear Channel's chairman, Lowry Mays, was on its board. Under Mr. Hicks, Utimco placed much of the university's endowment under the management of companies with strong Republican Party or Bush family ties. In 1998 Mr. Hicks purchased the Texas Rangers in a deal that made Mr. Bush a multimillionaire.*[49]

It is, of course, always threatening to free expression when a public media company enjoys this degree of intimacy with any government agency, let alone the White House. The question is how such relationships affected popular music and culture in the post-9/11 context.

Country Music Goes to War

From the buildup to the war in Afghanistan to the invasion of Iraq, the attention of the American national audience was captured by a number of songs from the country end of the spectrum that followed a rough trajectory from thoughtful reflection to strident fighting. They appeared all the more audacious as dissent was systematically suppressed iin the United States in the name of national security and oppositional popular music was eliminated from the national airwaves.

On 28 October 2001—he remembers the exact date—Alan Jackson penned "Where Were You (When the World Stopped Turning)," which went straight to number one on the country singles chart and crossed over to the Top Thirty on the pop charts. "Where Were You" was a thoughtful rumination on the kinds of things people might have been doing when the twin towers were struck; it recalled the notion that most people remembered exactly what they were doing when they heard John F. Kennedy was assassinated. Aaron Tippin weighed in with "Where the Stars and Stripes and the Eagle Fly," which became the ninth most popular song of 2001. Lee Greenwood's "God Bless the USA"—which appeared on four different compilations by the end of 2001—came in at number six for the year. Both talked of pride in America and expressed a willingness to pay a price to defend the nation's freedom. It is remarkable that these songs found their way into the year-end Top Ten with only a couple of months of sales.

Greenwood had actually written his anthem in 1984; it became the title song on his 1990 album of the same name, during the buildup to the first Gulf War. At that time, Greenwood had turned to patriotism to bolster a flagging career. According to one biographer, "Though he tried to retain his audience through patriotic work during the 1991 Gulf War—even earning the Congressional Medal of Honor Society's Patriot Award and a Points of Light Foundation Award—he couldn't successfully battle the onslaught of harder-edged, contemporary country artists that overtook country radio in the early 1990s. By the middle of the decade, he was no longer charting singles."[50] The 9/11 attacks propelled "God Bless the USA" (and Greenwood) back into the upper reaches of the pop charts, and the war in Afghanistan provided the hit single with enough momentum to finish 2002 as the eleventh most popular song of the year.

In a similar way, Aaron Tippin began his career as a recording artist in 1991, releasing "You've Got to Stand for Something," from his debut album of the same name, in the wake of the first Gulf War. The song became a Top Ten hit, and Tippin was invited to join Bob Hope's USO tour. A decade later, "Where the Stars and Stripes and the Eagle Fly" was a crossover hit that reached the pop Top Twenty. A number of other artists also had patriotic entries that dated back to the first Gulf War. In 1990 Hank Williams Jr. released "Don't Give Us a Reason," which told "old Saddam" that "you figured wrong." Billy Ray Cyrus contributed "Some Gave All," from the 1992 album of the same name, which also included his blockbuster "Achy Breaky Heart." Indeed, it was the patriotic fervour of the first Gulf War that propelled Whitney Houston's "The Star Spangled Banner" into the Top Twenty the first time it was released.

If the sheer tragedy and disorientation of 9/11 produced a somewhat restrained and reflective patriotism in American pop country, the rhetoric surrounding the war in Afghanistan and the increasing demonization of Iraq as part of the "axis of evil" set a different tone. It was Toby Keith's "Courtesy of the Red, White and Blue (The Angry American)," from *Unleashed* (2002), that captured the new vengeful attitude more than any other song. With a number of platinum releases to his name, Keith was no stranger to stardom, but it was "Courtesy"—which warns anyone who messes with the United States that "We'll put a boot in your ass/It's the American

If the sheer tragedy and disorientation of 9/11 produced a somewhat restrained and reflective patriotism in American pop country, the rhetoric surrounding the War in Afghanistan and the increasing demonization of Iraq as part of the "axis of evil" set a different tone.

Way"—that made him a household name. On the strength of the hit single, *Unleashed* hit number one in 2002 and had been certified double platinum by year's end. In the countdown to the war in Iraq, Darryl Worley's "Have You Forgotten" went to the top of the country chart in five weeks, reminding listeners "about bin Laden/Have you forgotten?" Pat Garrett, inspired by one of Secretary of State Colin Powell's warnings to Saddam Hussein, continued in this vein with "Saddam Stomp," which made an explicit connection between the Iraqi leader and Osama bin Laden. In fact, both songs provided Bush with a sorely needed link between Iraq and bin Laden, which he was having great difficulty demonstrating in reality. These were followed by Clint Black's "I Raq and Roll," which warned the enemies of the United States to "be careful where you tread," and Lynyrd Skynyrd's "Red, White, and Blue," whose message was summed up by singer Johnny Van Zant as "love it or leave it" and which provided the group with its first hit in years.

The fact that many of these songs became year-end bestsellers suggested that they hit a nerve among the U.S. populace. Indeed, domestic support for official U.S. foreign policy was very strong at the time. The momentum created by these songs encouraged artists from other genres to get on board. R. Kelly, whose career was in need of a boost following his twenty-one-count indictment for having sex with a minor, contributed "A Soldier's Heart." Ray Stevens seized the opportunity to score with a novelty track, "Osama—Yo' Mama," which criticized bin Laden's mother for not raising him correctly. (Unbeknownst to most younger fans, this was the same Ray Stevens who had a Top Five hit with "Ahab, the Arab" back in 1962.) Neil Young weighed in with "Let's Roll," in honour of the passengers who reportedly fought the hijackers on Flight 93. While Young had provided the only hint of protest in selecting "Imagine" for his performance at America: A Tribute to Heroes, this song presented his more liberal rock fans with something of a dilemma, as it provided President Bush with one of his classic one-liners. As critic John Metzger put it:

> Part of the problem with "Let's Roll" is its uncomfortable lyricism. While it pays tribute to those on ill-fated Flight 93—the plane which crashed into a Pennsylvania field after its passengers struggled with hijackers—it's also impossible not to take it as supportive of the current Administration and their poorly planned war-run-amuck. To be fair, at the time of the song's writing, America was in shock and was more willing to concede to its leaders' whims. But with lines like, "We're goin' after Satan/On the wings of a Dove," the song now stands as an odd statement from someone like Young, who long has rallied against war and unjust government policy. Then again, Young also spent a portion of the '80s speaking in support of Ronald Reagan.[51]

If Young expressed the ambivalence and confusion of some mainstream rockers, the more conservative artists at the country end of the spectrum were resolute in their defence of official U.S. policy. It wasn't that their hits were patriotic or even pro-war—popular culture had been able to accommodate different points of view since Barry McGuire's "Eve of Destruction" went head-to-head with Barry Sadler's "Ballad of the Green Berets" in 1965. The problem was that the response to these songs left no room for any other point of view. Steve Earle was a case in point. As much a rocker as a country artist, Earle had been compared to everyone from Randy Travis and Dwight Yoakam to Bruce Springsteen and John Mellencamp. Frequent bouts with substance abuse and a number of failed marriages contributed to a tumultuous personal life, just as years of label-hopping made for a challenging career. His songwriting is sharp and edgy, tending toward outlaw country, and his progressive political point of view has seldom won him friends in Nashville. As concerned and confused as anyone about the events of 9/11, Earle attempted a complex consideration of the issues at a time when country music was moving toward a more strident patriotism. On "John Walker's Blues,"—about John Walker Lindh, the "American Taliban"—from *Jerusalem* (2002), he attempted to get inside Lindh's head to explore from his point of view what might have led an American youth searching for truth in Islam to take up arms with the Taliban. While *Jerusalem* was a Top Ten country album that crossed over to pop, Earle was routinely denounced as a traitor by conservative commentators for his trouble.

The boycott of the Dixie Chicks was even more dramatic. The band rose to superstardom on the strength of their 1998 multiplatinum debut major label release, *Wide Open Spaces,* which promised and delivered solid material, great musicianship, and a female trio having a genuinely good time in concert; it offered little in the way of anything controversial. Their follow-up album, *Fly* (1999), which went to number one, continued in the same vein, except for the single

If Young expressed the ambivalence and confusion of some mainstream rockers, the more conservative artists at the country end of the spectrum were resolute in their defence of official U.S. policy.

"Goodbye Earl," about the murder of an abusive husband, which caused a stir at a number of country stations. For their September 2002 release, *Home,* the Chicks went deeper into their country roots with traditional instrumentation and few concessions to pop sensibilities. Nevertheless, *Home* debuted at number one on the *Billboard* 200 and garnered not only Country Music Awards but also American Music Awards, People's Choice Awards, and four Grammys. *Home* also included "Travellin' Soldier," a tender love song about a Vietnam-era casualty that was the group's commentary on war and its consequences. Riding the popularity of their blockbuster album, the Chicks were selected to sing the national anthem at the 2003 Super Bowl. For a time, it seemed that they were the darlings of the whole country. But while on tour in London in the spring of 2003, where anti-American sentiment was running high, lead singer Natalie Maines told her audience, "We're ashamed the president of the United States is from Texas," an obvious reference to her dissatisfaction with his foreign policy regarding the war in Iraq. Although Maines issued an apology to President Bush within days, calling her remarks "disrespectful," the Dixie Chicks were banned on some seventy-four country radio stations in the United States. The message was clear: it was not an option to criticize the president during a sensitive period of military engagement.

Intended to silence the Chicks, instead this action emboldened them. Like many women in country, the Dixie Chicks were made of strong stuff; they were no strangers to feminist or First Amendment values. At the very first show of the U.S. leg of their continuing tour, they addressed the controversy head on with the performance of "Truth #2," a song about standing up for one's beliefs, during which they showed video footage of civil rights and gay rights events and pro-choice demonstrations, in conjunction with slogans like "freedom" and "truth" projected on the screen. Maines was outspoken in her defence of First Amendment rights even in a time of crisis, at one point telling her concert audience, "If you're here to boo, we welcome that, because we welcome freedom of speech."[52] Despite the country radio boycott, the band's sixty-two-date U.S. tour nearly sold out. Natalie Maines also held her own, trading barbs with Toby Keith, whose "Courtesy of the Red, White and Blue" she had called "ignorant." The jousting reached its climax when Maines appeared on the Country Music Awards telecast wearing an F.U.T.K. T-shirt.

"Not Ready to Make Nice"

Artist: The Dixie Chicks

Music / Lyrics by the Dixie Chicks

Label: Sony, from the CD
Taking the Long Way (2006)

The Dixie Chicks' hit song "Not Ready to Make Nice" is Natalie Maines' defiant refusal to back down after receiving death threats for a comment she made to an English audience in 2003 just as the United States was about to invade Iraq. While the group suffered bans on radio airplay and their concert attendance declined, their May 2006 CD, *Taking the Long Way,* sold a half-million copies in the United States in the first week of its release.

Musical Style Notes

"Not Ready to Make Nice" features the Dixie Chicks' signature multiple vocals and country-rock instrumentation (acoustic and electric guitars, bass, drums, fiddle, keyboards). Its structure is straightforward but not simple. The verse-verse-chorus form, used frequently in a country ballad, is made more complex by the addition of a lyrically crucial bridge (this is where the death threats are referred to in very specific terms) and an instrumental section that functions as a transition from the bridge back to the chorus, with no intervening verse. The ending is a reprise of Verse 1, but it ends abruptly halfway through, driving home the message of the lyric and leaving the harmony unresolved. In other words, the song does not return at the end to the musical "tonic," or keynote, and this results in the absence of an aural perception of "finality."

Musical "Road Map"

TIMINGS	COMMENTS	LYRICS
0:00–0:11	Instrumental introduction; prominent acoustic guitar, keyboards	
0:11–0:36	Verse 1 Acoustic guitar still prominent	*Forgive—sounds good . . .*
0:36–0:58	Verse 2 Drums enter.	*I'm through with doubt . . .*
0:58–1:24	Chorus Multiple vocals enter.	*I'm not ready to make nice . . .*
1:24–1:48	Verse 3	*I know you said . . .*
1:48–2:14	Bridge section (This is the section that tells the actual story of the death threats made to Maines.)	*I made my bed . . .* *. . . or my life will be over . . .*
2:14–2:24	Instrumental transition Orchestral texture layered in	
2:24–2:48	Chorus Orchestral texture continues; multiple vocals	*I'm not ready to make nice . . .*
2:48–3:13	Chorus, repeated, with vocal *obligato* (additional sustained vocal part) added	
3:13–3:27	Transitional passage—same as introduction	*What it is you think I should . . .*
3:27–3:53	Verse 1	*Forgive—sounds good . . .*
3:53	Song ends abruptly at last line of verse.	*. . . but I'm still waiting.*

The rivalry between Toby Keith and the Dixie Chicks could be seen as a referendum on the extremes in country music for the next few years. Keith's *Shock'n Y'All*—a title seen by some observers as a clumsy play on "shock and awe" from the Iraq war—debuted at number one on the *Billboard* 200 in 2003 and placed him at the top of five year-end country charts in 2004. Having won a massive conservative country audience with *Unleashed,* Keith played to these same fans on *Shock'n Y'All,* but without the didactic rants and strident patriotism of "Courtesy of the Red, White and Blue." In some ways, Keith had established himself as an outlaw country musician in the tradition of Willie Nelson and Waylon Jennings, but with a conservative bent. On *Honkytonk University* (2005), Keith included a shout-out to his "boys in Afghanistan and Baghdad City" but remained focused for the most part on the hardcore country themes of hard drinking and failed relationships, a trend he continued with even more versatility on *White Trash with Money* (2006).

Whatever the Dixie Chicks lost at the conservative end of the country spectrum they more than made up for in pop. Thumbing their nose at Nashville tradition, the group underwent a folk-rock makeover for *Taking the Long Way* (2006), an album rooted in country but reflective of their new status and sophistication as international superstars. The album debuted at number one on both the pop and country charts, demonstrating a substantial country music fan base. Although their tour suffered in some conservative regions, the album's provocative first single, "Not Ready to Make Nice," made it clear that the Dixie Chicks were still not ready to back off from the controversy that surrounded them in 2003, no matter what the cost. "I'd rather have a smaller following of really cool people," said Martie Maguire, "than people who have us in their five-disc changer with Reba McEntire and Toby Keith."[53]

Dissent Unplugged

It was curious to many observers that while pro-war anthems emerged as year-end bestsellers, there was virtually no protest music heard on radio. The absence of protest was notable, especially by the time of the war in Iraq. While the war in Afghanistan was greeted with ambivalence in the peace movement, nothing approaching a consensus existed by the time the United States invaded Iraq. World opinion was clearly opposed to a unilateral invasion, and even in the United States the antiwar movement had established a significant national presence well before the war began. Many peace activists began to wonder aloud if protest music hadn't died. Writing for the University of Peace, Joseph Schumacher opined:

> *The sorry state of musical political protest is surprising given that the American, Australian and British Governments' joint invasion of Iraq galvanized global anti-war sentiment unlike any other single action since the Vietnam War. The millions of people who marched against the war in the weeks preceding and during the Iraq invasion sent a powerful message for peace across the world. What has been conspicuously missing is a soundtrack to the phenomenon.*[54]

In fact, there was plenty of protest music being produced; it simply wasn't being played on radio. Many observers blamed the 1996 Telecommunications Act. Noting that popular music and songs like Crosby, Stills, Nash & Young's "Ohio" had "played a crucial role in the national debate over the Vietnam War," Brent Staples argued in the *New York Times*, "A comparable song about George W. Bush's rush to war in Iraq would have no chance at all today. There are plenty of angry people, many with prime music-buying demographics. But independent radio stations that once would have played edgy, political music have been gobbled up by corporations that control hundreds of stations and have no wish to rock the boat."[55]

Other observers noted that a climate of intolerance for opposing viewpoints had caused many artists to censor themselves. "We've seen dozens of acts quietly bury their edgier songs," complained Jeff Chang in 2002. "The Strokes pulled a song called 'New York Cops' from their album and Dave Matthews decided not to release 'When the World Ends' as a single."[56] In 2003, Madonna reportedly withdrew a completed video for her "American Life" single because it portrayed her wearing Army fatigues, tossing a grenade at a President Bush–like figure. When artists performed controversial protest material during this period, they often paid a price, even if in small, obscure ways. Bruce Springsteen was bold enough to perform "41 Shots" at one of his New York dates, but it cost him his customary after-concert police escort to the airport. Jethro Tull was banned from classic rocker WCHR-FM in New Jersey for complaining that drivers who hung American flags from their cars and SUVs were confusing nationalism with patriotism. "As far as we're concerned," said program director and on-air personality Phil LoCascio, "this ban is forever."[57]

Still, a number of stalwarts continued to release antiwar material. Even before the invasion of Iraq, George Michael released a cover of Don McLean's "The Grave," after taking aim at British prime minister Tony Blair on "Shoot the Dog." Pearl Jam disparaged the U.S. president on "Bushleaguer," claiming "He's not a leader/He's a Texas leaguer." Public Enemy reinforced this notion on "Son of a Bush." On "Combat Rock," Sleater-Kinney's Carrie Brownstein shouts, "Where is the protest song . . . ? Dissent's not treason." Given the dearth of protest material, the album that garnered all the attention in the mainstream press was Bruce Springsteen's *The Rising*. The return of the E Street Band would have been cause for celebration in itself. But Springsteen's thoughtful, if measured, politics, which avoided the jingoism and vengefulness of the most popular songs about the war, strengthened the album further. On songs like "Into the Fire," "You're Missing," and "Lonesome Day," Springsteen tried to give voice to the unheard and build bridges among a diversity of groups. In the end, however, *The Rising* was a retrospective, if sensitive, engagement with the intense emotions of 9/11 more than it was a forward-looking political critique of current foreign policy. In the absence of radio play, many artists interested in protesting the war turned to the Internet, often posting protest songs as MP3s available for free download. A sampling of protest songs that were posted on the World Wide Web between spring 2002 and spring 2003 is included here

Protest Music on the Internet (Spring 2002–Spring 2003)

Beastie Boys, "In a World Gone Mad" (www.beastieboys.com)

Luka Bloom, "I Am Not at War With Anyone" (www.lukabloom.com)

Billy Bragg, "The Price of Oil" (www.billybragg.co.uk)

Chuck D, "A Twisted Sense of God" (www.slamjamz.com)

Zack de la Rocha (w/DJ Shadow), "March of Death" (www.marchofdeath.com)

Nanci Griffith, "Big Blue Ball of War" (www.nancigriffith.com)

Mick Jones, "Why Do Men Fight" (www.poptones.co.uk)

Lenny Kravitz, "We Want Peace" (www.rockthevote.org)

John McCutcheon, "We Know War" (www.folkmusic.com)

John Mellencamp, "To Washington" (www.mellencamp.com)

Meshell Ndegeocello, "Forgiveness & Love" (www.meshell.com)

Leslie Nuchow, "An Eye for an Eye (Will Leave the Whole World Blind)" (www.slammusic.com)

R.E.M., "The Final Straw" (www.remhq.com)

Spearhead, "Bomb the World" (www.spearheadvibrations.com)

Cat Stevens, "Peace Train" (www.yusufislam.org)

System of a Down, "Boom!" (www.systemofadown.com)

(although it should be noted that many of the links have probably expired). In an unfriendly radio climate, however, the Internet offered only limited possibilities for disseminating protest music.

From 9/11 until the 2004 presidential election, the most provocative anti-administration songs came from artists located in the more progressive sectors of punk and rap. Prior to the invasion of Afghanistan, Anti-Flag released "911 for Peace" (included on *Mobilize,* 2002), on whose chorus Justin Sane repeatedly shouted, "I don't wanna die, I don't wanna kill." Anti-Flag was founded in 1993 as an old-school, in-your-face punk band with explicitly left-wing politics. On *The Terror State* (2003), which opens with a direct assault on the veracity of the president, the group took on issues ranging from the war to the economy. That same year, NoFX weighed in with "The Idiot Son of an Asshole," taunting both Bush presidencies with an endless repetition of the song's title. Green Day delivered a certified antiwar blockbuster with *American Idiot* in 2004, with "Holiday" breaking ground by getting Adult Contemporary radio play.

Despite its penchant for violence, misogyny, and unabashed materialism, rap delivered the fullest, deepest, and most radical critique of U.S. foreign policy. One of the first responses of substance to 9/11 was "Makeshift Patriot," released by slam poet/rapper Sage Francis in October 2001. The song opens with a live audio track that was recorded by the artist at Ground Zero five days after the attacks. Its extended rap over a church-like organ captures all the horror ("Leaping lovers are making decisions to jump, while holding hands . . . to escape the brutal heat") and the contradictions ("We taught that dog to squat. How dare he do that shit in our own back yard!") of that fateful September day. He is clear, however, about the outcome. "Freedom will be defended," he acknowledges, but then quickly adds "at the cost of civil liberties."

> *Despite its penchant for violence, misogyny, and unabashed materialism, rap delivered the fullest, deepest, and most radical critique of U.S. foreign policy.*

Some of rap's responses were more circumspect, reflecting the ambivalence and confusion of the rap community itself. OutKast's "The Whole World" presented an impressionistic, gut-level response to the initial attacks set to an up-tempo beat, as Big Boi moaned, "Lookin' on the TV / Everything is looking Dismal." Talib Queli expressed contradictory feelings toward police and other officials on "The Proud," accusing them one minute of killing "my people everyday" and admiring them the next for their selflessness at Ground Zero. On Wu-Tang Clan's "Rules" Ghostface Killah, angry and bewildered over the bombings, shows respect toward Osama bin Laden when he says, "No disrespect, that's where I rest my head. I understand you gotta rest yours too nigga." But when he realizes that his people are dying as a result, he takes matters into his own hands as he intones, "Mr. Bush sit down, I'm in charge of this war."

As the war in Afghanistan began to segue into talk of invading Iraq, with little in the way of hard evidence or concrete connections to justify it, some of the more outspoken political rappers took a more radical stance. Boston's Mr. Lif opened "Home of the Brave" with a speech by one of the Kennedys, which established thoughtful political protest as "the basis of all human morality." Over the course of this extended rap, he accuses Bush of stealing the presidency, asserts the complicity of the media, and suggests that a war in the Middle East can only divert people's attention from other pressing issues, such as a recession at home. Paris had addressed the 1991 Gulf War with "Bush Killa." On "What Would You Do?," from *Sonic Jihad* (2003), whose cover depicts a speeding 747 about to crash into the White House, he took this analysis to its logical conclusion. On this cut, Paris names Bush as the person who has the most to gain from a war in the Middle East and accuses the administration of creating an enemy to justify its actions. Paris sputters, "It's plain to see / the oldest trick in the book is make an enemy / of phony evil now the government can do its dirt." On "Why?" (2004), Jadakiss asked pointedly, "Why did Bush knock down the towers?"

Even among higher-profile rap artists, there were hints of dissatisfaction about the post-9/11 world. On "Rule," from *Stillmatic* (2002), Nas asked Bush to "call a truce, world peace, stop acting like savages." The Black Eyed Peas scored a major Top Forty radio hit in 2003 with "Where Is the Love?," a collaboration with an uncredited Justin Timberlake that proclaimed, "A war is goin' on but the reason's undercover." Eminem included some critical verse in cuts like "Business" and "My Dad's Gone Crazy" on *The Eminem Show* (2002). The album's first video for "Without Me" featured the artist dressed as Osama bin Laden doing the "running man" dance in a cave. On "Square Dance," he cautions young people about joining the war effort. For *Encore* (2004), Eminem (and Dr. Dre) produced a Spartan album with straightforward lyrics. On "Mosh," he unleashed a barrage of criticism as he intoned, "Fuck Bush, until they bring our troops home." Clearly there were a variety of opinions being expressed about the Bush administration and its War on Terrorism. Many of these rap songs were released within the chart life of the country singles that dominated the national airwaves. They could have contributed to a national debate on the topic, but instead most received only limited exposure.

Musicians who were dissatisfied with this state of affairs decided to take a more activist stance by joining forces with the broad-based Win Without War coalition, an organization that came together to prevent war in Iraq, and whose members included the NAACP, the National Council of Churches, Physicians for Social Responsibility, and MoveOn, among many others. Musicians United to Win Without War described itself as "a loose coalition of contemporary musicians who feel that in the rush to war by the Bush administration the voices of reason and debate have been trampled and ignored."[58] The group included the usual suspects, ranging from David Byrne and Sheryl Crow to Ani DiFranco and Fugazi, as well as newcomers as diverse as Missy Elliot, Dave Matthews, and Bubba Sparxxx. Other musicians like Jackson Browne, Bonnie Raitt, and Michael Stipe were also active but listed themselves as members of a

sister organization, Artists United to Win Without War, which included mostly actors. At MUWWW's founding press conference on 27 February 2003, Russell Simmons and Ben Chavis of the Hip Hop Summit Action Network gave the new group an additional shot in the arm by committing themselves, in the name of the

Billy Bragg continued to promote the voice of protest in popular music.

hip hop community, to joining the fledgling coalition. Rockers and rappers launched an energetic voter registration campaign, signing up nearly 100,000 new voters in a matter of weeks. Punks took a more aggressive and partisan stance. Under the leadership of Fat Mike from NOFX, they formed Punkvoter (www.punkvoter.com), dedicated to building a "united front in opposition to the dangerous, deadly, and destructive policies of George Bush, Jr." As Fat Mike told *The Nation*, "It's time to get mad."[59]

Although the invasion of Iraq proceeded without interruption, all this activity revealed considerable antiwar sentiment and enabled progressive musicians to rediscover their historical voice of protest. Significantly, the partners in the Win Without War coalition were some of the same organizations and individuals protesting concentration in the mass media, the erosion of artists' and consumers' rights, and the restrictive globalization policies of the World Trade Organization. Attempting to pull these disparate strands of political activism into a united movement for social change, in November 2003, Billy Bragg launched the "Tell Us the Truth" Tour, which also featured Tom Morello (formerly of Rage Against the Machine) performing as the Nightwatchman, Steve Earle, Lester Chambers of the Chambers Brothers, and on some dates, rapper Boots Reilly of the Coup. The tour was sponsored by the AFL-CIO, Common Cause, the Future of Music Coalition, Free Press, and the Axis of Justice. At around the same time, a group of music industry liberals from Nashville formed Music Row Democrats to make the point that the conservative voice of country music did not speak for everyone associated with the country music business. While these developments represented a significant cross-section of centre-left U.S. political thought, they were neither loud enough to drown out the chorus of nationalist anthems that had conquered the charts nor sufficiently compelling to recapture the White House for the Democrats.

> *Although the invasion of Iraq proceeded without interruption, all this activity revealed considerable antiwar sentiment and enabled progressive musicians to rediscover their historical voice of protest.*

As the war in Iraq dragged on, with its mounting death toll, spiraling costs, and no apparent exit strategy, public opinion began to shift, putting the administration on the defensive and causing moderate Republicans to distance themselves from the White House in the run-up to the midterm elections. By this time, there was enough distance from and dissatisfaction with the war that a number of mainstream hitmakers felt comfortable criticizing it. Before 2005 was out, the Rolling Stones had chastised President Bush for his hypocrisy on "Sweet Neo-Con." System of a Down continued their successful activist prog rock career with the multiplatinum double album *Mesmerize/Hypnotize* (released in two parts), both halves of which entered the charts at number one. On "B.Y.O.B." from *Mesmerize*, frontman Seij Tankian asked pointedly, "Why don't presidents fight the wars?" In 2005, Anti-Flag made the previously unthinkable leap to a major label with their politics intact and in 2006 released *For Blood and Empire*, an album brimming with anti-Bush sentiment and criticism of the war in Iraq. That same year, expatriate Canadian Neil Young released *Living with War*, an album that brought the artist a full 180 degrees from his earlier pro-administration stance following the terrorist attacks of 9/11. *Living with War* was recorded in three days by a power trio (guitar, bass, and drums) and a 100-voice chorus. At the time, Young described the album on his website (www.neilyoung.com) as "a metal version of Phil Ochs and Bob Dylan . . . metal folk protest?" The media was immediately drawn to the album's most controversial cut, "Let's Impeach the President," a straight-ahead rocker that called the White House to task over "why we have to send our men to war." Around the time of Young's release, it seemed the floodgates opened to antiwar material by a broad range of artists, including Pink ("Dear Mr. President"), Pearl Jam ("World Wide Suicide"), the Pet Shop Boys ("I'm with Stupid"), the Flaming Lips ("Haven't Got a Clue"), and the Roots ("False Media"). Music Row Democrats released a country compilation album, the *MRD Song Pack,* featuring twenty songs, many of which were directly critical of the president and the war in Iraq, such as Billy Braddock's "Thou Shalt Not Kill" and Nanci Griffith's "Big Blue Ball of War." P. F. Sloan even recorded a new version of his classic antiwar song, "Eve of Destruction," which was a number one hit for Barry McGuire in 1965.

While *Living with War* caused a stir in the media and peaked at number fifteen on the pop charts, the album hovered in the lower reaches of the charts after its release. Bruce Springsteen's *We Shall Overcome: The Seeger Sessions,* a tribute album of Pete Seeger songs, entered the pop charts at number three and was certified gold within weeks. The album, which was recorded with more than a dozen musicians, featured old-time instrumentation (fiddle, banjo, accordion, washboards, and steel guitar), a large horn section, and a full vocal chorus. It showcased a broad range of Seeger material, including folktales like "John Henry" and "Jesse James," rollicking gospel like "Jacob's Ladder" and "O Mary Don't You Weep," spirited Cajun chants like "Pay Me My Money Down," and of course the title song. Quietly at work on the project since 1997, Springsteen claimed that it was not a product of the current political situation. Still, he chose to open the tour supporting the album in hurricane-ravaged New Orleans, performing not only most of the tunes from the album but also an updated version of Blind Alfred Reed's "How Can a Poor Man Stand Such Times and Live?" that included a pointed reference to "President Bystander." Interviewed about the response to Hurricane Katrina, Springsteen had words that echoed Neil Young's provocative single: "Obviously, get rid of the president," said Springsteen. "When you see the devastation [in New Orleans] and realize the kind of support the city will need to get back on its feet, there's no way to make sense of someone pushing for more tax cuts for the 1 percent of the 1 percent of the population. It's insanity and a subversion of everything America is supposed to be about."[60] There was also a Pete Seeger song, not included on the album, that Springsteen added to the tour in an updated version that summed up his feelings about the Iraq war—"(If You Love Your Uncle Sam) Bring 'Em Home."

As the twentieth century was coming to a close, the music industry had recovered from a period of flat sales and had resumed its journey toward further expansion and consolidation. But just as the major labels were expecting to cash in on the economies of scale that resulted from another round of mega-mergers, the industry was hit by a double whammy at the turn of the new millennium: Napster and its offspring ushered in an era of unauthorized digital music file swapping, and the events of 9/11 knocked the bottom out of the whole economy. While no one questioned that the future of music was going to be digital, downloadable, and customized for individual taste, the music industry remained obsessed with copyright protection and centralized control at the expense of user-friendly services. As a result, the major labels tended to lag far behind third-party services they should have been trying to emulate rather than eliminate. By inflating CD prices, demonizing the record-buying public, and failing to offer a convenient, affordable method of accessing music online, the music industry gave consumers considerable incentive to take matters into their own hands and feel righteous about doing so. Artists may have been caught in the middle on the copyright question, but record companies were clearly in it for themselves, going after revenues that most often accrued to the labels either as royalties or as artist payback of record company advances. Artists themselves tended to derive their income more from touring and merchandising. Meanwhile, the majors consolidated their control over a global market, all but eliminated the public domain, and narrowed fair use almost to extinction.

The tragedy of 9/11 and subsequent escalation of military engagement brought the more conservative elements of country music to the fore, as the push for a more patriotic popular culture captured the attention of the mainstream audience. The more liberal rock establishment seemed more ambivalent in its political responses, which ranged from outright protest to serious self-censorship. With the passage of time, however, the War in Iraq—indeed, the entire Middle East situation—seemed to spiral out of control, transforming public opinion in the process. As the Bush administration sank to its lowest approval ratings ever, protest music resurfaced across genres—including a compilation of antiwar country music—and the War in Iraq promised to become the pivotal issue in the next round of elections in the United States.

Getting Back to Business: Popular Music in the New Millennium

It has often been said by music industry executives that the business of music is *business.* Following a loss of more than 25 percent of the music industry's business over a three-year period, for a while it looked like 2004 was going to be the year that the business turned around. The first half of the year showed dramatic increases in CD sales, with a 7 percent overall gain as of September. By year's end, however, the expected boost from holiday sales had failed to materialize, and the final figures showed only a modest increase of 1.6 percent. The downward spiral continued throughout 2005, which ended with a net loss of about 8 percent in CD sales, marking a return to the dismal 2003 figures.[1] Were it not for an increase in authorized digital downloads taking up some of the slack, the results would have been even more devastating. Needless to say, such a situation was discouraging for an industry that had been accustomed to posting double-digit annual growth figures for most of its history.

In Canada, the music business also experienced a slight increase in sales from 2003 to 2004, growing 2.7 percent from 58.6 million units to 60.2 million units. Despite this increase in the total number of units sold, dollar volume decreased by 4.7 percent because of discounting in the retail sector. This was the sixth straight year of declining dollar volume in the Canadian music industry. Despite this, the sales of recordings by Canadian artists increased between 2001 and 2004 by a stunning 25.3 percent (11.2 percent between 2003 and 2004 alone), while sales in Canada by foreign artists fell 20.2 percent in the same period. The total share of the market by Canadian artists in Canada increased from 16.5 percent in 2001 to 25 percent in 2004. French-language recordings accounted for approximately one-third of all Canadian sales.

In the post-9/11 period, there was a great need to get back to business as usual in the music industry, as elsewhere. But with the advances of peer-to-peer technology and the devastation of the American economy, it was no longer quite clear what "usual" was. Instead of taking a serious look at its core business model, the music business flailed about, concentrating externally on laws and lawsuits that would staunch its revenue hemorrhage, and internally on jockeying for position amidst a new round of mergers, changing label configurations, and the threat of being downsized. In 2004, Sony and BMG merged, reducing the Big Five to four and cutting the ranks of music industry personnel by 2,000 positions.[2] Edgar Bronfman, Jr., the heir to the Seagrams fortune who had sold Universal to Vivendi, reentered the business with a consortium that bought the Warner Music Group for $2.6 million after Time Warner cut its music division loose from the disastrous merger that was AOL-Time Warner. Warner's restructuring plan called for the elimination of another 1,000 jobs.[3] Looking to compete on a more equal footing with Universal and Sony-BMG, Warner had plans to become a publicly traded company and to buy EMI, the other free-floating major label group, in a move that finally would have reduced the majors still further to a Big Three. But the WMG IPO, which fell short of its target, derailed those plans and actually raised questions about which company would be the buyer in a WMG-EMI merger.

> In the post-9/11 period, there was a great need to get back to business as usual in the music industry, as elsewhere.

Meanwhile, all the "cost-saving" measures and administrative realignments created a period of dizzying staff turnover, a sample of which is reported here simply to make the point. For years, *Billboard* has run a weekly column called "The Executive Turntable," which tracks staff changes in the music business. During this period, the turntable spun as never before. Sony and BMG had merged mostly in name only; their new operating structure kept the respective label groups separate, with executives from each company splitting the roles in the new joint company more or less equally. Still, the company was plagued by infighting for eventual dominance. At BMG, for example, Arista label head Antonio "L.A." Reid, having delivered multiplatinum releases by OutKast, Usher, and Avril Lavigne, was unceremoniously fired to make room for industry veteran Clive Davis to take over BMG's North American operations. But Reid landed on his feet, heading up Universal's Island/Def Jam group (and then hiring Jay-Z to run Def Jam itself) when Lyor Cohen left the position to become head of the new Warner Music Group. In Warner's restructuring plan, Atlantic and Elektra were to be merged, with Jason Flom as co-chair and Atlantic founder Ahmet Ertegun reduced to the largely ceremonial position of founding chairman. Flom was then fired the following year; he resurfaced as CEO of EMI's Virgin imprint. When Universal dropped Bad Boy, label head Puffy Combs made a $30 million deal with Cohen to move his operation to WMG. Universal also closed its Dream Works Nashville operation when executives learned that Toby Keith had left to form his own Show Dog Nashville label. If all this movement, which barely scratches the surface, sounds like rearranging the proverbial deck chairs, then welcome to the music business. For all the major labels' complaining about file swapping and piracy, it was a wonder that they could find the time to sell CDs at all. And these executives are some of the most creative administrators in the business. Imagine if all that energy had been put into developing music!

And Now for Something Completely Familiar

The days and weeks immediately following 9/11 were marked by a departure from business as usual. In the mass media, there was a (short-lived) return to hard news and substantive reporting, and popular music was consciously deployed to create a desired effect, be it mourning the victims, calling the nation to arms, or, to a lesser extent, protesting the buildup to war. Ironically, as the terrorist attacks threatened to disrupt the normal flow of everyday life and an already flagging economy, getting back to business as usual took on a perverse urgency. For a time our ability to go shopping became the measure of a nation unbowed by terrorism. In popular music, it was almost as if the sound of loud rock bands at the *Concert for New York City* offered some reassurance that the nation was moving toward some kind of normalcy. And just as surely as the news returned to coverage of celebrity trials and the latest American Idol, the music industry soon witnessed a resurgence of the familiar sounds of guitar-based rock. For many in the music industry, getting back to business rested not only on recovering lost revenues, but also on restoring the dominance of rock. This vision, however, often overlooked the gains made by country music, and it raised the age-old spectre of racism in undervaluing the degree to which rap and hip hop had become the foundation of U.S. popular culture.

> *That the label* post-grunge *was variously applied to all these groups had more to do with the fact that they had formed in the mid-1990s after the peak of the Seattle scene than with the similarity of their sound.*

The Return of Rock

By early 2002, a number of guitar-based bands that had been successful since before 9/11 had seemingly reasserted the primacy of rock. "With Creed, Linkin Park, and Nickelback all at the top of the charts," reported *Rolling Stone* in February 2002, "record companies are getting back to the business of rock."[4] These multiplatinum mainstream rockers were the most visible segment of an even broader range of guitar-based rock sounds that was also developing at the club level. That the label *post-grunge* was variously applied to all these groups had more to do with the fact that they had formed in the mid-1990s after the peak of the Seattle scene than with the similarity of their sound. Linkin Park, for example, routinely incorporated not just classic rock, but old school rap and electronic influences as well in their debut album, *Hybrid Theory* (2000), which sold eight times platinum by 2002. Linkin Park continued in the same vein for the multiplatinum *Meteora* in 2004. Indeed, the post-grunge appellation was attached to guitar-based bands from Blink 182 (*Take Off Your Pants and Jackets,* 2001) and the Canadian group Sum 41 (*All Killer No Filler,* 2001) to Staind (*Break the Cycle,* 2001) and Lifehouse (*No Name Face,* 2001). In fact, Lifehouse's "Hanging by a Moment" (2001) marked the first time since 1988 that a male rock group had the number one song of the year. In 2002, it was "How You Remind Me," by Alberta's Nickelback, that had captured the number one slot for the year and marked the apex of the trend that *Rolling Stone* had identified.

If Lifehouse and Nickelback had momentarily reached the pop peak, Creed had already demonstrated its staying power. The year 2001 was the first time in four years that Creed did not finish the year as the top mainstream rock artists. Florida-based Creed was formed in 1995 as a Seattle-influenced grunge metal outfit by singer/lyricist Scott Stapp and guitarist/composer Mark Tremonti. Stapp grew up in a Christian fundamentalist home. His stepfather prohibited rock music in the house, preferring instead psalms and proverbs for inspiration and corporal punishment when rules were sidestepped. Stapp's experience with religion definitely had an influence on his writing. As to the songs on the first album, Stapp says: "I was still dealing with guilt issues about all the Ten Commandments and all the other things the Bible says that I wasn't living in my life."[5] As a result, the group has often been taken to be an alternative Christian band, a label which they have only halfheartedly denied. The group's debut album, *My Own Prison* (1997), generated four number one singles on *Billboard*'s mainstream rock radio charts— "My Own Prison," "Torn," "What's This Life For," and "One"—and sold 5 million copies over the next two years. Their follow-up, *Human Clay* (1999), entered the pop charts at number one and sold 10 million copies over the next two years. Their next three singles, "Higher," "What If," and "With Arms Wide Open," topped the charts as well, providing the group with seven number one radio singles in a row. *Weathered,* released in November 2001, also entered the charts at number one, and sold 5 million copies in its first two months. Throughout Creed's career, the band have received nothing but critical disdain as a hopelessly derivative and formulaic group. Fortunately for them, this has always been a surefire indicator of massive sales among hard rock groups.

Creed was certainly the best-positioned group to carry the rock banner into the future, but a car accident in early 2002 in which Stapp sustained a back injury ultimately caused the group to disband. It was left to other guitar-based bands with a diversity of styles to carry on. Early on, Matchbox Twenty had been typecast as a stereotypic post-grunge rock band with a steady stream of Top Ten albums, including *More Than You Are* in 2002. That same year, Lifehouse continued their post-grunge angst on *Stanley Climbfall,* Linkin Park reprised its marriage of buzzsaw guitar riffs and elements of hip hop on its second number one multiplatinum album, *Meteora* (2003). Staind also scored a second multiplatinum number one pop entry, *14 Shades of Grey,* in 2003 and followed it with *Chapter V* (2005), its third number one album in a row. Hoobastank's 2003 post-grunge entry *The Reason* went to number three on the album charts. From Biloxi, Mississippi, 3 Doors Down parlayed their first Top Ten single, "Kryptonite," into a run of Top Ten albums, peaking with *17 Days,* which hit number one in 2005. Nickelback crafted the most stable, if undistinguished, career for themselves, following up 2001's "How You Remind Me" with "Someday," from *The Long Road* (2003), and six U.S. Top Thirty hits from *All the Right Reasons* (2005): "Photograph," "Savin' Me," "Far Away," "If Everyone Cared," "Rockstar," and "Into the Night." By the end of its run, *All the Right Reasons* had sold 6.7 million copies in the United States and 9.5 million worldwide. In the summer of 2007, lead singer Chad Kroeger was featured on a duet with 1960s guitarist Carlos Santana on a remake of "Into the Night," from the latter's *Ultimate Santana* album, providing Kroeger with yet another Top 30 hit.

These coliseum-level acts were joined by a resurgence of guitar-based garage rock bands at the club level as well. Throughout 2002, groups like the Strokes (*Is This It?*) from New York, the White Stripes (*White Blood Cells*) from Detroit, the Hives (*Veni, Vidi, Vicious*) from Sweden, and the Vines (*Highly Evolved*) from Australia generated a significant buzz in international music centres such as New York and London.

At the same time, Canada retained an extremely active and increasingly internationally successful independent rock scene led by the recent success of Arcade Fire, Broken Social Scene, and Feist. Arcade Fire was formed in Montreal by husband-and-wife team Win Butler and Régine Chassagne in mid-2003. Releasing their first album, Funeral, in 2004, on Merge Records, the band was championed by veteran rock artists such as David Bowie and Robbie Robertson. With very little radio or television play, *Funeral* sold over 500,000 copies worldwide, went gold in Canada, and was nominated for a Grammy in the Best Alternative Rock Album category. Despite major label interest, Arcade Fire elected to remain independent, and in 2007 released their sophomore effort, *Neon Bible*, on Merge. The album debuted at number one on the Canadian and Irish album charts and number two on both *Billboard's* Top 200 chart in the United States and Britain's Top 40 Album Chart. In 2008, *Neon Bible* garnered Arcade Fire another Grammy nomination in the Best Alternative Music Album category and won a Juno for the band as Alternative Album of the Year.

If Arcade Fire were the darlings of the Montreal independent scene, Broken Social Scene were Toronto's great alternative hope in the first decade of the twenty-first century. Formed by Kevin Drew, Brendan Canning, and Justin Peroff in 1999, the group records and often tours as a collective, at times totaling some fifteen musicians, virtually all of whom record and tour with other bands or as solo artists. In 2006, the group's third album, the eponymous *Broken Social Scene*, won a Juno as Alternative Album of the Year.

Broken Social Scene's most successful part-time member is Leslie Feist. Born in Amherst, Nova Scotia, Feist grew up in Regina and Calgary before relocating to Toronto in 1996. Feist's second solo album, *Let It Die*, sold 500,000 copies worldwide, earned platinum status in Canada, and won Juno Awards in the categories of Best New Artist and Best Alternative Rock Album. The follow-up album, 2007's *The Reminder*, included the hit single "1234." Featured in an iPod nano commercial, "1234" became a Top Ten hit in the United Kingdom, the United States, and Canada, a remarkable achievement for a single released by an independent label, Toronto-based

Arts and Crafts. At the 2008 Juno Awards, Feist won in five categories: Songwriter of the Year, Artist of the Year, Pop Album of the Year, Album of the Year, and Single of the Year. She was also nominated for four Grammies: Best Female Pop Vocal, Best New Artist, Best Pop Vocal Album, and Best Short Form Music Video.

It was an iPod nano commercial that propelled Feist's "1234" to mega-commercial success.

But why this sound? Why at this time? One commentator interviewed by *Rolling Stone* in early 2002 pointed out that "you can't ignore what's happened in this country since September 11th. There's been a change of tenor in the music scene."[6] Another noted that pop sales had declined substantially and opined that "Rock has started to fill that void."[7] By the end of the year, *Billboard*'s Larry Flick reported, "One growing form of expression has been simple guitar-based rock, which has swept aside the squeaky-clean pop that dominated the U.S. market in recent years."[8] Given such commentary, it is perhaps not too far-fetched to suggest that in the disorientation produced by the aftereffects of 9/11, many mainstream fans found comfort in the familiar sounds of guitar-based rock. Further, in the buildup to the war in Afghanistan, which enjoyed tremendous popular support, it is not difficult to imagine that the more aggressive sounds of hard rock might have been the preferred sounds. Finally, in a war that was often framed in terms of Christianity vs. Islam, with the Bush White House repeatedly invoking Christian references to defend its position, the misperception of Creed as a Christian band probably did nothing to diminish the group's immense popularity.

It is perhaps not too far-fetched to suggest that in the disorientation produced by the aftereffects of 9/11, many mainstream fans found comfort in the familiar sounds of guitar-based rock.

This is not to suggest an easy homology between rock and war—indeed, in the sixties, rock was perceived, if anything, as antiwar. Nor is it to suggest that the groups mentioned above were particularly identified with the war effort, as was the case with some conservative country acts. If anything, these groups tended to focus inward, turning away from the problems of the world. Rather, the point of this speculation is to wonder why certain production styles become popular when they do and to reflect on the functions of music qua music in a given social context. To complicate the analysis still further, this music was not the only trend that had the effect of displacing saccharine teen pop. While this notion of guitar-based rock filling a void may have been one part reality-based, it was also at least one part wishful thinking, perhaps reflecting the needs and desires of the rock critics who wrote about the music. In fact, there were other trends that rivaled, even eclipsed, these post-grunge sounds in popularity and sales.

Singer/Songwriters Emote

As if to provide a balance to the male-dominated, angst-ridden, post-grunge sounds of the period, there was also a new generation of female singer/songwriters—Alicia Keys, Norah Jones, Michelle Branch, Vanessa Carlton, Canadian Nelly Furtado, and to some extent Avril Lavigne and Pink—that eclipsed teen pop with a more soulful brand of introspection. All of these women can be described as disarmingly attractive, albeit in sometimes unconventional ways. This fact alone might suggest that they were simply a next generation of teen queens being groomed to fill a market niche. But these young women were not creations of Disney World or products of the recording studio. All were serious artists, gifted songwriters, and talented performers. Some, like Branch, Lavigne, and Pink, were signed to recording contracts before they were out of their teens. Others were musical prodigies with an impressive pedigree of artistic training, even at their young ages. Alicia Keys had graduated as valedictorian from the High School for the Performing Arts in Manhattan before entering Columbia University at age 16. Norah Jones studied at the High School for Performing and Visual Arts in Dallas. Vanessa Carlton attended the School of American Ballet before embarking on a music career. Their music was recognized as something of a trend in 2002, the year Vanessa Carlton released her platinum debut, *Be Not Nobody*, and its best-selling single, "A Thousand Miles." As *Billboard*'s Melinda Newman reported:

> *A new crop of female pop singer/songwriters emerged this year. They were as young as Britney Spears and Christina Aguilera, but instead of showing off their belly buttons and abs, they flexed their songwriting muscles. Avril Lavigne, Vanessa Carlton, Michelle Branch, and Norah Jones all climbed to the upper reaches of the charts. It was refreshing to see attractive women who didn't have to take off their clothes or talk about their body piercings to get their music heard.[9]*

While this trend peaked in 2002, its beginnings could be seen in Michelle Branch's *The Spirit Room* (2001) or even in Nelly Furtado's *Whoa, Nelly!* (2000), but it was defined by the tastefully stunning debut of Alicia Keys' *Songs in A Minor*, released in the summer of 2001. Powered by the ubiquitous gospel-inflected hit single "Fallin'," the album hit number one and sold four times platinum before the year was out. Born of an interracial couple and raised by her white mother, Keys nevertheless self-identified as black and displayed a maturity and self-confidence well beyond her years. Influenced by everyone from Marvin Gaye to Prince to Biggie Smalls to Chopin—"Chopin is my dawg," she says—Keys was also blessed with a manager who was loyal to a fault and a record company that learned—albeit the hard way—to let a sixteen-year-old write and produce her own tracks. She conquered the *Tonight Show* and the *Oprah Winfrey Show*, and generated significant buzz on MTV with the video for "Fallin'"—hand delivered by Clive Davis—before the album was

As if to provide a balance to the male-dominated, angst-ridden, post-grunge sounds of the period, a new generation of female singer/songwriters appeared and that eclipsed teen pop with a more soulful brand of introspection.

Alicia Keys' tasteful debut CD defined the new sound of female singer/songwriters.

Norah Jones' sultry delivery produced incredible sales for someone signed to a jazz label.

released. When the tragedy of 9/11 struck, it was fitting that she be invited to perform at *America: A Tribute to Heroes.* Keys performed a soulful version of Donny Hathaway's classic "Someday We'll All Be Free," which displayed a sensitivity appropriate to the occasion. But hers was not a knee-jerk patriotism. Describing her ambivalence toward the tragedy, she told one reporter: "All day I been seein' everyone rockin' flags in they hats and on the street and I'm torn. . . . I see lies in that flag. I can't suddenly be all patriotic. But this is about human life beyond any country or flag."[10]

In a country preoccupied with race, Alicia Keys clearly takes her place among other soul divas like Jill Scott and India.Arie, but it is not a stretch to see her also as the artist who helped carve out the cultural space occupied by singer/songwriters like Norah Jones and Vanessa Carlton. Her long-awaited second album, *The Diary of Alicia Keys,* wasn't completed until 2003. With expectations running high—perhaps too high—*Diary* didn't so much break new ground as confirm the staying power of the youthful singer. With tracks ranging from the waltz-time "If I Ain't Got You" to the reggae-inflected "You Don't Know My Name," Keys demonstrated the same sophisticated musicality and soulful delivery that had made her first album the defining moment of a new trend. Not unlike its predecessor, *Diary* went to number one and multiplatinum certification and finished 2004 as the fourth most popular album of the year. In the time between Keys' two blockbuster releases, Jones and Carlton, as well as Avril Lavigne and Pink, enjoyed platinum releases.

Norah Jones—who, like Keys, listed Chopin as an influence—took the music forward into the terrain of pop jazz and what she described somewhat tongue-in-cheek as "soft cock rock." After a period of waitressing by day and playing low-paying club dates at night in Manhattan, she scored a contract with Blue Note. Her mellow, sultry delivery on *Come Away with Me* propelled her debut album to eight times platinum certification and netted Jones an impressive five Grammy Awards, including "Album of the Year," "Record of the Year" (for "Don't Know Why"), and "Best New Artist." "Don't Know Why," never a blockbuster hit single, nevertheless became an instant classic. Interestingly, it never occurred to Jones to trade on her good looks or the fact that she had a famous father (sitar master Ravi Shankar) because she was expecting— hoping, really—to sell 10,000 copies of the album, just enough to convince Blue Note to let her make another one. When all was said and done, *Come Away with Me* had logged some three years on the album charts. While it was still a best-seller, Jones released *Feels Like Home* in early 2004. Her sophomore effort expanded her musical palette somewhat, but it was not a major

"Don't Know Why"

Artist: Norah Jones

Music / Lyrics by Jesse Harris

Label: Blue Note, from the CD *Come Away With Me* (2002)

The media makes much of the fact that Norah Jones is the daughter of Indian sitar master Ravi Shankar, but Jones paved her own musical path, and her style is firmly rooted in American popular music genres. Her music contains elements of jazz, soul, and even country, and her mellow, sensuous vocal style recalls a number of great female jazz and soul singers (she has cited Billie Holiday as an important early influence). In 2004, *Time* magazine listed her as one of the year's most influential artists, stating that "in an age when knob-twiddling producers rule and lip-synching pop tarts stalk the stage, she has reintroduced the world to the human voice."

Musical Style Notes

> **Music Terminology Demystifed: What Is a "Bridge"?**
>
> A "bridge" is a section of a song that usually occurs after at least two repetitions of the main verse melody. Its tune differs from that of the verse, providing a contrasting section that then connects back once again to the main verse melody, which usually features either a new lyric verse or a repeat of Verse 1.

Structurally, "Don't Know Why" is classic pop ballad: verse / verse / bridge / verse / bridge / verse, with the final line of each verse serving as a lyric refrain. Stylistically, it features a folk- and jazz-influenced acoustic flavour. Songwriter Jesse Harris played guitar on the track; the other players are bassist Lee Alexander, violinist Jenny Scheinman, organist Sam Yahel, and Norah Jones on acoustic and electric piano and vocals.

Musical "Road Map"

TIMINGS	COMMENTS	LYRICS
0:00–0:11	Introduction—instrumental guitar, piano, bass, drums	
0:11–0:38	Verse 1	*I waited 'til I saw the sun . . .*
0:38–1:00	Verse 2	*When I saw the break of day . . .*
1:00–1:22	Bridge	*My heart is drenched in wine . . .*
1:22–1:44	Verse 3	*Out across the endless sea . . .*
1:44–2:06	Bridge 2	*My heart is drenched in wine . . .*
2:06–2:27	Instrumental over bridge—piano, guitar, bass, drums	
2:27–3:06	Verse 4 with extra last line "don't know why . . ."	*Something has to make you run . . .* *I don't know why I didn't come.*

departure from her signature sound, which her guitarist Adam Levy described as "this cocktail of Ray Charles and Etta James, and Bill Evans on piano, and these simple country vocals, the way Loretta Lynn sings, so direct you can't ignore it."[11] With expectations for the album running "very high," as label head Bruce Lundvall put it, *Feels Like Home* did not disappoint, selling 1 million copies in its first week and finishing 2004 as the fifth most popular album of the year, just one notch down from Alicia Keys.

Avril Lavigne, a small-town Canadian teen from Napanee, Ontario, was positioned as the Britney slayer—a guitar-carrying teen icon who did not appear manufactured. As a precocious and talented young artist signed to Arista at sixteen, however, she was equally capable of looking like a brat with chops. Presented as a singer/songwriter—there are conflicting stories about how much of her music she actually writes—her music ranged from teen pop to some hard rockers. Her debut album, *Let's Go,* was produced by label head Antonio L. A. Reid. Propelled by three Top Ten singles—"Complicated," "Sk8er Boi," and "I'm with You"—written in collaboration with the Matrix songwriting team in Los Angeles, *Let's Go* achieved sales of 4 million in half a year. It lent credence to Lavigne's ability to topple teen pop, clearly demonstrated her potential for future growth, and established her as a major player in the new singer/songwriter trend. *Under My Skin* (2004), released while she was still in her teens, debuted at pop number one and revealed a somewhat more mature Lavigne. Not the blockbuster of her first release, *Under My Skin* nevertheless remained on the charts for over a year, selling over 8 million copies worldwide, and yielded her biggest single in the United States, "My Happy Ending." Lavigne then took a break from music, branching out into film and a contract with the Ford modeling agency. In 2005, Lavigne won the Juno Fan Choice Award as well as the Junos for Artist and Pop Album of the Year. In April 2007, her third album, *The Best Damn Thing,* debuted at number one on Billboard's album chart. Its first single, "Girlfriend," reached number one on Billboard's Hot 100 chart and became the second-most-watched video in YouTube history. By December 2007, *The Best Damn Thing* had sold 4.1 million copies worldwide.

> *A*vril Lavigne was positioned as the Britney slayer—a guitar-carrying teen icon who did not appear manufactured. As a precocious and talented young artist signed to Arista at sixteen, however, she was equally capable of looking like a brat with chops.

Label-mate Pink started her career earlier than Lavigne and, having toured as the opening act for 'N Sync, was in danger of becoming just another teen pop act. Her debut album was a dance pop assemblage of well-crafted songs that sold double platinum but offered her little in the

By 2007, Avril Lavigne had shed her teenage neo-punk image and had been reborn as a mature pop star.

way of distinctiveness. Pink, however, was fiercely independent and deeply distrustful of all authority figures, from parents and teachers to the police and federal officials. She has argued that "teachers should be paid more so that they care more about their jobs and should be screened better so that they're not biased, prejudiced, racist, sexist assholes that get to shape your children."[12] Apparently that spirit applied to recording executives as well. For her second outing, she teamed up with Linda Perry (of 4 Non Blondes) to write most of the material for *M!ssundaztood,* fought hard for artistic control over the objections of her label, and delivered an unlikely product that offered everything from dance/pop ("Get the Party Started") and mainstream rock ("18 Wheeler") to deeply personal confessionals like "Family Portrait," "Dear Diary," and "My Vietnam." By the end of 2002, *M!ssundaztood* had been certified four times platinum and had established Pink as her own person.

For her third outing, Pink teamed up with Rancid's Tim Armstrong to produce *Try This* (2003), a mostly rock-based but very eclectic mix of everything from ska to electronica. She returned in 2006 with *I'm Not Dead,* cranking up the dance rhythms and taking shots at everyone from Paris Hilton ("Stupid Girls") to George W. Bush ("Dear Mr. President"). Neither album duplicated the sales of *M!ssundaztood,* but both hit the Top Ten and confirmed Pink as a talented risk taker who was not afraid to buck a trend or follow her muse wherever it might lead her.

While Avril Lavigne was preparing to enjoy marital bliss with Deryck Whibley, of Canadian punk group Sum 41, her big-city Canadian sister and single mom from Toronto, Nelly Furtado, was busy rescuing her career from a failed second album. Furtado's career bracketed the trend of female singer-songwriters in the early 2000s, with *Whoa, Nelly!* (2000) at one end and *Loose* (2006) at the other. Conscious of her working-class background and Portuguese roots, Furtado speaks four languages and says she loves living in Toronto because of its multicultural character, support for gay marriage, and commitment to grassroots political activism.[13] These are perhaps the main traits that contributed to the adventurous eclecticism of her musical tastes, which are even more wide-ranging than Pink's, running from r&b/hip hop and alternative to Portuguese fado, Brazilian bossa nova, and Indian raga, including unlikely combinations of all of them. On *Whoa, Nelly!,* Furtado received critical acclaim for her adventurous genre blending, and the album generated two Top Ten singles, "Turn Off the Light" and "I'm Like a Bird," which earned a Grammy for Best Female Pop Vocal Performance. Following the disappointment of *Folklore* (2002), Furtado took some time off to raise her daughter. She returned in 2006 with *Loose*, a (mostly) Timbaland-produced album that hit number one and further showcased her ability to incorporate global cultural influences into a pop sound. Furtado also followed an innovative marketing plan in which four singles were released in different regions of the world to maximize the album's appeal to a diversity of cultural groups. These included the reggaeton-influenced "No Hay Igual," recorded with members of Calle 13; the Latin-tinged "Te Busqué" (featuring Juanes); the pop-oriented "Maneater"; and the hip-hop-influenced "Promiscuous" (featuring Timbaland), which went to number one in the United States and Canada.

If Pink and Furtado stretched the role of singer/songwriter and took the practice in new directions, a new generation of male singer/songwriters returned the craft to its early 1970s roots.

If Pink and Furtado stretched the role of singer/songwriter and took the practice in new directions, a new generation of male singer/songwriters returned the craft to its early 1970s roots. These included John Mayer (*Heavier Things*), Jack Johnson (*On and On*), Jason Mraz (*Waiting for My Rocket to Come*), David Gray (*A New Day at Midnight*), Pete Yorn (*Day I Forgot*), Howie Day (*Stop All the World Now*), and others. All of these artists enjoyed chart successes in 2003. Jon Pareles commented on the significance of their music for the period: "It doesn't require the Council of Economic Advisers to recognize that the United States is having economic troubles. All it takes is turning on a pop radio station or MTV to get the strange feeling that the mid-1970's have returned: the days of post-Vietnam and post-Watergate letdown, oil crisis, unemployment and soothing soft rock to provide consolation for it all."[14] As if to consecrate the link to the 1970s, not only did period icon James Taylor release a new album, but Ben Taylor, his and Carly Simon's son, debuted with *Famous Among the Barns.*

As introspective as any singer/songwriter, Dave Matthews has assembled an integrated rocking band and become politically engaged.

Interestingly, just about all these artists have been associated in one way or another with Dave Matthews, whom Pareles describes as "a brooding songwriter strumming an acoustic guitar."[15] Both John Mayer and Jason Mraz have worked with John Alagia, who had produced Matthews in the past. Jack Johnson exhibited some stylistic similarities. Howie Day named Matthews as an influence. And David Gray got his big push in the United States after opening for Matthews. Although Matthews has spent a fair amount of time exploring the darker side of life, he is more than just a "brooding songwriter"; he is also an international superstar. The fact that he was born in apartheid South Africa makes it all the more interesting that he put together a band composed of three black musicians (Boyd Tinsley, Carter Beauford, and LeRoi Moore) and two white ones (Stefan Lessard and himself) and that such an outfit achieved international fame. Signed to RCA in the mid-1990s, the Dave Matthews Band released three platinum or better major label studio albums before canning long-time producer Steve Lillywhite in favour of the more mainstream Glen Ballard for the release of the double platinum *Everyday* (2001), a move that upset many loyal fans. *Busted Stuff* (2002) remixed much of the unused material from the Lillywhite sessions. Both *Everyday* and *Busted Stuff* could be found among the year-end bestsellers for 2002. In addition to being one of the most successful touring acts in the business—grossing over $80 million in 2001—Matthews and the other band members continued to produce platinum live albums. Some moved on to solo projects as well. Matthews also became very active in the movement to remove George Bush from the White House.

Among the new crop of singer/songwriters, none has achieved Dave Matthews' celebrity or adopted his activist politics; John Mayer and Jack Johnson have come the closest to being stars. After a stint at the Berklee College of Music in Boston, Mayer headed for Atlanta, where he enjoyed indie success before getting signed to Columbia. On the strength of his major label debut, *Room for Squares* (2002), Mayer walked off with the 2003 Grammy for Best Male Pop Vocalist, besting Elton John, Sting, and James Taylor. In 2003, his second major label effort, *Heavier Things,* went all the way to number one and platinum certification. All three of his albums could be found among *Billboard*'s most popular albums of the year for 2003. Mayer considered his third major label album, *Continuum* (2006), the third of a trilogy that he recorded with a pared-down trio of guitar, bass and drums. Jack Johnson was an accomplished surfer in Hawaii before he moved into songwriting and filmmaking while attending the University of California at Santa Barbara. His *On and On* hit number three in 2003, catapulting him to the upper reaches of touring acts. By then, even his debut release, *Brushfire Fairytales* (2001), had gone platinum, confirming his star power. Johnson's sunny disposition and feel-good sound defined his work, even when he addressed topical issues such as materialism ("Gone") and war ("Traffic in the Sky"). *In Between Dreams* (2005) fared best of all, peaking at number two on the album charts; naturally, it delivered more of the same.

Other singer/songwriters of note include Toronto's Ron Sexsmith, heralded by no less a figure than Bob Dylan, and the three Canadian singer/songwriters Colin Linden, Stephen Fearing, and Tom Wilson, who collectively record as roots-rock icons Blackie and the Rodeo Kings and as solo artists in their own right.

It is fair to say that the music of this group of artists is sensitive, direct, and heartfelt. Still, descriptions of it in places like the *All Music Guide* offer less than flattering insights into its social functions. A review of *On and On* noted that "Fans will enjoy Johnson's soothing ballads and boy-next-door charms, never looking beyond the surface of the songs themselves."[16] John Mayer's *Heavier Things* was described as "songs that are melodic without being truly catchy" and "music that floats through the speakers nicely and never leaves much of a lasting impression."[17] This is music that was designed to soothe while shielding the listener from the problems of the world. In the words of Jon Pareles: "Mr. Mayer and his fellow songwriters often play the same comforting role as their forebears. Turning away from the bad news of the outside world, they focus on personal affairs: mostly romance, but also the endless processes of self-invention and finding a place in the world."[18] As if to challenge Pareles' earlier assessment, for *Continuum* Mayer claimed on his website (www.johnmayer.com) that he was ready to tackle "big themes." Nevertheless, on "Waiting for the World to Change," a jaunty but ultimately disempowering rocker from the album, Mayer elevated political inactivity to the level of ideology as he abdicated all personal agency to act while waiting for the world to magically change, in effect confirming Pareles' views. As Mayer explained on his website, "It's meant to shed a little light on inactivity and inaction because I don't believe that inaction is disinterest; I think inaction is preservation."

Idol Worship

If the most recent crop of singer/songwriters tended to insulate their audiences from pressing world problems, there was another post-9/11 popular culture phenomenon that offered similar diversions, ironically in the name of "reality"—that is, "reality TV," with its signature music program, *American Idol*. The model for *American Idol* went back to a television show called *Popstars* that aired in New Zealand in the late 1990s. Producer Jonathan Dowling marketed the idea to producers in other countries, notably Australia and Great Britain. The British version of *Popstars*, in turn, was the inspiration for a talent search called *Pop Idol*, which debuted in 2001. In the hands of media Svengali Simon Fuller and his colleagues Simon Cowell and Simon Jones, the *Pop Idol* format became an international franchise, spawning dozens of national versions of the show in countries all over the world, including *Canadian Idol*, which debuted in June 2003. In the United States, a company called Fremantle North America, owned by the German conglomerate Bertelsmann, produced the show. After being turned down by all of the U.S. networks, *American Idol* was picked up by Fox, which is owned by media mogul Rupert Murdoch's conservative News Corporation, headquartered in Australia. Acting on a tip

American Idol *quickly became the number one Nielsen-rated television show in the country, averaging as many as 31.6 million viewers a week in 2006.*

from his daughter in England, Murdoch reportedly told his executives, who were eyeing the program from a distance, "Don't look at it. Buy it! Right now!"[19] *American Idol* quickly became the number one Nielsen-rated television show in the country, averaging as many as 31.6 million viewers a week in 2006.[20] Given the size of the U.S. market, the show easily became the most popular in the international *Idol* series. As of 2006, it was being aired in over 100 countries, including some that had their own national versions of the show.[21]

The contest begins with enormous public auditions in major cities all over the country. Thousands of would-be performers in the eligible age range of sixteen to twenty-eight (initially, sixteen to twenty-four) parade their talents (or lack of same) before three judges: the irascible Simon Cowell (who came over from *Pop Idol* in Britain) at one extreme, singer and sympathetic panelist Paula Abdul at the other, and, in the middle of the road, musician/producer Randy Jackson. In each season, these early sessions have produced endless fodder for celebrity gossip columnists, *Saturday Night Live* skits, and culture vultures across the blogosphere, keeping the show constantly in the public eye. The legions of contestants eventually get whittled down to a group of semifinalists and then finalists, and audience voting becomes the mechanism for progressing toward victory. In addition to the $1 million first prize, the winners (and, in some cases, other finalists) are typically offered record contracts with one of Sony-BMG's affiliated labels because of the show's connection with Bertelsmann. They are also signed to management contracts with 19 Entertainment, Simon Fuller's massive international artist development company, headquartered in Britain. This company oversees not just the Idols' record deals, but also their live shows, merchandising, endorsements, and movie deals. Initially, the show was regarded with some skepticism as a kind of amateur hour for the masses. But within only a few years, naysayers had to admit that although *American Idol* may have provided viewers with countless hours of mindless celebrity wannabe drama, it had also produced a group of democratically elected superstars who had proven themselves in the marketplace.

Kelly Clarkson's versatility, ease with her audience, and success in the marketplace made it more difficult for critics to dismiss American Idol out of hand.

Beginning with the first season in 2002, *American Idol* veterans steadily built their presence in the popular market (see table). First-season winner Kelly Clarkson scored the best-selling single of the year in 2002 with "A Moment Like This," later included on her debut album, *Thankful*. At home in front of the camera and able to handle everything from Aretha Franklin covers to middle-of-the-road pop, Clarkson's first-season victory made it more difficult to simply dismiss the show out of hand. *Thankful* was strategically released in the spring of 2003, timed to coincide with the second season of *American Idol* auditions and with the release of the film *From Justin to Kelly*, starring Clarkson and runner-up Justin Guarino. The film was an utter flop (as was Guarino's subsequent career), and while *Thankful* didn't bowl anybody over, it showcased Clarkson's versatility to advantage and eventually rose to number one on the pop charts. On her aptly named second effort, *Breakaway* (2004), Clarkson shed the trappings of *American Idol* and established herself as an artist with staying power. On the strength of a number of hit singles, ranging from pop balladry ("Because of You") to arena rockers ("Since U Been Gone"), the album sold more than 5 million copies and netted Clarkson two Grammys in 2006.

In 2003, second-season runner-up Clay Aiken and winner Ruben Studdard entered the Hot 100 Single Sales chart at numbers one and two, respectively, and held onto the Top Two position for *Billboard*'s year-end tally. By this time, Clarkson's *Thankful* and Aiken's *Measure of a Man* had hit number one on the album charts, selling millions of copies each, and Studdard's long-awaited *Soulful* debuted in the number one slot at the end of the year. Studdard had narrowly edged Aiken aside for the second season crown in a controversial photo finish that separated the two contestants by only 134,000 votes out of 24 million cast. But Aiken beat Studdard to the punch in the popular market, achieving better chart and sales positions on both his single and his album, as well as beating the winner to the cover of *Rolling Stone,* becoming, in effect, the season's champion. The extra time it took for Studdard to finish his first album, however, was time well spent. *Soulful* had a cohesive r&b/hip hop feel to it, and its distinctive sound served to separate Studdard from the MOR pop sound that had defined the Clarkson and Aiken releases—and *American Idol* generally—at the time.

In 2004, *American Idol* contestants were responsible for the three best-selling singles of the year and four of the top six—including third-season winner Fantasia (Barrino) at number one with "I Believe," which set a record as the first time a new artist had debuted at number one on the *Billboard* Hot 100 with her first single. Fantasia, as she is billed, is a soul/gospel powerhouse, from a solidly gospel family, with a booming Broadway voice and a story to tell, which led to a best-selling autobiography and a made-for-TV movie, *The Fantasia Barrino Story: Life Is Not a Fairy Tale*. An early favourite among the judges, Fantasia may have solidified her hold on the top slot with her electrifying and tearful performance of "Summertime" during the competition. Although there were voting irregularities along the way, some leading to charges of racism, in the end Fantasia captured the majority of the 65 million votes cast, triumphing over second-place winner Diane DeGarmo. Fantasia's debut album, *Free Yourself,* reached the Top Ten and sold 2 million copies.

American Idol Best-Selling Singles of the Year (Source: *Billboard*)

Year/Position	Artist	Song
2002 — #1	Kelly Clarkson	"A Moment Like This"
2003 — #1	Clay Aiken	"This Is the Night"/"Bridge over Troubled Water"
#2	Ruben Studdard	"Flying Without Wings"/"Superstar"
2004 — #1	Fantasia	"I Believe"
#2	Clay Aiken	"Solitaire"/ "The Way"
#3	Diana DeGarmo	"Dreams"
#6	Kimberly Locke	"8th World Wonder"
2005 — #1	Carrie Underwood	"Inside Your Heaven"
#2	Bo Brice	"Inside Your Heaven"/ "Vehicle"

By 2005, the idols had made inroads into audience demographics across the board. Fourth-season winner Carrie Underwood, the first "country" idol, had the best-selling pop single and best-selling country single of the year with "Inside Your Heaven." And fourth-season runner-up Bo Brice was right behind her, scoring the second bestselling single of the year with his version of "Inside Your Heaven"/"Vehicle." Kelly Clarkson placed two singles in the year-end Hot 100 Songs—"Since You Been Gone" and "Behind These Hazel Eyes"—and scored the number one Adult Contemporary hit with "Breakaway" from her second album of the same name. Ruben Studdard had the number one Gospel album of the year with his second entry, *I Need An Angel,* and Clay Aiken finished the year with the number one Christian album, *Merry Christmas with Love*. Fantasia emerged as the number one Adult R&B Artist and New R&B/Hip Hop Artist. When all was said and done, *American Idol* winners (or runners-up) had walked off with seventeen number one honours on *Billboard*'s year-end tallies, with Kelly Clarkson racking up nine of them herself. By the time Taylor Hicks and Katharine McPhee won the top positions for season five in 2006, Clarkson, Aiken, Studdard, and Fantasia were all hard at work on new albums, with no end in sight.

Hip Hop: The New Rock

If the return of guitar-based rock signaled the need for familiarity during a period of profound social dislocation, the overwhelming social function of the new singer/songwriters and television idols (with a few notable exceptions) was to protect their audiences from the bitter injustices and difficult political choices that swirled about them daily. Clearly, the success of these groups indicated that there was an emotional need (and, therefore, a market) for music that offered comfort and diversion amidst the turbulence. But if it began to appear as if these trends had captured more than a small segment of the popular music audience, that impression was more than laid to rest when it was reported in the 11 October 2003 issue of *Billboard* that, for the first time in the magazine's fifty-year history, all ten of the Top Ten songs in the country were by black artists, nine of them rappers, with Beyoncé in the number one slot (see table, right). Once again, most observers had failed to notice the elephant in the room until it stared them in the face. Critic Nelson George was quick to claim the ultimate victory. "The battle's been won," said George. "Hip-hop is the new American music."[22] That statement may have been a bit over the top, but there certainly was a germ of truth to it. Indeed, it echoed David Toop's statement of some twenty years earlier. "Hip hop," said Toop, "was the new music by virtue of its finding a way to absorb all other music."[23]

What had happened was that hip hop singles had made the transition from urban radio to Top Forty radio, which reflected the broadest audience demographic and

Billboard Top Ten Singles October 11, 2003

1.	Baby Boy—Beyoncé, Featuring Sean Paul
2.	Shake Ya Tailfeather—Nelly, P. Diddy & Murphy Lee
3.	Get Low—Lil Jon & The East Side Boyz, Featuring Ying Yang Twins
4.	Right Thurr—Chingy
5.	Frontin'—Pharrell, Featuring Jay-Z
6.	Damn!—YoungBloodZ, Featuring Lil Jon
7.	P.I.M.P.—50 Cent
8.	Into You—Fabolous, Featuring Tamia/Ashanti
9.	Stand Up—Ludacris, Featuring Shawnna
10.	Where Is the Love?—Black Eyed Peas

With his fabled penchant for violence and strong rhyming and production skills, 50 Cent emerged as the most popular artist of 2003, a feat he repeated in 2005.

formed the basis for *Billboard*'s *Hot 100* chart. But the Hot 100 is more heavily weighted to radio play than to sales. It is the *Billboard* 200, the mainstream album chart, that reflects the bulk of sales. Had black artists captured the Top Ten album positions, George's statement would have been unassailable. Still, he was correct when he said that "The reason radio stations are playing it is simple: it keeps listeners on their station listening to the McDonald's ads."[24] In addition, even the hardest rappers have become more oriented toward the crossover market, and hip hop aesthetics have exerted a defining influence on other styles, from teen pop to r&b. Artists like Bubba Sparxxx and Nappy Roots even offer country rap. In the final analysis, hip hop may not have achieved the final victory in CD sales, but it was the music that most influenced other styles and it was the music that sold the most other products. It is in that sense that one might think of it as "the new American music" or, at the very least, a new paradigm that may have surpassed rock in cultural importance.

The media splash created by black artists occupying the first ten positions on the pop charts simultaneously might have generated more heat than light at the time, but it marked the beginning of a pattern of continued growth that many in the music industry found troubling. Their concerns were blunted for a time because black artists were still sharing top honours with artists from other genres at year's end, including Shania Twain, the Dixie Chicks, and Tim McGraw in country, singer/songwriters Norah Jones and Avril Lavigne, and rockers Nickelback and Evanescence, whose *Fallen* had remained on the album charts for nearly two years. Still, it would not have been a stretch even in 2003 to say that rap and hip hop were first among equals— certainly in mainstream influence, but also in popularity and sales. Indeed, *Billboard*'s first three Top Pop Artists of the Year were black, and six of the ten most popular songs of 2003 were by black artists. More important, this was a baseline from which their presence only expanded.

If the year was owned by any single artist, it was 50 Cent. *Rolling Stone*'s April 3 cover pictured him as buff and as mean as he could be. By this time, he had become the most controversial figure in rap, if not in popular culture generally. His exploits had already generated so much buzz that when his much-anticipated debut, *Get Rich or Die Tryin'*, was finally released, it sold a record-breaking 872,000 units in five days, powered by the ubiquitous feel-good single "In Da Club." He closed the year with the number one single of the year from the number one album of the year, making him *Billboard*'s Top Pop Artist of the Year, with two other black artists—R. Kelly (*Chocolate Factory*) and Sean Paul (*Dutty Rock*)—in positions two and three, respectively. The same year, 50 Cent's G-Unit posse released the platinum-selling *Beg for Mercy*. All in all, it was a good year for 50 Cent. But although he was nominated for an impressive five Grammy Awards, he was completely shut out of the winner's circle. Particularly angered at not being named Best New Artist of the Year, he actually tried to block Evanescence from receiving the award.

50 Cent may have been locked out of his expected Grammy victories, but three other rap or r&b/hip hop acts—Jay-Z, OutKast, and Beyoncé—bested all artists in nominations for the 2003 calendar year, with six nominations each. Beyoncé opened the February 2004 Grammy Awards telecast with a stunning medley of Prince tunes and her hit single "Crazy in Love," accompanied by none other than Prince himself. At the end of the night, Beyoncé went home not only with her boyfriend Jay-Z, who won two Grammys of his own for his guest appearance on "Crazy In Love," but also with five of the six awards for which she was nominated. Given the momentum of the evening, it was considered odd by many that she lost out to Coldplay's *Clocks* for Record of the Year. The year 2003 was something of a breakout for Beyoncé, who called the curtain on Destiny's Child and struck out on her own as a solo artist, releasing *Dangerously in Love* in June. By year's end, the album had sold 2 million copies and, before running its course, had generated five Top Ten pop singles, including two at number one: the funky dance pop track "Crazy in Love" with Jay-Z and "Baby Boy," enhanced by the staccato dance hall verse of Sean Paul. The Jamaican rapper himself scored the third most popular single of the year with "Get Busy." Beyoncé reunited with Destiny's Child the following year to record their farewell album, *Destiny Fulfilled*, whose title sounded like the state of her own career path.

OutKast had followed up their triple-platinum *Stankonia* (2000) with *Speakerboxxx/The Love Below* (2003), for which they won three Grammys, as well as becoming the first rap artists ever to win the coveted Album of the Year award. The double album was also one of the few hip hop albums ever to be certified diamond (10 million units sold or, as in this case, 5 million for each CD). *Speakerboxxx/The Love Below* was essentially two albums: the first a Big Boi compilation that continued OutKast's adventurous Dirty South hip hop; the second, an eccentric André 3000 (a.k.a. Dré) foray into funk and soul. Each CD generated a number one hit single: Big Boi's "The Way You Move" and André's "Hey Ya!," which became one of the standout singles of the year. For the Grammys, OutKast was booked for two performances: Big Boi did "The Way You Move" as a medley with George Clinton's P-Funk ensemble and Robert Randolph's Family Band and Dré closed the show with "Hey Ya!" Both performances approached the high bar set by Beyoncé earlier in the evening, although Dré's set offended many in the Native American community for its use of dancers in feathered headdresses and matching hot pants gyrating wildly after emerging from a giant green teepee. CBS, already on the hook for Janet Jackson's Superbowl "wardrobe malfunction," apologized immediately. OutKast did not.

"In Da Club"

Artist: 50 Cent

Music / Lyrics by Curtis James Jackson III (50 Cent), with Mike Elizondo and Andre Young (Dr. Dre)

Label: Shady / Aftermath / Interscope, from the CD *Get Rich or Die Tryin'* (2002)

In the wake of the archetypal Brooklyn hip hop of Run–D.M.C. and the Afrocentric rapping of Queen Latifah, hip hop made a breakthrough into white radio with so-called "gangsta" rap. Often focusing, like "In Da Club," on both bicoastal (New York vs. Los Angeles) and interpersonal rivalries, gangsta rappers have crafted a much harder, even more minimalist, "outlaw" approach. As with many gangsta rap songs, "In Da Club" was released in both an "explicit" version and a "clean" version. The explicit version is much more direct in its references to drug use and specific feuds and more liberal in its use of language that some might find offensive.

Musical Style Notes

"In Da Club" is in classic hip hop style: Layers of interlocking rhythms create a compelling, repetitive "groove" over which the rap is foregrounded. Altogether, the rhythm features a steady "sixteenth note" pattern (each large beat is subdivided into 4 smaller beats); a syncopated drum track; a syncopated chord progression that repeats throughout the piece; and a synthesized hand-clap track that accentuates the backbeat, forming an interlocking pattern.

large beat			1	2	3	4	1	2	3	4
syncopated beat (chords)	1 2 3 **4**	1 2 **3** 4	1 2 3 **4**	1 2 3 **4**	1 2 3 **4**	1 2 **3** 4	1 2 3 **4**	1 2 3 **4**	1 2 3 **4**	1 2 3 **4**
handclaps			X		X			X		X
large beat subdivided into 4	1 2 3 4	1 2 3 4	1 2 3 4	1 2 3 4	1 2 3 4	1 2 3 4	1 2 3 4	1 2 3 4	1 2 3 4	1 2 3 4

The vocals alternate between spoken voice—a combination of "chanted" speech on one note, which may alternate slightly by one tone—and passages that are sung.

Musical "Road Map"

TIMINGS	COMMENTS	LYRICS
0:00–0:15	Verse 1 (spoken) Keyboards and prominent bass (See *Musical Style Notes* for interlocking rhythm pattern.)	*Go, Go, Go, Go, Go, Go, Go Shorty It's your birthday . . .*
0:15–0:26 0:26–0:36	Chorus (chanted on a single note, with occasional variation by one or two tones) Note additional layer of sampled "orchestral" sound. Chorus repeats.	*You can find me in da club Bottle full of bub . . . (etc.)*
0:36–1:19	Verse 2 (chanted, "sung-speech"; changes to a focus on speech as the verse continues; the last lines are sung) "Orchestral" sound drops out and returns at 0:59.	*When I pull up out front . . . (etc.)*
1:19–1:30 1:30–1:42	Chorus (chanted on a single note, with occasional variation by one or two tones) Chorus repeats.	*You can find me in da club . . . (etc.)*
1:42–1:52	Bridge (sung) (Whistle heard way in the background)	*My flow, my show . . .*
1:52–2:23	Verse 3 (chanted—sung speech)	*You should love it . . . (etc.)*
2:23–2:34	Chorus (chanted on a single note, with occasional variation by one or two tones)	*You can find me in da club . . . (etc.)*
2:34–2:45	Chorus repeats. "Orchestral sample" is mixed up a little more prominently here.	
2:45–3:12	Ending verse—spoken Chord progression continues; music fades out, ends at 3:12.	*Ha ha—Don't try to act like you don't know . . . . . . (laughter)*

In retrospect, the separate CDs and separate Grammy performances may have signaled a split for OutKast. *Speakerboxxx/The Love Below* worked well enough within the OutKast brand only because the album as a whole stayed true to the experimental spirit fans expected from the duo. In fact, Big Boi and Dré had been moving in different directions both personally and artistically for some time. At one point, Dré moved to Los Angeles to try his hand at films. During this period, he refused to tour, so Big Boi took to the road alone. "At first, it was kinda weird," commented Big Boi, "because I'm used to turning around and he's right there." Revealing his true feelings, he then mumbled under his breath, "That shit's fucked up, for real."[25] After some minor success in Hollywood, Dré returned to Atlanta, at which point HBO approached OutKast with the idea of doing a musical. They decided to go for it. Although they reportedly had fun filming *Idlewild*, by the time their Prohibition-era feature film was completed, they had appeared only in three scenes together, and they worked in separate studios to create the accompanying soundtrack of the same name.

Black dominance in popular music continued the following year with seven of the first ten Top Pop Artists of the Year and eleven of the thirteen most popular singles being by rap or r&b/hip hop artists. In addition to artists already mentioned, like Alicia Keys, OutKast, Beyoncé, and Jay-Z (whose *Black Album* marked his retirement from performing, as he moved to the administrative side of the business), there were also newcomers like Twista (*Kamikazi*) and Kanye West (*The College Dropout*). It was Usher who ruled 2004 in much the same way that 50 Cent dominated the previous year, only more so. Usher finished the year with the most popular album of the year (*Confessions*) as well as the top two singles ("Yeah!" and "Burn"). *Confessions* sold an incredible 1.1 million units in its first week. The album's first single, "Yeah!" (featuring L'il Jon and Ludacris), which married Dirty South crunk beats to an r&b sound, occupied the number one position on *Billboard*'s Hot 100 for a record-tying twelve weeks. It was replaced by "Burn," an r&b/hip hop song built around Usher's gentle falsetto. This held the top spot for another seven weeks, giving Usher an unprecedented nineteen-week run at pop number one. After being displaced by Fantasia's "I Believe" for one week, "Burn" came back for another week at number one. The album also generated two other number one singles— "Confessions Pt. 2" and "My Boo," a duet with Alicia Keys—placing Usher at the top of the Hot 100 for twenty-eight weeks of the year. Signed to La Face Records by L. A. Reid when he was just fourteen, Usher released his first album while he was still in high school and the platinum-selling *My Way* (1997) shortly after graduating. *Confessions* (2004) was his fourth studio album; it was certified eight times platinum before the year was out.

This was also the year that producer Kanye West stepped out from behind the mixing board and into the studio as rapper Kanye West. West was not your average MC. Looking more like someone from the pages of *GQ* than the *Source* in his pink Polo shirts and Gucci loafers, he graced the cover of *Time* magazine before *Rolling Stone* gave him the cover on which he is pictured as Jesus Christ with a crown of thorns. West invited controversy wherever he went and he went everywhere. At the *American Music Awards,* he threw a fit after country singer Gretchen Wilson bested him for the Best New Artist award. The controversy he was best-known for was the time he abandoned the teleprompted script at a benefit for Hurricane Katrina victims and launched into a nervous anti-government rant that climaxed with the pronouncement that "George Bush doesn't care about black people," with a stupefied co-host Mike Myers standing motionless, like a deer caught in the headlights. As difficult as that moment was for West, however, he considered it second to the time he spoke out against homophobia in rap in an MTV interview.

West was raised mostly in the middle-class South Shore suburb of Chicago by his mother, Donda, a former chair of the English Department at Chicago State University. He spent summers with his father, a former Black Panther, who had since done stints as a photographer, a Christian marriage counselor, and a sociology professor at the College of Southern Maryland. Clearly college bound, West dropped out after one year to try his hand at music. Creating beats for local Chicago rappers soon led to gigs at Bad Boy and Roc-A-Fella in New York, where he built a solid reputation as a producer, working with top-tier artists like Alicia Keys ("You Don't Know My Name"), Twista ("Slow Jamz"), Ludacris ("Stand Up"), and Jay-Z ("Izzo [H.O.V.A.]," "Takeover," and "03 Bonnie & Clyde"). But when he told his colleagues at Roc-A-Fella that he wanted to rap, his request was first met with an awkward standoffishness. "It was obvious we were not from the same place or cut from the same cloth," said Jay-Z. "We all grew up street guys who had to do whatever we had to do to get by. Then there's Kanye, who to my knowledge has never hustled a day in his life. I didn't see how it could work."[26]

Jay-Z's reluctance to let West grab the microphone was born of a limiting stereotype that rappers had to look and act (and speak) in a certain way to be successful. But an earlier generation of New York rappers from Run-D.M.C. to Public Enemy had long since demonstrated that a college education was not necessarily an impediment to fame. Fearing that one of their hottest producers might jump ship to another label, Roc-A-Fella ultimately decided to sign West to a contract. It was a smart move. His first effort, aptly titled *The College Dropout*, debuted at number two and sold nearly 3 million copies; West also earned ten Grammy nominations for that year, of which he won three. The album had been delayed by a near-fatal car accident, which West chronicled on his hit single "Through the Wire" while his jaw was still wired shut. This plus "Slow Jamz," his hilarious ode to romantic r&b singers, a collaboration with Twista and Jaime Fox, kept West in the public eye while the album was being released. *Dropout* then generated other hit singles like "All Falls Down" and the gospel-based "Jesus Walks." For his second album, *Late Registration* (2005), West used another approach, collaborating with Fiona Apple's producer Jon Brion, who added horns and strings to the rapper's sample-heavy beats. *Late Registration* went to number one and platinum certification, and won

An unlikely hip hop hero in his upscale, preppy attire, Kanye West proved to be a top-selling rapper and an outspoken political commentator.

the Grammy for Best Album of the Year. Singles from the album included the topical "Diamonds from Sierra Leone" and "Gold Digger" (featuring Jaime Fox in his Ray Charles persona), which went to pop number one.

By 2005, black dominance on the pop charts had reached such proportions that those in the industry who get concerned about such things were moved to action. In February, *Billboard*, seemingly out of nowhere, introduced a brand new chart called the Pop 100. To the uninitiated, this move first appeared to be, at best, a duplication of effort. The Hot 100 had been *Billboard*'s pop singles chart since 1958. It was the chart that the radio program *American Top 40* used to create its weekly playlist from 1970 to 1995. It had been modified over the years to keep pace with new phenomena like digital downloads, but it remained *Billboard*'s main chart for the most popular individual songs throughout. What, then, was the Pop 100? The answer to this question began to reveal itself after one noticed that every record to reach number one on the Hot 100 in 2004 was by a black artist (see table). Simply put, the Pop 100 was created to remedy this situation. While the Hot 100 was based on sales and airplay data from songs played on all radio formats, the Pop 100 limited its data collection to a narrower range of mainstream Top 40 stations to track what *Billboard* called "mass-appeal mainstream hits," as if that phrase didn't describe rap.[27] Explained journalist and music librarian Bill Lamb, "By the beginning of the new century, many fans and members of the music industry became concerned that the Hot 100 had become biased in favour of r&b and hip hop music. It was becoming more and more difficult for rock and mainstream pop songs to do well on the Hot 100."[28]

What was really going on was that hard-core rap and r&b/hip hop had captured the taste preferences of white suburban teenagers to the degree that other categories were overshadowed, and many music executives didn't like that. Put another way, the runaway success of rap and hip hop had allowed numerous street-toughened black entrepreneurs to become multimillionaires on their own terms, and this challenged narrow mainstream conceptions of the American Dream. When one stripped away the racism associated with this state of affairs, it was clear that the Hot 100 was still a more accurate measure of popular taste. The Pop 100 was designed to give white artists in pop, rock, and country a better chance to claim a number one hit song. The system was far from flawless; ironically, the first song to hit number one on the new Pop 100 chart was Ciara's "1, 2 Step," a dance-oriented r&b/hip hop single featuring Missy Elliott. Still, the new chart enabled Kelly Clarkson's "Since U Been Gone" to top the year-end recap. Other than that, the two charts were remarkably similar in practice. This was because rap and r&b/hip hop had already made inroads into Top 40 radio territory and because many white artists had adopted hip hop

> *By 2005, black dominance on the pop charts had reached such proportions that those in the industry who get concerned about such things were moved to action.*

Billboard Number One Songs on the Hot 100 in 2004

Starting Date at No. 1	Song	Artist
January 3	"Hey Ya!"	OutKast
February 14	"The Way You Move"	OutKast featuring Sleepy Brown
February 21	"Slow Jamz"	Twista featuring Kanye West and Jamie Foxx
February 28	"Yeah!"	Usher featuring Lil' Jon and Ludacris
May 22	"Burn"	Usher
July 10	"I Believe"	Fantasia
July 17	"Burn"	Usher
July 24	"Confessions Part II"	Usher
August 7	"Slow Motion"	Juvenile featuring Soulja Slim
August 21	"Lean Back"	The Terror Squad
September 11	"Goodies"	Ciara featuring Petey Pablo
October 30	"My Boo"	Usher and Alicia Keys
December 11	"Drop It Like It's Hot"	Snoop Dogg featuring Pharrell

aesthetics and rap styles in their own music. Gwen Stefani's "Hollaback Girl"—a jaunty dance pop single with rapped verses—scored number two for the year on both charts.

Even with the new chart, there was no denying that black artists dominated the year; 50 Cent returned to claim 2005 with a vengeance, and Mariah Carey resuscitated a flagging career with blockbuster success. 50 Cent's *The Massacre* (2005) made the rapper the Top Artist of the Year for the second time in three years. Four singles from the album—"Disco Inferno," "Candy Shop," " Just a Lil Bit," and "Outta Control"—hit the Top Ten not only on the Hot 100 but, interestingly, on the Pop 100 as well. 50 Cent's radio presence was extended on his collaborations with the Game on "How We Do It" and "Hate It or Love It." The Game was a Compton rapper who had joined 50 Cent's G-Unit in 2004, across rap's geographical divide. By the time the singles caught fire, however, the relationship had already gone bad, and 50 Cent unceremoniously dismissed the Game from G-Unit on New York's Hot 97 radio station. Rival posses gathered in front of the building, a skirmish ensued, and a member of the Game's posse was shot in the leg. But, then, that kind of violence had always been a career booster for 50 Cent. Extending his image further, the rapper finished the year with an aptly named video game, *50 Cent: Bulletproof*, and a starring role in a loosely autobiographical film, *Get Rich or Die Tryin'*.

Mariah Carey was the comeback story of the year. Carey had hit rock bottom in the early 2000s (which for her meant mere gold CD sales), complete with suicide notes and erratic behaviour—all in all, a rather public and highly publicized breakdown. After signing with Virgin for a reported $80-million-deal, her film musical, *Glitter,* and its accompanying sound-track album of the same name did so poorly critically and commercially that the movie failed to recover its production costs in its initial U.S. release, and the album barely broke gold sales. Adding insult to injury (but enhancing her financial situation considerably), Virgin then paid her $28 million to go away. Moving to Island/Def Jam to set up her own label in 2002, Carey's first outing,

Mariah Carey's return demonstrated the resilience of the artist and the centrality of hip hop aesthetics to mainstream success.

Charmbracelet, an unsuccessful attempt to recapture the pop mainstream, failed to lift her career out of the doldrums. Three years later, on *The Emancipation of Mimi,* Carey again embraced hip hop and returned to an r&b-based dance pop groove that finally put the early 2000s behind her. The album hit number one and was still riding the charts a year later, having been certified six times platinum; it was her best-selling album

Canadian r&b diva Jully Black finally broke through in 2007 with her stunning cover of Etta James' "Seven Day Fool."

in more than a decade. It also generated a number of hit singles, including "We Belong Together," which spent fourteen weeks at number one, and "Don't Forget About Us," which became her seventeenth number one hit. Only Elvis Presley at eighteen and the Beatles at twenty had more. Carey's return demonstrated the resilience of the artist and the centrality of hip hop aesthetics to mainstream success.

While Mariah Carey was enjoying her comeback, Toronto's Jully Black was getting poised to record her breakthrough album. As early as 1996, Black, then nineteen, was being featured on seminal Canadian hip hop tracks by Choclair and Kardinal Offishall. Two years later, she recorded "Rally'n" under her own name. In 2005, Black issued her first full CD, *This Is Me*, from which "Sweat of Your Brow" and "5x Love" stormed their way into the Canadian Top Thirty. In 2007, Black's propulsive cover of Etta James' "Seven Day Fool" was released ahead of her second album, *Revival*. Recasting Black as a big-voiced soul chanteuse, "Seven Day Fool" reached number nine on the Canadian charts and was awarded the Juno for R&B/Soul Recording of the Year in April 2008. It is important to note that the success that Black has enjoyed would not have been possible prior to the establishment of urban radio in Canada in 2001.

Reggaeton: The New Hip Hop?

Given the importance of hip hop to U.S. culture and the particular characteristics of U.S. immigration in the early 2000s, when a group of (mostly) island-based Puerto Rican artists merged hip hop style with a selective mixture of Caribbean influences to create a musical hybrid called reggaeton (or *reguetón,* as it is sometimes called in Latin America), the stage was set for it to find a national audience and possibly mainstream acceptance, even though it was delivered in Spanish. If the U.S. dance club scene in 2004 and 2005 was any indicator, reggaeton had become the first music with Spanish vocals ever to find a national mainstream audience in the United States.

Between 1990 and 2005, according to census data, the number of immigrants in the United States (documented and undocumented) rose from 19.8 million to 35.7 million, "a number larger than the population of California."[29] More of these immigrants—about 11 million—came from Mexico than any other country. As a result, this pattern has been referred to as "the Mexicanization of U.S. immigration." As of 2004, the U.S. Census Bureau listed more than 40 million residents of the United States as being of "Hispanic Origin."[30] By this time, they had surpassed African Americans as the country's largest minority ethnic group. As important for our purposes, is the fact that new arrivals no longer limited themselves to the historical points of entry like California, New York, Texas, and Florida. Less-expected places saw dramatic increases: Indiana, 34 percent; South Dakota, 44 percent; Delaware, 32 percent; Missouri, 31 percent; Colorado, 28 percent; and New Hampshire, 26 percent.[31] The result was a nationally dispersed immigrant population, the largest group of which was Latino. Just as internal migration during World War II created national markets for what had been regional musics, international immigration to the United States in the age of globalization and the resulting settlement patterns had profoundly altered the U.S. cultural landscape once again.

But if the largest percentage of Latinos were of Mexican extraction, why was it that a music with a Caribbean character was the one that caught fire? According to Wayne Marshall:

As a modern sound, a sound intimately related to hip-hop and reggae, reggaeton gives Latino youth a way to participate in contemporary urban-American culture without abandoning important aspects of their heritage. This may help to explain why a Latin-Caribbean form—and not, say, a Mexican or Chicano style—has managed to captivate young Latinos in a way that norteño *never has, despite Mexican-Americans constituting well over 60% of the U.S. Hispanic population.*[32]

A cursory examination of the historical development of reggaeton reveals a study in the international circulation and synthesis of traveling cultures. The simple answer to the question of where reggaeton started is that it was born in Panama and raised in Puerto Rico. But, as one might expect, that answer borders on the simplistic. The more complicated answer involves the interweaving of disparate sonic elements across national boundaries, linguistic barriers, and separate (and unequal) marketing structures.

Prior to the birth of reggaeton, Jamaican reggae had traveled not only to major sites of international migration like London and New York, but also to Puerto Rico and Panama, where descendants of Jamaican workers, who had moved there to help build the canal, had begun performing what came to be called *reggae en español*. During the same time frame, through the circular travels of New York-based Puerto Ricans, who had grown up with and participated in the development of hip hop from the beginning, rap found its way to Puerto Rico, where it was soon indigenized as *rap en español* by artists like Vico C, who used the local vernacular and island-specific themes. By the late 1980s, Panamanian artists like El General ("Tu Pum Pum," 1988), considered by many to be the father of reggaeton, had adapted the insistent bounce of dance hall reggae for Latin American audiences. Significantly, El General was living in New York when he recorded many of his hits. With lyrics in Spanish, this music had enormous appeal in Puerto Rico, where Jamaican dance hall had already achieved widespread popularity. Indeed, as Puerto Rican DJs like Playero and DJ Nelson developed the sound further, they were so drawn to a Shabba Ranks song called "Dem Bow," with its minimalist dance hall beat punctuated by snare drum accents, that this "riddim," initially created by producer Bobby Digital, became a defining characteristic of the music. Around the mid-1990s, the music that combined these elements coalesced into what came to be known as reggaeton. The distinctive Puerto Rican variant of the music developed further over the next few years in the Puerto Rican club scene and gradually found acceptance in pan-Latino centres like New York. But it wasn't until New York-based N.O.R.E.'s "Oye Mi Canto" (2004)—a driving appeal to inclusiveness and pan-Latino identity—opened the door to reggaeton in the States and Daddy Yankee's *Barrio Fino* with its ubiquitous hit single, "Gasolina," flooded the market that reggaeton became a mainstream phenomenon.

From 2004 into 2005, *Billboard* reported that the only category of music to register growth was Latin music.[33] While it was clear that the bedrock of Latin music sales remained regional Mexican musics, the magazine attributed the expansion to two phenomena: Shakira and reggaeton. Following an ambitious touring schedule to support her 2001 album *Laundry Service*, Shakira took an extended break, during which she wrote about sixty songs in English and Spanish. A selected number of these were released six months apart in 2005 in two albums divided by language: *Fijacion Oral, Vol. 1* and *Oral Fixation, Vol. 2*. Both albums hit the Top Five on the pop album charts and earned Shakira a massive crossover audience. On "La Tortura," a duet with Alejandro Sanz from *Vol. 1,* Shakira included a version that incorporated a reggaeton

Daddy Yankee had been a pivotal artist in the Puerto Rican underground for more than a decade before his ubiquitous single, "Gasolina," conquered the mainland mainstream.

sound. The video for the song was reportedly the first in Spanish to go into regular rotation on MTV. *Vol. 2* was rereleased in 2006 to include her runaway hit single "Hips Don't Lie" (featuring Wyclef Jean), the video for which portrayed Shakira at her sensual best, combining erotic but tasteful dance moves from her Middle Eastern heritage with a hot Latin dance groove. By 2006, Shakira had become a truly global pop star, incorporating influences ranging from pop, rock, and disco to cumbia, tejano, and reggaeton into a coherent bilingual musical project that was as ambitious and well executed as any in the business.

Meanwhile, on the reggaeton front, summer 2005, according to *Billboard*, was "the summer of reggaeton." On 30 July 2005, all ten of the Top Ten songs on the Latin Tropical Airplay chart had some connection to reggaeton. Seven of them were outright reggaeton songs, and of the three that weren't, two had reggaeton remixes, and Aventura's "Ella y Yo" featured reggaeton star Don Omar.[34] Also at this time, Daddy Yankee's *Barrio Fino* was the best-selling Latin album in the country and the first reggaeton album to debut at number one on the Latin charts, a position it held on and off for nearly a year. Daddy Yankee had been one of the most important figures in the Puerto Rican underground since the early nineties and had started building a more high-profile presence in the island reggaeton scene later in the decade. With the promotional clout of Universal behind him for *Barrio Fino* in 2004, he was first coming out of the gate in the competition for the crossover crown of mainstream U.S. acceptance. Although "Gasolina"—a bouncy dance track that was a playful metaphor for sex—was the single that caught on in the U.S. market, the album also contained a number of other well-produced songs, including "Lo Que Pasó, Pasó" and "No Me Dejes Solo" (featuring Wisin & Yandel), that received significant exposure on Latin radio, and "Like You," which crossed over to pop. Daddy Yankee stayed in the game with a couple of reissues and live albums, including *Barrio Fino: En Directo* (2006), which also hit number one on the Latin charts and then crossed over to pop.

As reggaeton made more and more inroads into mainstream America, many listeners reported a certain sameness to "all, not some" reggaeton tunes, as the *Village Voice* put it.[35] Part of that perception could easily have been attributed to the fact that reggaeton had been dominated by a single production team, known as Luny Tunes. Luny (Francisco Saldana) and Tunes (Víctor Cabrera) were born in the Dominican Republic and raised in Peabody, Massachusetts, where they became interested in music production. Moving to Puerto Rico at the invitation of DJ Nelson, they quickly became the "Neptunes" of reggaeton, eclipsing all other reggaeton producers in their uncanny ability to generate hits. They worked intensely, producing some of the genre's biggest hits, including Daddy Yankee's "Gasolina," Don Omar's "Dale Don Dale," and Wisin & Yandel's "Rakata." Their compilation albums, *Mas Flow* (2003), *La Trayectoria* (2004), and *Mas Flow, Vol. 2* (2005), became some of reggaeton's most popular and best-selling albums.

Regarding the sameness of the Luny Tunes production style, Wayne Marshall argued that their inclination "to rehash the same synth-patches, the same riffs and basslines, and the same drum patterns . . . reflects the tradition of creative re-use that takes the Jamaican example of 're-licked' riddims as a model."[36] Among Luny Tunes' many accomplishments, one of the innovations they could be credited with was the incorporation of Dominican elements of bachata and *merengue* into reggaeton. According to Deborah Pacini Hernandez, Tego Calderón's "Métele Sazón," for example, "exhibits both bachata's signature guitar arpeggios and merengue's characteristic piano riffs."[37] A well-known hip hop DJ in Puerto Rico put the cultural significance of these developments in perspective when he stated: "In the same way you can mark reggaeton before and after Tego, there's a before and after Luny Tunes. . . . Luny Tunes contributed something very positive, because they solidified the marriage between bachata and reggaeton. It made it what it is, a tropical music; in that way it distinguished it from hip hop."[38] Beyond the apparent uniformity of reggaeton's production, closer examination revealed enough rhythmic variation within the bedrock boom-ch-boom-chick foundation to offer difference and enough staccato bursts of snare drum samples to break the monotony. Beyond that it was the richness of the producer's electronic palette and the effectiveness of the artist's flow that made reggaeton infectious.

Reggaeton was a club music first and foremost, and its gut-level appeal was most apparent on the dance floor, where uninhibited partygoers routinely gave their bodies over to the prevailing dance style perreo (doggystyle), which invited sexualized movements that went well beyond suggestive.

Reggaeton was a club music first and foremost, and its gut-level appeal was most apparent on the dance floor, where uninhibited partygoers routinely gave their bodies over to the prevailing dance style perreo (doggystyle), which invited sexualized movements that went well beyond suggestive. Explained one male participant in no uncertain terms: "Sex is a feeling like what you experience when you listen to reggaeton. Not only because the lyrics talk about sex, but also because of the sensation one feels from the Dembow. It's the same sensation you feel when you are having sex with a woman."[39] In the course of its development, reggaeton had been criticized for many things—for violence, for misogyny, for being inferior music. But it was criticized most severely for its overt sexuality. Such criticism, of course, only served to confirm its outlaw status, which was the dominant narrative that helped make the music and the scene so attractive in the first place.

The ability of reggaeton to generate hits (and sales) from the dance floor—like disco before it—ultimately forced radio to take the music more seriously. At first, stations that were formatted for hip hop and r&b began adding a few individual reggaeton cuts like "Oye Mi Canto" and "Gasolina." Then, some of the more adventurous (or desperate) Spanish-language stations began moving toward a new reggaeton-centric format that was eventually dubbed

"Hurban" (for Hispanic urban). History was made when KXOL-FM in Los Angeles switched from easy-listening to reggaeton in the summer of 2005 and the station went from eighteenth in market share to second place overall and first among listeners twelve to twenty-four years old.[40] Immediately following, Univision flipped eight of its major market stations to a reggaeton-centred format they called La Kalle (slang for "the street"), and Clear Channel followed suit with four conversions. There were others as well, including KFMR in Phoenix, KZZA in Dallas, and WYUU in Tampa. "We've found that the appeal of reggaeton is universal," said Clear Channel senior vice president for programming Tom Poleman. "It's not just about Latin listeners; white suburban kids have a lot of passion for it."[41]

By 2006, some of these stations had begun to slip in the ratings. It was not clear at the time whether reggaeton was simply a novelty that had run its course or whether it was still a vibrant new form awaiting an influx of new talent and material. Any number of artists and industry professionals were betting on the latter. Jennifer Lopez had commissioned a full-length documentary of the music. And Luny Tunes' cell phones were ringing constantly, as everyone from Jay-Z, Alicia Keys, and R. Kelly to Sean Paul, Ricky Martin, and Ja Rule (not to mention Paris Hilton) came calling for remixes. Whether or not reggaeton turned out to be the Next Big Thing in itself, it could certainly be seen as an indicator of how global cultural flows would affect the character of our popular culture in the future.

The drive to return to business as usual in the post-9/11 period precipitated yet another round of serious mega-mergers, leading to even more concentration in the music industry, and prompted a return to the familiar sounds of guitar-based rock and the introspections of earnest singer/songwriters. Amidst all this activity, there was the continuing momentum of a significant paradigm shift toward hip hop as the foundational template for U.S. popular music and a crossing of the language barrier with the introduction and success of reggaeton, which confirmed that Latino immigration in the United States had reached some sort of critical mass. What remained unclear, however, was how all these developments would proceed into the future. While it was certain that the major labels would keep their antennae attuned to potential blockbuster hits in the near term, there was mounting evidence that suggested that the future of the music business would be as much about niches as about hits. The combination of more powerful computers, broadband connectivity, inexpensive storage capacity, and democratic avenues of viral communication held out the possibility that lots of artists selling a few thousand songs each could, in the aggregate, rival the market for hits. In such a future, major companies might be motivated to experiment with new models for developing and disseminating music. Or they might simply share the marketplace with inventive new companies that catered to independent artists on a more loosely defined, revenue-sharing basis. Either way, the prospects for a vibrant musical culture seemed well within reach.

Notes

INTRODUCTION

1. It could be argued that rap music may yet necessitate a shift in the paradigm.

2. It should be noted that this discussion concerns cultural development as it occurred in European societies. There are, of course, any number of other societies that developed according to different cultural patterns, but the cultural forms and values of the "New World" were informed by those of the European colonial powers; thus an understanding of cultural development in European societies is relevant to understanding the tensions and complexities of contemporary U.S. culture.

3. This analysis was developed most forcefully by the members of the Frankfurt School, a group of Jewish intellectuals in Germany who were rightly disturbed by Hitler's effective use of the mass media in advancing the cause of fascism in the 1930s and 1940s.

4. Oscar Handlin, "Comments on Mass and Popular Culture," in *Culture for the Millions? Mass Media in Modern Society,* ed. Norman Jacobs (Princeton, N. J.: D. Van Nostrand, 1959), 66.

5. Stuart Hall and Paddy Whannel, *The Popular Arts* (New York: Pantheon Books, 1965), 67–68.

6. Carl Belz, *The Story of Rock,* 2d ed. (New York: Harper Colophon, 1971), 1.

7. Simon Frith, *Sound Effects: Youth, Leisure and the Politics of Rock 'n' Roll* (New York: Pantheon Books, 1981), 54.

8. Charlie Gillett, *The Sound of the City: The Rise of Rock and Roll* (New York: Outerbridge and Dienstfrey, 1970), i.

9. Ibid.

10. Frith, *Sound Effects,* 203.

11. Peter Wicke, *Rock Music: Culture, Aesthetics and Sociology* (Cambridge, Eng.: Cambridge University Press, 1990), 12.

12. Richard Middleton, "Reading Popular Music." Unit 16 of Open University course U203 *Popular Culture.* Milton-Keynes: The Open University, 1981, p. 17.

13. Charles Hamm, *Yesterdays: Popular Song in America* (New York: W. W. Norton, 1983), 358.

14. H. F. Mooney, "Popular Music Since the 1920s: The Significance of Shifting Taste," in *The Age of Rock,* ed. Jonathan Eisen (New York: Vintage Books, 1969), 10, 11.

15. Ibid.

16. Ibid., 10.

17. Christopher Small, *Music of the Common Tongue: Survival and Celebration in Afro-American Music* (New York: Riverrun Press, 1987), 25.

18. Iain Chambers, *Urban Rhythms: Popular Music and Popular Culture* (New York: Macmillan, 1985), 10.

19. Wicke, *Rock Music,* 16–17.

20. The use of the terms *race* and *hillbilly* as marketing categories for music was initiated by producer Ralph Peer. The origin of the terms is explained in detail in the next chapter.

21. David Brackett, "The Politics and Practice of 'Crossover' in American Popular Music, 1963 to 1965," *The Musical Quarterly* (Winter, 1994), 777.

22. Arnold Shaw, *Honkers and Shouters: The Golden Years of Rhythm and Blues* (New York: Collier Books, 1978), 524.

23. "Billboard Adopts 'R&B' As New Name for 2 Charts," *Billboard,* 27 October 1990, 35.

24. Ibid., 6.

25. See Arnold Shaw, *The Rockin' '50s* (New York: Hawthorne Books, 1974), 145.

26. Shaw, *Honkers and Shouters,* 215.

27. Ben Fong-Torres, "The Rolling Stone Interview: Ray Charles," *Rolling Stone,* 18 January 1973, 18.

28. Nick Tosches, *Country: Living Legends and Dying Metaphors in America's Biggest Music* (New York: Charles Scribner's Sons, 1985), 55.

29. Shaw, *Honkers and Shouters,* 497.

30. "To Censor Popular Songs," *Literary Digest* (24 May 1913), 1181.

31. Ibid.

CHAPTER 1

1. Russell Sanjek, *American Popular Music and Its Business: The First Four Hundred Years, Volume II from 1790 to 1909* (New York: Oxford University Press, 1988), 377. Sanjek further states: "The production of pianos and player pianos reached its all-time high in 1899, when more than 365,000 were manufactured, and it continued to average 300,000 annually until just after World War I" (p. 296).

2. Charles Hamm, *Yesterdays: Popular Song in America* (New York: W. W. Norton, 1983), 285. Ian Whitcomb puts the figure at 10 million copies over a twenty-year period. See Ian Whitcomb, *After the Ball: Popular Music from Rag to Rock* (Baltimore: Penguin Books, 1974), 4.

3. Sanjek, *American Popular Music,* 2: 365.

4. Jerrold Northrop Moore, *A Matter of Records: Fred Gaisberg and the Golden Era of the Gramophone* (New York: Taplinger Publishing Co., 1976), 6.

5. Whitburn, *Pop Memories.*

6. It is interesting to note that at this point, the term *gramophone* was dropped from the language in the United States (but not in Europe), and phonograph became the generic term for all record players.

7. As if to complement the gentility of the series, Johnson then introduced the Victrola, the first console record player, which featured an enclosed turntable, tone arm, and playback horn, and a price tag of $200.

8. Whitcomb, *After the Ball,* 98–99.

9. C. A. Schicke, *Revolution in Sound, A Biography of the Recording Industry* (Boston: Little, Brown and Co., 1974), 67–68.

10. Sanjek, *American Popular Music,* 2: 297.

11. Eileen Southern, *The Music of Black Americans: A History* (New York: W. W. Norton, 1971), 347.

12. Hamm, *Yesterdays,* 290.

13. Ibid., 325.

14. "The Birth of Our Popular Songs," *Literary Digest* (7 October 1916), 892.

15. *Irving Berlin's America,* PBS documentary produced by Joann G. Young, 1986.

16. Hamm, *Yesterdays,* 340.

17. Gunther Schuller, *Early Jazz: Its Roots and Musical Development* (New York: Oxford University Press, 1968), 24.

18. Whitcomb, *After the Ball,* 26.

19. It is interesting to note that Joplin never recorded. The recordings attributed to him were actually made from piano rolls he cut. Given the popularity of player pianos at the beginning of this century, piano rolls became a vehicle for introducing the music of some black artists to mainstream listeners. However, since there are no recordings of Joplin himself, there remains no definitive statement as to the tempo at which he played his compositions.

20. Gilbert Seldes, *The Seven Lively Arts* (1924; reprint New York: A. S. Barnes, 1957), 71.

21. Hamm, *Yesterdays,* 321.

22. Schuller, *Early Jazz,* 38.

23. LeRoi Jones [Amiri Baraka], *Blues People* (New York: William Morrow, 1963), 69.

24. Ibid., 148.

25. William Barlow, "Cashing In," in *Split Image: African Americans in the Mass Media,* 2d ed., ed. Jannette L. Dates and William Barlow (Washington, D.C.: Howard University Press, 1993), 31.

26. There is actually a more complicated history here than meets the eye. Apparently, a number of black jazz musicians, including New Orleans trumpeter Freddie Keppard, were asked to record by recording companies. They declined because they feared that if recorded, their styles could be studied and stolen. As the innovators of jazz styles, African American artists apparently felt that they had more to lose than to gain by engaging with the new technology.

27. Seldes, *The Seven Lively Arts,* 94.

28. Sanjek, *American Popular Music,* 2: 339.

29. Hamm, *Yesterdays,* 288.

30. Russell Sanjek, *American Popular Music and Its Business: The First Four Hundred Years, Volume III from 1900 to 1984* (New York: Oxford University Press, 1988), 23.

31. Southern, *The Music of Black Americans,* 353.

32. For more information on the early history of radio see Gleason L. Archer, *History of Radio to 1926* (New York: American Historical Society, 1938) and Erik Barnouw, *A Tower in Babel: A History of Broadcasting in the United States to 1933* (New York: Oxford University Press, 1966).

33. Melhuish, 30.

34. Archer, *History of Radio,* 178.

35. Ibid., 85.

36. Ibid., 112.

37. Barnouw, *The Golden Web,* 33.

38. Lee de Forest, *Father of Radio* (Chicago: Wilcox and Follett, 1950), 442–43.

39. Sanjek, *American Popular Music,* 3: 81.

40. It should be noted that due to a loophole in the 1909 Copyright Act, novels and plays could be read on the air without infringing copyright. This loophole was not plugged until 1952. Much of the classical music that was performed was already in public domain; thus, no royalty payments were required.

41. Sanjek, *American Popular Music,* 3: 166.

42. Barnouw, *The Golden Web,* 6.

43. Donald Clarke, ed., *The Penguin Encyclopedia of Popular Music* (New York: Viking, 1989), 301.

44. Sanjek, *American Popular Music,* 3: 155.

45. Ibid., 110–11.

CHAPTER 2

1. Charles Hamm, *Yesterdays: Popular Song in America* (New York: W. W. Norton, 1983), 379.

2. William Barlow, "Cashing In," in *Split Image: African Americans in the Mass Media,* 2d ed., ed. Jannette L. Dates and William Barlow (Washington, D.C.: Howard University Press, 1993), 43.

3. Samuel Charters, *The Country Blues* (New York: Rinehart and Company, 1959), 34.

4. Following the failure of reconstruction and the replacement of legal slavery with economic dependence and political disenfranchisement, work songs reappeared with a new intensity and in a more basic style, "and in the next decades a crude blues form developed, still largely unaccompanied, and linked together in irregular, freely improvised patterns. This blues was still more in the realm of sung speech rather than song per se" (Gunther Schuller, *Early Jazz: Its Roots and Musical Development* [New York: Oxford University Press, 1968], 37). This is the music that gradually evolved into what is called the country blues.

5. Charters, *The Country Blues,* 27.

6. Schuller, *Early Jazz,* 36.

7. Bill C. Malone, *Country Music U.S.A.: Revised Edition* (Austin: University of Texas Press, 1985), 4.

8. Christopher Small, *Music of the Common Tongue: Survival and Celebration in Afro-American Music* (New York: Riverrun Press, 1987), 36.

9. LeRoi Jones [Amiri Baraka], *Blues People* (New York: William Morrow, 1963), 70.

10. Malone, *Country Music U.S.A.,* 24.

11. John W. Work, *American Negro Songs* (New York: Crown Publishers, 1940), 34.

12. While Rodgers tested what would become his characteristic yodel on "Sleep, Baby, Sleep" in 1927, he was not the first to yodel on record. According to Nick Tosches, that honour probably goes to Riley Puckett, the blind guitarist of the Skillet Lickers, who yodeled on the group's Columbia recording of "Rock

All Our Babies to Sleep" three years earlier. Bessie Smith cut a song called "Yodeling Blues" in 1923 but did not yodel on the record. The elusive Emmett Miller may have beat them all to yodeling, but he did not record one until 1925 on "Lovesick Blues." See Nick Tosches, *Country: Living Legends and Dying Metaphors in America's Biggest Music* (New York: Charles Scribner's Sons, 1985), 110–11.

13. Tosches, *Country,* 194.

14. Jones [Baraka], *Blues People,* 105.

15. Charters, *The Country Blues,* 48.

16. Over the course of their careers, boogie pianists appeared everywhere, from dives to fashionable society restaurants. One of their major social functions during the Great Depression was to provide entertainment for "rent parties."

> In Harlem, as in other large ghetto areas of northern cities, the only way that many blacks could cope with the problem of paying the excessive rents charged for their apartments was to give parties where "guests" were invited to contribute toward the rent. It was the job of the pianist "to draw people in"—into the barroom or café or the apartment itself—and the vitality and vigor of his playing was his drawing card. The playing of the best pianists could be heard for a considerable distance away. It was very important that a piano should have the correct "barroom" sound; sometimes it would have to be "doctored," by placing newspapers behind the hammers and putting tin on the felts, in order to obtain the effect wanted.

See Eileen Southern, *The Music of Black Americans: A History* (New York: W. W. Norton, 1971), 404–05.

17. Robert Palmer, *Deep Blues* (New York: Viking Press, 1981), 100.

18. Many observers, myself included, have written disparagingly about the implications of the term *race music.* It is likely, however, that Ralph Peer, the man who created the term, simply took his cue from the African American newspapers in which his company, OKeh Record Company, advertised—the *Chicago Defender* and the *Pittsburgh Courier,* which themselves referred to the members of the African American community as "the race."

19. Jones [Baraka], *Blues People,* 99.

20. Ibid., 89.

21. TOBA stood for Theater Owners Booking Association, but the performers often translated it as "Tough On Black Artists," or more crudely, "Black Asses."

22. Charters, *The Country Blues,* 46.

23. Howard W. Odum and Guy B. Johnson, *Negro Workaday Songs* (Chapel Hill: University of North Carolina Press, 1926), 38.

24. Southern, *The Music of Black Americans,* 398.

25. Charters, *The Country Blues,* 67.

26. Malone, *Country Music U.S.A.,* 39.

27. Ibid., 40.

28. Ibid., 42.

29. One study conducted by Anne and Norm Cohen concluded that between 1922 and 1924 only 2 percent of country performers' repertoires were of British origin. See Malone, *Country Music U.S.A.,* 44.

30. Ibid., 52.

31. Green, http://thecanadianencyclopedia.com.

32. Thomas Cripps, "Film," in *Split Image: African Americans in the Mass Media,* 2d ed., ed. Jannette L. Dates and William Barlow (Washington, D.C.: Howard University Press, 1993), 146.

33. Nelson George, *The Death of Rhythm & Blues* (New York: Pantheon Books, 1988), 11.

34. Ibid.

35. *CBC Times,* 11–17 April 1964.

36. Malone, *Country Music U.S.A.,* 152.

37. John Hammond, *On Record* (New York: Penguin Books, 1981), 163.

CHAPTER 3

1. Ian Whitcomb, *After the Ball: Pop Music from Rag to Rock* (Baltimore, MD: Penguin Books, 1974), 199.

2. Russell Sanjek, *American Popular Music and Its Business: The First Four Hundred Years, Volume III from 1900 to 1984* (New York: Oxford University Press, 1988), 176. The dramatic increase of ASCAP's revenues from 1932 to 1937 came about when eleven music publishing houses controlled by Warner Brothers and representing 20 to 40 percent of the music played on the radio returned to ASCAP's fold. Dissatisfied with their share of publishing revenues, they had decided to collect their own royalties independently and had left ASCAP in 1935. They returned August 1936, freeing up some 36,000 songs, including works by George Gershwin and Jerome Kern, which had been out of circulation since January of that year.

3. Nat Shapiro, *Popular Music: An Annotated Index of American Popular Songs: Volume 2, 1940–1949* (New York: Adrian Press, 1965), 6.

4. "ASCAP Defied," *Business Week,* 16 November 1940, 50.

5. Minna Lederman, "Music and Monopoly," *The Nation,* 28 December 1940, 656.

6. Bill C. Malone, *Country Music U.S.A.,* rev. ed. (Austin: University of Texas Press, 1985), 179.

7. Arnold Passman, *The Deejays* (New York: Macmillan, 1971), 64.

8. Sanjek, *American Popular Music,* 3: 128.

9. D. Dexter, "1935–1945, Disk Jockey: Origin of the Species," *Billboard,* 27 December 1969, 58.

10. According to the terms of the 1909 Copyright Act, only the underlying composition of a recording could be copyrighted; the recording itself could not. As a result, only writers and publishers received royalties from the broadcast of recorded music.

11. Passman, *The Deejays,* 80. Whiteman and RCA Victor had initiated the suit that led to the lower court decision.

12. Using Ralph Peer's international business connections, the companies had also attempted to record U.S. pop in Latin America, but the attempt failed. In Cuba the language barrier prevented English-language recordings of broadcast quality. In Mexico the progressive Mexican musicians' union refused to participate in the strikebreaking strategy.

13. Arnold Shaw, *Honkers and Shouters: The Golden Years of Rhythm and Blues* (New York: Collier Books, 1978), 124.

14. Charlie Gillett, *The Sound of the City: The Rise of Rock and Roll* (New York: Outerbridge and Dienstfrey, 1970), 3.

15. Unlike Sinatra, many Italian American performers anglicized their names. Frankie Lane began life as Frank Paul LoVecchio, Vic Damone as Vito Rocco Farinola, Tony Bennett as Anthony Dominic Benedetto, and Dean Martin as Dino Crocetti.

16. Whitcomb, *After the Ball,* 200.

17. Gillett, *The Sound of the City,* 9.

18. LeRoi Jones [Amiri Baraka], *Blues People* (New York: William Morrow, 1963), 168. Rhythm and blues, of course, developed in the blues tradition of African retentions superimposed on a European melodic and harmonic structure. For a more detailed discussion see: Portia K. Maultsby, "Africanisms in African American Popular Music," in *Africanisms in American Culture,* ed. Joseph E. Holloway (Bloomington: Indiana University Press, 1990); Reebee Garofalo, "Crossing Over, 1939–1992," in *Split Image: African-Americans in the Mass Media,* 2d ed., ed. Jannette L. Dates and William Barlow (Washington, D.C.: Howard University Press, 1993).

19. George Lipsitz, *Class and Culture in Cold War America: "A Rainbow at Midnight"* (South Hadley, MA: J. F. Bergin, 1982), 195–96.

20. Nelson George, *The Death of Rhythm & Blues* (New York: Pantheon Books, 1988), 10.

21. Jones [Baraka], *Blues People,* 160.

22. George, *The Death of Rhythm & Blues,* 9.

23. Jones [Baraka], *Blues People,* 171.

24. Shaw, *Honkers and Shouters,* 278–79.

25. Malone, *Country Music, U.S.A.,* 209.

26. Shaw, *Honkers and Shouters,* 289.

27. Donald Clarke, *The Penguin Encyclopedia of Popular Music* (New York: Penguin Books, 1989), 1217.

28. Edward Zwick, "An Interview with the Father of Hi-Fi: Dr. Peter Goldmark," *Rolling Stone,* 27 September 1973, 44–45.

29. Ibid., 44.

30. Unable to bend like the AM signal, FM waves move in a straight line; transmission, therefore, suffers from a "line of sight" problem, in that irregular topography and the curvature of the earth prevent transmission over long distances. However, the quality of the signal in terms of frequency response and suppression of interference is far superior to AM transmission.

31. Sanjek, *American Popular Music,* 3: 173.

32. *That Rhythm, Those Blues,* PBS documentary produced by George T. Nierenberg, 1988.

33. ABC *20/20,* segment on rap produced by Danny Schechter, 1981.

34. George, *The Death of Rhythm & Blues,* 41.

35. Ibid.

36. Shaw, *Honkers and Shouters,* 509.

37. Ibid., 518.

38. Passman, *The Deejays,* 175.

39. George, *The Death of Rhythm & Blues,* 41.

40. Passman, *The Deejays,* 185.

41. Ibid., 176.

42. Ibid.

43. Steve Chapple and Reebee Garofalo, *Rock 'n' Roll Is Here to Pay: The History and Politics of the Music Industry* (Chicago: Nelson-Hall, 1977), 56.

CHAPTER 4

1. Charlie Gillett, *The Sound of the City: The Rise of Rock and Roll* (New York: Outerbridge and Dienstfrey, 1970), 1.

2. Nick Tosches, *Country: Living Legends and Dying Metaphors in America's Biggest Music* (New York: Charles Scribner's Sons, 1985), 32.

3. Jim Dawson and Steve Propes, *What Was the First Rock 'n' Roll Record?* (Boston: Faber and Faber, 1992), xvi–xvii.

4. Tosches, *Country,* 28.

5. Robert Palmer, "The Fifties," *Rolling Stone,* 19 April 1990, 48.

6. George Lipsitz, *Class and Culture in Cold War America* (South Hadley, MA: J. F. Bergin, 1982), 214.

7. Steve Perry, "Ain't No Mountain High Enough: The Politics of Crossover," in *Facing the Music,* ed. Simon Frith (New York: Pantheon Books, 1988), 67–68.

8. Greil Marcus, *Mystery Train: Images of America in Rock 'n' Roll* (New York: Dutton, 1975), 166.

9. In *San Antonio Rose: The Life and Music of Bob Wills* (Urbana: University of Illinois Press, 1976), Charles R. Townshend suggests that Walker and his friend Charlie Christian (who was to electric jazz guitar what Walker was to electric blues) were themselves influenced by white western-swing electric guitarists Bob Dunn, who played for Milton Brown and His Musical Brownies, and Leon McAuliffe, who was a steel guitarist for Bob Wills and His Texas Playboys. In "The Church of the Sonic Guitar," *South Atlantic Quarterly* 90, no. 4 (Fall 1991), Robert Palmer argues that Walker's style is derived from Blind Lemon Jefferson and jazz licks he learned from Christian.

10. Palmer, "The Church of the Sonic Guitar," 652.

11. John Storm Roberts, *The Latin Tinge: The Impact of Latin American Music on the United States* (Tivoli, N.Y.: Original Music, 1985), 136.

12. Gillett, *The Sound of the City,* 42.

13. For a more detailed discussion of the concentration of the music industry during this period, see Richard A. Peterson and David C. Berger, "Cycles in Symbol Production: The Case of Popular Music." *American Sociological Review* (April 1975).

14. Erik Barnouw, *The Golden Web: A History of Broadcasting in the United States, 1933–1953* (New York: Oxford University Press, 1966), 221.

15. Arnold Shaw, *The Rockin' '50s* (New York: Hawthorne Books, 1974), 66.

16. Ibid., 235.

17. Richard A. Peterson, "Why 1955? Explaining the Advent of Rock Music," *Popular Music* (January 1990), 113.

18. Langdon Winner, "The Sound of New Orleans," in *The Rolling Stone Illustrated History of Rock 'n' Roll,* ed. Jim Miller (New York: Rolling Stone Press, 1976), 42.

19. Gillett, *The Sound of the City,* 148.

20. John Broven, *Rhythm and Blues in New Orleans* (Gretna, LA: Pelican Publishing Co., 1988), 29.

21. Ibid., 64.

22. Ibid., 14.

23. Winner, "The Sound of New Orleans," 46.

24. Arnold Shaw, *Honkers and Shouters: The Golden Years of*

Rhythm and Blues (New York: Collier Books, 1978), 190.

25. Shaw, *The Rockin' '50s,* 210.

26. Ibid. Since then, Richard has tried to manage the tension between his ministry and his music career. Invariably, his irrepressible rock 'n' roll spirit shows through.

27. Steve Chapple and Reebee Garofalo, *Rock 'n' Roll Is Here to Pay: The History and Politics of the Music Industry* (Chicago: Nelson-Hall, 1977), 233.

28. Johnny Ace was the first major rock 'n' roll fatality. He died playing with a loaded gun on tour on Christmas day in 1954, just before "Pledging My Love" hit the pop charts.

29. Preston Love, preface to *Listen to the Lambs,* by Johnny Otis (New York: W. W. Norton, 1968).

30. Michael Lydon, *Rock Folk: Portraits from the Rock 'n' Roll Pantheon* (New York: Dell, 1968), 10.

31. Gillett, *The Sound of the City,* 96–97.

32. Nelson George, *The Death of Rhythm and Blues* (New York: Pantheon Books, 1988), 68.

33. Lydon, *Rock Folk,* 20.

34. Robert Pruter, *Chicago Soul* (Urbana: University of Illinois Press, 1992), 25.

35. John W. Rumble, "Roots of Rock 'n' Roll: Henry Glover at King Records," *Country Music Journal* (Vol. 14, No. 2, 1992): 38.

36. Robey also bought Duke Records from founder James Mattis, who was a deejay for WDIA in Memphis, thus forming the Duke/Peacock complex.

37. Shaw, *Honkers and Shouters,* 479.

38. Peter Guralnick, *Sweet Soul Music: Rhythm and Blues and the Southern Dream of Freedom* (New York: Harper and Row, 1986), 26.

39. Ray Charles and David Ritz, *Brother Ray: Ray Charles' Own Story* (New York: DaCapo Press, 1992), 149.

40. Guralnick, *Sweet Soul Music,* 50.

41. Ibid., 66.

42. Shaw, *Honkers and Shouters,* 444.

43. Wilson suffered a heart attack on stage in 1975 and remained in a coma until he died in 1984.

44. Tony Heilbut, *The Gospel Sound: Good News and Bad Times* (New York: Simon and Schuster, 1971), 76.

45. Gillett, *The Sound of the City,* 182.

46. Greil Marcus, "Is This the Woman Who Invented Rock & Roll?: The Deborah Chessler Story," *Rolling Stone,* 24 June 1993, 41.

47. Ibid., 43.

48. Doo wop groups with predominantly Italian American membership included the Mello-Kings ("Tonight, Tonight," 1957), the Elegants ("Little Star," 1958), the Mystics ("Hushabye," 1959), and the Capris ("There's a Moon Out Tonight," 1961), and at the periphery of the style, the Royal Teens ("Short Shorts," 1958) and the Regents ("Barbara Ann," 1961).

49. Buck Ram added Zola Taylor to the Platters largely for show. Both the Skyliners ("Since I Don't Have You," 1959) and the Cleftones ("Heart and Soul," 1961) also performed with female vocalists who had no readily distinguishable roles.

50. Among the groups that could still be associated somewhat with the style were the Duprees ("You Belong to Me," 1962), the Tymes ("So Much in Love" and "Wonderful, Won-derful," 1963), the Vogues ("Five O'Clock World," 1965), and the Fortunes ("You've Got Your Troubles," 1965).

51. Peter Guralnick, *Feel Like Going Home: Portraits in Blues and Rock 'n' Roll* (New York: E. P. Dutton, 1971), 140.

52. Gillett, *The Sound of the City,* 38.

53. Ibid., 30.

54. Shaw, *Honkers and Shouters,* 64.

55. *Blackboard Jungle* was the first Hollywood film to include a rock 'n' roll record in its soundtrack, which might not have happened without the advocacy of its Tin Pan Alley composers. Either *Rebel Without a Cause,* starring James Dean and released that same year, or *The Wild One,* released in 1954 with Marlon Brando in the lead role, would have been equally obvious choices for rock 'n' roll soundtracks, but both films used big-band soundtracks, which tended to contradict their themes of youth rebellion.

56. Guralnick, *Feel Like Going Home,* 140.

57. Peter Guralnick, *The Listener's Guide to the Blues* (New York: Facts on File, 1982), 80.

58. Guralnick, *Feel Like Going Home,* 149–50.

59. Lydon, *Rock Folk,* 32.

60. Gillett, *The Sound of the City,* 36.

61. Peter Guralnick, "Elvis Presley," in *The Rolling Stone Illustrated History of Rock 'n' Roll,* ed. Jim Miller (New York: Rolling Stone Press, 1976), 35.

62. Guralnick, *Feel Like Going Home,* 142.

63. Guralnick, "Elvis Presley," 35.

64. Ibid., 36.

65. Ibid., 36, 38.

66. Presley died on 16 August 1977 in Memphis, a bloated, drugged-out caricature of his former self.

67. Dawson and Propes, *What Was the First Rock 'n' Roll Record?,* 192.

68. Ibid.

69. Tosches, *Country,* 82.

70. Ibid., 95.

71. Ibid.

72. Ted Fox, *Showtime at the Apollo* (New York: Holt, Rinehart and Winston, 1983), 207.

73. For an excellent discussion of these unsung female rockabillies, see David Sanjek, "Can a Fujiyama Mama Be the Female Elvis? The Wild Wild Women of Rockabilly," in *Sexing the Groove,* ed. Shiela Whitely (New York: Routledge, 1996).

74. *Rock and Roll: The Early Days,* video documentary produced by Patrick Montgomery, 1985.

CHAPTER 5

1. For a more detailed analysis of this, see Steve Chapple and Reebee Garofalo, *Rock 'n' Roll Is Here to Pay: The History and Politics of the Music Industry* (Chicago: Nelson-Hall, 1977), 300–04; and Peter Wicke, *Rock Music: Culture, Aesthetics and Sociology* (New York: Cambridge University Press, 1990), 30–34.

2. Charlie Gillett, *The Sound of the City: The Rise of Rock and Roll* (New York: Outerbridge and Dienstfrey, 1970), 360.

3. Russell Sanjek, "The War on Rock," *Downbeat Music '72 Yearbook* (Chicago: Maher Publications, 1972).

4. This situation was complicated when Frank Sinatra charged Miller with trying to foist BMI material on him while he was still with Columbia in 1956. In response Miller produced statistics that disproved Sinatra's allegation.

5. Just as Columbia did through its subsidiary OKeh, Victor maintained a presence in the r&b market through its Groove subsidiary, which was founded in 1953. One memorable Groove recording that hit rock 'n' roll pay dirt was the eerie "Love Is Strange" (1957) by Mickey and Sylvia. Mickey was the experienced session guitarist Mickey "Guitar" Baker; Sylvia was Sylvia Robinson, who went on to form Sugar Hill Records, the first rap label of note, in the late 1970s.

6. Gillett, *The Sound of the City,* 74.

7. Ibid.

8. For a reasonably exhaustive listing of pop/r&b covers, including label and release date, see Philip Ennis, *The Seventh Stream: The Emergence of Rock 'n' Roll in American Popular Music* (Hanover, NH: Wesleyan University Press/University Press of New England, 1992), 223–26.

9. Dot achieved the status of a major when it was purchased by ABC-Paramount in 1957.

10. Gillett, *The Sound of the City,* 76.

11. Chapple and Garofalo, *Rock 'n' Roll Is Here to Pay,* 49–52; 246–48.

12. Gillett, *The Sound of the City,* 127.

13. Ed Ward, Geoffrey Stokes, and Ken Tucker, *Rock of Ages: The Rolling Stone History of Rock & Roll* (New York: Rolling Stone Press, 1986), 166.

14. Gillett, *The Sound of the City,* 127.

15. Russell Sanjek, *American Popular Music and Its Business: The First Four Hundred Years, Volume III from 1900 to 1984* (New York: Oxford University Press, 1988), 444.

16. Arnold Shaw, *The Rockin' '50s* (New York: Hawthorne Books, 1974), 176.

17. Henry Schipper, "Dick Clark," *Rolling Stone,* 19 April 1990, 70.

18. Ibid.

19. Shaw, *The Rockin' '50s,* 197.

20. Linda Martin and Kerry Segrave, *Anti-Rock: The Opposition to Rock 'n' Roll* (New York: DeCapo Press, 1993), 24–25.

21. Shaw, *The Rockin' '50s,* 218–19.

22. Gillett, *The Sound of the City,* 360.

23. Shaw, *The Rockin' '50s,* 267.

24. Trent Hill, "The Enemy Within: Censorship in Rock Music in the 1950s," *South Atlantic Quarterly* (Fall 1991): 677.

25. Sanjek, *The War on Rock,* 18.

26. Ibid., 11, 19.

27. Ibid., 62.

28. Ibid.

29. Lillian Roxon, *Lillian Roxon's Rock Encyclopedia* (New York: Grosset and Dunlap, 1971), 477.

30. Chapple and Garofalo, *Rock 'n' Roll Is Here to Pay,* 52.

31. Greg Shaw, "Instrumental Groups," in *The Rolling Stone Illustrated History of Rock & Roll,* ed. Jim Miller (New York: Rolling Stone Press, 1976), 108.

32. Arnold Shaw, *Black Popular Music in America* (New York: Schirmer Books, 1986), 207.

33. Gillett, *The Sound of the City,* 218.

CHAPTER 6

1. Bernice Johnson Reagon, "Songs That Moved the Movement," *Civil Rights Quarterly* (Summer 1983).

2. At the time, mass culture was considered to be a sign of capitalism at its worst. Thus it was viewed as an irredeemably debased culture, produced only for profit, with no possibility for resistance or opposition rather than as an arena for cultural struggle. By the end of the decade, politically minded people had begun to rethink this position.

3. Nelson George, *The Death of Rhythm & Blues* (New York: Pantheon Books, 1988), 69.

4. *Hail! Hail! Rock 'n' Roll,* film documentary, prod. Taylor Hackford, 1987.

5. David Hinckley, Liner Notes, *Phil Spector Back to Mono (1958–1969),* Phil Spector Records, 7118-2.

6. Tom Wolfe, "The First Tycoon of Teen," *The Kandy-Kolored Tangerine-Flake Streamline Baby* (New York: Farrar, Straus, and Giroux, 1965), 69.

7. Love has gone on to become an accomplished actress, who is perhaps best known for her role as Danny Glover's wife in the *Lethal Weapon* films.

8. Richard Farrar, "Da Doo Ron Ron," *Rolling Stone,* 11 May 1968, 18.

9. Jay Grossman, "Let There Be Dancing in the Streets," *Rolling Stone,* 23 May 1974, 22.

10. Michael Lydon, "Smokey Robinson," *Rolling Stone,* 28 September 1968, 21.

11. Gerri Hersey, *Nowhere to Run: The Story of Soul Music* (New York: Penguin Books, 1984), 190.

12. *The Garland Encyclopedia of World Music: The United States and Canada,* (2001).

13. George, *The Death of Rhythm & Blues,* 85.

14. Lester Bangs, "The British Invasion," in *The Rolling Stone Illustrated History of Rock 'n' Roll,* ed. Jim Miller (New York: Random House, 1976), 164.

15. Steve Chapple and Reebee Garofalo, *Rock 'n' Roll Is Here to Pay: The History and Politics of the Music Industry* (Chicago: Nelson-Hall, 1977), 70.

16. Burdon went on to front the African American ensemble War in the late 1960s, an association that lasted through the release of the painfully titled LP *Black Man's Burdon.* The group then left Burdon, going on to record fifteen hit albums of its own.

17. For a developed discussion of white blues controversy, see Chapple and Garofalo, *Rock 'n' Roll Is Here to Pay,* 250–257.

18. These two shows, currently available on a single home video as *Born to Rock* (UPA Productions of America, 1982), also included such African American artists as Chuck Berry, Bo Diddley, Ray Charles, James Brown, the Ronettes, and Ike and Tina Turner.

19. Hersey, *Nowhere to Run,* 185.

20. Anthony Scaduto, *Bob Dylan* (New York: Signet Books, 1973), 203–04.

21. Although it is not hard to imagine that they took this occasion to toke up, it seems quite unlikely that they had not encountered the mind-altering substance during their hard day's nights in Hamburg, where they flirted with the German art school scene through the influence of Stuart Sutcliffe's girlfriend Astrid Kirchherr.

22. Scaduto, *Bob Dylan,* 204.

23. Ibid.

24. Lillian Roxon, *Lillian Roxon's Rock Encyclopedia* (New York: Grosset and Dunlap, 1971), 78.

25. Ibid., 187.

26. After Vietnam Sadler worked as a mercenary, hiring himself out to more than half a dozen battles around the world. In September 1988 he took a bullet in the head in Guatemala City.

27. Todd Gitlin, *The Sixties: Years of Hope, Days of Rage* (New York: Bantam Books, 1993).

28. George, *The Death of Rhythm & Blues,* 86.

29. Jim Delahunt, "Whatever Success I Had Was Through the Help of the Good Lord," *Rolling Stone,* 20 January 1968, p. 13.

30. Peter Guralnick, *Sweet Soul Music: Rhythm and Blues and the Southern Dream of Freedom* (New York: Harper and Row, 1986), 169.

31. Ibid., 332.

32. Hettie Jones, *Big Star, Fallin' Mama* (New York: Viking Press, 1974), 41. The term *Rap* in Jones' quote refers to H. Rap Brown, the militant black leader whose poetic, fiery speeches may well have been one of rap music's formative influences.

33. Robert Palmer, "James Brown," in *The Rolling Stone Illustrated History of Rock & Roll,* ed. Jim Miller (New York: Rolling Stone Press, 1976), 136.

34. Roxon, *Lillian Roxon's Rock Encyclopedia,* 210.

35. Ibid., 209.

36. David Crosby, *The Monterey International Pop Festival,* boxed set, Rhino R2 70596.

37. Roxon, *Lillian Roxon's Rock Encyclopedia,* 229.

38. "The Rolling Stone Interview with Eric Clapton," *Rolling Stone,* 11 May 1968, 12.

39. Roxon, *Lillian Roxon's Rock Encyclopedia,* 228–29.

40. George, *The Death of Rhythm & Blues,* 98.

41. Gitlin, *The Sixties,* 287.

42. *Woodstock,* film directed by Michael Wadleigh, 1970.

43. *Gimme Shelter,* film directed by David Maysles, Albert Maysles, and Charlotte Zwerin, 1970.

CHAPTER 7

1. Michael Lydon, "Rock for Sale," in *The Age of Rock 2: Sights and Sounds of the American Cultural Revolution,* ed. Michael Lydon (New York: Vintage Books, 1970), 53.

2. Steve Pond, "The Seventies," *Rolling Stone,* 20 September 1990, 53.

3. For a detailed discussion of the merger movement, see Steve Chapple and Reebee Garofalo, *Rock 'n' Roll Is Here to Pay: The History and Politics of the Music Industry* (Chicago: Nelson-Hall, 1977), 82–87.

4. Peter Wicke, *Rock Music: Culture, Aesthetics and Sociology* (Cambridge: Cambridge University Press, 1990), 121.

5. Ben Fong-Torres, ed., *The Rolling Stone Interviews,* vol. 2 (New York: Warner Books, 1973), 292.

6. Wicke, *Rock Music: Culture, Aesthetics and Sociology,* 126.

7. Chapple and Garofalo, *Rock 'n' Roll Is Here to Pay,* 175.

8. Ibid., 109.

9. Ibid., 121.

10. Robert Draper, *Rolling Stone Magazine* (New York: Harper and Row, 1990).

11. Jann Wenner, "A Letter from the Editor," *Rolling Stone,* 9 November 1967, 2.

12. Michael Lydon, "The High Cost of Music and Love: Where's the Money from Monterey?" *Rolling Stone,* 9 November 1967, 1.

13. Jann Wenner, "A Letter from the Editor," 2.

14. Draper, *Rolling Stone Magazine,* 95.

15. Jann Wenner, "Musicians Reject New Political Exploiters," *Rolling Stone,* 11 May 1968, 1, 22.

16. Jann Wenner, Introduction to "The Sound of Marching Charging Feet," by Michael Rossman, *Rolling Stone,* Special Insert: "American Revolution 1969," 5 April 1969, 1.

17. Draper, *Rolling Stone Magazine,* 157.

18. Jann Wenner, "A Letter from the Editor: On the Occasion of Our Fourth Anniversary Issue," *Rolling Stone,* 11 November 1971, 34.

19. *The Compleat Beatles,* video documentary, produced by Patrick Montgomery, 1982.

20. Ibid.

21. Joe Smith, *Off the Record: An Oral History of Popular Music* (New York: Warner Books, 1988), 242.

22. Simon Frith, *Sound Effects: Youth Leisure and the Politics of Rock 'n' Roll* (New York: Pantheon, 1981), 53.

23. *The Compleat Beatles,* 1982.

24. Ralph Gleason, "Perspectives: Changing with the Money Changers," *Rolling Stone,* 20 January 1968, 9.

25. Ralph Gleason, "Stop This Shuck Mike Bloomfield," *Rolling Stone,* 11 May 1968, 10.

26. John Pidgeon, *Eric Clapton* (London: Panther, 1976), 65.

27. Dave Morse, *Motown* (London: Vista, 1971), 108.

28. Jon Landau, "Soul," *Rolling Stone,* 24 February 1968, 18.

29. "The Rolling Stone Interview: Keith Richards," *Rolling Stone,* 19 August 1971, 24.

30. Wicke, *Rock Music: Culture, Aesthetics and Sociology,* 95.

31. Simon Frith and Howard Horne, *Art into Pop* (New York: Methuen, 1987), 86.

32. Ibid., 109.

33. Ibid., 108.

34. Ibid., 107.

35. Iain Chambers, *Urban Rhythms: Pop Music and Popular Culture* (New York: Macmillan, 1985), 114–15.

36. Robert Walser, *Running with the Devil: Power, Gender, and Madness in Heavy Metal Music* (Hanover, NH: Wesleyan University Press, 1993), 61–62.

37. Irwin Stambler, *Encyclopedia of Pop, Rock & Soul* (New York: St. Martin's, 1977), 176.

38. Frith and Horne, *Art into Pop,* 98.

39. *Rolling Stone,* 28 May 1970, 17.

40. Ross, 3.

41. *RPM Weekly* reprint, 1.

42. April Wine was actually formed in Halifax in late 1969, but they moved to Montreal in early 1970 before their first recording and are generally regarded as a Montreal band.

43. www.crtc.gc.ca.

44. www.factor.ca.

45. Chambers, *Urban Rhythms,* 118.

46. "Wexler Attributes Greater R&B Volume to Black Buyer," *Billboard,* 20 November 1971, 8.

47. Paul Ackerman, "Gortikov Scorches Whitey Trade in NATRA Speech," *Billboard,* 17 July 1969, 1.

48. "New Black Hope," *Billboard,* 17 May 1969, 34.

49. John Lombardi, "Kenny Gamble and Leon Huff and the Resurrection of Jerry Butler and Philly Soul," *Rolling Stone,* 30 April 1970, 39.

50. Nelson George, *The Death of Rhythm & Blues* (New York: Pantheon Books, 1988), 145.

51. Jim Miller, "The Sound of Philadelphia," in *The Rolling Stone Illustrated History of Rock & Roll,* ed. Anthony DeCurtis and James Henke (New York: Random House, 1992), 518.

52. Of course, not all veteran r&b groups were this lucky. The Dells, the model for Robert Townshend's film *The Five Heartbeats,* had been together since 1953. The group's biggest success, "Oh, What a Night" (1969), was a remake of an r&b hit the group had recorded thirteen years earlier. The Dells' last Top Forty hit was in 1973.

53. Jon Landau, "The Motown Story," *Rolling Stone,* 13 May 1971, 42.

54. *Billboard,* 20 November 1971, 8.

55. Ray Brack, "James Brown," *Rolling Stone,* 21 January 1970, 12.

56. Peter Guralnick, *Sweet Soul Music* (New York: Harper and Row, 1986), 391.

57. Robert Christgau, *Any Old Way You Choose It: Rock and Other Pop Music, 1967–1973* (Baltimore: Penguin Books, 1973), 217.

58. Ibid., 211.

59. Chapple and Garofalo, *Rock 'n' Roll Is Here to Pay,* 80.

60. Katherine Orloff, *Rock 'n' Roll Woman* (Los Angeles: Nash Publishing, 1974), 11.

61. Gillian G. Gaar, *She's a Rebel: The History of Women in Rock & Roll* (Seattle: Seal Press, 1992), 123.

62. Orloff, *Rock 'n' Roll Woman,* 133.

63. Christgau, *Any Old Way You Choose It,* 212.

64. Stephen Holden, "The Evolution of the Singer-songwriter," in *The Rolling Stone Illustrated History of Rock & Roll,* ed. Anthony DeCurtis and James Henke (New York: Random House, 1992), 489.

65. Robin Denselow, *When the Music's Over: The Story of Political Pop* (Boston: Faber and Faber, 1989), 180.

66. Ellen Willis, "Beginning to See the Light: or Rock & Roll, Feminism, and Night Blindness," *Village Voice,* 27 March 1978, 21–22.

67. Christgau, *Any Old Way You Choose It,* 274.

68. Gaar, *She's a Rebel,* 138.

69. Ibid., 136.

70. Ibid., 139.

71. Cynthia M. Lont, "Women's Music: No Longer a Small Private Party," in *Rockin' the Boat: Mass Music and Mass Movements,* ed. Reebee Garofalo (Boston: South End Press, 1992), 242.

72. Gaar, *She's a Rebel,* 155–56.

73. Bill C. Malone, *Country Music, USA* (Austin: University of Texas Press, 1985), 386.

74. Stambler, *Encyclopedia of Pop, Rock & Soul,* 37.

75. Christgau, *Any Old Way You Choose It,* 269.

76. Anthony DeCurtis, "The Eagles," *Rolling Stone,* 20 September 1990, 92.

77. Malone, *Country Music, USA,* 404–05.

78. Deena Weinstein, *Heavy Metal: A Cultural Sociology* (New York: Lexington Books, 1991), 23.

79. Walser, *Running with the Devil,* 2.

80. Weinstein, *Heavy Metal,* 16.

81. Walser, *Running with the Devil,* 57–107.

82. Ibid., 10.

83. J. D. Considine, "Led Zeppelin," *Rolling Stone,* 20 September 1990, 59.

84. Stambler, *Encyclopedia of Pop, Rock & Soul,* 57.

85. Ibid.

86. Walser, *Running with the Devil,* 61, citing Mordechai, "Where There's Smoke . . . There's Fire." *Guitar World,* February 1991, 62.

87. Walser, *Running with the Devil,* 66.

88. Ibid., 68.

89. Christgau, *Any Old Way You Choose It,* 116.

90. Considine, "Led Zeppelin," 59, 109.

91. Smith, *Off the Record,* 273.

92. Chambers, *Urban Rhythms,* 113.

93. Ibid.

94. Frith and Horne, *Art into Pop,* 115.

95. Chambers, *Urban Rhythms,* 133.

96. Peter York, *Style Wars* (London: Sidgwick and Jackson, 1980). Cited in Chambers, *Urban Rhythms,* 138.

CHAPTER 8

1. Charles M. Young, "Rock Is Sick and Living in London: A Report on the Sex Pistols," *Rolling Stone,* 20 October 1977, 68.

2. Mikal Gilmore, "Disco," *Rolling Stone,* 19 April 1979, 54.

3. Robert Christgau, "A Cult Explodes—and a Movement Is Born," *Village Voice,* 24 October 1977, 57.

4. Jon Savage, *England's Dreaming: Anarchy, Sex Pistols, Punk Rock, and Beyond* (New York: St. Martins Press, 1992), 138.

5. Andrew Kopkind, "The Dialectic of Disco," *Village Voice,* 12 February 1979, 11.

6. Simon Frith, "Beyond the Dole Queue: The Politics of Punk," *Village Voice,* 24 October 1977, 78.

7. Ibid.

8. Kopkind, "The Dialectic of Disco," 11.

9. Abe Peck, "Disco! Disco! Disco! Four Critics Address the Musical Question," *In These Times,* 6–12 June 1979, 20.

10. Gilmore, "Disco," 54. It should also be noted that a good deal of the "disco sucks" mentality had to do with the fear of and hostility toward technology replacing live music.

11. Savage, *England's Dreaming,* 200.

12. Young, "Rock Is Sick and Living in London," 70.

13. Savage, *England's Dreaming,* 87.

14. Clinton Heylin, *From the Velvets to the Voidoids: A Pre-Punk History for a Post-Punk World* (New York: Penguin Books, 1993), 87–88.

15. Ibid., 38.

16. Ibid., 120.

17. Ibid., 123.

18. Ibid., 172.

19. Ibid., 174.

20. Savage, *England's Dreaming,* 202.

21. Frith, "Beyond the Dole Queue," 78.

22. Savage, *England's Dreaming,* 330.

23. Ibid., 63.

24. Ibid., 188.

25. Christgau, "A Cult Explodes," 70.

26. Ibid.

27. Lester Bangs, "The White Noise Supremacists," *Village Voice,* 30 April 1979, 45–46.

28. Ibid., 46.

29. Savage, *England's Dreaming,* 242.

30. David Widgery, *Beating Time: Riot 'n' Race 'n' Rock 'n' Roll* (London: Chatto and Windus, 1986), 53.

31. Savage, *England's Dreaming,* 398.

32. Widgery, *Beating Time,* 80.

33. Ibid., 64.

34. Savage, *England's Dreaming,* 442.

35. Gillian G. Garr, *She's a Rebel: The History of Women in Rock & Roll* (Seattle, WA: Seal Press, 1992), 277.

36. Robert Palmer, "New Rock from the Suburbs," *New York Times,* 23 September 1984, 23.

37. Vic Bondi, "Feeding Noise Back into the System: Hardcore, Hip Hop, and Heavy Metal" (paper presented at the New England American Studies Association Conference, Brandeis University, Boston, Mass., 1 May 1993), 5.

38. Heylin, *From the Velvets to the Voidoids,* 314.

39. Stephen Holden, "The Evolution of a Dance Craze," *Rolling Stone,* 19 April 1979, 29.

40. Tom Smucker, "Disco," in *The Rolling Stone Illustrated History of Rock & Roll,* ed. Anthony DeCurtis and James Henke (New York: Random House, 1992), 562.

41. Barbara Graustark, "Disco Takes Over," *Newsweek,* 2 April 1979, 59.

42. Ibid., 58–59.

43. Kopkind, "The Dialectic of Disco," 14.

44. George Clinton quoted in Joe McEwen, "Funk," in *The Rolling Stone Illustrated History of Rock & Roll,* ed. Anthony DeCurtis and James Henke (New York: Random House, 1992), 521.

45. Graustark, "Disco Takes Over," 64.

46. Kopkind, "The Dialectic of Disco," 11.

47. Holden, "The Evolution of a Dance Craze," 30.

48. James Henke, "Record Companies Dancing to a Billion Dollar Tune," *Rolling Stone,* 19 April 1979, 46.

49. Among the most popular acts were Brick ("Dazz"), Dr. Buzzard's Original Savannah Band ("Whispering/Cherchez La Femme/Se Si Bon"), the Emotions ("Best of My Love"), Thelma Houston ("Don't Leave Me This Way"), Rose Royce ("Car Wash"), Hot ("Angel in Your Arms"), Chic ("Dance, Dance, Dance (Yowsah, Yowsah, Yowsah)"), Heatwave ("Boogie Nights"), Peter Brown ("Do Ya Wanna Get Funky With Me," "Dance with Me"), and Taste of Honey ("Boogie Oogie Oogie").

50. http://thecanadianencyclopedia.com.

51. Kopkind, "The Dialectic of Disco," 16.

52. Russell Sanjek, *American Popular Music and Its Business: The First Four Hundred Years, Volume III* (New York: Oxford University Press, 1988), 514.

53. David Ansen, "Rock Tycoon," *Newsweek,* 31 July 1978, 41.

54. Ibid., 41.

55. Jay Merritt, "Disco Station Number One in New York," *Rolling Stone,* 22 March 1979, 11.

56. Kopkind, "The Dialectic of Disco," 11.

57. Don McLeese, "Anatomy of an Anti-Disco Riot," *In These Times,* 29 August–September 4 1979, 23.

58. Graustark, "Disco Takes Over," 58.

59. Dave Marsh, "The Flip Sides of 1979," *Rolling Stone,* 27 December 1979, 28.

60. Georgia Christgau, "Disco! Disco! Disco! Four Critics Address the Musical Question," *In These Times,* 6–12 June 1979, 21.

61. McLeese, "Anatomy of an Anti-Disco Riot," 23.

62. Robert Hilburn, "Musical Lessons from 1983's First Half," *Cape Cod Times,* 16 July 1983, 12.

63. N. R. Kleinfeld, "FM's Success Is Loud and Clear," *New York Times,* 26 October 1979, Dl.

64. Marsh, "The Flip Sides of 1979," 30.

65. Pablo Guzman, "On the Radio, Part Two," *Rock & Roll Confidential,* January 1984, 2.

CHAPTER 9

1. Recording Industry Association of America (RIAA), *Inside the Recording Industry: A Statistical Overview, Update '86* (New York: Recording Industry Association of America, 1986), 4.

2. Michèle Hung and Esteban Garcia Morencos, *World Record Sales 1969–1990: A Statistical History of the World Recording Industry* (London: International Federation of the Phonogram Industry, 1990), 85.

3. Paul Grein, "Unemployment Lines: LA Industrial Personnel Face Major Challenges to Rebuild Their Careers," *Billboard,* 19 May 1979, 3.

4. Simon Frith, "Picking Up the Pieces: Video Pop," in *Facing the Music,* ed. Simon Frith (New York: Pantheon Books, 1988), 93.

5. "Record Business Sees Light Ahead—On Video Screen," *Chicago Tribune,* 26 April 1983, p. 5.

6. RIAA, *Inside the Recording Industry,* 5.

7. Russell Sanjek, *American Popular Music and Its Business: The First Four Hundred Years, Volume III* (New York: Oxford University Press, 1988), 602.

8. Frith, "Picking Up the Pieces," 117.

9. Sanjek, *American Popular Music and Its Business,* 641.

10. Andrew Goodwin, *Dancing in the Distraction Factory: Music Television and Popular Culture* (Minneapolis: University of Minnesota Press, 1992), 133.

11. Eric Gelman, "Rocking Video," *Newsweek,* 18 April 1983, 98.

12. Goodwin, *Dancing in the Distraction Factory,* 132–39.

13. Ibid., 134.

14. Ibid.

15. Parke Peterbaugh, "Anglomania: America Surrenders to the Brits—But Who Really Wins?" *Billboard,* 10 November 1983, 31.

16. *Rock and Roll Confidential,* July 1983, p. 6.

17. Rebecca Bricker, "Take One," *People,* 4 April 1983, 31.

18. Steven Levy, "Ad Nauseam: How MTV Sells Out Rock & Roll," *Rolling Stone,* 8 December 1983, 37.

19. Bricker, "Take One," 31.

20. Gelman, "Rocking Video," 98.

21. Michael Shore, *The Rolling Stone Book of Rock Video* (London: Sidgwick and Jackson, 1985), 86.

22. See, for example, E. Ann Kaplan, *Rocking Around the Clock: Music Television, Postmodernism, and Consumer Culture* (New York: Routledge, 1987); L. Lewis, *Gender Politics and MTV: Voicing the Difference* (Philadelphia: Temple University Press, 1990); and Susan McClary, *Feminine Endings: Music, Gender, and Sexuality* (Minneapolis: University of Minnesota Press, 1991).

23. Gelman, "Rocking Video," 97.

24. Barclay, Jack, Schneider, 55–56.

25. Pegley dissertation, 3.

26. Pegley in *The Garland Encyclopedia of World Music: The United States and Canada.*

27. Goddard and Kamin (1989), 100.

28. *Saturday Night,* June 1972.

29. Steve Morse, "Can American Bands Beat the British Blitz?" *Boston Globe,* 1 January 1984, p. A4.

30. Paul Grein, "AOR Programmers Plan More Variety," *Billboard,* 14 January 1984, 66.

31. Laurence Kenneth Shore, "The Crossroads of Business and Music: A Study of the Music Industry in the United States and Internationally" (Ph.D. Diss., Stanford University, 1983), 248; Hung and Morencos, *World Record Sales, 1969–1990,* 85.

32. Paul Grein, "'83 RIAA Tally: Fewer Biggies," *Billboard,* 14 January 1984, 4.

33. Jeffrey Zaslow, "Music and Money," *Wall Street Journal,* 21 May 1985, 1.

34. Jim Miller, "State of the Art," *Newsweek,* 18 April 1983, 97.

35. Ted Fox, *In the Groove* (New York: St. Martin's Press, 1986), 322.

36. Frith, "Picking Up the Pieces," 97.

37. Stephen Holden, "Musical Odyssey," *New York Times,* 9 December 1987, p. C33.

38. Frith, "Picking Up the Pieces," 102–03.

39. Paul Grein, "Charts '86," *Billboard,* 27 December 1986, Y-4.

40. Steve Gett, "Rock '86," *Billboard,* 27 December 1986, Y-4.

41. Frith, "Picking Up the Pieces," 90.

42. John Rockwell, "Leftist Causes? Rock Seconds Those Emotions," *New York Times,* 11 December 1988, 23.

43. David Breskin, "Bob Geldof: The Rolling Stone Interview," *Rolling Stone,* 5 December 1985, 34.

44. Mark Coleman, "The Revival of Conscience," *Rolling Stone,* 15 November 1990, 71.

45. Griel Marcus, "Rock for Ethiopia" (panel presentation at the Third International Conference on Popular Music Studies, Montreal, Quebec, July 1985), 17.

46. Pete Hamill, "A Day to Remember," *Rolling Stone,* 29 August 1985, 28.

47. Ibid., 74.

48. Will Straw, "Rock for Ethiopia" (panel presentation at the Third International Conference on Popular Music Studies, Montreal, Quebec, July 1985), 28.

49. Breskin, "Bob Geldof: The Rolling Stone Interview," 28.

50. Simon Frith, "Crappy Birthday to Punk," *In These Times,* 23–29 April 1986, 20.

51. *Rock & Roll Confidential,* 1985 September, 1.

52. Stan Rijven, "Rock for Ethiopia" (panel presentation at the Third International Conference on Popular Music Studies, Montreal, Quebec, July 1985), 3–7.

53. Jack Healy, "Mass Concerts/Mass Consciousness: The Politics of Mega-Events" (panel discussion at the New Music Seminar, New York, 17 July 1989).

54. Coleman, "The Revival of Conscience," 80.

55. The bill included Whitney Houston, Sting, Stevie Wonder, Dire Straits, Tracy Chapman, Peter Gabriel, The Fat Boys, Jackson Browne, Natalie Cole, Little Steven, Eurythmics, Freddie Jackson, Phil Collins, UB40, Al Green, Midge Ure, Miriam Makeba, Hugh Masakela, Simple Minds, Sly and Robbie, Aswad, The Bee Gees, Youssou N'Dour, Salt-n-Pepa, and more.

56. Anthony DeCurtis, "Rock & Roll Politics: Did the Nelson Mandela Tribute Make Its Point," *Rolling Stone,* 11 August 1988, 34.

57. Danny Schechter, "Why We Didn't See Wembley," *Africa Report* (July–August 1990): 66.

58. *Rock & Roll Confidential,* September 1985, p. 1.

59. Simon Frith and John Street, "Party Music," *Marxism Today* (June 1986): 29.

60. *The Making of Sun City,* MTV documentary produced by Steve Lawrence and Vinny Longabardo, Karl-Lorimar Home Video, 1985.

61. Steven Feld, "Notes on World Beat," *Public Culture Bulletin* (Fall 1988): 33–34.

62. Ibid., 32.

63. Susan Nunziata, "'90 Label Tally: Units Up 7.3%, $ Jump 14.6%," *Billboard,* 6 April 1991, 1, 80.

64. Michèle Hung and Esteban Garcia Morencos, *World Record Sales 1969–1990: A Statistical History of the World Recording Industry* (London: International Federation of the Phonogram Industry, 1990), 60.

65. Simon Frith, ed. *Facing the Music* (New York: Pantheon Books, 1988), 129.

66. Ted Fox, *In the Groove* (New York: St. Martin's Press, 1986), 334–36.

CHAPTER 10

1. Tricia Rose, *Black Noise: Rap Music and Black Culture in Contemporary America* (Hanover, NH: University Press of New England, 1994).

2. Philip Bashe, *Heavy Metal Thunder: The Music, Its History, Its Heroes* (Garden City, NY: Doubleday, 1985); Deena Weinstein, *Heavy Metal: A Cultural Sociology* (New York: Lexington Books, 1991).

3. Weinstein, *Heavy Metal,* 44.

4. Robert Walser, *Running with the Devil: Power, Gender, and Madness in Heavy Metal Music* (Hanover, NH: Wesleyan University Press, 1993), 12.

5. Ibid., 94.

6. Ibid., 76.

7. Gillian G. Garr, *She's a Rebel: The History of Women in Rock & Roll* (Seattle, WA: Seal Press, 1992), 415.

8. Andrew Goodwin, *Dancing in the Distraction Factory: Music Television and Popular Culture* (Minneapolis: University of Minnesota Press, 1992), 135.

9. Ibid., 135.

10. Greg Ptacek, "Majors Return to Nuts and Bolts of pre-MTV Metal Marketing Days," *Billboard,* 27 April 1985, p. HM 15.

11. Linda Martin and Kerry Segrave, *Anti-Rock: The Opposition to Rock 'n' Roll* (New York: DaCapo Press, 1993), 232.

12. Ptacek, "Majors Return to Nuts and Bolts," HM 3.

13. Ibid., HM 15.

14. Goodwin, *Dancing in the Distraction Factory,* 136.

15. E. Ann Kaplan, *Rocking Around the Clock: Music Television, Postmodernism, and Consumer Culture* (New York: Routledge, 1987), 102–03.

16. Roberta Smoodin, "Crazy Like David Lee Roth," *Playgirl,* August 1986, p. 43, quoted in Walser, *Running with the Devil,* 129.

17. Walser, *Running with the Devil,* 111.

18. Ibid., 121.

19. Weinstein, *Heavy Metal,* 48.

20. Ibid., 50.

21. Jim Miller, "It's Not Only Rock 'N' Roll," *Boston Globe,* 23 August 1991, p. 94. There were parallel developments in post-punk. Thrash metal was to classic metal what the hardcore sound of Black Flag and SS Decontrol was to new wave. By the time Black Flag leader Henry Rollins left to form his new group, the Rollins Band, its music was defined by yet another fusion category called thrashcore, which included a group called Suicidal Tendencies.

22. Weinstein, *Heavy Metal,* 51.

23. Sue Cummings, "Road Warriors," *Spin,* August 1986, quoted in Weinstein, *Heavy Metal,* 160.

24. Paul Grein, "The Year in Charts," *Billboard,* 26 December 1987, Y-4.

25. J. D. Considine, "Metal Mania," *Rolling Stone,* 15 November 1990, 104.

26. See Weinstein, *Heavy Metal,* 66; Walser, *Running with the Devil,* 17.

27. Weinstein, *Heavy Metal,* 67.

28. Walser, *Running with the Devil,* 17.

29. Laurel Fishman, "Lita Ford," *Metal,* May 1988, quoted in Walser, *Running with the Devil,* 132.

30. Tim Carr, "Talk That Talk, Walk That Walk," *Rolling Stone,* 26 May 1983, p. 22.

31. David Toop, *The Rap Attack 2: African Rap to Global Hip Hop* (London: Serpent's Tail, 1991), 14.

32. Ibid., 154.

33. For an excellent explication of the (primarily) Puerto Rican involvement in early rap as a conjunctive (rather than merely additive) experience, see Juan Flores, *From Bomba to Hip Hop: Puerto Rican Culture and Latino Identity* (New York: Columbia University Press, 2000). See also Raquel Z. Rivera, "Boricuas from the Hip Hop Zone: Notes on Race and Ethnic Relations in New York City," *Centro Journal* (Spring 1996): 202–15.

34. Steven Hager, *Hip Hop: The Illustrated History of Break Dancing, Rap Music, and Graffiti* (New York: St. Martin's Press, 1984), 91.

35. Stephen Holden, "Pop Records Turn to Hip Hop," *New York Times,* 23 September 1984, 78.

36. Toop, *The Rap Attack 2,* 149.

37. Ibid., 179.

38. Brian Cross, *It's Not About a Salary: Rap, Race and Resistance in Los Angeles* (New York: Verso, 1993), 50.

39. Alex Henderson, "Active Indies," *Billboard,* 24 December 1988, R-16.

40. Ibid., R-8.

41. Dan Stuart, "Black Radio," *Billboard,* 17 June 1989, B-12.

42. Henderson, "Active Indies," R-21.

43. Jon Pareles, "There's a New Sound in Pop Music: Bigotry," *New York Times,* 10 September 1989, Arts and Leisure, 1.

44. Ibid., 33.

45. Harry Allen, "Hip Hop Madness: From Def Jams to Cold Lampin', Rap Is Our Music," *Essence,* April 1989, p. 117.

46. Ibid.

47. Toop, *The Rap Attack 2,* 200.

48. For an excellent discussion of this complexity, see Rose, *Black Noise,* 146–82.

49. Toop, *The Rap Attack 2,* 201.

50. Cross, *It's Not About a Salary,* 55.

51. David Nathan, "Rap," *Billboard,* 24 December 1988, R-5.

52. Stuart, "Black Radio," B-12.

53. Kristal Brent Zook, "Reconstructions of Nationalist Thought in Black Music and Culture," in *Rockin' the Boat: Mass Music and Mass Movements,* ed. Reebee Garofalo (Boston: South End Press, 1992), 262.

54. Toop, *The Rap Attack 2,* 185.

55. Cross, *It's Not About a Salary,* 58.

56. Ibid.

57. Herman Gray, "Popular Music as a Social Problem: A Social History of Claims Against Popular Music," in *Images of Issues,* ed. Joel Best (Hawthorne, NY: De Gruyter, 1989).

58. See Lawrence Grossberg, *We Gotta Get Out of This Place: Popular Conservatism and Postmodern Culture* (New York: Routledge, 1992). For an abbreviated treatment of this discussion, see Lawrence Grossberg, "The Framing of Rock: Rock and the New Conservatism," in *Rock and Popular Music: Politics, Policies, Institutions,* ed. Tony Bennett et al. (New York: Routledge, 1993), 195.

59. Nan Levinson, "Shut Up," *Boston Globe,* 20 February 1994, p. 79.

60. Susan McClary and Robert Walser, "Start Making Sense: Musicology Wrestles with Rock," in *On Record: Rock, Pop, and the Written Word,* ed. Simon Frith and Andrew Goodwin (New York: Pantheon Books, 1990), 278.

61. Linda Martin and Kerry Segrave, *Anti-Rock: The Opposition to Rock 'n' Roll* (New York: DaCapo Press, 1993), 292.

62. U.S. Congress, Senate, Committee on Commerce, Science, and Transportation, *Record Labeling,* 99th Cong., 1st sess., 1985, 11, quoted in Herman Gray, "Rate the Records: Symbolic Conflict, Popular Music, and Social Problems," *Popular Music and Society* (Fall 1989): 6–7.

63. Steven Dougherty, "Parents Vs. Rock," *People,* 16 September 1985, 50.

64. Simon Frith, *Sound Effects: Youth, Leisure, and the Politics of Rock 'n' Roll* (New York: Pantheon Books, 1981), 175.

65. Dougherty, "Parents Vs. Rock," 50.

66. Gray, "Rate the Records," 9.

67. Frank Zappa, "The Porn Wars," *Penthouse,* May 1989, 78.

68. Editorial, *Rolling Stone,* 7 November 1985, 10.

69. PMRC Video, *Rising to the Challenge,* produced by Teen Vision, Inc., 1989.

70. Ibid.

71. Ibid.

72. Walser, *Running with the Devil,* 139.

73. Dougherty, "Parents Vs. Rock," 52.

74. Walser, *Running with the Devil,* 140.

75. Dave Marsh, "What's Being Sold in Country?" *New York Times,* 24 May 1992, p. 20.

76. Ibid.

77. Robin Denselow, *When the Music's Over: The Story of Political Pop* (Boston: Faber and Faber, 1989), 267.

78. U.S. Congress, Senate, Committee on Commerce, Science, and Transportation, *Record Labeling,* 99th Cong., 1st sess., 1985, 11, quoted in Gray, "Rate the Records," 10.

79. David Thigpen, "Up Against the Wall," *Rolling Stone,* 24 February 1994, 16.

80. Jello Biafra, "The Far Right and the Censorship of Music," *Harvard Law Record,* 17 April 1987, 11.

81. Marjorie Heins, *Sex, Sin and Blasphemy: A Guide to America's Censorship Wars* (New York: The New Press, 1993), 90.

82. Ibid., 89.

83. Ibid., 92.

84. Walser, *Running with the Devil,* 150.

85. ABC, *20/20,* Segment on heavy metal, produced by Danny Schechter, 1987.

86. Lynn Minton, "Is Heavy Metal Dangerous?" *Parade,* 20 September 1992, 12.

87. K. Zimmerman, "Priest Ruling Gives Unclear Message," *Variety,* 3 September 1990, 8, quoted in Steve Jones, "Ban(ned) in the USA: Popular Music and Censorship," *Journal of Communication Inquiry,* Winter, 1991, 77.

88. The editors of *Rock & Roll Confidential, You've Got a Right to Rock* (Los Angeles: Duke and Duchess Ventures, Inc., 1990), 6.

89. Richard N. Ostling, "No Sympathy for the Devil," *Time,* 19 March 1990, 56.

90. Robert J. Barry, "Satanism: The Law Enforcement Response," *The National Sheriff,* February/March 1987, 40.

91. David Alexander, "Giving the Devil More Than His Due." *The Humanist,* March/April 1990, quoted in Walser, *Running with the Devil,* 199–200.

92. Barry, "Satanism," 39.

93. Ibid., 41.

94. Dougherty, "Parents Vs. Rock," 46.

95. Ostling, "No Sympathy for the Devil," 56.

96. Peter Steinfels, "Surge in Satanic Activity Alarms O'Connor," *New York Times,* 6 March 1990, B6.

97. Reuters, "Of Hard-Rock Demons: A Cardinal Speaks Out," *Boston Globe,* 6 March 1990, 23.

98. Steinfels, "Surge in Satanic Activity Alarms O'Connor," B6.

99. Pareles, "There's a New Sound in Pop Music: Bigotry," 1, 32–33.

100. Dennis Wharton, "D.C. Bluebloods Want X Rating for Porn Rock," *Variety,* 22 May 1985, quoted in Martin and Segrave, *Anti-Rock,* 293.

101. Biafra, "The Far Right and the Censorship of Music," 12.

102. Ibid.

103. Heins, *Sex, Sin, and Blasphemy,* 22–24.

104. Henry Louis Gates, Jr., "2 Live Crew, Decoded." *New York Times,* 9 June 1990, p. A23.

105. Brechner Center for Freedom of Information, *The Brechner Report* (Gainesville: University of Florida, 1992), 2.

106. David Mills, "Rap as Politics: The Sayings of Sister Souljah," *Essence,* September 1992, 20.

107. Alan Light, "Ice," *Rolling Stone,* 20 August 1992, 30.

108. Charlene Orr et al., "Texas Police Pursue 'Cop Killer,'" *Billboard,* 27 June 1992, 79.

109. Greg Sandow, "Fire & Ice," *Entertainment Weekly,* 14 August, 1992, 32.

110. Havelock Nelson, "Music and Violence: Does Crime Pay?" *Billboard,* 13 November 1993, 109.

111. Havelock Nelson, "The Rap Column," *Billboard,* 4 December 1993, 30.

112. Touré, "Snoop Dogg's Gentle Hip Hop Growl," *New York Times,* 21 November 1993, 32.

113. Toop, *The Rap Attack 2,* 170.

114. Phyllis Stark et al., "Gangsta Rap Under the Gun," *Billboard,* 18 December 1993, 141.

115. Bill Holland, "Senate Hearing Examines Gangsta Lyrics," *Billboard,* 5 March 1994, 10.

116. Ibid., 89.

117. Ibid., 10.

CHAPTER 11

1. Mikal Gilmore, "The Year in Music," *Rolling Stone,* 13–27 December 1990, 13.

2. Ibid., 17.

3. Ibid.

4. Ibid.

5. Kim Neely, "Into the Unknown," *Rolling Stone,* 16 June 1994, 117.

6. Anthony DeCurtis, "Kurt Cobain, 1967–1994," *Rolling Stone,* 2 June 1994, 30.

7. David Fricke, "Kurt Cobain," *Rolling Stone,* 27 January 1994, 36.

8. Donna Gaines, "Suicidal Tendencies: Kurt Did Not Die for You," *Rolling Stone,* 2 June 1994, 67.

9. "k.d. lang," in *Encyclopedia of Music in Canada* (online), www.thecanadianencyclopedia.com.

10. Steve McLean, "Ashley MacIsaac," in *Encyclopedia of Music in Canada* (online), www.thecanadianencyclopedia.com.

11. Glenn Colton, "Great Big Sea," in *Encyclopedia of Music in Canada* (online) www.thecanadianencyclopedia.com.

12. Jim Sullivan, "Lollapalooza: The Sound of Success," *The Boston Globe,* 2 August 1992, B25.

13. Jon Pareles, "Howls of Rage, Nine Hours Worth, at Waterloo Village," *New York Times,* 13 August 1991, C13.

14. Peter Watrous, "Good Things Happen to Lollapalooza," *New York Times,* 5 August 1992, C13.

15. David Fricke, "Red Hot Chili Peppers' Naked Truth," *Rolling Stone,* 25 June 1992, 29.

16. Ibid., 29.

17. Steve Pond, "The Trick Is to Be Loved but Not Embraced," *New York Times,* 26 June 1994, sec. 2, 28.

18. Anthony DeCurtis, "Ropin' the Whirl Wind," *Rolling Stone,* 1 April 1993, 35.

19. Anthony DeCurtis, "The Year in Music," *Rolling Stone,* 10–24 December 1992, 26.

20. Michael Erlewine et al., eds., *All Music Guide to Rock* (San Francisco: Miller Freeman Books, 1997), 5.

21. Ibid., 436.

22. Ibid., 871.

23. Rich Cohen, "Southern Comfort," *Rolling Stone,* 10 August 1995, 43.

24. "1990 Yearbook," *Rolling Stone,* 13–27 December 1990, 72.

25. Fred Goodman, "Big Deals: How Money Fever Is Changing the Music Business," *Musician,* January 1992, 42.

26. Neil Strauss, "For Record Industry, All Signs are Gloomy," *New York Times,* 4 December 1996, A-1.

27. Among the best of these are Sarah Thornton, *Club Cultures: Music, Media and Subcultural Capital* (Hanover, NH: University Press of New England, 1995); Matthew Collin, *Altered States: The Story of Ecstasy Culture and Acid House* (New York: Serpent's Tail, 1997); Hillegonda C. Rietveld, *This Is Our House: House Music, Cultural Spaces and Technologies* (Brookfield, VT: Ashgate, 1998); Simon Reynolds, *Generation Ecstasy: Into the World of Techno and Rave Culture* (New York: Routledge,

1999); Dan Sicko, *Techno Rebels: The Renegades of Electronic Funk* (New York: Billboard Books, 1999); Kai Fikentscher, *You Better Work: Underground Dance Music in New York City* (Hanover, NH: University Press of New England, 2000).

28. Because these styles are often presented ahistorically, the listening public has been deluged with a smorgasbord of over 300 sub-sub-genres of which Kembrew McLeod ("Genres, Sub-Genres, Sub-Sub-Genres and More: Musical and Social Differentiation Within Electronic-Dance Music Communities," *Journal of Popular Music Studies,* Spring 2001) has distilled an edited list that includes "Abstract Beat, Abstract Drum-n-Bass, Acid House, Acid Rave, Acid-Beats, Acid-Funk, Acid-Techno, Alchemic House, Ambient Dance, Ambient Drum-n-Bass, Amyl House, Analogue Electro-Funk, Aquatic Techno-Funk, Aquatic-House, Atomic Breaks, Avant-Techno, Bass, Big Beat, Bleep-n-Bass, Blunted Beats, Breakbeat, Chemical Beats, Chicago Garage, Chicago House, Coldwave, Cosmic Dance, Cyber Hardcore, Cybertech, Dark Ambient, Downtempo Funk, Downtempo Future Jazz, Drill-n-Bass, Dronecore, Drum-n-Bass, Dub, Dub-Funk, Dub-Hop, Dub-n-Bass, Electro, Electro-Acoustic, Electro-Breaks, Electro-Dub, Freestyle, Future Jazz, Futuristic Breakbeat, Futuristic Hardbeats, Futuristic Hardstep, Gabber, Garage, Global House, Global Trance, Goa-Trance, Happy Hardcore, Hardcore Techno, Hard Chill Ambient, Intelligent Drum-n-Bass, Intelligent Jungle, Intelligent Techno, Miami Bass Minimal Techno, Minimal Trance, Morphing, Mutant Techno, Mutated Minimal Techno, Mystic-Step, Neurofunk, Noir-House, Nu-Dark Jungle, Old School, Organic Chill Out, Organic Electro, Organic Electronica, Progressive House, Progressive Low Frequency, Progressive Trance, Ragga, Ragga-Jungle, Rave, Techstep, Techxotica, Trance, Trancecore, Trance-Dub, Tribal, Tribal Beats, Tribal House, Tribal Soul, Trip-Hop, Tripno, Twilight Electronica, Two-Step, UK Acid, UK Breakbeat, Underground, World-Dance."

29. Simon Reynolds, *Generation Ecstasy: Into the World of Techno and Rave Culture* (New York: Routledge, 1999), 24.

30. Hillegonda C. Rietveld, *This Is Our House: House Music, Cultural Spaces and Technologies* (Brookfield, VT: Ashgate, 1998), 23.

31. It is interesting to note that "Alleys" was released concurrently with Afrika Bambaataa's "Planet Rock," also heavily indebted to Kraftwerk, which typified the New York hip hop sound called *electro.*

32. Reynolds, *Generation Ecstasy,* 60.

33. Sarah Thornton, *Club Cultures: Music, Media and Subcultural Capital* (Hanover, NH: University Press of New England, 1995), 76.

34. Reynolds, *Generation Ecstasy,* 13.

35. Thornton, *Club Cultures,* 73.

36. Matthew Collin, *Altered States: The Story of Ecstasy Culture and Acid House* (New York: Serpent's Tail, 1997), 254.

37. Reynolds, *Generation Ecstasy,* 260.

38. Ibid., 341.

39. Ibid., 330.

40. Ethan Smith, "Organization Moby," *Wired,* May 2002, 91.

41. Marilyn Gillen, "The Year in Business: Ups, Downs, and Rebounds," *Billboard,* 27 December 1999, YE 14.

42. Steve Morse, "In Pop, Women Took New Ground All Over," *Boston Globe,* 29 December 1996, N6.

43. James Sullivan, "Three's the Charm as the Last Lilith All-Women Music Festival Loses Its Sensitive Side," *San Francisco Chronicle,* 15 July 1999, reported on Geocities.com. www.geocities.com/SunsetStrip/Stage/8151/990713.htm.

44. Ibid.

45. Ibid.

46. From Ruffhouse Records' Official Website, www.lauryn-hill.com/history.html.

47. Joan Anderman, "Shut Up," *Boston Globe,* 3 December 2000, K1.

48. Rob Sheffield, "Rage Against the Latrines," *Rolling Stone,* 2 September 1999, 54.

49. Joan Anderman, "The Female Fans Say They're in It for the Catharsis," *Boston Globe,* 16 July 2000, P1.

50. "Readers Poll," *Rolling Stone,* 20 January 2000, 51.

51. Neil Straus, "The Hit Girl: Christina Aguilera," *Rolling Stone,* 6–20 July 2000, 82, 151.

52. Anthony Bozza, "NSynchronicity," *Rolling Stone,* 30 March 2000, 55.

53. Touré, "True Tales of the Pop Life: 'N Sync," *Rolling Stone,* 16 August 2001, 66.

54. Ibid., 70.

55. Steven Daly, "Britney Spears: Inside the Heart and Mind (and Bedroom) of America's New Teen Queen," *Rolling Stone,* 15 April 1999, 65.

56. Peter Kafka, "The Queen of Teen," *Forbes,* 20 March 2000, 162.

57. Chris Heath, "Has Anyone Seen Christina," *Rolling Stone,* 14 November 2001, 55.

58. Ibid.

59. Ibid.

60. Joseph P. Kahn, "Musical Chairs Coming Up for the White House," *Boston Globe,* 20 January 2001, C2.

61. Chris Heath, "The Epic Life of Carlos Santana," *Rolling Stone,* 16 March 2000, 41.

62. Mim Udovitch, "Shakira," *Rolling Stone,* 31 October 2002, 102.

63. LARAS, "Universe of Rhythms: The Grammys Guide to Latin Music," 2000. www.grammy.com/press/guide_eng.html.

64. Deborah Pacini Hernandez, "Race, Ethnicity and the Production of Latin/o Popular Music," in *Global Repertoires: Popular Music Within and Beyond the Transnational Music Industry,* ed. Andreas Gabesmair and Alfred Smudits (Burlington, VT: Ashgate Publishing Ltd., 2001).

65. N.A. "R. Kelly," Wall of Sound. http://wallofsound.go.com/artists/rkelly/home.html.

66. Lola Ogunnaike, "Caught in the Act," *Vibe,* May 2002, 93.

67. Ibid., 92.

68. Keith Negus, *Music Genres and Corporate Cultures* (New York: Routledge, 1999), 85.

69. Mikal Gilmore, "Puff Daddy," *Rolling Stone,* 7 August 1997, 72.

70. Fred Schruers, "Master P," *Rolling Stone,* 29 October 1998, 42.

71. Keith Negus, *Music Genres and Corporate Cultures,* 96.

72. Nelson George, *Buppies, B-Boys, Baps and Bohos: Notes on Post-Soul Black Culture* (New York: HarperCollins, 1992), 80.

73. Tony Green, "The Dirty South," in *The VIBE History of Hip Hop,* Alan Light, ed. (New York: Three Rivers Press, 1999).

74. Murray Forman, "'Represent': Race, Space and Place in Rap Music," *Popular Music,* January 2000, 68–69.

75. David Bry, "The Song of the South," *Vibe,* June 2002, 94.

76. Ibid., 100.

77. Renée Graham, "Is Some Hatred More Acceptable Than Others?" *Boston Globe,* 5 January 2001, C1.

78. N.A., "The Hip-Hop 50," *Rolling Stone,* 29 October 1998, 45–57.

79. Touré, "DMX Reigns as the Dark Prince of Hip Hop," *Rolling Stone,* 13 April 2000, 85.

80. Nathaniel Welch, "Hit Man," *Rolling Stone,* 22 August 2002, 54.

81. Touré, "The Life of a Hunted Man," *Rolling Stone,* 3 April 2003, 46.

82. John Bush, "Outkast," *All Music Guide,* 2003. http://www.allmucis.com/cg/amg.dlle

83. Vanessa E. Jones, "Whose Word Is It Anyway?" *Boston Globe,* 7 July 1999, D1.

CHAPTER 12

1. Vito Peraino, "The Law of Increasing Returns," *Wired,* August 1999, 144.

2. Rachel Konrad, "Napster Among Fastest-Growing Net Technologies," CNET News.com, 5 October 2000. http://news.cnet.com/news/0-1005-200-2938703.html.

3. U.S. Constitution: art. 1, § 8, cl. 8.

4. William Fisher, "Theories of Intellectual Property," Draft of 11 April 2000. www.law.harvard.edu/Academic_Affairs/coursepages/tfisher/iptheory.html#_ftnref10.

5. H.R. Rep. No. 609, 100 Congress, 2nd session 23, 1988. Cited in L. Ray Patterson and Stanley W. Lindberg, *The Nature of Copyright: A Law of User's Rights* (Athens, GA: University of Georgia Press, 1991), 49.

6. Kenneth Cohen et al., "No Electronic Theft Act: Policy Development Team Report," Washington, D.C.: U.S. Sentencing Commission, February 1999, 2.

7. Reuters, "Prince Voices Support for Napster," CNET News.com, 9 August 2000, http://news.cnet.com/news/0-1005-200-2482624.html.

8. Statement of Roger McGuinn, Senate Judiciary Committee Hearing on the Future of Digital Music: Is There an Upside to Downloading?, 11 July 2000, http://www.senate.gov/~judiciary/7112000_rm.htm.

9. Ibid.

10. See Ron Harris, "Metallica to Napster: Cut Users,"

Boston Globe, 4 May 2000, E4, and Steve Morse, "Napster Strikes Dissonant Chords," *Boston Globe,* 5 May 2000, D18.

11. John Borland, "Napster Says 30,000 Metallica Fans Appeal Ban," CNET, 16 May 2000, http://yahoo.cnet.com/news/0-1005-200-1883655.html?pt.yfin.cat_fin.txt.ne.

12. P. J. Huffstutter, "Music Makers at Wits' End in Battle with Internet Takers," *Los Angeles Times,* 29 May 2000, A14.

13. Reuters, "BMG Says It Discussed Business Models with Napster," CNET News.com, 3 October 2000, http://news.cnet.com/news/0-1005-200-2927330.html

14. Mark Latonero, "Survey of MP3 Usage: Report on a University Consumption Community," The Norman Lear Center, Annenberg School for Communication, University of Southern California, June 2000, 2.

15. N.A., "Playboy Poll: Napster Users Buy CD's." MP3 Newswire, 17 August 2000, www.mp3newswire.net/stories/2000/playboy.html.

16. RIAA Press Release, "Compact Disc Shipments at All-Time High," Washington, D.C., 25 August 2000, www.RIAA.com/PR_Story.cfm?id=312.

17. Bloomberg News, "FTC Slams Record Labels on CD Sales Practice," 10 May 2000, http://yahoo.cnet.com/news/0-1005-200-1851819.html?pt.yfin.cat_fin.txt.ne.

18. Janelle Brown, "Crack SDMI? No Thanks!" Salon.com, 14 September 2000, www.salon.com/tech/log/2000/09/14/hack_sdmi/index.html.

19. Hiawatha Bray, "Hackers Go One Up," *Boston Globe.* 26 October 2000, C1.

20. Jim Hu, "Web, Music Giants March to Different Tunes," CNET News.com, 13 July 2001, http://news.cnet.com/news/0-1005-200-6561339.html?tag=dd.ne.dtx.nl-sty.0.

21 Reuters, "Music Industry Still in First Gear Online," 7 January 2002, http://news.com/2100-1023802359.html.

22. Amy Harmon, "Music Industry in Global Fight on Web Copies," *New York Times,* 7 October 2002, www.nytimes.com/2002/10/07/technology/07SWAP.html?ex=1035021589&ei=1&en=8f37d36c94fe6e8e.

23. John Borland, "Judge: File-Swapping Tools Are Legal," CNET News.com, 25 April 2003, http://news.com.com/2100-1027-998363.html?tag=nl.

24. Sue Zeidler, "Music Industry Sends Warning to Song Swappers," Yahoo News, 29 April 2003, http://sg.news.yahoo.com/030429/3/3akqc.html.

25. NA, "Senator: Trash Illegal Downloaders' PCs," CNN.Com, 18 June 2003, www.cnn.com/2003/TECH/internet/06/18/download.music.ap/index.html.

26. Andy Sullivan, "Music Firms, DJ Offer to Pay 12-Year-Old's Fine," Reuters, 11 September 2003, www.reuters.com/newsArticle.jhtml;jsessionid=GJHB5ZIZY5BACRBAEKSFFA?type=topNews&storyID=3431108.

27. *RIAA v. The People: Two Years Later,* Electronic Frontier Foundation, 2005, www.eff.org.

28. Staff and Agencies, "Music Industry Counts the Cost of Online Piracy," *The Guardian,* 4 April 2006, http://arts.guardian.co.uk/netmusic/story/0,,1746741,00.html.

29. Bruce Gain, "RIAA Takes Shotgun to Traders," *Wired News,* 4 October 2005, www.wired.com/news/digiwood/0,1412,68951,00.html.

30. Brian Garrity, "Grokster Blasts RIAA Anti-Piracy Tactics," *Billboard.com,* 27 June 2003. posted on Free-Republic.com, http://209.157.64.200/focus/f-news/936821/posts.

31. "New P2P File Sharing Stats," *p2pnet.net News,* 22 October 2004, http://p2pnet.net/story/2797.

32. Neil Strauss, "File-Sharing Battle Leaves Musicians Caught in Middle," *New York Times,* 14 September 2003, www.nytimes.com/2003/09/14/technology/14MUSI.html.

33. John Schwartz, "A Heretical View of File Sharing," *New York Times,* 5 April 2004, www.nytimes.com/2004/04/05/technology/05music.html?ex=1083124800&en=585a8241cab4c298&ei=5070.

34. Beth Potier, "File Sharing May Boost CD Sales: Study Defies Traditional Beliefs About Internet Use," *Harvard Gazette Archives,* 15 April 2004, www.news.harvard.edu/gazette/2004/04.15/09-filesharing.html.

35. Editorial, "The Sound of Lawsuits," *San Jose Mercury News,* 9 September 2003, www.bayarea.com/mld/mercurynews/news/opinion/6727444.htm.

36. Justice David Souter, *MGM v. Grokster.* Supreme Court of the United States, No. 04–480, 27 June 2005.

37. Ibid.

38. Ibid.

39. Ibid.

40. N.A., "Roxio Buys pressplay, to Relaunch Napster," Salon.Com, 19 May 2003, www.salon.com/tech/wire/2003/05/19/roxio_pressplay/index.html.

41. Matthew Yi, "One Billion Songs Sold on iTunes," *San Francisco Chronicle,* 24 February 2006, http://sfgate.com/cgi-bin/article.cgi?file=/chronicle/archive/2006/02/24/BUG9THDRI31.DTL.

42. N.A., "I Heard the News Today . . . ," *Rolling Stone,* 25 October 2001, 32.

43. David Fricke, "Imagine," *Rolling Stone,* 27 December 2001–3 January 2002, 38–41.

44. Cynthia Cotts, "Telecom for Dummies, *Village Voice,* 5–11 September 2001, cited by MediaChannel.org, www.mediachannel.org/news/indepth/fcc/

45. Greg Kot, "What's Wrong with Radio," *Rolling Stone,* 16 August 2001, 25.

46. Ray Waddell, "Touring Strong, But Some Numbers Cause Concern," *Billboard,* 28 December 2002, 77.

47. Tim Jones, "Media Giant's Rally Sponsorship Raises Questions," *Chicago Tribune,* 19 March 2003, www.chicagotribune.com/news/showcase/chi-0303190157mar19.story.

48. Ibid.

49. Paul Krugman, "Channels of Influence," *New York Times,* 25 March 2003, www.nytimes.com/2003/03/25/opinion/25KRUG.html.

50. Tom Roland, "Lee Greenwood," *All Music Guide,* ND., www.allmusic.com/cg/amg.dll?p=amg&uid=CASS80310101206&sql=B3srz286c054a.

51. John Metzger, "Neil Young Are You Passionate?"

The Music Box, May 2002, Vol. 9, No. 5, www.musicbox-online.com/ny-pass.html.

52. Jenny Eliscu, "Chicks Triumph," *Rolling Stone,* 29 May 2003, 10.

53. Joan Anderman, "Dixie Chicks: A Brief History of an Outspoken Band," *Boston Globe,* 28 July 2006, www.boston.com/news/globe/living/articles/2006/07/28/dixie_chicks_a_brief_history_of_an_outspoken_band.

54. Joseph Schumacher, "Is Protest Music as Dead as Disco?" *Peace and Conflict Monitor,* 12 May 2003, www.monitor.upeace.org/innerpg.cfm?id_article=5.

55. Brent Staples, "The Trouble with Corporate Radio: The Day the Protest Music Died," *New York Times,* 20 February 2003, www.nytimes.com/2003/02/20/opinion/20THU4.html.

56. Jeff Chang, "Is Protest Music Dead?" AlterNet.org, 16 April 2002, www.alternet.org/story.html?StoryID=12880.

57. N.A., "N.J. Rock Station Won't Play Jethro Tull," Associated Press, 13 November 2003, http://apnews.excite.com/article/20031113/D7UPO1981.html.

58. Posted on the MoveOn website, www.moveon.org/musiciansunited.

59. Kristin V. Jones, "Rocking the Hip Hop Vote," *The Nation,* 1 December 2003, 8.

60. Edna Gundersen, "For Springsteen, 'Seeger Sessions' Sends a Message," *USA Today,* 7 June 2006, 3d.

CHAPTER 13

1. Brian Garrity, "Anticipated Boom Was a Bust," *Billboard,* 24 December 2005, 28.

2. Brian Garrity, "Music Biz Gets a Makeover," *Billboard,* 25 December 2004, YE-53.

3. Ibid.

4. Fred Goodman, "Will Rock Trounce Teen Pop," *Rolling Stone,* 28 February 2002, 19.

5. Chris Heath, "Creed's Stairway to Heaven," *Rolling Stone,* 28 February 2002. 40.

6. Goodman, "Will Rock Trounce Teen Pop," 20.

7. Ibid.

8. Larry Flick, "Declining Sales in 2002 Trigger Desire for Less Hype, Better Records, Fresh Blood," *Billboard,* 28 December 2002, 17.

9. Melinda Newman, "The Good, Bad, and Mostly Ugly of 2002 Remembered," *Billboard,* 28 December 2002, 15.

10. Touré, "The Next Queen of Soul," *Rolling Stone,* 8 November 2001, 84.

11. Mark Binelli, "The Accidental Superstar," *Rolling Stone,* 18 March 2004, 54.

12. Mim Udovitch, "Pink Fights the Power," *Rolling Stone,* 4–11 July 2002, 60.

13. Austin Scaggs, "Why Is Nelly Furtado's New Album So Loud?" *Rolling Stone,* 19 June 2006, www.rollingstone.com/news/story/10603268/why_is_nelly_furtados_new_album_so_loud.

14. John Pareles, "Music; So Sweet, So Sensitive, So Self-Absorbed, So 70's," *New York Times,* 18 May 2003. URL: http://query.nytimes.com/search/restricted/article?res=F10A14F63A5B0C7B8DDDAC0894DB404482.

15. Ibid.

16. MacKenzie Wilson, "On and On," *All Music Guide,* www.allmusic.com/cg/amg.dll?p=amg&uid=UIDSUB040312201828452281&sql=Allf8zfi3eh2k.

17. Stephen Thomas Erlewine, "Heavier Things," *All Music Guide,* www.allmusic.com/cg/amg.dll?p=amg&uid=UISUB04031220182.

18. Pareles, "Music; So Sweet, So Sensitive, So Self-Absorbed, So 70's."

19. Bill Carter, "How a Hit Almost Failed Its Own Audition," *New York Times,* 30 April 2006, 1.

20. Paul R. La Monica, "No False 'Idol' for Fox," CNN Money.com, 24 May 2006, http://money.cnn.com/2006/05/22/news/companies/idol_fox/index.htm.

21. "President Bush Invites Idol Contestants to White House," *CBC Arts,* 21 July 2006, www.cbc.ca/story/arts/national/2006/07/21/americanidol-bush.html?ref=rss.

22. Joan Anderman, "Hip-Hop Setting the Beat," *Boston Globe,* 4 October 2003, www.boston.com/news/local/articles/2003/10/04/hip_hop_setting_the_beat?mode=PF.

23. David Toop, *The Rap Attack: African Jive to New York Hip Hop* (New South Wales, Australia: Pluto Press, 1984), 154.

24. Anderman, "Hip-Hop Setting the Beat."

25. Margeaux Watson, "The End of OutKast?" EW.com, retrieved on 24 August 2006, www.ew.com/ew/report/0,6115,1195670_4_0_,00.html.

26. Josh Tyrangiel, "You Can't Ignore Kanye," *Time,* 29 August 2005, 54.

27. Silvio Pietroluongo, Minal Patel, and Wade Jessen, "Singles Minded: Hot 100 Adds Digital Sales; Pop 100 Debuts," *Billboard,* 12 February 2005, 64.

28. Bill Lamb, "How to Read the Billboard Charts," About.com, retrieved on 26 August 2006, http://top40.about.com/od/popmusic101/a/billboardcharts.htm.

29. Rick Lyman, "New Data Shows Immigrants' Growth and Reach," *New York Times,* 15 August 2006, 1.

30. U.S. Census Bureau, "Table 1.1 Population by Sex, Age, Hispanic Origin, and Race: 2004," www.census.gov/population/socdemo/hispanic/ASEC2004/2004CPS_tab1.1a.html.

31. Lyman, "New Data Shows Immigrants' Growth and Reach."

32. Wayne Marshall, "The Rise of Reggaeton," *Boston Phoenix,* 19 January 2006, www.thephoenix.com/article_ektid1595.aspx

33. Leila Cobo, "Reggaeton Broke Out But Regional Mexican Acts Drove Latin Biz," *Billboard,* Special Section, 24 December 2005, 20.

34. Leila Cobo, "Reggaeton Rules," *Billboard,* 30 July 2005, 32.

35. Jon Caramanica, "Grow Dem Bow," *Village Voice,* 12 January 2006, www.villagevoice.com/music/0603,caramanica,71722,22.html

36. Marshall, "The Rise of Reggaeton."

37. Deborah Pacini Hernandez, "Dominicans in the Mix: Reflections on Dominicans and Reggaeton," in Raquel Z. Rivera, Deborah Pacini Hernandez, and Wayne Marshall, eds., *Reading Reggaeton: Historical, Aesthetic and Critical Perspectives* (Raleigh, NC: Duke University Press, in press).

38. Interview with DJ Velcro, Deborah Pacini, and Reebee Garofalo, San Juan, Puerto Rico, 10 May 2006.

39. *Chosen Few: El Documental*, video documentary produced by Manuel Alejandro Ruiz ("Boy Wonder"), 2004.

40. Agustin Gurza, "The Reggaeton Craze Saw a Quick Burnout with Fans and Radio," *Chicago Tribune,* 19 April 2006, 3.

41. Leila Cobo, "Radio Flips for Reggaeton," *Billboard,* 10 September 2005, 47.

Bibliography

Ackerman, Paul. "Gortikov Scorches Whitey Trade in NAFTRA Speech." *Billboard* (17 July 1969).

Alexander, David. "Giving the Devil More Than His Due." *The Humanist* (March–April 1990).

Allen, Harry. "Hip Hop Madness: From Def Jams to Cold Lampin', Rap Is Our Music." *Essence (*April 1989).

"American Revolution 1969." *Rolling Stone* (special insert) (5 April 1969).

Anderman, Joan. "Dixie Chicks: A Brief History of an Outspoken Band." *Boston Globe* (28 July 2006). www.boston.com/news/globe/living/articles/2006/07/28/dixie_chicks_a_brief_history_of_an_outspoken_band/.

———. "The Female Fans Say They're in It for the Catharsis." *Boston Globe* (16 July 2000).

———. "Hip-Hop Setting the Beat." *Boston Globe* (4 October 2003). www.boston.com/news/local/articles/2003/10/04/hip_hop_setting_the_beat?mode=PF

———. "Shut Up." *Boston Globe* (3 December 2000).

Ansen, David. "Rock Tycoon." *Newsweek* (31 July 1978).

Archer, Gleason L. *History of Radio to 1926.* New York: American Historical Society, 1938.

"ASCAP Defied." *Business Week* (16 November 1940).

Bangs, Lester. "The White Noise Supremacists." *Village Voice* (30 April 1979).

Barclay, Michael, Ian A. D. Jack, and Jason Schneider. *Have Not Been the Same: The CanRock Renaissance.* Toronto: ECW Press, 2001.

Barlow, William. "Cashing In." In *Split Image: African Americans in the Mass Media.* 2d ed., eds. Jannette L. Dates and William Barlow. Washington, D.C.: Howard University Press, 1993.

Barnouw, Erik. *The Golden Web: A History of Broadcasting in the United States, 1933–1953.* New York: Oxford University Press, 1968.

Belz, Carl. *The Story of Rock.* 2d ed. New York: Harper Colophon, 1971.

Bennett, Tony, Simon Firth, Lawrence Grossberg, John Shepard, and Graeme Turner, eds. *Rock and Popular Music: Politics, Policies, Institutions.* New York: Routledge, 1993.

Berry, Robert J. "Satanism: The Law Enforcement Response." *The National Sheriff* (February–March, 1987).

Biafra, Jello. "The Far Right and the Censorship of Music." *Harvard Law Record* (17 April 1987).

Binelli, Mark. "The Accidental Superstar." *Rolling Stone* (18 March 2004).

"The Birth of Our Popular Songs." *Literary Digest* (7 October 1916).

Bloomberg News. "FTC Slams Record Labels on CD Sales Practice" (May 10, 2000). http://yahoo.cnet.com/news/0-1005-200-1851819.html?pt.yfin.cat_fin.txt.ne

Bondi, Vic. "Feeding Noise Back into the System: Hardcore, Hip Hop, and Heavy Metal." Paper presented at the New England American Studies Association Conference, Brandeis University, Boston, Mass. (1 May 1993).

Borland, John. "Judge: File-Swapping Tools are Legal." CNET News.com (25 April 2003). http://news.com.com/2100-1027-998363.html?tag=nl.

———. "Napster Lawyer Turns Antitrust Experience on RIAA." CNET News.com (July 20, 2000). http://news.cnet.com/news/0-1005-200-2295301.html.

———. "Tech Giants Slam Napster Injunction." CNET News.com (25 August 2000). http://news.cnet.com/news/0-1005-200-2612001.html.

———. "U.S. Sides with RIAA against Napster." CNET News.com (8 September 2000). http://news.cnet.com/news/0-1005-200-2731198.html.

Bowman, Rob. *Capitol Records-EMI of Canada: Portrait of a Company on the Rise.* Toronto: EMI Publishing, 1989.

Bozza, Anthony. "NSynchronicity." *Rolling Stone* (30 March 2000).

Brack, Ray. "James Brown." *Rolling Stone* (21 January 1970).

Brackett, David. "The Politics and Practice of 'Crossover' in American Popular Music, 1963 to 1965." *The Musical Quarterly* (Winter, 1994).

Bray, Hiawatha. "Hackers Go One Up." *Boston Globe* (26 October 2000).

Breskin, David. "Bob Geldof: The Rolling Stone Interview." *Rolling Stone* (5 December 1985).

Bricker, Rebecca. "Take One." *People* (4 April 1983).

Broven, John. *Rhythm and Blues in New Orleans.* Gretna, La.: Pelican Publishing Co., 1988.

Brown, Janelle. "Crack SDMI? No Thanks!" Salon.com (14 September 2000). www.salon.com/tech/log/2000/09/14/hack_sdmi/index.html.

Browne, David. "Turn That @#!% Down: The Complete Idiot's Guide to the Future of Rock & Roll." *Entertainment Weekly* (21 August 1992).

Bry, David. "The Song of the South." *Vibe* (June 2002).

Caramanica, Jon. "Grow Dem Bow." *Village Voice* (12 January 2006). http://www.villagevoice.com/music/0603,caramanica,71722,22.html.

Carr, Tim. "Talk That Talk, Walk That Walk." *Rolling Stone* (26 May 1983).

Carter, Bill. "How a Hit Almost Failed Its Own Audition." *New York Times* (30 April 06).

"To Censor Popular Songs." *Literary Digest* (24 May 1913).

Chambers, Iain. *Urban Rhythms: Popular Music and Popular Culture.* New York: Macmillan, 1985.

Chang, Jeff. "Is Protest Music Dead?" AlterNet.org (16 April 2002). www.alternet.org/story.html?StoryID=12880.

Chapple, Steve, and Reebee Garofalo. *Rock 'n' Roll Is Here to Pay: The History and Politics of the Music Industry.* Chicago: Nelson-Hall, 1977.

Christgau, Georgia. "Disco! Disco! Disco! Four Critics Address the Musical Question." *In These Times* (6–12 June 1979).

Christgau, Robert. *Any Old Way You Choose It: Rock and Other Pop Music, 1967–1973.* Baltimore, Md.: Penguin Books, 1973.

———. "A Cult Explodes—and a Movement Is Born." *Village Voice* (24 October 1977).

Clarke, Donald, ed. *The Penguin Encyclopedia of Popular Music.* New York: Viking, 1989.

Cobo, Leila. "Radio Flips for Reggaeton." *Billboard* (10 September 2005).

———. "Reggaeton Broke Out but Regional Mexican Acts Drove Latin Biz." *Billboard,* Special Section (24 December 2005).

———. "Reggaeton Rules." *Billboard* (30 July 2005).

Cohen, Kenneth, Tom Brown, Jim Gibson, Paul Hofer, Vanessa Locke, Sharon Long, Cynthia Matthews, and Courtney Semisch. "No Electronic Theft Act: Policy Development Team Report." Washington, D.C.: United States Sentencing Commission (February 1999).

Cohen, Rich. "Southern Comfort." *Rolling Stone* (10 August 1995).

Coleman, Mark. "The Revival of Conscience." *Rolling Stone* (15 November 1990).

Collin, Matthew. *Altered States: The Story of Ecstasy Culture and Acid House.* New York: Serpent's Tail, 1997.

Considine, J. D. "Led Zeppelin." *Rolling Stone* (20 September 1990).

———. "Metal Mania." *Rolling Stone* (15 November 1990).

Cotts, Cynthia. "Telecom for Dummies." *Village Voice* (5–11 September 2001). Cited by MediaChannel.org. URL: www.mediachannel.org/news/indepth/fcc.

Cripps, Thomas. "Film." In *Split Image: African Americans in the Mass Media.* 2d ed., eds. Jannette L. Dates and William Barlow. Washington, D.C.: Howard University Press, 1993.

Cross, Brian. *It's Not About a Salary: Rap, Race and Resistance in Los Angeles.* New York: Verso, 1993.

Cummings, Sue. "Road Warriors." *Spin* (August 1986).

Daly, Steven. "Britney Spears: Inside the Heart and Mind (and Bedroom) of America's New Teen Queen." *Rolling Stone* (15 April 1999).

Dates, Jannette L., and William Barlow, eds. *Split Image: African Americans in the Mass Media.* 2d ed. Washington, D.C.: Howard University Press, 1993.

Dawson, Jim, and Steve Propes. *What Was the First Rock 'n' Roll Record?* Boston: Faber and Faber, 1992.

DeCurtis, Anthony. "The Eagles." *Rolling Stone (*20 September 1990).

———. "Kurt Cobain, 1967–1994." *Rolling Stone* (2 June 1994).

———. "Ropin' the Whirl Wind." *Rolling Stone* (1 April 1993).

———. "The Year in Music." *Rolling Stone* (10–24 December 1992).

DeCurtis, Anthony, and James Henke, eds. *The Rolling Stone Illustrated History of Rock & Roll.* New York: Random House, 1992.

de Forest, Lee. *Father of Radio.* Chicago: Wilcox and Follett, 1950.

Denisoff, R. Serge, and Richard A. Peterson, eds. *The Sounds of Social Change: Studies in Popular Culture.* New York: Rand McNally, 1972.

Denselow, Robin. *When the Music's Over: The Story of Political Pop.* Boston: Faber and Faber, 1989.

Dexter, D. "1935–1945, Disk Jockey: Origin of the Species." *Billboard* (27 December 1969).

Draper, Robert. *Rolling Stone Magazine.* New York: Harper and Row, 1990.

Eisen, Jonathan, ed. *The Age of Rock.* New York: Vintage Books, 1969.

Eliscu, Jenny. "Chicks Triumph." *Rolling Stone* (29 May 2003).

Ennis, Philip. *The Seventh Stream: The Emergence of Rock 'n' Roll in American Popular Music.* Hanover, N.H.: Wesleyan University Press/University Press of New England, 1992.

Erlewine, Michael, et al., eds. *All Music Guide to Rock.* San Francisco: Miller Freeman Books, 1997.

Farrar, Richard. "Da Doo Ron Ron." *Rolling Stone* (11 May 1968).

Farrell, Allen. *The CHUM Story: From the Charts to Your Hearts.* Toronto: Stoddart Publishing Co., 2001.

Feld, Steven. "Notes on World Beat." *Public Culture Bulletin* (Fall, 1988).

Felder, Rachel. *Manic Pop Thrill.* Hopewell, N.J.: Echo Press, 1993.

Fikentscher, Kai. *You Better Work: Underground Dance Music in New York City.* Hanover, N.H.: University Press of New England, 2000.

Fisher, William. "Theories of Intellectual Property." Draft of 11 April 2000. www.law.harvard.edu/Academic_Affairs/coursepages/tfisher/iptheory.html#_ftnref10.

Flick, Larry. "Declining Sales in 2002 Trigger Desire for Less Hype, Better Records, Fresh Blood." *Billboard* (28 December 2002).

Flores, Juan. *From Bomba to Hip Hop: Puerto Rican Culture and Latino Identity.* New York: Columbia University Press, 2000.

Fong-Torres, Ben, ed. *The Rolling Stone Interviews.* 2 vols. New York: Warner Books, 1973.

———. "The Rolling Stone Interview: Ray Charles." *Rolling Stone* (18 January 1973).

Forman, Murray. "'Represent': Race, Space and Place in Rap Music." *Popular Music* (January 2000).

———. "Soundtrack to a Crisis: Music, Context, Discourse." *Television and New Media* (May 2002).

Fox, Ted. *In the Groove.* New York: St. Martin's Press, 1986.

———. *Showtime at the Apollo.* New York: Holt, Rinehart and Winston, 1983.

Fricke, David. "Imagine." *Rolling Stone* (27 December 2001–3 January 2002).

———. "Kurt Cobain." *Rolling Stone* (27 January 1994).

———. "Red Hot Chili Peppers' Naked Truth." *Rolling Stone* (25 June 1992).

Frith, Simon. "Beyond the Dole Queue: The Politics of Punk." *Village Voice* (24 October 1977).

———. "Crappy Birthday to Punk." *In These Times* (23–29 April 1986).

———, ed. *Facing the Music.* New York: Pantheon Books, 1988.

———. *Sound Effects: Youth, Leisure and the Politics of Rock 'n' Roll.* New York: Pantheon Books, 1981.

Frith, Simon, and Andrew Goodwin, eds. *On Record: Rock, Pop, and the Written Word.* New York Pantheon Books, 1990.

Frith, Simon, and Howard Horne. *Art into Pop.* New York: Methuen, 1987.

Frith, Simon, and John Street. "Party Music." *Marxism Today* (June 1986).

Gaar, Gillian G. *She's a Rebel: The History of Women in Rock & Roll.* Seattle, Wash.: Seal Press, 1992.

Gain, Bruce. "RIAA Takes Shotgun to Traders." *Wired News* (4 October 2005). www.wired.com/news/digiwood/0,1412,68951,00.html.

Gaines, Donna. "Suicidal Tendencies: Kurt Did Not Die for You." *Rolling Stone* (2 June 1994).

Garofalo, Reebee. "Crossing Over, 1939–1992." In *Split Image: African Americans in the Mass Media,* 2d ed, eds. Jannette L. Dates and William Barlow. Washington, D.C.: Howard University Press, 1993.

———. "The Impact of the Civil Rights Movement on Popular Music." *Radical America* (March 1989).

———. "Nelson Mandela, the Concert: Mass Culture as a Contested Terrain." *In Re-Imaging America: The Arts of Social Change,* eds. Mark O'Brien and Craig Little. Philadelphia: New Society Publishers, 1990.

———, ed. *Rockin' the Boat: Mass Music and Mass Movements.* Boston: South End Press, 1992.

———. "Setting the Record Straight: Censorship and Social Responsibility in Popular Music." *Journal of Popular Music Studies.* Vol. 6 (1994).

———. "Understanding Mega-Events: If We Are the World, Then How Do We Change It?" In *Technoculture,* eds. Constance Penley and Andrew Ross. Minneapolis: University of Minnesota Press, 1991.

Garrity, Brian. "Anticipated Boom Was a Bust." *Billboard* (24 December 2005).

———. "Grokster Blasts RIAA Anti-Piracy Tactics." Bill-Board.com (27 June 2003). Posted on FreeRepublic. com. http://209.157.64.200/focus/f-news/936821/posts.

———. "Music Biz Gets a Makeover." *Billboard* (25 December 2004).

George, Nelson. *Buppies, B-Boys, Baps and Bohos: Notes on Post-Soul Black Culture,* New York: HarperCollins, 1992.

———. *The Death of Rhythm & Blues.* New York: Pantheon Books, 1988.

Gett, Steve. "Rock '86." *Billboard,* 27 December 1986.

Gillen, Marilyn. "The Year in Business: Ups, Downs, and Rebounds." *Billboard* (27 December 1999).

Gillett, Charlie. *The Sound of the City: The Rise of Rock and Roll.* New York: Outerbridge and Dienstfrey, 1970.

Gilmore, Mikal. "Disco." *Rolling Stone* (19 April 1979).

———. "The Year in Music." *Rolling Stone* (13–27 December 1990).

Gitlin, Todd, *The Sixties: Years of Hope, Days of Rage.* New York: Bantam Books, 1993.

Gleason, Ralph. "Perspectives: Changing with the Money Changers." *Rolling Stone* (20 January 1968).

———. "Stop This Shuck Mike Bloomfield." *Rolling Stone* (11 May 1968).

Goddard, Peter, and Philip Kamin, eds. *Shakin' All Over: The Rock'n'Roll Years in Canada.* Toronto: McGraw-Hill Ryerson Ltd., 1989.

Goldberg, Michael. "Bill Graham: The Rolling Stone Interview." *Rolling Stone* (19 December 1985).

———. "The Spending Begins." *Rolling Stone* (24 October 1985).

Goodman, Fred. "Big Deals: How Money Fever Is Changing the Music Business." *Musician* (January 1992).

———. "Will Rock Trounce Teen Pop." *Rolling Stone* (28 February 2002).

Goodwin, Andrew. *Dancing in the Distraction Factory: Music Television and Popular Culture.* Minneapolis: University of Minnesota Press, 1992.

Graham, Renée. "Is Some Hatred More Acceptable Than Others?" *Boston Globe* (5 January 2001).

Graustark, Barbara. "Disco Takes Over." *Newsweek* (2 April 1979).

Gray, Herman. "Popular Music as a Social Problem: A Social History of Claims Against Popular Music." In *Images of Issues,* ed. Joel Best. Hawthorne, N.Y.: De Gruyter, 1989.

———. "Rate the Records: Symbolic Conflict, Popular Music, and Social Problems." *Popular Music and Society* (Fall, 1989).

Green, Tony. "The Dirty South." In *The VIBE History of Hip Hop,* ed. Alan Light. New York: Three Rivers Press, 1999.

Grein, Paul. "AOR Programmers Plan More Variety." *Billboard* (14 January 1984).

———. "Charts '86." *Billboard* (27 December 1986).

———. "'83 RIAA Tally: Fewer Biggies." *Billboard* (14 January 1984).

———. "The Year in Charts." *Billboard* (26 December 1987).

———. "Unemployment Lines: LA Industrial Personnel Face Major Challenges to Rebuild Their Careers." *Billboard* (19 May 1979).

Grossberg, Lawrence. "The Framing of Rock: Rock and the New Conservatism." In *Rock and Popular Music: Politics, Policies, Institutions,* eds. Tony Bennett et al. New York: Routledge, 1993.

———. *We Gotta Get Out of This Place: Popular Conservatism and Postmodern Culture.* New York: Routledge, 1992.

Grossman, Jay. "Let There Be Dancing in the Streets." *Rolling Stone* (23 May 1974).

Gundersen, Edna. "For Springsteen, 'Seeger Sessions' Sends a Message." *USA Today* (7 June 2006).

Guralnick, Peter. *Feel Like Going Home: Portraits in Blues and Rock 'n' Roll.* New York: E. P. Dutton, 1971.

———. *The Listener's Guide to the Blues.* New York: Facts on File, 1982.

———. *Sweet Soul Music: Rhythm and Blues and the Southern Dream of Freedom.* New York: Harper and Row, 1986.

Gurza, Agustin. "The Reggaeton Craze Saw a Quick Burnout

with Fans and Radio." *Los Angeles Times* (19 April 2006). www.chicagotribune.com/features/lifestyle/chi-0604190022apr19,1,3467652.story?coll=chi-leisuretempo-hed&ctrack=1&cset=true.

Guzman, Pablo. "On the Radio, Part Two." *Rock & Roll Confidential* (January 1984).

Hager, Steven. *Hip Hop: The Illustrated History of Break Dancing, Rap Music, and Graffiti.* New York: St. Martin's Press, 1984.

Hall, Ron. *The CHUM Chart Book: 1957–1983.* Toronto: Stardust Productions, 1984.

Hamill, Pete. "A Day to Remember." *Rolling Stone* (29 August 1985).

Hamm, Charles. *Yesterdays: Popular Song in America.* New York: W. W. Norton, 1983.

Hammond, John. *On Record.* New York: Penguin Books, 1981.

Harmon, Amy. "Music Industry in Global Fight on Web Copies." *New York Times* (7 October 2002). www.nytimes.com/2002/10/07/technology/07SWAP.html?ex=1035021589&ei=1&en=8f37d36c94fe6e8e.

Harris, Ron. "Metallica to Napster: Cut Users." *Boston Globe,* (4 May 2000).

Heath, Chris. "Creed's Stairway to Heaven." *Rolling Stone* (28 February 2002).

———. "The Epic Life of Carlos Santana." *Rolling Stone* (16 March 2000).

———. "Has Anyone Seen Christina." *Rolling Stone* (14 November 2001).

Heilbut, Tony. *The Gospel Sound: Good News and Bad Times.* New York: Simon and Schuster, 1971.

Heilemann, John. "David Boies: The Wired Interview." *Wired* (October 2000). www.wired.com/wired/archive/8.10/boies_pr.html.

Heins, Marjorie. *Sex, Sin, and Blasphemy: A Guide to America's Censorship Wars.* New York: The New Press, 1993.

Henderson, Alex. "Active Indies." *Billboard* (24 December 1988).

Henke, James. "Record Companies Dancing to a Billion Dollar Tune." *Rolling Stone* (19 April 1979).

Hersey, Gerri. *Nowhere to Run: The Story of Soul Music.* New York: Penguin Books, 1984.

Heylin, Clinton. *From the Velvets to the Voidoids: A Pre-Punk History for a Post-Punk World.* New York: Penguin Books, 1993.

Hilburn, Robert. "Musical Lessons from 1983's First Half." *Cape Cod Times* (16 July 1983).

Hill, Trent. "The Enemy Within: Censorship in Rock Music in the 1950s." *South Atlantic Quarterly* (Fall, 1991).

"The Hip-Hop 50." *Rolling Stone* (29 October 1998).

Holden, Stephen. "The Evolution of a Dance Craze." *Rolling Stone* (19 April 1979).

———. "Musical Odyssey." *New York Times* (9 December 1987).

———. "Pop Records Turn to Hip Hop." *New York Times* (23 September 1984).

Holland, Bill. "Senate Hearing Examines Gangsta Lyrics." *Billboard* (5 March 1994).

Holloway, Joseph E., ed. *Africanisms in American Culture.* Bloomington: Indiana University Press, 1990.

Hu, Jim. "Web, Music Giants March to Different Tunes." CNET News.com (13 July 2001). news.cnet.com/news/0-1005-200-6561339.html?tag=dd.ne.dtx.nl-sty.0.

Huffstutter, P. J. "Music Makers at Wits' End in Battle with Internet Takers." *Los Angeles Times* (29 May 2000).

Hung, Michèle, and Esteban Garcia Morencos. *World Record Sales 1969–1990: A Statistical History of the World Recording Industry.* London: International Federation of the Phonogram Industry, 1990.

"I Heard the News Today . . ." *Rolling Stone* (25 October 2001).

Jacobs, Norman, ed. *Culture for the Millions? Mass Media in Modern Society.* Princeton, N.J.: D. Van Nostrand, 1959.

Jennings, Nicholas. *Before the Gold Rush: Flashbacks to the Dawn of the Canadian Sound.* Toronto: Viking, 1997.

Jones, Hettie. *Big Star, Fallin' Mama.* New York: Viking Press, 1974.

Jones, Kristin V. "Rocking the Hip Hop Vote." *The Nation* (1 December 2003).

Jones, Leroi [Amiri Baraka]. *Blues People.* New York: William Morrow, 1963.

Jones, Steve. "Ban(ned) in the USA: Popular Music and Censorship." *Journal of Communication Inquiry* (Winter, 1991).

Jones, Tim. "Media Giant's Rally Sponsorship Raises Questions." *Chicago Tribune* (19 March 2003). www.chicagotribune.com/news/showcase/chi-0303190157mar19.story

Jones, Vanessa E. "Whose Word Is It Anyway?" *Boston Globe* (7 July 1999).

Kafka, Peter. "The Queen of Teen." *Forbes* (20 March 2000).

Kahn, Joseph P. "Musical Chairs Coming Up for the White House." *Boston Globe* (20 January 2001).

Kaplan, E. Ann. *Rocking Around the Clock: Music Television, Postmodernism, and Consumer Culture.* New York: Routledge, 1987.

Kennedy, Ted. *Top 40 Canadian Chart Mistakes.* Toronto: self-published, no date.

Kleinfeld, N. R. "FM's Success Is Loud and Clear." *New York Times* (26 October 1979).

Konrad, Rachel. "Napster Among Fastest-Growing Net Technologies." CNET News.com (5 October 2000). http://news.cnet.com/news/0-1005-200-2938703.html.

Kopkind, Andrew. "The Dialectic of Disco." *Village Voice* (12 February 1979).

Koskoff, Ellen. *The Garland Encyclopedia of World Music: The United States and Canada.* New York: Garland Publishing, Inc., 2001.

Kot, Greg. "What's Wrong with Radio." *Rolling Stone* (16 August 2001).

Krugman, Paul. "Channels of Influence," *New York Times* (25 March 2003). www.nytimes.com/2003/03/25/opinion/25KRUG.html?ex=1052452800&en=30da303a6b8fd49e&ei=5070.

Lamb, Bill. "How To Read the Billboard Charts." *About.Com* (retrieved on 26 August 2006). URL: http://top40.about.com/od/popmusic101/a/billboardcharts.htm

LaMonica, Paul R. "No False 'Idol' for Fox." *CNN Money.com* (24 May 2006). http://money.cnn.com/2006/05/22/news/companies/idol_fox/index.htm.

Landau, Jon. "The Motown Story." *Rolling Stone* (13 May 1971).

———. "Soul." *Rolling Stone* (24 February 1968).

Latonero, Mark. "Survey of MP3 Usage: Report on a University Consumption Community." The Norman Lear Center, Annenberg School for Communication, University of Southern California (June 2000).

Lax, Roger, and Frederick Smith. *The Great Song Thesaurus.* New York: Oxford University Press, 1989.

Lederman, Minna. "Music and Monopoly." *The Nation* (28 December 1940).

Levinson, Nan. "Shut Up." *Boston Globe* (20 February 1994).

Levy, Steven. "Ad Nauseam: How MTV Sells Out Rock & Roll." *Rolling Stone* (8 December 1983).

Lewis, L. *Gender Politics and MTV: Voicing the Difference.* Philadelphia: Temple University Press, 1990.

Light, Alan. "Ice." *Rolling Stone* (20 August 1992).

Lipsitz, George. *Class and Culture in Cold War America: "A Rainbow at Midnight."* South Hadley, Mass.: J. F. Bergin, 1982.

———. *Time Passages: Collective Memory and American Popular Culture.* Minneapolis: University of Minnesota Press, 1990.

Lombardi, John. "Kenny Gamble and Leon Huff and the Resurrection of Jerry Butler and Philly Soul." *Rolling Stone* (30 April 1970).

Lont, Cynthia M. "Women's Music: No Longer a Small Private Party." In *Rockin' the Boat: Mass Music and Mass Movements,* ed. Reebee Garofalo. Boston: South End Press, 1992.

Lydon, Michael, ed. *The Age of Rock 2: Sights and Sounds of the American Cultural Revolution.* New York: Vintage Books, 1970.

———. "The High Cost of Music and Love: Where's the Money from Monterey?" *Rolling Stone* (9 November 1967).

———. *Rock Folk: Portraits from the Rock 'n' Roll Pantheon.* New York: Dell, 1968.

———. "Smokey Robinson." *Rolling Stone* (28 September 1968).

Lyman, Rick. "New Data Shows Immigrants' Growth and Reach." *New York Times* (August 15, 2006).

Malone, Bill C. *Country Music U.S.A.* Rev. ed. Austin: University of Texas Press, 1985.

Marcus, Greil. "Is This the Woman Who Invented Rock & Roll? The Deborah Chessler Story." *Rolling Stone* (24 June 1993).

———. *Mystery Train: Images of America in Rock 'n' Roll.* New York: Dutton, 1975.

———. "Rock for Ethiopia." Panel presentation at the Third International Conference on Popular Music Studies, Montreal, Quebec, Canada (July 1985).

Marsh, Dave. "The Flip Sides of 1979." *Rolling Stone* (27 December 1979).

———. "What's Being Sold in Country?" *New York Times* (24 May 1992).

Marshall, Wayne. "The Rise of Reggaeton." *Boston Phoenix* (19 January 2006). www.thephoenix.com/article_ektid1595.aspx.

Martin, Linda, and Kerry Segrave. *Anti-Rock: The Opposition to Rock 'n' Roll.* New York: DeCapo Press, 1993.

Maultsby, Portia K. "Africanisms in African-American Popular Music." In *Africanisms in American Culture,* ed. Joseph E. Holloway. Bloomington: Indiana University Press, 1990.

McClary, Susan. *Feminine Endings: Music, Gender, and Sexuality.* Minneapolis: University of Minnesota Press, 1991.

McClary, Susan, and Robert Walser. "Start Making Sense: Musicology Wrestles with Rock." In *On Record: Rock, Pop, and the Written Word,* eds. Simon Frith and Andrew Goodwin. New York: Pantheon Books, 1990.

McGuinn, Roger (Statement of). Senate Judiciary Committee Hearing on "The Future of Digital Music: Is There an Upside to Downloading?" (11 July 2000). www.senate.gov/~judiciary/7112000_rm.htm.

McLeese, Don. "Anatomy of an Anti-Disco Riot." *In These Times* (29 August–4 September 1979).

McLeod, Kembrew. "Genres, Sub-Genres, Sub-Sub-Genres and More: Musical and Social Differentiation Within Electronic-Dance Music Communities." *Journal of Popular Music Studies* (Spring 2001).

Melhuish, Martin. *Oh What a Feeling: A Vital History of Canadian Music.* Kingston: Quarry Press, 1996.

Merritt, Jay. "Disco Station Number One in New York." *Rolling Stone* (22 March 1979).

Metzger, John. "Neil Young Are You Passionate?" *The Music Box* (May 2002), Vol. 9, No. 5. www.musicbox-online.com/ny-pass.html.

Miller, Jim. "It's Not Only Rock 'n' Roll." *Boston Globe* (23 August 1991).

———, ed. *The Rolling Stone Illustrated History of Rock 'n' Roll.* New York: Rolling Stone Press, 1976.

———. "State of the Art." *Newsweek* (18 April 1983).

Mills, David. "Rap as Politics: The Sayings of Sister Souljah." *Essence* (September 1992).

Minton, Lynn. "Is Heavy Metal Dangerous?" *Parade* (20 September 1992).

Mooney, H. F. "Popular Music Since the 1920s: The Significance of Shifting Taste." In *The Age of Rock,* ed. Jonathan Eisen. New York: Vintage Books, 1969.

Moore, Jerrold Northrop. *A Matter of Records: Fred Gaisberg and the Golden Era of the Gramophone.* New York: Taplinger Publishing Co., 1976.

Morse, Dave. *Motown.* London: Vista, 1971.

Morse, Steve. "Can American Bands Beat the British Blitz?" *Boston Globe* (1 January 1984).

———. "In Pop, Women Took New Ground All Over." *Boston Globe* (29 December 1996).

———. "Napster Strikes Dissonant Chords." *Boston Globe* (5 May 2000).

Nathan, David. "Rap." *Billboard* (24 December 1988).

Neely, Kim. "Into the Unknown." *Rolling Stone* (16 June 1994).

Negus, Keith. *Music Genres and Corporate Cultures.* New York: Routledge, 1999.

Nelson, Havelock. "Music and Violence: Does Crime Pay?" *Billboard* (13 November 1993).

"N.J. Rock Station Won't Play Jethro Tull," *Associated Press* (13 November 2003). http://apnews.excite.com/article/20031113/D7UPO1981.html.

"New Black Hope." *Billboard* (17 May 1969).

Newman, Melinda. "The Good, Bad, and Mostly Ugly of 2002 Remembered." *Billboard* (28 December 2002).

"New P2P File Sharing Stats." *p2pnet.net News* (22 October 2004). URL: http://p2pnet.net/story/2797.

Nunziata, Susan. "'90 Label Tally: Units Up 7.3%, $ Jump 14.6%." *Billboard* (6 April 1991).

Odum, Howard W., and Guy B. Johnson. *Negro Workaday Songs.* Chapel Hill: University of North Carolina Press, 1926.

"Of Hard-Rock Demons: A Cardinal Speaks Out." *Boston Globe* (6 March 1990).

Ogunnaike, Lola. "Caught in the Act." *Vibe* (May 2002).

O'Neil, Thomas. *The Grammys for the Record.* New York: Penguin Books, 1993.

Orloff, Katherine. *Rock 'n' Roll Woman.* Los Angeles: Nash Publishing, 1974.

Orr, Charlene, et al. "Texas Police Pursue 'Cop Killer.'" *Billboard* (27 June 1992).

Ostling, Richard N. "No Sympathy for the Devil." *Time* (19 March 1990).

Pacini Hernandez, Deborah. "Dominicans in the Mix: Reflections on Dominicans and Reggaeton." In Raquel Z. Rivera, Deborah Pacini Hernandez, and Wayne Marshall, eds., *Reading Reggaeton: Historical, Aesthetic and Critical Perspectives* (Raleigh, NC: Duke University Press, in press).

———. "Race, Ethnicity and the Production of Latin/o Popular Music." In *Global Repertoires: Popular Music Within and Beyond the Transnational Music Industry,* ed. Andreas Gabesmair and Alfred Smudits. Burlington, VT: Ashgate Publishing Ltd., 2001.

Palmer, Robert. "The Church of the Sonic Guitar." *South Atlantic Quarterly* 90, no. 4 (Fall, 1991).

———. *Deep Blues.* New York: Viking Press, 1981.

———. "The Fifties." *Rolling Stone* (19 April 1990).

———. "New Rock from the Suburbs." *New York Times* (23 September 1984).

Pareles, Jon. "Howls of Rage, Nine Hours Worth, at Waterloo Village." *New York Times* (13 August 1991).

———. "Music; So Sweet, So Sensitive, So Self-Absorbed, So 70's." *New York Times* (18 May 2003). http://query.nytimes.com/search/restricted/article?res=F10A14F63A5B0C7B8DDDAC0894DB404482.

———. "There's a New Sound in Pop Music: Bigotry." *New York Times* (10 September 1989).

Passman, Arnold. *The Deejays.* New York: Macmillan, 1971.

Patterson, L. Ray, and Stanley W. Lindberg. *The Nature of Copyright: A Law of User's Rights.* Athens, GA: University of Georgia Press, 1991.

Peck, Abe. "Disco! Disco! Disco! Four Critics Address the Musical Question." *In These Times* (6–12 June 1979).

Pegley, Kip. *Coming to You Wherever You Are: MuchMusic, MTV, and Youth Identities.* Middleton, CT: Wesleyan University Press, 2008.

Peraino, Vito. "The Law of Increasing Returns." *Wired* (August 1999).

Perry, Steve. "Ain't No Mountain High Enough: The Politics of Crossover." In *Facing the Music,* ed. Simon Frith. New York: Pantheon Books, 1988.

Peterbaugh, Parke. "Anglomania: America Surrenders to the Brits—But Who Really Wins?" *Rolling Stone* (10 November 1983).

Peterson, Richard A. "Why 1955? Explaining the Advent of Rock Music." *Popular Music* (January 1990).

Peterson, Richard A., and David C. Berger. "Cycles in Symbol Production: The Case of Popular Music." *American Sociological Review* (April 1975).

Pietroluongo, Silvio Minal Patel, and Wade Jessen, "Singles Minded: Hot 100 Adds Digital Sales; Pop 100 Debuts." *Billboard* (12 February 2005).

"Playboy Poll: Napster Users Buy CD's." *MP3 Newswire* (17 August 2000). www.mp3newswire.net/stories/2000/playboy.html

Pond, Steve. "The Seventies." *Rolling Stone* (20 September 1990).

———. "The Trick Is to Be Loved but Not Embraced." *New York Times* (26 June 1994).

Potier, Beth. "File Sharing May Boost CD Sales: Study Defies Traditional Beliefs About Internet Use." *Harvard Gazette Archives* (15 April 2004). www.news.harvard.edu/gazette/2004/04.15/09-filesharing.html

"President Bush invites Idol contestants to White House." *CBC Arts* (21 July 2006). www.cbc.ca/story/arts/national/2006/07/21/americanidol-bush.html?ref=rss.

Pruter, Robert. *Chicago Soul.* Urbana: University of Illinois Press, 1992.

Ptacek, Greg. "Majors Return to Nuts and Bolts of Pre-MTV Metal Marketing Days." *Billboard* (27 April 1985).

"Readers Poll." *Rolling Stone* (20 January 2000).

Reagon, Bernice Johnson. "Songs That Moved the Movement." *Civil Rights Quarterly* (Summer, 1983).

"Record Business Sees Light Ahead—On Video Screen." *Chicago Tribune* (26 April 1983).

Recording Industry Association of America. *Inside the Recording Industry: A Statistical Overview, Update '86.* New York: Recording Industry Association of America, 1986.

Reuters. "BMG Says It Discussed Business Models with Napster." CNET News.com (3 October 2000). http://news.cnet.com/news/0-1005-200-2927330.html.

———. "Music Industry Still in First Gear Online." (7 January 2002). http://news.com.com/2100-1023-802359.html.

———. "Prince Voices Support for Napster." CNET News.com (9 August 2000). http://news.cnet.com/news/0-1005-200-2482624.html.

Reynolds, Simon. *Generation Ecstasy: Into the World of Techno and Rave Culture.* New York: Routledge, 1999.

RIAA Press Release. "Compact Disc Shipments at All-Time High," Washington, D.C. (25 August 2000). http://www.RIAA.com/PR_Story.cfm?id=312.

RIAA v. The People: Two Years Later. Electronic Frontier Foundation, 2005. URL: http://www.eff.org.

Rietveld, Hillegonda C. *This Is Our House: House Music, Cultural Spaces and Technologies.* Brookfield, VT: Ashgate, 1998.

Rijven, Stan. "Rock for Ethiopia." Panel presentation at the Third International Conference on Popular Music Studies, Montreal, Quebec, Canada (July 1985).

Roberts, John Storm. *The Latin Tinge: The Impact of Latin American Music on the United States.* Tivoli, N.Y.: Original Music, 1985.

Rock & Roll Confidential, the editors of *You've Got a Right to Rock.* Los Angeles: Duke and Duchess Ventures, Inc., 1990.

Rockwell, John. "Atwater's Other Hat: Stealing an Inaugural Show." *New York Times* (23 January 1989).

———. "Leftist Causes? Rock Seconds Those Emotions." *New York Times* (11 December 1988).

Rose, Tricia. *Black Noise: Rap Music and Black Culture in Contemporary America.* Hanover, N.H.: University Press of New England, 1994.

Ross, Gord. Unpublished chapter of Ph.D. dissertation. York University, 2007.

"Roxio Buys Pressplay, to Relaunch Napster," Salon.Com (19 May 2003). www.salon.com/tech/wire/2003/05/19/roxio_pressplay/index.html.

Roxon, Lillian. *Lillian Roxon's Rock Encyclopedia.* New York: Grosset and Dunlap, 1971.

Sanjek, David. "Can a Fujiyama Mama Be the Female Elvis? The Wild Wild Women of Rockabilly." In *Sexing the Groove,* ed. Sheila Whitely. New York: Routledge, 1996.

Sanjek, Russell. *American Popular Music and Its Business.* 3 vols. New York: Oxford University Press, 1988.

———. "The War on Rock." In *Downbeat Music '72 Yearbook.* Chicago: Maher Publications, 1972.

Saunders, Michael. "Getting Hip to Pop." *Boston Globe* (9 May 1993).

Savage, Jon. *England's Dreaming: Anarchy, Sex Pistols, Punk Rock, and Beyond.* New York: St. Martin's Press, 1992.

Scaduto, Anthony. *Bob Dylan.* New York: Signet Books, 1973.

Scaggs, Austin. "Why Is Nelly Furtado's New Album So Loud?" *Rolling Stone* (19 June 2006). www.rollingstone.com/news/story/10603268/why_is_nelly_furtados_new_album_so_loud.

Schechter, Danny. "Why We Didn't See Wembley." *Africa Report* (July–August 1990).

Schicke, C. A. *Revolution in Sound: A Biography of the Recording Industry.* Boston: Little, Brown and Co., 1974.

Schipper, Henry. "Dick Clark." *Rolling Stone* (19 April 1990).

Schruers, Fred. "Master P." *Rolling Stone* (29 October 1998).

Schuller, Gunther. *Early Jazz: Its Roots and Musical Development.* New York: Oxford University Press, 1968.

Schumacher, Joseph. "Is Protest music as Dead as Disco?" *Peace and Conflict Monitor* (12 May 2003). www.monitor.upeace.org/innerpg.cfm?id_article=5.

Schwartz, John. "A Heretical View of File Sharing." *New York Times* (5 April 2004). www.nytimes.com/2004/04/05/technology/05music.html?ex=1083124800&en=585a8241cab4c298&ei=5070.

Seldes, Gilbert. *The Seven Lively Arts.* 1924. Reprint. New York: A. S. Barnes, 1957.

"Senator: Trash Illegal Downloaders' PCs." CNN.Com (18 June 2003). www.cnn.com/2003/TECH/internet/06/18/download.music.ap/index.html.

Shapiro, Nat. *Popular Music: An Annotated Index of American Popular Songs: 1940–1949.* Vol. 2. New York: Adrian Press, 1965.

Shaw, Arnold. *Black Popular Music in America.* New York: Schirmer Books, 1986.

———. *Honkers and Shouters: The Golden Years of Rhythm and Blues.* New York: Collier Books, 1978.

———. *The Rockin' '50s.* New York: Hawthorne Books, 1974.

Sheffield, Rob. "Rage Against the Latrines." *Rolling Stone* (2 September 1999).

Shore, Laurence Kenneth. "The Crossroads of Business and Music: A Study of the Music Industry in the United States and Internationally." Ph.D. diss., Stanford University, 1983.

Shore, Michael. *The Rolling Stone Book of Rock Video.* London: Sidgwick and Jackson, 1985.

Sicko, Dan. *Techno Rebels: The Renegades of Electronic Funk.* New York: Billboard Books, 1999.

Small, Christopher. *Music of the Common Tongue: Survival and Celebration in Afro-American Music.* New York: Riverrun Press, 1987.

Smith, Ethan. "Organization Moby." *Wired* (May 2002).

Smith, Joe. *Off the Record: An Oral History of Popular Music.* New York: Warner Books, 1988.

"The Sound of Lawsuits." Editorial, *Mercury News* (9 September 2003). www.bayarea.com/mld/mercurynews/news/opinion/6727444.htm.

Souter, Justice David. "MGM v. Grokster." Supreme Court of the United States, No. 04-480 (27 June 2005).

Southern, Eileen. *The Music of Black Americans: A History.* New York: W. W. Norton, 1971.

Staff and agencies. "Music Industry Counts the Cost of Online Piracy." *The Guardian,* 4 April 2006. http://arts.guardian.co.uk/netmusic/story/0,,1746741,00.html.

Stambler, Irwin. *Encyclopedia of Pop, Rock & Soul.* New York: St. Martin's Press, 1977.

Stark, Phyllis. "Gangsta Rap Under the Gun." *Billboard* (18 December 1993).

Staples, Brent. "The Trouble With Corporate Radio: The Day the Protest Music Died." *New York Times* (20 February 2003). www.nytimes.com/2003/02/20/opinion/20THU4.html?th=&pagewanted=print&position=bottom.

Steinfels, Peter. "Surge in Satanic Activity Alarms O'Connor." *New York Times* (6 March 1990).

Strauss, Neil. "File-Sharing Battle Leaves Musicians Caught in Middle." *New York Times* (14 September 2003). www.nytimes.com/2003/09/14/technology/14MUSI.html?th=&pagewanted=print&position=.

———. "For Record Industry, All Signs Are Gloomy." *New York Times* (4 December 1996).

———. "The Hit Girl: Christina Aguilera." *Rolling Stone (*6–20 July 2000).

Straw, Will. "Rock for Ethiopia." Panel presentation at the Third International Conference on Popular Music Studies, Montreal, Quebec (July 1985).

Stuart, Dan. "Black Radio." *Billboard* (17 June 1989).

Sullivan, Andy. "Music Firms, DJ Offer to Pay 12-Year-Old's Fine." *Reuters* (11 September 2003). www.reuters.com/newsArticle.jhtml;jsessionid=GJHB5ZIZY5BNACR-BAEKSFFA?type=topNews&storyID=3431108.

Sullivan, James. "Three's the Charm as the Last Lilith All-Women Music Festival Loses Its Sensitive Side." *San Francisco Chronicle,* 15 July 1999, reported on Geocities.com. www. geocities.com/SunsetStrip/Stage/8151/990713.html.

Sullivan, Jim. "Lollapalooza: The Sound of Success." *The Boston Globe* (2 August 1992).

The Toronto Star files.

Thigpen, David. "Up Against the Wall." *Rolling Stone* (24 February 1994).

Thornton, Sarah. *Club Cultures: Music, Media and Subcultural Capital.* Hanover, N.H.: University Press of New England, 1995.

Toop, David. *The Rap Attack 2: African Rap to Global Hip Hop.* London: Serpent's Tail, 1991.

Tosches, Nick. *Country: Living Legends and Dying Metaphors in America's Biggest Music.* New York: Charles Scribner's Sons, 1985.

Touré. "DMX Reigns as the Dark Prince of Hip Hop." *Rolling Stone* (13 April 2000).

———. "The Life of a Hunted Man." *Rolling Stone* (3 April 2003).

———. "The Next Queen of Soul." *Rolling Stone* (8 November 2001).

———. "Snoop Dogg's Gentle Hip Hop Growl." *New York Times* (21 November 1993).

———. "True Tales of the Pop Life: 'NSync." *Rolling Stone* (16 August 2001).

Townshend, Charles R. *San Antonio Rose: The Life and Music of Bob Wills.* Urbana: University of Illinois Press, 1976.

Tyrangiel, Josh "You Can't Ignore Kanye." *Time* (29 August 2005).

Udovitch, Mim. "Pink Fights the Power." *Rolling Stone* (4–11 July 2002).

———. "Shakira." *Rolling Stone* (31 October 2002).

U.S. Census Bureau. "Table 1.1 Population by Sex, Age, Hispanic Origin, and Race: 2004." www.census.gov/population/socdemo/hispanic/ASEC2004/2004CPS_tab1.1a.html.

Yorke, Ritchie. *Axes, Chops and Hot Licks: The Canadian Rock Music Scene.* Edmonton: M. G. Hurtig, 1971.

Waddell, Ray. "Touring Strong, but Some Numbers Cause Concern." *Billboard* (28 December 2002).

Walser, Robert. *Running with the Devil: Power, Gender, and Madness in Heavy Metal Music.* Hanover, N.H.: Wesleyan University Press, 1993.

Warhol, Andy, and Pat Hackett. *POPism: The Warhol '60s.* New York: Harcourt Brace Jovanovich, 1980.

Watrous, Peter. "Good Things Happen to Lollapalooza." *New York Times* (5 August 1992).

Watson, Margeaux, "The End of Outkast?" EW.Com (retrieved on 24 August 2006). www.ew.com/ew/report/0,6115,1195670_4_0_,00.html.

Weinstein, Deena. *Heavy Metal: A Cultural Sociology.* New York: Lexington Books, 1991.

Welch, Nathaniel. "Hit Man." *Rolling Stone* (22 August 2002).

Wenner, Jann. "A Letter from the Editor." *Rolling Stone* (9 November 1967).

———. "A Letter from the Editor: On the Occasion of Our Fourth Anniversary Issue." *Rolling Stone* (11 November 1971).

———. "Musicians Reject New Political Exploiters." *Rolling Stone* (11 May 1968).

"Wexler Attributes Greater R&B Volume to Black Buyer." *Billboard* (20 November 1971).

Wharton, Dennis. "D.C. Bluebloods Want X Rating for Porn Rock." *Variety* (22 May 1985).

Whitburn, Joel. *The Billboard Book of Top 40 Albums.* New York: Billboard, 1991.

———. *The Billboard Book of Top 40 Hits.* 7th ed. New York: Billboard, 2000.

Whitcomb, Ian. *After the Ball: Popular Music from Rag to Rock.* Baltimore, Md.: Penguin Books, 1974.

Wicke, Peter. *Rock Music: Culture, Aesthetics and Sociology.* Cambridge, Eng.: Cambridge University Press, 1990.

Widgery, David. *Beating Time: Riot 'n' Race 'n' Rock 'n' Roll.* London: Chatto and Windus, 1986.

Wilkinson, Francis. "More Washington Show Talk." *Rolling Stone* (9 December 1993).

Willis, Ellen. "Beginning to See the Light: Or Rock & Roll, Feminism, and Night Blindness." *Village Voice* (27 March 1978).

Wolfe, Tom. "The First Tycoon of Teen." In *The Kandy-Kolored Tangerine-Flake Streamline Baby.* New York: Farrar, Straus, and Giroux, 1965.

Work, John W. *American Negro Songs.* New York: 1960.

Yi, Matthew. "One Billion Songs Sold on iTunes." *San Francisco Chronicle* (24 February 2006). http://sfgate.com/cgi-bin/article.cgi?file=/chronicle/archive/2006/02/24/BUG9THDRI31.DTL

York, Peter. *Style Wars.* London: Sidgwick and Jackson, 1980.

Yorke, Ritchie. *Axes, Chops and Hot Licks: The Canadian Rock Music Scene.* Edmonton: M.G. Hurtig, 1971.

Young, Charles M. "Rock Is Sick and Living in London: A Report on the Sex Pistols." *Rolling Stone* (20 October 1977).

Zappa, Frank. "The Porn Wars." *Penthouse* (May 1989).

Zaslow, Jeffrey. "Music and Money." *Wall Street Journal* (21 May 1985).

Zeidler, Sue. "Music Industry Sends Warning to Song Swappers." *Yahoo News* (29 April 2003). http://sg.news.yahoo.com/030429/3/3akqc.html.

Zimmerman, K. "Priest Ruling Gives Unclear Message." *Variety* (3 September 1990).

Zook, Kristal Brent. "Reconstructions of Nationalist Thought in Black Music and Culture." In *Rockin' the Boat,* ed. Reebee Garofalo. Boston: South End Press, 1992.

Zwick, Edward. "An Interview with the Father of Hi-Fi: Dr. Peter Goldmark." *Rolling Stone* (27 September 1973).

Subject Index

100 Club, London, 308, 311
101ers, 304
112, 472
1910 Fruitgum Company, 328
1984, 304
2 Live Crew, 416, 417
2-Tone records, 315
20/20 (tv program), 413
2001: A Space Odyssey (movie), 278
3 Doors Down, 522
33 rpm record (LP), 74, 232, 245
   sleeve designers, 238–239
3M. *See* Minnesota Mining and Manufacturing Company (3M)
4 Hero's Reinforced, 452
4 Non Blondes, 529
42nd Street (movie), 36
45 rpm record (single), 74–75, 87, 245
   twelve-inch, 329
"5" Royales, 105, 109
50 Cent (Curtis James Jackson III), 480–481, 537, 538, 539, 542
54-40, 262
77 Sunset Strip, 150
78 rpm record, 63, 75, 87
8 Mile (movie), 478, 480
808 State, 451, 455
98 Degrees, 462

A

A&M Records, 190, 309, 373, 409, 426, 485
A-Ha, 12
Aaliyah, 483
Aaron, Lee, 385
ABBA, 12
ABC, 339, 340
ABC-Paramount Records, 93, 104, 131, 141, 149, 151, 157
ABC-TV, 149, 157
Abdul, Paula, 533
Abner, Ewart, 104
Above the Rim (movie), 420
Abrams, Lee, 333
Abramson, Herb, 70
AC. *See* radio, Adult Contemporary (AC)
AC/DC, 284, 377, 414, 443, 505
Ace of Base, 444
Ace of Cups, 265
Ace Records, 92
Ace, Johnny, 98
acid house music, 450
acid rock music, 208–209, 212–213

Ackerman, Paul, 154
Acquaviva, John, 455
Acuff, Roy, 50, 56, 58, 270
Acuff-Rose Music, 58, 65, 132
Adam, Margie, 267
Adams, Bryan, 248, 365
Adams, Faye, 106
Adams, Stanley, 155
Ade, King Sunny, 366
Adler, Bill, 398
Adler, Lou, 158, 211, 257, 258
Adventures of Ozzie and Harriet, The, 151
Adverts, 313
Aeolian Hall, New York, 26
Aerosmith, 276, 279, 377, 393, 394, 396, 422, 446, 466
Afghan Wigs, 425
Afghanistan, war in, 507, 512, 514, 524
AFM. *See* American Federation of Musicians (AFM)
African American music, 5–9, 16
   alternative, 424–425
   by women, 41
   consumers of, 57, 66
   development of, 43
   discrimination against, 11, 13, 17
   folk artists in, 183–184
   incorporated into popular culture, 23–26
   influence of popular culture, 2–3
   influence on British invasion, 192–193
   jazz and, 25
   markets for, 48–49
   militancy in, 200–203
   Motown and, 173–174
   producers, 358
   superstars, 357–358
   Talking Heads and, 302
   teen pop and, 462–463
   Tin Pan Alley and, 23–24
   working class, 67
African National Congress (ANC), 366, 368
Africville (prev. Campbell River), 177
Afrika Bambaata, 366, 390–391, 392, 461
Afro-Cuban music, 222–223
Afrocentricity, 395
After Hours Swing Session radio program, 79
After the Fire, 340
AFTRA. *See* American Federation of Television and Radio Artists (AFTRA)
Against All Odds (movie), 357
Aglukark, Susan, 350
Aguilera, Christina, 461, 462, 463–464, 465, 501
Ahlert, Fred, 35

Aiken, Clay, 534
Air Supply, 291
Alabama White Citizens Council, 134
Alabama, 366
Aladdin records, 68, 90, 93, 95, 98, 140
Alagia, John, 531
Alberta, 47, 349
album-oriented rock (AOR), 333, 339, 344, 351, 380, 384
Aldon Music, 152, 170, 259
Ales, Barney, 173
Alexander, David, 414
Alexander, J. W., 109
Alexander, Lee, 527
Ali (movie), 471
Ali, Muhammed, 391, 503
Alice in Chains, 425, 426, 427, 440
All Music Guide to Rock, 444, 467, 481, 532
Allen, Chad, 194
Allen, Harry, 398
Allen, Lee, 84, 91, 92
Allen, Lillian, 179, 269
Allen, Steve, 124, 154
Allen, Woody, 257
Allman Brothers, 274, 275
Allman, Duane, 274, 275, 386
Allman, Greg, 274
Almanac Singers, 180
Altamont festival (1969), 224–225
alternative music, 4, 422–424
   in Canada, 432–437
   in Seattle, 425–427
   women in, 430–431
Alternative Nation, 440
Alternative Tentacles, 416
AM. *See* radio, amplitude modulation (AM)
Amadeus (movie), 411
Amandla: Festival of Unity, 264
ambient music, 451
Ameriarchi sound, 190
America, 261
America: A Tribute to Heroes (tv program), 502
American Bandstand (prev. *Bandstand*), 98, 119, 149–150, 338
American Dream, 160
   questioning of, 166
American Express Company, 338
American Family Association, 413–414
American Federation of Musicians (AFM), 59, 60
   calypso and, 143–144
   radio and, 60–61
American Federation of Television and Radio Artists (AFTRA), 61, 192

American Idol (tv program), 521, 532–534
American Marconi, 29, 30, 31
American Music Awards, 539
American Negro Songs, 39
American Record Company, 53, 54
American Revolution (1775-1783), 177
American Society of Composers, Authors, and Publishers (ASCAP), 28, 33, 34, 36, 59, 77, 120, 124, 138
   BMI and, 61, 154–156
   NAB and, 58
   royalties and, 57
American Telephone and Telegraph (AT&T), 30, 34
American Tobacco Company, 33
Ames Brothers, 136
AMI. *See* Automatic Musical Instrument Company (AMI)
Ammons, Albert, 54, 91
Amnesty International, 318, 366, 367–268, 370, 425
Amos 'n' Andy (radio program), 33
Amos, Tori, 456
Analysis of the Construction of National, Racial, and Gendered
   Identities on MuchMusic (Canada) and MTV (US), An, 348
ANC. *See* African National Congress (ANC)
Anderman, Joan, 460, 461
Andersen, Signe, 207
Anderson, Ian, 240–241
Anderson, Jon, 242
André 3000 (*a.k.a.* Dré), 537
Andrea True Connection, 327
Angelwitch, 377
Animal Rights, 473
Animals, 188, 189, 192–193, 195, 196, 212, 213
Anka, Paul, 130, 145, 147, 151–152
Annette (Funicello), 146
Annihilator, 383, 385
Ansen, David, 330
Ant, Adam, 237, 308, 311, 340
Anthem Records, 282
Anthem, 284
Anthony, Marc, 465
Anthony, Michael, 282
Anthrax, 383
anti-establishment lyrics, 212–213
Anti-Flag, 514, 516
Anti-Nazi League, 313
anti-war movement, 227
Anton, Alan, 435
Anvil, 385

AOL/Time-Warner, 485–486, 520
AOR. *See* album-oriented rock (AOR)
Apex record company, 51, 131
Apocalypse Now (movie), 411
Apollo music, 106, 109
Apollo Theatre, 100, 111, 115, 130
Appel, Mike, 263
Apple iPod, 500
Apple iTunes, 499
Apple Records, 257
Apple, Fiona, 457, 458, 540
April Wine, 247, 385
Aquatones, 117
Arc Sound, 232
Arcade Fire, 432, 523
Archies, 229
Archies, The (tv program), 338
Areas, José Chepitó, 222
Argo records, 69, 93
Arista records, 298, 325, 354, 400, 466, 520, 528
Aristocrat Records, 69, 70
Arlen, Harold, 147
Armed Forces Radio Network, 56
Armstrong, Edwin H., 75–76
Armstrong, Lillian, 46
Armstrong, Louis, 35, 40, 41, 46, 49, 67, 69, 138
Armstrong, Tim, 529
Arnold, Jimmie, 118
Arrested Development, 440
Arsenio Hall Show, The (tv program), 445
Art into Pop, 237
art rock music, 238–239, 242, 279, 300
  construction of, 240–241
  difference between black music and, 244–245
Arthur, Charlene, 133
artist and repertoire (a&r), 19
As the World Turns (tv program), 459
Asbury, Charles, 21
ASCAP. *See* American Society of Composers, Authors, and Publishers (ASCAP)
Ashanti, 480
Asher, Peter, 257
Asheton, Ron, 296, 310, 311
Asheton, Scott, 296
Ashford and Simpson, 366
Ashford, Nick, 176
Association, The, 206
Astaire, Fred, 342
Astronauts, 159
Aswad, 313
Asylum Records, 229, 256, 311
At Close Range (movie), 357
AT&T *See* American Telephone and Telegraph (AT&T)
Atkins, Chet, 124, 126, 273
Atkins, Cholly, 173
Atkins, Juan, 448, 450
Atlanta Journal, 50

Atlanta Old Time Fiddler's Convention, 44
Atlantic Canada, 177
Atlantic Records, 68, 70–71, 72, 90, 105, 106, 107, 112, 114–115, 130, 149, 170, 200, 201, 221, 229, 230, 239, 242, 249, 250, 252, 254, 278, 325, 330
Atlee, John Yorke, 18, 19
Attica State Prison uprising (1971), 217
Austin, Ray, 2
auteur theory, 235–236
Automatic Musical Instrument Company (AMI), 53
Autry, Gene, 48, 50, 51, 52, 64
Avalon Ballroom, San Francisco, 233
Avalon, Frankie (*nee* Francis Avalone), 93, 145, 147, 149–150, 158, 164
Avco records, 251, 252
Aventura, 545
Average White Band, 323
Axton, Estelle, 200
Axton, Hoyt, 10
Ayler, Albert, 297

B

B-52s, 433
B-Real, 404
B. Bumble and the Stingers, 159
B. T. Express, 326
Baader-Meinhoff group (Germany), 310
Babes in Toyland (movie), 36
Babes in Toyland, 430, 440
baby boomers, 4
Babydoll (movie), 445
Bach, Johann Sebastian, 240, 276, 279
Bach, Sebastian, 385
Bachman, Randy, 131, 194, 195, 276
Bachman, William, 74
Bachman-Turner Overdrive, 276, 385
Bachrach, Burt, 176
back catalogues, 446–447
Back to the Future (movie), 357
Backlash magazine, 425
Backstreet Boys, 461, 462, 463, 501
Backwoods Breakdown, 51
Bad Boy Entertainment, 472
Bad Boy Family, 475–476
Badu, Érykah, 458
Baez, Joan, 180, 181, 183, 220, 264, 271, 363
Bagdikian, Ben, 505–506
Bailey, Deford, 50
Bailey, Mildred, 62
Bailey, Philip, 324, 359
Baker, Anita, 356, 358, 369
Baker, Arthur, 371
Baker, Bob, 436

Baker, Carroll, 365, 445
Baker, Ginger, 192, 209–210
Baker, James, 408
Baker, LaVern, 71, 85, 138, 152
Baker, Susan, 408, 409, 414
Bakke, Alan, 312
Baldry, Long John, 209
Ball, Kenny, 189
Ballard, Florence, 174, 175, 343
Ballard, Glen, 531
Ballard, Hank, 98, 110
Ballet High, A, 244
Baln, Marty, 225
Baltimore, Charli, 482
Band Aid concerts, 360, 361
Band fur Ethiopia, 365
Band, 132, 184, 219, 245, 270–271, 274, 349
Bandstand. See American Bandstand (prev. *Bandstand*)
Bangles, 266, 505
Bangs, David C., 21
Bangs, Lester, 187, 233, 276, 312
Bar-Kays, 329
Baraka, Amiri (LeRoi Jones), 24, 40, 66, 67
barbershop harmonies, 111
Barclay, Michael, 347, 349, 432, 436
Barenaked Ladies, 350, 436–437
Baretto, Ray, 366
Barn Dance (radio program), 50
Barnet, Charlie, 62
Barnouw, Erik, 31, 34
Barraud, Francis, 19
Barrel House club, 98
Barrett, Pat, 118
Barrett, Syd, 240
Barretto, Ray, 11
Barron, Steve, 343
Barrow, Geoff, 452
Barry Boyd and the Frantics, 131
Barry records, 131
Barry, Claudja, 329
Barry, Jeff, 152, 170, 171
Barry, Robert J., 414
Bartholomew, Dave, 90, 91, 92, 93, 96, 126
Bartók, Béla, 239
Bashe, Philip, 378
Basie, Count, 54, 63, 78, 138
Bass, Ralph, 105
Baxter, Les, 136
Bays, Nora, 28
BBC. *See* British Broadcasting Corporation (BBC)
BBG. *See* Broadcast Board of Governors (BBG)
Beach Blanket Bingo (movie), 158
Beach Boys, 158, 160–161, 228, 408
Beach Party (movie), 158
beach party movies, 158–159
Beals, Jennifer, 392
Bean, Frances, 427
Beastie Boys, 394, 441, 502
Beat Factory Productions, 405
beat music, 192
Beat poets, 287

Beat Street (movie), 392
Beatles, 3, 43, 105, 127, 131, 161, 164, 165, 187–195, 194, 195, 206, 214, 215, 217, 218, 228, 235, 236, 238, 274, 278, 282, 307, 324, 330, 338, 354, 360, 363, 386, 390, 504, 543
  in Canada, 189
Beats by the Pound, 472–473
Beau Brummels, 190
Beau Dommage, 186
Beauford, Carter, 531
Beck, Jeff, 210, 237, 277
Beck, Martin, 26
Becker, Walter, 291
Bee Gees, 327, 330–331, 356
Beethoven, Ludwig van, 276, 332
Beetle Magazine, 232
Beiderbecke, Bix, 67
Belafonte, Harry, 144, 183, 361
Beliveau, Veronique, 365
Bell Laboratories, 74
Bell, Al, 201, 254, 255
Bell, Alexander Graham, 16
Bell, Chichester, 17
Bell, Freddie, 125
Bell, Thom, 250, 251, 252
Bell, William, 178
Belleville Kilties Band, 19
Belli, Melvin, 225
Bellknap, Ray, 413
Bells of Joy, 106
Belmonts, 117
Belz, Carl, 3
Benatar, Pat, 345, 346
Benjamin, Benny, 175
Bennet, Prime Minister R. B., 246
Bennett, Tony, 63, 65, 140
Bennett, Veronica, 170
Benson, Al, 79, 104
Benson, George, 244, 333
Bently Rhythm Ace, 453
Berg, Moe, 347, 434
Bergman, Art, 320
Berkeley, Busby, 36
Berklee College of Music, Boston, 531
Berle, Milton, 124
Berlin, 357
Berlin, Irving (Israel Baline), 16, 22, 23, 24, 26, 28, 35, 36, 58
Berliner Corporation, 19
Berliner, Emile, 18–19, 20
Berlioz, Hector, 411
Berne Convention Implementation Act (1988), 488
Bernhard, Sarah, 458
Bernie, Ben, 30
Berry, Chuck, 7, 10, 83, 84, 99–101, 102–103, 128, 132, 150, 157, 160, 161, 167, 188, 191, 192, 193, 198, 276
Berry, Ivan, 405
Berry, Jan, 163
Bertei, Adele, 315

Bertelsmann, 373, 490, 532
Best, Pete, 191
BET. *See* Black Entertainment
	Television (BET)
Betts, Dickie, 274, 275
Beverly Hills Cop (movie), 357
Bey, Salome, 365
Beyoncé, 537, 539
Biafra, Jello, 320, 416
big band era, 54
	decline of, 61–62, 63
big beat music, 453–454
Big Boi, 537, 539
Big Bopper, 99, 129, 157, 273
Big Broadcast, The (movie), 35
Big Brother and the Holding
	Company, 206, 208, 210,
	211
Big Champagne, 496
Big Chill, The (movie), 357
Big Pun(isher), 465
Bihari, Jules, 122
Bihari, Saul, 122
Bikini Beach (movie), 158
Biko, Steven, 395
Bilk, Mr. Acker, 189
Bill Haley and His Comets, 82,
	85, 120–121, 153
Billboard (magazine), 8, 9, 53,
	62, 68, 70, 81, 118, 119,
	126, 131, 136, 146, 154,
	155, 189, 233, 282, 291,
	327, 329, 331, 341, 346,
	352, 358, 373, 380, 381,
	384, 394, 395, 400, 401,
	419, 422, 427, 441, 449,
	456, 471, 482, 520, 522,
	524, 535, 536, 539, 541
	Hot 100, 189, 332
Billboard 200, 476
Billy J. Kramer and the Dakotas,
	189, 190
Billy Ward and the Dominoes,
	105
bin Laden, Osama, 508, 509,
	514, 515
Birchmount Records, 179
Birdsong, Cindy, 174
birth control, 206
Bishop, Ferron, 268
Bishop, Heather, 268
Bit Torrent, 499
Bizarre records, 228
Björk, 453, 455
Black and Tan Fantasy (movie),
	48
Black Crowes, 501
Black Entertainment Television
	(BET), 339, 419
Black Eyed Peas, 515
Black Flag, 319, 320, 425, 438
black liberation, 217, 250–251
Black Light Orchestra, 329
black music, 9
	in Canada, 177–178
	influences on, 358
Black Noise, 376
Black Panther Party, 200, 210,
	216–217, 218, 224, 225
Black Patti records, 42

Black Power movement, 165,
	202–203, 210
black power, 200
Black Rob, 472
Black Rock Coalition, 385
Black Sabbath (prev. Earth),
	229, 277–278, 284, 381,
	413
Black Swan records, 42, 49, 53
Black, Bill, 123, 125, 159
Black, Cilla, 190
Black, Clint, 412, 443, 508
Black, Jully, 350, 543
Blackboard Jungle (movie), 121,
	452
Blackie and the Rodea Kings,
	262
Blackmore, Ritchie, 239, 279,
	280, 282
Blackwell, Bumps, 93, 94, 96,
	108, 109
Blackwell, Chris, 264, 314, 342,
	356
Blackwell, Otis, 126
Blades, Rubén, 322, 366, 465,
	468
Blake, Arthur "Blind", 43
Blake, Peter, 238
Bland, Bobby, 90, 122
Blasters, 366
Blige, Mary J., 469, 470, 471,
	472, 501
Blink 182, 521
Block, Martin, 59–60
Blondie, 295, 296–297, 298,
	301, 302, 315, 316, 321,
	334, 335, 392
Blood, Sweat, and Tears, 208,
	241, 244
Bloomfield, Mike, 70, 208, 210
Blossoms, 169
Blue Cheer, 277
Blue Hawaii (movie), 157
Blue Network, 31
Blue Note Records, 527
Blue Öyster Cult, 284, 297
Blue Rodeo, 247, 248, 432, 435,
	437
blue-eyed soul music, 170–171
bluegrass music, 177
Blues Brothers, 209
Blues Incorporated, 192
blues music, 6, 23, 37, 110, 204,
	276, 282, 291, 305
	African American origins,
		38–39, 41, 66
	classic, 40
	country, 40, 42–43
	definition of, 38
	distinction between jazz and,
		67
	evolution of, 38
	in Canada, 208–209
	instrumentation, 39
	on radio, 49
	psychedelics and, 210–211
	revival of, 206–207
	roots of rock 'n' roll, 83–84
	Tin Pan Alley and, 24–25
	vocal styles, 39

	white revivalists, 192
	women vocalists, 41
Blues Project, The, 208
Bluesbreakers, 192, 210, 290
BMG, 520
BMI. *See* Broadcast Music Incor-
	porated (BMI)
Bob and Earl (Robert Byrd and
	Earl Nelson), 98
Bob and Wisdom, 179
Bob B. Soxx & the Blue Jeans,
	169, 171
Bob Marley and the Wailers, 264
Bob Seger and the Silver Bullet
	Band, 291
Bob Wills and His Texas Play-
	boys, 48, 52, 120, 121
Bobettes, 117
Body Count, 438
Bogart, Neil, 328
Bohemian Embassy, Toronto,
	178
Bolan, Marc, 286
Bolduc, La, 185
Bomb Squad, 395
Bon Jovi, 381, 382, 503, 504
Bon Jovi, Jon, 502
Bondi, Vic, 320
Bonds, Gary "U.S.", 149, 164
Bonham, John, 28, 277
Bono, 366, 501, 502, 504
Boo Yah Tribe, 404, 439
Boogie Down Productions, 371,
	394, 399, 402
boogie woogie music, 6, 40–41,
	69
Booker-T and the MGs, 200
boom boxes, 376
Boomtown Rats, 292, 361, 366
Boone, Pat, 91, 92, 97, 141,
	142–143, 167
Booth, James, 347
bootleg, 271
Boots Reilly, 516
Bootsy's Rubber Band, 325
Bossmen, 244
Bosstown sound, 229
Bostic, Joe, 79
Boston Arena, 157
Boston Globe, 351, 383, 438, 456,
	460
Boston Tea Party, 231, 302
Boston, 290
Boswell Sisters, 35
Bouchard, Lucien, 186
Bound for Glory, 180
Bourbon Tabernacle Choir, 432,
	435
Bowen, Jimmy, 129, 411
Bowie, David (*nee* David Jones),
	237, 286–287, 296, 313,
	324, 334, 341, 342, 472,
	503, 523
Box, 433
Boyd Bennett and the Rockets,
	141
Boyd, Liona, 365
Boyz II Men, 444, 445, 469, 470
Boyz N the Hood (movie), 401
Bracken, James, 104

Brackett, David, 9
Braddock, Billy, 517
Bradford, Perry, 41
Bradley, Owen, 129
Bradshaw, Tiny, 68
Bragg, Billy, 369, 516
Bramlett, Bonnie, 317
Branca, Glenn, 430
Branch, Michelle, 525
Brando, Marlon, 461
Brandy and Monica, 458
Brandy, 462
Branson, Richard, 446
Brantford, Ontario, 22
Braxton, Toni, 421, 456, 469,
	470
break dancing, 293, 342, 389
break-beat music, 390
Breakin' (movie), 392
Breaking and Entering (movie),
	393
Breeders, 441
Brenston, Jackie, 80, 84, 99,
	120, 122
Brewer, Teresa, 136, 140
Brice, Bo, 535
Brides of Frankenstein, 325
bridge, 527
Brill Building, 1619 Broadway,
	New York, 152–153, 170,
	171, 176, 257, 258, 259
Brinkley, "Doc", 59
Brion, Jon, 540
British art schools, 237
British Broadcasting Corporation
	(BBC), 240
British Gramophone Company,
	19
British invasion (1964), 130,
	133, 151, 152, 159, 160,
	164, 170, 187–195
	African American influences
		on, 192–193
	after the, 172
	blues revival and, 192
	class and culture effects of,
		193–194
	effect on Canadian musicians,
		194–195
	of Canada, 189
	second wave, 206–207, 220,
		229
	women in, 191–192
Broadcast Board of Governors
	(BBG), 246
Broadcast Music Incorporated
	(BMI), 58, 59, 77, 124
	ASCAP and, 61, 154–156
broadcasting, 77
Broadway Melody (movie), 34
Brockman, Polk, 38, 44, 50
Broken Social Scene, 432, 523
Bromberg, David, 261
Bronfman, Jr., Edgar, 520
Brooklyn Academy, 194
Brooklyn Bridge (show band),
	117
Brooks and Dunn, 501
Brooks, Diane, 179

Brooks, Garth, 411, 412, 441–442, 444
Brooks, Shelton, 22
Broonzy, Big Bill, 55, 70, 99, 123
Brother D and Collective Effort, 391
Brother Records, 228
Brothers Four, 145
Brown Berets, 218
Brown v. Board of Education, 1954 (school desegregation decision), 165, 167
Brown, Bill, 106
Brown, Buster, 178
Brown, Charles, 95, 115
Brown, David, 222
Brown, Foxy, 482, 483
Brown, Governor Jerry, 272, 320
Brown, James, 90, 105, 109, 202–203, 204, 206, 216, 253, 322, 324–325, 344, 388, 390, 391, 404, 419, 451, 482
Brown, Nappy, 140
Brown, Roy, 59, 83, 90
Brown, Ruth, 70–71, 72–73, 85
Brown, Toni, 265
Browne, Jackson, 229, 263–264, 272, 361, 366, 370, 371, 515
Brownstein, Carrie, 513
Bruce records, 111
Bruce, Jack, 192, 209–210
Bruford, Bill, 242
Brunswick records, 44, 53, 54, 107, 130, 139
Bryan, Alfred, 22
Bryan, Mark, 445
Bryans, Billy, 269
Bryant, Anita, 328
Bryant, Willie, 79
Bubba Sparxxx, 515, 536
Buck 65, 406
Buckingham, Lindsay, 290
Buddah records, 252, 328
Buddy Holly and the Crickets, 130, 139, 191
Buffalo Springfield, 179, 211, 212, 221
Buggles, 340
Bullwhip Brothers, 268
Bumstead Records, 436
Burdon, Eric, 192, 193, 195, 196, 253
Burks, "Spider", 78
Burleigh, Harry, 28
Burnette, Dorsey, 151
Burnette, Johnny, 151
Burning Spear, 314
Burr, Henry (Harry McClaskey), 18
Burroughs, William, 276, 290–291, 297, 427
Burton, James, 151
Burton, Ray, 258
Bush, George, 411, 516, 524, 531
Bush, Kate, 434
Busseri, Frankie, 118

Butler, Jerry, 104, 250
Butler, Win, 523
Butterfield, Paul, 70, 208
Butthole Surfers, 438
Buziak, Bob, 356
Buzzcocks, 293, 304, 308, 309
Byrds, 197–198, 199, 206, 211, 212, 221, 271=272, 431, 489
Byrne, David, 302, 321, 371, 515
Byrnes, Ed "Cookie", 150

C

Cadence Weapon, 406
Cadet records, 69
Cadillacs, 110
Café Tacuba, 465
Cage, John, 295
Calderón, Tego, 546
Cale, John, 295, 296, 298
Calgary, 47, 247, 523
California Alliance shows, 264
call-and-response style, 24, 106
Calle 13, 530
Calloway, Cab, 317
calypso music, 143–144
Camberwell Art School, 240
Cambodia bombings, 225
Cameo/Parkway Records, 146, 148, 149, 250
Camp Naivelt, Ontario, 183
Campbell, Arthur, 18
Campbell, Glen, 99, 273, 366
Campbell, Luther, 416, 474
Campbell, Mayor Larry, 320
Camps, 312
Can, 340
Canada,
  African American musicians in, 349
  alternative music in, 432–437
  broadcast controls in, 246
  cable television in, 346–347
  Canadian music, 349–350
  Celtic rock in, 437
  content (CanCon) regulations in, 247–248, 346–347, 435
  electronica music in, 455–456
  heavy metal music in, 385–386
  Jamaican music influences, 178–179
  multiculturalism in, 246–247
  music industry in new millennium in, 519–520
  musicians in, 245–246
  new millennium music in, 523–524
  regional music, 350
  second wave of punk in, 320
  star system in, 248
  women's liberation music in, 268–269

Canadian Academy of Recording Arts and Sciences (CARAS), 248
Canadian Broadcasting Company (CBC) (prev. CRBC), 32, 47, 51, 77, 89, 177
Canadian Confederation, 32
Canadian Copyright Act (1921), 27
Canadian Country Music Association (CCMA) Awards (prev. Big Country Awards), 248
Canadian Full Tilt Boogie Band, 220
Canadian immigration laws, discriminatory, 178
  restrictions removed, 179
Canadian Marconi Co., 30
Canadian Music Hall of Fame, 248, 436
Canadian National Railways (CNR), 32
Canadian Performing Rights Society (CPRS), 28–29
Canadian Phonograph, 19
Canadian Radio and Television Commission (CRTC), 246, 248, 346, 347, 406
Canadian Radio Broadcasting Company (CRBC), 32, 47, 51, 246
CanCon. *See* Canada, content (CanCon) regulations in
Canned Heat, 208, 211
Cannibal and the Headhunters, 190
Canning, Brendan, 523
Cannon, Freddy (*nee* Frederick Picariello), 146, 150
CanRock Renaissance, The, 347, 349
CAPAC. *See* Composers, Authors and Publishers Associated of Canada Limited (CAPAC)
Capeman, The (musical), 465
Capital Q, 405
Capitol Canada, 189, 247
Capitol Records, 23, 60, 64, 86, 100, 105, 128–129, 132, 133, 139, 141, 145, 159, 160, 161, 189, 208, 212, 228, 373, 401
Capitol-EMI Records, 229
Capote, Truman, 332
cappella, 113
Capricorn records, 275
Captain and Tenille, 289, 410
Carabello, Mike, 222
CARAS. *See* Canadian Academy of Recording Arts and Sciences (CARAS)
Cardinals, 110
Carefree (movie), 36
Carey, Mariah, 445, 456, 463, 502, 542
Carlisle, Belinda, 370
Carlton, Vanessa, 464, 525, 526

Carmichael, Stokely, 200
Carnegie Hall, 21, 54, 183, 435
Carol Pope and Rough Trade, 262, 268
Carpenter, Mary Chapin, 443
Carpenters, 289
Carr, Leroy, 95
Carroll, Ray, 79
Cars, 443
Carson, Fiddlin' John, 44, 50
Carter Family, 45–46, 48
Carter, Asa, 134
Carter, Calvin, 104
Carter, Jay, 117
Carter, Jimmy, 235, 275, 293, 335
Carter, Maybelle, 270
Carter, Nick, 462
Carter, Rubin "Hurricane", 271
Carter, Vivian, 104
Carter, Wilf, 47, 48, 50
Cartola, Bobby, 148
Caruso, Enrico, 20, 29
Casa Loma Orchestra, 52
Casablanca records, 325, 328, 329, 331, 337
Casey, Harry Wane, 327, 328
Cash Box magazine, 233, 239
Cash, Johnny, 121, 122, 128, 138, 270, 501
Castle, Irene, 21, 28
Castle, Vernon, 21, 28
Castor, Jimmy, 390, 391, 392, 439
Cat records, 112, 140
Cavern, Liverpool, 191
CBC Television, 183
CBC. *See* Canadian Broadcasting Company (CBC) (prev. CRBC)
CBGB Festival of Unsigned Bands (1975), 198, 304, 311
CBGB. *See* Country Blue Grass and Blues (CBGB) bar, New York
CBL radio station, 89
CBS Records, 212, 228, 229, 231, 234, 250, 254, 255, 309, 310, 336, 337, 345, 351, 374
CBS, Inc., 230
CBS. *See* Columbia Broadcasting System (CBS)
CBTV, 51
CCMA. *See* Canadian Country Music Association (CCMA)
CDs. *See* compact discs (CDs)
Celler, Congressman Emmanuel, 155–156
Celtic mysticism, 278
Celtic-rock music, 437
Cerrone, 329
Cervenka, Exene, 315
CFAC radio station, 47
CFBO radio station, 51
CFCF (prev. XWA) radio station, 30
CFCN radio station, 47

CFCY radio station, 51
CFRB radio station, 32, 89
Chad and Jeremy, 190
Chad Mitchell Trio, 183
Chambers Brothers, 516
Chambers, Iain, 7, 238, 249, 286
Chambers, Lester, 516
Chambers, Paul, 451
Champs, 99, 159, 261
Chance Records, 115
Chancellor records, 146
Chandler, Chas, 213
Chandler, Gene, 104, 164
Chang, Jeff, 513
Change of Heart, 432, 435
chansonnier tradition, 185–186,
    350
    rock orientated, 186
    separatism and, 186
Chantays, 159
Chantels, 117
Chanteurs sans Frontières, 365
Chapel Jean (a.k.a. Mattie
    O'Neill), 133
Chapin, Harry, 260
Chapman, Mike, 301, 321
Chapman, Tracy, 268, 367, 369,
    425
Chapple, Steve, 158
Chariglioni, Leonardo, 492
charity rock, 361–363
    in Canada, 365–366
Charlatans, 206, 236
Charlebois, Robert, 186, 241,
    365
Charles, Ray (a.k.a. Ray Charles
    Robinson), 10, 71, 85,
    107–108, 108, 149, 193,
    249, 269, 317, 361, 401,
    528, 541
Charlie Daniels Band, 274, 366
Charlie Poole and his North Car-
    olina Ramblers, 44–45
Charlottetown, 51
Charms, 105, 116, 140, 141
Charters, Samuel, 38, 40, 43
Chase, Charlie, 391
Chassagne, Régine, 523
Chateau records, 131
Chatham, Ontario, 184
Chavis, Ben, 484, 515
CHBY-TV, 51
CHCH-TV, 51
Checker records, 69, 140
Checker, Chubby, 148
Checkmates, 169
Cheeba, Eddie, 390
Cheetah magazine, 233, 234
Chelsea Hotel, New York, 294,
    297
Chemical Brothers (prev. Dust
    Brothers), 453–454
Cher, 198, 331, 332
Cherry Vanilla, 318
Cherry, Eagle Eye, 466
Cherry, Neneh, 453
Chess Records, 10, 68, 69–70,
    79, 90, 93, 99–100, 100,
    102, 104, 115, 122, 229,
    324

Chess, Leonard, 10, 69, 87, 99,
    101, 122
Chess, Phil, 69, 122
Chessler, Deborah, 111
Chesters. See Little Anthony and
    the Imperials (prev.
    Chesters)
Chi-Lites, The, 217
Chic, 391
CHIC-AM radio station, 329
Chicago Eight, 218, 224, 225
Chicago State University, 540
Chicago Sun-Times, 471
Chicago Tribune, 31, 506
Chicago Women's Liberation
    Rock Band, 265
Chicago, 99–101, 104–105, 208,
    241, 244, 290
Chicano rock, 99, 190
Chiffons, 168, 170, 171, 172
child abuse, 370–371
Children, The, 261
Childs, C. G., 20
Chilliwack, 247
Chin, Ken (a.k.a. Mr. Chi Pig),
    320
Chinn and Chapman, 301
CHNS radio station, 47
Choclair, 406, 543
CHOM radio station, 232
Chopin, Frédérick, 107, 108,
    525
Chords, 71, 85, 112–113, 114,
    118, 140
Chotem, Neil, 241
CHR. See radio, Contemporary
    Hits Radio (CHR)
Christgau, Robert, 233, 256,
    257, 258, 261, 265, 272,
    283, 292, 312, 332
Christian, Meg, 266–267
Chrysalis Records, 228, 301, 373
Chuck D., 376, 395, 487
Chudd, Lew, 93
CHUM AM radio station, 77,
    89, 178, 194
CHUM FM radio station, 232
CHUM, 346
Ciara, 541
Cimarrons, 313, 314
Cincinnati, 105–106
    doo wop music in, 116
Cinderella, 384, 442
CIQC (prev. CFCF) radio sta-
    tion, 30
Circle Jerks, 319
CityLimits (tv program), 347
Civil Rights movement, 145,
    160, 165
    assimilation in early stages of,
    172
    British invasion and, 193
    decline of, 227, 249
    folk music and, 180–181
    integrationist approach by,
    193
    Motown music and,
    173–174, 177
    music and, 166–170,
    169–170, 171

social consciousness from,
    217–218
CKEY radio station, 89
CKLG radio station, 232
Clanton, Jimmy, 92–93
Clapton, Eric, 192, 209–210,
    212, 213, 236, 237, 274,
    277, 313, 315, 466, 503
Clark, Dave, 192
Clark, Dee, 104
Clark, Dick, 98, 148, 149–150,
    157, 160, 206
Clark, Maggie, 22
Clark, Petula, 192
Clark, Steve, 378
Clarke, Gene, 272
Clarkson, Kelly, 541
Clarson, Kelly, 534
Clash (prev. London SS), 293,
    304, 307, 308, 309–310,
    311, 312, 313, 314, 316,
    334
Class records, 98
class, 21, 37
    see also middle class; working
    class
classical music, 2, 20, 282, 295,
    378, 386
    influences, 278–279
Claton-Thomas, David, 244
Clear Channel, 505, 506, 547
Clef Club, The, 20, 21
Cleftones, 114
Clegg, Johnny, 369
Clemmons, Clarence, 358
Cleveland Arena, 157
Cleveland, James, 106
Cliff, Jimmy, 314
Cline, Patsy, 133, 273, 435, 436
Clinton, George (a.k.a. Dr.
    Funkenstein, Maggot
    Overload, Uncle Jam),
    324–325, 328, 388, 537
Clooney, George, 46
Clooney, Rosemary, 65, 85, 138
Clovers, 71, 114
Clowns, 92
Club 47, Philadelphia, 185
Club Blue Note, Toronto, 178
Club Jamaica, Toronto, 179
Club Tijuana, 91
Club Trinidad, Toronto, 179
Club Tropics, Toronto, 179
CNFY-FM radio station, 437
CNR. See Canadian National
    Railways (CNR)
CNRO radio station, 32
Coasters, 84, 114–115
Cobain, Kurt, 426, 427–429,
    431, 441, 446
Cobra Records, 179
Cochran, Eddie, 129
Cochrane, Tom, 365
Cockburn, Bruce, 185, 261, 349,
    365, 370
Cocker, Joe, 184, 220, 248
Coed Records, 117
Coffey, Cath, 453
Coffin, Gerry, 152, 153, 171
Cohan, George M., 22, 24, 28

Cohen, Leonard, 245, 261, 262,
    350
Cohen, Lyor, 520
Cohen, Marshall, 338
Cohn, Nik, 475
COINTELPRO. See FBI's
    Counter-Intelligence Pro-
    gram (COINTELPRO)
Cold Chillin' Records, 400
Coldarini, Connie, 118
Coldplay, 37
Cole, Cozy, 159
Cole, M. M., 58
Cole, Nat "King", 63, 95, 105,
    107, 108
Cole, Natalie, 369
Cole, Paula, 457
Cole, Stranger, 179
Coleman, Ornette, 422
College Humor (movie), 35
Collin, Matthew, 451
Collins, Arthur, 21
Collins, Bootsy, 204, 325
Collins, Judy, 256
Collins, Phil, 342, 345, 356,
    357, 358, 363
Collins, Tim, 446
Color Me Badd, 469
Colpix records, 146
Colter, Jessie, 273
Coltrane, John, 297
Columbia Broadcasting System
    (CBS) laboratories, 74
Columbia Broadcasting System
    (CBS), 31, 41, 43, 47, 49,
    54, 61, 86
Columbia Graphaphone Co., 19,
    20, 28
Columbia Male Quartet, 18
Columbia Phonograph Broad-
    casting System, 31
Columbia Phonograph Com-
    pany, 17–18, 31
Columbia Records, 118, 128,
    130, 132, 138–139, 141,
    143, 145, 180, 182, 183,
    201, 220, 222, 247, 262,
    271, 279, 316, 400, 426,
    446, 447, 465, 531
    calypso music, 144
Columbia University, 75, 525
Colvin, Doug (Dee Dee), 298
Colvin, Shawn, 456, 457
Combo records, 140
Combs, Sean "Puffy", 421, 466,
    469, 471=472, 520
Commodores, 354
communication technologies, 3
Como, Perry, 63, 127, 136, 140,
    142
compact discs (CDs), 262, 357,
    373, 486
    copy proof, 495
    downloading effect on,
    497–498
    MAPS and, 492
Companion records, 111
Company Segundo, 465
Composers, Authors and Pub-
    lishers Associated of

Canada Limited (CAPAC) (prev. CPRS), 29
Concert for Bangladesh (1972), 315, 363
Conger, Laurie, 269
Congress on Racial Equality (CORE), 166
Conley, Arthur, 200, 249
Connors, Stompin' Tom, 51, 349
Conqueror Record Time (radio program), 52
Constellation records, 104
Continentals, 110
Contortions, 315
Cooder, Ry, 465
Cook, Paul, 294, 305
Cook, Will Marion, 28
Cooke, Sam, 7, 85, 108–109, 149, 186, 187, 193, 200, 257
Cookies, 170, 171, 188
Coon, Caroline, 293
Cooper, Alice, 285, 286, 378
Cooper, Gary, 131
Cooper, Jack L., 59, 78
Copas, Cowboy, 64, 68
Copeland, Miles, 318
Copeland, Stewart, 318
Coppola, Francis Ford, 411
copyright, 487–488
Coq d'Or, Le, Toronto, 178, 179
Coral records, 119, 130, 139, 140
CORE. *See* Congress on Racial Equality (CORE)
Cornell, Chris, 440
Correll, Charles, 33
Cosby (tv program), 401
Cosmic Force, 391
Costa, Don, 151
Costandinos, Alec, 329
Costello, Elvis (*nee* Declan Patrick McManus), 316–317, 308, 318
Cotton Club, 49, 68
Cotton, James, 70, 99, 122
Cougars, 179
Count Basie Orchestra, 55
Count Matthews' West Oakland House Rockers, 98
counterculture, 203, 206–207, 210
    comercializing, 211–212
    deterioration of, 235–236
    drugs and, 206
    individual consciousness-raising, 217–218
    political action, 217–219
    press, 233–234
country and western (c&w) music, 9, 16, 37, 68, 69
    on radio, 49–50
    commercial, 444–45
    fusion with r&b, 120
    influences on, 38–39
    music instrumentation, 39
    on cable, 339
    on Canadian radio, 50–51
    record companies and, 64–65

roots of rock 'n' roll, 83–84
    values of, 84
    vocal styles, 39
    Western influences, 48
Country Blue Grass and Blues (CBGB) bar, New York, 296, 297, 298, 300, 301, 302, 308, 309, 312, 425
Country Joe (McDonald) and the Fish, 206, 211, 212, 220
country music, 441–445
    patriotism in, 507–509
country rock music, 269–274
Country, 39
Coup, 516
Coury, Al, 336
cover records, 139–141, 143
Cowboy Junkies, 262, 432, 435
Cowboy Mouth (play), 297
Cowboy Songs (sheet music), 47
Cowboy Songs by Hank the Yodelling Ranger (sheet music), 47
cowboys, singing, 52
Cowell, Simon, 532
Cox, Ida, 41
CPRS. *See* Canadian Performing Rights Society (CPRS)
Cramer, Floyd, 124
Cramps, 131, 433
Cranberries, The, 456
Crash 'n' Burn club, Toronto, 303
Crawdaddy! magazine, 233
Cray, Robert, 425
Crazy World of Arthur Brown, 239
CRBC. *See* Canadian Radio Broadcasting Company (CRBC)
Cream, 192, 208, 209–210, 212, 229, 234, 277, 282, 360
Creatore, Luigi, 108
Cree-Lo, 466
Creed, 521–522, 524
Creed, Linda, 251
Creedence Clearwater Revival, 219, 272
Creem magazine, 233, 297, 412
Creme, Lol, 341
Crests, 117
Crew Cuts, 112, 118–119, 140
Crewe, Bob, 178
Crickets, 129, 130
Crimson records, 250
Criss, Peter, 286
Croce, Jim, 260
Crocker, Frankie, 326
Crofts, Dash, 99
Crombie, Mayor David, 244
Cromwell, Harry, 177
Cropper, Steve, 201
Crosby, Bing, 12, 35, 48, 52, 54, 61–62, 62, 142, 154
Crosby, David, 197, 212, 216, 221, 224, 256
Crosby, Stills & Nash, 212, 221, 229–230, 264
Crosby, Stills, Nash & Young, 212, 224, 349, 363, 512

Cross, Brian, 395, 404
Cross, Christopher, 472
cross-genre influences, 422
Crossover Dreams (movie), 322, 468
crossover media, 330, 351
crossover, 9
Crow, Sheryl, 447, 487, 491, 502, 515
Crowbar, 132, 209, 247
Crowe, Cameron, 427
Crows, 85, 110, 114
CRTC. *See* Canadian Radio and Television Commission (CRTC)
Crudup, Arthur "Big Boy", 59, 123
Crystals, 12, 147, 164, 168, 170, 171, 198
Cub records, 141
Cubanos Melloman Ace, 404
Cuddy, Jim, 435
Culture Club, 341
culture war, 423–424
culture,
    folk, 2
    high, 2, 22
    mass, 3
    popular, 2
    two-tiered system of, 2
    youth, 4
Cummings, Burton, 194, 195, 365
Cummings, John (Johnny), 298
Current Records, 269
Curse, 303
Curtis Mayfield and the Impressions, 216
Curtis, King, 84
Curtola, Bobby, 145
Cybotron records, 449, 450
Cypress Hill, 404, 439, 461
Cyrus, Billy Ray, 443, 508

D

D'Arby, Terrence Trent, 425
D-Mob, 450
D.J. Jazzy Jeff & the Fresh Prince, 401
D.O.A., 320
Da Brat, 445, 482
Daffodil Records, 209, 247
Dahl, Steve, 333
Dale, Dick, 161
Dalhart, Vernon, 45
Dallas Conservatory of Music, 45
Daltrey, Roger, 220
Daly Steven, 463
Dames (movie), 36
Damned, 293, 307–308, 308
Damone, Vic, 63
Damrosh, Walter, 30
Danae, 322
Dance Fever (tv program), 331
dance music, 355, 389
    black, 326

jacking, 449
Dance Parade (radio program), 62
Dancing in the Distraction Factory, 339
Danderliers, 119
Danforth, John, 409
Daniels, Charlie, 275
Daniels, Ray, 282
Danko, Rick, 270
Danleers, 140
Danny and the Juniors, 134, 250
Dante, Alighieri, 411
Darin, Bobby (*nee* Walden Robert Cassotto), 146, 147, 152
Darling, Eric, 180
Darren, James (*nee* James Ercolani), 146, 153, 158
DAT. *See* digital audio tape (DAT)
Daughterty, Jay Dee, 298
Dave Carroll Orchestra, 119
Dave Clark Five, 189, 192
Dave Matthews Band, 531
David, Hal, 176
Davies, Ray, 192, 237
Davis, Angela, 399
Davis, Clive, 212, 255, 354, 466, 520, 525
Davis, Mac, 179, 260
Davis, Miles, 214, 244, 366
Davis, Rik, 449
Dawson, Jim, 82, 127
Day, Bobby (Robert Byrd), 98
Day, Doris, 85, 138
Day, Howie, 530, 531
Dayglo Abortions, 320, 434
de Forest, Lee, 29, 32, 34
De Fries, Tony, 287
de la Rocha, Zac, 461
De Luxe records, 90, 91, 116
De Sylva, Brown, and Henderson (music publishers), 35
De Sylva, Buddy, 60
Dead Boys, 299, 302, 311
Dead Kennedys, 319, 320, 415–416, 425
Deadly Nightshade, The, 265
Dean, James, 461
Dean, Larry, 78
Death Row Records, 421
Decca (U.K.), 54, 230
Decca (U.S.), 54, 66, 68, 86, 111, 120, 129, 133, 139, 141, 151, 153, 168, 373
    cover records, 140
Decline of Western Civilization, The (movie), 319
DeCurtis, Anthony, 426, 444
Dee, Sandra, 158
deejays. *See* disc jockeys (deejays)
Deep Purple, 229, 239, 240, 277, 278–279, 280–281, 377, 381
Deep River Hour (radio program), 49
Deep Space records, 449
Def Comedy Jam (tv program), 478

Def Jam records, 394, 396, 400, 474, 475–480, 484, 520
Def Jeff, 391
Def Leppard, 377, 381, 384, 443
Definition (tv program), 406
DeGarmo, Diane, 534
Deja Voodoo, 347, 432, 433
Dekker, Desmond, 314
DeKnight, Jimmy, 120
Del-Fi records, 99
Del-Satins, 117
Delfonics, 250, 251
Delicious Vinyl records, 401
Dell-Vikings, 117, 143
Dellesandro, Joe, 238
Dells, 104
Delmore Brothers, 68, 69, 105
Delta records, 131
DeMann, Freddy, 467
Demics, 303
Democratic National Convention, Chicago, 1968, 218–219, 234
Denselow, Robin, 264
Densmore, John, 215
Denver, John, 273, 409
Depêche Mode, 340
Derek and the Dominoes, 386
Destiny's Child, 462, 465, 469–470, 471, 479, 501, 503, 537
Destri, Jimmy, 301
Detroit Symphony Orchestra, 449–450
Deutsche Grammophon, 373
Devo, 302–303, 321
Dew Drop Inn, 91
Dewald, Tony, 433
DGC records, 426, 428, 430
Diallo, Amadou, 423
Diamond Head, 377
Diamond, Neil, 289
Diamonds, 119, 140
Dibango, Manu, 11, 326, 366
Dick Dale and the Del-tones, 159
Dickinson, Bruce, 378
Dictators, 311
Diddley, Bo (*nee* Elas Bates; raised as Ellas McDaniel), 83, 85, 99, 150, 153
Different World, A (tv program), 401
DiFranco, Ani, 456, 515
Digital Audio Home Recording Act (1992), 488, 489
digital audio tape (DAT), 374
Digital Millennium Copyright Act (1998), 488, 495
Digital Rights Management (DRM), 499
digital video disc (DVD), 497
Digital, Bobby, 544
Dimension records, 149
Dinosaur, Jr., 425, 440
Diodes, 303
Dion (DiMucci) and the Belmonts, 117, 118
Dion (DiMucci), 117, 216

Dion, Celine, 12, 247, 455, 456, 458–459, 470, 502, 503
Direction and Rio Records, 329
Dirty Dancing (movie), 356
disc jockeys (deejays), 27, 68, 88, 112, 232, 342, 390, 452, 455
  best known, 80–81
  black, 78, 79
  definition of, 59
  disco and, 326–327
  history of, 59–60
  individual, 77
  payola hearings and, 156–157
  Puerto Rican, 544
  see also individual disc jockeys,
Disco Magic (tv program), 331
disco music, 5, 8, 11, 250, 252, 321–323
  black artists in, 326
  commercialism of, 331–332
  differences between punk and, 291–292
  Euro, 329
  hard rock reaction to, 332–333
  in Canada, 329
  independent producers, 329–330
  Latin side of, 331
  mainstream, 330–334
  on radio, 326–327
  popularity of, 327–328
  racial and class divisions in, 292–293
  see also dance music
Disco Tex and his Sex-O-Lettes, 322
Disney Company, 150
Disques Parapluies, Les, records, 329
Dixie Chicks, 458, 502, 509–511, 512, 536
Dixie Cups, 171
Dixie Hummingbirds, 106
Dixieland music, 120
Dixon, Luther, 167, 168
Dixon, Willie, 69–70, 283
DJ Hollywood, 390
DJ International, 449
DJ Nelson, 545
DJ Shadow, 452, 453
DJ Terminator X, 376, 395
DMX, 476, 477, 479, 480
DNA, 315
Do the Right Thing (movie), 371, 401
Dobson, James, 413
Doc Hauer's Medicine Show, 50
Doe, John, 315
Dogg, Sen, 404
Dogg, Snoop Doggy, 418, 419, 445
Doggett, Bill, 105, 159
Doherty, Dennis, 199
Dokken, 379, 380
Dolby, Thomas, 340
Dolca, Vita, La (movie), 415
Dolgay, Sid, 183

Dolphin's Hollywood Record Shop, Los Angeles, 79
Domino, Fats, 41, 59, 80, 84, 85, 91–92, 93, 94, 95, 96, 140, 141, 142, 148, 151, 167, 193
Dominoes, 82, 106, 107
Dommage, Bo, 241
Don Messer and His Islanders, 51
Don Messer Show, The (tv program), 51
Don Messer's Jubilee (tv program), 51, 177
Don't Fence Me In (movie), 52
Donahue, "Big Daddy" Tom, 232
Donegan, Lonnie, 189, 190
Donovan, 184, 198, 261
doo wop groups, 7, 110, 111, 114
  all female, 117–118
  as distinct from vocal harmony groups, 115
  gender balance in, 117
  racially integrated, 117
  white, 117
doo wop music, 85, 110–119, 175
  contrasted to gospel music, 110
  in Canada, 118–119
  in Cincinnati, 116
  New York City as centre of, 111–112, 115
  period, 119
  roots of, 111
  song structure, 112–113
Doobie Brothers, 264, 290
Doors of Perception, The, 215
Doors, 212, 215–216, 218, 229, 244, 296, 360
Dopsie, Rockin', 372
Doroschuk, Ivan, 432, 433
Dorough, Howie, 462
Dorsey Brothers, 54, 124
Dorsey, Jimmy, 6
Dorsey, Tommy, 62
Dot Records, 117, 142–143
  cover records, 140–141
Double Trouble, 390
Doughboys, 433
Dovells, 148
Dowling, Jonathan, 532
Downchild Blues Band, 208–209
Downey, Thomas, 409
Downie, Gord, 436
Doyle, Alan, 437
Dozier, Lamont, 174, 175, 176, 252
Dr. Dre (Andre Young), 400, 419, 421, 474, 477, 490, 501, 515, 538, 539
Dr. Feelgood, 304
Dr. Music, 179
Drake, Bill, 232
Draper, Robert, 233, 234
Dream Warriors, 350, 405–406
Dresser, Paul, 16
Drew, Kevin, 523

Drifters, 71, 106, 114–115, 116–117, 138, 153, 167, 168, 193
DRM. *See* Digital Rights Management (DRM)
drugs, 206, 215, 219, 225, 231, 240, 296–297, 322, 450
  see also ecstasy, lysergic acid diethylamide (LSD)
drum and bass, 452
Duane Eddy and the Rebels, 160
dub poetry, 179
Dubin, Al, 36
Dubmatique, 406
Dubois, Claude, 186, 365
Duke/Peacock records, 68, 98
Dukes, Amboy, 206, 279
Dunn, James, 251
Dupree, Champion Jack, 91
Dupri, Jermaine, 501
Duran Duran, 341, 345
Durst, Fred, 460, 461
Dutch Mason Trio, 208–209
DVD. *See* digital video disc (DVD)
Dylan, Bob (*nee* Robert Zimmerman), 3, 54, 180–183, 184, 185, 187, 195, 196, 198, 199, 213, 214, 217, 262, 264, 270, 271, 274, 287, 290, 360, 361, 363, 516, 532

E

E. B. Marks, 58
E. Street Band, 513
Eagles, 229, 272, 273, 279, 290, 442
Ealing Art College, London, 237
Earle, Steve, 509, 516
Earth, Wind & Fire, 323–324, 358, 472
East Bolton, Quebec, 29
East Coast Music Awards (prev. Maritime Music Awards), 248
Easton, Edward D., 17
Easy Rider (movie), 225, 276
Easy Riders, 144
Easy-E, 395
Ebony magazine, 78, 192
Eckstein, William, 23
Eckstine, Billy, 69
Ecstasy, 450
Ed Sullivan Show, 100, 124, 194, 216, 217
Eddie and the Hot Rods, 304
Eddy, Duane, 150
Edison Speaking Phonograph Company, 15, 19, 28, 45, 53
Edison, Thomas, 15, 16–17, 18, 19
Edmonton folk festival, 184
Edmonton, 131, 195, 320, 436
  alternative music in, 432, 434
Edmunds, Dave, 316

Edmunds, Kenneth "Babyface", 358, 469
eDonkey, 499
Edsels, 110
Edwards, James, 112
Edwards, Jonathan, 260
Eels, 310–311
Egan, Raymond, 22
Egyptology, 324
Eisenhower, President Dwight D, 135, 167
El Dorados, 104, 110, 115, 141
El General, 544
Electric Circus, New York, 231
Electric Circus, Toronto, 231
Electric Eels, 302
Electric Factory, Philadelphia, 231
Electric Flag, The, 206, 210
Electric Kool-Aid Acid Test, The, 207
Electric Ladyland studios, 214
Electronic Frontier Foundation, 496
electronica music, 448, 453–454
   in Canada, 455–456
Elektra records, 215, 229, 296, 315, 386, 434, 446, 453, 454
Elektra-Asylum records, 230
Elizondo, Mike, 538
Elliman, Yvonne, 331
Ellington, Duke, 6, 28, 35, 48, 49, 54, 62, 63, 67, 90, 138, 204, 411
Elliott, Cass, 199
Elliott, Ken, 78
Elliott, Missy "Misdemeanour", 445, 458, 482–483, 515, 541
Ellis, Alton, 179
ELO, 442
Emerson, Keith, 239
Emerson, Lake & Palmer, 238, 239, 241, 244
EMI Records, 191, 230, 305, 308, 351, 373, 389, 426
Eminem (Marshall Mathers III), 461, 474, 477–478, 515
Emmerson, Darren, 454
Emperor Jones, The (movie), 48
Empire State Building, 75
En Vogue, 469
Enchanted Forest, 265
End records, 114, 115
English Beat, 315
Eno, Brian, 288, 302
Enterprise records, 254
Epic records, 342, 344, 426
Epstein, Brian, 188, 191, 194, 330
Erdelyi, Tom (Tommy), 298
Eric Burdon and the Animals, 211
Eric's Trip, 425, 432, 434
Erik B. & Rakim, 394
Ertegun, Ahmet, 70, 114, 221, 230, 520
Ertegun, Nesuhi, 70, 230
ESG, 449

Esquerita, 141
Essex, The, 168
Estefan, Emilio, 466–467
Estefan, Gloria, 12, 456, 465
Estes, Sleepy John, 43
Esther, Little, 98
Ethel Walters Show (radio program), 49
Eurodisco, 323, 448
Europe, James Reese, 20, 21, 28
Eurythmics, 340=341, 359
Eva, Little (*nee* Eva Narcissus Boyd), 149
Evanescence, 537
Evans, Bill, 528
Evans, Dale, 52
Evans, Earnest, 148
Evans, Faith, 421, 472
Evans, George, 22
Eve, 483
Everett, Betty, 104
Everlast, 466
Everly Brothers, 132, 154
Everly, Don, 132
Everly, Phil, 132
Evers, Medgar, 180
Evita (movie), 330
Excelsior records, 98
Exclusive records, 95
Exit Wounds (movie), 479
Exodus, 383
Exploding Plastic Inevitable, 295
Eyes, 265

F

Faber, Dr. Shane, 402
Fabian (*nee* Fabiano Forte), 93, 145, 149, 164
Fabio, 452
Faces, 229
FACTOR. *See* Foundation to Assist Canadian Talent on Record (FACTOR)
Factory (Andy Warhol's), 295
Fagan, Donald, 291
Faith No More, 422, 439
Faith, Percy, 136, 332
Falcons, 110
Fame records, 200, 201, 274
Famous Flames, 105, 109
Famous Ward Singers, 106
Fania records, 322
Fanning, Shawn, 486–487
Fanny, 265–266
Fantasia (Barrino), 534, 539
Fantasia Barrino Story, The: Life Is Not a Fairy Tale (tv program), 534
Farina, Johnny, 159
Farina, Santo, 159
Farm Aid, 366, 370, 425
Farner, Mark, 283
Farrakhan, Louis, 484
Farrar, Richard, 170
Farrell, Perry, 438, 440, 441
Fat Boys, The, 392, 394
Fat Mike, 516

Fatback Band, 391
Fatboy Slim, 453
Fats Waller's Rhythm Club (radio program), 49
Fay, Johnny, 436
FBI's Counter-Intelligence Program (COINTELPRO), 249, 391
FBI. *See* Federal Bureau of Investigation (FBI)
FBOA. *See* Film Booking Offices of America (FBOA)
FCC. *See* Federal Communications Commission (FCC)
Fear, 319
Fearing, Stephen, 262, 532
Fearless Four, 392
Feaster, Carl, 112, 113
Feaster, Claude, 112
Feathers, 110
Federal Bureau Of Investigation (FBI), 249
Federal Communications Commission (FCC), 31, 60, 76, 87, 158, 232, 506–507
Federal records, 105, 106, 109, 116
Federal Trade Commission (FTC), 492
Feist, 349, 432, 523
Feist, Leslie, 523
Feld, Steven, 371
Félix Awards, Quebec, 185, 248, 458
Fellini, Frederico, 415
Felten, Edward, 492
feminism, 218, 227, 258, 264–265
   heavy metal and, 377
Fender, Leo, 159
Ferguson, Jay, 434
Ferland, Jean-Pierre, 186
Ferrer, Ibrahim, 465
Ferris, Tom, 434
Ferry, Bryan, 288
Fessenden, Reginald, 29
Fiedler, Bernie, 185
Fields, Danny, 296
Fifth Column, 269
Fifth Dimension, 152
Fillmore Auditorium, San Francisco, 231
Fillmore East, New York, 308
Film Booking Offices of America (FBOA), 34
Finch, Richard, 327, 328
Finkelstein, Bernie, 261
Fiori, Serge, 241
First Choice, 449
Fishbone, 440
Fisher, Eddie, 136, 139
Fisher, William, 488
Fisk Jubilee Singers, 38
Fitzgerald, Ella, 62, 63, 69, 401
Five Blind Boys of Mississippi, 106, 107
Five Canadians, 195
Five Crowns, 115
Five Rogues, 178
Five Satins, 111

Flack, Roberta, 254
Flames, 98
Flaming Lips, 517
Flamingos, 110, 115, 140, 141
Flashdance (movie), 356, 392
Flavor Flav, 418
Fleetwood Mac, 192, 290
Fleetwood, Mick, 192, 290
Fleetwoods, 110, 118
Flick, Larry, 524
Flock of Seagulls, A, 340
Flom, Jason, 520
Flow-97, 406
flower power movement, 210–211
Fly to France, 435
Flying Burrito Bothers, 272
FM Broadcasters Association, 76
FM rock radio, 228, 232–233, 332–333
FM. *See* radio, frequency modulation (FM)
Focus on the Family, 413, 414
Foghat, 290, 291
folk music, 2, 9
   authentic *vs.* commercial, 180–181
   Civil Rights movement and, 180–181
   in Canada, 183–186
   origins of, 179–180
   race of artists, 183–184
   social voice of, 177, 186–188
folk rock music, 197–198, 206–207, 271
   social consciousness of, 198–200
Follow the Fleet (movie), 36
Fong-Torres, Ben, 233
Fontana, D. J., 125, 127
Fontane Sisters, 141
Foot in Cold Water, A, 247, 282
Footlight Parade (movie), 36
Footloose (movie), 356, 357
Force Inc. records, 455
Force MDs, The, 392
Ford, Frankie, 92
Ford, Lita, 266, 380, 388–389
Ford, Mary, 23, 136
Foreigner, 291
Forgotten Rebels, 303
Forman, Murray, 474
Formby, George, 189
Forrester Research, 496–497
Fort MacLeod, Alberta, 256
Forty-Second Street Harlots, 286
Foster, David, 365
Foundation to Assist Canadian Talent on Record (FACTOR), 248
Four Aces, 62
Four Knights, 111
Four Lads, 118
Four Lovers, 119
Four Seasons, 104, 119, 178
Four the Moment, 178
Four Tops, 173, 176, 252, 343
Four Tunes, 111
Fowley, Kim, 266
Fox Studios, 34, 35

Fox, Jaime, 540, 541
Foxx, Charlie, 257
Foxx, Inez, 257
Foxy, 322
Frampton, Peter, 279, 289–290, 326
Francis, Connie (*nee* Concetta Franconero), 85, 146, 147, 152
Francis, Sage, 514
Frank Marino and Mahogany Rush, 385
Frank Motley and the Hitchhikers, 178
Frankie Lymon and the Teenagers, 114, 117, 119, 140, 141
Franklin Institute, Philadelphia, 19
Franklin, Aretha, 13, 54, 153, 201–202, 216, 217, 228, 229, 249, 253–254, 259, 274, 359, 534
Franklin, Irma, 210
Franklin, Kirk, 470
Frantz, Chris, 302, 392
Fratto, Russ, 101
Fraunhofer Institute, Germany, 486
Freddie and the Dreamers, 189, 191
Free, 192
Freed, Alan, 80–81, 101, 111, 114, 128, 149, 156–157, 194, 326
Freedman, Max, 120
Freenet, 486–487
Frehley, Ace, 286
French-language recordings, 336
Fresh Prince of Bel Air, The (tv program), 401
Frey, Glenn, 272
Friar's Tavern, Toronto, 178
Fricke, David, 439
Friday Night Videos (tv program), 339
Fringe Records, 320–321
Frith, Simon, 3, 4, 237, 238, 292, 307, 356, 360, 370, 374, 408
Frizzell, Lefty, 48, 271, 442
From Here to Eternity (movie), 62, 151
From Spirituals to Swing (concert), 54
Front 242, 440
Frost, Kid, 404
FTC. *See* Federal Trade Commission (FTC)
Fugazi, 319, 425, 515
Fugees, 456, 459
Full Tilt Boogie Band, 132
Fuller, Simon, 532, 533
Funicello, Annette, 150, 158
Funk Brothers, 175
Funk Doobiest, 404
funk music, 179, 203, 317, 322–323
Funk, Farley "Jackmaster", 449

Funkadelic, 325, 333, 393, 439, 449
Funky Four Plus One, 390
Fuqua, Harvey, 115
Furious Five, 390, 392
Furtado, Nelly, 525, 529–530
fusion. *See* jazz-rock (fusion) music

G

G. Ricordi & Co., 58
Gaar, Gillian, 260, 267
Gabler, Milt, 120
Gabriel, Peter, 358, 367, 368, 369, 371, 434
Gaines, Cassie, 275
Gaines, Donna, 430
Gaines, Steve, 275
Gaisberg, Fred, 19
Gallagher, Noel, 454
Gallen, Joe, 502
Gamble, Kenny, 250
Game, 542
Gang Related (movie), 420
Gang Starr, 405
garage band, 292
garage music, 449–450
Garcia, Gerry, 207
Gardner, Freddy, 189
Gardner, Taana, 449
Gardner, Ted, 438
Garfunkel, Art, 198
Garner, Kay, 267
Garnett Amplifiers, Winnipeg, 232
Garret, Pat, 508
Garrett, Bobby, 98
Garrett, Peter, 366
Garrett, Siedah, 401
Garrity, Freddie, 191
Garthwaite, Terry, 265
Garvey, Marcus, 395
Gasken, George J., 18, 19
Gass, Glen, 112
Gauthier, Claude, 185
Gaye, Marvin, 173, 176, 193, 217, 249, 252–253, 257, 322, 343, 459, 501, 525
Gaynor, Gloria, 322, 326, 329
Gayten, Paul, 91
GBX, Toronto, 232
GE. *See* General Electric
Gee records, 114
Geffen Records, 370, 373, 409, 434, 446, 447
Geffen, David, 221, 229, 230, 256, 271, 426, 430
Gehr, Richard, 386
Geiger, Marc, 438
Geldof, Bob, 361, 362, 364, 370
gender, 12–13
Gene and Eunice, 119, 140
General Electric (GE), 30, 31, 34
General Hospital, 465
generation gap, 212
Generation X, 308, 313, 314, 428

Genesis, 238, 240, 241
Genet, Jean, 287
Genius (GZA), 476
George Clinton and Parliament Funkadelic, 179
George Clinton and the P-Funk All Stars, 441
George White's Scandals (movie), 35
George, Boy, 341, 345
George, Nelson, 49, 67, 78, 101, 166, 186, 200, 216, 250, 399, 473, 535, 536
Gerde's Folk City, New York, 185
Gere, Richard, 370
Germs, 319
Gerry and the Pacemakers, 189, 190, 193
Gershwin, George, 16, 26, 28, 58, 152
Gershwin, Ira, 152, 154
Get Rich or Die Tryin' (movie), 542
Ghostface Killah, 514
Gibb, Andy, 331
Gibb, Barry, 330
Gibb, Maurice, 330
Gibb, Robin, 330
Gibbons, Beth, 452
Gibbs, Georgia, 110, 140
Gibson, "Jockey Jack", 78
Gibson, Debbie, 462
Gibson, Don, 10, 133
Gibson, Luke, 261
Gidget (movie), 158
Giger, H. R., 416
Gil, Vince, 443
Gilbert, L. Wolfe, 28
Gilkyson, Terry, 144
Gillan, Ian, 280
Gillen, Marilyn, 456
Gillett, Charlie, 4, 62, 82, 90, 101, 120, 138, 139, 143, 146, 167
Gilmore, Mikal, 291, 293, 422, 423
Gilmour, David, 240
Gimme Shelter (movie), 225
Ginsberg, Arnie, 163
girl groups, 118, 158
    classic songs, 171
    end of, 170–171
    men behind, 167–170
    music writers for, 170–171
    obstacles, 172
    production formula for, 170
Girlschool, 379
Gitlin, Todd, 199, 218
Gladiolas, 119, 140
Gladys Knight and the Pips, 104, 252
Gladys Music, 124
glam (glitter) rock music, 285–289, 290
    in England, 286–287
Glaser, Tompall, 273
Glass Tiger, 291
Glass, Louis, 17
Glazier, Mitch, 491

Gleason, Ralph, 233–234, 236
Glitter (movie), 542
glitter rock music. *See* glam (glitter) rock music
Glitter, Gary, 286
Glover, Henry, 68, 105
Glover, Roger, 280
Gnutella, 486–487
Go Records, 434
Goddo, 385
Godfrey, Arthur, 111
Godley, Kevin, 341, 345
Godspeed! You Black Emperor, 432
Goffin, Jerry, 149, 170, 257, 259, 266–267
Going Hollywood (movie), 35
Gold Diggers (movie), 36
Goldberg, Whoopi, 459
Golden Dogs, 262
Golden Horseshoe area, Ontario, 79
Golden, Billy, 21
Goldie and the Gingerbreads, 265
Goldie, 452, 455
Goldmark, Dr. Peter, 74
Goldner, George, 114
Goldstein, Richard, 233
Gone records, 114
Good News (movie), 35
Goodman, Benny, 54, 62, 63, 262
Goodman, Mark, 342
Goodman, Steve, 261
Goodwin, Andrew, 339, 380, 381
Gordon, Bill, 78
Gordon, Kim, 430, 431
Gordon, Phil "Dr. Jive", 79
Gordy, Berry, 107, 115, 167, 168, 172–177, 193, 212, 252–253, 324
Gore, Al, 375, 409
Gore, Leslie, 147, 148
Gore, Tipper, 375, 408, 414
Gorme, Eydie, 153
Gorog, Chris, 500
Gortikov, Stan, 249, 408, 409, 410, 412
Gosden, Freeman, 33
gospel music, 106–110, 186, 204
    contrasted to doo wop music, 110
Gospel Starlighters, 109
Gotham records, 106
Gotti, Irv (Irv Lorenzo), 479
Gough, Tommy, 117
GQ magazine, 539
Gracie, Charlie, 146
Graduate, The (movie), 199
graffiti art, 389, 391
Graham Bond Organisation, 209
Graham, Bill, 231, 361
Graham, Renée, 477
Grammy Awards, 199, 258, 259, 331, 340, 342, 354, 367, 372, 384, 385, 388, 401, 432, 436, 458, 459, 467, 483, 523, 529, 537

Gramophone Co., Ltd., The, 19
gramophone, 19
Grand Funk Railroad, 283, 390
Grand Master Flash and the Furious Five, 334
Grand Ole Oprey Show (prev. *Barn Dance*), 47, 50, 105, 123, 127, 133
Grand Ole Oprey, 272
Grand Terrace club, Chicago, 49
Grande Ballroom, Detroit, 231
Grandmaster Flash, 390, 392
Grandmaster Melle Mel, 392, 401
Grandmixer Muggs, 404
Grannan, Nancy, 413
Grant, Eddie, 351
Grant, Peter, 277, 279
Grapes of Wrath, 434
graphophone, 17
Grateful Dead (prev. Warlocks), 39, 79, 206–207, 211, 212, 225, 228, 229, 235, 274
Graustark, Barbara, 322
Gravenites, Nick, 70
Graves, Claud L., 23
Gray, David, 530, 531
Gray, Glen, 52
Gray, Herman, 406
Gray, Jerry, 183
Gray, Macy, 464
Gray, Tony, 395
Grealis, Walt, 246
Grease (movie), 330
Great Big Sea, 248, 350, 432, 437
Great Depression, 29, 34, 42, 48, 49, 56, 136
  effect on recording industry, 53–54
  folk music and, 179–180
Great Speckled Bird, The, 184
Green Day, 514
Green, Peter, 192, 220
Green, Richard, 47
Green, Tony, 474
Greenberg, Florence, 168
Greenfield, Howard, 152
Greenpeace, 370
Greenwich, Ellie, 152, 170, 171
Greenwood, Lee, 501, 507–508
Greg Kihn Band, 346
Gregory, Dick, 264
Grein, Paul, 351, 358
Gridlock (movie), 420
Grieg, Edvard, 159
Griffith, Nanci, 517
Grohl, Dave, 26, 428
Grokster, 493, 494, 496, 497, 498
Grooverider, 452
Grossberg, Lawrence, 407
Grossman, Albert, 184, 270
GRT tape company, 229, 244
Gruen, Bob, 295
Gruesomes, 432, 433
Grundy, Bill, 308, 309
grunge music, 426–428
Grunt records, 228

Guarino, Justin, 534
Guess Who (prev. Chad Allen and the Expressions), 178, 194, 245, 276–277, 349
Guinness Book of World Records, 352
Guira, Lou, 347
Guitar Player magazine, 283, 378
Gulf and Western, 229
Guns 'n' Roses, 379, 385, 388, 415, 441
Guralnick, Peter, 106, 122, 127, 201, 233
Guru, 405
Guthrie, Arlo, 230, 352
Guthrie, Woody, 179–180, 182
Gutshall, Jack, 87
Guy Called Gerald, A, 452
Guy, 469
Guy, Buddy, 70
Guzman, Pablo, 334

H

H.O.R.D.E., 441
Hager, Sammy, 366
Hager, Steven, 392
Haggard, Merle, 206, 366, 442
Haight-Ashbury district, San Fransisco, 208
Hair (musical), 326
hair bands, 380
Hale, James, 436
Haley, Bill, 7, 84, 91, 99, 129, 139, 140, 141
Halifax, 47, 51, 177, 195, 425
  alternative music in, 432, 434
  hip hop scene in, 405
Hall (Daryl) and Oates (John), 334, 342, 363
Hall, John, 263, 264
Hall, Stuart, 3
Hallett, Bob, 437
Hallmark Records, 183
Hamill, Pete, 364
Hamilton, Ontario, 51, 131, 189, 209, 247, 269, 303
Hamm, Charles, 6, 22, 23, 24, 27, 37
Hammer (prev. M.C. Hammer), 401, 404, 441
Hammerstein, Oscar, 27, 62, 154
Hammett, Kirk, 386
Hammond, John, 54, 55, 180, 262
Hammond, Tommy, 416
Hamon, Clarence "Poppa Stoppa", 78
Hampton, Fred, 224
Hampton, Lionel, 69
Hampton, Mike, 325
Hancock, Herbie, 244, 370, 392
Hancock, Hunter, 79
Hand, Judge Learned, 60
Handlin, Oscar, 3
Handsome Ned (*a.k.a.* Robin Masyk), 435

Handy, W. C., 24–25, 28, 41, 42, 49
Haney's Big House, 122
Hank Ballard and the Midnighters, 105, 148
Hanks, Tom, 502
Hanson, 462
Happy Days (tv program), 266
Hard Day's Night, A (movie), 191
hardcore funk music, 390
Harder They Come, The (movie), 314
Hardesty, Herb, 84, 91
Hardship Post, 425, 434
Haring, Keith, 369
Harlan Leonard and the Kansas City Rockets, 98
Harlem Frolics revue, 41
Harlem Music Shop radio program, 79
Harmonium, 12, 186, 241, 350
Harmonizing Four, 104
Harold Melvin and the Blue Notes, 250
Harpo, Slim, 193
Harptones, 111
Harris, Charles K., 16
Harris, Emmylou, 10, 272, 274, 442
Harris, Jesse, 527
Harris, Oren, 156, 157
Harris, Thurston, 98
Harris, Wynonie, 59, 67, 68, 69, 83, 90
Harrison, George, 190, 214, 257, 315, 363
Harrison, Jerry, 302
Harrison, Wilbert, 164
Harrow, Ontario, 178
Harry, Deborah, 296–297, 301, 392
Hart, Corey, 365
Hart, Lorenz, 28, 36, 117
Hart, Mickey, 207
Harvard Business School, 497
Hatch, Orrin, 495
Hathaway, Donny, 254, 526
Haunted, 195
Have Not Been the Same: The Can-Rock Renaissance, 432
Havens, Richie, 220
Hawaiian Eye, 150
Hawkins, Coleman, 67
Hawkins, Hawkshaw, 64, 68
Hawkins, Ronnie, 131–132, 209, 270, 365
Hawkins, Screamin' Jay, 139, 141
Hawks, 270
Hawtin, Richie (Plastikman), 455
Hay, George D., 50
Hayden, Tom, 181
Hayes, Isaac, 249, 254, 322
Hays, Lee, 180
Haywire, 385
Hazel, Eddie, 325
Hazelwood, Lee, 150
Headbanger's Ball (tv program), 380

Headpins, 385
Healey, Jeff, 209
Healy, Jack, 367, 368
Hear Music, 256
Hearst, Patti, 298
Heart Records, 179
Heart, 283–284, 379, 388
Heartbreakers, 297
Heavy D. & the Boyz, 394
heavy metal music, 4, 5, 275–286
  African American, 381, 385, 388
  categories of, 381
  challenges masculinity, 284–285
  Christian fundamentalists and, 380–381
  context for, 283–284
  death, 381
  elements of, 276
  glam, 381
  in Canada, 385–386
  influences on, 277–279
  lack of industry support for, 283–284
  lack of women in, 283–284
  lite (pop), 381–382
  MTV and, 380–381
  new wave, 377–378
  on radio, 381–382
  origins of, 276
  PMRC and, 375–376
  psychedelics and, 279
  racism in, 388
  romance in, 382–383
  technology and, 376
  thrash (speed), 381, 383–384
  white, 381
  women in, 379, 388–389
Heilbut, Tony, 108
Heinemann, Otto, 38
Helix, 385
Hell's Angels, 225
Hell, Richard (*nee* Richard Meyers), 297, 298
Helm, Levon, 270
Helms, Chet, 233
Hemingway, Ernest, 269
Henderson, Fletcher, 41, 54, 67, 138
Henderson, Jocko, 77
Hendrix, Jimi, 5, 206, 209, 211–212, 212–214, 220, 226, 228, 244, 277, 324, 352, 376, 388, 393, 396, 425, 460, 501
Hendryx, Noma, 321
Henley, Don, 272, 273, 366, 491
Henry Rollins Band, 438
Henry, Clarence "The Frogman", 93
Herald/Ember records, 68, 111
Herb Alpert and the Tijuana Brass, 190
Herbert, Victor, 27
Heritage Foundation, 408
Herman's Hermits, 189, 191

Hernandez, Deborah Pacini, 467, 546
Hershey, Gerri, 176
Hertz, Heinrich, 29
Heston, Charlton, 418
Hetfield, James, 386
Heylin, Clinton, 297
Heywood, Earl, 47, 65
Hi-Fi's, 435
Hi-Fives, The, 131
Hide magazine, 269
high fidelity, 74
High School of Performing Arts, New York, 260, 525
high-fidelity stereo records, 230
Highway QCs, 104
Highwaymen, 145
Hilburn, Robert, 333, 435
Hill Billies, 44
Hill, Big Bill, 79
Hill, Chippie, 41
Hill, Dan, 260–261, 365
Hill, Faith, 443, 502
Hill, George Washington, 33
Hill, Lauryn, 456, 458, 459, 466
Hill, Trent, 155
hillbilly music, 9, 37, 38, 52, 64
    definition of, 44
    myths, 120
Hillman, Chris, 197, 272
Hilton, Paris, 547
Hinckley, David, 169
Hinds, Hayden & Eldridge, 58
Hines, Earl "Fatha", 40, 49
hip hop music, 11, 282, 389, 390
    disc jockeys, 390
    geography of, 471–474
    global, 403–405
    in Canada, 350
    Latino in, 391
    sexism in, 398–399
    Southern, 481–482
    style, 538
    women in, 399
hip hop soul music, 468–470
Hip Hop Summit Action Network, 484, 515
History of Rock Music, A: The Rock and Roll Era, 112
Hit Parader magazine, 233, 298, 410
Hitsville USA studio, 173
Hives, 522
Hoboken Four, 62
Hoffert, Paul, 244
Hoffman, Abbie, 219
Hoffman, Ben, 321
Hold Everything (movie), 35
Holden, Stephen, 261, 321, 392
Hole, 427, 430
Holiday Inn (movie), 35
Holland, Brian, 174, 175, 176, 252
Holland, Eddie, 174, 175, 176, 252
Holliday, Billie, 54, 202, 262, 527
Hollies, 189, 191, 221, 341
Hollings, Fritz, 409

Holloway, Nicky, 448
Holly, Buddy, 84, 99, 110, 129–130, 150, 157, 273
Hollywood Canteen (movie), 52
Hollywood Flames (*a.k.a.* Satellites), 98
Holzman, Jac, 215, 229, 296
Hondells, 160
Honeycombs, 192
Honeymoon Suite, 291
Hoobastank, 522
Hooker, John Lee, 43, 44, 67, 83, 99, 104, 193, 275
Hootie and the Blowfish, 444, 447
Hope, Bob, 508
Hopkins, Al, 44
Hopkins, Lightnin', 43
Horn, Bob, 149
Horne, Howard, 237, 238
Hornsey Art College, London, 237, 240
Horny Horns, 325
Horseshoe Tavern, Toronto, 436
Horton, Walter, 122
Hot 97 radio station, 542
Hot Band, 274
Hot Chocolate, 327
Hot Tracks (tv program), 339
house music, 448, 449
House of Pain, 404
House Party (movie), 401
House, Son, 43
Houston, Cissy, 354
Houston, Whitney, 354, 356, 358, 369, 463, 470, 501, 508
How I Won the War (movie), 234
Howar, Pam, 408, 415
Howe, Steve, 242
Howlett, Liam, 453
Hudson, Garth, 270
Hues Corporation, 326
Huey Lewis and the News, 356, 357
Huff, Leon, 250
Huffstutter, P. J., 490
Hughes, Howard, 171
Hullabaloo (tv program), 338
Human Be-In Festival, San Francisco, 1967, 211
Human League, 340
Humanist, The, 414
Humble Pie, 279, 289–290
Humphrey, Hubert, 218
Hunter, George, 236
Hunter, Ivory Joe, 59, 105, 141
Hunter, Meredith, 225
Hunter, Tab, 146
Hunter, Tommy, 365
Hunting, Russell, 18, 19
Hurban music, 547
Hurley, Steve Silk, 449
Hurt, Mississippi John, 43
Hüsker Dü, 319, 425
Husky, Ferlin, 132
Huxley, Aldous, 215
Hyde Park concert (1968), 225
Hyde, Paul, 365
Hyland, Brian, 148

Hyman, Jeff (Joey), 298
Hynde, Chrissie, 318–319

I

I Got the Hook-Up! (movie), 473
Ian and Sylvia (Ian Tyson and Sylvia Tyson (*nee* Sylvia Fricker)), 184
Ian, Janis, 217
Ice Cube, 400, 401, 411, 439, 440, 477
Ice-T, 393, 394, 398, 401, 417, 418, 419, 438, 439, 440
Idlewild (movie), 539
Idol, Billy, 308, 314, 340
Ienner, Don, 445
Ifield, Frank, 189
IFPI. *See* International Federation of the Phonographic Industry (IFPI)
Iggy Pop and the Stooges, 287, 295, 297
    see also Pop, Iggy
Iglesias, Enrique, 465, 468, 502, 503
Iglesias, Julio, 11, 351, 359
Ike and Tina Turner, 171
Illegal records, 318
Images in Vogue, 434
Impalas, 110, 141
Imperial Opera (Russia), 20
Imperial records, 68, 90, 93, 95
Imperials, 110
Impressions, 104, 186
In Old Santa Fe (movie), 52
Incredible Bongo Band, 390
Index on Censorship journal, 407
India.Arie, 526
Industrial Revolution, 2, 3
Inferno, 411
Ingram, James, 359, 401
Ink Spots, 63, 111, 116
Inner City records, 450
Innocents, 117
Institute for the Study of American Religion, 414
Inter-Global records, 329
International Federation of the Phonographic Industry (IFPI), 336, 485
International Monetary Fund, 261
International Talent Management (ITM), 173
internationalization, 352
Internet Service Provider (ISP), 495, 496
Internet, 486–487, 493–494
    protest music on, 513–514
Interview magazine, 294
Intruders, 250
Inuit musicians, 350
Invictus records, 252
Invisibl Skratch Piklz, 455
Iraq, invasion of, 507, 512, 516
Iron Butterfly, 278
Iron Maiden, 377–378, 378

IRS records, 431
IRS. *See* U.S. Internal Revenue Service (IRS)
Irwin, May, 18
Isis, 265
Island Records, 264, 309, 342, 373, 401, 542
Isle of Wight Festival, 244
Isley Brothers, 149, 188, 191, 213
ISP. *See* Internet Service Provider (ISP)
Italian Americans, 117–119, 146–147
ITM. *See* International Talent Management (ITM)
Ives, Burl, 159

J

J&M Studio, 90
J. Geils Band, 276, 345
Ja Rule, 466, 479, 480, 547
Jack Benny Show (radio program), 49
Jack, Ian, 347, 349, 432, 436
jacking, 449
Jackson Five, 252, 329, 342, 343, 390, 445, 462
Jackson State University, 226
Jackson, Alan, 507
Jackson, Brian, 264
Jackson, Bullmoose, 67, 68, 69
Jackson, Chuck, 188
Jackson, George, 217
Jackson, Hal, 79
Jackson, Janet, 356, 358, 446
Jackson, Joe, 317
Jackson, Li'l Son, 83
Jackson, Mahalia, 106
Jackson, Michael, 334, 335, 342–343, 344, 345, 351, 352, 354, 356, 357, 361, 401, 404, 425, 431, 437, 441, 444, 446, 467, 470, 501
Jackson, Papa Charlie, 43
Jackson, Paul, 344
Jackson, Randy, 533
Jackson, Reverend Jesse, 201, 254, 419
Jackson, Wanda, 133
Jacquet, Illinois, 84
Jagger, Mick, 192, 193, 194, 225, 284, 363, 503
Jaime records, 150
Jale, 425, 434
Jam and Spoon, 455
Jam Master Jay, 396, 481
Jam, 292, 293, 309, 312
Jam, Jimmy, 358
Jamaican influences, 350
Jamerson, James, 173, 175
James Gang, 178, 279
James, Colin, 209
James, Curtis, 538
James, Darryl, 420
James, Elmore, 122, 275

James, Etta, 98, 110, 140, 528, 543
James, Harry, 62
James, Mark (DJ Mark the 45 King), 402
James, Rick, 179, 333, 342
James, Skip, 210
James, Sonny, 132, 146
Jan (Berry) and Dean (Torrence), 158, 163
Jane Fonda's Workout (movie), 345
Jane's Addiction, 438
Jardine, Al, 160
Jarreau, Al, 401
Jarvis, Al, 60
Javits, Senator Jacob, 249
Jay and the Americans, 148
Jay-Z, 445, 470, 476, 478–479, 480, 503, 520, 537, 539, 540, 547
Jayhawks, 110
jazz music, 6, 23, 90, 110, 256, 282, 290, 317
   African American influences, 63
   distinctions between blues and, 67
   New Orleans, 25
   origins of, 25–26
   social voice of, 177
   Tin Pan Alley and, 24
Jazz Singer, The (movie), 34, 35
jazz-rock (fusion) music, 244–245
Jazzy Five, 391
JC Chasez, 462
Jean, Wyclef, 459, 501, 502, 545
Jeff Beck Group, 210
Jefferson Airplane, 206–207, 208, 211, 212, 218, 220, 221, 225, 228
Jefferson, Blind Lemon, 43, 127
Jellyfishbabies, 434
Jennings, Waylon, 10, 273–274, 512
Jerry Butler and the Impressions, 104
Jerry Jerry and the Sons of Rhythm Orchestra, 433–434
Jesse, Young, 132
Jesus and Mary Chain, The, 439, 440
Jethro Tull, 228, 238, 241, 245, 385, 513
Jett, Joan, 266
Jewel of the Nile (movie), 357
Jewel, 456
Jewish influences, 23, 183
Jim Kweskin's Jug Band, 260
Jimi Hendrix Experience, 208, 213, 428
Jive Records, 400, 462, 474
Jo-Jo and the Fugitives, 179
Joan Jett and the Blackhearts, 388
Jobete Publishing, 173
Jodeci, 469

Joe Liggins and the Honeydrippers, 67, 95
Joel Plaskett Emergency, 434
Joel, Billy, 290, 361, 366, 502, 503
Joey Dee and the Starlighters, 321
Johansen, David, 286
Johanson, Jai Johanny "Jaimo", 274
John, Elton, 290, 359, 447, 503
John, L'il, 539
John, Little Willie, 98, 105
John, Prakash, 179
Johnny and the Hurricanes, 159
Johnny and the Moondogs, 191
Johnny Kidd and the Pirates, 194
Johnny Maestro and the Crests, 117
Johnny Moore's Three Blazers, 95
Johnny Otis Show, 98
Johnny Thunders' Heartbreakers, 308
Johnson, Charles "the Electrifyin' Mojo", 449
Johnson, Eldridge R., 19
Johnson, George Washington, 18, 21, 22
Johnson, Jack, 530, 531, 532
Johnson, James P., 40
Johnson, James Weldon, 28
Johnson, Lyndon, 166, 199, 218
Johnson, Marv, 192
Johnson, Pete, 54–55, 91
Johnson, Robert, 43, 44, 138
Johnson, Simone, 402
Johnson, Stovepipe, 39
Jolliffe, C. B., 76
Jolson, Al, 12, 27, 28, 34, 35, 45, 53
Jon Lee and the Checkmates, 178
Jones, "Hoppy", 111
Jones, Ada (First Lady of Phonograph Records), 21
Jones, Casey, 39
Jones, George, 442
Jones, Grandpa, 68
Jones, Hettie, 202
Jones, Jimmy, 141, 164, 257
Jones, John Paul, 277
Jones, Mick, 304
Jones, Norah, 464, 525, 526–527, 536
Jones, Quincy, 333, 342, 344, 352, 358, 361, 401, 406
Jones, Simon, 532
Jones, Steve, 294, 305, 308
Jones, Tim, 506
Jones, Vanessa, 483
Jonquiére, Quebec, 385
Joplin, Janis, 13, 132, 184, 210, 211, 212, 214, 217, 220, 226, 228, 248
Joplin, Scott, 24
Jordan, Louis, 66, 95, 120, 317, 337
Jordan, Michael, 470

Jordanaires, 126
Joseph, Curtis, 179
Journey, 291
Journeymen, 145
Jowett, Mark, 434
Joy Division, 311
Joy of Cooking, 265
Jr. Gone Wild, 432, 434
Juanes, 530
Jubilee Records, 86, 111, 144
Judas Priest, 279, 284, 366, 377, 379, 413
Judson, Arthur, 31
Juice (movie), 401, 420
jukebox, 53, 68, 74–75, 79, 88
   video, 338
Julio 204, 391
Julliard School, The, 152
Juneau, Pierre, 246, 248, 435
Jungle Fever (movie), 452
jungle music, 451–452
Junior Walker and the All Stars, 173
Juno Awards (prev. RPM Gold Leaf Awards), 178, 248, 269, 282, 523, 528, 543
Justis, Bill, 159
Juvenile, 477

K

K-Os, 406
K. C. and the Sunshine Band, 327
Kags Music, 109
Kaipo, Joe, 46
Kalin Twins (Herbie and Hal), 132
Kallen, Kitty, 85
Kane, Arthur, 294
Kane, Big Daddy, 401
Kansas City Six, 55
Kansas, 290, 442
Kantner, Paul, 221
Kaplan, E. Ann, 381–382
Kapp, Jack, 54
Kardinal Offishall, 406, 543
Karenga, Ron, 216
Karloff, Boris, 277
Karnes, Kim, 359
Kashtin, 350
Katz, Steve, 208
Kaye, Lenny, 235, 297
Kaye, Sydney M., 155
Kaye, Tony, 239
KaZaA, 493, 494, 496, 497
KC and the Sunshine Band, 322
KCFJ radio station, 59
KCMU radio station, 425
KDAY radio station, 393
KDKA radio station, 30
Keelor, Greg, 435
Keen records, 108
Keene, Bob, 99, 108, 109
Keisker, Marion, 119
Keith, Toby, 508, 510, 512, 520
Keith-Albee theatres, 26–27
Keithley, Joey "Shithead", 320

Kelly, R., 470, 479, 509, 537, 547
Kelowna, British Columbia, 434
Kelvington, Saskatchewan, 349
Kendricks, Eddie, 252, 363
Kennedy, President John F., 166, 187, 507
   assassination of, 212
Kennedy, Robert, 216, 234
Kennedy, Steve, 179
Kenner, Chris, 192
Kenner, Roy, 178
Kenny and the Be-Bops, 131
Kenny, Bill, 111, 116
Kensington Market, 195, 261
Kent State University, 224, 302, 318
   student killings, 226
Kenton, Stan, 62
Kern, Jerome, 16, 36, 62, 117, 152
Kerner Commission on Civil Disorders (1968), 216
Kerr, Jim, 319
Kesey, Ken, 207
Ketjak Balinese Monkey Dance, 392
Key, cEvin (Kevin Crompton), 434
Keyes, James, 112
Keys, Alicia, 502, 525, 526, 539, 540, 547
KFMR radio station, 547
KFVD radio station, 79, 179
KFWB radio station, 52
Khan, Chaka, 264, 392, 401
Kid Frost, 393
Kid Koala, 455
Kid N Play, 401
Kid Rock, 459, 461
Kiedis, Anthony, 439, 440
Killer Dwarfs, 385
Kim, Lil', 482, 483
Kimberleys, 274
Kinetic Playground, Chicago, 231
Kinetoscope, 18
King Beezz, 195
King Biscuit Time (radio program), 49
King Crimson, 239
King Lou, 405
King Oliver's band, 25
King Records, 10, 64, 68, 69, 105, 116, 121, 153, 204
King's X, 388
King, B. B., 43, 44, 78, 84, 90, 122, 236, 276
King, Ben E., 115, 168, 188, 360
King, Carole, 149, 152, 153, 170, 171, 257–258, 259, 266, 505
King, Earl, 92
King, Jr., Reverend Martin Luther, 166, 181, 183, 234, 395
   assassination of, 216
King, Rodney, 417, 442
Kingston Trio, 144–145, 180
Kingston, Ontario, 23, 189, 436

Kinks, 192, 237, 277, 318, 341
Kinney Corporation, 229
Kirschner, Don, 152
Kiss, 285–286, 328, 377, 379, 442
Kitchener, Lord, 144
KJET radio station, 425
Klees, Stan, 178, 246
Kleinbard, Annette, 118
KLF, 451
KLIF radio station, 88
KMET radio station, 232, 333
KMIC radio station, 59
KMPX radio station, 232
KMS records, 450
Knight, Gladys, 359
Knight, Marion "Suge", 421
Knight, Terry, 283
Knowles, Beyoncé, 470, 479
Knox, Buddy, 129
Knuckles, Frankie, 448–449, 449
Kokomo, 159
Kool and the Gang, 323, 324, 358, 359, 391
Kool Here, 390, 391
Kool Moe Deer, 401
Kooper, Al, 208, 275
Kopkind, Andrew, 292, 326, 330
Korn, 459, 460, 461
Korner, Alexis, 192, 208
Kostash, Myrna, 349
Kotchmar, Danny "Kootch", 259
Kowalski, Ted, 119
KOWH radio station, 88
KPLA radio station, 59
KPRC radio station, 52
Kraftwerk, 340, 390, 392, 433, 449, 450
Kragen, Ken, 354, 361
Kral, Ivan, 298, 301
Kreutzmann, Bill, 207
Krieger, Robby, 215
Kristal, Hilly, 295, 302, 311
Kroeger, Chad, 522
KRS-One, 395, 405
Krugman, Paul, 507
Krupa, Gene, 62
KSAN radio station, 79, 232
KSFA radio station, 65
Ku Klux Klan, 44, 414
Kudlets, Harold, 131
Kunkel, Russ, 259
Kurtis Blow, 334, 390
KVOO radio station, 48, 52
KXLW radio station, 78
KXOL-FM radio station, 547
KYA radio station, 232
KYNO radio station, 232
KYW radio station, 59
KZZA radio station, 547

L

L.L. Cool J., 394, 398
L7, 425, 430
La Bostrie, Dorothy, 94, 96
LA Luv (Phillip Gayle), 405
La Rock, Scott, 395, 405

LA Times, 490
LaBelle, Patti, 264, 321, 358, 366, 458
Ladysmith Black Mambazo, 371–372
LaFace records, 474
Lahara, Preteen Brianna, 495
Laine, Frankie, 63, 64, 65, 136, 138
Laing, Corky, 385
Lake, Greg, 239
Lamb, Bill, 541
Lance, Herb, 72
Landau, Jon, 233, 234, 236, 263
Landis, John, 345
lang, k.d. (nee Kathryn Dawn Lang), 434, 435, 436, 455
Lange, Mutt, 378, 443
Langley, Jeff, 267
language, 11–12
Lanier, Allen, 297
Lanois, Daniel, 269, 349, 367
Lantree, Honey, 192
Lanza, Mario, 126
LARAS. See Latin Academy of Recording Arts and Sciences (LARAS)
Larks, 110
Last Poets, 391
"Last Waltz" concert, 1976, 184
Last Waltz, The (movie), 271
Latent Records, 435
Latin Academy of Recording Arts and Sciences (LARAS), 465
Latin beat, 143
Latin dance music, 121
Latin music, 11
  growth of, 544–545
Latin polyrhythms, 222
Latin rock music, 220
Latin-American music, 23
Latino music, 327, 331, 339, 363, 464–469, 543–544
  hip hop music and, 391
  Spanish and, 468–469
Lauper, Cyndi, 345–346, 361
Laurie records, 117
Lavigne, Avril, 464, 520, 525, 526, 536
Lawrence, Vince, 449
Le Bon, Simon, 341
Le Face Records, 539
Leachman, Silas, 21
Leadbelly (Huddie Ledbetter), 43, 44, 59, 105, 183
Leadon, Bernie, 272
Leary, Timothy, 207
Leavitt, Phil, 119
LeBlanc, Keith, 422
Leclair, Marc (a.k.a. Akufen), 455
Leclerc, Félix, 185
Led Zeppelin (prev. New Yardbirds), 192, 208, 229, 240, 277, 278, 279, 280, 282, 283, 284, 363, 377, 381, 392, 428, 472
Lee, Barbara, 117

Lee, Brenda (nee Brenda Mae Tarpley), 133, 269
Lee, Geddy, 279, 365
Lee, Peggy, 62, 152
Lee, Spike, 371, 401, 452
LEF Interactive, Australia, 497
LeFace Records, 469
Leiber, Jerry, 98, 114–115, 116, 118, 124, 125, 167, 168, 250
Lemay, Jacqueline, 268
Lennon, John, 190, 191, 214, 215, 217, 218, 224, 234, 262, 305, 501, 505
  murder of, 335
Lennon, Julian, 363
Lennon-McCartney songs, 190–191
Lennox, Annie, 340, 341, 345
Lesage, Premier Jean, 185
lesbian music, 267–268
  in Canada, 268–269
Lesh, Phil, 207
Letterman, David, 365
Levan, Larry, 448
Levinson, Nan, 407
Levy, Adam, 528
Lewis, E. R., 54
Lewis, Huey, 361
Lewis, Jerry Lee, 10, 41, 68, 84, 94, 121, 122, 127–128, 150, 157, 300
Lewis, Meade Lux, 54, 91
Lewis, Peter, 125
Lewis, Ramsey, 324
Lewis, Rudy, 115
Lewis, Smiley, 91, 93, 126, 141, 316
Lewis, Terry, 358
LFO, 462
Liberty Belles revue, 41
Liberty Records, 106, 411
Lifehouse, 521, 522
Lifeson, Alex, 279
Liggins, Joe, 95
Lightfoot, Gordon, 184, 185, 230, 245, 261, 349, 365
Lighthouse, 241, 244
Lightin' Rod (nee Jalal Nurindin), 391
Lil' Kim, 472
Lilith Fair, 434, 441, 457–458, 459
Lillywhite, Steve, 531
Limeliters, 145
Limp Bizkit, 459, 460, 461, 502
Linden, Colin, 262, 532
Linkin Park, 521, 522
Linna, Miriam, 312
Lippincott, Jesse, 17
Lipsitz, George, 66, 84
Liskiw, Greg, 195
Listen to the Lambs, 98
Literary Digest, 23
Little Anthony and the Imperials (prev. Chesters), 114
Little Caesar and the Romans, 119
Little Feat, 272
Little Lulu comic strip, 129

"Little Nipper" logo, 19
Little Rock, Arkansas, 167
Live Aid concerts, 315, 360, 362, 363, 370
Liverpool College of Art, 237
Liverpool, 282
Living Color (tv program), 401
Living Colour, 385, 388, 422, 424, 438, 439, 444
Living Single (tv program), 401
LLoyd, Richard, 295
LMR Records, 405
LoCascio, Phil, 513
Loch Ness, Scotland, 242
Lockhart, Eugene, 23
Lockie, Steven (a.k.a. Nazi Dog), 303–304
Lockwood, Robert, 49
Loew's theatres, 26
Logan, Karen, 413
Loggins, Kenny, 357
Lollapalooza festivals, 308, 425, 436, 437–438, 457
Lomax, Alan, 43, 70
Lomax, John, 43
Lombardo, Guy, 6, 54, 63, 248
London Blues and Barrelhouse Club, 192
London Festival Orchestra, 239
London Philharmonic Orchestra, 239
London records, 131
London School of Economics, 194
London Symphony Orchestra, 240
London, Ontario, 23, 189, 303, 385, 455
Lone Star Rangers, The (radio program), 52
Long & McQuade, 231
Long, Jack, 231
Longhair, Professor, 85, 91
Lont, Cynthia, 267
Loose Joints, 449
Lopez, Jennifer, 465, 466, 468, 480, 547
Lopez, Trini, 180, 183
Lopez, Vincent, 30
Lord of the Rings (movie), 244
Lord, Jon, 239, 279, 280
Lorenz, George "Hound Dog", 79, 88, 178
Los Angeles Times, 277, 435
Los Angeles, 95–96, 98–99
Los Fabulosos Cadillacs, 465
Los Lobos, 11, 372
Lou, Mammy, 39
Loud records, 476
Louis Armstrong Show (radio program), 49
Louisiana Hayride, 123
Louisville Jug Band, 46
Love Me Tender (movie), 124
Love Unlimited Orchestra, 254, 472
Love Unlimited, 254
Love, Airrion, 251
Love, Courtney, 427, 430
Love, Darlene, 169, 171

Love, Mike, 160, 408, 409
Love, Monie, 399, 401, 402
Loverboy, 291, 365, 385
Lovin' Spoonful, 198, 199, 270
Lowe, Nick, 308, 316
Lowe, Ruth, 62
Lox, 472
LP. *See* 33 rpm record (LP)
LSD. *See* lysergic acid diethy-
    lamide (LSD)
Lucky Millinder Orchestra, 83
Ludacris, 539, 540
Lukather, Steve, 344
Luke Records, 416
Luman, Bob, 123
Lundvall, Bruce, 528
Luny (Francisco Saldana) Tunes
    (Víctor Cabrera),
    545–546, 547
Lush, 439, 440
Lydon, Michael, 227, 234
Lymon, Frankie, 234
Lynn, Loretta, 366, 528
Lynn, Vera, 189
Lynyrd Skynyrd, 274, 275, 442
lysergic acid diethylamide
    (LSD), 207, 240, 324

M

M/A/R/R/S, 450
Mabon, Willie, 99
MacIsaac, Ashley, 350, 437
Mack, Cecil, 28
Mack, Greg, 393
MacKaye, Ian, 319
Mackenzie King, Prime Minister
    William Lyon, 32
MacNeil, Rita, 268
Macola Records, 393
Macomba nightclub, 69
Macon, Uncle Dave (David Har-
    rison), 50
Mad Dogs and Englishmen tour,
    220
Mad magazine, 229
Mad Max: Beyond Thunderdome
    (movie), 357
Maddox, Rose, 133
Madison Square Garden, 263,
    503
Madness, 315
Madonna, 345, 354–355, 356,
    357, 358, 359, 361, 408,
    415, 446, 447, 454, 467,
    513
Maestro, Johnny (John Mas-
    trangelo), 117
magnetic tape, 71–72
magnetophone, 71
Mahavishnu Orchestra, 244
Mahler (movie), 311
Maines, Natalie, 510, 511
Major Bowes Amateur Hour (radio
    program), 62
Make Believe Ballroom (radio pro-
    gram), 59
Makeba, Miriam, 183, 372

*Making of Michael Jackson's
    Thriller, The* (movie), 345
Malcolm X (*nee* Malcolm Little),
    187, 200, 395, 422
Mallory's Music, New Orleans,
    80
Malmsteen, Yngwye, 378
Malone, Bill C., 38, 39, 44, 52,
    270, 274
Malopoets, 366
Mama Quilla II and the Para-
    chute Club, 269, 349
Mamas and the Papas, 199, 211,
    212
Mammy (movie), 36
Mana, 465, 466
Manchester, Melissa, 260
Mandala, 178
Mandela, Nelson, 366, 368, 395
Mandela, Winnie, 395, 399
Mandy (Moore), 462
Manero, Tony, 330
Manfred Mann, 189, 191, 210
Mangione, Chuck, 244
Manilow, Barry, 289
Mann Act (White-Slave Traffic
    Act of 1910), 101, 157
Mann, Barry, 152, 170
Mann, Herbie, 331
Manson, Charles, 224, 312
Manta Sound, 179
Manuel, Richard, 270
Manzarek, Ray, 215, 315
MAPL. *See* Maple Leaf System
    (MAPL)
Maple Leaf Gardens, Toronto,
    153
Maple Leaf System (MAPL), 246
MAPP. *See* minimum advertising
    price programs
Mapplethorpe, Robert, 297
Maratime musicians, 350
March on Washington, 1963,
    180
March, Little Peggy, 148
Marchan, Bobby, 92
Marconi, Guglielmo, 29, 30
Marcucci, Bob, 146
Marcus, Greil, 84, 110, 111,
    234, 235, 361
Mardi Gras parade, 90
Mardin, Arif, 330
Mariposa Folk Festival (orig.
    Orillia, Ontario), 184,
    185, 256
marketing, 8–11
Marketts, 159
Marley, Bob, 264–265, 314,
    315, 326, 459, 501, 505
Marley, Rohan, 459
Mars, 315
Marsalis, Branford, 368
Marsh, Dave, 233, 332, 370,
    411
Marshall Tucker Band, 274–275
Marshall, Laurie, 329
Marshall, Wayne, 543, 546
Martha and the Muffins, 269
Martha and the Vandellas, 168,
    173, 175, 176, 252

Martin, Dean, 63, 126
Martin, George, 191, 214, 235,
    236
Martin, Janis, 133
Martin, John, 346
Martin, Linda, 154, 380
Martin, Mary, 270
Martin, Max, 462
Martin, Miss Halloween, 59
Martin, Ricky, 12, 465, 547
Martin, Sarah, 41
Martin, Vince, 144
Martinex, Eddie, 393, 396
Martino, Al, 63
Marvelettes, 73, 164, 168, 175,
    252
Marvin and Johnny, 140
Marx, Karl, 311
Masakela, Hugh, 212, 366, 372
Mase, 472
Mashmakan, 241
Massey Hall, Toronto, 435
Massive Attack, 452
Mastrangelo, John. *See* Maestro,
    Johnny (John Mas-
    trangelo)
Matall, John, 192
Matassa, Cosimo, 90, 91, 92, 93,
    96
Matchbox Twenty, 466, 522
Mathias, Charles, 409
Mathis, Johnny, 108, 139, 152
Matlock, Glen, 294, 305
Matsushita records, 172
Matthews, Count, 98
Matthews, Dave, 466, 502, 513,
    515, 530–531
Matthews, Shirley, 178
Maugeri, Rudy, 118
Max Webster, 282, 385
Max's Kansas City bar, New
    York, 295, 298, 308
May, Derrick, 448, 450
Mayall, John, 290
Mayer, John, 530, 531
Mayfield, Curtis, 104, 186–187,
    249
Mays, Willie, 79
MBE. *See* Members of the British
    Empire (MBE)
MC Flavor Flav, 395
MC Lyte, 399
MC Ren, 477
MC5, 218, 296
MCA Records, 51, 172, 409,
    436, 485
McBride, Bob, 244
McBride, Terry, 434
McCann, Sean, 437, 457
McCarthy era, 144, 157
    folk music in, 180
McCarthy, Senator Gene, 218
McCarthy, Senator Joe, 135
McCartney, Paul, 23, 97, 190,
    191, 214, 257, 298, 343,
    358, 363, 489, 502, 503,
    504
    see also Paul McCartney and
    Wings
McClary, Susan, 407

McCullom, John, 412
McDaniels, Darryl (MDC), 393,
    396
McDonald, Michael, 359
McEntire, Reba, 443, 455, 512
McFerrin, Bobby, 401
McGhee, Brownie, 183
McGhee, Stick, 70
McGraw, Tim, 443, 536
McGuinn, Roger (*nee* Jim
    McGuinn), 197, 199, 489
McGuire Sisters, 130, 140
McGuire, Barry, 198, 199, 509,
    517
MCing, 390
McKenna Mendelson Mainline,
    208–209
McKenna, Mike, 208–209
McKenzie, Scott, 210, 211, 214
McKernan, Phil, 79
McKernan, Ron "Pigpen", 79,
    207
McKinley, Larry, 78
McLachlan, Sarah, 248, 432,
    434, 437
McLaren, Malcolm, 294, 299,
    304, 308, 309, 311, 318
McLauchlan, Murray, 185, 261,
    349, 365
McLaughlin, John, 214, 244
McLean, Don, 513
McLendon, Gordon, 88
McLuhan, Marshall, 362
McMaster, Natalie, 437
McNeely, Big Jay, 67, 84
McNeil, Legs, 292
McPhatter, Clyde, 85, 106, 107,
    152
McRae, Floyd "Buddy", 112
McRae, George, 326, 327
MCs, 390, 391
McTell, Blind Willie, 43
McVie, Christine, 290
McVie, John, 192, 290
Media Monopoly, The, 505
Mee, Michie (Michelle McCul-
    loch), 350, 405
Megadeath, 383, 442
Meisner, Randy, 272
Melanie, 220
Mellencamp, John Cougar, 366,
    370, 458, 503, 509
Mellers, Wilfred, 235, 236
Mello-Tones, 114
Melody Maker magazine, 293,
    316
Melton, J. Gordon, 414
Meltzer, Richard, 284
Members of the British Empire
    (MBE), 194
Memphis Commercial-Appeal, 50
Memphis Horns, 200
Memphis Recording Service,
    122, 126
Men Without Hats, 432–433,
    433
Mendehlson, John, 277
Mendelson, Joe, 208–209
Mercer Art Center, New York,
    286, 294, 297

Mercer, Johnny, 60, 147
Merchant, Natalie, 456
Mercury News, 497
Mercury records, 64, 100, 111, 112, 116, 117, 118, 119, 139, 140, 229, 373
    cover records, 140
Mercury, Freddie, 237
Merge Records, 523
Meritt records, 42
Merry Widow, The (movie), 36
Messer, Don, 50–51
Messina, Joe, 173
Metal magazine, 389
Metallica, 320, 383, 384, 385, 386–387, 413, 490, 501, 505
Metro-Goldwyn-Mayer (MGM), 34
Metropolitan Opera, 20, 29, 31
Metzger, Tom, 414, 509
Mexican influence, 190
MFSB (Mother Father Sister Brother), 252, 322
MGM Records, 64, 65, 133, 139, 141, 229, 253
MGM. *See* Metro-Goldwyn-Mayer (MGM)
Mia-X, 482
Miami sound, 328
Miamis, 286
Michael, George, 358, 359, 513
Michaelangelo, 235
Michel, Jacques, 186
Michel, Prakazrel "Pras", 459
Michigan Women's Music Festival, 267
Mickey Mouse Club, 150, 462
Microsoft Network (MSN), 493
middle class, 1, 15
    surf music, 158
Middleton, Richard, 6
Midler, Bette, 264, 289
Midnight Oil, 366, 370
Midnighters, 109, 110
Midnights, 110
Midwestern Hayride (radio program), 68
Milburn, Amos, 67, 95
Miles, Buddy, 210
Miles, Lynn, 262
Milestone Communications, 406
Miller, Bruce, 78
Miller, Glenn, 62, 63, 332
Miller, Jim, 234, 252, 353
Miller, Max, 62
Miller, Mitch, 138
Miller, Percy (*a.k.a.* Master P), 472–473
Miller, Steve, 210, 211
Milligan, Jeff (DJ Algorithm), 455
Millinder, Lucky, 68
Millington, Jean, 265
Millington, June, 265–266
Mills Brothers, 35, 54, 63, 111
Milton, Roy, 67, 95
Minglewood, Matt, 209
Mingus, Charles, 256

minimum advertising price programs (MAPP), 492
Ministry, 439, 440
Minnesota Mining and Manufacturing Company (3M), 71, 74
Minor Threat, 319
Mintz, Leo, 80
Minutemen, 319, 425
Miracles, 173, 188, 252
Mirrors, The, 302, 310
Miseducation of the Negro, The, 459
Miserables, Les, 465
Mission Impossible II (movie), 490
Misty in Roots, 314
Mitch Ryder and the Detroit Wheels, 170
Mitchell's Christian Singers, 55
Mitchell, Guy, 65, 132
Mitchell, Joni, 184, 185, 221, 224, 229, 230, 245, 256, 257, 259, 260, 365, 459
Mitchell, Kim, 365
Mitchell, Mitch, 213
Mitoo, Skatalite Jackie, 179
Mizzell, Jason (Jam Master Jay), 393, 396
Mo'Wax records, 453
Moby (Richard Melville Hall), 453, 454–455, 502
Moby Grape, 206, 208
Modern Lovers, 302
Modern records, 67–68, 79, 95, 140
Modern/RPM records, 122
Moev, 432, 434
Mojo-Navigator R&R News magazine, 233
Molly Hatchett, 274, 275
Molotov, 465
Moncton, New Brunswick, 434
Mondale, Walter, 354
Money, H. F., 6
Monica, 462
Monkees, 153, 213, 229, 286, 390
Monkees, The (tv program), 338
Monroe, Bill, 123
Monroe, Marilyn, 301
Monroe, Vaughn, 62, 139
Monterey International Pop Festival, 211–212, 213, 234
    psychedelics and, 214–215
Montez, Chris, 190
Montgomery Ward, 39
Montreal Symphony Orchestra, 241
Montreal, 18, 19, 30, 47, 65, 186, 195, 209, 233, 247, 291, 385, 523
    alternative music in, 432, 433
    disco in, 329
    electronica music in, 455
    hip hop scene in, 405
    rap scene in, 406
Monument records, 128, 130
Moody Blues, 190, 238–239, 245
Moog synthesizer, 239

Moon Dog House Rock 'n' Roll Party, The (radio program), 80
Moon Records, 282
Moon, Keith, 277, 428
Moonglows, 115, 140
Moore, LeRoi, 531
Moore, Melba, 332
Moore, Peter, 435
Moore, Scotty, 123, 125, 127
Moore, Thurston, 430, 431
Morali, Jacques, 328
morality, 13–14
More Cowboy Songs (sheet music), 47
Morello, Tom, 461, 516
Morgan, Jane, 85
Morisette, Alanis, 248, 456, 458, 459, 460
Moroder, Georgio, 323, 326, 328, 329
Morpheus, 493, 494, 497, 498
Morrison, Jim, 212, 215, 216, 226, 297
Morrison, Junie, 325
Morrison, Sterling, 295, 296
Morrison, Val, 186, 248–249, 262
Morrison, Van, 230, 352
Morse, Dave, 236
Morse, Steve, 351, 456
Morton, George "Shadow", 170, 171
Moss Def, 502
Mothers of Invention, 230, 238
Motion Picture Association of America (MPAA), 493
Motion Pictures Export Group (MPEG), 486, 492
Mötley Crüe, 284, 379, 381, 384, 411, 446
Motörhead, 284, 377, 378, 379
Motown 25 (tv program), 343
Motown music, 158, 168, 172–174, 175, 342
    British invasion and, 193
    civil rights movement and, 173–174, 177
    competition for, 200
    end of, 252–253
    social voice of, 177
Motown Records, 104, 107, 115, 226, 232, 236, 252, 329, 342, 373, 462
    black pride and, 200–201
    tour of UK, 193
Motown sound, 173–177
Mott the Hoople, 287
Mottola, Tommy, 445
Mountain, 385
Mouvement, 406
movies,
    history of, 34–36
    music and, 356–357
    see also individual movie titles
    soundtracks, 356–357
Moxy, 385
Moyet, Alison, 453
Mozart, Wolfgang Amadeus, 276, 411

MP3 (MPEG 1—Audio Layer 3), 486–487, 492
    players, 493–494
    protest songs on, 513–514
MP3 players, 488–489
MP3.com, 487, 489
MP4 format, 499
MPAA. *See* Motion Picture Association of America (MPAA)
MPEG. *See* Motion Pictures Export Group (MPEG)
Mr. Lif, 514
Mraz, Jason, 530, 531
Ms. magazine, 229
MSN. *See* Microsoft Network (MSN)
MTV Unplugged (tv program), 445, 467, 502
MTV, 337, 338–339, 341–342, 343, 346, 351, 359, 363, 375, 380, 381, 384, 401, 422, 425, 441, 443
    and MuchMusic, 348–349
MuchMusic, 339, 346–347, 369, 434
    MTV and, 348–349
Mud Honey, 425
Mugwumps, 199
Muir, Lewis F., 28
Mulan (movie), 463
Mulcahy, Russel, 341
Muldaur, Maria, 260
Mullen, Don, 438, 439
Mullican, Moon, 64, 68, 69, 105, 128
multiculturalism, 83
Murcia, Billy, 294
Murderrecords, 434
Murdoch, Rupert, 532
Murphy, Chris, 434
Murphy, Dudley, 48
Murray the K, 214
Murray, Anne, 273, 365
Murrell, Herbie, 251
Murvin, Junior, 314
MUSE. *See* Musicians United for Safe Energy (MUSE)
Music Box, 339
music industry,
    commercialsim of, 227–228
    copyright legislation for, 488–489
    discrimination in, 249–250
    in Canada, 289
    in new millennium, 519–521
    infrastructure, 231–232
    international sales, 373
    internet and, 485–487, 493–494
    marketing of, 228–229, 444–445
    merger era of, 289–290
    mergers, 229–230
    military connections, 230
    more mergers, 485
    music videos and, 338–339
    piracy and, 491–494
    recession in, 335–337, 351

responses to culture war, 423–424
Music Max, 348
music press,
    different reaction to black music, 248–249
    rock, 232, 233–234
music production, 230–231
Music Row Democrats, 517
Music Without Borders: Live, 504
Musical Clock (radio program), 59
musical theatre. *See* vaudeville
Musicians United for Safe Energy (MUSE), 263
Musicians United to Win Without War (MUWWW), 515
MusiquePlus, 348
Mussorgsky, Modest, 239, 411
Mutual Broadcasting System, 31
MUWWW. *See* Musicians United to Win Without War (MUWWW)
Muzio, 406
Myers, Mike, 539
Mynah Birds, 179
Mystikal, 482

N

N'Dour, Youssou, 365–366, 367, 371
N.O.R.E., 544
N.W.A. (Niggas With Attitude) (prev. World Class Wrecking Cru), 393, 395, 399, 400, 418, 419, 474
N.Y.C. Peech Boys, 449
NAACP. *See* National Association for the Advancement of Colored People (NAACP)
NAB. *See* National Alliance of Broadcasters (NAB)
Naked Lunch, 276, 291
Napanee, Ontario, 528
Nappy Roots, 536
Napster, 486–487, 490, 491, 492, 493, 498, 499, 500
NARAS. *See* National Academy of Recording Arts and Sciences (NARAS)
Nas, 478, 515
Nash, Graham, 191, 221, 224, 256
Nash, Johnny, 314
Nashville Network, The (TNN), 339, 422, 443
Nashville Rebel (movie), 274
Nashville Teens, 190
Nashville, 132
Nathan, David, 400
Nathan, Syd, 20, 68, 69, 105, 109, 116, 121
Nation of Islam, 484
Nation, The, 516

National Academy of Recording Arts and Sciences (NARAS), 384, 385, 401, 465
National Alliance of Broadcasters (NAB), 31, 33, 57, 59
    AFM and, 59
    ASCAP and, 58
National Association for the Advancement of Colored People (NAACP), 61, 137, 166, 418, 484, 515
National Association of Television and Radio Announcers (NATRA), 249
National Barn Dance (radio program), 18, 50, 52
National Black Police Association, 418
National Broadcasting Company (NBC), 30, 31, 33, 47, 49, 62
National Electric Signaling Company, 29
National Federation of Music Clubs, 13
National Front Party, 304, 312, 313, 314, 316
National Organization for Women (NOW), 217, 505
National Political Congress of Black Women (NPCBW), 419
National Rainbow Coalition, 419
National Records, 70, 111
National Sheriff, The, 414
Native Americans, 183
    folklore, 272
NATRA. *See* National Association of Television and Radio Announcers (NATRA)
Nazario, Ednita, 465
Nazi paraphernalia, 284, 292, 310–313
NBC-TV, 213, 339
NBC. *See* National Broadcasting Company (NBC)
Ndegéocello, Me'Shell, 458
Neal, Bob, 124
Near, Holly, 267
Neely, Kim, 426
Negro Hour, The (radio program), 59
Negus, Keith, 471, 473
Neil, Vince, 411
Nelly, 482
Nelson, Havelock, 418
Nelson, Rick (Ricky), 92, 146, 147, 151, 272
Nelson, Sandy, 159
Nelson, Willie, 11, 273, 274, 359, 366, 502, 512
NEMS company, 330
Neon Rome, A, 432, 435
Neptunes, 463
Nettwerk Records, 434, 457
Nevins, Al, 152

Nevius, Sally, 408, 414
New Brunswick Lumberjacks, 51
New Brunswick, 18, 52
New Christy Minstrels, 180
New Cowboy Songs (sheet music), 47
New Edition, 462
New England Conservatory, 49
New Haven Women's Liberation Rock Band, 265
New Hormones records, 309
New Jack City (movie), 401
New Kids on the Block, 462
New Left, 218, 227, 234
New Musical Express magazine, 298, 318
New Order magazine, 312
New Order, 311, 340
New Orleans, 89–95, 95, 96
new romantic movement, 339–340
New Voice records, 171
new wave music, 282
New York City,
    doo wop centre, 111–112
New York Dolls, 286, 294–295, 297, 311, 379
New York Symphony Orchestra, 30
New York Times, 319, 360, 398, 414, 415, 419, 438, 447, 507, 512
New York's Academy of Music, 194
Newell, Richard "King Biscuit Boy", 209
Newfoundland, 437
Newman, Randy, 230, 261
Newport Folk Festival, 104, 181, 184, 197
News Corporation, 532
Newsted, Jason, 413
Newsweek magazine, 198, 263, 322, 330, 353, 417
Newton, Wayne, 465
Newton-John, Olivia, 345
Nice, 239
Nickelback, 248, 521, 522, 536
Nicks, Stevie, 290, 346
Nico, 295, 296, 312
Nielsen SoundScan, 497
Night Flight (tv program), 339
Night Tracks (tv program), 339
Nightengale, Maxine, 327
Nightwatchman, 516
Nils, 433
Nimbus Nine Productions, 195, 245, 303
Nine Inch Nails, 438
Ninja Tune records, 455
Nirvana, 425, 426, 427, 428–430, 440, 441, 442, 444, 466
Nitty Gritty Dirt Band, 270
Nitzsche, Jack, 159
Nixon, Richard M., 136, 218, 224, 234, 250, 253, 272, 273
No Doubt, 456, 462

No Electronic Theft Act (1997), 488
No Limit Army, 472, 473
No Nukes concerts, 263–264
Nobel Peace Prize, 364
Nobles, Gene, 78
Noetix Records, 434
NoFX, 514, 516
Nolan, Bob, 52
Nolan, Faith, 178
Nolan, Jerry, 294
Norman Lear Center, University of Southern California, 491
North American Phonograph Company, 17
North Bay, Ontario, 131
Northeastern Law School, 52
Northern Lights, 365
Notorious B.I.G., 461
Notting Hill carnival, London, 307
Nova Express, 276
Nova Scotia, 47
    black population, 178
Novoselic, Krist, 426, 428
NOW. *See* National Organization for Women (NOW)
NPCBW. *See* National Political Congress of Black Women (NPCBW)
'N Sync, 461, 462, 465, 528
Nuclear Assault, 383
Nugent, Ted, 279, 290, 377
Numan, Gary, 340
Number of Names, A, 449
Nutmegs, 111, 119
Nutty Professor, The (movie), 478
Nyro, Laura, 211

O

O'Casey, Michael, 18
O'Connor, Billy, 301
O'Connor, Cardinal John J., 414
O'Connor, Sinéad, 422, 444, 458
O'Day, Anita, 62
O'Hara, Geoffrey, 23
O'Hara, Mary Margaret, 435
O'Jays, 250
O'Neill, Eugene, 48
O'Riordan, Dolores, 456
O, 268
Oakenfeld, Paul, 448
Oakley, Berry, 274
Oasis, 454
obscenity laws, Canadian, 320–321
Ocean, Billy, 356, 357, 358
Ochs, Phil, 181, 183, 198, 218, 516
October Game, 434
Ode Records, 257, 259
Odetta, 183
ODJB. *See* Original Dixieland Jazz Band (ODJB)
Offenbach, 186, 241

Office de la langue Française, L'
(The Office of the French
language) (Quebec), 185
Officer and a Gentleman, An
(movie), 184
Offord, Eddie, 242
Og Records, 433
Ogre, Nivek (Kevin Ogilvie), 434
Ohio Express, 328
Ohio Players, 323–324
OKeh Record Company, 38, 41,
43, 53, 70, 138, 139
Ol' Dirty Bastard, 476
Olatunji, 264
Old Gold Show, The (radio pro-
gram), 49
Oldham, Andrew Loog, 194
Oliver, George, 178
Olivia Records, 266–267, 267,
268
Olsen, George, 30
Olympics, 115
Omar, Don, 546
Omega Equities, 229
On the Avenue (movie), 36
Once Upon a Time (mini opera),
328
one hit wonders, 111
Ono, Yoko, 218
Ontario Place, Toronto, 304
Ontario, 349
black population in, 178
Opera House, Bowery, New
York, 26
Oprah Winfrey Show, The (tv pro-
gram), 525
Orb, 451
Orbison, Roy, 128, 130–131,
133, 269, 436
Original Dixieland Jazz Band
(ODJB), 22, 25
Original Lockers, 390
Orillia, Ontario, 185
Orioles, 85, 86, 87, 106, 110,
111
Orleans, 263
Orloff, Katherine, 258
Orlons, 148, 168
Orpheum theatres, 26, 27
Orwell, George, 304
Osborne, Joan, 456, 457
Osbourne, Ozzy, 284, 285, 366,
378, 379, 384, 389, 412,
413, 414
Osbourne, Sharon, 389
Osburne, Marg, 51
Oshawa, Ontario, 385
Osmond, Donny, 409
Ostin, Mo, 229, 230
Otis, Johnny, 59, 95, 98, 100,
110, 114, 125
Ottawa, 32, 261
doo wop music in, 118
Out of Sight (movie), 466
OutKast, 481–482, 514, 520,
537, 539
Owen, William Barry, 19
Owens, Buck, 10
Owens, Harry, 35
Oxford, "Jumpin'" George, 79

P

P-Funk vocal chorus, 325, 537
P2P. *See* peer-to-peer (P2P) ser-
vices
Pace, Harry, 25, 42
Pacific Phonograph Company,
17
Packard, Vance, 156
Page, Jimmy, 220, 277, 283, 472
Page, Patti, 85, 88, 112, 136
Page, Steven, 436
Pagliaro, Michel, 241, 350
Paice, Ian, 280
Paiment, Rachel, 365
Palevsky, Max, 235
Paley, William S., 31, 32–33, 54
Palmer, Bruce, 179, 211
Palmer, Carl, 239
Palmer, Earl, 90
Palmer, Robert, 41, 83, 84, 202,
319, 345, 358
Palmieri, Eddie, 264
Panagoniuk, Charley, 350
Pantages theatres, 26
Parade magazine, 413
Paradise records, 111
Paramount Studios, 34, 43, 53,
229
Pareles, Jon, 398, 438, 530, 531,
532
Parent/Teacher Association
(PTA), 408
Parents Music Resource Center
(PMRC), 375, 407,
408–421
Paris Sisters, 118
Paris, 514–515
Parizeau, Premier Jacques, 186
Parker, Colonel Tom, 124
Parker, Graham, 308
Parker, Kris (KRS-One), 402
Parker, Little Junior, 122
Parker, Maceo, 204, 325
Parks, Rosa, 167, 395
Parlet, 325
Parliament, 321, 324, 325, 328,
439, 449
Parrish, Maxfield, 236
Parsons, Gram, 272
Parton, Dolly, 274, 331
Partridge Family, The (tv pro-
gram), 338
Pastor, Tony, 26
Patel, Judge Marilyn Hall, 490
patronage, 2
Patti LaBelle and the Blue Belles,
174
Patti Smith Group, 298
see also Smith, Patti
Patton, Charlie, 43
Paul and Paula, 148
Paul Butterfield Blues Band, 181
Paul McCartney and Wings, 289
Paul Revere and the Raiders, 206
Paul, Les, 23, 136
Paul, Sean, 537, 547

Paupers, The, 195, 211, 244,
261
Pavitt, Bruce, 425
payola hearings (1959–1960),
27, 154, 156–158, 409
Payolas, 365
Peaches and Herb, 329
Peacock Records, 93, 106
Peaks, Anthony, 402
Pearl Jam, 425, 426, 427, 439,
440, 447, 501, 513, 517
Pearlman, Lou, 462
Pearson, Prime Minister Lester
B., 179
Peart, Neal, 279, 282
Peck, Abe, 292
Peel, John, 308
Peer, Ralph, 41, 43, 46, 58
Peer-Southern Music, 130
peer-to-peer (P2P) services, 494,
496, 498, 499
Peerless Quartet, 18
Pegley, Karen, 348, 504
Pelicans, 110
Peltier, Leonard, 460
Penguins, 85, 110, 116, 119,
140
Pennies from Heaven (movie), 35
Penny, Hank, 68, 69
Pentangle, 192
Pentland, Patrick, 434
People magazine, 332, 342, 411
People, Ishan, 179
Peppermint Lounge, New York,
321
Pere Ubu, 302, 311
Peretti, Hugo, 108
Performing Rights Society
(Britain), 28
Perkins, Carl, 10, 43, 88, 121,
122, 127, 128, 138, 150
Perkins, John, 118
Perkins, Ray, 118
Peroff, Justin, 523
Perren, Freddie, 329
Perry, Joe, 393
Perry, Lee "Scratch", 314
Perry, Linda, 529
Perry, Richard, 265
Perry, Steve, 84
Pet Shop Boys, 517
Peter and Gordon, 190
Peter, Paul & Mary, 180, 181,
183, 185, 198, 206, 261,
264
Peterborough, Ontario, 385
Peters, Dan, 413
Peters, Steve, 413
Peterson, Oscar, 248, 365
Peterson, Richard, 88
Petrillo, James C., 60
Pettinicchio, Darlyne, 414
Petty, Norman, 129, 130
Petty, Tom, 264, 466, 501, 502,
503
Phantom Empire, The (movie), 52
Philadelphia International
Records (PIR), 228, 250
Philadelphia Ledger, 149
Philadelphia,

schlock rock in, 146
Philips Electronics, 229, 357,
373
Philles Records, 170
Phillinganes, Phil, 344
Phillips, Dewey, 78, 123
Phillips, John, 199, 211
Phillips, Michelle, 199
Phillips, Sam, 87, 99, 119–120,
121–122, 123, 125, 127,
146
Philly Groove records, 250
Phoenix, River, 431
Phonofilm Company, 34
phonograph, 16
Phuture, 450
Piche, Paul, 186
Pickett, Wilson, 190, 200, 201,
249, 274
Pickwick Records, 295
Pilgrim Travelers, 106, 109
Pinckney, Bill, 107
Pink Floyd, 228, 240, 245, 451
Pink Panther (movie), 390
Pink, 464, 517, 525, 526,
528–529
PIR. *See* Philadelphia Interna-
tional Records (PIR)
piracy, 336–3337, 491–493
Pirroni, Marco, 308
Pitney, Gene, 147, 171
Pitofsky, Robert, 492
Pittman, Barbara, 133
Pittman, Robert, 338, 339, 346
Plant, Robert, 277, 283, 284
Plaskett, Joel, 434
Plastic Ono Band, 218
Platters, 84, 116
Playboy magazine, 491
Pleiades records, 267
PLP. *See* Progressive Labor Party
(PLP)
Plus 8 records, 455
PMRC. *See* Parents Music Re-
source Center (PMRC)
Poco, 272
Poetic Justice (movie), 418, 420
Poindexter, Buster, 286
Pointer Sisters, 355, 356, 357,
358
Poison, 379–380, 384
Poleman, Tom, 547
Poles, 303
Police, 316, 317–318, 368, 472
politicos, 218–219
polka music, 64
Polydor Records, 309, 373
PolyGram Music, 485
Polygram records, 331, 351, 373,
388, 453, 485
polyrhythms, 72
Pomus, Doc, 152
Pond, Steve, 228, 440
Poneman, Jon, 425
Poni-Tails, 117
Pop Idol (tv program), 532, 533
Pop, Denniz, 462
Pop, Iggy (*nee* James Osterberg),
296, 303

see also Iggy Pop and the Stooges
Pope, Carol, 268, 365
Popstars (tv program), 532
Porcaro, Jeff, 344
Porcaro, Steve, 344
Porno for Pyros, 438
Port Hilford, Nova Scotia, 47
Port Huron Statement, The, 181
Porter, Cole, 28, 58, 409, 411
Portishead, 452
Posey, Sandy, 217
Possessed, 383
post-grunge music, 521–522
poster art, 236–237
postmodernism, 339–340
postwar prosperity, 137–138
Powder Blues Band, 209
Powell, Enoch, 313
Powell, Maud, 13–14
Powell, Maxine, 173
Powell, Michael, 506
Power Station, 339
Power, Darrell, 437
Powers, Tony, 171
Pranksters, 207
Pratt Institute, New York, 297
Presley Music, 124
Presley, Elvis, 7, 10–11, 65, 83, 84, 91, 92, 94, 120, 121–127, 128, 138, 139, 141, 146, 150, 151, 157, 159, 188, 191, 216, 300, 307, 330, 411, 501, 543
Presley, Gladys, 123
Presley, Vernon, 123
Pressplay, 493
Preston, Jimmy, 120
Preston, Johnny, 183
Pretenders, 299, 316, 318–319, 458
Price, Alan, 192
Price, Lloyd, 80, 84, 91, 93, 141
Price, Sam, 38
Pride, Charlie, 10
Primus, 440
Prince (*nee* Prince Rogers Nelson), 204, 333, 342, 344, 351, 352–353, 357, 408, 446, 447, 449, 458, 489, 501, 505, 525, 537
Prince Ayman, 406
Principle, Jamie, 449
Prine, John, 261
Priority records, 395, 401
Prism, 291
Private Stock records, 301
Proctor, F. F., 27
Procul Harum, 228, 240
Prodigy, 451, 453, 454
"Professor Bop," 78
Professor Griff, 395, 398
Progressive Labor Party (PLP), 218
progressive rock music, 228, 231, 238, 242
    in Quebec, 241
    segregation in, 236–237
Prohibition, 44, 53, 60
Prokop, Skip, 244

promo clips, 339–340
Propes, Steve, 82, 127
Protestant work ethic, 137
proto metal music, 280
Pryor, Richard, 254
psychedelics, 210–211, 231, 236–237, 240, 276, 278, 321
    heavy metal music and, 279
    Monterey International Pop Festival and, 214–215
Psychedlic Stooges, 296
psychographics, 338
PTA. *See* Parent/Teacher Association (PTA)
Public Enemy, 371, 376, 394–395, 398, 399–400, 401, 415, 418, 474, 513, 540
Puente, Tito, 220, 222
Puff Daddy, 402, 489
Punk magazine, 292
punk music, 8, 287, 288, 326, 383
    aims of, 292
    differences between disco and, 291–292
    fascism and, 310–313
    first wave of, 295–296
    history of, 293–295
    in Britain, 304–310
    in Canada, 303–304, 320
    in London, 299, 301
    new (second) wave, 316–318
    reggae convergence, 313–314
    women in, 315–316
Punk Rock Festival (1976), 308
Purple Rain (movie), 353
Pursey, Jimmy, 314
Pursuit of Happiness, 347, 434
Puttin' on the Ritz (movie), 36
Pyramids, 159
pyrotechnics, 284

Q

Q'Part, Jack, 89
Quality Records, 131, 194
Quarreymen, 190
Quartette, 184
Quatro, Suzi, 266
Quebec sovereignty referendum (May, 1980),
Quebec sovereignty referendum (October 1995), 186
Quebec, 12, 131
    CanCon regulations in, 248
    chansonnier tradition, 350
    folk music in, 185–186
    French language law (Bill 101), 406
    French rock music in, 186
    progressive music in, 241
    recession in music industry in, 336
    separatism, 186
Québécois, 185

Queen Latifah (*nee* Danah Owens), 399, 400, 401, 402–403, 458, 482, 538
Queen records, 68
Queen, 237, 338
Queli, Talib, 514
? (Question Mark) & the Mysterians, 190
Quicksilver Messenger Service, 206, 208, 211, 212
Quiet Revolution, Quebec, 185
Quiet Riot, 378, 379, 380, 381
Quinn, Dan, 18
Quinn, Martha, 363
Quinones, Lee, 391
Quintones, 117

R

R.E.M., 425, 430, 431, 432, 439, 446, 447
Rabbit's Foot Minstrels, 41
Rabble, 195
race music, 8–9, 21, 37, 38, 64, 67
    field recording, 43, 44
race riot, Detroit (1967), 185
race tensions, 216–217
racism, 8–11, 153, 224, 333, 342, 345–346, 354, 376, 388, 415
    British invasion and, 193–194
    institutionalized, 167
Radio Corporation of America (RCA), 30, 34, 47, 54, 65, 74, 75–76, 86, 93, 108, 138, 141, 153, 212, 228, 229, 351
    calypso music, 143, 144
    cover records, 140
radio,
    Adult Contemporary (AC), 380
    amplitude modulation (AM), 75
    black, 79, 333–334, 398
    commercial, 32–33
    Contemporary Hits Radio (CHR), 380
    disco on, 326–327, 331
    end of network, 76
    frequency modulation (FM), 75, 76
    heavy metal music on, 381–382
    history of, 29–31, 232–233
    in Canada, 32, 77, 89
    independent, 77
    network, 87
    no segregation on, 79–80
    patriotism on, 504–505
    punk music on, 292
    r&b, 78–80
    reggaeton on, 546–547
    see also individual radio stations
    Top Forty, 88

Urban Contemporary (UC), 333–334, 351, 380
radio, amplitude modulation (AM), 174, 232
radio, ownership of, 505–506
Radio-Keith-Orpheum (RKO), 34
Rage Against the Machine, 423, 460–461, 505, 516
rage rockers, 459–460
ragtime music, 6, 23
Raiders of the Lost Ark (movie), 345
Rainbow, 279
Rainey, Gertrude (Ma), 41, 44, 193
Raitt, Bonnie, 12, 260, 263, 264, 352, 366, 369, 458, 515
Ram, Buck, 116, 117
Rama records, 114
Ramirez, Richard, 414
Ramones, 296–297, 298–301, 302, 305, 311, 312, 433, 440
Rampling, Danny, 448
Rampling, Jenni, 448
Ranaldo, Lee, 430
Rancid, 529
Rand, Ayn, 279, 284
Randy and the Rainbow, 301
Raney, Wayne, 68, 69
Ranks, Shabba, 544
rap music, 4, 5, 8, 329, 371, 375, 389, 390, 482
    gangsta, 394, 404, 480–481, 538
    in Canada, 405
    message, 394–395
    movies and, 401
    roots of, 391
    second wave, 392–393
    styles of, 483–484
    technology and, 376
    television and, 401
    violence of, 399–400
    women in, 482–483
Rap Sheet magazine, 419, 420
Rapaport, David, 331
RAR. *See* Rock Against Racism (RAR)
Rascals, 216
Rascalz, 406
Rational Youth, 433
Ratt, 379, 380
rave music, 451
Ravens, 110, 111
Rawls, Lou, 212
Ray Condo and his Hardrock Goners, 433
Ray, Johnny, 4, 118, 138–139
Rays, 119, 140
Raze, 449
RCA Photophone, 34, 53
RCA Records, 244, 265, 273, 373, 389, 400, 446, 462, 464, 531
RCA-Victor records, 124, 125, 126, 127, 130, 133
RCA. *See* Radio Corporation of America (RCA)

Ready Steady Go! (tv program), 193
Reagan, Nancy, 320
Reagan, Ronald, 320, 335, 354, 364
Reagon, Bernice Johnson, 166
RealNetworks, 493
Rebels, 150
Reclines, 436
record companies,
    contradictions, 141, 143
    cover records, 143
    disco and, 326–327
    diversions, 143–144
    independents, 67–68, 87
    major, 86–87, 138
    reaction to backlash, 153–154
    schlock rock and, 146–147
    see also individual record companies
record pools, 327, 332
Record Rendevouz radio program, 80
Record Rendevouz Shop, Cleveland, 80
Record World magazine, 233
Recording Artists Coalition, 491
Recording Industry Association of America (RIAA), 249, 408, 409, 410, 488, 489, 490, 491, 493, 494, 495, 496
recording technology, 5
Records Tropical, 179
records, 16
    as inexpensive medium, 74–75
    see also LPs, singles
Red Brains, 320
Red Brigades (Italy), 310
Red Hot Chilli Peppers, 439, 460
Red Label series, 20
Red Leaf Records, 178
Red Network, 31
Red River theatres, 26
Red Seal series, 20
Red, Tampa, 39
Reddick, Paul, 209
Redding, Otis, 200, 201, 211, 212, 214, 249
Reddy, Helen, 217, 258, 260
Reding, Noel, 213
redneck music. *See* southern boogie (redneck) music
Redwood Records, 267
Reed, Bill, 119
Reed, Blind Alfred, 517
Reed, Jimmy, 99, 104
Reed, Lou, 287, 288, 295, 369, 406, 430, 435
Reeves, Martha, 173
Regency records, 131
Regent Street Polytechnic, 240
reggae music, 179, 282, 313–314, 317, 326
    in US, 314–315
    migration of, 544
    punk convergence, 313–314

reggaeton music, 543–544
Regina, 209, 523
Reid, Antonio "L.A.", 358, 469, 520, 528, 539
Reid, Vernon, 385, 388, 425
Reisman, David, 136
René, Leon, 98
René, Otis, 98
Reno, Mike, 365
Reo records, 131
REO Speedwagon, 291
Reprise Records, 185, 229, 265
Request Review radio program, 80
Respighi, Ottorino, 292
Revilot records, 324
Revolution, 353
Revolutionary Youth Movement (RYM), 218
Rex Records, 92
Reyes, Rico, 222
Reynolds, Debbie, 85
Reynolds, Simon, 449, 450, 452, 453
Reznor, Trent, 438
Rheostatics, 262, 349, 432
Rhino records, 300, 373
Rhoads, Randy, 378, 384
Rhode Island School of Design, 302
Rhodes, Bernie, 304, 307
Rhodes, Todd, 68, 80
Rhythim Is Rhythim, 449
rhythm 'n' blues music, 290, 317
    fusion with c&w, 120
    gospel music and, 106–110
    in Canada, 350
    in Toronto, 178–179
    loss of edge, 253–254
    punk new wave and, 321
    southern, 167
    uptown, 167–168
    values of, 84
rhythm and blues (r&b) music, 9, 64, 66, 68, 69, 82
    style example, 72–73
Rhythm Boys, 35
Rhythm Heritage, 327
Rhythm Method, 117
Rhythm Orchids, 129
RIAA. *See* Recording Industry Association of America (RIAA)
Rice, Captain Gitz, 23
Rich, Charlie, 128
Richard Hell and the Voidoids, 299
Richard, Cliff, 189
Richard, Keith, 503
Richard, Little (nee Richard Penniman), 41, 84, 85, 88, 90, 93–95, 95, 96–97, 108, 129, 141, 142, 157, 167, 180, 188, 189, 191, 213, 352
Richards, Keith, 194, 209, 230, 237, 363
Richardson, Jack, 195, 245, 268
Richbourg, John, 78
Richie, Lionel, 345, 351, 354, 356, 357, 358, 361

Richman, Jonathan, 302
Ricks, Jimmy, 111
riff, 386, 396
Righteous Brothers, 153, 170, 171
Riley, Teddy, 469, 479
Rimes, LeAnn, 443, 456
Rip Chords, 160
Ripoll, Shakira Isabel Mebarak, 466–467, 544, 545
Ripperton, Minnie, 264
Rising to the Challenge (video), 410, 412
Risque Disque records, 435
Ritter, Woodward Maurice (Tex), 52
Riverboat Coffeehouse, Toronto, 185
Rivers, Johnny, 10
Riviera, Jake (nee Andrew Jakeman), 308
RKO. *See* Radio-Keith-Orpheum (RKO)
Roadracer Records, 385
Roadwork Inc., 267
Robbie Lane and the Disciples, 195
Robbins, Marty, 132, 261
Robert Randolph's Family Band, 537
Roberts, Bob, 21
Roberts, Eliot, 229
Roberts, Luckey, 40
Robertson, Ed, 436
Robertson, Robbie, 270, 271, 349, 523
Robeson, Paul, 48, 183
Robey, Don, 106
Robins, 110, 114, 115
Robinson, Dave, 308
Robinson, Glen, 506
Robinson, Smokey, 174, 175, 212, 232, 252, 334, 409
Robinson, Sugar Ray, 107
Robinson, Tom, 315
Robinson, Vicki Sue, 327
Robitaille, Linda, 269
Roc-a-Fella music, 478, 540
Rock 'n' Roll Hall of Fame, 44, 47, 54, 149
    50 Songs That Shaped Rock and Roll, 161
rock 'n' roll music, 3, 81, 291
    African American influences on, 2, 4, 6–9, 11, 16
    backlash against, 153–154
    beginning of, 82–83
    country influences on, 132–133
    culture war in, 423–424
    death of, 152–153
    definitions of, 82–83
    instrumental, 159–160
    major record companies reaction to, 137–139
    music industry changes from, 86–87
    reaction to, 135–136
    relationship to youth, 5
    roots of, 83–86

sexism in, 264–265
    style, 85
    technology and, 5
    urban sound of, 89–90
    women in, 85–86, 260–261
Rock Against Racism (RAR), 313–314, 315–316
rock music, 290
    all-female bands, 265–266
    as art, 235–237
Rock Scene magazine, 298
Rock Steady Crew, 391, 392
Rock, Bob, 248, 320
rockabilly music, 10–11, 119–120, 151, 269, 270, 304, 436
    in Canada, 131–133
    women in, 133
Rocket from the Tombs, 302, 310, 311
Rockola Company, 53
Rockola, David, 53
Rockwell, John, 292, 360
Rocky IV (movie), 253
Rodeo record company, 51
Rodgers, Jimmie, 39, 45–47, 47, 48, 65, 127
Rodgers, Richard, 28, 36, 117, 152
Roger, Jolly, 450
Rogers, Kenny, 274, 354, 359, 361, 366
Rogers, Nile, 358, 374
Rogers, Roy, 52
Rogers, Ted, 32
Rogers, Will, 31
Rolfe, B. A., 30, 33
Rolie, Gregg, 222
Rolling Stone magazine, 170, 228, 232, 233–235, 236, 244, 250, 253, 291, 294, 297, 332, 361, 369, 385, 410, 412, 422, 426, 430, 431, 441, 455, 464, 466, 471, 478, 505, 521, 524, 537, 539
Rolling Stones Readers Poll (1999), 461
Rolling Stones, 70, 188, 192–193, 193, 194, 195, 206, 208, 217, 218, 224–225, 230, 237, 238, 272, 279, 286, 290, 292, 297, 303, 307, 331, 388, 390, 446, 461, 516
Rollins, Henry, 319, 438
Romeo and Juliet, 411
Romeo Must Die (movie), 479
Romeos, 250
Rondstadt, Linda, 10, 11–12
Ronettes, 12, 168, 170, 171, 172
Ronnie Hawkins and the Hawks, 132, 209
Ronnie Laine and the Disciples, 178
Ronny & the Daytonas, 160
Ronstadt, Linda, 260, 272, 290, 359
Rooftop Singers, 180
Roosters, 104

Roots, 517
Rosamond, J., 28
Rose, Axl, 385
Rose, Fred, 58, 65
Rose, Tricia, 376
Ross, Diana, 11, 174, 175, 176, 252, 322, 345, 358, 359, 361
Ross, Steve, 229, 230
Rosso, Wayne, 496
Roth, David Lee, 282, 378, 382
Rotten, Johnny (*nee* John Lydon), 292, 293, 294, 305
Roulette records, 129, 130, 229
Rounder Records, 265
Roundhouse, London, 299
Rowland, Kelly, 470
Rowlands, Tom, 454
Roxio, 493, 499–500
Roxon Lillian, 158, 197, 198, 208, 213
Roxy club, London, 309
Roxy Music, 288, 294
Roy Acuff's Smoky Mountain Boys, 48
Roy Hall's Blue Ridge Entertainers, 48
Royal Academy of Music, London, 239
Royal Albert Hall, London, 239, 279
Royal Commission on Broadcasting (Aird Commission) (1929), 32
Royal Commission on Broadcasting (Fowler Commission) (1957), 246
Royal Sons, 109
Royal Winnipeg Ballet, 244
Royals, 109
RPM Weekly magazine, 246, 247, 248
RSO records, 330, 331, 337, 366
Rubin, Rick, 393
Ruby and the Romantics, 168
Rudolph, Larry, 463
Ruffin, David, 252, 363
Ruffo, Titta, 31
Rufige Cru (*a.k.a.* Metalheadz), 452
Rumble, John W., 105
Rumour, 308, 317
Run-D.M.C., 363, 366, 386, 392, 394, 396–397, 398, 422, 480, 538, 540
Runaways, 266, 388
Rundgren, Todd, 286
Rupe, Art, 93, 94, 108
Rush, 247, 279, 282, 284, 290, 346, 385
Russell, Leon, 220
Rutsey, John, 282
Rydell, Bobby (*nee* Robert Ridarelli), 93, 145, 147, 148, 150, 164
RYM. *See* Revolutionary Youth Movement (RYM)

S

S'Express, 451
Sadler, Barry, 509
Sadler, Eric "Vietnam", 395
Sadler, Sgt. Barry, 199
Saga, 385
Sahm, Doug, 190
Saint John, New Brunswick, 51
Sainte-Marie, Buffy, 183, 184, 270
Sakamoto, Kyu, 11
Sales, Soupy, 80
salsa music, 317, 322, 366
Salt-N-Pepa, 394, 399
Sam and Dave, 109, 179, 200, 249
Sam the Sham and the Pharaohs, 190
Sambora, Richie, 502
San Francisco Chronicle, 233
San Francisco State College, 236
Sands, Tommy, 132, 146, 150
Sanjek, Russell, 27, 138, 149
Santana, 11, 220, 222–223, 465–466, 468
Santana, Carlos, 222, 244, 465, 522
Santangelo, Patricia, 496
Santiago, Herman, 117
Santiago, Maria Elena, 130
Sanz, Alejandro, 544
Sapphire Club, Toronto, 178
SAR (Sam and Alex) Records, 109
Sarnoff, David, 31, 32–33, 34, 53, 54, 74, 75–76, 139
Saskatoon, 241, 256
Satanism, 285, 413–414
satellite transmission, 337–338
Satherley, Art, 50, 52
Saturday Night Fever (movie), 324, 330, 331, 353, 356
Saturday Night Live (tv program), 244, 533
Saturday Night magazine, 349
Saunders, Jesse, 449
Saunders, Wallace, 39
Saunderson, Kevin, 448, 450
Savage, Jon, 295, 309, 313
Savoy club, Harlem, 49
Savoy records, 68, 90, 106, 114
Saxon, 377
Scaduto, Anthony, 195, 196
Scaggs, Boz, 210, 290
Scales, Harvey, 178
scats (sings nonsense syllables), 113
Scepter Records, 168, 176
Scheinman, Jenny, 527
Schicke, C. A., 21
Schiffman, Frank, 130
Schirmer, E. C., 58
schlock rock music, 145–149, 150
   Italian influences, 146–147
   women in, 147–148

Schneider, Jason, 347, 349, 432, 436
School of American Ballet, 525
Schoolly-ID, 394
Schubert, Franz, 411
Schuller, Gunther, 23, 24
Schumacher, Joseph, 512
Schumann, Robert, 411
Schwarz, Brinsley, 308
Scientific American magazine, 15
SCLC. *See* Southern Christian Leadership Conference (SCLC)
Scorpions, 379, 380
Scorsese, Martin, 271
Scotch tape, 74
Scott, Andrew, 434
Scott, Bon, 377
Scott, Jack (*nee* Jack Scafone Jr.), 131
Scott, Jill, 526
Scott-Heron, Gil, 264, 391
Screaming Trees, 425, 440
Scribner, Ron, 179
Scruggs, "Bugs", 78
Scruggs, Earl, 270
SDMI. *See* Secure Digital Music Initiative (SDMI)
SDS. *See* Students for a Democratic Society (SDS)
Seal, 501
Seale, Bobby, 225
Seals and Crofts (Jim Seals and Dash Crofts), 99, 261
Seals, Arthur, 24
Seals, Jim, 99
Searchers, 190, 305
Sears Roebuck, 39, 50
Sears, Zenas "Daddy", 78
Seattle Rocket, 425
Sebastian, John, 199
Seburg Company, 53
Second Fiddle (movie), 36
Second Wave records, 268
Secure Digital Music Initiative (SDMI), 492, 493
Security of the First World, 395
Sedaka, Neil, 147, 152
Seeger, Pete, 179–180, 181, 182, 183, 224, 517
Seekers, 190
Segal, Steven, 479
Segato, Lorraine, 269, 349, 365
Segrave, Kerry, 154, 380
Seitz, Ernest, 23
Seldes, Gilbert, 24
Selecter and the Specials, 315
Selective Phonograph, 53
Selena (movie), 465
Sensations, 168
September 11, 2001 attacks, 501, 504, 507, 514
Sepultura, 383
Seraw, Mulugeta, 414
Serendipity Singers, 180
Seven Arts film company, 229
Sex Pistols, 292, 293, 294, 295, 298, 299, 300, 304, 305–306, 307, 308, 309,

310, 312, 313, 318, 425, 426
Sex, 447
sexism, 345=346
Sexsmith, Ron, 349, 532
sexual ambiguity, 286–287
sexual revolution, 217–218
sexuality, 172
   Victorian view of, 165
Sgt. Pepper's Lonely Hearts Club Band (movie), 324, 330
Shadow Morton, 286
Shady/Aftermath/Interscope records, 538
Shaffer, Paul, 365
Shaft (movie), 249
Shaggy, 482
Shaheed, Malik, 406
Shakespeare, William, 83, 411
Shakira. *See* Ripoll, Shakira Isabel Mebarak
Shakur, Tupac, 418, 419, 420–421, 468, 471
Sham 69, 314
Shane, Jackie, 178
Shangri-Las, 168, 170, 171, 172
Shankar, Ravi, 214, 527
Shannon, Del, 147
Shanté, Roxanne, 398–399
Shapiro, Helen, 189
Shapiro, Nat, 58
Sharkbait, 439
Sharman Networks, 497
Sharp, Dee Dee, 149
Sharpe Records, 320
Shaw, Arnold, 9, 11, 61, 68, 69, 79, 94, 120, 149, 155
Shaw, Artie, 49
Shaw, Greg, 160
Sheeley, Sharon, 129
sheet music, 2, 15–16, 18, 75
shellac, 63–64, 74–75
Shepherd Sisters, 117
Shepherd, Sam, 297
Shider, Gary, 325
Shindig (tv program), 338
Shire, David, 331
Shirelles, 109, 164, 168, 170, 171, 188, 257, 259
Shirley and Lee (Shirley Goodman and Leonard Lee), 91, 93, 193
Shocklee, Hank, 395
Shore, Dinah, 62, 139
Shore, Howard, 244
Show Dog Nashville records, 520
Shrek the Third (movie), 406
Shuman, Mort, 152
Shut Up and Dance, 451, 452
Sibbles, Leroy, 179
Siberry, Jane, 365, 435
Sidcup Art School, 237
Sideburns magazine, 315
Sigma Studios, 252, 288
Silhouettes, 111
Silk, 469
Sill, Lester, 170
Sills, Beverley, 418
Silver Beatles, 191
Silver Convention, 327

Silver Echoes, 106
Silver Spurs (movie), 52
Silver, Al, 111
Silver, Liberty, 365
Simmons, Ed, 454
Simmons, Gene, 285
Simmons, Joseph (Run), 393, 396
Simmons, Russell, 479, 484, 515
Simon (Paul) and Garfunkel (Art) (prev. Tom and Jerry), 198–199, 211, 228, 234, 257, 501
Simon, Carly, 257, 260, 264, 352, 530
Simon, Paul, 198, 199, 234, 260, 315, 371–372, 465, 502
Simone, Nina, 193, 200, 217
Simonon, Paul, 304
Simple Minds, 319, 366
Simpson, Jessica, 462
Simpson, Valerie, 176
Sims Twins, 109
Sinatra, Frank, 4, 12, 56, 62, 126, 147, 151, 154, 156, 157, 229, 285
Sinatra, Nancy, 217
Sinclair, Gord, 436
Sinclair, Jim, 218
Sinclair, John, 296
Singing Idol, The, 150
Singing Nun, 11
single. *See* 45 rpm record (single)
Singles (movie), 427, 441, 447
Singleton, Charlie, 72
Sinnreich, Aram, 493
Sioux, Siouxsie, 308
Siouxsie and the Banshees, 308, 311, 315, 316, 438
Sir Douglas Quintet, 190
Sire Records, 299, 311, 436, 437
Sister Act II (movie), 459
Six Teens, 117
Skaggs, Ricky, 442
Skatemaster Tate, 404
Skid Row, 385
skiffle music, 190
Skillet Lickers, 44–45
skinheads, 314
Skinny Puppy, 432, 434
Skylight Singers, 106
Slaughter and the Dogs, 304
slavery, 11
    escape to Canada, 177–178
Slayer, 383
Sleater-Kinney, 513
Sledge, Percy, 200, 249
Slick, Grace, 12, 206–207, 217, 220
Slits, 315
Sloan, 432, 434
Sloan, P.F., 517
Slovak, Hillel, 439
sludgeabilly music, 433
Sly and Robbie, 371
Sly and the Family Stone, 206, 216, 220–221, 322, 352, 353, 388, 390
Small, Ambrose, 26
Small, Christopher, 7

Small, Millie, 314
Smalls, Biggy (Notorious B.I.G.), 420–421, 468, 471, 482, 525, 672
Smalls, Tommy, 79
Smashing Pumpkins, 425, 441
Smilin' Buddha Cabaret club, Vancouver, 320
Smith, Bessie, 41–42, 44, 48, 54, 138
Smith, Bob "Wolfman Jack", 78
Smith, Clara, 41
Smith, Clarence "Pine Top", 40
Smith, Fred, 301
Smith, Huey "Piano", 41, 91, 92
Smith, James, 251
Smith, Joe, 229, 230, 231, 235
Smith, Kate, 35
Smith, Larry, 396
Smith, Mamie, 41, 44
Smith, Patti, 295, 296–297, 297–298, 299, 300, 301, 312
    see also Patti Smith Group
Smith, Trixie, 41, 83
Smith, Warren, 128
Smith, Will, 401, 503
Smith, Willie-the-Lion, 40
Smokey Robinson and the Miracles, 173, 188, 193
Smucker, Tom, 322
SNCC. *See* Student Non-Violent Coordinating Committee (SNCC)
Snedker, Jacqui, 269
SNFU, 320, 434
Snider, Bob, 435
Snider, Dee, 409
Snow, Hank, 47, 48, 50, 59
So It Goes (tv program), 304
SOCAN. *See* Society of Composers, Authors and Music Publishers of Canada (SOCAN)
Soccio, Gino, 329
Socialist Workers Party, 313
Society of Composers, Authors and Music Publishers of Canada (SOCAN) (prev. CAPAC), 29
Soft Cell, 340
soft rock music, 255–258, 276
    in Canada, 261–262
    personal communication of, 260–261
    singer/songwriters in, 261
    women in, 260
soft soul music, 250, 252
Sohl, Richard, 297
SoHo Weekly magazine, 298
Solé, 482
Somerville, Dave, 119
Song of the Gringo (movie), 52
Songwriters of America, 155
Songwriters Protective Association, 156
songwriting teams, 152
Sonic Youth, 425, 430, 431
Sonny and Cher, 198

Sonny Bono Copyright Term Extension Act (1998), 488
Sonny Til and the Orioles, 140
Sons of the Pioneers, 52
Sony Canada, 247
Sony Music, 373
Sony, 357
Sopwith Camel, 206
Soul Assassins records, 404
Soul Asylum, 440
soul music, 9, 109, 204, 228, 249, 276, 278
Soul Stirrers, 106, 108, 109
Soul Survivors, 250
Soul Train Awards (tv program), 421
Soulsonic Force, 391, 392
Sound of the City, The, 4
Soundgarden, 425, 426, 439, 440
Sounds magazine, 377
Source, The magazine, 471, 539
Sousa, John Philip, 18, 22, 27
Souter, Justice David, 498
southern boogie (redneck) music, 274–275
Southern Christian Leadership Conference (SCLC), 183
Southern Music Publishing Company, 46, 58
Southern, Eileen, 21
Space Jam (movie), 470
Spandau Ballet, 334, 340
Spaniels, 104, 115
Spark records, 115
Sparrow, Mighty, 144
Spartan records, 131
Spears, Britney, 461, 462, 463, 464
Special Extermination Night (1974), 310
Speciality records, 68, 90, 92, 93, 94, 95, 96, 106, 108
Spector, Phil, 104, 118, 163, 167–168, 168–170, 171
Spencer, Len, 21
Spheeris, Penelope, 319, 379
Spice Girls, 444, 456, 462
Spiders, 91, 93
Spier, Henry C., 38
Spin Doctors, 440
Spinners, 249, 252
Spirit of the West, 437
Spivey, Victoria, 41
Springfield, Dusty, 191
Springsteen, Bruce, 54, 261, 262–263, 264, 290, 298, 326, 337, 353–354, 356, 358, 361, 366, 367, 423, 502, 509, 513, 517
Sputnik (Soviet Union satellite), 166
Squire, Chris, 242
SST records, 319, 425, 426
St. Augustine School for the Blind and Deaf, Florida, 107
St. Bruno, Quebec, 385
St. Catherines, Ontario, 282
St. Louis Blues (movie), 42, 48

St. Martin's School of Art, London, 237
St. Michael's Cathedral, Toronto, 118
Stafford, Jo, 62, 65, 138
Staind, 521, 522
Stampeders, The, 247
Stanley, Paul, 286
Staple Singers, 104, 186–187
Staples, Brent, 512
Staples, Kevan, 268
Stapp, Scott, 522
Star Search, 462
Stardust, Alvin, 286
Starr, Edwin, 226
Starr, Kay, 62
Starr, Maurice, 462
Staton, Candi, 330
Stax records, 104, 178, 187, 228, 254
Stax-Volt Records, 200, 201, 229
Steel Pulse, 313, 316
Steele, Micki, 266
Steely Dan, 290–291
Stefani, Gwen, 456, 483, 542
Stein, Chris, 301
Stein, Seymour, 299
Stephenson, Cal, 434
Stephney, Bill, 395
Steppenwolf, 245, 276, 277
Sterling records, 65
Sterling Trio, 18
Stetsasonic, 371, 399
Steve Miller Band, 212
Steven, Little, 366
Stevens, Cat, 261
Stevens, Connie (*nee* Concetta Ingolia), 146, 150
Stevens, Ray, 509
Stewart, Bill, 88
Stewart, Dave, 340
Stewart, Jim, 200, 201, 255
Stewart, Rod, 210, 248, 290, 331
Stiff Records, 307–308, 309, 316
Stigwood, Robert, 324, 330, 353
Stiles, Danny "Cat Man", 79
Stilettos, 301
Still, William Grant, 49
Stills, Stephen, 179, 191, 212, 221, 224
Sting, 317–318, 363, 367, 368, 370, 502
Stipe, Michael, 431, 432, 501, 502, 515
Stitch in Tyme, The, 195
stock market crash (1929), 59
Stockhausen, Karlheinz, 295
Stoller, Mike, 98, 114–115, 116, 118, 124, 125, 167, 168, 250
Stoloff, Morris, 88
Stone Canyon Band, 272
Stone Poneys, 260
Stone, Sly, 438
Stony Creek, Ontario, 22, 435
Stony Plain Records, 184, 209
Stooges, 310, 311

Storer Broadcasting, 87
Storer, George, 87
Storm, Gale, 141
Storz, Tod, 88, 89
Straight Arrow magazine, 233
Straight Outta Brooklyn (movie), 401
straightedge music, 319–320
Strait, George, 412, 443
Strand, 294
Stranglers, 304, 309
Strauss, Neil, 447
Stravinsky, Igor, 332
Straw, Will, 329, 364
Strawbs, 241
Stray Cats, 346
StreamCast Networks, 497, 498
Street, John, 370
Streisand, Barbra, 289, 328
Strokes, 513, 522
Strong, Barrett, 164, 173, 188, 191
Strummer, Joe, 304, 310
Stuart, Dan, 400
Studdard, Ruben, 534
Student Non-Violent Coordinating Committee (SNCC), 166
Students for a Democratic Society (SDS), 181
    1969 National Convention, 218
Studio 54, 332
Sturman, Susan, 269
Stylistics, 251, 252
Styrene, Poly, 315
Styx, 291, 442
Sub Pop magazine, 425
Sub Pop records, 425, 426, 434, 446
suburbia, 165
Sue Records, 178
"Sugar Daddy", 78
Sugar Hill Band, 334, 391
Suicidal Tendencies, 383
Sullivan, Ed, 124, 216
Sullivan, James, 457–458
Sullivan, Jim, 438
Sultans of Swing, 80
Sum 41, 521, 529
Summer of Love (San Francisco, 1967), 210–211
Summer, Donna, 292, 322, 323, 326, 328, 329, 333, 341, 345, 346, 351
Summers, Andy, 318
Summus Records, 179
Sun Records, 68, 99, 119–120, 120, 122, 123, 124, 125, 128, 133, 139, 159
Sunday Ramparts magazine, 233
Sunday Times, 193, 292
Sunny Side Up (movie), 35
Sunshine records, 42
Superfly (movie), 186, 249
superstars, 351–353, 357–358, 447–448
    female, 456–457
Supertramp, 241

Supremes, 168, 173, 174–175, 176, 193, 252, 278, 342, 343
Sure, Al B., 401
surf music, 158–159, 160–163
    instrumental, 159–160
Surfaris, 159
Surfers, 439
Sutcliffe, Stuart, 190
Swallows, 110
Swan records, 146
Swann Silvertones, 104
Sweet Honey in the Rock, 264
Sweet, The, 286
swing music, 61–62
Swinging Blue Jeans, 189, 190
Swingtime Records, 107
Swollen Members, 406
Sword, 385
Sylvain, Sylvain, 294
Sylvers, 327, 329
Sylvia, Margo, 117
Symionese Liberation Army, 298
Syncopated Society Orchestra, 20, 21
syncopation, 73
Syracuse University, 149
System of a Down, 516

T

T. Rex (prev. Tyrannosaurus Rex), 286
T.A.M.I. (tv program), 193
Tagus, Toronto, 232
Tainter, Charles Sumner, 16–17
Take 6, 401
Taki 138, 391
Talking Heads, 295, 296–297, 299, 302, 303, 316, 321, 325, 370, 392
Tamla music, 173
Tankian, Seij, 516
tape recorder, 74
    portable, 336
Taste of Honey, 11
Tate, Sharon, 224
Tatum, Art, 107
Taupin, Bernie, 290
Tavares, 326, 329, 331
Taylor, Ben, 530
Taylor, James, 230, 256, 257, 259, 260, 261, 264, 442, 530
Taylor, Johnny, 109, 327
Taylor, Mike, 225
Taylor, Sam, 84, 112, 113
Tchaikovsky, Peter, 3, 108, 159
techno music, 448, 449, 450
technology,
    advances in, 53–54
Teddy Bears, 118
Tee Tot (Rufe Payne), 65
teen pop, 461–643
Teen Queens, 117, 141
Teenage Head, 303–304
Teenage Lust, 286
Teenage Wasteland, 430

telephony, 29
Television, 285, 297, 298, 301, 302
television, 75, 149–151, 285
    cable, 338–339
    deregulation of, 338
    development of, 76
    in Canada, 346–347
    popular music and, 338–339
    reality, 532–533
    rigged quiz shows on, 155
    see also individual television programs,
Temptations, 173, 176, 208, 216, 252, 322, 343, 363
Ten Years After, 220
Terrell, Tammy, 176
Terriers, 144
Terry, Sonny, 55, 183
Testament, 383
Thank God It's Friday (movie), 328
Tharpe, Sister Rosetta, 55, 83
Thatcher, Margaret, 304, 316, 370
Thau, Marty, 294
The Mamas and The Papas, 109
Theatre Owners Booking Association (TOBA), 41
Them, 190, 262
Thiele, Bob, 130, 139
Thin Lizzy, 388
Third Base, 404
Third World, 314, 321, 333
Thomas, Rob, 465, 466
Thomas, Rufus, 78, 122, 193
Thomkins, Jr., Russell, 251
Thompson Twins, 341
Thompson, Hunter, 235
Thompson, Sue, 148
Thornton, Sarah, 450, 451
Thornton, Sir Henry, 32
Thornton, Willie Mae "Big Mama", 98, 115, 122, 125, 210
THP Orchestra, 329
Three Cheers (movie), 35
Three Degrees, The, 252
Three Mile Island nuclear disaster, 263
Three Suns, 117
Thrush Hermit, 434
Thrust, 406
Thundermug, 385
Thunders, Johnny, 294, 311
Tiger Beat magazine, 412
Til, Sonny, 86, 87
Tillotson, Johnny, 148
Tim Dogg, 391
Timbaland, 483, 530
Timberlake, Justin, 462, 515
Time magazine, 192, 263, 414, 527, 539
Time, 353
Time-Warner, 373
Timmins, Margo, 345
Timmins, Michael, 435
Timmins, Peter, 435
Tinsley, Boyd, 531
Tippin, Aaron, 507, 508

Titanic (movie), 456, 458
Titanic disaster, 29, 31
TK Records, 327
TLC, 469
TNN. *See* Nashville Network, The (TNN)
TNT (tv program), 193
TOBA. *See* Theatre Owners Booking Association (TOBA)
Today (tv program), 308
Toles, Michael, 329
Tom Robinson Band, 316
Tom Tom Club, 392, 445
Tommy (movie), 330
Tommy Boy records, 399, 400, 402
Tommy Dorsey Orchestra, 62
Tommy James and the Shondells, 217
Toni (Brown) and Terry (Garthwaite), 265
Tonight Show, 151, 525
Tony Torrez and the Latin Rascals, 393
Too Much 4 Much (tv program), 348
Too Short, 391
Toop, David, 389, 390, 392, 395, 404, 419, 535
Toorish, Bernie, 118
Top Gun (movie), 357
Top Hat (movie), 36
Top of the Pops (tv program), 340
Torin, "Symphony Sid", 79
Tornadoes, 159
Toronto (band), 385
Toronto Conservatory of Music, 23
Toronto Star, The, 153
Toronto, 22, 26, 32, 77, 112, 132, 184, 195, 209, 244, 247, 269, 276, 279, 303, 320, 347, 348, 349, 523, 529, 532, 543
    alternative music in, 432, 435–436
    Beatles in, 189
    Caribbean peoples in, 350
    disco in, 329
    doo wop music in, 118–119
    hip hop scene in, 405
    r&b in, 178, 179
    radio stations in, 89
Torres, Harold, 117
Tosches, Nick, 11, 39, 82, 83
Tosh, Peter, 314
Toto, 344
Toussaint, Allen, 92
Tower of power, 323
Townsend, Graham, 51
Townshend, Pete, 237, 238, 363
Traffic, 210
Tragically Hip, The, 247, 248, 349, 350, 432, 435, 436, 437
Trainspotting (movie), 454
Trammps, 327, 331
transistor, 74
Transmat Records, 449

transnational music corporations, 351–352
trash rock music, 294–295
Travellers, 183
Travers, Pat, 385
Travis, Merle, 270
Travis, Randy, 411, 412, 509
Travolta, John, 330, 331, 332, 356
Trax records, 449
Traynor, Pete, 231
Treacherous Three, 390
Treadwell, George, 115
Tremonti, Mark, 522
Tres Dessos (Three Wishes), 456
Tribe Called Quest, A, 391, 399
Tricky, 452, 453
trip hop music, 452–453
Trips Festival, 207
Tritt, Travis, 443
Triumph, 291, 379, 385
Troiano, Dominic, 178
Troopers Saga, 291
Troubleman (movie), 249
Trucks, Butch, 274
Trudeau, Margaret, 332
Trudeau, Prime Minister Pierre, 246, 433
True North Records, 261, 268
Truth, Sojourner, 399
Tubb, Ernest, 48, 52, 59, 65
Tucker, Dr. C. DeLores, 420
Tucker, Maureen, 295
Tucker, Sophie, 28, 41, 49
Tuesday Records, 179
Tumbling Tumbleweeds (movie), 52
Tune Weavers, 117
Tupac, 461
Tupperaros Records, 269
Turbans, 111
Turk, Roy, 35
Turner, Big Joe, 55, 71, 80, 85, 120, 140, 153, 209
Turner, Brian, 395
Turner, Ike, 99
Turner, Tina, 170, 249, 356, 357, 358, 363
Turtles, 198
Twain, Ellen "Shania", 443, 456, 536
Twain, Shania, 47
Twaist, Laymen, 406
Tweedside, Nova Scotia, 50
Twin Peaks (movie, tv program), 454
twist dance, 148, 149
Twista, 539, 540
Twisted Sister, 332, 380, 409
Twitty, Conway (*nee* Harold Jenkins), 128, 133, 139
Two Nice Girls, 268
Tyers, Will, 28
Tyler, Red, 91, 92
Tyler, Steve, 279, 393
Tympany Five, The, 66, 121
Tyson, Ian, 349
Tyson, Sylvia, 365

U

U.S. Census Bureau, 543
U.S. Civil Rights Act of 1964, 187, 312
U.S. Communications Act of 1934, 31, 57, 505
U.S. Constitution, 488
U.S. Copyright Act (1909), 27, 28, 33, 57
U.S. Department of Justice, 493
U.S. Internal Revenue Service (IRS), 129
U.S. Library of Congress, 43, 70
U.S. Marine Band, 18
U.S. Radio Act of 1927, 31
U.S. Supreme Court, 165, 167, 497–498
U.S. Telecommunications Act (1996), 505, 512
U.S. Voting Rights Act (1965), 200
U.S.A. *See* United Support for Artists (U.S.A.)
U2, 366, 367, 370, 441, 454, 502, 504
UA. *See* United Artists
UB 40, 315
UBO. *See* United Booking Office (UBO)
UC. *See* radio, Urban Contemporary (UC)
UCLA. *See* University of California, Los Angeles (UCLA)
Uggams, Leslie, 130
Ugly Ducklings, 195
Ulrich, Lars, 386
Ultravox, 340, 361
Umbrella Records, 268
UMG. *See* Universal Music Group (UMG)
Uncle Jam's Army, 393
Underground Railroad, 178
Underwood, Carrie, 535
Underworld, 453
Unique 3, 451
United Artists (UA), 34, 114, 253
United Booking Office (UBO), 27
United Independent Broadcasters, 31
United Support for Artists (U.S.A.), 361
United Wireless Company, 29
Universal Music Group (UMG), 485
Universal Records, 482
Universal Studios, 34
University of California, Los Angeles (UCLA), 215
University of California, Santa Barbara, 531
University of Minnesota, 180
University of North Carolina, 497
University of Texas, 52
University of Virginia, 506

Up in Smoke tour, 477–478
Urban Cowboy (movie), 442
urban/dance-oriented rock music, 358–359
Ure, Midge, 361
Uriah Heep, 279
USA Cable Network, 339
Usher, 520, 539
UTFO, 394, 399

V

V and the Satellites, 179
Valdy, 260
Valee, Rudy, 117
Valens, Ritchie (Ritchie Valenzuela), 11, 99, 129, 157, 183, 190, 197, 273
Valentinos, 109
Vallance, Jim, 365
Valli, Frankie (*nee* Francis Castelluccio), 119
Valli, June, 106, 140
Van Alstyne, Egbert, 22
Van Halen, 282–283, 345, 378, 379, 381, 382
Van Halen, Alex, 282
Van Halen, Eddie, 282–283, 343, 344, 352, 366, 376
Van Herk, Gerard, 433
Van McCoy and the Soul City Orchestra, 326
Van Zant, Johnny, 508
Van Zant, Ronnie, 275
Vance, Ray, 413
Vancouver folk festival, 184
Vancouver, 131, 189, 209, 232, 247, 385, 406
  alternative music in, 432, 434
Vandross, Luther, 358, 469
Vanelli, Gino, 291
Vanguard Records, 184, 212
Vanilla Fudge, 278
Vanilla Ice, 404
Vanity, 352
Varèse, Edgar, 49
Variety magazine, 53, 153
Vaudeville Managers Association (VMA), 27
vaudeville, 16
  in Canada, 26–27
  Tin Pan Alley and, 26–27
Vaughan, Sarah, 78, 401
Vaughan, Stevie Ray, 396
VCR. *See* video cassette recorder (VCR)
Vedder, Eddie, 440, 502
Vee Jay records, 68, 99, 104–105, 110, 115, 188
Vee, Bobby, 114, 148
Vega, Suzanne, 370–371, 456, 457
Veliotes, Alexander, 98
Veliotes, Irene, 98
Velvet Underground, 238, 295–296, 296, 302, 430, 435
Venom, 377

Ventures, 160, 425
Venus and Adonis, 83
Verlaine, Tom, 295, 297
Verne, Larry, 183
Verse to Vinyl records, 269
Verve Records, 151
very high frequency (VHF), 75–76
VH-1 cable tv station, 339, 348, 370, 375
VHF. *See* very high frequency (VHF)
Via Afrika, 366
Vibe magazine, 471
Vibranaires, 111
Vibrators, 307, 308
Vicious, Sid, 308, 311
Vico C., 544
Victor Gramophone Company, 28, 43, 45, 46, 53, 54, 61
Victor Talking Machine Company, 19, 20, 25
Victoria Times Colonist, 320
Victoria, British Columbia, 184, 320
video cassette recorder (VCR), 337
video games, 337
Video Soul (tv program), 339
video, music, 338
  African American, 341–342
  AOR and, 339
  in Europe, 339–340
  interracial, 359
  objectification of women in, 345–346
  performance clip, 381–382
  politics and, 407–408
Vietnam Moratorium (November, 1969), 224
Vietnam War (1959–1975), 199, 206, 217, 218, 234, 273, 354
  anti-war lyrics, 212–213
  Tet offensive, 216
Vigneault, Gilles, 185, 186
Viletones, 303–304, 435
Village People, 328–329
Village Voice magazine, 298, 326, 431, 545
Vincent, Gene (*nee* Vincent Eugene Craddock), 128–129, 139
Vincent, Johnny (Vincent Imbragulio), 92
Vines, 522
Vinson, Eddie "Cleanhead", 67
Vintage Records, 179
Vinton, Bobby, 114, 148
vinylite, 63–64, 74–75
Virdon, Manitoba, 53
Virgin Records, 303, 309, 310, 446, 450, 520, 542
Viscounts, 159
vitaphone, 34
Viva Las Vegas (movie), 157
Vivaldi, Antonio, 276, 378
Vixen, 380, 388–389
VMA. *See* Vaudeville Managers Association

vocal harmony groups, 115
Vocalion records, 43
Voidoids, The, 297
Voisine, Roch, 350
Voivod, 385
Von Tilzer, Harry, 16, 22, 23

W

W.A.S.P., 379, 409
WABC (prev. WJZ) radio station, 31, 157, 232
Wagner, Richard, 411
Waikiki Wedding (movie), 35
Wailers, 315
Wainwright III, Loudon, 261
Waiting to Exhale (movie), 456
Waitts, Tom, 261
Wakeman, Rick, 239, 240, 242
WAKR radio station, 80
Walden, Narada Michael, 358
Walden, Phil, 275
Walker, Aaron "T-Bone", 43, 95
Walker, C. P., 26
Walker, Jack, 79
Walker, Mel, 98
Walker, T-Bone, 84
wall of sound, 118, 163
Wall Street Journal, 352
Wallace, Governor George, 224
Wallace, John, 72
Wallace, Michelle, 470
Wallace, Sippie, 41
Waller, Fats, 40–41, 49, 68
Wallerstein, Ted, 54, 74
Wallichs, Glenn, 60
Walser, Robert (Bob), 239, 276, 277, 279, 283, 378, 382, 388, 407, 410, 412
Walsh, Donnie "Mr. Downchild", 209
Walsh, Joe, 279
Walter Murphy and the Big Apple Band, 327
Walter, Little, 122, 209
Wand, Hart, 24
War of 1812, 177
War, 208, 249, 253
WAR. *See* White Aryan Resistance (WAR)
Ward, Billy, 106
Ward, Ed, 146, 233
Warhol, Andy, 238, 287, 288, 294, 295, 296, 297
Warner Brothers Records, 34, 35–36, 53, 54, 146, 212, 228, 229, 257, 280, 282, 285, 325, 342, 351, 352, 400, 431, 446
Warner Communications, 229, 230, 235, 247, 337, 338
Atari division, 337
Warner Music Canada, 437
Warner Music Group, 519–520
Warner-Elektra-Atlantic Records (WEA), 229, 435

Warner-Reprise records, 230
Warner-Seven Arts, 229
Warnes, Jennifer, 184
Warp, 451
Warren, Diane, 458, 469
Warren, Harry, 36
Warwick, Dionne, 176, 354, 359, 420
Washington, Denzel, 418
Waters, Alan, 89
Waters, Muddy (*nee* McKinley Morganfield), 43, 44, 70, 79, 84, 99, 100, 208, 276, 305
Waters, Roger, 240
Watson, Doc, 270
Watts Prophets, 391
Watts rebellion (1965), 98, 200
Watts, Charlie, 192, 194
Wattstax benefit concert (1972), 254
Wavy Gravy and the Hog Farm Commune, 219
Wayne County, 286
Wayne Fontana and the Mindbenders, 191
WBAP radio station, 50
WBBM radio station, 232
WBCN radio station, 232
WBLK radio station, 178, 406
WBLS radio station, 326, 419
WBNX radio station, 79
WCBS radio station, 49
WCHR-FM radio station, 513
WCKY radio station, 68
WDIA radio station, 78, 153
We Five, 184
WEA. *See* Warner-Elektra-Atlantic Records (WEA)
WEAF radio station, 30
Weathermen, 218, 224
Weavers, 180, 183
Webb, Chick, 49, 62
Webster, Max, 247
Weeping Tile, 349
Weil, Cynthia, 152, 170
Weill, Kurt, 147
Weinstein, Deena, 276, 378, 383, 388
Weir, Bob, 207
Welk, Lawrence, 63, 130
Weller, Freddy, 10
Weller, Paul, 312
Wells, Junior, 70
Wells, Kitty, 133
Wells, Mary, 173
Wenner, Jan, 233, 234, 235
WERD radio station, 78
Wesley, Fred, 325
West Coast Cotton Club, 49
West Indian Federation Club, Toronto, 179
West, Kanye, 539–540
Westbrook, Uncle John, 127
Western Electric, 34
western swing, 48
Westinghouse, 30

Westwood, Vivienne, 294, 311, 318
Wexler, Jerry, 9, 70, 201, 249, 253
Weymouth, Tina, 302, 392
WFIL-TV, 149
WGPR radio station, 449
Whalen, Terry, 185
Wham!, 356
Whannel, Paddy, 3
What Was the First Rock 'n' Roll Record?, 127
Where the Action Is (tv program), 206
Whibley, Deryck, 529
Whitcomb, Ian, 20, 24, 63, 190
White Aryan Resistance (WAR), 414
White Lion, 380
White Nights (movie), 357
White Panther Party, 218
White Stripes, 522
White, Barry, 254, 322, 401, 469
White, George, 78
White, Josh, 183
White, Maurice, 324
White, Paul, 189
Whiteman, Paul, 25, 26, 28, 35, 49, 60, 147
Whitesnake, 384
Whitfield, Norman, 176
Whitney theatres, 26
Who, 24, 208, 211, 212, 219–220, 238, 241, 277, 292, 297, 330, 363, 428, 503
Whodini, 392, 394
WHOM radio station, 79
Wicke, Peter, 5, 7, 231, 237
Wide Women/Urana records, 267
Widgery, David, 313
Wild Cherry, 324
Wild Style (movie), 392, 393
WILD. *See* Women's Independent Labels Distributors (WILD)
Wilde, Oscar, 287
Wildmon, Reverend Donald, 413
Williams, Bert, 21
Williams, Billy, 21
Williams, Brent, 177
Williams, Charles, 90, 92
Williams, Hank, 59, 65, 127, 147, 435, 442
Williams, Jr., Hank, 508
Williams, Larry, 93
Williams, Mayo (Ink), 42, 43, 70
Williams, Nat D., 78
Williams, Otis, 119
Williams, Peter, 230
Williams, Tex, 64
Williams, Tony, 116
Williams, Trudy, 117
Williams, Wesley (Maestro Fresh Wes), 405

Williamson, Cris, 266–267
Williamson, Sonny Boy (Rice Miller), 49, 99, 209
Willis, Ellen, 233, 264–265, 266
Willows, 119
Wills, Bob, 35, 48, 65
Wilson, Ann, 283
Wilson, Brian, 160, 161, 163
Wilson, Carl, 160
Wilson, Dennis, 160
Wilson, Gretchen, 539
Wilson, Jackie, 90, 98, 106, 107–108, 172
Wilson, Mary, 174, 176
Wilson, Nancy, 283
Wilson, President Woodrow, 30
Wilson, Tom, 198, 532
Wilson, Vic, 282
Wimbish, Doug, 425
Wimbledon College of Art, London, 237
Win Without War coalition, 515
Wind in the Willows, 301
Windsor, Ontario, 22, 131, 178, 443, 455
Wine, Toni, 169
Winner, Langdon, 90, 92, 234, 325
Winnipeg folk festival, 184
Winnipeg, 26, 131, 189, 194
WINS radio station, 61, 79, 80, 157
Winslow, Vernon, 78
Winter, Johnny, 234
Winter, Kurt, 195
Winterhalter, Hugo, 139
Winwood, Steve, 209, 210, 220, 356, 358
Wired magazine, 454, 455, 487
Wireless Telegraph and Signal Company, Ltd., 29
Wireless Telegraph Co. of Canada, 29
Wisconsin Chair Company, 42
Wisin & Yandel, 545, 546
Witherspoon, Jimmy, 10
WJW radio station, 80
WJZ radio station, 31
WKBW radio station, 88
WKNR radio station, 232
WKTU radio station, 331, 333, 448
WLAC radio station, 131
WLIB radio station, 79
WLS radio station, 50, 52
WLUP (the "Loop") radio station, 333
WLW radio station, 68
WMCA radio station, 79
WNBC (prev. WEAF) radio station, 31, 49
WNEW radio station, 59, 60, 62, 157, 232
WNEW-TV, 157
WNOX radio station, 50
WOKJ radio station, 78
Woldemarian, Philip, 418

Wolf, Howlin', 43, 44, 70, 99, 122, 208, 276
Wolfe, Tom, 169, 207
Wolfer, Bill, 344
Womack, Bobby, 109, 425
WOMAD. *See* World of Music, Arts and Dance Festival (WOMAD)
Women's Independent Labels Distributors (WILD), 267
women's liberation movement, 165, 260, 267
women's music, 266–267
Wonder, Stevie, 173, 228, 249, 252–253, 264, 290, 322, 333, 334, 343, 344, 358, 359, 502, 503
Wonderlove Band, 344
Wood, Randy, 140
Wood, Ron, 210, 237, 363
Woodson, Carter G., 459
Woodstock '99 concert, 460
Woodstock Music and Art Fair, The (1969), 219–221, 224, 231, 274, 363, 379, 441
    African Americans at, 220–222
    women at, 220
WOPA radio station, 79
WOR radio station, 52
Work, John W., 39, 70
working class, 1, 4, 5, 194
    African American, 67

black, 66
    rock 'n' roll and, 84
World of Music, Arts and Dance Festival (WOMAD), 368
World War I, 19, 21, 22, 28, 29, 40, 42, 154, 157
    post, 41
World War II, 1, 4, 9, 15, 35, 61, 63, 71, 76, 87, 135–136, 207
    exodus from South during, 57, 63
    immigration to US, 468, 543
    military buildup before, 56
    worst recession in UK since, 304
Worley, Darryl, 508
Worrell, Bernard, 321, 325
Worth, Bobby, 2
Wosniak, Steve, 379
WOV radio station, 77, 79
WQAM radio station, 89
Wright, Johnny, 462
WRKS radio station, 395
WROL radio station, 50
WSB radio station, 50
WSBC radio station, 59
WSM radio station, 50
WSOK radio station, 78
WTBS cable station, 339
WTIX radio station, 88
Wu-Tang Clan, 461, 476, 514
Wurlitzer Company, 53
WWRL radio station, 79

Wyman, Bill, 194
WYUU radio station, 547

X

X, 315, 319, 366
X-ecutioners, 455
X-Ray Spex, 316
XWA radio station, 30
XXX (movie), 483

Y

Yahel, Sam, 527
Yahoo, 493
Yancey, Jimmy, 40
Yankee, Daddy, 544, 545, 546
Yanovsky, Zal, 199
Yardbirds, 189, 210, 237
Yasgur, Max, 219, 225
Yearwood, Trisha, 443
Yes, 238, 239–240, 241, 242–243, 245
Yippies, 234
Yo! MTV Raps (tv program), 401
Yoakam, Dwight, 443, 509
Yogi, Maharishi Mahesh, 215
York, Peter, 288
Yorkville Records, 195
Yorkville Sound, 231

Young Black Teenagers, 404
Young Canadians, 320, 434
Young Lords, 218
Young Rascals, 170
Young, Angus, 377
Young, Charles M., 291, 294, 413
Young, Kathy, 117
Young, La Monte, 295
Young, Malcolm, 377
Young, Neil, 179, 184, 185, 211, 212, 221, 224, 230, 245, 272, 275, 349, 365, 366, 369, 439, 502, 503, 505, 509, 516–517
Young, Owen D., 30
Your Hit Parade (radio program), 8, 34, 62, 88
YouTube, 528

Z

Zappa, Frank, 238, 282, 285, 324–325, 409, 410, 411
Ziegfeld, Flo, 27
Zircon records, 131
Znaimer, Moses, 346
Zombies, 190
Zook, Kristal Bent, 404
Zubot and Dawson, 262
ZZ Top, 209, 274, 275–276, 345, 446

Music Index

Note: Song titles are in Roman typeface; Album titles are in italics.

03 Bonnie & Clyde, 540
12 Play, 470
14 Shades of Grey, 522
17 Days, 522
18 Wheeler, 529
1977, 307
1984, 378, 381
1999, 352–353
1999's Decks, 454
19th Nervous Breakdown, 297
2-4-6-8 Motorway, 215
2pacalypse Now, 420
3 Years 5 months & 2 days in the Life of …, 440
400 Degreez, 477
431Green Shirt, 317
5-10-15 Hours, 70
52nd Street, 290
5x Love, 543
634-5789, 201
7800° Fahrenheit, 382
911 for Peace, 514
96 Tears, 190
9mm, 394

A

ABC, 252
Abraham, Martin, and John, 216
Abraxas, 220, 222
Acadian Driftwood, 349
Acadie, 367
Ace of Spades, 378
Achy Breaky Heart, 508
Acid Man, 450
Acid Trax, 450
Across the Great Divide, 271
Across the Valley from the Alamo, 63
Addicted to Love, 345
Africville, 178
After the Ball, 16
Aftermath, 453
Again, 63
Against All Odds (Take a Look at Me Now), 357
Age Ain't Nothing But a Number, 470
Ahab the Arab, 509
Ain't 2 Proud 2 Beg, 469
Ain't Got No Home, 93
Ain't No Mountain High Enough, 176
Ain't Nobody Better, 450
Ain't Nobody Here but Us Chickens, 66
Ain't Nothing Like the Real Thing, 176
Ain't That a Shame, 85, 91, 93, 141
Ain't That Peculiar, 173
Ain't We Got Fun?, 22

The Air I Breathe, 250
Aja, 291
Aladdin Sane, 287
Albert Flasher, 195
Alberta Waltz, 65
Alexander's Ragtime Band, 23, 24, 28
Alice in Hell and Never Neverland, 385
Alive, 501
All Along the Watchtower, 213
All Day and All of the Night, 192
All Eyez on Me, 420
All Falls Down, 540
All Hail the Queen, 399, 402
All I Have to Do Is Dream, 132
All I Really Want to Do, 198
All I Want for Christmas Is You, 445
All Killer No Filler, 521
All My Loving, 189
All Night Long (All Night), 354
All of You, 11, 359
All Shook Up, 126
All the Right Reasons, 522
All the Young Dudes, 287
All Touch, 268
All Women are Bitches: Repeat, 269
All You Need is Love, 217
Alla en Al Rancho Grande, 99
Allegheny Moon, 88
Alleys of Your Mind, 449
Almost Blue, 317
Alone, 117
Alone at Last, 108
Along Came Jones, 115
Along Comes Mary, 206
Amazing Grace, 188
Amen, 186
America Eats Its Young, 179
America the Beautiful, 502
American Idiot, 514
American Skin (41 Shots), 423
American Woman, 194, 195, 276
Amerikka's Most Wanted, 400
Anarchy in the U.K., 304, 305–306, 308, 311, 313
… And Justice for All, 383, 384, 386–387
And Now, The Legacy Begins, 405
… And Then There Was X, 479
Angel Eyes, 86, 209
Angel with a Lariat, 436
Angry Young Woman, 269
Animal (F**k like a Beast), 379
Animal Rights, 454
The Animals, 192
Annie Had a Baby, 110
Annie Pulled a Humbug, 110
Annie's Answer, 110
Annie's Aunt Fanny, 110
Anniversary Song, 62

Another Brick in the Wall, 240
Another Saturday Night, 109
Any Other Way, 178
Anyone Who Had a Heart, 176
Apache, 390
Apollo: Atmospheres & Soundtracks, 367
Appetite for Destruction, 385
April in Portugal, 136
April Love, 141
Are We Not Men? We Are Devo!, 303
Are You Experienced, 213
Are You Lonesome Tonight, 126
Argh Fuck Kill—Die Sinner Die, 320
Arnold Layne, 240
Around and Around, 193
Artificial Intelligence, 451
As Nasty as They Wanna Be, 399, 416
Asia Minor, 159
Asthma Attack, 296
Astral Weeks, 262
At My Front Door, 115, 141
At the Feet of the Moon, 269
At the Hop, 250
A-Tisket A-Tasket, 62
Atlantic City, 353
Aura Lee, 126
Autobiography of a Crackhead, 452
Automan, 320
Automatic for the People, 431, 432

B

B.Y.O.B., 516
Baby, Baby, Baby, 469
Baby Boy, 537
Baby Don't Do It, 109
Baby I Love You, 171, 202
Baby, I Love Your Way, 290
Baby I Need Your Loving, 176
Baby I'm Burnin', 331
Baby It's You, 115, 168, 188
Baby Let Me Follow You Down, 197
Baby, Let Me Take You Home, 197
Baby Let's Play House, 124
Baby Love, 174, 176
… Baby One More Time, 462, 463
Baby Please Don't Go, 70
Baby Seals' Blues, 24
Baby Talk, 163
Baby Wants to Ride, 449
Baby What You Want Me to Do, 104
Back Down, 480
Back for the Attack, 379
Back in My Arms Again, 174

Back in the High Life, 356
Back in the U.S.A., 10
Back on the Block, 401
Back on the Chain Gang, 319
Back Stabbers, 250
Back to Mono, 169
Backlash Blues, 200
Backside of the Moon, 451
Bad, Bad Whiskey, 67
Bad Boy for Life, 472
Bad Girls, 328
Bad Luck, 250
Bad Manors, 209
Badlands, 263
Badmotorfinger, 426, 439
Bailamous, 465
Ball and Chain, 210
Ball of Confusion (That's What the World Is Today), 216
Ballad of the Green Berets, 199, 509
The Ballad of Wendell Clark, 349
Ballroom Blitz, 286
Banana Boat (a.k.a. Day-O), 14
The Banana Boat Song, 144
The Band, 271
Bang a Gong (Get It On), 286
Bang Your Head (Metal Health), 379
Barbara Allen, 39
Barracuda, 284
Barrio Fino, 544, 545
Barrio Fino: En Directo, 545
Barry Manilow Live, 289
The Basement Tapes, 271
The Battle of Evermore, 278
The Battle of Los Angeles, 461
Be My Baby, 168, 171
Be My Guest, 91
Be My Yoko Ono, 437
Be Not Nobody, 525
Be True to Your School, 160
Beale Street Blues, 25
Bear Cat, 122
Beat Crazy, 317
Beat It, 343, 344, 345, 361
Beatnik Fly, 159
Beauty and the Beast, 458
Beauty Is Only Skin Deep, 173
The Beavis and Butt-Head Experience, 430
Be-Bop Baby, 151
Be-Bop-A-Lula, 129
Because of You, 63, 534
Because the Night, 298
Because They're Young, 150
Before the Flood, 271
Beg for Mercy, 537
Behind These Hazel Eyes, 535
Believe What You Say, 151
Belsen Was a Gas, 311
Bennie and the Jets, 290
Best of Both Worlds, 471, 479

The Best Damn Thing, 528
Betcha by Golly, Wow, 252
Beyond the Season, 441
Big Blue Ball of War, 517
Big Cheese, 426
Big Circumstance, 261
Big Feeling, 350
Big Fun, 450
Big Fun, 450
Big Time Sensuality, 455
Big Town Boy, 178
Big Yellow Taxi, 256
Bigger and Deffer, 394
Billie Jean, 343, 345, 361
Billion Dollar Babies, 285
Biograph, 214
Big Boy Pete, 115
Bird Dog, 132
Bird in a Gilded Cage, 22
The Birds Do It, The Bees Do It, 409
Birds of Fire, 244
Birth Poem, 269
Birthday, 386
A Bit of Liverpool, 193
Bitches Brew, 244
Bits and Pieces, 192
Black Album, 539
Black Angel's Death Song, 295
Black Day in July, 185
The Black Donnellys, 349
Black Magic Woman, 219
Black Pearl, 168, 169
Black Secret Technology, 452
Black Snake Blues, 43
Black Sunday, 404Blackened, 383
Blame It on the Bossa Nova, 153
Bleach, 426, 446
Blitzkrieg Bop, 311
Blonde on Blonde, 270
Blood on the Tracks, 271
Blood Sugar Sex Magik, 439
Bloodshot Eyes, 69
Blow at High Dough, 436
Blowin' in the Wind, 173, 176, 181, 187, 363
Blowin' Your Mind, 262
Blue Angel, 130
Blue Lines, 452
Blue Monday, 91
Blue Moon, 86
Blue Moon of Kentucky, 123, 124
Blue Moves, 290
Blue on Blue, 148
Blue Suede Shoes, 88, 127
Blue Tail Fly, 159
Blue Velvet, 114, 148, 149
Blue, 256, 459
Blue, 443, 456
Blue Yodel No. 9, 46
Blueberry Hill, 85, 91
The Blueprint, 479
Blues for Moon Dog, 80
Blues Stay Away from Me, 105
Bo Diddley, 85, 100
Bo Weevil, 140
Bobbitt, 320
Bobby Sox to Stockings, 147
Bobcaygeon, 349
Bodies in the Wall, 320
Body Count, 417, 440
Bodyrock, 385
Bohemian Rhapsody, 338

Bombardin', 455
Bomber, 378
Bony Maroney, 93
Boogie Chillen, 67
Boogie Fever, 327, 329
Boogie Woogie Dancin' Shoes, 329
The Book of Taliesyn, 278
Boom Boom, 193
Bootylicious, 471
Borderline, 35
Born a Woman, 217, 268
Born in the U.S.A., 353, 356
Born in the U.S.A., 354
Born into the 90s, 470
Born Slippy, 454
Born to Be Wild, 276, 277
Born to Run, 263, 354
Born Too Late, 117
Boston, 290
Both Sides Now, 256
The Boy is Mine, 458
Boys, 188
Boys N the Hood, 394
Brainwashed, 244
Brass in Pocket, 318
Brave Wolfe, 184
Break on Through (To the Other Side), 215
Break the Cycle, 521
Break Up to Make Up, 252
Breakaway, 534
Breakaway, 535
Breaking Up Is Hard to Do, 147
Breakout, 356
Breakthrough, 370
Breathe, 443
Breathless, 128
Brian Wilson, 437
Bridge Over Troubled Water, 19, 501
Briefcase of Blues, 209
Bring It on Home to Me, 183
Bring the Noise, 376
Bringing It All Back Home, 181
Bristol Stomp, 148
Britney, 463
Broken Social Scene, 523
Brooklyn's Finest, 478
Brothers and Sisters, 274
Brown Eyed Girl, 262
Brown Sugar, 217
Brown-Eyed Handsome Man, 10, 101, 198
Brushfire Fairytales, 531
The Buena Vista Social Club, 465
Built for Speed, 346
The Bully, 18
Bumble Boogie, 159
Bump N' Grind, 470
Burn, 539
Burn That Candle, 120
Burning Bridges, 131
Bus Stop, 191
Bush Killa, 514
Bushleaguer, 513
Business As Usual, 28
Business, 515
Busted Stuff, 531
But I Do, 93
Butterfly, 445
Butterfly, 86, 146
Buttons and Bows, 62

Buzz, Buzz, Buzz, 98
By Any Means Necessary, 395
By the Time I Get to Phoenix, 254
Bye Bye Love, 132

C

C'mon, Let's Go, 99
Calendar Girl, 147
California Dreaming, 199
California Girls, 162, 163
California Uber Alles, 320
Call It Democracy, 261
Call It Stormy Monday, 84
Calypso, 144
Can I Get a Witness, 193
Can't Buy Me Love, 191
Can't Get Enough of Your Love Babe, 254
Can't Get Enough, 279
Can't Slow Down, 354, 356
Can't Stand Losing You, 318
Can't You Feel My Heart Beat, 329
Canadian Railroad Trilogy, 185, 349
Canciones de mi Padre, 12
Candy Shop, 542
The Cannibal Café, 320
The Capture of Albert Johnson, 47
Cara Mia, 148
Career Opportunities, 307
Carefree Highway, 185
Carol, 193
Carole King: Writer, 257
Castles, 265
A Casual Look, 117
Cat Scratch Fever, 279
Cathy's Clown, 132
Celebration, 324
Celine Dion, 458
Centerfold, 345
A Century of Song, 183
Chain Gang, 109, 187
Chain of Fools, 202
Chains, 170, 171, 188
Chains of Love, 71, 80
Chances Are, 139
A Change is Gonna Come, 187, 200
The Changer and the Changed, 267
Changes, 287
Chapel of Love, 171
Chapter V, 522
Charity Ball, 265
Charlie Brown, 115
Charly, 451, 453
Charmbracelet, 542
The Chase, 441
Chattanooga Choo-Choo, 332
Cheek to Cheek, 23
Cheep, 28
Cherry Bomb, 266
Chicago, 224
Chill Out, 451
Chimes of Freedom, 199
Chips-Chicken-Banana Split, 179
Chocolate Factory, 537
Choice of Colors, 216

Choo Choo Ch'Boogie, 66
Chop Chop Boom, 119
Christina Aguilera, 464
The Chronic, 400, 474
Church Bells May Ring, 119
Cindy, Oh Cindy, 144
The Cisco Kid, 253
Clear, 449
Clicks and Cuts, 455
Clocks, 537
Close My Eyes Forever, 389
Closer to the Ground, 265
Clouds, 256
CN Tower, 303
Cock the Hammer, 404
Codeine, 183
Cold Sweat, 202
Cold Turkey, 262
Cold, Cold Heart, 63, 65
The College Dropout, 539, 540
Combat Rock, 309, 513
Come a Little Bit Closer, 148
Come and Get These Memories, 168
Come Away With Me, 526, 527
Come Back Baby, 107
Come Back to Sorrento, 126
Come Go with Me, 117, 143
Come into My House, 399
Come Josephine in My Flying Machine, 22
Come On Little Angel, 117
Come On Over, 443, 457
Come On Over Baby (All I Want is You), 464
Come on Pretty Baby, 131
Come See About Me, 174
Come Softly to Me, 118
Complete Control, 310, 314
Complicated, 528
Concerto for Group and Orchestra, 239, 279
Conditions Critical, 269
Confessions Pt. 2, 539
Confessions, 539
Continuum, 531, 532
Control, 356, 358
Cop Killer, 417, 418, 419, 438, 440
Could It Be I'm Falling in Love, 252
Country Boy, 91
Country Grammar, 482
Country Life, 288
Country Road, 257
Courtesy of the Red, White and Blue (The Angry American), 508, 510
Cowboys to Girls, 250
Cracked Rear View, 444, 447
Crackin' Up, 100
Crazy, 133, 273
Crazy Blues, 41, 44
Crazy in Love, 537
Crazy Man Crazy, 82, 120
CrazySexyCool, 469
Creep, 469
Crimes of Passion, 268
Criminal, 457
Criminal Minded, 394
Crocodile Roc, 290
Crosby, Stills & Nash, 220
Cross Country, 265
Cross over the Bridge, 112

Crossover, 322
Cruel to Be Kind, 316
Cry of the Wild Goose, 65
Cry, 118, 138
Crying, 130, 436
Crying in the Chapel, 85, 86, 106, 140
Cum on Feel the Noize, 379
Cup of Life, 465
Cut the Cake, 323
Cuts Both Ways, 12

D

Da Doo Ron Ron, 168, 171
Da Game Is to Be Told, Not to Be Sold, 473
Da Real World, 483
Da Ya Think I'm Sexy?, 331
Dale Don Dale, 546
Dallas Blues, 24
Damaged, 319
Damned, Damned, Damned, 309
Dance for Me, 399
The Dance of Romance, 296
Dance to the Bop, 129
Dance to the Music, 220
Dance with Me Henry, 110, 140
Dance with Me, 115, 167, 263
Dancer, 329
Dancing in the Street, 173
Dancing on the Ceiling, 354
Dancing on the Ceiling, 354
Danger Zone, 357
Dangerous, 425
Dangerously in Love, 537
Danny Boy, 133
Dark Side of the Moon, 240
Darkness on the Edge of Town, 263
Darktown Strutters' Ball, 22
Dat Draggy Rag, 24
Date Rape, 399
Day After Day, 435
Day I Forgot, 530
A Day in the Life, 214
Daydream, 199
Daydream, 445, 456
Daydream Believer, 213
Days of Future Past, 238
Deacon's Hop, 67
Dead Man's Curve, 163
The Deadly Nightshade, 265
Dear Diary, 529
Dear Lady Twist, 149
Dear Mr. President, 517, 529
Death Certificate, 400, 439
Dede Dinah, 146, 147
Dedicated Follower of Fashion, 192
Dedicated to the One I Love, 109, 164, 168
Deep Cover, 419
Deep Purple in Rock, 277
Deep Purple, 106
Deep Six, 426
Deguello, 276
Déjà vu, 221
Delirious Rag, 23
Dem Bow, 544
Demolition, 379
Denis, 301
Denise, 301

Desire, 271
Destiny Fulfilled, 537
Devil in Disguise, 85
Devil or Angel, 114, 148
Devilish Blues, 39
Diamond Dogs, 287
Diamond Mine, 435
Diamonds from Sierra Leone, 541
Diana, 85, 147, 151
The Diary of Alicia Keys, 526
Different Drummer, 260
Difficult to Cure, 279
Dig Your Own Hole, 545
Dim, Dim the Lights, 120
Dirrty, 464
Dirt, 427
Dirty, 430
Dirty Mind, 352
Disco Inferno, 331, 542
Disco Lady, 327
Disco Spaceship, 329
Disco Sucks, 320
Disraeli Gears, 210
Dizzy Miss Lizzy, 93
Do It ('Til You're Satisfied), 326
Do Something for Me, 106
Do That to Me One More Time, 410
Do the Bird, 149
Do the Freddie, 191
Do the Twist with Ray Charles, 149
Do They Know It's Christmas, 361
Do You Believe in Magic?, 195, 199
Do You Feel Like We Do, 290
Do You Love What You Feel, 450
Do You Really Want to Hurt Me?, 341
Doctor My Eyes, 263
Document, 431, 432
Does Your Chewing Gum Lose Its Flavour (on the Bedpost Over-night), 189
Dogfarts, 320
Doggie in the Window, 85, 136
DoggyStyle, 419
Doin' It Right, 209
Dominique, 11
Domino, 262
Don't, 124, 139
Don't Be Angry, 140
Don't Be Cruel, 124, 125, 126
Don't Call Me Nigger, Whitey, 221, 438
(Don't Fear) The Reaper, 284
Don't Forget About Us, 543
Don't Give Us a Reason, 508
Don't Hang Up, 168
Don't Know Why, 526, 527
Don't Let Me Be Misunderstood, 193
Don't Let the Rain Come Down, 180
Don't Let the Stars Get in Your Eyes, 136
Don't Let the Sun Catch You Crying, 190
Don't Make Me Wait, 449
Don't Mess with Bill, 173
Don't Say Nothin' Bad About My Baby, 170, 171

Don't Think Twice, It's Alright, 181
Don't Tread on Me, 501
Don't Wanna Lose You, 11
Don't Worry Baby, 162
Don't Worry, 132
Don't You Just Know It, 92
Don't You Know I Love You, 114
Don't You Know, 107
Don't You Want Me, 340
Dónde Están Los Ladrones? (Where Are the Thieves?), 466–467
Donna, 99
Doo Wah Diddy Diddy, 191
Doo Wop (That Thing), 458
The Doors, 215
Double Crossing Blues, 115
Down by the Henry Moore, 349
Down by the Riverside, 166
Down Low (Nobody Has to Know), 470
Down the Aisle of Love, 117
Down Went McGinty, 18
Downhearted Blues, 42
Downtown, 192
Dr. Dre—2001, 477
Drag City, 163
Dream Baby, 130
Dream Lover, 86
The Dream of the Blue Turtles, 368
Dreamboat Annie, 283
Driftin' Blues, 95
Drinkin' Wine Spo-dee-o-dee, 70
Dropout, 540
Dub Poet: The Poetry of Lillian Allen, 269
Dubnobasswithmyheadman, 454
Duke of Earl, 104, 164
Dummy, 452
Dutty Rock, 537
The Dynasty: Roc la Familia, 479

E

E.A.T. (East African Tragedy), 365
Early in the Morning, 130
Early Morning Rain, 185
Earth Angel, 85, 116, 119, 140
Easier Said Than Done, 168
Easter Parade, 23
Easter, 298
Easy Lover, 359
Eat a Peach, 274
Ebony and Ivory, 358
Eddie My Love, 117, 141
Efil4zaggin, 400
EFX & 909, 545
Eight Miles High, 206
Eighteen, 285
El Loco, 276
El Paso, 132
El Rancho Rock, 99
El Watusi, 11
Eleanor Rigby, 278
Elements of Style, 405
Ella y Yo, 545
The Emancipation of Mimi, 542
Emergency, 359

The Eminem Show, 515
Emotions, 445
Encore, 515
The End, 215
Endtroducing, 453
The Enemy Within, 346
Enter the Wu-Tang: 36 Chambers, 476
Enter, 449
Entropy, 453
Epic, 422
Eruption, 283
Ethiopie, 365
Eve of Destruction, 195, 199, 509, 517
Even Now, 289
Eve-Olution, 483
Every Breath You Take, 318, 472
Every Little Thing She Does Is Magic, 318
Every Night About This Time, 91
Everybody in the Place, 451
Everybody's Doin' It, 28
Everybody's Somebody's Fool, 147
Everybody's Trying to Be My Baby, 127
Everyday, 130
Everyday, 531
Everyday I Write the Book, 317
Everyday People, 216, 220, 221
Everything Is Wrong, 454
Evil Empire, 461
Evil Ways, 220
Exit Planet Dust, 454
Exodus, 264
Experimental Jet Set, Trash and No Star, 430
Express, 326
Expressway to Your Heart, 250

F

Facelift, 427
Fade to Black, 413
Fairweather Johnson, 447
Fall on Me, 432
Fallen, 536
Fallin', 525
Falling into You, 456, 458
False Media, 517
Fame, 288
Family Affair, 220, 221
Family Portrait, 529
Family Reunion, 250
Famous Among the Barns, 530
Fan Mail, 469
Fandango!, 276
Fanny Hill, 265
Fannie Mae, 178
Fantasy, 445
Far Away, 522
Fascination, 85
The Fat Man, 80, 91
The Fat of the Land, 453
Fear of a Black Planet, 395
Fear of Music, 321
Feed U.S.A. Fetus, 320
Feel Like Makin' Love, 254
Feels Like Home, 526, 528

Ferry Cross the Mersey, 190
Fever, 105
A Fifth of Beethoven, 327
Fifth Symphony, 332
Fight the Power, 371
Fijacion Oral, Vol. 1, 544
Final Solution, 302, 311, 399, 401
Fine Malt Lyrics, 404
Fingertips—Part 2, 173
Fire and Rain, 257
Fire, 323, 460
Firebird Suite, 332
Firestarter, 453
The First Time Ever I Saw Your Face, 254
The Fish, 148
Fish Cheer, 220
Fit as a Fiddle, 437
Five Days in July, 435
Five Long Years, 209
Five to One, 218
Flash Light, 325
Fleetwood Mac, 290
Flesh of My Flesh, 476, 479
The Flight of the Bumble Bee, 159
The Flight of the Valkyries, 411
Flip Flop and Fly, 209
Fluffy Little Clouds, 451
Fly, 509
The Fly, 148
Fly, Robin, Fly, 327
Flying Home, 84
Folklore, 520
Folsom Prison Blues, 128
Fool, Fool, Fool, 114
Footloose, 357
For Blood and Empire, 516
(For God's Sake) Give More Power to the People, 217
For Lovin' Me, 185
For Sentimental Reasons, 63, 85
For Those About to Rock, We Salute You, 377
For What It's Worth (Stop, Hey What's That Sound), 212
For You, 352
For Your Love, 210
For Your Pleasure, 288
For Your Precious Love, 104, 186
Forty Days, 132
Forty Miles of Bad Roads, 150
Four Strong Winds, 184, 349
Fox on the Run, 286
Fragile, 139, 240, 242
Frampton Comes Alive!, 289, 290
Frampton, 290
Frankenchrist, 415
Frankie, 152
Frankie and Johnny, 39
Frantic City, 304
Freak Out, 238
Freaky Styley, 439
Free Your Mind and Your Ass Will Follow, 324
Free Yourself, 534
Freebird, 275
Freedom, 220, 504
Freeway of Love, 254
The Freewheelin' Bob Dylan, 180
Freeze, 334
Fresh Cream, 210

Fresh Fruit for Rotting Vegetables, 320
From Justin to Kelly, 534
From Me to You, 191
From South Africa to South Carolina, 264
F-U-C-K Like a Beast 409
Fuck Your Society, 320
Fulfillingness' First Finale, 252
Full Throttle, 453
Fully Completely, 436
Fumbling Towards Ecstasy, 434, 457
Fun, Fun, Fun, 162
Funeral, 523
Funhouse, 401
Funky and Western, 265
Funky Broadway, 201
Funky Stuff, 324
Funky Worm, 323
The Future, 261

G

G. I. Jive, 66
G.T.O., 160
Gallows Pole, 278
Galveston, 273
Game Face, 473
The Game of Love, 191
Garden Party, 272
Garth Brooks, 441
Gasolina, 544, 545, 546
Gaucho, 291
Gee, 85
Genie in a Bottle, 464, 465
Genius of Love, 392, 445
George Jackson, 217
Get Dancin', 322
Get Down Tonight, 328
Get Happy!!, 316
Get Off, 322
Get on the Good Foot, 390
Get Rich or Die Tryin', 480, 537, 538
Get the Party Started, 529
Get Up and Boogie, 327
Get Up, Stand Up, 264
Get Ur Freak On, 483
G-Force, 453
Ghetto Child, 149
The Ghetto Is Trying to Kill Me, 473
Ghetto Postage, 473
Ghost in the Machine, 318
Ginger Bread, 147
Girl (Why You Wanna Make Me Blue), 176
Girl from the North Country, 270
The Girl Is Mine, 343, 359
Girls Just Wanna Have Fun, 346
Girls on Film, 341, 345
Girls, Girls, Girls, 384
Give My Regards to Broadway, 22, 34
Give Peace a Chance, 218, 224
Glad All Over, 192
Glad to Be Gay, 215
The Globe Sessions, 458
Gloria, 190
Glory Days, 354

Go, 454
Go! Now, 190
Go, Jimmy, Go, 93
God Bless America, 23, 503
God Bless the USA, 501, 507, 508
God Save the Queen, 309, 310, 312
Goin' Home to Memphis, 131
Goin' Out of My Head, 114
Gold Digger, 541
Golden Teardrops, 115
Gone, 132, 532
Gone, Gone, Gone, 127
Good Golly, Miss Molly, 94
Good Life, 450
Good Lovin', 170
Good Night Irene, 105
Good Rockin' Tonight, 67, 83, 85, 90, 124
Good Times, 391
Good Timin', 141, 164
Good Vibrations, 161, 163
Goodbye Bozos, 296
Goodbye Cruel World, 146
Goodbye Earl 510
Goodbye Sunshine, Hello Moon, 23
Goodbye Sweet Liza Jane, 45
Goodbye to Romance, 378
Goodbye Yellow Brick Road, 290
Goodnight, It's Time to Go, 115
Goody Goody, 114
Gordon, 437
Got a Woman, 85, 107
Got My Mojo Working, 70, 84
Got to Get You into My Life, 195, 324
Graceland, 371, 372
The Grateful Dead, 207–208
The Grave, 513
Grave Dancer's Union, 440
Great Balls of Fire, 86, 128
The Great Depression, 479
The Great Pretender, 116
Great Speckled Bird, 50
Greatest Hits (Connie Francis), 147
Green, 431, 432
Green, Green, 180
Greenfields, 145
Greenhouse Effect, 383
Greetings from Asbury Park, N.J., 262
Groove Me, 469
Groovin', 170
Guava Jelly, 314
Gum Drop, 116, 119, 140
The Gypsy, 63
Gypsy Woman, 186

H

Half as Much, 65
Hallelujah, I Love Her So, 85, 107, 193
Hand Me Down World, 195
Handy Man, 141, 164, 257
Hang On to Your Life, 195
Hanging by a Moment, 521
Happy Birthday Sweet Sixteen, 147

Happy, Happy Birthday Baby, 117
Harbor Lights, 117
A Hard Day's Night, 191
Hard Knock Life, 479
Hard Times, 115
Hardcore '81, 320
Harlem Nocturne, 98, 159
Hasten Down the Wind, 290
Hate It or Love It, 542
Hats Off (To the Stranger), 244
Hats Off to Larry, 147
Hava Nagila, 332
Have I the Right?, 192
Have Mercy Baby, 106
Have You Forgotten, 508
Haven't Got a Clue, 517
He Hit Me (It Felt Like a Kiss), 170, 171
He Was a Friend of Mine, 212
He's a Rebel, 147, 164, 168, 169, 171
He's So Fine, 168
He's Sure the Boy I Love, 169, 171
Head, 253
Headhunters, 244
Heart Like a Wheel, 260
Heart of Glass, 321
Heartaches by the Number, 132
Heartbeat, 449
Heartbreak (It's Hurtin' Me), 105
Heartbreak Hotel, 124, 127
Heartbreaker, 445
Hearts of Stone, 105, 116, 141
Heat Wave, 168, 173, 176
Heaven Knows, 329
Heaven Must Be Missing An Angel, 329
Heaven, I Need a Hug, 471
Heavier Things, 530, 531, 532
Hell to Pay, 209
Hello, 345, 354
Hello Mary Lou, 147, 151
Help Me Somebody, 109
Help Me, 256
Helpless, 349
Helter Skelter, 224
Henry's Got Flat Feet (Can't Dance No More), 110
Her Royal Majesty, 153
Here Comes the Night, 190
Here in My Heart, 63
Here Today, Guano Tomorrow, 320
Here We Are, 12
Here's to the State of Mississippi, 181
Hero, 503
Heroin, 295
Hey Good Lookin', 65
Hey Joe, 213, 298
Hey Jude, 218
Hey Little Cobra, 160
Hey Little Girl, 104
Hey Paula, 148
Hey There, 85
Hey Ya!, 537
Hi, How Are You Today?, 437
High 'n' Dry, 377
High Noon, 64
High School Confidential, 268–269
Higher, 522

Highly Evolved, 522
Highway Star, 279
Highway to Hell, 377
Hippy Hippy Shake, 190
Hips Don't Lie, 545
His Band and the Street Choir, 262
Hispanic Causing Panic, 404
History Lesson, 422
Hit 'Em Up, 478
Hit Me with Your Rhythm Stick, 316
Hit the Road, Jack, 193
Hitchhike, 193
Ho in Here, 482
The Hockey Song, 349
Hojita de Limon, 183
Holiday, 355, 514
Holiday in Cambodia, 320
Hollaback Girl, 542
Hollywood Swinging, 324
Home, 510
Home for a Rest, 437
Home Sweet Home, 18
Honest I Do, 104
Honey, 445
Honey Chile, 66
Honey Don't, 127
Honey Hush, 71, 80
Honeydripper, 67
Honky Tonk, 105, 159
Honky Tonk University, 512
Honky Tonk Woman, 217
Hoochie Coochie Man, 70
A Horse with No Name, 261
Horses, 298
Hot Boyz, 458, 483
Hot Buttered Soul, 254
Hot for Teacher, 345
Hot Fun in the Summertime, 220
Hot Legs, 331
Hot Line, 327
Hot Shot, 482
Hot Stuff, 323, 328
Hot, Cool & Vicious, 394, 399
Hotel California, 272, 273, 290
Hound Dog, 115, 122, 124, 125–128
Hound Dog Man, 147
House of the Rising Sun, 192, 195, 197
How Can a Poor Man Stand Such Times and Live?, 517
How Can You Mend a Broken Heart, 330
How Deep Is Your Love, 330
How I Could Just Kill a Man, 404, 461
How Jesus Died, 107
How Sweet It Is to Be Loved by You, 173, 257
How to Rob, 481
How We Do It, 542
How We Gonna Make the Black Nation Rise, 391
How Will I Know, 354
How You Remind Me, 521, 522
Howlin' Wind, 308
The Hucklebuck, 67, 148
A Huge Evergrowing Pulsating Brain That Rules from the Centre of the Ultraworld, 451

Hully Gully, 149
Human Clay, 522
The Hunchback of Notre Dame, 329
Hungry Like a Dog, 341
Hunky Dory, 287
Hurricane, 271
Hurts So Bad, 114
Hush, 278
Hustle, 326
Hustler's Convention, 391
Hybrid Theory, 521
Hyperspeed, 453

I Ain't Marching Anymore, 181
I Almost Lost My Mind, 141
I Am with You, 106
I Am Woman, 217, 258
I Believe I Can Fly, 470
I Believe in Music, 179
I Believe, 136, 534, 539
I Can Never Go Home Anymore, 172
I Can See Clearly Now, 314
I Can't Be Satisfied, 70
I Can't Help It, 65
I Can't Help Myself, 173, 176
I Can't Sleep Baby (If I), 470
I Can't Stop Loving You, 10
I Didn't Raise My Boy to Be a Soldier, 22
I Didn't Want to Do It, 91, 93
I Dig Rock and Roll Music, 198
I Do Not Want What I Haven't Got, 422
I Don't Care If the Sun Don't Shine, 124
I Don't Care, 198
I Don't Have to Ride No More, 111
I Don't Wanna Be Learned, I Don't Wanna Be Tamed, 298, 300
I Don't Wanna Go Down to the Basement, 298
I Don't Want To, 456
I Fall to Pieces, 133
I Feel For You, 392
I Feel Free, 360
I Feel Like Goin' Home, 70
I Feel the Earth Move, 505
I Forgot to Remember to Forget, 124
I Get Around, 163
(I Got Everything I Need) Almost, 209
I Got the Feelin', 202
(I Got the) Rockin' Pneumonia and the Boogie-Woogie Flu, 92
I Got You Babe, 195
(I Got You) I Feel Good, 204–205
I Got You, 202
I Have but One Heart, 63
I Hear You Knocking, 91, 93, 141, 316
I Heard It Through the Grapevine, 176
I Just Wanna Stop, 291

I Just Want to Make Love to You, 70
I Knew You Were Waiting for Me, 359
I Know a Place, 192
(I Know) I'm Losing You, 173, 176
I Know You Know, 267
I Like It Like That, 192
I Like to Score, 454
I Love How You Love Me, 118
I Love Music, 250
I Met Him on a Sunday, 168
I Need an Angel, 535
I Need to Know, 465
I Never Loved a Man (The Way I Love You), 200
I Only Have Eyes for You, 115
I Only Want to Be with You, 191
I Put a Spell on You, 139
I Quit My Pretty Mama, 105
I Raq and Roll, 508
I Say a Little Prayer, 176
I Shall Be Released, 271
I Shot the Sheriff, 315
I Think We're Alone Now, 217
I Took Your Name, 432
I Waited Too Long, 152
I Walk the Line, 128
I Wanna Get High, 404
I Wanna Hold Your Hand, 195
(I Wanna) Testify, 324
I Want a Bow-Legged Woman, 67
I Want to Be Wanted, 133
I Want to Hold Your Hand, 191
I Want to Walk You Home, 91
I Want You Back, 252
I Want You to Be My Girl, 114
I Will Follow Him, 148
I Will Survive, 326, 329
I Won't Back Down, 503
I Wonder Why, 117
I'll Be Around, 252
I'll Be Doggone, 173
I'll Be Home, 142
I'll Be Missing You, 421, 472
I'll Be Satisfied, 173
I'll Be There, 252, 445
I'll Be Watching You, 402
I'll Never Find Another You, 190
I'll Never Smile Again, 62
I'll Take You There, 187
I'll Tumble 4 Ya, 341
I'll Walk Alone, 62
I'm a Believer, 213
I'm a King Bee, 193
I'm a Man, 100, 305
I'm a Slave 4 U, 463
I'm an Adult Now, 347
I'm Gone, 91
I'm Gonna Be a Country Girl Again, 270
I'm Gonna Be Strong, 147
I'm Gonna Get Married, 93
I'm Gonna Love You Just a Little More Baby, 254
I'm Henry VIII, I Am, 191
I'm in Love Again, 85, 91, 141, 193
I'm Left, You're Right, She's Gone, 124
I'm Like a Bird, 529

I'm Moving On, 47
I'm Not a Girl, Not Yet a Woman, 463
I'm Not Angry, 316
I'm Not Dead, 529
I'm Okay, 464
I'm Ready for Love, 173
I'm Real, 466
I'm So Bored with the U.S.A., 307
I'm So Glad, 210
I'm So Lonesome I Could Cry, 435
I'm Sorry, 133
I'm Stickin' with You, 129
I'm Talking About You, 193
I'm Telling You Now, 191
I'm Walkin', 92, 151
I'm Walking Behind You, 136
I'm Weak but I'm Willing, 67
I'm with Stupid, 517
I'm With You, 528
I'm Your Angel, 470
I'm Your Boogie Man, 328
I'm Your Man, 261
I've Been Loving You Too Long, 200
I've Got Friends in Low Places, 411
I've Got My Love to Keep Me Warm, 23
I've Got the Big River Blues, 105
Iceberg, 394
Ida Red, 10, 100
The Idiot Son of an Asshole, 514
Idlewild South, 274
If a Tree Falls, 161
If Everyone Cared, 522
If I Ain't Got You, 526
If I Can't Have You, 331
If I Didn't Care, 111
If I Had a $1 000 000, 437
If I Had a Hammer, 180, 183
If I Had a Rocket Launcher, 261, 370
If It Weren't for the Music, 266
If You Could Read My Mind, 185
If You Don't Know Me By Now, 250
If You Had My Love, 465, 466
If You're Ready (Come Go with Me), 187
I-Feel-Like-I'm-Fixin'-to-Die Rag, 212, 219
Ignoreland, 432
Ill Communication, 441
Illmatic, 478
Imagine My Surprise, 267
Imagine, 218, 501, 503, 505, 509
Immigrant Song, 278
Immigration Man, 224
In Between Dreams, 532
In Da Club, 480, 537, 538
In Flux, 453
In God We Trust, Inc., 320
In My Life, Vol. I, 479
In My Room, 160
In Pieces, 441
In the Ghetto, 216
In the Good Old Summer Time, 22
In the Jungle Groove, 451

In the Midnight Hour, 200, 201
In the Name of Love, 341
In the Navy, 329
In the Shade of the Old Apple Tree, 22
In Utero, 427
In-A-Gadda-Da-Vida, 278
In-A-Gadda-Da-Vida, 278
Independent Woman, 399
Ingenue, 436
Inherited Hell, 383
Inner City Blues, 217
Inner Mounting Flame, 244
Innervisions, 252
Inside Your Heaven 535
Into the Fire, 513
Into the Night, 522
Introduce Yourself, 422
Introducing … The Beatles, 188
Iron Flag, 476
Is It All over My Face, 449
Is She Really Going Out with Him, 317
Is This It?, 522
Is This the End, 472
Is This What I Get for Loving You?, 171
Is You Is, or Is You Ain't My Baby?, 66
The Israelites, 314
It Ain't Me Babe, 198
It Came from Canada, 433
It Doesn't Matter Anymore, 130
It Hurts to Be in Love, 147
It Keeps on A-Hurtin', 148
It Matters to Me, 443
It Might as Well Rain until September, 257
It Only Takes a Minute, 326
It Still Ain't Easy, 209
It Takes a Nation of Millions to Hold Us Back, 395
It Wasn't God Who Made Honky Tony Angels, 133
It's a Man's Man's Man's World, 202
It's All About the Benjamins, 472
It's All Right, 186
It's Dark and Hell Is Hot, 476, 479
It's Just Begun, 390, 392
It's Late, 151
It's My Party, 148
It's Not for Me to Say, 139
It's Now or Never, 126
It's Only Make Believe, 133, 139
It's So Easy, 129
It's the Same Old Song, 173
It's Too Soon to Know, 111
Italian Favourites, 147
Itchycoo Park, 217
Itsy Bitsy Teenie Weenie Yellow Polkadot Bikini, 148
Ivory Tower, 116, 141
Izzo (H.O.V.), 540

J

J. Lo, 466
Jack the Groove, 449
Jack Your Body, 449

Jacob's Ladder, 517
Jagged Little Pill, 456
Jailhouse Rock, 124
Jam, 427
Jamaica Farewell, 144
Jambalaya, 65
The Japanese Sandman, 22, 28
JC, 430
Je m'en souviens, 406
Jean Genie, 287
Jenny from the Block, 466
Jenny Lee, 163
Jenny, Jenny, 94
Jeopardy, 346
Jerusalem, 509
Jesse James, 517
Jesus Christ Superstar, 330
Jesus Walks, 540
Jim Dandy, 71, 85
Jive Talkin', 330
Jocko Homo, 303
Joe Hill, 219
Joe Turner Blues, 25
Johannesburg, 264
John Henry, 517
John Lennon/Plastic Ono Band, 262
John Walker's Blues, 509
John Wesley Harding, 270, 272
Johnny B. Goode, 10, 84, 101
Johnny's Theme, 151
Jole Blon, 105
The Joshua Tree, 367
Journey to the Centre of the Earth, 240
Journey to the Centre of the Mind, 206
Joy of Cooking, 265
Judy's Turn to Cry, 148
Jump, 378, 382
Jump Around, 404
Jumpin' Jack Flash, 206
Jumpin' Jive, 317
Jungle Boogie, 324
Jungle Techno, 451
Jungleland, 263
Junker Blues, 91
Just a Dream, 93
Just a Lil Bit, 542
Just a Little, 190
Just Can't Get Enough, 340
Just Once in My Life, 170
Justify My Love, 415

K

Kamikazi, 539
Kansas City, 164
Karma Chameleon, 341
Keep a Knockin', 94
Keep on Pushing, 186
Keep on the Sunny Side, 46
Keep Ya Head Up, 418
Keep Your Eyes on the Prize, 166
Kick Out the Jams, 218
Kicks, 206
Kid, 318
Kill the Poor, 320
Killing Me Softly with His Song, 254, 459
King Heroin, 206
King of Rock, 393

King Tim III (Personality Jock), 391
The Kiss, 18
K-K-K-Katy (The Stammering Song), 23
Ko Ko Mo (I Love You So), 119, 140
Kookie, Kookie (Lend Me Your Comb), 150
Kryptonite, 522

L

L'Heptade, 141
L'Ostidcho, 241
La Bamba, 11, 99, 197
La La Means I Love You, 250
La Moitié du monde est une femme, 268
La Tortura, 544
La Trayectoria, 546
Ladies First, 399, 402–403, 458
Ladies Night, 324
Lady Isabel and Elf-Knight, 40
Lady, 266
Land of 1000 Dances, 190, 201
Land Speed Record, 319
Landlord Blues, 105
Last Dance, 328
Last of the Red Hot Burritos, 272
The Last Temptation, 480
Last Train to Clarksville, 213
Late Registration, 540
Laughing, 195
The Laughing Song, 18
Laundry Service, 467, 544
Lawdy Lawdy Blues, 43
Lawdy Miss Clawdy, 80, 91, 93
Lay Lady Lay, 270
Layla, 274, 386
Le Boyfriend, 406
Leader of the Pack, 168, 170, 171
Leave Home, 299
Leaving Home, 45
Led Zeppelin II, 277, 283
Led Zeppelin III, 278
Led Zeppelin IV, 278, 284
Legs, 345
Less Than Zero, 317
Let It Bleed, 24
Let It Die, 523
Let It Snow, Let It Snow, Let It Snow, 62
Let Me In, 168
Let the Good Times Roll, 93, 193
Let There Be Drums, 159
Let There Be Eve … Ruff Ryders First Lady, 483
Let There Be Rock, 377
Let's Dance, 190, 341, 472
Let's Face the Music and Dance, 23
Let's Get It On, 253
Let's Get Ready, 482
Let's Go Crazy, 353
Let's Go Trippin', 159
Let's Go, 528
Let's Have a Party, 133
Let's Impeach the President, 516
Let's Roll, 509

Let's Shake, 304
Let's Talk About Love, 457, 458
Lethal Injection, 400
Lethal, 394
Leven Zonder Honger, 365
Licensed to Ill, 394
Life After Death, 421
Life in the Fast Lane, 273
Life Is but a Dream, 111
Life Stinks, 302
Life's Rich Pageant, 432
Lifted by Love, 455
Light My Fire, 215, 216
Lightfoot!, 185
Lighthouse Live!, 244
Like a Virgin, 345, 355, 408, 415
Like a Virgin, 354–355, 356
Like You, 545
Limbo Rock, 148
Limon Tree, 183
Lindy Lou, 131
Ling Ting Tong, 116
The Lion and the Cobra, 422
Lipstick on Your Collar, 147
Lit' Red Riding Hood, 190
Lita, 389
Little Annie Rooney, 18
Little Big Band, 209
Little Bitty Pretty One, 98
Little Children, 190
Little Darlin', 119, 140
Little Deuce Coup, 160
Little Girl, 9
Little Honda, 160
Little Johnny Jewel, 297
The Little Old Lady (From Pasadena), 163
The Little Old Log Cabin in the Lane, 44
Little Red Corvette, 342, 353
Little Red Rooster, 70
Little Star, 86
Little Things Mean a Lot, 85
Little Willy, 286
Live and More, 329
Live to Tell, 357
Live! One Night Only, 458
Lives in the Balance, 370, 371
Livin' La Vida Loca, 12, 465
Livin' on a Prayer, 383
Living for the City, 249
Living in America, 253
Living in the USA, 260
Living Large, 394
Living with War, 516, 517
Lo Que Pasó, Pasó, 545
The Loco-Motion, 149
London Calling, 309
London's Burning, 307
Lonely Avenue, 107
Lonely Blue Boy, 133
Lonely Boy, 147
The Lonely Surfer, 159
Lonely Teardrops, 107, 172
Lonely Weekends, 128
Lonesome Blue Yodel, 47
Lonesome Day, 513
The Lonesome Death of Hattie Carroll, 180
Long Ago and Far Away, 63
Long Black Veil, 271
The Long Road, 522
The Long Run, 273

Long Tall Sally, 85, 88, 94, 141, 188
Long Time Coming, 216, 221
Look What the Cat Dragged In, 384
Looking Out for #1, 277
Loose, 529, 530
Lord Lovel, 39
Losing My Religion, 432
Lost and Found, 453
Lotta Lovin', 129
Louder Than Love, 426
Lovable, 108
Love and Kisses, 329
Love Buzz, 426
Love Can't Turn Around, 449
Love Devotion Surrender, 244
Love Don't Cost a Thing, 466
Love for Sale, 411
Love Goes to Building on Fire, 302
Love in C Minor, 329
Love Is a Battlefield, 346
(Love is Like a) Baseball Game, 150
Love is Like Oxygen, 286
Love Is the Drug, 288
Love Letters in the Sand, 141
Love Me Do, 189, 191
Love Me Tender, 126
Love Potion No. 9, 114
Love Rollercoaster, 324
Love Takes Time, 445
Love the One You're With, 224
Love to Love You Baby, 326, 328
Love Train, 250
Love Will Keep Us Together, 289
The Love You Save, 252
Love, Love, Love, 114
Love's in Need of Love Today, 503
Love-Itis, 178
A Lover's Question, 85, 107
Lovers in a Dangerous Time, 261
Lovers Never Say Goodbye, 115
Lovers of Today, 318
Lovin' Sound, 184
Lucille, 94, 107
Lucky Lips, 71, 85
Lucky Star, 355
Lucy in the Sky with Diamonds, 214
Ludi, 405
Luka, 370, 457

M

M!ssundaztood, 529
M.R.F. est arrive, 406
MacArthur Park, 274, 328, 329
Machine Head, 279
Macho Man, 329
Mack the Knife, 147
Mademoiselle from Armentieres, 23
Magic Carpet Ride, 277
Magnificent Seven, 334
The Maid Freed from the Gallows, 39
Main Course, 330

Make It Big, 356
Makeshift Patriot, 514
(Mama), He Treats Your Daughter Mean, 70, 72–73
Mama Look-a Boo Boo, 144
Mama Said, 168
Mama's Pearl, 252
Mambo Rock, 121
Man of Words, Man of Music, 287
(The Man Who Shot) Liberty Valence, 147
The Man Who Sold the World, 287
Maneater, 530
Manifest Destiny, 311
Mannish Boy, 70
Mantra for a State of Mind, 451
Maple Leaf Rag, 24
Marianne, 144
Marie from Sunny Italy, 23
Marquee Moon, 297
Marrakesh Express, 221
The Marshall Mathers LP, 477
Mary Lou, 132
Mas Flow, 546
Mas Flow, Vol. 2, 546
Mashed Potato Time, 149
The Massacre, 542
Master of Reality, 277
Master of Puppets, 384
Match Box Blues, 43
Matchbox, 127
Material Girl, 345, 355
Matters of the Heart, 425
Maxinquaye, 453
Maybe, 117
Maybellene, 10, 101
Me Against the World, 420
Me and Bobby McGee, 210
Me So Horny, 416
Mean Old Woman, 131
Measure of a Man, 534
Mellow Yellow, 206
Memphis, 10
Memphis Blues, 24
Merry Christmas with Love, 535
Merry Christmas, Baby, 95
Mesmerize/Hypnotize, 516
Mess Around, 193
The Message, 392
Message in a Bottle, 318
Metal Health, 379, 381
Métele Sazón, 546
Meteora, 521, 522
Mi Reflejo (My Reflection), 464
Mickey's Monkey, 173
Midnight at the Oasis, 260
Midnight in Moscow, 189
Midnight Shift, 110
Midnight Train to Georgia, 252
Milagro, 465
Milkcow Blues Boogie, 124
Millennium, 462
Milwaukee Blues, 45
Mingus, 256
Mirrorball, 457
The Miseducation of Lauryn Hill, 459
Misled, 455
Miss E ... So Addictive, 483
Miss You, 331
Mississippi Goddam, 200
Mobilize, 514
Mockingbird, 257
The Mockingbird, 18

Modern Sounds in Country and Western Music (Volume I), 10
Modern Sounds in Country and Western Music (Volume II), 10
A Moment Like This, 534
Moments to Remember, 118
Mon pays (My Country), 185
Mona Lisa, 105
Monday, Monday, 199
Money, 164, 173, 188, 191
Money Honey, 107
Monster, 431, 447
The Mooche, 411
Moody, 449
Moody River, 141
Moody Woman, 250
Moondance, 262
Moonglow and Theme from Picnic, 88
More Italian Favourites, 147
More, More, More, 327
More Songs About Buildings and Food, 302
More Than a Woman, 331
More Than You Are, 522
Mosh, 515
The Most Happy Fella, 118
Mother, 262
Mother and Child Reunion, 315
Mother's Little Helper, 206
Mother's Milk, 439
Mountain Moving Day, 265
Move Something, 399, 416
MP Da Last Don, 472
Mr. Blue, 118
Mr. Crowley, 378
Mr. Custer, 183
Mr. Johnson, Turn Me Loose, 18
Mr. Kite, 214
Mr. Lee, 117
Mr. Lonely, 148
Mr. Tambourine Man, 198
Mr. Tambourine Man, 198
MRD Song Pack, 517
Mrs. Brown, You've Got a Lovely Daughter, 191
Mrs. Robinson, 199
Mrs., 269
Mule Train, 63, 64, 65
Murmur, 431
Muscles, 345
Music for the Gilted Generation, 453
Music from Big Pink, 271
Music of My Heart, 465
Music of My Mind, 252
My Aim Is True, 316
My Boo, 539
My Boy Lollipop, 314
My Boyfriend's Back, 168
My Country 'Tis of Thy People You're Dying, 183
My Dad's Gone Crazy, 515
My Daddy Rocks Me (With One Steady Roll), 83
My Definition of a Bombastic Jazz Style, 405
My Ding-a-Ling, 101
My Generation, 210, 212, 297
My Girl, 173
My Guy, 173
My Happiness, 63, 126, 147

My Happy Ending, 528
My Heart at thy Sweet Voice, 107–108
My Heart Belongs to Only You, 148
My Heart Will Go On, 458
My Hometown, 354
My Kind of Christmas, 464
My Old Man, 256
My Own Prison, 522
My Own Prison, 522
My Prayer, 111, 116
My Sugar Is So Refined, 111
My Swiss Moonlight Lullaby, 47
My True Love, 131
My Vietnam, 529
My Way, 151
Mystery Train, 124
The Myths and Legends of King Arthur and the Knights of the Round Table, 240

N

Nackt im Wind, 365
Naked, 471
Nashville Cats, 270
Nashville Skyline, 270
Natural Woman, 153, 202
Nearly God, 453
Nearly Lost You, 441
Nebraska, 353, 354
Needles and Pins, 190, 305
Nellie Belly Swelly, 269
Nellyville, 482
Neon Bible, 523
Neutron Dance, 257
Never Can Say Goodbye, 252, 326
Never Mind the Bullocks, Here's the Sex Pistols, 284, 425
Never, Never Gonna Give Ya Up, 254
Nevermind, 425, 426, 427, 428, 431
New Adventures in Hi-Fi, 447
A New Day at Midnight, 530
New Jole Blon, 105
New Orleans, 146
New Orleans Is Sinking, 436
New Rose, 307
New York Dolls, 286
New York Mining Disaster 1941/Have You Seen My Wife Mr. Jones, 330
New York State of Mind, 503
Nicaragua, 261
Night, 107
Night & Day, 317
Night Fever, 331
The Night Has a Thousand Eyes, 148
The Night They Drove Old Dixie Down, 271
Nights in White Satin, 245
Nights on Broadway, 330
Nikki Darling, 408
Ninth Symphony, 279
Nkosi Sikelel' iAfrica, 366
No Code, 447
No Fences, 441
No Hay Igual, 530

No Jacket Required, 356
No Me Dejes Solo, 545
No Money Down, 101
No More Drama, 471
No More Tears (Enough Is Enough), 328
No Name Face, 521
No, Not Much, 118
No Other Love, 136
No Protection, 452
No Sell Out, 422
No Sleep Till Hammersmith, 378
No Sugar Tonight, 195
No Way Out, 421, 472
No Woman, No Cry, 264
Nobody Knows You When You're Down and Out, 42
Nobody Loves Me Like You, 115
Norman, 148
Northern Touch, 406
Norwegian Wood, 214
Nos braves habitants (Our Brave People), 185
Not a Moment Too Soon, 443
Not Fade Away, 130
Not Ready to Make Nice, 511, 512
Not Too Young to Get Married, 171
Nothing Compares 2 You, 422
… Nothing Like the Sun, 368
Nothingface, 385
Now I Wanna Sniff Some Glue, 298
Now That the Buffalo's Gone, 183
Now That We Found Love, 321
Nowhere Man, 214
Nowhere to Run, 173
'N'Sync, 462
Nude Photo, 449
The Number of the Beast, 378
Nut Rocker, 159
The Nutcracker, 159

O

O Dio Mio, 147
O Mary Don't You Weep, 517
O Sole Mio, 126
Ode to Joy, 279
Odyssey, 378
Off the Wall, 342
Official Music, 209
OG, 394
Oh Bondage! Up Yours, 216
Oh Boy!, 130
Oh Mercy 367
Oh What a Difference Since the Hydro Came, 23
Oh What a Feeling, 247
Oh You Beautiful Doll, 22
Oh! Carol, 147
Oh, Carolina, 482
Oh, Lonesome Me, 133
Oh, Pretty Woman, 130
Oh, That Beautiful Rag, 24
Oh, What a Dream, 70–71
Oh! You Pretty Things, 287
Ohio, 224, 512
Okie from Muskogee, 206
Ol' Man River, 62

Old Man River, 111
Old Shep, 123
The Old Hen Cackled and the Rooster's Going to Crow, 44
Oliver's Army, 317
On and On, 449, 458, 530, 531, 532
On Broadway, 115
On My Own, 359
On the 6, 466
On the Road Again, 208
On This Mike, 405
On Through the Night, 377
Once Upon a Time, 329
One, 384, 522
One Fine Day, 168, 170, 171
One Fine Morning, 244
The One I Love, 432
One in a Million, 385, 388
One Love, 501, 505
One Mint Julep, 114
One Minute Man, 483
One More Night, 345
One Nation under a Groove, 325
One Night of Sin, 126
One Night, 126
One of the Boys, 287
One of Us, 457
One Summer Night, 140
One Sweet Day, 445
One Week, 437
The One Who Really Loves You, 173
Only a Pawn in Their Game, 180
Only God Can Judge Me, 473
Only in America, 148, 501
Only Love Can Break a Heart, 147
Only the Lonely, 130
Only the Strong Survive, 250
Ooby Dooby, 128
Ooh! My Soul, 94
Ooooooohhh … On the TLC Tip, 469
Oops! … I Did It Again, 462, 463
Open Sesame, 324
Open Sesame, 394
Open the Door, Richard, 63
Oral Fixation, Vol. 2, 544, 545
Ordinary Day, 350
Osama—Yo' Mama, 509
Our Day Will Come, 168
Out for Blood, 388
Out of Step, 319
Out of the Cellar, 379
Out Of the Womb, 320
Out of Time, 431, 432
Outskirts, 435
Outta Control, 542
Over There, 22
Overkill, 378
Overprotected, 463
Oxford Town, 180
Oye Como Va, 11, 219, 222–223
Oye Mi Canto, 544, 546

P

P***y, 471
Pacific State, 451
Paid in Full, 394

Pain Is Love, 480
Pain, 472
Palisades Park, 147
Papas Got a Brand New Bag, 202
Paper Thin, 399
Paradise City, 385
Parallel Lines, 301
Parallel Play, 434
Parallel Universe, 452
Paranoid, 277
Part-Time Lover, 359
Party Doll, 86, 129
Pay Me My Money Down, 517
Pearl, 210
Peg o' My Heart, 22
Peggy Sue, 130
Penetration, 159
Penis Landscape, 415–416
Penny Lane, 214, 338
People Get Ready, 196
People Got to Be Free, 216
People Gotta Move, 291
The People's Album, 231
Peppermint Twist, 321
Peppermint, 434
Perfidia, 160
Permanent Waves, 282
Perpetual Rag, 23
Personality, 93
Pet Sounds, 161, 163
Phases and Stages, 273
Photograph, 522
Physical, 345
Piano Concerto No. 1, 2, 108
Pick Up the Pieces, 323
Pictures at an Exhibition, 239
Piece of My Heart, 210
Pieces of You, 456
Pies Descalzos (Bare Feet), 466
Pine Top's Boogie Woogie, 40
Pipeline, 159
Piss Factory, 297
A Place in the Sun, 173
Planet Rock, 392
Planet Waves, 271
Plastic Letters, 301
Play Some Ragtime, 24
Play that Funky Music, 324
Play, 454
Playboy, 168, 173
Pleasant Valley Sunday, 153
Please Don't Go, 328
Please Hammer Don't Hurt 'Em, 401
Please Mr. Postman, 164, 168, 173
Please, Please Me, 191
Pledging My Love, 98
A Pocket Full of Kryptonite, 440
Poetry in Motion, 148
Point of Light, 411
Poison Ivy, 115
Police and Thieves, 307, 314
Political, 437
Pony Time, 148
Poor Little Fool, 151
Pop, 454
Porgy and Bess, 26
Power, 263
Power, 384
The Power of Love, 12, 357
Power to the People, 217, 218
Precious, 318
Predator, 400

Pre-Millennium Tension, 453
Presto, 282
The Pretender, 263
Pretenders II, 318
A Pretty Girl Is Like a Melody, 23
Pretty Hate Machine, 438
Pretty Lady, 24
Pretty Vacany, 307
Pretzel Logic, 291
Pride, 422
Pride (In the Name of Love), 367
Pride and Joy, 173, 176
The Prisoner Cowboy, 47
The Prisoner's Song, 45
Private Dancer, 356
Private Life, 318
Private Property, 178
Problems of the World, 392
Problems, 307
The Prodigy Experience, 453
Promiscuous, 530
Promised Land, 10
The Promised Land, 263
Protection, 452
The Proud, 514
Proud to Be a Canadian, 320
Psalm 69, 439
Proud to be Black, 404
PSK, 394
Psycho Killer, 302
Puff the Magic Dragon, 206
Pump Up the Volume, 450
Punky Reggae Party, 315
Puppy Love, 147
Purple Haze, 206
Purple Rain, 353
The Pusher, 277
Put a Light in the Window, 118
Put Your Head on My Shoulder, 147
Puttin' on the Ritz, 23
Pyromania, 381

Q

Quadrophenia, 241
Quarter to Three, 164
Quentin Tarantino Can't Act, 320
Quicksand, 168, 173

R

R., 470
R. Kelly, 470
Radio Ethiopia, 298
Radio, Radio, 317
Rag, Mama, Rag, 271
Ragged Old Flag, 501
Rags to Riches, 63
Ragtime Violin, 24
Rain on the Scarecrow, 370
Rainbow, 445
Rainbow Warriors, 370
Raindrops, 104
Raising Hell, 393, 394
Rakata, 546
Rally'n, 543

Ramblin' Man, 274
The Ramones, 299
Rapper Chic, 406
Rapper Delight, 391
Rappin' Black in a White World, 391
Rapture, 334, 392
Rapture, 356
Rastaman Vibration, 264
Raunchy, 159
Rave On, 130
Raving I'm Raving, 451, 452
Raw Power, 287
Ray of Light, 458
Reach, 456
Reach Out I'll Be There, 173, 176
Ready for Love, 279
Ready to Die, 421
The Real Slim Shady, 461
The Real Thing, 422
The Reason, 522
Reasonable Doubt, 478
Rebel-'Rouser, 150
Red Headed Stranger, 273
Red River Rock, 159
Red River Valley, 159
Rednecks, 261
Reelin' and Rockin', 192
Reet Petite, 107, 172
Reflection, 463
Regatta de Blanc, 318
Remain in Light, 321
The Reminder, 523
Remote Control, 310
Renegades of Funk, 461
Renegades, 461
Respect, 202
Restless Heart, 93
Reveille Rock, 159
Revival, 543
Revolution, 218, 360
Revolutionary Tea Party, 269
Revolver, 214
Rhapsody in Blue, 26
Rhyme Pays, 394
Ricky Martin, 465
Riders on the Storm, 216, 360
Right Back Where We Started From, 327
Rio, 341
Riot in Cell Block No. 9, 115
Rip It Up, 85, 94
The Rise and Fall of Ziggy Stardust and the Spiders from Mars, 287
Rise Up, 269
The Rising, 513
Ritual de lo Habitual, 438
River Deep—Mountain High, 171
Road Apples, 436
Rock 'n' Roll, 83
Rock & Roll Music, 84, 101, 102–103
Rock & Roll Nigger, 312
Rock Against Racism, 314
Rock Around the Clock, 82, 120, 121
Rock Box, 386, 393, 396–397
Rock Island Line, 190
Rock Me All Night Long, 111
Rock Me Baby, 277
Rock Me, 83

Rock Star, 522
Rock the Boat, 326
Rock the Casbah, 309
Rock the Joint, 120
Rock This Town, 346
Rock Your Baby, 326, 327, 328
Rocka Rolla, 279
Rock-A-Billy, 132
Rocket 88, 80, 84, 99, 120, 122
Rocket Man, 290
Rocket to Russia, 299
Rockin' and Rollin', 83
Rockin' Robin, 98
Rockit, 392
Rocks and Gravel, 195
Rocky Mountain High, 273, 409
Roll Over Beethoven, 101, 188, 189
Roll the Bones, 282
Roll with Me Henry, 110, 140
Rolling Stone, 70
Romeo and Juliet, 329
Ronald McRaygun, 320
Room for Squares, 531
Ropin' the Wind, 412, 441, 442
Rosalita, 263
Roses are Red, 148
Rough Trade Live!, 268
Roundabout, 240, 242–243
Roxanne, 318
Roxanne, Roxanne, 399
Roxanne's Revenge, 399
Rubber Ball, 148
Rubber Soul, 214
The Rubberband Man, 252
Rudolph, the Red-Nosed Reindeer, 64
Rule, 515
Rule 3:36, 480
Rules, 514
Rum and Coca Cola, 62
Rumours, 290
Run for the Hills, 378
Run to Him, 148
Runaround Sue, 117
Runaway, 147
Runaway Train, 441
Run-D.M.C., 393, 396
Running Back to Saskatoon, 349
Running Bear, 183
Running On Empty, 263
Running Scared, 130

S

Sabbath Bloody Sabbath, 284
Sad Wings of Destiny, 279
Saddam Stomp, 508
Safety Dance, 432
The Saga Continues, 472
Sail Away, 261
Sally Can't Dance, 288
Salsation, 331
Samen, 365
Samson and Delilah, 108
San Antonio Rose, 35, 48
Sandanista!, 309
Satisfaction, 303
Saturday Night Fishfry, 66
A Saucerful of Secrets, 240
Save the Last Dance for Me, 115, 167

Save This House, 437
Save This House, 437
Saving Me, 522
Say it Loud—I'm Black and I'm Proud, 203
Say it With Music, 23
Say Man, 85, 100
Say My Name, 470
Say You, Say Me, 354, 357
Say, Say, Say, 359
Scarlet Ribbons, 144
School Day, 84, 101, 167
School's Out, 164, 285
The Score, 456, 459
Screamin Fist, 304
Sea Cruise, 92
Sea of Madness, 378
Sealed with a Kiss, 148
Search and Destroy, 296
Searchin', 115
Second Toughest in the Infants, 454
Secret Love, 85
See Saw, 115
See See Rider, 193
See That My Grave Is Kept Clean, 43
See the Light, 209
See You Later, Alligator, 120
Seek and Destroy, 505
Self-Destruction, 400
Setting Sun, 454
Seven Day Fool, 543
Seven Deadly Finns, 288
Seventeen, 141, 307
Seventh Son, 70
Sex and Drugs and Rock and Roll, 316
Sex Me (Parts I and II), 470
Sexuality, 455
Sexy Ways, 110
Sgt. Pepper's Lonely Hearts Club Band, 3, 5, 161, 163, 214, 230, 232, 235, 236, 238, 355, 452
Shadow Dancing, 331
Shadowland, 436
Shake, 109, 193
Shake a Hand, 106
Shake Your Bon Bon, 465
Shake Your Booty, 327, 328
Shake Your Groove Thing, 329
Shake, Rattle and Roll, 71, 120–121, 140
Shakin' All Over, 194
Share the Land, 195
Sharevari, 449
Sh-Boom, 71, 85, 112–113, 114, 118, 140
She Cried, 148
She Loves You, 191
She Works Hard for the Money, 341, 346
She's a Bitch, 483
She's a Fool, 148
She's About a Mover, 190
She's All I Ever Had, 465
She's Not There, 190
She's So Unusual, 345
Sheena Is a Punk Rocker, 299
Shenandoah, 144
Sherry, 119
Sheryl Crow, 447
Shining Star, 323, 324
Ship A'Hoy, 250

Shock'n Y'All, 512
The Shoop Shoop Song (It's in His Kiss), 104
Shoot the Dog, 513
Shop Around, 173
Short Fat Fanny, 93
Short People, 261
Shot Down In Flames, 505
Shot Gun Blues, 209
Shotgun Willie, 273
Shotgun, 173
Shout at the Devil, 379
Shout, 149, 321
Show Me the Way, 290
Shut Down, 160
Siamese Dream, 441
The Sign, 444
Silhouettes, 119, 140
Silk Degrees, 20
Silly Little Love Songs, 289
Simple Dreams, 260
Sin After Sin, 284
Since I Met You Baby, 105
Since U Been Gone, 534, 535, 541
Since You've Been Gone, 152
Sincerely, 115, 140
Singing the Blues, 132
Sister Hold On, 269
Sister Morphine, 206
Sister Ray, 296
Sisters Are Doin' It for Themselves, 359
(Sittin' on) The Dock of the Bay, 212
Six in the Morning, 394
The Six Wives of Henry the VIII, 240
Sixteen Candles, 117
Sixteen Reasons, 146
Sixty Minute Man, 82, 86, 106, 153
Sk8er Boi, 528
Skin Tight, 323
Skokiaan, 118
Slave Driver, 264
Sleep, 105
Sleep, Baby, Sleep, 46
Sleep Walk, 159
Sleepy Maggie, 437
Sleepy Time Gal, 22
The Slim Shady LP, 477
Slip It In, 319
Slippery When Wet, 382, 383, 384
Slippin' and Slidin', 94
Slippin' into Darkness, 253
Slow Jamz, 540
Smeared, 434
Smells Like Teen Spirit, 425, 428–429
Smiley Smile, 163
Smoke Gets in Your Eyes, 117
Smoke on the Water, 279, 280–281
Smoke That Cigarette, 64
Smokey Joe's Café, 115
Smooth, 465, 466
Snowbird, 273
So, 368
So It Goes, 308
So Long, 70
So Long, I'm Gone, 128
Society's Child, 216, 217

Sock It to Me, Baby, 170
Soft and Wet, 352
Solace, 434
Soldier Boy, 168
A Soldier's Heart, 509
The Soldiers' Sweetheart, 46
Some Gave All, 508
Some of These Days, 22
Somebody to Love, 206–207, 225
Someday, 522
Someday Soon, 184
Someday We'll All Be Free, 526
Somethin' on My Mind, 304
Somewhere Out There, 359
Son of a Bush, 513
Song from Moulin Rouge, 136
Songs From a Room, 261
Songs in A Minor, 525
Songs in the Key of Life, 252, 290
Songs of Leonard Cohen, 261
Songs to a Seagull, 256
Sonic Jihad, 514
Sonic Reducer, 302
Sorry (I Ran All the Way Home), 141
Soul Bossa Nova, 406
Soul Makossa, 11, 326
Soul Man, 200
Soul Sacrifice, 219
Soulful, 534
Sounds of Joy, 179
Sounds of Silence, 195, 198
Sour Times, 453
South Bronx, 394
South Carolina (Barnwell), 264
South Street, 168
The South's Gonna Do It Again, 275
Southern Hospitality, 105, 482
Southern Man, 224, 275
Spanish Fever, 322
Spanish Harlem, 168
Spank Thru, 426
Speakerboxxx/The Love Below, 537, 539
Spice, 444, 456
Spin Age Blasters, 311
Spinning Wheel, 244
Spiral Scratch, 309
The Spirit Room, 525
Spirits in the Material World, 318
Sports, 356
Square Dance, 515
St. Louis Blues, 25
St. Theresa of the Roses, 106
Stage Fright, 271
Stagger Lee, 93
Stained Class, 377, 413, 414
Stairway to Heaven, 147, 278, 280, 284, 363
Stand!, 221
Stand Back, 346
Stand By Me, 360
Stand Up, 540
Standing n the Shadows of Love, 173
Standing on the Corner 118
Stankonia, 481, 537
Stanley Climbfall, 52
Star Dust, 106
The Star-Spangled Banner, 220, 501, 508

Star Wars, 332
State of Shock, 363
Stayin' Alive, 220, 356
Stealing Fire, 261
Steppin' Out, 317
Sticky Fingers, 238
Still Not a Player, 465
Still the One, 263
Stillmatic, 478, 515
Stink, 208
Stir It Up, 314
Stood Up, 151
Stop All the World Now, 530
Stop That Rag, 24
Stop the War, 226
Stop Your Sobbing, 318
Stop! In the Name of Love, 174, 175, 176, 177
A Story Untold, 119
Straight Outa Compton, 395, 400
Straight Up, 209
The Stranger, 290
Stranger in a Strange Land, 378
Stranger in Paradise, 63
Stranger on the Shore, 189
Strawberry Fields, 214, 338
Stray Cat Strut, 346
Street Fighting Man, 218, 461
Street Songs, 342
Strictly for my N.I.G.G.A.Z., 420
Strings of Life, 449
Stripped, 464
The Stroll, 119
Stunt, 459
Stupid Cupid, 152
Stupid Girl, 217
Stupid Girls, 529
Stupid Songs, 320
Stupid World, 320
Sub Pop 200, 426
Submission, 307
Subterranean Homesick Blues, 181
Such a Night, 106, 138
Sudbury Saturday Night, 349
Suddenly, 356
Suicide Solution, 378, 412, 413
Suite: Judy Blue Eyes, 221
Sukiyaki, 11
Summer Breeze, 261
Summer Came Home, 457
Summer in the City, 199
Summertime Blues, 129, 220, 277
Summertime, 26, 34
Sunday Bloody Sunday, 367, 504
Sunday Kind of Love, 111
Sundown, 185
Sundown, 261
Sunny Days, 244
Sunshine of Your Love, 210, 277
Sunshine on My Shoulders, 273
Sunshine Superman, 195, 206
Supa Dupa' Fly, 483
Superfreak, 342
Superman, 331
Supernatural, 465, 466
Superstition, 438
Superunknown, 426
Surf City, 163
Surfacing, 434, 457
Surfer Girl, 160
Surfer's Stomp, 159

Surfin' Safari, 160
Surfin' U.S.A., 160–162
Surfin' U.S.A., 162
Surfin', 160
Surrender, 126
Survivor, 470, 471
Swanee, 28
Swastika Girl, 303
Sweat of Your Brow, 543
Sweet Baby James, 257
Sweet Dreams Are Made of This, 340, 341
Sweet Home Alabama, 275
Sweet Jane, 287, 435
Sweet Leilani, 35
Sweet Little Sixteen, 84, 160, 161
Sweet Neo-Con, 516
Sweet Nothin's, 133
Sweet Oblivion, 440
Sweet Sixteen, 71, 80, 101
Sweet Soul Music, 200
Sweet Talkin' Guy, 172
Sweethearts of the Rodeo, 272
Swimsuit Issue, 430
Swingin' on a Star, 62
Swinging School, 147
Symphonie Fantastique, 411
Symphony in Effect, 405
Synchronicity, 318

━━━━━

T

Tainted Love, 340
Take Good Care of My Baby, 148
Take It Easy, 272
Take Me Home, Country Roads, 273
Take Me Home, 331
Take Me to the River, 302
Take My Breath Away, 357
Take Off Your Pants and Jackets, 521
Take On Me, 12
Take Over, 540
Takin' Care of Business, 276–277
Taking the Long Way, 511, 512
Talahassee Lassie, 147
Talk Back Trembling Lips, 148
Talk to Me, Talk to Me, 105
Talkin' 'bout Jesus, 107
Talkin' 'bout You, 107
Talking Book, 252
Talking Heads '77, 302
Tall Paul, 147
Tam Tam Pour L'Ethiopie, 366
Tammy, 85
Tapestry, 257–258, 259
Tarantula, 482
Ta-ra-ra Boom Der-e, 18
Tattooed Love Boys, 318
Taxman, 214
Te Busqué, 530
Tea for the Tillerman, 261
Tear the Roof off the Sucker (Give Up the Funk), 325
Teardrops from My Eyes, 70
Tears Are Not Enough, 365
Tears of St. Anne, 65
Tears on My Pillow, 114

Techno: The Dance Sound of Detroit, 450
Teddy's Jam, 469
Teen Beat, 159
Teen-age Crush, 132, 146, 150
A Teenager in Love, 117
A Teenager's Romance, 151
Tejas, 276
Tell Me Why, 117
Telstar, 159
Ten, 439
Ten Commandments of Love, 115
Tequila, 99, 159
Terminator, 452
The Terror State, 514
Test for Echo, 282
Thank God I'm a Country Boy, 273
Thank You, 472
Thank You (Falletinme Be Mice Elf Agin), 219
Thankful, 534
That Lucky Old Sun, 63
That Old Black Magic, 147
That'll Be the Day, 129, 130
That's All Right, 123, 124
That's Amore, 63
That's My desire, 63
That's My Little Susie, 99
That's the Way I Like It, 327, 328
That's the Way of the World, 324
That's What Friends Are For, 359
That's When Your Heartaches Begin, 126
That's Why (I Love You So), 107, 172–173
The Theme, 451
Theme from S.W.A.T., 327
Then He Kissed Me, 168, 171
There Goes My Baby, 115, 167
There I've Said It Again, 148
There'll Be No Tears Tonight, 65
There's a Riot Goin' On, 221
There's Only One of You, 118
There's Your Trouble, 458
These Boots Are Made for Walkin', 217
These Eyes, 195, 276
They Dance Alone, 370
(They Long to Be) Close to You, 289
Think, 109, 202
Thirty Days, 101
Thirty Seconds over Tokyo, 302
This Is Me ... Then, 466
This is Me, 543
This is My Country, 216
This Land Is Your Land, 166, 179, 183
This Little Girl of Mine, 107
This Little Light of Mine, 107, 166
This Magic Moment, 115, 167
This Ones for You, 289
This Tear, 458
This Train Is Bound for Glory, 179
Those Lonely, Lonely Nights, 92
Those Oldies but Goodies, 119
Thou Shalt Not Kill, 517
A Thousand Miles, 525

A Thousand Stars, 117
Three Blind Mice, 243
Three O'Clock Blues, 84
Three Rows Over, 147
Three Stars, 129
Three Times a Lady, 354
The Thrill Is Gone, 84
Thriller, 342–343, 344, 352, 353, 356, 361, 431, 444
Thriller, 345, 354
Through the Wire, 540
Thunder Road, 263
The Thunder Rolls, 442
The Tide is High, 315
Tiger, 147
Till I Am Myself Again, 435
Till I Waltz Again with You, 136
Till We Meet Again, 22
Tillsonburg, 349
Time Out of Mind, 367
Time's Up, 422
Timeless, 452
The Times They Are A-Changin', 180
The Times They Are A-Changin', 182, 360
Ting-a-Ling, 114
Tired of Waiting for You, 192
To All the Girls I've Loved Before, 11, 359
To Cut a Long Story Short, 340
To Know Him Is to Love Him, 118
To Sir with Hate, 269
To the Extreme, 404
Tobacco Road, 190
(Today I Met) The Boy I'm Gonna Marry, 169, 171
Today Your Love, Tomorrow the World, 311
Tom, 522
Tom Dooley, 145
Tommy, 219–220, 238
Tonight We Love, 2
Tonight We're Settin' the Woods on Fire, 65
Too Hot, 324
Too Hot for Love, 329
Too Much Monkey Business, 10, 101
Too Much Too Soon, 286
Tooth and Nail, 379
Topsy (part I), 159
Topsy (part II), 159
Touch, 457
Touch a Hand, Make a Friend, 187
Touch me, feel me ..., 219–220
Toulyev, 434
Toys in the Attic, 279
TP-2.com, 470
Tra La La, 71
Traffic in the Sky, 532
Tragedy, 118
Tragic Kingdom, 456
Trans Europe Express, 392
Transformer, 287
Travellin' Man, 151
Travellin' Soldier, 510
Treasure of Love, 85, 107
Tres Hombres, 276
Tribute, 378, 384
The Trinity Sessions, 435
True Blue, 355, 356

A Truly Western Experience, 436
Truth #2, 510
Try, 435
Try This, 529
TSOP (The Sound of Philadelphia), 252
Tu peux raveler ta romance (You Can Take Back Your Romance), 186
Tu Pum Pum, 544
Tuesday Night Music Club, 447
Tumbling Tumbleweeds, 52
Turn Me Loose, 147
Turn Off the Light, 529
Turn the Beat Around, 327
Turvy (part II), 159
Tush, 276
Tusk, 290
Tutti-Frutti, 85, 94, 95–97, 141, 142
Tweedlee Dee, 71, 85
The Twelfth of Never, 139
Twice Removed, 434
Twilight Time, 117
The Twist, 148
Twist and Shout, 149, 188, 191
Twist, Twist Senora, 149
Twistin' the Night Away, 109, 149
Two Little Hitlers, 317
Two Lovers, 173

U

Ubangi Stomp, 128
Über Alles, 320
Ultramega OK, 426
Un Canadien errant, 184
Un-break My Heart, 456, 469
Uncle Jam Wants You, 393
Under My Skin, 528
Under My Thumb, 217, 225
Under the Boardwalk, 115, 193
Under the Bridge, 439
Underwhelmed, 434
Undun, 195
The Unforgettable Fire, 367
Unison, 12, 458
Universal Soldier, 184
Unleashed, 508, 512
Until You Come Back to Me (That's What I'm Gonna Do), 253–254
Up Against the Wall, 215
Up on Cripple Creek, 271
Up on the Roof, 115, 153
Up to Here, 436
Up Where We Belong, 184
Up Your Alley, 388
Up, 437
The Uplift Mojo Party Plan, 439
Uptight (Everything's Alright), 173
Uptown, 171, 198
Use Ta Be My Girl, 252
Use Your Illusion I, 385
Use Your Illusion II, 385

V

V'la Le Bon Vent, 184
Valley of Tears, 91
Van Halen, 282
Vaya Con Dios, 136
The Velvet Underground and Nico, 295
The Velvet Underground, 296
Veni, Vidi, Vicious, 522
Venni, Vetti, Vecci, 480
Venus, 85, 147
Venus in Blue Jeans, 93
Venus in Firs, 295
Victory is Calling, 405
Video Killed the Radio Star, 340
Vietnow, 461
Virginia Plain, 288
Vision of Love, 445
Vitalogy, 447
Vivid, 388
Vol. 2 ... Hard Knock Life, 476, 479
Vol. 3 ... Life and Times of S. Carter, 479
Volare, 11, 147
Volunteers, 220
Voodoo Thing, 209
Vs, 427, 448

W

The W, 476
The Wabash Cannonball, 46, 50
The Wah Watusi, 148, 168
Waif Me, 430
Wait 'Til My Bobby Gets Home, 169, 171
Waiting for My Rocket to Come, 530
Waiting for the Robert E. Lee, 28
Waiting for the World to Change, 532
Waiting for Tonight, 465
Wake Up America, 320
Wake Up Everybody, 250
Wake Up Little Susie, 132, 154
Walk Like an Egyptian, 505
Walk on By, 171
Walk on the Wild Side, 287, 406
Walk Right In, 180
Walk This Way, 393, 396, 422
Walk-Don't Run, 160
Walkin in the Rain, 171
Walking After Midnight, 133, 435
Walking on the Moon, 318
Walking the Dog, 193
Walking the Razor's Edge, 385
Walking to New Orleans, 91
The Wall, 240
Wallflower, 110, 140
Wanted Dead or Alive, 504
Wanted: The Outlaws, 273
War, 26
War, 367
War/We Don't Need No Trouble, 264

Wash Your Face in My Sink, 405
Watch Your Step, 28
Watching the Detectives, 317
Waterfalls, 469
Watershed, 436
Way Down Yonder in New Orleans, 147
The Way I Walk, 131
The Way We Were, 289
The Way You Move, 537
Waylon and Willie, 273
We Almost Lost Detroit, 264
We Are the World, 359, 360, 361, 366, 372, 501
We Belong Together, 543
We Call It Acieed, 450
We Can Be Together, 218
We Care a Lot, 422
We Don't Need Another Hero (Thunderdome), 357
We Got Love, 147
We Gotta Get Out of This Place, 212
We Shall Be Free, 442
We Shall Overcome, 166, 180, 186, 362
We Shall Overcome: The Seeger Sessions, 517
We Vibrate, 307
We're a Winner, 216
We're All in the Same Gang, 400
We're an American Band, 283
We're Only in It for the Money, 238
We've Got a Bigger Problem Now, 320
Weathered, 522
The Wedding Song of the Painted Doll, 34
Wee Wee Hours, 100, 101
Welcome to the Occupation, 432
Well-O, Well-O, Well-O, Baby, 92
A Well Respected Man, 192
Western Movies, 115
Westray, 349
What a Girl Wants, 464, 465
What a Wonderful World, 257
What About Love, 388
What About Me, 359
What About Your Friends, 469
What Does Your Soul Look Like?, 453
What Have I Done to Make You Go Away, 105
What If, 522
What in the World's Come Over You, 131
What is Hip, 323
What Made You Say That, 443
What More Can I Give, 501
What Will I Tell My Heart, 111
What Would You Do, 514
What'd I Say, 107
What's Goin' On, 252, 459, 501
What's Going On, 217
What's My Name, 307
What's the 411?, 469
What's the Use of Breaking Up, 250
What's This Life For, 522
What's Your Fantasy, 481
Wheels of Fire, 210
When, 133

When a Man Loves a Woman, 200
When Doves Cry, 353, 501, 505
When I Grow Up (To Be a Man), 162
When the Blue of the Night Meets the Gold of the Day, 35
When the Going Gets Tough, the Tough Get Going, 357
When the Swallows Come Back to Capistrano, 98
When Will I See You Again, 252
Whenever, Wherever, 467
Where Did Our Love Go, 174, 176
Where Do Broken Hearts Go, 354
Where Have All the Cowboys Gone, 457
Where Have All the Flowers Gone, 180
Where Is the Love?, 515
Where or When, 117
Where the Stars and Stripes and the Eagle Fly, 507, 508
Where Were You When the World Stopped Turning, 507
Which Side are You On, 166
Whip It, 321
Whispering Bells, 117, 143
Whispering, 28
The Whistling Coon, 18
White Album, 218, 386
White Blood Cells, 522
White Christmas, 35, 106
White Light/White Heat, 296
White Lines (Don't Do It), 392
White Nights, 354
White Rabbit, 206, 207
White Riot, 307, 312
A White Sport Coat (and a Pink Carnation), 132
White Trash with Money, 512
White White World, 452
A Whiter Shade of Pale, 240
Whites off Earth Now, 435
Whitesnake, 384
Whitney Houston, 356, 358
Whitney, 354
Who Are You, 504
Who Dunit, 329
Who Needs You, 118
The Who Sell Out, 238
Who's Sorry Now, 85, 146, 147
Whoa, Nelly!, 525, 529
Whole Lotta Love, 283

Whole Lotta Lovin', 91
Whole Lotta Shakin' Goin' On, 128
The Whole World, 514
Why, 514
Why Do Fools Fall In Love, 114, 119, 140, 141
Why Do Lovers Break Each Others' Hearts, 169, 171
Why Don't We Do It in the Road, 217
Why Don't You Haul Off and Love Me, 69
Why'd You Lie, 209
Wichita Lineman, 273
Wide Open Spaces, 509
Wild Boys, 341
Wild Night, 458
Wild One, 147
The Wild, the Innocent, and the E Street Shuffle, 262
Wild World, 261
Wildwood Flower, 46
Will the Circle Be Unbroken?, 270
Will the Circle Be Unbroken?, 46, 187
Will You Love Me Tomorrow, 164, 168, 170, 171, 257, 258
Willie and the Hand Jive, 98, 100
Willy, 256
Winner in You, 358
Wipe Out, 159
Wishbone, 179
With a Little Help from My Friends, 214, 220
With a Little Help from My Friends, 220
With Arms Wide Open, 522
Without Love (There is Nothing), 107
Without Me, 515
Without You, 148
Woman Love, 129
The Woman in Me, 443, 456
Won't Get Fooled Again, 504
Wooden Ships, 220
Woodstock, 224
Wooly Bully, 190
Wop Bop Aloo Bop, 94
Word of Mouf, 482
Words of Love, 199
Wordy Rappinghood, 392
Work with Me Annie, 109, 110, 153
Working Class Hero, 262

Working My Way Back to You/Forgive Me, Girl, 252
Works, Volume I, 239
Works, Volume II, 239
The World is a Ghetto, 249
The World is Waiting for the Sunrise, 23
World of Wonders, 261
World Wide Suicide, 517
A World Without Love, 190
The World's Greatest, 471
Worried Devil Blues, 39
Worried Man Blues, 46
The Worst Thing That Could Happen, 117
The Wreck of the Edmund Fitzgerald, 185
The Wreck of the Old 97, 45
The Writing's on the Wall, 470
Wu-Tang Clan Forever, 476

Y

Y.M.C.A., 329
Yah Mo B There, 359
Yakety Yak, 115
Yeah!, 539
Yellow Submarine, 206
The Yellow Tape, 436
The Yes Album, 239
Yesterday's Gone, 190
Yo! Bum Rush the Show, 395
You, 117
You Ain't Seen Nothing Yet, 277
You Always Hurt the One You Love, 93
You and I were Young, Maggie, 22
You Are My All in All, 23
You Are My Destiny, 147
You Beat Me to the Punch, 173
You Can't Hurry Love, 342
You Didn't Have to Be So Nice, 199
You Don't Have to Say You Love Me, 191–192
You Don't Know My Name, 526, 540
You Don't Own Me, 147
You Got What It Takes, 192
You Keep Me Hanging On, 278, 456
You Make Me Feel Brand New, 251, 252
You Make Me Feel Like a Natural Woman, 159

You Need Love, 283
You Never Can Tell, 10
You Oughta Know, 459
You Really Got Me, 192
You Remind Me of Something, 470
You Send Me, 85, 108
You Sexy Thing, 327
You Should Be Dancing, 327, 330
You Stepped into My Life, 332
You Turn Me On, I'm a Radio, 256
You Turn Me On, 190
You Were Meant for Me, 34
You Were on My Mind, 184
You, You, You, 136
You'll Be Mine (Party Time), 456
You're a Heartbreaker, 124
You're Breaking My Heart, 63
(Your Love Kept Lifting Me) Higher and Higher, 108
You're Making Me High, 456, 469
You're Missing, 513
You're My Everything, 176
You're My World, 190
You're No Good, 260
You're Still the One, 458
You're the Apple of My Eye, 119
You're the First, the Last, My Everything, 254
You've Got a Friend, 257, 259
You've Got to Fight for Your Right to Party, 394
You've Got to Stand for Something, 508
You've Lost That Loving Feeling, 153, 170
You've Made Me So Very Happy, 244
You've Really Got a Hold on Me, 173, 188
Young Americans, 288
Young Blood, 115
Young Love, 132, 146
Young, Gifted, and Black, 216, 217
Your Body's Callin', 470
Your Cheatin' Heart, 65
Your Time Is Gonna Come, 278

Z

Zip-A-Dee Doo-Dah, 169